International Directory of
COMPANY
HISTORIES

International Directory of
COMPANY
HISTORIES

VOLUME 95

Editor

Jay P. Pederson

ST. JAMES PRESS

A part of Gale, Cengage Learning

GALE
CENGAGE Learning™

Detroit • New York • San Francisco • New Haven, Conn • Waterville, Maine • London

International Directory of Company Histories, Volume 95

Jay P. Pederson, Editor

Project Editor: Miranda H. Ferrara

Editorial: Virgil Burton, Donna Craft, Louise Gagné, Peggy Geeseman, Julie Gough, Linda Hall, Sonya Hill, Keith Jones, Lynn Pearce, Holly Selden, Justine Ventimiglia

Production Technology Specialist: Mike Weaver

Imaging and Multimedia: Lezlie Light

Composition and Electronic Prepress: Gary Leach, Evi Seoud

Manufacturing: Rhonda Dover

Product Manager: Jenai Mynatt

For product information and technology assistance, contact us at **Gale Customer Support, 1-800-877-4253.**
For permission to use material from this text or product, submit all requests online at **www.cengage.com/permissions.**
Further permissions questions can be emailed to **permissionrequest@cengage.com**

Gale
27500 Drake Rd.
Farmington Hills, MI, 48331-3535

LIBRARY OF CONGRESS CATALOG NUMBER 89-190943
ISBN-13: 978-1-55862-616-4
ISBN-10: 1-55862-616-6

This title is also available as an e-book
ISBN-13: 978-1-4144-2979-3   ISBN-10: 1-4144-2979-7
Contact your Gale, a part of Cengage Learning sales representative for ordering information.

BRITISH LIBRARY CATALOGUING IN PUBLICATION DATA
International directory of company histories, Vol. 95
Jay P. Pederson
33.87409

Printed in the United States of America
1 2 3 4 5 6 7 12 11 10 09 08

Contents

Preface

The St. James Press series *The International Directory of Company Histories* (*IDCH*) is intended for reference use by students, business people, librarians, historians, economists, investors, job candidates, and others who seek to learn more about the historical development of the world's most important companies. To date, *IDCH* has covered more than 9,500 companies in 95 volumes.

INCLUSION CRITERIA

Most companies chosen for inclusion in *IDCH* have achieved a minimum of US$25 million in annual sales and are leading influences in their industries or geographical locations. Companies may be publicly held, private, or nonprofit. State-owned companies that are important in their industries and that may operate much like public or private companies also are included. Wholly owned subsidiaries and divisions are profiled if they meet the requirements for inclusion. Entries on companies that have had major changes since they were last profiled may be selected for updating.

The *IDCH* series highlights 25% private and nonprofit companies, and features updated entries on approximately 35 companies per volume.

ENTRY FORMAT

Each entry begins with the company's legal name; the address of its headquarters; its telephone, toll-free, and fax numbers; and its web site. A statement of public, private, state, or parent ownership follows. A company with a legal name in both English and the language of its headquarters country is listed by the English name, with the native-language name in parentheses.

The company's founding or earliest incorporation date, the number of employees, and the most recent available sales figures follow. Sales figures are given in local currencies with equivalents in U.S. dollars. For some private companies, sales figures are estimates and indicated by the abbreviation *est*. The entry lists the exchanges on which the company's stock is traded and its ticker symbol, as well as the company's NAICS codes.

Entries generally contain a *Company Perspectives* box which provides a short summary of the company's mission, goals, and ideals; a *Key Dates* box highlighting milestones in the company's history; lists of *Principal Subsidiaries*, *Principal Divisions*, *Principal Operating Units*, *Principal Competitors*; and articles for *Further Reading*.

American spelling is used throughout *IDCH*, and the word "billion" is used in its U.S. sense of one thousand million.

SOURCES

Entries have been compiled from publicly accessible sources both in print and on the Internet such as general and academic periodicals, books, and annual reports, as well as material supplied by the companies themselves.

CUMULATIVE INDEXES

IDCH contains three indexes: the **Cumulative Index to Companies**, which provides an alphabetical index to companies profiled in the *IDCH* series, the **Index to Industries**, which allows researchers to locate companies by their principal industry, and the **Geographic Index**, which lists companies alphabetically by the country of their headquarters. The indexes are cumulative and specific instructions for using them are found immediately preceding each index.

SUGGESTIONS WELCOME

Comments and suggestions from users of *IDCH* on any aspect of the product as well as suggestions for companies to be included or updated are cordially invited. Please write:

The Editor
International Directory of Company Histories
St. James Press
Gale, Cengage Learning
27500 Drake Rd.
Farmington Hills, Michigan 48331-3535

St. James Press does not endorse any of the companies or products mentioned in this series. Companies appearing in the *International Directory of Company Histories* were selected without reference to their wishes and have in no way endorsed their entries.

Notes on Contributors

M. L. Cohen
Novelist, business writer, and researcher living in Paris.

Jeffrey L. Covell
Seattle-based writer.

Ed Dinger
Writer and editor based in Bronx, New York.

Jodi Essey-Stapleton
Writer based in Illinois.

Paul R. Greenland
Illinois-based writer and researcher; author of two books and former senior editor of a national business magazine; contributor to *The Encyclopedia of Chicago History, The Encyclopedia of Religion,* and the *Encyclopedia of American Industries.*

Robert Halasz
Former editor in chief of *World Progress* and *Funk & Wagnalls New Encyclopedia Yearbook*; author, *The U.S. Marines* (Millbrook Press, 1993).

Frederick C. Ingram
Writer based in South Carolina.

Kathleen Peippo
Minnesota-based writer.

Nelson Rhodes
Editor, writer, and consultant in the Chicago area.

Carrie Rothburd
Writer and editor specializing in corporate profiles, academic texts, and academic journal articles.

David E. Salamie
Part-owner of InfoWorks Development Group, a reference publication development and editorial services company.

Ted Sylvester
Photographer, writer, and editor of the environmental journal *From the Ground Up.*

Mary Tradii
Colorado-based writer.

Frank Uhle
Ann Arbor-based writer; movie projectionist, disc jockey, and staff member of *Psychotronic Video* magazine.

List of Abbreviations

¥ Japanese yen
£ United Kingdom pound
$ United States dollar

A

AB Aktiebolag (Finland, Sweden)
AB Oy Aktiebolag Osakeyhtiot (Finland)
A.E. Anonimos Eteria (Greece)
AED Emirati dirham
AG Aktiengesellschaft (Austria, Germany, Switzerland, Liechtenstein)
aG auf Gegenseitigkeit (Austria, Germany)
A.m.b.a. Andelsselskab med begraenset ansvar (Denmark)
A.O. Anonim Ortaklari/Ortakligi (Turkey)
ApS Amparteselskab (Denmark)
ARS Argentine peso
A.S. Anonim Sirketi (Turkey)
A/S Aksjeselskap (Norway)
A/S Aktieselskab (Denmark, Sweden)
Ay Avoinyhtio (Finland)
ATS Austrian shilling
AUD Australian dollar
ApS Amparteselskab (Denmark)
Ay Avoinyhtio (Finland)

B

B.A. Buttengewone Aansprakeiijkheid (Netherlands)
BEF Belgian franc

BHD Bahraini dinar
Bhd. Berhad (Malaysia, Brunei)
BRL Brazilian real
B.V. Besloten Vennootschap (Belgium, Netherlands)

C

C.A. Compania Anonima (Ecuador, Venezuela)
CAD Canadian dollar
C. de R.L. Compania de Responsabilidad Limitada (Spain)
CEO Chief Executive Officer
CFO Chief Financial Officer
CHF Swiss franc
Cia. Companhia (Brazil, Portugal)
Cia. Compania (Latin America [except Brazil], Spain)
Cia. Compagnia (Italy)
Cie. Compagnie (Belgium, France, Luxembourg, Netherlands)
CIO Chief Information Officer
CLP Chilean peso
CNY Chinese yuan
Co. Company
COO Chief Operating Officer
Coop. Cooperative
COP Colombian peso
Corp. Corporation
C. por A. Compania por Acciones (Dominican Republic)
CPT Cuideachta Phoibi Theoranta (Republic of Ireland)

CRL Companhia a Responsabilidao Limitida (Portugal, Spain)
C.V. Commanditaire Vennootschap (Netherlands, Belgium)
CZK Czech koruna

D

D&B Dunn & Bradstreet
DEM German deutsche mark
Div. Division (United States)
DKK Danish krone
DZD Algerian dinar

E

EC Exempt Company (Arab countries)
Edms. Bpk. Eiendoms Beperk (South Africa)
EEK Estonian Kroon
eG eingetragene Genossenschaft (Germany)
EGMBH Eingetragene Genossenschaft mit beschraenkter Haftung (Austria, Germany)
EGP Egyptian pound
Ek For Ekonomisk Forening (Sweden)
EP Empresa Portuguesa (Portugal)
E.P.E. Etema Pemorismenis Evthynis (Greece)
ESOP Employee Stock Options and Ownership
ESP Spanish peseta
Et(s). Etablissement(s) (Belgium,

France, Luxembourg)
eV eingetragener Verein (Germany)
EUR euro

F
FIM Finnish markka
FRF French franc

G
G.I.E. Groupement d'Interet Economique (France)
gGmbH gemeinnutzige Gesellschaft mit beschraenkter Haftung (Austria, Germany, Switzerland)
G.I.E. Groupement d'Interet Economique (France)
GmbH Gesellschaft mit beschraenkter Haftung (Austria, Germany, Switzerland)
GRD Greek drachma
GWA Gewerbte Amt (Austria, Germany)

H
HB Handelsbolag (Sweden)
HF Hlutafelag (Iceland)
HKD Hong Kong dollar
HUF Hungarian forint

I
IDR Indonesian rupiah
IEP Irish pound
ILS new Israeli shekel
Inc. Incorporated (United States, Canada)
INR Indian rupee
IPO Initial Public Offering
I/S Interesentselskap (Norway)
I/S Interessentselskab (Denmark)
ISK Icelandic krona
ITL Italian lira

J
JMD Jamaican dollar
JOD Jordanian dinar

K
KB Kommanditbolag (Sweden)
KES Kenyan schilling
Kft Korlatolt Felelossegu Tarsasag (Hungary)
KG Kommanditgesellschaft (Austria, Germany, Switzerland)
KGaA Kommanditgesellschaft auf

Aktien (Austria, Germany, Switzerland)
KK Kabushiki Kaisha (Japan)
KPW North Korean won
KRW South Korean won
K/S Kommanditselskab (Denmark)
K/S Kommandittselskap (Norway)
KWD Kuwaiti dinar
Ky Kommandiitiyhtio (Finland)

L
LBO Leveraged Buyout
Lda. Limitada (Spain)
L.L.C. Limited Liability Company (Arab countries, Egypt, Greece, United States)
L.L.P. Limited Liability Partnership (United States)
L.P. Limited Partnership (Canada, South Africa, United Kingdom, United States)
Ltd. Limited
Ltda. Limitada (Brazil, Portugal)
Ltee. Limitee (Canada, France)
LUF Luxembourg franc

M
mbH mit beschraenkter Haftung (Austria, Germany)
Mij. Maatschappij (Netherlands)
MUR Mauritian rupee
MXN Mexican peso
MYR Malaysian ringgit

N
N.A. National Association (United States)
NGN Nigerian naira
NLG Netherlands guilder
NOK Norwegian krone
N.V. Naamloze Vennootschap (Belgium, Netherlands)
NZD New Zealand dollar

O
OAO Otkrytoe Aktsionernoe Obshchestve (Russia)
OHG Offene Handelsgesellschaft (Austria, Germany, Switzerland)
OMR Omani rial
OOO Obschestvo s Ogranichennoi Otvetstvennostiu (Russia)
OOUR Osnova Organizacija Udruzenog Rada (Yugoslavia)

Oy Osakeyhtî (Finland)

P
P.C. Private Corp. (United States)
PEN Peruvian Nuevo Sol
PHP Philippine peso
PKR Pakistani rupee
P/L Part Lag (Norway)
PLC Public Limited Co. (United Kingdom, Ireland)
P.L.L.C. Professional Limited Liability Corporation (United States)
PLN Polish zloty
P.T. Perusahaan/Perseroan Terbatas (Indonesia)
PTE Portuguese escudo
Pte. Private (Singapore)
Pty. Proprietary (Australia, South Africa, United Kingdom)
Pvt. Private (India, Zimbabwe)
PVBA Personen Vennootschap met Beperkte Aansprakelijkheid (Belgium)

Q
QAR Qatar riyal

R
REIT Real Estate Investment Trust
RMB Chinese renminbi
Rt Reszvenytarsasag (Hungary)
RUB Russian ruble

S
S.A. Société Anonyme (Arab countries, Belgium, France, Jordan, Luxembourg, Switzerland)
S.A. Sociedad Anónima (Latin America [except Brazil], Spain, Mexico)
S.A. Sociedades Anônimas (Brazil, Portugal)
SAA Societe Anonyme Arabienne (Arab countries)
S.A.B. de C.V. Sociedad Anónima Bursátil de Capital Variable (Mexico)
S.A.C. Sociedad Anonima Comercial (Latin America [except Brazil])
S.A.C.I. Sociedad Anonima Comercial e Industrial (Latin America [except Brazil])
S.A.C.I.y.F. Sociedad Anonima Comercial e Industrial y Finan-

ciera (Latin America [except Brazil])

S.A. de C.V. Sociedad Anonima de Capital Variable (Mexico)

SAK Societe Anonyme Kuweitienne (Arab countries)

SAL Societe Anonyme Libanaise (Arab countries)

SAO Societe Anonyme Omanienne (Arab countries)

SAQ Societe Anonyme Qatarienne (Arab countries)

SAR Saudi riyal

S.A.R.L. Sociedade Anonima de Responsabilidade Limitada (Brazil, Portugal)

S.A.R.L. Société à Responsabilité Limitéc (Francc, Bclgium, Luxembourg)

S.A.S. Societá in Accomandita Semplice (Italy)

S.A.S. Societe Anonyme Syrienne (Arab countries)

S.C. Societe en Commandite (Belgium, France, Luxembourg)

S.C.A. Societe Cooperativa Agricole (France, Italy, Luxembourg)

S.C.I. Sociedad Cooperativa Ilimitada (Spain)

S.C.L. Sociedad Cooperativa Limitada (Spain)

S.C.R.L. Societe Cooperative a Responsabilite Limitee (Belgium)

Sdn. Bhd. Sendirian Berhad (Malaysia)

SEK Swedish krona

SGD Singapore dollar

S.L. Sociedad Limitada (Latin America [except Brazil], Portugal, Spain)

S/L Salgslag (Norway)

S.N.C. Société en Nom Collectif (France)

Soc. Sociedad (Latin America [except Brazil], Spain)

Soc. Sociedade (Brazil, Portugal)

Soc. Societa (Italy)

S.p.A. Società per Azioni (Italy)

Sp. z.o.o. Spólka z ograniczona odpowiedzialnoscia (Poland)

S.R.L. Sociedad de Responsabilidad Limitada (Spain, Mexico, Latin America [except Brazil])

S.R.L. Società a Responsabilità Limitata (Italy)

S.R.O. Spolecnost s Rucenim Omezenym (Czechoslovakia

S.S.K. Sherkate Sahami Khass (Iran)

Ste. Societe (France, Belgium, Luxembourg, Switzerland)

Ste. Cve. Societe Cooperative (Belgium)

S.V. Samemwerkende Vennootschap (Belgium)

S.Z.R.L. Societe Zairoise a Responsabilite Limitee (Zaire)

T

THB Thai baht

TND Tunisian dinar

TRL Turkish lira

TWD new Taiwan dollar

U

U.A. Uitgesloten Aansporakeiijkheid (Netherlands)

u.p.a. utan personligt ansvar (Sweden)

V

VAG Verein der Arbeitgeber (Austria, Germany)

VEB Venezuelan bolivar

VERTR Vertriebs (Austria, Germany)

VND Vietnamese dong

V.O.f. Vennootschap onder firma (Netherlands)

VVAG Versicherungsverein auf Gegenseitigkeit (Austria, Germany)

W–Z

WA Wettelika Aansprakalikhaed (Netherlands)

WLL With Limited Liability (Bahrain, Kuwait, Qatar, Saudi Arabia)

YK Yugen Kaisha (Japan)

ZAO Zakrytoe Aktsionernoe Obshchestve (Russia)

ZAR South African rand

ZMK Zambian kwacha

ZWD Zimbabwean dollar

Abril S.A.

Avenida das Nações 7221
São Paulo, São Paulo 05425-902
Brazil
Telephone: (55 11) 3037-2000
Fax: (55 11) 037-5855
Web site: http://www.abril.com.br

Private Company
Incorporated: 2001
Employees: 7,440
Sales: BRL 2.3 billion ($943 million) (2005 est.)
NAIC: 323110 Commercial Lithographic Printing; 511120 Periodical Publishers; 511130 Book Publishers; 515210 Cable and Other Subscription Programming; 517110 Wired Telecommunications Carriers; 517212 Cellular and Other Wireless Telecommunications; 517510 Cable and Other Program Distribution; 518111 Internet Service Providers; 551112 Offices of Other Holding Companies

■■■

Abril S.A. is the holding company for a giant Brazilian communications conglomerate. Its main subsidiary, Editora Abril S.A., is Latin America's largest publishing company. This company dominates magazine publishing in Brazil and also includes the nation's largest textbook publisher, printing company, and database marketing company. Yet Abril is even more. It is a power in electronic media through TVA Sistema de Televisão S.A. (TVA), Brazil's second largest subscription cable televi-

sion company, which also takes in Ajato, for broadband Internet access, and TVA Voz for Internet telephone service. TVA also acts as an Internet service provider and offers many portals and Internet wireless service. Also within Abril is the MTV network in Brazil.

MAGAZINE MOGUL: 1950–80

Abril was founded by Victor Civita in 1950. He was born in New York City to Italian immigrants but brought back to Italy in childhood. With war clouds gathering in Europe, Civita returned to New York in 1939, taking with him his wife and children. He worked in the graphics field, becoming vice-president of a firm producing quality packaging, until 1949, when he moved to Brazil. In this way he was following in the footsteps of his brother César, who had also returned to the United States but had moved to Argentina, where he had founded the publishing company Editora Abril S.A. in Buenos Aires. César told Victor that Brazil was virgin territory: a country of 50 million people who never read anything.

Editora Abril got its start by publishing Portuguese-language editions of Donald Duck and other Disney comic books, under license, in São Paulo. Abril became the world's major center, outside the United States, of comic books based on Disney characters. "We create much more Disney material than Disney itself—about 2,000 pages of comics a year," Civita told Laurel Wentz for an *Advertising Age* article in 1984. Abril's own printing plant, Impressora Brasiliera, began work the following year. "To be a publisher, I had to build my own printing plant," Civita explained to Wentz.

1

In 1952 Abril entered the magazine field with *Capricho,* which offered romance novels in photo form. *Manequin* (1959) was a fashion magazine. In 1960 the company came out with one of its most popular magazines, *Quatro Rodas,* aimed at auto buffs. The following year the company introduced *Claudia,* a women's magazine that proved to be the nation's most popular in its field. That year Abril established its own distribution company, Dinap S.A.–Distribuidora Nacional de Publicações.

Also in 1961, Civita introduced something novel: "Partworks," which involved publishing a book-length reference type topic in weekly installments of 15 to 24 pages, sold inexpensively on newsstands. Abril scored a big hit by introducing the Bible in such installments in 1965. The following year Abril began publishing an encyclopedia in installments. Other Partworks series included great painters, gardening, cooking, computers, motherhood, and sex. Abril was exploiting the practice by Brazilian newsstands of stocking not only newspapers and magazines but popular novels, textbooks, and classical records. In 1966 the company introduced the first travel guide in Brazil, *Guia Quatro Rodas.*

However, it was the magazines that made Abril a power. The company was adept at launching magazines that would exploit a particular segment of the market. In 1965 Civita's son Roberto created *Realidade,* a general interest monthly. This whetted his appetite to establish a weekly news magazine based on *Time.* This magazine, *Veja* ("Look"), made its debut in 1968 and promptly sank like a stone, because, a company executive later explained, people expected such a publication to be a large-format picture magazine like *Paris Match.*

Veja survived only by selling subscriptions. This was anathema to the newsstand vendors, who had a monopoly on magazine distribution, but Abril used its considerable influence to persuade newsstand owners to make an exception. *Veja* lost money for its first six years but eventually became not only Abril's chief magazine moneymaker but the world's largest news weekly outside the United States. Another start-up of this period was *Exame,* in 1967. *Exame* became Brazil's best selling business magazine.

PUBLISHING PLUS TELEVISION: 1980–99

By the 1980s Abril was getting almost half of its revenues from businesses outside publishing, including hotels, farms, packaging, warehouses, and frozen foods. Roberto and his brother Richard could not work together, so in 1982 the family enterprise was divided. Richard received the nonpublishing enterprises in addition to Partworks, book publishing, and Circulo do Livro, the first and leading book club in Brazil. Roberto received Editora Abril, which embraced the magazines, the printing plant, and the direct marketing division.

Editora Abril's roster of magazines included nine of Brazil's top ten in circulation. Three were comic books. The others included *Veja, Claudia, Quatro Rodas,* and two under license: *Playboy* and *Nova* (the Brazilian version of *Cosmopolitan*). However, not all of Abril's ventures were successful: *TV Guia* failed twice because a rival media empire, Organizações Globo, dominated the nation's airwaves with three popular *telenovelas* (serial dramas) each night and the evening news, so there was little incentive to buy the magazine.

Abril also invested in Portugal, forming in 1995 an association with Controjornal, the nation's largest publishing company, which printed and distributed such Abril titles as *Exame* and *Casa Claudia.* The company was less successful in Spanish-speaking media, although in 1991 it joined with Editorial Perfil S.A. to establish Editorial Primavera in Argentina.

Globo had close ties to the military governments that ruled Brazil from 1964 to 1985. Resentful of criticism by Editora Abril, they denied the company a license to own an over-the-air television station. However, in 1983 Abril Video was created as a producer turning out two hours of programming per day for a São Paulo station. The intention was for Abril to learn the business in preparation for the day when cable television reached Brazil. By 1995 Abril Video was Brazil's largest manufacturer and distributor of videos. In 1990 Abril became the partner of Viacom Inc. in MTV Brasil, the first over-the-air television station to operate round the clock.

In 1991 Abril and the consumer electronics marketer Machine Group introduced TeleVisão por Assinatura (TVA), the first important subscription television network in Brazil. The startup consisted of five cable channels: one a movie channel, another showing documentaries and travel programs, and three U.S.-based channels, offering Cable News Network, Turner

KEY DATES

1950: Victor Civita begins publishing comic books in Brazil.

1951: Editora Abril opens its own printing plant for its publications.

1952: Abril introduces its first magazine, *Capricho.*

1961: Debut of *Claudia,* which becomes Brazil's best-selling women's magazine.

1968: Abril launches *Veja,* which eventually outsells all weekly news magazines outside the United States.

1983: Establishment of Abril Video as a producer of programs for television.

1991: The company introduces TVA, a subscription television service via cable.

1996: Abril introduces Brazil's first Internet service provider.

1999: Abril and a partner purchase Brazil's two largest publishers of educational books.

2005: TVA introduces bundled television, telephone, and broadband Internet access service.

Network Television, and ESPN. By 1995 TVA had 350,000 subscribers and a number of other channels, including Discovery, Disney, and Playboy. Later it added HBO. TVA won 40 percent of Brazil's subscription TV market, but remained second to Globo, which held the other 60 percent.

The Globo conglomerate, perhaps annoyed by Abril's entry into its bailiwick, established *Época* as a rival to *Veja* in 1998. In addition, Editora Tres had another entry in the field. Although *Veja* had a large lead on its competitors, Larry Rohter wrote in the *New York Times* in 1999, "The magazines are engaged in an old fashioned, bare-knuckles battle, the likes of which have rarely been seen in publishing circles here." *Veja* had a bigger staff and the prestige that came from exposés of corruption such as the ten cover stories in 1992 that contributed to the impeachment and resignation of President Fernando Collor de Mello. *Época* chose to run shorter stories and use more graphics and photos than *Veja.*

Still intent on diversifying its business, Abril introduced Brazil's first CD-ROM in 1994 and established the nation's first Internet service provider, Brasil On-Line, in 1996. BOL was soon incorporated into Universo Online (UOL), created in collaboration with Folha de S. Paulo, publisher of São Paulo's largest newspaper. UOL also functioned as a portal for Abril's more than 200 magazines. Also in 1996, Abril introduced DirecTV Brasil, a joint venture with the holding company Galaxy Latin America. This was the direct-to-home satellite television service in Brazil. Also that year, Abril founded Datalistas S.A., its database marketing company. Music was the next entertainment field to receive the Abril treatment. The company introduced its own record company, Abril Music, in 1998. Abril Music enjoyed brief success producing, marketing, and distributing a variety of compact discs, but the parent company folded the enterprise in 2003.

Abril's expansion came to a halt in 1999, when Brazil had to devalue its currency by half, and an economic recession ensued. The company sold its DirecTV stake to Galaxy for $300 million and TVA's programming assets as well. It also withdrew from Portugal. However, it joined with the French media group Havas/Vivendi Communication to acquire Editora Ática and Editora Scipione, the leading Brazilian publishers of educational books. Between them, the two held the largest share of textbook publishing in the nation. Abril bought out its French partner (now Vivendi Universal Publishing) in 2004 for about $40 million.

ABRIL IN THE 21ST CENTURY

Publications accounted for 70 percent of Abril's net sales, compared to only 13 percent from television and 9 percent from entertainment. However, UOL was by 2000 the world's largest non-English-language Internet service provider, one of the world's ten most-visited Internet sites, and the leading Brazilian portal. UOL had 600,000 subscribers, a search engine, and almost two million home pages visited on a daily basis. Abril owned 44 percent of UOL in 2001 and all of Usina Do Som, an interactive web site that allowed 40,000 songs to be accessed over the Internet. The company had also introduced Ajato, the first broadband Internet access service in Brazil, in 1999, and Abril Sem Flo, which introduced wireless service, in 2001.

A reorganization in 2001 established Abril S.A. as the holding company for Editora Abril and the subsidiary that held the cable company. Roberto Civita appointed Ophir Toledo as its chief operating officer. Toledo sought to reorganize the group so that the executives in each of the units would start to talk to each other and, it was hoped, eventually collaborate to achieve goals such as establishing multimedia advertising packages. However, he soon left the company.

In 2004, Abril improved its financial position by selling 13.8 percent of the holding company to funds operated by Capital International, Inc., a U.S.-based private equity firm, for $150 million. The debut of TVA Voz in 2005, which provided telephone service via cable modem, enabled Abril to offer a bundled "triple play": cable television via TVA, broadband Internet access via Ajato, and telephone and other voice services via TVA Voz.

By this time, however, it was clear that Abril lacked the resources to compete meaningfully in subscription television in Brazil, which had become dominated by multinational firms with deeper pockets. TVA's share of this market, consisting of a little more than 300,000 cable customers in São Paulo, Rio de Janeiro, and five other cities, had fallen to only 7 percent. In 2006, a Brazilian subsidiary of Telefónica S.A., the Spanish-based telecommunications group, acquired 49 percent of the common stock of TVA's cable operations in São Paulo and three other cities and all of its wireless cable business based on MMDS technology in São Paulo, Rio de Janeiro, and two other cities. Telefónica paid about BRL 1 billion ($539 million), part of which Abril applied to reducing debt.

Abril also bettered its financial position in 2006 by selling 30 percent of its shares to the South African media company Naspers Limited for $422 million. The sale included the stake previously held by Capital. Abril's net revenues in 2005 were estimated at BRL 2.3 billion ($943 million), of which Editora Abril accounted for 70 percent and TVA 14 percent. In 2006, Editora Abril had net revenues of BRL 1.48 billion ($678.9 million).

Robert Halasz

PRINCIPAL SUBSIDIARIES

Editora Abril S.A.

PRINCIPAL DIVISIONS

Abril Digital; Abril Educaçao; Magazines; TV Group.

PRINCIPAL COMPETITORS

Brasil Net; Globo Comunicação e Participações S.A.

FURTHER READING

Aquino, Cleber, *História empresarial vivida,* São Paulo: Gazeta Mercantil, 1988, Vol. 4, pp. 203–56.

"Brazil Publisher Abril Sells TVA Stake to Telefonica," *Dow Jones International News,* October 29, 2006.

Fagan, Perry L., "Editora Abril S.A.," *Harvard Business School Cases,* October 26, 2000.

Gomes, Tom, "Abril Closure Leaves Void in Brazil," *Billboard,* March 1, 2003, p. 27.

Kelly, Caitlin, "Brave New Brazil," *Folio,* March 1, 1998, pp. 72, 74.

Loukos, Panos, "Brazilian Regulator Approves Telefônica's Acquisition of TVA with Restrictions," *Global Insight Daily Analysis,* July 19, 2007.

McKegney, Margaret, "BIG in Brazil," *AdAgeGlobal,* August 2001, p. 20.

Panteado, Claudia, "Brazil Publisher Abril Advances with Civita," *Advertising Age,* June 19, 1995, International supplement, p. I13.

Rohter, Larry, "A News Magazine War in Brazil," *New York Times,* August 30, 1999, p. C11.

"Telefônica adquire parte da TVA," *Valor Econômico,* October 30, 2006.

Turner, Rik, "Brazil Plugs into Pay TV," *Advertising Age,* October 21, 1991, p. 36.

Wentz, Laurel, "He Wrote the Book on Brazilian Publishing," *Advertising Age,* July 5, 1984, pp. 28–30.

Abt Associates Inc.

Abt Associates Inc.

55 Wheeler Street
Cambridge, Massachusetts 02138-1192
U.S.A.
Telephone: (617) 492-7100
Fax: (617) 492-5219
Web site: http://www.abtassociates.com

Private Company
Incorporated: 1965
Employees: 1,000
Sales: $193 million (2006 est.)
NAIC: 541618 Other Management Consulting Services;
541910 Marketing Research and Public Opinion
Polling

■ ■ ■

Abt Associates Inc. is an employee-owned government and business research and consulting company based in Cambridge, Massachusetts. It ranks among the top global research firms and U.S. market research firms according to the American Marketing Association. The firm maintains seven U.S. offices in Massachusetts, Maryland, Illinois, and North Carolina, and more than 40 project sites in about 30 countries. In addition to companies and federal, state, and local government agencies, Abt serves international organizations, nonprofit associations and institutions, and foundations. Clients range from the U.S. Department of Agriculture and the Department of Defense to the World Bank, the Bill and Melinda Gates Foundation, the Salk Institute, and such corporate clients as Ford Motor Company, Ap-

plied NeuroSolutions, American Airlines, Marriott International, American Express Company, AT&T, Eastman Kodak, and Abbott Laboratories. Sectors served are varied and numerous, including agriculture, brand and image, customer acquisition and retention, education, environment, healthcare, homeland security, homelessness, product development and pricing, survey research, welfare, and workforce development.

FLEEING NAZI GERMANY

The founder of Abt Associates, Clark Claus Abt, was born in Cologne, Germany, in 1929. After the Nazi Party came to power, his family fled the country, making their way to the United States in 1937. Abt became a naturalized citizen in 1944. He was a young man of varied interests, part entrepreneur, part scholar, part scientist. At the age of 12 he was building ship models to be sold at Saks Fifth Avenue. He worked as a typesetter for the *New York Times* and as a draftsman in Connecticut for United Aircraft before enrolling in the Massachusetts Institute of Technology (MIT) in 1947 to study aeronautical engineering. After graduating in 1951 he indulged his love of ships by serving as an ordinary seaman during a four-month stint in the Merchant Marine. Abt then spent a year teaching English at Johns Hopkins University while earning a master's degree, followed by two years working as a power plant engineer in San Francisco. Abt was also in the U.S. Air Force Reserve, on active duty as a navigator and intelligence officer, involved in electronic countermeasures, from 1953 to 1957. He then joined Raytheon Company's Missile and Space Division, where he held a number of engineering and management positions until 1964. He then earned a Ph.D. in political science from MIT in 1965 and in that same year launched Abt Associates.

Abt's concept for his new research company was to foster an academic atmosphere yet engender an entrepreneurial spirit while transferring the technology and systems employed by Raytheon and other defense contractors to the needs of private industry and public programs. Thus, the company would apply such tools as systems analysis and computer modeling and simulation to the problems of housing, education, and criminal justice. In the beginning the firm set up shop above a Cambridge, Massachusetts, machine shop and next door to the One-Two Club, a bar that could prove distracting to researchers working into the night. By the end of the first year, Abt Associates posted revenues of $205,000, enough to warrant the company moving into its present-day headquarters in 1966. Revenues doubled each year through the rest of the decade.

WASHINGTON, D.C., OFFICE
OPENS: 1968

The firm's early work came from the Office of Economic Opportunity (OEO), a federal agency established to help in the evaluation and planning of antipoverty programs using such social science research techniques as cost-benefit analyses, consumer surveys, and case studies. Abt Associates was able to successfully employ these methods for OEO in such areas as training programs for unemployed workers, migrant workers, Native Americans, and the disabled. Thus, the company established a reputation for social service program evaluation that would become a staple of the company's business. In 1968 Abt Associates opened an office in Washington, D.C., to serve government clients. Other projects the company took on during this period included cost-effectiveness models for public schools, the evaluation of Native American schools in several tribal lands, completion of a multimodal transportation model for the New England corridor, and water studies for the western United States. In addition, the company assisted

in the development of international socioeconomic projects in Latin America, Africa, and Asia.

Some of the solutions which it advocated for society, Abt Associates applied to itself. In 1968, for example, a pilot women's Job Corps center was established at the corporate headquarters where single mothers lived with their children while receiving training in computer programming, social work, and child care. Growing out of this experiment was an interest in day-care research, leading in 1971 to Abt Associates opening one of the United States' pioneering corporate day-care centers. During this period, Dr. Abt also developed the idea of "social accounting," a way to determine the positive and negative impact Abt Associates, and by extension other companies, had on employees, clients, shareholders, and society in general. This effort led to his 1976 book, *The Social Audit for Management.*

By the start of the 1970s revenues increased to $3.2 million. In the first half of the decade, Abt Associates conducted research on housing subsidies that led to the Section 8 federal program of subsidized housing for low-income families and individuals. Studies were also done for the Office of Education on the Head Start and Follow-Through education programs for disadvantaged children. The company also established a National Drug Abuse Training Center for the National Institute on Drug Abuse, provided research to help set Medicaid rates, and was involved in urban and rural employment projects. Revenues increased to $16.4 million in 1974.

The international scope of Abt Associates expanded in the second half of the 1970s. A subsidiary was established in West Germany, Abt Forschung, and work was done elsewhere in Europe and Japan as well as for the United Nations. A Canadian subsidiary was also formed and later sold. Eventually the German subsidiary would also be closed. At home, Abt Associates became involved in a prisons and jails study that helped refine projections for future prison populations and stimulated a national debate on the relationship between prison and punishment. In addition, another evaluation of the Head Start program was conducted, and a day-care services study was done on behalf of the federal government that for many years would have a major influence over states' child-care regulations. The company's in-house graphic design department became Abt Books in the late 1970s, used to publish the results of the company's work but also to produce a newsletter, *Findings.* Abt Associates closed the 1970s with $27 million in annual revenues and 800 employees, a number that would soon reach 1,100 when revenues reached $30 million in fiscal 1980.

KEY DATES

1965: Clark Abt founds company.
1968: Washington, D.C., office opens.
1986: Abt leaves company to run for Congress; after losing race, he returns to assume the post of chairman.
1987: Employees gain controlling stake in company.
1992: Wendell Knox is named CEO.
1997: Abt Associates Clinical Trials is established.
2005: Clark Abt retires as chairman.

FUNDING CUTS DURING REAGAN ADMINISTRATION

With the arrival of the Reagan administration in Washington in 1981, funds for social research, the backbone of Abt Associates, were slashed. Employment fell to just 300 and in 1983 the company was lucky to break even. It sought more business from the private sector, establishing the Business Strategy Group to conduct consulting work for corporations, such as studying ways to keep down healthcare costs for Ford Motor Company. The new unit also studied ways to measure customer satisfaction and customer segmentation in the automotive field, work that influenced product design and marketing campaigns. Moreover, after a few years some of the federal social research projects returned as the Reagan administration sought to find more efficient ways to make use of the funds that remained after a major military buildup. In fiscal 1985 revenues topped the $30 million level, 25 percent of which came from corporate clients, which also provided half the $1.3 million in operating profits.

Some competitors suggested that many of the government contracts were awarded to Abt Associates because it was located in Massachusetts's Eighth Congressional District, home of House Speaker Thomas "Tip" O'Neill. Important government research projects of the mid-1980s included an evaluation of the Food Stamp Program and the development of policy guidelines for dealing with AIDS in prisons. The company developed a public education campaign for the National Crime Prevention Council that introduced McGruff the dog character and the "Take a Bite Out of Crime" tagline. Abt Associates also began work on a long-term effort for the U.S. Agency for International Development (USAID) to improve agricultural policies and rural development programs around the world.

Clark Abt decided to run for Congress in 1986, seeking the seat vacated by Democrat Tip O'Neill, and took a leave of absence from the company. He was replaced as CEO by Walter R. Stellwagen, the company's chief social scientist. Running as a Republican, Abt lost to Joseph P. Kennedy II, son of Robert F. Kennedy. Rather than return to his old post, Abt was content to remain chairman of Abt Associates and leave Stellwagen in charge. Abt devoted much of his time to running Apt Books and teaching at Boston University, where he became a professor of international relations. Having already sold a large percentage of Abt Associates to its employees, in 1987 he sold the controlling stock to them as well.

Under Stellwagen's leadership, Abt Associates enjoyed especially strong growth in its international business in the latter half of the 1980s, much of it related to USAID. Domestic projects included an evaluation of the Job Training Partnership Act for the U.S. Department of Labor; a study on the use of electronic funds transfer technology in the Food Stamp Program and other assistance programs; and evaluations of elementary, secondary, and vocational education programs. When the decade came to a close, revenues had increased to $46 million and a backlog of work twice that amount had accumulated.

WENDELL KNOX NAMED CEO: 1992

New contracts in the early 1990s swelled the backlog further as revenues reached the $100 million mark in four years. During much of this time, the company would be led by a new CEO, Wendell J. Knox, who replaced Stellwagen as chief executive in 1992, becoming one of the highest ranking African American executives in New England. The son of the head porter of a New Orleans Sears, Roebuck store and a mother who was a domestic worker, Knox had begun working for Abt Associates part-time in 1969 while completing his degree at Harvard University. After graduation he joined the company full-time and never left. In 1982 he was assigned the task of starting up the corporate consulting practice, and over the course of the next decade grew it into a $15 million business. According to the *Boston Globe* in a 1992 profile, "a business acquaintance warned him that companies would be hesitant to accept advice from a black consultant. 'I found that very energizing,' Knox says today. 'There was a real opportunity to slam dunk that one.' In fact, he adds, he soon found in his relationships with clients 'the main color they were focusing on was green.'" Abt Associates had always been known for promoting minorities and women. At the time Knox took charge, two of the eight practice groups were headed by black women and one-third of the company's 36 vice-presidents were women.

Knox sought to continue to grow the private-sector work of Abt Associates, becoming involved in several new industries and expanding internationally, but public-sector contracts continued to provide the lion's share of revenues. The company received the master contract to oversee the HIV Network of Prevention Trials that covered nearly 20,000 subjects. It performed work for Medicare and Medicaid that was used to determine payment calculations for patient services. Abt Associates was also involved in a number of environmental projects, including a cost-benefit study on the risks of exposing children to residual lead in paint, soil, and dust. In addition, the fall of communism and other political changes opened up a number of international opportunities. The company was doing work in more than 100 countries by the mid-1900s, including projects in Africa to help rural healthcare facilities develop ancillary revenue streams to help pay for much needed drug and medical supplies. Work on privatized housing in the formerly communist countries of Eastern Europe was also conducted.

FORMATION OF ABT ASSOCIATES CLINICAL TRIALS: 1997

Housing efforts in Eastern Europe continued in the final years of the 1990s, and healthcare finance and service delivery consulting contracts were won in Russia, Ukraine, and the Central Asian Republics, leading to the opening of offices in Moscow, Kiev, and Almaty. Other offices were opened in Johannesburg, South Africa, and Cairo, Egypt. Domestic work also continued in such areas as child care, education, criminal justice, and the environment. In 1997 the company took advantage of its access to major healthcare databases related to its Medicare and Medicaid, hospital, and homecare work to form Abt Associates Clinical Trials, a contract research organization that shepherded pharmaceuticals and medical devices through the development and regulatory process and then helped introduce them into the marketplace.

Abt Associates began the new century with more than $173 million in annual revenues and profits of $6.5 million. Abt Associates Clinical Trials achieved profitability in 2001. In that same year, the terrorist attacks of September 11, 2001, against the United States prompted Abt Associates to establish a homeland security program, in which Clark Abt became actively involved. The new practice quickly won contracts from the Federal Bureau of Investigation, the Transportation Security Administration, the U.S. Department of Transportation, and others. Two years later the war in

Iraq led to a USAID contract to build up the Iraqi health systems. Elsewhere around the globe, Abt Associates' contracts included the Agriculture-Led Export Business Project in Cairo to help Egypt spur exports to Europe, the Central Asia Sport and Health Education Program, a watershed project in Costa Rica, a disaster mitigation program in the Dominican Republic, and the USAID Partnership for Health Reformplus project that helped mostly rural African communities establish risk-sharing healthcare financial pools.

Also during the 1990s Abt Associates established a behavioral health practice, conducting such work as a public school mental health service survey. Social research work continued through the National Evaluation of Child Care Subsidy Strategies study in which the company developed experiments intended to help states determine the best way to fund child-care initiatives. In housing, Abt Associates worked with the Department of Housing and Urban Development on evaluating the Moving to Opportunity Demonstration Program to assist low-income families in moving out of high-poverty urban neighborhoods through the use of vouchers rather than housing development subsidies. In 2005 Clark Abt turned over the chairmanship to John A. Shane and became chairman emeritus. A venture capitalist, Shane had been a director of Abt Associates since 1967 and had served as chairman of the company's audit and compensation committees.

Abt Associates grew through acquisitions in the second half of the first decade of the 2000s. In 2006 it added the International Group consulting practice of IBM's Business Consulting Services Public Sector unit, which performed international economic development work for USAID. A year later, Abt Associates acquired Schulman, Ronca & Bucuvalas, Inc. (SRBI), a 26-year-old, New York City-based full-service survey and market research firm, serving both the public and private sectors with offices in Maryland, Florida, Kentucky, New Jersey, Arizona, and West Virginia. The addition of SRBI gave Abt Associates greater heft, allowing it to not only increase its overall market share but to also bid on a wider range of contracts.

Ed Dinger

PRINCIPAL SUBSIDIARIES

Abt Associates Clinical Trials; Schulman, Ronca & Bucuvalas, Inc.

PRINCIPAL COMPETITORS

Booz Allen Hamilton Inc.; McKinsey & Company; Westat, Inc.

FURTHER READING

"Abt Associates Inc.," *Marketing News,* June 10, 2002, p. H26.

Connolly, Allison, "Abt Uses Social Research to See Why Drugs Don't Sell," *Boston Business Journal,* March 9, 2001, p. 25.

Hemp, Paul, "Knox Named President of Abt," *Boston Globe,* May 5, 1992, p. 43.

Therrien, Lois, "Clark Abt Even Sells Social Research to Reaganites," *Business Week,* January 27, 1986, p. 114.

ACCURAY®
Accuray Incorporated

1310 Chesapeake Terrace
Sunnyvale, California 94089
U.S.A.
Telephone: (408) 716-4600
Toll Free: (888) 522-3740
Fax: (408) 716-4601
Web site: http://www.accuray.com

Public Company
Incorporated: 1990
Employees: 450
Sales: $140.45 million (2007)
Stock Exchanges: NASDAQ
Ticker Symbol: ARAY
NAIC: 339112 Surgical and Medical Instrument Manufacturing

■ ■ ■

Accuray Incorporated designs, develops, and sells radio-surgery systems that treat solid tumors. The company's flagship product, the first of its kind in the world, is the CyberKnife Robotic Radiosurgery System, which uses image guidance technology, a linear accelerator, and a robotic arm to destroy tumor cells anywhere in the body. CyberKnife, which sells for $4.2 million, is approved for use in the United States, Europe, and Asia. Accuray also develops and sells a number of other devices that are designed to be used with its CyberKnife system. The company's Synchrony Respiratory Tracking System monitors and tracks a patient's respiratory motions in real time, correlating tumor motion with respiratory motion. The Xsight Lung Tracking System and the Xsight Spine Tracking System help track tumor movement.

FOUNDER'S BACKGROUND

Accuray was founded by John Rodenbeck Adler, M.D., whose advancements in the field of radiosurgery marked a breakthrough in treating cancer. Born in Yonkers, New York, Adler earned his medical degree at Harvard University in 1980 at age 26. After earning his degree, he served his residency at a teaching affiliate of Harvard, Brigham and Women's Hospital, rising to the status of chief resident of neurosurgery in 1986. The year also marked the conclusion of his work in Sweden, financed by the Von L. Meyer Traveling Fellowship, which introduced Adler to the man who invented radiosurgery.

Lars Leksell was in the last year of his life when Adler arrived at the Karolinska Institute in Stockholm. The 79-year-old physician and professor of neurosurgery could count many accomplishments in his life, including a new surgical approach to treat Parkinson's disease, but his groundbreaking work in harnessing the destructive power of radiation was his single greatest achievement. Scientists had known for years that radiation could destroy cancer cells, but in 1951 Leksell developed a device that could deliver a high dose of radiation in a precise manner that minimized damage to surrounding tissues. His technique employed a cyclotron, a type of particle accelerator, that directed beams of ionizing radiation at a small, specific area of the brain, which irradiated and destroyed the targeted tumor. He called the technique *strålkniven*, or "ray knives," which became the basis of radiosurgery and the Leksell Gamma Knife. His work clearly made an impression on Adler, who returned to the United States and began developing what would become known as CyberKnife.

Leksell's pioneering work represented a major leap forward in treating cancer. Radiosurgery was noninvasive and, because of its precision, large doses of radiation could be targeted at a tumor, thereby increasing the probability of tumor cell death. There were shortcomings in the technique, however. Because of the precision of the procedure and the high amounts of radiation involved, the patient needed to be entirely immobilized. Not a movement could be tolerated, which meant tumors in soft tissue organs such as the lung, liver, pancreas, and prostate could not be assaulted because of movement caused by normal bodily functions. The technique was practical only for destroying intracranial tumors, a procedure that required a rigid frame to be attached to the patient's head by inserting four screws into the skull. Further, because of the difficulty in precisely repositioning the head frame for multiple treatments, radiosurgery rarely was used when more than one dose of radiation was required.

A VISION OF COMPREHENSIVE RADIOSURGERY

Adler intended to advance the capabilities of the technique developed by his Swedish mentor. He wanted to develop a radiosurgery system capable of treating tumors anywhere in the body. He developed the concept for CyberKnife in 1987, one year after he left Stockholm and the same year he was hired as acting assistant professor of neurosurgery at Stanford University. The path from concept to commercialization was a lengthy one, involving numerous design changes, a series of prototypes, and the long wait for approval from the U.S. Food and Drug Administration (FDA) and the regulatory agencies of other countries, but the essence of Adler's initial work represented a major technological

leap from Leksell's work. Leksell, the "father" of radiosurgery, was a pioneer, and so too was Adler, whose CyberKnife system offered an impressive way to combat the second-leading cause of death in the United States and the cause of 13 percent of all deaths worldwide. For Adler, cancer was the enemy and CyberKnife was his weapon.

Adler's system used image-guiding technology and a compact linear accelerator to free radiosurgery from its frame-based constraints. The system autonomously tracked, detected, and corrected for tumor and patient movement on a real-time basis, delivering high dosages of radiation within a millimeter of the target identified by its image-guidance technology, which continuously acquired images to track a tumor's location. The linear accelerator, or linac, used microwaves to accelerate electrons, creating high-energy X-ray beams that a robotic arm directed at the targeted tumor. The Cyber-Knife procedure required no anesthesia and it could be performed on an outpatient basis. Most important, it extended the benefits of radiosurgery to the entire body.

FORMATION OF ACCURAY: 1990

Back in 1987, work was just beginning to make Cyber-Knife a reality. After his initial conceptual designs, Adler enlisted the help of a group of Stanford scientists and a manufacturer of linac technology and founded Accuray in 1990. The long and arduous road to commercialization began in Sunnyvale, California, where Adler and his team began developing the first prototypes of CyberKnife. Financially, the enterprise relied on individual private investors to fund its operations, which were not considered active until 1992. In 1992, the company developed a prototype system it sold to Stanford University Hospital, giving it a much needed infusion of capital. In 1994, Accuray's prototypes were granted an Investigational Device Exemption by the FDA, which marked the first time CyberKnife was used to treat patients.

JAPAN GIVING ITS NOD OF APPROVAL IN 1996

A major milestone in the company's history occurred in 1996. Japan became the first country in the world to approve the commercial sale of CyberKnife, granting regulatory clearance for the device's use to treat tumors in the head and neck. Using a distributor named Meditec Corporation, Accuray sold its first CyberKnife in 1997, counting the Konan St. Hill Hospital in the city of Ube as its first customer. During the next three years, CyberKnife would be used to treat nearly 300 patients for brain tumors and other lesions, impressing physi-

KEY DATES

1987: John R. Adler develops the design for the CyberKnife Robotic Radiosurgery System.

1990: Accuray Incorporated is formed.

1992: Company commences operation.

1994: U.S. Food and Drug Administration (FDA) awards an Investigational Device Exemption for CyberKnife.

1996: Regulatory officials in Japan approve the use of CyberKnife.

1999: FDA approves CyberKnife to treat tumors in the head and base of the skull.

2001: FDA approves CyberKnife to treat tumors anywhere in the body.

2002: Regulatory officials in Europe approve CyberKnife to treat tumors anywhere in the body.

2003: Korean regulatory agencies approve CyberKnife to treat tumors anywhere in the body.

2004: FDA approves Accuray's Synchrony Respiratory Tracking System.

2005: FDA approves the Xsight Spine Tracking System.

2006: FDA approves the Xsight Lung Tracking System.

2007: Accuray completes its initial public offering of stock.

cians with its capabilities. "We waited four years to acquire the CyberKnife system, and I believe it was worth the wait," a Japanese neurosurgeon remarked in an April 12, 2000, interview with *AsiaPulse*. "My first experience using the system to treat a brain tumor patient is still vivid. One month after the treatment, the follow-up visit showed that approximately 90 percent of the tumor disappeared, which is very impressive."

Japan became the first notch on Adler's belt, but he would have to wait five years before he realized the ultimate objective of his original vision. Accuray depended on funding secured through several rounds of private financing, bridge loans, and the contributions from individual investors as it refined and upgraded CyberKnife. Sales from Japan provided a welcome stream of cash, helping the company finance the further development of CyberKnife as Adler sought regulatory approval from other countries. No nod of approval meant more than the one the company received three years after gaining acceptance from the Japanese.

FDA CLEARS CYBERKNIFE IN 1999

In 1999, the FDA approved CyberKnife for the treatment of tumors in the head and base of the skull. Accuray gained access to the largest healthcare market in the world. Within a year, there were five CyberKnife systems installed in the United States. The radiosurgery devices were installed at Stanford University Medical Center, The Cleveland Clinic Foundation, University of Texas–Southwestern Medical Center in Dallas, University of Pittsburgh/Shadyside Hospital, and the Newport Radiosurgery Center in Newport, California.

Adler's crowning achievement, the goal he had been pursuing since he left Stockholm in 1986, occurred in 2001. After making several improvements in Cyber-Knife, Adler received permission from the FDA to use CyberKnife on tumors located anywhere in the body. That same year, Korea and Taiwan approved Cyber-Knife for treating tumors in the head and neck, giving Accuray a wealth of new business opportunities to explore.

NEW LEADERSHIP IN 2002

The task of turning Accuray's technological achievement into a financial success was handed to a new leader in 2002. In March, Euan S. Thomson was hired as Accuray's chief executive officer, adding the title of president in October. Before joining Accuray, Thomson, who earned his doctorate in physics with an emphasis on stereotactic brain radiotherapy from the University of London, practiced as a medical physicist with the U.K. National Health Service. For the three years immediately preceding his appointment as Accuray's new leader, he served as president and chief executive officer of Photoelectron Corporation, a publicly held medical device company.

Thomson inherited control over a company with great prospects. Acceptance of CyberKnife was spreading, giving him numerous markets to exploit. The year he joined the company, European regulatory agencies approved CyberKnife for treating tumors anywhere in the body. At the start of 2003, the first CyberKnife site in Europe opened, debuting at Vicenza Hospital in Vicenza, Italy. The year also saw Korea remove its restriction on CyberKnife, clearing the device for use on tumors anywhere in the body, a decision also made by Taiwanese regulatory officials in 2004.

PRODUCT LINE EXPANSION

Once regulatory approval had been received, Thomson began fleshing out his company's product line to take advantage of the CyberKnife system's wide range of capabilities. The new products were designed to be integrated with the CyberKnife system. In 2004, Accuray received FDA clearance for the Synchrony Respiratory Tracking System, which allowed clinicians to continuously track, detect, and correct tumor movement caused by respiration. Use of the Synchrony System allowed patients to breathe normally during treatment of tumors in the lung, liver, and pancreas. In 2005, when the fourth-generation CyberKnife was released, the FDA approved the Xsight Spine Tracking System, which tracked, detected, and corrected for tumor movement without implanting radiographic markers. The following year the company introduced a similar system, the Xsight Lung Tracking System, which also earned approval from the FDA.

A FOCUS ON MANUFACTURING

As the new products rolled out, Accuray invested in its infrastructure and vertically integrated its manufacturing operations, preparing for what was expected to be an exponentially higher volume of business. In 2005, the company acquired the linear accelerator assets owned by the High Energy Systems Division of American Science and Engineering Inc. The purchase gave the company ownership of the technology and production of the linac systems that played an integral role in the operation of CyberKnife systems. "With this transaction Accuray gains increased control over its supply chain and enters in a new phase of growth," an Accuray executive said in a January 17, 2005, interview with *Wireless News.* "Bringing this production capability in-house will lower our cost of doing business and allows us to optimize product performance." The following year, the company's new manufacturing might was put to use in a new manufacturing and research and development facility in Sunnyvale.

Financially, Accuray was recording robust growth during the first years of the decade, although a lack of profits continued to plague the company. Sales shot upward, rising from $2.7 million in 2003 to $52.8 million in 2006 before nearly tripling to $140.4 million in 2007. The use of CyberKnife (there were more than 100 systems in use by mid-2007) was proliferating, creating a community of more than 40,000 patients who had been treated with the system. Adler's desire to extend the benefits of radiosurgery throughout the body created what was fast becoming a standard clinical approach to treating tumors in a variety of locations. In April 2007, Accuray announced the number of lung tumor patients treated with CyberKnife had surpassed 2,000. By November 2007, CyberKnife had been used to treat more than 4,000 lung cancer patients as well as 1,000 men diagnosed with prostate cancer.

Jeffrey L. Covell

PUBLIC DEBUT IN 2007

Accuray celebrated the 20th anniversary of CyberKnife in 2007, choosing to start a new era of existence as it threw itself headlong into the commercialization phase of its development. The new era officially began on February 13, 2007, when the company completed an initial public offering (IPO) of stock and began operating as a publicly held company. More than 18 million shares were sold for $18 per share in the IPO, raising $171.3 million in net proceeds.

PRINCIPAL SUBSIDIARIES

Accuray International SARL (Switzerland); Accuray Europe SARL (France); Accuray UK, Ltd.; Accuray Asia Ltd. (Hong Kong); Accuray Japan K.K.; Accuray Spain, S.L.U.

PRINCIPAL COMPETITORS

Integra Life Sciences Holding Corporation; Varian Medical Systems, Inc.; TomoTherapy Incorporated.

FURTHER READING

"Accuray Acquires Technology and Manufacturing Capability from AS&E," *Wireless News,* January 17, 2005.

"Accuray and Siemens to Develop Enhanced Radiosurgery and Radiotherapy Products," *Wireless News,* October 6, 2006.

"Accuray Announces 3 New CyberKnife Installations in Japan," *AsiaPulse News,* April 12, 2000, p. 33.

"Accuray Closes Out Fiscal Year with Profitable Quarter and Strong Momentum in Sales Growth," *PR Newswire,* September 4, 2003.

"Accuray Incorporated Reports Second Consecutive Profitable Quarter and Continued Business Growth," *PR Newswire,* November 14, 2003.

"Accuray Introduces Radiosurgery Products Designed for the Non-Invasive Treatment of Lung Tumors," *Wireless News,* November 8, 2006.

"Accuray Named As Technology Pioneer 2008 by the World Economic Forum," *Wireless News,* December 2, 2007.

"Accuray Says CyberKnife System Shows Momentum As Treatment Option for Prostate Cancer," *Wireless News,* October 2, 2007.

"Accuray Surpasses 4,000 Lung Cancer Patients Treated with CyberKnife," *Wireless News,* November 25, 2007.

"Vicenza Hospital in Italy Opens First CyberKnife Radiosurgery Center in Europe," *PR Newswire,* March 31, 2003.

Adams Childrenswear Ltd.

Attleborough House, Townsend Drive
Nuneaton, CV11 6RU
United Kingdom
Telephone: (+44-24) 7635-1000
Fax: (+44-24) 7634-5583
Web site: http://www.adams.co.uk

Private Company
Founded: 1933
Employees: 3,200
NAIC: 422330 Women's, Children's, and Infants'
    Clothing and Accessories Wholesalers; 448130
    Children's and Infants' Clothing Stores; 454111
    Electronic Shopping

■ ■ ■

Adams Childrenswear Ltd. is one of the leading specialty retailers of children's clothing in the United Kingdom. Under the brand Adams Kids, the company designs, produces, and markets its clothing for children from newborn through ten years of age. The company also sells skiwear and a variety of clothing accessories, such as backpacks, hats, umbrellas, and sunglasses. A selection of schoolwear is available for children five to 16 years of age. Adams operates more than 270 retail shops in England, Wales, Scotland, and Ireland, and the company owns or franchises more than 100 stores internationally, including locations in India, Spain, Greece, Cyprus, Russia, Slovakia, Iceland, Saudi Arabia, and the Middle East. Adams designs and produces the Mini Mode, Molly n' Jack, and JCB Junior brands of clothing for Boots, a leading general goods merchant in the United Kingdom.

BECOMING A NATIONAL RETAILER

Adams Childrenswear Ltd. originated in 1933, when Amy Adams started sewing baby linens in her home in Kings Heath, a suburb of Birmingham, England. Success in selling the linens led Adams to begin making clothing for newborns and children up to seven years of age. Adams succeeded by providing value-priced children's clothing for low- and middle-income families. The cottage business evolved into a growing family enterprise with the opening of a retail store in Kings Heath. Stores in other Birmingham suburbs, including Bearwood, Sparkhill, Solihuli, and Northfield, soon followed.

Amy's son Michael Adams became president of the company in 1960, and he continued in that position through an expansion period and successive ownership changes. Adams Childrenswear merged with menswear retailer Foster Brothers Clothing Company in 1973. Foster Brothers invested heavily and rapidly in new store development, opening 30 stores during the first two years after acquisition. Expansion led to relocation of the office to Nuneaton in the summer of 1980, where the company built a new warehouse to accommodate widespread distribution. Sears Group plc purchased Foster Brothers in 1985. Michael Adams eventually took a position on the Sears board of directors, then retired in October 1991.

COMPANY PERSPECTIVES

Adams Kids' mission is to ensure its products are always of the highest quality, design and fashionability. By the very fact that it is a brand that specializes purely in childrenswear, Adams Kids is confident in its knowledge and understanding of what today's children and mums demand.

The Sears acquisition and its subsequent expansion of Adams Childrenswear coincided with a period of substantial growth in the children's clothing market. A rise in the birthrate throughout Great Britain coupled with a cultural shift toward dressing children in a more fashion-conscious manner supported the company's growth. Moreover, dual income households and fashion-oriented grandparents provided the financial stimulus for higher sales volumes. Competition in children's clothing increased as new specialty retailers, such as Jacardi and Hennes, entered the childrenswear market. Also, established retailers, including Mothercare, Ladybird, Woolworths, Marks and Spencer, and C&A Department Stores, allocated more floor space for children's clothing to accommodate rising demand.

With financial support from Sears Group, Adams widened its geographical reach to meet competition and demand in children's fashions. Between 1986 and 1993 the company expanded at the rate of 20 to 40 new stores per year. By the close of the fiscal year ending January 31, 1993, Adams operated 289 stores in England, Scotland, Wales, and Ireland. In addition to suburban and regional shopping centers, Adams emphasized establishment of new stores on the high streets, England's city center shopping districts. Sales increased 29 percent in 1992 alone, and overall sales reached £155 million during the 1993 fiscal year. The company's market share increased from 2.3 percent in 1987 to 10.7 percent in 1993. That year Adams became the top specialty U.K. retailer of children's clothing for the newborn to age eight group.

INTERNATIONAL EXPANSION

Anticipating market saturation in childrenswear in the United Kingdom, with the expectation of a decline in the birthrate by 1995, Sears and Adams were prompted to seek international expansion opportunities. New free trade agreements encouraged the company's ambition, and Sears contributed some experience with women's clothing and shoe stores in Holland and Germany. An extensive study of European market opportunities for children's clothing led Adams to launch its brand in Spain. A specialty retailer for children's clothing did not exist in Spain at the time, and overall competition was less than other European countries, such as France and Italy. Moreover, a young population with growing families assured a ready market.

Local market researchers in Spain facilitated market development in terms of region and city locations. To replicate the typical Spanish children's clothing shopping experience, the researchers employed mothers of children from newborn to eight years of age to visit stores in Barcelona, Madrid, Seville, Bilbao, and Valencia. The women visited different kinds of retail environments, at shopping centers, city centers, and hypermarkets, in order to determine the appeal of each option. They evaluated product choices based on emotional and rational factors as well as price concerns. The study indicated Bilbao and Madrid as the places to begin operations, and in the autumn of 1992 Adams opened a store in each city. Sales exceeded expectations, prompting Adams to open a store in Barcelona in March 1993, followed by another nine stores throughout Spain by the end of the year.

While Adams owned and operated the stores in Spain, the company preferred to expand through franchise development. Hence, Adams initiated its first franchise for store development in Saudi Arabia. The store opened in 1997, and ten additional stores were established in Saudi Arabia, the Gulf States, and Cyprus by early 1999.

In the United Kingdom, Adams expanded through a partnership with Sainsbury's Savacenter, a hypermarket retailer that combined the grocery store and general store formats. Sainsbury sought to compete with other superstores that carried children's clothing. The partnership benefited Adams by providing new outlets of operation at less expense than new store development. Beginning in July 1999, Adams opened outlets in 48 Sainsbury stores.

1999 MANAGEMENT BUYOUT OPENS COMPANY TO NEW STRATEGIES

By the end of the 1990s, Adams garnered approximately £200 million in annual revenues from its 350 national and international retail outlets. However, the maturity of the children's clothing market in the United Kingdom impacted Adams' market share. Related profitability issues created an environment conducive to the sale of the company. After several months of consideration, Managing Director Michael Hobbes led a

KEY DATES

1933: Amy Adams begins making infant linens from her home near Birmingham, England.

1960: Michael Adams becomes president of the company.

1973: Adams Childrenswear is purchased by Foster Brothers Clothing Company.

1985: Sears Group plc acquires Foster Brothers and begins major expansion.

1999: Management buyout marks beginning of diversified expansion strategy; Adams opens concessions at several Sainsbury's supermarkets.

2003: Adams launches Mini Mode brand in partnership with Boots stores.

2005: New brand identity, Adams Kids, includes new logo and store concept.

2007: Financial problems lead to store closures and new ownership.

management buyout in 1999. Commercial Director Dean Murray, Marketing Director Philip Walker, Operations Director Stuart Dickerson, and Human Resources Director Claire Shale participated in the buyout. Adams' management acquired 25 percent interest through the backing of Natwest Equity Partners, and Bridgeport Capital purchased a 75 percent stake in the company. The total purchase price was £87 million ($126 million).

While conducting a review of business operations, the new owner-managers pursued existing plans for retail development in the United Kingdom and abroad. International expansion involved a new store opening in Malta and two new stores in Cyprus. The total number of stores in Saudi Arabia increased to 23 by the fall of 2000. In early 2001, the company announced that its concessions in Sainsbury stores would expand to another 100 outlets. One year after the buyout, Adams operated 400 stores and concession outlets in the United Kingdom and 42 international outlets. Moreover, the operations review, which evaluated product range and pricing and also materials sourcing, generated effective cost management and positive growth in profit margins. Hence, for the fiscal year ended July 31, 2001, overall profit rose 34 percent, while profits from international trade increased 49 percent. Sales increased 10 percent, to £217 million.

Adams sought to regain market share in the United Kingdom, in particular to compete with Marks and Spencer, then the largest children's clothing retailer. Hence, marketing and merchandising initiatives involved development of multiple brands and multiple channels of distribution. The company launched a line of higher-quality clothing for four- to ten-year-olds. The Top Quality brand featured Lycra fabric blends to provide parents with more durable clothing for this active age group. To improve its footwear selection, Adams acquired Start-rite in 2001. The company offered a limited range of products through Littlewoods, a retail store and mail-order catalog company. Also, Adams took advantage of the dissolution of C&A Department Stores to introduce a line of children's skiwear, satisfying the new gap in demand for ski pants, jackets, gloves, and hats. Launched in November 2001 under the brand name Trespass, the line provided skiwear for children ages three to ten. Adams entered the market for school uniforms, introducing the B line for 8- to 16-year-olds. In 2002, Adams offered a limited range of clothing online through J.D. Williams, a mail-order company.

As part of its brand development strategy, Adams formed its first product design and retail partnership. Adams and Boots, a British retailer known on the high streets for its mother and baby products, began a collaboration on a line of baby clothes and accessories designed for the midprice market. The innovative line, given the brand name Mini Mode, replaced the existing line of children's clothing at Boots. Mini Mode offered products for three age groups: newborns up to six months, babies up to 18 months, and toddlers from one to four years old. In-store promotions and a £150,000 advertising campaign launched Mini Mode at 260 Boots stores in the United Kingdom and Ireland in February 2003.

International growth continued with new franchise expansion and development. In April 2002, a new franchisee, Shasbank International, opened its first store in New Delhi, India. Adams adjusted the product mix for the climate in India, but retained the store format, brand strategy, and product line in the style of the U.K. brand. With economic growth fostering a taste for international brand clothing in India, Shasbank planned to open six stores over three years. While the first Adams Childrenswear franchise opened in Greece in late 2002, franchisee Fashion Link planned to open 30 stores over six years. The number of franchises in Cyprus increased to eight and the total in Saudi Arabia rose to 30 locations. Locations in the Gulf States increased to 18, including new stores in Kuwait, the United Arab Emirates, Bahrain, and Dubai. Difficulty finding appropriate-sized facilities in Ireland prompted Adams to seek a partnership with Roches, a rapidly growing retailer with locations in downtown, suburban, and regional retail locations. The in-store outlets fit well with other prominent European brands carried by Roches. Adams continued the search for locations for full stores in Ireland.

FUNDING RENOVATIONS AND IMPROVEMENTS

In order to remain competitive and to improve operating efficiency, Adams required an infusion of capital. The company needed to reorganize its warehousing and distribution, older stores needed renovation, and the Adams brand needed to be updated. Adams found new investment funding through Lloyd TSB Development Capital in 2002. Lloyd TSB acquired a 15 percent stake from Bridgeport and obtained an additional £77.5 million in credit financing to fund system and store upgrades.

New funding supported a two-year renovation and reorganization project at the Nuneaton warehouse and distribution center. The company implemented new methods of supply chain management that significantly increased the facility's capacity for warehousing and product movement to nearly 1,000 stores and outlets. These included more than 330 Adams stores in Great Britain and Ireland, 160 Sainsbury stores, over 300 Boots stores, 86 international outlets, plus a handful of smaller outlets. Also, Adams installed the necessary computer systems to accommodate the complex organization of warehousing product from several Asia manufacturers for multibrand, multichannel distribution.

By early 2004, the evolution of Adams' multibrand strategy required the company to restructure its marketing department with the formation of three subsidiaries. One unit oversaw Adams' primary retail marketing. A second unit handled a new partnership with Sainsbury, as Adams developed an exclusive children's clothing brand. The new brand, TU, would replace Adams brand clothing at the company's 160 Sainsbury outlets. Another marketing unit handled Boots' Mini Mode brand and developed other new brands and collections for Boots stores. These included the Mini Essentials line, which supplied basic, low-priced clothing to 100 Boots stores, and the Junior line of back-to-school clothing for school-age children up to 12 years old.

Another new channel of distribution involved entry into New Look, fashion retail stores for women and men. New Look chose Adams Childrenswear as its brand of choice in testing the market for the inclusion of children's clothing in its stores. By selling an established brand, rather than developing a new brand,

New Look gained immediate availability of product with an established reputation as well as the flexibility of the Adams' wide assortment of goods. In September 2004, New Look tested Adams' clothing in five stores with a stock of merchandise for the newborn to ten-year-old age range.

With Dean Murray as the company's new chief executive officer, Adams unveiled a new brand strategy for its principal retail market in 2005, creating the Adams Kids concept to connote familiarity through a more accessible, contemporary moniker. Also, the new name enabled Adams to expand into other children's products, such as toys and educational products, without forming a separate brand. Adams' marketing team designed a new logo, a colorful line drawing of the upper half of an apple with stem and leaf placed above "Adams" in the Adams Kids name. The company applied the logo and brand concept to its web site, launched with a full availability of stock for the first time in August 2006.

Continued success with the Boots collaboration led to a five-year extension of the contract for the Mini Mode brand. Moreover, Adams developed two new labels for Boots. Molly n' Jack, launched in 100 Boots stores, featured fashionable clothing for girls and boys to age four. JCB Junior, for boys up to age four, offered masculine themes and launched at 50 Boots outlets in September 2006. The company also designed layettes for underweight babies and clothing for small children with special medical needs.

International expansion involved new store openings of one store each in Iceland in 2004, and in Slovakia and Finland in 2005. Adams opened two stores in St. Petersburg, Russia, in the fall of 2006. Store development in the Middle East included Jordan and Lebanon, while franchisees planned an additional eight stores for India and entry into Malaysia.

SAVING ADAMS FROM DISSOLVING

Unfortunately, financial troubles arose due to too many discounts, which created cash flow problems, particularly during the Christmas sales season. Adams entered bankruptcy reorganization in early 2007. Administrators closed 59 stores, but the remaining 273 stores and 3,200 jobs were saved due to a buyout by John Shannon. A retail entrepreneur and former chairman of Stead & Simpson shoe stores and of Country Casuals clothing stores, Shannon acquired Adams Kids for £20 million. Operations at Myriad Holding Company, which had been formed as an umbrella company, and at the TU subsidiary, were not affected by the acquisition.

The resulting management turnover included the hiring of a new chief executive officer, David Carter-Johnson, who held the lead position at Adams during Sears' tenure as owner. Carter-Johnson immediately streamlined to reduce costs, removing a layer of management and lowering overhead costs at the Nuneaton facilities.

The primary goal of Adams at this time involved competing with grocery stores. The convenience of one-stop shopping in the hypermarket format served to increase grocery store market share for children's clothing, which rose from 14 percent in 2003 to 21 percent in 2007. Volume discounters such as ASDA further eroded market share for specialty retailers. Moreover, Sainsbury's appropriated control of the TU brand, becoming another Adams competitor. New Look began in-house production of children's clothing design and production as well.

An alternative scheme involved developing higher priced goods, with fashion as the company's primary attraction rather than price. Hence, initial product changes involved new clothing designs using higher-quality fabrics. With this strategy Adams planned to compete with high-end specialty retailers, such as New Zealand's Pumpkin Patch and France's Petit Bateau.

Mary Tradii

PRINCIPAL SUBSIDIARIES

Adams Kids; Mini Mode.

PRINCIPAL COMPETITORS

ASDA Stores Ltd.; Benetton Retail Ltd.; Gap UK Ltd.; H&M Hennes Ltd.; Marks and Spencer plc; Mothercare plc; New Look plc; Petit Bateau; Pumpkin Patch Ltd.; J Sainsbury plc; Tesco plc; Woolworths plc.

FURTHER READING

"Adams," *Euroweek*, August 31, 2001, p. 16.

"Adams and Boots Launch New Baby Clothes Brand," *Birmingham Post*, April 2, 2002, p. 15.

"Adams Axes Director in Restructure," *Marketing*, February 12, 2004, p. 3.

"Adams Chain Reveals Plans to Go Greek," *In-Store Marketing*, October 2002, p. 15.

"Adams Children's Ski Range Attempts to Fill Gap Left by C&A," *Marketing Week*, July 19, 2001, p. 7.

"Adams' Expansion," *Kid's Marketing Report*, January 31, 2001, p. 2.

"Adams Figures Back on Track After Buyout," *Retail Week*, September 8, 2000, p. 2.

"Adams Goes to India," *Birmingham Post*, April 30, 2002, p. 24.

"Adams Highlights Practicality in TV Work by Still Price," *Campaign*, May 29, 1992.

"Adams in Argos Points Deal," *In-Store Marketing*, November 2001, p. 7.

"Adams Is 'TU' Good," *Birmingham Post*, June 3, 2004, p. 24.

"Adams Kids to Launch Year-Round Costumes and Schoolwear Ranges," *Retail Week*, August 4, 2006.

"Adams Review Pays Off in Profits Hike," *In-Store Marketing*, October 2001, p. 49.

"Boots Partners Up on Kids Clothes," *In-Store Marketing*, February 2003, p. 6.

Carter, Sue, "Adams Planning Major Expansion: The British Childrenswear Chain, with 18 Stores in the Republic, Has Lifted Profits 34 Percent and Identified 10 Key Targets for New Outlets Here," *Irish Times*, September 5, 2001.

Cavazza, Manfreda, "New Look Teams up with Adams for Kidswear Push," *Retail Week*, September 24, 2004, p. 1.

"Child's Play at Adams," *In-Store*, April 5, 2005, p. 6.

"European Role at Sears," *Financial Times*, August 31, 1990, p. 34.

"Healthcheck—Adams," *Retail Week*, July 19, 2002, p. 31.

Hobday, Nicola, "UK Kid Clothier Ponders IPO, Merger," *Daily Deal*, August 28, 2001.

"International News—Adams Plots Debut in India and Promises to Be Faithful to UK Brand," *Retail Week*, May 3, 2002, p. 6.

"Jobs Rescued in Adams' Buyout; Retail Deal: Hundreds Saved from Redundancy at Tots' Clothing Giant," *Coventry Evening Telegraph*, February 3, 2007, p. 2.

Johnson, Maureen, and Bill Allen, "Taking the English 'Apple' to Spain: The Adams Experience," *International Journal of Retail & Distribution Management*, November–December 1994, p. 3.

"Management Buyout for Adams Childrenswear," *CWN*, August 28, 1999, http://www.cwn.org.uk/business/a-z/a/adams-childrenswear/1999/08/990828-buyout.html.

"More Good News for Bridgepoint," *European Venture Capital Journal*, June 2002, p. 27.

Morrell, Liz, "Childrenswear—A Brand by Any Other Name," *Retail Week*, September 24, 2004, p. 14.

"New Kid on the Block Hopes to Save Adams," *Daily Mail*, February 2, 2007, p. 79.

Price Brown, Jessica, "Managers Exit Adams As New Chief Recruited," *Retail Week*, March 30, 2007.

Thompson, James, "Adams Board Shake-up Signals Global Ambition," *Retail Week*, October 13, 2006.

Tomilson, Heather, "Adams on Eve of Bid for World Domination of Children's Wear," *London Independent*, June 9, 2002, p. 3.

"Touch of Irish for Adams," *Coventry Evening Telegraph*, November 7, 2002, p. 28.

"U.K.: Adams Names Head of International Operations," *just-style.com,* July 19, 2004.

"'Transport and Logistics Are Core to Retail; Because Stock Is the Lifeblood of the Stores, and, for That Reason, We Would Never Dream of Contracting the Whole Thing Out,'" *Motor Transport,* July 7, 2005, p. 1.

"U.K.: Dean Murray Takes Over As Adams Chief Executive," *just-style.com,* February 8, 2005.

Vickers, Emma, "Adams Chain to Grow Up; Financial: Childrenswear Retailer Needs to Adapt if It Is to Cope with New Foes," *Sunday Express,* September 9, 2007, p. 6.

Young, Jo, "Adams Sets a 300-Store Target for Global Growth," *Retail Week,* October 13, 2000, p. 2.

AeroGrow International, Inc.

6075 Longbow Drive, Suite 200
Boulder, Colorado 80301
U.S.A.
Telephone: (303) 444-7755
Toll Free: (800) GrowNow (800) 476-9669
Fax: (303) 444-0406
Web site: http://www.aerogrow.com

Public Company
Incorporated: 2002 as Magneticare, Inc.
Employees: 75
Sales: $35.2 million (2006)
Stock Exchanges: NASDAQ
Ticker Symbol: AERO
NAIC: 333112 Lawn and Garden Tractor and Home
 Lawn and Garden Equipment Manufacturing

■■■

AeroGrow International, Inc., produces aero-hydroponic systems for the consumer market. Billed as the "world's first kitchen garden appliance," the company's signature AeroGarden circulates air, water, and nutrients over plants' roots to make them grow more than twice as fast as possible in soil.

Founded by entrepreneur Michael Bissonnette in 2002, the company has used television ads, infomercials, and prominent placement with national retailers to achieve large sales volumes quickly. These marketing efforts, and the years of testing and development that have gone into developing the AeroGarden, represent a substantial investment. Escalating demand has also

prompted the company to invest in increasing its manufacturing capabilities. (The products are manufactured under contract in China, with the exception of the seed kits, which are assembled in Colorado.)

While AeroGrow has excelled at growing plants quickly, as well as saturating the marketplace, profits have required more patience. AeroGrow has nevertheless attracted hundreds of investors, many of them from Colorado. It became a public company in 2006 via a reverse merger.

COLORADO ROOTS

Michael Bissonnette established AeroGrow International, Inc., in July 2002. (The entity was actually incorporated in March 2002 as Magneticare, Inc., but changed its name to Aero Grow International, Inc., several months later. It finally adopted AeroGrow International, Inc., as its name upon the February 2006 reverse merger that made it a public company.) AeroGrow was originally controlled by the investment group Mentor Capital Consultants, Inc., of which Bissonnette was CEO and president. Start-up capital was $5 million.

Already an experienced entrepreneur, Bissonnette included among his previous ventures Shagrila Carpets, Inc., a small carpeting chain; consumer security products manufacturer Knight Protective Industries, Inc.; and Voice Powered Technology International, Inc., a maker of voice recognition software for handheld electronics.

Bissonnette and an associate, future marketing chief and investor relations head John Thompson, sifted

COMPANY PERSPECTIVES

AeroGrow is a publicly traded company specializing in the research, development, manufacturing and marketing of consumer products for the emerging "Kitchen Garden" product category, and the developer of the world's first Kitchen Garden Appliance, the AeroGarden. The AeroGarden is a revolutionary kitchen appliance that grows abundant harvests of garden fresh lettuce, tomatoes and herbs year-round, right on the kitchen counter. The AeroGarden uses NASA-tested aeroponic technology to grow plants faster and more reliably than with any other method, with no dirt, weeds or mess. The resulting appliance is so simple to use that anyone, with or without gardening experience, can enjoy great-tasting, healthy, homegrown food. AeroGrow also develops, manufactures and markets a variety of recurring revenue, repeat sales products, including seed kits, lights and nutrients.

through hundreds of ideas for a new enterprise before settling on aeroponics, a soilless method of growing plants. It had been found that increasing the flow of oxygen around the roots boosted growth incredibly. Bissonnette was inspired by the technology on exhibit at Disney's EPCOT Center, and he persuaded one of its developers to join his advisory board.

SEED MONEY

With his track record, Bissonnette was able to raise nearly $9 million in AeroGrow's first two and a half years. According to the *Boulder Daily Camera*, most of AeroGrow's several hundred early shareholders were small local investors.

AeroGrow became a public company in February 2006 via a reverse merger with a five-year-old shell corporation called Wentworth I, Inc. It started trading shares over-the-counter in early 2007 under the ticker symbol "AGWI." Its listing soon moved to the NASDAQ, landing the symbol "AERO."

The vast size of the potential market was one reason for the stock's appeal. The National Gardening Association reckoned gardening to be the most popular hobby in the United States, with more than 70 million participants. There were many other types of potential buyers, including gardening wannabes, foodies, even

parents interested in teaching a bit of life science to their children or office workers who wanted to brighten up their dreary corporate cubicles.

The AeroGarden would move hydroponics out of the realm of the serious hobbyist and make it accessible to virtually anyone. Previously, an indoor growing setup required a series of buckets, tubes, lights, nutrients, and a not inconsiderable amount of skill. The AeroGarden promised spectacular results by going beyond standard hydroponics; in essence, it was delivering state-of-the-art agricultural science.

AN ANCIENT OASIS

The practice of hydroponics dates back as far as the Hanging Gardens of Babylon, one of the Seven Wonders of the World. The innovation known as "aeroponics" also springs from an ancient land. It is perhaps appropriate that the science that inspired the AeroGarden grew out of work at Ein Gedi, Israel, a lush desert oasis mentioned in Song of Songs. In the early 1980s Dr. Hillel Soffer, a researcher at the Volcani Institute there, found that increasing oxygen to the roots of plants greatly increased their growth. (He later conducted further experiments at the University of California at Davis.)

Making a viable consumer appliance out of the idea took AeroGrow more than three years and $9 million. The resulting design featured powerful fluorescent grow lights and modular "seed pods," which sandwiched the seeds in a foam plug. With water trickling over them, the roots grew down through a layer of humid air into a nutrient bath below. All the components for the novel product were custom engineered, including the lightbulbs.

AeroGarden's first prototype did not include its own lights. It was meant to be placed in a sunny window. The addition of powerful fluorescent bulbs made the AeroGarden a year-round, virtually foolproof proposition, one of the key promises of the brand. (A March 2008 piece in the *Boulder Daily Camera* details some of the company's early experiments.)

Another key component was the nutrient tablets AeroGrow developed. In traditional hydroponics, chemicals had to be carefully measured and stored. AeroGrow reduced the procedure to merely dropping a tablet or two into the basin. They were added at pre-scheduled intervals for the original units, but the company soon added a computer-controlled indicator light as a cue for operators.

Even the controlled environment of the AeroGarden was not capable of nurturing every type of plant, however. The company tested hundreds of varieties to find the ones best suited for success. The first available seed kits included herbs, salad greens, cherry tomatoes, and chili peppers.

NATIONAL LAUNCH

AeroGardens made their national retail debut in March 2006 via Sur la Table, an upscale cooking chain. The units were priced at about $150 each. Like many new consumer goods, the AeroGarden's path to mass-market awareness included spots on QVC beginning in July 2006. Television commercials and infomercials were also soon underway.

Promotional efforts received an unexpected boost when producers featured an AeroGarden in the apocalyptic thriller *I Am Legend*, released just a couple weekends before Christmas in 2007. "In the movie, pretty much the only things left on earth are Will Smith, his dog and his AeroGarden," noted Bissonnette.

Revenues for calendar year 2006 were nearly $7 million, but the company posted a net loss of $8.4 million. By this time, the company had accumulated a deficit of almost $28 million. AeroGrow still had fewer than 70 employees, but many of its functions were outsourced. It relied on outside contractors for distribution and handling telephone orders as well as manufacturing.

In 2005 AeroGrow had contracted manufacturing of the lights to Mingkeda Industries Co. Ltd., via an arrangement with Alabama's Source Plus, Inc. AeroGrow traded some of its shares for tooling and price concessions. A few years later, an additional manufacturer, Main Power Electrical Factory Ltd., signed on. AeroGrow made its seed pods in-house at an 1,800-square-foot facility in Longmont, Colorado.

A STREAM OF NEW PRODUCTS

AeroGrow had several products in development even as the original AeroGarden Classic was being launched. It was able to introduce a steady stream of new growing devices, accessories, and seed kits. By early 2008 there were nearly two-dozen different varieties of plants available. With the Master Gardener kit, growers could assemble their own grow pods at home using seeds of their choice. For the experienced gardener, AeroGarden made available a tray with space to start 70 seedlings for transplanting.

The company started shipping live plants in 2007, beginning with strawberries. This was an ambitious undertaking in itself, requiring the company to design a whole supply chain that would enable it to be the first year-round shipper of live strawberry plants. However, it was necessary to ensure consistent results for plants that took months to bear fruit. Another popular product shipped live was the miniature rose garden.

New devices extended AeroGrow's market toward both serious hobbyists and those seeking few demands on their space and time. The Pro100 featured more sophisticated controls while the AeroGarden Pro200 incorporated brighter lights and a longer lamp arm for growing taller plants such as full-sized tomatoes. The SpaceSaver6 was 30 percent smaller than the AeroGarden Classic and specially designed to fit in corners, while the even more compact AeroGarden 3 was the size of a coffeemaker.

WIDESPREAD GROWTH

AeroGrow's President and Chief Operating Officer Jerry Perkins took over the CEO position from Michael Bissonnette in March 2008. Perkins had previously been an executive with Johnson Outdoors Inc. and Brunswick Corporation.

The transition was described as the typical scenario of the creative entrepreneur passing the baton to more professional management. Bissonnette remained onboard as chairman. He had forecast the industry AeroGrow had created, and still had largely to itself, would be a $1 billion one within ten years.

A company official told *Equities* AeroGrow was trying to occupy as much retail space as possible to prevent potential competitors from taking root. It went as far as producing a separate brand called the "Ultimate Kitchen Gardener" for sale through alternate retail channels such as the Home Shopping Network (while QVC had the original AeroGarden brand). The Ultimate Kitchen Gardener was a little smaller, with six pods instead of seven, and saved space by cutting the air layer out of the basin. It sold for a little less than the original AeroGarden.

The company was already active on multiple international fronts. In 2007 it introduced the AeroGarden concept to the United Kingdom, Germany, Austria, and Switzerland via a distribution arrangement with Best Direct (International) Ltd. It also had Japan in its sales territory by the end of the year and signed a Korean distribution deal in early 2008.

The company began mailing out its own catalogs to encourage orders of replacement seed kits and lights as well as accessories for preparing herbs and blending them into salad dressings. By 2008 it was putting out several catalogs annually, five million copies in all.

The concept continued to make its way into more retail storefronts. The AeroGarden was available at 4,000 locations and the company was preparing to enter mass-market channels such as Wal-Mart, Target, and Costco.

Frederick C. Ingram

PRINCIPAL COMPETITORS

General Hydroponics, Inc.; American Hydroponics, Inc.; Green Fortune AB; SMEG S.p.A.; W. Atlee Burpee & Co.; Gardener's Supply Company.

FURTHER READING

"AeroGrow Due for Some Pruning, Vertical Branding Waiting to Fly," *Seeking Alpha,* March 12, 2007.

Africano, Lillian, "AeroGarden: A Farmer's Market in My Kitchen," *Spa Review Worldwide,* November/December 2006.

Avery, Greg, "AeroGrow Finds Market for Countertop Garden," *Boulder (Colo.) Daily Camera,* February 5, 2007.

———, "Boulder, Colo., Businessman Hopes to Market Indoor Plant Machines," *Knight-Ridder/Tribune Business News,* September 12, 2004.

Brooke, Lawrence, "Aero-Hydroponics: The Method of the Future," *MySecretPantry.Com,* 2007.

Gillen, Sharon, "AeroGrow Plants a Bloomin' Good Idea," *Denver Business Journal,* May 21, 2007.

Gresham, Aimie, "A Garden on the Countertop," *Equities,* January 2008, pp. 100+.

Harlan, Jessica Goldbogen, "Built to Produce," *HFN,* March 6, 2006.

Tierney, Jim, "AeroGrow Sprouts Mail Order Arm," *Multichannel Merchant,* September 1, 2007, p. 8.

Wallace, Alicia, "Boulder's AeroGrow Sows Seeds for Expansive Future," *Boulder (Colo.) Daily Camera,* March 3, 2008.

———, "Space-Age Gardening Takes Off," *Denver Rocky Mountain News,* Bus. Sec., March 6, 2008.

Allegis Group, Inc.

7301 Parkway Drive
Hanover, Maryland 21076
U.S.A.
Telephone: (410) 579-4800
Toll Free: (877) 388-3823
Fax: (410) 540-7556
Web site: http://www.allegisgroup.com

Private Company
Incorporated: 1993
Employees: 5,000
Sales: $4.4 billion (2006 est.)
NAIC: 561310 Employment Placement Agencies;
   541611 Administrative Management and General
   Management Consulting Services

■ ■ ■

Allegis Group, Inc., is a privately owned, Hanover, Maryland-based holding company for a global family of personnel staffing and recruitment agencies. U.S. subsidiaries include Aerotek, serving technical, professional, and industrial needs, ranging from laborers to architects; Stephen James Associates, a recruitment company focusing on accounting and finance, banking, human resources, sales, and marketing personnel; and TEKsystems, specializing in the staffing and recruitment of information technology personnel. Aerotek units are also located in Puerto Rico, Canada, the Netherlands, and Germany, while TEKsystems maintains offshoots in Canada, the Netherlands, and Germany. In addition, Allegis Group India offers staffing services to Bangalore,

India, and nearby areas, and Allegis Group United Kingdom does the same for the United Kingdom and Ireland. The cofounder and primary owner of Allegis Group, Stephen J. Bisciotti, is also the owner of the Baltimore Ravens franchise of the National Football League (NFL).

MOVING TO BALTIMORE AREA: 1961

Born in Philadelphia, Pennsylvania, in 1960, Steve Bisciotti moved with his family a year later to the Baltimore suburb of Severna Park, where he grew up an avid sports fan, dedicated to the NFL's Baltimore Colts and the Baltimore Orioles of Major League Baseball. His father, Bernard, worked in construction sales, until his death from leukemia in 1969. His grandfather helped support the family while Bisciotti chipped in as a teenager, learning the value of hard work by pumping gas, mowing lawns, working in a restaurant kitchen, and babysitting. He played sports but his passion for athletics far outpaced his talent. Bisciotti was also a poor student. He was told he lacked focus, but was more than likely the victim of an undiagnosed learning disorder. Nevertheless, his mother urged him to attend college, and despite his grades he was accepted by Salisbury State College in Maryland. After failing statistics and managerial economics in his junior year, Bisciotti gave up on a business degree and instead switched to psychology as a way to prepare himself for a career in sales like his father and grandfather. He graduated from Salisbury in 1982 with a less than stellar 2.05 GPA.

FORMATION OF AEROTEK: 1983

Bisciotti returned home and took a job with a Baltimore firm that placed contract engineers, but just 15 months later the company went out of business, leaving him unemployed. He turned for advice to his future father-in-law, Jim Foote, who suggested the 23-year-old start his own business. When Bisciotti pointed out his age and lack of finances, just $3,500 in the bank, Foote countered with the argument, "Well, you ain't got far to fall." Persuaded to give entrepreneurship a try, Bisciotti decided in 1983 to start his own engineering placement service under the name Aerotek Inc.

So that he could concentrate on sales and marketing, Bisciotti brought in his cousin, James Davis, regarded as the cofounder of Allegis Group, to handle the business aspects of the company. They set up shop in the basement of the townhouse Bisciotti shared with two roommates in Annapolis, Maryland, furnishing the office with a pair of desks bought from Goodwill Industries and an orange shag carpet held together by duct tape. To make sure he took the venture seriously, Bisciotti put on a suit and tie before walking down the stairs to start his day in the basement.

After visiting the engineering managers of all the area companies, Bisciotti was able to land a pair of aerospace clients, allowing him to take a weekly salary of $100. The company enjoyed strong growth, partly the result of good timing. A technology boom was underway, but another key factor was Bisciotti's commitment, hard work, and willingness to take chances. He hired new college graduates based on their aggressiveness rather than experience and was not afraid to borrow money to grow the business. He also proved to be a good leader, acting like a football coach or baseball manager, able to stroke people when they deserved compliments but more than willing to confront and challenge underachievers. In this way he was able to develop a team of employees who shared his vision for Aerotek and dedicated themselves to growing the company.

At the end of the first year, Aerotek posted sales of $1.5 million, but that was just the start. The company built on its strong start and grew at a fast pace. In the late 1980s Bisciotti decided to expand beyond the contract engineer business by launching a new subsidiary, Data Temps, to provide data entry services. The name was later changed to Maxim Group. In 1990 Aerotek sought to take advantage of the increasing need for communications services personnel and formed Aerotek Telecommunications Services. Soon Bisciotti and Davis were ready to take their business international.

ESTABLISHMENT OF ALLEGIS GROUP: 1993

In 1993 Allegis Group was formed to serve as a holding company for the growing family of staffing and recruitment companies. Dedicated to information technology infrastructure and staffing, Aerotek Data Service Group was also established in 1993, as was Aerotek Europe in the United Kingdom in November of that year. At the same time, a number of Aerotek divisions were formed in Europe, including Maxim, Telecoms, Engineering, and TEKsystems. In short order, TEKsystems, with operations in the United States and Europe, became the leading name in staffing for the applications, infrastructure, and communications fields.

The Allegis companies thrived in the mid- to late 1990s. Aerotek Europe also enjoyed strong growth. A Netherlands company was acquired in June 1995, and in that same month the Petrochemical division was formed. A German division was established in 1999, as was a Managed Service division in the United Kingdom.

BISCIOTTI RELINQUISHES CONTROL: 1997

In 1997 Bisciotti decided to lessen his time commitment to Allegis Group. After years of traveling 40 weeks out of the year, he relinquished day-to-day control of the company in order to spend more time with his family. "It just got to the point where I was wealthier than I ever thought I would be and knew I didn't need to make more money," he explained to the *Baltimore Sun.* "And my boys were of the age that my brother and I were when I didn't have a father. It was just the right time." He stayed on as co-chairman of Allegis, involved in big-picture strategy that kept him busy about one day a week.

Bisciotti soon had another pursuit, one that could involve his two sons: sports ownership. When the

```
┌─────────────────────────────────────────┐
│                                         │
│              KEY DATES                  │
│                 ■                       │
│                                         │
│  1983:  Stephen Bisciotti and James Davis found │
│         Aerotek.                        │
│  1990:  Aerotek Telecommunications Services is │
│         formed.                         │
│  1993:  Allegis Group is established as a holding │
│         company for related staffing companies. │
│  1997:  Bisciotti relinquishes day-to-day control. │
│  2002:  Aerotek Europe becomes Allegis Group Ltd. │
│  2006:  Stephen James Associates is established. │
│  2008:  Major, Lindley & Africa is acquired. │
│                                         │
└─────────────────────────────────────────┘
```

Orioles were acquired by a local businessman in 1993 it became apparent to Bisciotti that he too had enough money to own a sports franchise. In 1998 he was presented with a chance to acquire the Florida Marlins baseball team, and considered it only because the Marlins and his beloved Orioles played in different leagues. In the end, he passed on the opportunity, but a year later sports deal maker John Moag suggested he try to buy the Baltimore Ravens, whose owner, Art Modell, was in financial trouble and needed to sell the franchise that a few years earlier he had moved from Cleveland. In debt to the NFL, Modell was on the verge of having the league take over the franchise and sell it on the open market. Although Bisciotti could have purchased the team outright, he bought 49 percent of the Ravens in 1999 for $275 million and an option to acquire the rest five years later. In this way, Modell was able to leave football after a 40-year tenure with a measure of grace and Bisciotti was able to become accustomed to the role of team owner. Some of the cash he brought to the Ravens was used on free agents that helped to bring a Super Bowl championship to Baltimore in January 2001. Bisciotti, who remained close to his childhood and college friends, spent more of the money he made from Allegis to charter a plane to take them and their families, more than 150 in all, to watch the Super Bowl victory in Tampa, Florida. In 2004 he paid Modell another $325 million to become majority owner of the Ravens at age 44. Not only one of the youngest, Bisciotti was one of the more low-key NFL owners, engaged in all the major decisions but far from meddlesome. "I left Allegis because I didn't want to work 60 or 70 hours a week anymore. I was real good being those people's bosses. I'm not qualified to be the boss of the Ravens," he told the *Annapolis (Md.) Capital.* "I earned the right to be the boss of Allegis, I bought my way into the Ravens."

The management team Bisciotti put in place at Allegis maintained the company's steady growth rate while he turned his attention to the Ravens. Because the company was privately held, sales figures were not readily available, but due to Bisciotti's sudden celebrity the little-known firm drew some attention from the Maryland media. In 1998 the *Sun* estimated that Aerotek generated revenues of $894 million in 1998, while TEKsystems Inc. brought in $602 million, Maxim Group $529 million, Maxim Healthcare Services another $119 million, and Onsite Engineering and Management Inc. $374 million. A year earlier the Aerotek Data Services Group had been folded into TEKsystems to offer both staffing and managed services. The subsidiary grew even larger in 2002 when Maxim Group was added, creating a one-stop shop for IT staffing, infrastructure, applications, and telecommunications services.

In the late 1990s Allegis Group attempted to become a consolidator in the accounting industry and acquire a number of other professional-services companies in such areas as human resources, asset-management, and technology consulting. In 1998 Allegis acquired the Baltimore accounting firm of Stout, Causey & Horning to serve as a consolidation vehicle, but only a few months later Allegis ended the effort when it was unable to attract enough desirable accounting firms to sell out.

AEROTEK EUROPE: 2000

The new century brought especially strong growth to the European operation, which was repositioned as a full-service solutions company. In 2000 the United Kingdom's Barclay Personnel was acquired and re-branded Aerotek Europe. Another U.K. firm, Genesis Recruitment & Stone Personnel, was also bought in April 2000. An Aerotek Europe operation was then established in the Republic of Ireland in February 2001, and in that same month Aerotek Europe Managed IT Solutions was launched. Two months later Aerotek Europe was rebranded as Allegis Group Ltd., while the IT & Telecoms division was renamed IT&C Strategic Staffing and the Engineering division became Engineering Staffing Solutions. An Education Staffing Solutions division was established in the United Kingdom in early 2002, and more changes followed in 2003. The Petrochemical division was renamed Oil & Gas Staffing Solutions, and Managed IT Services became Allegis Group IT Solutions. Also, in July 2003, Allegis Europe formed the Business Services division.

Allegis Group generated total revenues of $2.6 billion in 2003. A year later the company struck a deal that it hoped would be a blueprint for the future. In May 2004 Aerotek won a four-year contract with California-based Solectron Corp., global provider of electronics manufacturing and integrated supply chain services. The deal called for Aerotek to staff 18 Solectron facilities in the United States and Canada with as many as 4,000 manufacturing, light technical, and administrative contract employees. Aerotek hoped to prove itself to Solectron in order to win the company's global business, conducted in more than 20 countries.

While subsidiaries grew through the opening of new offices around the world, Allegis also expanded through start-ups and acquisitions. In 2006 the chairman of the Maryland Stadium Authority, Carl A. J. Wright, launched Stephen James Associates for Allegis, the name drawn from the first names of the Allegis cofounders. A recruiting firm, Stephen James started out with offices in the Baltimore area; Boston; Charlotte, North Carolina; and northern Virginia. Subsequent offices were opened in Ft. Lauderdale, Boca Raton, and Miami, Florida, and Cincinnati, Ohio. Wright's goal was to grow the firm into a $1 billion company with 50 offices in 12 years. In 2008 Allegis acquired the 26-year-old legal placement firm Major, Lindley & Africa, the

largest search firm of its kind in the world, with offices in the United States, London, and Hong Kong.

Ed Dinger

PRINCIPAL SUBSIDIARIES

Aerotek; Stephen James Associates; TEKsystems; Allegis Group India; Allegis Group United Kingdom.

PRINCIPAL COMPETITORS

Adecco S.A.; CDI Corp.; MPS Group, Inc.

FURTHER READING

Apperson, Jay, "It Was Baltimore or Nothing for Buyer," *Baltimore Sun,* December 20, 1999, p. 1A.

Hensley, Jamison, "New Raven Majority Owner Steve Bisciotti Still Clings to His Boyhood Values, Friends," *Baltimore Sun,* July 25, 2004, p. 1E.

Smith, Jamie, "Hanover, Md., Staffing Firm to Provide 4,000 Workers for Electronics Maker," *Baltimore Sun,* May 18, 2004.

Unger, Mike, "Ravens' Owner a Self-Made Man," *Annapolis (Md.) Capital,* May 16, 2004, p. A1.

Anadolu Efes Biracilik ve Malt Sanayii A.S.

———— ■ ————

Bahcelievler Mah Adnan Kahveci Bulvari No. 5
Istanbul, 34870
Turkey
Telephone: (+90 212) 449 36 00
Fax: (+90 212) 641 96 44
Web site: http://www.efesbev.com

Public Company
Incorporated: 1969
Employees: 1,006
Sales: TRL 3.03 billion ($1.5 billion) (2007)
Stock Exchanges: Istanbul
Ticker Symbol: AEFES
NAIC: 312120 Breweries; 312111 Soft Drink Manu-
    facturing

■ ■ ■

Anadolu Efes Biracilik ve Malt Sanayii A.S. (Anadolu Efes) is Turkey's leading beer and soft-drinks producer, the sixth largest in Europe, and ranks 16th in the world. The Istanbul-based company operates breweries, as well as bottling and malting companies in 13 countries, including Turkey, Russia, Kazakhstan, Serbia, and Moldova. The company's 17 breweries reached a total brewing capacity of 34.5 million hectoliters in 2007. Efes's six malteries produce more than 236,000 tons per year, while its 12 bottling facilities have a capacity of 670 million cases per year. Anadolu Efes's beer portfolio includes nearly 70 brands, including flagship Efes; Beliy Medved, Stary Melnik, Krasny Vostok, and Zhigu-levskoe in Russia; Sokol, Kragandinskoe (Kazakhstan),

Chisinau, Vitanta (Moldova); Pils Plus, Standard, Zaje-carsko (Serbia); as well as a number of licensed brands, such as Miller Genuine Draft, SOL, and Warsteiner. Anadolu Efes's international brewery operations are conducted through its 70 percent stake in publicly listed, Netherlands-based Efes Breweries International.

Beer sales in Turkey represent 32 percent of Ana-dolu Efes's annual sales of TRL 3.03 billion ($1.5 bil-lion), while international beer sales account for 36 percent. Overall Turkey remains the company's largest single market, generating a total of 57 percent of its an-nual revenues, beer and soft drinks included. Soft drinks, particularly Anadolu Efes's 50.3 percent stake in Coca-Cola İçecek A.S. (CCI) represent 32 percent of the group's sales. CCI is one of the world's largest Coca-Cola bottling companies, holding the franchise for seven countries and a potential population of more than 120 million. Anadolu Efes was founded in 1969 as part of Anadolu Endüstri Holding, one of Turkey's largest conglomerates, controlled by the Yazici and Özilhan families. Anadolu Efes is listed on the Istanbul Stock Exchange. Kamil Yazici is the company's chairman; Ale-jandro Jimenez is president of the Efes Beer Group, and Michael O'Neill is president of the Efes Soft Drinks Group.

CHALLENGING THE GOVERNMENT BEER DOMINANCE IN 1969

The Turkish market for beer had been dominated by the country's government-owned breweries into the 1960s. Beer drinkers were offered little choice other than the

COMPANY PERSPECTIVES

Our vision is: to become one of the leading beer systems in the world with core strengths generated in Eurasia. Our mission is: To maximize sustainable stakeholder value. To make our flagship brand "Efes" global.

government's beer brands, with the exception of a joint venture producing the Tuburg brand under license.

This situation changed in the late 1960s when a rising industrial conglomerate owned by Kamil Yazici and Izzet Özilhan became interested in the sector. Yazici and Özilhan had founded the company, later known as Anadolu Endüstri, in the 1950s in order to invest in developing a range of trade and industrial companies. In 1966, Anadolu formed a new company, known as Efes, and began construction of its first two breweries, in Erciyas and Ege. Production at both breweries commenced in 1969, followed by the launch of the Efes Pilsen brand.

In order to impose the brand on the Turkish market, Efes devised a three-pronged strategy. The group focused on developing a strong distribution network, while at the same time adopting an aggressive pricing approach. Importantly, Efes also recognized the potential of adapting Western-styled advertising campaigns for the Turkish market. The company's strong investment in advertising, especially television advertising, quickly helped develop its brand throughout the country. Efes would become one of Turkey's most well-known brands, with a recognition level approaching 100 percent.

The company also invested in developing its infrastructure through the 1970s and 1980s. In 1971, the company inaugurated its own hops processing facility in Tarbes; this was followed by the construction of a malting plant, in Afyon, completed in 1973. With its sales rising, the company built a third brewery, in Guney, which launched production in 1974.

Efes added a second malting factory in 1984. The company also became the first in Turkey to launch sales of canned beer, in 1986. By then, Efes had also established a dedicated marketing and distribution subsidiary, Efes Pazarlama, as its sales spread to a national basis. Efes also took a number of its operations public, including its four breweries.

SOFT DRINKS IN 1993

By the early 1990s, Efes had captured a significant percentage of the Turkish beer market, a level that was to top 80 percent by 2000. With future growth in the beer sector becoming more limited, the company eyed an expansion into other drinks categories. Turkey's status as a Muslim country naturally led the company to seek to develop a nonalcoholic branch. While Turkey's secularism remained anchored in the country's constitution, the large population of religious Muslims, for whom alcoholic beverages were proscribed, meant that Efes was unable to reach this consumer segment. An attempt to launch an alcohol-free beer had failed, however.

Instead, the company sought entry into the soft-drinks market. Its first step toward this effort was to create a new company, Efes Sinai Yatirim Holding, in 1993. Also known as Efes Invest, this company then began acquiring Coca-Cola bottling franchises within the markets of the newly created Commonwealth of Independent States (CIS). In order to raise investment capital, the company sold a 25 percent stake in Efes Invest to outside investors the following year.

The company's first investment, in Kazakhstan, began bottling Coke in 1995. This was soon followed by bottling plants in Kyrgyzstan and Azerbaijan in 1996. That same year, Efes acquired a 33 percent stake in four Coca-Cola bottling companies operating in Turkey. This acquisition placed Efes in partnership with the Coca-Cola Company, and gave it control of 80 percent of that company's franchise network in Turkey.

Efes continued developing its brewery operations at the same time, inaugurating its fourth and most modern brewery in Ankara in 1995. The company then acquired rival Toros Biracilik, including its Marmara brand and its brewery in Lüleburgaz, in 1998.

INTERNATIONAL EXPANSION

Efes's dominance of the Turkish brewery market meant that its only choice to continue building its brewery business was to turn to the international market. The company took a first step toward establishing its foreign presence by acquiring the Karaganda Brewery in Kazakhstan, as part of the country's privatization program. The new brewery added 400,000 hectoliters of brewing capacity, as well as its own malting facility, while also enabling Efes to roll out its own flagship brand into that market.

Under CEO İlker Kerimoğlu, Efes developed an ambitious international growth strategy. For this, the company incorporated a new subsidiary, Efes Breweries

```
╔══════════════════════════════════════╗
║              KEY DATES               ║
║                 ■                    ║
╠══════════════════════════════════════╣
```

1966: Kamil Yazici and Izzet Özilhan found Efes and begin building two breweries in Turkey.

1969: Breweries launch production; company begins building hops processing and malting plants.

1986: Company becomes first in Turkey to market canned beer.

1993: Company forms soft drink subsidiary Efes Sinai Yatirim Holding (later Efes Invest), acquires Coca-Cola franchise.

1995: Company acquires first international Coca-Cola franchise in Kazakhstan.

1998: Efes Breweries International (EBI) is formed in the Netherlands as part of international brewery expansion.

2001: Company restructures soft-drink operations into Coca-Cola Içecek A.S. (CCI).

2003: EBI goes public on London stock exchange.

2007: Company acquires Krasny Vostok Brewing Group, becoming one of top five brewers in Russia.

International (EBI), headquartered in the Netherlands, in 1998. By the end of that year, EBI had overseen the launch of Efes's first newly constructed brewery outside of Turkey, in Ploieşti, Romania. This was quickly followed by the company's entry into Russia, one of the world's top five beer consumption markets, with the construction of a modern brewery and a malting plant in Moscow. Built in partnership with the Moscow government, the new brewery launched its first brand, Stary Melnik, in 1999. In just two years, Stary Melnik succeeded in establishing itself as the leading premium beer in the Moscow market.

With its international operations well underway, Efes launched a restructuring at home. Part of this involved merging its four publicly listed breweries, along with the malting operations, into a single company, which became Anadolu Efes. This process was completed in 2000, with the new company retaining its public listing.

The company next began reorganizing its Coca-Cola bottling franchise in Turkey. This process created two new subsidiaries, one for production, the other for sales and marketing. The restructuring of the company's soft-drinks operations was to continue into the early 2000s, resulting in the creation of Coca-Cola Içecek A.S. (CCI), held at 50.3 percent by Efes, in 2002.

MOVING INTO THE EUROPEAN LEAD IN THE NEW CENTURY

Efes's international operations were also growing strongly. The company added a brewery in Ukraine in 2001, constructed as part of a joint venture with IN-VESCO CEAM. The company also began adding a number of licensed brands, including Miller Genuine Draft in 2000, and Becks in 2002, both for the Turkish market, then Warsteiner Premium for the Russian market in 2002. Other foreign brands added through the middle of the decade included Czech brand Zlatoprament, introduced into Russia, and Fosters, introduced into Turkey, in 2005; the Dutch Bavaria brand, in Russia, and Mexico's SOL, both in 2006. Efes also launched a number of new labels under its own brand, including Efes Ice in 2006 and, in 2007, the wheat beer Gusta as well as a lemon and agave flavored beer called Mariachi.

This brand growth was supported by an ambitious expansion of the group's international brewery network. The company bought Moldova's leading brewer and soft-drinks group, Vitanta Intravest, in 2003, then bought control of Belgrade, Serbia-based Pancevo Brewery (renamed as Efes Weifert) that year. The company strengthened its presence in Russia, buying the Amstar Brewery, in Ufa, in the Urals region. One year later, Efes claimed the number three spot in Serbia, after buying majority control of Zajecar Brewery there. Also in that year, Efes Breweries International went public, listing its shares on the London Stock Exchange in order to generate investment interest from a wider community. Efes's stake in EBI then dropped to 70 percent.

The public offering came in support of a new investment campaign by EBI in the first half of the first decade of the 2000s. The company built new breweries, including a brewery in Rostov, Russia, and one in Amaty, Kazakhstan. The company also launched the expansion of a number of its existing facilities, including the breweries in Ufa, Moldova, and Rostov in 2005. By the end of that year, the company's total brewery capacity neared 12 million hectoliters.

Efes soft-drinks wing was also growing strongly, following the group's announcement in 2003 that it intended to spend more than $150 million on its expansion. The company added a new market when it acquired 90 percent of The Coca-Cola Bottling Company of Jordan in 2005. Efes Invest, soon to be acquired by CCI, also founded a 50-50 joint venture to establish the Coca-Cola Bottling Company of Iraq FZCO that year. CCI then added a spring water brand, Mahmudiye, acquired in 2006.

While Efes continued to build up its presence in the Baltic region and among the members of the CIS, Russia, the world's third largest beer-drinking market, clearly retained Efes's strongest attention. The company continued to seek to expand its market share there, and in 2007 landed its biggest fish. In that year, the company bought Krasny Vostok Brewing Group, the seventh largest brewer in Russia. The acquisition catapulted Efes itself into the top five, and added another strong, national brand to its portfolio there.

Efes remained on the lookout for new markets and opportunities. In early 2008, the company launched a joint-venture agreement with Heineken to build two breweries in Uzbekistan. Efes and Heineken also agreed to merge their operations in Kazakhstan and Serbia. Efes remained the majority partner in all three businesses. Continuing its expansion in the region, Efes also completed the acquisition of Lomisi, the leading brewer in Georgia. The acquisition gave Efes a 42 percent market share. In just ten years since the launch of its international expansion, Efes had grown into Europe's sixth largest brewery and soft-drinks group, and the 16th largest in the world.

M. L. Cohen

PRINCIPAL SUBSIDIARIES

Coca-Cola Içecek A.S. (50.3%); Efes Breweries International N.V. (Netherlands; 70%); Efes Pazarlama ve Dagitim Tic. A.S.; Tarbes Tarim Ürünleri ve Besicilik San. Tic. A.S.

PRINCIPAL COMPETITORS

Allied Domecq PLC; SABMiller PLC; Whitbread PLC; Aachener und Munchener; Guinness Ltd.; Anheuser-Busch; Heineken NV; Bass Brewers; Interbrew SA; Brau und Brunnen; Nestlé SA; Brauerei BECK; Paulaner Salvator Beteiligungs; Budvar; PepsiCo, Inc.; Carlsberg; Plzensky Prazdroj; Central European Distribution Corporation; South African Breweries; Coca-Cola Company; Tucher Bräu; Danone SA.

FURTHER READING

Conway, Edmund, "Turkish Brewer in Float Plan," *Daily Telegraph,* May 15, 2004.

"Efes Breweries Completes Lomisi Acquisition," *just-drinks.com,* February 22, 2008.

"Heineken, Efes Breweries Enter Joint Venture," *Beverage World,* February 15, 2008, p. 12.

"Efes Breweries International Sees Volumes up in '07," *just-drinks.com,* January 21, 2008.

"Efes Confirms Consolidation of Krasny Vostok Stake," *just-drinks.com,* November 21, 2007.

"Moscow-Based Efes Brewery Has Made a Significant Move to Capture Some of the Regional Beer Markets," *Moskovski Novosti,* June 27, 2000.

"Russian Thirst Slaker to Float in London," *Guardian,* May 15, 2004, p. 29.

Spain, William, "Ilker Keremoglu: Efes Pilsen," *Advertising Age,* December 8, 1997, p. S12.

Auvil Fruit Company, Inc.

21902 State Route 97
Orondo, Washington 98844
U.S.A.
Telephone: (509) 784-1033
Fax: (509) 784-1712
Web site: http://www.auvilfruit.com

Private Company
Incorporated: 1928
Employees: 100
Sales: $32.2 million (2007)
NAIC: 111331 Apple Orchards

■ ■ ■

Auvil Fruit Company, Inc., grows Granny Smith, Fuji, Gala, and Pink Lady apples on its 1,385 acres in the Pacific Northwest and markets them under the brand names Elite, Gee Whiz, and Topaz in the United States and Canada. The company also grows Rainier and Bing cherries. Founder Grady Auvil has been recognized many times over for promoting innovation in the tree fruit-growing industry and for being willing to take risks and plant new varieties of fruit.

STARTING A SMALL FAMILY ORCHARD: 1928–50

In 1928, Grady Auvil, his wife, Lillie, and Auvil's two brothers, Robert and David, started an apple orchard in Orondo, Washington. The Auvils bought 150 acres of land that "was nothing but sagebrush" or "new country,"

according to Grady Auvil in a 1992 *Oregonian* article; on it, they planted 22 fruit trees. The Auvil family had relocated to the Pacific Northwest from West Virginia in 1908; the three young Auvil brothers learned tree fruit growing when their father began raising apples along the Entiat River in Washington State.

Auvil Fruit Company remained relatively small through its first two decades. In the mid-1940s, Grady Auvil began to promote his philosophy of providing the best possible quality fruit no matter the price. Although this might have put him at odds with retailers, whose interests lay in lower costs, Auvil impressed his business partners by staying on the experimental edge of new varieties of production. As he explained in an article that appeared in the *Oregonian* in 1992, his commitment was to live in a "constant effort to do better and be better—not only for you but for everyone around you."

Auvil was, according to those who knew him, both a visionary and a genius when it came to planting fruit trees, a man with a sense of his own destiny and little time to waste. Auvil took the doors off his cars so that he could get in and out of them more quickly; he developed a method for tying his shoes with one hand and taught those around him to do so as well. The center of Auvil Fruit was Grady Auvil's kitchen table where he met with fruit farmers and brokers from around the world.

In 1948, Auvil Fruit built a packing house with state-of-the-art equipment (that it would later update with newer cold-storage capacity and continue to use until 1995). Then, in the mid-1950s, the company

COMPANY PERSPECTIVES

One bad apple may not spoil the barrel, but it can spoil consumer confidence. That's why crisp, crunchy, good-tasting apples have always been the ultimate goal at Auvil Fruit Company. Few growers in Washington State, or anywhere else for that matter, have gone further to consistently deliver premium quality apples. Auvil's ongoing internationally recognized support of research and development has resulted in many innovations in the fruit growing industry.

began to expand. With the pending creation of the Rocky Reach Dam in Wenatchee, Washington, Auvil Fruit sold its land west of old Highway 97 and the Columbia River, which was flooded when the dam was filled in 1958. It planted new orchards to the east of both.

EXPLORING CHERRIES AND NECTARINES: THE SIXTIES AND SEVENTIES

Auvil also built Daroga Park, a public park named for the three brothers, on high ground on its land around 1960. The park had camping stalls and a swimming area and boat launch, and remained open to the public throughout the sixties. In the seventies, the company converted the park area to provide housing for summer help and, in 1980, it sold the property to the state and federal government for a minimal sum.

However, the park proved successful for another reason. The company used the park land for planting Bing and Rainier cherry trees and Red Gold nectarines starting in the mid-sixties. Although the Rainier cherry trees were originally intended only as pollinizers, Auvil noticed that if the fruits were allowed to ripen, they got large and sweet. After closing the park in the mid-seventies, Auvil invested more heavily in planting cherries and nectarines. In 1975, the company brought Rainier cherries to the commercial market, introducing its field packing program to accommodate the white Rainier cherry's easily bruised flesh. It contracted with Raley's grocery chain of California to become their main supplier of cherries, nectarines, and apples.

The price of nectarines peaked through the sixties and then topped out in the seventies. During the same time period, bitter winters caused severe damage to Auvil's nectarine and cherry trees in 1964 and 1969. These

two factors led to the company's decision to exit the nectarine market and to focus once again on apples, beginning with the Granny Smith, which Grady Auvil traveled to New Zealand to investigate in the early seventies.

EXPANSION IN THE EIGHTIES

The 1970s were in other ways, too, a time of new directions for Auvil Fruit Company. The relationship among the three brothers had always been rocky and, after David Auvil died in 1968 and Robert Auvil sold his share in the company in 1973, Grady Auvil increased his experiments with new varieties of apples.

The apple industry standard since the 1920s had been the Red Delicious, but beginning in 1972, Auvil Fruit started planting Granny Smith apples. Since 1915, Washington had been the nation's leading apple producer, and, in 1969, Grady Auvil played a key role in establishing the Washington Tree Fruit Research Commission (WTFRC). The purpose of this commission, according to the WTFRC web site, was to "support researchers in their efforts to explore ways to improve fruit storage, decrease insect effects on fruit and grow better fruit which will increase the revenues of the growers of Washington State." The commission also administers "specific industry service programs ... which will or may benefit the planting, production, harvesting, handling, processing or shipment of tree fruit" of Washington State.

In 1980, when the company added 1,000 acres in Vantage, Washington, it began what Auvil Fruit referred to as its "big expansion." Between 1980 and 1992, Auvil Fruit Company tripled in size. In 1988, it started planting Fuji apples, smuggling in bud wood from Japan through Canada. During this decade, too, Auvil planted an additional 30 acres of Rainier cherries after arranging, through Horizon, a fruit brokerage company that specialized in shipping produce to Japan, to provide gift boxes of Rainier cherries to the Japanese market.

INVESTING IN NEW VARIETIES OF APPLES

Meanwhile, changes were afoot among the Pacific Northwest's tree fruit growers. By 1990, Washington, the nation's leading apple producer since 1915, produced 60 percent of the nation's apple crop. The Red Delicious, still the nation's favorite apple in 1994, covered more than 120,000 of the state's 160,000 acres of apple orchards. By 1990, however, the preceding three years of poor prices (due in part to the Alar pesticide scare) were causing growers to reassess their options.

```
┌─────────────────────────────────────────┐
│                                         │
│            KEY DATES                    │
│               ■                         │
│  ─────────────────────────────────      │
│                                         │
│  1928:  Grady Auvil and his brothers    │
│         found Auvil Fruit Company.      │
│  1948:  The company builds a packing    │
│         house with state-of-the-art     │
│         equipment.                      │
│  1973:  Robert Auvil sells his share    │
│         in the company to Grady Auvil.  │
│  1980:  The company buys 1,000 acres    │
│         at Vantage, Washington.         │
│  1995:  The company completes its new   │
│         packing warehouse and fruit     │
│         storage facility in Orondo,     │
│         Washington.                     │
│  1998:  Grady Auvil dies and Paul King  │
│         becomes president; Jim Wright   │
│         becomes general manager.        │
│  2003:  Jim Wright becomes chief        │
│         executive.                      │
│                                         │
└─────────────────────────────────────────┘
```

By this time other growers were investing heavily in the dull red and yellow Fuji, originally developed in Japan, which brought a much higher wholesale price and had a longer shelf life. Growers were also planting Granny Smith, Gala, and Braeburn stock and taking advantage of new dwarf stock and denser planting methods to shorten the time between putting new stock in the ground and harvesting fruit and to allow for more fruit per acre. Dwarf root stocks could tolerate up to 1,500 trees per acre by the late 1990s and brought orchards to full production in four years' time. They also lowered labor costs because workers could pick trees from the ground. "You used to grow apples so they would come into production in 10 to 15 years' time and keep producing for 70 years," according to a horticulturist quoted in the *Seattle Times* in 1994. "Now an orchard should be in production four years from planting. The life of an orchard is 12 to 15 years. Not because the trees are dying. It's because the varieties are changing rapidly."

Auvil, always on the forefront of new ways of doing things, had in mind planting even more densely. "We're working on growing up to 4,000 trees to the acre," he announced in the 1992 *Oregonian*. "I don't know how that's going to work out, but it's an idea." This number of trees bore no comparison to the "30 to 50 or 60 trees to the acre" in a mature orchard that he recalled from the days when he was starting out in the apple business. Although high-density planting cost up to $27,000 an acre to put in, "[t]here's never been a chance like there is right now to make money—$40,000 to $50,000 an

acre in a four-year-old orchard. ... If you make $20,000 an acre net, that's more than the orchard sells for," he explained.

In 1995, Auvil Fruit doubled its apple-packing capacity with the opening of a $5 million, 60,000-square-foot packing house with computerized controls in Orondo, Washington. This represented its first addition since 1948. The new Van Doren and Aweta equipment it had purchased was able to pack up to 12,000 boxes of apples in a workday. The packing house also included a new transport system, the first of its kind in North America, that handled the apples more gently than before. The addition made it easier to process Auvil's 400 acres of Granny Smith, 425 acres of Fuji, and 100 acres of Gala and to supply its customers in a timely manner. The company also had 30 acres of Rainier cherries in Orondo.

The year 1996 produced a bumper crop of apples. Then in 1997, Washington growers, who accounted for 25 percent of the world's apple market, faced multiple challenges. Sales of apples were flat domestically, while sales in many Pacific Rim countries, the state's second largest market, had dropped by 50 percent from 1996 totals as foreign currencies lost value against the dollar. In addition, growers faced losing Washington's largest export market when Mexico slapped a tax on imported American apples in 1997. To make matters worse, the U.S. Border Patrol stepped up enforcement against illegal aliens, worsening a labor shortage as unions attempted to organize the packers and pickers. Damage from hail and fewer blossoms led to a crop that was 10 percent smaller as overseas shipments declined 40 percent in all.

PERPETUATING GRADY AUVIL'S LEGACY: 1996

Around 1996, Paul King became general manager of Auvil Fruit. Despite larger crops in 1998, the tighter global market put the apple industry in a precarious position and left profits slim to nonexistent for many growers. Auvil continued to be a steady presence at his warehouse or in his orchards until he died in December 1998. After Auvil's death at age 93, Paul King became president and Jim Wright became general manager. Paying tribute to Auvil, the president of the Washington Apple Commission was quoted in a December 1998 *Yakima Herald Republic* article as saying, "The legacy of Grady Auvil has been innovation. You look at all the varieties in the state, and he was the first one. He had his eye on the future." Among Auvil's many honors, in 1998 he received the Washington Medal of Merit, awarded by the legislature to a citizen whose achievements have benefited others.

Also contributing to orchardists' woes was consolidation among apple retailers. As the latter decreased in number and increased in size, big-box sellers, such as Wal-Mart, were making forays into selling produce; together the two had the power to set prices for the producers and squeeze the smaller out of business. Further complicating the picture was the demise of the Washington Apple Commission when a district judge ruled that the commission's mandatory assessment on growers of 25 cents for each 42-pound box of apples to fund itself was unconstitutional. The demise of the commission shifted the marketing of apples to retailers and packing houses.

Auvil Fruit persevered through these hard times as it did through a suit filed by 28 employees shortly before Wright assumed leadership of the company. The workers claimed that they had been discriminated against after they struck to protest their lack of job security and the firing of workers who bruised apples. Auvil, one of the first companies to offer its workers shares in the business, said the suit was a publicity ploy on the part of the United Farm Workers of America, which supported the work stoppage. However, the workers insisted that their hire dates had been changed to the date on which they returned from the strike. They also said that Auvil had hired replacement workers without disclosing the existence of the strike in violation of the federal Migrant and Seasonal Agricultural Worker Protection Act and that the company had harassed and intimidated striking workers, threatening termination. In September 1998, Auvil settled with the workers, agreeing to hire back those who wanted to return and paying them a lump sum of $40,000.

In the early years of the new decade, Jim Wright became president of Auvil Fruit, succeeding Paul King. By 2003, there were 3,000 commercial apple farmers left in Washington, down from 4,000 in the mid-1990s; one out of four apple farmers had gone bankrupt, and

the industry as a whole had lost $1.7 billion during the preceding five years. Cheaply grown foreign apples and inexpensively produced juice penetrated the domestic market, and the federal government offered direct cash subsidies to apple farmers for the first time.

During the next five years, the company continued to pursue Grady Auvil's philosophy of providing exceptional fruit of proven and new varieties. As Auvil himself expressed it in a 1992 *Oregonian* article, "Anything new, I plant it and try it. But, if we can't deliver quality fruit, we will cut it down and plant something else." Auvil Fruit Company was committed to perpetuating Grady Auvil's vision and legacy.

Carrie Rothburd

FURTHER READING

Barnard, Jeff, "Shiny Future for New Apples—New Zealand Imports Gaining Acreage in Northwest Orchards," *Seattle Times,* August 27, 1994, p. D1.

Eskenazi, Stuart, "The Other Rainier—The Making and Marketing of Washington's Celebrity Fruit," *Seattle Times,* June 27, 2004, p. 12.

"Fruit Growers Lament Passing of Pioneer—Grady Auvil," *Yakima Herald Republic,* December 30, 1998, p. B1.

Gee Whiz: The Story of Grady Auvil, documentary, directed by Jamie Howell, Wenatchee, Wash.: Howell at the Moon Productions, 2008.

Mapes, Lynda V., "The Polish Is Off the Apple—The Fruit Is Sweeter and the Crop Is Smaller, but Trade Troubles Overseas Is Likely to Bruise Washington Growers' Profits," *Seattle Times,* November 2, 1997, p. J1.

Senior, Jeannie, "Growing for the Future," *Oregonian,* June 21, 1992, p. E1.

Stucke, John, "Slim Pickings; Apple Orchards, Packing Houses Attempt to Reverse Industry's Disastrous Downturn," *Spokesman Review,* October 19, 2003, p. D1.

Axcelis Technologies, Inc.

108 Cherry Hill Drive
Beverly, Massachusetts 01915-1053
U.S.A.
Telephone: (978) 787-4000
Fax: (978) 787-3000
Web site: http://www.axcelis.com

Public Company
Incorporated: 1995 as Eaton Semiconductor Equipment
  Inc.
Employees: 1,755
Sales: $404.8 million (2007)
Stock Exchanges: NASDAQ
Ticker Symbol: ACLS
NAIC: 333295 Semiconductor Machinery Manu-
  facturing

■ ■ ■

A public company based in Beverly, Massachusetts, Ax-celis Technologies, Inc., is a leading provider of ion implantation devices, used to introduce ions into semiconductor chips in order to modify conductivity. The company also offers rapid thermal processing, another semiconductor manufacturing process, used to quickly heat silicon wafers and prepare them for ion implantation; ultraviolet (UV) curing devices used to improve yield and chip performance; and dry strip cleaning devices used to remove chip impurities and improve performance. Axcelis also sells parts, services its equipment, and offers other support services, including the planning of equipment installation, start-up,

optimization, and training, either computer-based or onsite at Beverly. Manufacturing and product development is conducted in Beverly as well as in Tokyo through SEN Corp., a joint venture between Axcelis and Sumitomo Heavy Industries. In addition, Axcelis maintains a network of more than 50 service offices in a dozen states and about ten other countries. Major customers include IBM, Motorola, Micron, NEC, Texas Instrument, and Toshiba.

INCORPORATION AS EATON SUBSIDIARY

Axcelis was incorporated in 1995 by Eaton Corporation as Eaton Semiconductor Equipment Inc. and then spun off five years later. Eaton itself was established in Bloomfield, New Jersey, by Joseph Oriel Eaton as a small machine shop under the name Torbensen Gear and Axle Co., producing heavy-duty truck axles based on a patent received by his brother-in-law Henning O. Taube and Viggio V. Torbensen. In order to be closer to vehicle makers, the company was relocated to Cleveland and in 1917 sold to Republic Motor Truck Co. Joseph Eaton bought back the company in 1922, renaming it Eaton Axle and Spring Co. With the addition of other automotive parts to its product offerings, the company became Eaton Manufacturing Co. in 1932.

Ten years after Eaton's death in 1949 the company began diversifying through a spate of acquisitions. Some of the new products were automotive-related, such as the addition of heavy-duty truck transmissions, but others were in entirely new fields, intended to free the company from the cyclical nature of the auto industry.

In 1963 Eaton merged with Yale & Towne Manufacturing Co. to become involved in locks, hardware, and materials handling equipment, while Dole Valve Co. added appliance as well as automotive valves to the mix. In 1966 the company took the name Eaton Yale & Towne and five years later changed it to Eaton Corporation.

EATON CORP. ENTERS SEMICONDUCTOR INDUSTRY: 1970

Because the addition of Yale & Towne offered meager profits and Eaton remained overly dependent on Detroit, Chairman E. Mandell de Windt plotted a new course in the late 1970s to move the company in a new direction. In 1979 Eaton paid $382.3 million to acquire Culter-Hammer, Inc., an electronics company involved in defense avionics, industrial control and power distribution equipment, and semiconductor testing and manufacturing equipment. Semiconductor equipment, spurred by the rise of personal computers, became a growth vehicle for Eaton. Ion implantation products were introduced in 1980 and soon became a major product of the semiconductor unit. In order to increase manufacturing capacity and make inroads with the Japanese semiconductor equipment industry, Eaton in 1982 formed a 50/50 joint venture with Sumitomo Heavy Industries, Sumitomo Eaton Nova, which became SEN Corp. to produce ion implanters. By the mid-1980s the Eaton unit generated more than $200 million in annual sales, making it the world's fourth largest semiconductor equipment manufacturer. However, the company had made a number of poorly executed mergers that led to divestitures and a recasting of the company as a niche ion implantation device maker rather than broadline equipment supplier.

In 1994 Eaton unveiled a line of high-energy ion implanters that quickly became the market leader. A year later Eaton packaged its semiconductor business into a wholly owned subsidiary, Eaton Semiconductor Equipment Inc., which in 1995 accounted for $385

million in sales and net income of $48.6 million, a more than 50 percent increase over the previous year. A year later a very-high-energy implanter was added to the mix and manufacturing plants were opened in Austin, Texas, for medium-energy implanters (replacing an older facility) and in South Korea to serve semiconductor manufacturers in that country, including Hyundai, LG Semicon, and Samsung. Eaton Semiconductor also began to take steps to grow beyond niche status. Late in 1996 Eaton formed a group to develop ion implantation devices for use in the rapidly growing flat-panel manufacturing industry, the first products shipped to a Japanese manufacturer in May 1997. Furthermore in 1996, Eaton Semiconductor expanded beyond ion implantation devices through the acquisition of Peabody, Massachusetts-based High Temperature Engineering Corporation (HTE), maker of rapid thermal processor furnaces and small batch vertical furnaces which were being increasingly used in conjunction with ion implantation. Moreover, the market for the company's profit was $1.5 billion and growing, and with less than $10 million in annual revenues in 1995, HTE had only scratched the surface of its potential.

HTE was renamed Thermal Processing Systems and was so successful for Eaton Semiconductor that the company added a fourth division and became involved in photoresist removal (performed with either a "dry strip" or "wet strip") and photostabilization products in 1997 through the acquisition of Rockville, Maryland-based Fusion Systems Corporation for $201.5 million. Fusion Systems had pioneered the development of photostabilization in 1983 and then was taken public in 1994. A second product line, UV curing equipment, was sold in 1996 in order to focus on the semiconductor manufacturing equipment business. The semiconductor industry suffered an immediate downturn, however. Although Fusion Systems rebounded in short order and the price of its stock began to rise, the industry was consolidating and the company, which was generating about $85 million in annual sales, concluded it needed to merge with a larger partner with a global reach to remain competitive. It had been involved in low-level technical collaborations with Eaton Semiconductor for several years. In late 1996 there were discussions about further collaboration, but by early 1997 the two companies began discussing a possible merger, which came to fruition in the summer.

A financial crisis in Asia led to a severe slump in the semiconductor industry that adversely impacted Eaton Semiconductor. Revenues fell from $460 million in 1997 to $265.7 million in 1998, when the subsidiary lost nearly $138 million. Business rebounded in 1999 and Eaton Semiconductor returned to profitability, netting $12.3 million on sales of $397.3 million. Although

KEY DATES

∎

1980: Eaton Corporation begins manufacturing ion implantation products.
1982: Joint venture is established with Sumitomo Heavy Industries.
1995: Eaton Semiconductor Equipment Inc. is formed as subsidiary.
1996: High Temperature Engineering is acquired.
1997: Fusion Systems Corporation is acquired.
2000: Eaton Semiconductor is spun off as Axcelis Technologies, Inc.
2002: Mary Puma is named CEO.
2008: Sumitomo makes unsolicited bid to acquire Axcelis.

the parent company continued to maintain Eaton Semiconductor was a future platform for growth, the division contributed just 5 percent of Eaton's total sales of $8.4 billion. Furthermore, it enjoyed no synergy with the rest of the company and grew further apart in 1999 with the $1.7 billion acquisition of Aeroquip-Vickers, Inc., producer of hydraulic pumps, cylinders, motors, drives, fittings, and hoses for the automotive, aerospace, and industrial markets. Following a subsequent reorganization, Eaton Semiconductor had little in common with its sister divisions: automotive components, truck components, fluid power, and industrial and commercial control.

SPINNING OFF AXCELIS TECHNOLOGIES: 2000

It became apparent that spinning off Eaton Semiconductor would not only unlock unrecognized value and spur the growth of the business but also maximize value for Eaton shareholders. Hence, in April 2000 the Eaton board of directors agreed to take Eaton Semiconductor public with a partial (about 20 percent) stock offering to raise equity, build awareness of the company, and help pay down debt. The rest of the stock would be distributed to Eaton Corporation shareholders. By having stock available, the independent company would also be in a better bargaining position in the hiring and retention of talented workers. In preparation of the split, Eaton Semiconductor changed its name to Axcelis Technologies Inc. at the end of June 2000. A month later shares in Axcelis were sold at $22 each. The remaining shares were then distributed to Eaton shareholders in December 2000. Installed as chief execu-

tive officer in May 2000 was Brian R. Bachman, who for the previous five years had served as senior vice-president and group executive for Eaton's Hydraulics, Semiconductor Equipment, and Specialty Control units. Prior to that he was the general manager of the Standard Products Business Group of Philips Semiconductor.

For the year 2000, Axcelis reported sales of $680.4 million, about a 75 percent increase over the previous year, and net income of $99.1 million. However, with the semiconductor industry entering a downturn due to a deteriorating economy, the worst in a quarter-century, Axcelis could not hope for similar results during its first full year as an independent company. Indeed, revenues fell to $365.3 million and the company lost $20.2 million. Nevertheless, Axcelis continued to invest in the future to position itself for an eventual recovery in the market. Not only did it complete an array of ion-implant tools by adding a very-high-energy tool to complement its medium-energy and high-energy tools, Axcelis introduced a new dry strip tool and a new rapid thermal processing (RTP) tool.

Difficult business conditions did require some belt tightening, however. Measures taken included voluntary furloughs, executive pay freezes, and temporary plant shutdowns. More drastic steps were also taken, as about one-fifth of the workforce was terminated in 2001 when curing and cleaning manufacturing operations were moved from Rockville, Maryland, to Beverly, Massachusetts, taking advantage of an 80,000-square-foot expansion that had been added to the Beverly facility in 1999, the process not completed until well into 2002. Research and development, marketing, and customer support functions continued to be conducted in Maryland.

NEW CEO TAKES CHARGE: 2000

In January 2002 Axcelis received a new CEO, Mary G. Puma, who had served as the company's president and chief operating officer since the split from Eaton. She had come to Eaton in 1996 after 15 years with General Electric Company to become general manager of the Commercial Controls Division. Two years later she joined Eaton Semiconductor as general manager of the Implant Systems Division. When she took charge of Axcelis, the semiconductor industry continued to experience a challenging environment. Although sales fell to $309.7 million and the company lost $26.1 million, Axcelis continued to position itself for future growth. Work was completed on a new 135,000-square-foot Advanced Technology Center, used to facilitate advanced process development, product demonstration, and customer training operations. Axcelis also launched a number of new products in 2002, including the Ultra low-energy ion implantation device that quickly found several customers. Axcelis also looked to strengthen its position in the fast-growing Asia-Pacific market. A major new office was opened in Shanghai, and one of China's leading capital equipment distribution and support companies, Tritek International, was acquired.

Ultra continued to make inroads in its market in 2003, and Axcelis added to its dry strip offerings with the launch of a new product, followed by the acquisition of Matrix Integrated Systems, a dry strip capital equipment manufacturer, that brought with it a robust slate of dry strip technology. The company continued to trim overhead and returned to profitability in the fourth quarter as the semiconductor equipment industry began to recover. Overall, Axcelis generated sales of $322 million and posted a net loss of $113.9 million. Improved business conditions led to solid gains in 2004, when revenues increased to $508 million. SEN also enjoyed a record year, bringing worldwide revenue for the year to $837.7 million. Axcelis netted $74.2 million, the margins helped in part by integrating all Maryland operations with the Beverly location and other efforts to eliminate redundancies. The company also introduced the Optima implant platform that kept Axcelis as the leader in the ion implantation market, and set the stage for future growth in curing and cleaning with the launch of new products in this arena.

Axcelis's performance was something of a roller coaster ride over the next three years. Poor demand resulted in a decrease in the number of semiconductors produced in 2005, leading to a significant loss in business for semiconductor equipment manufacturers such as Axcelis, which experienced a decrease in sales to $372.5 million and a net loss of $3.86 million. The company rebounded nicely in 2006, returning to profitability by netting $40.8 million on revenues of $461.7 million, but the following year once again proved challenging. In 2007 revenues dipped to $404.8 million and Axcelis returned to red ink, losing $11.4 million.

PARTNER MAKING UNSOLICITED OFFER: 2000

Because Axcelis was faring poorly financially and losing market share, longtime Japanese partner Sumitomo made an unsolicited bid for the company in February 2008, rare for a Japanese company in this sector, offering approximately $5.20 per share for a total of $544 million. The Axcelis board declined the offer, but Sumitomo was not ready to concede defeat and increased the offer to $6 per share. Again, in March 2008, the Axcelis board unanimously rejected the proposal, maintaining that $6 per share significantly undervalued the company, which the board insisted was well positioned with its deep product portfolio and global market reach to enjoy a prosperous future.

Ed Dinger

PRINCIPAL SUBSIDIARIES

Fusion Systems Corporation; High Temperature Engineering Corporation; Axcelis Technologies Semiconductor Trading (Shanghai) Co., Ltd.

PRINCIPAL COMPETITORS

Mattson Technology, Inc.; Veeco Instruments Inc.; Aviza Technology Inc.

FURTHER READING

Aeppel, Timothy, "Eaton Expects to Exceed Earnings Projections," *Wall Street Journal*, July 16, 1999, p. 1.

Chappell, Jeff, "Axcelis Product Blitz Continues," *Electronic News*, June 25, 2001, p. 30.

Erkanat, Judy, and Gale Bradley, "Eaton Semiconductor Acquires HTE," *Electronic News*, June 17, 1996, p. 54.

Fasca, Chad, "Eaton, Fusion Tying Knot in $292M Transaction," *Electronic News*, July 7, 1997.

Gold, Howard, "Eaton Redux," *Forbes*, June 3, 1985, p. 166.

LaPedus, Mark, "Hostile Takeover Bid Hits Chip-Equipment Sector," *Electronic Engineering Times*, February 18, 2008, p. 20.

Livingston, Sandra, "Eaton to Spin Off the Rest of Axcelis Stockholders," *Cleveland Plain Dealer*, October 26, 2000, p. 1.

Stoughton, Stephanie, "Beverly, Mass.-based Semiconductor-Equipment Maker to Cut Staff by 4 Percent," *Boston Globe*, November 14, 2001.

Baidu.com Inc.

12/F Ideal International Plaza
No. 58 West-North 4th Ring
Beijing, BEJ 100080
China
Telephone: (+86-10) 82621188
Fax: (+86-10) 82607007
Web site: http://www.baidu.com

Public Company
Incorporated: 1999
Employees: 3,113
Sales: RMB 838.84 million ($107.36 million) (2006)
Stock Exchanges: NASDAQ
Ticker Symbol: BIDU
NAIC: 514191 Online Information Services

■ ■ ■

Baidu.com Inc. develops and operates the largest Chinese-language search engine in the People's Republic of China. The company commands more than 60 percent of the fast-growing advertising-based search market, beating out closest competitors Yahoo! and Google. Baidu—the name, which translates as "one hundred times," was inspired by an ancient Song dynasty poem about the search for love amid chaos—has rolled out its brand into a variety of online products. One of its most popular is the online encyclopedia Baidu Baike, a user content-generated

encyclopedia pioneered by Wikipedia. Baidu's encyclopedia features more than one million entries, making it the largest online Chinese-language encyclopedia. Another popular Baidu product is Baidu Knows, in which users post questions and answers, generating a vast online knowledge base. Baidu Post Bar features the company's own technology and connects users to other users conducting similar search queries, in this way creating instant online communities.

More controversially, Baidu enables users to search for and retrieve MP3s and videos directly from its search interface. The company also operates Baidu Space, a social networking site similar to MySpace. Other products include a voice search service, featuring live operators answering users' queries, and an instant messaging service. In addition, the company offers a variety of subject-specific search engines, including Baidu Ancient Chinese History Search; Baidu Map Search; and Baidu Movie and TV Search. The company also launched mobile telephone search services in early 2008. Nearly all of Baidu's revenues, which neared RMB 840 million ($108 million) in 2007, are generated through advertising revenues. The company was one of the pioneers of the "pay-for-performance" advertising model, in which advertisers pay rates vary according to the number of clicks generated by their ads. Founded in 1999 by CEO and Chairman Robin Yanhong Li, Baidu went public on the NASDAQ in one of the most successful Chinese Internet initial public offerings (IPOs). The company's share price, which tripled through 2007, valued the company at more than $12 billion in early 2008.

BRINGING SEARCH TO CHAOS IN THE NINETIES

Born in 1968, Li Yanhong (Robin Li) was raised in a poor city south of Beijing. Li proved an able student, and won admission to the prestigious Beijing University. Li studied library science, while also taking classes in computer science, and graduated at the beginning of the 1990s.

China, still reeling from the repressive crackdown following the Tiananmen Square demonstrations of 1989, offered few prospects for Li at the time. Instead, Li began applying to graduate schools in order to study computer science in the United States. By 1991, Li had succeeded in winning a fellowship to the State University of New York at Buffalo. There, Li joined the Center of Excellence for Document Analysis and Recognition, which focused on developing search and sorting tools using pattern-recognition technologies, as a research assistant.

Li initially intended to pursue a Ph.D. in computer science. After completing his master's degree in 1994, however, Li decided to leave the campus and enter the workforce. Li's first job took him to New Jersey and Dow Jones & Co., where he became part of the team developing the online edition of the *Wall Street Journal.*

While working on that project, Li recognized the importance of developing methods for sorting the massive amounts of information available not only at the WSJ site, but throughout the Internet. Li began to develop his own search technologies. By 1996, he had created his "link analysis" system, which ranked web sites according to the number of links they shared with other web sites.

Li's bosses at Dow Jones, however, were not interested in the technology. Undaunted, Li signed up for a Silicon Valley computer conference, renting space for his own table in order to present the technology. Li attracted the attention of William Chang, who served as chief technology officer at Infoseek, at that time one of the leaders in the already bustling online search market. Chang offered Li a job overseeing development of Infoseek's own search engine.

FOUNDED IN 1999

At Infoseek, Li devised a number of search technologies that were to become standards in the growing search industry. However in 1999, Infoseek's major shareholder, Disney, took full control of the company and made the decision to reorient Infoseek as a content provider. Part of the reason for this was the emergence of a new heavyweight in the search market, Google.

Disillusioned by the turn of events at Infoseek, Li nonetheless remained committed to developing his own search technologies. In 1999, he joined with friend and fellow Chinese national Eric Xu, also a veteran of the Silicon Valley biotech industry, to set up his own search company, called Baidu. Xu and Li quickly attracted an initial $1.2 million from Peninsula Capital and Integrity Partners.

Instead of attempting to compete in the already crowded U.S. market, the partners decided to return to China, where Internet usage remained in its infancy. Li and Xu set up shop in a hotel room in Beijing, near the city's university, in 1999.

Baidu originally began developing search services for third parties. The model proved successful, as early Chinese web portals sought to expand the range of content and services of their sites. By the end of 2000, Baidu had attracted another $10 million in start-up funding from IDG Technology and Draper Fisher Jurvetson. The latter soon became the company's largest shareholder, with 28 percent. Xu, in the meantime, left Baidu to pursue other opportunities.

The success of another company, California-based Overture, provided Baidu with new inspiration. That company had developed a means of correlating searches with advertising content; for the first time, users conducting searches were greeted by advertisements related to their search terms. Li recognized the potential of adapting that technology for the Chinese market.

In order to pursue this objective, Li decided to lead Baidu into developing its own search engine and portal. While the change in strategy met with some resistance from the company's investors, Li pushed ahead, and by 2001 had launched Baidu.com.

Featuring a sparse interface borrowed heavily from Google, Baidu appeared just as China experienced its first surge in Internet use. Baidu also rolled out its pay-for-performance advertising system. This system enabled advertisers to bid for available advertising space, and then pay according to the number of clicks their ads received. While open to abuse, notably from so-called click fraud, by which the number of clicks could be artificially boosted, the advertising model proved highly popular. By 2002, the company's revenues had topped RMB 11 million ($1.4 million).

KEY DATES

1999: Robin Li and Eric Xu establish Baidu in Beijing to provide online search services for the Chinese market.
2001: Baidu changes strategy and launches its own search portal, Baidu.com, which becomes wildly successful.
2005: Baidu goes public on the NASDAQ.
2008: Baidu launches new range of search products for the mobile telephone market.

CHINA'S GOOGLE

Baidu was aided early on by the Chinese government's adoption of the Internet as a means of stimulating the country's economic growth. As a result, the government adopted policies favoring the growth of a domestic, Internet-based industry, while putting up entry barriers to larger international players. One example was the move by the government to cut off access to the Chinese and English versions of the popular user-generated online encyclopedia, Wikipedia.

Baidu more successfully navigated the Chinese government's strict censorship regulations, avoiding political content and instead focusing on the entertainment market. The youthful online market in China, where average users were much younger than their Western counterparts, meant that the role of the Internet in the country was especially as an entertainment medium. Among the services offered by the company, for example, was a dedicated music search function that allowed users to locate and download songs and other files in a variety of file formats.

The shutdown of Wikipedia presented the company with the opportunity to launch its own online encyclopedia in 2005. Baidu Baike, as the site was called, resembled Wikipedia in that users were responsible for developing its content. However, Baidu required that its contributors be registered, and the site's content was policed in order to keep within the boundaries of the government's censorship regulations. Nonetheless, the site became immensely popular. By the middle of the decade, Baidu Baike boasted more than one million entries.

A major part of Baidu's success was its commitment to developing technologies that incorporated the idiosyncrasies of the ideogram-based Chinese language. As such, the company successfully combined the simplified mainland system with that of the more traditional system still in use in Hong Kong, Taiwan, and Singapore.

GOING PUBLIC IN 2005

Baidu turned its first profit in 2004, generating RMB 12 million on sales of RM 117.5 million. By then, the Internet market in China had begun to explode. By the middle of the decade, the country counted more than 130 million online users, making the country the world's second largest online market behind only the United States. Yet China's potential for as many as a billion online users placed the country at the center of Internet, and investor, interest in the middle of the first decade of the 2000s.

A number of Chinese Internet groups had already completed highly successful IPOs in the first half of the decade. With its own profits and revenues building strongly, Baidu decided to join them. In 2005, the company launched its public offering on the NASDAQ. The offering, priced at $27 per share, raised more than $109 million for the company. The offering became one of the most successful of the Chinese IPOs. Indeed, by the end of the first day in trading, the group's shares had grown by nearly 350 percent. Just two years later, Baidu's share price had hit highs of more than $350 per share, giving the company a market capitalization of $12 billion, beating out even Google.

That company, which had grown to dominate every market it had entered, was nonetheless forced to take a back seat to Baidu in China. Despite massive investments by both Google and Yahoo!, the two U.S. giants were unable to make much impact against Baidu's dominance. With more than 60 percent of the search market in China, Baidu remained the outright leader there. At the same time, and because of the size of the Chinese market, the company had grown into one of the world's top search groups.

ADDING MOBILE SERVICES IN 2008

Internet penetration continued to grow strongly in China. By early 2008, the company was estimated to have more than 220 million online users, as the country appeared poised to overtake the United States as the world's largest single Internet market. However the even stronger penetration of mobile telephone use in the country, with more than 500 million users, represented a new market for the company. With many Chinese preferring to access the Internet through their telephones, Baidu launched development of its own mobile search technologies.

Baidu looked beyond China, setting up a subsidiary in Japan to enter the search market there. The company's primary impulse into that market, which was already dominated by the presence of Yahoo!, Google, and others, was to provide a portal connecting Japanese businesses with an entry into the Chinese market.

China represented the group's main growth center. Baidu continued expanding its brand family, rolling out a range of social networking and community building services such as Baidu Post Bar, Baidu Knows, and Baidu Space. In early 2008, the company debuted its own instant messaging service. At the same time, Baidu rolled out a new voice-based search service, available to mobile telephone users, which featured live operators providing responses to user queries.

Baidu's growth reflected the surge in the Chinese Internet market in general. By 2005, the company's revenues had neared RMB 320 million. Just one year later, Baidu posted sales of RMB 838 million ($107 million), and by the end of 2007, the company's revenues appeared on their way toward doubling again.

Despite its dominance of the Chinese search market, Baidu could not afford to rest. The push by other search players, especially Google, into China had seen the beginnings of a slowdown in Baidu's own growth. Nonetheless, with its industry-leading technology and its appeal as a truly Chinese brand, Baidu appeared certain to maintain its position as China's favorite search engine.

M. L. Cohen

PRINCIPAL SUBSIDIARIES

Baidu (China) Co., Ltd.; Baidu.com Times Technology (Beijing) Co., Ltd.; Baidu Holdings Limited; Baidu Inc. (Japan); Baidu Online Network Technology (Beijing) Co. Ltd.

PRINCIPAL COMPETITORS

Google Inc.; Yahoo! Inc.

FURTHER READING

"Baidu Starts Voice Search Service," *China Business News,* March 6, 2008.

Barboza, David, "The Rise of Baidu (That's Chinese for Google)," *New York Times,* September 17, 2006.

Bremner, Brian, "Gizmo," *New Scientist,* May 20, 2006, p. 29.

"Chinese Music Industry Groups File Suit Against Baidu," *Reuters,* February 28, 2008.

Einhorn, Bruce, "Baidu Thinks It Can Play in Japan," *Business Week Online,* February 16, 2007.

————, "Big Numbers Give Baidu a Bump," *Business Week Online,* April 30, 2007.

"A Fallen Net Star Stages a Comeback," *Business Week Online,* March 1, 2006.

Greenburg, Zach O'Malley, "China's Google," *Forbes,* January 28, 2008, p. 104.

Liu, John, "Put Off by Mainland Rules, Baidu Won't Pursue IPO," *International Herald Tribune,* September 5, 2006, p. 14.

Rowland, Kara, "Beijing Search Engine Drubs Google in China," *Washington Times,* July 10, 2007, p. C08.

Thaw, Jonathan, and John Liu, "Baidu.com Sees Sales Slowing Down," *International Herald Tribune,* February 16, 2007, p. 15.

"UB Grad from China Cofounded a Chinese Version of Google," *Buffalo News,* August 5, 2005, p. D7.

Woo, Eva, "Baidu's Censored Answer to Wikipedia," *Business Week Online,* November 14, 2007.

Bassett Furniture Industries, Inc.

3525 Fairystone Park Highway
P.O. Box 626
Bassett, Virginia 24055
U.S.A.
Telephone: (276) 629-6000
Toll Free: (877) 525-7070
Fax: (276) 629-6332
Web site: http://www.bassettfurniture.com

Public Company
Incorporated: 1902 as Bassett Furniture Co.
Employees: 1,450
Sales: $295.4 million (2007)
Stock Exchanges: NASDAQ
Ticker Symbol: BSET
NAIC: 337122 Nonupholstered Wood Household
    Furniture

■ ■ ■

Bassett Furniture Industries, Inc., leverages its strong brand name to retain a place among top makers and retailers of home furnishings. Along with other American furniture companies, Bassett has turned away from domestic to foreign production to bring down costs. The company relies on its dedicated retail store program to drive sales growth of its midpriced furniture and accessories.

19TH-CENTURY ORIGINS

As the 19th century came to a close, the Bassett family of Henry County, Virginia, owned two sawmills that had been built to provide track ties and bridge timbers to the Norfolk & Western railroad. However, ever since the railroad from Roanoke to Winston-Salem was completed in 1892, the Bassetts had been looking for new buyers for the abundant hardwood in the area. Much of the marketing was done by John D. Bassett, who negotiated the family's first nonrailroad contract with the Turner-White Coffin Co. in Winston-Salem. From there, he went to High Point, North Carolina, where he was able to obtain two minor contracts with small furniture companies. That success led him to Jamestown, New York, and Grand Rapids, Michigan, two of the major furniture-producing areas of the day.

For the next half dozen years, J. D. Bassett continued to develop relationships with Northern furniture makers. Then in 1902, Bassett, 36, called a family meeting that was attended by two brothers, Samuel and Charles C. Bassett, and a brother-in-law, Reed L. Stone. At the meeting, J. D. Bassett proposed that the family go into the business of making furniture. As he recalled years later, "Here I was, shipping raw lumber from Henry County to Jamestown, New York, and to Grand Rapids, Michigan, where factories converted that lumber into finished furniture to be shipped everywhere, including the South. It seemed to me that furniture certainly could be made in Henry County at a tremendous advantage."

At the time, the Southern economy was still recovering from the Civil War, and the Bassetts knew almost nothing about making furniture. However, J. D. Bassett figured the savings in freight alone would give them an advantage over Northern manufacturers. "I was convinced that the time for such a venture in Henry

County was ripe because the South was then recovering rapidly," Bassett recalled. "Among the necessary commodities, furniture was in growing demand. I believed that this demand would continue for many years to come."

The four family members raised $27,500—somewhat less than J. D. Bassett figured they needed—and formed Bassett Furniture Co. They decided to start with basic bedroom furniture because it seemed less complicated to make and none of them really knew anything about the business, except J. D. Bassett, who had absorbed what he could on the road. Up to that point, J. D. Bassett had also been a teacher, a tobacco farmer, and a drummer for a wholesale grocery business. He also owned his own grocery, Bassett Mercantile Co., that doubled as the local post office, which later resulted in the small, western Virginia community becoming known as Bassett.

Bassett Furniture Co. was set up in a wooden shed, later to be sheathed in metal. J. D. Bassett, president of the fledgling company, paid a traveling designer from Grand Rapids $100 to develop working prints, and hired about 50 of his rural Virginia neighbors, who were paid five cents an hour to work in the factory, which was soon turning out beds, dressers, washstands, and chifforobes made of oak. He also signed contracts to sell the furniture through stores in Virginia, West Virginia, and North Carolina. Company records show that beds originally wholesaled for $1.50 each.

In its first year, Bassett Furniture Co. earned $15,000 on sales of $76,000. The next year, 1903, the company earned $25,000 on sales of a little more than $100,000. By the end of the third year, the family members had recouped their entire investment and the company was debt free. Even in 1907, with the nation in the grip of a financial panic, Bassett Furniture Co. reported net income of $606. That same year, the

company made its first outside acquisition, buying the American Furniture Co. of Martinsville, Virginia, for 10,000 shares of Bassett stock. J. D. Bassett also established his own bank, Bank of Bassett Inc., capitalized at $13,000, which later became First National Bank of Bassett.

By 1911, the economy had recovered and Bassett Furniture Co. added sales representatives in several major Northern cities, including New York, Detroit, and Chicago. The company also paid its first dividends to shareholders, declaring a 5 percent dividend in February and an additional 5 percent in July.

Six years later, on December 31, 1917, disaster struck when fire destroyed the Bassett Furniture Co. factory. However, the company soon resumed operations in a modern brick building with motor-driven woodworking equipment, abandoning the belt-driven line-shaft system that had been a hallmark of the industrial revolution. In 1920, the board of directors voted to increase capital stock to $1 million; Bassett Furniture Co. had become a million-dollar business in 18 years. J. D. Bassett was then earning $5,000 a year as president.

BASSETT VERSUS BASSETT

In 1921, J. D. Bassett took the unusual step of forming a second furniture business, J.D. Bassett Manufacturing Co., apparently to test the abilities of his oldest son, William M. Bassett. J. D. Bassett was president of both companies, but his son was named vice president of J.D. Bassett Manufacturing Co. and was largely responsible for day-to-day operations. J.D. Bassett Manufacturing Co. developed its own sales staff and retail distribution network but, confusingly, both companies used the same trade name, "Bassett."

In 1923, William Bassett succeeded his father as president of J.D. Bassett Manufacturing Co., while J. D. Bassett's second son, John Douglas Bassett (later known as J. D. Bassett Jr.) became vice-president. By then, the Bassett furniture businesses had become totally self-sufficient. In 1920, J.D. Bassett and his partners in Bassett Furniture Co. had purchased Valley Veneer Co. to produce veneers exclusively for Bassett furniture. In 1923, J. D. Bassett formed Bassett Mirror Co., which set up operations in a 15,000-square-foot building next to Bassett Furniture Co.

Fire struck again in 1925, this time destroying a large part of the J.D. Bassett Manufacturing Co. plant. When the business was rebuilt, it added a facility to manufacture dining room furniture, marking the first time the Bassett name would venture outside bedroom furnishing.

KEY DATES

1902: Sawmill operation turns to furniture making.
1907: Company acquires its first outside business.
1911: Shareholders receive first dividends.
1917: First of two fires (the second struck in 1925) destroys factory.
1930: Holding company is established.
1940: Common stock offering raises more than $2 million.
1945: End of World War II leads to plant modernization and new products.
1960: Company ranks as world's largest manufacturer of wood furniture.
1967: First retail outlet opens.
1971: Begins series of purchases to expand line.
1984: Company creates cooperative marketing program to gain exclusive space in retail shops.
1995: Company moves toward vertical integration with Bassett Direct Plus Dealership program.
1997: New leadership takes charge, begins cutbacks.
2001: Plants are shuttered in response to industry downturn.
2007: Soft market contributes to losses.

Two years later, in 1927, William Bassett, apparently unhappy with his prospects in the growing Bassett family of businesses, left his job as head of J.D. Bassett Manufacturing Co. John Douglas Bassett succeeded him as president. William Bassett then bought Craig Furniture Co. in nearby Martinsville, which he renamed W.M. Bassett Furniture Co.

Other family members had also left the fold to form their own furniture companies, including J. D. Bassett's son-in-law, Thomas Bahnson Stanley, a future governor of Virginia, who started Stanley Furniture Co. in 1924 on land adjacent to the Bassett plants. That same year, J. Clyde Hooker, the son-in-law of J. D. Bassett's brother, Charles, formed Hooker-Bassett Furniture Co. in Martinsville, which later became Hooker Furniture Corp.

J. D. Bassett also backed another son-in-law, Taylor Vaughan, and his brother, B. C. Vaughan, when they formed their respective furniture businesses, Vaughan Furniture Co. and Vaughan-Bassett Co. Cabell Philpott, the son of a Bassett Furniture Co. board member, also worked for Bassett before leaving to form United Furniture Co. in Lexington, North Carolina.

In *Foresight, Founders and Fortitude: The Growth of Industry in Martinsville and Henry County, Virginia,* Dorothy Cleal and Hiram H. Herbert noted, "At first J. D.'s attitude about competition appears paradoxical. With a strong wedge in the southern furniture field, why did he risk weakening his position by inviting competition, even in his own family?" They go on to suggest that Bassett was more consumed by a "personal struggle" to establish the South as the dominant furniture-making region in the United States. "If this is so," the authors concluded, "then it must be deduced that J. D. Bassett, Sr., had phenomenal foresight. By the time he died in 1965 at the age of 98 he was able to see dramatic changes taking place in America's preference for furniture produced in the South as opposed to furniture produced in the North, the cradle of the American furniture industry."

FORMATION OF BASSETT FURNITURE INDUSTRIES: 1930

Two years after William Bassett bought his own furniture business, and John Douglas Bassett rose to the presidency of J.D. Bassett Manufacturing Co., J. D. Bassett called another family meeting. With the Great Depression beginning, he suggested the three Bassett furniture businesses could be more efficiently run as a single enterprise. Readily agreeing with that assessment, in 1930, the Bassetts and their investors formed Bassett Furniture Industries, Inc., a holding company for all three furniture manufacturers.

The accounting firm of Ernst & Ernst conducted an inventory of each business and placed a value of $1.875 million on the consolidated companies, which issued 187,500 shares of preferred stock. J. D. Bassett was named president of the new corporation. John Douglas Bassett, by then known as J. D. Jr., was vice-president, and William Bassett, secretary-treasurer. Later that year, J. D. Bassett was elected chairman of the board and William Bassett succeeded to the presidency.

Despite the rigors of the Depression, the new corporation adopted an aggressive position in the industry. In 1931, Bassett Furniture Industries formed Bassett Chair Co. Three years later, it acquired Ramsey Furniture Co., later to be known as Bassett Superior Lines, in a public auction for $117,000. Bassett Furniture Industries, although forced to cut back on its workers' hours and wages, continued to operate throughout the Depression, at one point bringing in a railroad carload of Virginia hams for its employees.

In 1938, Bassett Furniture Industries introduced its massive and elaborate Waterfall design. Two years later, with the nation in the midst of an economic boom following the outbreak of war in Europe, the company raised more than $2 million in an offering of common stock. The proceeds were used to retire the preferred stock in Bassett Furniture Co., J.D. Bassett Manufacturing Co., and William M. Bassett Furniture Co., making them wholly owned subsidiaries of the holding company. Later that year, the three furniture companies, along with Bassett Chair Co. and Bassett Superior Lines, were merged into a single enterprise.

The following year, when the United States entered World War II, Bassett Furniture Industries realized that furniture was not going to be a high priority item in a time of government rationing. As they did when the market for railroad ties dried up in 1892, the Bassetts had to find another market. Although the company was unsuccessful in its efforts to obtain government contracts, J. D. Bassett Jr. negotiated a sizable contract with Yellow Cab and Coach Co. in Detroit to manufacture wooden truck bodies.

When the war ended in 1945, the nation experienced another economic boom, and rising expectations. Cleal and Herbert explained: "Throughout the nation there had been countless war-time marriages, and now the couples wanted homes of their own. ... With the new homes came demands for furniture to fill them." Bassett Furniture Industries invested $6 million to modernize its plants, all internally financed. Bassett Chair Co. also began manufacturing coffee tables and other occasional pieces to fit the changing American lifestyle, culminating in 1957 with the formation of Bassett Table Co. By 1960, corporate-wide sales had reached $60 million, employment had risen to more than 3,000, and Bassett Furniture Industries had become the world's largest manufacturer of wood furniture.

Marketing, however, was beginning to pose headaches for the growing company. In 1959, there were still four separate marketing organizations for Bassett products: Bassett Furniture Co., J.D. Bassett Manufacturing Co., William M. Bassett Furniture Co., and Bassett Table Co. All three organizations handled sales for Bassett Superior Lines. As a result, a salesman for one Bassett line often found himself vying for retail space with another. Differences in design were usually minor, which left furniture dealers confused and often angry.

William Bassett, then chairman and chief executive of Bassett Furniture Industries, also worried that Bassett-branded furniture would find its way into cut-rate discount stores, a new force in American retailing, if the internal competition continued. Under his direction, top salesmen from the three companies were organized into a single sales force to represent the entire Bassett line in a three-state trial area. The test was so successful that the program was expanded nationwide within a year. William Bassett also died in 1960, after 30 years at the helm of Bassett Industries, and was succeeded as chairman and chief executive by his younger brother, J. D. Bassett Jr.

In 1960, Bassett Furniture Industries also initiated its first nationwide marketing campaign, advertising in consumer magazines with a combined readership of 70 million to establish the Bassett image. By 1964, when Bassett Furniture Industries became the first furniture manufacturer to advertise in *Reader's Digest,* the marketing program was reaching more than 445 million readers. In addition to *Reader's Digest,* with its 22 million readers, Bassett advertised in *Ebony, Seventeen, Brides Magazine, Better Homes & Gardens, Sunset, Modern Bride, Good Housekeeping,* and *Bride & Home.* In 1963, Bassett Furniture Industries had also rounded out its product line by acquiring Prestige Furniture Corp. in Newton, North Carolina, which made upholstered furniture. Afterward, Bassett Industries could claim to make and sell furniture for every room of the house.

J. D. Bassett Jr., then 65, died unexpectedly in 1966. He was succeeded as chairman and chief executive by John Edwin Bassett Sr., a cousin and the son of Charles C. Bassett, one of the original founders of Bassett Furniture Co. in 1902.

EXPANSION THROUGH ACQUISITIONS

In 1967, Bassett Furniture Industries opened its first retail outlet, a freestanding showroom on Interstate 85 between High Point and Thomasville, North Carolina. That same year, the company formed Bassett Furniture Industries of North Carolina, a wholly owned subsidiary, to manufacture juvenile furniture in Statesville, North Carolina. Two years later, Bassett Furniture Industries acquired Art Furniture Manufacturing Co. in Macon, Georgia, and Art Table Co. in Barnesville, Georgia. Those companies were reorganized as Bassett Furniture Industries of Georgia. The expansion continued in 1969 with the purchase of Taylorcraft Furniture Co. in Taylorsville, North Carolina, which became a subsidiary of Prestige Furniture Corp. Bassett Furniture Industries' sales topped $139 million in 1969.

Bassett Furniture Industries continued to expand through acquisitions during the 1970s. In 1971, the company entered the mattress market by purchasing E.B. Malone Bedding Co. That same year, it purchased National Mount Airy Furniture Co., a manufacturer of upscale furniture in Mount Airy, North Carolina, followed by acquisition of Weiman Co., a manufacturer of heirloom-quality furniture in Christianburg, Virginia, in 1979.

In 1984, Bassett Furniture Industries launched its Bassett Gallery program, a cooperative marketing program for retail dealers who were willing to set aside a portion of their floor space exclusively for settings of Bassett Furniture. The company also acquired Impact Furniture Inc., a manufacturer of low-end occasional and bedroom furniture in Hickory, North Carolina, followed by the purchase of Motion Chair Inc., a maker of recliners, in 1986.

TRYING NEW AVENUES

In 1993, Bassett Furniture Industries built the first U.S. finishing plant for 100 percent polyester furniture in Catawba County, North Carolina. The furniture was marketed under the brand names Vision One by Bassett and Nova by Impact.

Two years later, Bassett Furniture Industries introduced its first ready-to-assemble line of furniture, a line of home-office furniture that was carried by the Staples chain of office superstores. Matt Johnson, then national sales manager for the division launching the home-office line, said the growth of home-based businesses convinced Bassett Furniture Industries that consumers would pay more for a better grade of furniture than traditional ready-to-assemble products. However, Johnson said the company had no plans to expand its ready-to-assemble line. In 1995, the company also launched its Bassett Direct Plus Dealership program of franchised furniture superstores that carried only the Bassett line.

Bassett generated 14 percent of its revenue from J.C. Penney stores in 1995. Beyond major retailers, the company sold its wares in more than two dozen Bassett Direct Plus Galleries. In addition to the Bassett brand, the company was making furniture under the Impact, Weiman, and Mount Airy labels. Its manufacturing operations were located in 15 states. Bassett Furniture Industries posted earnings of $22.9 million on sales of $490.8 million for the year.

NEW LEADERSHIP: 1997–2000

Paul Fulton, University of North Carolina–Chapel Hill business school dean and former president of Sara Lee Corporation, was tapped as CEO and chairman in 1997. Fulton, a board member since 1993, would succeed Robert H. Spilman, who was stepping down after 40 years with the company. His son, Robert (Rob) H. Spilman Jr., executive vice-president of marketing and merchandising, was named president and chief operating officer. The younger Spilman had sparked a move to update the company.

"Fulton is an outsider, yet he had a very good track record at Sara Lee, where among other things, he was instrumental in the rollout of the Coach Leather stores, and did so successfully, while Coach continued to sell to independent dealers," John Baugh, managing director of the Wheat First Butcher Singer investment firm, told *HFN*. Fulton and the younger Spilman had their work cut out for them. Sales, down 3.9 percent in 1995, fell an additional 8.2 percent in 1996 to $450.7 million. Faced with a fading product image, Bassett pumped money into manufacturing, communication, and brand enhancement.

The company sharpened its focus in 1997. The promotional goods line Impact Furniture was cut entirely. The high-end furniture business, in which Bassett had never become a major player, also was phased out, although the company planned to retain the Louis-Philippe style furniture made by National/Mt. Airy.

Manufacturing operations were also restructured. One plant was closed with production transferred to existing plants, including the Mt. Airy facility, which was one of the company's best, according to *HFN*.

The moves reduced sales by about 10 percent but were expected to improve operating earnings. Some industry watchers applauded the company's efforts to return to its core product line.

"These moves make sense," Bud Bugatch, senior vice-president of investment firm Raymond James and Associates, told *HFN*. "Bassett's most significant asset is the Bassett name so the smartest thing they can do is to take steps to maximize that asset."

To translate name recognition into sales, Bassett set out to place its goods in reach of consumers. The company opened new stores, including a westward expansion. An online program to link customers with the company's independent retailers, Bassett Furniture Direct (BFD) stores, and At Home With Bassett galleries was also in the works, according to a July 1999 *HFN* article. Pleased with the success of its first national ad campaign, introduced in November 1998, Bassett planned a second push in 2000.

Meanwhile, the company had another problem to resolve. In August 1999, Bassett struck an agreement with the U.S. Environmental Protection Agency and the Justice Department over Clean Air Act violation notices occurring in 1997 and 1998. Bassett agreed to pay a $575,000 penalty and spend $1.6 million on pollution prevention. Boilers tied to excess particulate emissions had been renovated or retired to fix the problem. The company was also required to implement an environmental management plan as part of the agreement. Beyond the required actions, Bassett intended to take additional steps to mitigate particulate pollution, *Wood & Wood Products* reported.

Bassett President Rob Spilman Jr. succeeded Paul Fulton as CEO in 2000. Fulton continued as nonexecutive chairman of the board. "Fulton wasn't going to run this forever," First Union Securities Managing Director John Baugh explained to *HFN*. "The plan all along was for Rob to see the company through this transition period. Rob was the CEO heir apparent all along." Baugh added that the tough decision to downsize had been made, and the marketing strategy was set.

TOUGH TIMES IN THE 21ST CENTURY

Spilman soon faced another wave of challenges, however. Sales weakened in 2000. An industry downturn forced plant closures and layoffs in 2001. The economy remained depressed into 2002 and another plant was shuttered. In doing so, the hundred-year-old company stepped further away from its roots as a product manufacturer and closer to a new identity as product marketer.

As the economy began turning around, the centenarian firm endeavored not to act its age. Ad spending was upped in 2004, targeting a younger customer as well as the working woman, according to *Brandweek*. Yet while profits for the year were $8.2 million, sales remained flat at $316 million.

In August 2006, Bassett sent out its first direct-to-consumer catalog, targeting 1.2 million U.S. households. The company, among the country's top 20 furniture producers and retailers, had 111 licensed and 25 company owned stores. In addition to touting its furniture and accessories, Bassett highlighted its design consultation services and 30-day delivery on custom-built furniture.

Economic conditions again conspired against the furniture industry in 2007. A housing meltdown stunned the country and its financial institutions. In addition, consumers faced more bad news at the gasoline pump.

During 2007, Hooker Furniture, Stanley Furniture, and Bassett all shut down domestic wood furniture plants, according to the *Roanoke Times*. Industry survivors depended increasingly on foreign production and smaller, more efficient domestic operations to stay in the game.

Publicly traded furniture companies received a shot in the arm from the government in early 2008. A cut in the interest rate by the Federal Reserve and an economic stimulus proposal from the Bush administration helped drive up stock prices.

Housing sales contributed to approximately 20 percent of furniture purchases, according to a *Roanoke Times* article by Duncan Adams. Other precipitating factors included marriage, divorce, and the birth of a baby.

Reporting on its 2007 results, Bassett attributed a sales drop-off of 10 percent to the soft market. The company was also stung by a crib recall late in the year. On the earnings front, Bassett fell into the red, posting a net loss of $9.9 million versus a net gain of $5.4 million the prior year.

Dean Boyer
Updated, Kathleen Peippo

PRINCIPAL SUBSIDIARIES

Bassett Furniture Industries of North Carolina, L.L.C.; The E.B. Malone Corporation; Bassett Direct Stores, L.L.C.; Bassett Direct NC, L.L.C.; Bassett Direct SC, L.L.C.

PRINCIPAL COMPETITORS

Stanley Furniture Company, Inc.; Ethan Allen Interiors Inc.; Hooker Furniture Corporation.

FURTHER READING

Adams, Duncan, "Feds Cut Check for Furniture Makers," *Roanoke Times & World News,* December 19, 2006, p. C6.

———, "Furniture Industry Polishes Its Image," *Roanoke Times,* January 24, 2008, p. C8.

Allegrezza, Ray, "Bassett Breaks into RTA," *HFN—The Weekly Newspaper for the Home Furnishing Network,* June 26, 1995, p. 11.

———, "Sharp Focus for Bassett," *HFN—The Weekly Newspaper for the Home Furnishing Network,* May 26, 1997, pp. 1+.

"Bassett Furniture to Pay $575,000 Fine for EPA Violations," *Wood & Wood Products,* August 1999, pp. 13+.

Bishop, Susan, "Bassett Names Rob Spilman Jr. CEO," *HFN— The Weekly Newspaper for the Home Furnishing Network,* April 3, 2000, p. 6.

Buchanan, Lee, "Bassett Emerging As Retail Power Next Year, Company Plans to Step Up Its National Advertising Campaign," *HFN—The Weekly Newspaper for the Home Furnishing Network,* July 12, 1999, p. 32.

Cleal, Dorothy, and Hiram H. Herbert, *Foresight, Founders and Fortitude: The Growth of Industry in Martinsville and Henry County, Virginia,* Bassett, Va.: Bassett Printing Corp., 1970.

O'Loughlin, Sandra, "Bassett Furniture Polishes Message to Floor Rivals: Company Breaks from Tradition to Attract New Customers," *Brandweek,* June 14, 2004, p. 15.

Wray, Kimberly, "Bassett Helm to Outsider," *HFN—The Weekly Newspaper for the Home Furnishing Network,* May 12, 1997, pp. 1+.

the beautiful foods company™

Bellisio Foods, Inc.

525 South Lake Street
Duluth, Minnesota 55802
U.S.A.
Telephone: (218) 723-5555
Fax: (218) 723-5577
Web site: http://www.bellisiofoods.com

Private Company
Incorporated: 1990 as Luigino's Inc.
Employees: 1,670
Sales: $650 million (2006 est.)
NAIC: 311412 Frozen Specialty Food Manufacturing

∎∎∎

Bellisio Foods, Inc., another entry by convenience food entrepreneur Jeno Paulucci, has successfully challenged established names in the frozen entrée sector. The company claims the number three spot among U.S. frozen entrée makers with such brands as Michelina's, Howlin' Coyote, Charrito's, Arden Kitchens, and Fusion Culinary. Aggressive expansion has taken Bellisio's products from North America across the globe to Australia, Russia, and China.

STAR OF THE NORTH: 1945–85

Early in the 20th century, Michelina and Ettore Paulucci made their way from Italy to the iron mining region of northeastern Minnesota to carve out a living. Son Luigino (Jeno) Francesco was raised in Hibbing (later home of basketball's Kevin McHale and music's

Bob Dylan). His early experience as a vegetable vendor catapulted Jeno Paulucci into a career that would span a lifetime.

Paulucci, seeing Chinese vendors selling bean sprouts, was inspired to do the same. "It quickly became a local, though somewhat oddball, success story. Here was an Italian American selling Chinese foods in a region populated mostly by Scandinavians," Andrew E. Serwer wrote for *Fortune.* "Jeno soon decided to go national, and his timing couldn't have been better. With returning GIs looking for new foods and Mom wanting the convenience of easy-to-prepare dinners, Chun King took off." Paulucci sold Chun King Foods in 1963 to R.J. Reynolds for $63 million in cash, according to *Fortune.* He then put his egg roll machine to use in another food venture, Jeno's Inc.

By 1972, the Jeno's Pizza brand was the leader in frozen pizza and frozen hot snacks. Yet the pizza business, held in trust for the Paulucci children, faced a stiff challenge from Totino's. The competition forced some changes. The Duluth plant, hindered by inefficiencies and rising transportation costs, lost jobs to Ohio in 1981. The move was a blow to the port city of Lake Superior, already weighed down by a severe downturn in the region's iron ore industry.

Paulucci, meanwhile, had engaged in a slew of other activities ranging from banking and Florida real estate to restaurants and a grocery delivery service. They produced mixed results. He sold Jeno's Inc. in 1985 to competitor Pillsbury for approximately $150 million.

Attempts to bring jobs back to his native northeastern Minnesota, as promised, had fallen flat. A legal battle with the city of Duluth over an old Chun King plant site created further dissonance. However, once that issue was resolved out of court, new opportunities for the city and Paulucci emerged.

RETURN TO ROOTS IN 1990

Eager to start his next product line, Paulucci negotiated time off his five-year noncompete contract with Pillsbury and established Luigino's Inc. in 1990. At the time, the 72-year-old ranked among *Forbes* magazine's 400 richest Americans, holding a personal net worth estimated at $500 million.

The Michelina's brand of frozen Italian entrées, based on his mother's recipes and carrying her name and likeness, came to market during an economic downturn. However, Paulucci priced his offerings below the competition, betting his timing would once again be good, as strapped consumers looked for a bargain.

Paulucci kept close tabs on the new operation, sampling sauces, watching for waste, and scrutinizing production. Well known among buyers, the onetime chairman of R.J. Reynolds Foods (later RJR-Nabisco) leveraged "his name and reputation by personally pitching his product in tough markets," Jane Brissett wrote in *Corporate Report—Minnesota.*

To start the new venture, Paulucci had put up $8 million of his own money, according to Brissett. The proceeds from $2.2 million in industrial revenue bonds, a $1 million loan from Minnesota Power Economic Development Fund, and loans of $500,000 each from the Minnesota Small Cities Program and St. Louis County provided additional capital. The Duluth 1200 Fund, established on the heels of the loss of Jeno's Inc. jobs, chipped in another $250,000 in loans. However,

the new operation returned just a fraction of the jobs lost to Duluth, when Jeno's had shifted production to Ohio a decade earlier.

Besides the single-serving Italian entrées, Luigino's produced Italian sauces for commercial and military operations. The products found early acceptance and Paulucci quickly moved to double plant capacity, investing several million dollars more. Paulucci intended to take the brand national, a daunting task for a small company. Newman's Own, the salad dressing and sauces entry of actor Paul Newman, was among the rare success stories, according to *Corporate Report—Minnesota.* Moreover, Paulucci planned on doing the national rollout sans advertising, a shift from his strategy with the Jeno's and Chun King brands.

Instead of sinking a percentage of sales into ads, he subsidized retailers' in-store promotions, such as displays and samples. The strategy went against conventional wisdom and the merits in touting the qualities of a food product, in this case one which was low-calorie and preservative free. The veteran food producer also cut costs by instating a 600 case minimum order policy, cutting down warehousing of back stock. While facing off against Stouffer's, Weight Watchers, and Budget Gourmet brands, Michelina's quickly found its way to shelves of chains such as Safeway, Winn-Dixie, and Dominick's.

POPULAR ITEM

After three years on the shelves, Michelina's was winning the battle against much larger competitors. Tactics such as separating the sauce from the pasta and gaining discounts from utilities added up to a winning combination of taste and value. In 1993 sales climbed more than 60 percent, topping $175 million, according to *Fortune.* Employees had grown to about 500 at the Duluth headquarters and plant, with an additional 1,200 at the Jackson, Ohio, plant. A line of Yu Sing Chinese entrées had been added, and the company's first ad campaign was being planned.

Despite chances to sell, Paulucci held onto Luigino's Inc. Paulucci cited reluctance to see Duluthians lose jobs another time should he sell, according to a July 1998 article by Jane Brissett. Paulucci had been the city's largest private employer prior to the exit of Jeno's Inc. Workers had also been displaced, earlier on, when Chun King was sold.

However the temptation to sell would likely continue. The popularity of branded foods had created a profitable niche, generating good cash flow. Mrs. Paul's and Gorton's brands had been sold by Campbell Soup Co. and General Mills Inc., respectively. "'A company

KEY DATES

1990: Jeno Paulucci launches Michelina's, an Italian convenience food line.

1993: Sales for the parent company, Luigino's, top $175 million.

1999: Luigino's expands into southwestern food offerings.

2001: Company buys All-American Gourmet Company.

2002: Production capacity is added.

2004: Paulucci steps away from day-to-day management.

2005: Renamed Michelina's, company is put up for sale.

2007: Operations are consolidated under umbrella company Bellisio Foods.

like Luigino's would be an attractive buy,' said Leonard Teitelbaum, managing director of Merrill Lynch & Co. Inc. in New York City. 'There seems to be an appeal for branded foods whose franchises can be expanded,'" he told Brissett.

FROZEN FOODS HEATING UP

Luigino's won a four-year-old trademark infringement case in 1999. Stouffer Corp., owned by Nestlé, had attempted to thwart the use of the words Lean 'N Tasty. The U.S. Eighth Circuit Court of Appeals said the Michelina's entry was not infringing on Lean Cuisine and "trademark law does not give Stouffer the exclusive right to use a mark that consumers associate with tasty, low-fat frozen entrées," the *Duluth News-Tribune* reported in March.

Also in 1999, Luigino's acquired Minneapolis-based Paradise Kitchens, maker of southwestern-style frozen chili and shelf-stable salsa. Luigino's, aiming to double its sales within the next five years, saw expanded southwestern offerings as a key part of its growth, according to *Quick Frozen Foods International*. Prior year sales for retail and foodservice were an estimated $185 million and $285 million, respectively.

Meanwhile, eager to drive sales of Michelina's new premium entrées, Paulucci was prepared to invest $20 million of his own money on advertising, according to *Supermarket News*. A member of the Frozen Food Hall of Fame, Paulucci previously had challenged branded frozen food makers to spend more on promoting their industry as a whole, as other types of food producers had done.

Luigino's acquired All-American Gourmet Co. from Heinz Frozen Food Co. in 2001. The deal included Budget Gourmet and the Budget Gourmet Value Classics brands. Michelina's held about 13 percent of the U.S. frozen entrée market and Budget Gourmet about 11 percent. The two brands would continue to be marketed separately.

Michelina's was sold in the United States, Canada, the United Kingdom, Australia, New Zealand, and elsewhere. The brand produced sales of about $350 million in 2000, Luigino's President and CEO Ron Bubar told *Frozen Food Digest*.

While the purchase of All-American Gourmet boosted revenue by more than 30 percent in 2001, according to *Refrigerated & Frozen Foods*, a 2002 purchase expanded Luigino's production. Arden International Kitchens, located south of the Twin Cities in Lakeville, Minnesota, had been operating at less than half of annual capacity, packaging food for restaurants and private-label products for retailers.

Luigino's pulled the plug on further production expansion during 2003, the *Duluth News-Tribune* reported. Although a West Virginia site was set to go, Luigino's backed out of the deal. Earlier proposed plants in northeastern Minnesota and Butte, Montana, also failed to come to fruition. Luigino's Jackson, Ohio, plant, located within 500 miles of 50 percent of the country's population, was producing about a million frozen entrées a day.

Although the company was owned by the family, Jeno Paulucci held the only voting shares of Luigino's and was known to keep a tight rein on operations. However, as the national and international expansion grew increasingly complex Paulucci decided to step back from day-to-day management, a 2004 *Duluth News-Tribune* article explained. He planned to continue as an adviser while developing his next venture, microwaveable food products. Bubar succeeded Paulucci as chairman. Joel Conner, former senior executive vice-president of marketing and international sales, stepped in as president.

GOODBYE AGAIN, MAYBE

Paulucci placed the company, renamed Michelina's Inc., up for sale in 2005. The Michelina's line was moved to Jackson, Ohio. A scaled-back number of Duluth workers began making microwaveable hot subs. Yet Duluth lost even those production jobs in 2006, when the aging plant was deemed unsuitable for expansion and shut down. Production shifted to Lakeville while Duluth retained its headquarters status, albeit shared with Sanford, Florida, Paulucci's other home.

In 2007, the frozen entrée operation saw another name change, to Bellisio Foods, Inc. Paulucci's maternal hometown was Bellisio Solfare and son Michael operated a Duluth restaurant under the name Bellisio. "The Beautiful Foods Company" planned to consolidate several companies under one umbrella, including Luigino's International, the microwaveable food operation, and Fusion Culinary, a research and development center established in Lakeville, where new products were in the works. The consolidation also was expected to facilitate overseas sales to Russia, China, and India, Brissett reported for the *Duluth News-Tribune.*

The Ohio plant was at capacity, so Bellisio Foods tapped a town in Georgia as the site of the next production plant. The company was preparing a Joy of Cooking line of frozen meals, having licensed the name from the grandson of cookbook author Irma S. Rombauer, according to *Forbes.*

Bellisio brands included Michelina's, Michelina's Budget Gourmet, Michelina's Lean Gourmet, BUNdino's, Fusion Culinary, Arden Kitchens, Howlin' Coyote, and Charrito's. Among its customers were retailers Albertson's, Food Lion, Kroger, Supervalu, and Wal-Mart and national restaurant chains Bennigan's and Applebee's.

Bellisio's 2006 operating income (Ebitda) was $105 million on $650 million in sales, according to a January 2008 *Forbes* article. Regarding Paulucci, Emily Schmall told readers the businessman had been lauded for his hiring practices, employing people with disabilities, criminal records, and other "black spots" that might prevent them from being hired elsewhere. Equally true, his company benefited from tax credits linked to such hiring. Also well versed in state and local incentives for job creation, Paulucci leveraged his knowledge to keep his own costs down. During 2007, however, one significant opportunity did evade him, a $700 million deal with a private equity firm for the sale of Bellisio Foods failed to close.

Kathleen Peippo

PRINCIPAL DIVISIONS

Michelina's Canada; Michelina's Australia.

PRINCIPAL COMPETITORS

The Schwan Food Company; Southeast Frozen Foods Inc.; Windsor Quality Food Co. Ltd.; H. J. Heinz Company; Nestlé USA, Inc.

FURTHER READING

Brissett, Jane, "Frozen Food Company Has a Change of Name," *Duluth News-Tribune,* September 27, 2007.

———, "Frozen Food King Hands Over Company Reins," *Duluth News-Tribune,* July 7, 2004, p. 7B.

———, "Head of Minnesota-Based Luigino's Turns Down Buyout Offers," *Knight Ridder/Tribune Business News,* July 17, 1998.

———, "Jeno's Homecoming," *Corporate Report—Minnesota,* June 1991, pp. 48+.

———, "Michelina's, a Longtime Duluth Presence, Closes," *Duluth News-Tribune,* January 6, 2006.

———, "Paulucci Expects to Sell Luigino's by End of 2005," *Duluth News-Tribune,* July 16, 2005, p. 1A.

———, "Soup's On," *Duluth News-Tribune,* October 23, 2005, p. 1A.

"Duluth, Minn.-based Frozen-Food Company Cancels Expansion," *Knight-Ridder/Tribune Business News,* April 8, 2003.

Egerstrom, Lee, "Frozen Food Magnate Presses President Bush for Grand Jury on Corporate Crime," *St. Paul Pioneer Press,* July 24, 2002.

Harris, John, "Jeno's Next Course," *Forbes,* May 27, 1991, p. 358.

Lincoln, Craig, "Founder of Jeno's Breaking the Ice with New Frozen Foods Firm," *Knight-Ridder/Tribune Business News,* January 9, 1994.

"Luigino's Buys Frozen Chili Outfit, Looks to Double Sales Volume," *Quick Frozen Foods International,* April 1999, p. 173.

"Luigino's Doubles Pasta Plant Capacity, Hopes to Reach Sales of $50 Million," *Quick Frozen Foods International,* July 1991, p. 127.

"Luigino's Inc. Acquires the All-American Gourmet Co.," *Frozen Food Digest,* April–May 2001, p. 16.

"Luigino's Profile," *Duluth News-Tribune,* November 9, 2003, p. 7A.

Meeks, Fleming, "Full Plate," *Forbes,* November 27, 1989, pp. 286+.

Meyer, Ann, "Jeno's Back in Business," *Prepared Foods,* January 1991, pp. 15+.

Murray, Barbara, "Michelina's Gets $20M Boost from Luigino's CEO," *Supermarket News,* May 3, 1999, p. 150.

Passi, Peter, "Duluth-Minn.-Based Frozen Food Company Acquires Heinz Subsidiary," *Knight-Ridder/Tribune Business News,* February 10, 2001.

"Paulucci's Frozen Food Empire Expands, Again," *Refrigerated & Frozen Foods,* May 2002, p. 10.

"Sanford, Fla.-based Luigino's Wins Trademark Case," *Knight-Ridder/Tribune Business News,* March 17, 1999.

Schmall, Emily, "Gimme a Break," *Forbes,* January 28, 2008, pp. 78–79.

Serwer, Andrew E., "Head to Head with Giants—And Winning," *Fortune,* June 13, 1994, p. 154.

The Will and the Way, Duluth, Minn.: Manley Goldfine and Donn Larson, 2004, pp. 145–52.

Blish-Mize Co.

223 South 5th Street
Atchison, Kansas 66002
U.S.A.
Telephone: (913) 367-1250
Toll Free: (800) 995-0525
Fax: (913) 367-7483
Web site: http://www.blishmize.com

Private Company
Incorporated: 1871 as Blish, Mize & Silliman
Employees: 175
Sales: $67.4 million (2007)
NAIC: 423710 Hardware Merchant Wholesalers

■ ■ ■

Blish-Mize Co. is a wholesaler and distributor of hardware and building materials, selling more than 50,000 different types of products to hardware stores, retail home centers, building materials dealers, lumberyards, and paint stores. Blish-Mize serves roughly 1,400 customers in a 13-state territory in the Southwest and Midwest. The company's merchandise includes hand tools, lawn and garden supplies, plumbing products, power tools and accessories, fasteners, paint and paint sundries, heating and cooling products, electrical goods, toys and sporting goods, and household and houseware supplies. Blish-Mize operates a 350,000-square-foot distribution center near its main offices in Atchison, Kansas, and a smaller distribution center in Denver, Colorado. Blish-Mize, under the fourth generation of family ownership and management, also fulfills

orders online, serving customers who shop on Amazon.com, Cornerhardware.com, and several other web sites.

BORN ON A FRONTIER TOWN

In the great westward migration of the 19th century, the town of Atchison, in the northeastern section of Kansas, figured as a prominent waypoint for the waves of settlers heading to the Rocky Mountains and beyond. Existing as a French trading post early in the century, the location served as the embarkation point for the Lewis and Clark Expedition in 1804, establishing a precedent followed by generations of settlers destined for the West. When the town site was staked a half-century later, its steamboat landing on the banks of the Missouri River enabled the newly incorporated town to flourish as one of the region's leading commercial centers. As many as five steamboats per day stopped at Atchison, which was farther west than many other river towns. The U.S. Post Office selected the town as the headquarters and starting point for mail headed to the West. The stagecoach line from Atchison to Placerville, California, ranked among the most important and longest lines in the country. Further, the wagon road that headed west was regarded as one of the most ideal routes for settlers to use.

The establishment of the Atchison, Topeka, and Santa Fe Railroad in 1859 cemented the town's usefulness as a stopping point to prepare for the trek west. The arrival of the Chicago, Rock Island, and Pacific Railroad in 1872 made Atchison the termination point for eight different railroad lines, not including four railroad lines whose eastern terminus was located on the other side of the Missouri River. Crowds of fortune seekers and adventurers created a mass of humanity in the town, enabling Atchison to flourish as a hub of commerce. Covered wagons converged on the town, stopping to take on the provisions required for the months of travel ahead. Merchants and outfitters thrived off the frenzy of commercial activity, including one hardware-outfitting firm that attracted the attention of a Chicago businessman, John B. Silliman.

A BAND OF BROTHERS-IN-LAW

Silliman left Chicago to survey business opportunities in Atchison roughly a decade after the Atchison, Topeka, and Santa Fe Railroad was established. Once in Atchison, Silliman came across a business for sale. He liked what he saw and, after returning to Chicago, he informed his brothers-in-law, David P. Blish and Edward A. Mize, that he had found a promising investment opportunity. In 1871, Blish and Mize followed Silliman to Atchison, where the three men purchased the outfitting business that would bear their names. Blish, Mize & Silliman hitched its growth to the wagon trains pausing before embarking west, selling axle grease, shovels, guns, tools, and other goods to the town's itinerant community.

Atchison's rise to prominence lost traction after the town delayed building a bridge across the Missouri River. Its usefulness as a launching point for settlers headed to the West diminished as well, usurped by the infrastructures and capabilities of far larger cities. After the bustle of commerce related to expeditions to the West died down in Atchison, the three transplanted Chicagoans faced their first crisis, one they responded to quickly and deftly. Well before the end of the century, the three entrepreneurs began distributing merchandise to general stores, greatly expanding their operating territory beyond the confines of Atchison. Blish, Mize & Silliman struck deals with general store proprietors throughout Kansas and four neighboring states, supplying nearly 2,000 products to roughly 800 general stores

in a five-state region. Geographically, the firm's boundaries were set, establishing the operating territory for Blish, Mize & Silliman until the late 20th century.

FROM GENERAL STORES TO HARDWARE STORES

Having demonstrated an ability to change with the times after Atchison's economy weakened, the three business owners and their descendants showed they were able to respond to changing market dynamics in subsequent years. General stores, as a retail format, gradually disappeared, giving way to Blish, Mize & Silliman's new breed of customers: hardware stores. In some cases, the hardware store customers the company dealt with were the same customers that it had served before. Its clients had converted to a different format, and Blish, Mize & Silliman responded by adapting to the needs of its clientele. The company prided itself on its attention to customer service, which was exemplified in a profound instance when it switched from catering to general stores to supplying hardware stores. The process occurred gradually, but by the mid-1930s the company was focused exclusively on hardware retailers.

Blish, Mize & Silliman faced many challenges during its lengthy history. Through four generations of family ownership and management, the company withstood pernicious economic conditions, none greater than the national financial crisis that raged during the 1930s. It faced assaults on its way of doing business, confronted by competitors who threatened to make regional wholesalers and distributors obsolete. Blish, Mize & Silliman experienced its first significant struggle with a competitor when Sears, Roebuck & Company began mailing its catalog. In later years, particularly after World War II, the company battled to survive amid industry consolidation that saw national distributors acquire smaller distributors to maximize their size. Beginning in the 1980s and 1990s, the company also faced the rise of big-box retailers, a new breed of giants with massive stores and their own distribution infrastructure. Through all the trials and tribulations—fluctuating economic conditions, encroaching competitors, changing industry dynamics—the company credited its success with its tireless dedication to customer service. Further, it remained focused on what it did best, keeping an even keel as it navigated through more than a century of often times tempestuous waters. The company's name changed on several occasions, from Blish, Mize & Silliman Hardware Co. to BM&S in the 1970s and to Blish-Mize Co. a decade later, but its mission remained the same, one expressed on its web site 137 years after its founding: If we don't take care of our customer, "someone else will."

KEY DATES

1871: Brothers-in-law John B. Silliman, David P. Blish, and Edward A. Mize buy an outfitting business in Atchison, Kansas.

1930s: The company's customer base of general store operators complete their conversion to the hardware store format.

1985: The acquisition of DuttonLainson makes paint and paint sundries Blish-Mize's single largest line of merchandise.

1999: Blish-Mize enters Texas, New Mexico, and Arizona through the acquisition of Galbraith Wholesale Supply Co.

2001: Blish-Mize adds 51,000 square feet to its distribution center in Atchison.

2007: Sales reach $67.4 million for the year.

BLISH-MIZE IN THE EIGHTIES

The philosophy espoused by Blish-Mize was embraced by the fourth generation of the family, John Mize Jr., who presided over a company that generated $36 million in sales by the end of the 1980s. "You ought to be good at what you do and not stray from that," he said in a February 1989 interview with *Chilton's Hardware Age.* "A wholesaler like us should stay in its niche and region and watch its costs and provide service—that's how we have survived." By the time Mize offered his thoughts to the trade publication, Blish-Mize served 1,200 customers, a number he purposely had cut in half during the previous two years. "We're calling on fewer accounts by choice," he informed *Chilton's Hardware Age.* "We can't economically serve a dealer unless it gives us enough volume."

Mize halved his customer base, expressed no desire to extend the company's reach beyond its existing nine-state operating territory, and stressed to *Chilton's Hardware Age* his intent to stay "in our own niche," but he did not sit back as Blish-Mize's president and chief executive officer. Several acquisitions were completed during the 1980s, including the purchase of F.C. Stearns in 1984, which gave Blish-Mize an Arkansas-based hardware wholesaler. The following year the company acquired DuttonLainson, a Nebraska-based paint manufacturer and distributor. The purchase of Dutton-Lainson substantially expanded Blish-Mize's paint offerings and marked its entry into paint production, making paint and sundries the company's single largest line of merchandise. In 1986, Blish-Mize entered the Dallas,

Texas, market by acquiring a bankrupt, Louisville, Kentucky-based wholesaler named Belknap. The most important addition of the period was a distribution center in Denver, which figured as Mize's most aggressive move.

ACQUISITIONS IN THE NINETIES

During the 1990s, Mize brokered several more deals, fleshing out the company's presence in its existing markets. After noticing the merchandising mix of his retail customers increasingly favored paint and paint sundries, Mize realized he needed to step up Blish-Mize's ability to the meet the rising demand. In 1997, as a follow-up to the purchase of DuttonLainson a decade earlier, he purchased Denver-based Eastern Slopes Distributing. "We saw the need to be broader in paint and paint sundries," Mize explained in a February 2001 interview with *Do-It-Yourself Retailing.* "It's a growing area with hardlines retailers who are finding a successful niche in that department. The Eastern Slopes acquisition helped us learn more about the paint and sundries business and how we could better serve our customers."

At the end of the decade, Mize completed another major acquisition, one that marked a rare move for his company: expanding geographically. In 1999, Mize acquired Lubbock, Texas-based Galbraith Wholesale Supply Co., a hardware and building materials wholesaler. The purchase extended Blish-Mize's reach into the Southwest, giving it the ability to provide full-service distribution to customers in Texas, New Mexico, and Arizona. The acquisition also provided a major boost to Blish-Mize's business volume, adding Galbraith Wholesale's estimated annual sales of $27 million, which represented a 40 percent increase to the annual total collected by the Atchison-based organization. Galbraith Wholesale served more than 500 retail customers, including 60 building centers owned by Dallas-based Foxworth-Galbraith Lumber Company. As part of the transaction, the $300-million-in-sales retailer agreed to use Blish-Mize as its primary hardlines supplier.

BLISH-MIZE IN THE 21ST CENTURY

Blish-Mize celebrated its 130th anniversary in 2001. The company carried more than 40,000 different products by the time the date arrived, having expanded its roster of products substantially during the previous decade. The company added 51,000 square feet to its main distribution facility in Atchison during the year, and it also could celebrate its ability to incorporate new technology into its century-old business. Blish-Mize began fulfilling orders online through its web site, a new facet to its business, the company explained, that grew out of its perpetual drive to satisfy its customers. "Everybody has seen how valuable computers and the Internet technology is and what we can do with it," Blish-Mize's vice-president of sales and marketing explained in a February 2001 interview with *Do-It-Yourself Retailing*. "These technologies have really strengthened our business. Our customers came to us saying, 'When are you going to be on the Internet?' We listened to them again and now it is another area that we are strong in." The statement was delivered by the chief executive officer's son, Jonathan Mize, the fifth generation of family leadership.

As Blish-Mize plotted its future course, the years ahead promised to see the company adhere to its disciplined approach to expansion. It did not harbor desires to become a nationally oriented distributorship; instead, it remained focused on excelling within the territory it operated. Blish-Mize exuded stability, a trait earned by surviving decades of enormous changes and challenges and one that likely would sustain the company for decades to come.

Jeffrey L. Covell

PRINCIPAL SUBSIDIARIES

Galbraith Wholesale Supply Co.

PRINCIPAL COMPETITORS

Saint-Gobain Corporation; Orgill, Inc.; Moore-Handley, Inc.

FURTHER READING

"Blazing New Trails," *Do-It-Yourself Retailing*, February 2001, p. 71.

"Blish-Mize Company Acquires Galbraith Wholesale Supply," *Do-It-Yourself Retailing*, March 1999, p. 17.

"Blish-Mize Offers Dealers Industrial Supplies Niche," *Do-It-Yourself Retailing*, November 2001, p. 80.

Shuster, Laurie A., "Interview: John Mize," *Chilton's Hardware Age*, February 1989, p. 79.

Boise Cascade Holdings, L.L.C.

1111 West Jefferson Street, Suite 300
Boise, Idaho 83702-5389
U.S.A.
Telephone: (208) 384-6161
Web site: http://www.bc.com

Private Company
Incorporated: 1931 as Boise Payette Lumber Company
Employees: 5,000
Sales: $5.4 billion (2007 est.)
NAIC: 321210 Veneer, Plywood, and Engineered Wood Product Manufacturing; 421310 Lumber, Plywood, Millwork, and Wood Panel Wholesalers; 421330 Roofing, Siding, and Insulation Material Wholesalers; 421390 Other Construction Material Wholesalers

■ ■ ■

Boise Cascade Holdings, L.L.C., through its operating unit, is one of the largest building materials distributors in the United States. Wholly owned subsidiary Boise Cascade, L.L.C., also manufactures plywood, lumber, particleboard, and engineered wood products. Madison Dearborn Partners IV holds an 80 percent stake in the company, with OfficeMax retaining the other 20 percent.

LUMBER BEGINNINGS

The firm was established under the name Boise Cascade Corporation in 1957 through the merger of Boise Pay-ette Lumber Company and Cascade Lumber Company of Yakima, Washington. Boise Payette had been one of Idaho's top lumber producers since its formation in 1931; however, the building boom following World War II had seriously depleted its timberlands. Cascade Lumber Company had been in operation since 1902, when it was founded by George S. Rankin, the owner of several other businesses in the Yakima Valley. Rankin had been joined in this new venture by a business associate, Fred V. Pennington, and other individuals experienced in lumber operations in the Midwest. Initially, Cascade owned timberland at the headwaters of the Yakima River, which it had purchased for $100,000, and also operated several retail lumberyards in the area in addition to its Yakima mill. These yards were closed in 1914 and consolidated into one lumberyard at the Yakima sawmill, which continued operating even after the merger with Boise Payette.

Robert V. Hansberger, who had joined Boise Payette in 1956 as president, saw the merger of the two companies as an opportunity for Boise Payette to replenish its timber supply. More importantly, combining the resources of the two firms would enable the resulting company to build a base of raw materials large enough to allow it to expand beyond lumber production into the manufacture of paper and pulp products.

In 1958 the company, now known as Boise Cascade, built a kraft pulp and paper mill in Wallula, Washington, and corrugated container plants at both Wallula and Burley, Idaho. The paper and pulp area grew rapidly over the next five years with further expan-

COMPANY PERSPECTIVES

We are proud, persistent, passionate, participative people. As we focus on delivering the best return for our investors, we can be trusted to do what we say and take responsibility for our actions, which we base on the following Values & Principles: Integrity: We are our word. That is the foundation of all our relationships. Safety: It is our way of life. Communication: We talk straight, really listen, and share our knowledge across the company. Quality: We meet or exceed the expectations of our customers and are committed to helping them enhance their businesses. Stewardship: We manage our businesses to sustain environmental resources for future generations. Innovation: We are creative and nimble and look worldwide for better ways to do things. Recognition: We value one another. We recognize one another's responsibility to participate actively, and we respect one another for our ideas and contributions. Growth: we support an environment of continuous learning where our people can take on new challenges and build successful careers.

sion of the company's paper and wood production capacity. In spite of this success, Hansberger and his management team recognized how vulnerable the company was because of the cyclical nature of the wood and paper industries. They decided to diversify into other areas as a hedge against possible downturns in demand for its forest products.

DIVERSIFICATION: 1964–69

Since joining the company, Hansberger had filled the company's top management ranks with graduates of the country's leading business schools. He permitted these executives to operate independently and expand the company's operating divisions as they saw fit. In 1964 Boise Cascade entered the office products distribution business. By 1969 Boise Cascade had completed over 30 mergers and acquisitions and had become the third largest forest products company in the United States. Its operations encompassed such diverse activities as residential and mobile home construction, recreational vehicle production, publishing, and cruise management.

One of the company's major interests during the mid-1960s was the field of real estate speculation and recreational land development. In 1967 alone, Boise

Cascade acquired U.S. Land Company, Lake Arrowhead Development Company, and Pacific Cascade Land Company, and amassed real estate holdings of 126,000 acres in more than 12 states, with the majority of the land in California. Hoping to sell this property to large investors, the company met with little success and was forced to revise its strategy and develop the land itself into residential and recreational areas.

Although the company experienced greater success with this approach and sales were brisk, the new business division encountered several unanticipated problems. For example, Boise Cascade became a prime target for a growing ecological movement, particularly on the West Coast, which was concerned about the impact of the company's plans on the environment. Activist groups often hampered the company's efforts to gain approval for its developments from local planning agencies. Another major setback resulted from a series of lawsuits brought against Boise Cascade by the California attorney general. These legal actions were filed in response to complaints from prospective buyers about the tactics used by the company's salesmen, many of whom had been inherited in the course of the company's acquisitions of realty projects. The suits were eventually settled at a cost of $59 million.

In addition to these problems, Boise Cascade also experienced serious cash-flow difficulties related to its land development business. In this industry, the developer was responsible for paying the costs of constructing a community's sewer and water systems. These costs, typically, were high and had to be paid immediately, yet the developer was unable to collect its revenues until up to seven years after its sales were made. In an attempt to infuse the firm with fresh capital to fund the land development business on an ongoing basis, Boise Cascade acquired Ebasco in 1969. Ebasco and its subsidiaries were in the engineering and construction business and provided engineering services to major utilities. It was particularly attractive to Boise Cascade because it was rich with cash. It held millions of dollars worth of Latin American bonds, payable in U.S. dollars, that had been gained through the sale of Ebasco's utility operations in Argentina, Brazil, Chile, Colombia, and Costa Rica. By 1970 it was clear the company's land development business was in serious trouble, accumulating losses that placed the entire organization in jeopardy.

Upon the 1968 purchase of Princess Cruises, the company shifted its marketing efforts away from independent travel agencies, which had originally spurred the growth of the cruise line. Instead, it instituted a direct-mail campaign that was developed

KEY DATES

1902: Cascade Lumber Company of Yakima, Washington, is founded.

1931: Boise Payette Lumber Company is founded.

1957: Boise Cascade Corporation is created through the merger of Boise Payette Lumber and Cascade Lumber.

1958: The company's first pulp and paper mill and first corrugated container plants are built.

1964: Boise Cascade enters the office products distribution business.

1969: Diversification program results in various activities, including land development, recreational vehicle production, and cruise management.

1972: John Fery takes the helm, focusing the company on core areas: paper, building products, and office products distribution.

1987: Company sells its consumer packaging division.

1990: Recession hits Boise Cascade hard.

1992: Wholesale segment of office products distribution business is sold.

1994: Paper division begins three-year refocusing, with five paper mills sold or shut down.

1995: Company sells minority stake in Boise Cascade Office Products, retaining an 82.7 percent interest.

1999: Billerica, Massachusetts-based Furman Lumber, Inc., is acquired and merged into the company's wholesale building products unit.

2003: Boise Cascade buys and merges OfficeMax with office products business.

2004: Madison Dearborn Partners purchases the paper and forest products operations and retains the Boise Cascade name; the office products business begins operating under the OfficeMax name.

2005: Initial public offering of Boise Cascade is halted due to lack of interest.

2008: Private equity investors complete purchase of paper, packaging, and newsprint businesses.

DIVESTMENTS AND RESTRUCTURING

In an attempt to reverse its losses, Boise Cascade wrote off a significant portion of its real estate holdings and divested its residential housing operation, along with other assets judged to be inadequate performers or lying too far outside the company's core business areas. In light of the land-development reversals, Robert Hansberger, the architect of the company's rapid growth, resigned in 1972 and was replaced as president and chief executive officer by John Fery. Fery had been hired as Hansberger's assistant in 1957 and had ascended to executive vice-president and director within ten years.

After taking the helm, Fery immediately placed tighter controls on the company's internal management structure. He began selling off additional subsidiaries, including several Latin American investments gained in the Ebasco purchase, in order to reduce debt and refocus the firm's energies on forest products. As a result of these measures, Boise Cascade moved from a $171 million net loss to a $142 million net profit in just one year. Fery also instituted a five-year, billion-dollar capital spending program that was intended to help reduce the company's dependence on areas with correlating demand cycles, such as lumber and plywood, in favor of businesses with higher and more consistent growth potential. Fery's strategy placed greater emphasis on the manufacture of products for the construction industry and on paper products that could be marketed directly to end users in business form printing, data processing, and publishing.

This initiative propelled Boise Cascade into the 1980s as a specialized and efficient manufacturer of forest products and owner of timberland. By 1982 the company encountered sluggish demand for its products on two key fronts. The housing industry was badly depressed, reducing the demand for building products. The company's pulp and paper operation, intended to help Boise Cascade weather downturns in its other markets, experienced similar problems as industrial firms cut back expenditures in response to the weakening economy. Over the next two years, the firm closed a number of inefficient or unprofitable mills and consolidated its marketing operations. In 1987 Boise Cascade sold its consumer packaging division, which had manufactured containers for various products, and a chain of retail building materials centers that had been acquired from Edwards Industries in 1979. Labor contracts with union employees were renegotiated in an attempt to reduce the company's overall cost structure.

At this time, the Federal Trade Commission accused Boise Cascade of violating the Robinson-Patman Act and the Federal Trade Commission (FTC) Act. In its

internally and proved less effective in generating business. As a result, the cruise line went from profits to losses within a matter of months.

suit, filed in 1980, the FTC claimed that the company had purchased office products for resale to commercial users and retailers at prices below those available to competitors. The FTC subsequently issued a cease and desist order to the firm in 1986. In 1988, however, an appeals court reversed this directive, determining that the FTC had not effectively substantiated its claim that the company's purchasing practices had adversely affected competition. The case was reargued before the FTC, resulting in a renewed finding of violation.

FACING RECESSION IN THE NINETIES

When the paper industry rebounded in 1986, Boise Cascade and other manufacturers began construction to increase both production and capacity to meet the demand. By 1990, however, this response to the market upswing resulted in an oversupply of paper and excess industry capacity that caused prices and profits to drop. Boise Cascade again found itself vulnerable to the peaks and valleys of another cyclical industry.

Although periods of recession were not new to Boise Cascade, the severity of this economic slump, coupled with the company's large investment in facility renovation and expansion, presented formidable challenges unrivaled in the company's history. Within the paper industry, the grades of paper most severely affected by the recession were newsprint and uncoated business and printing papers, the two grade categories in which Boise Cascade was most heavily committed. To make matters worse, preservation limits on the harvesting of timber in the Pacific Northwest, where the company maintained a greater presence than its competitors, reduced the supply of timber and consequently negatively affected operating costs. Expansion costs, especially the company's $550 million modernization program at its International Falls, Minnesota, paper mill, which was funded by borrowed money, raised its debt level, adding to the economic woes of the company. Boise Cascade's office products division also felt the brunt of the recession, suffering substantial losses in sales and profits.

To mitigate losses during the downturn, Boise Cascade formulated a business plan in 1990 to respond to the debilitating economic situation. The company decided to retain only those mills that could be upgraded to compete on a worldwide basis, to lessen its dependence on timber in the Pacific Northwest, and to sell assets that did not fit within its new strategic plan.

By the following year, the nation was still mired in a recession, and the paper industry continued to suffer from an oversupply of paper. Conditions at Boise Cascade were not much better. Facing its most difficult year ever, Boise experienced a drop in sales from 1990 levels; operating costs continued to rise due to timber supply reductions in the Pacific Northwest. The company, however, continued to invest heavily toward the expansion and modernization of its facilities, spending $2.2 billion on such programs over a three-year period. The combination of lower prices, increased operating costs, and the high interest payments stemming from capital investment projects resulted in a net loss of over $79 million, a considerable drop from a profit of $267 million two years earlier. In an effort to streamline the company, Boise Cascade announced the sale of $250 million of assets it no longer deemed strategically prudent to own. In July 1991, Boise Cascade sold its 50 percent interest in Durapack AG, a corrugated container manufacturer in Europe, for $50 million. Also in 1991, the company sold 29,500 acres of timberland in western Oregon and by January 1992 had sold the wholesale segment of its office products distribution business.

Despite its efforts to recover from the downturn, Boise Cascade suffered even greater losses in 1992. Sales dropped to $3.7 billion from nearly $4 billion in 1991, and the company recorded a net loss of $227 million. Still plagued by the same problems that had affected the company since the beginning of the recession in 1989, Boise Cascade responded by expanding its production of specialized papers and increasing the breadth of its office products distribution business. After divesting its wholesale operations, the company expanded its commercial distribution channels by opening new facilities in South Carolina and Florida, and acquired an existing office products distribution business in Minnesota. A year earlier, Boise Cascade had attempted to tap into the growing trend for recycled products by converting its Vancouver, Washington, mill into a recycled white paper facility. However, none of these endeavors could wrest Boise Cascade from the grip of the recession.

ACTION-PACKED END TO DECADE

Boise Cascade continued to be troubled into 1994, suffering from the prolonged slump in paper prices and burdened by a $2 billion debt load. The company paid down some of the debt by issuing almost $500 million in preferred stock in 1992 and 1993. Overall sales were on the rise in 1993 and 1994, growing to $3.96 billion and $4.14 billion, respectively, but Boise Cascade continued in the red, posting net losses of $77 million in 1993 and $63 million in 1994. In April 1994 Fery retired from his position as CEO, remaining chairman, with George J. Harad, who had been president and chief operating officer, moving into the CEO slot. Harad soon took on the chairmanship as well.

During 1995 Boise Cascade rode a sharp increase in paper prices to record sales of $5.07 billion and net income of $352 million, which resulted in the company's first profitable year since 1990. That year the company was also in the midst of a three-year restructuring of its paper division, in which five paper mills were sold or shuttered and the division shifted to a primary focus on office, printing and converting, packaging, and value-added uncoated white papers. In 1995 the company sold its remaining stake in its Canadian newsprint unit, Rainy River Forest Products Inc. During the following year came the sale of a coated-paper mill in Rumford, Maine, and 667,000 acres of woodlands to Mead Corporation for about $650 million. Meanwhile, in April 1995 Boise Cascade also sold 17.3 percent of its office products subsidiary, Boise Cascade Office Products (BCOP), to the public in an initial public offering (IPO) of 10.6 million shares at $12.50 per share. Immune to the ups and downs of the paper industry, BCOP had been a consistent bright spot for Boise Cascade since it exited from the wholesale sector in 1992. Revenues for BCOP increased from $672 million in 1992 to $1.99 billion in 1996 while net income increased from $19 million to $102 million during the same period.

Boise Cascade faced additional challenges in its wood products manufacturing unit, as prices for lumber were flat at the same time that timber sales from federal lands were dwindling, driving up production costs. Unable to operate them at acceptable levels of profitability, the company closed sawmills in Horseshoe Bend, Idaho, and Fisher, Louisiana, during 1998 and a sawmill in Elgin, Oregon, in 1999. A plywood plant in Yakima, Washington, had also been slated for closure but remained open following a major fire in September 1998 at the company's plywood plant in Medford, Oregon. In October 1999 Boise Cascade also sold 56,000 acres of timberland in central Washington to U.S. Timberlands Yakima, L.L.C., for about $60 million.

In September 1999 Boise Cascade completed the acquisition of Furman Lumber, Inc., based in Billerica, Massachusetts. The purchase added 12 regional building materials distribution centers in the East, Midwest, and South to the company's wholesale building products unit, which boasted 16 such centers, most of which were located in the West. Boise Cascade thereby became a national distributor of various commodity and value-added building products. Furman had recorded fiscal 1999 sales of $574 million, while the company's building products distribution unit had posted sales of $861 million in 1998.

Boise Cascade did not fare as well with an attempted bid for Le Groupe Forex Inc., Canada's leading maker of oriented strand board, a product similar to plywood in strength but less expensive to produce. In a battle with Louisiana-Pacific Corporation waged in the summer of 1999, Boise Cascade lost a bidding war despite making two separate offers for Forex, of $470 million and $500 million.

Through the first nine months of 1999, Boise Cascade appeared headed for a possible turnaround year, with sales of $5.08 billion, an increase of almost 10 percent over the same period during 1998, and net income of $124.3 million, a vast improvement over the net loss of $25.9 million recorded in 1998. In a period of consolidation brought about by industry-wide excess production, Boise Cascade, despite its improved performance, appeared vulnerable to a takeover by a larger forest products rival. In addition to Louisiana-Pacific's takeover of Forex, International Paper Company acquired Union Camp Corporation, and Weyerhaeuser Company took over MacMillan Bloedel Ltd. Potential suitors of Boise Cascade could view the company's stake in Boise Cascade Office Products as a potential post-takeover cash-raising divestment, increasing the likelihood of a takeover. Boise Cascade Office Products Corporation produced record net income and record sales for 1999. The next year, Boise Cascade repurchased minority shares in the business, once again taking full ownership of the distributor.

NEW CENTURY

The September 11, 2001, terrorist attacks on the United States precipitated a steep decline in the stock market. Consequently, many companies suffered a drop in valuation and were considered good buys. Of Boise Cascade, Kenneth L. Fisher wrote in a September 2002 *Forbes:* "Its 2.4 million acres of real estate are worth a lot—perhaps $1,300 an acre. By that measure the land alone is worth, after due allowance for other assets and debt, $21 a share—so the rest of the operations cost you just $7. The company is dirt cheap in another way: It is selling at 20% of annual revenue and 4.5 times cash flow, with a 2.2% dividend yield."

In a marketing move during the year, the company took on a new trade name: simply Boise. The company retained its legal name but renamed the divisions. Office products changed to Boise Office Solutions, the paper unit to Boise Paper Solutions, and the timber and wood products and building materials operations consolidated under the name Boise Building Solutions.

Also during 2002, Boise Cascade agreed to a $4.35 million penalty and to fund $15 million in air emission control improvements at eight plywood and particleboard plants in Idaho, Louisiana, Oregon, and Washington. The mediated agreement with the Environmental Protection Agency and the Justice Department forestalled Clean Air Act litigation against the company.

Despite an ongoing tweaking under George Harad's leadership, Boise Cascade remained lackluster. Harad had bought and sold paper-related businesses, entered and exited international markets, closed tree processing plants, and cut research and development spending. "The results have been less than impressive," Steven Pearlstein observed in the *Washington Post*. "In the nine years since Harad took over, Boise lost money in four years, posted puny profits in two and started 2003 off in the red. In that time, Boise shares fell 15 percent." Competitor Weyerhaeuser, meanwhile, stayed the course with its core business, earned money each year, and grew in value, Pearlstein added.

Hoping to cash in on its one consistent performer, the office products business, Boise Cascade made another purchase: OfficeMax. Envisioning increased operating efficiency and marketing clout, Boise was ready to pay a 25 percent premium for the chain of office supply superstores despite its slim margins, according to Pearlstein.

Combined with the complementary Boise operation, OfficeMax hoped to gain ground on Staples, Inc., and Office Depot, Inc. The two larger companies used tactics including international expansion, mail order, and product delivery to drive up sales. In contrast, OfficeMax pushed to improve its U.S. store productivity, generating industry leading same-store sales, according to *DSN Retailing Today*.

Staples, leader of the multibillion-dollar industry, generated sales of $11.6 billion, and Office Depot followed closely behind with $11.4 billion. Ohio-based OfficeMax came in a distant third with $4.8 billion. Moreover, the number three player had been contending with stock price stagnation. OfficeMax sought to increase shareholder value through the merger, according to the August 2003 *DSN Retailing Today* article.

Coinciding with the $1.2 billion OfficeMax purchase, Boise Cascade altered its environmental policy. The forest products company had lost Kinko's, Patagonia, and L.L. Bean accounts and faced pressure from environmental groups. Boise Cascade said it planned to stop cutting timber from old growth forests, stop buying wood from endangered forests, give preference to suppliers using wood from certified forests, and track the

origin of wood products, the *Columbian* reported in September 2003.

The fifth largest public U.S. forest products company left the business in 2004 and culminated its transformation from forest products manufacturer to office products distributor. Chicago-based Madison Dearborn Partners paid Boise Cascade $3.7 billion for its paper, forest products, and timberland assets. The 100-year-old company began operating under the OfficeMax name.

Madison Dearborn Partners, in turn, formed Boise Cascade L.L.C. Former MacMillan Bloedel Ltd. CEO W. Thomas Stephens was tapped to head the pulp and paper mills and the building products manufacturing and distribution businesses. The timberland unit was sold to Forest Capital Partners L.L.C. for $1.65 billion.

NEW OWNERSHIP

Madison Dearborn Partners was no novice to the industry. "Past investments in the sector include, most notably, the firm's $6.06 billion acquisition of Jefferson Smurfit Group plc in 2002 (a deal that won *Buyouts'* European Deal of the Year), as well as other investments in Packaging Corp. of America, Graphic Packaging Corp., and Bay State Paper Holding Corp.," Kenneth MacFadyen reported in *Buyouts*.

The new incarnation of Boise Cascade faced dual challenges early in 2005. On the one hand rising energy costs pressured its margins; on the other, its largest customer, OfficeMax, was faltering.

Not only did OfficeMax hold a minority share in Boise Cascade, by way of the paper and wood products operations sale, it had promised significant paper purchases from the company. In addition, with a big OfficeMax investor disgruntled and floating the idea of a company breakup or sale, Boise's future was clouded, Robert Barker explained in *Business Week*.

Madison Dearborn, nevertheless, endeavored to take Boise Cascade public. Despite a lowered asking price—$17 to $19 a share, down from $24 to $25 a share—interest lagged. Consequently, the IPO was canceled. Continuing as a privately held company, Boise Cascade reported net income of $71.6 million on sales of $5.8 billion in 2006.

In 2007, year-over-year sales fell, as building materials and wood products businesses were hampered by the housing industry slowdown. The newsprint segment faced its own challenges, which included falling prices and rising raw material costs. However, corrugated products and linerboard saw improvements in pricing, helping to offset newsprint's income decline.

Paper sales also benefited from higher prices. Paper and the Packaging & Newsprint segments also benefited from lower depreciation and amortization costs toward year's end. In September 2007, Boise Cascade announced plans to sell the operations. "Madison Dearborn, whose chairman, John A. Canning Jr., is leading an investor group that hopes to buy the Chicago Cubs from the Tribune Company, is now shedding divisions of Boise Cascade two years after the investment company failed in its bid to sell shares of the wood products company because of lack of interest," the *New York Times* reported.

Aldabra 2 Acquisition Corp. planned to change its name to Boise Inc. following closure of the $1.6 billion deal. Boise Cascade, L.L.C., would retain 100 percent ownership of the building materials and wood products businesses and own up to 49 percent of Boise Inc.'s shares. The purchase was completed in February 2008.

Sandy Schusteff
Updated, Jeffrey L. Covell; David E. Salamie;
Kathleen Peippo

PRINCIPAL SUBSIDIARIES

Boise Cascade, L.L.C.

PRINCIPAL OPERATING UNITS

Boise Building Materials Distribution; Boise Wood Products.

PRINCIPAL COMPETITORS

BlueLinx Corp.; Georgia-Pacific Corporation; International Paper Company; Louisiana-Pacific Corporation; Potlatch Corporation; Temple-Inland Inc.; UPM Kymmene Oyj; Weyerhaeuser Company.

FURTHER READING

Anderson, Steven, "Price Slump, Market Woes Prompt Boise Cascade Cuts," *Idaho Business Review*, January 4, 1999, p. 9.

Barker, Robert, "What's Looming Over Boise Cascade," *Business Week*, April 11, 2005, p. 108.

Bary, Andrew, "No Paper Tiger," *Barron's*, January 29, 1996, pp. 20–21.

Benoit, Ellen, "Late Bloomer in the Forest," *Financial World*, September 8, 1987.

"Boise Cascade Halts Stock Sale," *Chicago Tribune*, May 20, 2005, p. 3.

"Boise Cascade Sells Unit to a Private Equity Firm," *New York Times*, September 8, 2007, p. C4 (L).

"Boise Cascade Shifts Toward Tighter Control," *Business Week*, May 15, 1971.

"Boise Cascade to Cut 1,100 Jobs," *Deseret News*, March 3, 2004, p. E3.

"Boise Won't Use Old-Growth," *Columbian*, September 4, 2003, p. E1.

Carlton, Jim, "Boise Cascade Bids About $470 Million for Timber Firm," *Wall Street Journal*, July 29, 1999, p. A6.

———, "Boise Cascade Bows out of Bidding War for Forex After Rival Increases Offer," *Wall Street Journal*, August 16, 1999, p. B12.

———, "OfficeMax CFO Quits," *Wall Street Journal*, January 13, 2005, p. A3.

Chipello, Christopher J., "Stone-Consolidated Offers to Acquire Rainy River Forest for $552 Million," *Wall Street Journal*, August 18, 1995, p. A5.

"Cinderella," *Forbes*, November 15, 1972.

Downs, Tim, "New Uncoated Free-Sheet Capacity Starts Up at Boise's I-Falls Mill," *Pulp & Paper*, May 1991, p. 98.

Eyriey, Nick, "Maxed Up! Now You See It, Now You Don't," *Office Products International*, September 2004, p. 31.

Fischl, Jennifer, "Mead and Boise: The Long and the Short," *Financial World*, November 18, 1996, p. 24.

Fisher, Kenneth L., "A Beautiful Market," *Forbes*, September 16, 2002, p. 160.

Gonzalez, Jason, "Boise, L-P Battle It Out for Groupe Forex," *National Home Center News*, August 9, 1999, pp. 9, 278.

Heiman, Grover, "Getting Back to Basics," *Nation's Business*, January 1983.

Johnson, Jim, "Boise Cascade Resolves Dispute over Emissions," *Waste News*, April 1, 2002, p. 12.

———, "Boise Joins Climate Club," *Waste News*, October 10, 2005, p. 11.

MacFadyen, Kenneth, "Madison Dearborn Re-enters the Forest," *Buyouts*, August 9, 2004, pp. 1, 42.

"Madison Dearborn Taking Boise Private in Buyout," http://www.paperloop.com, September 2004.

Narisetti, Raju, "Mead to Buy Coated-Paper Mill, Woods from Boise Cascade for $650 Million," *Wall Street Journal*, October 1, 1996, p. A4.

Pearlstein, Steven, "Boise Learned the Folly of Vertical Growth," *Washington Post*, July 16, 2003, p. E1.

Richards, Bill, "Boise Cascade May Be out of the Woods in First Period," *Wall Street Journal*, April 12, 1993, p. B4.

Rosmarin, Rachel, "Out of the Woods and into the Office," *Business 2.0*, January/February 2005, p. 49.

Taylor, John H., "Fery on the Defensive," *Forbes*, November 12, 1990, pp. 52–58.

Troy, Mike, "Boise, OfficeMax Merger Creates Larger No. 3," *DSN Retailing Today*, August 4, 2003, pp. 5+.

Tucker, John, "Wood Products Companies Contemplating Their Futures: Boise Cascade, TJI Face Choices As Consolidation Comes to Industry," *Idaho Statesman*, June 27, 1999, p. 1D.

Valentin, Erhard K., "Anatomy of a Fatal Business Strategy," *Journal of Management Studies,* May 1994, pp. 359+.

"Will Quality Tell?" *Forbes,* July 15, 1970.

Yang, Dori Jones, and Phillip L. Zweig, "Boise Has a Lot of Paper Work to Do," *Business Week,* May 9, 1994, pp. 78–79.

Breeze-Eastern
Corporation

—■—

700 Liberty Avenue
Union, New Jersey 07083-8198
U.S.A.
Telephone: (908) 686-4000
Toll Free: (800) 929-1919
Fax: (908) 686-9292
Web site: http://www.breeze-eastern.com

Public Company
Incorporated: 1962 as Space Ordnance Systems Inc.
Employees: 206
Sales: $73.3 million (2007)
Stock Exchanges: American
Ticker Symbol: BZC
NAIC: 332995 Other Ordnance and Accessories
    Manufacturing; 336419 Other Guided Missile and
    Space Vehicle Parts and Auxiliary Equipment
    Manufacturing; 336413 Other Aircraft Parts and
    Auxiliary Equipment Manufacturing

■ ■ ■

Breeze-Eastern Corporation is a leading manufacturer of hooks, hoists, winches, and other motion control products for helicopters, cargo planes, and weapons systems. A pioneer in the field of rescue hoists and cargo winches, Breeze-Eastern has long held leadership of the global market with a greater than 50 percent market share. Breeze-Eastern was known as TransTechnology Corporation before 2006, when the parent company renamed itself after its main division.

ORIGINS IN ORDNANCE

Breeze-Eastern Corporation's predecessor company was formed in California in January 1962 as Space Ordnance Systems, Inc. (SOS). It was reorganized as a Delaware corporation in 1986.

SOS's early products included igniters used to start rocket and missile engines and components for ejection seats. Later, the company began making flares carried by combat aircraft as a decoy against heat-seeking missiles, and chaff (metallic strips used to confuse enemy radar).

Annual revenues were about $17 million in the late 1960s, but the company was beginning to post consistent losses. In 1969, Arch Scurlock, whose investment group Research Industries was the largest shareholder, took over. Dan McBride was named chief executive officer, a position he would hold for two decades. Scurlock's tenure was even longer, ending in 1992. The pair had previously worked together at Atlantic Research Corp., a maker of solid fuel engines for missiles that Scurlock had founded.

BUILDING A SMALL CONGLOMERATE

Space Ordnance adopted the name TransTechnology Corporation in January 1974. By this time, it was operating nationally, and had begun to expand beyond its traditional business into a number of different fields.

TransTechnology quickly built up a textile equipment and supplies business made up of Gessner Co. (finishing machines), Howard Brothers (textile processing machinery), Curtis & Marble, and Lloyd

COMPANY PERSPECTIVES

Breeze-Eastern products are considered the leaders in their respective fields, often specified by the world's leading manufacturers of helicopters, weapon handling systems, military and civilian aircraft, and spare parts distributors. Breeze-Eastern's sophisticated lifting and restraining products are used in cargo transport and on rescue missions by most military and civilian helicopters and aircraft throughout the world. We believe that what separates Breeze-Eastern from the competition is that all our personnel, from talented engineers to skilled factory craftsmen, are dedicated to meeting our customers' precise design specifications. Our employees, dedicated to defense and aerospace products, have an uncommon "can-do" spirit, a fierce pride and belief in the mission of our products, and a sincere dedication to customer service and product improvement which are the foundation of our continued success and growth.

Manufacturing Co. (elastic fibers). It also bought the country's biggest manufacturer of meteorological instruments, Belfort Instrument Co.

Around 1973, TransTechnology acquired Eastern RotorCraft, a maker of helicopter hoists and cargo hooks based in Doylestown, Pennsylvania. The company had been formed in 1947 by J. Richard Huber and Julian P. "Cap" Perry.

1982 BREEZE BUY

By 1980, TransTechnology was reporting revenues of $36 million a year. Government work accounted for about half its business. A key acquisition and liberal defense spending under President Ronald Reagan would help the company nearly triple in size within a couple of years.

In 1982 TransTechnology bought Breeze Corp., Inc., a smaller, publicly owned conglomerate based in Union, New Jersey. Breeze was profitable on fast-rising sales of nearly $35 million a year. Its product lineup had some striking similarities to that of the acquiring company.

Breeze's Federal Laboratories, Inc., unit also produced flares, but for the law enforcement market. It also made tear gas grenades and bulletproof vests. The Electro-Mechanical division produced winches and

hoists for helicopters and other aircraft, dominating the market for smaller units.

Breeze Corp. was founded in 1926 by a prolific and successful inventor and salesman named Joseph J. Mascuch. As a young man, Mascuch had reportedly consulted with Thomas Edison on one of his first key creations, the engine ignition shielding that allowed aircraft and automobiles to carry radios. He continued to lead the company until its sale, when he was 85.

Breeze Corp. originally specialized in aircraft components. Its sales were $136,805 in 1927, according to a rather unflattering piece in a 1939 issue of *Time* magazine. The same article points out that the company's newly acquired subsidiary Federal Laboratories, Inc., made a good deal of its money selling weapons to stifle labor protests; this was not to be Federal Labs' last brush with controversy.

In 1983 Breeze Corp. was combined with TransTechnology's Eastern RotorCraft division to form Breeze-Eastern. The new profit center employed 350, about two-thirds of them from Breeze, and had revenues of $34 million in 1981. The addition helped push fast-growing TransTechnology's total annual sales to $100 million.

ACQUISITIONS AND DIVESTITURES

TransTechnology continued to add aerospace companies. It bought Los Angeles-based Flight Connector Corp. for $5 million in 1985. By this time, TransTechnology had plants at about a dozen sites across the United States.

The company diversified by acquiring Lundy Electronics & Systems for $46 million in 1986. Lundy made sorting equipment used by the banking industry. With net sales of $100 million, it helped push TransTechnology's total revenues beyond $200 million.

By this time, problems at the company's original business had made it a serious drain on income. Thousands of gallons of toxic waste were found to be improperly stored at two of the California sites of its Space Ordnance Systems unit, Placerita Canyon and Mint Canyon. In May 1990 TransTechnology sold Space Ordnance Systems to Phoenix-based Universal Propulsion Co. Inc. (a company formed by a former SOS executive).

TransTechnology's shares migrated from the American Stock Exchange to the New York Stock Exchange in February 1988. Revenues were about $235 million for the year. Ralph E. Hutchins, formerly general manager of the Eastern RotorCraft unit, succeeded Dan McBride as TransTechnology president and

KEY DATES

1926: Prolific inventor Joseph J. Mascuch forms Breeze Corp., Inc.

1947: Eastern RotorCraft is established to produce helicopter hoists.

1962: Space Ordnance Systems, Inc., is established in El Segundo, California.

1969: Entrepreneur Dr. Arch Scurlock becomes Space Ordnance chairman.

1974: Space Ordnance takes the name TransTechnology Corporation as it diversifies.

1982: TransTechnology acquires Breeze Corp., Inc., of Union, New Jersey.

1990: TransTechnology sells its California defense ordnance business to Universal Propulsion Co. Inc.

1992: After securing the top job in a proxy battle, new Chairman Michael Berthelot heads restructuring drive.

2003: Robert L. G. White becomes TransTechnology's fourth CEO to date.

2006: TransTechnology takes the name Breeze-Eastern Corporation.

CEO in January 1990. It was to be a short tenure. The company posted an $8 million loss on revenues of less than $200 million.

MANAGEMENT TRANSITION AND RESTRUCTURING

Although the company had begun to turn a profit after unloading money-losing units such as a computer graphics business, a major restructuring was in order. As part of this effort, in 1992 new CEO Michael Berthelot relocated the company headquarters from California to Union, New Jersey, site of its key Breeze subsidiary.

The end of the Cold War was making TransTechnology's defense businesses unpopular with investors. Nevertheless, the company shed some of its civilian-oriented lines. The bank automation equipment business was sold to Dallas's Recognition Equipment Inc. in 1992 for $38 million. TransTechnology also divested textile machinery unit Gessner/Howard Brothers/Miller, and the elastomer product line of its Lloyd Manufacturing division during the year. Meteorology equipment maker Belfort Instrument was sold in January 1993.

After a successful proxy fight, Michael J. Berthelot succeeded Dr. Arch C. Scurlock as chairman in October

1992. Berthelot, an accountant, had become a director the previous year and soon convinced the board to confer control of the company to him as it began to post serious losses while Scurlock dealt with health issues. When the board after a few months stripped Berthelot's titles over perceived arrogance, he put the matter directly to shareholders, promising to turn the company around and including a special dividend to sweeten the deal. They voted him in. (Scurlock died in 2002. He had also led his Research Industries investment group and Washington, D.C., information technology contractor Halifax Corp.)

The early 1990s divestments reduced TransTechnology's total sales to about $100 million a year. TransTechnology then set out to bulk up its remaining, core business segments: Industrial Products and Aerospace Products.

The $1.7 million acquisition of Electrical Specialties Company in July 1993 added a manufacturer of heavy equipment wiring products. TRW's Palnut unit, a leading maker of metal fasteners for the automotive and industrial markets, was added the next month in a deal worth $22 million.

There were more sell-offs. TransTechnology sold Federal Laboratories to Mace Security International in March 1994. Federal Laboratories had developed a successful metal detector business in the 1970s and remained a leader in the law enforcement tear gas market. However, it drew protests after Israel used its products on Palestinian demonstrators. The parent company also sold its chaff business. This went to Tracor Aerospace Inc., a unit of Marconi Corp. PLC, in 1995.

Acquisitions continued in 1997 with the purchase of automotive fastener manufacturer TCR Corp. Based in the Minneapolis area, TCR had annual revenues of $23 million and fewer than 200 employees. The next year TransTechnology added another specialty manufacturer, Aerospace Rivet Manufacturers Corp. (ARM) of Santa Fe Springs, California. It paid $27 million for ARM, which had 140 employees and annual revenues of $15 million.

UNFASTENING SOME UNITS

At the beginning of the 2001 calendar year, the company's total debt was around $250 million. It had 15 operating units and total annual revenues of about $350 million. In fiscal 2001, TransTechnology began a sell-off of its specialty fastener business. This was completed in February 2003 when Marathon Power Technologies Company, a division of TransDigm Inc., bought the Norco, Inc., unit.

Robert L. G. White, formerly head of the aerospace business, was named TransTechnology's fourth CEO in February 2003. At this time the slimmed down company had about 200 employees. Annual revenues were $55 million for the 2003 fiscal year.

U.S. military activity spurred demand, and the company was involved in a new generation of weapon systems that used its hoists to lift pods filled with rockets. Revenues were more than $64 million by 2004 and after a couple of flat years reached $73 million in 2007.

STILL EVOLVING

Although it had settled on a comfortable niche, there were more corporate changes. After trading on the Big Board, the company's shares listed on the American Stock Exchange in August 2006 (ticker symbol BZC). TransTechnology was renamed Breeze-Eastern Corporation, after its main operating company, in October 2006.

The Union, New Jersey, headquarters was sold in February 2008 for $10.5 million. The building had been in the company since 1953. Breeze-Eastern continued to lease it until a more suitable location could be found.

Frederick C. Ingram

PRINCIPAL SUBSIDIARIES

TTERUSA, Inc.; TT Connecticut Corporation; Rancho TransTechnology Corporation; Retainers, Inc.; SSP Industries; SSP International Sales, Inc.; TT Minnesota Corporation; TransTechnology International Corporation (U.S. Virgin Islands); TransTechnology International Corporation; TransTechnology Germany GmbH.

PRINCIPAL OPERATING UNITS

Hoist and Winch; Cargo Hooks; Weapons Handling.

PRINCIPAL COMPETITORS

Goodrich Corporation.

FURTHER READING

"CEO Interview: Michael J. Berthelot, Chairman and CEO, Discusses the Outlook for TransTechnology Corp.," *Wall Street Transcript Digest,* May 12, 1997.

DeMaria, Lawrence J., "A Solid Military Supplier," *New York Times,* Sec. 3, April 24, 1988, p. 8.

Gordon, Mitchell, "Flaring Up: Outlook at TransTechnology Brightened by a Key Defense Product," *Barron's,* February 22, 1982.

———, "Lucky Lundy; Acquisition to Help TransTechnology Book Record Profits," *Barron's,* September 1, 1986, pp. 48–49.

"Inventor Lives in Luxury," *Oakland (Calif.) Tribune,* July 6, 1969, p. 2D.

Marcial, Gene G., "Weaning a Defense Baby," *Business Week,* May 28, 1990, p. 98.

McMenamin, Brigid, "TransTechnology's Trojan Horse," *Forbes,* January 17, 1994, p. 110.

Mehlman, William, "Breeze, TransTech Feel Each Other Out in Preliminary Talks," *Insiders' Chronicle,* December 21, 1981.

Peterson, Robert, "Life Begins at Forty," *Great Bend (Kans.) Daily Tribune,* Editorial Sec., March 21, 1965, p. 4.

Stern, Gabriella, "Berthelot Is Ousted After Lengthy Fight over TransTechnology Corp.'s Fortunes," *Wall Street Journal,* August 17, 1992, p. B6.

"TransTechnology Buys Aero Rivet Firm," *Electronic News (1991),* September 28, 1998, p. 52.

"War Babies," *Time,* October 30, 1939.

Watson, E. Ronald, "Eastern RotorCraft Praised by Parent Firm," *Intelligencer* (Montgomery County, Pa.), May 29, 1983, p. D1.

Wolcott, Denis, "SOS to Leave Santa Clarita; Defense Contractors Cite Losses in Wake of Contamination Disclosures As Reason for Sale," *Los Angeles Daily News,* Santa Clarita Sec., March 21, 1990, p. 1.

CANADIAN PACIFIC

Canadian Pacific Railway Limited

——————————■——————————

Gulf Canada Square
401 – 9th Avenue SW, Suite 500
Calgary, Alberta T2P 4Z4
Canada
Telephone: (403) 319-7000
Toll Free: (888) 333-6370
Fax: (403) 319-7567
Web site: http://www.cpr.ca

Public Company
Incorporated: 1881 as Canadian Pacific Railway
    Company
Employees: 15,382
Sales: CAD 4.71 billion (2007)
Stock Exchanges: Toronto New York
Ticker Symbol: CP
NAIC: 482111 Line-Haul Railroads; 488210 Support
    Activities for Rail Transportation; 488510 Freight
    Transportation Arrangement; 487110 Scenic and
    Sightseeing Transportation, Land

■ ■ ■

Canadian Pacific Railway Limited is the smallest of the
"Big Six" North American railways, known as Class 1
railways. Its 13,300-mile network includes a
transcontinental main line in Canada extending from
Vancouver to Montreal, as well as a number of collector
and feeder lines; the Canadian network extends for
about 8,750 miles. In the United States, the company's

rail lines consist of 3,250 miles in the Midwest operated
by Soo Line Railway Company, a subsidiary; and 1,300
miles in the Northeast operated by another subsidiary,
Delaware and Hudson Railway Company, Inc. Alliances
with Union Pacific Corporation and other rail firms
extend Canadian Pacific's rail services throughout the
other areas of the United States and into Mexico as well.
Canadian Pacific's core business is the transport of bulk
cargo, including grain, coal, sulfur, and fertilizers; intermodal containers; and industrial and consumer
products, automobiles and automotive products, and
forest products. The company also offers intermodal
services through a network of intermodal terminals and
major rail yards.

Canadian Pacific Railway Company—the principal
subsidiary of Canadian Pacific Railway Limited—was
formed in 1881, making it one of Canada's oldest
companies. Four years after its incorporation, it
completed construction of the first transcontinental
railway in Canada. Over the succeeding decades, the
company expanded into a number of other industries,
including hotels, steamships, oil and gas, mining,
airlines, telecommunications, and shipping services. In
1971 a new holding company was formed called
Canadian Pacific Limited, with Canadian Pacific
Railway and the other businesses becoming subsidiaries
of the new parent. On October 1, 2001, Canadian
Pacific Limited was broken up into five separate publicly
traded companies, one of which was called Canadian
Pacific Railway Limited and consisted of the original
railway (Canadian Pacific Railway Company) and
related operations.

Canadian Pacific Railway Limited

COMPANY PERSPECTIVES

Our strategy is to create long-term value for customers, shareholders, communities and employees primarily by profitably growing within the footprint of CPR's premier core rail franchise. We seek to accomplish our strategy by: (1) Generating quality revenue growth—realizing the benefits of demand growth in bulk, intermodal and merchandise business segments with targeted infrastructure capacity investments linked to global trade opportunities; (2) Improving productivity—by leveraging strategic marketing and operating partnerships, executing a scheduled railway (our Integrated Operating Plan), and improving fluidity to drive more value from existing assets; and (3) Continuing to develop a dedicated, professional and knowledgeable workforce—committed to safety and sustainable financial performance through steady improvement in profitability, increased free cash flow and an adequate return on investment.

LATE 19TH CENTURY: FOUNDING OF CPR AND COMPLETION OF TRANSCONTINENTAL RAILWAY

The building of the Canadian Pacific Railway was a demanding battle, both physically and politically. After negative reports from both explorers and surveyors, a long and sometimes bitter parliamentary dispute, and threats of refusal by British Columbia to become part of the Canadian Dominion, a contract to build the rail line was finally approved by royal assent on February 15, 1881. The following day, the Canadian Pacific Railway Company (CPR) was incorporated. The company established its headquarters in Montreal. A group of railroad professionals, known as The Syndicate, who had come to Canada from Scotland as fur traders, headed the railroad's first management team. The Syndicate chose George Stephen, a former president of the Bank of Montreal and one of the principals involved in the organization of the St. Paul, Minneapolis and Manitoba Railway, as CPR's first president. Stephen was assisted by CPR Vice-President Duncan McIntyre, who left his post as president of the Canada Central Railway to help build the country's first and only transcontinental railroad.

Under the terms of the government contract, CPR received CAD 25 million in investor-subscribed funds

and 25 million acres of timberland, which eventually included the land's subsurface resources. These important assets provided the basis for the company to raise more capital. Several stock issues were floated, and large loans were made to further finance the project. In 1882 the company issued CAD 30 million worth of CPR stock to various New York investment syndicates, followed by the sale of 200,000 shares of common stock on the New York Stock Exchange (NYSE) the following year, becoming in the process the first non-American firm to be listed on the NYSE (CPR shares were first listed on the Toronto Stock Exchange in 1892). To complete the project, CPR floated a CAD 15 million bond issue through a London-based investment house. Although the company's contract allowed CPR ten years to complete the railroad's construction, the project took less than half that time. Construction of the main line was completed on November 7, 1885. At the time the Canadian Pacific Railway was the longest and costliest railroad line ever built. The first regular passenger train to use the new line, the "Pacific Express," departed from Montreal on June 28, 1886, arriving in Port Moody, British Columbia, on July 4.

The completion of the line had many effects on both the company and the Canadian economy. The subsurface resources acquired in the land deal with the Canadian Parliament put the company into the coal, zinc, lead, gold, silver, and, later, gas businesses. The railway opened the prairies for settlement, and CPR was involved in agricultural development, including irrigation and wheat farming. A rail connection from the more industrialized eastern regions to the Pacific Coast enabled the company to expand into the export shipping business and opened up many opportunities in the Far East. It was also believed that the railway's consolidating effect on the Canadian provinces stifled further northern expansion by the United States. The company, then known to most Canadians as the CPR, continued its steady growth well into the mid-1900s.

EARLY DEVELOPMENT OF RELATED ACTIVITIES

Moves into related activities began as early as 1886 when the company chartered seven ships to carry tea and silk from Asia to the West Coast of Canada, thereby providing eastbound freight for the railway. This marked the beginning of CPR's steamship services, later known as CP Ships. In 1903 CP Ships began serving the transatlantic market. CP Ships became renowned in the early decades of the 20th century for its luxury passenger liners: the famous Canadian Pacific Empress class ships. These boats sailed the world's oceans from 1891 to 1970. The speed and reliability of the CP Ships fleet

KEY DATES

1881: Canadian Pacific Railway Company (CPR) is formed to build a transcontinental railway; headquarters are established in Montreal.

1883: CPR stock is listed on the New York Stock Exchange.

1885: The company completes construction of Canada's first transcontinental railway.

1886: CPR charters seven ships to carry tea and silk from Asia to Canada, marking the beginning of steamship operations, later known as CP Ships; the company's first hotel, Mount Stephen House, is completed, initiating what will later be called Canadian Pacific Hotels.

1958: Canadian Pacific Oil and Gas Limited is formed as a subsidiary.

1971: A new parent company, Canadian Pacific Limited (CPL), is formed, with CPR and the company's other operations becoming subsidiaries; CP Oil and Gas merges with Central Del Rio Oils to form PanCanadian Petroleum Limited.

1990: CPL takes full control of Soo Line Corporation.

1991: Delaware and Hudson Railway Company, Inc., is acquired.

1995: Company headquarters are moved to Calgary.

1999: CP Hotels acquires Fairmont Hotels, leading to the eventual creation of Fairmont Hotels & Resorts Inc.

2001: CPL demerges into five separate publicly traded companies: Canadian Pacific Railway Limited, PanCanadian Energy Corporation, CP Ships, Fording Inc., and Fairmont Hotels.

2007: Canadian Pacific Railway acquires Dakota, Minnesota & Eastern Railroad Corporation, a regional railway based in Sioux Falls, South Dakota.

led to lucrative mail contracts on both transpacific and transatlantic routes. In 1922 CP Ships entered the cruise market.

CPR also began building hotels and dining rooms along the railway in order to provide passengers with food and shelter. The architect of this strategy was American railroader William Cornelius Van Horne, who had joined the company as general manager at the beginning of 1882. Van Horne had previously served as general manager of the Chicago, Milwaukee & Saint Paul Railroad. He would succeed Stephen as second president of CPR in 1888. Envisioning a string of grand hotels along the railway, Van Horne built the company's first hotel, Mount Stephen House, high in the Canadian Rockies in 1886. Two years later came the opening of the famed Banff Springs hotel, located in the Canadian Rockies of Alberta. Next came Chateau Lake Louise, completed in 1890, and Le Chateau Frontenac, which opened its doors in 1893. Most of the hotels were modeled on French chateaus and eventually achieved landmark status. These operations formed the basis for Canadian Pacific Hotels, which eventually was running hotels and resorts in every major city serviced by the railway.

CPR's involvement in the oil and gas industry also had an early start, although it would be many more years before energy became a significant part of the company operations. In 1883 a CPR crew drilling for water near Medicine Hat made the first natural gas discovery in Alberta. This was the Milk River formation, which remains one of the largest discoveries in western Canada. Initially, when CPR sold parts of its vast land holdings it would sell the mining and mineral rights as well. By 1912, however, this policy was reversed and CPR began reserving rights to "all mines and minerals under the lands" for property that it sold. This made possible the company's later activities in both mining and energy.

The company in its early years added to its rich natural resource holdings. In 1898 it acquired British Columbia Smelting and Refining Company, and in 1906 merged this and other properties into the Consolidated Mining and Smelting Company of Canada Limited, later known as Cominco Limited. In 1905 CPR purchased the Esquimalt and Namaimo Railway and 1.5 million acres of timber on Vancouver Island.

Another nonrailroad activity was undertaken in 1942 when CPR merged ten local airlines to form Canadian Pacific Air Lines (CP Air). In 1955 this airline pioneered the polar route when it began flying from Vancouver to Amsterdam over the North Pole. It would eventually become, for a time, Canada's second largest airline.

As early as 1920 CPR began using all-steel railroad cars. In many instances these units weighed nearly 60 tons, which limited the number of cars that could be pulled by a steam-powered locomotive. The Great Depression and then World War II slowed the introduction of diesel-powered engines to the railroad industry. By 1954, however, CPR completed the conversion of its locomotives to diesel power. Because of the ruggedness of much of the terrain over which CPR operated, the company used some of the largest diesel-powered trains in the world. Eventually, these units were capable of hauling 10,000 tons of cargo and were powered by as many as 11 diesel engines.

ORGANIZING AND FURTHER EXPLOITING NONRAILROAD ASSETS

Throughout its first 75 years in business, CPR's explosive growth resulted in poor record-keeping, and only in 1956 did the company institute a comprehensive inventory of its assets. The inventory took seven years. It quickly became apparent that the CPR's vast holdings warranted further exploitation and development. CPR formed a wholly owned subsidiary, Canadian Pacific Oil and Gas Limited, in 1958 to develop and explore its mineral rights on more than 11 million acres of company-held western Canada land. With the completion of the CPR's forest and real estate surveys, two more subsidiaries were formed. Marathon Realty Company Limited was incorporated to manage and develop the company's vast, nationwide real estate holdings. Pacific Logging Company Limited was to be responsible for reforestation and the development of tree farming on CPR's timberlands.

As the survey of company holdings reached completion, it became clear that the development of the CPR's nonrailroad assets needed to be centralized under a separate holding company. CPR formed Canadian Pacific Investments Limited in 1962 to administer the development of CPR's natural resources and real estate holdings and to operate as an investment holding company.

During most of CPR's first 80 years, the company was owned by foreign interests, primarily English, French, and American. The transition to a majority of Canadian ownership began after the end of World War II and was completed in 1965. In that year, Ian Sinclair, CPR's chairman, assumed control of the company's burgeoning enterprises. Sinclair brought to bear his influence and power to finally reverse the flow of foreign investment into the company.

1971 REORGANIZATION UNDER CANADIAN PACIFIC LIMITED

In November 1967 the company offered to the public CAD 100 million in convertible preferred shares of CPR stock. At the time, it was the largest single stock issue in Canadian history and provided an opportunity for Canadians to share more directly in the resource development of their country. In a major reorganization in 1971, a new parent company was formed called Canadian Pacific Limited (CPL), with Canadian Pacific Railway becoming a subsidiary of the new company, as did the various other operations. In 1980 Canadian Pacific Investments Limited changed its name to Canadian Pacific Enterprises Limited (CP Enterprises).

There were also significant changes at Canadian Pacific Oil and Gas. In 1964 CP Oil and Gas purchased a stake in Central Del Rio Oils, based in Alberta. Central Del Rio had a large production base stemming from its discovery of the 1.5 billion barrel Weyburn oil pool in southeast Saskatchewan. In 1969 CP Oil and Gas became a wholly owned subsidiary of Central Del Rio, giving CPR a stake in the publicly traded Central Del Rio. Two years later CP Oil and Gas and Central Del Rio were merged to form PanCanadian Petroleum Limited, one of Canada's largest gas and oil companies. The publicly traded PanCanadian was now majority owned by Canadian Pacific Limited.

Sinclair took the company into the hotel business in the United States and to locations as distant as Jerusalem. An airline catering business in Mexico City was also purchased. Sinclair's railroading focused on the transportation of goods and raw materials rather than people. In 1976 the Canadian government formed Via Rail Canada Inc. as a nationwide passenger rail service. Via Rail gradually began taking over responsibility for passenger train operation from both CPL and archrival Canadian National Railway Company (which had been formed by the Canadian government in 1917), a process largely complete by 1979. At the close of Sinclair's tenure in 1981, CPL's railroad inventory comprised 69,000 freight cars, 1,300 locomotives, 3,600 maintenance and equipment cars, and only 57 passenger cars.

A DEEPLY DIFFICULT DECADE

Sinclair was succeeded by Frederic Burbidge in 1981. Burbidge acquired leadership of a company that was about to have the worst decade in its history. A worldwide recession coupled with extremely poor crop years in the early 1980s in both Canada and the midwestern United States resulted in thousands of empty Canadian Pacific and Soo Line boxcars. Many of CPL's nonrailroad businesses were highly cyclical. PanCanadian Petroleum helped compensate for the rail operations' poor performance for a time, but with the collapse of oil prices in 1986, the company was faced with profound difficulties.

William Stinson replaced Burbidge as CPL's chairman in 1985. Stinson, who had been with the company for 30 years, starting as a management trainee in 1955, was the youngest chairman in the company's history. He set out to streamline the company's operations.

Stinson oversaw the sale to Teck Corporation of CPL's 52 percent interest in Cominco Limited, which had become one of the world's largest zinc producers. By selling what had been a money loser since 1981, Stinson raised CAD 472 million and removed an expensive liability. On the heels of the Cominco sell-off, the company divested itself of CP Air in a CAD 300 million deal with Pacific Western Airlines in 1987. CP Air had not shown any profits since 1980; the sale also eliminated nearly CAD 600 million in long-term debt. On December 6, 1985, with the consent of both companies' stockholders, CPL and CP Enterprises merged into one company. Under the terms of the merger, CP Enterprises became a wholly owned subsidiary of CPL.

After the sale of Cominco and CP Air, Stinson worked to turn around three of CPL's other subsidiaries: AMCA International Limited, a producer of structural steel, the Soo Line, and Algoma Steel Corporation, an Ontario-based steel manufacturer. Stinson's plan was to focus CPL in four major core businesses: freight transportation, natural resources, real estate, and manufacturing. Stinson's cutbacks, sales, and restructuring had a positive effect, and the company showed a profit of a little more than CAD 58 million in 1987. One project that Stinson did not attempt to curtail was the construction of the longest railway tunnel in North America. The Macdonald Tunnel, located in British Columbia's Selkirk Mountains and more than nine miles in length, was completed in 1988. That same year, CP Hotels bought the hotel chain of Canadian National Railway, gaining such properties as the Chateau Laurier in Ottawa and Jasper Park Lodge in Alberta and becoming the largest hotel operator in Canada. CPL also purchased a 47.2 percent voting interest in Laidlaw Inc., a school bus operator and waste management company, for CAD 499.3 million. There was one further divestment in the late 1980s, however, that of the company's steel production operations, including Algoma Steel and AMCA International.

The years 1988 and 1989 showed little improvement for CPL's financial outlook. The Canadian economy was in a weakened condition. The company's forest products division reported a net operating loss of more than CAD 190 million in 1989 because of the depressed market for paper products. Marathon Realty showed a net operating loss that same year of more than CAD 17 million. The company's rail division held its own in 1989, however, and Laidlaw had a record-breaking year.

1990–95: RESTRUCTURING AND RECOVERY

As CPL entered the 1990s, the company's restructuring efforts suffered a major setback in a ruling by the Supreme Court of Ontario. Under the court's decision, CPL was prohibited from spinning off Marathon Realty as a separate public company. CPL had planned to distribute 80 percent of the shares of Marathon Realty to its common stockholders while retaining a 20 percent interest itself. The court ruled that the transaction would penalize CPL's preferred stockholders. At the same time, it appeared that CPL's performance would be further hindered by the lingering weakness in the company's forest products division.

The company's rail business increased in 1990, largely because of a resurgence in grain shipments. That year CPL acquired the 44 percent of Soo Line that it did not already own. CPL officials expected the transaction to make possible greater integration of the rail systems. Early in 1991 CPL bought another rail company, the Delaware and Hudson Railway, operating in the northeastern United States. This bolstering of the U.S. rail operations was an important development given the increased U.S.-Canada trade that was occurring as a result of the Canada-U.S. Free Trade Agreement of 1989.

CPL suffered during the economic downturn of the early 1990s. After posting net income of CAD 744 million in 1989 and CAD 354 million in 1990, the company began to lose money. Part of the problem was a decline in rail traffic. That lull was augmented by weak prices for oil and gas and a major slump in real estate markets, among other problems. Furthermore, the CPL organization was relatively bloated and inefficient, despite attempts to boost productivity. CPL executives responded to mounting losses by intensifying efforts to reorganize and increase efficiency. To that end, CPL jettisoned several poorly performing operations, including several lackluster rail lines. The company also sold its troubled forest products division, consisting of a 60.7 percent stake in Canadian Pacific Forest Products Limited, to a group of underwriters for CAD 697.8 million in 1993. At the same time, it beefed up its investments in its more successful divisions, particularly its shipping group.

Despite gains in its shipping division and a few other segments, CPL suffered losses totaling more than CAD 1.5 million between 1991 and 1993, which was partly the result of restructuring write-offs and accounting changes. By 1994, though, restructuring initiatives were beginning to bear fruit. Indeed, CPL had slashed its workforce from more than 75,000 in the late 1980s to fewer than 40,000 by 1994, reflecting a significant liquidation of assets. Meanwhile, company sales plunged from more than CAD 10 billion in 1990 to roughly CAD 6.5 billion in 1993. Finally, in 1994, CPL returned to profitability with a net income of nearly CAD 400 million.

In September 1994 CPL offered to pay CAD 1.4 billion ($1.04 billion) for the Canadian National Railway's rail operations in eastern Canada and the United States. CPL believed that the deal would benefit both companies, each of which had been racking up heavy losses in eastern Canada. The combination would eliminate excess rail capacity in eastern Canada. Canadian National opposed the unsolicited proposal, and in December 1994 the Canadian government blocked the deal.

By 1995, CPL had reorganized all of its operations into eight different companies. Transportation-related businesses, including rail (CPR) and container-shipping (CP Ships) operations, accounted for about 57 percent of total company revenues. Energy-related businesses, which included oil and gas (PanCanadian Petroleum) and coal (Fording Coal) segments, made up about 29 percent. Finally, hotel (CP Hotels) and real estate (Marathon Realty) businesses accounted for 14 percent of CPL's sales. CPL also continued to hold a 47.2 percent interest in Laidlaw and a 48 percent stake in Unitel Communications Holdings Inc.

Unitel was a new name for CPL's telecommunications arm, which had been known as CNCP Telecommunications Limited. Rogers Communications Inc. had acquired a 40 percent stake in CNCP in 1989. In June 1992 Unitel received permission from the Canadian Radio-Television and Telecommunications Commission to provide public long-distance telephone service. The following year, AT&T Corporation purchased a 20 percent stake in Unitel, reducing CPL's stake to 48 percent and Rogers' stake to 32 percent.

1996–2001: END OF CONGLOMERATE UNDER O'BRIEN

David O'Brien became president of CPL in 1995 and then chairman and CEO, succeeding Stinson, the following year. Dramatic changes would take place under what would turn out to be his short tenure of leadership. O'Brien had begun his career as a trial lawyer in Montreal, before moving into the oil and gas industry in western Canada, eventually becoming executive vice-president of Petro-Canada Limited. In 1990 he became head of PanCanadian Petroleum. As president of CPL, O'Brien began shaking things up by moving the company's headquarters from Montreal to Calgary in 1995. As chairman and CEO, O'Brien quickly jet-

tisoned the firm's three main noncore assets: the stakes in Unitel and Laidlaw were sold in 1996 and 1997, respectively, and in 1996 CPL sold Marathon Realty for CAD 952 million ($693.2 million) to a partnership formed by Oxford Properties Group Inc. and General Electric Capital Corporation. At this point, CPL consisted of five wholly or majority owned subsidiaries: Canadian Pacific Railway, CP Ships, PanCanadian Petroleum, Fording, and CP Hotels.

O'Brien believed that in the new era of free trade and globalization, CPL's structure (a holding company for several companies that were major players in the Canadian market) no longer made sense. Increasingly powerful shareholders were demanding "pure plays" that could compete on an international basis. Thus, O'Brien reasoned that eventually CPL would need to be broken up. The separate operating companies, however, would need to be strengthened first before being left to fend for themselves.

The last years of the 20th century were therefore spent expanding and improving the profitability of the five businesses. CPR, for example, embarked on a multi-year program of jettisoning about 5,400 miles of underperforming track, aided by changes in Canadian regulations that made it easier to dispose of rail lines. At the same time it launched a massive capital improvement program to bring the railroad up to international standards. A number of new locomotives were purchased, bringing the average age down to 18 years, from 22. An impetus behind the increased investment in the railroad was the 1995 privatization of Canadian National Railway, which meant that CPR would no longer have to compete with a government-owned company that did not have shareholders clamoring for profits.

From 1997 to 2000 CP Ships completed several acquisitions, including Lykes Lines, Contship Containerlines, Ivaran Lines, and CCAL. Revenues during this period increased from $1.6 billion to $2.6 billion. The second largest energy producer in Canada, PanCanadian Petroleum completed the largest acquisition in its history in 2000, the oil and gas division of Montana Power Company.

A number of developments were also occurring at CP Hotels, the largest hotel operator in Canada. In 1997 CP Hotels spun off 11 of its hotels, mainly those located in large cities, into a real estate investment trust (REIT) called Legacy Hotels. The company continued to run the hotels and kept a one-third interest in the REIT. CP Hotels maintained ownership of 16 hotels, particularly its historic resort properties. The Legacy deal raised almost CAD 600 million in capital for expansion. In early 1998 CP Hotels bought Delta Hotels Limited, a Canadian chain, for about CAD 94 million. This doubled the number of rooms under management and gave the company a moderately priced chain to go along with its traditional high-end properties. CP Hotels also gained its first properties outside of Canada in 1998 by paying $540 million for Princess Hotels International Inc., an operator of seven resorts in sunny destinations in Barbados, Bermuda, Mexico, and Arizona. Continuing to seek international growth, CP Hotels in October 1999 acquired Fairmont Hotels, owner of seven high-end properties in the United States, including the Fairmont San Francisco (the first Fairmont hotel, having opened in 1907) and the Plaza in New York. This acquisition led to the eventual creation of Fairmont Hotels & Resorts Inc. and the addition of the Fairmont name to the CP Hotels (e.g., the Fairmont Banff Springs).

THE 2001 BREAKUP OF CANADIAN PACIFIC LIMITED

By late 2000, strong performances by all five of the CPL subsidiaries led O'Brien to conclude that the time had come to act. In February 2001 the company announced that it would split itself into five publicly traded independent companies: CPR, CP Ships, PanCanadian Energy Corporation, Fording Inc., and Fairmont Hotels & Resorts. The demerger was completed on October 1, 2001, with holders of CPL stock receiving various amounts of stock in the first four of these companies. Canadian Pacific Limited retained the hotel business and renamed itself Fairmont Hotels & Resorts Inc.

Following the demerger all five of the Canadian Pacific offspring initially had listings on the Toronto and New York stock exchanges. Within half a decade, however, only Canadian Pacific Railway remained intact. PanCanadian, headed by O'Brien as chairman, merged with Alberta Energy Company Limited in April 2002 to form EnCana Corporation. Fording was converted in 2003 into an income trust called Fording Canadian Coal Trust. In October 2005 TUI AG acquired CP Ships and merged the container shipper into its Hapag-Lloyd AG subsidiary. Fairmont merged with Raffles Hotels in 2006 to form the privately held Fairmont Raffles Hotels International Inc.

EARLY 21ST CENTURY: NEWLY INDEPENDENT CANADIAN PACIFIC RAILWAY

In the meantime, the railroad unit, through which the CPL conglomerate had been built, returned to its roots as a stand-alone publicly traded company called Canadian Pacific Railway Limited, with a principal

subsidiary of Canadian Pacific Railway Company. Robert J. Ritchie was president and CEO of the company, a position he had held since 1995. Canadian Pacific began its new era of independence as a much stronger company than just a few years previous, thanks to the heavy capital investments and the efficiency initiatives of the 1990s. In addition to its own rail network, the company also counted among its strengths an alliance with Union Pacific called Can-Am Corridor that facilitated the exchange of traffic between the two railroad's networks and thereby extended Canadian Pacific's reach deeper into the United States and into Mexico as well. Although speculation about mergers among the Class 1 railroads continued to arise, it was alliances such as Can-Am Corridor that were actually implemented during this period of increased traffic between and among Canada, the United States, and Mexico that had been set in motion by the North American Free Trade Agreement (NAFTA), which took effect in 1994.

In 2002, its first full year as a newly independent firm, Canadian Pacific managed to achieve record earnings of nearly CAD 500 million on revenues of CAD 3.67 billion despite a drop in coal traffic and the impact on its core grain-hauling operations of a prolonged drought in western Canada. The difficult operating environment continued into 2003, when grain volumes remained depressed and the company also contended with surging fuel costs and a meteoric rise of the Canadian dollar. The latter resulted in lower revenues when U.S. sales were translated into Canadian currency.

By mid-2003 Canadian Pacific had responded to these challenges with a cost-cutting initiative that involved the slashing of more than 800 jobs and an after-tax charge of CAD 141.4 million covering the restructuring and a write-down in the value of its investment in the underperforming Delaware and Hudson Railway. The job cuts were intended to yield annual savings of as much as CAD 50 million. Canadian Pacific took another blow in November 2003 when it lost out in the CAD 1 billion bidding for BC Rail Ltd., the third largest railway in Canada, to its main rival Canadian National Railway.

After unsuccessfully shopping Delaware and Hudson to other Class 1 and short-line rail companies, Canadian Pacific in 2004 instead entered into a cooperation agreement with Norfolk Southern Corporation intended to improve the operations of the northeastern U.S. railway and enhance its customer service. The alliance involved a number of agreements to share track, freight haulage, and yard services across the two companies' northeastern U.S. operations. A key component provided Canadian Pacific with the right to use Norfolk Southern trackage between Detroit and Chicago over a route much shorter than one previously used via an agreement with CSX Corporation.

At this same time, trade between Canada and China was booming in both directions—consumer goods coming into Canada and various resources, including coal from the interior of British Columbia and grain and potash from the Canadian prairies, going out. To help reduce congestion at the Port of Vancouver, Canadian Pacific in the spring of 2005 launched a CAD 160 million expansion of its western rail network. By the end of the year, nearly 27,000 feet of new track had been installed and various other infrastructure improvements had been implemented. As a result, Canadian Pacific increased its capacity by 1,500 trains per year. A further effort to ease the West Coast rail gridlock arose in January 2006 when Canadian Pacific and Canadian National entered into a cooperation agreement to share certain tracks in the Vancouver region.

The Asian trade bonanza helped Canadian Pacific post its best results ever in 2005. Revenues were up more than 12 percent to CAD 4.39 billion, operating income topped the CAD 1 billion mark for the first time, and net income surged 31.5 percent to a record CAD 543 million. The firm's efficiency efforts had helped lower its operating ratio to 77.2 percent in 2005, compared to the 79.3 percent figure for 2003. The operating ratio was a key yardstick of a railway's efficiency, and profitability, that compared expenses with revenues (the lower the figure the better). The cost-containment drive continued in early 2006 with the announcement of plans to cut nearly 400 management and office support jobs, a 15 percent reduction in Canadian Pacific's white-collar employee ranks.

2006 AND BEYOND: THE GREEN ERA

Ritchie retired from the CEO post in May 2006 and was succeeded by Fred Green. The new leader had been with the company since 1978 and had been instrumental in the implementation of the important initiatives of the early 21st century, serving as executive vice-president of operations and marketing starting in 2004 and as president and chief operating officer in November 2005. After leading Canadian Pacific through another stellar year in 2006, Green faced a new challenge in mid-2007 when a private-equity consortium began preparing a takeover attempt. Canadian Pacific opposed the bid, which quickly evaporated as the credit crunch that began that year dried up funding for leveraged buyouts.

In September 2007, shortly after this takeover bid dissolved, Canadian Pacific turned acquisitive itself,

reaching an agreement to buy Dakota, Minnesota & Eastern Railroad Corporation (DM&E), a regional line based in Sioux Falls, South Dakota, with 2,500 miles of track in South Dakota, Wisconsin, Minnesota, Illinois, Missouri, Iowa, Nebraska, and Wyoming. DM&E was particularly attractive for its energy-related traffic. The railway's midwestern network was heavily involved in shipping grain to ethanol producers and then shipping ethanol to various markets. DM&E was also in the midst of a long-planned expansion into Wyoming's coal-rich Powder River Basin, another potential energy-related shipping goldmine. Canadian Pacific agreed to pay $1.48 billion for DM&E, but the deal also included contingency payments totaling another $1.05 billion should the Powder River Basin expansion be completed.

The transaction to acquire DM&E was completed in October 2007, but Canadian Pacific did not immediately gain operational control over the railway because the U.S. Surface Transportation Board launched an in-depth regulatory review of the deal with a plan to release its ruling in October 2008. Opposition to the deal had been raised in particular by the Mayo Clinic, which objected to the Powder River Basin expansion, which was expected to lead to a substantial increase in train traffic through the clinic's home base of Rochester, Minnesota. As the regulatory review commenced, DM&E's shares were placed into an independent voting trust. In the meantime, Canadian Pacific continued to struggle to keep up with the surging demand for freight-hauling stemming from the burgeoning Canada-Asia trade, and this demand helped keep the firm's financial results on the positive side: 2007 results showed a 7 percent increase in net income (after the elimination of extraordinary items) and a 3 percent gain in revenues to CAD 4.71 billion.

William R. Grossman
Updated, Dave Mote; David E. Salamie

PRINCIPAL SUBSIDIARIES

Canadian Pacific Railway Company; Soo Line Corporation (U.S.A.); Soo Line Railroad Company (U.S.A.); Delaware and Hudson Railway Company, Inc. (U.S.A.); Mount Stephen Properties Inc.

PRINCIPAL COMPETITORS

Canadian National Railway Company; Burlington Northern Santa Fe Corporation; Union Pacific Corporation; CSX Corporation; Norfolk Southern Corporation.

FURTHER READING

"Another Rail Way," *Forbes,* March 1, 1972, p. 28.
Barker, Robert, "Green Light for Canadian Pacific," *Barron's,* May 26, 1986, pp. 13+.

Bary, Andrew, "From Sleepy to Sleeper: Canadian Pacific's Revival Is Apparent Everywhere but in Its Stock Price," *Barron's*, May 18, 1998, pp. 30, 32–33.

Berton, Pierre, *The Impossible Railway: The Building of the Canadian Pacific*, New York: Knopf, 1972, 574 p.

———, *The Last Spike: The Great Railway, 1881–1885*, Toronto: McClelland and Stewart, 1971, 478 p.

———, *The National Dream: The Great Railway, 1871–1881*, Toronto: McClelland and Stewart, 1970, 439 p.

Binkley, Alex, "In Canada: Shrinking for Growth," *Railway Age*, February 1998, pp. 47–48.

Blaszak, Michael W., "Canadian Pacific Railway on Its Own," *Trains*, May 2001, pp. 18–19.

Bliss, Michael, "The Company That Built a Country: Canada's Most Storied Company Is About to Be Broken Up," *Globe and Mail*, August 31, 2001, p. 46.

Byrne, Harlan S., "Parting Ways: Canadian Pacific Units Seek Fulfillment on Their Own," *Barron's*, October 29, 2001, pp. 17–18, 21.

"Canadian Pacific Runs Off the Rails—and into Prosperity," *Financial Times of London World Business Weekly*, July 21, 1980, p. 10.

Clark, Marc, "The Remaking of a Household Name," *Maclean's*, January 20, 1986, p. 39.

"CP + DM&E = New PRB Line?" *Railway Age*, October 2007, p. 10.

"CPR Sets a Restructuring Strategy," *Railway Age*, July 2003, p. 14.

Davies, Charles, "The Long Haul," *Globe and Mail Report on Business Magazine*, March 31, 2006, p. 65.

Eagle, John A., *The Canadian Pacific Railway and the Development of Western Canada, 1896–1914*, Kingston, Ont.: McGill-Queen's University Press, 1989, 325 p.

Eliot, Jane, *The History of the Western Railroads*, New York: Bison Books, 1985.

Freeman, Alan, "Canadian Pacific Overhaul Boosts Profits," *Wall Street Journal*, October 12, 1988.

———, "Canadian Pacific Plans a Merger with Subsidiary," *Wall Street Journal*, September 9, 1985.

Freeman, Kenneth D., et al., *The Growth and Performance of the Canadian Transcontinental Railways, 1956–1981*, Vancouver, B.C.: Center for Transportation Studies, University of British Columbia, 1987, 345 p.

Gallagher, John, "Not For Sale: CP Chooses Trackage, Haulage Agreement with NS Instead of Selling Its Underperforming D&H Railway," *Traffic World*, July 12, 2004, pp. 27–28.

Gormick, Greg, "Canada's Troubled Railroads," *Railway Age*, February 1991, pp. 62–68.

———, "For CP, a Long, Long Trail," *Railway Age*, November 1994, pp. 35–37.

Hallman, Mark, "CP President Calls It Quits," *Financial Post*, December 14, 1994, sec. 1, p. 3.

———, "CP Surges Back to $393M Profit from $191 M Loss," *Financial Post*, February 7, 1995, sec. 1, p. 9.

———, "New CP Executives Face Difficult Times As Strike Looms," *Financial Post*, February 14, 1995, sec. 1, p. 3.

"How—and Why—CP Rail Is Reorganizing," *Railway Age*, December 1995, p. 20.

"Is CP in Play?" *Railway Age*, August 2007, p. 10.

Jang, Brent, "CP Rail Cuts Jobs to Keep Pace with CN," *Globe and Mail*, January 16, 2006, p. B1.

———, "CPR Eyes Big League of U.S. Carriers," *Globe and Mail*, September 6, 2007, p. B1.

———, "CPR Plans $160-Million Expansion of Western Rail," *Globe and Mail*, April 19, 2005, p. B5.

———, "Ritchie Retiring After 11 Years at CPR Helm; Company Veteran Fred Green Taking Over," *Globe and Mail*, February 23, 2006, p. B5.

Kimelman, John, "O Canada!: How Long Will We Have to Wait for Things to Improve at Canadian Pacific?" *Financial World*, January 19, 1993, pp. 22+.

Koch, George, "Full Throttle: Canada's Railroads—and Their Profits—Come Steaming Back," *Barron's*, September 13, 1999, p. 24.

Kozma, Leslie S., and Charles W. Bohi, "Canada's New Rail Barons: Shortline Pioneers Have Expanded Nationwide," *Trains*, February 1999, pp. 38–44.

Lamb, W. Kaye, *History of the Canadian Pacific Railway*, New York: Macmillan, 1977, 491 p.

Machalaba, Daniel, "Canadian Pacific Bets on Energy: Like Its U.S. Rivals, Railroad Focuses More on Coal and Ethanol," *Wall Street Journal*, October 3, 2007, p. A8.

Masters, John, "Time Passages: The CPR and the Future," *Canadian Business*, November 1985, pp. 10+.

McKee, Bill, and Georgeen Klassen, *Trail of Iron: The CPR and the Birth of the West, 1880–1930*, Vancouver, B.C.: Glenbow-Alberta Institute in association with Douglas & McIntyre, 1983, 192 p.

McMurdy, Deirdre, "Breaking Up Is Good to Do," *Canadian Business*, October 15, 2001, p. 15.

———, "Canada Inc.: Canadian Pacific's Struggle to Reinvent Itself Mirrors That of the Entire Canadian Economy," *Maclean's*, May 17, 1993, pp. 30–32.

McMurdy, Deirdre, and Barbara Wickens, "A Corporate Diet: CP Slims Down by Selling Off the Forests," *Maclean's*, August 23, 1993, pp. 36–37.

Meyer, Richard, "Blurred Image," *Financial World*, February 7, 1989, pp. 22+.

Murray, Tom, *Canadian Pacific Railway*, St. Paul, Minn.: Voyageur Press, 2006, 160 p.

Nemeth, Mary, and Liz Warwick, "Down the Line: CP Rail Announces a Move to Calgary—and Another Wave of Layoffs," *Maclean's*, December 4, 1995, pp. 52–53.

Newman, Peter C., "CP Ltd.: Betting on the West's Dominance," *Maclean's*, May 20, 1996, p. 44.

Ryans, Leo, "CP Undergoing Major Restructuring," *Journal of Commerce*, February 27, 1987.

Sheppard, Robert, "The Very Last Spike," *Maclean's,* February 26, 2001, pp. 48+.

Simon, Bernard, "Canadian Pacific Plots Its Demise," *New York Times,* September 26, 2001, p. W1.

Vantuono, William C., "Rob Ritchie Leads CPR Down an Independent Path" (Railroader of the Year), *Railway Age,* January 2004, pp. 31–32+.

———, "Westward Expansion," *Railway Age,* November 2005, pp. 26–29.

Verburg, Peter, "New Kid on the Beach," *Canadian Business,* February 12, 1999, pp. 52–54, 56.

Willis, Andrew, "Brookfield Abandons Plan to Buy CPR," *Globe and Mail,* August 21, 2007, p. B1.

Wilson-Smith, Anthony, "Putting CP on a Different Track: A Tough Competitor Reshapes His Company," *Maclean's,* November 16, 1998, pp. 46–47.

Ytuarte, Christopher, "Turning a Corner," *Railway Age,* October 2001, pp. 31–33.

CARPENTER

Carpenter Technology Corporation

2 Meridian Boulevard
Wyomissing, Pennsylvania 19610-3202
U.S.A.
Telephone: (610) 208-2000
Toll Free: (800) 338-4592
Fax: (610) 208-3716
Web site: http://www.cartech.com

Public Company
Incorporated: 1889 as Carpenter Steel Company
Employees: 4,152
Sales: $1.95 billion (2007)
Stock Exchanges: New York
Ticker Symbol: CRS
NAIC: 331111 Iron and Steel Mills; 331222 Steel Wire Drawing; 331491 Nonferrous Metal (Except Copper and Aluminum) Rolling, Drawing, and Extruding

■ ■ ■

Carpenter Technology Corporation produces and distributes specialty steel and structural ceramics worldwide for consumer and industrial applications. Formed as a steel company in the late 19th century, it was a pioneer of stainless steel and its emphasis on research and development has led to some of the world's most advanced alloys.

The company's products are used in demanding applications in the aerospace, automotive, consumer product, energy, industrial, and medical markets. In 2007, Carpenter employed more than 4,100 workers throughout the world; its headquarters and main plant remained in the Reading, Pennsylvania, area where it was originally founded.

ORIGINS

The man whose name the present company bears, James Henry Carpenter, served in the Navy during the Civil War, then embarked on a career as a construction engineer, developing an interest in metallurgy and the manufacture of tool steel. A New Yorker, Carpenter was encouraged to found a steelmaking enterprise in Reading, Pennsylvania, by a visionary city councilman who, realizing that the region's bustling iron industry would naturally support such a venture, foresaw a boon to the city's economy. Incorporated in New Jersey on June 7, 1889, Carpenter Steel Company leased a rail-making plant in Reading and soon received its first order for 3,000 tons of steel. Within five months, the fledgling company had outgrown the rail-making plant and acquired a facility known as Union Foundry, which over 100 years later still functioned as company headquarters and a specialty steel mill.

Carpenter's branching into specialty steel operations began with a May 1890 contract with the U.S. Secretary of the Navy. Having found Carpenter's tool steels to be of superior quality, the Navy was betting, correctly as it turned out, that the company could develop armor-piercing projectiles. The fulfillment of the Navy contract was enabled by a patent granted to James Carpenter for an "air-hardening steel" manufacturing process. In November 1896, the Navy informed Congress that Carpenter's projectiles had tested successfully, calling them "the first made that would pierce improved armor plate." In the Spanish-American War of 1898, the routing of the Spanish fleet at Manila Bay was credited in part to Carpenter projectiles.

Unfortunately, the preeminence Carpenter achieved through its wartime armaments proved to be a curse when the Spanish-American War, and the contracts it fostered, ended. Complicating the decline in business was the death in March 1898 of founder James Carpenter. By 1903, the company had fallen into receivership. However, the court-appointed receiver, Robert E. Jennings, was a former vice-president of a rival steel company and would soon oversee a dramatic resurgence at Carpenter. Elected president of a reorganized Carpenter Steel Company the following year, Jennings possessed expertise in marketing; for the remainder of the decade he presided over innovations resulting in a variety of steel grades broad enough for almost every extant tooling application, including heavy-duty cutting tools, high-speed cutting tools, and hot heading.

Early in the 20th century, the nascent automobile industry afforded the single most auspicious market for Carpenter's innovations in specialty steel. In 1905, the company developed a prime grade chrome-nickel steel; by 1908 it had created ten other steels that were used to make automobile chassis. Most of the "runabout" vehicles of the day ran on Carpenter steel, and "Old 16," the racer that won the Vanderbilt Cup in 1908, comprised front and rear axles, crankshaft, gears, and other parts fabricated from Carpenter steel. Affinity with automobile manufacturers gave rise to a hallmark of Carpenter's distribution system: maintaining service centers where its customers were based. The beginnings of its modern regional service center system began with the opening of branch warehouses in Cleveland and Hartford, then the centers of automobile production, in 1907 and 1909.

With the 1917 entrance of the United States into World War I, wartime munitions and supplies overtook automotive steel as Carpenter's principal product. The Reading plant operated on around-the-clock shifts, producing everything from tool steels to soldiers' safety razor blades. Accelerated production levels, however, did not distract Carpenter from technical and metallurgical innovation. During the war, the company put into operation four new electric-arc furnaces, which allowed greater control over the melting process than had the old crucible furnaces. It also turned out its first batch, in December 1917, of what would become its principal product: stainless steel. The first applications of this new high-strength, chemical-resistant steel were airplane engine components, cutlery, and spark plugs.

Continuing its quest to improve what was already a successful product line, Carpenter unveiled its "rustless steel," an alloy of 0.3 percent carbon, 20 percent chromium, and one percent copper, in December 1920. Throughout the 1920s, Carpenter spent much effort in improving the fabricability, into parts, of its stainless steel. In 1928, it brought out the first free-machining, "antifriction" stainless steel, sulfur being the component responsible for the breakthrough. The introduction of stainless steel strip in the mid-1920s reestablished Carpenter as an important supplier to the automobile industry; in 1929, the company trumpeted the statistic of 24 pounds of automotive trim on each Pierce Arrow car. Strip also began to be welded into tubing, and in 1927, Carpenter's Welded Alloy Tube Division became the earliest commercial supplier of stainless tubing, with applications in chemical processing, oil refining, generation of electricity, and food and beverage processing.

Another historical milestone that demonstrated Carpenter's preeminence was Charles Lindbergh's pioneering nonstop flight from New York to Paris in May 1927. The gears, shafts, and fasteners of the engine of the *Spirit of St. Louis,* Lindbergh's legendary plane, were all made from Carpenter steel. An identical engine had powered Richard Byrd's flight to the North Pole the previous year. Even the Wright brothers' maiden flight

KEY DATES

1889: Construction engineer James H. Carpenter begins steelmaking operation in Reading, Pennsylvania.

1907: Carpenter establishes nationwide warehouse and service center system.

1920: Carpenter introduces an early type of stainless steel.

1937: Carpenter becomes a public company.

1968: Carpenter Steel Company is renamed Carpenter Technology Corporation to reflect its emphasis on R&D.

1994: Carpenter enters structural ceramics business via acquisition of Certech, Inc.

1997: Acquisition of the Talley Industries conglomerate adds an advanced minimill to Carpenter's assets.

1998: Revenues exceed $1 billion; Carpenter begins developing its own online direct selling exchange.

2006: Company plans to increase capacity and make more acquisitions.

in 1903 had been achieved with Carpenter steel-based engine components. The aircraft industry, like the earth-bound automobile industry, owed much of its success to Carpenter.

DOWNSIZING IN THE DEPRESSION

The Great Depression, particularly during the early 1930s, caused Carpenter to operate at a loss for three consecutive years and forced it to downsize. Still, the company's penchant for new product development continued virtually unabated. The Depression years saw the introduction of new stainless steels with additives of selenium, tellurium, and chrome and nickel. For the first time, Carpenter began licensing other manufacturers to produce some of its stainless steels. Also during the 1930s, increasingly high wear-resisting varieties of tool steel were introduced, and in 1937 Carpenter brought out *Tool Steel Simplified,* a book of diagrams to assist customers in choosing the proper tool steel for a specific application, depending on toughness and hardening properties. The book would remain a standard industry reference work through the 1970s. In June 1937, Carpenter Steel Company went public.

The most obvious challenge to Carpenter in the 1940s, as for the country as a whole, was World War II. In March 1941, with U.S. entrance into the war looking increasingly probable, the U.S. Office of Production Management summoned Carpenter's president to Washington, D.C., to discuss expanding the company's production capacity on an urgent basis. Carpenter's board of directors responded by voting an immediate capital investment program of nearly $1 million. During the course of the war, the company's numerous varieties of stainless steel found their way into virtually every conceivable wartime application: engine parts, steel fasteners, and cockpit instruments for fighter planes and bombers; components of Sherman tanks and submarines; radio masts for PT boats and radio equipment for battle fronts; and medical supplies such as hypodermic needles and surgical implements.

After the war, Carpenter returned to stable, profitable operations. The 1950s brought significant technological advances in melting, particularly with the process of vacuum arc remelting in a consumable-electrode furnace, which allowed unprecedented high purity in steel alloys—and none too soon, since applications in the embryonic aerospace field required immaculate degrees of purity. During the same decade, Carpenter introduced "Stainless 20," an alloy which by virtue of rare earth element additives could withstand harsh, corrosive chemicals. Expansion of infrastructure and capacity continued apace. In 1951, Carpenter bought a wire redrawing plant in New Jersey, thus acquiring the capability to produce extremely fine wire for applications such as surgical sutures and knitting machines. The year 1954 saw the addition of a new mill in Reading which allowed Carpenter to become extremely competitive in the manufacture of specialty alloy wire. When, in the mid-1950s, the company found itself having to turn down orders despite operating at full capacity, it purchased Northeastern Steel Corporation in Bridgeport, Connecticut, enabling a 100 percent increase in the production of ingots.

EMPHASIZING RESEARCH AND DEVELOPMENT

Research and development (R&D) and technology were the dominant themes of the 1960s; the company changed its name in 1968 to reflect this, becoming Carpenter Technology Corporation and reincorporating in the state of Delaware. The company also announced that it was spending five times as much on R&D as were other steel manufacturers, and proudly opened a new $3 million R&D center in Reading in 1967. Carpenter began to cast a wide technological net through three strategic acquisitions: NTH Products,

Inc., of El Cajon, California, in 1961; a 50 percent share in Gardner Cryogenics Corporation, Bethlehem, Pennsylvania, in 1969; and a 50 percent share in Titanium Technology Corporation, Pomona, California, also in 1969.

NTH Products eventually became Carpenter's special products division, responsible for making metal and specialty steel products such as tubular components, precision-rolled solid shapes, and photoetch sheets. It also made fuel channels for nuclear reactor cores. Gardner Cryogenics (taking its name from the science of low-temperature phenomena) facilitated the company's entrance into making storage and transport equipment. Titanium Technology Corporation supplied the aerospace and other industries with titanium castings.

Infrastructure enhancements in the 1960s included the installation of a 15,000-pound vacuum induction furnace, which permitted the melting of alloys of unprecedented purity, and of a mill capable of rolling thin electronic alloy strip used in transistors and semiconductors. Then, in the early 1970s, installation of two varieties of increasingly sophisticated furnaces enabled additional improvements to the product line. First, two 25-ton ElectroSlag Remelting furnaces, which had their world premiere at Carpenter, allowed ingots to be remelted in molten slag, reducing overall amounts of microscopic impurities. Then the Argon-Oxygen Decarburizing unit accomplished, as its name implied, efficient removal of carbon through a process of blowing argon and oxygen through the steel bath.

Carpenter managed to ride out the two national recessions of the 1970s, with sales and profit figures consistently breaking records throughout the decade. Separate multimillion-dollar capital expansion plans were put into action in 1976 and 1979. Beginning in 1970, the company had implemented a pollution control plan, installing ducts, exhaust fans, and 2,400 filter bags to trap exhaust fumes and iron oxide dust that would otherwise escape into the atmosphere.

POST-DIVERSIFICATION DIVESTITURES

The 1970s also saw Carpenter reverse course after its earlier aggressive pursuit of diversification. Many previously acquired enterprises were sold during the decade, including the New Jersey wire redrawing plant, Titanium Technology Corporation, Gardner Cryogenics, and affiliates in Brazil and Mexico. According to Howard O. Beaver Jr., who was then president, the divested enterprises "did not fit Carpenter's long-range goals and objectives," and the proceeds from the sales would be "more effectively employed" in enhancements to the stainless steel product line.

The 1981–82 recession was one of the deepest ever to afflict the U.S. economy, and steel companies were especially hard-hit due to fierce competition and price undercutting from foreign producers. To combat such severe economic buffetings, the bulk of the domestic industry began selling off tangential operations and trying to diversify by branching into insurance or retail—but not Carpenter. Even though its fiscal 1982 earnings fell significantly below the previous year, the company was proceeding unflinchingly with its 1979 capital investment plan. The new president, Paul Roedel, conceded that Carpenter's previous efforts in diversification had caused return on capital to plummet and vowed the same mistake would not be repeated.

Factors that tended to immunize Carpenter better than most steel producers against recession were noted in a 1982 *Forbes* magazine article. Its highly specialized steels were selling at ten times the average price per ton of the rest of the industry, and its share of the specialty steel market was 25 percent. Company philosophy was to broaden the market base, which it had done successfully, rather than diversify the product line. Its nationwide warehouse and service center system, begun in 1907, numbered 21 facilities, and had put Carpenter in the unique position of hearing its customers' conundrums first-hand; this allowed the company to develop custom markets for itself.

100 IN 1989

By fiscal 1989, when Carpenter marked its 100th anniversary, the 1982 recession was just a memory as net sales reached an all-time high of $634.3 million, and net income was 19 percent higher than in the previous year. Market forces had reduced the number of publicly traded specialty steel companies to four at this point, but these entities, Carpenter included, were regarded by financial analysts as highly efficient and high in quality. Consumer demand for specialty steel had risen faster than the economy in general since the early 1960s, and over the same period, the amount of specialty steel in cars had risen from ten to 70 pounds.

Carpenter had made two significant acquisitions during the 1980s—Eagle Precision Metals Corporation of Fryeburg, Maine, and AMAX Specialty Metals Corporation of Orangeburg, South Carolina—and had sold the Bridgeport, Connecticut, steelmaking facility after market growth rate had slowed. Eagle, a precision drilling facility, beefed up Carpenter's ability to produce high-quality hollow steel bars, while AMAX was a wire-finishing plant, capable of redrawing steel wire to extremely fine sizes.

Economic cycles continued to affect Carpenter's balance sheet; the 1991 recession once again forced restructuring and downsizing, and as with many basic-industry companies, recovery seemed more elusive than with the economy as a whole. However, at the end of fiscal 1994, Carpenter President Robert W. Cardy exulted that net sales had been second only to 1989 and observed that the company was operating virtually at full capacity. The dual goals of the year ("to strengthen and grow specialty metal operations worldwide, and to expand strategic business opportunities worldwide") had been achieved.

INTO CERAMICS IN 1994

Especially important during 1994 were two acquisitions destined to fulfill Carpenter's aspirations as a worldwide steel distributor. First, a joint venture with Walsin-Lihwa, a Taiwanese cable and wire manufacturer, resulted in the company's first presence in Asia. Second, the acquisition of Aceros Fortuna, Mexico's number one specialty steel distributor, resulted in the bulk of Carpenter's increased 1994 sales. On the domestic front, Carpenter bought Certech, Inc., a Woodridge, New Jersey, maker of structural ceramics. According to a senior vice-president, "Some customers who traditionally bought steel had switched to structural ceramics for some applications. To keep its customers, Carpenter decided to broaden its product line."

According to *American Metal Market,* structural ceramics had high temperature properties and high corrosion resistance, and were "used to make precision valves, components for electrical and fiber optic connectors, special wear inserts, and critical application components for the plasma spray industry." Carpenter accelerated its push into this new field in 1995 with the acquisition of Technical Ceramics Laboratories, Inc., (TCL) of Alpharetta, Georgia. TCL's specialty, ceramics research, was expected to complement the ceramics manufacturing capability provided by Certech.

As its second century of operation unfolded, Carpenter was poised to become increasingly influential as a global supplier of specialty steels, structural ceramics, and specialty materials complementing applications that were formerly the exclusive domain of metals. This emphasis, together with its far-reaching warehouse and service center system, indicated that Carpenter planned to bolster and broaden its market niches and customer bases.

Carpenter continued to grow through acquisitions, such as the 1997 addition of Dynamet Incorporated, a maker of titanium bar, wire, and alloys. It also built up its burgeoning ceramics business by buying ICI Advanced Ceramics. The company made a very large purchase in February 1997, buying a controlling interest in Talley Industries, Inc., for $312 million. This added an advanced minimill and a distributorship to Carpenter's assets; the rest of Talley's operations were put up for sale since they did not mesh with Carpenter's existing business lines.

A BILLION-DOLLAR COMPANY

This purchase helped push Carpenter's total revenues past $1 billion in 1998. The company then had 5,100 employees, more than half of them in Reading. During the year, Carpenter began a retooling of its distribution network, reducing its 23 warehouses to seven as it developed its own Internet site to sell directly to its thousands of customers, many of them quite small, rather than going through third-party online metals exchanges.

Robert W. Cardy, CEO since 1992, was succeeded by the company's president and chief operating officer, Dennis M. Draeger, in 2001. The next year, Draeger was replaced by Robert J. Torcolini. Their challenge was making Carpenter Technologies a truly global company capable of thriving in a rapidly changing industry.

GLOBALIZATION

The steel industry remained true to its notoriously cyclical nature. Involvement in foreign markets provided some hedging, as different countries tended to follow different cycles. However, sometimes the down periods converged, making business especially difficult. Aviation industry customers in the United States were cutting back in the late 1990s even as inexpensive imported steel flooded the market as a result of the Asian financial crisis.

Carpenter postponed capital projects and let its workforce shrink largely through attrition. While the company lobbied for protection from dumping in the form of trade tariffs, it reported little benefit after they were implemented in 2002. Layoffs of hundreds of people ensued as the company slipped into the red.

Globalization opened up the company to dozens of new competitors, but it also provided opportunity for Carpenter to expand abroad, in some cases following its existing customers who were setting up shop overseas. In 1999, Carpenter established a manufacturing and distribution joint venture with Kalyani Steels Ltd. in India. The company also bought Mexico's Aceromex Atlas SA de CV and the advanced ceramics business of ICI Australia Ltd. In 2000 Carpenter added the Anval Group, a powder tool steel manufacturer based in Sweden, from France's Vallourec Group. The price was a little less than $9 million including assumed debt.

Carpenter continued to focus its operations on high-value materials. In 2005 it sold a medical components business, Carpenter Special Products Corp., to WHI Capital Partners of Chicago for $19.5 million. (The unit was then renamed Veridiam Inc.)

Revenues exceeded $1.5 billion in fiscal 2006. The company was operating profitably again after a lapse earlier in the decade and boasted more than 100 years of consecutive quarterly dividend payments. It was planning to continue buying companies while adding more furnaces. In October 2006 the board hired Anne Stevens, formerly an executive vice-president with Ford Motor Co., to be the company's CEO and chairperson. She was a native of Reading, Pennsylvania.

Val Holley
Updated, Frederick C. Ingram

PRINCIPAL SUBSIDIARIES

Carpenter Investments, Inc.; CRS Holdings, Inc.; CRS Investments, Inc.; Dynamet Incorporated; Talley Industries, Inc.

PRINCIPAL DIVISIONS

Specialty Metals; Engineered Products.

PRINCIPAL OPERATING UNITS

Carpenter Specialty Alloys; Carpenter Specialty Wire Products; Carpenter Technology U.K.; Carpenter Powder Products; Dynamet; Shalmet Corp. Tally Metals; Aceros Fortuna.

PRINCIPAL COMPETITORS

Allegheny Technologies, Inc.; Titanium Metals Corporation; RTI International Metals, Inc.; Haynes International, Inc.; AK Steel Holding Corp.; Steel Dynamics, Inc.; Universal Stainless & Alloy Products, Inc.

FURTHER READING

Ahles, Andrea, "Reading Firm Is Riding Out Slump in Steel: Foreign Competition and a Drop in Domestic Business Have Strained Carpenter Technology; It Has Retrenched and Innovated to Keep Its Specialty Alloys Line Alive," *Philadelphia Inquirer,* April 26, 1999, p. F1.

Brubaker, Harold, "Specialty Metals Firm to Cut 500 Jobs; Carpenter Technology Said Most Layoffs Would Be at Its Reading Facility," *Philadelphia Inquirer,* October 1, 2002, p. E11.

Building a New Growth Model for Carpenter, Reading: Carpenter Technology Corporation, 1994.

Building on 100 Years of Progress, Reading: Carpenter Technology Corporation.

Byrne, Harlan S., "Carpenter Technology: 109 Years Young," *Barron's,* April 6, 1998, p. 25.

Byrne, John A., "Three Numbers," *Forbes,* April 12, 1982, p. 121.

"Carpenter Bypasses Steel Exchanges to Sell Directly to Its Disparate Customers," *Manufacturing News,* November 15, 2000, pp. 1, 7.

"Carpenter Meets Financial Goals, Continues Expansion in FY94," *Business Wire,* October 25, 1994.

"Carpenter Reports Record Sales and Higher Earnings for the Year Ended June 30, 1989," *PR Newswire,* July 28, 1989.

"Carpenter Sales Rise 21 Percent," *PR Newswire,* April 24, 1980.

Fernandez, Bob, "Ford Alum to Drive Reading Firm; Anne Stevens Will Be Carpenter Technology CEO," *Philadelphia Inquirer,* October 19, 2006, p. C1.

"From Carrier Decks to Off-Road Biking," *Machine Design,* April 6, 1995, p. 36.

Guzzo, Maria, "Carpenter Growth to Come via Buys, Capacity Builds," *American Metal Market,* September 22, 2006, pp. 1, 2.

Hershey, Robert D., "In One City, Signs of an Upturn," *New York Times,* June 13, 1991, p. D1.

McClenahen, John S., "Making a Material," *Industry Week,* June 22, 1998, p. 36.

Ozanian, Michael K., "Today's Steals," *Financial World,* September 5, 1989, p. 49.

Sacco, John E., "Carpenter Technology Focuses on Global Expansion," *American Metal Market,* pp. 5A, 17A.

Welch, David T., "Carpenter Inks Deal to Buy Ceramic Firm," *American Metal Market,* March 6, 1995, p. 4.

Central National-Gottesman Inc.

3 Manhattanville Road
Purchase, New York 10577-2110
U.S.A.
Telephone: (914) 696-9000
Fax: (914) 696-1066
Web site: http://www.cng-inc.com

Private Company
Incorporated: 1886 as M. Gottesman & Company
Employees: 1,000
Sales: $3 billion (2006 est.)
NAIC: 422130 Industrial and Personal Service Paper
    Wholesalers

■ ■ ■

Based in Purchase, New York, Central National-Gottesman Inc. is the world's largest privately owned pulp and paper distributor and among the top 150 largest private companies according to *Forbes* magazine. The company sells wood pulp, newsprint, paper and paperboard, and fine paper, as well as providing such marketing and management services as market research and consulting, sales, invoicing, transportation, and financing. One of the strengths of Central National-Gottesman is its longstanding ties to major paper suppliers, including Weyerhaeuser and International Paper. The company also has reliable relationships in all of the world's important fiber-producing areas, allowing it to be a dependable one-stop source for all grades of wood pulp to a global base of customers. All told, Central National-Gottesman operations include 14 U.S. warehouses, and 26 U.S. and 17 international sales offices, as well as representatives in more than 40 countries. The company does not, however, maintain any retail distribution facilities and stores, preventing it from supplying small-quantity orders. Aside from North America, major markets include Brazil, the United Kingdom, Portugal, South Africa, South Korea, Thailand, Russia, and China. The company's business is divided between two main divisions. The focus of the Central National-Gottesman division is marketing and other services related to wood pulp, newsprint, publication papers, and packaging. The Lindenmeyr Division contains four entities: Lindenmeyr Book Publishing serves publishers, printers, and packagers; Lindenmeyr Central serves magazine and catalog publishers; Lindenmeyr Munroe distributes printing paper to commercial printers, business form manufacturers, graphic designers, and on-demand printing operations, and communication paper for business use to wholesale stationers, resellers, facility management companies, and retailers; and CNG Specialty Papers offers a full range of paper management services. Lindenmeyr also operates a fleet of trucks to provide prompt delivery. Gottesman's chief executive officer, Kenneth L. Wallach, is the great-grandson of the company's founder.

19TH-CENTURY HERITAGE

Central National-Gottesman Inc. was established in New York City in 1886 as M. Gottesman & Company by Mendel Gottesman. Born in Hungary in 1859, he came to the United States in the same year that he founded his wood-pulp firm that served the paper industry. In 1899 he was joined by his 14-year-old son, David Samuel Gottesman, who was also born in Hungary and usually went by the name D. Samuel Gottesman or Samuel Gottesman. The firm became known as M. Gottesman & Son. and in time the younger man became a partner, while his father also became president of the Credit Utility Banking Corporation and pursued a number of philanthropic endeavors related to his Jewish faith, including serving as treasurer of Yeshiva College and establishing an endowment fund for the school, contributing to the Federation of Jewish Charities and United Jewish Appeal, and in 1917 organizing the Gottesman Tree of Life Foundation to carry on his charitable work. He would die in 1942 at the age of 83.

OPENING OF CENTRAL NATIONAL BANK: 1926

D. Samuel Gottesman followed a similar path as his father, acting as a financier as well as a wood pulp merchant, while supporting a number of philanthropies. He became president of M. Gottesman, which under his guidance became a major importer of wood pulp from Europe. In 1926 he spearheaded the organization of Central National Bank of the City of New York and became its chairman. The bank opened its offices in January 1926 at 40th Street and Broadway, the primary purpose to serve the needs of the businesses located in the Times Square area. Other positions Gottesman held at this time included treasurer and director of the Broadway-Fortieth Street Corporation. the Central National Safe Deposit Company, and the Gottesman Company Aktiebolag of Stockholm, Sweden. In February 1928 Central National Bank formed a subsidiary called Central National Corporation to deal in securities and underwrite stock offerings. A year later the stock market crash would lead to the Great Depression of the 1930s, and while Central National Bank fell by the wayside, Central National Corporation continued on, serving as the investment securities arm of Gottesman & Co., Inc.

IRA WALLACH TAKES OVER AS CEO: 1954

Samuel Gottesman was acting as president and director of Gottesman, Central National, Aktiebolag, and Allied International Corporation (an aviation export sales company), as well as serving as a director of Eastern Corporation and Rayonier, Inc., when he died at the age of 71 in 1956. Succeeding him as chief executive at Gottesman & Co. and Central National was Ira D. Wallach, his son-in-law. Wallach was a native New Yorker, born in the city in 1909. He later enrolled at Columbia University to earn a bachelor's degree and law degree. Following a stint in the Navy during World War II, he joined Gottesman & Co. in 1946, becoming executive vice-president.

When Wallach took over Gottesman & Co. it was a modest wood pulp distributor. Under his leadership the firm began opening sales offices in Europe and South America, so that by the end of the 1970s the company maintained operations in 18 countries. In 1979 he turned over the reins to his son, James G. Wallach, staying on as chairman and later senior vice-chairman. He would live until early 2007, when he passed away at the age of 97.

James Wallach was in his early 30s when he succeeded his father as president and CEO in 1979. He had been with Gottesman & Co. since 1966 after receiving a master's degree in business administration from the University of California at Berkeley. After taking the reins at Gottesman and Central National, he brought them together as Central National-Gottesman, and in the early 1980s responded to changes in the pulp and paper industry to expand quickly in the increasingly important Asian market, opening new offices in Pacific Rim countries.

ACQUISITION OF LINDENMEYR PAPER: 1984

The early 1980s also saw Central National-Gottesman diversify, becoming involved in the distribution of fine paper to the publishing industry through the 1984 acquisition of the Lindenmeyr Paper Corporation. The Lindenmeyr name possessed an even deeper connection to the New York paper trade than Gottesman. The patriarch of the family was Henry Lindenmeyr who was born in Germany in 1830 and immigrated to the United States as a young man. In 1859 he established a paper dealership in lower Manhattan, which took the name Henry Lindenmeyr & Sons after his sons Henry and Gustave joined the firm. After he died, his children carried on the business, serving as president until 1931 when Fritz Lindenmeyr, deep in debt, committed

KEY DATES

1886: Mendel Gottesman forms M. Gottesman & Company.

1899: D. Samuel Gottesman joins his father in the business.

1926: Samuel Gottesman forms Central National Bank.

1928: Central National Corporation is formed.

1942: Mendel Gottesman dies.

1956: Son-in-law Ira Wallach becomes Gottesman's president following Samuel Gottesman's death.

1979: James Wallach succeeds father as Gottesman's CEO.

1984: Lindenmeyr Paper Corporation is acquired.

1988: D.F. Munroe Company is acquired.

1991: Communication Paper Corporation is acquired.

1998: James Wallach dies, replaced by uncle, Kenneth Wallach.

2002: Chicago assets of WWF Paper Corp. are acquired.

suicide. In 1950 the firm merged with Charles F. Hubbs & Co., an industrial paper merchant established in New York in 1855. The combined operation did business in Long Island City, Queens, as Lindenmeyr Paper Corporation, enjoying strong growth in the 1960s and 1970s as the company benefited from the installation of computerized inventory and invoicing systems.

The addition of Lindenmeyr made Central-National Gottesman a $1 billion company. The company added to Lindenmeyr in 1988 when D.F. Munroe Company, a Massachusetts-based regional paper distributor, was acquired. More specialty acquisitions followed in the 1990s. In 1991 Communication Paper Corporation, supplier of communication and printing papers to Long Island, was purchased. Then in 1998 Central-National acquired Perkins & Squier Company, a wholesale distributor of book publishing papers. During this period Lindenmeyr also expanded its operations to the south, encompassing the Baltimore; Washington, D.C.; and Richmond, Virginia markets.

While the Lindenmeyr Division was growing into one of the largest fine paper distributors in the United States, Central National-Gottesman was expanding its international operations, especially focusing on emerging markets in both Eastern Europe and Asia. It was also a

time of transition in the top ranks of management. In 1997 James Wallach succeeded his father as chairman, while continuing to serve as CEO. Just a year later, however, the 55-year-old Wallach died from a cerebral aneurysm. His brother, Kenneth L. Wallach, succeeded him as CEO.

GAINING ACCESS TO CHICAGO: 2002

As Central National-Gottesman entered the 2000s, it was generating $2 billion in annual sales. In 2002 the Lindenmeyr Division was expanded further when Pennsylvania-based competitor WWF Paper Corp. was forced to liquidate. Lindenmeyr added WWF's Midwest division, including offices and a warehouse in Itasca, Illinois, giving the company access to Chicago, the country's largest print market.

The new century was a time of both opportunity and challenges. Because of its global footprint, Central National-Gottesman was able to take advantage of the emerging markets in Eastern Europe, as the free market economies of the former members of the Soviet Union came to fruition. The company's diversity also allowed it to exploit the branded coated fine paper market, which had become the fastest-growing sector of the paper industry, as well as the promising environmentally preferable paper market, the growth of which was spurred by consumer concerns and the advocacy of environmental groups. On the other hand, Central National-Gottesman was concerned about electronic equivalents to paper, including e-books and e-newspapers. The rising popularity of mobile telephones also threatened to reduce the need for printed directories, which could be replaced by accessible electronic databases and curtail the demand for newsprint used by directory publishers. Moreover, Internet job sites such as Monster.com were also having an effect on newspaper want ad sections, reducing page counts and the need for newsprint. The growth of discount chains, in particular Wal-Mart, which did little newspaper advertising, was also a problem because they were driving out other retailers, including department stores and supermarkets, who printed a great deal of newsprint retail ads.

The paperless office and other electronic threats to the wood pulp and paper industry never seemed to materialize, however. By 2007 Central National-Gottesman had increased revenues to the $3 billion mark. The company was especially optimistic about the prospects of the Chinese paper market, which over the next few years was expected to enjoy increasing demand in all areas: more than 5 percent a year in fine paper, 8 to 11 percent in coated fine paper, 12 percent in printed advertising, 11 percent in the magazine and newspaper market, and more than 8 percent in packaging. The company also looked to take advantage of growing demand for packaging materials in India, Russia, and Central and Eastern Europe. North America, on the other hand, was a mature market with modest growth in packaging expected. Furthermore, the corrugated container market in the United States was also expected to experience tepid growth, due to a struggling economy, increased foreign competition, and substitute materials including reusable plastic containers and intermediate bulk containers.

There were other areas of concern as well for Central National-Gottesman. Pulp prices surged, and while the company was not a paper manufacturer, its profits were adversely impacted by the higher production costs of suppliers. The fact that the company was only a distributor was also a concern because the bulk of its competitors were integrated, manufacturing and distributing forest products. Without that manufacturing capability, Central National-Gottesman would likely find it difficult to increase market share. In addition, competitors such as International Paper Company and Domtar Corporation were establishing retail stores and distribution facilities, creating a capability to cater to the needs of quick printers and graphic designers who generally ordered small quantities of paper.

In addition, retail stores were able to develop relationships with customers, allowing them to browse for products and pick up samples. The lack of retail operations had the potential to cost the company business. On the other hand, Central National-Gottesman had been operating successfully for well over a century and had adjusted to changes in the marketplace before. In the middle of the first decade of the 2000s, for example, the company took advantage of e-commerce to provide greater services to customers and drive sales. There was every reason to expect the company's seasoned management team to make the adjustments necessary to keep Central National-Gottesman a competitive company in the pulp and paper industry for many years to come.

Ed Dinger

PRINCIPAL DIVISIONS

Central National-Gottesman; Lindenmeyr.

PRINCIPAL COMPETITORS

Domtar Corporation; Midland Paper Company Inc.; Ris Paper Company, Inc.

FURTHER READING

"Central National-Gottesman Inc.: Company Profile," http://www.datamonitor.com, July 16, 2007.

"D. Samuel Gottesman, Merchant, Dies; President of a Wood Pulp Concern Here," *New York Times,* April 22, 1956.

"Fritz Lindenmeyr, Ill, Tries Suicide in Hotel," *New York Times,* March 19, 1931.

"Henry Lindenmeyr," *New York Times,* September 12, 1895.

"James G. Wallach, 55, Head of Paper Company," *New York Times,* June 23, 1998.

"M. Gottesman, 83: A Philanthropist," *New York Times,* December 17, 1942.

McFadden, Robert D., "Ira D. Wallach, 97, a Philanthropist, Dies," *New York Times,* January 8, 2007.

"Say Central Bank Will Fill New Need," *New York Times,* January 24, 1926.

"2 Paper Concerns Are Consolidated," *New York Times,* September 7, 1950.

The Charmer Sunbelt Group

60 East 42nd Street
New York, New York 10165
U.S.A.
Telephone: (334) 323-4472
Toll Free: (866) 455-3971
Fax: (334) 270-5983
Web site: http://www.charmer-sunbelt.com

Private Company
Incorporated: 1944 as Blue Crest Wine & Spirits Corp.
Employees: 6,550
Sales: $4.1 billion (2006 est.)
NAIC: 424820 Wine and Distilled Alcoholic Beverage Merchant Wholesalers

■ ■ ■

Maintaining its headquarters in New York City, The Charmer Sunbelt Group is one of the United States' largest wholesale distributors of wine, spirits, beer, bottled water, and other beverages. Through subsidiaries and partnerships, the privately held Charmer operates in Alabama, Arizona, Colorado, Connecticut, Delaware, Florida, Illinois, Maryland, Mississippi, New Jersey, New York, North Carolina, Pennsylvania, South Carolina, Virginia, and Washington, D.C. Wholly owned subsidiaries include Connecticut Distributors, Inc.; Washington Wholesale Liquor Co. Inc., serving the District of Columbia; Bacchus Importers, Ltd., also serving the District as well as Maryland and Delaware; Reliable Churchill, serving Maryland; Florida's Premier Beverage Co.; North Carolina's Prestige Wines Distribu-

tors, LLC; Capital Wines & Spirits Co. of Pennsylvania; and Service-Universal Distributors Inc., serving New York. Charmer serves its home territory, the New York City metropolitan area, through a joint venture, Empire Merchants. Charmer Sunbelt is owned and operated by the third generation of the Merinoff family.

FORMATION OF PREDECESSOR COMPANY: 1944

Charmer Sunbelt began modestly in 1944 when 43-year-old Charles Merinoff started a small beverage distributorship in Brooklyn, New York, under the name Blue Crest Wine & Spirits Corp. He was just one of a multitude of distributors in the city. Three years later he joined forces with Brooklyn-born James G. Scileppi, a man who was somewhat familiar with the spirits trade: As a U.S. Attorney based in New York City from 1935 to 1946, he broke up three major bootleg liquor rings. Merinoff and Scileppi formed Blue Crest Wine and Spirits Distributing Company to act as a Manhattan wholesaler. A year later Scileppi left for booming Long Island, where he became a residential housing developer. Merinoff stayed in the city and nurtured the business, gaining a toehold upstate by acquiring a Rochester, New York, distributor, Universal Liquors, in 1957.

HERMAN MERINOFF JOINS COMPANY: 1959

Merinoff was joined by his son, Herman I. Merinoff, in 1959. Born in Manhattan in 1928, the younger Merinoff received a degree from Syracuse University before earning a law degree from Harvard Law School, where he graduated magna cum laude and was an editor of the law review. After Harvard he returned to New York to take a position with the law firm of Chadbourne, Parke, Whiteside, Wolff & Brophy. He later became an assistant federal prosecutor in Manhattan.

In 1966 the Merinoffs formed Charmer Industries, based in Astoria, Queens, to serve as a holding company for their distributorships. The name was a combination of "char" from Charles and "mer" from Merinoff. Charles Merinoff would serve as chairman of the concern until his death in 1972 at the age of 71. Herman Merinoff carried on the family business and also became chairman and chief executive officer of Renfield Importers, Ltd., primarily a distributor of such brands as Gordon's and Martini & Rossi. Renfield also took a major stake in Sonoma Vineyard and in 1984 Merinoff became chairman, president, and CEO of that company as well.

THIRD GENERATION JOINS CHARMER: 1980

A third generation of the Merinoff family became involved with Charmer in 1980 after Charles Merinoff, the founder's namesake, graduated from the University of Wisconsin with a degree in finance and marketing. He did not, however, come in as an executive. Instead, he began as a driver's helper and systematically learned the different operations of the company, holding various posts in operations, sales, and purchasing. Finally, in 1991, he was named president of Charmer Industries.

In the mid-1980s there were about a dozen large distributors in New York City, Charmer's core market, but because consumers were becoming increasingly health-conscious, wine and spirits were no longer a growth business and new business would have to be taken from competitors. The field would begin to shake out as consolidation resulted in fewer, but larger, distributors. Queens-based Charmer and Brooklyn-based Peerless proved to be the most nimble and aggressive and grew apace over the next decade, while at the same time Charmer expanded outside of the city. In 1986 Connecticut Distributors was acquired. A year later Service Universal of New York City was added as was Washington Wholesale, serving Washington, D.C. In 1991 Charmer acquired Service Universal serving upstate New York, and in 1994 Bacchus Importers became part of Charmer, serving Washington, D.C., Maryland, and Delaware.

In 1994 Charmer generated sales of $500 million, making it the third largest liquor and wine wholesaler in the country. Although it had three warehouses with a combined 500,000 square feet, the company was hard pressed to effectively meet demand. In addition to consolidation in liquor distribution, another trend that had emerged in recent years was customers placing smaller orders, a just-in-time approach to doing business that required suppliers to make more frequent deliveries. Charmer was still geared toward filling large orders and lacked a warehouse management system that could allow it to simultaneously fill full pallet, case, and in some cases individual bottle orders. As a result, customer service suffered and through inefficiency the company incurred extra labor costs. The problem was especially acute during the busy holiday season, November and December, when about 40 percent of all liquor sales took place each year. To address the problem Charmer automated its warehouse operations with real-time inventory control and a flexible pick-pack operation that greatly increased space utilization and productivity, translating into higher margins and more satisfied customers.

By the start of 1997, according to *Crain's New York Business,* Charmer had "begun to emerge as the dominant player in New York by wresting away key business accounts from Brooklyn-based Peerless." According to industry projections, Charmer had generated $715 million in sales in 1996, a significant increase over the $640 million posted a year earlier, while Peerless dropped from $635 million to $590 million. As a result, Charmer was the fourth largest distributor in the United States and Peerless the seventh.

ACQUISITION OF SUNBELT BEVERAGE: 1997

Charmer was not content with merely dominating the metropolitan New York City market, however. In 1997 it extended its national footprint when the Merinoff and Drucker families (Herman Merinoff's sister Ruth had

KEY DATES

1944: Charles Merinoff forms Blue Crest Wine & Spirits Corp. in Brooklyn, New York.

1947 Merinoff begins wholesale distribution to Manhattan.

1959: Herman Merinoff joins company.

1966: Merinoff family forms Charmer Industries.

1972: Charles Merinoff dies.

1980: Grandson Charles Merinoff joins company.

1997: Sunbelt Beverage is acquired, creating The Charmer Sunbelt Group.

2002: Charles Merinoff is named Group's CEO.

2006: Herman Merinoff dies.

married Maurice Drucker) acquired a controlling interest in Sunbelt Beverage Corp., a Baltimore, Maryland-based operation with facilities in a number of states where Charmer was not represented. The combined entity assumed the name The Charmer Sunbelt Group.

Sunbelt Beverage started out as McKesson Wines & Spirits, a unit of McKesson Corporation, a major pharmaceutical wholesaler. McKesson had been established in New York City in 1933 as a wholesale and drug import company by John McKesson and his partner Charles Olcott. The McKesson family left the business in the 1890s and in 1926 Frank D. Costner bought the company, then known as McKesson & Robbins. Costner appeared to be the owner of a hair tonic company but in truth was an inveterate criminal, Philip Musica, who had been a bootlegger, among other illicit activities. He rapidly expanded McKesson's wholesale drug operations, and in 1934, after the repeal of Prohibition, he became involved in the legal liquor business, launching McKesson Wines & Spirits.

Costner's identity came to light in 1938 due to financial irregularities that drew the attention of the McKesson treasurer, resulting in an investigation that revealed Costner had been embezzling funds to pay off a blackmailer threatening to expose him. In the end, the blackmailer was sent to jail and Costner ended his life by gunshot. McKesson was taken private and its affairs, as well as those of McKesson Wine & Spirits, avoided the newspapers until 1967 when San Francisco-based Foremost Dairies acquired the company in a hostile takeover and the conglomerate moved its headquarters to San Francisco.

McKesson was an unwieldy collection of businesses and starting in 1980 management began to divest assets

to concentrate on pharmaceuticals and healthcare items, shedding companies involved in home building, chemicals, and food, including Foremost Dairies. In 1988 a controlling stake in McKesson Wine & Spirits was sold for about $115 million to the company's management team with financial backing from the New York investment firm of Weiss, Peck & Greer. In fiscal 1988 the McKesson division had recorded sales of about $540 million, operating 11 wholesale operations in eight states: Arizona, Arkansas, Florida, Georgia, Hawaii, Maryland, Texas, and South Carolina. Because of the orientation of most of the locations toward the South and Southwest, the independent company assumed the name Sunbelt Beverage Corporation and established headquarters in Baltimore, Maryland, headed by Ray Herrmann, the former president of McKesson's Wine & Spirits group, which included other assets that McKesson would soon sell.

By this time an independent company, Sunbelt Beverage continued to expand. Over the next four years it added distributorships throughout Florida. It also forged a joint venture with Ben Arnold Co. in 1993 to create Ben Arnold Sunbelt Beverage Company, the largest wholesale distributor of wine, spirits, and nonalcoholic beverages in South Carolina. In 1995 Sunbelt entered the Pennsylvania market by acquiring Philadelphia-based Capital Wines & Spirits. Two years later these assets would become part of an even larger enterprise, The Charmer Sunbelt Group.

Herman Merinoff served as chairman and CEO of Charmer Sunbelt and led it through the early years of integration and further growth. In 1998 a pair of acquisitions were completed, Mississippi Sales Company and Alabama Sales Company, and a joint venture, Alliance Beverage Distributing, was created in Arizona. In 2001 Charmer moved into the Colorado market with the acquisition of Beverage Distributors company. A year later Reliable Churchill of Maryland and North Carolina's Prestige Wines Distributors were added to the group.

DEATH OF HERMAN MERINOFF: 2006

Also in 2002 Charles Merinoff, who two years earlier had become chairman of the board of Charmer Industries, became CEO of Charmer Sunbelt. His father stayed on as co-chairman until June 2006 when at the age of 77 he died of pancreatic cancer. Charmer Sunbelt continued to expand under the new chief executive. Illinois-based Distinctive Wines & Spirits was acquired in 2003, as was Delaware's First States Distributing Group. A year later R&R Marketing LLC of West Caldwell, New Jersey, was added, and in 2005 Prestige Wines expanded in North Carolina through a merger with Charlotte-based Blue Ridge Wholesale Wine Company, Inc., the combined company taking the name Blue Ridge Wholesale Wine Company, LLC. During this period the company also signed exclusive distribution agreements for many of its territories with Allied Domecq Spirits & Wine North America, whose stable of brands included Kahlua, Stolichnaya Vodkas, Sauza Tequilas, Beefeater, Malibu flavored rum, Canadian Club, Courvosier, Maker's Mark, Buena Vista, Clos Du Bois, Bancott, and Perrier Jouet and Mumm champagne.

Associated Distributors of Virginia joined Charmer Sunbelt in 2006, and First State Distribution Group in Delaware created a joint venture with Century Wine & Spirits and Delaware Beverage Co., creating United Distributors of Delaware, LLC. Also in 2006, in a deal that would consummate in 2007, longtime competitors Charmer Industries and Peerless Importers joined forces to dominate the metropolitan New York City market, creating Empire Merchants, LLC. Later in 2007 Empire Merchants North was formed with the merger of Service Universal and Colony Wine & Spirits. In that same year, Commonwealth Wine & Spirits of Massachusetts was acquired, and in 2008 Distinctive Wines & Spirits, LLC, of Illinois was sold to Southern Wine & Spirits of America, Inc. After five years of effort, Charmer Sunbelt had been unable to make enough inroads in the Illinois

market and elected to devote its resources to more promising markets.

Ed Dinger

PRINCIPAL SUBSIDIARIES

Connecticut Distributors, Inc.; Washington Wholesale Liquor Co. Inc.; Bacchus Importers, Ltd.; Reliable Churchill; Premier Beverage Co.; Prestige Wines Distributors, LLC; Capital Wines & Spirits Co.; Service-Universal Distributors Inc.

PRINCIPAL COMPETITORS

Glazer's Wholesale Drug Company, Inc.; National Wine & Spirits Inc.; Southern Wine & Spirits of America Inc.

FURTHER READING

"Charles Merinoff," *New York Times,* September 1, 1972.

Evenson, Laura, "McKesson Sells Wine, Spirits Unit," *San Francisco Chronicle,* June 8, 1988, p. C1.

Kaplan, Andrew, "Mixed Drinks," *Beverage World,* July 15, 2007, p. 26.

"McKesson Will Sell Wine, Spirits Business to Group of Managers," *Wall Street Journal,* June 8, 1988, p. 1.

Saul, Stephanie, "Herman I. Merinoff, 77, Liquor Business Executive, Dies," *New York Times,* June 29, 2006.

Walsh, Mark, "NY Distributors Locking Horns over Liquid Assets," *Crain's New York Business,* January 6, 1997, pp. 3+.

Cinemark Holdings, Inc.

—■—

3900 Dallas Parkway, Suite 500
Plano, Texas 75093
U.S.A.
Telephone: (972) 665-1000
Toll Free: (800) 246-3637
Fax: (972) 665-1004
Web site: http://www.cinemark.com

Public Company
Incorporated: 2006
Employees: 16,700
Sales: $1.68 billion (2007)
Stock Exchanges: New York
Ticker Symbol: CNK
NAIC: 512131 Motion Picture Theaters (Except
  Drive-Ins)

■ ■ ■

Cinemark Holdings, Inc., is the third largest operator of
movie theaters in the United States, trailing industry
leader Regal Entertainment Group and AMC Entertainment Holdings, Inc. Cinemark operates 408 theaters
and 4,665 screens in 38 states, one Canadian province,
and 12 Latin American countries. The company's
properties are located in midsized markets where they
typically hold sway as the dominant theaters in their
market. More than 80 percent of Cinemark's theaters
feature stadium seating and first-run feature films. In the
United States, its greatest concentration of theaters is
located in the company's home state of Texas, where 78

theaters house 1,054 screens. Internationally, the
company operates in Mexico, Brazil, Chile, Argentina,
Colombia, Peru, Ecuador, Honduras, El Salvador,
Nicaragua, Costa Rica, and Panama.

FOUNDER, LEE ROY MITCHELL

Lee Roy Mitchell tried to get out of the movie theater
business twice in his life, but he was lured back into the
industry on both occasions. His decision to remain in
the business resulted in a career spanning a half-century
whose crowning achievement was Cinemark Holdings.

Mitchell grew up in the movie theater business. His
father ran three cinemas in the small Texas towns of
Forney, Bastrop, and Smithville, which served as a training ground for Mitchell during his youth. As a teenager,
he helped his father run the businesses, spending time at
each location popping popcorn, sweeping the floors, and
running the projectors. As a young adult during the
1950s, he made his first break with the cinema business
when he began selling cars. Mitchell enjoyed success as a
Ford dealer, but before the end of the decade, he was
back helping his father, whose three theaters were beginning to show their age.

ACQUIRING HIS FIRST PROPERTY

Mitchell made his first move on his own in the cinema
business in 1960. He purchased a drive-in located in
Ennis, Texas, that became the foundation of his first
business empire. A series of acquisitions followed Mitchell's initial purchase, as he bought property after
property and built his first chain of movie theaters.

COMPANY PERSPECTIVES

We apply a disciplined growth strategy, selectively building or acquiring new theatres in markets where we can establish and maintain a strong market position. Our portfolio of modern theatres provides a superior movie-going experience to patrons, contributing to our consistent cash flows and high operating margins. Our significant presence in the U.S. and Latin America has made us an important distribution channel for movie studios, particularly as they look to increase revenues generated in Latin America. Our market leadership and track record of strong financial performance is attributable in large part to our senior executives, who average approximately 33 years of industry experience and have successfully navigated us through multiple business cycles.

Mitchell focused his investments on properties located in small Texas towns before expanding into neighboring states, keeping his sights restricted to small markets. He spent a quarter century building his company into a recognizable regional player in the Southwest, eventually stringing together 80 screens in his chain before tiring of the daily rigors of running his company. Mitchell decided to retire. In 1984, he sold his chain of theaters to movie-house mogul Henry Pitt, gaining $12 million from the sale, and used a pittance of the proceeds to buy a new mobile home. Mitchell had decided to begin his retirement by taking a lengthy tour of the United States. His retirement and his trip lasted no longer than the drive from Texas to Utah.

Mitchell was ready to begin a new chapter in his life. He had a new wife, Tandy, and a new mission, to explore the country, but the seduction of the movie theater business altered his plans for the second time. His about-face came in the form of an epiphany, one that struck him as he wended his way through one small town after another in his mobile home. "There were no more drive-ins," he recalled in an October 12, 1992, interview with *Forbes*. From his years helping his father run his small-town theaters and presiding over his own collection of small-town properties, Mitchell knew drive-ins offered an inexpensive alternative for families to go to the movies. He sensed that some people were being priced out of the moviegoing experience, and by the time he parked his mobile home in Salt Lake City, his retirement was over.

LAUNCHING A SECOND CHAIN IN 1985

After Mitchell saw an advertisement for three movie houses in Salt Lake City, he began building his second chain. In 1985, he paid $1 million for the three properties. Mitchell reopened two of the theaters as discount houses that charged customers $1 to see films that had yet to be released on videotape. Mitchell's roadside epiphany had not led him to start a chain of drive-ins, but it had led him to focus on serving a demographic that he perceived to be underserved. He focused on communities with populations ranging between 30,000 and 100,000, looking for locations where his properties would be the dominant movie house in the area. After the purchase of the Salt Lake City theaters, Mitchell took on a partner, Paul Broadhead, who invested $5 million. Broadhead, a Mississippi-based shopping mall developer, had sold his real estate company in 1984. With Broadhead sharing in the financial risk, Mitchell acquired additional screens closer to his home, developing a strong presence in the Sun Belt region as he pushed forward with his concept of "dollar houses."

Whether it was the influence of Broadhead or some midlife burst of ambition, there was a distinct difference between the chains created before and after Mitchell's short-lived retirement. His second company, which adopted the Cinemark name in 1987, was decidedly more aggressive than was his first company. By 1989, four years after Mitchell had shelved plans for retirement, Cinemark operated 663 screens in 18 states. The company ranked as the seventh largest movie house chain in the country. Mitchell, by that point, was shooting for 1,000 screens by 1992. "We feel we need to get to that size to be recognized as a major distributor," he said in an April 16, 1990, interview with the *Dallas Business Journal*.

TWO CHAINS FUELING RAPID GROWTH

Part of the reason for the tremendous growth of Cinemark stemmed from a change in Mitchell's strategy. As he and his staff scoured the countryside for suitable locations for dollar houses, they came across locations where the real estate was too expensive to support a discount house but the market was ideal for a first-run theater. Mitchell could not pass up the opportunities and began building a chain of traditional movie theaters alongside his discount chain. By 1992, his chain of first-run theaters was larger than his discount chain, spreading Cinemark's presence into more than 20 states. The company rose to be the sixth largest chain in the country, catapulting up the industry rankings within its

KEY DATES

1960: Lee Roy Mitchell acquires his first movie theater.

1984: After decades of building a chain of theaters, Mitchell sells his 80-screen operation and retires.

1985: Mitchell acquires three properties in Utah, establishing the foundation for Cinemark.

1992: Mitchell begins expanding internationally by establishing a presence in Mexico.

2002: Plans for an initial public offering of stock are canceled.

2004: Cinemark is acquired by Madison Dearborn Partners, LLC, a Chicago-based private equity firm.

2006: Cinemark acquires Century Theatres, Inc., adding more than 1,100 screens to its holdings.

2007: Cinemark completes its initial public offering of stock.

first seven years of business, but far more was yet to come.

CINEMARK ENTERING FOREIGN MARKETS IN 1992

In early 1992, Broadhead cashed out on his investment for $20 million, not the last time someone would profit substantially from Cinemark's growth. The year also marked the beginning of Mitchell's boldest expansion campaign, the exportation of his cinema strategy across international borders. In July 1992, Mitchell formed Cinemark Mexico (USA) Inc. as a subsidiary to spearhead the development and acquisition of theaters in Mexico, the beginning of an international expansion plan that would see Cinemark stake a presence throughout Central America and into South America.

As Cinemark marched into international markets, its operations in the United States took on a new look. Mitchell's initial emphasis on discount houses had given way to a chain primarily comprising first-run theaters, theaters described as "flashy" and "glitzy" by the business press that embraced the popular format of the 1990s, the multiplex. Cinemark, which achieved much of its growth through new theater development, grew rapidly by building theaters that housed multiple screens. Although the company replaced its neon-bright décor with an art deco design at the end of 1998, the same

year it moved its headquarters from Dallas to Plano, Texas, its reliance on the multiplex format did not change. By the end of the 1990s, Cinemark ranked as the fifth largest chain in the country. It operated more than 2,100 screens in 38 states and nine countries, generating roughly $500 million in annual revenue. Cinemark entered the 21st century ready to establish a presence in Europe, with properties under development in Northampton, England, and Düsseldorf, Germany.

PUBLIC DEBUT PROVING DIFFICULT

The new millennium proved to be a difficult time for movie theater chains in the United States. Overexpansion during the late 1990s forced several high-profile operators to declare bankruptcy, which triggered a new wave of industry consolidation during the first years of the century. Cinemark persevered through the difficult years, but it did experience problems executing its corporate strategy. Mitchell wanted to take the company public, filing with the Securities and Exchange Commission for a July 2002 initial public offering (IPO) of stock. He hoped to raise approximately $230 million from the offering, but when July arrived the company delayed the IPO indefinitely, citing lackluster conditions in the stock market. Cinemark scheduled a second attempt for May 2003, but again the IPO was canceled. By the beginning of 2004, another, far more profound, move was being contemplated.

At the beginning of 2004, reports surfaced that Cinemark had hired two investment firms to ascertain interest in the sale of all or part of the company's operations. Cinemark was weighed down heavily by debt, which it had attempted to reduce by completing an IPO, but after aborting two attempts to become a public company, it turned to other options. The company, ranking as the third largest competitor in the industry, officially announced it was on the auction block on January 23, 2004.

NEW OWNERSHIP IN 2004

Industry observers foresaw a major consolidation within the industry when Cinemark revealed it was up for sale. The industry's two largest competitors, Regal Entertainment Group and AMC Entertainment Holdings, Inc., were seen as Cinemark's most likely suitors, but Mitchell's influence made a megamerger improbable. He was demanding too high of a price for his 3,156 screens, and he wanted to remain at the helm of the company, which was an unlikely scenario if Regal or AMC acquired Cinemark.

Speculation about Cinemark's fate ended in April 2004, when Madison Dearborn Partners, LLC, acquired

83 percent of Cinemark. Madison Dearborn, Chicago's largest private equity firm, paid $1 billion and assumed $560 million of debt to become Cinemark's majority owner, agreeing to let Mitchell remain as the company's chairman and chief executive officer.

As part of the $1.56 billion deal, Cinemark parted ways with one of its major investors. Back in March 1996, New York-based Cypress Group LLC acquired a 44.8 percent stake in Cinemark for $139.2 million. When Madison Dearborn completed its transaction, Cypress Group netted nearly a 200 percent profit on its eight-year-old investment.

CINEMARK SWALLOWING CENTURY THEATRES IN 2006

The next major event in Cinemark's development occurred slightly more than two years after the new ownership arrangement was finalized. In August 2006, Cinemark Holdings, Inc., was formed as the holding company for Cinemark, Inc., a corporate maneuver executed to facilitate the purchase of a major movie theater chain. The same month the holding company was formed, Cinemark acquired San Rafael, California-based Century Theatres, Inc., an operator with more than 1,100 screens in 12 states. Founded in 1940, Century Theatres restricted its expansion to the western United States for its first half-century of business, but it began to expand eastward in the decade leading up to its acquisition by Cinemark. The company, like Cinemark, favored stadium seating and modern, multiplex theaters. Together, Cinemark and Century Theatres operated 391 theaters with 4,395 screens in 37 states and 13 countries.

PUBLIC DEBUT IN 2007

Once the two companies were organized into a cohesive whole, Mitchell succeeded in executing the move he had been attempting for five years. In April 2007, Cinemark completed its IPO, giving investors the opportunity to participate financially in the future growth of the chain. The company ended the year with $1.68 billion in revenue, 408 theaters, and 4,665 screens. Looking ahead, the totals were expected to increase as Mitchell endeavored to make the industry's third largest participant a formidable competitor for years to come.

Jeffrey L. Covell

PRINCIPAL SUBSIDIARIES

Cinemark, L.L.C.; Sunnymead Cinema Corp.; Trans Texas Cinema, Inc.; Cinemark Properties, Inc.; Greeley Holdings, Inc.; Greeley, Ltd.; Cinemark International, L.L.C.; Cinemark Mexico (USA), Inc.; Cinemark Leasing Company; Cinemark Partners I, Inc.; Cinemark Partners II, Ltd.; Cinemark Investments Corporation; Multiplex Properties, Inc.; Canada Theatre Holdings, Inc.; CNMK Brazil Investments, Inc.; CNMK Delaware Investments I, L.L.C.; CNMK Delaware Investments II, L.L.C.; CNMK Delaware Investment Properties, L.P.; CNMK Texas Properties, LLC; Brainerd Cinema, Ltd.; Laredo Theatre, Ltd.; Brasil Holdings, L.L.C.; Cinemark Media, Inc.; Century Theatres, Inc.; NBE, Inc.; Marin Theatre Management, LLC; Century Theatres NG, L.L. C.; CineArts, L.L.C.; CineArts of Sacramento, L.L.C.; Corte Madera Theatres, L.L.C.; Novato Theatres, L.L. C.; San Rafael Theatres, L.L.C.; Northbay Theatres, L.L.C.; Century Theatres Summit Sierra, L.L.C.; Century Theatres Seattle, L.L.C.; Cinemark Argentina, S.R.L.; Prodecine S.R.L. (Argentina); Bulnes 2215, S.R.L. (Argentina); Cinemark Brasil S.A. (Brazil); Cinemark Theatres Canada, Inc.; Cinemark Holdings Canada, Inc.; Century Theatres of Canada, ULC; Cinemark Panama, S.A.; Cinemark Equity Holdings Corporation (British Virgin Islands); Cinemark Costa Rica, S.R.L.; Cinemark El Salvador, Ltda de C.V.; Cinemark Nicaragua y Cia, Ltda.; Cinemark Honduras S. de R.L.; Cinemark Chile S.A.; Inversiones Cinemark, S.A. (Chile); Worldwide Invest, Inc. (British Virgin Islands); Cinemark Colombia S.A.; Cinemark del Ecuador S.A.; Cinemark Germany GmbH; Cinemark Holdings Mexico S. de R.L. de C.V.; Cinemark de Mexico, S.A. de C.V.; Servicios Cinemark, S.A. de C.V.; Cinemark del Norte, S.A. de C.V.; Cinemark del Peru S.R.L.; Cinemark Holdings Spain, S.L.

PRINCIPAL COMPETITORS

Regal Entertainment Group; AMC Entertainment Holdings, Inc.; Carmike Cinemas, Inc.

FURTHER READING

Carey, David, "Cypress Triples Money on Cinemark," *Daily Deal,* March 16, 2004.

Cecil, Mark, "Cinemark Screens Strategic Options," *Mergers & Acquisitions Report,* February 2, 2004.

"Cinemark Acquires Century Theatres Chain," *Dallas Morning News,* August 8, 2006.

DiOrio, Carl, "Cinemark Is on the Block," *Daily Variety,* January 14, 2004, p. 1.

———, "Cinemark Yanks IPO," *Daily Variety,* July 24, 2002, p. 6.

Fairchild, Lori, "Lee Roy Mitchell: Cinemark USA Inc.," *Dallas Business Journal,* June 27, 1997, p. C5.

Gubernick, Lisa, "Dollar House Mitchell," *Forbes,* October 12, 1992, p. 118.

Kirkpatrick, John, "Chicago Firm Would Pay $1 Billion for Texas-Based Cinema Chain, Newspaper Says," *Dallas Morning News,* March 11, 2004.

————, "Plano, Texas-based Cinemark Holds Off on Initial Public Offering," *Dallas Morning News,* July 24, 2002.

Mann, Jennifer, "Dallas-Based Movie Theater Chain Cinemark Plans Initial Public Offering," *Kansas City Star,* May 21, 2002.

Ricketts, Chip, "Cinemark Targets 150 New Screens in '90 Expansion Drive," *Dallas Business Journal,* April 16, 1990, p. 11.

————, "Two Deals Help Cinemark Corp. Take Its Act Nationwide," *Dallas Business Journal,* September 18, 1989, p. 3.

Sayewitz, Ronni, "Cinemark USA Moving Headquarters to Plano," *Dallas Business Journal,* December 4, 1998, p. 5.

Scott, Dave, "Cinemark Expansion Turns South: $27M War Chest to Fund Big Push into Mexico," *Dallas Business Journal,* December 17, 1993, p. 7.

Strahler, Steven R., "Seeing Gold on the Silver Screen," *Crain's Chicago Business,* May 3, 2004, p. 4.

The Coffee Beanery, Ltd.

3429 Pierson Place
Flushing, Michigan 48433
U.S.A.
Telephone: (810) 733-1020
Toll Free: (800) 728-2326
Fax: (810) 733-1536
Web site: http://www.coffeebeanery.com

Private Company
Incorporated: 1976
Employees: 140
Sales: $17 million (2007 est.)
NAIC: 311423 Dried and Dehydrated Food Manufacturing; 311930 Flavoring Syrup and Concentrate Manufacturing; 424490 Other Grocery and Related Product Merchant Wholesalers; 445299 Other Specialty Food Stores; 522110 Owners and Lessors of Other Non-Financial Assets

■■■

One of the largest retail coffee shop chains in the United States, The Coffee Beanery, Ltd., owns and franchises more than 135 specialty coffee shops and kiosks in 28 states, as well as 25 locations in seven countries. The company offers more than 50 varieties of coffee, all roasted in small batches to unique specifica-tions that release the particular characteristics of various coffee beans. The Coffee Beanery imports Arabica beans from growers in Colombia, Kenya, Costa Rica, Guatemala, Ethiopia, Sumatra, Jamaica, Hawaii, and other locations worldwide. Basic coffee flavors, "straight" or decaffeinated, include Colombia Supremo and Bean-ery Blend. Decaffeinated coffee is produced using the chemical-free, Swiss-water method of decaffeination. The company's proprietary Espresso Perfecto lends a slightly sweet flavor to lattes, cappuccinos, and iced smoothies. All coffee drinks can be sweetened and flavored with a variety of syrups, such as chocolate, caramel, almond, English toffee, hazelnut, and Irish cream. The Coffee Beanery offers regular and decaffein-ated coffee roasted in many special flavors, such as Vanilla Nut, Crème Brulee, Butter Rum, Café Caramel, Amaretto, and Double Dutch Fudge. The Coffee Bean-ery offers whole-bean coffee in one-pound packages at stores and franchises and in one-, two-, or three-pound bags through the company's web site. All coffee is roasted, hand-flavored, and packaged at the company's production and warehouse facility in Flushing, Michigan.

In addition to coffee, Coffee Beanery cafés and kiosks offer a variety of herbal and flavored teas and a selection of baked goods, such as bagels, scones, muf-fins, cinnamon rolls, and cookies. The larger cafés provide a variety of egg sandwiches for breakfast, salads, soup, and sandwiches for lunch, and cheesecake, pie, and cake for dessert. Coffee-related accessories include French presses, drip coffeemakers, coffee grinders, travel coffee mugs, and gift sets.

COMPANY PERSPECTIVES

Coffee Beanery opened its first stores in the United States in 1976, before the American public knew the term "specialty coffee." In the 30 years that have followed, Coffee Beanery continues to build its brand and franchise organization on the principles of time-tested and honored traditions and values. Exceptional coffee, a warm relaxing environment, and a corporate culture that embraces its franchisees with every opportunity to succeed exemplify these values.

OFFERING A GOOD CUP OF COFFEE

Many years before gourmet coffeehouses became ubiquitous in U.S. cities and towns, JoAnne Shaw learned of people's dissatisfaction with the standard, freeze-dried coffee found in grocery stores. During the early 1970s, Shaw provided coffee and snack distribution services to offices on a monthly basis. Although Shaw built the business, started by her husband Julius, to 225 customers, she was surprised to find it difficult to find a buyer for the operation. People liked the aroma of coffee but not the taste, so they did not want the business.

Believing that many people had not tasted good coffee, JoAnne and Julius Shaw began exploring the possibility of opening a gourmet coffee shop in 1975. They brought an extensive background in restaurant and catering management to this endeavor. The Shaws found an ideal location at the Fairlane Towne Center, an upscale shopping mall in Dearborn, Michigan, then under construction. They obtained $90,000 to fund the venture by obtaining a second mortgage on their home and using the family's two cars as additional collateral. Managed by JoAnne, the first Coffee Beanery opened in 1976.

The Coffee Beanery offered fresh-brewed coffee, flavored coffee, espresso drinks, and packaged coffee. To educate customers about the taste of good coffee, Shaw provided free tasting samples. Complementary products sold at the store included coffeemakers, coffee mugs, and kitchen products, such as spices and salad spinners. Shaw continually refined the store concept, eliminating the kitchen products and adding coffee grinders, espresso machines, and drip filters. The Coffee Beanery began making iced coffee drinks in the early 1980s. By leasing equipment and other creative measures, Shaw

managed to open another eight stores in suburban malls in southeast Michigan by 1985.

CORPORATE AND FRANCHISE EXPANSION FOLLOWING EARLY SUCCESS

From the beginning, Shaw expected the gourmet coffee concept to expand. The first franchise operation opened in November 1985 and developed quickly from there. Shaw provided franchisees with a store design, marketing plan, and coffee and coffee products. Franchisees purchased dairy products, including milk, butter, and cream cheese for bagels, as well as baked goods from local suppliers.

Confronted with an unreliable supply of gourmet coffee from vendors, The Coffee Beanery began to roast its own coffee beans in 1987. Over the course of several months, Shaw and her employees learned how to roast, flavor, grind, and package coffee beans. In addition to ensuring an adequate supply of gourmet coffee for expansion, the change provided franchises with a wider selection of coffee. The company obtained coffee beans from growers around the world and developed more than 50 fresh-roasted varieties of coffee, including flavored coffee, such as the popular Hazelnut and Swiss Chocolate Almond. The unique roasting requirements of each type of coffee bean inspired the marketing tagline, The Right Roast. In 1989, the company purchased new packaging equipment that allowed The Coffee Beanery to offer coffee in different sized and shaped bags for retail sale or use by the coffee shops. Because the idea of gourmet coffee was still so revolutionary, the one-pot, sample bags of flavored coffee were popular among new patrons.

In further preparation for new store development, Shaw hired staff for franchise support and continued to do so in pace with growth. She set a goal to double the number of stores/franchises every year over the next two years. The company's marketing strategy included a new design for the store interior, adding oak, brass, and marble fixtures. By the end of 1989, the company and its franchisees operated 23 shops at shopping malls in five states, generating approximately $7 million in sales. Moreover, developers began to approach Shaw about opening Coffee Beanery stores in shopping malls under construction.

The cost to start a franchise, at $90,000 to $180,000, included the $17,500 franchise fee paid to The Coffee Beanery. The fee included an intensive, two-week training course covering all phases of managing a business that Shaw herself had to learn. In addition to the basics, such as budgeting and hiring, the training

KEY DATES

1976: The first Coffee Beanery store opens in Dearborn, Michigan.

1985: With nine stores in operation, the company initiates franchising opportunities.

1987: To ensure a stable supply of gourmet coffee, the company begins to roast its own coffee beans.

1992: New storefront cafés offer seating and a selection of foods for breakfast and lunch.

1999: New store design adopts a tropical West Indies theme.

2001: International development begins with the opening of a Coffee Beanery in Qatar.

2003: Coffee Beanery franchises open in Chengdu, in China.

2007: Two franchises open on island of Cyprus.

included proper brewing techniques, finding a location based on demographic studies, negotiating a lease, and determining construction costs. The marketing segment involved an understanding of promotions, advertising, signage, and informational brochures. The franchise fee included a complete starting inventory of coffee, training at a company store, and onsite assistance for the first two weeks of a store's operation. For franchisees with cash and good credit, The Coffee Beanery provided as much as 40 percent of financing. Also, Shaw developed a franchise leasing package to provide equipment and store fixtures to reduce start-up costs.

GOURMET COFFEE WEATHERS RECESSION

During the recession of the early 1990s, Coffee Beanery continued to grow and attract new customers. Although the average price of a pound of coffee was $9, gourmet coffee became a small luxury, even when people stopped spending money on big purchases. Aggregate revenues of 66 franchises reached $14 million in 1991. Sales filled through the company's warehouse generated an additional $7 million.

Rapid growth required The Coffee Beanery to relocate to a 31,000-square-foot warehouse, production, and office facility in Flushing, Michigan. The facility provided space for a new roaster, capable of roasting 1,000 pounds of coffee beans per hour. The new equipment allowed the company to increase its coffee selection to nearly 100 varieties. Each store carried about 70

kinds of coffee and brewed six varieties each day for immediate consumption. For people who did not drink coffee, the company introduced "Teas of the World," a selection of 30 varieties of hot tea.

The Coffee Beanery diversified its coffee outlet design, to both smaller and larger formats. In late 1991, the company successfully launched its first coffee cart in the Renaissance Center in Detroit. The coffee cart offered brewed coffee, espresso drinks, hot tea, and baked goods to office workers. Conversely, the company began opening larger, storefront units outside of urban malls in areas such as Manhattan and Washington, D.C. These café's provided seating and offered a wider array of baked goods, as well as soup, salads, and sandwiches for lunch. By September 1993, 104 Coffee Beanery shops were in operation, including 24 company-owned units.

PROMOTIONS BUILDING CONSUMER AWARENESS

With a limited budget, The Coffee Beanery initiated several low cost promotional projects to improve company and store sales. In 1992, the company experimented with a direct-mail service and each of ten stores sent 10,000, 12-page catalogs offering coffee and accessories for sale. Also, the company cooperated with Pressman Toy Corporation to provide sample card packs for the adult trivia game Mind Trap at Coffee Beanery stores. Conversely, the games sold elsewhere included coupons for the purchase of packaged coffee from any Coffee Beanery shop.

In late 1993, The Coffee Beanery entered into a joint venture with Sanders Systems, an established, Detroit favorite for chocolate and ice cream. Sanders began to serve Coffee Beanery products at Sanders lunch counters and restaurants and to sell packaged, whole-bean coffee at its chocolate shops.

Educating customers about the finer qualities of coffee acted as a low-key form of product promotion. New packaging for whole-bean coffee included a description of each coffee's cultural and geographic origins. Color coding for different types of coffee—red for flavored, brown for blends, and ivory for rare varieties—helped customers identify coffee specialties. Hands-on education involved "cupping" demonstrations, which taught customers everything about identifying good coffee beans and tasting coffee for body, flavor, acidity, and finish. The quality of coffee beans could be determined by the aroma the coffee emits during the steeping process. At the cupping, fresh roasted beans were ground fresh, then steeped in water in front of participants. The Coffee Beanery celebrated the spring 1996 opening of the company's largest shop, a 2,400-

square-foot storefront in Birmingham, Michigan, with a cupping demonstration. The event garnered positive response from participants.

In 1996 The Coffee Beanery combined celebration of its 20 years in operation with a sample promotion. That year the company produced a special 20th Anniversary Blend and attached one-pot sampler packages to 65,000 large-sized bottles of Hiram Walker's Drambuie liquor.

A particularly successful promotion, the "flavor poll," became an annual event. Started in 1996, the event offered customers a $1 coupon for the purchase of a pound of coffee beans in exchange for a completed ballot. More than 7,000 people voted for their favorite flavors. Furthermore, customer suggestions resulted in the introduction of three new flavored coffees the following year: cinnamon-almond macaroon, white chocolate chiffon, and English toffee and cream.

WIDE-RANGING MARKETING STRATEGIES BUILDING ON SUCCESS

The Coffee Beanery expanded by opening in a variety of new venues, in part a result of outsourcing foodservices. In 1996 the company opened coffee bars in several entertainment venues, such as the Andy Williams theater in Branson, Missouri, All American Sports Park in Las Vegas, and in the Magic on Ice and Euro Circus venues in Myrtle Beach, South Carolina, Other new venues included a car dealership that purchased a license to offer Coffee Beanery products to customers. Spec's Music Store in Florida opened a similar operation.

The Coffee Beanery opened a corporate store at a new Kroger Co. grocery store in the upscale West Bloomfield Township, Michigan, area. The Coffee Beanery leased space from Kroger for a 24-foot counter and seating for 15 people. Kroger viewed the inclusion of the coffee bar as convenient service to customers. The location, with a supply of 24 packaged coffee varieties for sale in addition to a full menu of coffee drinks, tended to sell more packaged coffee than other units, given its location in a grocery store.

With extensive expansion plans for south Florida, The Coffee Beanery employed a more attention-getting promotion to celebrate the store opening at North Miami. Billed as the "world's longest coffee break," the festivities included fire jugglers, Caribbean stilt dancers in colorful costumes, and a street artist who used raw (green) coffee beans to replicate a Picasso painting. A prototype for street front cafés, the coffeehouse provided seating for 50 inside the 1,800-square-foot store, and an additional 30 seats outdoors. Other new locations in

south Florida included Ft. Lauderdale, Hollywood, West Palm Beach, Coral Springs, and Pembroke Pines.

In November 1998 The Coffee Beanery aired its first national advertisement in 30 states on CNN, The Weather Channel, and the Food Network. The 30-second spot, "Use Your Bean," featured Colombian music as it highlighted The Coffee Beanery's philosophy of coffee roasting.

The company's small advertising budget required creativity in achieving public exposure. Toward that end, The Coffee Beanery obtained product placement in movies and television shows. Frequently, the movie studios contacted The Coffee Beanery. In *Deep Impact,* Coffee Beanery cups were placed across a conference table during a long scene. In *Jackie Brown,* actress Pam Grier stood in front of a Coffee Beanery shop where promotional posters prominently advertised white-chocolate mocha. Popular television shows *Ally McBeal, ER,* and *Everybody Loves Raymond* also helped publicize the chain.

Although coffee and espresso drinks became increasingly popular during the late 1990s, growth at Coffee Beanery stagnated as competition from Starbucks and independent coffee shops sharpened. At the end of 1996 the company and its franchisees operated 187 stores in 30 states, but only 190 at the end of 1999. Likewise, systemwide sales hovered in the $51 million to $54 million range. At the same time, espresso drinks became more popular, especially the café mocha (a latte with chocolate sauce), and the check average rose from $1.85 in 1993 to $3.30 in 1996. The company sold more than two million pounds of coffee each year, equivalent to about 23 million cups of coffee.

COFFEE BEANERY COMPETING WITH STORE AND PRODUCT DEVELOPMENT

The Coffee Beanery sought to enliven its coffeehouse concept by introducing a new store design, beginning with the opening of the first Little Rock store in October 1999. The 2,000-square-foot café featured colors and elements evocative of a coffee plantation in the colonial West Indies. Decorative elements included animal print upholstery for booths and banquettes, cherrywood-stain tables and chairs, silk coffee trees, ceiling fans with natural leaf blades, tiled walls, and slate floors. Multiple clocks showed the times of prominent coffee-growing regions, such as Jamaica, Costa Rica, Kenya, Hawaii, Tanzania, and Sumatra. New stores that opened in 2000, including locations in Tennessee, Ohio, and New York, incorporated the new plantation motif. Remodeling of all stores began in the spring of 2000.

The new style succeeded in increasing sales and attracted the interest of potential franchisees.

With the growing popularity of espresso drinks, The Coffee Beanery designed its own proprietary blend. The new "Espresso Perfecto" combined Central American, South American, and African coffee. The Coffee Beanery intensified and refined the flavor and deepened the color by roasting more beans per liquid measure of the ultimate cup of espresso. Also, the company enhanced the texture of the milk foam by reducing the amount of air injected into the milk during frothing. The technique created a creamier, silkier texture. The overall effect of the changes involved creating a sweeter espresso drink that would not require as much sugar.

The company offered its first premium estate and organic coffees. Guatemalan Finca Dos Marias was grown at a family-owned plantation dating to 1870, and Organic Aztec Pluma was grown by a cooperative in southern Mexico.

FRANCHISES IN GROWING INTERNATIONAL MARKETS

Although the company opened its first international unit in 1998, in Guam, further expansion took a few years to germinate. Shaw's involvement in the International Franchise Association, along with overseas interest in American coffee culture, attracted franchisees to The Coffee Beanery. Three franchise agreements played a role in The Coffee Beanery's international expansion to the Middle East and Asia. The Sterling Group, which operated A&W and Ponderosa franchises in the Middle East, agreed to open Coffee Beanery cafés in Kuwait, Qatar, Bahrain, and the United Arab Emirates. The group opened its first store in Qatar in 2001.

A franchise agreement with the Jun family led to the opening of a Coffee Beanery in Seoul, South Korea, in April 2002. The 4,000-square-foot unit, located in a densely populated business district, was an immediate success, leading to the opening of a second location.

The Coffee Beanery franchisee in China opened its first store in Chengdu, in Sichuan province, in 2002, quickly followed by four additional stores. The Coffee Beanery signed a master franchise agreement with four Chinese firms to open 17 coffee shops in Shanghai beginning in 2004.

Other international locations included Puerto Rico and Cyprus. Three locations opened in Cyprus during 2007.

SHAW CONCENTRATING ON RENEWING DOMESTIC FRANCHISING

The contribution of domestic franchises to The Coffee Beanery's overall success shifted, as a number of locations closed and new franchises opened in other locations. However, the company did not maintain its peak 1999 level of 190 stores. By the end of 2006, the company counted 150 stores in 28 states, 90 percent of which were franchise operations. The company maintained a concentration of coffeehouses in the Northeast, particularly in New York and New Jersey, and in the Midwest, such as Michigan. Nevertheless, Shaw maintained an optimistic attitude. She focused on building a concentration of stores in the Northeast, thereby maximizing the benefits of advertising and marketing costs. During the summer of 2007, she promoted The Coffee Beanery franchise throughout Michigan and visited the 26 franchises in the state as a show of support as the economy faltered.

During the fall of 2007, the company's Christmas holiday promotion offered customers a chance to win a vacation in Jamaica. Customers received a Scratch-and-Win promotion game ticket with a minimum purchase of $9.99. The grand prize was a one-week vacation for two at an all-inclusive resort in Jamaica. Another ten winners received a year's supply of specialty coffee. With 250,000 tickets distributed, The Coffee Beanery provided many opportunities for customers to win free coffee drinks.

Mary Tradii

PRINCIPAL COMPETITORS

Caribou Coffee Company, Inc.; Starbucks Corporation.

FURTHER READING

Bakri, Lama, "Business Is Perky," *Detroit Free Press,* July 8, 1996.

Cebrzynski, Gregg, "Hollywood Plays Role in Coffee Beanery Ad Budget," *Nation's Restaurant News,* January 11, 1999, p. 6.

"The Coffee Beanery Adds Unique Coffees," *Specialty Coffee Retailer,* May 2001, p. 8.

"The Coffee Beanery Celebrates 30 Years," *Display & Design Ideas,* March 16, 3007.

"Coffee Beanery Creates 'Espresso Perfecto,'" *Tea & Coffee Trade,* September 20, 2000, p. 94.

"Coffee Beanery Embraces a West Indies Theme," *Tea & Coffee Trade Journal,* March 2000, p. 92.

"The Coffee Beanery Gains Widespread Notice," *Specialty Coffee Retailer,* September 2001, p. 8.

"Coffee Beanery Launches First Ad Campaign; Challenges Consumers to Use Their Bean," *Business Wire,* November 11, 1998, p. 1144.

"The Coffee Beanery Named One of the Best Coffee Franchises," *Business Wire,* January 29, 1999, p. 1197.

"The Coffee Beanery Opened Two Units in a Columbia, SC Airport and Plans to Open Another Unit," *Food Institute Report,* October 8, 2007, p. 3.

"Coffee Beanery Opens Store in Seoul Korea," *Gourmet Retailer,* April 2002, p. 10.

"The Coffee Beanery Places Its Beans on Screens," *Tea & Coffee Trade,* April 20, 2001, p. 128.

"Coffee Beanery Secures Credit Facility," *Nation's Restaurant News,* May 18, 1998, p. 50.

"Coffee Beanery Signs Mideast, S. Korea Expansion Pacts," *Nation's Restaurant News,* May 14, 2001, p. 76.

"Coffee Beanery to Air First National TV Ads," *Nation's Restaurant News,* November 9, 1998, p. 18.

"Coffee Beanery Unveils New Store Design," *Nation's Restaurant News,* February 14, 2000, p. 34.

Deck, Cecilia, "Grounds for Optimism; Chain of Gourmet Coffee Bean Stores Expects Upscale Brews Will Stay Hot," *Detroit Free Press,* November 28, 1990, p. 1G.

Eberwein, Cheryl, "The Queen of Java," *Corporate Detroit,* January 1992, p. 50.

"Franchise Coffee Shop Gears Up for National Expansion," *Tea & Coffee Trade Journal,* September 1989, p. 66.

Harper, Roseanne, "Kroger Is Brewing Up Its First In-Store Coffee Beanery," *Supermarket News,* February 10, 1997, p. 37.

Harrison, Sheena, "Program Offers Veterans a Discount on Franchise Fee," *Crain's Detroit Business,* August 9, 2004, p. 12.

"JoAnne Shaw," *Nation's Restaurant News,* January 2000, p. 164.

Patterson, Pat, "Coffee Beanery: Grinding Out Beans for the Mall," *Nation's Restaurant News,* September 17, 1993, p. 15.

Rodgers, Jodi, "Coffee Chains Buzzing: Growth Opportunities Are Hot," *South Florida Business Journal,* November 27, 1998, p. 14A.

Shaw, JoAnne, "Franchising in China; Growing Opportunities," *Franchising World,* April 2004, p. 27.

Strauss, Karyn, "Coffee Beanery's Redesign Sparks Sales, Growth Plans," *Nation's Restaurant News,* March 13, 2000, p. 33.

Verhages, Kris, "Coffee Beanery," *Specialty Coffee Retailer,* August 2007, p. 47.

Wagner, Karen L., "The Coffee Beanery Limited," *Specialty Coffee Retailer,* January 2007, p. 46.

Walkup, Carolyn, "Coffee Beanery Gets Creative with Low-Cost Promotions," *Nation's Restaurant News,* March 10, 1997, p. 18.

———, "Coffee Beanery to Open in Car Dealership, Other Venues Planned," *Nation's Restaurant News,* May 6, 1996, p. 7.

Whittmore, Meg, "Franchising's Appeal to Women," *Nation's Business,* November 1989, p. 63.

Coffee Holding Co., Inc.

4401 1st Avenue, Suite 1507
Brooklyn, New York 11232
U.S.A.
Telephone: (718) 832-0800
Toll Free: (800) 458-2233
Fax: (718) 832-0892
Web site: http://www.coffeeholding.com

Public Company
Incorporated: 1971
Employees: 83
Sales: $57.42 million (2007)
Stock Exchanges: American
Ticker Symbol: JVA
NAIC: 311920 Coffee and Tea Manufacturing

∎ ∎ ∎

Coffee Holding Co., Inc., is a diversified wholesale coffee roaster and dealer operating in the United States and Canada. Coffee Holding conducts its business through three segments: private-label coffee, branded coffee, and wholesale green coffee. The company's private-label business involves roasting, blending, and packaging coffee for customers who want to sell coffee under their own name but who do not want to blend and roast their own coffee. Coffee Holding supplies coffee under more than 400 private labels to wholesalers and retailers, including the three largest grocery wholesalers in North America, Supervalu Inc., C&S Wholesale Grocers, Inc., and Nash-Finch Company. Coffee Holding's branded coffee business includes products roasted and blended

according to the company's recipes. The company sells its brands, which are Café Caribe, S&W, Café Supremo, Don Manuel, Fifth Avenue, Via Roma, and Il Classico, to supermarkets, wholesalers, and individually owned stores. Coffee Holding's wholesale green coffee business includes more than 90 varieties of unprocessed beans the company imports and sells to small roasters and coffee shop operators. The company's order sizes range from 132-pound bags to 44,000-pound truckloads. Coffee Holding operates roasting and packing facilities in New York City and La Junta, Colorado.

ORIGINS

Coffee Holding, a generic name for a company in a specialty business, entered the coffee-roasting industry at a time when it was possible to know every roaster in the country by name. The company was founded in January 1971 by Sterling Gordon, who based his operations in Brooklyn, home to the company for more than the next 35 years. During his first decade in business, Gordon was one of fewer than 50 roasters in the United States, a fraction of the total his sons would compete against in the coming decades. The growth of the industry, which began to accelerate rapidly during the 1990s, would fuel the rapid expansion of the family business, dividing the company's development into two distinct eras.

For the most part, Gordon led Coffee Holding during the years before coffee shops and roasters proliferated across the country. Although his tenure encompassed the period when Coffee Holding maintained a low profile, his accomplishments were significant, establishing the company's foundation and putting it in a position to reap the rewards of the market's eventual expansion. During the initial phase of the company's development, Gordon derived much of his business from Coffee Holding's branded coffee business, specifically from the sale of the company's Café Caribe brand. Café Caribe was a specialty espresso coffee tailored for a specific clientele, Latin American coffee drinkers. Market research later revealed Gordon had identified an ideal target customer. Latin American customers consumed as much as four times more coffee than other drinkers; they also demonstrated a tendency to be more loyal to a particular brand than other drinkers.

Coffee Holding also depended heavily on its private-label business during its first decade of existence. Through the company's roasting operations in Brooklyn, Coffee Holding roasted, blended, packaged, and distributed coffee to customers. The private-label business catered to customers who wanted to sell coffee under their own brand name, but who did not want to assume the responsibility and cost of manufacturing their own coffee. Coffee Holding sold its private-label products in cans, brick packages, and as instants in a variety of sizes.

A SECOND GENERATION OF GORDONS

Gordon was joined by his sons a little more than a decade after starting his business. David Gordon was the first to join the company, hired during the early 1980s. David Gordon became a charter member of the Specialty Coffee Association of America, an organization formed in 1982 by a small group of coffee professionals. His brother, Andrew Gordon, joined the company in the mid-1980s, arriving at Coffee Holding after earning a business degree at Emory University. Both brothers took on various responsibilities at the company, learning the nuances of the coffee business under the tutelage of their father. David Gordon served as operating manager for a six-year term beginning in 1989, eventually rising to the posts of executive vice-president and chief operating officer. He was responsible for overseeing all aspects of the company's roasting and blending operations. Andrew Gordon served as vice-president from 1993 to 1997 before earning promotion to the posts of president and chief executive officer. In 2004, he added the duties of chief financial officer to his responsibilities.

MARKET GROWTH IN THE NINETIES ENCOURAGING EXPANSION

As the Gordon brothers began to exercise their control over Coffee Holding, the company began to adopt a more aggressive posture. Beginning in 1991, the company sought to shed its regional competitor status and transform into a national player in the industry. Conditions in the coffee market had changed considerably since Sterling Gordon first opened his doors in Brooklyn, and his sons looked to take advantage of the fertile environment. When Sterling Gordon started his business, there were only 50 specialty coffee shops in the country. By 1995, there were 5,000 specialty shops in operation. A mere four years later, there were 12,000 specialty stores catering to the premium tastes of the country. From there, the numbers continued to mushroom.

The most visible of the companies taking advantage of the trend toward specialty coffee was Seattle, Washington-based Starbucks Corporation. Starbucks was founded in 1971, the year Coffee Holding was formed, beginning with one shop. Starbucks did not add a coffee bar to sell drinks until the company's marketing director, Howard Schultz, championed the concept. Schultz left the company the following year, but purchased Starbucks from its owners in 1987 and began to build a chain of immense size. By 1992, he had 165 stores in operation. By the end of the decade, when Schultz was opening a new store nearly every day, there were 2,800 Starbucks in operation. By 2002, the size of the chain had more than doubled.

Coffee Holding, in essence, wanted to emulate Starbucks, but without the retail-oriented influence of Schultz. The company, as it stated years later in an April 1, 2008, filing with the Securities and Exchange Commission, preferred to make its profit by selling "one bag at a time rather than one cup at a time." Throughout the 1990s, the Gordons plowed back profits into the business, improving the company's roasting, packaging, and fulfillment infrastructure. The capital investments

```
┌─────────────────────────────────────────────┐
│                                             │
│              KEY DATES                      │
│                  ■                          │
│ ─────────────────────────────────────────── │
│                                             │
│ 1971:  Sterling Gordon establishes Coffee   │
│        Holding Co., Inc.                     │
│ 1998:  Coffee Holding merges with a         │
│        corporate shell, Transpacific         │
│        International Group Corp.             │
│ 2004:  Coffee Holding acquires a roaster in │
│        La Junta, Colorado.                   │
│ 2005:  Coffee Holding completes its initial │
│        public offering (IPO) of stock.       │
│ 2006:  Coffee Holding forms a joint venture │
│        company with Caruso's Coffee.         │
│ 2007:  Coffee Holding signs a licensing     │
│        agreement with Entenmann's Products  │
│        Inc.                                  │
│                                             │
└─────────────────────────────────────────────┘
```

were made to enable the company to produce and to distribute large quantities of coffee products on a national basis.

STRATEGIC MERGER IN 1998

In a corporate maneuver aimed at gaining financial assistance in its expansion efforts, Coffee Holding completed a merger during the coffee market's robust growth phase of the 1990s. In February 1998, Coffee Holding merged into Transpacific International Group Corp. Transpacific had been incorporated three years earlier for the sole purpose of acquiring or merging with another business. The company was a corporate shell. Transpacific owned no assets when it completed a "blind pool" stock offering in 1996 that raised $18,000 in gross proceeds from 35 investors. When Coffee Holding merged into Transpacific, Transpacific emerged as the surviving entity and subsequently changed its name to Coffee Holding Co., Inc.

The most discernible evidence of the fantastic growth of the coffee market was seen in Coffee Holding's wholesale green coffee segment. The enormous growth in the number of coffee shops and small roasters created a wealth of new business for suppliers of unprocessed beans. While some independent operators forged their own relationships with farmers, most of the smaller entities did not import green coffee beans. The specialty green coffee market became the fastest-growing area of the coffee industry, and it also became the fastest-growing segment of Coffee Holding's business. Between 1998 and 2007, the number of the company's wholesale green coffee customers increased 129 percent, jumping from 150 customers to 344 customers.

By the time Coffee Holding celebrated its 30th anniversary in 2001, it was generating $20 million in annual revenue. The company's private-label coffee business accounted for 50 percent of its revenue, serving 35 wholesale and retail customers. Its branded coffee business continued to rely on Café Caribe as its leading brand, but the company had a roster of other brands to address the needs of its customer base. Coffee Holding roasted and blended Café Supremo, a specialty espresso designed to introduce coffee drinkers to the tastes of dark-roasted coffee. It sold Don Manuel, a 100 percent Colombian coffee. The company also roasted and blended two other brands, Fifth Avenue and Via Roma, shipping the varieties directly from its facilities in Brooklyn to supermarkets, wholesalers, and independent coffee shops.

EXPANSION INTO COLORADO IN 2004

A momentous event in Coffee Holding's aspirations for national coverage took place in 2004, occurring at a point when annual revenues continued to hover at $20 million. Revenues began to swell after the event, nearly tripling during the ensuing three years as the company recorded the greatest financial growth in its history. Since 1991, the Gordon brothers had been pursuing a national profile for their company, but they had done so without establishing a physical presence outside of Brooklyn. In January 2004, they were approached by the chief executive officer of La Junta, Colorado-based Premier Roasters LLC and a representative of La Junta Development Inc. with an offer that led to the first geographic expansion in their company's history.

Premier Roasters opened in 2003 and soon began to struggle. Its roasting and packing business gained a major customer when the supermarket chain Safeway Inc. began placing orders with the fledgling company, but when Safeway severed its ties to the roaster in late 2003, it was unable to sustain its operations. Premier Roasters' chief executive officer, Tom Paper, and La Junta Development's Allison Cortner asked the Gordons to purchase Premier Roasters, presenting the brothers with an opportunity they could not pass up. The Gordons submitted a bid for Premier Roasters' equipment, customer lists, and packaging assets in January 2004 and acquired the company the following month, paying $825,000 for the assets. The transaction legitimized Coffee Holding's efforts to become a nationally oriented concern, one hailed by Andrew Gordon in a February 19, 2004, interview with the *Pueblo Chieftain*. "We are going to produce for our existing customer base out of the La Junta facility," he said, "and, in addition, there is a lot of business out there that we are going to be able to pick up because we will be on the West Coast and achieve certain efficiencies that we could not achieve from the East Coast."

Concurrent with the Premier Roasters acquisition, Coffee Holding brokered another important deal. The company signed a licensing agreement with Del Monte Corporation for the exclusive right to use S&W and Il Classico trademarks in the United States. The right to produce and to sell roasted whole bean and ground coffee under the S&W label, in particular, represented a potential boost to the company's business, giving it a premium canned coffee established in 1921. The licensing agreement covered numerous S&W and Il Classico lines, including Premium, Premium Decaf, French Roast, Colombian, Colombian Decaf, Swiss Water Decaf, Kona, and Mellow'd Roast.

PUBLIC DEBUT IN 2005

Sales began to increase energetically after Coffee Holding gained control of the La Junta facility. Between 2004 and 2006, revenues increased from $28 million to $51 million. The growth occurred at an ideal time, coinciding with the company's initial public offering (IPO) of stock. In mid-2005, Coffee Holding sold 1.4 million shares at $5 per share, debuting on the American Stock Exchange under the symbol "JVA."

To ensure revenues continued to climb, the Gordons searched for new sources of growth as they plotted Coffee Holding's future course. In 2006, they formed a jointly owned business with Caruso's Coffee, a Brecksville, Ohio-based company. The business, Generations Coffee Company, LLC, was formed to roast, package, and sell private-label specialty coffee in small batches. From a manufacturing standpoint, Coffee Holding was not equipped to produce specialty beans in small quantities. Another deal, consummated in August 2007, involved a three-year licensing agreement with Entenmann's Products Inc., a Montebello, California-based bakery product company. Under the terms of the agreement, Coffee Holding was to manufacture and distribute a line of coffee products under the Entenmann's label. In the years ahead, further deals were expected, as the Gordons labored to make their company a permanent fixture in the coffee industry.

Jeffrey L. Covell

PRINCIPAL SUBSIDIARIES

Generations Coffee Company, LLC (60%).

PRINCIPAL COMPETITORS

Starbucks Corporation; Nestlé S.A.; The Procter & Gamble Company.

FURTHER READING

Bartz, Alicia, "Make Mine Organic," *Specialty Coffee Retailer,* August 2002, p. 16.

Booth, John, "Caruso's Coffee, Brooklyn Co. Brew Business Partnership," *Crain's Cleveland Business,* May 22, 2006, p. 13.

"Coffee Holding Co. Inc., Brooklyn, N.Y. Entered into a Three-Year Licensing Agreement with Entenmann's Products Inc., Montebello, Calif.," *Beverage Industry,* August 2007, p. 27.

"DJ Coffee Holding Co. Announces Initial Public Offering," *FWN Select,* May 3, 2005.

"Entenmann's Adds Coffee to Its Roster," *Promo,* July 6, 2007.

Mestas, Anthony A., "New York-based Coffee Roasting Firm Warms Up La Junta, Colo., Market," *Pueblo Chieftain,* February 19, 2004.

Compagnie Maritime Belge S.A.

De Gerlachekaai 20
Antwerp, B-2000
Belgium
Telephone: (+32 03) 247 59 11
Fax: (+32 03) 248 09 06
Web site: http://www.cmb.be

Public Company
Incorporated: 1895 as Compagnie Belge Maritime de Congo
Employees: 615
Sales: EUR 424.27 million ($499.1 million) (2007)
Stock Exchanges: NYSE Euronext
Ticker Symbol: CMB
NAIC: 483111 Deep Sea Freight Transportation; 488320 Marine Cargo Handling

■ ■ ■

Compagnie Maritime Belge S.A. (CMB) is a holding company focused on the international shipping industry. The company's shipping operations are carried out primarily through Bocimar, a dry bulk goods specialist founded in 1973. Bocimar owned and operated a fleet of 15 Capesize, three Panamax, and two Handymax vessels at the beginning of 2008. The company either fully owns or partially owns these vessels. In addition, the company charters six Capesize and two Panamax vessels, bringing its total fleet to 28 ships. In 2007, the company carried a total of nearly 37 million dry tons of cargo throughout the world. Bocimar especially targets the Asian sector, including Japan, which accounts for 30

percent of revenues, and the booming Chinese market, which accounts for 40 percent. In order to respond to the growing demand in these markets, the company has 24 new buildings on order. Bocimar operates from offices in Antwerp, Tokyo, Shanghai, and New Delhi.

The company also has a series of partnerships in place, notably with Nippon Steel in Japan, NCSC in Israel, FMO in Venezuela, and CLP/Ho Ping in Taiwan. In addition to Bocimar's fleet, CMB owns two 50 percent stakes in two additional vessels, the Farwah oil tanker, and the Hong Kong-based Panamax Moonlight Ventures. The company also has 50 percent stakes in two chemical carriers under construction from 2007. In addition to its shipping, CMB's other activities include Hessenatie Logistics, a leading player in the Antwerp logistics sector; 50 percent of the Reslea real estate group; and 50 percent of Air Contractors Group, which operates a fleet of 50 airplanes. CMB is listed on the NYSE Euronext Stock Exchange and is led by Chairman Etienne Davignon and Managing Director Marc Saverys. CMB's revenues in 2006 neared EUR 425 million ($500 million).

THE ROUTE TO CONGO IN 1895

CMB was founded as Compagnie Belge Maritime de Congo (CBMC) in 1895. Until then, there was no regular shipping between Belgium and Congo. As Belgium extended its colonial control over that part of Africa, King Leopold II sought a permanent link between Belgium and the colony. Attempts by Belgium interests to found a line failed, however; instead, Leopold turned to two foreign shippers, British African

COMPANY PERSPECTIVES

CMB's aim is to ensure that our shareholders receive a satisfactory and growing level of dividend and share value; care for the well-being of our employees, for the safety of our seafarers, in a spirit of personal responsibility and mutual respect; provide our customers with a level of service ahead of their expectations at market conditions; respect the seas, the stage of our activities, with a strong concern for safety and protection of the environment.

Steam Ship Company, part of England's Elder Dempster group, and Woermann Linie, through a subsidiary Société Maritime du Congo (SMC), of Germany. The two companies agreed to provide alternate monthly service between Antwerp and Congo, with each supplying ships to the new operation. CBMC's first ship, called the *Leopoldville*, set sail in February 1895.

The partnership between the British and German shipping companies lasted into the dawn of the twentieth century, with both companies providing liner service on a three-weekly basis between Antwerp and the port of Matabi. In 1901, however, SMC left the partnership. British African Steam Ship Company became the sole operator of the CBMC line. Woermann Linie nonetheless remained a major company shareholder.

The full transfer of Congo to Belgian rule led to the takeover of majority control of CBMC by Belgian interests. The Belgian bank, Banque d'Outremer, took over majority control of the company in 1911. Both Elder Dempster and Woermann remained shareholders in the company. By the beginning of World War I, CBMC's service had been expanded to three vessels, which served as both passenger and cargo carriers, as well as providing postal shipping between Belgium and its colonies.

The outbreak of World War I led the company to transfer its headquarters and its small fleet to London. The company then set up its operations in the headquarters of its shareholder, British African Steam Ship Company. That company retained its stake in CBMC following the end of the war; however, Belgian interests took over the shares of Woermann Linie, and eventually gained full control of CBMC.

The boom in trade between Africa and Europe after World War I brought significant expansion to CBMC, particularly in cargo transport. The company created a new subsidiary for these operations in 1920, called Compagnie Africaine de Navigation (CAN). That company soon built up a strong fleet of cargo ships, with 14 ships in operation by the end of the decade. This fleet expansion enabled CAN to expand its routes beyond the Congo-Antwerp and ports along the West African coastline to serve East African ports as well.

BELGIAN SHIPPING LEADER IN THE THIRTIES

Société Generale de Belgique (SBC) had acquired Banque Outremer, becoming CBMC's primary shareholder in the early 1920s. The backing of this powerful parent permitted the company to grow strongly. In particular, CBMC began developing more diversified operations in the shipping industry. During this period, the company entered the port services market, principally through its subsidiary Agence Maritime Internationale (AMI). Through a series of acquisitions, CBMC became a major port services group in Antwerp and elsewhere.

SBC's financial clout also allowed CBMC to develop its shipping operations. In 1930, the company bought Lloyd Royal Belge. That company, founded only in 1916, had rapidly built up a fleet of more than 80 vessels in the immediate post–World War I era. However, when cargo prices dropped in the 1920s, Lloyd Royal itself neared collapse. Following a rescue orchestrated between the Belgian government and SBC, Lloyd Royal was merged into CBMC in 1930.

The newly enlarged company changed its name to Compagnie Maritime Belge (Lloyd Royal). The company became the single largest shipper in Belgium, with a fleet of 38 vessels and control of nearly 45 percent of the total shipping market. CMB began to expand its operations beyond its African lines; over the next decade, the company dropped a number of its African routes, in favor of routes to the Americas and to Asia.

CMB was able to weather the crisis years of the Depression in part because of its importance to the Belgian shipping industry. Through government assistance, CMB restructured its fleet. This included the sale of most of its older vessels, and their replacement by a smaller number of larger and more modern ships. By the outbreak of World War II, the company's total fleet numbered 31 ships.

REBUILDING IN THE POSTWAR ERA

World War II had dramatic consequences for CMB's fleet. By the end of the war, the company had lost 23

KEY DATES

∎

1895: Compagnie Belge Maritime de Congo (CBMC) is founded by British and German shipping companies in order to provide liner service between Belgium and Congo.

1908: Banque Outremer (later part of Société Generale de Belgique, or SBC) of Belgium buys majority control of CBMC.

1920: Company founds Compagnie Africaine de Navigation (CAN) cargo liner subsidiary.

1930: CBMC acquires Lloyd Royal Belge, becoming largest shipper in Belgium and changes name to Compagnie Maritime Belge (CMB).

1960: Company acquires second largest Belgian shipper, Armement Deppe.

1974: Company acquires 40 percent of Bocimar, part of Almabo, as part of expansion of dry bulk business.

1982: Company acquires full control of Bocimar.

1991: SBC sells its 49.5 percent stake in CMB to Almabo, which becomes majority shareholder.

2007: CMB refocuses as a holding company around Bocimar dry bulk business, and launches subsidiary in Hong Kong.

---

ships, and nearly 300 of its crew had been killed. During the war, those of the group's ships that had managed to escape Belgium before the German invasion were put into service providing cargo and troop transport for the Allied forces. Other CMB vessels were pressed into service by the Germans. CMB's headquarters in Antwerp, in the meantime, were destroyed by one of Germany's V2 rockets.

The surge in shipping demand following World War II enabled CMB to quickly rebuild its fleet. By the early 1950s, the company had expanded its cargo fleet to 24 vessels, nearly all of which were modern newbuilds. The company also operated five passenger vessels. This latter activity, however, came to play less and less importance for the company, especially with the growth of the passenger airline industry in the late 1950s and into the 1960s.

As a result, CMB focused its efforts in developing its cargo operations. Through the 1950s, the company launched a new and highly ambitious newbuild program, adding another 21 vessels. The African markets, especially the Congo, remained the group's primary market. However, pressure was growing from

most of the European colonies, including Congo, for independence. In preparation of this, CMB once again sought to expand its range of destinations. The company opened dedicated lines to both North and South American markets; through the 1950s, the company also launched a new line linking Congo and India to the United States. At the same time, CMB had been building a fuller range of shipping services, adding operations including ship repair, insurance, and inland navigation.

The independence of Congo in 1960 forced CMB to step up its effort to broaden its operations. The company took a major step forward in reducing its reliance on the African markets that same year through the takeover of its main Belgian rival, Armement Deppe. That company brought CMB its focus on the South and Central American markets, helping to fill the gap created by the loss of CMB's Congo operations. CMB also expanded its shipping services wing that year, adding towing and the production of navigation instruments through the takeover of Ufmar.

DEVELOPING DRY BULK IN THE SIXTIES

The early 1960s also marked another significant milestone for the company. Starting in 1962, CMB began building up operations in the dry bulk market. For this the company focused on the coal and iron ore markets. The company began a new building program, and by the end of the decade had taken delivery of five dedicated dry bulk vessels.

The move into dry bulk helped the company overcome the new pressures on its traditional liner business. That shipping sector faced new competition from the development of the containership. By the early 1970s, containerships had started to dominate the freight shipping industry. CMB joined in this trend, launching the DART consortium in partnership with a number of British shipowners, in 1968. CMB directly controlled the Dart Europe, at the time the world's largest containership. Through Dart, CMB also invested heavily into support operations for the containership sector. As a result, the company built up its own park of 17,000 containers and trailers by the early 1970s.

The success of the DART partnership led CMB to pursue a number of other partnerships over the next decade. This enabled the group to develop operations in new markets in Asia, the Middle East, and elsewhere. The company also entered a partnership with fellow Belgian firm Almabo, which operated the shipping sector through Exmar, and its dry bulk subsidiary, Bocimar. In 1974, CMB acquired a 40 percent stake in Bocimar. This was raised to 100 percent in 1982.

The Bocimar purchase corresponded with the company's entry into the tanker market, following the addition of a liquid natural gas tanker in 1978. In the meantime, the oil crisis on the one hand, and the rising strength of the containership market on the other, had caused a sharp drop in the liner sector. As a result, CMB was forced to restructure its own liner operations. While the liner market was to pick up again in the late 1980s, CMB's shipping future lay more firmly in the dry bulk market.

FOCUSING ON DRY BULK FOR THE FUTURE

The late 1980s saw significant growth in CMB's port services wing. The company acquired two companies, Stevedoring Gylsen, and the Stocatra bulk good handler. In 1988, the company acquired Hessenatie, the leader in the Antwerp port services sector. CMB itself emerged as a leader in the European cargo and container handling sector.

This era also saw other significant changes for the company. For one, CMB launched a massive fleet upgrade, adding 11 new bulk carriers to its Bocimar operations. For another, the company's ownership structure changed, following the acquisition of SBC by France's Suez financial group. As part of the restructuring following that merger, SBC sold its 49 percent stake in CMB to Almabo-Exmar. That company, owned by the Saverys family, held 3 percent of CMB.

Initially, the company's new owners focused on revamping the company's liner business. The company launched a new round of acquisitions in the late 1980s and into the 1990s. These included Woermann Linie, one of CMB's founding shareholders, and Deutsche Ost-Africa Linie, both purchased in 1990. In that same year, the company also scored a major purchase, buying the maritime division of Andrea Merzario SpA based in Milan, Italy.

By 2000, however, CMB had launched the restructuring of its business. Selling its liner operations, the company also moved to spin off its tanker businesses, which were regrouped into two companies, Euronav and Exmar. Both then were taken public. The company also shed its AMI shipping services in Africa, which were sold to Bollore in 1999. Then, in 2002, the company merged Hessenatie's cargo handling operations with those of Noord Natie, also based in Antwerp, creating Hesse-Noord Natie (HNN). Soon after, CMB sold its stake in HNN to Singapore-based PSA.

By the middle of the first decade of the 2000s, CMB's restructuring had left the group's primary focus on its Bocimar dry bulk business. Part of the reasoning behind this new focus was the surge in growth in the dry bulk market as a result of the economic boom in China. In order to consolidate its position in that market (the group had built a strong presence in Japan as well) Bocimar opened an office in Shanghai in 2004. In 2007, the company launched a dedicated Hong Kong subsidiary. China by then represented 40 percent of the group's turnover, which neared EUR 425 million. The company further strengthened its position in the Asian market, buying 27 percent of Anglo-Eastern Group. In early 2008, CMB formed a joint venture with Drylog to acquire a new ship, the *Mineral Monaco,* from Japan's Imbari group. After more than 110 years, CMB remained one of Belgium's leading shipping companies.

M. L. Cohen

PRINCIPAL SUBSIDIARIES

Bocimar Belgium NV; Bocimar Far East Holdings Limited (Liberia); Bocimar International NV; Bocimar Lux SA (Luxembourg); Bocimar NV (Belgium); Bylot Shipping Limited (Liberia); CMB International NV (Belgium); CMB Japan Limited; CMB Services SA (Luxembourg); Entarco NV; Hessenatie Logistics Kortrijk NV; Hessenatie Logistics NV; International Barge Operators NV; JBOC Pte Ltd. (Singapore); Labaco Investment Ltd. (Hong Kong); Sakura International KK (Japan); Transportimmo NV (Belgium).

PRINCIPAL COMPETITORS

Sumitomo Corp.; Brega Marketing Co.; Jardine Pacific Ltd.; A P Moller-Maersk A/S; TUI AG; Marubeni Corp.; Louis Dreyfus S.A.S.; ThyssenKrupp Services AG; Nippon Yusen KK; Danzas Group.

FURTHER READING

"Bocimar International Goes Full Steam Ahead in Asia," *South China Morning Post,* February 28, 2007.

"Bollore Buys AMI from CMB," *Les Echos,* June 17, 1999, p. 23.

Bray, Julian, "CMB Responds to the Demands of the Marketplace," *International Freighting Weekly,* March 12, 1990, p. 4.

"CMB Buys into Anglo Eastern," *Journal of Commerce Online,* July 10, 2007.

"Compagnie Maritime Belge," *Euroweek,* March 7, 2003, p. 20.

Mulder, Yvonne, "CMB Buy Musters Africa Core," *International Freighting Weekly,* February 12, 1990, p. 1.

———, "CMB Transport Buys Merzario Maritime Assets," *International Freighting Weekly,* January 8, 1990, p. 2.

———, "Saverys Family Buys CMB Stake," *International Freighting Weekly,* June 24, 1991, p. 1.

Crete Carrier Corporation

400 Northwest 56th Street
Lincoln, Nebraska 68528
U.S.A.
Telephone: (402) 475-9521
Toll Free: (800) 998-4095
Fax: (402) 479-2075
Web site: http://www.cretecarrier.com

Private Company
Incorporated: 1966
Employees: 6,100
Sales: $1 billion (2006 est.)
NAIC: 484121 General Freight Trucking, Long-Distance, Truckload

■ ■ ■

Crete Carrier Corporation is the family-owned Lincoln, Nebraska-based holding company for three trucking concerns: Crete Carrier, Shaffer Trucking, and Hunt Transportation, Inc. The Crete Carrier unit offers dry van service to the 48 contiguous states, Canada, and Mexico, focusing on the midwestern and southeastern states. With its home base in Lincoln, it maintains more than 20 terminals. Based in New Kingston, Pennsylvania, Shaffer Trucking concentrates on temperature-sensitive truckload services. Hunt Transportation, operating out of Omaha, Nebraska, also serves the 48 contiguous states, handling specialized flat-bed loads such as heavy agricultural and construction equipment. Crete is family owned and operated, headed

by chairman Duane Acklie and his son-in-law, CEO Tonn M. Ostergard.

FORMATION OF CRETE CARRIER: 1966

Crete Carrier was founded in Crete, Nebraska, in 1966 by Kenneth R. Norton. It started out as a contract carrier, its customers including the Alpo pet food plant in Crete. Norton's attorney was Duane Acklie. Born in Nebraska in 1931 and raised on a family farm, Acklie earned an undergraduate degree from the University of Nebraska in 1953 and two years later received a bachelor of laws degree from the school. Following a two-year stint in the military, during which Acklie served in Europe as a lieutenant in counter intelligence, he returned to the university to earn his J.D. in 1959. He then entered private practice with the firm of Acklie and Peterson, serving as a trial lawyer and often representing the transportation industry and such clients as Crete Carrier.

In June 1971 Norton telephoned Acklie at his lakeside vacation cabin and offered to sell Crete Carrier because he was moving his family to Salt Lake City, Utah, where he had started a new trucking company. After considerable pacing around the lake, Acklie agreed to buy the business and three days later he and his wife Phyllis borrowed $8,000 to acquire Crete from Norton. "I wasn't sure I could get the money, and I wasn't sure, if I got the money, whether I could run a trucking company," Acklie confessed to the *Commercial Carrier Journal.* Fortunately, Acklie was able to draw income from some work he was wrapping up for his law firm, allowing him to refrain from taking a salary during the crucial first year of running Crete. His wife, a former teacher, also worked for Crete at no salary. The company was very much a shoestring affair. It had few if any assets beyond the operating authority for six contracts, dependent on owner-operator truck drivers and leased trailers.

NEW HEADQUARTERS IN LINCOLN: 1973

In 1973 Acklie moved Crete's headquarters to Lincoln, a location that proved beneficial to a trucking company. Not only was Lincoln perfectly positioned between both coasts as well as Canada and Mexico, Interstate 80 and U.S. 77 ran through it, and relatively close by were Interstates 29, 35, 70, and 90. Moreover, the area was well served by railroads, making Lincoln a natural transportation hub. A year after moving from its hometown, Crete Carrier expanded by acquiring Shaffer Trucking Inc., a temperature-sensitive hauler based outside of Harrisburg, Pennsylvania, that brought with it several regional authorities. Established in 1937 it had originally served as an irregular route, general commodities truckload carrier. At the time of the Shaffer acquisition, the trucking industry was heavily regulated and the Interstate Commerce Commission (ICC) decided that Crete had grown large enough for the moment and barred Acklie from making any further acquisitions for three years.

The next step in Crete's growth took place in 1979, when the company acquired Sunflower Carriers Inc., a York, Nebraska-based refrigerated truck fleet that was a subsidiary of meatpacker Sunflower Beef. While Shaffer served customers coast to coast, Sunflower limited its operations to midwestern states. Also in 1979 Crete forged a backhaul alliance with Tennessee-based Hilt Truck Service in which trucks having completed their deliveries were used to carry other shipments on their return trips. It was an arrangement that played a role in the deregulation of the trucking industry.

HILT MERGER: 1980

Hilt, an authorized meat hauler, had wanted to backhaul lard from meatpackers but had always been denied

permission by the ICC. Hilt tried to haul lard on Crete's authority and applied to the ICC for a rate. Not surprisingly the railroads regularly protested trucking requests and typically prevailed. This time Hilt applied for permission to haul yak fat, a commodity with limited if any demand in the United States, triggering an immediate protest from the railroads, who were put in the awkward position of arguing that their yak fat business would be put in jeopardy if authority was granted to Hilt. Not only did the railroads take the bait, the ICC agreed with their arguments and denied Hilt's request to haul yak fat. Hilt contacted the press, and a number of major publications, including *Business Week* and *U.S. News & World Report,* carried the yak fat controversy to the embarrassment of the ICC and railroads. Drawing the ire of the ICC, Hilt was charged with being an unfit carrier, prompting Acklie to step in as an attorney to represent Hilt. Eventually the charges were dropped and in 1980 Hilt was merged into Crete. More importantly, in that year the trucking industry was deregulated.

Unfettered and no longer needing to fight for operating authority to serve a potential customer, Crete enjoyed strong growth in the 1980s. "After deregulation," Acklie told *Heavy Duty Trucking,* "I was like a kid in a candy store." In the first half of the 1980s Crete enjoyed an annual growth rate of 10 to 15 percent. It was also during this period that Acklie's daughter, Holly, and her husband, Tonn Ostergard, joined the company.

After Holly Acklie had graduated from the University of Nebraska–Lincoln in 1980 with a degree in education, she moved to Dallas where she worked in sales for two years. She then earned her trucking license and was driving 18-wheelers, hauling auto parts for her father when a mutual friend introduced her to Ostergard. He was a fourth-generation member of a Nebraska farm family, who was also a graduate of the University of Nebraska, where he had studied business. The couple married in 1984 and Holly gave up the steering wheel of a truck to take a position in the Crete offices, working in the fuel-tax section before moving into operations/dispatch. Ostergard, in the meantime, worked as an accountant for Coopers & Lybrand and KPMG Peat Marwick in Lincoln. In 1985 he quit to become Crete's chief financial officer and learn the trucking business under the tutelage of Duane Acklie. Aside from being married to the boss's daughter, Ostergard was well suited to joining the family business because of his financial experience. "It seemed like in those early years in post de-regulation," he recalled in an interview with the *Trucker News,* "a lot of companies were taking advantage of the opportunities presented by deregulation and were hiring people with backgrounds such as mine." In 1988 Ostergard became Crete's execu-

KEY DATES

1966: Company is founded in Crete, Nebraska.
1971: Duane Acklie acquires Crete.
1974: Shaffer Trucking is acquired.
1979: Sunflower Carriers is acquired.
1985: Tonn Ostergard is named chief financial officer.
1999: Hunt Transportation (no relation to J.B. Hunt Transport Services) is acquired.
2006: Revenues top $1 billion.

tive vice-president and chief operating officer. He also continued his classroom education, graduating from the Owner/President Management Program of the Harvard Business School in 1991.

BEGINNING OF INTERMODAL SERVICE: 1993

To spur further growth, Crete acquired Council Bluffs, Iowa-based HTL Truck Line Inc., a dry van operator. By the start of the 1990s Crete's annual revenues reached $200 million and continued to climb at an annual rate of 15 to 20 percent. In 1993 Crete joined forces with its longtime foe, the railroads, creating Crete Intermodal Service in conjunction with Union Pacific Railroad. The new unit hauled intermodal containers that were standardized for use on ships, trains, or trucks. By the mid-1990s Crete was operating out of 15 terminals and a 16th was soon opened in Allentown, Pennsylvania. With Acklie past retirement age, Ostergard took over as chief executive officer, although his predecessor continued to serve as chairman and remained very much involved in the business.

The Acklie-owned companies had always operated independently, each responsible for such areas as operations, maintenance, insurance, and marketing. However, increased competition following deregulation had resulted in falling rates, forcing the subsidiaries to consolidate functions and take advantage of economies of scale to remain competitive. Redundant operations were weeded out, the first being risk management. Crete was able to implement a single insurance program that saved money for all the carriers. This success was followed by a program to use the company's size to receive the best prices on tractors, trailers, and other equipment. To better manage the company's growing fleet of trucks, Crete began discussing a way to streamline its maintenance operations as well. In early

1998 plans began in earnest to establish a unit called Acklie Maintenance System (AMS), intended to serve all of Crete's trucking companies, the combined assets of which included 5,200 tractors and 12,000 trailers (2,500 of them refrigerated). On the first day of 1999 AMS became operational and began serving all four of the Acklie-owned carriers.

ACQUISITION OF HUNT TRANSPORTATION: 1999

Late in 1999 a fifth carrier was added to the family, Hunt Transportation, Inc. (no relation to J.B. Hunt Transport Services), acquired when Crete bought the stock of Butler Holdings Inc., whose only subsidiary was Hunt. The Omaha, Nebraska-based trucking company had been in business since 1927 when L. S. Hunt began hauling livestock. It later turned its focus to the hauling of flatbed trailers, serving such agricultural and construction equipment manufacturers as Deere & Co., Valmont Industries Inc., New Holland NV, and Caterpillar Inc. Hunt's son-in-law Ben Butler took over after the founder's death, and after Butler died in 1992 his son, Matt Butler, assumed control through Butler Holdings. Crete took over a fleet of 335 trucks and 700 trailers, generating nearly $40 million in annual revenues. The business had been operating successfully, but Butler recognized that in the years to come trucking companies would require greater size in order to better control costs and remain viable, and concluded that Hunt would be better off as a part of a larger concern like Crete than to try to go it alone.

Crete ended the 1990s with combined revenues of $577 million. The new century was a time of continued growth, punctuated by fresh challenges. Sales reached $745 million in 2003. In that same year, the Sunflower operation was folded into Shaffer, creating one of the United States' largest refrigerated truck fleets. A major customer driving sales was Wal-Mart, which used Crete as a dedicated carrier for distribution centers in North Platte, Nebraska, and Bartlesville, Oklahoma. Crete then became a dedicated carrier for a new Wal-Mart distribution center that opened in Sterling, Illinois, in 2006. This additional Wal-Mart business helped Crete to top the $1 billion mark in revenues in 2006.

The decade was not without challenges, however. Escalating fuel costs tightened margins, forcing the company to look for ways to trim overhead. In late 2007 the company announced that Shaffer's York facility would be closed and its operations transferred to Crete's Lincoln headquarters. In addition, the New Kingston, Pennsylvania, office would become the regional center for both Shaffer and Crete Carrier. The company also had difficulty in finding enough qualified drivers. Crete had always relied on hiring and keeping good drivers, who tended to remain with the company for long stints because of profit sharing and other benefits. The average age was 47, resulting in better safety records and lower insurance rates. To develop a new source of truck drivers Acklie helped start a driver training program at Lincoln's Southeast Community College, targeting farming children, who, as Acklie well knew from personal experience, were generally familiar with driving trucks and farm equipment.

At the start of 2008 Acklie was 76 years old and ready to spend more time traveling as well as living in Florida for several months out of the year. After serving for 26 years he resigned from the Nebraska Highway Commission. He continued to serve as chairman of Crete, but his involvement in day-to-day decisions would also diminish as Ostergard assumed greater control.

Ed Dinger

PRINCIPAL SUBSIDIARIES

Shaffer Trucking Inc.; Hunt Transportation, Inc.

PRINCIPAL COMPETITORS

J.B. Hunt Transport Services, Inc.; Schneider National, Inc.; Werner Enterprises, Inc.

FURTHER READING

Cayton, Rodd, "Lincoln's Location Beneficial in Transport," *Lincoln Journal Star,* May 21, 2003, p. 4.

"Crete Carrier Corp. Continues Growth but Needs Drivers," *Lincoln Journal Star,* February 27, 2005, p. 5.

"Crete Carrier's Acklie: Customer Service Is the Key," *Fleet Owner,* February 1984, p. 65.

Finney, Lyndon, "Crete Carrier: Philosophy of Crete's Tonn Ostergard Permeates All Levels of Company," *Trucker News Service,* September 1, 2006.

Loza, Josefina, "Queen's Family Driven to Serve," *Omaha World-Herald,* October 14, 2007.

Richards, Paul, "A Chairman Among Chairmen," *Commercial Carrier Journal,* October 1, 2000, p. 139.

Taylor, John, "Acklie Group Buys Hunt from Butler," *Omaha World-Herald,* November 2, 1999, p. 16.

Whistler, Deborah, "Duane Acklie," *Heavy Duty Trucking,* January 2005.

Wilkinson, Melanie, "Shaffer Trucking to Move Operations to Lincoln," *York (Neb.) Times,* November 7, 2007.

D&H Distributing Co.

2525 North 7th Street
Harrisburg, Pennsylvania 17110
U.S.A.
Telephone: (717) 236-8001
Toll Free: (800) 877-1200
Fax: (717) 255-7838
Web site: http://www.dandh.com

Private Company
Incorporated: 1918 as Economy Tire and Rubber Co.
Employees: 850
Sales: $1.77 billion (2006)
NAIC: 423620 Electrical and Electronic Appliance, Television, and Radio Set Merchant Wholesalers; 423430 Computer and Computer Peripheral Equipment and Software Merchant Wholesalers

∎∎∎

D&H Distributing Co. is a privately held, Harrisburg, Pennsylvania-based distributor of electronic products, serving resellers, retailers, system builders, and college bookstores. In the home technology sector D&H offers HDTVs, DVD recorders, gaming systems and accessories, digital cameras, computers and peripherals, printers, GPS devices, audio products, and select housewares such as vacuums and indoor grills. D&H serves business and institutional technology with a wide variety of servers and storage products, server racks and enclosures, software, both wired and wireless networking products, office computers and peripherals, printing and document imaging products, presentation and display products, and mobile products, including computing, communication, navigation, and storage products. D&H also sells a range of products to the campus bookstore market, including computing, mobile, electronics, and entertainment products. In addition to its mid-Atlantic distribution hub located in Harrisburg, D&H maintains regional hubs in Bolingbrook, Illinois; Jacksonville, Florida; Coppell, Texas; and Fresno, California. Canada is served through subsidiary D&H Canada.

ORIGINS AS TIRE BUSINESS: 1918

The men who contributed their initials to the D&H name were David Schwab, who immigrated from Russia with his family in 1906, and his brother-in-law Harry Spector. In 1918 they went into business together in Williamsport, Pennsylvania, 30 years before the Little League World Series began to make the town famous. The partners were originally involved in tire retreading, doing business as Economy Tire and Rubber Co. In 1921 the company expanded by distributing wholesale auto parts, and in 1926 began distributing RCA radios at the behest of the owners' close friend and fellow Russian Jew David Sarnoff, the head of the Radio Corporation of America (RCA) and founder of the National Broadcasting Company. The move into electronics led to a name change in 1929, when Economy Tire and Rubber became D&H Distributing Co., although the retreading business continued under its old name.

COMPANY PERSPECTIVES

From small independent resellers to large national accounts, D&H delivers individualized, personal attention for each and every customer. Whether you're a VAR, Solution Provider, System Integrator, Reseller, Retailer, eTailer, Dealer, Installer, Education Reseller, Campus Reseller, College Bookstore or K12 School, we have solutions for you.

COMPANY SURVIVING GREAT DEPRESSION

In time, D&H would grow to be one of the United States' largest distributors of RCA products, but the company was fortunate to survive the Great Depression that encompassed the 1930s. Were it not for the forbearance of banks and manufacturers such as RCA, D&H would have gone out of business in 1936 after a major flood destroyed its warehouse.

The Depression did not end until the United States' entry into World War II in late 1941 and massive defense spending fueled an economic recovery. In 1943 D&H took advantage of improved conditions to expand aggressively into consumer electronics, which appeared to have a promising future in television after that medium made its debut in the late 1930s. The Economy Tire and Rubber business was sold and the proceeds spent to open new distribution centers in Harrisburg and Baltimore, Maryland. The war years also proved difficult for D&H. David Schwab's son, Israel ("Izzy"), recalled years later, "During World War II, we couldn't get anything. We were a radio distributor, and we had no radios. All of the factories were turning into defense contractors. We sold wooden toys."

POSTWAR GROWTH IN ELECTRONICS

Shortages soon became a memory after the war came to an end in 1945 and the economy, after a brief recession, continued to roar in the postwar years when the United States emerged as the world's economic powerhouse and American consumers eagerly bought houses, raised families, and purchased vast amounts of the consumer goods D&H had to offer. Not only was D&H a major distributor of RCA radios and televisions by the early 1950s, it was also distributing phonograph records, Gibson refrigerators, and other home appliances (many of them supplied by Whirlpool), Lewyt Vacuum cleaners,

and Vornado fans. As demand outstripped the company's facilities, a new distribution building was opened in the summer of 1952 in Harrisburg, the site of the company's present-day headquarters.

It was also during the 1950s that Izzy Schwab joined the family business. After graduating from Penn State University with a degree in business administration in 1957, Schwab started out in the Baltimore office, working at the sales desk and occasionally sweeping the floors despite being the son of the boss. Before the decade was over, however, he emerged as one of the top sales representatives for RCA. Then in 1961 he moved to the Harrisburg office to become operations manager. D&H made Harrisburg its headquarters, owing to the city's close proximity to major highways (Interstates 76, 78, 81, and 83) and rail lines that gave it access to all the major markets of the East Coast. A dozen years later Schwab became vice-president of sales for the Harrisburg branch as well as an office in Altoona, Pennsylvania.

When D&H celebrated its 50th anniversary in 1968, annual revenues reached $45 million. The company's top brands, accounting for the majority of sales, were RCA and Whirlpool. They would remain dominant in the 1970s, although D&H expanded its electronic offerings, resulting in an electronic specialty products division. It was during this period that D&H became involved with the video-game market, distributing products from the likes of Atari Games Corp. and Mattel Inc. In 1979 the company entered the home computer business. One of the first products it carried was the Atari 800, which grew out of the Atari game consoles.

In 1980 D&H posted sales of $125 million, with home computers accounting for less than 1 percent of that total. Nevertheless, D&H continued to expand its offerings in this area, adding products from Texas Instruments, Commodore Computers, and Corona Data Systems. A major factor in the company's growth in home computers was Izzy Schwab, who had a personal affection for electronics. A joke that made the rounds at D&H was that the company would never have to worry about zero sales for any product: Izzy would buy at least one. In 1984 he became president of the company and played a key role in transforming D&H from a regional distributor to a national one.

RECASTING BUSINESS MODEL: 1987

Izzy Schwab was also at the helm at a time when D&H faced a very uncertain future. In 1987 the French government-run company Thomson SA acquired the

```
┌─────────────────────────────────────────────┐
│                                             │
│              KEY DATES                      │
│                    ■                        │
│   1918:  Company is founded as Economy Tire │
│          and Rubber Co.                     │
│   1929:  Company is renamed D&H Distributing│
│          Co.                                │
│   1943:  Warehouses open in Harrisburg and  │
│          Baltimore.                         │
│   1957:  Izzy Schwab joins company.         │
│   1961:  Headquarters move to Harrisburg.   │
│   1979:  D&H begins distributing home       │
│          computers.                         │
│   1984:  Izzy Schwab is named president.    │
│   1989:  Company loses RCA distribution     │
│          rights.                            │
│   1995:  D&H becomes Microsoft distributor. │
│   1998:  Employee ownership plan is launched│
│   2007:  Canadian subsidiary is formed.     │
│                                             │
└─────────────────────────────────────────────┘
```

RCA consumer products line. A year later D&H was informed that RCA would soon eliminate its regional distributors, including D&H. Formal notice came in March 1989, and a month later RCA products were sold and D&H lost 60 percent of its sales revenues in one stroke. For many years the company had been dependent on RCA and catered to the needs and whims of the manufacturer. "RCA was a bear," Izzy Schwab told trade publication *CRN* in 2002. Mixing his metaphors, he added, "They ruled the roost. They came in every June and said, 'Here's your order. Sign here.' We had no choice. You either signed or you lost the line. ... We were an independent company but very highly controlled." To make matters worse for D&H, after losing RCA it soon received a letter from Whirlpool severing its relationship as the distributor's second largest revenue producer.

For some time Schwab and his chief lieutenant, Gary Brothers, had toyed with the idea of moving in the direction of national distribution because it was becoming increasingly difficult to operate as a regional concern. Out of sheer necessity, they decided to pursue the national stage, using the company's RCA parts operations as a platform. This unit had distributed circuit boards and other electronic components, and D&H leveraged it to persuade some peripheral manufacturers to grant distribution rights. Later it would gain rights to distribute computer systems from Packard Bell Electronics Inc., Leading Edge Technologies Inc., and Swan Technologies Inc.

At the same time, D&H began to establish a national distribution footprint, opening regional hubs. The first was in the Chicago area, followed by Seattle, California, Dallas, Boston, and Jacksonville, Florida.

D&H also had to find new customers, bidding farewell to RCA and Whirlpool dealers and the sales rep that had long served these accounts. The fresh team of sales reps drummed up hardware sales from techies they tracked down, and because those customers proved uninterested in the softer goods, the ribbons and other accessories, they found a greeting-card chain to carry those items. By 1992 the distribution network was in place and D&H was finding success transferring decades of experience in creating product demand, not just providing fulfillment, and providing the kind of service to vendors and customers (many of whom were new to merchandising) that other distributors in the field were either unwilling or unable to deliver. Despite the difficulties created by the shift in business model, D&H managed to remain profitable throughout the transition.

D&H posted sales of $300 million in 1993, and continued to look for ways to grow the business. In 1994 it opened a personal computer configuration center to save suppliers time and effort by loading software, conducting bench tests, and shipping the systems to end customers. In addition, the center assembled computer systems from off-the-shelf parts, marketed under a D&H brand, Majestic. The company also continued to look for higher-profile branded product lines to carry. In 1994 it was able to add a large number of IBM products, NEC Technologies Inc. for printers, and AT&T Global Information Systems for PCs. After sales improved to $375 million in 1994, D&H looked to expand its line of software products. A year later it scored a major coup when it became a Microsoft Corporation Delivery Service Partner, able to sell the Windows 95 operating system as well as various hardware components.

ORGANIZATIONAL CHANGES: 1999

The Microsoft business helped D&H to post $550 million in sales in 1997 despite refraining from growth through acquisitions, unlike other large distributors. In that same year the company rewarded its employees by establishing an employee-ownership plan, and within a year the employees owned a 10 percent stake in the company. An organizational change took place in 1999, when Gary Brothers was named president and Izzy Schwab assumed the chief executive officer and chairman titles. His sons, in the meantime, had also assumed prominent positions in the organization. Dan Schwab was vice-president of marketing while brother Michael served as vice-president of purchasing.

Always searching out new channels of revenues, D&H launched a web site in October 1999, and within a month it accounted for 1 percent of total orders. By the end of the fiscal year it contributed 8 percent of all orders, an amount that would grow to 20 percent by 2008. In the new century, D&H looked to build a new source of sales, catering to the federal government by securing a General Services Administration schedule contract, which listed the approved prices of D&H's product lines, made available to government users and agencies.

BEGINNING OF CANADIAN OPERATIONS: 2007

D&H also drove sales by adding an expanded line of audio, video, and other electronic products that were enjoying strong demand, such as flat-panel televisions, digital cameras, wired and wireless routers, and GPS devices. In 2005 D&H landed important distribution deals with Cisco, maker of computer networking equipment, and Lenovo, offering desktops, computer workstations, and notebooks. In addition, D&B looked to new markets to drive sales. The company's first international warehouse opened in Ontario, Canada, in the summer of 2007.

D&H celebrated its 90th anniversary in 2008. By this time, sales were approaching the $2 billion mark. The company remained nimble as always, ready to adapt to changing conditions. Izzy Schwab, 72 years of age, remained very much in charge, exhibiting no inclinations toward retirement, although succession plans were reportedly in the works.

Ed Dinger

PRINCIPAL SUBSIDIARIES

D&H Canada.

PRINCIPAL COMPETITORS

Arrow Electronics, Inc.; Ingram Micro Inc.; Tech Data Corporation.

FURTHER READING

Campbell, Scott, "Izzy Schwab—Distribution Magician," *CRN*, November 13, 2002.

Chudoin, Joseph, "Growth in a New Direction," *Business Credit*, June 1999, p. 23.

Lahey, Liam, "Distributor Pays Homage to One of Its Founding Fathers," http://www.echannelline.com/usa/story.cfm?item=22744, December 12, 2007.

Mitchell, Robert W., "D&H in Business for Eight Decades," *Computer Reseller News*, March 23, 1998, p. 65.

O'Heir, Jeff, "Convergence Is Key at D&H," *Dealerscope*, July 2007, p. 60.

Pereira, Pedro, "81-Year-Old D&H Knows Its Place," *Computer Reseller News*, August 16, 1999, p. 49.

———, "Tradition of Taking Risks Pays Off," *Computer Reseller News*, April 24, 1995, p. 223.

Ryan, Jim T., "D&H Leader Celebrates Half Century with Firm," *Central Penn Business Journal*, January 4, 2008.

Daniel Thwaites Plc

Star Brewery
Syke Street
Blackburn, BB1 5BU
United Kingdom
Telephone: (+44 01254) 686868
Fax: (+44 01254) 681439
Web site: http://www.danielthwaites.plc.uk

Public Company
Incorporated: 1807
Employees: 2,351
Sales: £162.7 million ($329.9 million) (2007)
Stock Exchanges: London OFEX
Ticker Symbol: THW
NAIC: 312120 Breweries; 722410 Drinking Places (Alcoholic Beverages); 721110 Hotels (Except Casino Hotels) and Motels

■ ■ ■

Daniel Thwaites Plc is one of the United Kingdom's oldest independent brewers. The Blackburn-based company, founded in 1807, has traditionally focused on its northern region. There the group produces and distributes a strong catalog of cask and bottled ales, lagers, bitters, and other products. The company's brand portfolio includes Daniel Thwaites Original, Daniel's Hammer, Lancashire Brown Ale, Lancaster Bomber, Liberation Ale, Playmaker, Stein Pils, Strong Brown Ale, Wainwright's Fine Ale, and Premium Thoroughbred. The company also produces seasonal and other limited edition ales, including several, such as Double Century,

Golden Jubilee Celebration Ale, and Good Elf, as part of its 200th anniversary celebrations in 2007. All told, the company brews more than 320,000 barrels of beer each year. In addition to its brewery business, Daniel Thwaites operates approximately 450 pubs throughout the north of England and distributes its draft and bottled beers to another 1,000 locations in the northwest, as well as the Midlands, Wales, and Yorkshire. The company also operates a hotels division, which includes seven Shire Hotels, as well as the Stafford Hotel in London. Daniel Thwaites Plc is listed on the London Stock Exchange's OFEX market, but remains controlled by the founding family. Ann Yerburgh is the current chair of the board. The group's managing director duties are shared by B. C. Hickman, in the Brewery division, and A. H. Spencer, who oversees the Hotels division. In 2007, Daniel Thwaites Plc posted revenues of £162.7 million ($329.9 million).

FROM TAXMAN TO TAP MAN

Daniel Thwaites was born in 1777 and by the year 1800 had been working as an excise officer in Blackburn. Thwaites' duties involved among other things collecting beer taxes from local breweries and pubs. This brought him into contact with two local brewers, Edward Duckworth and William Clayton, who operated the Eanam Brewery in Blackburn. Thwaites joined the pair as a partner in the business in 1807. A year later, Thwaites married Duckworth's daughter.

Edward Duckworth died in 1822, leaving his share of the business to his daughter. Two years later, the Thwaiteses bought out Clayton's share as well, gaining sole proprietorship of the growing brewery. By then, the brewery's bitter, later known as Thwaites' Original, had become a popular local favorite among Blackburn's working class.

Three of the 12 Thwaites children joined the family business. Yet it was the sixth-born, Daniel Thwaites II, who took over as head of the brewery following his father's death in 1843. Born in 1817, Daniel Thwaites II did not marry until 1859. By then, he had gained full control of the brewery, following the death of his mother and the retirement of the two brothers who had been active in the business. Thwaites' first child died as an infant; the couple's daughter, Elma Amy Thwaites, was to assure the succession of the family's ownership of the Blackburn brewery.

Elma Thwaites married Robert Armstrong Yerburgh, and joined the operations of the company. The Thwaites brewery grew in prominence in the Blackburn market especially after 1863, when the company took over rival Snig Brook Brewery that year. Soon after, Daniel Thwaites II entered politics, becoming a member of Parliament and gaining recognition across the United Kingdom. The brewer's operations, however, remained a regional business. Into the later 19th century, the Thwaites brewery built up a strong network of pubs throughout Blackburn and the surrounding region. The notion of the "tied" pub, in which pubs were directly owned by breweries and served primarily their production, remained the dominant feature of the U.K. brewing industry until the end of the 20th century.

REGIONAL EXPANSION IN THE TWENTIES

Daniel Thwaites II died in 1888, leaving the company to Elma and Robert Yerburgh. Ten years later, the company incorporated as a limited company. Thwaites grew steadily into the World War I era. Following the war, the company entered a new and more ambitious expansion phase. Acquisitions played a major role in the company's growth in the 1920s, starting with the purchase of the James Pickup Wines & Spirit Company that year.

The Daniel Thwaites company next purchased Henry Shaw & Co. and its control of the New Brewery, located in Salford. In 1927, the company acquired another brewery, the Fountain Free Brewery. Another significant milestone for the brewery was the launch of bottled beer production in 1925. This allowed the company to expand its distribution beyond the traditional pub and restaurant circuits into the grocery sector.

Elma Yerburgh remained at the head of the company until her death in 1946. The family had already prepared its succession, however, and leadership of the company passed to her grandson, John Yerburgh. The postwar era saw new growth for the company, starting in 1946 with the acquisition of the Bury Brewing Company. This was followed by another local brewery purchase, the Preston Brewery Company, in 1956.

Throughout this period and into the 1960s, Thwaites continued to extend its number of company-owned pubs. The company also extended its reach into the East Lancashire region during the 1960s. As a result of this growth, the company carried out an expansion of its original Eanam Brewery. Upon completion, the newly enlarged complex was given the new name Daniel Thwaites' Star Brewery.

RAISING ITS PROFILE IN THE SEVENTIES

Under John Yerburgh, the Daniel Thwaites brewery steadily built its reputation from a largely local basis to a regional and even national level. The purchase of Yates & Jackson, a Lancaster-based brewer, in the 1970s, played a strong part in boosting the company's reputation regionally. Meanwhile, the company had been developing a number of new beer and ale recipes. Among these was Thwaites Best Mild, which gained national attention in 1978 when it won that year's Champion Beer of Britain award. Two years later, the company proved that the award had not been a fluke, when its Best Mild once again was named the country's best beer. The feat was all the more remarkable in that only three ales had ever won the title of Champion Beer of Britain.

Expansion of the company's pub operations continued to play a key role in the group's growth into the end of the 20th century. By the end of the 1980s, Thwaites operated a strong portfolio of company-owned pubs, which were grouped under its Thwaites Inns division. In addition to its own pubs, the company also supplied the growing free agent circuit of pubs, bars, clubs, and other drinking establishments. At the same time, Thwaites also operated a strong hotel division, boasting seven Squire Hotels into the 2000s.

KEY DATES

1807: Daniel Thwaites becomes partner in Eanam brewery.

1824: Thwaites acquires full control of brewery.

1863: Company acquires rival Snig Brook Brewery.

1925: Company launches production of bottled beer.

1946: Bury Brewing Company is acquired.

1956: Company purchases Prestong Brewery Company.

1960s: Company completes expansion of the Eanam brewery, which is renamed Thwaites' Star Brewery.

1978: Thwaites Best Mild ale wins Champion Beer of Britain award.

1991: Daniel Thwaites acquires nine pubs from Bass.

1999: Lancaster Bomber ale brand is acquired from Mitchells Brewery.

2000: Daniel Thwaites purchases 27 pubs from Bass as part of expansion into Midlands region.

2002: Company adds licenses to produce and distribute Warsteiner and Kaltenberg brands for the U.K. market.

2007: Company acquires LCL Pils brand from Scottish & Newcastle as part of expansion into northeast region.

As noted, the United Kingdom's brewery market was long dominated by the tied-house system. At the beginning of the 1990s, however, the British government took steps to break up the system, in large part to end the dominance of the national brewing groups, including Bass and Guinness. This resulted in a massive sell-off of pubs as well as the creation of a number of dedicated pub operators in the early 1990s. Thwaites itself profited from the breakup. In 1991, the company announced that it had completed the purchase of 27 north England pubs from Bass.

NITRO KEGS IN THE NINETIES

Thwaites appeared to have lost its way somewhat during the 1990s, earning itself the reputation as the "sleeping giant of the North." Part of the reason for this was the group's decision to convert a large part of its production to pasteurized, nitro-based kegs. The move came in part to respond to shifting consumer tastes in northern England, especially in the club circuit, where the more

youthful consumers favored keg beers. However, Thwaites found itself outpaced by rival brands, and especially John Smith Smooth. At the same time, Thwaites' focus on keg beers helped alienate the group with the fast-growing Campaign for Real Ale (Camra), which had launched a major effort to preserve traditional British ales in the face of pasteurized and bottled beers. As a result, its sales to the traditional pub circuit slowed as well.

By the end of the 1990s, however, Thwaites took steps to get itself back on track. The company returned its attention to cask ale, boosting its production to more than 320,000 barrels by the middle of the first decade of the 2000s, or about 10 percent of the company's total output. Another important step came with the acquisition of the Lancaster Bomber brand of cask ale in 1999. The company acquired the rights to produce and market that local and regional favorite from the Mitchells Brewery in Lancaster, which had shut down its own brewery operations that year. The Bomber brand continued to grow strongly for the company throughout the first half of the first decade of the new century.

BICENTENNIAL CELEBRATIONS

Thwaites continued to seek to expand its pub estate operations in the new century as well. While the group remained committed to its northern England market, Thwaites increasingly sought to shed its image as a purely regional brewer. This led the group to target expansion into neighboring regions, especially the Midlands. In Lichfield, for example, the company spent £1 million developing a new pub, called Just One of Those Things, or Joott.

The company's effort to crack the Midlands market took a major step forward in 2000. In that year, the company completed its largest-ever acquisition, buying 27 pubs from Bass. The acquisition brought Thwaites a number of prime locations, including three pubs in Sutton Coldfield, two in Solihull, two Birmingham region pubs, and a site in Coventry, among others. Described as a "secret multi-million pound deal," the purchase helped boost the company's total pub holdings past 400.

By 2007, the company had succeeded in raising that total to 450. At the same time, Thwaites had extended its distribution circuit to include nearly a thousand free agents. At the same time, Thwaites moved to extend its operations beyond the pub and club circuit, targeting stronger penetration of the retail bottled beer market. Among the brands the group sought to develop for the retail channel was its Lancaster Bomber, launched in bottled form in 2002.

Thwaites also kept on the lookout for new beer and ale brands during the decade. The company targeted an extension into German lagers, adding production of a premium lager brand, Warsteiner. In 2002, the group acquired the license to brew and distribute a second German brand, Kaltenberg, from the Bavarian brewer Crown Prince Luitpold of Kaltenberg. The agreement also gave Thwaites the rights to Kaltenberg's lager, Pils, and wheat beers.

Thwaites celebrated its 200th birthday in 2007, and its position as one of the few remaining family-owned breweries in the United Kingdom. As part of the celebration, the company launched a number of limited edition brews, including Wainright real ale, a cask ale named after a celebrated Blackburn playwright. The success of the limited run of the new ale was such that the company decided to launch permanent production of the brew in 2008. By then, Thwaites had acquired another important brand for its portfolio, LCL Pils brand, from Scottish & Newcastle. The addition of LCL was especially significant in that it provided the group with a new springboard into the northeast region. The LCL label joined Thwaites' growing stable of beers, including its Original, still going strong after more than 200 years.

M. L. Cohen

PRINCIPAL SUBSIDIARIES

Shire Hotels Ltd.

PRINCIPAL DIVISIONS

Brewery; Hotels.

PRINCIPAL COMPETITORS

Enterprise Inns Plc; Spirit Group Limited; Compass Group PLC; Whitbread PLC; Compass Roadside Ltd.; J D Wetherspoon PLC; Wolverhampton and Dudley Breweries PLC; Mitchells & Butlers plc; Greene King PLC; Luminar PLC; Ascot PLC; SFI Group PLC.

FURTHER READING

"Blackburn Brewer Daniel Thwaites Has Ordered a Quick Fire Launch of a Bottled Version of Its Lancaster Bomber Draught Beer After Its Successful Revival of the Brand," *Grocer,* July 20, 2002, p. 50.

"Brewer Fights for Right to Extend Hours," *Daily Post,* March 5, 2008, p. 9.

"Brewery Celebration," *Grocer,* March 17, 2007, p. 70.

Morley, Chris, "Brewer's Deal Not Small Beer," *Birmingham Evening Mail,* June 14, 2000, p. 11.

Protz, Roger, "Thwaites of Blackburn," *Beer Pages.com,* August 2006.

"Raising a Glass to 200 Years," *Lancashire Telegraph,* January 6, 2007.

"S&N Agrees Sale of LCL Pils to Thwaites," *just-drinks.com,* December 5, 2007.

"Thwaites Adds to Its Brews," *Grocer,* October 5, 2002, p. 77.

"Thwaites Unveils Logo," *Grocer,* November 18, 2006, p. 67.

Walsh, Dominic, "Bicentenary Cheers for Family Brewer," *Times,* April 13, 2007, p. 52.

Diana Shipping Inc.

Pendelis 16, Palaio Faliro
Athens, 17564
Greece
Telephone: (+30) 210-947-0100
Fax: (+30) 210-942-2995
Web site: http://www.dianashippinginc.com

Public Company
Incorporated: 1999 as Diana Shipping Investments Corp.
Employees: 365
Sales: $149.6 million (2007)
Stock Exchanges: New York
Ticker Symbol: DSX
NAIC: 483111 Deep Sea Freight Transportation

■ ■ ■

Diana Shipping Inc. is a Greek ship-owning company focused on the dry bulk shipping market. Diana operates a fleet of 19 vessels. Thirteen of these vessels are Panamax class vessels (up to 75,000 dryweight tons, or dwt, freight capacity), and six are of the Capesize class, the largest of the dry bulk shipping vessels, with a capacity exceeding 150,000 dwt. By concentrating its fleet on the two largest vessel classes, Diana has become one of the largest ship-owning companies, with a total capacity of more than two million dwt per year. The company also operates one of the industry's youngest fleets, with an average age of just 3.5 years, compared to ten years and as much as 20 years for many of its competitors. The company took delivery of a Capesize vessel in February 2008, with two Capesize-class new-

buildings expected for delivery by 2010. Like most ship-owning companies, Diana's operations consist of chartering its vessels to third-party corporations. The company's fleet management operations are carried out through subsidiary Diana Shipping Services. The youthfulness of Diana's fleet enables the company to attract many of the world's largest names in international trade, such as Cargill International, the Australian Wheat Board, China National Charting Corp., Bocimar International, Rio Tinto Shipping, Bunge, and Swissmarine. Typically, a small number of customers account for the majority of Diana's revenues, with its largest customer generating more than 25 percent of revenues. Diana Shipping, with sales of nearly $150 million in 2007, has been listed on the New York Stock Exchange since 2005. The company is led by founder, CEO, and Chairman Simeon P. Palios and COO Andreas Michalopoulus.

FROM SHIPPING AGENT TO SHIP OWNER IN 1999

While incorporated in 1999, Diana Shipping inherited three decades of shipping experience. The company's origins trace back to 1972, when Simeon P. Palios founded the shipping agent Diana Shipping Agencies, a Malta-registered company based in Greece. Palios had earned a bachelor's degree in marine engineering at Durham University, becoming a qualified naval architect and engineer. Palios then served the Greek Navy as an ensign attached to the Merchant Marine ministry. In that capacity, Palios was responsible for inspecting passenger and other vessels.

COMPANY PERSPECTIVES

Among the distinguishing strengths that we believe provide us with a competitive advantage in the dry bulk shipping industry are the following: we own a modern, high quality fleet of dry bulk carriers; our fleet includes four groups of sister ships, providing operational and scheduling flexibility, as well as cost efficiencies; we have an experienced management team; we benefit from strong relationships with members of the shipping and financial industries.

Following his service, Palios established his own ship's agency, providing brokering and chartering services to the fast-rising Greek shipping industry. By the early 1970s, Greece had established a central role for itself in the global shipping market. The country's dominance over the sector gave rise to a growing number of billionaire shipping magnates, and the Greek shipping industry was to retain its leading presence into the next century.

In 1979, Palios was joined by Andreas Michalopoulus, later to become Diana Shipping Inc.'s chief financial officer. Michalopoulus oversaw various financial aspects of Diana's shipping agency operations, particularly its insurance arrangements. In 1987, Diana Shipping Agencies changed its name to Diana Shipping Services (DSS).

The 1990s offered new horizons for the international shipping industry. The shift of the manufacturing sector toward lower-wage developing markets in the Far East intensified during the decade. This trend was further stimulated by the emerging economic might of China as its economic reform policies were put into action. Demand for shipping services increased steadily through the 1990s, particularly in the containership sector, transporting goods from China and other Asian Pacific locations to the West and elsewhere.

At the same time, the booming Asian economies created new demand for raw materials, such as iron ore, grains, and other dry bulk goods, as well as petroleum and natural gas. While pipelines partially competed with the oil tanker sector, no such rival existed for the dry bulk shipping sector. The dry bulk sector, which had seen modest growth through the decade, became swept up in the demand for iron ore, grains, coal, and other commodities fueling the new Chinese and Asian economies. Demand quickly strained capacity of the existing global fleet of ships. At the same time, the

relatively long lead times necessary to build new carriers, especially the larger Panamax and Capesize classes, sent prices soaring.

In 1999, Palios and Michalopoulus decided to move more directly into the dry bulk shipping sector, founding Diana Shipping, originally called Diana Shipping Investments Corp., as a ship-owning company separate from Diana Shipping Services. The latter company then became the exclusive agent for Diana Shipping; into the early 2000s, all of DSS's operations were focused on Diana Shipping's growing fleet.

BUILDING CAPACITY

The company set out to build its fleet. In 1999, Diana incorporated several subsidiaries, including Husky Trading, Panama Compania Armadora, Skyvan Shipping Company, and Buenos Aires Compania Armadora, in order to purchase a series of newbuildings. Skyvan, for example, acquired the Panamax class *Nirefs,* with a capacity of more than 75,000 dwt, taking delivery in 2001. Husky Trading took delivery of the *Triton* that year, while Panama Compania Armadora and Buenos Aires Compania Armadora added the *Oceanis* and *Alcyon,* respectively. Like the *Nirefs,* these vessels too were in the Panamax class.

The decision to focus on the larger carrier categories became a central part of Diana's growth strategy. While the smaller Handymax and other vessel classes provided greater flexibility, particularly in the choice of ports, the larger classes provided the potential for far greater economies of scale. In its earliest years in operation, Diana limited itself to the Panamax class, so named because it was the largest class of vessel capable of making the passage through the Panama Canal.

With its first vessels in operation in 2001, Diana posted revenues of $11 million. The company was hit by the drop-off in international trade, sparked by a global economic slump exacerbated by the September 11 terrorist attacks on the United States that year.

Nonetheless, Diana remained committed to its fleet expansion, adding several more ship-owning subsidiaries through 2002 and 2003. One feature of Diana's fleet expansion was its focus on developing its fleet as groups of "sister ships," that is, ships built to the same design. As an example, the *Nirefs, Triton, Alcyon,* and *Oceanis* were all part of a group of six sister ships. In this way, sister ships shared similar maintenance and operating requirements, helping to drive down costs. The use of sister ships also provided the company with greater flexibility in fulfilling its charter contracts. By the end of 2004, Diana had seven Panamax vessels in operation.

PUBLIC OFFERING IN 2005

Diana's strong investment in its fleet expansion paid off quickly as the market once again began expanding toward the middle of the decade. By 2003, the company's revenues had topped $25 million. That figure soared the following year, past $68 million, as chartering rates reached historic levels. Driving this trend was the surge in Chinese commodities exports, especially iron ore. From fewer than 75 million tons in 2000, China's demand for iron ore more than doubled by 2004, and topped 250 million tons by 2005.

Diana, like its major competitors, began laying out plans to increase its fleet size. These plans coincided with a highly buoyant investors market, which had identified the dry bulk sector as one of the most attractive investment areas in the middle of the decade. The availability of ready capital, backed by steady demand, encouraged shipping companies in their fleet expansion objectives. As a result, the year 2005 saw a run of initial public offerings (IPOs) from shipping companies.

Diana too joined this trend, backed by Fortis Bank, which had taken a sizable shareholding in the company, and launched its own IPO on the New York Stock Exchange in March 2005, changing its name to Diana Shipping Inc. Ahead of its offering, Diana had already completed a new phase in its fleet expansion, taking delivery of two newbuild Panamax carriers in February of that year. At the same time, Diana made its first move to extend its fleet beyond the Panamax category, buying the *Pantelis SP,* a Capesize class carrier with more

than 150,000 dwt capacity from Louis Dreyfuss Armateurs. Diana's IPO was successful, enabling Fortis to sell down its own holding to 12.6 percent. Palios, who sold no shares during the offering, remained the company's majority shareholder, with nearly 52 percent of shares.

The public offering enabled the company to pay off its debts, while providing the foundation for the group's future fleet expansion. The company also declared its intention to absorb Diana Shipping Services, which remained controlled by Palios. While the deal appeared on the surface to fit in with the notoriously incestuous dealings elsewhere in the closely knit, and often family-owned Greek shipping sector, Diana's position as DSS's sole customer, and DSS's role as Diana's exclusive shipping agent, made the deal a natural fit. The merger of DSS into Diana Shipping was completed in 2006, at a cost of $20 million.

MAJOR SHIPPING PLAYER IN THE NEW CENTURY

Diana continued to broaden its shipping capacity into the second half of the decade. The company took delivery of several more ships through 2006, raising its total fleet to 15 by the end of the year. These included the company's second Capesize vessel, and its first newbuild in this class, added in November 2006. That vessel, called the *Sideris GS,* cost the company $91 million, and added more than 174,000 dwt to the group's total capacity. The *Sideris* was immediately chartered to BHP Billiton, with a four-year contract.

Diana remained highly active in developing its fleet through 2007. In particular, the group sought to differentiate itself from its competitors by building one of the youngest fleets in the industry. While the sector's average ship age hovered at over 12 years, Diana worked at steadily reducing the age of its own fleet by selling its older vessels. These included its first Capesize vessel, the *Pantelis,* built in 2001.

Instead, the company replaced that vessel with the first of two newbuild Capesize ships from Shanghai Waigaoquiao Shipbuilding Co. in China, for $98 million in mid-2007. The second of these ships was delivered in November of that year. Also during that year, the company took delivery of a number of other vessels, including a secondhand Capesize, with a capacity of more than 180,000 dwt built in 2005. That ship was chartered out to Cargill International, under a four-year contract.

By the beginning of 2008, Diana's fleet boasted a total of 19 ships, including 13 Panamax carriers and six Capesize vessels. The latest of these, renamed the

Norfolk, was bought from Corus UK for $135 million in February of that year. At the same time, the company placed orders for two new Capesize carriers, to be built in China, with expected delivery by 2010. With one of the youngest fleets in the industry, and a capacity of more than two million dwt, Diana Shipping had grown into one of the dry bulk shipping sector's leaders in the new century.

M. L. Cohen

PRINCIPAL SUBSIDIARIES

Bikini Shipping Company Inc. (Marshall Islands); Buenos Aires Compania Armadora S.A. (Panama); Cerada International S.A. (Panama); Changame Compania Armadora S.A. (Panama); Chorrera Compania Armadora S.A. (Panama); Darien Compania Armadora S.A. (Panama); Diana Shipping Services S.A. (Panama); Eaton Marine S.A. (Panama); Husky Trading, S.A. (Panama); Jaluit Shipping Company Inc. (Marshall Islands); Panama Compania Armadora S.A.; Skyvan Shipping Company S.A. (Panama); Texford Maritime S.A. (Panama); Urbina Bay Trading, S.A. (Panama); Vesta Commercial, S.A. (Panama); Bulk Carriers (USA) LLC United States.

PRINCIPAL COMPETITORS

Sumitomo Corporation; Brega Marketing Co.; Jardine Pacific Ltd.; A P Moller-Maersk A/S; TUI AG; Marubeni Corp.; Alghanim Industries; Companhia Vale do Rio Doce; Louis Dreyfus S.A.S.; ThyssenKrupp Services AG; Dryships Inc.

FURTHER READING

Alva, Marilyn, "Shipper of Dry Goods to Dock at Wall Street," *Investor's Business Daily,* March 16, 2005, p. A06.

"Diana Shipping," *Investor's Business Daily,* July 17, 2007.

"Diana Shipping Enters into Time Charter Contract with Cargill," *Logistics Business Review,* February 12, 2008.

"Diana Shipping Files for IPO," *Journal of Commerce Online,* March 1, 2005.

"Diana Shipping Gets New Vessel," *Pacific Shipper,* December 5, 2005.

"Diana Shipping Signs Time Contract with Japanese Charterer for Capesize Carrier," *Logistics Business Review,* February 27, 2008.

DiBenedetto, Bill, "Sailing to Wall Street," *Traffic World,* April 11, 2005, p. 33.

———, "Strong Dry Bulk Market Brings IPO Wave," *Pacific Shipper,* April 1, 2005.

Gallagher, Thomas L., "Diana Shipping Profit Soars," *Traffic World,* February 19, 2008.

———, "Diana Triples Net," *Traffic World,* November 14, 2007.

Willoughby, Jack, "Making Waves," *Barron's,* September 21, 2005.

DryShips Inc.

—■—

80 Kifissias Ave., Marousi
Athens, 15125
Greece
Telephone: (+30) 210-809-0570
Web site: http://www.dryships.com

Public Company
Incorporated: 2004
Employees: 2
Sales: $583.56 million (2007)
Stock Exchanges: NASDAQ
Ticker Symbol: DRYS
NAIC: 483111 Deep Sea Freight Transportation

■ ■ ■

DryShips Inc. is a leading specialist in the dry bulk shipping market. The company owns a fleet of nearly 50 vessels. This fleet includes five Capesize vessels, 31 Panamax, two Supramax, as well as three Handymax vessels. Together, the company's fleet has a total carrying capacity of more than four million deadweight tons (dwt). DryShips' fleet is fairly young, with an average age of just over ten years. The company has, however, enacted an active fleet renewal program. As part of this effort, the group sells off its older vessels, replacing them with younger secondhand vessels. The company has also made a number of newbuilding purchases, including two Chinese-built Panamax vessels expected for delivery by 2010.

The variety of DryShips' fleet allows the company to position itself across the full range of the dry bulk

shipping sector, the largest category in the global shipping trade. DryShips, which has just two employees, does not itself operate its vessels, instead chartering them out to its customers. Management for these operations are carried out by Cardiff Marine Inc., a privately held and closely affiliated group. Founder George Economou is DryShips' CEO, COO, and chairman, and its largest shareholder. Economou, one of the most powerful figures in the Greek shipping industry, also controls Cardiff Marine. DryShips has been listed on the NASDAQ since 2005.

BIRTH OF A GREEK SHIPPING EMPIRE: 1986

Like many of Greece's shipping tycoons who made their fortunes toward the turn of the 21st century, George Economou built his empire from the ground up. The Athens-born Economou's father owned a small paper products business; yet Economou's own career goals turned to the shipping sector. By the mid-1970s, Greece had gained prominence as a center of the global shipping industry. A handful of Greek billionaires emerged as dominant players in this crucial component of the increasingly global trade market.

Economou graduated from Athens College at the beginning of the 1970s, then went to the United States, where he studied at the Massachusetts Institute of Technology. There he earned a bachelor's degree, then went on to complete two master's degrees, in naval architecture and marine engineering, and in shipping and shipyard management. Upon graduation in 1976, Economou returned to Greece, where he took up the

COMPANY PERSPECTIVES

We are focused on maximising shareholder value by maximising returns on our investments while at the same time ensuring our vessels adhere to the highest safety and environmental standards.

position of superintendent of engineering for Thenamaris Ship Management. In 1981, Economou changed jobs, returning to the United States to become general manager of New York-based Oceania Maritime Agency.

By the middle of the 1980s, Economou had begun developing plans to take a more direct role in the shipping business. In 1986, he bought his first ship, and founded his first shipping company. Over the next several years, Economou acquired several more vessels and created a number of new companies for these holdings. In 1991, Economou brought all of his ships and their operating companies under a single holding company, Cardiff Marine. Joining Economou in the business was his sister, Chryssoula Kandylidis, who took a 30 percent share of the company, to George Economou's 70 percent. Cardiff then began developing its own operations as a ship management company, including creating a Liberia-registered subsidiary, DryBulk SA, which handled the family's charter and ship trading brokering business.

Cardiff grew into one of the largest of Greece's shipping empires, boasting a fleet of vessels with a total of more than six million dwt capacity. Economou himself was transformed into a billionaire, and gained a place among the Greek shipping industry's top five magnates.

NOTORIETY IN 1998

Economou would also gain a good deal of notoriety among the global investment community. The rising growth of global trade in the 1990s, especially with the emergence of China, India, and other Asian markets in the second half of the decade, had brought a new upswing in the traditionally cyclical shipping industry. Into the second half of the decade, a growing number of shipping companies launched ambitious plans to expand their fleets. As a result, the market quickly became flooded with a wave of high-yield shipping bonds.

Economou recognized an opportunity to expand and rejuvenate his own fleet of vessels. A vessel's age played an important role in ship management

companies' ability to charter the vessel at profitable rates. The older a vessel, the less efficient and more costly it was to run, thereby lowering demand. A number of ships in Economou's fleet were more than 20 years old, considered "elderly" in the sector.

In order to take advantage of the surge in investor interest in the shipping sector, Economou formed a new company, Alpha Shipping, in 1998, placing himself as that company's general manager. In February of that year, Alpha Shipping floated junk bonds worth more than $175 million in order to raise capital to acquire a fleet of shipping vessels. The float, for ten-year, 9.5 percent unsecured bonds, was backed by Credit Suisse First Boston and SBC Warburg Dillon Read. Neither had much prior experience in the shipping sector.

Alpha Shipping went on a spending spree, and quickly acquired a fleet of 26 vessels. All of these came from Cardiff and other Economou shipping holdings, and of the 26, fully 20 vessels were over 20 years old. Indeed, investors later charged that Alpha had overpaid for the vessels. The company paid $46 million, for example, to acquire six ships owned directly by Economou. The other ships were acquired from Cardiff and other Economou companies. All together, Alpha paid nearly $100 million for the fleet of 26 ships. At the same time, Alpha was said to have paid "exorbitant" ship management fees of $6 million to Cardiff Marine and DryBulk SA.

The bottom soon fell out of the shipping industry's junk bond market. The economic crisis that swept through Asia in 1998 led to a new downturn in the global shipping trade. As a result, most of the bond issues were severely downgraded. Alpha Shipping's bond issue soon revealed itself as one of the largest flops. By 1999, Alpha Shipping had defaulted on its interest payments, and neared bankruptcy.

Economou quickly negotiated a restructuring of the company's debt, however, paying just 37 cents on the dollar. The terms of the deal also left most of Alpha Shipping's fleet intact. With the restructuring complete, Economou began selling off Alpha Shipping's fleet. While half of the fleet was sold to outside companies, Economou, through his various companies, himself regained control of the other half, buying back 13 vessels at heavily discounted prices.

As one investor told *Institutional Investor:* "Uniquely among the bonds that have blown up, or will, this bond deal has resulted in enormous personal benefit to the owner, somewhere in the area of $35 million." Economou defended himself, however, stating: "We have done nothing wrong. Those who are talking about me, about Alpha, are particularly jealous people. They're self-serving and have their own agenda."

KEY DATES

1986: George Economou acquires his first dry bulk shipping vessel.
1991: Economou combines various vessels and operating companies into Cardiff Marine.
1998: Economou forms Alpha Shipping, which raises $175 million through a junk bond offer, then goes bankrupt.
2004: Company forms DryShips Inc., a dry bulk specialist, which acquires first six vessels.
2005: DryShips goes public on the NASDAQ.
2007: DryShips acquires 30 percent stake in Ocean Rig, of Norway, which owns and operates deepwater drilling vessels.

DRYSHIPS TO NASDAQ IN 2005

The upturn in the global shipping sector in the middle of the first decade of the 2000s provided Economou with a new opportunity to raise capital from the investment community. China's emergence as one of the world's largest economies, its central position in the global manufacturing industry, and the rapid buildup of its infrastructure, as well as the boom in its construction industry played a major role in the shipping industry's fresh vigor. At the same time, China's own expansion was reflected in the strong growth throughout the Asian Pacific region. The booming economies created a new surge in demand for raw materials, such as iron ore, steel, and petroleum and related products.

Economou once again spotted the potential to open part of his shipping empire to public investment. In 2004, he founded a new ship-holding company, Entrepreneurial Spirit Foundation, based in Liechtenstein, which became owner of six dry bulk shipping vessels. The Liechtenstein company then became a 70 percent owner of the newly created DryShips Inc., itself based in Greece. Economou's sister again joined her brother, with a 30 percent stake through her own Liberia-registered Prestige Finance SA. Entrepreneurial Spirit then transferred control of its six ships to DryShips.

Economou soon raised eyebrows when he announced his intention to launch DryShips' stock on the NASDAQ through an initial public offering (IPO). The choice of venue alone appeared to surprise some investment analysts. As one investor told *Barron's:* "It was surreal. When someone asked why he was doing the deal, here—now, [Economou] actually said, basically,

'Because Americans are the dumbest investors around, and there's lots of liquidity in this market.'"

Others criticized the offering, or rather investor interest in the offering, as well. As some observers pointed out, apart from Economou's prior involvement in the Alpha Shipping debacle, the IPO quite clearly spelled out a number of other risk factors. Among these was the company's intention to pay out nearly $70 million, nearly all of its accumulated earnings, to Economou-controlled companies prior to the IPO. Another highlighted the fact that the company had just three employees, Economou, who served as CEO and chairman, and a COO and corporate secretary. All of the company's operations otherwise were to be conducted through Cardiff Marine.

Economou remained in control not only of Cardiff Marine, but also other competing dry bulk shipping companies. As the company's prospectus openly acknowledged: "In particular, Cardiff may give preferential treatment to vessels that are beneficially owned by related parties because Mr. Economou and members of his family may receive greater economic benefits."

In addition, among the IPO's objectives was to finance the company's plan to buy six vessels recently acquired by Economou's sister through her own company. While the sale of most of these vessels was completed at cost, Kandylidis herself was paid a $3 million fee for the transaction.

BUILDING A DRY BULK FLEET FOR THE NEW CENTURY

Despite these "red flags," as some observers called them, the NASDAQ IPO was completed successfully. Indeed, DryShips' IPO success sparked a run on the investment market, with nearly a dozen Greek dry bulk shippers seeking listings on the New York markets over the next two years. These included Ocean Freight, a company established by Economou's nephew, Antonios Kandylidis. In all, these offerings raised more than $4 billion in investment capital.

DryShips quickly began building up its fleet, spending over $900 million over the next three years. The company put together a highly varied portfolio of ships, ranging from the massive Capesize, the largest category, to smaller and highly versatile Handymax ships. The bulk of the group's fleet nonetheless remained in the more standard and profitable Panamax size, which presented the advantage of being able to navigate both the Suez and Panama canals.

Unlike the case with Alpha, a major feature of DryShips' fleet expansion was its emphasis on rejuvenating the fleet. By the end of 2007, the company could boast a fleet with an average age of just over ten years. While most of the group's purchases remained on the secondhand market, DryShips also launched a number of newbuilding contracts that year. The company's 2007 purchases included three Korean-built Capesize vessels, with delivery expected between 2009 and the beginning of 2010. The company also placed orders for two Kamsarmax vessels, each with a tonnage of 82,000 dwt, from shipyards in China, also slated for delivery in 2010.

DryShips also posted strong revenue gains through the middle of the decade. Aided by surging Asian demand for raw materials, especially the booming demand for petroleum and other energy products, the company saw its daily charter rates surge by more than five and a half times between 2006 and 2007. As a result, the company's annual revenues jumped from under $64 million in 2004 to more than $248 million in 2006. By the end of 2007, the company's revenues had more than doubled again, topping $580 million.

Once again Economou was raising eyebrows. As *Forbes* stated: "DryShips is a public company. But the way George Economou runs the place, you'd hardly know it." What had sparked this statement was DryShips' sudden decision, at the end of 2007, to move beyond the dry bulk shipping sector. In November of that year, DryShips announced its decision to pay $405 million to acquire a 30 percent stake in Norwegian deepwater drilling rig group Ocean Rig. As part of that deal, DryShips agreed to pay a $4 million brokering fee to Cardiff Marine, which itself had just placed a $1.4 billion order for two drill ships from Samsung Heavy Industries. Economou himself bought a 4 percent stake in Ocean Rig, leading to concerns that he might use his shareholder position to pressure Ocean Rig to acquire the new drill ships on order from Cardiff. Soon after, DryShips' COO announced his resignation, leaving Economou to add that position, in addition to his role as CEO and chairman.

DryShips' decision to veer into the deepwater drilling market prompted at least one institutional investor to dump his stake in the company, telling *Forbes:* "I am not going to be part of anything where a chief executive is self-dealing." As if in answer, Economou told *Forbes:* "Listen guy, if you don't like it, you don't have to be here. Sell the stock." DryShips' Economou remained one of the global shipping industry's most powerful, most controversial, and most successful figures.

M. L. Cohen

PRINCIPAL SUBSIDIARIES

Annapolis Shipping Company Limited; Blueberry Shipping Company Limited; Helium Shipping Company Limited; Hydrogen Shipping Company Limited; Oxygen Shipping Company Limited; Silicon Shipping Company Limited; Wealth Management Inc. (Marshall Islands).

PRINCIPAL COMPETITORS

Sumitomo Corp.; Brega Marketing Co.; Jardine Pacific Ltd.; A P Moller-Maersk A/S; TUI AG; Marubeni Corp.; Alghanim Industries; Companhia Vale do Rio Doce; Louis Dreyfus S.A.S.; ThyssenKrupp Services AG.

FURTHER READING

"DryShips Buys Eight Vessels," *Journal of Commerce Online,* August 7, 2007.

"DryShips Buys Three Bulkers," *Journal of Commerce Online,* April 18, 2007.

Ellis, Stephen, "DryShips: An Investing Shipwreck," *Motley Fool,* September 1, 2006.

"Full Speed Ahead at DryShips?" *Business Week,* January 21, 2008, p. 75.

"New Bulker for DryShips," *Journal of Commerce Online,* April 19, 2006.

Quinn, Lawrence Richter, "Shipwrecked," *Institutional Investor International Edition,* August 1999, p. 23.

Vardi, Nathan, "Curious George," *Forbes Global,* March 10, 2008, p. 32.

Welling, Kathryn M., "The Golden Fleece?" *Barron's,* February 28, 2005.

Ergon, Inc.

2829 Lakeland Drive
Jackson, Mississippi 39232-9798
U.S.A.
Telephone: (601) 933-3000
Toll Free: (800) 824-2626
Fax: (601) 933-3355
Web site: http://www.ergon.com

Private Company
Incorporated: 1954 as Lampton Oil Company
Employees: 2,500
Sales: $4.11 billion (2006 est.)
NAIC: 324110 Petroleum Refineries; 423191 Petroleum
Lubricating Oil and Grease Manufacturing

■ ■ ■

Ergon, Inc., is a private holding company based in Jackson, Mississippi, controlling more than 60 companies involved in six business segments, mostly related to energy. Involved in the refining and marketing area are two key subsidiaries. Lion Oil Company, a familiar retail gasoline brand from the 1920s into the early 1980s, provides the bulk of Ergon's revenues. Not only does it produce consumer gasoline and diesel fuels at its El Dorado, Arkansas, refinery, Lion also offers asphalt products to highway contractors and other customers in Arkansas and parts of Texas and Louisiana. A second subsidiary, Ergon Refining, Inc., operates refineries in Newell, West Virginia, and Vicksburg, Mississippi, producing naphthenic oils used in lubricants, tanning, and a wide variety of products, including

adhesives, coatings, hoses and belts, water sealants, pigments, printing inks, shoe soles, tennis balls, and tires. Ergon also wholly or partially owns five subsidiaries involved in the asphalt and emulsions business: Ergon Asphalt & Emulsions, Inc.; Paragon Technical Services, Inc.; Ertech, Inc.; Crafco Inc.; and Tricor Refining, LLC. The transportation and terminaling division includes Ergon Trucking, Inc., a transporter of oils, emulsions, and chemicals to the 48 contiguous states and Canada; Magnolia Marine Transport Company, which moves asphalt products on the Mississippi River and the intercoastal waterways of the Gulf Coast; Ergon Terminaling, Inc., operating nine southern liquid bulk terminals; Specialty Process Fabricators, Inc., a custom fabricator of storage tanks, pressure vessels, and other equipment used in the oil and gas, petrochemical and refining, power generation, and paper and pulp industries; and ISO Panels, Inc., maker of heated tanks using pre-engineered thermal insulation panels. Ergon is involved in the retail propane industry through Lampton-Love, Inc., serving parts of Mississippi, Alabama, Louisiana, Georgia, and Tennessee. Ergon's different business interests have also taken the company into the embedded computing field. Through Diversified Technology, Inc. Ergon provides single board computers and system platforms to the commercial, communications, and government and military markets.

In addition, Ergon has a myriad of real estate interests, including commercial and industrial properties, condominiums, and the Kearney Park shooting preserve in central Mississippi where hunters can stay and participate in quail shoots and take advantage of a sporting clay range. Ergon is also involved in NASCAR racing, its Ergon Racing unit mostly taking part in the Craftsman Truck Series. Ergon is owned by the Lampton family, headed by the founder and patriarch, Leslie B. Lampton Sr., a member of *Forbes'* top 400 richest Americans.

LAMPTON OIL: 1954

Forbes describes Leslie Lampton as the "intensely private oil tycoon." What little is known about him is that he was born in 1926 and graduated with an engineering degree from the University of Mississippi in 1947. He then spent two stints, 1949 to 1951 and 1953 to 1954, with Joe T. Dehmers Distributors, a Jackson, Mississippi-based company. In 1954 Lampton struck out on his own, starting Lampton Oil Company as a petroleum retailer, setting up shop on Farish Street in Jackson with a single employee. Lampton supplied bulk lube oil to southern and central Mississippi oil drilling operations. In 1957 he expanded his business further by starting Magnolia Marine Transport Company with Mark Shurden of Greenville, Mississippi. Operating out of Shurden's home, the company used three barges and one leased vessel to supply No. 6 oil to power plants and paper plants. It was also in the 1950s that Lampton-Love, Inc., was launched to distribute propane gas.

FORMATION OF ERGON: 1970

It was not until 1970 that Lampton formed Ergon, Inc., to hold his growing slate of businesses. Along the way his businesses made use of computers and in 1971 Ergon took advantage of those capabilities to launch Diversified Technology, Inc., to work in the embedded computing industry, producing computer systems that performed specialized functions. Three years later the subsidiary made its mark in the field by introducing an all-CMOS passive backplane, single board, slot card computer. In 1977 Lampton added to his business

empire, launching Ergon Exploration, Inc., to pursue oil and gas exploration, development, and production. By this time his four sons were coming on board and taking on increasing levels of responsibility within the organization.

ACQUISITION OF LION OIL STAKE: 1985

Ergon became involved in oil refining through the 1985 participation in the acquisition of Lion Oil Company. Lion Oil was founded in 1923 in the oil boom town of El Dorado, Arkansas, a modest business until it was acquired by Colonel Thomas H. Barton who turned it into a major regional oil company, whose lion logo adorned gas stations throughout the South. Barton sold it to Monsanto Chemical Company in 1956 and served on the Monsanto board until his death in 1960. The Lion Oil name was dropped and the El Dorado refinery and pipeline system was sold to Santa Monica, California-based Tosco Corporation in 1976. The operation struggled, the last Lion Oil filling station closed in the early 1980s, and by mid-decade the business was on the verge of being shut down. While there was a bidder interested in buying the company for the pipeline, the refinery was slated to be closed. Arkansas Governor Bill Clinton then engineered a sale to another group of investors, which included Ergon, along with four Arkansas companies, Continental Ozark Inc. and three crude-oil producers: Long Brothers Oil Company, Shuler Drilling Company, and Max Delong.

The ownership group revived the Lion Oil name, calling the new enterprise Lion Oil Company. It continued to operate the El Dorado refinery, although at the time, with oil selling for just $6 a barrel, the refinery business was a money-losing proposition and a number of small refiners went out of business. As part of the deal Ergon managed Lion Oil for a fee of 20 percent of net profits. The owners were also responsible for obtaining a letter of credit, $2 for each $1 par value subscribed in stock, which was needed to purchase large lots of crude oil. Charles Long of Long Brothers Oil Co. served as chairman, but when he suffered some financial reversals in 1989 and could no longer provide the letter of credit, Leslie Lampton replaced him and engineered a recapitalization plan that allowed Ergon to take a larger position in Lion Oil. In time Ergon would acquire all of the company and make substantial investments in the El Dorado refinery, which would become more profitable in the 1990s, minus some tough patches during down cycles in the price of oil.

In the 1990s Ergon added to its refinery business while making other adjustments to its business mix and operations. In an effort to protect employees as well as

KEY DATES

1954: Leslie Lampton starts Lampton Oil Company.
1957: Magnolia Marine Transport Company is launched.
1970: Ergon, Inc., is created to house Lampton's interests.
1977: Ergon Exploration, Inc., is formed.
1985: Company acquires stake in Lion Oil Company.
1997: Newell, West Virginia, refinery is acquired.
2001: Ergon purchases ISO Panels, Inc.
2006: Company paves Talladega Speedway Track.

the environment, the company in 1991 formed the Corporate Environmental Health & Safety Department. It had been started seven years earlier in the Engineering department with just one person. In other developments in the 1990s, Diversified Technology moved into a state-of-the-art research and manufacturing facility in 1997. In that same year, another subsidiary, Ergon Nonwovens, maker of melt-blown roll goods, used in the manufacture of materials to soak up oil spills, was sold to Denver-based Schuller Corp.

PURCHASE OF NEWELL REFINERY: 1997

A more significant transaction later in 1997 was the acquisition of the Newell, West Virginia, refinery from Quaker State, which became the heart of Ergon Refining, Inc. Over the next five years Ergon would invest $70 million to increase capacity at the facility located in the panhandle of West Virginia with terminals in Ohio and Pennsylvania. To take advantage of increased refining capacity, Ergon in early 2000 arranged to purchase or lease all of the crude-oil gathering facilities and equipment in the region of Pennzoil-Quaker State Company.

A variety of other deals would transpire in the new century for Ergon and its family of companies. ISO Panels Inc. was purchased in 2001. The maker of insulated tank panels was started in 1975 by Otis Heard as Heat & Frost Insulation. Given the large surface area of heated storage tanks, the insulated sidewalls developed by Heard provided dramatic cuts in utility bills. After Heard retired in 2001, Ergon was quick to snap up the niche business. Also in 2001 Paragon Technical Services, Inc., was incorporated. Growing out of Ergon Technical Development, the new subsidiary developed new products for Ergon Asphalt & Emulsion.

FORMATION OF ERGON ENERGY PARTNERS: 2001

With the price of oil and gas on the rise in the first decade of the 2000s, Ergon expanded its energy business on a number of fronts. In 2001, Ergon Exploration formed Ergon Energy Partners to develop the acreage it had acquired on the Wolf Creek Prospect in the Woodville, Texas, area, along with seismic data. Further investments were also made at the Newell refinery in West Virginia and the Lion Oil refinery in Arkansas to remove sulfur from diesel fuel in order to meet the standards for ultralow sulfur diesel that went into effect in 2006. Ergon also sought to take advantage of growing interest in ethanol. In 2006 subsidiary Ergon Ethanol, Inc., and its grain handling partner, Bunge North America, Inc., broke ground on a new $100 million ethanol plant in Vicksburg, Virginia, expected to be the largest ethanol plant in the Deep South. Also in Vicksburg in the early 2000s, Ergon Refining, Inc., invested in its refinery to increase the production of naphthenic base oils. In 2006 another capital improvement program was launched to build three major new units and add storage tank capacity to increase the production of oil used to support the expected growth in the rubber and electrical insulating oil industries. The work would cost more than $100 million and was slated for completion in 2008.

On other fronts in the 2000s, Diversified Technology, which in 1999 had become a member of the Intel Applied Computing Platform Provider Program, joined the Intel Communications Alliance in 2003. Building on this platform, the company expanded internationally by opening distribution offices in Germany, Israel, the Benelux and Nordic countries, and the United Kingdom. In 2007 the company added to its capabilities by acquiring Tier Electronics, LLC, a Wisconsin company that specialized in power electronics designs, including embedded microcontrollers. In another acquisition in 2007, Ergon Asphalt & Emulsions, Inc., acquired Kansas City, Kansas-based Innovative Adhesives Company, manufacturer of specialty asphalt coatings and adhesives.

It was through Ergon Asphalt & Emulsions that Ergon became involved in racing. In 2006 the company was contracted to pave the track at NASCAR's largest facility, the Talladega Speedway in Alabama, featuring a notoriously dangerous surface. The new asphalt was universally praised and introduced the Ergon name to much of the public. The company increased its recognition further in 2007 when it agreed to sponsor a promising young driver, Marc Mitchell, in 11 races in NASCAR's 2007 ARCA series. In 2008 it joined forces with Billy Ballew Motorsports to sponsor Mitchell in the NASCAR Craftsman Truck Series.

While Leslie Lampton preferred to keep himself and his companies out of the spotlight, he could not avoid receiving attention for his business success. Ergon was listed by *Forbes* magazine among the largest 100 private companies in the United States with estimated sales of $2.68 billion in 2005. "They just guess at that," Lampton told the *Arkansas Democrat Gazette,* in a rare telephone interview, conducted because the octogenarian had no secretary and answered his own phone. The money he saved was negligible compared to his estimated personal worth of $2 billion, an amount that also landed him on the *Forbes* list of the 400 richest Americans.

Ed Dinger

PRINCIPAL SUBSIDIARIES

Lion Oil Company; Ergon Refining, Inc.; Ergon Asphalt & Emulsions, Inc.; Paragon Technical Services, Inc.; Ertech, Inc.; Crafco Inc.; Tricor Refining, LLC; Magnolia Marine Transport Company; Ergon Terminal-ing, Inc.; Specialty Process Fabricators, Inc.; ISO Panels, Inc.; Lampton-Love, Inc.; Diversified Technology, Inc.

PRINCIPAL COMPETITORS

Ferrellgas Partners, L.P.; Koch Industries, Inc.; Marathon Oil Corporation.

FURTHER READING

Emmerich, Wyatt, "Disappearing Companies," *Northside Sun,* July 14, 2006.

"Energy Billionaires," *Forbes,* February 21, 2008.

Minton, Mark, "Small Player in State's South," *Arkansas Democrat Gazette,* March 19, 2006.

Muzzi, Doreen, "Ergon and Bunge Join Forces," *Delta Business Journal,* December 4, 2006.

Petzer, Alan, "State of N. Appalachian Oil," *Oil & Gas Journal,* March 4, 20002, p. 17.

"Tosco Plans to Sell Refinery in Arkansas," *Wall Street Journal,* March 12, 1985, p. 1.

Exponent, Inc.

———— ■ ————

149 Commonwealth Drive
Menlo Park, California 94025
U.S.A.
Telephone: (650) 326-9400
Toll Free: (888) 656-3976
Fax: (650) 326-8072
Web site: http://www.exponent.com

Public Company
Incorporated: 1968 as Failure Analysis Associates, Inc.
Employees: 835
Sales: $168.49 million (2006)
Stock Exchanges: NASDAQ
Ticker Symbol: EXPO
NAIC: 541611 Administrative Management and General Management Consulting Services

■ ■ ■

Exponent, Inc., is a science and engineering consulting firm that assists clients in solving technical problems. The company's services range from analyzing and reconstructing major disasters, such as plant explosions or aviation accidents, to researching health or environmental issues related to product development. The majority of the company's revenues are derived from litigation support. Exponent's staff includes scientists, physicians, engineers, and regulatory consultants regarded as experts in more than 90 different technical disciplines. The company serves clients in a variety of industries, including automotive, aviation, chemical, construction, consumer products, energy,

health, and manufacturing. Exponent also counts the U.S. Department of Defense as a client. The company operates through 18 offices in the United States and overseas through subsidiary companies in the Netherlands, Poland, the United Kingdom, and China.

ORIGINS

The founding of Exponent was analogous to the start of a poker game. Instead of poker chips, each of the five founders of the company anted $100 in the pot and used the money to start their own business, betting that they could succeed as consultants. The founders pooled their money in April 1967, forming a company they would incorporate in California the following year. The name of the business, one that would excite the curiosity of observers for years to come, was Failure Analysis Associates (FAA).

When FAA's founders came together in 1967, it was a gathering of intellectuals. Each individual possessed a Ph.D., bringing extensive knowledge in materials science, engineering mechanics, and structural analysis to the formation of the consultancy business. Although the methods of FAA's work were complex, the mission of the founders' consultancy business was straightforward: try to understand why things fail.

Initially, FAA focused its research on the energy industry. Customers employed the company to conduct research on stress and fracture mechanics, turning to the handful of scientists at FAA for help in understanding how materials crack and break. By the early 1970s, the company's initial line of business had earned it national recognition within industrial and government circles,

COMPANY PERSPECTIVES

The problems that Exponent tackles take many forms besides a disaster or accident involving a product or property. It may be a technical, health, or environmental issue related to a developing product, such as potential radiation from cell phones, whose resolution needs to be accurate, innovative, and cost effective. A regulatory issue may have a critical impact on a client's future business, and may turn on how the product can be sold or serviced. Very often, a client calls because a production facility is suffering unusual down time, or a production machine has failed, or the recently received component parts just don't seem to work right. We assist clients contemplating any business transaction that requires careful scientific research and analysis as part of the due diligence, including the value of intellectual property and patents.

which enabled it to branch out into the more broadly defined disaster-analysis industry. FAA was called upon to investigate and analyze accidents and failures resulting from fire, explosions, and earthquakes. The company's projects encompassed mundane and ordinary failures and the great catastrophes of its era, everything ranging from stress fractures in manufacturing equipment to major aviation disasters.

ROGER L. MCCARTHY ERA BEGINS: 1978

FAA grew slowly and steadily throughout the 1970s, never making a major leap in its financial stature, but rarely taking a step backward. The company, employee-owned, financed its expansion through cash flow. It gained solid leadership after Roger L. McCarthy joined the firm in 1978. McCarthy, who held five academic degrees including a doctorate in mechanical engineering from the Massachusetts Institute of Technology, was promoted to vice-president in 1980 and to president and chief executive officer two years later, taking over from one of the founders, Bernard Ross, who eventually became chairman emeritus (a distinction also awarded to McCarthy decades later).

Under McCarthy's stewardship, FAA changed substantially. The company's organizational structure was altered, new businesses were formed, and it converted from private to public ownership. Perhaps most important, the company cemented its reputation

as an expert in a variety of disciplines and in numerous infamous disasters and accidents. FAA's name was linked to nearly every catastrophe of the 1980s, the high-profile cases of failure that served as the firm's lifeblood. Once a disaster occurred, FAA scientists were called in to perform the complex task of determining what caused the incident, a painstaking process that required extensive scientific and engineering expertise. FAA projects during the 1980s reflected a decade of destruction, failure, and mishap, beginning with the collapse of indoor pedestrian walkways that killed 113 people in the Hyatt Regency Hotel in Kansas City, Missouri, in 1981. A host of FAA investigations followed, including the Delta Airlines crash that killed 137 people at the Dallas/Fort Worth Airport in 1985, the explosion of the *Challenger* space shuttle in 1986, the Du Pont Hotel fire in Puerto Rico in 1987, Suzuki Motor's safety problems with its Samurai model in 1988, and the *Exxon Valdez* oil spill in 1989.

PUBLIC DEBUT IN 1990

As FAA's business and reputation grew, McCarthy began to contemplate significant changes. He first began to consider taking the company public in 1988 because expansion could no longer be financed from cash flow, as it had for the previous 20 years. He took the first step toward completing an initial public offering (IPO) of stock in 1989 by forming The Failure Group, Inc., as a holding company for FAA. The following year, he filed with the U.S. Securities and Exchange Commission to sell 2.3 million shares, hoping to raise $22 million for the company and $12 million for investors. Failure Group, a name lampooned by a fair number of industry observers, completed its IPO in 1990, and added to the amusement of onlookers when the company began trading under the ticker symbol, "FAIL."

Failure Group's public debut opened its operations to scrutiny for the first time. The company ended 1990 with $59 million in revenue, a total generated by its 445 employees, 270 of whom possessed advanced degrees. The company's average project billed out at $20,000, but some of its largest projects brought in $4 million or more. The company was staffed with experts trained in disciplines such as biomechanics, physics, anatomy, and computer modeling. Despite its robust growth (revenues doubled and profits tripled between 1987 and 1990s) the company was exceptionally methodical in adding new personnel to its payroll, usually hiring new talent by consulting with professors at the most prestigious schools for referrals. When the company hired a new toxicologist in 1990, the job offer ended a six-year search for the right person. Failure Group, despite its name, feared mistakes in the disaster analysis and

KEY DATES

1967: Five scientists form Failure Analysis Associates, the predecessor to Exponent, and incorporate the next year.
1978: Roger L. McCarthy is hired and is promoted to chief executive officer four years later.
1989: The Failure Group is formed as a holding company.
1990: The Failure Group completes its initial public offering of stock.
1996: Michael R. Gaulke replaces McCarthy as chief executive officer.
1997: The company acquires Performance Technologies, Inc.
1998: The Failure Group changes its name to Exponent.
2002: Exponent acquires Novigen Sciences, Inc.
2005: A subsidiary in China is established.
2007: Gaulke is named Exponent's chairman.

reconstruction work it performed and assiduously tried to maintain its sterling reputation.

MICHAEL R. GAULKE HIRED AND ACQUISITIONS

The 1990s, like the 1980s, witnessed profound changes at the San Mateo, California-based company (it later relocated to Menlo Park). McCarthy had spearheaded expansion efforts and guided the company through its conversion to public ownership, and his successor would preside over equally important initiatives. Michael R. Gaulke joined Failure Group in 1992, hired as the company's executive vice-president and chief financial officer, the same positions he held at his former employer, Raynet Corp., a subsidiary of electronics and telecommunications manufacturer Raychem Corp. Gaulke was promoted to president in 1993 and to chief executive officer in 1996, when McCarthy ended his 14-year term as Failure Group's leader. McCarthy remained chairman, a title he had held since 1986 and would continue to hold until 2005.

Under Gaulke's rule, Failure Group began to expand its capabilities beyond its core competency in failure analysis. The diversification was accomplished largely through acquisitions, which began the year Gaulke was named chief executive officer. Late in 1996, the company acquired Environmental Health Strategies,

Inc., a company founded in 1989 that applied epidemiology, a branch of medicine dealing with the transmission and control of disease in populations, and medical expertise to health issues in the workplace. Next, in mid-1997, Failure Group purchased Performance Technologies, Inc., a company that operated under the name PTI Environmental Health Strategies. The acquisition of the ten-year-old company enabled Failure Group to offer analysis of environmental problems affecting a variety of industries. (Failure Group also had a fourth subsidiary, BCS Wireless, Inc., which specialized in the design, installation, and maintenance of wireless communications networks. BCS was sold in 2000 for $2 million.)

NAME CHANGE IN 1998

After expanding its operations into the medical and environmental fields, Failure Group stood as a larger, more comprehensive provider of analytical services. By 1998, the company and its three consulting organizations had 25 offices in four countries. Revenues reached $80 million during the year, from which the company posted $4 million in net income. Aside from increasing the company's stature and expanding its capabilities, the acquisitions, Gaulke decided, necessitated a name change. In March 1998, The Failure Group, Inc., became Exponent, Inc. FAA changed its name from Failure Analysis Associates to Exponent Failure Analysis Associates. PTI Environmental Services became Exponent Environmental Group. Environmental Health Strategies was recast as Exponent Health Group. The company's ticker symbol changed from "FAIL" to "EXPO." In a press release published in the March 6, 1998, issue of *PR Newswire,* Gaulke explained the reasoning behind the name change. "Over the past two years," he said, "as we began to implement our growth strategy through both internal development and acquisitions, we recognized the need for a name that would reflect the full scope of our integrated services. Although analysis of failure and accidents will always be an important part of our business, increasingly our clients require a broader range of scientific research and analysis of product development, regulatory compliance, and risk management."

As Exponent entered the 21st century, its more broadly based business began to embrace a fundamental alteration in focus. Since its inception, the company had concentrated primarily on providing analysis of failures and disasters after they occurred. With new resources at his disposal after the acquisitions of the late 1990s, Gaulke began to promote his company's ability to provide preventative services. "Traditionally," he said in a July 2000 interview with *Failure* magazine, "our business has been very event driven—when a plane crashes or a chemical plant explodes. We're now doing more work before the failure, and in that case we're more proactive."

EXPONENT IN THE EARLY 21ST CENTURY

The first years of the new century saw Exponent grow financially at the greatest pace in its history. After 33 years of business, the company reached the $100 million mark in revenues in 2000. By 2006, the company's volume had increased to $168 million. Its ability to turn a profit also demonstrated strength, with profits rising each year between 1998 and 2006.

Several notable events occurred as Exponent recorded its encouraging growth. In 2002, the company completed another acquisition, purchasing Novigen Sciences, Inc. Novigen was a specialist in regulatory issues related to food, pesticides, chemicals, biochemicals, microbials, and products of biotechnology. Exponent rebranded the company as Exponent Food & Chemicals.

The company also made a significant international move in the years leading up to its 40th anniversary. McCarthy's crowning achievement on the international front had been the formation of Failure Analysis B.V. in 1990, a Dutch subsidiary the company used to attract clients in Europe. In 2005, Gaulke scored his overseas success by opening an office in China. The office operated as Exponent Science and Technology Consulting Co. Ltd., an operation also known as Exponent China Ltd. Through the subsidiary, Exponent provided engineering and scientific consulting services to U.S. and international companies operating in East Asia.

EXPONENT TURNS 40 IN 2007

Exponent's 40th anniversary celebration in 2007 coincided with Gaulke's appointment as the company's chairman. Under his control as both chief executive officer and chairman, the company faced a promising future. For four decades, Exponent demonstrated an admirable constancy in its consulting work. In the years ahead, fortified with its armada of scientists, engineers,

and medical doctors, there was every indication the company would continue to enjoy the level of success that described its past.

Jeffrey L. Covell

PRINCIPAL SUBSIDIARIES

Failure Analysis Associates B.V. (Netherlands); Failure Analysis Associates, Spolka z.o.o. (Poland); Exponent Realty LLC; Exponent International Ltd. (U.K.); Exponent Science and Technology Consulting (Hangzhou) Co. Ltd. (China).

PRINCIPAL DIVISIONS

Exponent Failure Analysis Associates; Exponent Health Sciences; Exponent Environmental; Exponent Food & Chemical.

PRINCIPAL COMPETITORS

National Technical Systems Inc.; Bureau Veritas; SGS SA.

FURTHER READING

Autry, Ret, "Failure Group," *Fortune,* October 8, 1990, p. 140.
Calbreath, Dean, "Failure Group Succeeding in Buyout," *San Francisco Business Times,* July 16, 1993, p. 3.
Carlsen, Clifford, "Firm Simulates Failure; Files Public Offering," *San Francisco Business Times,* July 9, 1990, p. 4.
Cook, Dan, "The Failure Group Inc.: An Innovative Blend of Idiosyncrasy, Convention," *California Business,* May 1991, p. 9.
"Exponent Announces Sale of BCS Wireless," *PR Newswire,* May 4, 2000, p. 3254.
"Exponent Appoints Michael Gaulke, Chairman & CEO," *PR Newswire,* May 29, 2007.
"Exponent, Inc. Opens Subsidiary in China," *PR Newswire,* July 18, 2005.
"The Failure Group, Inc. Changes Its Name to Exponent, Inc.," *PR Newswire,* March 6, 1998.
Lewis, Seth, "Failures, Name Change Breed Success for Menlo Park, Calif., Failure Analysts," *Knight-Ridder/Tribune Business News,* October 25, 2004.
Marcial, Gene G., "Exponent: A Rising Power in Consulting?" *Business Week,* April 9, 2007, p. 99.
Zasky, Jason, "Exponent: The Company That Failure Built," *Failure,* July 2000.

F.W. Webb Company

160 Middlesex Turnpike
Bedford, Massachusetts 01730
U.S.A.
Telephone: (781) 272-6600
Fax: (781) 275-3354
Web site: http://www.fwwebb.com

Private Company
Incorporated: 1900 as F.W. Webb Manufacturing
    Company
Employees: 1,400
Sales: $650 million (2007 est.)
NAIC: 421720 Plumbing and Heating Equipment and
    Supplies (Hydronics) Wholesalers; 421730 Warm
    Air Heating and Air-Conditioning Equipment and
    Supplies Wholesalers; 421740 Refrigeration Equip-
    ment and Supplies Wholesalers

■ ■ ■

F.W. Webb Company is the largest distributor of
plumbing, heating, cooling, and piping products in the
northeastern United States. The company carries approximately 100,000 products it distributes through 64
locations in seven states, using a more than 400,000-
square-foot distribution facility in Amherst, New
Hampshire, as its hub of operations. Family-owned and
-managed, F.W. Webb supplies plumbing, heating,
ventilation, air conditioning, refrigeration, pumps, and
fittings, among scores of other products, for industrial
and residential use. Through Webb Bio-Pharm, the

company supplies sanitary piping for pharmaceutical
and biotechnology customers.

ORIGINS

A fixture in the New England area for a century-and-a-
half, F.W. Webb achieved its dominance through
decades of expansion and acquisitions. The company
traces its origins to 1866, the year Stultz and Mansur
was founded in Boston. The company, a small brass
shop, became the city's first wholesaler of plumbing
fixtures.

The link that connected the brass shop in Boston
with the company that eventually became F.W. Webb
was tied in 1888, the year an industrialist from
Baltimore set his acquisitive sights on the business
founded by Stultz and Mansur. Henry McShane, owner
of The McShane Company, was a man of means, presiding over a large brass foundry with distribution operations in Washington, Philadelphia, and New York City.
His company was well known as a manufacturer of
church bells, bells whose peal still could be heard more
than a century later in belfries dotting the northeastern
United States.

FRANK WEBB TAKES CONTROL IN
1900

McShane added Boston to his operating territory with
the purchase of Stultz and Mansur. To manage the
operations in Boston, McShane selected his brother-in-
law, Frank Wooten Webb. McShane's death a year after
the acquisition, a passing that attracted a procession of

COMPANY PERSPECTIVES

The objective of the F. W. Webb Company is to grow our distribution business by constantly and consistently improving Customer Service. Through the research and implementation of better and improved methods of performing all facets of "delighting" the customer, we ensure our growth, profitability, and survival. Doing right by the customer once means we've earned the right to try a second time, and that's all it means. We must prove to that customer that we're better than the next guy every time out if we want to be the supplier of choice.

1,000 mourners through the streets of downtown Baltimore, gave Frank Webb his chance for advancement. In 1900, he purchased the Boston operations that he had managed and renamed it F.W. Webb Manufacturing Company.

Although Frank Webb's ownership term encompassed little more than a decade, his name would fly on the company's corporate banner for more than the ensuing century. F.W. Webb, the corporate title, not the man, would become familiar to generations of New Englanders. Frank Webb spent his time in charge of manufacturing brass fittings, faucets, and accessories. He also struck a deal with a pottery manufacturer to produce china and enameled iron plumbing fixtures that were sold under the F.W. Webb label.

POPE OWNERSHIP ERA BEGINNING IN 1933

After Frank Webb died in 1912, ownership of the company was held by a consortium of investors from Baltimore. Under new ownership, there were few changes at F.W. Webb. The company continued to manufacture the same types of products, limiting its operating territory to the confines of Boston. Sales began to decline as the Great Depression exacted its toll, but the cataclysmic financial conditions were not enough to dissuade Roger D. Pope from buying the company at a time when few individuals could entertain buying anything beyond basic necessities.

Pope acquired F.W. Webb in 1933 when he was 32 years old. Annual sales at the time of the acquisition had dipped below $350,000. His purchase of the company marked the beginning of constancy, ushering in a lengthy period of ownership and managerial stability at

F.W. Webb. More than seven decades later, the company continued to be owned by the Pope family, headed by Roger Pope's son, John D. Pope.

EXPANSION COMMENCING IN 1945

Once Roger Pope had acquired F.W. Webb, his ambitious nature had to be checked. Any plans for transforming the brass works into something larger had to be shelved, delayed until economic conditions improved. The wait was prolonged by the United States' entrance into World War II, but after a dozen years of biding his time, Pope found ideal market conditions greeting him in 1945. He moved quickly during the year, establishing distribution facilities in a handful of Massachusetts communities, extending F.W. Webb's reach into Fitchburg, Greenfield, Hyannis, Pittsfield, and Salem. He also crossed state lines for the first time, setting up offices in Nashua, New Hampshire, the first of many moves that would spread the company's business throughout New England.

Roger Pope died in 1962 after nearly 30 years of guiding F.W. Webb, leaving behind him a company with seven locations and annual sales exceeding $5 million. His son, John Pope, took command of the operations, marking the beginning of a leadership era that would stretch into the next century.

ACQUISITION CAMPAIGN

A lull in expansion activity characterized John Pope's first decade in charge, but the young executive would more than make up for the lack of physical growth by orchestrating impressive expansion in the decades to follow. F.W. Webb's acquisition campaign began in 1972, signaling the beginning of a 32-year period during which the company would acquire 28 companies with 34 locations. The result was a company whose annual revenue volume increased by a factor of 100 under John Pope's control.

F.W. Webb's acquisition campaign began with the purchase of Atlantic Pipe, a Boston-based company, and Crane Supply, a company with offices in Portland, Maine, and Springfield, Massachusetts. The company combined its external means of expansion with internal means, establishing its own facilities in Dover, New Hampshire, and Bangor, Maine, as it blossomed into a regional force. In 1978, when the company broke ground on a 60,000-square-foot distribution facility in Merrimack, New Hampshire, it entered Vermont for the first time by purchasing Shepard Supply, which operated in Barre, Rutland, and St. Johnsbury.

KEY DATES

1866: The establishment of a small brass shop in Boston represents the origins of F.W. Webb Co.

1888: The McShane Company acquires the Boston brass shop and appoints Frank W. Webb as its general manager.

1900: Frank Webb purchases the Boston brass shop and renames it F.W. Webb Manufacturing Company.

1933: Roger D. Pope acquires F.W. Webb.

1962: Roger Pope dies, leaving his son, John D. Pope, to take the reins of command.

1972: F.W. Webb embarks on an acquisition campaign.

1998: A three-year buying spree ends after the purchase of 13 companies.

2000: Webb Bio-Pharm is formed.

2003: The company begins constructing a new distribution center in Amherst, New Hampshire.

2006: F.W. Webb celebrates its 140th anniversary.

JACK HESTER JOINS COMPANY

As F.W. Webb marched across New England, Pope gained a valuable partner to help conduct the company's expansion drive. Jack Hester, a 1961 business graduate of Boston College, joined F.W. Webb in 1969 after spending the previous seven years working in the finance department of a General Motors division in Framingham, Massachusetts. Hester was hired as an office manager, earned a promotion to the position of treasurer in 1972, and after a decade managing F.W. Webb's finances, was named president in 1983. Hester and Pope would work alongside each other for the next two decades, spearheading the company's development into the largest wholesaler of its type in the Northeast.

F.W. Webb's acquisition campaign resumed during the second half of the 1980s. The company acquired four businesses during the period, adding six locations in Massachusetts, Maine, and Vermont. Internally, the company opened offices in New York, establishing branches in Albany, Plattsburgh, and Queensbury. An eight-year gap separated the company's last purchase in the 1980s from its first purchase in the 1990s, but once Pope and Hester acquired Boston-based Braman Dow in 1995 they went on a buying spree. Within three years, the pair purchased 13 companies, adding 14 locations in Massachusetts, Maine, New Hampshire, Rhode Island, New York, and Connecticut.

NEW DIVISIONS ADDED DURING LATE NINETIES

The acquisitions completed between 1995 and 1998 included several major transactions, giving F.W. Webb assets it used to form divisions. The acquisition of Kentrol, Inc., in 1998, was one such example, leading to the formation of the F.W. Webb division, Kentrol Process Control Solutions. Incorporated in 1982, Kentrol supplied control valve, flow, level, pressure, and temperature and analytical measurement equipment from facilities in Winslow, Maine; Warwick, Rhode Island; and Queensbury, New York. Another division was formed from the 1998 acquisition of Victor Manufacturing, a purchase that provided entry into the liquid propane and natural gas market. Victor Manufacturing was formed in 1935 to produce oil burners and oil space heaters. During the 1940s, as propane and natural gas use increased, the company discontinued its manufacturing operations and concentrated on distributing gas appliances and equipment. A third division, Sevco, Inc., was formed from the acquisition of a company with the same name in 1998. Incorporated in 1968, Sevco operated as a pressure relief valve assembly and repair facility.

F.W. WEBB IN THE 21ST CENTURY

After decades of steady expansion, F.W. Webb entered the 21st century exuding considerable strength. The company operated in 57 locations throughout New England and upstate New York, possessing 1.4 million square feet of distribution space and carrying 96,900 different products. The company was generating $329 million in revenue at the start of the century, having climbed to the top of its industry within its operating territory. Although Pope and Hester determined the company's strategy, they relied on the general managers of 31 full-service offices to help run the company. Each of the general managers reported to Pope's son, Jeffrey Pope, F.W. Webb's vice-president of operations, giving the company a decentralized managerial structure.

"We want to become our customers' single source for everything they need," Hester said in an October 2001 interview with the trade publication *Supply House Times*. To achieve Hester's goal, the company continuously expanded its capabilities. The formation of Webb Bio-Pharm, a division established in February 2000 to supply sanitary piping to pharmaceutical and biotechnology companies, was one example of the company's commitment to diversification. Nothing was more important, however, than the company's ability to move products from one location to another. At its core, F.W. Webb was a distributor, which meant its central distribution facility played a critical role in the company's success. In June 2003, the company took an important step toward ensuring its future success by announcing it was constructing a new primary distribution complex. Located on a 42-acre site in Amherst, New Hampshire, the facility was designed with 420,000 square feet of space and scheduled to be completed in the first half of 2004.

While construction was underway in Amherst, Pope focused his expansion efforts in Connecticut. "There's a bunch of people [in Connecticut]," Pope matter-of-factly noted in a November 3, 2003, interview with the *Waterbury Republican-American.* "They buy stuff. You can't sell stuff if there's nobody around to buy." Propelled by that simple observation, Pope ordered the purchase of Colonial Supply, a 30-year-old, family-owned distributor based in Waterbury, Connecticut, F.W. Webb's first acquisition in the Nutmeg State in five years. With plans to increase its volume of business fourfold in Connecticut, the company followed the purchase of Colonial Supply with the acquisition of New Haven Plumbing Supply, a 30,000-square-foot operation in New Haven, and the former Fordham Distributors building next to its existing facilities in Hartford.

F.W. Webb celebrated its 140th anniversary in 2006 as the premier competitor in its field. The company operated out of 64 locations in seven states, generating more than $500 million in annual revenue. Jeffrey Pope had taken on the duties of president by the time celebrations were underway, giving the company the energies of an eager, young executive to purse its lofty goal. F.W. Webb wanted to reach $1 billion in sales by 2011, an objective that would require the company to continue the acquisition campaign begun in 1972. After decades of demonstrating the ability to integrate smaller distributorships into its fold, the company chased its financial target with an air of confidence. Provided a sufficient number of acquisition opportunities existed, F.W. Webb, the most ambitious consolidator in the Northeast, stood poised to reach $1 billion in sales well before its 150th anniversary.

Jeffrey L. Covell

PRINCIPAL SUBSIDIARIES

Victor Manufacturing; Sevco, Inc.; Kentrol, Inc.

PRINCIPAL DIVISIONS

Webb Pump & Service; Kentrol Process Control Solutions; Sevco, Inc.; Fire Protection; Utilities Supply; Webb Bio-Pharm; Victor Manufacturing.

PRINCIPAL COMPETITORS

MSC Industrial Direct Co., Inc.; W.W. Grainger, Inc.; WESCO International, Inc.

FURTHER READING

"F.W. Webb Co.," *Supply House Times,* June 2003, p. 10.

"F.W. Webb Signs Distributor Agreement," *Air Conditioning, Heating & Refrigeration News,* August 21, 2006, p. 6.

"F.W. Webb to Supply York Products," *Snips,* October 2006, p. 94.

Hester, Jack, "Source ASA+ Is the Future," *Supply House Times,* November 2000, p. 4.

Olsztynksi, Jim, "Taking Care of Business," *Supply House Times,* October 2001, p. 42.

Petersen, Chris, "A Changing Legacy," *US Business Review,* February 2006, p. 12.

Smith, David A., "Plumbing, Ventilation Firm F.W. Webb Expands into Connecticut," *Waterbury Republican-American,* November 3, 2003.

Spoth, Tom, "F.W. Webb Is a Hit with Sox," *Sun,* February 8, 2006.

First Solar, Inc.

———————————■———————————

4050 East Cotton Center Boulevard, Building 6
Phoenix, Arizona 85040
U.S.A.
Telephone: (602) 414-9300
Fax: (602) 414-9400
Web site: http://www.firstsolar.com

Public Company
Incorporated: 2006
Employees: 1,462
Sales: $503.97 million (2007)
Stock Exchanges: NASDAQ
Ticker Symbol: FSLR
NAIC: 334413 Semiconductor and Related Device
   Manufacturing

■ ■ ■

First Solar, Inc., designs and manufactures solar modules using a proprietary thin-film technology that differs from traditional crystalline silicon modules. First Solar uses a thin layer of cadmium telluride semiconductor material as a coating to convert sunlight into electricity, which enables the company to use approximately 1 percent of the semiconductor material used by crystalline silicon module manufacturers. The result is one of the lowest manufacturing costs in the world, enabling the company to pursue its goal of offering solar electricity on a non-subsidized basis at a price equal to the cost of retail electricity. First Solar manufactures its solar panels in Perrysburg, Ohio, and in Frankfurt, Germany.

The company is constructing a third manufacturing facility in Malaysia.

THE GLASS GENIUS

First Solar's founder, the prolific inventor and industrialist Harold A. McMaster, found his calling at the age of six. After his father gave him a set of tools, McMaster treated the gift not as mere playthings, but as instruments to help his father run the tenant farm he and his family lived on in Deshler, Ohio. By age eight, he had used the tool set to build a collection of farm machinery. By age ten, McMaster had created a threshing machine capable of husking corn. By the time he was 12 years old, he had begun to build his own automobile motors.

McMaster's curiosity and skill earned him more than 100 patents during his life. He combined his flair for inventiveness, an aptitude that earned him a place in the Engineering and Science Hall of Fame, with an entrepreneurial zeal, excelling as both a technological pioneer and businessman. McMaster, one of 13 children from an impoverished family, was awarded a scholarship by Defiance College; later, he transferred to Ohio State University, and earned degrees in nuclear physics, astronomy, and mathematics in 1939. After working for Libbey-Owens-Ford, where he invented a rear-vision periscope for fighter aircraft, McMaster began his career as an entrepreneur.

While working for Libbey-Owens-Ford, McMaster was selected to manage the company's optical glass laboratory. Glass became his focus of scientific work, as

COMPANY PERSPECTIVES

First Solar is committed to improving the global environment and the health and safety of our employees, customers and communities. We are accomplishing this by: producing cost effective solar energy solutions that displace fossil fuels and other conventional energy solutions; managing our product life cycle—from raw material sourcing through end of life collection and recycling—in a perpetually renewable cycle that continually reduces hazardous air emissions and removes solid waste from the environment; and striving for continuous improvement in our environmental, health and safety management systems and in the environmental quality of our products, processes and services.

it was the focus of the community in which he lived. Toledo was known as the "Glass City," home to Owens-Illinois, Owens Corning, Libbey Glass, and Libbey-Owens-Ford, and McMaster became known as "The Glass Genius." His first company, formed in 1948, was named Permaglass, which became a leading supplier of glass plates for television sets before directing its energies toward the booming automobile industry. In 1969, McMaster merged the company with Guardian Industries, a union that created the third largest glass company in the world.

McMaster left Permaglass two years after the merger to start another glass business. In 1971, he collaborated with another Toledo inventor, Norman Nitschke, and formed Glasstech, Inc., basing the company in the Toledo suburb of Perrysburg, the future home of First Solar. With a handpicked research and development team, McMaster began pursuing a goal that had eluded glassmakers for 2,000 years, one discussed by the ancient Roman author Pliny the Elder. According to its molecular profile, glass was five times stronger than steel, but internal defects and irregularities that occurred during production limited its potential. McMaster, through Glasstech, wanted to unleash the potential of glass and set his sights on making the world's strongest and clearest tempered glass. Although the company struggled financially, the goal was achieved. More than 30 years after its founding, an estimated 80 percent of the world's automotive glass and 50 percent of its architectural glass was manufactured using Glasstech's machine.

MCMASTER'S FIRST SOLAR PANEL BUSINESS

While Glasstech was making its mark in the tempered glass market, McMaster embarked on another glass-related project. In 1984, he formed Glasstech Solar, a company dedicated to producing solar arrays. The company marked McMaster's first attempt at developing thin-film technology for solar panels, an approach that involved applying thin coatings over a special glass panel. Chemical coatings could change glass's color or its ability to pass light, which, combined with glass's quality of acting as an electrical insulator, provided two essential ingredients for making photovoltaic cells, the solar cells that changed sunlight directly into electricity. Traditional solar panels were made with silicon, but several alternative, thin-film strategies involved using different materials, such as copper indium gallium selenium (CIGS), cadmium telluride, or amorphous silicon. With Glasstech Solar, McMaster chose to use amorphous silicon.

FORMATION OF FIRST SOLAR'S PREDECESSOR: 1990

McMaster's first attempt at making inexpensive, commercial-scale solar panels foundered. After exhausting $12 million in funding, he abandoned Glasstech Solar and his amorphous silicon research, but he did not give up on his goal of using thin-film technology in the commercial-scale production of electricity. In 1990, McMaster raised $15 million to establish Solar Cells, Inc., First Solar's predecessor, a company that would use cadmium telluride instead of amorphous silicon to make its solar panels.

The formation of Solar Cells marked the beginning of a long and, often times, frustrating research and development phase. The goal of developing a technique to manufacture solar panels for large-scale use by electric utilities would require years of painstaking research and large amounts of capital. The process would test the perseverance of McMaster, his successors, and investors, one of whom included John Walton, heir to the Wal-Mart Stores fortune, who took a major stake in the project.

By 1993, a prototype production machine had been built. In 1997, a breakthrough year for Solar Cells, the company's research team realized great strides in the manufacturing technique it was developing, demonstrating the superiority of cadmium telluride thin-film technology over amorphous silicon techniques. The company was able to coat glass panels measuring two feet by four feet at the rate of one panel every 30 seconds, thoroughly besting its closest competitor, who

```
┌─────────────────────────────────────────┐
│                                           │
│             KEY DATES                     │
│              ───■───                      │
│                                           │
│  1990:  Harold A. McMaster forms Solar    │
│         Cells, Inc., First Solar's        │
│         predecessor.                      │
│  1999:  Solar Cells is reorganized as     │
│         First Solar, LLC, and begins      │
│         constructing a manufacturing      │
│         plant in Perrysburg, Ohio.        │
│  2002:  Commercial production at the      │
│         Perrysburg plant commences.       │
│  2003:  First Solar forms a German        │
│         subsidiary to aid its sales       │
│         efforts in Europe.                │
│  2006:  First Solar converts to public    │
│         ownership and records its first   │
│         annual profit.                    │
│  2007:  First Solar begins building a     │
│         manufacturing plant in Malaysia.  │
│                                           │
└─────────────────────────────────────────┘
```

needed six hours to coat a similarly sized panel. Improvements in Solar Cells' manufacturing capabilities promised to bring the cost of solar panel production close to $1 per watt, but, as the company frequently learned, expectations often fell short of actuality.

NEW OWNERSHIP IN 1999

A new era began for the company at the end of the decade. In 1999, Arizona-based True North Partners LLC (later renamed JWMA Partners LLC) acquired a controlling stake in the company and reorganized it as a limited liability company named First Solar, LLC. The year also marked a turning point in the company's research and development phase. Investors put up $16 million to help finance the construction of a manufacturing facility in Perrysburg that promised to usher in the commercial phase of the company's development. The announcement of the plant's construction triggered frenzied excitement, as First Solar revealed it was building the largest solar panel manufacturing facility in the world. Capacity was slated to be 100 megawatts annually, an amount equal to the total production of solar panels worldwide in 1999.

With its first profits tantalizingly close, First Solar's years of struggle appeared to be at an end. JWMA Partners' president, Michael J. Ahearn, assumed the duties of president and chief executive officer in August 2000, taking the helm as the company's moment of glory neared. Unfortunately for Ahearn and the rest of First Solar's staff, the company's ordeal was not over. Construction of the plant ran into difficulties, delaying the company's commercial debut. Further, Ahearn conceded First Solar had jumped too quickly into the construction of the facility before resolving problems with its proprietary manufacturing process.

FIRST SOLAR'S COMMERCIAL DEBUT IN 2002

Commercial production did not begin until 2002, nearly 20 years after McMaster had first delved into making solar panels and one year before his death at age 87. Production began at a lower rate than initially had been forecasted, but the discrepancy did little to dampen the exuberance in Perrysburg and among the small staff at the company's Arizona headquarters. First Solar was making 600 panels per week during the first part of the year with plans to manufacture as many as 1,000 per week by late summer. The company was expecting to generate $6 million in sales in 2002, a projected total to be collected by selling 50-watt, two foot by four foot, panels for $130 each.

Once commercial production commenced, First Solar began to enjoy itself, putting behind it the years of exhausting research and development. Although the company's solar panels produced electricity for $2.60 per watt, substantially higher than the $1 per watt needed to make solar energy competitive with other energy sources, there was an air of confidence exuded by the company, an attitude backed by rising financial figures posted by the company. In June 2003, the company broke ground on a $20 million expansion program at the Perrysburg facility. Concurrently, the company formed a new subsidiary, First Solar, GmbH, to support the needs of major solar product distributors and solar plant project developers in Germany, a primary market for the company.

First Solar's prospects brightened with each passing year as it made its first serious assault on the $7 billion market for solar panels. In May 2005, the company broke ground on a second, $74 million production facility in Perrysburg, a plant that was expected to be completed in 2007. The addition of the second plant would nearly triple capacity to roughly one million solar panels annually, enabling it to produce 75 megawatts of power. As construction of the new plant began, First Solar could celebrate McMaster's decision to rely on cadmium telluride to make solar panels. The price of silicon, the element used in the technology for 92 percent of the solar panels on the market, had nearly tripled during the previous two years, putting silicon-based manufacturers in dire straits.

INITIAL PUBLIC OFFERING IN 2006

While everything was working in First Solar's favor, Ahearn sought to convert the company's growing esteem into financial gain. In 2006, First Solar shed its status as a limited liability company and incorporated as First Solar, Inc. Next, in November, the company completed its initial public offering (IPO) of stock, selling 20 million shares at $20 per share. First Solar's public debut occurred at an ideal time, coinciding with an announcement that undoubtedly excited Wall Street. The company ended the year with its first annual profit, recording $4 million in net income from $135 million in sales, a 181 percent increase from the previous year's total.

Once First Solar turned the corner on profitability, it began to record fantastic financial growth, which, in turn, fueled explosive growth in the company's stock value. The company ended 2007, a year in which it broke ground on a manufacturing facility in Malaysia, with a staggering $158.3 million profit, more than it had generated in sales the previous year. Revenues soared to $504 million for the year, exponentially higher than the $3.2 million it had generated just four years earlier. The company's stock value leaped upward as a result, rising from its debut price of $20 per share to $228 per share by early 2008.

BRIGHT PROSPECTS AHEAD

As First Solar plotted its future course, it occupied an enviable position. The company was demonstrating stellar financial performance, confirming McMaster's conviction that cadmium telluride offered the best chance for solar panels to succeed commercially. Looking ahead, the company planned to focus its efforts on the U.S. market (most of its panels were being sold to customers in Germany, Spain, and other European countries). Ahearn wanted to begin targeting U.S. utilities in 2008 and beyond, telling financial analysts, "that's the next move for us," as quoted in the December 4, 2007, edition of the *Toledo Blade*. Toward that end, First Solar paid $34 million for Turner Renewable Energy, LLC, in November 2007, gaining a company skilled at constructing solar installations for U.S. customers. The acquisition also was part of First Solar's plans to expand beyond the production of solar panels into the design, construction, and operation of solar installations.

Jeffrey L. Covell

PRINCIPAL SUBSIDIARIES

First Solar GmbH (Germany); First Solar Holdings GmbH (Germany); First Solar Manufacturing GmbH (Germany); Minera Teloro S.A. de C.V. (Mexico); First Solar FE Holdings Pte. Ltd. (Singapore); First Solar Malaysia Sdn. Bhd.; First Solar Electric, LLC; FSE Blythe I. LLC.

PRINCIPAL COMPETITORS

Q-Cells AG; Sharp Corporation; Suntech Power Holding Co., Ltd.

FURTHER READING

Chavez, Jon, "First Solar Stock Leaps $57 a Share," *Toledo Blade*, November 9, 2007.

———, "First Solar Surges on Profit Report," *Toledo Blade*, February 14, 2008.

———, "Investors in First Solar Sunny," *Toledo Blade*, March 16, 2007.

"Company in Perrysburg Township, Ohio, Plans to Increase Solar Panel Production," *Toledo Blade*, April 26, 2002.

"First Solar Announces Closing of IPO and Exercise of Over-Allotment Option," *PrimeZone Media Network*, November 22, 2006.

"First Solar Announces Groundbreaking of Malaysian Plant," *PrimeZone Media Network*, April 20, 2007.

"First Solar Announces New Management Team," *Renewable Energy Today*, June 24, 2003, p. 1.

"First Solar Establishes New German Subsidiary," *Renewable Energy Today*, June 26, 2003, p. 1.

"First Solar Expands Manufacturing Plant in OH," *Renewable Energy Today*, June 6, 2003, p. 1.

"First Solar Inc. Orders Solar Simulators from Spire Corp. for German Manufacturing Facility," *Energy Resource*, August 10, 2006.

"First Solar LLC Breaks Ground on a Solar Panel Plant in Ohio," *EC&M Electrical Construction & Maintenance*, June 3, 2005.

"First Solar: Scorching Hot," *Business Week Online*, February 15, 2007.

"First Solar to Get $5 Million Loan to Expand Plant near Toledo," *Toledo Blade*, November 4, 2003.

"First Solar to Offer Public Stock, Possibly Monday," *Toledo Blade*, November 9, 2006.

"Interview with Pierre-Yves Le Borg, First Solar," *European Report*, October 9, 2007.

McKinnon, Julie M., "First Solar Posts 1st Profit in 20-Year History," *Toledo Blade*, February 14, 2007.

Pakulski, Gary T., "Analysts Give First Solar Edge in Race for Cost Efficiency," *Toledo Blade*, July 15, 2007.

———, "First Solar Prepares to Boost Output As Cost Crunch Hits Rivals," *Toledo Blade*, May 24, 2005.

———, "First Solar Stock Sale Garners $618M," *Toledo Blade*, August 11, 2007.

————, "First Solar Will Focus on U.S. Market," *Toledo Blade,* December 4, 2007.

————, "Governor's Visit Puts Focus on Toledo, Ohio, High-Tech Solar-Panel Plant," *Toledo Blade,* May 1, 2007.

————, "Wanted: First Solar Headquarters," *Toledo Blade,* July 10, 2007.

Vellequette, Larry P., "First Solar's Stellar Results Vault 2 Teams to Top Ranks," *Toledo Blade,* February 19, 2008.

for those of us who have a love/hate
relationship with our sexy shoes

Foot Petals L.L.C.

6615 East Pacific Coast Highway, Suite 150
Long Beach, California 90803
U.S.A.
Telephone: (562) 795-1700
Toll Free: (866) Tip-Toes (847-8637)
Fax: (562) 795-7700
Web site: http://www.footpetals.com

Private Company
Founded: 2002
Employees: 14
Sales: $9 million (2007 est.)
NAIC: 315999 Other Apparel Accessories and Other
Apparel Manufacturing

■ ■ ■

Foot Petals L.L.C. was inspired, not surprisingly, by sore feet. After 11 years in the fashion industry and more than double the time coping with foot pain, Tina Aldatz Norris fabricated a fashionable insole for women's shoes. Surviving her start-up years, Aldatz Norris took the line from foot cushions into accessories, gift sets, legwear, slippers, and men's shoe pads, with more ideas in the works. Sold in the United States and abroad, Foot Petals products have won the praise of red carpet walking celebrities and fashion and industry watchers alike.

PAINFUL BEGINNING

Born in Travers City, Indiana, in 1968, Tina Aldatz grew up in Orange County, California. A youthful encounter with the hot coals of a beach bonfire yielded months of painful walking and years of foot-related problems. A troubled home life led to other difficulties.

Aldatz dropped out of school at 15 years of age. Living with a family friend, she bagged groceries to pay her expenses. "The rent was simply to show me you have to work for things," she explained in *Forbes*. At 16, she earned a high school equivalency diploma.

Along with a willingness to work hard, Aldatz had a propensity for fashion and business. In 1987 she started recycling Levi's jeans and exporting them to Europe and Japan. A few years later, in 1990, she opened a Long Beach vintage clothing store, drawing in some celebrity customers.

In 1991 she joined Victoria's Secret, as assistant manager of a mall store in Costa Mesa, California. A promotion sent her to the flagship Manhattan store. Staying in New York, Aldatz moved to BCBG Max Azria, a manufacturer and retailer of young women's apparel, in 1998. As director of special events and merchandising, she put a lot of mileage on her fashionable feet. Seeking relief from the pain, she tried to adapt orthopedic insoles for her heels and pumps. The bulky blue drugstore offering clashed with her fashion sense, but the only other option was the unacceptable skirt and sneaker combo seen on the street. Her solution was less than perfect, though. "I'd slip off my stilettos on a date and the guy would notice all this blue gel and padding. It was embarrassing," she revealed in *Forbes*.

IDEA BLOSSOMING: 2001–02

Having made her way back to California, Aldatz began working for an Internet start-up. When the operation folded in 2001, she started an all-out search for insole materials, intent on coming up with a better fix for her foot problem. A high performance urethane, produced by Rogers Corp., a Connecticut-based company, and used in automobile and electronics manufacturing, fit the bill. Poron mitigated odor, bacteria, and moisture, provided for some shock absorption, and came in a variety of colors.

Four credit cards and a 401(k) funded Aldatz's travel expenses and product samples. A friend's father-in-law provided additional backing of $10,000. Armando DuPont, owner of a land survey firm, later invested $250,000 for a 50 percent stake in the endeavor, according to *Forbes*.

Knowledgeable about potential pitfalls of foreign production from her retailing days, Aldatz decided on domestic manufacturing. The foot cushion would cost $1 to produce and retail for $7. Attractive colors, pleasing shapes, and flowery packaging would differentiate the cushion from others on the market. Aldatz distributed 200 pairs of the ball-of-the-foot insoles at an apparel show in May 2001. The move generated $100,000 in orders for the Tip Toes, according to *Forbes*.

A *Self* magazine "A" rating also gave the product a significant boost. Unfortunately, a retail slowdown at the end of 2001 resulted in order cancellations. Aldatz countered by selling to smaller stores and agreeing to ac-

cept unsold merchandise. The bet paid off; only a fraction of the insoles were returned. In a year, she would have 300 accounts and $630,000 in sales.

In 2002, Aldatz established Foot Petals L.L.C. She moved the business out of her home and into a Culver City office. Aldatz also had begun promoting a second product, Heavenly Heelz. Intended to stop slippage and protect the heel from blisters, the insole could also be worn at the top of the shoe to improve fit.

PIVOTAL MOMENT

Foot Petals sold its products primarily to small businesses, such as boutiques, shoe stores, or sock shops. Consequently, small orders were the norm. Thus, when Stein Mart requested 30,000 pairs of Tip Toes, Aldatz had reason to celebrate. The retailer's $75,000 order was her largest to date.

However, the victory dance was short-lived. Not only did she owe $150,000 to her manufacturer, Remington Products, she had a sizable percentage of customers behind on their payments to her. "In a stiffly worded letter Remington threatened to halt shipments. 'I was in a panic,'" Aldatz recounted in *Forbes*.

Aldatz jumped on a plane to Ohio. In a deal with the manufacturer, she gave up a fifth of her 50 percent stake in the company, according to *Forbes*. Her lone investor sold Remington most of his shares, forgoing a profit. The new owner de-emphasized brand building and told Aldatz to pull the plug on delinquent retailers, even those with celebrity clientele.

Foot Petals turned to Pennaco, the legwear division of Danskin Inc., to broaden its distribution. "We cater to specialty stores, but we feel it's time to expand our brand," Aldatz explained in an August 2003 *WWD* article. She said, at the time, Foot Petal products were carried in 1,500 stores.

Pennaco expected Foot Petals to pull in roughly a half million dollars in sales during the first year of the department store push, according to *WWD*. The alliance with Pennaco also included Foot Petals' entry into legwear.

Sales to high-end department stores, meanwhile, had been impeded by free footpad giveaways, Murphy Barret explained in the *Forbes* article. Yet as a bare-legged fashion trend took hold, the retailers looked for other products to replace falling hosiery sales. Customer response to a trial run, in late 2003, sold Nordstrom on Foot Petals.

DESIGNING WOMAN

Aldatz and Foot Petals put product development into high gear. In 2003, Strappy Strips, thin strips for high heel and sandal straps, and Petal Plusheez, a spa-like sock, were introduced. The company also had begun selling gift sets, a "petal pouch" travel bag, and toe rings, *WWD* reported. New prints and colors for Tip Toes and Heavenly Heelz livened the established offerings.

Previously participating in gift and bridal shows, Foot Petals debuted at the 2004 WSA (World Shoe Association) convention. The product line had found acceptance among hosiery buyers, but not so with the shoe industry, according to *Footwear News.*

The company's premier product, Tip Toes, had cushioned more than one million pair of feet. *Footwear News* said about 2,500 stores, in 12 countries, carried Foot Petal products. "I see Foot Petals becoming a household name, like the next Band-Aid," Aldatz told the publication in September. "I plan to infiltrate the mass markets; I want to sell in stores like Target."

New products added in 2004 included Killer Kushionz, insoles for strappy, backless, or open-toe shoes; Sole Stopperz; and a men's line, Sole Kings. The three-quarter-length Jack and full-length King were fabricated from 100 percent Poron, featured tapered edges, and were affixed with 3M adhesive.

The men's insole received the stamp of approval by the American Podiatric Medical Association (APMA), joining Foot Petals' best-selling products Tip Toes, Heavenly Heelz, and Strappy Strips. The APMA endorsement paved the way for the sale of those insoles through chiropractor and podiatrist offices.

Half of the company's business was through department stores, 30 percent from specialty and branded boutiques, and 20 percent from its web site, Sarah Taylor reported for *Footwear News.* Stores ranged from JCPenney to Saks Fifth Avenue.

Those retailers could expect some new Foot Petal products for their consideration. A shoe care line was already in the works, and a designer shoe line was shopping for a licensing or partnership arrangement, according to Taylor.

STAYING ON HER TOES

As the company celebrated a year of strong growth, in 2004, Foot Petals also had to keep an eye on increased competition. The Kayser-Roth entry, Foot Cloud, was "indistinguishable from Foot Petals' Tip Toes," according to *Forbes.* For her part, Aldatz intended to stay focused on bringing customers innovative products. Aldatz entered into some related coursework in 2005. The study led toward certification as a Pedorthist, someone who fits and modifies footwear and orthotics per medical prescription. On a more personal note, Aldatz married during 2005, becoming Tina Aldatz Norris. The nuptials inspired a new product targeting brides.

The company, relocated to West Los Angeles, was flying high. Foot Petals had "cornered the market on designer in-shoe cushions," the *St. Louis Post-Dispatch* declared in July 2006. Foot Petals had successfully tapped into consumers' desire to continue their heel wearing ways, despite warnings to the contrary.

"It's not a normal position to bear weight. The foot is not meant to do that," Christian Wunderlich, a podiatrist, told the *St. Louis Post-Dispatch.* However, women continued to wear painful and potentially bone damaging footwear, creating a wealth of opportunity. Perennial drugstore entry Dr. Scholl's wanted to cash in. Schering-Plough had begun selling For Her, a fashion-oriented foot pad containing massaging gel. In addition, Summer Soles, a suede insole to pad the foot and reduce slippage, entered the market through the e-tail channel.

BEST FOOT FORWARD: 2007–08

Undaunted, the company moved to a larger Long Beach office in 2007 and also set up shop on the East Coast, in New Jersey. In addition to earning fashion-related accolades during the year, Foot Petals landed spots on the *Entrepreneur* and *Inc.* lists of fastest-growing companies.

In December 2007, a deal was struck with online shoe retailer Zappos to have Foot Petals pads built into their shoes. The Foot Petals logo would gain added exposure, as the Zappos-branded shoes rolled out in the spring of 2008.

For 2007, the company recorded $1.9 million in pretax income on $9 million in sales. This amounted to increases over the prior year of 53 percent and 70 percent, respectively, according to *Forbes.*

The number of U.S. retailers carrying Foot Petals exceeded 5,000, according to the company's web site. Dillard's was among them. With Nordstrom prepared to sell Foot Petals' lotions, soaps, and deodorants, the founder envisioned entry into cosmetic stores. However, "Aldatz-Norris is realistic about her prospects as a small player fighting bigger companies with more clout in mainstream stores. She wants to sell. 'The right company could take this brand farther than I can. Plus, I have a million ideas where this one came from.' Her price: $20 million," according to *Forbes*.

Kathleen Peippo

PRINCIPAL COMPETITORS

Dr. Scholl's.

FURTHER READING

"Back with a Style Vengeance," *Footwear News,* February 12, 2004, p. 12.

Barret, Victoria Murphy, "She's Got Sole," *Forbes,* January 28, 2008, pp. 58–59.

Bass, Debra D., "The Time Has Come for Padded High Heels," *St. Louis Post-Dispatch,* July 20, 2006, p. F3.

Kletter, Melanie, "Bring in the New," *WWD,* August 11, 2003, p. 10.

"New Petals," *Women's Wear Daily,* May 6, 2002.

Taylor, Sarah, "Cushy Job," *Footwear News,* September 20, 2004, p. 16.

Force Protection Inc.

9801 Highway 78, Building No. 1
Ladson, South Carolina 29456
U.S.A.
Telephone: (843) 740-7015
Fax: (843) 329-0380
Web site: http://www.forceprotection.net

Public Company
Incorporated: 1996 as Boulder Capital Opportunities III,
    Inc.
Employees: 1,000
Sales: $196.01 million (2006)
Stock Exchanges: NASDAQ
Ticker Symbol: FRPT
NAIC: 423110 Automobile and Other Motor Vehicle
    Merchant Wholesalers

■■■

Force Protection Inc. is a manufacturer of heavy armored vehicles designed to protect soldiers from mines and other battlefield dangers. Customers include all branches of the U.S. military as well as allied foreign governments such as the United Kingdom and Iraq. Leading products include the massive Buffalo, typically assigned to minesweeping duty, and the Cheetah, a lighter, more general-purpose vehicle. Before 2004, the company was known as Sonic Jet Performance Inc. Once a maker of high-performance watercraft, it acquired Technical Solutions Group and its armored vehicle business after the September 11, 2001, terrorist attacks on the United States (9/11). Its mine-resistant ambush-protected (MRAP) vehicles became very sought after during the war in Iraq due to their success in dealing with roadside bombs. Calls to bring this type of vehicle into more general purpose roles promised much larger orders to come. Force Protection pioneered the MRAP category in the United States but it has had to share the expanding market with a number of larger military contractors.

FROM THE MOUNTAINS TO THE SEA

The company that eventually became known as Force Protection, Inc., was formed by Colorado consultant and real estate broker Robert Soehngen. Originally called Boulder Capital Opportunities III, Inc., it was incorporated in Colorado in November 1996 and listed shares publicly soon after.

The company was renamed Sonic Jet Performance, Inc., in 1998 after it acquired the high performance watercraft business of Alex Mardikian. It made some of the fastest vessels on the waters, capable of speeds in the vicinity of 60 knots, intended for police and emergency workers.

This operation was based in Huntington Beach, California, but farmed out fiberglass fabrication to Chinese contractors. Within a couple of years the growing company unsuccessfully attempted to add a site in Florida. Although sales were nearly $1 million by 1999, the company was losing money at an increasing rate. A subsequent bid to make speedboats for the luxury market floundered in a slowing economy. Sonic Jet went through a succession of CEOs around the turn of the millennium as it struggled with steep fluctuations in its share price.

TECHNICAL SOLUTIONS GROUP

With little hope for a rebound in pleasure boats in the post-9/11 environment, the company began shopping around for defense and government contractors. It bought Technical Solutions Group (TSG), a Charleston, South Carolina, armored vehicle manufacturer, in June 2002, making it a wholly owned subsidiary (later renamed Force Protection Industries, Inc.).

Garth Barrett formed TSG in San Diego, California, in 1996 to build South African–style mine-protected vehicles. Barrett had previously led commando units in Rhodesia and South Africa before joining anti-mining specialist Mechem (Pty.) Ltd. TSG paid fees to Mechem and South Africa's Council for Scientific and Industrial Research for exclusive rights to the technology used in its Buffalo, Cougar, and Tempest models.

The vehicles were built atop the drivetrains and frames of commercially available trucks, their custom bodies armored with steel and composite plates. One of the most striking features of their design was the wedge shape of the hull, which directed the impact of explosions away from the occupants.

Originally consigned to minefield duty, the company's six-wheel-drive Buffalo was a massive beast indeed, weighing in at 24 tons (compared to up to five tons for armored Humvees). It was fitted with a remotely operated arm for unearthing and disabling mines.

The company had a handful of other designs. One of the more popular was the Cougar. Available in 4x4 and 6x6 versions, it weighed in at a relatively svelte 13 to 19 tons and could carry a dozen or more troops. The Tempest favored by U.K. forces was a heavier version of the Cougar.

TSG relocated to South Carolina's Charleston Naval Shipyard in 1998. It moved into a former General Electric jet engine plant in nearby Ladson a few years later. Revenues tripled to $6 million in 2003 as defense-related orders began to pour in. The company ended the year with about 40 employees. The tiny company was struggling to fill orders for even a dozen or two vehicles, and also struggling to make money on them.

AN ANSWER TO IEDS

Massive mine-protected vehicles did not figure heavily into the Rumsfeld Doctrine of a fast and trim fighting force such as the one that so rapidly overcame Saddam Hussein's army. However, in the occupation that followed, the U.S. military's trucks and Humvees proved susceptible to improvised explosive devices (IEDs), usually made by wiring a cell phone or other trigger to an artillery shell. Although crude, IEDs could toss five-ton Hummers in the air like toys, and soon were producing casualty counts in the hundreds.

Force Protection's vehicles were originally pressed into service seeking out and destroying IEDs. The company had the market nearly all to itself, as far as U.S. manufacturing capability was concerned (a couple of domestic defense contractors did produce mine-protected vehicles through overseas units). Capacity was Force Protection's chief constraint.

Sonic Jet was renamed Force Protection Inc. in 2003 to reflect its new specialty. It traded its boat business for shares in Rockwell Power Systems, Inc., later Challenger Powerboats, Inc. TSG's revenues were $6.2 million in 2003 and grew to $10.3 million in 2004, when the company posted a net loss of $12 million. At this time, it was taking the company up to five weeks to produce a single Buffalo.

The company had swiftly increased its workforce to 250 employees by the end of 2005 and was still hiring at a frantic pace. Revenues were $49.7 million (as restated) for the year and the company had a loss of $14.4 million. The Colorado corporation Force Protection, Inc., had been replaced by a new Nevada corporation of the same name in January 2005. The subsidiary TSG was renamed Force Protection Industries, Inc., later in the year.

By 2006 revenues were $196 million and the company was beginning to show a profit, $18.2 million

KEY DATES

1996: Garth Barrett forms Technical Solutions Group (TSG) in California to build South African–style mine-protected vehicles; Boulder Capital Opportunities III, Inc., is created.

1998: TSG moves to Charleston, South Carolina; Boulder Capital Opportunities is renamed Sonic Jet Performance, Inc.

1999: Sonic Jet revenues approach $1 million.

2002: Sonic Jet acquires TSG.

2003: Sonic Jet is renamed Force Protection Inc.

2006: Revenues approach $200 million as Force Protection begins to post a profit.

2007: Force Protection sets up additional plant in Roxboro, North Carolina, to meet rising demand and acquires R&D center in Edgefield, South Carolina.

for the year. The most incredible statistic was the success rate of its products in the field. Its vehicles had by then been involved in more than 1,000 explosions in Iraq, yet none had resulted in a fatality.

After trading over-the-counter, the company's shares were listed on the NASDAQ in January 2007. Force Protection was expecting to more than quadruple annual revenues in 2007 to $875 million.

A NEW SCALE OF MAGNITUDE

The success of mine-resistant ambush-protected (MRAP) vehicles prompted calls to expand their use beyond specialized duties such as minesweeping. There was talk of using smaller varieties as a replacement for the Humvee, the Army's workhorse. This would represent a new scale of magnitude, with potential orders totaling in the tens of thousands of units. To handle such an increase, Force Protection entered a partnership with General Dynamics Land Systems, Inc., called Force Dynamics, LLC.

While Force Protection had pioneered the MRAP concept in the United States, it was suddenly faced with competition from a host of much larger rivals, including Armor Holdings (owned by British defense conglomerate BAE Systems plc), Oshkosh Corporation, Navistar International Corp. (through its International Military & Government unit), and Force Protection's own partner General Dynamics. General Dynamics and Textron Marine & Land Systems were making these

vehicles overseas in South Africa and Germany. While Force Protection did not have the name recognition of some of these giant defense contractors, it was getting some exposure via Hollywood. Its towering Buffalo model made an appearance as a villain in the mechanistic sci-fi flick *Transformers*.

The company continued to expand its production capacity as fast as it could. In 2007 it established an operation in a 435,000-square-foot former automotive components plant in Roxboro, North Carolina, to meet rising demand for the Cheetah, the lightweight of the family at eight tons. It also added a research facility in Edgefield, South Carolina, during the year.

There was change at the top in this phase of Force Protection's growth. In January 2008 Gordon McGilton retired as CEO after a couple of years with the company. He was succeeded by Michael Moody. The company was also getting a new chief operating officer and chief financial officer.

LOOKING AHEAD

While Force Protection's MRAPs appeared to have mastered the IED challenge, there was a new generation of threats on the horizon: explosively formed projectiles (EFPs). Force Protection responded by designing a supplemental armor kit.

Frederick C. Ingram

PRINCIPAL SUBSIDIARIES

Force Protection Industries, Inc.; Force Protection Technologies, Inc.

PRINCIPAL COMPETITORS

Navistar International Corp.; Armor Holdings Inc.; General Dynamics Land Systems, Inc.; Textron Marine & Land Systems; Oshkosh Corporation; Krauss-Maffei Wegmann & Co. KG.

FURTHER READING

Axe, David, "Hand-Built Armored Vehicles Save Lives," *Military.com,* November 27, 2006.

Buettner, Michael, "Ladson Company Carries Soldiers Through Combat," *Charleston (S.C.) Post & Courier,* April 12, 2004.

"CEO Interview: Albert Mardikian—Sonic Jet Performance Inc. (SJET)," *Wall Street Transcript Digest,* July 9, 2001.

Cole, August, "Troop-Truck Supplier Confronts Own Battles—Force Protection Sees Shares Slump As Dominance Falls," *Wall Street Journal,* August 31, 2007, p. C5.

Dreazen, Yochi J., and August Cole, "How a Safer Iraq Endangered One Firm; Force Protection Geared Up to Build Armored Trucks; New Orders Will Soon Halt," *Wall Street Journal,* February 6, 2008, p. B1.

Eisler, Peter, "The Truck the Pentagon Wants and the Firm That Makes It," *USA Today,* August 1, 2007.

Eule, Alexander, "This War Horse Looks Like a Winner," *Barron's,* August 27, 2007, p. 51.

"Force Protection Shuffles Management; Armored Vehicle Maker Force Protection Hires New Managers Amid Accounting Woes," *CNNMoney.com,* March 3, 2008.

Grant, Greg, "An Answer to IEDs," *Defense News,* September 12, 2005.

Hull, Peter, "Make Way for One Big, Bad Movie Star," *Charleston (S.C.) Post & Courier,* July 10, 2007, p. B7.

———, "Pentagon Orders 358 Cougars: Force Protection Gets $379M Contract, Loses Ground to Rivals," *Charleston (S. C.) Post & Courier,* December 20, 2007, p. B7.

Johnson, Jessica, "Wars in Middle East Lead to Record Year for Armored-Vehicle Maker," *Charleston (S.C.) Post & Courier,* March 23, 2007.

Knap, Chris, "Huntington Beach, Calif., Jet-Ski Firm Has Shaky Start," *California,* April 18, 2000.

Parker, Jim, "Sonic Jet's Sales Benefit from Purchase of Company," *Charleston (S.C.) Post & Courier,* November 21, 2002, p. B10.

Phillips, Noelle, "Force Protection Expands to N.C.: Armored-Vehicle Manufacturer Might Still Proceed with Pee Dee," *Columbia (S.C.) State,* July 14, 2007.

Smith, Bruce, "Three Years On, Hundreds Make Mine-Protected Vehicles," *Associated Press,* June 3, 2006.

Smith, W. Thomas Jr., "Buffalo Roams the Battlefield to Protect Soldiers from Mines," *Washington Times,* August 29, 2005.

"Sonic Jet Signs Letter of Intent to Acquire Mine-Protected Vehicle Maker TSG," *Defense Daily,* May 31, 2002.

Stock, Kyle, "Ladson Company Snares $490M Marine Contract," *Charleston (S.C.) Post & Courier,* April 25, 2007, p. B11.

West, William F., "Community's Spirits Soar at Opening," *Durham (N.C.) Herald-Sun,* December 1, 2007.

G&K Holding S.A.

Avenida Rui Barbosa 3450
São José dos Pinhais, Paraná 83005-260
Brazil
Telephone: (55 41) 3381-7000
Fax: (55 41) 3381-7001
Web site: http://www.boticario.com.br

Private Company
Incorporated: 2006
Employees: 950
Sales: BRL 780 million ($357.8 million) (2006)
NAIC: 325620 Toilet Preparation Manufacturing; 446120 Cosmetics, Beauty Supplies, and Perfume Stores; 533110 Lessors of Nonfinancial Intangible Assets (Except Copyrighted Works); 551112 Offices of Other Holding Companies

■ ■ ■

G&K Holding S.A. is the holding company for the enterprises that manufacture, commercialize, and distribute products, chiefly cosmetics and fragrances, sold in O Boticário stores and that administer the franchising of such stores. G&K is the world's largest franchiser of cosmetics stores and has blanketed Brazil with over 2,400 O Boticário outlets. The company has a much smaller presence abroad—it is in 20 other countries—chiefly through points of sale in larger stores but also in its own O Boticário retail outlets and kiosks.

AT HOME AND ABROAD: 1977–89

O Boticário ("The Apothecary") was founded in 1977 by Miguel Gellert Krigsner. The son of Holocaust survivors, Krigsner was born in Bolivia but became a citizen of Brazil, where he studied biochemistry and became a pharmacist. He opened a pharmacy in Curitaba, the capital of the state of Paraná, in collaboration with a university colleague according to one account (or two dermatologists, according to another). They invested $3,000 in the start-up. This was not the usual drugstore but a user friendly space with carpets, couches, coffee, and magazines for the customers to enjoy while they waited for their prescriptions to be filled. A second store opened in 1979 in a tiny space in Curitaba's airport terminal. The business flourished not by filling prescriptions but from O Boticário's own line of cosmetics, especially its perfume, Acqua Fresca.

Over the next 15 years, O Boticário developed a wide range of proprietary cosmetics made from natural materials, most of them grown for the company as specialty crops. These included avocado, cinnamon, ginseng, mallow, marine algae, mint, sweet almond, and wheat germ. The ingredients were used in O Boticário's lines of toilet water, skin care items, fragranced body and bath goods, shampoos, and tanning and sun block products for women; fragrances and grooming products for men; and toiletries and toilet water for children.

These products could not be distributed and marketed through O Boticário's own resources. The key to the company's success was selling the company's brands through franchising of retail outlets. The first franchised outlet made its appearance in 1980. During the next five years, the number of franchised stores reached 500. In 1986, O Boticário made its first appearance outside Brazil, in a Lisbon shopping center. By midsummer 1989, there were six franchised stores in Portugal. The company was planning to open a laboratory and a local manufacturing facility in the country for further expansion. It also had a franchised outlet in a shopping center in Bergen, Norway, and was planning to open a second in Oslo.

O Boticário also had established franchise stores in two of Brazil's neighboring countries: Bolivia and Paraguay, and one in a Miami shopping center, which it had opened in order to conduct test marketing in the United States. Krigsner said that of the 84 products being sold abroad, deodorant-colognes were the most popular, with perfumes, soaps, and shampoos next, and, after that, a line of skin care items.

There were no less than 1,100 O Boticário franchised outlets in Brazil by this time—so many that Krigsner, president of the company, had put a halt on further expansion in the home country. His plan was to consolidate O Boticário's gains by upgrading the outlets, in order to preserve the brand name and image. The company was establishing training courses for thousands of personnel so that there would be a common sales approach. It also formed partnerships with universities and research centers for the development of products in the marketplace. Dozens, eventually hundreds, of new products were offered each year to a fickle public.

RESTRUCTURING AND RENEWAL: 1990–2002

By the end of 1991, the number of O Boticário outlets in Brazil had fallen to about 900; later, the number dropped to 800. International expansion, on the other hand, was booming, with franchised outlets having opened in Great Britain, the Netherlands, and Chile. The first British store made its debut in 1990 in Glasgow as a temporary test outlet. The second opened in London's Canary Wharf in 1991, with a full 320-item range of products due the next spring.

The internationalization of O Boticário proved a thorny road, however. In Portugal, where the initial effort was made, the company thought little adjustment would be needed because people spoke the same language as in Brazil. In fact, however, Brazilian advertising was not always comprehensible in Portugal. Moreover, Portuguese tastes turned out to be European in character: shoppers were unsettled by the tropical perfume essences and bright makeup colors favored by Brazilians. Franchisees complained that the company was not providing assistance and did not understand local problems.

Within Brazil, O Boticário made a major change in its way of doing business in the late 1990s. The company dismissed 24 of its 27 distributors, took on the job itself, and began monitoring its franchisees, training staff in sales methods. During an arduous process of change in which company managers visited each store periodically, the various outlets adopted a common stock of items and common labor and accounting practices. O Boticário stopped filling prescriptions to concentrate its focus on health and beauty items. The sales counters of the stores were removed and replaced with self-service product displays that allowed customers to make their own choices. A Fidelity Card program was introduced to reward loyal customers. As a result of these initiatives, sales rose dramatically. Franchisees not bringing in healthy profits or unwilling to adjust to the chain's new profile were dropped.

O Boticário established a foundation in 1990 to support studies and projects to preserve the environment. It commissioned hundreds of research and education projects and established, in 1994, a nature reserve on 4,239 acres off the northern coast of Paraná. This reserve, declared a Natural Heritage Site in 1999, was intended to protect an area of rain forest. A second reserve, Serrado Tombador, was established in 2007. The company also pledged 1 percent of its net income to social-responsibility programs.

By 2001, after being named best company in its field the previous year by the Brazilian business magazine *Exame,* O Boticário had 1,900 points of sale, linked to headquarters by a radio communications system. Approximately 450 items were available, divided into perfumes (for which O Boticário was still best known), face and body lotions, hair care, deodorants, and makeup. The company had doubled the size of its factory, near Curitiba, and it was turning out 50 million units a year. By 2002 O Boticário was the world's leading cosmetics store franchiser. The combined sales volume of its outlets had reached $430 million the previous year. Also that year, the company entered Mexico for the first time.

KEY DATES

1977: O Boticário is founded by Miguel Gellert Krigsner.

1980: The company begins franchising its retail outlets.

1986: O Boticário first appears outside Brazil, in a Lisbon shopping center.

1989: The number of O Boticário franchised outlets in Brazil has reached 1,100.

1991: The number of such outlets has fallen to 900, as the company upgrades its image.

1996: O Boticário begins a restructuring that includes self-service product displays in the stores.

2002: The company has become the world's leading franchiser of cosmetics stores.

2004: First U.S. store exclusively devoted to O Boticário products opens.

2006: O Boticário is chosen International Retailer of the Year.

2007: A new store design emphasizes soft lighting, warm colors, and changes in display.

CORPORATE AND STORE CHANGES: 2004–07

By the fall of 2004 there were 70 units in seven countries outside Brazil, including 50 in Portugal and a few in Mexico, Bolivia, Paraguay, Peru, and Uruguay. The first store in the United States exclusively devoted to O Boticário products opened in Newark, New Jersey (a city with a large Brazilian population), in December 2004. By early 2006 a second O Boticário store had opened in a Rochester, New York, shopping mall, and there were about 50 retailers authorized to sell the company's products in New York, New Jersey, and Pennsylvania.

O Boticário also had 438 sales counters in Japanese department stores and a number of department store kiosks in Mexico, Uruguay, Angola, Mozambique, Saudi Arabia, and the United Arab Emirates as well. The concept of establishing points of sale (within larger stores) abroad was an attractive one for O Boticário, which was distributing its products in more than 1,200 such locations, as well as 61 stores and 17 kiosks, in 20 countries in 2007, including Australia, South Africa, and Egypt. Even so, sales volume abroad was minuscule compared to the amount spent in O Boticário's 2,240 outlets in 1,415 Brazilian communities.

The company was continuing to focus on internationalization because it considered the home market to be close to saturation. It was still having a hard time, however, presenting its products to countries and peoples very different in culture and habits. Sales abroad were comprising only about 1 percent of the total.

In the United States, O Boticário received an award in 2006 from the National Retail Foundation as International Retailer of the Year. The company offered 600 stockkeeping units for men, women, and children, all under its own brand. It also had begun fielding a satellite based network linking its stores with headquarters. This network enabled O Boticário to beam audio, video, and IP multicasts for product launches, advertisements, and management communications with staff. Net sales for O Boticário and its franchised outlets reached about $1 billion in 2005. The Fidelity Card program now had over 3.2 million people registered.

O Boticário introduced a new design for its stores in 2007. It featured what the company called a "sensorial experience," with lighting to establish colors at the warm end of the spectrum and a wave effect ceiling for a soft look. Products were no longer to be displayed by brand but sorted into three sections: Basic Care in front (soaps, oil, deodorants, and shampoos); Transform in the largest, central area (cosmetics and fragrances); and Prepare in the back (skin and sun care). The company also changed its logo and its slogan, which became "You can be what you want."

For a new line of cosmetics aimed at teenagers, O Boticário market researchers recruited 21 girls in the São Paulo metropolitan area between the ages of 12 and 19 and escorted them around town rather than assembling them in a focus group. They attended "fun" events such as an MTV program, a surfing class, and a fashion show sponsored by a boutique but also were put to work evaluating the 16 items of the new Cores line. The girls selected the names for three items, defined the color tones of the makeup items and the aromas used, and rejected the glittery packaging as "tacky." They also suggested smaller packaging that could be fit into a purse.

In 2006 O Boticário changed its corporate structure, establishing G&K Holding to take in several subsidiaries. The "K" stood for Krigsner and the "G" for Artur Grynbaum, the vice-president and Krigsner's brother-in-law. Before then, manufacturing was by Botica Comercial Farmacêutica Ltda., distribution and administration by Cálamo Distribuidora de Produtos de Beleza Ltda., and logistics by Embralog Ltda., enterprises that were under the holding company O Boticário Franchising S.A. Early in the year, the company sold a shopping center it bought in 2000 and a convention center it acquired in 2004, both poor performers, for about $70 million.

In December 2006, a fund of the group GP Investimentos became the first outsider investor within the private company. For an investment of BRL 50 million (about $23 million), the group received 2.4 percent of the shares and a seat on the board of directors.

Robert Halasz

PRINCIPAL SUBSIDIARIES

Botica Comercial Farmacêutica S.A.; Cálamo Distribuidora de Produtos de Beleza S.A.; Embralog Ltda.; O Boticário Franchising S.A.

PRINCIPAL DIVISIONS

Commercial; Franchises; Industrial; Logistics.

PRINCIPAL COMPETITORS

Avon Cosméticos Ltda.; Natura Cosméticos S.A.

FURTHER READING

Alexander, Antoinette, "O Boticário Resonates with Ethnic Consumers," *Drug Store News/DSN Retailing Today,* April 24, 2006, p. S4.

"Boticário: A New Sensorial Experience," *ICN/International Cosmetics News,* June 1, 2007.

"Brazilian Beauty Migrates to America," *Drug Store News/DSN Retailing Today,* April 24, 2006, p. S14.

"Brazil's Best Opens in Britain," *Cosmetics International,* December 15, 1991, p. 4.

"Brazil's O Boticario Rolls Out to International Markets," *Cosmetics International,* August 15, 1989, p. 7.

Brookman, Faye, "Brazil's O Boticario on the Rise," *WWD/Women's Wear Daily,* October 3, 2003, p. 13.

Fonseca, Olga, "Franquiciamania!" *AméricaEconomía,* May 2, 2002, pp. 20–21.

Fontes, Laura, "Equilíbrio entre expansáo e solidez," *Exame Melhores e Majores,* July 2001, pp. 188, 190.

Kepp, Michael, "Best Face Forward," *Latin Trade,* June 2005, p. 25.

Mano, Cristiane, "Uma indústria boa de varejo," *Exame,* March 29, 2006, p. 58.

Mautone, Silvana, "Adolescentes que mandam," *Exame,* May 23, 2007, pp. 128–29.

Naiditch, Suzana, "Vinte e um anos de erros," *Exame,* October 10, 2007, pp. 70–71.

"O Boticário muda estrutura e facilita entrada de investidores," *Valor Econômico,* April 3, 2007.

Santos, Cristiane Martins, "O Boticário's Formula for Success," *Global Cosmetic Industry,* September 2004, pp. 24–26.

Toscano, Joseph, "O What a Feeling!" *Soap & Cosmetics,* May 2000, p. S25.

Glu Mobile Inc.

1800 Gateway Drive, 2nd Floor
San Mateo, California 94404
U.S.A.
Telephone: (650) 571-1550
Fax: (650) 571-5698
Web site: http://www.glu.com

Public Company
Incorporated: 2001 as Cyent Studios, Inc.
Employees: 200
Sales: $46.2 million (2006)
Stock Exchanges: NASDAQ
Ticker Symbol: GLUU
NAIC: 511210 Software Publishers; 541511 Custom Computer Programming Services

■ ■ ■

Glu Mobile Inc. is a developer of games designed to be played on mobile phones. The company sells more than 100 original and branded titles through more than 150 wireless carriers and distributers throughout the world. Glu Mobile's product offerings include software titles such as "Deer Hunter," "Sonic the Hedgehog," "Battleship," "Hoyle Solitaire Pro," "Diner Dash," and "Who Wants to Be a Millionaire?" Glu Mobile derives slightly more than half its annual sales from business overseas. Domestically, the majority of the company's business is conducted through Verizon Wireless, AT&T Wireless, and Sprint Nextel. Glu Mobile, based in San Mateo, California, operates offices in England, Hong Kong, France, Germany, and Brazil.

THE WORK OF SCOTT ORR

Glu Mobile represented the efforts of a gaming industry veteran testing his skills in a new branch of the industry. Scott Orr had little else to prove in the industry mainstream when he founded Glu Mobile's predecessor. In the market for games developed to play on consoles and personal computers, he was regarded as a titan. "A monster in the game business," *Game Developer* wrote of Orr in its April 2003 issue, referring to him as "a bona fide hit-making machine," whose commercial success racked up "nearly $2 billion in sales over the course of his 20-year career."

Orr's early experience in the video-game industry perhaps best equipped him to tackle the challenges presented by mobile gaming. He started in the early 1980s when he founded a video-game publishing company that developed games for the Atari VCS console (later rebranded as the Atari 2600), and IBM computers. The games he developed were well before three-dimensional graphics and a host of technological developments would put the games of the 1980s to shame in terms of their visual appeal. With Glu-Mobile, Orr would have to forget nearly all the technological skills he had honed for the previous two decades. Mobile gaming demanded a return to the early days of video-game development.

Few other game developers could point to careers as successful as Orr's career. When another, much larger video-game developer, Activision, purchased his company, Orr took a job at another game developer, Electronic Arts, joining the company in 1990. At Electronic Arts, Orr became a recognized force in the

COMPANY PERSPECTIVES

We believe that improving quality and greater availability of mobile games are increasing end-user awareness of and demand for mobile games. At the same time, carriers and branded content owners are focusing on a small group of publishers that have the ability to produce high-quality mobile games consistently and port them rapidly and cost effectively to a wide variety of handsets. Additionally, branded content owners are seeking publishers that have the ability to distribute games globally through relationships with most or all of the major carriers. We believe we have created the requisite development and porting technology and have achieved the requisite scale to be in this group. We also believe that leveraging our carrier and content owner relationships will allow us to grow our revenues without corresponding percentage growth in our infrastructure and operating costs.

industry. He developed the first Madden football game in 1990, a game that drew upon the appeal of the former Oakland Raider's coach, John Madden. The game spawned a revenue-generating franchise that would fill Electronic Arts' coffers for years to come. While presiding over the development of the Madden franchise, Orr also developed other moneymakers for Electronic Arts, spearheading the creation of "NHL Hockey," "NASCAR Racing," and "Andretti Racing."

Within Electronic Arts, Orr was a resource to be used wisely. His developmental efforts, as *Game Developer* had calculated, had helped Electronic Arts collect nearly $2 billion in sales. Unfortunately, and unwittingly, for Electronic Arts, the company used one of its prized resources unwisely, planting the seed that would prompt Orr to leave Electronic Arts. Electronic Arts selected Orr to work for its online gaming business, EA.com, asking him to develop sports games that Internet users could use to play against each other online, a branch of the gaming industry known as "multiplayer."

FORMATION OF SORRENT: 2001

When the Internet sector imploded at the turn of the millennium, Electronic Arts drastically reduced its involvement in online gaming, but Orr had developed a desire to see online gaming succeed. "I started thinking about wireless gaming during the latter half of 2000,"

Orr said in an article published in the April 2003 issue of *Game Developer*. He resigned as an Electronic Arts vice-president and began pursuing his own interests. Orr secured funding from New Enterprise Associates and Sienna Ventures and started his own company in April 2001, forming Cyent Studios, Inc., a San Mateo, California-based developer of games for mobile phones. Cyent Studios changed its name to Sorrent, Inc., before the end of the year.

By setting his sights on the nascent mobile gaming market, Orr took on numerous challenges. Much of his knowledge about advanced gaming technology had little applicability in his new business. Instead of trying to create experiences that would promote hours, if not days, of game play, the objective for mobile gaming developers was to occupy a player's interest for five to ten minutes, 15 minutes at the most. Further, the technological limitations demanded a new approach to game development, one that harkened back to Orr's early days developing games for the Atari console. Mobile phones had small screens, low power, and slow transmission speeds, transferring data at rates that demanded simple games. "These are challenges that, from our perspective, require a fresh look," Orr said in a March 31, 2003, interview with *RCR Wireless News*. "How do we create an immersible experience that is fun to play and easy to play?" he asked.

As Orr and his team of designers began developing games, they primarily used BREW and Java technology. BREW, the acronym for Binary Runtime Environment for Wireless, was an application development platform created by Qualcomm for mobile phones. Java, developed by Sun Microsystems, was application software designed for use in a cross-platform environment.

During its first two years in business, Sorrent recorded substantial progress, developing a portfolio of content that could be transmitted to wireless users. The company signed agreements with wireless carriers such as Nextel Communications, AT&T Wireless Service, Cingular Wireless, Verizon Wireless, and Sprint PCS. The company's 19-person staff, 14 of whom were engineers, developed a collection of games that included a racing title, a puzzle game using billiard balls, and basketball and football games for FoxSports.com.

NEW CEO, L. GREG BALLARD: 2003

Several important announcements were made toward the end of 2003. In September, Orr announced he was giving up his duties as chief executive officer to serve as

KEY DATES

2001: Scott Orr resigns as vice-president of Electronic Arts to found Sorrent (the company was known as Cyent Studios initially), a mobile gaming company.
2003: L. Greg Ballard is hired as president and chief executive officer.
2004: Sorrent acquires Macrospace Limited.
2005: Sorrent changes its name to Glu Mobile Inc.
2006: Glu Mobile acquires iFone Holdings Limited.
2007: Glu Mobile completes its initial public offering of stock.

Sorrent's chairman. He was replaced by an industry veteran named L. Greg Ballard. Before joining Sorrent, Ballard had served as a senior executive for numerous companies, including Digital Pictures, Inc., and Capcom Entertainment, Inc., each a video-game developer, Warner Custom Music Corp., a division of Time Warner, Inc., and 3dfx Interactive, Inc., a manufacturer of advanced graphics chips. During the years immediately preceding his arrival at Sorrent, Ballard served as chief executive officer of MyFamily.com, a subscription-based Internet service, from 2000 to 2001. After spending nearly a year working as a consultant, Ballard joined SONICblue Incorporated, a manufacturer of ReplayTV digital video recorders and Rio digital music players. Ballard spent one year at SONICblue, leaving as the company's chief executive officer in April 2003 to work as a consultant for Virgin USA, Inc., for the five months leading up to his appointment as Sorrent's president and chief executive officer.

At roughly the same time Ballard joined the company, Sorrent announced it had expanded its deal with Fox Sports Interactive Media. The agreement called for Sorrent to produce 12 new Fox Sports games in the coming year. The company also announced the introduction of its gaming character service, which it had been promising for months. Called Mobile Persona, the service enabled players to register a gaming character on Sorrent's web site and use the same character in a variety of Sorrent games. Gamers, playing through their mobile avatar, could record high scores and accumulate experience points and skills that could be transferred to other games. The company planned to release ten Mobile Persona games by the end of 2004.

JOINING FORCES, SORRENT AND MACROSPACE: 2004

When the end of 2004 arrived, there was much bigger news than the deployment of Mobile Persona to discuss. In December, Sorrent announced the acquisition of Macrospace Limited, an award-wining mobile games publisher based in London, England. Macrospace's products and services were available through more than 90 mobile carriers and 70 service providers, reaching more than 700 million wireless subscribers. The company had developed and published more than 40 mobile games, including "Fatal Force: Earth Assault," winner of the Mobile Consumer Choice award for the best game of 2004. The combination of Macrospace and Sorrent created a global force in the wireless gaming segment, one hailed by Ballard in a statement published in the December 1, 2004, issue of *AsiaPulse News.* "Macrospace is one of the most highly regarded mobile gaming companies in Europe and is a true culture fit with Sorrent," he said. "Their exceptional management team, innovative portfolio of games, and extraordinary technology and distribution significantly enhances our position in Europe and will be a substantial asset to Sorrent as we seek to become the leading mobile entertainment publisher in the world."

Ballard wasted little time before adding to the business of the new, much larger company. In January 2005, he reached an agreement with Twentieth Century Fox, one of the world's largest producers and distributors of motion pictures. Under the terms of the agreement, Sorrent was named as the exclusive publisher of mobile games for selected feature films. The deal was slated to launch with the release of a computer-animated feature film, *Robots,* and the concurrent release of a mobile game and a console title.

SORRENT BECOMES GLU MOBILE IN 2005

At the annual BREW Conference in June 2005, Ballard used the opening night of the event to make an important announcement. Attendees were the first to learn that Sorrent would be renamed Glu Mobile Inc. to give a single, worldwide identity to the combined assets of Sorrent and Macrospace. "We realized very quickly that we had a great opportunity to combine the two companies to create a global publisher and bring it all under one brand," a company executive explained in the June 6, 2005, issue of *RCR Wireless News.* "The reality is that neither Sorrent nor Macrospace was a great consumer-facing name; neither company was really seen as a global franchise."

During the months following the name change, Ballard busied himself by forging partnerships that expanded the company's portfolio of products. Setting out, he had more than 100 original and branded titles, including market winners such as "DRIV3R" and "Deer Hunter," as well as an array of ringtones and custom screens. To this collection, he added mobile games for Hoyle-branded products. The multiyear, multigame agreement was signed in March 2006 with Encore Software, an interactive publisher that operated as a subsidiary of Navarre Corporation. The deal for the Hoyle brand, one of the stable of brands owned by the United States Playing Card Co., was launched with the release of "Hoyle 6-in-1 Solitaire Pro." At roughly the same time the Hoyle deal was brokered, Ballard reached an agreement with Hasbro Properties Group, the intellectual property development arm of Hasbro, to develop a mobile Transformers game to coincide with the release of a feature film of the same name that was scheduled for release in July 2007. One month after negotiating the two deals, Ballard announced the acquisition of Manchester, England-based iFone Holdings Limited, a wireless entertainment publisher with titles such as "Lemmings," "Atari Classics," and "Monopoly."

GLU MOBILE'S PUBLIC DEBUT IN 2007

Investors were given their first chance to take part in the expansion being orchestrated by Ballard when Glu Mobile filed for an initial public offering (IPO) of stock in early 2007. The company had relationships with more than 150 wireless carriers and other distributors by the time it announced it intended to go public, conducting business with carriers in North America, Latin America, Europe, and the Asia Pacific region. According to figures submitted to the U.S. Securities and Exchange Commission, Glu Mobile generated $25.6 million in revenue in 2005 (a 265 percent increase from the previous year's total), deriving 58 percent of its revenues from domestic business. During the first nine months of 2006, the last period of financial results reported before its IPO, the company generated $31.8 million, a substantial increase from the $18.8 million collected during the first nine months of 2005. Glu Mobile completed its IPO in March 2007, debuting at $11.50 per share. The company raised $84 million from the stock offering.

In the months after its conversion to public ownership, the company continued to add to its collection of entertainment content, a focus it likely would maintain for years to come. Glu Mobile expanded its relationship with Sega Europe Ltd. in September 2007, gaining the rights to offer up to ten mobile versions of Sega games to customers in Europe, the Middle East, Africa,

Australia, and New Zealand. In November 2007, the company signed an agreement with Indiagames to distribute Glu Mobile games, wallpapers, and ringtones in India, providing access to a massive wireless market. Further deals were expected in the years ahead, as Glu Mobile pursued its goal of becoming the largest mobile games developer in the world.

Jeffrey L. Covell

PRINCIPAL SUBSIDIARIES

Macrospace Limited; iFone Holdings Limited.

PRINCIPAL COMPETITORS

Digital Chocolate, Inc.; Electronic Arts Inc.; Gameloft S.A.; Namco Bandai Holdings Inc.; THQ Inc.

FURTHER READING

Calica, Ben, "Sorrent: The Big Orr Dips into Mobile Gaming," *Game Developer,* April 2003, p. S2.

Dano, Mike, "Sorrent's Orr Aims to Connect Wireless Users with Games," *RCR Wireless News,* March 31, 2003, p. 14.

"Fox Sports Gets Mobile with Sorrent," *Online Reporter,* September 11, 2004.

"Gamers, Now Investors, Surf Wireless Waves," *IPO Reporter,* March 11, 2002.

Glasner, Joanna, "Glu Mobile Debuts As IPO Boom Sticks," *Private Equity Week,* March 26, 2007, p. 1.

"Glu Mobile Acquires UK-Based Mobile Entertainment Publisher iFone," *Wireless News,* April 4, 2006.

"Glu Mobile, Encore Software Ink Pact to Create Hoyle Games for Mobiles," *Wireless News,* March 29, 2006.

"Hasbro and Glu Mobile Sign Global Licensing Deal for 'Transformers' Franchise," *Wireless News,* March 26, 2006.

"Indiagames and Glu Mobile Partner to Bring Glu Mobile Content to India," *Wireless News,* November 24, 2007.

"Sorrent and Macrospace Unite As Glu Mobile," *AsiaPulse News,* June 2, 2005.

"Sorrent Buys Macrospace; New Company Will Reach 800m Users," *Online Reporter,* December 4, 2004, p. 5.

"Sorrent, European Mobile Publisher Macrospace Join Forces," *AsiaPulse News,* December 1, 2004.

"Sorrent Expands in Asia, Europe and North America," *AsiaPulse News,* July 30, 2004.

"Sorrent Names New Chief, Expands Offerings," *RCR Wireless News,* October 20, 2003, p. 22.

"Twentieth Century Fox and Sorrent Announce Global Partnership," *AsiaPulse News,* January 25, 2005.

Wolverton, Troy, "Glu Mobile Strengthens Ties with Sega," *San Jose Mercury News,* September 5, 2007.

Guangzhou R&F Properties Co., Ltd.

10–15/F R and F Properties Bldg.
19 Jiaochangdong Rd.
Guangzhou, 510055
Hong Kong
Telephone: (+852 020) 8730 2328
Fax: (+852 020) 8732 9029
Web site: http://www.rfchina.com

Public Company
Incorporated: 1994
Sales: RMB 10.19 billion ($1.35 billion) (2006)
Stock Exchanges: Hong Kong
Ticker Symbol: 027777
NAIC: 233110 Land Subdivision; 233220 Multi-Family Housing Construction; 233320 Commercial and Institutional Building Construction

■ ■ ■

Guangzhou R&F Properties Co., Ltd., is one of China's largest and fastest-growing real estate developers, and one of only a few capable of operating on a national level. The Guangzhou-based, Hong Kong–listed company is also one of the mainland's most integrated property development groups, handling all phases from land selection and acquisition, to project design and development, construction and sales, and financing and post-sales services. R&F has focused on the middle- to high-end residential sector, which has seen a surge in demand since 2000. The company has developed a number of prestige residential properties in Guangzhou, Beijing, Tianjin, Xian, Chongqing, and Hainan. R&F also develops mixed-use and nonresidential properties, including office buildings and shopping centers. As part of a shift from high turnover developments to long term investment properties, the company has also entered the hotel sector, launching construction of two hotels in partnership with the Hyatt and Ritz Carlton companies in 2007. R&F has been listed on the Hong Kong Stock Exchange since 2005. Cofounders Li Sze Lim and Zhang Li are chairman and co-chairman and CEO, respectively. In 2006, R&F posted revenues of RMB 10.19 billion ($1.35 billion).

GUANGZHOU PROPERTY GROUP FOUNDED IN 1994

Guangzhou R&F Properties was founded in 1994 by Li Sze Lim and Zhang Li. Li had earned a bachelor's degree in mathematics from the Chinese University of Hong Kong in 1978, before launching a career as a merchant. The early development of Guangzhou as part of China's economic reform policies led Li to take an interest in the real estate market. In 1993, Li founded his own business. Zhang too entered the real estate market in 1993, after having gained experience in the construction industry, before becoming the general manager of Guangzhou's Meihua Town Hotel.

The development of Guangzhou as a free trade zone led to a leap in demand for new residential housing. In 1994 Li and Zhang decided to join forces, and founded a new real estate company, Tianli Properties. Soon after, Zhang and Li recognized the potential of launching their own property development operations as well. This led to the creation of Guangzhou R&F Properties.

From the start, the company targeted the residential market with large-scale apartment complexes. The company began developing its first property, positioned toward the higher end of the growing middle- and upper-middle-class housing sector. By 1995, the first project, R&F Court, built on a former factory site, had been completed. The project was a success, selling out quickly. The success of R&F Court encouraged the company to focus on converting Guangzhou's many industrial areas into residential complexes.

The company's next large-scale project came in 1996, when it launched the R&F Plaza development, located in the East and West areas of Guangzhou. The company continued to pick up steam into the late 1990s. In 1998, for example, the company launched three major residential properties—R&F Peninsula Garden, R&F West Garden, and R&F Fortune Garden—in the same year.

By the beginning of the 2000s, R&F was a major developer in the Guangzhou region. The company launched a number of new major projects in 2000 and 2001, with such names as R&F Aristocratic House, R&F American Dream Island, and R&F Sunny Sky Court. The completion of these projects transformed R&F into Guangzhou's largest property development group in the early 2000s. In 2001, the company reincorporated as a joint stock limited company as it prepared for its next growth phase.

ENTERING BEIJING IN 2002

One particularity of the Chinese real estate market was that each of the country's major cities functioned as distinct markets, each following separate development cycles. Expansion as a national, rather than local or regional, developer, held a great deal of appeal, providing developers with a means of diversifying their operations. In this way, national property developers found a degree of protection from downturns in a particular local or regional market.

Having established itself as a major developer in Guangzhou, R&F set out to build itself into a national group. For this, the company targeted an entry into the Beijing market in 2002. Like Guangzhou, Beijing offered a midlevel residential market with strong growth potential. At the same time, the northern location of Beijing provided a diversification for the company away from its southern Guangzhou base. Beijing offered strong growth perspectives in advance of the Olympic Games to be held there in 2008. At the same time, its proximity to two other major city markets, Tianjing and Shenyang, appealed to R&F's future growth goals.

R&F began building up a strong land bank in the Beijing area. The group's first effort was a success, as it outbid its rivals to win the right to develop a site near the city's central business district, one of the first major sites put up for tender by the Beijing government. For this R&F agreed to pay RMB 3.18 billion, or roughly RMB 2,200 per square meter. The company launched development of a new residential complex, dubbed R&F City, that year.

Upon completion, the site was projected to have a total gross floor area of 1.56 million square feet, accommodating nearly 7,500 residential apartments, as well as two office towers and a 133,000-square-meter shopping center. R&F's gamble quickly appeared to pay off, and by 2004 the group had achieved presales revenues of RMB 2.35 billion. An encouraging sign for the company was the steady rise in the site's value, which jumped from RMB 6,800 per square meter during Phase 1 of the project, to more than RMB 10,500 per square meter at Phase 3.

This success allowed R&F instant access to the top ranks of the Beijing property development market, as the company continued to build up both its brand name and its land bank. By 2004, the company had launched three additional projects in Beijing, including Xinran Court, R&F Another City, and R&F Edinburgh Apartments. R&F had not neglected its core Guangzhou market, however, and in 2003 began construction of a new flagship project there, the R&F Peach Garden. That project was slated for completion by 2008.

PUBLIC OFFERING IN 2005

R&F quickly spread its success to Tianjin, where it won the bid to develop a major site in Nankai District. The complex under development was named Tianjin R&F Properties City. From Tianjin, R&F next turned to Xi'an City, paying RMB 436 million in October 2005 to acquire a nearly 45-hectare site in the city's Chang'an district. This project, called Xi'an R&F City, was expected to serve as the company's flagship for its future

KEY DATES

1994: Li Sze Lim and Zhang Li found real estate company Tianli Properties in Guangzhou, China.

1995: Enters property development market, forming Guangzhou R&F Properties, and completes first major project, R&F Court.

2001: Reincorporates as joint stock limited company in preparation for entry into Beijing market.

2005: R&F goes public on Hong Kong Stock Exchange.

2007: Completes vertical integration with acquisition of Guangzhou Tianli Construction Company.

growth in the Xi'an region. In the meantime, R&F had successfully completed a public offering on the Hong Kong Stock Exchange that helped raise founders Li and Zhang to the top ranks of the newly wealthy in China.

The public offering allowed R&F to expand its geographic focus again. In 2006, the company entered the Chongqing market, launching development of its Chongqing R&F City, a massive project covering three sites with a total ground surface of 2.4 million square meters, and a total floor space of 6.8 million square feet. R&F also made preparations to enter Hainan, acquiring its first sites there.

By then, R&F had also begun a shift in its operating strategy. Throughout its first decade of growth, the company had focused especially on the residential sector. This focus was accompanied by a concentration on short-term, high-turnover projects. Into the middle of the first decade of the 2000s, R&F increasingly began to develop an interest in the commercial property development sector. At the same time, the company adopted a new strategy of developing long-term property investment interests.

The company began implementing its new strategy in 2004, when it began developing two new luxury hotels in Guangzhou in partnership with the Hyatt and Ritz Carlton brands. The company also added eight more sites in Guangzhou destined for the development of office and commercial projects.

With a landbank of nearly 18 million square meters, primarily in Guangzhou and Beijing, but also in Tianjin, Chongqing, Hainan, and Xi'an, R&F stood as

one of China's leading property development groups. The company was also one of the market's most integrated, with operations spanning most of the development spectrum, from land selection and acquisition, to project design and development, as well as sales and post-sales services. In 2007, the company completed its vertical integration, when it acquired Guangzhou Tianli Construction, a major construction group in south China. In this way, R&F gained control of the last major phase, and one of the most important, in its property development. Guangzhou R&F Properties by then had become one of the leaders of China's property development boom in the 2000s.

M. L. Cohen

PRINCIPAL SUBSIDIARIES

Beijing Honggao Ltd. (75%); Ease Glory International Limited (British Virgin Islands); East Global Enterprises Limited (British Virgin Islands); Easycross International Limited (Hong Kong); Link City Limited (British Virgin Islands); Longxi Shunjing Ltd.; Project Charter Enterprises Limited (Hong Kong); R&F Properties (HK) Company Limited (Hong Kong); R&F Properties (British Virgin Islands) Co., Ltd. (British Virgin Islands); Smart Keen International Limited (British Virgin Islands).

PRINCIPAL COMPETITORS

Wheelock Properties Limited; Synergis Holdings Limited; China Properties Group Ltd.; Pan Hong Property Group Limited; Zhong An Real Estate Limited; Agile Property Holdings Limited; China Aoyuan Property Group Limited; Greentown China Holdings Limited; Shimao Property Holdings Limited; Country Garden Holdings Company Limited.

FURTHER READING

"Guangzhou R&F Properties IPO Set to Reach $250m Goal," *Euroweek,* July 8, 2005, p. 23.

"In the Mix," *Contract,* September 1, 2007.

"R&F Properties Plans Purchase of Constructor," *Alestron,* June 11, 2007.

"R&F Properties Targets 25.9% Net Profit Margin for 2008," *Alestron,* September 10, 2007.

"Shunned by Retail Buyers, Guangzhou R&F Debuts Strongly," *Euroweek,* July 15, 2005, p. 19.

"Sun Hung Kai Properties to Set up JV," *Alestron,* December 13, 2007.

Headlam Group plc

P.O. Box 1
Gorsey Ln.
Coleshill
Birmingham, B46 1LW
United Kingdom
Telephone: (+44 01675) 433000
Fax: (+44 01675) 433030
Web site: http://www.headlam.com

Public Company
Incorporated: 1992
Employees: 2,062
Sales: £509.89 million ($1.03 billion) (2006)
Stock Exchanges: London
Ticker Symbol: HEAD
NAIC: 423220 Home Furnishing Merchant Wholesalers; 551112 Offices of Other Holding Companies

■ ■ ■

Headlam Group plc is the United Kingdom's leading distributor of floor coverings, and one of the largest such firms in Europe. The Birmingham-based company supplies and distributes a full range of floor coverings, including commercial and residential carpet, vinyl floor coverings, floor tiles, and wood and laminated wood flooring. Residential carpet sales generate more than 50 percent of Headlam's total revenues, while commercial flooring represents 27 percent of revenues. Altogether, Headlam sells approximately 50 brand names. The company's U.K. operations are grouped into five primary categories: Regional Multiproduct; National Multiproduct; Commercial Specialist; Residential Specialist; and Regional Commercial. Together these operations represent more than 35 businesses throughout the United Kingdom. Headlam Group's customer base consists primarily of smaller retailers and independent contractors.

Headlam led the consolidation of the flooring distribution sector in the United Kingdom in the 1990s and early 2000s, and has built up a market share of more than 50 percent. The company is also the leading distributor in France, through subsidiary La Maison du Sol and its two warehouses and 19 regional branches. The company's Belcolor subsidiary is a leading distributor in eastern Switzerland. In the Netherlands, the company is the fourth largest flooring distributor through Lethem-Vergeer. The United Kingdom remains the group's primary market, however, generating more than 85 percent of its sales of £510 million ($1.03 billion) in 2006. Headlam is led by CEO Tony Brewer and is listed on the London Stock Exchange.

ROOTS IN THE FADING U.K. FOOTWEAR INDUSTRY

While Headlam could legitimately trace its origins back to the late 19th century, the company's modern operations stem from Headlam's difficulties at the start of the 1990s. Headlam originated as a manufacturer of footwear founded by Robert Coggins in 1887. That company produced high-end sports footwear, ranging from soccer and rugby shoes to hockey and ice skates, ski boots, and golf shoes. Following Coggins' death, the company incorporated as R. Coggins & Sons in 1908.

COMPANY PERSPECTIVES

Headlam has a clear and focused strategy based on the creation of a diverse and autonomous structure. The group operates through 47 separate businesses in the UK and a further three in Continental Europe.

A key factor contributing to the group's success is the individuality of experienced management teams who are responsible for the market presence, development and ultimate profitability of their businesses.

Each business is supported by the commitment to continued investment in people, product, facilities and IT. This commitment has provided the basis for the group's growth and subsequent performance enabling it to develop into Europe's leading floor-covering distributor.

Over the next 50 years, Coggins extended its footwear range to include military footwear, which became its largest operation during the years of World War II. The company also added more casual footwear for the general market.

Coggins merged with noted British footwear factor and distributor Headlam and Sims Limited in 1948. Headlam had been founded by W. Headlam and G. Sims in 1932 before formally incorporating in 1935. The company, which operated a showroom in London, handled a wide range of shoes, including sports shoes. Headlam and Sims targeted principally the midrange to high-end segments. By the end of World War II, Headlam and Sims had grown into a national supplier to the country's department stores and specialist retailers.

Headlam and Sims' factoring business brought it into contact with Coggins, and through the 1940s the two companies developed a close working relationship. By the end of the war, Coggins and Headlam had launched a successful sports shoe collaboration with the specialized sports brand of Simlam. In 1948, this collaboration led the two companies to join forces, creating Headlam, Sims & Coggins Limited. The company went public that same year. The Coggins operation remained the group's manufacturing wing, and by the 1980s had focused its production on the sports and industrial footwear categories. The group's distribution business, regrouped as Simlam, similarly focused on the sports and leisure markets.

The 1980s, however, marked the beginning of the long decline of the British footwear industry. This was in large part due to the increasing levels of lower-priced imported shoes that entered the United Kingdom during the decade. At the same time, the sports footwear market was undergoing a sea change, as a rising number of heavily marketed brands, such as Nike, adidas, Puma, and Reebok, came to dominate the sports shoe market. Changing consumer tastes, particularly the massive adoption of sport shoes as everyday footwear, added new pressures for traditional footwear producers. By the early 1990s, the appearance of still less expensive Asian imported footwear sounded the death knell for the British footwear sector.

NEW STRATEGIES FOR THE NINETIES

Headlam attempted to adapt to these developments. The company launched its own retail operation in the early 1980s, called Centre Sports Ltd. That operation proved a loss maker. By 1984, Headlam had been forced to shut down its retail branch. Instead, in 1988, Headlam attempted to branch out into the textiles sector, acquiring Phipps Faire Limited. That company specialized in the distribution of synthetic and other materials used in footwear production.

By the beginning of the 1990s, Phipps had come to represent more than 60 percent of Headlam's operating profit. Yet Phipps was also under heavy pressure from the rising tide of imported Asian shoes. At the same time, Headlam was forced to reorient the R. Coggins operation, which came to specialize in the industrial footwear market.

These efforts, however, proved too little too late for Headlam. By the early 1990s, the company's management began looking for a new strategy. This came in early 1991, when Headlam's board resigned in favor of a new board of directors and management team led by Graham Waldron, Ian Kirkham, and Tony Brewer. The new team, which also acquired stakes in the company, then refocused Headlam entirely on the distribution market, shedding its production business.

The arrival of Graham Waldron played an especially important role in Headlam's new direction. Waldron had founded Midland Carpet Distributors (MCD) in 1977. Under Waldron's leadership, that company grew into the leading distributor of carpets in the United Kingdom within a decade. Waldron sold that company in 1987, then traveled to the United States, where he helped turn around LD Brinkman Inc., a flooring distributor that had slipped into losses in that decade. That company was subsequently taken over by Coloroll.

Returning to the United Kingdom, Waldron set out to build a new distribution giant, once again targeting

```
┌─────────────────────────────────────────┐
│                                         │
│           KEY DATES                     │
│              ─■─                        │
│                                         │
│  1991:  Headlam, with roots tracing back to 1887,  │
│         takes over temporary management of Hickson │
│         Flooring Distributors (HFD) as part of     │
│         transformation into distribution group.    │
│  1993:  Company completes acquisition of most      │
│         profitable parts of HFD, then launches sector │
│         consolidation strategy.                    │
│  1996:  First international expansion occurs with   │
│         acquisition of Lethem-Vergeer.             │
│  1999:  Headlam acquires La Maison du Sol and      │
│         becomes French market leader.             │
│  2000:  Headlam acquires Belcolor of Switzerland.  │
│  2001:  Company refocuses as flooring distribution │
│         specialist.                               │
│  2007:  Company continues U.K. consolidation with  │
│         acquisition of Rug Company.               │
│                                         │
└─────────────────────────────────────────┘
```

the flooring market. Headlam quickly found a way into that market, when the management of Hickson Flooring Distributors Ltd. (HFD) approached the company with an offer to turn over the operation of HFD's business on a three-month consultancy basis.

HFD was part of Hickson International, one of the United Kingdom's leading chemicals groups. Hickson had originated as a producer of sulfur black, used in the tanning process, founded in 1893. Incorporated as Hickson & Welch in 1931, Hickson became the leading producer of DDT in the United Kingdom by the 1940s. The company also launched production of a line of timber preservatives and chemicals.

Over the next decades, Hickson diversified its range of operations, particularly with the acquisition of a distribution company, Alvin Morris & Co. (Timber) Ltd., in 1961. Alvin Morris, which operated from depots in Leeds, Manchester, and Sheffield, distributed a variety of timber and other construction materials, including plywood, fiberboard, and plastics. Under Hickson, the Alvin Morris operation grew into a major flooring distributor in the United Kingdom. This position was reinforced in 1984, when Hickson acquired Beds Flooring and Adhesives Distributors Ltd. and its sister company Beds Flooring Distributors Ltd. These operations were subsequently merged with Alvin Morris, creating HFD. HFD then went on a buying spree acquiring a number of flooring distributors. By the beginning of the 1990s, HFD operated from 16 loca-

tions throughout the United Kingdom and had emerged as one of the country's market leaders.

HFD remained just a small part of Hickson's overall operations, however. Worse, HFD's expansion drive had resulted in a highly inefficient business that slipped into losses at the beginning of the early 1990s. When Headlam agreed to the management consultancy, it was initially with a view toward acquiring the whole HFD operation, which by then had revenues of more than £87 million. However, the consultancy period enabled Headlam to recognize the full extent of HFD's problems, and to identify its healthiest components.

Instead of acquiring HFD outright, Headlam chose to cherry-pick the best of HFD's operations. This was completed in several phases between 1991 and 1993. Upon completion, Headlam (the company incorporated under the new name in 1992) had become the United Kingdom's second biggest floor covering distributor, with sales of nearly £65 million.

ACQUIRING THE U.K. LEAD IN 1997

Headlam disposed of its noncore operations, including its footwear and Faire Brothers textiles and materials operations, while refocusing as a distribution group. The company continued to target a somewhat diversified range, with operations including wall and window coverings. However, flooring quickly emerged as the company's primary focus.

Through the 1990s and into the 2000s, Headlam played a major role in the consolidation of the U.K. floor covering distribution sector. The company launched a new acquisition strategy, acquiring a number of prominent distributors, including Mercado in 1996. Headlam's consolidation strategy reached a new high point the following year, when the company bought MCD from investment group Cinven. This purchase gave Headlam the firm lead in the U.K. floor covering sector.

Other U.K. acquisitions included Florcraft, in 1997, which focused on the mail-order market, and commercial carpet supplier Joseph, Hamilton and Seaton, in 1999. The company bought Ossfloor, which specialized in printed carpets, in 2000, followed by commercial distributor Floorsales and residential tufted wool carpet specialist Georgian Carpets in 2001.

Parallel to its expansion in floor coverings, Headlam continued to seek growth in its other distribution categories. The company built up a Fabrics division through a series of acquisitions, including that of Gordon John Textiles, in 1993, then William O'Hanlon,

Edinburgh Weavers, and Sundour into the middle of the decade, and culminating with the purchase of window blinds group Eclipse Blinds, for £64.5 million, in 1999. These purchases allowed the company to claim a 25 percent share of the U.K. window-covering market. Yet the Eclipse purchase quickly turned sour, as Eclipse's sales and profits dropped within a year.

In 2001, Headlam appointed Tony Brewer as the group's new CEO. Brewer immediately launched Headlam on a new restructuring to refocus itself entirely around its core flooring distribution operations. As a result, the company carried out a wave of disposals, including of Eclipse, through 2002.

FOCUSING ON FLOOR COVERINGS IN THE NEW CENTURY

The decision to focus on floor coverings led Headlam to launch a new acquisition phase. The company carried out a number of new acquisitions of both regional and national distributors in the United Kingdom. These included Rikette AS, Crucial Trading, Wollimex, Wolffe Carpet Mills, and GAAS Flooring in 2002; Manx Carpets in 2003; DIY-channel specialist National Carpets in 2004; Kingsmead Carpets in 2005; and, in 2006, Tomkinson Carpets and Gaskell Wool Rich. By the middle of the decade, Headlam had built a network of more than 44 businesses throughout the United Kingdom, with a total market share of more than 50 percent.

With future growth in the rapidly maturing United Kingdom becoming increasingly limited, Headlam began preparing for expansion elsewhere. The floor coverings market in continental Europe remained highly fragmented, resembling in this way the U.K. market at the beginning of the 1990s. Headlam took its first step onto the continent in 1996, when it acquired Dutch flooring distributor Lethem-Vergeer. That purchase gave the company the fourth place ranking in the Dutch market.

Headlam stepped up its presence in Europe in 1999, with the acquisition of La Maison du Sol. That company, which operated two warehouses and a network of 19 showrooms, was the leading French floor covering distributor. Headlam paid £5.5 million ($10 million) for that business. From France, Headlam turned to Switzerland, where it acquired Belcolor, a leading floor covering distributor for the eastern Swiss region. That purchase was completed in 2000.

By 2007, Headlam's European operations accounted for 15 percent of the group's revenues, as the company promised to be a player in the coming consolidation of the floor covering market through the end of the decade. Headlam had no intention of neglecting its core U.K. market, however, continuing to seek new acquisition opportunities. New purchases made through the middle of the decade included Concept (Midlands) Limited, in 2006. In 2007, the company completed three acquisitions, of 3D Flooring Supplies, Florportec, and Plantation Rug Company. Through its steady string of acquisitions, Headlam signaled its clear intention to remain at the head of the U.K. floor coverings market.

M. L. Cohen

PRINCIPAL SUBSIDIARIES

Belcolor AG (Switzerland); DFA SA (France); HFD Limited; Lethem-Vergeer BV (Netherlands); MCD Group Limited.

PRINCIPAL COMPETITORS

Homestyle Group PLC; Stirling Group Ltd.; James Halstead PLC; Interface Europe Ltd.; AW (Europe) Ltd.; CWV Ltd.; Westbridge International Group Ltd.; Landsdon Ltd.; Mark Two Distributors Ltd.; Walker Greenbank PLC.

FURTHER READING

Davoudi, Salamander, "Appetite for Vinyl Helps Headlam to Make Progress," *Financial Times,* August 17, 2005, p. 22.

"Focused Headlam Group Forges Ahead," *Carpet/Flooring/Retail,* April 20, 2007, p. 14.

Goff, Sharlene, "Headlam Takes Bullish Approach in Acquiring Market Share," *Financial Times,* March 16, 2004, p. 26.

"Headlam Acquires Georgian Carpets," *Carpet/Flooring/Retail,* February 4, 2002, p. 6.

"Headlam Builds on Its Strengths," *Carpet/Flooring/Retail,* April 7, 2003, p. 4.

"Headlam Group Builds on Growth," *Carpet/Flooring/Retail,* July 19, 2007, p. 7.

"Headlam Has It Covered," *Investors Chronicle,* September 12, 2007.

Jolliffe, Alexander, "Carpet Comfort for Headlam," *Financial Times,* August 15, 2002, p. 25.

"New Name Follows Sale," *Carpet/Flooring Retail,* April 12, 2005, p. 8.

"Plantation Boosts Headlam Empire," *Carpet/Flooring/Retail,* September 14, 2007, p. 14.

Urquhart, Lisa, "Headlam Hurt by Reverse at Windows Unit," *Financial Times,* March 28, 2001, p. 30.

Voyle, Susanna, "Headlam Has £30m for Purchases," *Financial Times,* March 17, 1999, p. 22.

Henkel KGaA

Henkelstrasse 67
Düsseldorf, 40589
Germany
Telephone: (+49 211) 797-0
Fax: (+49 211) 798-4008
Web site: http://www.henkel.com

Public Company
Incorporated: 1876 as Henkel & Cie
Employees: 53,000
Sales: EUR 12.74 billion ($16.78 billion) (2006)
Stock Exchanges: Frankfurt Bayerische Borse Berlin
Ticker Symbol: HEN
NAIC: 551112 Offices of Other Holding Companies; 325320 Pesticide and Other Agricultural Chemical Manufacturing; 325520 Adhesive Manufacturing; 325611 Soap and Other Detergent Manufacturing; 325612 Polish and Other Sanitation Goods Manufacturing; 325613 Surface Active Agent Manufacturing; 325620 Toilet Preparation Manufacturing; 325998 All Other Miscellaneous Chemical Product and Preparation Manufacturing

■ ■ ■

Based in Germany, Henkel KGaA is a globally oriented manufacturer and marketer of a variety of branded products and technologies. The company focuses on three main areas: laundry and home-care products (approximately 32 percent of overall sales), personal care products (23 percent), and adhesives, sealants, and surface treatment products (44 percent). In the first two of these areas, Henkel's products are aimed at consumers; in the case of the latter, the company is involved not only in the consumer market but also in the industrial and engineering markets.

Among Henkel's top brands are Persil and Purex laundry detergents, Pril and Somat dishwashing soaps, Bref and Soft Scrub household cleaning products, Schwarzkopf hair-care products, Fa body-care products, Dial soaps, Right Guard deodorants, Theramed dental-care products, and Loctite, Pattex, and Pritt adhesive products. Henkel also holds a stake of nearly 30 percent in Ecolab Inc., a St. Paul, Minnesota-based supplier of cleaning, sanitizing, pest elimination, maintenance, and repair products and services for the global hospitality, foodservice, healthcare, and industrial markets. With operations in around 75 countries and sales in more than 125, Henkel derives approximately 80 percent of its revenues outside of Germany, making it one of the most internationally active German companies. More than one-fifth of the firm's sales are generated in North America. After more than 130 years in business, Henkel is still controlled by descendants of the founding Henkel family, who hold more than 51 percent of the company's voting rights.

LATE 19TH-CENTURY ROOTS

Henkel's roots go back to September 26, 1876, when Fritz Henkel founded Henkel & Cie, a three-man company based in Aachen, Germany, engaged in making a "Universal Detergent." Henkel was from the Hesse region and was then 28. Two years later, the company launched one of the first German consumer products to

COMPANY PERSPECTIVES

Our vision is to be a leader with brands and technologies that make people's lives easier, better and more beautiful. We research the markets and analyze the needs of our customers and consumers in order to utilize our insights in the development of new, high-quality products and superior technologies. Innovation is the basis for success—in our World of Brands.

bear a brand name. This was Henkel's Bleich-Soda (bleaching soda). The packet bore the company's early trademark, a benevolent-looking lion in front of a halo of sunbeams. The same year, 1878, saw the young firm's move to a new factory in Düsseldorf, where the company still has its headquarters. The actual site changed in 1899, when Henkel transferred production to a much larger plant at Düsseldorf-Holthausen. Convenient for transporting goods either by railway or on the Rhine, this was to be Henkel's permanent home. (Over the years, however, it would grow from 600,000 square feet to 16.2 million square feet.) In 1877 and 1879 Fritz Henkel bought out his two cofounders, and from then on control was kept firmly in the family.

From the start Henkel appreciated the power that the control of raw materials conferred. Not only did such control insulate the manufacturer from the vagaries of third-party suppliers; it also placed control of ingredient quality into its hands. Sodium silicate, or water glass, was one of the main ingredients of Henkel's detergents; accordingly, in 1884 Henkel acquired the Rheinische Wasserglasfabrik and started to make its own water glass. Already the importance of research and development was appreciated; the process for making water glass was improved upon to the point where, in 1898, Henkel was to patent its own process.

The drive to control as much of the production process as possible continued to be apparent. In 1908 and 1909 Henkel opened soap factories for detergent production and a fat-splitting plant for fatty acid production, which in turn went into the soap. In 1910 came a plant to process glycerol, a byproduct of the manufacture of fatty acids.

In 1893 Fritz Henkel had welcomed his elder son, 18-year-old Fritz Henkel, Jr., into the firm as an apprentice. In due course, Fritz was to play a key role in developing the company's innovative policy of marketing under brand names. Fritz Henkel, Jr.'s brother, Hugo Henkel, a trained chemist, joined the family firm

12 years later. While contributing to the company's technological side in particular, he helped Henkel to diversify into a well-rounded chemical business.

Henkel was already demonstrating a forward-looking concern for the welfare of its 80 employees: it provided free staff lunches from 1900. A few years later Henkel became involved in a building cooperative providing rental housing for workers' families and low-cost mortgages for executives. Recreational facilities such as gyms were supplied by the firm, as were the washrooms, which factory workers needed in order to comply with the company stipulation that they bathe at least once a week. Some early staff benefits might strike the modern reader as overly paternalistic: for example, female workers who announced their intention of getting married were offered a trousseau and a cookery and domestic-science course to be taken at the firm's expense.

1907 INTRODUCTION OF PERSIL

The year 1907 was exceptionally important for product development. It marked the launch of Henkel's arguably most famous brand, the revolutionary detergent Persil. The name came from two of its most important ingredients, hydrogen *per*oxide and sodium *sil*icate. The product, Henkel's own invention, was almost simultaneously invented by two Stuttgart chemists. To be on the safe side, Henkel acquired the chemists' patent but never used it. Three years later, after further intensive research on Henkel's part, the product was registered as Persil. The product was a breakthrough in labor-saving because no rubbing or bleaching was required to clean clothes.

Since those early days, the brand name Persil caused some confusion. In 1909 the English firm of Joseph Crosfield & Sons acquired the patent rights and trademarks of Persil for the United Kingdom and various British, Dutch, and Danish colonies. Crosfield was later absorbed by Lever Brothers, which in turn became part of Unilever. Both Henkel and Unilever continued to market a product named Persil in the early 21st century. In Western Europe, for example, Unilever owned the trademark Persil in Britain and France, while Henkel had Germany, Belgium, Luxembourg, the Netherlands, Italy, and Denmark.

In the early 20th century, Henkel's use of brand names was innovative. Its products were easy to spot by their packaging and were widely distributed. Henkel felt that there was more to be gained by informative advertising than from what would now be called hype. The objectives were to make the Henkel name synonymous with quality and reliability, and to keep

KEY DATES

1876: Fritz Henkel founds Henkel & Cie in Aachen, Germany.

1878: Company moves to Düsseldorf and introduces its first consumer brand, Henkel's Bleich-Soda.

1907: Henkel introduces the revolutionary detergent Persil.

1913: The first foreign subsidiary is established, in Switzerland.

1922: Company starts manufacturing glues, initially for internal use.

1924: Marketing of institutional cleaning products begins.

1930: Acquisition of Thompson-Werke GmbH takes Henkel into the production of household care products.

1947: Production of personal hygiene and cosmetic products begins.

1960: First U.S. company, Standard Chemical Products, Inc., is acquired.

1974: Henkel patents Sasil, a phosphate substitute later used in detergents; the company purchases a minority stake in The Clorox Company.

1975: Henkel KGaA is established as the holding company for the Henkel Group.

1983: Dixan, the first phosphate-free detergent, is introduced.

1985: Company goes public through an offering of preferred, nonvoting shares.

1991: Henkel and the U.S. firm Ecolab Inc. combine their European institutional cleaning and sanitizing businesses into a joint venture, Henkel-Ecolab.

1995: Via acquisition of Hans Schwarzkopf GmbH, Henkel becomes a leader in the European hair-care sector.

1996: Henkel lists its common, voting shares on the stock exchange for the first time; Henkel family retains controlling stake.

1997: Hostile takeover of Loctite Corporation is completed.

1999: Chemical operations are spun off into a new, Henkel-owned entity called Cognis.

2001: Company sells Cognis and its interest in the Henkel-Ecolab joint venture; Henkel continues to hold a significant minority stake in Ecolab.

2004: Henkel acquires The Dial Corporation; the firm's 29 percent stake in The Clorox Company is exchanged for $2.1 billion in cash, the Soft Scrub cleaning brand, and other assets.

reminding the public of Henkel's presence by having its goods and name on display everywhere. As early as 1911, motorized delivery vans bearing the Henkel livery were to be seen in Düsseldorf. There was a famous slogan, "Persil bleibt Persil" (Persil remains Persil), first used in 1913. By 1914, Henkel had 120 salesmen out in the field.

Henkel had been quick to set up marketing operations in Germany's neighbor countries. In 1913 Henkel opened a foreign subsidiary, the first of many, at Basel-Pratteln in Switzerland, a country whose appetite for Persil and bleaching soda had proved particularly healthy. Four years later it was to acquire another subsidiary, this time German, when it bought Matthes & Weber, operator of a soda factory in Duisburg.

ACTIONS DURING AND IMPACT OF WORLD WAR I

Henkel played a patriotic part in World War I. Jobs of workers who went to the defense of their country were kept open for their return, although 71 never returned. A hospital was set up for the employees who were wounded. Henkel employees fighting in the German trenches continued to receive not only food parcels but also copies of the company newspaper, which had begun to be published in 1914.

Rationing of oils and fats made it necessary in 1916 to bring in a low-soap version of Persil. In general, the war had less effect on Henkel's business than did the Allied occupation of the Rhineland from 1919 onward. Some of the effects of the occupation were positive. The danger that the Holthausen plant would be cut off from its customer base led to the construction of a new factory at Genthin in central Germany, which opened in 1921. The extra capacity would be valuable later on.

INTERWAR EXPANSION AND DIVERSIFICATION

The war was followed in Germany by a period of hyperinflation. At its peak, in November 1923, a packet of Persil cost 1.25 billion marks. Once this situation was brought under control, Henkel's expansion continued apace, in line with a general Western European trend toward higher standards of living, and in particular of personal and domestic hygiene. In Germany, soap products were becoming affordable, and thanks in part to Henkel's advertisements, their virtues were well known. For most of its first half-century the company had focused on the manufacture of detergent and cleaning products. A period of vigorous diversification began in the 1920s under the guidance of Hugo Henkel, supported not only by his sons but by a board of eight directors. This activity continued throughout the interwar period, but the stimulus to diversify again came from the occupation of the Rhineland. In 1922, fearing that the occupying forces would restrict the supply of the adhesives it needed for detergent packaging, Henkel started to manufacture its own glues. With characteristic opportunism, it was soon putting the glue department's products on the market.

Henkel's next move, in 1924, was to start marketing cleaning products aimed at institutional and industrial markets. In 1929 the P3 phosphate-based cleaning agents were added to Henkel's product lines for industrial machinery and food production. By buying Thompson-Werke GmbH in 1930 and Deutsche Hydrierwerke AG in 1932, it acquired an interest in the market for household care products, such as polishes and scouring powders, and increased its capacity to manufacture the fatty alcohols needed for its detergents.

Henkel's acquisition of Böhme-Fettchemie GmbH, Chemnitz, in 1935, followed the latter's launch of a new type of detergent named Fewa three years earlier. This synthetic product, designed to wash delicate fabrics, was the first of its kind. The year 1935 also saw the foundation by Henkel of a German whaling association that sent a fleet to the Antarctic Ocean three times in the prewar years. The fleet's catches were of relevance to oleochemical production. By 1939 Henkel could boast of 15 European plants in addition to the main factory in Düsseldorf.

OTHER INTERWAR DEVELOPMENTS

Henkel's expansion of its product range between the wars meant more research and development. A laboratory had existed since the early 1900s, but in 1920 a test department for new products was set up. At first the focus was inorganic chemistry, but later on other branches of chemistry were included. Further new laboratories were built and equipped during the 1930s, culminating in a major laboratory that opened on the Deutsche Hydrierwerke site at Rodleben, shortly before the outbreak of World War II, designed to support all of Henkel's products. Cash-starved Germany could ill afford to import natural fats, and so one important object of research was the development of soapless washing powders. By 1936 Henkel was producing powders using fatty acids derived from coal. Meanwhile, improvements had been made in the manufacturing process: packaging of detergents became fully automatic in 1926. Always keen to take advantage of new technology in management as well as production, Henkel installed an automatic telephone exchange in 1928, and in 1935 became the first subscriber to the Düsseldorf teleprinter service.

Alongside its policy of expansion and diversification in the interwar period, Henkel maintained an imaginative approach to advertising. Skywriting planes emblazoned the name of Persil far above the heads of astonished German spectators, and in an interesting variation on the sandwich board, six men carried through the streets snow-white umbrellas bearing the name "Persil." Henkel continued to forge ahead in the field of staff management and welfare. First-aid facilities, the precursor of later Henkel staff medical centers, had arrived in 1912. A pension plan began three years later. In 1925 a training structure for specialist staff was established, and two years later Henkel became the first member of the German chemical industry to appoint a safety engineer to reduce the risk of accidents.

Jost Henkel, son of Hugo Henkel, had joined the company in 1933, and it was under his leadership that Henkel weathered World War II. The war itself had relatively little impact on the Düsseldorf works, although 259 employees were lost in action, prison camps, and air raids. Henkel had to abandon Persil in favor of basic, state-approved products during wartime. Once again the aftermath of war was more serious. The occupying British forces removed the Henkel family from the head of the firm, and did not allow it to return until 1947. The Genthin plant was expropriated by the communists in 1946. In line with the German economy, which began to recover at that time, Henkel was able to get back on a level footing in time for its 75th anniversary in 1951.

POST–WORLD WAR II INTERNATIONAL GROWTH

After World War II, Henkel, under first Jost Henkel and then his brother Konrad Henkel, who took over in 1961, did not simply set about rebuilding what it had before, but entered one new market after another, diversifying its products through innovation and acquisition, and gaining representation in parts of the world not previously penetrated. In 1946 the Düsseldorf factory started to manufacture chemical products for use in the textile and leather industries, and the Poly hair-care brand was launched. The following year, personal hygiene and cosmetic products were added to the range. During this period, Henkel's production facilities for oil-related chemicals were brought together at the Düsseldorf-Holthausen plant, giving a greatly increased capacity for the manufacture of ingredients for soaps, detergents, cosmetics, and pharmaceutical products. In 1951 Pril dishwashing liquid was introduced. During the 1950s, the company set up manufacturing plants in Japan and Brazil, gaining its first footholds in the East Asian and South American marketplaces.

The first acquisition of a U.S. company, Standard Chemical Products, Inc., in 1960, heralded the two decades of Henkel's most dramatic expansion (Standard, a maker of chemicals for the textile industry based in Hoboken, New Jersey, was renamed Henkel Corporation in 1971). To give a solid foundation to its growth program, the Henkel Group opened a state-of-the-art research center in 1962 at the main Düsseldorf plant. This laboratory complex had been in phased construction since 1959 and was not completed until 1967. Pritt, the solid glue in a cylindrical tube, was launched in 1969, contributing to Henkel's lead in the European adhesive market.

By the 1970s, there was mounting concern about the environmental impact of the chemical industry in general, and specifically about the use of phosphates in detergents. In 1974 Henkel patented a compound known as Sasil, which was to prove a good substitute for the offending phosphates. Now there could be a phosphate-free Persil; Henkel introduced Dixan, the first phosphate-free detergent, in 1983. The discovery of Sasil helped Henkel gain the leading position in the European detergent market. Henkel also began collecting license fees from other users of Sasil or related products.

A biological institute was added to Henkel's group of laboratories in 1974. The scientists and technologists who worked there concentrated on the protection of the consumer and the environment. Also in 1974, Henkel purchased a minority stake in The Clorox Company, a U.S.-based consumer products firm; Clorox in turn gained access to Henkel's research-and-development capabilities and acquired manufacturing and marketing rights to Henkel-developed products in the United States, Canada, and Puerto Rico. In 1975 Henkel KGaA was established as the holding company for the Henkel Group. Seven years later, the group's U.S. activities were concentrated within Henkel Corporation.

When the founder, Fritz Henkel, died in 1930, ownership of the company had been divided between the families of his three children. By 1985, control was held by 66 family members who in that year decided, together with president Helmut Sihler, that it was time to go public. Thus Henkel shares were issued at last to an eager market. At the same time steps were taken to guard against excessive outside interference; the issue was of nonvoting preferred shares, and all ordinary shares were to belong to the family at least until the year 2000.

CONTINUED EXPANSION

Expansion continued through the 1980s, most notably with the acquisition of Union Générale de Savonnerie in France and three U.S. companies: Parker Chemicals, maker of metal surface treatments; Oxy Process Chemicals; and Emery Group, a base-materials and chemicals company, in the United States. Emery, based in Cincinnati, was the leading maker of oleochemicals in the country. An important new production plant opened in Malaysia in 1984. The following year Henkel acquired a minority stake in Hartford, Connecticut-based Loctite Corporation, a leading adhesives and sealants firm. By the end of the 1980s, the expansion in the United States was particularly noteworthy, having led to a quadrupling of revenues over just the last few years of the decade.

Henkel succeeded in maintaining a sound balance sheet throughout all its acquisition activities. Although outsiders sometimes regarded the group as overdiversified, its management was satisfied with the mix. It had clear rules for acquisition: not to diversify through acquisition, to retain acquired companies' existing management, and to purchase companies that complied with their profit requirements. Unprofitable companies, or those that did not fit in, were rejected. Strategic relationships were formed, and minority shareholdings bought as the least risky and cheapest way of getting a foothold in a new market. The *Wall Street Journal Europe,* on November 25, 1988, described Henkel's business approach as "a blend of America's short-term emphasis on profit and West Germany's long-term emphasis on the future." Certainly, Henkel's consistently healthy results gave credibility to its strategies.

In its research and development, Henkel continued to target environmental and consumer protection issues. DM 282 million was spent on this area in 1989 alone, while DM 30 million was earmarked for related capital expenditure. In addition to measures to develop safer and more environmentally sound products in all ranges, there were programs to minimize the pollution generated by the manufacturing plants. Henkel claimed that environmental damage caused by its parent plant had been reduced by between 50 and 75 percent between 1984 and 1990.

On the marketing and production front in the late 1980s, Henkel was preparing intensively for the planned single European market. It was designing its branding concepts with Europe in mind and was reviewing its distribution and production facilities. Management development programs too were being specifically targeted at international business. Language classes were offered to staff throughout the group.

LATE 20TH-CENTURY ACQUISITIONS AND RESTRUCTURING EFFORTS

Konrad Henkel, the grandson of founder Fritz Henkel, continued as chairman of the supervisory board and shareholders' committee until the end of 1990, when Albrecht Woeste, great-grandson of the founder, replaced him. Taking over as president and CEO in mid-1992 was Dr. Hans-Dietrich Winkhaus. Woeste and Winkhaus were thereby in charge for most of the 1990s, a decade in which Henkel's revenues nearly doubled and its international presence deepened through a number of acquisitions and joint ventures. Henkel also improved its profitability in the 1990s through streamlining and restructuring efforts, including the divestiture of noncore units and workforce layoffs.

The decade began, however, with the company's return to eastern Germany following the reunification of the country. In 1990 Henkel repurchased the laundry detergent plant in Genthin that had been expropriated in 1946. The following year Henkel and St. Paul, Minnesota-based cleaning and maintenance company Ecolab Inc. combined their European institutional cleaning and sanitizing businesses into a new 50-50 joint venture, Henkel-Ecolab. Henkel also received a 19 percent stake in Ecolab, while the U.S. firm acquired Henkel's cleaning and sanitizing operations in Latin America and Asia. The joint venture experienced some initial difficulties as a result of a poor European economy, but in a few short years became the leader in Europe in institutional and hospitality cleaning, sanitizing, and maintenance. Henkel-Ecolab, which was based in Düsseldorf, operated throughout Europe, including

Russia and other former republics of the Soviet Union.

In 1992 Henkel purchased the consumer goods division of Nobel Industries AB of Sweden, gaining its first foothold in Scandinavia. Asia became a main focus for the company in 1993 and 1994, with a particular emphasis on China, where Henkel had eight joint ventures in place by late 1994. Sales in China were about $100 million in 1994. A key step came in 1995 when Henkel established a Beijing-based holding company for its growing operations there, Henkel (China) Investment Co. Ltd., thereby enabling it to directly hire Chinese managers. Also in 1995 Henkel became a leading supplier of hair-care products in Europe through the purchase of a 77 percent stake in Hamburg-based Hans Schwarzkopf GmbH from Hoechst AG. Two years later Henkel purchased the remaining shares in Schwarzkopf from the founding family.

The company bolstered its surface technologies operations through the 1996 acquisition of Novamax Technologies Inc., an Atlanta-based specialist in products and systems for the treatment of metal surfaces. In November 1996 Henkel began a hostile takeover bid for the 65 percent of Loctite it did not already own. When Henkel increased its bid to $1.3 billion, Loctite agreed to be taken over, with the deal finalized in January 1997. At the time, this was the largest acquisition in company history. To help finance it, Henkel sold its 16 percent stake in Degussa AG, a German metals and chemical group, to German utility firm VEBA AG for DM 1.3 billion. Meanwhile, in an alteration to the Henkel family's 1985 agreement, the company listed its common, voting shares on the stock exchange for the first time in 1996. Nevertheless, the founding family continued to own 80 percent of the common stock into the early 21st century, and the new agreement ensured that the Henkel family would retain long-term control of more than 50 percent of the voting shares.

Acquisitions were again at the forefront in 1998, with the two most significant being U.S. firms: Manco Inc., a $111 million purchase, and DEP Corporation, for $93 million. Manco, a private company based in Avon, Ohio, had sales of $160 million and provided Henkel a much enhanced presence in the U.S. consumer adhesives market, including the Duck duct tape brand. With the purchase of DEP, a financially troubled firm based in Los Angeles with sales of $117 million, Henkel entered the U.S. personal care market for the first time and furthered its goal of fully globalizing its cosmetics/toiletries sector. Among DEP's brands were DEP, L.A., Looks, Agree, Halsa, and Lilt in hair care; Theorie, Porcelana, Cuticura, and Le Systeme in skin care; and Lavoris and Topol in dental care.

In 1999 Henkel spun off its chemicals unit—including the oleochemicals, care chemicals, and organic specialties operations—into a stand-alone, but fully Henkel-owned entity called Cognis. The separation was intended to provide Cognis with additional flexibility in regard to forming joint ventures, entering into mergers, or raising funds through an initial public offering (IPO). Cognis also gained the freedom to sell its products to competitors of Henkel in such areas as detergents and adhesives. Henkel intended to indefinitely retain at least a majority stake in Cognis.

Henkel entered into another significant joint venture in 1999. Marking a further move by Henkel into the U.S. consumer market, the company and Scottsdale, Arizona-based Dial Corporation formed a 50-50 venture to create new laundry detergent products under Dial's Purex brand. In early 2000 the two companies entered into a second detergent joint venture in Mexico, where they purchased an 80 percent stake in Fábrica de Jabón Mariano Salgado, S.A. de C.V., a leading maker of detergents and soaps in that country. Henkel's aggressive U.S. expansion helped make the company one of the most globally active German companies, with more than 70 percent of sales being generated outside the home market.

EARLY 21ST CENTURY: SHIFTING TO CONSUMER BRANDED PRODUCT EMPHASIS

In May 2000 Winkhaus retired and was replaced as president and CEO by 14-year company veteran Dr. Ulrich Lehner. The new leader made globalizing Henkel his top priority as the firm's core areas of detergents, cosmetics, and toiletries were dominated by the much larger and more internationally oriented Unilever and Procter & Gamble Company (P&G). Seeking to concentrate more of its attention on these consumer-brand sectors, and needing funds for major acquisitions to become more of a global player in these areas, Henkel elected to divest Cognis. The specialty chemical unit was sold to a consortium of private-equity firms for EUR 2.5 billion ($2.2 billion) in November 2001.

That same year, Henkel sold its share of the Henkel-Ecolab joint venture to its partner for EUR 484 million ($433 million). As part of a new agreement between the two companies, Henkel was allowed to increase its stake in Ecolab to a maximum of 35 percent, and in fact by the end of 2001 Henkel had pushed its holding up to 28.4 percent. Following these divestments, 70 percent of Henkel's revenues were tied to branded consumer goods (including consumer adhesives). Going forward, the company intended to focus on branded products in its core areas plus industrial and engineering adhesives and surface technologies. Late in 2001 the new emphasis on brands was highlighted through the introduction of a new corporate slogan: "Henkel—A Brand Like a Friend."

On the acquisition front, Henkel's initial ambitions for a blockbuster deal were thwarted. The company made a play for the Clairol hair-care business, which Bristol-Myers Squibb Company was selling, but P&G won the bidding in late 2001 with an offer of nearly $5 billion. Less than two years later, P&G once again topped Henkel, securing control of Wella AG, the German professional hair-care group, for $6.27 billion. Henkel's pursuit of the German cosmetics firm Beiersdorf AG in 2003 also came to naught. The company ended up settling for a number of smaller takeovers during this period, including OAO Pemos, the second largest detergents producer in Russia, bought in 2001; and the U.K.-based Sellotape consumer adhesive tapes business, purchased in 2002.

NORTH AMERICAN PUSH HEADLINED BY 2004 ACQUISITION OF DIAL

Henkel's fortunes on the acquisition trail brightened in 2004 when a string of deals fulfilled at least part of the company's global ambitions. The most significant of these, and the firm's largest to date, was the purchase that March of The Dial Corporation for EUR 2.4 billion ($2.9 billion). Adding Dial substantially increased Henkel's presence in the U.S. market and lessened the firm's reliance on the German and European markets. Dial, which had 2002 sales of $1.3 billion, produced such well-known brands as Purex laundry detergent, Renuzit air fresheners, and Dial and Coast soaps. Descended from meat processor Armour & Company, which had begun making soap from byproducts of meatpacking production, Dial was still producing canned meat products and ready meats under the Armour brand. This food business, an ill fit for Henkel's portfolio, was sold in March 2006 to Pinnacle Foods Group Inc. of Cherry Hill, New Jersey, for $183 million.

Two other 2004 acquisitions further bolstered Henkel's position in North America. In February the firm purchased Costa Mesa, California-based Advanced Research Laboratories (ARL) for roughly $250 million. ARL produced such hair-care brands as Citré Shine and got2b. In November, Henkel spent $575 million for Sovereign Specialty Chemicals Inc., a Chicago-based producer of adhesives, sealants, and coatings, mainly for industrial customers, that had annual sales of nearly $400 million. The previous month Henkel completed a significant deal that helped finance the purchase of Dial and also added to its portfolio of U.S. brands. The company swapped its 29 percent stake in Clorox for $2.1 billion in cash; the Soft Scrub line of cleaning products; Clorox's insecticides business, including the Combat brand; and Clorox's 20 percent stake in a joint venture with Henkel focusing on consumer products in Spain and Portugal. In June 2004, meanwhile, Henkel purchased the European professional hair-care business Indola from Alberto-Culver Company, gaining an operation with 2003 revenues of EUR 47 million.

The most visible short-term outcome of the 2004 acquisition spree was Henkel's much greater presence in North America. By 2005, 25 percent of the company's sales of EUR 11.97 billion and 27 percent of its operating profits of EUR 1.16 billion were derived in North America, substantially more than the 12 percent and 8 percent figures, respectively, for 2003. Furthermore, in 2005 the United States was Henkel's largest single market in terms of revenues, surpassing Germany for the first time in the company's history. Seeking to push its U.S. sales up to 30 percent of overall revenues, Henkel in April 2006 entered the deodorant/antiperspirant sector in North America by purchasing the Right Guard, Soft & Dri, and Dry Idea brands from P&G for $420 million. P&G was forced to divest the brands to gain regulatory approval of its acquisition of the Gillette Company. The acquired brands were generating combined annual sales of $275 million, 80 percent of which originated in North America with most of the remainder stemming from the United Kingdom.

During 2006, Henkel's sales increased 6.4 percent to EUR 12.74 billion ($16.78 billion), while its operating profits jumped 11.7 percent to EUR 1.3 billion ($1.7 billion). Late that year, a plan for management succession was put into place. Kasper Rorsted was named to succeed Lehner as company president and CEO effective in April 2008. The Denmark-born Rorsted, who had served as executive vice-president of information technologies, infrastructure services, human resources, and purchasing since April 2005, had previous management experience at several technology companies, including a stint serving as head of the European business of Hewlett-Packard Company.

Already the world leader in the global adhesives market, in August 2007 Henkel reached an agreement to acquire the adhesives and electronic materials businesses of National Starch and Chemical Company for nearly EUR 4 billion. National Starch, based in Bridgewater, New Jersey, was a subsidiary of the U.K. firm ICI plc, and Henkel's proposed acquisition was contingent upon the Dutch firm Akzo Nobel N.V. completing its proposed takeover of ICI, slated for completion in the second quarter of 2008. Adding the National Starch

businesses, which generated revenues of EUR 1.85 billion in 2006 and were particularly strong in the industrial adhesives sector, would mean that Henkel would derive roughly half of its total sales from adhesives. Annual cost savings from merging the businesses with the company's existing operations were estimated to total around EUR 250 million, with thousands of jobs likely to be eliminated and a number of plants and offices shut down. This latest Henkel blockbuster deal, which would be the firm's largest to that point, was likely to be financed through some combination of debt and/or equity capital and/or the divestiture of noncore assets.

Alison Classe and Olive Classe
Updated, David E. Salamie

PRINCIPAL SUBSIDIARIES

Elch GmbH; Hans Schwarzkopf & Henkel GmbH & Co. KG; Henkel Chemie Verwaltungsgesellschaft mbH; Henkel Fragrance Center GmbH; Henkel Genthin GmbH; Henkel Holding GmbH & Co. KG; Henkel Loctite-KID GmbH; Inter Beteiligungsverwaltungs-Gesellschaft mbH; Schwarzkopf & Henkel Production Europe GmbH & Co. KG; SHC Beauty Cosmetics GmbH; Henkel Algérie S.P.A. (Algeria); Henkel Argentina S.A.; Henkel Australia Pty. Ltd.; Henkel Austria GmbH; Henkel Central Eastern Europe GmbH (Austria); Henkel Belgium N.V.; Henkel Ltda. (Brazil); Henkel Canada Corporation; Henkel Consumer Goods Canada, Inc.; Henkel Chile Ltda.; Henkel Adhesives Co. Ltd. (China); Henkel Asia-Pacific Ltd. (China); Henkel (China) Co. Ltd.; Henkel (China) Investment Co. Ltd.; Henkel Huawei Electronics Co. Ltd. (China; 71.06%); Henkel Loctite (China) Co. Ltd. (71%); Henkel Colombiana SA (Colombia); Henkel Croatia doo; GPM-Henkel Ltd. (Cyprus; 51%); Henkel CR spol. s.r.o. (Czech Republic); Henkel PDC Egypt SAE (96.7%); Henkel Balti OÜ (Estonia); Henkel Makroflex AS (Estonia); Henkel Makroflex Oy (Finland); Henkel Norden Oy (Finland); Henkel France S.A.; Henkel Loctite France SAS; Henkel Technologies France SAS; Schwarzkopf S.A. (France); Henkel Hellas SA (Greece); Henkel Centroamericana S.A. (Guatemala); Henkel La Luz S.A. (Guatemala); Henkel Magyarország Kft (Hungary); Henkel Adhesives Technologies India Pvt. Ltd.; Henkel India Ltd.; PT Henkel Indonesien (Indonesia; 84.75%); Henkel Pakvash PJSC (Iran; 60%); Henkel Ireland Detergents Ltd.; Henkel Ireland Ltd.; Loctite (Overseas) Ltd. (Ireland); Notex Ltd. (Ireland); Henkel Soad Ltd. (Israel); Henkel Loctite Adesivi S.r.l. (Italy); Henkel S.p.A. (Italy); Loctite Italia S.r.l. (Italy); Schwarzkopf & Henkel Italia S.r.l. (Italy);

Henkel Japan Ltd.; Schwarzkopf & Henkel Ltd. (Japan; 85%); Henkel Lebanon S.A.L. (50%); Henkel Re S.A. (Luxembourg); Henkel (Malaysia) Sdn. Bhd.; Henkel Mexicana S.A. de C.V. (Mexico); Henkel Nederland B.V. (Netherlands); Loctite International B.V. (Netherlands); Henkel New Zealand Ltd.; Henkel Philippines, Inc.; Henkel Polska Sp. z o.o. (Poland); Henkel Romania Srl; OAO Henkel ERA (Russia; 98.04%); OAO Henkel Pemos (Russia; 95.82%); OOO Henkel Süd (Russia); ZAO Schwarzkopf & Henkel (Russia); Henkel Detergents Saudi Arabia Ltd.; Henkel Merima d.o.o. (Serbia; 91.77%); Henkel Singapore Pte. Ltd.; Henkel Slovensko spol. s.r.o. (Slovakia); Henkel Slovenija d.o.o. (Slovenia); Henkel South Africa (Pty.) Ltd. (74%); Henkel Home Care Korea Ltd. (South Korea); Henkel Korea Ltd. (South Korea); Henkel Loctite Korea Ltd. (South Korea); Henkel Iberica S.A. (Spain); Henkel Norden AB (Sweden); Henkel & Cie. AG (Switzerland); UMA AG (Switzerland); Henkel Syria S.A.S. (49.97%); Henkel Taiwan Ltd.; Henkel (Thailand) Ltd.; Henkel Alki S.A. (Tunisia; 66%); Türk Henkel Kimya Sanayi ve Ticaret A.S. (Turkey); Henkel Bautechnik (Ukraine) TOB (66%); Henkel Jebel Ali FZCO (U.A.E.); Chemtek Ltd. (U.K.); Henkel Loctite Adhesives Ltd. (U.K.); Henkel Ltd. (U.K.); Sellotape Holding Ltd. (U.K.); Sovereign Specialty Chemicals Ltd. (U.K.); Dexter Hysol Aerospace LLC (U.S.A.); Dial Brands Holding, Inc. (U.S.A.); Dial Brands, Inc. (U.S.A.); The Dial Corporation (U.S.A.); Dial International, Inc. (U.S.A.); Henkel Consumer Goods, Inc. (U.S.A.); Henkel Corporation (U.S.A.); Henkel of America Inc. (U.S.A.); Henkel Venezolana S.A. (Venezuela).

PRINCIPAL OPERATING UNITS

Laundry & Home Care; Cosmetics/Toiletries; Adhesives Technologies.

PRINCIPAL COMPETITORS

Unilever; The Procter & Gamble Company; Reckitt Benckiser plc; Beiersdorf AG; H.B. Fuller Company; 3M Company; Johnson & Johnson; Colgate-Palmolive Company; Church & Dwight Co., Inc.; BASF SE; Bayer AG; L'Oréal S.A.; S.C. Johnson & Son, Inc.

FURTHER READING

Alperowicz, Natasha, "Henkel to Separate Chemicals, Will Consider Mergers, IPO," *Chemical Week*, February 17, 1999, p. 9.

Bowtell, Maurice, "Henkel: 75 and Going Strong," *Adhesives Age*, May 30, 1998, pp. 56+.

Brockinton, Langdon, "Betting on a New U.S. Strategy at Henkel," *Chemical Week*, January 25, 1989, pp. 20+.

———, "For Emery, It's Henkel," *Chemical Week*, March 22, 1989, pp. 8+.

Buckley, Neil, "Henkel Reaches Agreement to Acquire ARL," *Financial Times*, December 22, 2003, p. 24.

Buckley, Neil, and Bettina Wassener, "Henkel Swaps Clorox Stake in U.S. Drive," *Financial Times*, October 8, 2004, p. 28.

Buckley, Neil, and Doug Cameron, "Henkel Agrees to Pay $2. 9bn for U.S. Soaps Rival Dial," *Financial Times*, December 16, 2003, p. 25.

de Guzman, Doris, "Clorox Swap Fortifies Henkel's U.S. Consumer Biz," *Chemical Market Reporter*, October 18, 2004, p. 20.

———, "Henkel Strengthens Deodorant Spot," *Chemical Market Reporter*, March 6, 2006, p. 21.

"Dial and Henkel Form North American JV for Laundry Detergents," *Chemical Market Reporter*, April 26, 1999, p. 3.

1876–1976 Hundert Jahre Henkel, Düsseldorf: Henkel, 1976.

"European Trimming Fills Henkel's China Sails," *Chemical Week*, February 9, 1994, pp. 20+.

Feiter, Wolfgang, and Alexandra Boy, *90 Jahre Persil: Die Geschichte einer Marke*, Düsseldorf: Henkel, 1997, 135 p.

Feldenkirchen, Wilfried, and Susanne Hilger, *Menschen und Marken: 125 Jahre Henkel, 1876–2001*, Düsseldorf: Henkel, 2001.

Fisher, Andrew, "Hoechst Sells Hair Care Arm to Henkel," *Financial Times*, August 12, 1995, p. 11.

Gibson, W. David, "Henkel Tightens Up Its U.S. Operations," *Chemical Week*, February 5, 1986, pp. 22+.

Goosmann, Cornelia, *Ein Jahrhundert Wasserglas von Henkel*, Düsseldorf: Henkel, 1985, 76 p.

Gow, David, "Jobs Threat As Persil Inventor Takes Over ICI Company," *Guardian* (London), November 8, 2007, p. 29.

Grant, Jeremy, "Henkel Buys Right Guard from Gillette in $420m Deal," *Financial Times*, February 21, 2006, p. 30.

"Henkel Enters U.S. Personal Care Market," *Chemical Market Reporter*, July 20, 1998, p. 3.

Henkel—Specialist in Applied Chemistry, Düsseldorf: Henkel, 1989.

Kerber, Ross, "Loctite Accepts New Henkel Offer of $1.3 Billion," *Wall Street Journal*, December 6, 1996, p. A12.

Kiesche, Elizabeth S., "In the U.S., Henkel Achieves Critical Mass, Focuses on Productivity," *Chemical Week*, February 9, 1994, pp. 20–21.

Layman, Patricia L., "A Rejuvenated Henkel Looking for New Markets," *Chemical and Engineering News*, February 10, 1986, p. 15.

Lerner, Ivan, "Henkel Buys Sovereign Specialty," *Chemical Market Reporter*, October 11, 2004, pp. 1, 11.

Lipin, Steven, "Loctite Sought by Henkel in Hostile Step," *Wall Street Journal*, November 6, 1996, p. A3.

Marsh, Peter, "The Secret Is in the Mix for Germany's Brightest," *Financial Times*, December 7, 1988.

Marshall, Matt, "Henkel Leaves German Fold to Go Global," *Wall Street Journal*, December 9, 1996, p. A9.

McCoy, Michael, "Henkel CEO Is Cautious on Outlook," *Chemical Marketing Reporter,* March 22, 1993, p. 9.

Milmo, Sean, "Henkel Acquires Leading Russian Soaper Pemos," *Chemical Marketing Reporter,* January 15, 2001, p. 6.

Milne, Richard, "Changing Habits in Shopping Force Henkel to Cut 3,000 Jobs," *Financial Times,* November 26, 2004, p. 15.

Minard, Lawrence, "A Man on the Move," *Forbes,* December 11, 2000, pp. 127+.

Morrison, Scott, "Henkel Wraps Up Sale of Cognis; Issues Another Profit Warning," *Chemical Week,* November 21/28, 2001, p. 17.

O'Boyle, Thomas F., "Henkel Makes Mark with Acquisitions," *Wall Street Journal Europe,* November 25, 1988.

Schöne, Manfred, *Stammwerk Henkel 80 Jahre in Düsseldorf-Holthausen,* Düsseldorf: Henkel, 1981, 148 p.

———, *Von der Leimabteilung zum grössten Klebstoffwerk Europas,* Düsseldorf: Henkel, 1979, 68 p.

Scott, Alex, "Henkel Shows Rivals a Green Pair of Heels," *Chemical Week,* January 19, 2000, p. 45.

Singer, Jason, "Akzo Nobel Brings in Henkel to Win a Deal for ICI," *Wall Street Journal,* August 6, 2007, p. A3.

Timeline 130 Years of Henkel, Düsseldorf: Henkel, 2006, 127 p.

Van Arnum, Patricia, "Did Dial Take Henkel to the Cleaners?" *Chemical Market Reporter,* January 26, 2004, pp. FR3–FR4, FR6.

Walsh, Kerri, "Free to Serve Henkel's Rivals," *Chemical Week,* September 8, 1999, p. 53.

———, "Henkel to Buy Sovereign; Sells Clorox Stake," *Chemical Week,* October 13, 2004, p. 8.

Walsh, Kerri, and Esther D'Amico, "Henkel to Acquire Dial for $2.9 Billion," *Chemical Week,* December 24/31, 2003, p. 25.

Wiesmann, Gerrit, "Brands That Stop at the Border," *Financial Times,* October 6, 2006, p. 13.

Highland Gold Mining Limited

26 New Street
Saint Helier, JE 3RA
United Kingdom
Telephone: (44 01534) 814202
Fax: (44 01534) 814815
Web site: http://www.highlandgold.com

Public Company
Incorporated: 2002
Employees: 3,616
Sales: $102.4 million (2006)
Stock Exchanges: London
Ticker Symbol: HGM
NAIC: 212221 Gold Ore Mining

■ ■ ■

Maintaining its headquarters in Jersey, the Channel Islands, a U.K. protectorate, Highland Gold Mining Limited is a U.K.-financed and Russian-led gold mining venture. Listed on the London Stock Exchange's Alternative Investment Market (AIM), Highland operates one fully functioning gold mine, the Mnogovershinnoye (MNV) mine, located in the far east of the Russian Federation in the Khabarovsk region. Mining is conducted underground and in an open-pit, and gold is processed at an onsite plant. Highland's portfolio also includes three development and six exploration projects. One project, Mayskoye, is among Russia's largest undeveloped gold deposits. Previously Highland oper-

ated another mine, Darasun, but it was a money-losing operation and was sold in 2007. Major Highland shareholders include Russian billionaire Roman Abramovich, who owns a 40 percent interest, and Canada's Barrick Gold Corporation, a 20 percent stakeholder.

MNV MINE: COLD WAR ORIGINS

At the height of the Cold War between the Soviet Union and the West, the Mnogovershinnoye deposit was discovered in an area close to China and Mongolia. Four years later an exploration effort was launched, but it was not until 1979 that construction was begun on the mine. Work on the processing plant was begun in 1990, and a year later MNV actually began to produce gold. The Soviet Union was coming unraveled during this period, a free market economy began to take shape, and the Russian Federation soon arose from the ashes of the former Communist power. The owners of MNV lacked the finances and technical expertise to fully exploit the mine and in 1997 it was shut down.

A year later, the MNV project was acquired by a group of investors led by Ivan Koulakov, an associate of Roman Abramovich. Koulakov was a new breed of Russian technocrat-capitalist, holding a degree in mechanical engineering from the Moscow State Technical University and a degree in economics from the Department of Finance and Banking at the Financial Academy of Government. Before forming Mnogovershinnoye SJC, he served as chairman of ZAO Oil Finance, part of Abramovich's Sibneft group of oil and gas companies.

COMPANY PERSPECTIVES

Highland's vision is to become the most profitable gold mining company in Russia and Central Asia with a firm commitment towards safety, health and the environment, and social responsibility towards employees and communities.

MNV RESUMES PRODUCTION: 1998

Koulakov's new company invested $57 million to rehabilitate MNV in 1998, and in July of the following year the mine produced its first gold for its new owner. By the end of the year it yielded 40,000 ounces, generating almost $10 million in sales. Production increased steadily over the next two years: to 107,000 ounces in 2000 and 153,000 ounces in 2001, making it the third largest operating Russian gold mine. Revenues topped $40 million and the company netted $11.8 million in profits. In the meantime, the company was converted in 2000 into a joint-stock company under the name ZAO MNV.

While MNV was ramping up production, events in the United Kingdom were taking place that would lead to the creation of Highland Gold Mining. In 2000 the venerable London-based merchant bank Robert Fleming & Co. was sold to Chase Manhattan Bank for about $7.7 billion, after a difficult stretch in the late 1990s when Fleming was hit hard by both scandal and the Asian financial crisis that led to a restructuring and a major loss of business. The Fleming family (one member of which had been Ian Fleming, the creator of James Bond) had owned about a 30 percent interest. After the sale to Chase, Roddie Fleming and others formed an investment company under the name Fleming Family & Partners (FF&P), catering to wealthy families. Brought on as a senior adviser in 2001 was Lord Peter Daresbury, a member of the Greenall brewing dynasty who had served as Greenall's chief executive until 1999. At Roddie Fleming's behest, the investment firm looked for investment opportunities in Russia, where it came upon Koulakov and the MNV mine.

FORMING HIGHLAND: MAY 2002

FF&P was interested in investing in MNV and other Russian gold projects and brought in as a partner South Africa's Harmony Gold Mining, which was interested in diversifying outside of its home country. Hence, in May

2002 Highland Gold Mining Limited was incorporated in Jersey, with FF&P taking a 36 percent interest, Harmony 31.6 percent, and Koulakov 20.4 percent after Highland acquired ZAO MNV. Koulakov also remained in charge of operating the mine as managing director, while Lord Daresbury was installed as executive chairman, both men appointed on June 18, 2002.

According to London's the *Evening Standard* in a December 2002 article, "The Russian mining industry has had a chequered history, with numerous foreign investors lured by vast mineral reserves leaving empty-handed after having a brush with the country's complicated and often unreliable legal system." Nevertheless, Russia had in recent years made enough progress in addressing investor concerns that Highland's backers quickly acquired other properties to stoke interest in an initial public offering of stock to be completed before the end of 2002.

In August 2002 OAO Novoshirokinskoye (Novo) was acquired, providing Highland with the right to develop the deposit at Novoshirokinskoye, located in the Chita region of eastern Siberia, which primarily contained zinc and lead but also offered gold and silver as byproducts. Discovered in 1951, it was explored for several years before mine construction began in 1970. The project was soon suspended, however, and after a new development plan was conceived in the late 1980s it too was terminated in 1994 due to changing conditions in the country. After acquiring the Novo mine, Highland commissioned a feasibility study to determine how best to exploit the deposit. In September 2002 Highland added another developmental project to the pipeline, acquiring OOO Darasun, which held licenses to develop deposits in Darasun, Teremki, and Talatui, located near Novo. The existing gold mining complex included open-pit and underground operations and mineral processing facilities that at the moment were not operational but which Highland hoped to return to production in the next year.

HIGHLAND TAKEN PUBLIC: DECEMBER 2002

With a slate of Russian gold projects in hand, Highland completed a stock offering in December 2002, netting $25 million for the company and another $14 million for its backers. The shares then began trading on AIM, immediately becoming the second largest company on the exchange in terms of market capitalization. When the year came to a close a few weeks later, Highland recorded revenues of $27.4 million from 178,000 ounces of gold produced at MNV and net earnings of $5.4 million.

```
╔══════════════════════════════════════╗
║                                      ║
║            KEY DATES                 ║
║                 ▪                    ║
║ ┌──────────────────────────────────┐ ║
║ │ 1999: Mnogovershinnoye (MNV) gold │ ║
║ │       mine resumes production     │ ║
║ │       under new ownership.        │ ║
║ │ 2002: Highland Gold Mining Limited│ ║
║ │       is formed to acquire MNV and│ ║
║ │       other Russian gold assets.  │ ║
║ │ 2004: Darasun mine begins         │ ║
║ │       production.                 │ ║
║ │ 2006: Fire at Darasun mine kills  │ ║
║ │       25.                         │ ║
║ │ 2007: Darasun mine is sold.       │ ║
║ └──────────────────────────────────┘ ║
╚══════════════════════════════════════╝
```

Another mining property was added in September 2003, JSC Mayskoye, which held the license to develop the Mayskoye gold deposit. Located in Russia's remote far northeast, Mayskoye was uncovered during a geological mapping effort in the area that was begun in 1953. The deposit was discovered in 1972, and a year later an exploration development program was launched and conducted in fits and starts over the next three decades. For about $35 million Highland was able to double its gold reserves, estimated to be as much as 525 tons. Two weeks later Highland purchased the MNV production assets it did not own but had previously leased.

With its position in the Russian gold sector bolstered, Highland was able to land a new investor and development partner in October 2003 when Barrick Gold Corporation of Canada acquired a 10 percent stake in the company from Harmony. In a press statement, Barrick's chief executive, Gregory Wilkins, explained, "We are making this investment due to the markedly improved investment climate in Russia and an abundance of quality gold targets in this region." Gold production increased to 194,000 ounces in 2003, resulting in revenues of $71.6 million and a net profit of $18 million.

In January 2004 Barrick deepened its commitment to Highland. It signed a four-year strategic partnership and invested $40 million, increasing its stake in Highland to 17 percent. The year would also bring the opening of the renovated Darasun mine, after an investment of $28 million, and by the end of the year it would produce 4,870 ounces of gold. Added to the 195,026 ounces produced by MNV, Highland's total gold production approached the 200,000-ounce level, but Darasun's contribution came at a high price: The mine suffered three fatalities in the workforce during the year. Also in 2004 Highland acquired licenses to mine the Talatui and Novoshirokinskoye deposits in the Chita Region; acquired an 80 percent interest in Investment Mining & Geology Company, license holder of the exploration of gold and silver deposits in the Kurile Region; and acquired the exploration and production rights for Taseevskoye deposit in the Chita region.

While Highland enjoyed some successes, investors were not satisfied with the company's performance. Darasun was expected to open earlier than it did, lowering the amount of production the company had counted on. Moreover, the MNV mine experienced higher than anticipated operating costs. Investors bid down the price of Highland's stock and in December Lord Daresbury resigned, offering no explanation beyond "the time is now right for new leadership." He was replaced as executive chairman by James Cross, a company director who had previously served as the senior deputy governor of the South African Reserve Bank, and had overseen the London trading desk for Swiss investment bank UBS. Two months later Koulakov was appointed deputy chairman and was succeeded as managing director by Dmitry Korobov.

Despite its problems, Highland was still able to attract new money in 2005. An April bond issue raised $26.8 million and a month later Barrick spent another $50 million for new shares of stock to increase its stake in Highlander to 20 percent, the money earmarked to lower short-term debt and finance development work. Later in the year Highland increased its potential plays by acquiring several more exploration projects, but the major development in 2005 was the significant drop in production from MNV, which fell to 140,038 ounces. Darasun, in the meantime, increased its production fivefold but could not make up the difference. As a result, Highland lost $7.2 million in 2005.

TRAGEDY STRIKES DARASUN: 2006

In February 2006 Korobov was replaced as managing director by Henry Horne, who possessed 25 years of mining experience. In that same month, Barrick strengthened its commitment to Highland, increasing its stake to 34 percent and exercising the right to acquire half-interests in three exploration projects. Barrick also placed a pair of its people on the board of directors and merged its Moscow office with Highland's office, bringing to bear the experience of more than 30 of their employees. While MNV enjoyed some improvement over the previous year, 2006 was marred by a fire at Darsun in September that took place 100 meters underground. Welding being done to repair a lift set some wood ablaze while 64 miners were working below ground. The welders failed to report the fire, despite spending at least an hour attempting to extinguish it. When the disaster was over 25 miners were left dead.

Darasun was put back into production later in 2006, but the operation was losing money, prompting management several months later to sell the property for $25 million to private mining company Yuzhuralzoloto. In connection to the fire, Highland took a charge of $79.3 million in 2006, a major cause of the $96.4 million the company lost in 2006.

Highland made strides in 2007 in integrating the Barrick personnel, improving operations at MNV, restructuring its finances, and progressing on its exploration projects. Perhaps the company's greatest asset, however, was the sheer scarcity of gold in the world, caused by decreasing production levels coupled with increasing demand. Roman Abramovich was optimistic enough in the future of Highland that late in 2007 he paid $400 million to acquire newly issued Highland shares to take a 40 percent interest. Not only did Highland have Barrick's expertise, it stood to benefit from Abramovich's considerable influence in Russia.

Ed Dinger

PRINCIPAL SUBSIDIARIES

ZAO Mnogovershinnoye; OAO Novoshirokinskoye; OOO Taseevskoye; OOO ZK Mayskoye.

PRINCIPAL COMPETITORS

Celtic Resources Holdings plc; Mining and Metallurgical Company Norilsk Nickel; Peter Hambro Mining PLC.

FURTHER READING

"British Company Expands Russian Gold Mine Holdings," *Interfax News Agency, Moscow,* September 4, 2003.

Chung, Joanna, "Canadians Stake Their Claim in Russian Gold," *Financial Times,* October 14, 2003, p. 25.

Cole, Robert, "Highland Gold Mining," *Times* (London), September 22, 2004, p. 24.

"Fire Kills 25 at Highland Gold's Darasun Gold Mine," *E&MJ,* October 2006, p. 18.

"Highland Surveys Its Golden Prospects," *Growth Company,* January 7, 2003.

Hill, Andrew, "Highland Gold Rush," *Financial Times,* December 5, 2007, p. 22.

Hotten, Russell, "Mining Gold Is Now More Precious Than Ever," *Daily Telegraph* (London), December 5, 2007.

Klinger, Peter, "Daresbury Quits As Highland Chairman," *Times* (London), December 10, 2004, p. 66.

Padgham, Jane, "Miners Counting on Lure of Russian Gold," *Evening Standard* (London), December 2, 2002, p. 36.

Stiff, Peter, "Abramovich Digs into Gold Mining," *Times Online,* December 4, 2007.

Sunderland, Ruth, "The Family with the Golden Touch," *Observer,* January 7, 2007.

Highlights for Children, Inc.

———■———

1800 Watermark Drive
P.O. Box 269
Columbus, Ohio 43216-0269
U.S.A.
Telephone: (614) 486-0631
Toll Free: (800) 255-9517
Fax: (570) 251-7847
Web site: http://www.highlights.com

Private Company
Founded: 1946
Employees: 75
Sales: $110 million (2007 est.)
NAIC: 511120 Periodical Publishers

■ ■ ■

Highlights magazine is the flagship publication of the Highlights for Children, Inc., fleet and a leader in American children's publishing. Family-owned and -operated, with a circulation of more than two million, *Highlights* surpasses the distribution of such magazines as *National Geographic for Kids* and *Nickelodeon,* whose parent organizations are multimillion-dollar conglomerates. The success of the over 60-year-old *Highlights* has been attributed to its unaltered focus on providing "Fun with a Purpose," the slogan adopted by founders Garry and Caroline Myers, and a reliance on a simple format and identifiable characters. Through acquisitions, the Highlights family has come to include Boyds Mills Press, Zaner-Bloser handwriting and spelling programs, Teachers' Publishing Group, educator

resource Staff Development for Educators, and *Teaching PreK–8* magazine.

FAMILY BEGINNINGS

Highlights founders Dr. Garry C. Myers and Caroline Clark Myers shared a passion for education and sought to spread their enthusiasm for learning. Both Garry and Caroline were born on farms in eastern Pennsylvania in the late 1880s and were well educated. Garry's educational background included a bachelor's degree from Ursinus College; a master's degree from the University of Pennsylvania; and a Ph.D. in psychology from Columbia University. He went on to teach at several universities and was an active member in professional organizations including the American Psychological Association and the National Society for the Study of Education.

Caroline, too, valued a good education. At a time when fewer than 10 percent of American women went to college, Caroline attended Ursinus College, Juniata College, Merrill-Palmer Institute, and Columbia University. She became an educator, tutoring illiterate World War I soldiers and joining the National Council on Family Relations. Garry and Caroline married on June 26, 1912.

The couple became nationally recognized for their involvement in child development studies. After the end of World War I, they moved to Cleveland, Ohio, to teach classes for educators and parents at Case Western Reserve University. In addition, Garry wrote a syndicated newspaper column called "Parent Problems," and together they authored several books about parenting. Much of the Myerses' advice helped parents understand and support children who were struggling academically. While living in Cleveland, the couple had three children: Jack, Garry Jr., and Elizabeth.

The Myerses' introduction to the children's magazine market began in the 1930s when they started working for a publication called *Children's Activities*. They gave lectures to children in classrooms and to parent groups on behalf of the magazine. Their lecture circuit began in 1941 and lasted for nearly five years, taking them across the nation. During their travels, the couple grew dissatisfied with the editorial process and managerial style of *Children's Activities*.

"FUN WITH A PURPOSE," 1946 TO SIXTIES

By 1946 the Myerses had raised their three children, witnessed the birth of six grandchildren, and moved to a family farm in Honesdale, Pennsylvania, where they planned to retire. However, instead of retiring to front porch rocking chairs, Garry and Caroline worked on plans for creating a new children's publication. Within a month they had designed a magazine similar in content to *Children's Activities*. Caroline then drove back to Ohio, delivering the first issue of *Highlights for Children* to a printer. With their motto "Fun with a Purpose" imprinted on the cover, they ordered an initial print run of 20,000 copies. For the new venture, Garry signed on as editor-in-chief and Caroline became managing editor, posts they held until their deaths.

Advertising and selling the magazine became a challenge early on. Early sales were handled through door-to-door contact; some of their first customers were doctors and dentists who caught on to the idea of a quality children's magazine and began displaying *Highlights* in

their waiting rooms. With this new audience came a unique marketing technique. Similar to other magazines, subscription cards were placed within the pages, inviting readers to tear out the card and subscribe to the magazine. Determining readers might be more inclined to remove a card if it seemed like others already had, *Highlights* began to take out the card that appeared first in the magazine. The marketing gambit worked and many parents subscribed to the magazine for their children.

The first issue ushered in a number of features, many of which are still seen by *Highlights* readers. One of *Highlights'* most popular activities, "Hidden Pictures," debuted in 1946. Hidden Pictures consisted of a full-page drawing with a number of hidden objects. Readers were challenged to find the simple, everyday items artfully concealed on the page. In 1948, two years after the first *Highlights* magazine was published, the Myerses introduced the antics of twins "Goofus and Gallant," who showed the good boy/naughty boy sides of all personalities. The twins started out as pointy-eared elves but changed into little boys. While their appearance changed over the years, the personalities remained the same: Goofus was the "naughty" boy and Gallant was the "good" one. A few years later, in 1951, readers were introduced to "Timbertoes," a family of wooden people who lived in a picture-world. The easy-to-follow pictures and simple words encouraged pre- and beginning readers to read the stories themselves.

The educational, entertaining, and visually stimulating content of *Highlights* was a priority from the start of the publication. With an emphasis on editorial content as a constant guiding factor, the publishers made the early decision to include no advertising (other than its own) throughout its pages. Subscriptions provided the sole means of revenue and the editors stuck to this child-centered philosophy throughout its publishing history. Much of the magazine's marketing success was attributed to Garry C. Myers Jr., son of the founders. In 1949 he assumed the president's office and held the position until he and his wife died tragically in a 1960 plane crash. His older brother, Jack, took on many of his business responsibilities as well as guardianship of the couple's five children.

FAMILY TRADITIONS, SEVENTIES AND EIGHTIES

By the early 1970s *Highlights* had proven itself to parents and educators, and had become a favorite of children. Thousands of young readers wrote letters every month, some asking questions about school, home, or friends. Each letter was answered with a personal response, and many of the stories, poems, and artwork

KEY DATES

1946: Husband-and-wife team Garry and Caroline Myers found *Highlights.*

1948: Popular "Goofus and Gallant" characters are introduced to readers.

1951: The wooden Timbertoes family makes their *Highlights* debut.

1971: Founder Garry Myers dies at age 87.

1972: Highlights Inc. acquires Zaner-Bloser Educational Publishers.

1980: At age 90, Managing Editor and founder Caroline Myers dies.

1985: *Teaching PreK–8*, a professional development classroom magazine, joins Highlights.

1990: The company launches a new book publishing division, Boyds Mills Press.

1991: Staff Development for Educators becomes part of Highlights.

1993: The company publishes its 500th issue of *Highlights* magazine.

2004: Boyds Mills Press acquires Front Street Inc.

2006: *Highlights* reaches two million readers per month; company publishes its one-billionth copy.

submitted were published on the magazine's "Our Own Pages." By 1971, nearly three decades after the original 20,000 copies were printed, paid circulation had grown to more than one million.

The child-centered traditions set up by the founders remained central to the magazine's ongoing success in the 1970s and 1980s. In 1971, at the age of 87, Garry Myers died while still employed as editor-in-chief of the magazine. Nine years later, in 1980, Caroline died at the age of 93. She, too, maintained her role as manager and adviser until a few years before her death. Their children, meanwhile, had taken over most of the magazine's management with daughter Elizabeth Myers Brown serving as senior editor, grandson Garry C. Myers III leading the company as chief executive officer, and grandson Kent L. Brown coming on board as an editor.

In addition to managerial changes, the era brought other advances, such as the company's expansion into other educational publishing arenas. In 1972 Highlights acquired Zaner-Bloser Educational Publishers, a company originally established as a college of penmanship in 1888. Zaner-Bloser had since become the nation's leading series of handwriting and spelling programs for children in kindergarten through eighth grade. While Highlights had always encouraged children's education, the company had also segued into supporting educators themselves. In 1985 the publishing company added a professional development magazine for teachers, *Teaching PreK–8,* to its line of publications. This magazine offered author interviews, classroom strategies and activities, teacher resources, and much more. The recipient of many "Excellence in Educational Journalism" awards, *Teaching PreK–8* became a valued asset to the Highlights line.

Since the Myerses saw their magazine and publishing company as an investment not only in children's education but their futures as well, the company established a foundation in 1987 to provide educational workshops to writers and illustrators committed to high-quality children's literature. The nonprofit organization offered classes and workshops as well as scholarships to deserving applicants.

NEW GENERATIONS, THE NINETIES

With its guiding principle of promoting a love for reading, Highlights continued to expand its reach in the 1990s. Boyds Mills Press, a publisher of picture books, fiction, nonfiction, poetry, and activity books for children of all ages was created in 1990. Similar to all Highlights publications, the book division avoided trendy, pop culture topics and strived to tell stories with lasting value. The following year, in 1991, the company began to offer professional development workshops and seminars through Staff Development for Educators (SDE) to help teachers of prekindergarten through 12th grade. As history had repeatedly shown, readers of Highlights publications still related to the content provided. In July 1993 *Highlights* magazine rolled out its 500th issue and remained the nation's largest-circulating children's magazine.

While rivals of *Highlights* had offered similar content for some time, many began publishing new magazines for the preteen audience. Publications such as *National Geographic for Kids* branched into *National Geographic World.* Other popular periodicals issued junior editions; these included *Sports Illustrated for Kids* and *Zillions (Consumer Reports* version for kids). In response to the competitive landscape, Highlights maintained the status quo, continuing to focus on quality for a general interest audience spanning preschoolers through 12-year-olds.

In 1996 *Highlights* was still the nation's leading children's magazine and its subscription base continued to grow. While most of its international subscribers had come from Canada, the mid-1990s saw an increase outside North America with 20,000 subscribers living in Europe, Asia, and other places. The company also sought to expand its nonmagazine holdings, acquiring the aptly named Teachers' Publishing Group, a publisher offering books and resources written by and for teachers. As the 20th century drew to a close, Highlights had reached sales of more than $100 million according to the February 5, 1999, issue of *Business First-Columbus.* The company joined the online revolution by launching a web site (www.highlights.com), complete with interactive games and various features, and began releasing educational CDs.

A NEW ERA, 2000 AND BEYOND

Highlights kicked off the new millennium with an international twist on an old idea: the magazine had been launched through direct contact with salespeople and teachers, and 60 years later, in January 2000, Highlights partnered with an Australian company to sell educational toys to parents and teachers through parties at schools and homes. This new direct-sales business, Highlights-Jigsaw Toy Factory, Inc., began testing markets in Ohio and by the end of the year had attracted more than 100 independent representatives worldwide.

Expansion continued in the early 2000s, keeping competition at bay. In 2004 Stephen Roxburgh's book publishing company Front Street Inc., became a direct imprint of Boyds Mills Press, run by Kent Brown, the founders' grandson. The acquisition relieved some of Roxburgh's administrative and production costs, freeing up time to focus on acquiring and publishing quality literature. Highlights benefited from the additional titles distributed through the distinguished Front Street line. In addition to the success of the book division, by August 2006 *Highlights* magazine had garnered more than two million monthly readers and printed its one-billionth copy.

Kent S. Johnson, chief executive and great-grandson of the founders, believed Highlights could stay true to its original mission of helping children learn through fun activities and thought-provoking stories while build-

ing upon its success in the 21st century. Johnson told *American Executive* in a June 2007 interview, "My great-grandparents felt that children have a greater capacity to learn than adults assume. They also felt that children should be taught by example, and those examples should convey purposeful messages related to morals and values." Johnson's words continued to resonate with *Highlights* readers of all ages, 60 years later.

Jodi Essey-Stapleton

PRINCIPAL OPERATING UNITS

Boyds Mills Press; Highlights for Children Magazine; Staff Development for Educators; Teachers' Publishing Group; Teaching PreK–8; Zaner-Bloser Educational Publishers, Inc.; Highlights-Jigsaw Toy Factory, Inc.

PRINCIPAL COMPETITORS

American Girl, Inc.; Disney Publishing Worldwide; Houghton Mifflin Harcourt Publishing Company; National Geographic Society; Nickelodeon Networks; RD School and Educational Services; Scholastic Corporation.

FURTHER READING

French, Liz, "Fun with a Purpose," http://www.AmericanExecutive.com, June 1, 2007.

"Magazines Spin Off Versions," *Christian Science Monitor,* November 1, 1994.

McCloud, Cynthia, "Highlights of Childhood: Fun with a Purpose," *Morgantown (W.Va.) Dominion Post,* July 13, 2006.

Milliot, Jim, "Front Street Merges with Boyds Mills Press," *Publishers Weekly,* August 23, 2004, p. 7.

Showalter, Kathy, "Making Its Play," *Business First-Columbus,* July 13, 2001, p. A1.

Wirfel, Courtney, "Caroline Elizabeth Clark Myers," *Contemporary Authors Online,* Detroit: Thomson Gale, 2007.

Woodard, Kathy L., "Kid's Fun Without Product Hype," *Business First-Columbus,* February 5, 1999, p. 21.

Zorn, Eric, "Goofus, Gallant Give Life Balance," *Chicago Tribune,* November 4, 1993, p. 1.

Home Inns & Hotels Management Inc.

Lane No. 421, Chang Ping Road
Jing An District
Shanghai, 200041
China
Telephone: (+8621) 3218-9988 2004
Web site: http://www.homeinns.com

Public Company
Incorporated: 2002
Employees: 6,300
Sales: $138.4 million (2007)
Stock Exchanges: NASDAQ
Ticker Symbol: HMIN
NAIC: 721110 Hotels (Except Casino Hotels) and Motels

■ ■ ■

Home Inns & Hotels Management Inc. has risen quickly to become the leading operator of economy hotels in the mainland Chinese market. Founded in 2002, Home Inns was operating nearly 270 hotels at the beginning of 2008. These included 195 hotels owned outright by the company, with the remainder operated as franchises under Home Inns' management. The company's network spans all of China's first-tier cities, including Shanghai and Beijing, as well as most of its second-tier cities, both on the eastern coastal region, and across the country. In all, Home Inns operates hotels in 66 cities across China, with more than 16,000 beds. The company also boasts one of the market's highest room occupancy rates, of more than 88 percent, and at times as high as 98 percent.

Part of the group's success has been its commitment to affordable, high-quality, and especially standardized accommodations. Home Inns hotels are highly formatted, featuring the same furniture and furnishings, particularly four-star quality bedding, across the chain. Rooms include free broadband Internet access, air conditioning, fresh drinking water and round-the-clock hot water, as well as modern bathrooms. Home Inns has also focused on acquiring prime property locations for its hotels. Following its listing on the NASDAQ in 2006, Home Inns announced its plans to expand to as many as 1,000 hotels by the end of the decade. Toward this goal, the company opened 100 hotels in 2007 alone; at the beginning of 2008, the group had another 115 hotels, in more than 80 cities, under development. Home Inns is led by CEO and Chairman David Sun. The company posted revenues of $138.4 million in 2007.

TARGETING THE CHINESE TRAVEL MARKET IN 1999

China's tourism market remained largely undeveloped at the end of the 20th century, in keeping with the low income levels of the vast majority of the country's population. The lack of discretionary spending meant that there was little impetus to develop the country's travel and tourism market. As a result, the hotel and lodgings market remained highly fragmented, with few national companies attempting to build Western-style branded chains. The vast majority of available accom-

COMPANY PERSPECTIVES

Company Highlights: Favorable industry fundamentals driving growth of economy hotel chains in China. Established leadership with broad national coverage and early mover advantage. Two pronged business model enables rapid expansion and penetration. Strong brand name and consistent product. Efficient and integrated operational infrastructure and information systems. Experienced management team and motivated staff. Outstanding track record of growth and profitability.

modations could be found in private homes, government-owned hostels, and similar settings, with extreme variability in furnishings and cleanliness.

While a growing number of star-rated hotels had appeared, only the luxury class four- and five-star hotels provided a degree of consistency, and profitability. The country's one-to-three-star hotel market struggled to avoid financial collapse; at the same time, the sector suffered from a reputation for low-quality accommodations. Meanwhile, the higher prices of the star-rated hotels reserved these accommodations to foreign travelers or business travelers from larger corporations.

The first economy hotels appeared in the late 1990s. These nonrated hotels, similar to U.S.-style motels, provided relatively simple accommodations at budget prices. The first economy hotels were introduced by Jin Jiang Inns in 1997. That company grew modestly before adopting a highly franchise-focused growth model.

The surge in China's economy by then had created a fast-growing middle class. The new availability of discretionary spending, consequently, led to an upturn in the domestic travel and tourism market. At the same time, the booming economy also stimulated the growth of a new class of business traveler. Another factor in the coming boom in the Chinese tourism industry was the new liberty of movement available to the Chinese population. Throughout much of the Communist era, the population movement was tightly controlled. Few Chinese were allowed to travel beyond their home provinces. The relaxing of these restrictions, and the increasing urban concentration of the population, brought about a new demand for budget travel accommodations.

Among the people to recognize the new opportunities in the country was Liang Jianzhang (James Liang). Liang had left China for the United States in the early 1990s, earning a computer engineering degree at Georgia Tech, before finding work in Silicon Valley. By the late 1990s, Liang had taken a position with Oracle that brought him back to the Chinese mainland. Liang's job was to convince companies of the need to adopt modern, Western-style management and administrative techniques.

Liang soon decided to put his own advice into action, and began looking for partners. In 1999, he met Ji Qi, when the latter applied for a license to sell Oracle software in China. The pair decided to go into business together, targeting the still largely undeveloped Chinese travel sector. Liang and Ji's idea was to introduce a Western-styled Internet-based consolidator model to the market, despite the relatively low levels of Internet penetration in China at the time. Liang and Ji then recruited additional partners. The first of these was Shen Nanpeng (Neil Shen) who brought a background working in the U.S. financial industry. The second was Min Fan, whose career experience included working in the top management at a state-owned travel corporation.

The new company, Ctrip, was launched that same year, backed by just $250,000 in startup funds. Yet the company's early entry allowed it to grow quickly, establishing itself as the market's dominant player just as Internet usage began to take off in China.

GETTING IN ON THE ECONOMY HOTEL GROUND FLOOR

The growth of Ctrip led Liang and his partners to investigate other opportunities within the travel and tourism field. The rising affluence of Chinese society enabled larger numbers of people, particularly those working in higher-wage, urban areas, to begin traveling for leisure. The appearance of large numbers of small, privately held companies at the same time created a new demand for accommodations especially suited to this market.

The growth of the budget hotel market, with Jin Jiang in the lead, attracted the attention of the Ctrip founders. In 2001, the company formed a new Hong Kong-based subsidiary, Home Inns & Hotels Management, in order to develop its own chain of hotels, to be called Home Inns. Joining Ctrip in the project was Beijing Capital Travel International Hotel Group Co., Ltd., part of Beijing Tourism Group, a state-owned holding company operating in the travel sector. In 2002, the partners launched Home Inns Beijing in order to open its first hotels in that all-important market. Ctrip initially controlled 55 percent of the company; over the

KEY DATES

2002: Home Inns is founded as subsidiary of travel consolidator Ctrips and opens first four hotels in Beijing.
2003: Home Inns & Hotels Management is spun off as separate company.
2004: David Sun is appointed CEO to lead expansion of Home Inns chain; first franchise hotels open.
2006: Home Inns & Hotels Management launches its IPO.
2007: Company acquires Shanghai Top Star Hotel Management Co., adding 25 hotels.

next year, however, Ctrip increased its stake in the company, buying part of Beijing Capital's 45 percent.

The Home Inn format was very much inspired by the hotels and motels of the 1950s in the United States, which spawned such noted brands as Holiday Inn and Howard Johnson. Home Inns developed a highly standardized format, outfitting its hotels with identical furniture and furnishings. Importantly, the company's room featured four-star quality bedding. Hotels were also painted bright yellow, in order to increase visibility in the crowded urban landscape. As part of its effort to cater to the small business traveler, the company offered free broadband Internet access in every room, as well as fresh drinking water and on-demand hot water. However, rates remained highly reasonable, at approximately $25 per night.

The company's commitment to quality, comfort, and cleanliness quickly attracted attention from the travel market, especially the growing number of business travelers. Through the early years of the 2000s, Home Inns' hotels boasted occupancy rates as high as 98 percent.

By the end of its first year, Home Inns operated four hotels in the Beijing market. The company then targeted the next largest Chinese market, Shanghai, opening its first hotels there. By the end of 2003, Home Inns operated ten hotels.

LEADING THE IPO WAVE IN 2006

Ctrip began planning its initial public offering (IPO) in 2003. As part of that effort, the company decided to spin off Home Inns as an independent company, Home Inns & Hotels Management Inc., that year. During that

process, Ctrip brought in a new group of equity investors, reducing its own stake in the company to 33 percent. At the same time, the company decided to bring in a new chief executive, David Sun, who had acquired experience in the retail sector as head of a ten-store chain of B&Q hardware stores, owned by Kingfisher of the United Kingdom, in the Shanghai region.

Home Inns continued to open new hotels in the Beijing and Shanghai markets. In addition the company also targeted expansion into the country's provincial regions, and its many second-tier and smaller cities. By the end of 2004, the company was present in ten cities, with 26 hotels in all. This figure nearly tripled the following year, as the group established a presence across 22 cities, with a total of 68 hotels. By then, the company had caught up with sector pioneer Jin Jiang.

Home Inns also enjoyed a strong reputation among travelers for the consistent quality of its hotels. This came in part due to the company's early decision to avoid adopting a franchise model, such as Jin Jiang, and instead maintain tight control over its hotel network. In this way, customers were assured of receiving a similar experience at all of the group's hotels, a model highly similar to that developed in the fast-food industry.

By the middle of the first decade of the 2000s, however, Home Inns was faced with a rising number of competitors. There were more than 100 economy hotel brands in operation across the country by 2006. In order to maintain its momentum, Home Inns was forced to step up its expansion rate. For this, the company took two approaches. The first was to develop its own franchise system. However, the Home Inns franchise, launched in 2004, exhibited significant differences from its competitors. The most important difference was the company's insistence that it appoint the hotel managers for the franchised properties, which were held to exactly the same format and standards as the group's own hotels.

With franchisees bearing the capital costs of new hotel openings, the company's network entered a new period of expansion. Home Inns, however, sought to maintain tight control over its hotel network, and as a result targeted a franchise rate of just 30 percent.

In keeping with this approach, the company turned to the international investment community, listing its stock on the NASDAQ in October 2006. The offering was a strong success, and signaled the start of a wave of Chinese hotel and tourism IPOs.

LARGEST ECONOMY HOTEL BRAND

Home Inns continued to add new properties as it stepped up its expansion drive. In 2006, the company opened nearly 70 new hotels. The following year, the company's new hotel openings topped 100, with another 115 in development as the company entered 2008.

At the same time, Home Inns' public offering provided it with a war chest to launch the first salvo in what many observers considered the inevitable consolidation of the highly fragmented economy hotel sector in China. Home Inns' first acquisition remained modest, however. In June 2007, the company bought the small Capital Sunshine Hotel group, which operated three budget hotels in Beijing.

The successful integration of these properties soon paved the way for what CEO Sun called the "formal start" of Home Inns' acquisition drive. In October 2007, Home Inns reached an agreement to acquire one of its larger rivals, Shanghai Top Star Management Co. Ltd., based in Shanghai, which operated a chain of 26 economy hotels. Top Star was established in 2005, and grew rapidly to claim the economy hotel sector's eighth place, with more than 4,200 rooms. Yet the chain's occupancy rates trailed significantly behind Home Inns, capping at 70 percent. This compared to Home Inns' own rates, which consistently neared 90 percent, and even peaked at nearly full capacity.

The purchase of the Top Star chain helped push the group's total hotel portfolio past 320 at the beginning of 2008. The company then began converting the Top Star properties to the Home Inns format. At the same time Sun signaled the group's intention to pursue a more aggressive acquisition strategy through the end of the decade, announcing plans for the chain to reach as many as 1,000 hotels by 2010.

Home Inns' ambitions nonetheless faced obstacles, as competition in the economy sector began to heighten at mid-decade. Of particular concern for the company was the announcement by global hotel giant Accor that it planned to develop its own chain of Ibis economy hotels in China. For the moment, however, the potentially vast and ever expanding Chinese hotel market provided plenty of optimism for Home Inns. With its early entry and fast-mover advantage, the company appeared certain to remain a leader in the Chinese economy hotel sector for years to come.

M. L. Cohen

PRINCIPAL SUBSIDIARIES

Hemei Hotel Management Company; Home Inns & Hotels Management (Hong Kong) Limited; Home Inns & Hotels Management Inc. (Cayman Islands); Home Inns Hotel Management (Beijing) Co., Ltd.; Home Inns Hotel Management (Shanghai) Co., Ltd.; Shanghai Huiju Hotel Equipment Lease Co., Ltd.

PRINCIPAL COMPETITORS

Shanghai Jinjiang International Hotels Development Co., Ltd.; Shanghai Motel Management Co., Ltd.; Zhejiang Xinyu Inn Co., Ltd.; Hotel Home Inc.; Super 8 Inc.; UTELS Inc.; Greentree Inns Inc.

FURTHER READING

Curtis, Glenn, "Time to Check into Home Inns (HIMN)," *Investopedia Advisor,* October 29, 2007.

"Economy Hotel Rank: Home Inns Outshines Peers," *Xinhua Economic News,* October 25, 2007.

"Home Inns Acquires Top Star Hotel Chain," *SinoCast, LLC China Financial Watch,* October 24, 2007.

"Home Inns Agrees to Acquire Top Star," *Alestron,* October 25, 2007.

"Home Inns Aims Expansion Through Property Acquisitions," *Xinhua Economic News,* July 2, 2007.

"Home Inns: China's No. 1 Economy Hotel," *Alestron,* October 19, 2007.

"Home Inns Expands Operating Scale Through Acquisitions," *Xinhua Economic News,* June 26, 2007.

"Home Inns Focuses on Its Own Hotels Rather Than Franchise Hotels," *Xinhua Economic News,* October 30, 2006.

"Home Inns' Hotel Chain Grows to 134 Hotels," *M2 Presswire,* January 26, 2007.

"Home Inns to Expand Hotels," *Alestron,* July 27, 2007.

"IDG-Backed Hotel Chain Files IPO on NASDAQ," *Private Equity Week,* October 16, 2006, p. 4.

"South China, Not Predominant Market for Home Inns, Says CEO," *Xinhua Economic News,* August 16, 2007.

Imperial Oil Limited

237 Fourth Avenue Southwest
Calgary, Alberta T2P 3M9
Canada
Telephone: (403) 237-3737
Toll Free: (800) 567-3776
Fax: (800) 567-3776
Web site: http://www.imperialoil.ca

Public Company, Majority-Owned by Exxon Mobil Corporation
Incorporated: 1880 as The Imperial Oil Company, Limited
Employees: 4,800
Sales: CAD 25.07 billion ($25.37 billion) (2007)
Stock Exchanges: Toronto American
Ticker Symbol: IMO
NAIC: 211111 Crude Petroleum and Natural Gas Extraction; 211112 Natural Gas Liquids Extraction; 324110 Petroleum Refineries; 324191 Petroleum Lubricating Oil and Grease Manufacturing; 325110 Petrochemical Manufacturing; 424710 Petroleum Bulk Stations and Terminals; 424720 Petroleum and Petroleum Products Merchant Wholesalers (Except Bulk Stations and Terminals); 447110 Gasoline Stations with Convenience Stores; 447190 Other Gasoline Stations; 486110 Pipeline Transmission of Crude Oil; 454311 Heating Oil Dealers; 486210 Pipeline Transportation of Natural Gas; Pipeline Transportation of Refined Petroleum Products

■ ■ ■

An integrated energy company, Imperial Oil Limited is one of Canada's largest producers of crude oil and natural gas, producing on average more than 350,000 barrels of oil equivalent each day. Its main exploration and production projects are situated onshore in Alberta and the Northwest Territories and offshore in the Beaufort Sea and in the North Atlantic off Canada's East Coast. In addition to its activities in conventional crude oil and natural gas, the firm has vast reserves of oil sands, from which it extracts heavy oil (or bitumen), which can be converted to crude oil or used for other purposes. Imperial, which is 69.6 percent owned by U.S. oil giant Exxon Mobil Corporation, is Canada's largest refiner of petroleum products, with the capacity to process 500,000 barrels of crude oil per day at its four refineries in Strathcona, Alberta; Dartmouth, Nova Scotia; and Sarnia and Nanticoke, Ontario. These refineries produce a wide variety of products and services that are marketed under the Esso and Mobil brand names at more than 1,900 Esso stations across Canada and also distributed through 27 primary distribution terminals and more than 90 secondary bulk terminals. The company also produces and markets various petrochemicals. Imperial has made itself known for its support of Canadian culture, health, education, and community services.

FORMATION FOLLOWING 1876 CANADIAN OIL BUST

In 1880, when Imperial Oil Company was founded in London, Ontario, oil actually did not look like a good business. The Canadian oil boom, triggered in 1857 with the sinking of the first oil well, had gone bust in

COMPANY PERSPECTIVES

Imperial Oil has been a major contributor to the growth of the petroleum industry and to Canada's economic and social development for more than 125 years. Today the company is well positioned to participate in some of the industry's most promising growth developments.

1876. Domestic overproduction and liberal free-trade policies had conspired to saturate the Canadian market. The industrial boom and rampant land speculation, begun in the 1850s, were coming to a halt. During the boom many Canadians had jumped to join the oil rush, which contributed to the flooding of the local market. This, coupled with a worldwide depression, resulted in deflated oil prices that were one-third of their former value. Thus, in 1876, Canadian refiners who had glutted their own market began to desert their businesses at bailout prices.

It was at this crisis point that 16 well-established Canadian businessmen from London and Petrolia, Ontario, banded together and decided to buy into the petroleum business. On September 8, 1880, with CAD 25,000, The Imperial Oil Company, Limited was formed. Its charter was "to find, produce, refine and distribute petroleum and its products throughout Canada." With two refineries, one in London and the other in Petrolia, the total capitalization was an impressive CAD 500,000.

Frederick A. Fitzgerald, a builder of the London Water Works who also dabbled in furniture, liquor, groceries, and oil, became Imperial's first president. The mastermind of the group's success, however, was its vice-president, Jacob Englehart, who by age 33 had 14 years experience in oil, having started his first refinery at age 19. William Spencer and Herman and Isaac Waterman also brought their knowledge of refineries to the association; Isaac Waterman's involvement in municipal politics and the railway, in particular, later proved to be a valuable asset to the group. John Geary, a lawyer-turned-refiner, and John Minhinnik, a plumber-turned-refiner, were more than ready to deal with the business's logistical and physical problems. Thomas Smallman and John Walker brought the experience they had gained when producing sulfuric acid with the first Canadian chemical company, while Walker was also experienced in federal politics. It was no accident that Thomas

Hodgens, a former wagon maker, and his brother Edward, a barrel maker, were brought into the deal. Edward Hodgens in 1879 had also patented a process that sweetened the odor of the rancid-smelling Canadian crude, making it more competitive with relatively odorless U.S. crude.

The group immediately began trying to set its products apart by improving their quality, as well as by trying to find new uses for the products and to increase distribution. Imperial acquired rights to Hodgens's patent and started deodorizing its oil. It began importing a new kerosene lamp that burned with a brighter, whiter light, from Germany. It sent dealers out into the previously unpenetrated west to hustle up sales. In the space of one year, Imperial was selling to Winnipeg, a frontier town of 8,000, as well as opening up an office in Montreal.

Imperial oil, carried in Imperial's handmade barrels, rode on Imperial-built wagons across the prairies of the Northwest Territories to Hudson's Bay Company posts. Imperial became so well known for its sturdy oak barrels, that, although the company offered a generous CAD 1.25 refund for each, most homesteaders chose to keep them and convert them to washtubs, rain barrels, and armchairs. By 1883 Walker's position as vice-president of Canadian Pacific Railway had helped Imperial to become the basic supplier not only of railroad construction crews but also of the settlers that squatted along the line as far as British Columbia.

After three years of growth, Imperial Oil suffered a major setback. During a thunderstorm in July, lightning hit an Imperial refinery, sparking a fire that burned its London processing operation to the ground. In 1884, when Imperial requested of the city of London a CAD 20,000 grant to build a new line to pipe crude from Imperial's Lambton wells into the city, its political connections were not enough. Londoners had had enough of the flash fires and the stench rising from streams of gasoline that ran from where it was dumped on the streets down to the river. Gasoline, a then-useless byproduct of kerosene, created problems elsewhere as well. Some refiners, trying to get the most dollars per barrel, illegally cut kerosene with gasoline, causing lamps not infrequently to explode when ignited. It is believed that gasoline mixed in with lamp kerosene started the Great Chicago Fire. Rather than rebuilding in what it felt to be a now-hostile London, Imperial moved its head offices first to Petrolia and then to Sarnia, Ontario. Within a short time, almost all related industries followed Imperial from London to Sarnia, which was becoming the new oil center.

KEY DATES

1880: A group of 16 well-established Canadian businessmen band together to form The Imperial Oil Company, Limited, based in London, Ontario.

1898: Needing capital for expansion, Imperial sells a majority interest to Standard Oil Company (New Jersey), later Exxon Corporation.

1899: As part of the previous year's deal, Imperial gains Standard Oil's Canadian assets, including its refinery in Sarnia, Ontario.

1907: In Vancouver, Imperial opens Canada's first service station.

1919: Company changes its name to Imperial Oil Limited.

1947: Imperial makes a major oil discovery at Leduc, Alberta, marking the beginning of western Canada's development into a major oil-producing region.

1978: The consortium Syncrude Canada Limited, 25 percent owned by Imperial, begins mining-based production of the Athabasca oil sands of Alberta.

1985: Company begins commercial production from an oil-sands recovery project at Cold Lake, Alberta.

1990: Imperial acquires Texaco Canada Inc. in a nearly CAD 5 billion deal.

1999: Exxon and Mobil Corporation merge to form Exxon Mobil Corporation, which inherits Exxon's majority stake in Imperial Oil.

2005: Imperial shifts its headquarters from Toronto to Calgary.

NEW PRODUCTS AND AFFILIATIONS

By 1893 Imperial had 23 branch offices spread from Halifax to Victoria. Imperial had done such a good job developing new markets that it could no longer supply the demands of the market. Imperial lacked the money necessary to expand to meet its consumers' needs, and feared losing market share to larger U.S. companies. Unable to convince Canadian or British banks or private investors to gamble with large amounts of capital, in 1898 Imperial turned to the U.S. Standard Oil Company (New Jersey), which had offered to purchase Imperial years earlier. On Dominion Day in 1898,

Standard Oil (later Exxon Corporation) assumed a majority interest in Imperial. Imperial took over Standard Oil's Canadian assets on February 23, 1899, including its refinery in Sarnia. Standard worked to keep its ownership of Imperial secret, giving Canadian government officials Imperial Oil stock as hush money.

After laying a pipeline to bring in its crude from Petrolia, Imperial was ready to start servicing all of Canada, producing 143 cubic meters per day at its Sarnia plant alone. Imperial's business got another boost with the growing popularity of the automobile. By 1910 there were about 6,000 of these gasoline-consuming machines prowling Canadian streets. Gasoline became a product in such demand that oil companies were not prepared to dispense it quickly enough. People bought gas in open buckets from grocery stores or even went to the oil companies' warehouses.

The first service station got its start in 1907 when a car pulled up to Imperial's Vancouver warehouse in between the horse-drawn oil wagons, and backfired. By the time the workers had gotten their horses settled, the foreman had banished automobiles forever. C. M. Rolston, Imperial's Vancouver manager, solved the problem the next day when he opened up Canada's first service station, a one-room metal shack with a garden hose and a water tank full of gasoline.

RAPID GROWTH DURING AND AFTER WORLD WAR I

Building a service station did not, however, meet all the demands that were awakened by automobiles. The use of automobiles increased so rapidly that Imperial was almost immediately forced to begin looking for ways to increase its supply of crude, simply to produce more gasoline. In 1914 Standard licensed Imperial to use its cracking technique, a process that yielded much more gasoline per barrel of crude, and installed the first units in its Sarnia refineries. Cracking involved the use of heat and pressure coils to chemically decompose the crude. That same year, Imperial formed the International Petroleum Company, Limited, to search for oil in South America; ordered an exploratory geological party to Turner Valley to confirm the discovery of crude near Calgary; laid a pipeline from Sarnia to Cygnet, Ohio, connecting Imperial refineries to some of the most productive oilfields in the United States; and built the first refinery in British Columbia, on Burrard Inlet. Before long, World War I broke out, creating a whole new market hungry for gasoline.

In 1919 the Imperial Oil Company, Limited changed its name to Imperial Oil Limited. To meet the new demands of war, Imperial grew rapidly. Within five years it quintupled the number of its refineries and doubled its refining capacity. By 1920 there were four times as many cars in Canada as five years prior, and once again Imperial began to search for more efficient ways to refine gasoline. In 1923 Imperial obtained Canadian rights to use pressure stills, which enhanced the cracking process, yielding a greater quantity and quality of gasoline.

Imperial in 1924 hired Reginald K. Stratford, its first research worker. He discovered that sulfur corrosion of the cracking coils could be prevented by adding lime to the crude. He also came up with a way to keep gasoline from gumming up engines by running the cracked product through a slurry of clay.

In 1926 Standard Oil began using the Esso brand name for most of its refined products (the name being derived from the initials for Standard Oil). Eventually, Standard's various affiliates around the world, including Imperial Oil, adopted the Esso name for their refined products. Imperial's service stations eventually began operating under the Esso banner as well.

The 1930s, for Imperial, were full of changes. Previously geologists searching for oil depended on a hammer, a chisel, maybe a pair of field glasses, and a lot of luck. In the 1920s, the rotary drill rig came along, and it became possible to drill deeper beneath the surface. Then, in the 1930s, Imperial started investigating the possibilities of seismology. Its geologists bounced shock waves off of underground rocks, and judging from the waves' reflection, the shape and size of possible oil formations could be determined. Imperial had started implementing these procedures before the outbreak of World War II, when the Allies needed all the fuel they could get.

CONTRIBUTIONS TO WAR EFFORT

Imperial was able to produce a large amount of the 87-octane aviation fuel that the Commonwealth Air Training Plan needed for its training aircraft by selecting crude oils containing the most useful fractions and by modifying its distillation equipment. Imperial also helped to produce 100-octane aviation fuel for combat aircraft. The company aided in the development of portable runways that could be rolled up, taken to a flat field almost anywhere, and laid in place. Imperial was a key player in Operation Shuttle, which kept oil flowing to Great Britain for a full two years before the United States entered the war.

Alaska's importance grew when Japan entered the war, and airports popped up there for U.S. defense. In 1942 the U.S. Army requested that Imperial build a refinery in the Yukon at Whitehorse, to supply the Alaskan airfields. Within two years, a ten-centimeter pipeline snaked out from the Whitehorse refinery to supply the much-needed fuel for a full year before the war ended.

When the war ended, Imperial welcomed back its employees who had served. Throughout the war, the company had made up the difference between military pay and the salaries at Imperial when military pay was lower. On enlistment, Imperial had given its employees one month's salary as a bonus.

In 1946 Imperial sold 6.275 million cubic meters of crude, more than any previous year. The company's officers, realizing that there had been no meaningful field discoveries since 1920, launched a full-scale exploration to assure supplies for the future.

LEDUC STRIKE IN 1947

At the end of the 1940s, 90 percent of all crude oil refined in Canada was imported. Imperial drilled 133 consecutive dry holes. The future looked so bad that Imperial was debating the expensive conversion of natural gas to gasoline. If things did not change, the company decided it would have to close its Sarnia refinery and rely on offshore crude shipped in to Montreal. Before Imperial shut down and began building in Montreal, however, the company's leadership decided to drill once more in the Hinge Belt, south of Edmonton. Seismograph crews picked a site in Leduc. On February 13, 1947, the Leduc well gushed oil in huge quantities. The extent of Leduc's success is best measured by the fact that the wells that quickly sprouted up in that area provided 90 percent of all oil produced in Canada; the strike is considered the starting point for western Canada's development into a major oil-producing region. With Leduc's success came the call for a neighboring refinery. Imperial dismantled the idled Whitehorse refinery and reassembled it in nearby Edmonton.

With the Leduc oil strike, domestic oil production was so greatly increased that Imperial began searching for ways to export it. To aid in exportation, Imperial and others joined to form Interprovincial Pipe Line Ltd. in 1949. Imperial owned 49.9 percent of Interprovincial's stock. By autumn of 1950, a pipeline had been laid from Edmonton, Ontario, to Superior, Wisconsin. In 1957 the line was extended to Toronto, then in 1976 it stretched to Montreal. Imperial sold its share of Interprovincial in 1990.

The surplus of oil in the 1950s and price wars that ensued led Imperial to analyze gasoline markets, eliminate unprofitable stations, and set up stations in the right places; some were simple gas stations, others were full-service auto "clinics." Imperial was responsible for introducing Canada's first car clinic, complete with electronic diagnosis. It was not long before highway service stations became a familiar sight, offering everything from gas to snacks. In 1970 self-service stations began popping up under the Esso name, Imperial's consumer brand name.

Canadian gas and oil reserves once again had begun to dwindle as demand continued to grow. Imperial began exploring the far northern waters off Canada's eastern coast, which was a costly operation. In January 1970, that extremely expensive search actually paid off when Imperial hit medium-gravity, low-sulfur crude at Atkinson Point, on the Beaufort Sea in the western Arctic, 1,700 meters deep. As a result of this and other offshore searches, Imperial pioneered the artificial island. The first artificial island, Immerl, was built by Imperial at the cost of CAD 5 million, not including the cost of the well, which turned out to be dry. The offshore oil search continued both in the farther north Queen Elizabeth Islands as well as in the Atlantic seabed.

In the 1960s and 1970s, Imperial Oil began developing the vast reserves of oil sands of northern Alberta, considered the world's largest single reserve of crude oil, a trillion and a half barrels worth. Unfortunately, it was both difficult and expensive to extract this heavy oil, or bitumen, from the sand to which it was embedded. The oil was extremely viscous and did not flow on its own. In the early 1960s Imperial began pilot programs at Cold Lake, where commercial production began in 1985, using a technique of recovering the bitumen from underground reservoirs without removing the sand in which it was embedded. In 1964 the company joined a consortium known as Syncrude Canada Limited, which began mining-based production of the Athabasca oil sands in 1978. By 1991 Syncrude had produced 500 million barrels of heavy oil, which could be converted to conventional crude oil or used to produce asphalt for roads, shingles, and roofing tar.

1990 ACQUISITION OF TEXACO CANADA

One of Imperial's most important steps toward growth happened in the late 1980s. In 1988 Imperial began talking to Texaco Canada Inc. about a possible merger, and in February 1989 Imperial bought the company for CAD 4.96 billion, making it the largest acquisition in Imperial's history and the second largest in Canada's. The actual merger did not take place until February 1990; it was held up awaiting approval from the Canadian competition authorities, who forced Imperial

to sell 638 retail stations, 14 oil terminals, and one refinery. (Following the merger Texaco Canada became known as McColl-Frontenac Petroleum Inc.; this name harkened back to the early history of Texaco Canada, which adopted the name McColl-Frontenac in 1927 upon the merger of McColl Brothers and Frontenac Oil Refineries Limited.)

Two consequences of this merger were immediately noteworthy. The sum of productivity and profits of both companies operating independently was surpassed by those of the two operating together as a whole, creating a synergy. Employees of both companies were looked to for answers to problems of operations and for suggestions about changes. One of the most remarkable features of the merger was the speed with which Imperial was able to reduce the initial debt incurred by the merger, taking it from CAD 4.96 billion to CAD 3.1 billion in 1989.

By this time, Imperial was much more than simply an oil producer, developer, and marketer, although it was Canada's largest petroleum company. From its beginning, Imperial's interests had branched through all aspects of the business, including the manufacture of wagons, barrels, and lamps, as well as chemicals for the treatment plants. Most of Imperial's sales were to industrial customers; it had developed into the leading manufacturer of aviation fuel, marine fuel, railway lubricants, and domestic heating fuels in Canada. In the late 1980s, Imperial stepped up its presence in the natural gas field, through the 1987 purchase of Calgary-based Sulpetro Limited and the 1988 acquisition of the Alberta oil and gas production assets of Ocelet Industries Ltd., and finally with the production capacity and reserves of natural gas gained through the addition of Texaco Canada. By 1989 the company was Canada's third largest producer of natural gas.

Imperial had also developed petrochemical interests, starting as early as 1955, and by the 1970s had developed into one of the largest chemical operations in Canada under the Esso Chemical Canada banner. Fertilizers were added to the manufacturing base in the 1960s, and were bolstered in 1989 with the purchase of Cascade Fertilizers Ltd., a western Canada-based maker of liquid fertilizers. Imperial also developed a natural resources business eventually known as Esso Resources, which at one time mined coal, zinc, and uranium. In the late 1980s all but the coal mining operations were sold (the company began production of coal in 1981 when Byron Creek Collieries Ltd. of British Columbia was acquired). Also divested in the late 1980s was Building Products of Canada Limited, a manufacturer of a wide variety of building materials that had been acquired in 1964.

Imperial's relationship with the environment had also changed since the early days, when it had dumped gasoline and suffered the flash fires in London. In 1989 its crisis-management team allocated CAD 8 million to be invested over three years to improve its response to oil spills at its offshore sites. That same year it simulated a large tanker spill to test its response capabilities. Imperial's relationship with the Canadian community was no less impressive. Imperial made news not for oil spills and environmental disasters, but for its support of education and innovative employee assistance programs.

LATE-CENTURY RESTRUCTURING AND DIVESTMENTS

In the early 1990s Imperial Oil was hurt both by continued high debt levels stemming from the acquisition of Texaco Canada and from a worldwide glut on the petroleum market. It consequently suffered the first operating loss in company history in 1991 (CAD 36 million). Long considered one of the least efficient petroleum companies in North America, Imperial was forced to make drastic changes. In 1992 it cut its workforce by 1,700, closed 1,000 service stations, and restructured its operations, absorbing its Esso Petroleum, Esso Chemical, and Esso Resources divisions into Imperial Oil proper. The following year it shut down its refinery at Port Moody, British Columbia. Imperial sold most of its fertilizer business in 1994 to Canadian mining, chemicals, and materials company Sherritt for CAD 408 million. As a result of these and other moves, Imperial was a much more profitable firm, logging a CAD 514 million profit in 1995, its largest since 1988. Profits in 1996 were aided by a CAD 843 million ($618 million) refund for tax overpayment between 1974 and 1990.

Meanwhile, Imperial was experiencing a steady decline in conventional crude oil production as conventional sources in Canada were quickly drying up. Rather than invest in the additional equipment required to extract more oil from old fields, Imperial decided to sell a number of these properties, including the historic Leduc oilfield. It was sold in 1997 to Calgary-based Probe Exploration Inc. for more than CAD 45 million. Also in 1997, the company sold three other Alberta oilfields to Calgary-based Pengrowth Gas Corp. for CAD 595 million ($463 million). To replace the loss of this conventional crude, Imperial stepped up production at the Cold Lake heavy oil project. By 1997 almost half of Imperial's net crude oil production came from Cold Lake, with an additional 21 percent deriving from the company's 25 percent interest in Syncrude. Imperial announced in 1997 that it would operate and hold a 58 percent interest in two parallel pipelines to be built for an estimated CAD 250 million between the Cold Lake area and Hardisty, Alberta, the site of a major pipeline terminal.

For the company's future, an emphasis on expensive-to-extract heavy oil ran the risk of the impact of low oil prices, such as the depressed level of early 1998, which led Imperial to temporarily suspend development work at Cold Lake. The company's natural gas operations were concurrently broadened through the May 1998 agreement between Imperial, Shell Canada, and Mobil Oil Canada Properties to explore for natural gas off the coast of Nova Scotia, where about 18 trillion cubic feet of natural gas was estimated to lie. Imperial took a 20 percent stake in the new venture. Imperial already had a 9 percent interest in an adjacent offshore development, the Sable Offshore Energy Project, which late in 1999 became the first project to begin producing offshore natural gas from Atlantic Canada.

Also in late 1999, Imperial Oil gained a much larger majority shareholder via the merger of Exxon and Mobil Corporation, which created Exxon Mobil Corporation. Although Imperial's relationship with its parent remained unchanged in the merger's immediate wake, the amalgamation did result in some significant actions. Most notably, in late 2000 Imperial and ExxonMobil Canada (formerly Mobil Oil Canada) entered into an agreement to share certain business and operational support services in a move designed to save the companies about CAD 40 million annually. The firms also agreed to jointly pursue opportunities for new oil and gas projects in Canada, with Imperial operating any resulting developments in northern Canada and ExxonMobil Canada doing so for developments in eastern Canada.

PURSUING MASSIVE NEW PROJECTS IN EARLY 21ST CENTURY

At the beginning of the 21st century, Imperial Oil's crude oil production operations remained centered on the Albertan oil sands. More specifically, about half of the company's crude oil production stemmed from Cold Lake, while the firm's interest in Syncrude accounted for another quarter. Major expansions were undertaken at both Cold Lake and Syncrude during the first years of the 21st century. Imperial was also at the beginning stages of developing a massive reserve of natural gas in the Mackenzie Delta region of the far northern Northwest Territories. Around six trillion cubic feet of gas had been discovered in the delta, with Imperial owning about half of these reserves. Imperial headed a consortium to develop the fields and the infrastructure necessary to bring the gas to southern markets. The most ambitious part of the project was a 1,220-kilometer (755-mile) natural gas pipeline along the Mackenzie Valley that would carry the natural gas from the fields south to the border with Alberta where it would interconnect with an existing pipeline network.

Inheriting responsibility for further development of the Mackenzie gas project was Tim Hearn, who succeeded Bob Peterson as company chairman and CEO in April 2002. Hearn had joined Imperial in 1967 and later had stints at Exxon/Exxon Mobil before returning to Imperial in late 2001 as company president.

Hearn saw through to completion a multiyear, CAD 600 million project to upgrade Imperial's refineries to comply with a federal regulatory order from Environment Canada stipulating a drastic reduction in the levels of smog-creating sulfur in gasoline. Imperial finished this project in 2003, more than a year ahead of the federally mandated deadline. At the same time, Imperial was in the midst of another multiyear effort aimed at upgrading and making more efficient and profitable the firm's network of around 2,000 Esso stations.

On the production side, Imperial Oil by 2003 was producing nearly 200,000 barrels per day from its Cold Lake operations and from its share of Syncrude's output. As expansions continued at both Cold Lake and Syncrude, Imperial had also begun to develop a major new oil-sands project, the Kearl project in northeastern Alberta near Fort McMurray. Kearl, developed in concert with ExxonMobil Canada with Imperial holding a 70 percent interest, was an oil-sands mining project similar to Syncrude. The project had an estimated total recoverable reserve of 4.6 billion barrels of bitumen and had the potential to produce more than 300,000 barrels per day over a 40-year life span. Imperial planned to build the project in stages, the first stage having a projected production capacity of 100,000 barrels per day upon completion in 2011 and a price tag as high as CAD 8 billion. By 2007 soaring petroleum prices and rising worldwide demand for energy had made the Albertan oil sands an even more viable oil production resource. Imperial gained regulatory approval for Kearl that year, but a federal court ruling in early 2008 that sided with environmental groups' concerns over the project's impact on climate change and greenhouse gas emissions had the potential to at least throw more obstacles in the project's potential path to completion.

In the meantime, with most of its major projects centered in western and northern Canada, Imperial Oil decided to relocate its headquarters closer to these endeavors. In 2005, then, the head office shifted from Toronto to Calgary. That year, near-record oil prices and a conservative approach to capital spending helped Imperial post record profits of more than CAD 2.6 billion ($2.23 billion). Profits soared further by 2007 to CAD 3.19 billion ($3.25 billion) thanks to a further surge in oil prices and improved refining margins. The firm's strong cash position enabled it to nearly extinguish its long-term debt.

When Hearn retired in the spring of 2008, therefore, he left the firm in a particularly strong position to pursue major projects. These included not only Kearl but also the Mackenzie natural gas project. A regulatory decision on the latter was expected in 2009, although the viability of the CAD 16 billion project was in some doubt because of a competing proposal for a pipeline that would ship natural gas south from an even larger reserve in Alaska's North Slope. Charged with overseeing these and other challenges was Bruce March, the new chairman and CEO. March joined Imperial from Exxon Mobil, where he was a longtime refining executive and had perhaps most notably served as director of that company's Baton Rouge, Louisiana, refinery, which he managed to keep operating when it was struck by Hurricane Katrina in 2005. This refining experience was seen as critical at a time when one of Imperial Oil's biggest challenges was expected to involve the integration of output from Kearl and other oil-sands projects with Exxon Mobil's vast network of U.S. refineries.

Maya Sahafi
Updated, David E. Salamie

PRINCIPAL SUBSIDIARIES

Imperial Oil Resources Limited; Imperial Oil Resources N.W.T. Limited; Imperial Oil Resources Ventures Limited; McColl-Frontenac Petroleum Inc.

PRINCIPAL COMPETITORS

EnCana Corporation; Petro-Canada; Suncor Energy Inc.; Shell Canada Limited; ConocoPhillips; Canadian Natural Resources Limited; Talisman Energy Inc.; BP Canada Energy Company; Nexen Inc.; Husky Energy Inc.

FURTHER READING

Baxter, Dennis, "Imperial Order," *Canadian Business,* March 31, 2003, pp. 51+.

Boras, Alan, "Imperial Gets Enormous Tax Refund Check," *Oil Daily,* April 1, 1996, p. 3.

———, "Imperial Gets Hot and Heavy over Plans to Double Spending at Canada's Cold Lake," *Oil Daily,* June 11, 1996, p. 2.

Brethour, Patrick, "ARC Buys Remnants of Old-Time Oil Patch: Imperial Gets $462-Million for Two Assets," *Globe and Mail,* December 7, 2005, p. B5.

———, "Imperial Oil Profit Soars to $2-Billion," *Globe and Mail,* January 26, 2005, p. B1.

Broadfoot, Barry, and Mark Nichols, *Memories: The Story of Imperial's First Century,* Toronto: Imperial Oil Limited, 1980, 148 p.

Broyles, Karen, "Imperial Plans $463 Million Property Sale," *Oil Daily,* August 21, 1997, p. 1.

Carlisle, Tamsin, "Exxon May Find Pipeline Self-Competing," *Wall Street Journal,* June 13, 2006, p. A18.

Ebner, Dave, "Imperial, Exxon Pumping Up to $6.5-Billion More into Oil Sands," *Globe and Mail,* July 13, 2005, p. B1.

———, "Imperial Oil Cites Proximity As Reason for Head Office Move," *Globe and Mail,* September 30, 2004, p. B1.

———, "Imperial Oil's Kearl Project Gets Green Light," *Globe and Mail,* March 1, 2007, p. B5.

Felton, Russell, "Bringing Energy to Canada for 125 Years," *Imperial Oil Review,* 2005, no. 1, pp. 4–9.

Jang, Brent, "Esso Brand Name to Remain Despite Ownership Change," *Globe and Mail,* December 3, 1999, p. B5.

———, "Imperial Stands to Gain from Exxon Deal," *Globe and Mail,* November 27, 1998, p. B1.

———, "Landmark Arctic Gas Pipeline Deal Reached," *Globe and Mail,* June 19, 2003, p. B1.

———, "Strong Succession Plans Pay Off for Imperial Oil," *Globe and Mail,* December 15, 2001, p. B9.

MacIsaac, Merle, "Born-Again Basket Case," *Canadian Business,* May 1993, pp. 38–44.

Malone, Mary, "Imperial Beginnings," *London Magazine,* December 1986.

McCarthy, Shawn, "Imperial Gains Right to Explore Arctic," *Globe and Mail,* July 20, 2007, p. B4.

McMurdy, Deirdre, "Running Out of Gas," *Maclean's,* January 13, 1992, p. 26.

Morritt, Hope, *River of Oil: The Founding of North America's Petroleum Industry,* Kingston, Ont.: Quarry Press, 1993, 194 p.

Morton, Peter, "Imperial Oil Ltd. to Lay Off 20% of Employees in Resource Division in Effort to Boost Profit," *Oil Daily,* June 29, 1994, p. 3.

———, "Imperial Switches Focus from Conventional to Heavy Oil," *Oil Daily,* April 5, 1995, p. 7.

Parkinson, David, "Imperial, Mobil Canada Tighten Business Ties," *Globe and Mail,* November 2, 2000, p. B3.

———, "Imperial to Pump $1-Billion into Oil Sands Project," *Globe and Mail,* February 21, 2001, p. B1.

Scott, Norval, "After the Storm, It's Off to the Oil Patch," *Globe and Mail,* December 12, 2007, p. B1.

———, "Value the Top Job for New Imperial Boss," *Globe and Mail,* March 27, 2008, p. B6.

Stevenson, James, "Imperial Posts Record Profit of $2.6-Billion," *Globe and Mail,* February 3, 2006, p. B3.

The Story of Imperial Oil, Toronto: Imperial Oil Limited, 1991, 48 p.

Taylor, Fabrice, "Imperial Oil's Success Could Tempt Exxon," *Globe and Mail,* September 12, 2007, p. B15.

IntercontinentalExchange, Inc.

———————— ∎ ————————

2100 RiverEdge Parkway, Suite 500
Atlanta, Georgia 30328
U.S.A.
Telephone: (770) 857-4700
Fax: (770) 857-4755
Web site: http://www.theice.com

Public Company
Incorporated: 2001
Employees: 506
Sales: $574.3 million (2007)
Stock Exchanges: New York
Ticker Symbol: ICE
NAIC: 523210 Securities and Commodity Exchanges

∎ ∎ ∎

IntercontinentalExchange, Inc., (ICE) is an Atlanta, Georgia-based online global commodity and financial products marketplace. The New York Stock Exchange–listed company divides its business into three segments: ICE Markets, ICE Services, and ICE Data. Under ICE Markets, the company operates three regulated derivatives exchanges—ICE Futures U.S., ICE Futures Europe, and ICE Futures Canada—where traders deal in energy commodities (including crude oil, coal, natural gas, and power); agriculture and soft commodities (including coffee, cotton, pulp, and sugar); indices for stock markets, the continuous commodity index, and the U.S. dollar; and foreign and U.S. currency futures and options. ICE Services provides clearing services through ICE Clear and electronic confirmation

services through ICE eConfirm, while ICE Education offers training in trading, hedging, commodity investing, and compliance. ICE Data products cover real-time commodity prices, historical prices, indices, market price valuations, and end-of-day settlements. In addition to its electronic trading platform, ICE Platform, the company also operates the ICE New York Trading Center at 2 World Financial Center in New York City to serve energy, agricultural, and financial products traders. Serving as chairman and chief executive officer is ICE's founder, Jeffrey C. Sprecher.

FOUNDER: A CHEMICAL ENGINEERING GRADUATE

Jeffrey Sprecher grew up in Wisconsin, the son of an insurance salesman. After earning a degree in chemical engineering from the University of Wisconsin at Madison in 1978, he left for sunnier climes, Southern California, where he earned a master's of business administration at Pepperdine University in Malibu. He then became involved in real estate development and also became a power plant operator in California, serving as president of the Western Power Group, Inc. As an operator he bought and sold power and natural gas at market-based prices but these markets were over-the-counter and far from transparent. With deregulation of electric power looming on the horizon in California in the 1990s, Sprecher found it difficult to sell his power on a long-term basis because no one wanted to get locked into 30-year contracts with so much future uncertainty. To protect his position, he conceived of a power exchange but no one in California was interested in supporting the idea.

Driven to be independent, Sprecher sold his stake in Western Power and looked for a way to gain an equal footing with the major power producers. He found an opportunity in Atlanta with Continental Power Exchange, Inc., a small technology outfit that used a hard-line network to allow 62 member utility companies to buy and sell small amounts of surplus electricity. Continental Power had been established in 1994 by an Iowa utility, MidAmerican Energy, controlled by Warren Buffett. Offering a deeper pool of information technology workers and fiber-optics resources than Iowa, Atlanta was selected to house the start-up exchange. Sprecher tried to convince Continental Power's member utilities to transform the operation into a much larger exchange, but they too rejected his idea.

ACQUIRING CONTINENTAL POWER EXCHANGE

Undeterred, Sprecher simply acquired a controlling interest in Continental Power in 1997. He then shut down the operation and brought in a technology team to adapt the architecture to the Internet and provide the exchange with global capabilities. In the meantime, he pitched his exchange idea to about 120 firms, only to find no one interested. That response would begin to change in 1999 when Enron Corporation launched the first online power exchange, EnronOnline. Before its spectacular demise, Enron was a Wall Street darling and its online exchange was embraced by investors, lending credibility to the concept that benefited Sprecher, as well as other online energy markets that cropped up. The Enron operation was hardly an open exchange, however. Members were limited to just one trading partner: Enron.

IPE TAKING SHAPE: 2000

Sprecher was able to sell the idea of an exchange that served as a neutral party, one that simply offered a place where investors could trade with one another. It was still by no means an easy sale, however. "One by one, we had to convince them the rest of the industry was going to be a part of this," he told *Business to Business* in a 2007 interview. "It was a sales job of triangulating around and playing on the benefits and the insecurities of not being at the start up of this." By the early months of 2000 Sprecher was able to recruit several heavyweight companies to join forces with him to establish the IntercontinentalExchange by acquiring the assets of Continental Power and its technology, which would serve as the platform for the new venture.

The ICE name was assumed because the founders planned to operate on more than one continent and not be limited to just power commodities. The seven partners were BP Amoco, Deutsche Bank, Goldman Sachs Group Inc., Morgan Stanley Dean Witter & Co., Royal Dutch/Shell Group, Societe Generale Investment Banking, and Totalfina Elf Group. In May 2000 IntercontinentalExchange, LLC, was formed in Delaware. (A year later it would be incorporated as IntercontinentalExchange Inc.) The partners also pledged $20 million in development money.

Sprecher became ICE's CEO and owned a stake in the business. Soon the exchange brought six natural-gas and electricity suppliers into the fold, many of whom had earlier negotiated to become part of ICE. Instead they formed a consortium, Energy Trading Platform Holding, just as ICE took shape. The consortium actually made it easier for ICE to bring in the energy companies because it could negotiate with just one entity. The new ICE members were American Electric Power, Aquila Energy, Duke Energy, El Paso Energy, Reliant Energy, and Southern Company Energy Marketing.

The first ICE trades that took place in August 2000 involved precious metals, both cash and derivatives, followed in October by energy trading in crude oil, electricity, and natural gas. Collecting fees on each transaction, the new exchange fared well, especially in comparison to fellow newcomers HoustonStreet and Tradecapture. ICE also took advantage of Enron's collapse, taking over much of its online business, and was soon profitable. However, ICE lacked a clearing arrangement, which, according to *Petroleum Economist*, meant that "in order to trade on ICE, counterparties have to enter into lengthy negotiations on the terms of bilateral international swaps and derivatives agreements to cover the terms of trade, including credit security." ICE would add a clearing arrangement in 2001 by acquiring London-based International Petroleum Exchange (IPE), which possessed an established clearing arrangement with the London Clearing House.

Launched in 1980, IPE initially traded gasoil futures and later added the trading of North Sea Brent crudes and options contracts on both. Natural gas futures were added to the mix in 1997 and earlier in 2001 trading began on U.K. electricity. Aside from gaining a clearing mechanism, the addition of IPE's futures operation brought together for the first time over-the-counter and futures markets. In effect, IPE was an analog version of the electronic ICE. The long-term plan, announced in 2002, was to replace the IPE's traditional exchange floor with an all-electronic platform. The result would be ICE Futures and ICE Futures Europe. When the conversion was completed in 2005 the trading floor closed.

TAKEN PUBLIC: 2005

ICE grew in spurts in the early years. Revenues increased to $125.5 million in 2002, when the company netted $20.3 million. The following year revenues dipped below $94 million while profits held fairly steady. Nevertheless, ICE was still a relatively small player in energy trading, accounting for less than 20 percent of the business the New York Mercantile Exchange handled in 2003. Focusing on energy, ICE was building momentum, however. Revenues improved to $108.4 million in 2004 and net income approached $22 million. Business was even better in 2005, when through the first nine months revenues were well above the pace set the prior year. The company filed for an initial public offering (IPO) of stock, not only taking advantage of its own growth but also other successful IPOs of futures exchanges: the Chicago Board of Trade's CBOT Holdings Inc., Chicago Mercantile Exchange Holdings Inc., and International Securities Exchange Inc. ICE's main business, energy futures, was also a

highly popular commodity at the time. When the stock offering was completed in November 2005, ICE grossed $478.4 million, the largest IPO ever for a Georgia-based company. Moreover, the opening price of $26 increased 67 percent on the first day of trading on the New York Stock Exchange.

ACQUISITION OF NYBOT: 2007

In 2005 ICE recorded revenues of $155.9 million and net income of $53.1 million. Having increased market share in all aspects of its business and successfully completed the conversion of ICE futures to electronic trading, ICE had clearly turned the corner. In 2006 revenue more than doubled to $313.8 million while net income almost tripled to $155.9 million. ICE also reached an agreement to acquire the 134-year-old New York Board of Trade (NYBOT) in a cash and stock deal worth about $1.1 billion that closed in early 2007.

The addition of NYBOT, which formed the basis of ICE Futures U.S., was important to ICE for two primary reasons. It provided diversification beyond energy, because NYBOT mostly traded in agricultural products, soft commodities including cocoa, coffee, cotton, frozen concentrated orange juice, and sugar contracts. ICE also obtained its first U.S. regulated futures market. In early February 2007 ICE was then able to quickly bring electronic trading to NYBOT, demonstrating the scalability and flexibility of the company's technology. Traders had their choice of the screen or the floor. A month later ICE made headlines when it interjected itself into an acquisition bid of the Chicago Mercantile Exchange (CME) for the Chicago Board of Trade (CBOT), offering more than $10 billion, far more than the offer of CME. Sprecher said he might even change ICE's name to help convince CBOT shareholders to support his bid. In the end, he was unable to pull off the deal, but at least forced up the price CME had to pay and received a bit of publicity for ICE.

In July 2007 ICE enjoyed better success with a less audacious acquisition, picking up the commodity trading business of ChemConnect, Inc. The ten-year-old ChemConnect operated the leading electronic marketplace for the $150 billion U.S. natural gas liquids (NGLs) industry, including propane and ethane, and chemical markets (including ethylene, propylene, and benzene). Because NGL prices dovetailed with natural gas and crude oil prices, ChemConnect's business was a natural complement to ICE. The ChemConnect operation was subsequently shifted to the ICE electronic platform, allowing both ICE and ChemConnect customers to take advantage of a single marketplace that offered a full range of energy commodities. A month later, August 2007, ICE paid $49.5 million for the Winnipeg Commodity Exchange, best known for its canola futures contract, as well as feed wheat and western barley. The 12-year-old exchange had converted to an electronic trading format, owned by CBOT, in December 2004, and before the end of 2007 made the successful switch to the ICE platform. The exchange was renamed ICE Futures Canada.

ICE enjoyed a strong year in 2007, generating revenues of almost $575 million and net income of $240.6 million. At the end of the year the company also took a step that promised to increase earnings further, announcing the closing of the NYBOT's futures pits in March 2008. While the decision may have upset some traditionalists, the truth was that business had been rapidly shifting to the electronic platform. Wall Street clearly approved the move, which promised to greatly reduce ICE's overhead, by bidding up the price of ICE's stock to record levels. Moreover, ICE's chief rival, the New York Mercantile Exchange (NYMEX), was under pressure to close its futures pits. NYBOT's options trading would remain on the trading floor for the time being, but ICE and NYMEX were pursuing an electronic options trading mechanism, the final step to building a complete electronic-screen trading platform, one that would soon make the trading floor a relic of the past.

Ed Dinger

PRINCIPAL DIVISIONS

ICE Markets; ICE Services; ICE Data.

PRINCIPAL COMPETITORS

CME Group Inc.; NASDAQ OMX Group Inc.; Regal One. Corp.

FURTHER READING

Bajaj, Vikas, "The Future of Futures," *New York Times*, October 13, 2006, p. C5.

Bossley, Liz, "Ice Reels in the IPE," *Petroleum Economist*, June 2001, p. 56.

Chambers, Matt, "ICE's Decision to Halt Futures Trade on the Floor Sits Well with Investors," *Wall Street Journal*, December 15, 2007, p. B5.

Ermenc, Drew, "The Wizard of ICE," *Business to Business*, October 2007.

Goodman, Leah McGrath, "Ice Capades," *Trader Monthly*, June/July 2007.

Lucchetti, Aaron, and Susan Buchanan, "ICE Agrees to Buy Nybot, Whose Members Will Meet to Weigh Offer," *Wall Street Journal*, September 15, 2006, p. C3.

McKay, Peter A., "Banks, Energy Firms Will Form Online Market," *Wall Street Journal*, March 21, 2000, p. 1.

———, "Six Firms Will Join IntercontinentalExchange," *Wall Street Journal*, July 26, 2000, p. 1.

McMahon, Chris, "Manhattan Melodrama," *Futures*, February 2007, p. 12.

Quinn, Matthew C., "Energy Trading Meets the Net," *Atlanta Constitution*, September 5, 2001, p. E1.

Walker, Tom, "The ICE That Sizzles," *Atlanta Constitution-Journal*, January 28, 2007, p. C1.

Wasendorf, Russell, Sr., "Hot Ice!" *Stock, Futures and Options Magazine*, October 2006.

Intertek Group plc

25 Savile Row
London, W1S 2ES
United Kingdom
Telephone: (+44-20) 7396-3400
Fax: (+44-20) 7396-3480
Web site: http://www.intertek.com

Public Company
Incorporated: 1996 as Intertek Testing Services Ltd.
Employees: 21,300
Sales: £775.4 million (2007)
Stock Exchanges: London
Ticker Symbol: IKTS F
NAIC: 926150 Regulation, Licensing, and Inspection of
   Miscellaneous Commercial Sectors

■ ■ ■

Intertek Group plc is a leading quality and safety services provider. According to the company, it tests, inspects, and certifies products, commodities, and systems for governments, manufacturers, retailers, and traders throughout the world in virtually every industry. Intertek has a broad spectrum of expertise in such areas as building, cargo scanning, electronics, food, heating, minerals, pharmaceuticals, petroleum, textiles, and toys.

PRE-HISTORY: 1885–1995

Intertek was officially formed on October 8, 1996, when the global investment firm Charterhouse Development Capital backed a £380 million management buy-out of Inchcape Testing Services Ltd. from Inchcape plc and renamed the company Intertek Testing Services Ltd. However, the company's origins can be traced back to the very formation of the modern testing industry. According to the company, its heritage encompasses the histories of many different organizations that, over the course of about 125 years, have combined to form the present-day Intertek.

Inchcape, Intertek's predecessor, entered the testing industry in 1973 when it formed Labest Hong Kong Ltd. as the in-house testing arm of Dodwell, a corporation Inchcape acquired in 1972. The company went on to establish itself as a testing leader, and by 1988 had sales of approximately $125 million and operations in about 60 countries. Inchcape's leadership position was secured through the acquisition of several industry pioneers. For example, in 1992 the company acquired the Warnock Hersey Co., which had roots dating back to 1888, when Milton Hersey first developed the concept of an independent testing laboratory and formed a fledgling chemical testing laboratory in Montreal, Quebec.

Inchcape added another industry pioneer to its ranks in 1988 when the company acquired Cortland, New York-based ETL Testing Laboratories Inc., which Thomas Edison had formed in 1896 as the Lamp Testing Bureau of the Edison Electric Illuminating Co. The Lamp Testing Bureau changed its name to Electrical Testing Laboratories (ETL) in 1904 and became an independent, employee-owned firm in 1942. Other major acquisitions by Inchcape included Albury Laboratories in 1992, as well as SEMKO and TestMark in 1994.

INITIAL GROWTH: 1997–2002

Following Charterhouse Development Capital's acquisition of Inchcape Testing Services Ltd., the assumption of the Intertek Testing Services Ltd. name was completed on April 2, 1997. At that point the company adopted a new identity and logo across all of its operations, which had grown to include 342 offices and 176 laboratories in 66 countries. On the strength of 7,500 employees, the company had become the largest product and commodities testing firm in the world.

Global Semiconductor Safety Services (GS3) was formed in 1997 when Intertek paired with Environmental Resources Management Ltd. (ERM) to establish a joint venture to serve capital equipment suppliers in the semiconductor industry. Two years later, Intertek bought ERM's stake in the venture and GS3 became a wholly owned subsidiary.

Intertek found itself in the midst of a difficult situation in 1998. Late that year, the company contacted a number of its clients, as well as the U.S. Environmental Protection Agency (EPA), and revealed that two defunct testing labs, which had operated under the Inchcape banner, had provided thousands of incorrect test results regarding hundreds of U.S. hazardous waste sites. The erroneous results, which were provided over the course of six years, posed a potential threat to public health. Intertek initially pegged the oversight on one employee, who reportedly had cut corners in order to expedite tests.

The testing results situation eventually resulted in the EPA launching a criminal investigation. By late 2000, the matter had broadened in scope. In its September 22, 2000, issue, the *Times* reported that six U.S. labs had provided incorrect water and soil toxicity data for approximately 59,000 landfill sites. While Intertek had closed two of the labs and sold four others, the U.S. Department of Justice brought criminal charges against 13 former staff members who were connected with the matter. In addition, Intertek faced lawsuits from some of its clients.

Intertek ultimately resolved the testing results situation in late 2001 when its defunct subsidiary, Intertek Testing Services Environmental Laboratories Inc., pleaded guilty to conspiracy and agreed to pay fines totaling $9 million. Despite the challenges it faced in 2001, Intertek generated an operating profit of £66.8 million that year on sales of £443 million. By this time the company's workforce had grown to 10,300 people who worked at labs in 99 countries worldwide.

On May 23, 2002, Intertek made its initial public offering (IPO) and listed on the London Stock Exchange, becoming Intertek Testing Services plc. At the time of the £600 million IPO, Charterhouse reduced its stake in Intertek from 84 percent to 30 percent. During its first year as a public company, Intertek expanded in Asia and China as more companies began shifting their manufacturing operations there.

GROWTH THROUGH ACQUISITIONS: 2003–08

On June 10, 2003, Intertek changed its name from Intertek Testing Services plc to Intertek Group plc. That year, the company made two acquisitions. Fastech Ltd. was acquired in September for £5.3 million, followed by Amtac Certification Services (Holdings) Ltd. in December for £1.6 million.

In September 2003, CEO Richard Nelson sold half of his shares in Intertek, generating £7.7 million. In the May 14, 2004, issue of the *Financial Times*, writer Maggie Urry explained that Nelson, a 30-year employee who had been CEO for more than two decades, was preparing to retire from the post. Nelson compiled a set of questions to make sure his successor would be a good fit with the company's culture, which he summarized as "very performance-oriented, decentralised, small head office, and very international."

Intertek kicked into high acquisition mode in 2004. The activity began when the company's ETL SEMKO and Labtest divisions made small acquisitions early in the year. Following these deals, Intertek's Caleb Brett arm snapped up Vestfold Telemark Metering for £1 million. In May, the Grand Rapids, Michigan-based automotive testing and engineering firm Entela Inc. was acquired for 256,622 shares of stock and $26.5 million in cash. The deal resulted in the formation of Intertek ETL Entela, which eventually was named Intertek Automotive Systems Certification.

Developments continued during the second half of 2004. In the fall, Allium LLC acquired two of Intertek's Labtest subsidiaries, with Intertek gaining a 40 percent stake in Allium. Intertek ended the year with a £5.3 million deal in which its Caleb Brett arm acquired Kelley Completion Services. For the year, Intertek's revenues increased 6 percent, reaching £499.6 million.

China held great promise for Intertek heading into the middle of the first decade of the 2000s. By this time

KEY DATES

1973: Inchcape Testing, Intertek's predecessor, enters the testing industry.

1996: Intertek is formed when Charterhouse Development Capital backs a £380 million management buyout of Inchcape Testing Services Ltd. from Inchcape and renames the company Intertek Testing Services Ltd.

1997: The Intertek Testing Services Ltd. name is adopted across all of the company's operations.

2002: Intertek makes its initial public offering and lists on the London Stock Exchange, becoming Intertek Testing Services plc.

2003: The company changes its name from Intertek Testing Services plc to Intertek Group plc.

2005: Wolfhart G. Hauser succeeds Richard Nelson as CEO, and Nelson becomes chairman.

the company employed approximately 2,100 employees in that country and enjoyed an estimated 50 percent share of the testing market there, according to the March 8, 2005, *Financial Times.* Intertek also had become the world's largest textiles inspector. In addition to increasing clothing imports on the part of retailers, Intertek eyed an opportunity to offer automotive component testing in China and pursued the construction of a new laboratory there.

In March 2005 Wolfhart G. Hauser was ultimately named as Intertek's new CEO, and Richard Nelson was named chairman. Hauser assumed the leadership post at a time of rapid growth, as Intertek continued to move forward along the acquisition path.

In addition to a Texas-based oil/gas exploration and production laboratory called Westport Technology Centre, several new companies were added to the Intertek fold in 2005. In a deal with Gemini Holdings Inc., the company acquired PARC Technical Services Inc. in August. That same month, the company's Caleb Brett arm acquired Louisiana Grain Services. Later in the year, Intertek parted with £20.1 million to acquire Texas-based Automotive Research Laboratory. It was around the same time that Caleb Brett acquired both Lintec Testing Services Ltd. and Lloyd's Register Lubricant Quality Scan.

The company ended the year with two important developments. First, Intertek ETL Entela announced plans to relocate its operations from Wyoming to Grand Rapids, Michigan, where $1.3 million in equipment was added to a 96,000-square-foot space that Intertek transformed at a cost of about $800,000. According to the December 15, 2005, *Grand Rapids Press,* Intertek designated the new building as a divisional headquarters site for China and Taiwan, as well as Boston and Detroit.

Another important development was the acquisition of KPMG's quality registrar business in India and the Middle East. The deal bolstered Intertek's workforce in India. Of 14,000 total employees, its Indian employee base had grown to about 500 people by this time.

Change came in the midst of the company's rapid growth. According to Intertek, an internal reorganization was carried out in 2005. The company's Caleb Brett business was placed within the Oil, Chemical & Agri division, while Labtest joined the new Consumer Goods division. ETL SEMKO was placed within the Commercial & Electrical division and Intertek's Foreign Trade Standards arm became part of a new division called Government Services.

In addition to the reorganization, Intertek was forced to contend with the aftermath of Hurricane Katrina in the United States, which impacted the Gulf of Mexico where many employees performed testing on oil rigs. In September 2005, London's *Daily Telegraph* reported that one week after the disaster, 50 employees were missing and lost revenues associated with the disaster were estimated at as much as £10 million. Despite these challenges, Intertek ended the year with before-tax profits of £79.4 million on sales of $580.1 million.

By 2006 Intertek was performing testing for many of the world's leading companies. Its client base included Wal-Mart, Nike, and Gap, among others. That year, growth continued through acquisitions. After purchasing Polychemlab's Dutch laboratory operations in a deal with DSM, Intertek acquired the California-based pharmaceutical testing firm Alta Analytical Laboratories Inc. in November for £14 million.

Intertek's growth continued into the later years of the first decade of the 2000s. In an effort to bolster its testing capabilities for the oil industry, the company's Caleb Brett arm acquired Manchester-based Umitek Ltd. in early 2007. As part of the $19.6 million deal, Caleb Brett also acquired Umitek's Smith Rea Energy and Capcis subsidiaries. It was around the same time that Intertek's ETL SEMKO business announced it was ready to relocate all of its Wyoming operations to the company's Grand Rapids facility.

In April, Intertek grew its commodities testing business via the acquisition of Maddington, Australia-based

Genalysis Laboratory Services Pty Ltd. in a deal potentially worth $56 million. Four months later, a new performance and safety testing facility was added to Intertek's 240,000-square-foot heating, ventilation, and air conditioning plant in Cortland, New York.

More acquisitions followed in the last quarter, beginning with Australia-based Northern Territory Environmental Laboratories in September. The following month Intertek added Canada's Ageus Solutions, which specialized in removing hazardous materials from products. Finally, the Pittsfield, Massachusetts-based plastics company Plastics Technology Laboratories Inc. was acquired in November. In all, Intertek spent £100 million to add 16 companies to its corporate family in 2007.

Growth continued into 2008, with Intertek acquiring five companies in the first quarter alone for £17.5 million. Among these was Aberdeen, Scotland-based CML Biotech, a microbiology testing lab and consulting enterprise serving the oil and gas industry. At this time the company announced that its annual profits had increased almost 16 percent in 2007, reaching £105.8 million on revenues of £775.4 million.

Heading into the 21st century's second decade, Intertek was benefiting from more stringent governmental standards regarding hazardous waste, strong demand for toy testing in the wake of safety-related recalls, and a growing focus on the environment. With 1,000 labs in more than 100 countries worldwide, the company appeared to be in a strong position to capitalize on these growth opportunities in the coming years.

Paul R. Greenland

PRINCIPAL SUBSIDIARIES

Allium LLC (U.S.A.; 40%); Caleb Brett USA Inc.; DE-KRA ITS Certification Services GmbH (Germany; 49%); Entela Inc. (U.S.A.); Intertek Finance plc; Intertek Holdings Ltd.; Intertek International Ltd.; ITS Hong Kong Ltd.; Intertek Testing Management Ltd.; Intertek Testing Services Holdings Ltd.; Intertek Testing Services Ltd. Shanghai (China; 85%); Intertek Testing Services Shenzhen Ltd. (China; 85%); Intertek Testing Services Taiwan Ltd.; Intertek Testing Services UK Ltd.; ITS NA Inc. (U.S.A.); ITS Testing Holdings Canada Ltd.; ITS Testing Services (UK) Ltd.; Kite Overseas Holdings BV (Netherlands); SEMKO-DEKRA Certification AB (Sweden; 49%); Testing Holdings France EURL; Testing Holdings Germany GmbH; Testing Holdings Sweden AB; SEMKO AB; Testing Holdings USA Inc.; Yickson Enterprises Ltd.

PRINCIPAL DIVISIONS

Commercial & Electrical; Consumer Goods; Government Services; Oil, Chemical & Agri.

PRINCIPAL COMPETITORS

Bureau Veritas; Det Norske Veritas Foundation; SGS SA.

FURTHER READING

Cole, Robert, "Intertek Appeal Lies Under Surface," *Times* (London), May 22, 2002.

"INCHCAPE; Inchcape Purchases ETL Testing Laboratories," *Business Wire,* October 3, 1988.

"Intertek Gets Tax Breaks for Move," *Grand Rapids (Mich.) Press,* December 15, 2005.

"Intertek Succeeds Against the Odds with £400m IPO After Punch's Aftermarket Rise," *EuroWeek,* May 24, 2002.

"Intertek Testing Services Environmental Laboratories Inc. Settles Litigation with the Department of Justice," *PR Newswire,* October 5, 2001.

"ITS Changes Identity Worldwide," *PR Newswire Europe,* April 2, 1997.

"Mission Statement," London: Intertek Group plc, March 19, 2008, Available from http://www.intertek.com.

Shah, Saeed, "False Data Charges Threaten Intertek Floatation," *Independent,* September 22, 2000.

Urquhart, Lisa, "Intertek Rises and Plans to Build on Chinese Growth," *Financial Times,* March 8, 2005.

Urry, Maggie, "Far-Flung Outfit Seeks Cultural Fit: Whoever Replaces Richard Nelson As Intertek Chief Must Have Certain Qualities to Lead the Company, Which Is Why the Current Incumbent Has Drafted a List of Questions to Weed Out the Wrong Candidates," *Financial Times,* May 14, 2004.

Wallop, Harry, "UK Oil Test Firm Lists 50 Missing After Hurricane," *Daily Telegraph,* September 6, 2005.

J Sainsbury plc

J Sainsbury plc

33 Holborn
London, EC1N 2HT
United Kingdom
Telephone: (+44-20) 7695-6000
Fax: (+44-20) 7695-7610
Web site: http://www.j-sainsbury.co.uk

Public Company
Founded: 1869
Incorporated: 1922 as J. Sainsbury Limited
Employees: 148,000
Sales: £17.15 billion ($33.76 billion) (2007)
Stock Exchanges: London
Ticker Symbol: SBRY
NAIC: 445110 Supermarkets and Other Grocery (Except Convenience) Stores; 445120 Convenience Stores; 454111 Electronic Shopping; 522120 Savings Institutions; 233110 Land Subdivision and Land Development

■ ■ ■

J Sainsbury plc, widely known in its home nation as Sainsbury's, is one of the largest operators of supermarkets in the United Kingdom. There are about 500 Sainsbury's supermarkets in the United Kingdom, the largest of which stock around 30,000 products, 50 percent of which carry the Sainsbury's brand. More than 100 of the stores offer Internet-based shopping with home delivery. The company also operates about 300 convenience stores under the Sainsbury's Local name, while Sainsbury's Bank is a joint venture with HBOS plc that runs in-store banks in the United Kingdom offering basic savings accounts, personal loans, credit cards, insurance, and other consumer-oriented financial products. The Sainsbury's chain was once the largest U.K. food retailer, but by the early 21st century it ranked number three behind Tesco PLC and ASDA Group Limited, the latter a subsidiary of U.S. giant Wal-Mart Stores, Inc. The founding Sainsbury family still maintains a 15 percent stake in the company.

EARLY HISTORY

Sainsbury's was off to a romantic but practical start in 1869 when two young employees of neighboring London shops met, married, and started a small dairy store in their three-story Drury Lane home. Mary Ann Staples, 19, had grown up in her father's dairy business. John James Sainsbury, 25, had worked for a hardware merchant and grocer. Their shop was a success from the start, as both John and Mary Ann had the business knowledge and capacity for hard work that it took to win the loyalty of the local trade. Their passion for order, cleanliness, and high-quality merchandise made the shop an inviting place, in contrast to the prevalent clutter of many tiny family-owned shops and the unsanitary conditions of the street vendors' stalls and carts.

Seven years later the Sainsburys opened a second shop in a newly developed section of town and moved into the upper portion of the building. Within a few years, they had opened several similar branches, planning to have a shop for each of their sons to manage. By the time their six sons were adults, the branches far

COMPANY PERSPECTIVES

Our objective is simple: to serve customers well and thereby provide shareholders with good, sustainable financial returns. We aim to ensure all colleagues have opportunities to develop their abilities and are rewarded for their contribution to the success of the business. Our policy is to work with all of our suppliers fairly, recognising the mutual benefit of satisfying customers' needs. We also aim to fulfil our responsibilities to the communities and environments in which we operate.

Our goal: At Sainsbury's we will deliver an ever improving quality shopping experience for our customers with great product at fair prices. We aim to exceed customer expectations for healthy, safe, fresh and tasty food making their lives easier everyday.

STEADY GROWTH IN THE EARLY 20TH CENTURY

By the beginning of the 20th century sons John Benjamin, George, and Arthur were working in the family business; they and other company employees were trained with equal care and attention to detail. Alfred and Paul went through the same training when they joined the company in 1906 and 1921, respectively. Frank, the third son, took up poultry and pork farming in 1902 and became a major supplier.

During this time, rivals seemed to be outdistancing Sainsbury's in terms of numbers. Lipton's, the largest, had 500 stores. It took Sainsbury's another 14 years to open its 115th branch. Nonetheless, Sainsbury's continued to place the highest priority on quality, taking the time to weigh each decision, whether it meant researching suppliers for a new product, assessing the reliability of a new supplier, or measuring the business potential of a new site.

The outbreak of World War I slowed expansion plans even further. Rationing and shortages of food, particularly fresh produce, led to the creation of grocery departments selling jams, spices, potted meat, and flour, all bearing Sainsbury's own label. Women began attending the training classes at the Blackfriars headquarters, to replace the male employees who had left for military service. Some worked in the packing plant for Sainsbury-label foods; others served as salespeople in the stores.

Eldest son John Benjamin took much of the initiative in the interwar years, adding new grocery lines while retaining his father's insistence on high quality. By 1922 there were 136 branches, many of them along the new suburban rail lines, and the firm was incorporated as J. Sainsbury Limited. Mary Ann died in 1927 and her husband in 1928, leaving John Benjamin in charge. By this time, so much public attention accompanied branch openings that when Sainsbury's opened a branch in Cambridge, it published an apology in the local newspaper for the impact of a huge opening day crowd. Altogether, 57 new branches were opened between 1919 and 1929, and the gilded glass Sainsbury sign had become a universal symbol of a spacious, orderly interior displaying foods of the finest quality.

There was an apparent break with tradition in 1936 when Sainsbury's bought the Thoroughgood stores, a chain of nine shops in Britain's Midlands. The purchase, however, was made with the same care and emphasis on quality that had distinguished all other Sainsbury branches. Stamford House, which had been built in 1912 as an extension of the headquarters at Blackfriars, was extended to provide more space for the centralized supply procurement and distribution that maintained

outnumbered the family size. Yet caution has always been characteristic of Sainsbury expansion; they regularly passed up opportunities to buy groups or chains of stores, preferring to develop each new store independently.

The passion for high quality led them to a turning point in 1882, when they opened a branch in Croydon. They used advanced design and materials that had an elegance not attempted in the other shops and that made the store easy to keep clean. The walls, floor, and counter fronts were tiled, while the countertops were marble slabs. Customers were seated on bentwood chairs. The store's cleanliness, still a rarity in food shops of that time, and elaborate decor helped attract more prosperous customers; it was an instant success. Several similar shops were added during that decade, while Sainsbury's also developed a less elaborate design for suburban branches opened during those years. In these, business could be done through open windows, as in the common market areas, but the design also attracted customers to come into the store to see a greater variety of food.

In 1890 Sainsbury's moved its headquarters to Blackfriars, where it remained throughout the 20th century. The location provided easy access to wholesale markets and transportation. To obtain the best quality in food, Sainsbury's always kept in close touch with suppliers, and it controlled and distributed stock from a central depot until the 1960s.

KEY DATES

1869: John James and Mary Ann Sainsbury open a small dairy store in their Drury Lane home.

1882: First branch outside London is opened in Croydon.

1922: Firm is incorporated as J. Sainsbury Limited.

1936: The Thoroughgood chain is acquired.

1950: First self-service Sainsbury's opens in Croydon.

1971: The period after the initial J is dropped from the company name.

1973: Company goes public as J Sainsbury plc.

1977: First Savacentre hypermarket opens.

1981: First Homebase home and garden center is opened.

1987: Sainsbury gains full control of the U.S. chain Shaw's Supermarkets.

1997: Sainsbury's Bank is launched.

1998: First Sainsbury's Local convenience store is opened.

1999: Savacentre outlets are converted into large-format Sainsbury's units.

2001: Sainsbury sells the Homebase chain.

2004: Company divests its U.S. supermarket operations; turnaround plan is launched by Justin King, the new chief executive.

2007: Two separate bids to take over Sainsbury come to naught.

quality control for all branches, which by this time numbered 244. Specially designed lightweight vans had replaced horse-drawn vehicles, further speeding deliveries.

World War II not only slowed Sainsbury's growth through shortages of food and labor but also brought the stores into the line of fire. Some branches were totally destroyed; others were extensively damaged. Vehicles carrying mobile shops kept up trade as far as possible in the areas affected by the Blitz. However, the evacuation of bomb-damaged areas made it impossible to continue the centralized procurement and distribution operation that had provided efficiency, economy, and standardization of products and services. Along with other wartime restrictions, this caused sales to dwindle to half the prewar level.

John Benjamin's sons Alan and Robert, who had shared the general manager's post since their father's retirement in 1938, became aware of the crucial role of

communications during the trying days of this wartime decentralization. The *JS Journal,* begun in 1946 (and its sister publication, the *Employee Report,* begun in the late 1970s), exemplified the thorough job of reporting that kept staff members abreast of company developments and business conditions. Both publications have won national awards for excellence.

POSTWAR RECOVERY

Long before the last of the wartime restrictions were lifted in 1954, the brothers had begun an aggressive recovery program. Basic operations were recentralized to regain the economies of scale that kept prices down while retaining a substantial profit margin. Alan studied the United States' burgeoning supermarkets and opened the first self-service Sainsbury's in June 1950 in Croydon, where his grandfather had opened his "turning point" store nearly 70 years earlier.

Expansion in the 1950s often meant converting existing stores to supermarkets in addition to adding new outlets. In 1955, the 7,500-square-foot Sainsbury's at Lewisham was considered the largest supermarket in Europe. By 1969, Sainsbury supermarkets had an average of 10,000 square feet of space. Supermarkets and hypermarkets in the 1980s would triple that amount.

John Benjamin and Arthur were the only two of the founders' sons whose own sons joined the family business. Arthur's son James, who had joined the company in 1926, was named Commander of the Order of the British Empire for his accomplishments. He created new factory facilities at Sainsbury's headquarters in 1936 and also set up the Haverhill line of meat products.

John Benjamin's sons Alan and Robert, and Alan's son John, were also honored for their work. Alan was made Baron Sainsbury of Drury Lane in 1962, and his son John was made Baron Sainsbury of Preston Candover in 1989. Robert was knighted in 1967. Alan and Robert shared the presidency of Sainsbury's, John was chairman, and Robert's son David was deputy chairman through the 1980s.

With typical caution, Sainsbury's did not actually use the word *supermarket* in its own communications until the late 1960s, even though it owned almost 100. Nonetheless, the company was at the forefront of new technology. In 1961, for example, Sainsbury's became Britain's first food retailer to computerize its distribution system. In the late 1980s, electronic cash registers at the checkout counter were replaced by scanners. Multibuy, a special feature of the scanning system, automatically applied a discount to multiple purchases of certain designated items. Spaceman, a microcomputer planning system, used on-screen graphics to plot the allocation of merchandise to specific shelf space in the stores. Electronic funds transfer at the point of sale allowed customers to use debit cards to make purchases.

DIVERSIFICATION

Sainsbury's centenary, 1969, sparked a series of rapid changes. Alan's son John, became chairman of a new management tier, which reported directly to the board of directors. Departmental directors were given greater responsibility for operating functions to strengthen the centralized control that had always been company policy. With ordering, warehousing, and distribution computerized, strict controls on the speeded-up activity were vital. Sainsbury's became a public company in 1973, two years after making a name change: the period after the initial J was dropped.

Personnel policies at Sainsbury's adhered closely to the principles established at its founding: thorough training, open communication, and continuing training on the job. The company recruited actively at schools and universities, preferring to "grow its own talent," but holding employees to high standards of performance. Along with other leading companies and the City University Business School, Sainsbury's conducted a practical management course, the Management M.B.A. Sainsbury's employees participated in profit sharing and share option schemes.

The company's community involvement was also active, taking many forms. John Sainsbury addressed the London Conference on saving the ozone layer early in 1989. The only retailer invited to take part in the conference and the associated exhibition, he presented details of the technological changes made in Sainsbury's aerosol products and plant operations to eliminate chlorofluorocarbons from their operations. Incubation of small start-up businesses, arts sponsorships, and grand-scale charity drives were other ongoing projects.

Forces within the grocery industry compelled Sainsbury's to begin a program of diversification within the retail category. Increased competition from discounters threatened to squeeze profit margins. Creeping market saturation and flat population growth combined to intensify competition as well. Sainsbury's began to make significant additions to its nonfood merchandise for the first time. The company's first petrol station, a convenience for shoppers, was opened in 1974 at a Cambridge store. To gain the economies of direct supplier-to-store deliveries, Sainsbury's formed a joint venture with British Home Stores in 1975, launching a chain of hypermarkets (huge stores combining grocery items and hard goods) called Savacentre; the first Sava-

centre opened in 1977 in Washington, Tyne and Wear. Sainsbury's retained control of all food-related operations, leaving nonfood lines to its partner until 1989, when Savacentre became a wholly owned subsidiary of Sainsbury's. Meanwhile, Sainsbury's opened a Savacentre hypermarket in Scotland in 1984.

Homebase, a chain of upscale do-it-yourself (DIY) stores, was in the planning stage by 1979. Sainsbury's owned 75 percent of this joint venture, and Grand Bazaar Innovations Bon Marché, Belgium's largest retailer (later known as GIB Group), owned the remaining 25 percent. The partners opened their first Homebase home and garden center in 1981, and had expanded the chain to 76 locations by the mid-1990s.

Sainsbury's looked to overseas markets for growth opportunities as well. In 1983 the company began to amass shares in Shaw's Supermarkets, a New England supermarket chain founded in 1860. Shaw's heritage of carrying high-quality food at the lowest prices meshed well with the ideals of the British firm. Moreover, like Sainsbury's, Shaw's had also been at the forefront of computer technology. By 1987, Sainsbury's had completed the purchase of 100 percent of the 60 stores in Massachusetts, Maine, and New Hampshire, and had plans to open additional stores in that area.

CHALLENGING TIMES IN ERA OF HEIGHTENED COMPETITION

The company boosted its holdings in the United States with the 1994 acquisition of a 50 percent voting stake and 16 percent nonvoting equity in Giant Food Inc., a Washington, D.C.–area chain with 159 stores. Sainsbury's increased its nonvoting equity to 20 percent in 1996 and was widely expected to purchase the remaining shares by the end of the decade, but Dutch retailer Royal Ahold N.V. stepped in during 1998 to acquire all of Giant Food.

Sainsbury's also developed a powerful private-label program. By the mid-1990s, its own-label products generated 66 percent of total sales. Three of the company's proprietary products in particular made headlines in the early 1990s. Novon, a laundry detergent introduced in 1992, marked Sainsbury's move into head-to-head competition with national brands. Within just six weeks of Novon's launch, the company's share of the detergents market doubled to 20 percent. In 1994 Sainsbury's changed the formulation and packaging of its own cola beverage, reintroducing it as "Classic Cola." The budget-priced cola featured red cans with italicized letters and a stripe; ads promoted the drink's "Original American Taste." Within just a few weeks, Classic Cola won 13 percent of Britain's total cola market, while sales of both Coca-Cola and Pepsi at Sainsbury stores plummeted. Not surprisingly, an incensed Coca-Cola demanded that Sainsbury's modify its packaging, claiming that the brands' similarity prevented customers from discerning between them. The supermarket chain acquiesced, but significantly decreased the rival brand's share of shelf space in stores.

Another highly successful, but less confrontational, private-label product also broke new ground for the category. In 1993 the company launched its own periodical, *Sainsbury's: The Magazine.* Like the publications it competed with, *Sainsbury's: The Magazine* featured illustrated pieces on fashion, health, and cooking, as well as national brand advertising. Sold only in Sainsbury's supermarkets, the magazine became "the most successful new magazine venture in Britain in many years," according to a November 1994 *Forbes* article.

Under the leadership of Chairman, CEO, and great-grandson of the founders David Sainsbury, who took over leadership from his cousin John in 1992, sales tripled from £3 billion in 1985 to £10.6 billion in 1994. During the early 1990s, however, Sainsbury's began losing ground to competitors ASDA, Safeway plc, and Tesco. Perhaps because of arrogance and complacency or the distractions of its forays into the U.S. market and the DIY sector, Sainsbury's core U.K. supermarket operations lost their edge in a number of areas, including price, customer service, and innovation. Customers began perceiving, rightly or wrongly, Sainsbury's as higher in price than the competition, as offering too many private-label products in comparison to name brands, as having insufficient staff to help customers in the aisles, and as having longer checkout lines. Both Tesco and Safeway gained sales through the introduction of loyalty cards, a new marketing practice initially scorned by Sainsbury's and then belatedly embraced through the June 1996 launch of the Reward Card. In 1995 Tesco displaced Sainsbury's from its perch as the top grocery retailer in the United Kingdom. For the fiscal year ending in February 1996 Sainsbury's posted its first profit decline in 22 years.

LATE-CENTURY TURNAROUND INITIATIVES

Among management's first moves aimed at turning the company's fortunes around was a mid-1995 customer service initiative that involved the addition of more than 5,000 staff to tend service counters, help customers in the aisles, and pack the groceries. Management changes were also afoot, including the replacement of the marketing director. On the DIY front, meantime, Sainsbury's completed the acquisition of the Texas Homecare

chain from Ladbroke Group PLC in March 1995 for £290 million. Texas Homecare held 7.6 percent of the U.K. DIY market. With the acquired units slowly being converted to the Homebase brand, Homebase by the late 1990s became the number two DIY chain in the United Kingdom, trailing only B&Q, which was owned by Kingfisher plc. In August 1996 Sainsbury's gained full control of Homebase when it bought out its partner in the venture, GIB Group, for £66 million.

In a new attempt at innovation, Sainsbury's launched Sainsbury's Bank in February 1997, becoming the first supermarket firm to open a fully licensed retail bank. A joint venture 55 percent owned by Sainsbury and 45 percent by Bank of Scotland, Sainsbury's Bank initially offered telephone banking services in Sainsbury supermarkets, including two credit cards and two savings accounts. By early 1998 the new bank had 700,000 customer accounts with £1.5 billion on deposit and had begun offering personal loans and mortgages. A whole host of additional financial services were introduced over the next few years. Sainsbury's Bank was profitable for the first time in fiscal 2000.

During 1997 Dino Adriano, who had joined Sainsbury in 1964 as a trainee accountant and had previously served as chairman of Homebase, was named group chief executive. Then, in a historic development, David Sainsbury in May 1998 announced his retirement as chairman in order to take on a political appointment as minister for science in Tony Blair's administration. In July 1998 George Bull, who had been serving as chairman of Diageo plc, took over as chairman of Sainsbury, becoming the first nonfamily member to head the company.

Under the new leadership, Sainsbury's continued to struggle and faced a new threat from ASDA following its 1998 acquisition by U.S. retailing giant Wal-Mart Stores, Inc. While Tesco had largely replaced Sainsbury's as the U.K. supermarket chain known for quality, and had thereby become the first choice for most middle- and upper-middle-class shoppers, ASDA began emphasizing the everyday-low-price scheme of its new parent, quickly becoming the price leader and gaining both working-class and middle-class customers in the process. Sainsbury's seemed to be lost between these two rivals and their respective niches. One response to the ASDA insurgency was Sainsbury's "low price guarantee" launched in October 1999, which promised to match the lowest prices on 1,600 commonly purchased products, including name-brand items. Sainsbury's also began adding nonfood items to its supermarkets' shelves, something its competitors had done several years previous. Needing funds to begin a store remodeling campaign, Sainsbury's cut 2,000 jobs from its workforce in 1999. Also that year, the company began a process of converting its 13 Savacentre outlets into large-format Sainsbury's units while also continuing to roll out a convenience-store format called Sainsbury's Local that had been launched in 1998.

In contrast to the difficulties of the U.K. supermarket operations, Sainsbury's Shaw's Homebase units were thriving. Shaw's was bolstered in June 1999 through the acquisition of Star Markets for $476 million. Star Markets operated more than 50 supermarkets in the Greater Boston and Cape Cod areas. A venture into a new foreign territory began in March 1999 when Sainsbury purchased a 25.1 percent stake in Edge SAE, a retail food chain based in Cairo, Egypt. Six months later the stake was increased to 80.1 percent and the company was later renamed Sainsbury's Egypt.

RESTRUCTURING AND COST-CUTTING UNDER DAVIS

Fiscal 2000 proved to be another difficult year for Sainsbury's. Profits fell 23 percent as the U.K. supermarkets operations suffered a significant profit decline that far outweighed the strong performance at Shaw's and Homebase. This prompted another management shakeup, and in March 2000 Peter Davis took over as chief executive from the retiring Adriano. Davis had been chief executive at Prudential plc, the largest life insurance firm in England, and had served as marketing director at Sainsbury's from 1976 to 1986.

Within months of the appointment of Davis, Sainsbury's appeared to be moving more quickly and decisively to engineer a turnaround. Davis quickened the pace of restructuring in the U.K. supermarkets, aiming to overhaul the entire store network within three years, rather than the eight years outlined previously. A major cost-cutting campaign that aimed at reducing annual operating expenditures by £600 million was initiated. Perhaps most importantly, Davis was attempting to fashion a successful niche for Sainsbury's aiming to tout the stores' quality and range of products and to not compete with Tesco and ASDA on price. This was a risky strategy, but Davis had apparently concluded that competing on price played into his competitors' strengths.

As this restructuring was being launched, Sainsbury also began pulling back from its diversification program, intending to concentrate on turning around the U.K. supermarkets. In mid-2000 Sainsbury began shopping Homebase around, and in December of that year reached an agreement to sell the home improvement chain for £975 million ($1.4 billion) in a complex three-way transaction. The deal closed in March 2001. Control of the Homebase chain itself went to Schroder Ventures, a U.K. private-equity firm, while 28 development sites were purchased by Kingfisher, owner of the rival B&Q chain. Sainsbury also reinvested £31 million in Homebase, resulting in a 17.8 percent stake. By retaining a stake, Sainsbury hoped to profit from a potential sale or public offering involving Homebase. Proceeds from the sale of Homebase went toward the supermarket remodeling program, an upgrade of Sainsbury's information technology systems as part of the efficiency drive, and debt reduction.

In 2001 Sainsbury sold its Egyptian supermarket chain to three Arab companies, who subsequently removed the Sainsbury name from the more than 100 stores. The venture was troubled from the start. Sainsbury had been the first international supermarket chain to enter the Egyptian market and was supported by the Egyptian government, but local supermarket owners were fearful of the new foreign competition and consumers began a boycott believing that Sainsbury would put local shops out of business. In October 2000 an outbreak of violence in the West Bank spread into Egypt when rumors that the Sainsbury chain was connected with Israel circulated, leading to the vandalizing of Sainsbury stores in Cairo. Sainsbury Egypt was also suffering mounting losses.

These disposals reduced the company to the Sainsbury's chain in the United Kingdom, the increasingly successful Sainsbury's Bank, and Shaw's in the United States, the 12th largest U.S. food retailer with annual revenues of about $4 billion. There was much speculation that Sainsbury would exit the U.S. market as well, but evidence to the contrary surfaced in November 2000 when the company agreed to purchase 18 Grand Union stores in Vermont and Connecticut. Following the March 2001 completion of this deal, the Grand Union outlets were rebranded under the Shaw's name. Also during 2001, Sainsbury moved its headquarters from the Stamford House complex at Blackfriars to Holborn Place in London. This development too was part of Davis's drive to make the company more efficient as the new site was more modern and enabled a consolidation of a number of key staff within one location. The relocation marked the end of an era as Sainsbury's headquarters had been in the Blackfriars area for more than 110 years.

By March 2004, the end of the 2004 fiscal year, Davis's multibillion-pound overhaul of the U.K. store network was largely complete, with mixed results. Significant cost savings had been achieved and profits had been shored up, but sales growth had yet to materialize. Most tellingly, comparable-store sales for the core U.K. supermarkets fell 0.2 percent during fiscal 2004.

With its market share continuing to erode, and with ASDA leapfrogging over it into second place among U.K. supermarket retailers during 2003, Sainsbury was keenly interested in acquiring Safeway, which had become the object of a bidding war among the major U.K. grocery retailers. In the fall of 2003, however, the U.K. government blocked Sainsbury, Tesco, and ASDA from purchasing Safeway for antitrust reasons. This cleared the way for Wm. Morrison Supermarkets PLC to take over Safeway, solidifying its position as the number four U.K. supermarket operator and making it a stronger Sainsbury competitor.

Morrison was forced to divest more than 50 stores to complete the takeover, and Sainsbury in May 2004 snapped up 14 of these stores, most of which were located in the Midlands and the north of England. Sainsbury also placed a further bet on the fast-growing convenience store sector by acquiring Bells Stores, a chain of 54 convenience stores in northeastern England, in February 2004. By that time, the company had opened more than 80 Sainsbury Local outlets. In August 2004 Sainsbury purchased Jacksons Stores Ltd., the leading independent, regional convenience store chain in the United Kingdom with 114 stores across Yorkshire and the North Midlands. This deal pushed Sainsbury's convenience store total past the 250 mark.

KING'S RECOVERY PLAN

In April 2004 Justin King was brought onboard to succeed Davis as chief executive. King had more than 20 years of experience in the grocery industry, including stints with ASDA and Marks and Spencer p.l.c. Davis briefly served as Sainsbury chairman, stepping down in July 2004 under pressure from shareholders incensed by what they considered an outsized bonus for fiscal 2004 given the company's poor performance. Philip Hampton was named chairman, having served as group finance director at Lloyds TSB Group plc.

In a deal negotiated under Davis but consummated in April 2004 under King, Sainsbury sold its U.S. supermarket operations, including the Shaw's and Star Markets chains, to Albertson's Inc. for $2.11 billion in cash and the assumption of about $368 million in capital leases. The deal was intended to help Sainsbury concentrate more fully on turning around its U.K. supermarket business.

After a six-month-long review of the business, King in October 2004 unveiled a three-year turnaround plan aimed at reversing Sainsbury's long slide. Overall, the plan emphasized sales growth, in contrast to previous re-

structurings' focus on profits, with a goal of boosting annual revenues by £2.5 billion by fiscal 2008. To jump-start sales, prices were cut on thousands of products to attract customers lost to low-price rivals such as Tesco and ASDA. At the same time, however, Sainsbury aimed to maintain its reputation for offering good, healthful food. Thus King's overall merchandising goal was to provide "great product at fair prices." In addition, an increasing emphasis on customer service was borne out by the hiring of 3,000 additional shop-floor staffers. The increase in staff was also part of a plan to address a critical issue with customers: keeping store shelves properly stocked. King blamed his predecessor for botching his overhaul of the supply chain, leading to the stocking problems. King's turnaround program placed less emphasis on cost-cutting than that of Davis, but the new chief executive did slash the headquarters staff by one-quarter, eliminating 750 jobs. One-time charges totaling roughly £510 million cut the pretax profits for fiscal 2005 to just £15 million.

By the end of the 2007 fiscal year in March 2007, Sainsbury had made great progress on its recovery. That year's revenues of £17.15 billion ($33.76 billion) amounted to an increase of roughly £1.9 billion over the figure for fiscal 2005, putting the company ahead of the pace needed to reach the three-year goal of a £2.5 billion sales boost. Also indicative of a turnaround were the nine straight quarters of comparable-sales growth recorded through the final quarter of fiscal 2007. Comparable sales for the full year of 2007 surged by a healthy 5.9 percent. The strong sales performance was also beginning to translate into bottom-line gains as pretax underlying profits jumped 42.3 percent to £380 million ($750 million). On the basis of this nascent turnaround, new three-year goals were set. By the end of fiscal 2010, Sainsbury aimed to increase its sales by an additional £3.5 billion. Toward this goal, the company sought to increase its Internet-based sales, expand 75 of its supermarkets particularly to include more nonfood offerings, and open 30 new supermarkets and 100 convenience stores. Overall sales space was to be increased by 10 percent to more than 19 million square feet. In addition, the convenience store operations were to be centered around the Sainsbury's Local brand as the Bells and Jackson's names were retired.

2007 FAILED TAKEOVER BIDS

As Sainsbury moved from recovery to growth, a consortium of private-equity firms led by CVC Capital Partners in early 2007 began pursuing a buyout of the company, a move that pushed its share price up to its highest level in eight years. A bid of £10.2 billion ($20.1 billion) eventually fell apart in April 2007 in part because of opposition from the Sainsbury family, which at the time continued to hold a stake of approximately 18 percent. Then by July 2007 Delta (Two) Ltd., a Qatari investment fund, had built up a 25 percent interest in Sainsbury. The Qataris proposed to take over Sainsbury for a total of £10.6 billion and invest billions of pounds in the firm to expand it into international markets. Talks between the Qataris and Sainsbury reached an advanced stage, but in November 2007 the Qataris dropped their bid, citing deteriorating credit markets and financial demands from Sainsbury's pension-fund trustees.

Sainsbury continued with its recovery and growth plans as these takeover bids played themselves out. Further optimism about the company's future was engendered by the March 2008 news that comparable-store sales had increased for the 13th straight quarter. By this time, however, members of the Sainsbury family had reduced their collective stake in the firm to around 15 percent, prompting further speculation about another takeover bid. The Qatari investment fund had maintained its 25 percent stake, and analysts considered a second bid from the fund a distinct possibility.

Betty T. Moore
Updated, April Dougal Gasbarre; David E. Salamie

PRINCIPAL SUBSIDIARIES

JS Insurance Ltd.; JS Information Systems Ltd.; Sainsbury's Supermarkets Ltd.; Swan Infrastructure Holdings Ltd.

PRINCIPAL COMPETITORS

Tesco PLC; ASDA Group Limited; Wm. Morrison Supermarkets PLC; John Lewis Partnership plc.

FURTHER READING

Adamy, Janet, and Erin White, "Albertsons to Acquire Shaw's Chain," *Wall Street Journal*, March 29, 2004, p. B4.

Bagnall, Sarah, "How King of the Grocers Was Eased Off Its Throne: Arrogance and Complacency Blamed for Sainsbury's Decline," *Times* (London), May 9, 1996.

Barnes, Rachel, "No Longer the Bad Apple?" *Grocer*, May 7, 2005, pp. 40–41.

Beck, Ernest, "Britain's Ailing Sainsbury Faces Stark Choice," *Wall Street Journal*, October 25, 1999, p. A49I.

Bernoth, Ardyn, and Matthew Lynn, "Counter Attack: Profile—David Sainsbury," *Times* (London), January 14, 1996.

Blackhurst, Chris, "Justin King," *Management Today*, May 2005, pp. 40+.

Braithwaite, Tom, and Elizabeth Rigby, "Sainsbury Eyes Life After Qatar," *Financial Times*, November 6, 2007, p. 21.

Brown-Humes, Christopher, "Humble Pie on Offer at Sainsbury," *Financial Times*, May 11, 1996, p. 5.

Buckley, Neil, "A Long Shopping List to Regain Lost Momentum: Sainsbury's Sales and Margins Have Caused Analysts Concern," *Financial Times*, November 2, 1995, p. 19.

———, "Super Service," *Financial Times*, June 16, 1995, p. 16.

Buckley, Sophy, and Bettina Wassener, "Counting the Cost: Can Justin King Put Sainsbury on the Right Track?" *Financial Times*, October 16, 2004, p. 11.

Cauchi, Marietta, "Sainsbury Bidders Falter As Blackstone, TPG Balk," *Wall Street Journal*, April 11, 2007, p. C3.

———, "Sainsbury Deal's Collapse Throws Focus on Rivals," *Wall Street Journal*, April 12, 2007, p. A10.

Churchill, David, "How Precision Boosts Sainsbury's Productivity," *Financial Times*, January 11, 1982, p. 10.

Cope, Nigel, "Checking Out," *Management Today*, February 2000, pp. 66–71.

Davidson, Andrew, "Dino Adriano," *Management Today*, March 1999, pp. 62+.

De Jonquieres, Guy, and John Thornhill, "Family Still Minding the Store," *Financial Times*, July 1, 1991, p. 30.

East, Robert, *The Anatomy of Conquest: Tesco Versus Sainsbury*, Kingston Upon Thames, U.K.: Kingston Business School, 1997.

The First 120 Years of Sainsbury's, 1869–1989, London: Sainsbury's, 1999.

Hollinger, Peggy, "Davis Heads for J Sainsbury Checkout," *Financial Times*, July 1, 2004, p. 24.

———, "Politic Departure Ends Six Years in the Chair and Rings Down the Curtain on Six Generations of Sainsburys at the Helm," *Financial Times*, May 7, 1998, p. 24.

———, "The Poser for the Pragmatist at Sainsbury's," *Financial Times*, May 31, 2000, p. 30.

———, "Sainsbury: Supermarkets, Super Margins, Superseded," *Financial Times*, October 30, 1996, p. 25.

———, "The Vision to Overcome a Mountain of Problems," *Financial Times*, June 1, 2000, p. 28.

Hunt, Jonathan, "Sainsbury' Innovative Traditionists," *Chief Executive*, October 1985, pp. 12+.

JS 100: The Story of Sainsbury's, London: J Sainsbury Ltd., 1969, 96 p.

Kennedy, Carol, *The Merchant Princes: Family, Fortune, and Philanthropy—Cadbury, Sainsbury, and John Lewis*, London: Hutchinson, 2000, 309 p.

———, "Public Company, Private Dynasty," *Director*, December 1992, p. 46.

Marcom, John, Jr., "Britain's Sainsbury to Buy Rest of Shaw's in a Cautious Approach to Growth in U.S.," *Wall Street Journal*, June 22, 1987.

McAllister, Sean, "King Jumps Ship," *Grocer*, November 22, 2003, pp. 24–25.

Mitchell, Alan, "Reinvention Is the Only Option Left for Sainsbury's," *Marketing Week,* October 28, 2004, pp. 30–31.

Nicholas, Ruth, "Sainsbury Cola Gives in to Coke," *Marketing,* May 12, 1994, p. 1.

Parkes, Christopher, "Fattened Up in Readiness for a New Boston Tea-Party: Sainsbury Set to Take Full Control of Shaw's," *Financial Times,* June 20, 1987, p. 8.

Raghavan, Anita, and Ernest Beck, "Sainsbury Enters Talks to Sell Homebase Stores," *Wall Street Journal,* November 29, 2000, p. A23.

Rigby, Elizabeth, and John Willman, "The Aristocrats of Retail," *Financial Times,* April 14, 2007, p. 9.

Rogers, David, "Britain's Supermarkets: An Industry in Turmoil," *Supermarket Business,* August 1989, p. 37.

Saigol, Lina, and Peter Smith, "How the Barons Beat the Barbarians: The Supermarket Chain's Fate Remains Firmly in the Hands of the Founding Sainsbury Family," *Financial Times,* April 14, 2007, p. 15.

Singer, Jason, "Qatar Drops Bid for Sainsbury," *Wall Street Journal,* November 6, 2007, p. B9.

Smith, Alison, "Sainsbury Looks for Convenience As It Buys 54-Strong Bells Chain," *Financial Times,* February 19, 2004, p. 20.

Stogel, Chuck, "The Once and Future King?" *Brandweek,* May 8, 1995, p. 34.

Tait, Nikki, "From High Road to Main Street," *Financial Times,* November 20, 1991, p. 20.

Urry, Maggie, "Developing 'Softly Softly' Outside the Mainstream," *Financial Times,* May 20, 1988, p. 12.

Voyle, Susanna, "Competitors Put the Squeeze on Sainsbury," *Financial Times,* July 21, 2003, p. 21.

———, "Customers Not Buying into Davis' Grand Plans," *Financial Times,* March 29, 2003, p. 16.

———, "Life Is Turning a Lot Tougher As the Problems Pile Up for King's Arrival," *Financial Times,* January 13, 2004, p. 22.

———, "Sainsbury Confirms King As New Chief," *Financial Times,* November 20, 2003, p. 23.

———, "Sainsbury's King Ready to Reign," *Financial Times,* March 27, 2004, p. 3.

———, "Strategy Under a Microscope," *Financial Times,* November 16, 2002, p. 13.

Williams, Bridget, *The Best Butter in the World: A History of Sainsbury's,* London: Ebury, 1994, 224 p.

Wilsher, Peer, "Housekeeping?" *Management Today,* December 1993, p. 38.

Zwiebach, Elliot, "Sainsbury to Buy 50 Percent of Giant's Voting Stock," *Supermarket News,* October 10, 1994, p. 1.

Keller Group PLC

Capital House
25 Chapel Street
London, NW1 5DH
United Kingdom
Telephone: (+44 020) 7616 7575
Web site: http://www.keller.co.uk

Public Company
Incorporated: 1990
Employees: 5,698
Sales: £920.2 million ($1.87 billion) (2006)
Stock Exchanges: London
Ticker Symbol: KLR
NAIC: 238910 Other Specialty Trade Contractors;
551112 Offices of Other Holding Companies

■ ■ ■

Keller Group PLC is one of the world's leading specialist ground engineering companies. The London-based company provides a full range of ground preparation and support services to the global construction and civil engineering industries. Keller provides ground improvement services using Vibro Stone columns, specialty grouting, piling, and other soil compensation technologies. These technologies stabilize the ground prior to the laying of foundations for large and small-scale construction and civil engineering projects. Keller is also a global leader in post-tension cable systems, which use reinforced concrete and structural spans as part of foundation slabs used in certain soil types and conditions. Since the mid-1990s, Keller has also built a leading position in the structural restoration market, providing concrete repair and other building refurbishment services. Part of Keller's success is its geographic diversity, with operations in 30 countries on five continents.

The United States has become the company's single largest market, accounting for more than 50 percent of annual revenues. Keller holds a leading position in the United States, where it operates through regional subsidiaries Hayward Baker, McKinney Drilling, Case Atlantic Company, Suncoast Post-Tension, and Anderson. The United Kingdom accounts for 13 percent of revenues, while the rest of Europe adds 27 percent. Subsidiaries in these markets include Keller Engineering Services and Keller Grundbau, and Makers, the U.K. refurbishment specialist. Keller is also active in Australia, where it is market leader through subsidiaries including Franki, Vibro-Pile, Piling Contractors, and Keller Ground Engineering. Keller Group was formed through a management buyout in 1990, and has been listed on the London Stock Exchange since 1994. The company is led by Chairman Michael West and CEO Justin Atkinson. In 2006, the company posted revenues of £920 million ($1.8 billion).

GKN UNIT IN THE FIFTIES

Keller Group's origins trace back to two sources. The oldest of the two was an engineering company founded in Germany in 1860 by Johann Keller. Based in Renchen, that company later specialized in the building foundation sector, and played an important role in developing foundation technologies in Europe. In 1974,

Keller was acquired by GKN Foundations, a subsidiary of U.K. conglomerate Guest, Keen and Nettlefolds Limited (later GKN). In the early 1950s, GKN had been forced to seek diversification beyond its core metals businesses, following the British nationalization of the country's steel industry in 1951. As a result, GKN targeted a number of new business areas, including the construction and civil engineering sector. The reconstruction of Britain in the post–World War II era provided a number of opportunities for GKN. Among them, the company built up its own specialist foundations and ground reinforcement subsidiary, GKN Foundations.

Ground reinforcement had long been an important component in the civil engineering and construction sectors, especially since the development of concrete had enabled the construction of ever-larger buildings, bridges, dams, and other construction projects. Techniques had long been employed to provide solid foundations for the increasingly heavy buildings; pilings, for example, had long been used to extend foundation support beneath the less solid upper layers of earth.

Other technologies were developed to improve soil composition, and to develop new drainage capacities and control. The creation of stone "columns," produced by compacting stone into holes dug in the ground, not only created a structure similar to piling, but also reinforced the surrounding soil. Grouting techniques enabled builders to control drainage, while also improving the soil. During the 1960s, engineers developed the post-tension cable system of foundation support, using reinforced concrete. This technology was especially useful in sandy and desert-like regions.

In 1976, GKN formally merged its U.K. and German foundations operations into a single company, which became GKN Keller. The company then became a significant specialty player in the European ground reinforcement market, while also benefiting from being part of the larger GKN group of companies.

GKN began its drive into the United States in the mid-1970s, establishing itself as a major supplier to the country's automotive industry. GKN's expansion set the stage for GKN Keller's own entry into the United

States. This was accomplished by the purchase of Hayward Baker Inc. in 1984. That company, based in Maryland, originally focused on the grouting sector. Under Keller, Hayward Baker expanded to include the full range of ground reinforcement technologies, becoming not only Keller's largest U.S. operation, but a leader in the U.S. market.

The move into the grouting market in the United States encouraged GKN Keller to seek further expansion in this construction services category. In 1986, the company reinforced its U.K. operations with the purchase of Colcrete, which specialized in grouting systems. This purchase helped reinforce GKN Keller's own foundations, as it grew to become the United Kingdom's leading ground reinforcement specialist.

MANAGEMENT BUYOUT IN 1990

In the meantime, GKN itself was carrying out its own transformation; by the beginning of the 1990s, the British conglomerate had restructured itself as a global automotive component supplier. GKN began shedding its noncore operations, with GKN Keller among them.

In 1990, GKN Keller's management team, led by future Chairman Michael West and Tom Dobson, led the buyout of GKN's global ground reinforcement operations. The company was then renamed Keller Group. Financial backing for the buyout was provided by venture capital group Candover.

Keller's early years were marked by the difficult economic period, as the world slipped into a global recession at the start of the 1990s. Especially troubling for the company was the slump in the global construction market, which, after a building boom in the 1980s, had collapsed at the end of that decade.

As the markets began to pick up again, Keller started preparing for its own expansion, preparing a strategy that was to see the group expand by nearly 1000 percent over the next decade. This transformation into a global leader was launched with the company's public offering on the London Stock Exchange in 1994.

ACQUIRING SCALE FROM 1994

Acquisitions formed the heart of Keller's growth strategy. The company first targeted new expansion in the U.S. market, which was just about to enter a new and extended economic growth phase. In 1994, the company acquired Chicago-based Case International. Founded in the 1950s, Case had grown into one of the United States' leading deep foundation specialists. The company was especially strong in the large-scale caisson pilings segment.

KEY DATES

1860: Johann Keller founds engineering company in Renchem, Germany.

1950s: GKN of the United Kingdom launches ground engineering subsidiary, GKN Foundations.

1974: GKN acquires Keller, which is subsequently merged into GKN Foundations, creating GKN Keller.

1984: Company enters United States through acquisition of Maryland's Hayward Baker.

1990: Spinoff of Keller Group is part of management buyout.

1994: Keller goes public and launches acquisition drive to become world leader.

2001: Company acquires Suncoast of the United States, adding post-tension cable systems expertise.

2007: HJ Foundations, based in Florida, is acquired.

The addition of Case gave Keller leading positions in two major ground support categories in the United States. In 1995, the company added a third, paying $3.3 million to acquire the global rights to soil mixing technology from Millguard. The company added to its U.S. operations again in 1997, buying another caisson group, Smith Drilling. That company was then merged with Case's operations in the south, creating Case Atlantic. The following year, Keller expanded its U.S. operations westward, with the purchase of Colorado-based Denver Grouting. As its name implied, this company focused on the grouting sector.

In England, the company targeted another important market, that of the refurbishment of the country's vast council housing sector. In 1996, the company bought Makers, the leading U.K. specialist provider of concrete repairing and related refurbishing services. However, the United Kingdom remained a difficult market for the company, in large part because most of its major competitors were subsidiaries of the country's leading construction groups. As such, Keller's rivals were supported by the parents' financial muscle, making it difficult for Keller to compete on price.

In response, Keller's ambitions turned increasingly international in the late 1990s. The company seized an opportunity to extend itself into the Australian market through the purchase of Franki Pacific Holdings (Frankipile) from Belgium's Franki in 1998. Frankipile

had been founded in 1953, and had become a leading foundation engineering group in Australia and New Zealand. The addition of Frankipile also extended Keller's reach to southeast Asia, particularly Indonesia, Papua New Guinea, and the Pacific Islands. That same year, Keller added its first North African operations, with the purchase of Egypt's Genco.

GLOBAL LEADER IN THE NEW CENTURY

Keller also expanded its European base as well. The company entered the Swiss market in 2000, buying MTS, which focused on provided soil nailing, micro piling, and similar ground reinforcement services. Keller then entered the Scandinavian market, acquiring a 50 percent stake in Göteborg, Sweden-based LCM. That company, with operations throughout the Nordic region as well as into Eastern Europe, had more than 20 years of experience in soil stabilization technologies.

However, Keller's largest market proved to be the United States. The company continued to target its expansion there, building its presence in most of the country's major regional markets. This led the company to its largest acquisition to date, of Suncoast. The purchase, which cost the company $90 million, gave it a significant presence in the southwestern markets, while also adding Suncoast's expertise in post-tension cable systems.

The Suncoast purchase was quickly followed by the acquisition of another important regional player, Catoh, which focused on heavy drilling technologies. In 2002, Keller reinforced its leadership position in the East Coast region with the purchase of caisson specialist McKinney Drilling. That purchase cost the company nearly $58 million. McKinney, founded in 1937, had been one of the pioneers of caisson piling technology.

By the middle of the first decade of the 2000s, Keller's U.S. operations accounted for more than half of the group's total revenues. These were further boosted by the acquisition of Anderson Drilling, a West Coast-based heavy foundations specialist, in 2006. The company then bought HJ Foundation, a piling specialist based in Florida, in 2007.

Nonetheless, Keller remained committed to expanding its global base. The company's European operations were lifted in the early 2000s, after much of Central Europe was devastated by floods. The company shored up its own operations there, buying Germany's Wannenwetsch, which focused on providing equipment for underwater concrete refurbishment.

Next, Keller looked toward Spain, where it became a 51 percent partner in a ground engineering joint venture, Keller-Terra. The company then completed its acquisition of LCM, buying the remaining 50 percent in 2004. In Australia, Keller cemented its leadership position with the acquisition of Piling Contractors, number two in the Australian market.

Back home, the group expanded its Makers subsidiary with the purchase of rival Phi, which brought expertise in retaining wall systems for the excavation and construction market in the United Kingdom. The group also extended its home base through the purchase of Systems Geotechnique. That company added its own grouting and drilling operations. By then, Keller's sales neared the £1 billion mark. From a small offshoot of GKN in the early 1990s, the company had grown to become a world-leading ground engineering specialist.

M. L. Cohen

PRINCIPAL SUBSIDIARIES

Case Atlantic Company (U.S.A.); Case Foundation Company (U.S.A.); Frankipile Australia Pty Ltd.; Geotechnical Engineering Contractor Ltd. (Egypt); Hayward Baker Inc. (U.S.A.); Hochdruckwassertechnik (Germany); Keller (Malaysia) Sdn. Bhd.; Keller Fondations Spéciales SAS (France); Keller Fondazioni S.r.l. (Italy); Keller Foundations (Southeast Asia) Pte Ltd. (Singapore); Keller Grundbau Ges.mbH (Austria); Keller Grundbau GmbH (Germany); Keller Limited; Keller Polska Sp. z o.o. (Poland); Keller Turki Company Ltd. (Saudi Arabia); Keller-Terra S.L. (Spain); Lime Column Method AB (Sweden); Makers Limited; McKinney Drilling Company (U.S.A.); Phi Group Limited; Piling Contractors Pty Ltd. (Australia); SJA Inc. (U.S.A.); Suncoast Post-Tension L.P. (U.S.A.); Vibro-Pile (Aust.) Pty Ltd. (Australia); Wannenwetsch GmbH.

PRINCIPAL COMPETITORS

VINCI Construction France S.A.S.; Trevi SpA; Bauer GmbH; Soletanche Bachy SAS.

FURTHER READING

Aldrick, Philip, "Keller Sees Foundation for Growth As Europe's Floods Subside," *Daily Telegraph,* August 23, 2002.

Davoudi, Salamander, "Strategy of Growth Through Bolt-ons," *Financial Times,* March 10, 2006, p. 4.

Gilchrist, Susan, "Keller Comes to Market with £72m Valuation," *Times,* April 20, 1994, p. 28.

Griggs, Tom, "Keller Enjoys Lift from Mideast Construction Boom," *Financial Times,* June 22, 2007, p. 20.

"Keller Acquires," *International Construction,* January–February 2004, p. 10.

"Keller Boosted by US Success," *Contract Journal,* August 24, 2005, p. 4.

"Keller Expects Flood of Work Across Europe," *Contract Journal,* August 29, 2002, p. 6.

"Keller Leads Way As Shares Hold up in Tough Market," *Contract Journal,* August 22, 2007.

Murray-West, Rosie, "Keller: One to Bury for a Rainy Day," *Daily Telegraph,* August 23, 2002, p. 40.

Stevenson, Rachel, "Foundations Solid at Keller, but Not the Time to Buy Yet," *Independent,* August 24, 2004, p. 41.

"US Operations Boost Keller," *Contract Journal,* March 8, 2006.

loans that change lives

Kiva

———————————■———————————

3180 18th Street, Suite 201
San Francisco, California 94110
U.S.A.
Telephone: (415) 358-7529
Web site: http://www.kiva.org

Nonprofit Organization
Incorporated: 2005
Employees: 16
Operating Revenues: $12.5 million (2007)
NAIC: 522310 Mortgage and Nonmortgage Loan
 Brokers

■ ■ ■

Kiva uses the Internet to connect entrepreneurs in more than 40 developing countries with lenders from around the world, who provide loans in $25 increments. The San Francisco-based nonprofit organization works with more than 85 microfinance institutions that disperse funds, collect payments, and help new borrowers post loan requests and update lenders. By carefully selecting these partners, Kiva has kept its default rate to less than two-tenths of a percent. The firm's overhead costs are primarily covered by an optional 10 percent loan surcharge donated by most of its lenders, and it also receives support from foundations and companies including PayPal, YouTube, Google, and Microsoft. In its first three years of operation Kiva has helped more

than 250,000 lenders invest over $25 million to fund nearly 40,000 loan requests.

BEGINNINGS

Kiva was founded in San Francisco by Matt and Jessica Flannery, whose inspiration can be traced to a 2003 talk given at Stanford University by Muhammed Yunus, who had founded the Grameen Bank in Bangladesh to make small loans to poor entrepreneurs. In less-developed countries interest rates from commercial banks or village money lenders could amount to several hundred percent or more, and Yunus, an economics professor, had founded the bank to give poor entrepreneurs a reasonably priced source of funds.

Deciding that she had found her calling, in early 2004 Jessica Flannery accepted an offer to spend three months in East Africa evaluating the effectiveness of a San Francisco-based organization called the Village Enterprise Fund, which provided loans and grants to small businesses there. She was joined for part of the time by Matt, himself a budding entrepreneur with a master's degree in analytical philosophy from Stanford who was working as an engineer at digital video recorder firm TiVo.

They were impressed by the way that tiny amounts of capital, by Western standards, could vastly improve the lives of villagers when invested in small businesses. It might cost just $500 to start a store in a community where residents otherwise would have to travel several miles on foot to buy basic goods, and even less than that to help a seamstress or animal herder expand their operations and better support their own family or create jobs for others.

Seeking a way to help more Africans grow their businesses, the couple at first tried to invest their money in a microfinance fund, but found that the minimum required was $50,000 or more. Undeterred, they decided to develop a new way to help by aggregating loans through a web site that Matt would develop. Starting with business plan software given to them by Jessica's father, they began seeking input from experts in the field. The venture was given the name Kesho, the Swahili word for "tomorrow."

During the latter half of 2004 and into 2005 the Flannerys spent their spare time wrestling with such legal issues as deciding whether to incorporate as a nonprofit—they ultimately registered as a 501(c) (3) organization—as well as sorting out the various hurdles to acting as an international, small-scale lending institution. After much searching they found a team of lawyers willing to help navigate these problems, which included the post-9/11 U.S. Patriot Act that sought to keep American money out of the hands of terrorists in foreign lands.

Although wary of attracting scrutiny from the Securities and Exchange Commission (SEC), Matt Flannery decided to call them and ask for help, and found to his surprise that the Office of Small Business Policy was able to offer significant assistance. Critically, its agents helped him decide not to pay interest to lenders, which avoided putting the firm in the category of securities issuer, which came with much stricter regulation.

ONLINE WITH BETA SITE IN MARCH 2005

After spending three-fourths of a year fine-tuning their plan, and with a number of problems still unresolved, the Flannerys decided to launch a warts-and-all "beta" version of the online lending site to test its functionality. Its goals would be fourfold: to let Internet users make small personal loans to specific borrowers around the world; to connect a network of microfinance institutions (MFIs) to the site and allow them to post loan applications online; to transact loans in which the lender assumed the risk of default; and to facilitate loans between people, not organizations, but which were administered by an MFI.

While working on their plans the Flannerys had become disenchanted with the name Kesho, and after consulting a Swahili dictionary changed it to Kiva, which meant "unity" or "agreement." After paying $600 to secure the already registered domain name, and trading Matt's electric guitar to a TiVo graphic artist for a distinctive green plantlike logo design, the site was ready to launch.

To find clients the Flannerys turned to Moses Onyango, a minister in Tororo, Uganda, whom Jessica had met while working there. He rounded up seven local entrepreneurs who needed loans, including a fishmonger, a goat herder, a cattle farmer, and a restaurateur. In March 2005 Kiva went online and the Flannerys sent e-mails to 300 of their wedding guests asking for help. Within a few days the $3,500 requested had been pledged.

Onyango soon began writing about the entrepreneurs' progress on the Kiva web site, and his reports were keenly read by the lenders. Over the next few months the Flannerys began receiving offers of help from a number of interested parties including Premal Shah, a Stanford economics graduate with a longstanding interest in microfinance who was working for eBay credit-processing subsidiary PayPal.

KIVA TAKES OFF IN OCTOBER 2005

While the seven initial loans were being repaid, the Flannerys asked Onyango to find 50 more prospective borrowers in preparation for a wider launch of the site. On October 12 a press release was issued announcing Kiva to the public at large, but there was little interest at first. However, two weeks later a blurb about the organization was posted on Daily Kos, one of the most popular political blog sites on the Internet, and within hours the new round of loans worth more than $10,000 was fulfilled. Thousands of e-mails also began pouring

KEY DATES

∎

2005: Matt and Jessica Flannery found web-based microlending organization Kiva.
2006: PayPal begins waiving credit card fees; *Frontline* exposure boosts lending tenfold.
2007: Bill Clinton and Oprah Winfrey promote Kiva; gift certificates, group loans debut.
2008: Cumulative lending reaches $25 million and lending partners top 85 by spring.

in, some offering assistance and others from MFIs in such countries as Bulgaria, Nicaragua, and Rwanda, seeking loans.

To attract even cash-strapped lenders, Kiva's loans were offered in $25 increments. Donors could view photos of borrowers and a brief description of their plans for using the money, and choose those they found appealing to support. Women tended to get funded first, as did agriculture-based businesses in the most undeveloped countries. Lenders were kept updated about loan repayments via e-mail and could get their money back after the debt was repaid, but the majority agreed to relend it, which helped the cumulative loan total grow exponentially.

Buoyed by the spike in loans, in December 2005 Matt Flannery decided to quit his TiVo job to concentrate on Kiva (Jessica Flannery had enrolled in Stanford's M.B.A. program). He quickly assembled a small staff of like-minded individuals, several of whom had experience in the world of finance, public relations, and technology. Although initially focused on Africa, the organization began to expand its loans to other parts of the globe.

In January 2006 Premal Shah left his job as product manager at PayPal to take the title of Kiva president, also providing his home as quarters for the firm's unpaid staff. He used his connections to secure PayPal's donation of free processing of loans (worth 3 percent of each transaction), making lending money through the site even easier. It was the first time the company had agreed to such a donation of service, and would prove a critical part of Kiva's financial picture.

In February the firm announced a new MFI partnership strategy and introduced its first five field partners, which were located in Uganda, Tanzania, Honduras/Nicaragua, Ecuador, and Gaza. Although as many as 10,000 such organizations existed, only about 200 were considered reliable by established banking standards, and it took time to sort out the best ones to work with, given that their typical clients were people with no credit record and little in the way of collateral.

Although lenders did not earn it, borrowers did pay interest, but this amount (which ranged from 4 to 50 percent and averaged 22 percent) went to support the local MFI's operation and its staff of field workers who helped post loans and collect payments. Challenges in getting the MFIs connected to the Internet were common, and in places such as rural Africa where the only way to go online was by telephone, it could take an hour to upload a photograph to the firm's web site.

By October 2006, one year after Kiva had issued the press release announcing itself to the world, the total amount lent had reached $430,000. It had come from 5,400 lenders and was disbursed to 750 entrepreneurs in 12 countries. The firm had 14 MFI partners in Africa, Asia, Eastern Europe, the Middle East, and Latin America. Overhead costs were low, with Kiva occupying rented quarters in San Francisco's gritty Mission District and using furniture and equipment donated by firms including Google and PayPal. Its total operating budget for 2006 was $125,000.

FRONTLINE REPORT LEADS TO LENDING SURGE IN LATE 2006

Despite its low overhead, by the fall Kiva had nearly used up the operating funds donated by board members and others, but Matt Flannery rejected options such as seeking venture capital. With money nearly depleted, on Halloween night a 15-minute report on Kiva's efforts ran on the Public Broadcasting Service show *Frontline*. The exposure set off a surge in interest that shut down the organization's computer servers for three days, but when the dust settled the amount lent had increased tenfold to $30,000 per day. With approximately 70 percent of lenders donating an optional 10 percent above their loan, operating funds soon reached a comfortable level. Other revenues came from "float," interest earned on banked money that was being repaid or awaiting dispersal.

In late 2006 YouTube cofounder Steve Chen contacted Kiva with another offer of support. The popular streaming-video site would run banner ads for Kiva 40 million times per month, and click-throughs to Kiva.org from YouTube soon accounted for 15 percent of the site's total traffic. Other assistance came from Google and Microsoft Research, which conducted a free study in East Africa to determine the best type of technology to use for the firm's microfinance projects.

By April 2007, two years after the first seven funding requests had been posted, Kiva had reached a cumulative loan total of $5.5 million. The number of prospective borrowers stood at about 6,000, 30 times the number of a year before.

In the summer of 2007 30 Kiva volunteers went into the field to observe the effects the organization was having, reporting in detail via the web site, and the firm also moved to new quarters on 18th Street in San Francisco's Mission District. By the fall Kiva was working with 62 MFIs in 39 countries, including partnerships in Iraq and Afghanistan, with lenders drawn from more than 50 countries worldwide. The firm's infrastructure was being supported by donations from the Kellogg Foundation, the Draper Richards Foundation, the DOEN Foundation, and Halloran Philanthropy.

With the organization's rapid growth the number of loan defaults had grown slightly to less than two-tenths of a percent, but this was still an insignificant amount. Each MFI's total default rate was shown online, which provided incentive to thoroughly vet their clients so they could attract more loans.

CEO Flannery expressed his desire to eventually pay optional interest to Kiva lenders, which he believed would facilitate the funding of more mundane proposals that sometimes had a hard time being chosen. It would also make the lender/client relationship more of a business one that relied less on emotional "do-gooder" motives that he believed perpetuated the stereotype of people in developing countries as helpless victims. The organization was continuing to work with its legal advisers to offer this option, but it would require SEC approval.

As the number of loans and donations grew Kiva was able to fund monitoring, auditing, and visitation programs that ensured the honesty of MFIs and borrowers. The firm also worked with MFIs to record data, in some cases holding the only record of loans as well as the MFI's bookkeeping. It simultaneously created a credit history for people who may never have had any records of their financial dealings compiled. Kiva staff also compiled a variety of data including social return on investment figures, depicting loans' impact on the regions served.

BILL CLINTON AND OPRAH TAKING KIVA HIGHER IN FALL 2007

During 2007 money lent grew at a rate of 30 percent per month, buoyed by increasing media exposure and such high-profile supporters as former President Bill Clinton, who praised Kiva in his book *Giving*. In early September the organization was featured on the

NBC-TV *Today* show, and cofounders Matt and Jessica Flannery appeared on *Oprah* with Clinton. Over the next few days Kiva attracted nearly 6,500 new lenders and $250,000 in new loans, which exhausted all requests for funding. Afterward the firm placed a $25 cap on the amount a person could lend to a single entrepreneur to help broaden the distribution of funds. The average loan request was filled less than a day after being added to the site.

In November Kiva announced the availability of gift certificates that allowed the recipient to make loans to a beneficiary of their choice, and more than $2.2 million worth were sold during the holiday season. In late 2007 the firm also began to offer group loans, in which a number of individuals with similar occupations banded together to request a single loan, mirroring the way funds were given out by many MFIs.

By the spring of 2008 Kiva, which was being hailed as one of the fastest-growing nonprofits in history, had lent more than $25 million since inception, with over 250,000 lenders taking part. More than 37,000 loans had been closed, with 99.86 percent paid back in full. The average loan was for $558.64, with each lender investing an average of $88.95. The organization anticipated a cumulative loan total of $100 million by 2010.

In the three years since the launch of its web site, Kiva had built up a stable of more than 85 lending partners in 42 countries and had attracted more than a quarter-million lenders. The loans it facilitated were helping bring a better life to many thousands around the world, and future growth looked certain.

Frank Uhle

PRINCIPAL COMPETITORS

Microplace, Inc.; DonorsChoose.org; The GlobalGiving Foundation; Network for Good; Modest Needs Foundation; Finca International; Accion International; theBigGive; Prosper Marketplace, Inc.; Zopa, Inc.

FURTHER READING

Crawford, Amy, "I, Lender," *Smithsonian,* September 22, 2007, p. 92.

Flannery, Matt, "Kiva and the Birth of Person-to-Person Microfinance," *Innovations,* Winter & Spring 2007, pp. 31–56.

Haven, Cynthia, "Small Change, Big Payoff," *Stanford Magazine,* November/December, 2007.

Hempel, Jessi, "A Little Money Goes a Long Way," *BusinessWeek,* July 31, 2006, p. 64.

Kristof, Nicholas D., "You, Too, Can Be a Banker to the Poor," *New York Times,* March 27, 2007, p. 19A.

Loizos, Constance, "Kiva Does Well, with Help from Friends," *Oakland Tribune,* March 26, 2007.

O'Brien, Jeffrey M., "The Only Nonprofit That Matters," *Fortune,* March 3, 2008, p. 37.

Pratt, Mary K., "Game Changer Kiva Harnesses IT to Revolutionize Microfinance," *Computerworld,* January 29, 2007.

Riley, Sheila, "Microcredit: Small Loans, Big Changes," *Investor's Business Daily,* April 30, 2007, p. A5.

Yollin, Patricia, "Microcredit Movement Tackling Poverty One Tiny Loan at a Time," *San Francisco Chronicle,* September 30, 2007, p. A1.

Klein Tools, Inc.

450 Bond Street
P.O. Box 1418
Lincolnshire, Illinois 60069-1418
U.S.A.
Telephone: (847) 821-5500
Toll Free: (800) 553-4676
Fax: (800) 553-4876
Web site: http://www.kleintools.com

Private Company
Founded: 1857 as Mathias Klein & Sons
Employees: 1,100
Sales: $180 million (2008 est.)
NAIC: 332212 Hand and Edge Tool Manufacturing

∎ ∎ ∎

Klein Tools, Inc., began in 1857 as the small forging shop of Mathias Klein, a German immigrant. Klein's initial claim to fame was a pair of newly forged pliers, the first known on record, which came to be known simply as "Kleins." Kleins quickly became the hand tool of choice among Chicago's early tradesmen during the city's transformation from a trading hub to industrial powerhouse. A wide range of finely crafted tools and accessories earned Mathias Klein & Sons a loyal following among the region's growing workers. Although the name has changed slightly, the family toolmaking tradition and emphasis on high quality and durability remain, more than 150 years later.

MID-19TH-CENTURY ORIGINS

Mathias Klein was born in 1826 in Worms, Germany. As a young man he apprenticed with a well-known locksmith to learn the trade. He was an excellent student and soon mastered the basics, hoping to earn a living as a locksmith. But Mathias dreamed of traveling, of going to faraway places. In 1851 he boarded a ship, bound for the exciting land of the United States, hoping like many before and after him to begin a new life.

Klein arrived in Philadelphia and all was not as he had hoped. Demand was low and several locksmiths were already established in the area. As luck would have it, he was offered another job, as a blacksmith on a whaling ship. Mathias set sail and found his skills in much demand. He created a variety of tools, but found he had a special affinity for blades and knives. When his ship came back to the United States, he decided to settle in the Midwest, in Chicago, Illinois.

The early 1850s were a time of extreme growth in Chicago as the city exploded with economic development. Located along the windy shores of Lake Michigan and a canal system connecting the Illinois and Chicago rivers, Chicago had become an established commerce center for fur traders, farmers, and a host of other purveyors of goods and services.

Klein was a blacksmith by trade, but an artisan at heart. He could fashion sturdy, beautifully made tools and implements and believed he could earn a good living. He opened a small shop and began forging tools. To sell his wares, he drove a horse-drawn wagon down the streets of the city and into the neighboring counties. Some of his tools proved rather popular with local

COMPANY PERSPECTIVES

A leading manufacturer of professional hand tools and occupational protective equipment, Klein Tools' product line has grown to include virtually every major type of hand tool used in the electrical and telecommunications markets, as well as for aviation, construction, electronics, mining and general industry. Since 1857, Klein Tools has been uniquely committed to providing only the finest professional-grade equipment. To this day, Klein Tools is owned and managed by members of the Klein family. Klein products are available worldwide through a well-established network of authorized agents and distributors who serve the professional tradesman.

workers in factories and shops, during Chicago's great transformation from a trading hub to an industrialized powerhouse. The "Second City" (as it was called, considered second to New York City) had become a thriving metropolis with numerous industries. From the stockyards to milling, brewing, printing, and publishing, Mathias lent his metalworking expertise to create, repair, and sell a wide range of products. One, in particular, would make the Klein name famous and produce a company synonymous with quality and durability.

In 1857 as the fledgling electronic communications industry gained a foothold in Chicago, a telegraph linesman came to Klein's shop with a partially broken plier-like tool. Klein fixed the side-cutting item by forging a new half. His customer went away happy but returned a few weeks later wanting the other half fixed in the same manner. These two halves became the first official pair of Klein pliers. They became known simply as "Kleins" and were soon the tool of choice among Chicago professional tradesmen.

PRODUCTION DURING THE CIVIL WAR AND BEYOND

The advent of the Civil War brought a boom in manufacturing. The telegraph took on increased importance and the need for reliable tools was paramount. "Kleins" were a linesmen's best friend and Mathias found that his small business, Mathias Klein & Sons, had become a rousing success. In addition to the original Klein pliers came screwdrivers, wire strippers, snippers, wrenches, and other handcrafted implements. For his loyal linesmen, Klein also designed and

produced tool belts, climbing pole straps, and other necessities. When the telegraph segued into the telephone and electricity began lighting homes and businesses, there were even more venues for durable, specialized tools.

Next came the railroads, stretching far and wide, and again Klein tools were at a premium. Mathias honed his craft and became indispensable to Chicago's burgeoning workforce. As the company continued to prosper, the world was wide open with possibilities. Then came the Great Chicago Fire of 1871, devastating the city and its inhabitants. Wooden buildings, windy conditions, and drought fueled the fire's intensity and it raged through the business district and along the Chicago River. While Klein was one of the lucky ones, many of his contemporaries were not. The disaster was costly, but brought Chicagoans together to rebuild the city. Klein tools were out in force.

During the next two decades, both Chicago and Klein Tools gained considerable prominence. The Windy City came back from its ashes and hosted the World's Columbia Exposition in 1893, bringing millions to the city's shores. Klein Tools had ushered in a new generation of family members, in Mathias's son and namesake, Mathias II. The company had earned a reputation for the best hand tools available in the Midwest, and its products had found their way throughout the nation. It was time to plan for international expansion, as well as other tools for an increasingly sophisticated workforce.

WORLD WARS AND GROWTH

As the second generation of Kleins, both the tools and family members, came of age, Klein Tools had become virtually indispensable. The company not only provided sturdy, quality tools but had continually expanded its product line to meet the needs of its customers. The Klein name came to represent the best in toolmaking, and the onset of two world wars served only to reinforce the claim. More and more professional tradesmen—electricians, utility workers, ironworkers, plumbers, and a host of others—discovered the quality of Klein's expertly made tools and were devotees for life. To keep up with demand, the company went north and opened a new steel forging plant on McCormick Road in Skokie, Illinois, in 1956. The following year Klein celebrated its centennial.

The 1960s ushered in the beginning of Klein's growth through acquisitions. In 1968 the company bought R.H. Burhke Company, Inc., a Chicago-based manufacturer of protective equipment and leather and canvas goods. Four years later came Klein's first

```
┌─────────────────────────────────────────────┐
│                                               │
│               KEY DATES                       │
│                    ▪                          │
│  ─────────────────────────────────────────    │
```

1852: Mathias Klein opens his own forging shop, creating hand tools.

1857: Klein fashions his first pair of custom pliers.

1871: Klein Tools survives the Great Chicago Fire.

1956: Klein begins operations at its McCormick Road plant in Skokie.

1957: The company celebrates its centennial.

1972: Klein establishes Herramientas Klein, S.A. de C.V., in Mexico.

1975: A new forging plant is opened in Moran, Kansas.

1978: Klein acquires leather-products firm William Warne Company.

1980: A new international distribution center is opened in Cedar Rapids, Iowa.

1986: Vaco Products Company of Jonesville, Michigan, is acquired.

1989: A new production plant is opened in Roselle, Illinois.

1991: Richard T. Klein Jr. is named president and chief operating officer.

1995: Klein begins radio advertising for the first time.

2001: Klein begins sponsoring aerial stunt pilot Michael Mancuso of Long Island, New York.

2003: Klein establishes the Tradesman Club and a newsletter for its longtime customers.

2005: The American LeMans Racing Series chooses Klein as their official hand-tool supplier.

2006: CEO Richard Klein is ousted from the family business.

2007: The company celebrates 150 years with the "Great Klein Tools Extravaganza."

international location with the establishment of a Mexican subsidiary, Herramientas Klein, S.A. de C.V., in 1972.

In 1975 Klein began building a new manufacturing facility to replace its Skokie plant. The McCormick Road plant had come under increasing fire for excessive noise. The source of the complaints, a new indoor tennis club, strenuously objected to the facility and went so far as to bring in the federal Environmental Protection Agency. Despite the area having been zoned for "heavy industry" at the time Klein took up residence, and the wealth of jobs created over 119 years in and around Chicago, neither the city nor the state seemingly had

any loyalty to Klein. Mathias Klein II, Klein's president, even wrote the governor, Dan Walker, but was rebuffed. "Encouraged" to leave, Klein stepped up the pace on its new state-of-the-art facility in Moran, Kansas, which welcomed the company. The new manufacturing plant sat on 154 acres near Moran, a tiny town with just over 500 residents who appreciated the new jobs.

Despite moving its primary manufacturing operations to Kansas, Klein's headquarters remained in northern Illinois, in Libertyville. The Kleins were still bitter over their treatment by the city of Skokie and its inhabitants, but decided success would be the best revenge. To this end, the company expanded its business with the acquisition of William Warne Company, a leather pouch manufacturer, in 1978. The leather pouches joined a growing line of accessories designed to house and protect a tradesman's best asset, his Klein tools.

RECOGNITION AND TURMOIL: EIGHTIES AND NINETIES

The Klein name, in any language, had come to represent the best in precision toolmaking. By the 1980s demand for "Kleins" led to a new international distribution center, built in Cedar Rapids, Iowa. The huge warehouse facility, which began operations in 1980 and was expanded in 1984, had state-of-the-art handling and shipping processes and helped get Klein tools and accessories to their destination faster than ever. The company also overhauled its Mexican subsidiary, Herramientas Klein. Its Arizona manufacturing plant, from its William Warne acquisition, was also renovated.

In 1986 Klein was once again in an acquisitive mood, buying Vaco Products Company of Jonesville, Michigan. Vaco produced a line of screwdrivers, nut drivers, hex-key wrenches, electrical terminals and connectors, and a host of similar products. Three years later, in 1989, Klein opened a new plant in Roselle, Illinois, to keep up with demand in the Midwest. The company's adjustable wrenches, like its sibling pliers, had become increasingly popular with tradesmen, and were produced primarily at the Roselle facility.

In 1991 Richard T. Klein Jr., a fifth-generation Klein, was named president and chief executive. Like his father before him, Richard Jr. believed he was destined to run Klein Tools. His father's tenure had ended abruptly in 1984 when the 49-year-old vice-chairman died suddenly. Richard Jr. and his brother Thomas were both involved in the family business, and had begun working their way up the corporate ladder. Working with Richard Jr. in Klein's management were Thomas (in materials and logistics) and two cousins: Michael Klein, chairman of the board, and Mathias Klein III, who served as executive vice-president.

As Richard Jr. took the helm, Klein renovated its midwestern headquarters, creating a tool museum and updating its 200,000-square-foot manufacturing facility in Libertyville. Designed by a Los Angeles architectural firm, the offices and plant were modernized, but the new 2,500-square-foot historic museum proved a stroke of genius. Klein tools from the earliest days of production were rounded up and tracked down, all placed within the exhibit for generations to see.

In 1992 the Klein name showed up in an unusual place: on an Indy car. Klein began sponsoring an Indy team for the Midwest's premier sporting event, the Indianapolis 500. In addition to this new advertising gambit, Klein initiated another first: radio advertisement of its products. Although the toolmaker had advertised in print venues, it had never promoted its wares over the airwaves. Both marketing strategies proved successful.

Klein opened another manufacturing plant in 1996 in nearby Schaumburg, southwest of its Libertyville headquarters. Reflecting the company's expansion in the Chicagoland area and the Midwest, Klein's workforce had reached 400 and revenues were reportedly just under $115 million.

Embracing the do-it-yourself trend of the late 1990s, Klein surprised its longtime wholesalers by inking a deal with national retailer Home Depot. Although Klein tools were high-end and far pricier than most of Home Depot's tools, Klein hoped the growing cadre of do-it-yourselfers would buy its products. The downside, however, was taking business away from wholesale distributors who were battling Home Depot for sales. Richard Klein felt the risk was worth taking, believing it would pay off in a wider clientele. "We remain a conservative company, but we've felt the need to identify new markets for our products," Klein told *Crain's Chicago Business* (July 9, 1996), "Our products have to be available where our customers want them." Though Klein produced well over 5,500 different tools, the company planned to sell only a few dozen of its top-selling designs at Home Depot.

THE NEW MILLENNIUM

By the early 2000s Klein operated six manufacturing plants in four midwestern states. Customers beyond its traditional tradesmen and utility workers were hearing the Klein name and buying its high-quality tools. In 2001 the company began sponsoring an aerobatics pilot named Michael Mancuso, placing the Klein name on his plane. Two years later, in 2003, Klein upped its exposure with the Indy circuit, sponsoring the well-known Andretti Green Racing team. The Klein logo was prominently displayed on Dan Sheldon's car and the driving suits of Michael Andretti and Tony Kanaan, according to *Electrical Wholesaling* magazine.

Klein also went further in its unusual marketing schemes in 2003, creating the Klein Tools Air Show, an official kickoff event of the Indy Racing League, with pilot Mancuso performing in his Klein-emblazoned plane. The year also marked the promotion of Richard Klein's brother Thomas, who was named executive vice-president of the company. Although the two purportedly worked well together, Thomas would later say Klein's work atmosphere was one of extreme "stress" during Richard's tenure.

In 2004 Klein sales were estimated at $165 million and the following year, in keeping with its recent racing promotions, the company became the official hand tool of the American Le Mans Series of sports car races based on the internationally known Le Mans endurance race. On the homefront, Klein was building another manufacturing plant, had created a comprehensive web site, and had reached sales of a reported $170 million for 2005.

The first quarter of 2006 brought major upheaval to the family-run Klein. With over 900 employees and estimated sales of $177 million, the firm entered choppy seas. In early April Richard Klein, chief executive since 1991, was asked to resign. When he refused, he was ousted from the company by cousin Mathias III, and Richard's brother Thomas. After the shakeup, Mathias took over the chairmanship and Thomas became the firm's president as they sought an outsider to fill Richard's shoes. Richard, who had worked at the family business for more than three decades and had no intention of leaving, filed a $25 million lawsuit in December against the company, Thomas, Mathias, and the firm's lawyers, accusing them of conspiracy, breach of contract, and fraudulent misrepresentation.

In 2007 Klein remained the top-selling brand of high-quality hand tools in the utility industry, and a leading seller in a myriad of other trades. As the company marked its 150th anniversary, it should have been a time of celebration; instead, it presaged an uncertain future. Only time would tell whether the family feud involving one of Illinois's oldest family-run businesses would resolve itself satisfactorily. One thing was certain though: Klein tools, which had proved their durability time and again, would far outlast the family firestorm.

Nelson Rhodes

PRINCIPAL SUBSIDIARIES

R.H. Burhke Company; Herramientas Klein, S.A. de C.V. (Mexico); William Warne Company.

PRINCIPAL COMPETITORS

Black & Decker Corporation; Cooper Industries, Ltd.; Danaher Corporation; Ideal Industries, Inc.; The Stanley Works.

FURTHER READING

Daniels, Steve, "Uncivil War: Richard Klein Says He Was Blindsided by Family …," *Crain's Chicago Business,* December 11, 2006, p. 3.

Geran, Monica, "Klein Tools: A Multi-Purpose Segment of the Firm's Chicago Spaces Designed by Gensler and Associates Architects/Los Angeles," *Interior Design,* November 1991, pp. 112+.

"Klein Plugs Tools to Racing Fans," *Electrical Wholesaling,* May 1, 2003.

"Klein Tools," *Industrial Distribution,* January 2000, p. 94.

"Klein Tools: A Tradition of Quality," *Industrial Distribution,* April 2002, p. 51.

"Klein Tools Introduces Tradesman Club," *Electrical Wholesaling,* July 1, 2003.

Mabley, Jack, "State Encourages Industry to Leave," *Chicago Tribune,* March 2, 1976, p. 4.

Murphy, H. Lee, "Pliers Poker: Retail Bet at Klein Tools," *Crain's Chicago Business,* July 8, 1996, pp. 1+.

"Summit Electric Promotes Klein Tools," *Electrical Wholesaling,* September 1, 2006.

Landec Corporation

3603 Haven Avenue
Menlo Park, California 94025
U.S.A.
Telephone: (650) 306-1650
Fax: (650) 368-9818
Web site: http://www.landec.com

Public Company
Incorporated: 1986
Employees: 107
Sales: $210.49 million (2007)
Stock Exchanges: NASDAQ
Ticker Symbol: LNDC
NAIC: 325211 Plastics Material and Resin Manufacturing

∎ ∎ ∎

Landec Corporation designs and manufactures temperature-activated polymers for customers involved in the food and agriculture industries. Landec's polymers are based on its proprietary Intelimer technology, which enables polymers to change their physical characteristics when heated or cooled through a predetermined temperature switch. For produce packers and marketers, Landec sells products that improve the shelf life and appearance of fruits and vegetables, such as the company's BreatheWay membranes that regulate temperature fluctuations and levels of oxygen and carbon dioxide. The company serves the agriculture industry by providing polymer seed coatings that enable farmers to plant two crops in one growing season and to plant their seeds before soil conditions are ideal for germination. Landec is based in Menlo Park, California, and maintains research and manufacturing facilities in Indiana.

A FOCUS ON POLYMERS

Polymers play a vital role in daily life, improving the quality, durability, and appearance of myriad products. Polymers, any of numerous compounds that have extremely high molecular weights, consist of up to millions of repeated, linked units, each a relatively light and simple molecule. They occur naturally in substances, including cellulose, amber, shellac, and natural rubber, and they are made synthetically, prized for their improved mechanical and thermal properties, such as strength and the ability to withstand high temperatures. Synthetic polymers, the compounds that provide the world with nylon fibers used in carpeting and clothing, coatings used in paints and finishes, plastics such as polyethylene, and elastomers used in automobile tires and latex gloves, helped usher in the modern age, replacing wood, natural fibers, and metal for numerous applications during the latter half of the 20th century.

Landec was focused on a special class of polymers called side chain crystalline polymers. Derived from natural fatty acids, side chain crystalline polymers were discovered by academic researchers in the mid-1950s. They were regarded important only as they related to polymer physics, and so their discovery did not inspire the drive toward commercialization that had given birth to nylon, polyethylene, Teflon, and silicone. The pioneer researchers, reportedly, treated their discovery as a scientific curiosity and nothing more. In the decades to follow, side chain crystalline polymers remained in the laboratory and out of the marketplace until Dr. Ray F. Stewart began thinking about their usefulness in the commercial world.

ENVISIONING LANDEC'S FUTURE IN POLYMERS

Stewart's interest in side chain crystalline polymers was piqued in the mid-1980s. At the time, he was employed by Raychem Corporation, where he presided over development efforts in the areas of adhesives, plastic electrodes, sensors, and, most important, synthetic polymer chemistry. A graduate of Northern Arizona University who had earned his doctorate in organic chemistry from the University of Minnesota, Stewart was in his early 30s when he began to envision commercial applications for side chain crystalline polymers.

What Stewart initially envisioned as the commercial application for side chain crystalline polymers would not be Landec's ultimate pursuit, but his curiosity did lead to the company's formation. Landec, incorporated in California in October 1986 and based in Menlo Park, was created to exploit a unique characteristic of side chain crystalline polymers. They could change properties rapidly at a specific temperature, a temperature that could be set during the polymer manufacturing process. Stewart was interested in using the temperature-activated permeability properties of the polymers to deliver various materials such as pharmaceuticals and pesticides, which became the original mission of Landec as it started out as a small research-and-development company.

LANDEC SETS OUT IN 1986

Landec's first years—nearly its first decade of existence—included the expected trials and tribulations experienced by a research-and-development company. There were no products to sell, no revenue to be collected. The time was spent in the laboratory, as Stewart and his small staff labored to bring new technology to market. Financial losses mounted, heightening the need for the company to produce something, anything that could generate income. During this initial phase in Landec's development, Stewart discovered different potential applications for temperature-activated polymers, establishing the foundation of Landec's proprietary Intelimer technology by creating polymers that could change their physical characteristics when heated or cooled through a preset temperature switch. There was great promise in the research being conducted at the company's laboratories, as Landec's team worked on polymers that could change attributes within the space of one or two degrees Celsius. The polymers could transform from a slick, nonadhesive state to a highly tacky adhesive state, from an impermeable state to a highly permeable state, or from a solid state to a viscous state. The dramatic changes, physical not chemical, were repeatedly reversible and could be tailored by Landec to occur at specific temperatures. Stewart's overriding objective was to find a profitable way to apply the technology to the marketplace.

FIRST PRODUCT IN 1994

Landec made its market debut in April 1994. The company's first product was targeted for the medical industry, a line of splints and casts marketed under the name QuickCast. Although an important first step, the release of QuickCast did not steer the company into the market that would sustain its operations in the future. QuickCast was sold to Bissell Healthcare Corporation three years later. Instead, the company found its mark in September 1995, when it released Intelimer packaging technology for the fresh-cut and whole produce packaging market. The product, launched as Intellipac and renamed BreatheWay in 1996, was a membrane that balanced the swing in temperatures during freight and regulated moisture to extend the shelf life of vegetables and fruit.

The debut of BreatheWay established the foundation for Landec's Food Product Technology business, one of two core businesses that supported the company during its first 20 years in business. The wrappings were ideal for packaging fresh vegetables and fruit, making the use of ice during distribution unnecessary. Landec began supplying its breathable membranes to Fresh Express Farms, selling the company a breathable label for film packages. A second, vitally important customer was added in early 1997, when Landec reached an agreement with Apio, Inc., one of the country's largest marketers and packers of produce and specialty packaged fresh-cut vegetables. Under the terms of the agree-

KEY DATES

1986: Dr. Ray F. Stewart forms Landec Corporation.
1994: Landec releases its first product, QuickCast splints and casts.
1995: Landec introduces packaging technology for produce marketers.
1997: A subsidiary, Landec Ag, is formed and Fielder's Choice Direct is acquired.
1999: Landec acquires Apio, Inc.
2003: Landec introduces Intellicoat Early Plant corn.
2004: Landec signs a development and supply agreement with Chiquita Brands International Inc.
2005: Landec's subsidiary, Landec Ag, acquires Heartland Hybrids, Inc.
2006: Landec sells Fielder's Choice Direct to Monsanto Company.
2007: Net income reaches a record high of $29.1 million.

ment, which involved fresh-cut broccoli and cauliflower, Landec began providing its breathable membranes in the form of package labels for premade film bags used in Apio's Eat Smart merchandising and distribution program for fresh-cut produce.

ACQUIRING APIO, INC., IN 1999

Apio quickly became Landec's largest customer in its Food Product Technology segment. The importance of the relationship with Apio became far more profound in 1999, when Landec acquired Guadalupe, California-based Apio. At the time of the purchase, Apio operated two major businesses. The company operated a "fee-for-service" business that included field harvesting and packing, cooling, and marketing of vegetables and fruit on a contract basis for growers primarily in California's Santa Maria, San Joaquin, and Imperial Valleys. Landec exited that business, selling certain assets to Beachside Produce, LLC, but it retained Apio's other core business, the specialty packaged fresh-cut and whole processed produce washed and packaged in BreatheWay packaging. The company also retained the Apio banner, which became the name of a new subsidiary responsible for Landec's Food Product Technology endeavors.

As Landec's Food Product Technology business developed into a new subsidiary named Apio, its other core business took shape. The origins of the company's

second primary business, Agricultural Seed Technology, came from research in the laboratory. Stewart discovered his polymer coatings could regulate water uptake into seeds according to temperature. By varying the length of the side chains, Stewart could set the polymer's switch temperature, which enabled seeds coated with the polymer to absorb water once the soil reached the predetermined switch temperature. The discovery meant farmers could widen the planting window, allowing them to plant seeds in cold conditions. Once the soil heated, creating ideal conditions for germination, the coatings changed physically, allowing the absorption of water. Stewart characterized the behavior as "intelligent," which inspired the name Intellicoat for the seed coatings.

Intellicoat was formed as a wholly owned subsidiary in 1997. Company executives immediately recognized the need for a national seed brand to help bring their seed coatings to market, which led to the acquisition of Fielder's Choice Direct in 1997. Fielder's Choice Direct ranked as the ninth largest hybrid seed company in the United States. The acquisition prompted a new name for the company's Agricultural Seed Technology business before the end of the year. Landec Ag, Inc., became the new name for the subsidiary responsible for developing commercial applications for the agricultural industry.

POLYMER SEED COATINGS GAIN ACCEPTANCE

Landec Ag registered its first commercial success in 2000. The subsidiary released Intellicoat Pollinator Plus, which substantially reduced production risk for seed companies. The following year, manufacturing and research facilities related to seed technology were moved from Menlo Park to Indiana to be closer to the subsidiary's customers. Meanwhile, a pilot program was underway for Intellicoat Early Plant corn, which allowed farmers to plant seeds as much as four weeks earlier than normal. The risk of chilling injury was eliminated because of the temperature-activated polymer seed coating. Before Intellicoat Early Plant was introduced to the market, Landec Ag released its second commercial product, Intellicoat Relay soybeans. The coating allowed farmers to double their crop by interplanting coated soybeans into winter wheat. In 2003, after two years of field trials with select customers, Landec Ag introduced Intellicoat Early Plant corn.

STRONG FINANCIAL PERFORMANCE

The growth of both Apio and Landec Ag contributed to rapid financial growth for Landec. The company, which had endured steady losses and meager revenues during its first decade of business, began to reap the rewards of its painstaking research. Revenues totaled $2.1 million in 1997, reached $21.4 million in 1999, and began to mushroom, leaping to $197 million in 2000.

As Landec progressed toward its 20th anniversary, both of its principal subsidiaries were adding to their commercial prowess. In 2004, Apio signed a joint technology development and supply agreement with Chiquita Brands International Inc., the titan of the banana industry. "We have been evaluating the Intelimer packaging technology for bananas for two years and, based on the results, we believe this product will effectively extend the shelf life of bananas," Chiquita's chairman and chief executive officer said in a September 13, 2004, interview with *Chemical Market Reporter*. On the agriculture side of Landec's business, Landec Ag cultivated relationships with six partner companies to promote the sale and distribution of Early Plant corn. In 2005, the subsidiary, which ranked as the largest direct marketer of seed corn, acquired Heartland Hybrids, Inc., the second largest direct marketer of seed corn. Based in Dassel, Minnesota, Heartland Hybrids served more than 3,000 farmers in 35 states.

20TH ANNIVERSARY IN 2006

In the years leading up to Landec's 20th anniversary, the company began to demonstrate consistent financial strength. The years of annual losses appeared to have ended. Between 2004 and 2006, the company's net income nearly tripled, increasing from $2.9 million to $8.6 million. Revenues during the period swelled from $192 million to $232 million. The company's anniversary year in 2006 was highlighted by two separate agreements with Monsanto Company, a giant seed and biotechnology company based in St. Louis, Missouri. In December, Monsanto's American Seeds Inc. subsidiary acquired Landec's direct marketing and seed sales company, Fielder's Choice Direct, paying $50 million for the company Landec had acquired nine years earlier. The second transaction involved a five-year, global technology license agreement that was expected to bring in $3.4 million per year in licensing fees for Landec. The agreement gave Monsanto an exclusive license for Landec's Intellicoat polymer technology, which it intended to use with corn, soybean, canola, and cotton seeds.

As Landec prepared for the future, it was entering an exciting period in its development. Its years of research and development were beginning to realize commercial success, fanning hopes that the years ahead would witness robust financial growth. After the company's net income leaped from $8.6 million to $29.1 million in 2007, the company's prospects only brightened, presenting an enticing opportunity for investors wishing to share in the future accomplishments of Landec. In the years ahead, Stewart's groundbreaking polymer technology was expected to make further inroads into the food and agriculture industries as well as find useful applications in other industries.

Jeffrey L. Covell

PRINCIPAL SUBSIDIARIES

Landec Ag, Inc.; Apio, Inc.

PRINCIPAL DIVISIONS

Food Products Technology; Agricultural Seed Technology.

PRINCIPAL COMPETITORS

Pioneer Hi-Bred International, Inc.; Seminis, Inc.; Cargill, Incorporated.

FURTHER READING

"Breathable Produce Film Goes 'Bananas,'" *Converting*, September 2000, p. 12.

"Chiquita Goes Bananas for Landec," *Chemical Market Reporter*, September 13, 2004, p. 28.

"Dock Resins Is Acquired by Emerging Firm Landec," *Chemical Market Reporter*, April 28, 1997, p. 5.

"Film Changes Permeability with Temperature," *Packaging*, February 1994, p. 14.

Guzman, Doris, "Landec Ag Sees Growth in Seed Coating Technology," *Chemical Market Reporter*, August 13, 2001, p. 18.

"Landec Ag Acquires Heartland Hybrids," *Corn and Soybean Digest*, July 6, 2005.

Materna, Jessica, "Fresh Harvest: Landec Sows Seeds for the Future," *San Francisco Business Times*, May 25, 2001, p. 53.

"Monsanto, Landec Announce Seed Agreements," *SciTech21*, December 4, 2006.

"Monsanto Licenses a Winter Coat for Seeds," *St. Louis Post-Dispatch*, December 5, 2006.

"Polymers Control Timing of Seed Germination," *Emerging Food R&D Report*, August 2000.

LLOYD AEREO BOLIVIANO S.A.

La línea aérea bandera de Bolivia

Lloyd Aéreo Boliviano S.A.

---■---

Avenida Heroínas 152
Aeropuerto Jorge Wilsterman
Cochabamba,
Bolivia
Telephone: (591 4) 459-0283
Fax: (591 4) 423-0325
Web site: http://www.labairlines.com.bo

Private Company
Founded: 1925
Employees: 1,800
Sales: $180 million (2006 est.)
NAIC: 481211 Nonscheduled Chartered Passenger Air Transportation

■ ■ ■

Lloyd Aéreo Boliviano S.A. (LAB), Bolivia's international airline, is a survivor. The second oldest continuing airline in South America, it has emerged intact from a series of rescues and resuscitations. Dogged by allegations of corruption and management, and bearer of a less-than-sterling safety record, LAB nevertheless continues to exist because Bolivia—although, per capita, the poorest country in South America—as a matter of national pride must show its flag to the world. Moreover, air transportation is vital to this virtually landlocked country (it shares Lake Titicaca with Peru), through which run some of the highest, most rugged mountains in the world, making rail and road links difficult. LAB also serves the main Bolivian

cities, although it has been losing ground to a wholly private competitor, AeroSur S.A.

AN EVENTFUL QUARTER CENTURY: 1925–50

LAB was founded in 1925, the centennial year of Bolivian independence from Spain, by the German community of Cochabamba. Wilhelm Kyllmann, its first director general, arranged for a single-engine Junkers F-13 to be shipped by rail in three pieces from Buenos Aires to Cochabamba, where it was assembled in the improvised landing field of a farm and presented to the nation. The craft, which had a two-man crew and room for four passengers, made a goodwill tour of the major Bolivian municipalities. LAB then offered shares to the public, in the proportion of three-quarters for Bolivian citizens and one-quarter to the German community of Cochabamba. The first commercial flight, from the Andes Mountains highlands to Santa Cruz, the chief settlement in the tropical lowland plains of eastern Bolivia, reduced the trip from four days by the fastest motor vehicles—and 15 days by muleback—to two and a half hours.

LAB ingratiated itself to the government by carrying official mail at no charge and offering a discount to high executive and legislative officials. The government took a stake in LAB in 1926, when the airline bought a second plane, which crashed on its delivery flight and was replaced a few months later. Later in the year the first Junkers crashed in Santa Cruz in bad weather. The five persons aboard were unhurt, however, and a replacement arrived early the next year. In 1928 LAB bought

KEY DATES

1925: Lloyd Aéreo Boliviano (LAB) is founded.

1930: LAB is serving 16 destinations in Bolivia.

1935: The Bolivian government takes a 48 percent interest in LAB.

1941: The government hires Panagra to manage LAB's operations.

1954: LAB makes its first international passenger flight.

1965: The Bolivian government resumes management of LAB.

1975: LAB begins service to the United States, flying in and out of Miami.

1995: VASP takes a 49 percent stake in financially troubled LAB.

2001: A majority interest in the airline is sold to a Bolivian entrepreneur.

2007: Flights halt for nine months because of a lack of funds.

three more Junkers and opened a school for its pilots and mechanics, which it maintained until 1953. Bolivia's first pilot graduated from this school. By the end of 1930 LAB was serving 16 cities either weekly or every two weeks.

LAB contributed its services to the ill-starred Gran Chaco War (1932–35), in which Bolivia disputed, but mostly lost to Paraguay, sovereignty over a vast, sparsely populated savanna tract mistakenly believed to hold large oil deposits. The airline flew thousands of flights and carried many thousands of passengers, some in three-engine Junkers transports. On its 25th anniversary, LAB received a "Condor of the Andes" decoration from the president of Bolivia for its contributions to the war effort. The government took a 48 percent interest in LAB in 1935.

By 1940 LAB was serving every major community in Bolivia and was an important link in German-managed air operations that connected Rio de Janeiro, on South America's east coast, to Lima, on the west coast. However, the United States, alarmed by the gains of the Axis powers following the fall of France, was about to intervene in the continent's affairs. In 1941 the Bolivian government, which held 64 percent of LAB's shares, dismissed all German employees and hired Pan American–Grace Airways (Panagra) to run the airline for five years in exchange for a 23 percent interest in the company.

Panagra ordered three Lockheed L-18s and destroyed all of LAB's tools and machinery of German design. It ordered a Douglas DC-3 in 1945 and made this craft the backbone of the LAB fleet, eventually acquiring 19. In 1949 it took possession of the first of eight Curtiss C-46 and C-47s, used to carry both passengers and cargo. In 1950 LAB acquired the first of 11 Boeing B-17 Flying Fortress bombers, which were converted to hold cargo. Like the aforementioned planes, they had previously been used by the U.S. Army Air Force and rebuilt to civil standards.

AN INTERNATIONAL CARRIER: 1950–90

Traveling by LAB required steady nerves on the part of both passengers and crew considering the relative paucity of navigational aids and the unforgiving nature of the Andean peaks. There were no less than 12 crashes that resulted in loss of life between 1951 and 1969. The last crash, into a mountain, killed all 74 aboard a DC-6B en route from Santa Cruz to La Paz. It was Bolivia's worst air accident. By this time LAB, which had established a mail run to the Brazilian border in 1928, was truly an international carrier. The airline inaugurated, in 1954, a multistop DC-3 flight from La Paz to Arica in neighboring northern Chile. Service to Brazil and Paraguay began in 1958. A route to and from Buenos Aires was opened in 1959, and one to São Paulo was started in 1963.

Panagra was replaced as LAB's manager in 1963 by North Central Airlines. The new team arrived to find that 4 of the 12 planes had been grounded in case parts for the other eight were needed. The airline was also lacking published flight and tariff schedules and a reservations system. The North Central contract was canceled in 1965, with the government taking over management. Whether to its credit or North Central's, LAB emerged from financial difficulties and actually balanced its budget in 1966.

International credits allowed LAB to order a Lockheed L-188A in 1967, a Boeing 727-100 in 1968, and two Fairchild FH-227Ms, which were delivered in 1969. French aid resulted in the purchase of two Caravelle jets. LAB rejected, however, a proposal by the Export-Import Bank that it divide into four companies. The proposal was widely considered in Bolivia as a plot by Braniff International Airways to enter the domestic market. Panagra and Braniff had international landing rights in La Paz but were not allowed to offer service within Bolivia; a Bolivian author claimed that as a consequence, the Export-Import Bank had prevented LAB from offering air service to Miami. In 1975, however, LAB began weekly service to Miami, with a stop in Panama City,

Panama. Another Miami route, by way of Manaus in Brazil's Amazon and Caracas, Venezuela, was introduced in 1978.

Lloyd Aéreo Boliviano joined the International Air Transportation Association in 1980. The airline struggled throughout the decade because of Bolivia's poor economic conditions. Passenger boardings peaked at 1.41 million in 1985 despite hyperinflation that reached 24,000 percent during the year.

A TURBULENT PASSAGE: 1990–2008

In 1990 LAB decided to replace some of its aging fleet, consisting mainly of Boeing jets, with three leased Airbus A300s and A310s. Service to and from Mexico City began in 1992. With the end of the Cold War and a trend toward free market policies, often called the "Washington Consensus" in Latin America, the government began considering partially privatizing LAB. However, the airline, saddled with high operational costs, was considered anything but a bonanza and attracted few suitors. Within Bolivia, a competitor, Aero-Sur S.A., had taken away much of its business with newer planes than LAB's Boeing 727s. In 1995 Viação Aéreo São Paulo, S.A. (VASP), the sole bidder in an auction, purchased a 49 percent stake in LAB for only $47.4 million, most of which consisted of the transfer of a Boeing 737 jet rather than cash. VASP also received a management contract.

VASP added LAB to an air system it had established with affiliates in Ecuador and Argentina as well as its own facilities in Brazil. In 1997, when LAB carried a record 1.73 million passengers, it was offering 150 flights a day and had 15 airplanes in operation. A year later, though, the airline was downgraded for failing to meet international safety standards and was banned from adding new routes to, or flying new equipment into, the United States.

By then the Bolivian government had alienated VASP by withdrawing LAB's exclusive right to operate international flights to and from the country. It also transferred most of its stake in the enterprise to Bolivia's two pension funds, an action VASP considered a violation of the agreement. VASP decided in 2000 to sell its share, now 50.3 percent, in LAB. It was purchased late the next year by a group headed by Ernesto Asbún, a Bolivian entrepreneur with interests in radio, television, and beer.

LAB, in 2002, took possession of the first of several Boeing 767s, which were introduced for the Miami and Mexican routes. These were the company's principal international markets. Also that year, the airline opened

an international center for the repair of airplanes and engines. LAB ended the year having carried 1.3 million passengers, with 45 daily flights and service to 26 destinations.

Nonstop service by Boeing 767 between Santa Cruz and Madrid, the airline's first European link, was introduced in 2003. A route to Washington, D.C., was opened in the same year. Operations resumed to Córdoba and Salta, Argentina; Manaus and Rio de Janeiro, Brazil; Arica, Chile; and Havana, Cuba. A more advanced computer system promised to make air travel via LAB more convenient for its customers. The airline had a frequent-flyer program and VIP halls, dubbed "Elite CLAB" in the Cochabamba, La Paz, and Santa Cruz airports.

LAB was, however, in desperate financial straits by early 2006, when employees went out on strike to protest the dismissal of a pilot and to denounce alleged irregularities in the management of the airline. President Evo Morales announced a 90-day government "intervention" to keep LAB flying while it investigated reports of corruption supposedly tied to Asbún. The airline was reported to have liabilities of perhaps $180 million and assets of only $2.5 million. Later in the year a Bolivian judge ordered Asbún's detention after he failed to appear at a hearing, but he had apparently fled the country. Only three of LAB's 12 airplanes were in operation because of lack of funds to pay for fuel.

Operations came to a complete halt in March 2007, when LAB canceled its flights to Spain because it was unable to pay for either the fuel or flight insurance. The airline remained grounded until December 24, when a charter flight left Cochabamba for Santa Cruz. By mid-January 2008 LAB had increased to 47 the number of charter flights to major Bolivian cities scheduled through February 10, and it was hoping to soon regain certification as a scheduled carrier. However, it suffered a setback February 1, when one of its planes was forced to make an emergency landing in a jungle clearing after apparently running out of fuel. No one was seriously hurt, but the 28-year-old Boeing 727 was severely damaged.

LAB's web site continued to display an international network consisting of flights to and from Miami and Washington in the United States; Mexico City and Cancún in Mexico; Madrid, Spain; Panama City, Panama; Caracas, Venezuela; Bogotá, Colombia; Guayaquil, Ecuador; Lima and Cuzco, Peru; Santiago, Chile; Buenos Aires, Córdoba, and Salta, Argentina; Asunción, Paraguay; and Manaus and São Paulo, Brazil. Within Bolivia, LAB listed stops in La Paz, Santa Cruz,

Sucre, Tarija, and Trinidad, as well as its home base, Cochabamba.

Robert Halasz

FURTHER READING

"Bolivia ordena prisão," *O Globo,* June 22, 2006.

Corral, Marcela, "'Acercan' a Sudamerica," *El Norte,* October 19, 2003, p. 9.

Davies, R. E. G., *Airlines of Latin America Since 1981,* Washington, D.C.: Smithsonian Institution Press, 1984, esp. pp. 317–32.

Ferro, Raúl, "Ave fénix?" *AméricaEconómia,* February 2002, p. 25.

Green, Philip Withers, "Lío en las alturas," *AméricaEconómia,* March 1998, p. 37.

"Interviene Morales aerolinea privada," *El Norte,* February 11, 2006, p. 18.

Orellana Vargas, Ignacio, *El L.A.B. y sus 45 años de vigencia,* Cocachamba: Editorial Serrano Hnos., 1970.

Peña, Jaime, "Choque aéreo," *AméricaEconómia,* December 1994, p. 30.

Smith, Myron J., Jr., *The Airline Encyclopedia 1909–2000,* Lanham, N.J.: Scarecrow Press, 2002, vol. 1, pp. 1661–65.

"U.S. Swiss TransAtlantic Takes Control of Bolivian LAB," *Latin America News Digest,* August 31, 2007.

Uphoff, Rainer, "Fuel Starvation Cited As 727 Makes Jungle Landing," *Flight International,* February 12, 2008.

Zalamea, Luis, "LAB Well on Its Way to Relaunching," *Aviation Daily,* January 16, 2008.

Loma Negra C.I.A.S.A.

Bouchard 680
Buenos Aires, C.F. C1106ABJ
Argentina
Telephone: (54 11) 4319-3000
Toll Free: (800) 555-1-555 (in Argentina)
Web site: http://www.lomanegra.com.ar

Wholly Owned Subsidiary of Camargo Corrêa Cimentos S.A.
Incorporated: 1926 as Loma Negra S.A.
Employees: 2,200
Sales: $394.2 million (2006)
NAIC: 327310 Cement Manufacturing; 327320 Ready-Mix Concrete Manufacturing; 327410 Lime Manufacturing; 482111 Line-Haul Railroads

■■■

Loma Negra C.I.A.S.A. is by far the largest producer of cement in Argentina. Its main activity is the manufacture of portland cement, masonry cement, concrete, and lime products in its nine plants. The company exports cements, portland clinker, and blast furnace slag. It also operates a railroad.

FIFTY YEARS OF MAKING CEMENT: 1926–76

Luciano Fortabat was a Basque sheepherder who came to Argentina in 1871, a time when, as in the United States, Indians were being cleared off their lands for the establishment of farms and ranches, and railroads were being built to link rural areas with cities. He flourished there, becoming a well-to-do landowner in Argentina's most important province, Buenos Aires, which surrounds the city of Buenos Aires on three sides. Local cattle were cross-bred on the Fortabat properties with Aberdeen Angus of British origin.

In the early years of the 20th century, a German living in Argentina discovered exploitable deposits of limestone, the basic raw material for cement, in the countryside around Olavarría, where Luciano Fortabat owned a farm. Nothing came of this discovery immediately, but in 1926 Alfredo Fortabat, the youngest of Luciano's three sons, decided to work the deposits, opening a cement plant two years later in the village of Loma Negra ("Black Hill"). In this enterprise he was encouraged by a big U.S.-based multinational company, Lone Star Cement Co. He also benefited from investment in the endeavor by the family of his first wife.

Cement is difficult to transport because of its great volume and weight, and the need to protect it from humidity, which will cause hardening and render it useless. In order to control costs, expansion required the business to establish new plants near other centers of consumption rather than carry the cement long distances by truck. A second Loma Negra plant opened in Frías, Santiago del Estero, in northern Argentina, in 1937. In 1956 a third one began production in the northwest, in Rivadivia, San Juan. Also in the 1950s, the company opened a cement plant in Barker, Buenos Aires. This facility was near Olavarría and added to the firm's capacity to supply the Buenos Aires metropolitan area; it became second to Olavarría in size and importance. In 1970 Loma Negra established a plant in

Zapala, Neuquén, in far western Argentina near Patagonia and the Chilean border.

Loma Negra grew large and profited greatly from public works construction grants. Seventy percent, perhaps even more, of the cement used in the public sector was provided by Loma Negra at a time of heavy expenditure and great optimism over Argentina's future. When Fortabat died in 1976, he owned not only the cement plants but 23 country estates occupying 160,000 hectares (395,000 acres), including a horse farm in Middleburg, Virginia, and 170,000 head of cattle.

The beneficiary of this wealth was Fortabat's second wife, Amalia Lacroze de Fortabat. As a 21-year-old soon to be married, she caught the eye of the industrialist, who was almost 30 years her senior. In 1947 they left their respective spouses and were married no less than three times in other Latin American countries, according to Luis Mujal's muckraking two-volume work on some of Argentina's wealthiest citizens. None of these ceremonies had any legal weight in Argentina, since the staunchly Catholic country forbade divorce, but in 1951 a law was passed with, according to Mujal, a clause especially designed for them, and almost immediately repealed. They were wed the next day in one of only six marriages under this law.

During her years living with her authoritarian husband, Amalita, as she was called, kept a low profile, concentrating on painting, sculpting, and other activities considered appropriately "feminine." On inheriting his estate, however, she quickly stepped to the fore, maintaining Loma Negra's almost feudal traditions at Olavarría, a company town where it was easy to find three generations working side by side at the plant. People were educated in the company's schools, lived in housing built by the company, and went to the company's medical dispensaries when ailing. Loma Negra owned the local radio station and sponsored the soccer team. It paid its employees better than average wages for the work entailed. Amalita kept up the tradition, dancing the tango at local fiestas and providing free tuition for illiterate or poorly educated mothers.

LOMA NEGRA UNDER AMALITA: 1976–2005

Holding the business together was another matter. Each of the five cement plants operated almost independently from the others, with different machinery and equipment, so that orders could not easily be shunted from one factory to another. Consequently, they were larger than needed and operated at considerably less than full capacity. Nevertheless, the late 1970s were a period of prosperity for the country and company. A sixth plant was added in Plata Yacyretá, Corrientes. Work began on another in Paraje La Calera (or El Alto), Catamarca, which, when it opened in 1982, became the most modern cement factory in South America. Plans were underway as well to expand the Olavarría and Frías plants.

Amalita enjoyed Loma Negra's success and profits to the hilt. In Buenos Aires she occupied a triplex apartment in the choicest part of town; almost next door were the premises of the Fortabat Foundation. She also had a house in the suburbs. A Lear jet carried her to Punta de Este, Uruguay, playground of the Argentine rich during the summer, where she had a house and an apartment. A helicopter took her from the house to the beach. She also had a house in Mar del Plata, the Argentine beach resort, and still another on a Greek island.

When Amalita traveled to New York in her jet, she stayed in an apartment she owned at the Pierre, a swank hotel on Fifth Avenue. She was a generous donor at New York benefits, and her acquaintances included Henry Kissinger and David Rockefeller. In 1980 she purchased the most expensive painting sold at auction to that date, by J. M. W. Turner, for $6.4 million. Her art collection also came to include paintings by Brueghel, Monet, Gauguin, Degas, Miró, Van Gogh, and Andy Warhol.

The 1980s, however, were a lost decade for Argentina. High interest rates imposed by the U.S. Federal Reserve Board from 1979 to 1980 ended double-digit inflation, but at the cost of a recession that spread around the world, including heavily indebted Argentina. The cement industry was among the first to suffer from reduced demand. By 1985 production was almost 50 percent lower than in 1980. The Catamarca plant, which may have cost $250 million, operated well below capacity, like the other facilities.

According to Mujal, however, this plant was, in effect, financed by the state, which also afforded Loma Negra tax breaks and allowed the company to import machinery tax-free. Argentina's cement companies also received a tax discount on purchases of natural gas by agreeing to concentrate production in the summer

KEY DATES

1928: Following two years of exploratory work, Alfredo Fortabat establishes a cement plant in the village of Loma Negra.

1970: Loma Negra, which dominates cement production in Argentina, opens its fifth plant.

1976: Alfredo Fortabat's widow, Amalia, inherits his estate, including Loma Negra.

1993: Loma Negra obtains the concession to operate a privatized railroad line, Ferrosur Roca.

1998: Loma Negra purchases four concrete companies.

2001: In the wake of Argentina's economic collapse, Loma Negra's debt rises to $450 million.

2005: Loma Negra is sold to a Brazilian company for $1.02 billion.

rather than winter, thereby relieving the seasonal demand for home heating. No company benefited more than Loma Negra, which was using as much gas as the nation's capital.

Señora Fortabat was an early backer of the successful presidential campaign of Carlos Menem, who was elected in 1989. The new president rewarded Amalita by appointing her a roving ambassador. The "Cement Queen," as newspapers and magazines called her, was generally acknowledged to be the wealthiest woman in Argentina, perhaps in Latin America, with a fortune estimated at $2 billion to $3 billion.

Prosperity returned to Argentina during Menem's first term. The new president tamed inflation by tying the currency's value to that of the U.S. dollar and privatized many state-owned firms. Foreign investment poured into the country. Loma Negra, in 1992, acquired Cementos San Martín S.A. from Lone Star Industries Inc. This purchase added three plants: a grinding plant in Paraná, Entre Rios, and two in Sierras Bayas, Buenos Aires, one of which turned out Plasticor, a high-resistance masonry cement, and another that produced concrete.

The following year Loma Negra secured a concession to operate Ferrosur Roca, a privatized rail freight line that carried the cement of four Loma Negra plants and extended to both the Atlantic Ocean and (by association with a Chilean line) to the Pacific. Loma Negra also acquired stock in two natural gas distribution companies that were supplying four of its cement plants

with fuel. In 1996 the company joined with others to acquire a distributor of electric power in Patagonia.

Loma Negra also initiated, with partners, the construction and operation of a recycling plant converting industrial waste into a fuel for use in its cement plants. The completed project became a subsidiary, Reycomb S.A. An unrelated venture, however, ended badly with Amalia Fortabat's purchase of the struggling Buenos Aires newspaper *La Prensa* in 1993. This had always been the paper she read, and she tried to make it profitable but eventually sold it to a hotel magnate.

Loma Negra purchased four concrete producers in 1998 and placed their output under the Hormigón Lomax brand. These enterprises, combined, held half the concrete market in the Buenos Aires metropolitan market. In December 1998 Loma Negra signed a marketing agreement with Uruguay's largest industrial firm, government-owned Administración Nacional de Combustibles, Alcohol y Pórtland (Ancap). They created Cementos del Plata S.A., in which Loma Negra took a 45 percent stake, for the purpose of marketing Ancap's cement in both Argentina and Uruguay. Loma Negra's products held 80 percent of the market in the Buenos Aires metropolitan area. It opened a third plant in Olvarría, La Amalí.

Not everyone was happy with Loma Negra's products, or those of its competitors. Two of the most prestigious Argentine architects said that because of poor quality they had to design more complicated structures, including supports three times as thick as those they employed in structures outside Argentina. Loma Negra said the problem was not the cement but the concrete promising to establish a center for technical assistance and to install mobile laboratories to improve the quality of the concrete.

The year 1998 was Loma Negra's last good one under Señora Fortabat. A small inner circle of executives was responsible for day-to-day administration under her supervision. One of these was Alejandro Bengolea, the son of her only child, a daughter from her first marriage. He was seen as the heir apparent to Loma Negra. In 1999, a deep recession gripped Argentina, which was no longer able to support the deflationary effect of keeping its currency at the same value as the U.S. dollar. The construction industry stalled, reducing demand for Loma Negra's building materials.

Loma Negra also faced a serious challenge from the merger of two competitors, Corcemar S.A. and Juan Minetti S.A. into Minetti S.A., which dominated the cement market in central Argentina. Minetti was backed and bankrolled by the powerful Swiss cement group Holderbank Financiere Glavis AG (later Holcim Ltd.), which took a one-third stake in the merged enterprise. Publicly, Loma Negra affected nonchalance, pointing out that Holderbank had not tried to dominate the market in other Latin American countries for fear of provoking antitrust legislation.

At the end of 2000 Argentina, unable to make payments on its debt, ceased to support its currency, which promptly fell two-thirds in value. This action had dire consequences for the nation's corporations, since their debts, generally to foreign banks and other outside investors, increased by a corresponding amount. Loma Negra's debt rose to $450 million. This was reduced to $270 million in 2003 with the aid of Morgan Stanley.

The Argentine economy was recovering, but Loma Negra's revenue in fiscal 2004 (the year ended August 31, 2004) was only $215 million, well below its pre-recession peak of $360 million. Loma Negra scrapped a plan to invest $63 million in the construction of a new cement plant in Uruguay and to renovate and expand the two existing Ancap plants. Ancap turned to Venezuela instead for help, and in 2008 Loma Negra reduced its participation in Cementos del Plata to 5 percent.

UNDER BRAZILIAN OWNERSHIP: 2005–07

In 2004 the business magazine *Apertura* ranked Amalia Fortabat fourth among the most influential business-people in Argentina. "At 82 years of age," it declared, "she continues to conduct with an iron (or should one say cement?) hand the company's destiny." Soon after, however, it became known that Loma Negra was up for sale. The company attracted much interest from foreign cement companies, because construction in Argentina was booming again, and Loma Negra held a 48 percent share of the cement market. In 2005 the company, which did not include the Fortabat farms and ranches or station Radio Coronel Olavarría, was sold for what was considered a premium price, $1.025 billion, to Camargo Corrêa Cimentos S.A., a subsidiary of the huge Brazilian conglomerate Camargo Corrêa S.A. This company's resources enabled Loma Negra to repay most of its negotiable debt of $295 million in 2006.

Loma Negra had sales of $394.2 million in fiscal 2006. It held 46 percent of the market that year and set

a production record of nine million metric tons. In view of a growing shortage of natural gas supplies in Argentina, the company was adapting its plants for the use of coal and petroleum coke as fuel. It also reopened an electricity generating turbine that had been closed in 2000. A subsidiary, Reycomb S.A., was recycling Loma Negra's industrial wastes as fuel for its furnaces. Camargo Corrêa pledged to invest $115 million in Loma Negra during 2007 and 2008. The company was being directed by Humberto Junqueira de Farias, a Brazilian.

Robert Halasz

PRINCIPAL SUBSIDIARIES

Ferrosur Roca S.A.; Reycomb S.A.

PRINCIPAL COMPETITORS

Minetti S.A.

FURTHER READING

"Ancap asumio control de sociedad con Loma Negra," *El País de Uruguay,* January 10, 2008.

Brooke, James, "New Peronist: Blending Grit with Wealth," *New York Times,* July 16, 1989, Sec. 1, p. 13.

Crespo, Mariana, "Argentina: The Powers That Be," *FW/ Financial World,* November 8, 1994, p. 68.

Dattilo, Sergio, "Nada es para siempre," *Apertura,* March 1999, pp. 44–48, 50, 52, 54.

"El imperio Fortabata," *Apertura,* December 1989/January 1990, pp. 62–63, 65–66, 68, 70, 72.

Majul, Luis, *Los dueños de la Argentina,* Buenos Aires: Editorial Sudamericana, 1993, Vol. 1, pp. 13–58.

"Los más influyentes empresarios de Argentina," *Apertura,* June 2004, p. 26.

Moyano, Julio, ed., *The Argentine Economy,* Buenos Aires: Julio Moyano Comunicaciones, 1997, pp. 556–57.

Pairone, Alejandro, "Venderían cementara en Argentina," *El Norte* (Monterrey, Mexico), September 15, 2004, p. 8.

Samor, Geraldo, "Argentine Cement Maker Seeks Buyer," *Wall Street Journal,* August 12, 2004, p. A8.

"El 2007, un buen año para el cemento," *La Nación,* November 5, 2006, Sec. 2, p. 6.

LOUD Technologies, Inc.

16220 Wood-Red Road NE
Woodinville, Washington 98072
U.S.A.
Telephone: (425) 487-4333
Fax: (425) 487-4337
Web site: http://www.loudtechinc.com

Public Company
Incorporated: 1988 as Mackie Designs Inc.
Employees: 533
Sales: $208.3 million (2007)
Stock Exchanges: NASDAQ OTC
Ticker Symbol: LTEC
NAIC: 334310 Audio and Video Equipment Manufacturing

■ ■ ■

LOUD Technologies, Inc., began its existence as Mackie Designs. The company is one of the world's largest pro audio and music products companies with brands that include Alvarez, Ampeg, Crate, EAW, Knilling, Mackie, Martin Audio, St. Louis Music, and TAPCO. LOUD offers a wide range of digital recording products, loudspeakers, commercial audio systems, audio and music software, guitars, guitar and bass amplifiers, and orchestral string instruments. These sell through retail outlets and a network of installed sound contractors in the United States and through distributors worldwide. LOUD also distributes pro audio and music accessories.

INTRODUCING AFFORDABLE, HIGH-QUALITY MIXERS TO A BROAD AUDIENCE: 1988–95

When he was in his late 30s in 1988, Gregory C. Mackie founded Mackie Designs Inc. in the bedroom of his Edmonds, Washington, condo with the purpose of producing a line of audio mixers. A former Boeing employee, Mackie had twice before turned his hobby of building custom guitar amplifiers and public address systems into a business. In 1970, he began Technical Audio Products Company (TAPCO), which pioneered professional multichannel live music mixers, and in 1978, he began Audio Control Corporation, which designed and manufactured equalizers and analyzers for the consumer electronics market. "It was very helpful that I had started TAPCO," Mackie recalled about the beginnings of Mackie Designs in a 1995 *Corpus Christi Caller Times* article, explaining that some of TAPCO's original customers ran music stores.

Until Mackie Designs came into being, the mixer market consisted either of high-priced boards used by professional studios or mass-market units made by giant electronics companies. There were no good-quality compact units at a reasonable price that would satisfy professional needs and would also appeal to a wider audience. Mixers adjust the volume, tone, and quality of sound sources before sending an audio signal to a broadcast, movie soundtrack, CD, tape, or speakers. Working alone with his own funding, Mackie developed the prototype of his first major product in 1989.

After attracting two investors, he began manufacturing his product in a 2,000-square-foot warehouse in

---

COMPANY PERSPECTIVES

LOUD competes primarily on the basis of product quality and reliability, price, ease of use, brand name recognition and reputation, ability to meet customers' changing requirements and customer service and support.

Redmond, Washington, in 1990, but his business quickly outgrew this space. Sales for 1990 totaled $558,000; in 1992, they were $12.4 million; and, in 1993, $21.9 million. By 1994, Mackie Designs was selling $50 million worth of mixers and related equipment annually. The company, which then employed 200 people, was adding about ten workers a week. Consequently, Mackie Designs made its fifth move in six years to much larger facilities in Woodinville, Washington. Export sales also increased steadily as a percentage of overall sales during the first half of the 1990s. By 1995, they were 30 percent of revenues of $63.9 million (triple 1993 levels), and by 1996, they were 37 percent.

Over the same period, the company achieved a number of important milestones. It received *Musical Merchandiser Review*'s "Dealer's Choice Mixer of the Year" in 1994. Mackie Designs held its initial public offering (IPO) the next year, selling 2.5 million shares on the NASDAQ under the ticker symbol MKIE. By then, the company had also moved beyond its originally defined market of corporate video departments, churches, schools, and would-be musicians performing in their home studios. Professional performers had begun touring with Mackie equipment, which sold for anywhere from $399 to $5,000. By 1996, the year Greg Mackie was named High Technology Entrepreneur of the Year, Mackie Designs mixers had become the industry standard with more than 200,000 units in use; other competitors marketed their products as "Mackie-type" mixers.

In fact, the company, had grown so fast that it had never been able to stockpile any of its components for assembly or to develop an inventory of finished goods. Intent on preserving its corporate culture of flat hierarchy, by mid-decade it consisted of only five supervisors for 350 employees whose pay was based partly on performance quality. However, Mackie Designs remained relatively unknown among non-audiophiles, and, as a result, investors did not particularly like Mackie Designs' stock. Despite the fact

the company shipped four new products during a profitable 1995, Mackie Designs shares closed at only about two-thirds of their IPO price half a year later. In 1997, the company began a stock repurchase program, which extended into 1998.

FROM SMALL ANALOG MIXER TO PRODUCER OF MULTIPLE TECHNOLOGIES: 1996–97

Despite the lack of enthusiasm among investors, revenues and the number of Mackie Designs' core products continued to grow during the late 1990s. Employees totaled 400. *Inc. Magazine* ranked Mackie Designs 78th in its 1996 list of the fastest-growing publicly owned companies, while the company was also named the tenth fastest-growing tech company in Washington for the previous five years. The following year, Deloitte and Touche named Mackie Designs to its Technology Fast 500 list.

Toward the end of 1996, Mackie Designs cast its net wider, deciding to pursue a course of aggressive expansion into related audio products, including studio monitors, amplifiers, digital recorders, desktop mixing systems, and public address systems aimed at film, multimedia, and recording studio professionals. These products represented a potential market for Mackie Designs more than double the size of its current niche, which at that point consisted of 11 percent of the $743 million-a-year world mixer market. The company's leadership also hoped this move would help enhance its visibility and reputation among still reluctant investors.

To this end, Mackie Designs added a web site and formed several partnerships in 1996 and 1997. It undertook joint product development for a low-cost hardware control surface with Digidesign, a division of Avid Technology, the leading digital audio production software and systems manufacturer for music, film, video, multimedia, and broadcast radio industries in 1996. In 1997, it also partnered with Radio Cine Forniture S.P.A. of Italy, a designer and manufacturer of professional audio products with a substantial customer base in European and overseas markets, to expand its acoustic product line. That same year, it signed partnering agreements with two leaders in sound-effects technology, Apogee Electronics Corporation and IVL Technologies Ltd.

The popularity of Mackie Designs products within the audio industry brought with it imitation, and in 1997 Mackie Designs sued Sam Ash Music Corporation, the leading retailer of Mackie Designs products, and Behringer Spezielle Studiotechnick, an audio equip-

KEY DATES

1988: Gregory C. Mackie founds Mackie Designs Inc.

1990: Mackie Designs begins manufacturing in Redmond, Washington.

1995: Mackie Designs holds its initial public offering on the NASDAQ under the ticker symbol MKIE.

1997: Company partners with Apogee Electronics Corporation, IVL Technologies Ltd., and Radio Cine Forniture S.P.A. of Italy; Mackie Designs sues Sam Ash Music Corporation and Behringer Spezielle Studiotechnick.

1998: Mackie Designs establishes storage warehouses in Europe, Asia, and South America; company also acquires Radio Cine Forniture and California-based Fussion Audio.

2003: Sun Capital Partners buys 74 percent of the company, which ends manufacturing operations in Woodinville; company is renamed LOUD Technologies Inc.

2005: LOUD Technologies transfers its stock to the National Association of Securities Dealers' OTC Bulletin Board under the ticker symbol LTLG; the company acquires St. Louis Music.

2006: LOUD Technologies rejoins the NASDAQ Capital Market under the symbol LTEC.

2007: LOUD Technologies purchases Martin Audio Ltd. of England.

represented the company's arrival in the sound delivery or speaker market. In 2000, the company created three new sales positions focused on the global market from the Pacific Rim to the Middle East. In 2002, the company opened its first direct-sales office in Japan.

At the same time, Mackie Designs was undergoing multiple internal changes. Although revenues rose to $156 million in 1999, the company laid off more than 50 employees, or 10 percent, of the Woodinville workforce as part of an internal restructuring. Roy Wemyss became chief executive and president in April 1999, but resigned from the position six months later. James T. Engen followed as chief executive and president in 2000, having served as the company's chief operating officer and, before that, as director of RCF upon its acquisition.

Finally, Mackie Designs continued to gain new acquisitions. In 2000, the company purchased Massachusetts-based Eastern Acoustic Works Inc. (EAW), the leading domestic high-end professional loudspeaker design and manufacturing firm, and Acuma Labs Ltd., of Victoria, Canada, which developed real-time embedded systems for professional audio applications, including digital signal processors, microprocessors, digital audio effects, analog and digital software, real-time operating systems, interfaces, and hardware design. Another acquisition occurred in 2001, that of Sydec n.v. of Belgium, an innovator of digital audio workstation technology products. Mackie Designs also entered into a partnership with Emagic to develop a family of hardware controllers and continued its expansion into the Chinese market by forming a partnership with Amoisonic Electronics Co. Ltd. to distribute its products there.

ment producer, for manufacturing and distributing copies of Mackie Designs audio products. Behringer stopped selling the infringing products following Mackie Designs' legal claims, and, in 1999, Mackie Designs settled out of court with each of the two companies. Sam Ash agreed to continue acting as a Mackie Designs dealer.

FOCUSING ON INTERNAL RESTRUCTURING AND GLOBAL EXPANSION: 1998–2000

Mackie Designs furthered its product diversification and global expansion in 1998 by setting up storage warehouses in Europe, Asia, and South America and by acquiring Radio Cine Forniture (RCF) and Fussion Audio of California. Fussion was a start-up formed by ex-RCF acoustic engineers. This double acquisition

HARD TIMES AND COURSE CORRECTIONS: 2001–03

However, the early years of the 21st century also signaled hard times. The year 2000 was Mackie Designs' last profitable year since its founding, with revenues of more than $207.4 million. Notwithstanding its acquisitions and expansions, revenue dropped to $206.5 million in 2001, and in 2002, the company experienced a $37.9 million loss even as the home integration market grew and Mackie equipment broadcast the events of the Salt Lake City 2002 Winter Olympics, the World Cup soccer tournament, and World Youth Day in Canada with Pope John Paul II.

When Sun Capital Partners bought more than 70 percent of the company and installed three new directors on its board in 2003, Mackie Designs stock was trading at $1 per share. The company underwent several contractions to try to correct its course that year. It laid off 200 workers and ended most of its manufacturing operations in Woodinville, moving production to China, although it maintained headquarters in Washington. Mackie Designs also sold RCF—Mackie Designs Italy, reducing the number of Mackie Designs brands to five: Mackie, TAPCO (entry level), EAW (high end), SIA, and Acuma Labs. In addition, Mackie Designs voluntarily delisted itself from the NASDAQ. By the summer of 2003, while the sale of consumer goods continued to be affected by the slow economy, the company began to feel, according to a *Seattle Post-Intelligencer* article, that it had "turned the corner" into better times. In September the company announced it had chosen a new corporate name: LOUD Technologies Inc.

RETURNING TO PROFITABILITY: 2004–07

By 2004, revenues had increased substantially to $123.4 million. In 2005, they rose 65.7 percent to $204.3 million. LOUD Technologies transferred its stock to the National Association of Securities Dealers' OTC Bulletin Board in 2005 under the new ticker symbol LTLG. It also underwent a 1-for-5 reverse split of common stock and acquired St. Louis Music, a maker and importer of musical and audio equipment. In early 2006, as sales rose still more to $215 million, LOUD Technologies succeeded in rejoining the NASDAQ under the symbol LTEC.

LOUD Technologies' restructuring seemed to have the desired effects when in 2006 the company's net sales increased more than 5 percent. Over the next two years, the company revamped its corporate infrastructure in a variety of ways. In 2006, it installed a new direct distribution system in North America. Individual sales teams focused on particular kinds of clients from large national chains to regional customers. In addition, LOUD Technologies formed a group of product specialists to support members of the distribution chain and developed a new system of online ordering.

In 2007, the company sold the sole manufacturing facility that it owned (it continued to lease other facilities in other states) in Yellville, Arkansas, laying off 226 workers. The sale was part of a move to shift domestic manufacturing operations overseas and thereby remain viable in an industry where its competitors were better financed and had a stronger market presence. LOUD Technologies also continued its strategy of acquisitions and global reach, purchasing Martin Audio Ltd. of England, which produced loudspeaker systems for touring entertainment groups, in 2007.

Carrie Rothburd

PRINCIPAL SUBSIDIARIES

St. Louis Music, Inc.; Mackie Designs S.P.A.

PRINCIPAL COMPETITORS

Electro-Voice; Fender Musical Instruments Company; Harman International Industries, Incorporated; Yamaha Corporation.

FURTHER READING

Park, Clayton, "Audio Guru Takes Firm Public," *Puget Sound Business Journal*, July 23, 1995, p. 1.

Virgin, Bill, "Mackie Designs Discovers the Right Mix for Success," *Corpus Christi Caller Times*, February 23, 1995, p. 6.

Wilhelm, Steve, "Mackie Designs Pushes into the Speaker Market," *Puget Sound Business Journal*, February 12, 1999, p. 7.

———, "Mackie Ready to Make Noise with New Lines," *Puget Sound Business Journal*, February 13, 1998, p. 4.

Macklowe Properties, Inc.

—■—

142 West 57th Street, 15th Floor
New York, New York 10019-3300
U.S.A.
Telephone: (212) 265-5900
Fax: (212) 554-5895
Web site: http://www.macklowe.com

Private Company
Incorporated: 1963 as Wolf & Macklowe Company
Employees: 310
Sales: $334 million (2006 est.)
NAIC: 531210 Offices of Real Estate Agents and
Brokers

■ ■ ■

Macklowe Properties, Inc., is the vertically integrated real estate firm privately held by controversial Harry Macklowe, chairman and chief executive, and his son, William, president and heir apparent. Focusing on midtown Manhattan, the company buys, upgrades, manages, and leases properties. All told, the company owns 900 apartment units and about 12 million square feet of office space. The flagship property is the General Motors Building located on the edge of Central Park at 59th Street and Fifth Avenue, acquired in a $1.4 billion deal. It was the most ever paid for a U.S. office building, elevating Harry Macklowe to the front ranks of Manhattan landlords.

Highly competitive and an avid sailor, Mackowe was once banned from yacht racing after the governing body of the sport ruled that he had made a threatening

run at another vessel during a race, leading to his disqualification. In the 1990s he feuded with Hamptons neighbor Martha Stewart over his shrubbery and a fence he built between the two properties. Over the years, Macklowe has skirted financial disaster on more than one occasion. In 2008 he again faced ruin after taking on considerable debt to finance a major deal, eight buildings at the cost of $7.5 billion, shortly before the subprime lending debacle unfolded. "He's Dracula," one New York real estate "figure" told the *New York Observer* in May 2000. "You have to drive a stake through his heart to kill him. Only he doesn't have a heart."

MACKLOWE TURNING TO REAL ESTATE: 1960

Raised in New Rochelle, New York, Harry Macklowe was the son of a Westchester County garment executive. After dropping out of the University of Alabama, New York University, and the School of Visual Arts he turned to real estate in 1960, becoming a broker for the Manhattan firm of Julien J. Studley, Inc. Macklowe became one of the firm's advertising specialists, leasing space to advertising agencies, which congregated between 34th and 59th streets, an area that would become the main focus of his career. His trademark aggressiveness paid off and he soon made assistant vice-president. In November 1962 he left to join a newly formed realty management and leasing concern, Brevoort Associates, Inc., as a principal and vice-president. Only a few months later, in May 1963, he teamed up with a former supervisor at Studley, Melvin D. Wolf, to form the predecessor to Macklowe Properties, Wolf & Macklowe Company. The realty company established offices at 342 Madison Avenue with Macklowe serving as president and Wolf as executive vice-president.

In the mid-1960s Macklowe expanded beyond leasing and management and began acquiring property in the SoHo district (South of Houston Street) as well as the Hotel Concord located at Lexington Avenue and 40th Street, which he converted into an office building. Another office building conversion was a 12-story loft building he acquired on 28th Street between Park and Madison avenues. He then tried his hand as a developer. Targeting a site on Second Avenue near 46th Street in the late 1960s, Macklowe cobbled together a parcel of land by acquiring three tenements, as well as a one-story building that he left in place but whose air rights were necessary for the construction of the three floors of the 16-story office building. At the time, the location was not ideal and when he began to rent the property he had trouble securing tenants because of a collapse in the rental market.

FIRST OFFICE BUILDING DEVELOPMENT: 1971

The 866 Second Avenue building opened in 1971. A decade would pass before Macklowe would try developing his next properties. He was not alone. Very few office or residential buildings were constructed in Manhattan during the 1970s. While a glut of space on the market curtailed the construction of new office properties, rent control and stabilization, high construction costs, tight money, and a difficult regulatory environment made apartment buildings an unattractive long-term investment. Conditions improved at the start of the 1980s. Macklowe and Wolf tried their first residential building, finding a desirable piece of property to construct the 38-story, $40 million River Tower with 324 apartments, located between 53rd and 54th streets and First Avenue and Sutton Place. It opened in 1981, the same time that Macklowe began construction on a new office building between Lexington and Third avenues from 44th to 45th streets.

ILLEGAL DEMOLITION LEADING TO CIVIL SUIT: 1985

Macklowe's ambitions increased as the decade wore on, but in the process he also gained notoriety. In the mid-1980s he developed the $150 million, 66-story residential and office high-rise Metropolitan Tower on West 57th Street overlooking Central Park and Carnegie Hall. Less savory was an incident in which a contractor he hired without permits, who failed to turn off the gas or electricity, demolished four Times Square single-room-occupancy hotels (SROs), used to house indigent people, in preparation for a major commercial redevelopment project he had planned. The work was done in the dead of night shortly before a new city ban on destroying SROs went into effect.

Many of the tenants became homeless, and politicians, including Mayor Ed Koch, were furious, while the newspapers branded Macklowe an outlaw developer. A grand jury considered the matter, and although Macklowe was not indicted he paid the city $2 million to settle a civil suit in 1985 and two years later paid another $2.7 million in fees levied for altering or demolishing SROs. One of his executives also pleaded guilty to a misdemeanor. Moreover, the city passed a new law that would have delayed construction on Macklowe's project by four years. Instead, the ban was mysteriously lifted after just two years when the legislation came up for renewal in 1987 and a city lawyer persuaded Mayor Koch that the provision affecting Macklowe was unconstitutional, a highly debatable conclusion. Without the mayor's top lawyer being consulted, the provision was removed and the city council was never told about the change to the legislation. Macklowe began construction two years early, saving millions of dollars, and only then did everyone realize that the construction ban had been lifted, setting off another political firestorm and a fresh round of negative publicity for Harry Macklowe.

WEATHERING FINANCIAL DIFFICULTIES

In late 1986 Macklowe and his partners acquired 15 buildings for $230 million. Just ten months later, on the eve of the October 1987 stock market crash, he sold the portfolio to Joseph Neumann for $350 million, pocketing a tidy profit while Neumann was left carrying a debt load just as the real estate market collapsed. The next few years were difficult times for the industry, and Macklowe looked to take advantage of conditions and continued to buy properties into the early 1990s when he too began to experience financial difficulties. In 1991 he gave up ownership of the Riverbank West apartment

KEY DATES

1963: Company is formed as Wolf & Macklowe, with Harry Macklowe as president.
1971: First Macklowe-built office building opens.
1981: First Macklowe-built residential building opens.
1985: Macklowe settles civil suit for illegally demolishing buildings.
1998: Bid to take Macklowe Properties public fails.
2003: General Motors Building is acquired.
2007: Seven Manhattan skyscrapers are acquired for $6.8 billion.

building in a prepackaged bankruptcy that turned over the title to his lender, Massachusetts Mutual Life Insurance Company. In July 1992 he defaulted on three loans, leading to a restructuring of the debt. A year later the three banks that aided sued him for defaulting on $13.5 million in promissory notes associated with the restructuring. He also defaulted on a $100 million mortgage on his prized Hotel Macklowe. Eventually he had to sell the property, which was renamed the Millennium Broadway, as well as divest several other properties.

In the mid-1990s, while the real estate market recovered, Macklowe made more news on the gossip pages than he did in the real estate or business section. For three years he feuded with Martha Stewart, the media personality and arbiter of style, over shrubs he planted between their East Hampton properties and "suburban" lighting he installed that she found tacky. After she was allowed to rip out the offending bushes, he tried building a fence, obscuring her view of a pond, and she supposedly assaulted one of his landscapers whom she mistakenly accused of erecting the fence, employing language not suitable for network television, and then backed her car to pin the man against a security gate control box, bruising his hip. The event was recorded at the police station but the Suffolk County district attorney elected not to file charges. Macklowe and Stewart's feud played itself out in the local city council meetings, the reports of their charges and countercharges amounting to several reams of paper before subsiding.

Macklowe fared better than Stewart in the public eye, but he would soon experience his own share of negative publicity after the New York real estate market came back to life in 1996. He secured new financial partners, including Credit Suisse First Boston, and resumed property development. A Seventh Avenue loft building was converted into the Chelsea Atelier, a luxury apartment building, and he paid $35 million for a mundane office building at 540 Madison Avenue, an amount considered too high, renovating it to provide greater retail space and dramatically increasing the value of the property. Unfortunately, part of the brick façade in December 1997 peeled away and crashed onto Madison, closing the street for weeks.

Although the city determined that the accident was the result of poor work done in 1970 when the building had been constructed, Macklowe's past was again revisited in the newspapers, as it was in the summer of 1997 when he was clearing a building site at Second Avenue and 53rd Street. According to the *New York Times,* Mayor Rudolph Giuliani "accused Mr. Macklowe of taking unfair advantage of a change in the state's new rent laws that allowed him to evict 13 rent-controlled tenants, including an 82-year-old blind man who said his removal would be the equivalent of a death sentence. 'If you can think of anyone with a bad history of abusing his position as a landlord and a developer, it's Harry Macklowe,' Mr. Giuliani said." Macklowe contended that he was "merely the 'windfall beneficiary' of a change in the rent laws."

CANCELING AN IPO

In May 1998 Macklowe filed to take his company public in hopes of raising $500 million, enough cash to cut his debt in half. Before the offering could be made, however, Asia was hit with a financial crisis with ripple effects that led to a difficult environment for real estate stocks and his initial public offering (IPO) was canceled. To make matters worse, Credit Suisse found itself overextended and called in $331 million in loans it had made to Macklowe, which he had planned to cover with the IPO, for a development site on Madison Avenue on which Macklowe planned to build a skyscraper overlooking Grand Central Station. Over the next two years Macklowe wrangled with Credit Suisse in a battle of maneuvers which at first blush appeared overwhelmingly in the favor of the bank. Macklowe was able to retain control of one of the parcels that made up the site, preventing Credit Suisse from completing a sale of the property. After two years Macklowe finally relinquished the property, but according to the *New York Times* the bank had to "give up valuable equity stakes it had in two of his buildings pledged as collateral."

While Macklowe sparred with Credit Suisse he also ousted his longtime chief lieutenant Warren Cole, president of the company since the late 1980s, and began grooming his son William to one day take charge.

Cole promptly filed suit, claiming Macklowe had cheated him out of $18 million and charging that his former boss would not even allow him to move into the apartment he had bought in one of Macklowe's buildings at a time when his wife was pregnant with their first child. In his early 30s, the younger Macklowe, a graduate of New York University, was "smoother around the edges than his father," in the words of the *New York Observer*, and "eager to improve the company's public image."

PURCHASE OF GENERAL MOTORS BUILDING: 2003

Despite wrangling with former partners, Harry Macklowe was able to secure new backers and continue to develop Manhattan properties. He built and sold out a condominium project at 76th Street and Lexington Avenue, renovated an office building at 400 Madison Avenue, and built a 300-unit apartment building in the Chelsea area. "Yet after decades in the business," opined *Fortune* in a 2008 profile, "he was still a second-tier player in New York's real estate oligarchy. In truth, the developer was better known for his late-night Times Square demolition than for his skills. That changed when he bought the General Motors Building from the bankrupt insurer Conseco in 2003." The price was a record $1.4 billion.

The initial reaction to the GM Building deal was that Macklowe had vastly overpaid for the property, but always creative he had a plan to increase the value of the 50-story building: adding an Apple store below ground with a glass entrance at street level. Not only did he sell Apple CEO Steve Jobs on the idea, he arranged to take a cut on the store's revenues. The GM Building, which Macklowe had coveted since watching its construction in the 1960s, increased dramatically, as did his reputation among his peers in the real estate field. "By the fall of 2006," according to the *New York Times*, "Mr. Macklowe was sitting pretty. ... He was putting together a premier development centered on what was once the site of the Drake Hotel, which he bought in 2006 for $418.3 million. He and his son were also building a hotel and apartment house at Madison and 53rd Street." Macklowe, now approaching 65, also proved he had not lost the creative touch. Because the residential market was beginning to slow he switched gears and turned the hotel and apartment complex into an office building catering to hedge fund firms, offering them the added amenities of a health club and swimming pool.

Not satisfied, Macklowe engineered another audacious deal in February 2007, in a manner of two weeks reaching an agreement to acquire seven Manhattan skyscrapers for $6.8 billion from Equity Office Proper-

ties trust, achieved with nearly no equity but a great deal of short-term debt. The Macklowes put up only $50 million and borrowed $7.6 billion, mostly from Deutsche Bank and hedge fund firm Fortress Investment Group, the extra cash needed to pay for closing and other fees. Given that the rental income was not expected to cover the interest payments for five years and that Harry Macklowe personally guaranteed $1.2 billion of the amount to Fortress, it was a bit of a high-wire act, one that turned into another potentially mystifying Macklowe escape trick as the market took a sudden turn for the worse because of the subprime crisis that greatly curtailed cash and prevented Macklowe from refinancing. In order to pay off the $1.2 billion, and avoid losing his personal wealth (including the homes in both Manhattan and the Hamptons, a cherished art collection, and a yacht), Macklowe was forced to put the GM Building up for sale in 2008. At the same time, he worked out an extension with Deutsche Bank that would likely lead to the sale of the seven properties the company bought just a year earlier.

Ed Dinger

PRINCIPAL DIVISIONS

Commercial; Residential.

PRINCIPAL COMPETITORS

Helmsley Enterprises, Inc.; SL Green Realty Corp.; The Trump Organization; Vornado Realty Trust.

FURTHER READING

Bagli, Charles V., "Without Renters in Place, Macklowe Plans a Manhattan Office Tower," *New York Times*, March 11, 1998, p. B1.

Bagli, Charles V., and Terry Pristin, "Harry Macklowe's $6.4 Billion Bill," *New York Times*, January 6, 2008, p. 3.

Finder, Alan, "Koch Disputed on a Benefit to Developer," *New York Times*, January 16, 1989, p. B1.

Forsyth, Jennifer S., "Macklowes on a Wire," *Wall Street Journal*, September 22, 2007, p. B1.

Grant, Peter, "Macklowe Defaults on Debts," *Crain's New York Business*, December 20, 1993, p. 1.

Koblin, John, "Macklowes Stomping Back Big with Buy," *New York Observer*, February 26, 2007, p. 40.

Leonard, Devin, "A Real Estate Mogul Risks It All," *Fortune*, March 3, 2008, p. 84.

Oser, Alan S., "Builder Finds the Times Are Trying," *New York Times*, November 15, 1970.

Pristin, Terry, "He'll Take Manhattan (or a Chunk of Midtown)," *New York Times*, February 21, 2007, p. C6.

Rice, Andrew, "Macklowe's Last Stand: Battles First Boston at 42nd and Madison," *New York Observer*, May 8, 2000, p. 1.

"2 Realty Men Form New Concern," *New York Times*, May 9, 1963.

Maurices Inc.

—■—

105 West Superior Street
Duluth, Minnesota 55802-2031
U.S.A.
Telephone: (218) 727-8431
Toll Free: (888) 255-1557
Fax: (218) 720-2102
Web site: http://www.maurices.com

Wholly Owned Subsidiary of Dress Barn, Inc.
Founded: 1931
Sales: $491.79 million (2007)
NAIC: 448120 Women's Clothing Stores

■ ■ ■

Maurices Inc., a specialty clothing retailer, has helped boost the earnings of parent company Dress Barn, Inc., since its 2005 acquisition. The company retains its Duluth-based headquarters and operates on a largely independent basis thanks to a strong management team. Although Maurices (the company lowercases its name) targets a younger customer than Dress Barn, in line with its parent company, the retailer is delving into the plus-sized segment of women's clothing.

DOWNTOWN DULUTH: 1931–59

E. Maurice Labovitz and his father operated a dry goods store in Duluth, Minnesota, during the 1920s. However, a bankruptcy in 1928 led to a change in tactics. In 1931, the younger Labovitz opened a merchandise business demanding a lower level of capital investment and higher level of inventory turnover. The store was located downtown on the same site as the Fair Store, not far from Lake Superior. Opened at the end of March, the store produced its first monthly profit, $4.12, in December. Sales for the year were $49,000.

"With hard work, a lot of imagination and good luck, the store slowly prospered. In 1933, Maurices moved to 120 W. Superior Street where it stayed until 1958. In 1937, my Dad had installed a new storefront there. In 1940, he installed fluorescent lights and air conditioning. These were certainly among the first, if not the first, such commercial installations in Duluth," Joel Labovitz recalled in a brief history of Maurices in The Will and the Way.

Ready to expand, Maurices established a shop in the town of Virginia, on the state's Iron Range. Two years later, in 1950, a Maurices store opened its doors in Superior, Wisconsin, just across the bay from Duluth.

Joel Labovitz began learning the workings of the family enterprise beginning in his early teens. He would graduate from the University of Minnesota–Duluth with a degree in business administration and work for a staple goods wholesaler before coming aboard as store manager in Virginia in 1950. Labovitz moved to the Duluth location in 1951. Teamed with store merchant Dan Blehart, an eventual partner in Maurices, Labovitz handled operations, marketing, and sales.

The 1958 move to a location across the street offered more sales floor, office, shipping, and storage space. Although sales and profits trended upward in the 1950s, the company needed to ratchet up its

COMPANY PERSPECTIVES

What started in 1931 as a small women's fashion shop in Duluth, Minnesota, has grown to nearly 600 stores in 42 states across the country. Maurices is the leading small town specialty store and authority for the savvy, fashion conscious consumer with a 20-something attitude.

performance to satisfy the needs of owners and employees alike.

CAPITALIZING ON CHANGING LIFESTYLES: 1960–81

As it had in the past, Maurices opened additional stores: Wausau, Wisconsin, in 1960; Green Bay and Appleton, in 1963; and Hibbing, in northeastern Minnesota, four years later. Its real growth spurt was yet to come.

In 1967, the year Joel Labovitz became CEO, Maurices entered the era of the shopping center. The retailer was initially reluctant to sign on the dotted line, facing what looked like steep rent. Once established, the Manitowoc, Wisconsin, store quickly produced a profit. Prior stores generally produced profits after two to three years of operation, Joel Labovitz revealed in *The Will and the Way.*

Recognizing changes in consumer habits, Maurices opened three more stores in shopping centers in 1969: Cedar Falls, Iowa; Mankato, Minnesota; and Sioux Falls, South Dakota. After success in these areas, Maurices strove to replicate the strategy "in similar communities." The company opened five more stores in 1970 and a like number in 1971.

By 1978, Maurices operated about 175 stores, with more in the pipeline. Smaller men's stores had been added to the mix, and some of the women's stores included men's shops. Labovitz shared credit for the company's success with the staff and management, most of whom were local and female.

Joel Labovitz, majority stockholder, directed the transition to new ownership in 1979. Maurices, operating in 18 states, was sold to the U.S. operating unit of a Netherlands-based privately held company. Labovitz stayed aboard until January 1981, "breaking in Hans Brenninkmeyer as the new CEO," he recalled in *The Will and the Way.* Mark and then Roland Brenninkmeyer would follow as chief officers. Thus, Maurices in

a manner continued as a family business, albeit part of a much larger family.

By the time Labovitz left Maurices behind for new endeavors, the company was 271 stores strong with about 750,000 total feet of sales floor space, according to the *Duluth News-Tribune.*

A NEW ERA FOR A.R.G. AND MAURICES: 1982–99

Maurices' parent company, Amcena Corp., changed its name to American Retail Group, Inc., (A.R.G.) in February 1994, according to the *Daily News Record.* The Brenninkmeyer family had established the U.S. operation, which consisted of eight retail chains, in the mid-1970s.

Headquartered in New York, its holdings over the years had included regional department stores Ohrbach's, Steinbach's, J. Byron's, and Upton's. Upton's, a 75-store chain established in 1985 in response to a booming Atlanta market, according to *WWD,* was due to be shuttered by the end of the decade. The 1990s did not prove kind, as it turned out, to the department store niche.

A retailer's growth depended on attracting new customers. Maurices, for example, introduced a prototype store offering entertainment as well as merchandise to lure in younger shoppers. The clublike Juxtapose stores opened in Minneapolis, Milwaukee, Portland, and Seattle in August 1997, coinciding with back-to-school shopping.

The growing Generation Y population held a lot of promise for retailers able to win them over. "This is a consumer who has a lot of expendable income. Last year, these consumers, girls ages 16 to 19, spent $37 billion," Diane Missel, Maurices president and COO, said in a September *WWD* article.

The 600-store Maurices specialty store chain, by and large, had been focusing on the buying patterns of women several years older. Other retailers, including Wet Seal/Contempo Casuals, Up Against the Wall, and Federated Department Stores were already in the fray for younger customers with entries named, respectively, Limbo Lounge, Commander Salamander, and Aeropostale.

Ron White, general manager of the Juxtapose concept, was named president and COO in 1998. A 13-year veteran of Maurices, White had also served as vice-president of marketing and regional sales manager, the *Duluth News-Tribune* reported in October.

Maurices' parent company, meanwhile, had been shifting its focus away from its fading department store

KEY DATES

1931: E. Maurice Labovitz establishes retail store in downtown Duluth.

1948: Second store is opened, in a town northwest of Duluth.

1950: Joel Labovitz joins business management ranks.

1967: Stores begin entering shopping center locations.

1979: Retail chain is sold to Amcena Corp. (later named American Retail Group), the U.S. operation of the Brenninkmeyer family of the Netherlands.

1997: Concept geared toward younger consumers is added.

2005: Sold to Dress Barn, Inc., Maurices remains largely independent.

2007: Duluth-based chain drops men's line and adds plus sizes for women.

business to its more robust specialty stores, which included Eastern Mountain Sports, Levi's and Docker's Outlets, as well as Maurices and Juxtapose. A.R.G.'s regional department stores had been losing out to national chains such as Sears, J.C. Penney, Wal-Mart, and Kohl's, *WWD* reported in July 1999. In line with its increased emphasis on the specialty stores, A.R.G. planned to tweak the Juxtapose start-up and add more stores. A more upscale Maurices format was also in the works, David Moin reported.

As for the Brenninkmeyers, Moin wrote, "The family is said to have a net worth of $4 billion, with 90 percent of the assets in retailing." Estimates had the privately held A.R.G. operation contributing about $1.5 billion in sales and the European C&A chain bringing in $5.5 billion.

NEW CENTURY SHAKEUPS

White stepped down from the posts of president and COO for personal reasons in June 2000, according to the *Duluth News-Tribune*. The company planned to divide his duties among other management team members. About 500 stores were in operation, primarily in small and midsized markets around the country.

Near the end of 2001, Maurices acquired most of the assets of Timbuktu Station, a 15-store women's clothing chain found in Minnesota, Michigan, Iowa, Colorado, Oregon, Utah, California, and Nevada.

A.R.G., out of the U.S. department store business as of 2000, saw a decline in total sales to an estimated $900 million in 2001, according to the *Daily Deal.* Change was in the works for its specialty stores as well. Some Miller's Outpost locations were being converted to the Anchor Blue brand, while others had been closed. Maurices locations had also been shut down. In 2003, talk of additional divestitures of U.S. holdings was in the air.

From a broader perspective, the September 11, 2001, terrorist attacks on the United States triggered an economic downturn with worldwide reverberations. The uncertainty of the times caused a downward pressure on consumption, challenging nearly every industry.

LIVING LARGER: 2005–07

Dress Barn Inc. moved to acquire the 464-store Maurices for $320 million, toward the end of 2004. For the fiscal year ended February 28, 2004, Maurices produced $342 million in sales.

Publicly traded Dress Barn recorded $754.9 million in sales for the year ending July 31, 2004. The clothing retailer operated 792 stores in 45 states, primarily in the Northeast. Maurices, expected to remain largely independent, had its strongest foothold in the Midwest and in smaller cities relative to Dress Barn.

Dress Barn planned to expand the Maurices chain at a rate of 30 to 40 stores a year for several years, according to the *Duluth News-Tribune* report by Peter Passi. In other projected changes, Maurices was likely to increase its private label offerings. Nearly all of Dress Barn's garments were in that higher margin category and often manufactured outside the United States.

The deal was completed in early January 2005, propelling Dress Barn into the reaches of billion-dollar companies. "More important, the Maurices retail brand is complementary to Dress Barn and will allow the maturing retailer to expand more rapidly and into new markets," Emily Scardino observed in a *Chain Store Age* article. Dress Barn customers were in the 35 to 55 age range while Maurices' were between 17 and 34 years old.

Dress Barn CEO David Jaffe, son of founder Roslyn Jaffe, also had begun to update the Dress Barn concept. During 2007, Maurices exited its men's business and entered the women's plus size segment. In-store shops within about 400 of its 587 stores carried sizes 16 to 24, according to a June *WWD* article. Dress Barn was well acquainted with the rapidly growing and profitable niche.

Maurices, meanwhile, had done wonders for Dress Barn's profit growth. Investors had yet to fully comprehend the change, however. "The stores are so far from major metropolitan areas, it's difficult for investors to kick the tires," an analyst for CL King & Associates in New York told the *Wall Street Journal.* "The average individual investor still probably doesn't even know what Maurices is," Mark Montagna added in the September 2007 article.

Maurices made the most of being located in small cities. Its relatively lower rental costs, for example, helped the chain generate healthy profits on more modest sales. That said, Jaffe had plans to introduce more Maurices stores in larger suburban and "metro-fringe" markets, areas where it had already had a taste of success. On the road to 1,000 stores, Maurices had embarked on rapid expansion in Texas and New York and planned to enter Florida and California.

Kathleen Peippo

PRINCIPAL COMPETITORS

J. C. Penney Company, Inc.; Kohl's Corporation; Sears, Roebuck & Co.

FURTHER READING

"Amcena Corp. Changes Name," *Daily News Record,* February 2, 1994, p. 5.

Brissett, Jane, "New Window on City History from Maurices West Superior Street Display Tells Story of Retailer's Corporate Hometown," *Duluth News-Tribune,* April 20, 1999, p. 1F.

Covert, James, "Dress Barn's Bold Wager Appears to Be Paying Off," *Wall Street Journal* (Eastern Edition), September 5, 2007.

Croft, Tara, and Heidi Moore, "American Retail Shops Two Units," *Daily Deal,* June 18, 2003.

"Dress Barn Completes Maurices Purchase," *Duluth News-Tribune,* January 4, 2005, p. 7B.

Hammond, Teena, "Trendy Offshoots," *WWD,* September 4, 1997, pp. 9+.

Kichera, Steve, and Peter Passi, "UMD Gets $4.5 Million," *Duluth News-Tribune,* May 14, 2003, p. A1.

"Maurices Buys Women's Clothing Chain—Timbuktu Station Purchase Adds 15 Stores to Duluth-Based Company," *Duluth News-Tribune,* December 11, 2001, p. 7C.

"Maurices Names White, East to Corporate Posts," *Duluth News-Tribune,* October 31, 1998, p. 1F.

"Maurices' President Resigns; White Cites Personal Reasons," *Duluth News-Tribune,* June 15, 2000, p. 1E.

Moin, David, "Maurices Adds Plus-Size, Drops Men's Wear Offerings," *WWD,* June 22, 2007.

———, "More Regional Fallout: ARG Plans to Shutter 75-Unit Upton's Chain," *WWD,* July 20, 1999, p. 1.

Passi, Peter, "After the Marriage, Blended Family's Doing Well," *Duluth News-Tribune,* December 17, 2007, pp. 1B, 3B.

———, "Dress Barn to Buy Maurices," *Duluth News-Tribune,* November 18, 2004, p. 1A.

Riell, Howard, "Barn Raising," *Retail Merchandiser,* November 2005, pp. 25–28.

Scardino, Emily, "Jaffe Opens the Door to Expansion," *Chain Store Age,* April 2005 (Supplement).

"Timbuktu Station Stores Sold to Duluth Chain," *Minneapolis (Minn.) Star Tribune,* December 12, 2001, p. 3D.

The Will and the Way: How a Generation of Activists Won Public and Private Achievements for Their Community and Region, Duluth, Minn.: Manley Goldfine and Donn Larson, 2004, pp. 7–8, 10, 79, 313.

Wilson, Marianne, "Positioned for the Teen Market," *Chain Store Age,* November 1997, pp. 136+.

May Gurney Integrated Services PLC

Trowse
Norwich, NR14 8SZ
United Kingdom
Telephone: (+44 01603) 727272
Fax: (+44 01603) 727400
Web site: http://www.maygurney.co.uk

Public Company
Incorporated: 1926 as May Gurney & Co.
Employees: 3,448
Sales: £406.4 million ($824.1 million) (2007)
Stock Exchanges: London AIM
Ticker Symbol: MAYG
NAIC: 237310 Highway, Street, and Bridge Construction; 237990 Other Heavy and Civil Engineering Construction

■ ■ ■

May Gurney Integrated Services PLC has long been a prominent name in the United Kingdom's engineering and construction sectors. Founded in 1926, the company has been focused from the start on the construction of water and sewage systems, road building, and related public works and infrastructure projects. Since the beginning of the 2000s, however, May Gurney has been transforming itself from a largely Norfolk-region-based engineering contractor into one of the United Kingdom's fastest-growing and most integrated engineering and construction services companies. A primary goal of the company has been to shift the bulk of its revenue stream to the development of long-term partnerships and contracts at the local, regional, and national level. As a result, May Gurney's engineering and construction operations accounted for just 25 percent of its 2007 revenues of £406.4 million ($824 million).

May Gurney operates through two primary divisions. Maintenance Services, the larger of the two, focuses on providing maintenance and other support services to the United Kingdom's highway and utilities systems. This division generated more than 62 percent of May Gurney's revenues in 2007. The second division, Engineering and Project Services, operates across the public and private sectors, including government-regulated private industries. This division's operations include infrastructure improvements for the road and rail systems, flood protection, ground and foundation support services, waste management, and other services, such as plant hire. May Gurney remained a privately held company for 80 years before going public on the London Stock Exchange's AIM market in 2006. The company is led by Chairman Tim Ross, CEO David Sterry, and COO Richard Dean.

SEWER BUILDER IN 1926

May Gurney was the brainchild of Roland May and Christopher Gurney. The former, born in Kent in 1873, had been active in the engineering industry since the mid-1890s. As a contractor's agent, and then as a managing engineer, May gained a background in a wide range of sectors, such as piling, water and sewer systems, and the construction of sea walls. Into the new century, May joined Robert Weals Ltd., a contractor focused on the public works sector. When that business failed, May moved to Norfolk, which was then faced with rebuilding its bridge system after flooding destroyed 30 bridges in 1912. Over the next decade, May worked for the county government, becoming its deputy surveyor. In 1923, however, he set out on his own, establishing a new business, RJ May Contractor, in Trowse, Norwich.

May soon found a financial complement to his engineering experience when he met Christopher Gurney. Gurney was part of the prominent Norfolk-based family behind the then 150-year-old Gurney Bank. Gurney, born in 1884, received a civil engineering degree at Trinity College in Cambridge; in World War I, Gurney served as part of the Royal Engineers. After a brief stint in London, Gurney returned to Norfolk as heir to the family fortune.

Gurney and May were introduced by Gurney's brother, and the pair quickly decided to go into business together, forming May Gurney & Co. in 1926. The company immediately began bidding for public works contracts in the Norfolk region. Among its first large-scale projects was the contract to construct the sewer system for the village of Thorpe, Norwich.

By the 1930s, May Gurney had also begun to compete for road-building and surfacing projects. Over the next two decades, the company continued to add new areas of expertise. Among these were flood protection, and dike, sea wall, and other systems to protect the coastline. Other areas included piling and ground preparation for construction and public works projects.

May himself led the company through the years of World War II. Gurney, in the meantime, had left May Gurney to join a timber company, before buying asphalt and aggregate supplier Ayton Asphalte. That company was to work closely with May Gurney as it expanded its road-building and surfacing operations. During World War II, as the construction sector fell off, May Gurney developed its operations elsewhere, notably in repairing damage caused by German bombing raids on the region's roadways and air raid shelters.

EXPANSION IN THE FIFTIES

Under Roland May, the company operated under a policy of maintaining a "reasonably small" size. This policy remained in effect in the immediate aftermath of World War II, even as Roland May retired to the chairman's seat in 1945. Nonetheless, under new Managing Director Ernest Cooke, the company showed the first signs of picking up its pace. In the late 1940s, May Gurney made its first major acquisition, of James Hobrough & Son, which complemented May Gurney's own operations, particularly with expertise in pipe laying.

Toward the end of the 1950s, as Roland May withdrew from an active role in the company (and died in 1959), May Gurney entered a new, more expansionistic phase. The company launched a new series of acquisitions, starting with the purchase of Richard Gurney's Ayton Asphalte. The purchase proved a major step toward May Gurney's later position as a highly integrated civil engineering group.

Into the 1960s, May Gurney completed several more acquisitions. These included Darby (Sutton) Ltd., a civil engineering company, and its subsidiary, Darby Plant Hitre. The company also acquired a dredging company, Blucher Thain, to support its sea defense and related works, in 1968. Into the beginning of the 1970s, the group bought Heyhoe Bros., which added demolition and land drainage operations, as well as plant hire and road surfacing, to May Gurney's mix of operations.

At the same time, May Gurney grew internally as well. The company launched a distribution wing, Farm and Domestic Oils, in 1962. That business distributed products from the Gulf Oil Company. In 1966, May Gurney added its own hauling operation, Georges Haulage, as part of its expanding Ayton Asphalte operation.

The arrival of a new chairman, Henry Utting, led to a new phase in May Gurney's growth at the beginning of the 1970s. In 1973, the company reorganized into a holding company for seven new subsidiaries, each focused on a specific area of operation. The new structure signaled the start of a new round of growth for the company. May Gurney began to build itself into a major regional player, with operations reaching into the London market.

MANAGEMENT BUYOUTS IN THE EIGHTIES AND NINETIES

As part of its expansion drive, the company added several new companies during the 1970s. These included Thames Plant Hire Ltd. and Butler & Sons Ltd., as well as Aubrey Wilson Ltd., based in Henley on

KEY DATES

1923: Roland May founds civil engineering business in Trowse, Norwich, England.

1926: Joined by Richard Gurney, May founds May Gurney & Co.

1937: Gurney leaves company to found Ayton Asphalte.

Late 1940s: May Gurney acquires James Hobrough & Son.

1959: Company acquires Ayton Asphalte as part of integration strategy.

1973: Company restructures into holding company and seven subsidiaries.

1989: First management buyout is completed.

1995: May Gurney wins first long-term services contract with Suffolk County Council.

2001: Second management buyout is completed; company launches restructuring to focus on long-term services contracts.

2006: May Gurney completes public offering on the London Stock Exchange's AIM.

Thames. The company also added a stake in Tate Pipelining Ltd., as part of its approach to the London market. Later in the decade, the company built up its home base, buying SA Cage Ltd., a builders merchant based in Norwich, in 1977. May Gurney also entered the Ipswich market, acquiring two companies, Ipswich Asphalt & Flat Roofing, and Moss Roofing, in 1978.

The shrinking market in the United Kingdom during the recession of the early 1980s led May Gurney to look abroad for growth during the decade. As part of this effort, the company formed a number of joint-venture partnerships. In this way, the company began carrying out contracts in such far-flung locations as Indonesia, Egypt, and Libya.

May Gurney's foreign moves were to remain only a small part of the company's business. This was especially true after 1989, when the group's management completed a buyout of the company from its existing shareholders. In this way the company retained its private status, while renewing its shareholder base. The company restructured once again in 1990, naming David Neale as the group's managing director. May Gurney then adopted a new strategy of expanding its civil engineering business on an increasingly national level. The company also changed its name, becoming May Gurney Construction Ltd.

The arrival of David Sterry into the group in the mid-1990s signaled the start of a new change of strategy for the company, however. While May Gurney remained predominantly a civil engineering and construction group, Sterry saw the potential for developing new operations in the services sector. The company was thus able to add a number of long-term contracts and partnerships, in contrast to the largely short-term nature of its civil engineering operations. The group's first public sector partnership contract was signed with Suffolk County Council in 1995.

Sterry was soon able to launch the group's new strategy in earnest. In 1999, most of the original buyout team announced their plans to retire. The company's management, led by Sterry, once again executed a buyout of the existing shareholders in 2000.

This placed Sterry in the chief executive's job, and in position to carry out a full restructuring of May Gurney's operations. As Sterry told *Contract Journal:* "When I came here, I knew that its good reputation was based on good relationships, as I heard that from customers. But two other things became apparent when I got here. First, there was an enormously wide skills base—much wider than I had anticipated and than most of our competitors had, especially during the 1990s—and I didn't feel we were making the best of our skills. Second, we were organised into traditional, separate subsidiaries, and developing slightly different cultures across those businesses, including some cases even when dealing with the same customers. The opportunity was there to not only look at the shareholding, but also the business's direction. We came up with two key strands for the business—a much more integrated approach and one which was going to be led totally by developing relationships and long-term partnerships."

FROM PRIVATE REGIONAL CONTRACTOR TO PUBLIC NATIONAL SERVICES GROUP

By then, May Gurney had won several more long-term service contracts, notably in the rail sector as the former Railtrack monopoly was privatized and broken up. In 1998, the company won a major highways contract with the Norfolk County Council. This was followed by the group's largest services contract, to maintain and expand the Essex highway system starting in 2000. This contract in particular signaled the coming of age of May Gurney's services operations.

In support of the Essex contract, and to expand its range of expertise and services, May Gurney acquired the Essex-based street-lighting specialist T. Cartledge Limited in 2002. May Gurney then set its sights on transforming the group from a regional contractor into a nationally operating, fully integrated services group. Among the company's new targets was a change in its revenue mix, with 75 percent of its annual revenues generated from its services operations. By 2004, the company had succeeded in boosting its services component to 60 percent of its sales.

Two years later, May Gurney completed a still more significant acquisition, that of rival TJ Brent. With its 18 regional offices, TJ Brent helped to catapult May Gurney from its regional focus to an increasingly national presence. Brent also brought May Gurney its own heavy focus on the services market, particularly in the utilities sector. The addition of Brent also allowed May Gurney to achieve its goal of a 75–25 services-to-contracting ratio. The group's focus on services was strengthened further in 2005, with the purchase of rail signaling design and testing specialist Hawthorns Project Management.

After 80 years as a privately held company, May Gurney began preparing for a public offering. As part of that effort, the company sold Ayton's Product division, including its asphalt, aggregate, and sand and gravel depots, generating £8.5 million for the company. The company's floatation came in June 2006, on the London Stock Exchange's AIM (alternative investment market) board. The public offering proved one of the most successful that year.

May Gurney continued to seek new acquisition prospects as it moved to cement its national presence. This led to the purchase of AC Chesters & Son Ltd. in March 2007, adding the Staffordshire company's expertise in mechanical and electrical engineering. In August of that year, the company added FDT, based in Manchester, which specialized in mobile telecom network inspection and maintenance. This purchase was followed by the addition of Willows Plant Limited in October 2007. Willows, based in Norfolk, focused especially on the gas utilities sector, bringing May Gurney its long-term maintenance contracts with the National Grid. The Willows acquisition cost May Gurney more than £14.6 million ($29 million).

May Gurney had clearly caught the momentum of the movement toward outsourcing of services in the United Kingdom. The group's revenues had been rising steadily, from less than £240 million in 2003 to more than £406 million in 2007. The company continued to win major new contracts, including the refurbishment and maintenance contract for the London and North East regions of the National Rail network. That contract, initially set for two years and extendable to five, held the potential to generate more than £100 million in revenues for May Gurney. After 80 years, the May Gurney name appeared certain to complete the leap from regional civil engineering group to national services powerhouse.

M. L. Cohen

PRINCIPAL SUBSIDIARIES

AC Chesters & Son Limited; May Gurney Estates Limited; May Gurney Limited; T. Cartledge Limited.

PRINCIPAL DIVISIONS

Maintenance Services; Engineering and Project.

PRINCIPAL COMPETITORS

Balfour Beatty PLC; Laing O'Rourke PLC; Kier Group PLC; AMEC PLC; Aggregate Industries Holdings Ltd.; Morgan Sindall PLC; GallifordTry PLC; Interserve PLC; Miller Group Ltd.; Alfred McAlpine PLC.

FURTHER READING

"Building on 80 Years of Success Is Key," *Eastern Daily Press,* October 11, 2006.

Davoudi, Salamander, "Nervous May Gurney's IPO Raises £44.1m on AIM and Is Almost Twice Subscribed," *Financial Times,* June 16, 2006, p. 19.

Feddy, Kevin, "May Gurney Snaps Up Rival," *Manchester Evening News,* October 19, 2007.

Fountain, Sam, "May Gurney Bags Its Third Acquisition This Year," *Business Weekly,* October 18, 2007.

Griggs, Tom, "May Gurney Seeks Expansion," *Financial Times,* May 31, 2007, p. 26.

———, "Public Contracts Buoy May Gurney," *Financial Times,* December 5, 2007, p. 25.

"May Gurney," *Investors Chronicle,* October 13, 2006.

"May Gurney Bags £100m Rail Deal," *Contract Journal,* March 5, 2008.

"Outsourcing Buoys May Gurney," *Investors Chronicle,* December 4, 2007.

Pesola, Maija, "May Gurney Ponders Listing," *Financial Times,* October 4, 2004, p. 22.

"Record Turnover of £410m for May Gurney," *Contract Journal,* June 6, 2007.

Wood, Tim, "May Gurney Acquires Lighting Firm," *Contract Journal,* July 17, 2002, p. 2.

MEDecision, Inc.

601 Lee Road
Chesterbrook Corporate Center
Wayne, Pennsylvania 19087
U.S.A.
Telephone: (610) 540-0202
Fax: (610) 540-0270
Web site: http://www.medecision.com

Public Company
Founded: 1988
Employees: 243
Sales: $44.2 million (2007)
Stock Exchanges: NASDAQ
Ticker Symbol: MEDE
NAIC: 511210 Software Publishers; 541512 Computer
Systems Design Services; 541519 Other Computer
Related Services; 541611 Administrative Manage-
ment and General Management Consulting
Services; 561110 Office Administrative Services

∎∎∎

MEDecision, Inc., is a leader in software design for
integrated information management and providing
products and services to regional and national healthcare
providers and managed care organizations. MEDecision
licenses several software options that are organized under
two brand categories, Alineo and NexAlign. Alineo
products are designed to retrieve, organize, and analyze
patient clinical information, while NexAlign service
provides secure transmittal of that data between the
healthcare organizations paying for care and healthcare

providers and their patients. The umbrella term "Collaborative Care Management" refers to MEDecision's
approach to information management, which is to
facilitate joint decision making between healthcare payers and healthcare providers. MEDecision's Collabora-
Care Consortium brings various software engineering
firms in cooperation with other concerned parties to create platforms for software compatibility.

IDEALS AND IDEAS PROVIDING FOUNDATION FOR NEW COMPANY

David St. Clair formed MEDecision in order to direct
his executive and strategic management experience into
a collaborative approach to information management for
the healthcare field. He hoped to apply his software
knowledge to modernize the workflow processes of managed care organizations. In particular, he sought to speed
communication between physicians and managed care
organizations through online channels. St. Clair believed
ready access to clinical data would improve the execu-
tion of healthcare services and, hence, reduce healthcare
costs overall. Moreover, by improving the timing of
medical decisions, such information management would
improve health results through patient safety and quality
of care. Also, St. Clair wanted to create an employee-
centered workplace by providing opportunities to succeed through respect for everyone's ideas, regardless of
their position in the company.

MEDecision's first priority involved the development of case management and services utilization
software for managed care organizations. During its first

year in operation, 1988, MEDecision introduced its first proprietary product, the Utilization Control System (UCS). The software provided managed care organizations with a tool for determining the necessity of healthcare treatments and for reviewing reliability of healthcare providers through analysis of hospital admissions, elective surgeries, high-tech diagnostic tests, medication, and other products and services. MEDecision continually improved the product, and in 1995, the company introduced WinUCS software, designed to be compatible with the Windows operating system. WinCMS (case management system), launched in 1998, provided oversight of individual patient care in situations that require multiple sites of care, such as after a substantial traumatic incident. WinReports provided summaries of patient care and results to healthcare payers. MEDecision found clients for its products among several Blue Cross and Blue Shield organizations, health maintenance organizations, Medicaid management organizations, and small and large insurance and managed care companies.

MARKETING PARTNERSHIPS AND AN ACQUISITION EXPANDING PRODUCT CAPABILITIES

Having established its credibility, MEDecision raised $3.5 million from a private issue of stock to support new marketing initiatives. To leverage its strengths through synthesis with complementary data technologies, MEDecision entered into a number of marketing partnerships during the late 1990s. In 1997, MEDecision signed an agreement to market InterQual's AutoBook2. The utilization management system provided criteria and guidelines for acute care, rehabilitation, subacute care, home care, surgery authorization and procedures, and other health services. The two companies engineered a process that simplified software access and operation so that clients could use AutoBook2 in conjunction with WinUCS and WinCMS. Thus, MEDecision and InterQual enhanced clinical productivity by integrating different tools needed to make healthcare decisions.

A marketing partnership with Patient InfoSYSTEMS, Inc., expanded MEDecision's software capabilities and provided new outlets for its case management software. By marketing the Personal Care Advisor to existing clients, MEDecision expanded the company's case management capabilities to include disease management, the oversight of healthcare services provided for chronic health conditions. Patient InfoSYSTEMS' Personal Care Advisor (PCA) comprised three disease management functions: to track symptoms, treatment compliance, and results of treatment, all determined through a timed schedule of patient interviews. PCA provided patients with materials that appropriately support their health condition and course of medical care, and it provided managed care organizations paying for treatment with reports on patient progress. By offering this service to their existing clients, MEDecision expanded its own database of patient information for case management.

An alliance with Health Systems Design Corporation combined that company's DIAMOND claims processing software with MEDecision's utilization, disease, and case management and reporting systems. Thus, MEDecision further integrated related managed care work processes.

Through the 1999 acquisition of Software Products Group, MEDecision expanded its information processing tools with the addition of the Practice Review System and the Management Review System. The software utilized artificial intelligence to provide managed care organizations with tools for analyzing patient treatment and billing schedules in conjunction with other case management systems. The software provided an overview of general practices across multiple cases, thus yielding information for better decisions regarding individual patients. In combination with WinReports, the technology enabled MEDecision to create a comprehensive data gathering and analytics module.

FACILITATING INFORMATION EXCHANGE

MEDecision's next phase of product development involved increasing the speed of information interchange among concerned parties. Toward that end, in June 1999, MEDecision introduced iEXCHANGE, an Internet communication software designed to facilitate the approval process for medical treatment and physician referral. By eliminating slower, paper-based systems of referral, such as facsimiles, iEXCHANGE offered clients a system capable of conducting the approval process before the patient left the physician's office. Moreover, the software provided access to case management files and other patient-approved information. Clients who

KEY DATES

1988: MEDecision introduces its first product.
1997: Marketing partnerships augment product capabilities.
1999: Decision to create new products leads to acquisitions, private stock offering.
2003: MEDecision launches the healthcare industry's first integrated medical management software.
2005: Patient Clinical Summary become available for electronic transmittal.
2007: Product offering is streamlined into two major brands, Alineo and NexAlign.

licensed the software included PacifiCare Health Systems, Blue Cross Blue Shield of Illinois, and Advanced Health Systems.

MEDecision generated funds to implement its iEX-CHANGE software, as well as to develop other products, through a second private stock issue. In June 2000, MEDecision sold convertible preferred stock to venture capitalists Grotech Capital Group and DWS Investments GmbH. Liberty Venture Partners and the State of Michigan Retirement Systems invested to a lesser degree than in the first stock issue. MEDecision received $30 million, enabling the company to release its collaborative data exchange module in 2001.

In preparation for further product development, MEDecision renamed its existing products in order to more effectively describe the purpose of the software as it evolved. WinUCS and WinCMS were combined under the CarePlanner name, and WinReports was renamed CarePlanner Reports.

New software addressed the requirements of the Health Insurance Portability and Accountability Act of 1996 (HIPPA). In April 2002, MEDecision introduced MEDInform 278, an electronic data interchange product, designed to work with CarePlanner. The software met rules set by HIPPA for secure transmission of important decisions, such as physician referrals and authorization for healthcare services.

CONSOLIDATING CARE MANAGEMENT WORKFLOW

In 2003 MEDecision introduced its Integrated Medical Management (IMM) software, the first comprehensive system of patient information in the healthcare field.

IMM contained three components, all based on consistent rules for information processing. The first component, Analytics and Disease Management, provided managed care organizations with tools to determine an appropriate course of treatment based on established criteria. MEDecision's Advanced Medical Management software, a tool for assessing care and its results, supported clinical staff efficiency at the point of care, but managed care organizations would have access to this information as well. The Transactions and Automated Authorizations component provided the electronic link between healthcare providers and payers for processing of healthcare transactions, such as specialist referrals and authorizations for care.

MEDecision improved the comprehensiveness of IMM's clinical case management capabilities through collaboration with IFI Health Solutions in 2004. By combining IFI's bank of clinical best practices and related data with IMM, MEDecision sought to facilitate payer and provider decision making in a manner that melded with existing workflow processes.

MEDecision refined its data organization and transmission software, and in 2005 the company introduced the healthcare industry's first software solution to consolidate all of the information available on a patient. The Patient Clinical Summary (PCS) included health history, data from doctors, testing laboratories, pharmacies, and other service providers covered by a patient's health insurance. IMM retrieved and organized the information for delivery, and MEDecision's Transactions and Information Exchange service enabled the electronic transfer of a PCS to a healthcare payer or provider. The introduction of PCS marked a new direction for MEDecision, to place more emphasis on providing data access at the point of care. Patients would have access to the information as well.

MEDecision's 2003 acquisition of OptiMed Medical Systems provided the foundation for another suite of software designed for clinical use, the Clinical Rules and Processes module. MEDecision automated Optima's data set of criteria for clinical care, thus adding standards of care proven reliable to the array of information available for decision making at the point of care. The Clinical Rules and Processes module was marketed under two brands, OptiCareCert and OptiCarePath, introduced in 2003 and 2004, respectively. In June 2005 MEDecision announced that a best practices component would be available through the OptiCare-Path software as well. The groundbreaking technology provided evidence-based, clinical knowledge to the point of care for case and disease management. Both of the new products were intended to create consistency in healthcare delivery.

In June 2005, MEDecision established the CollaboraCare Consortium, an association of several software companies specializing in healthcare. The consortium provided its 15 members an opportunity to share knowledge that would contribute to making different healthcare information technologies compatible. Hence, each company's products became more valuable to users by facilitating information access across a wide array of databases. The first project of the consortium involved combining CapMed's array of portable personal health records with IMM.

MOMENTUM BUILDING TOWARD 2006 STOCK OFFERING

By meeting the demands of healthcare professionals for streamlined data management tools, MEDecision experienced rapid growth. With 16 new contracts in 2003, MEDecision reached a market share of 14 percent among managed care organizations comprised of 70,000 or more members. Ten new customers included Blue Cross Blue Shield organizations, including those located in Delaware, Massachusetts, and Oklahoma. Other business came from Anthem West, Health Plus of New York, Berkshire Health Plan, South Central Preferred, Cambridge Integrated Services Group, Inc., Health New England, and Health Partners.

Such growth required MEDecision to expand its headquarters, and the company relocated to a 35,000-square-foot office space in August 2004. A year later, after signing another seven contracts, the company leased an additional 14,000 square feet in a neighboring building. In addition to accommodating 7 percent growth in staff, the new office space provided room for another 23 percent expected growth by end of the year. MEDecision obtained another 13 contracts between August and the end of the year; these included contract renewals for MEDecision product licenses. With a total of 20 contracts, revenues increased 41 percent in 2005 to $38.6 million.

While the momentum of growth continued, MEDecision prepared to take the company public in December 2006. The offering was priced at $10 per share and took place in December. The company applied $9.5 million of net proceeds to pay dividends to preferred stock shareholders, while the balance supported ongoing operations and software development.

SEEKING MAJORITY MARKET WITH PATIENT CLINICAL SUMMARY

Having gained a significant share of the market for care management tools, MEDecision sought to further improve its standing by promoting its PCS software. Toward that end, MEDecision funded a study to determine the actual economic benefits of information access. HealthCore conducted the study in the context of incorporating MEDecision's Patient Clinical Summary in the workflow process of the emergency department at Christiana Care Health System's Level-1 Trauma Center in Wilmington, Delaware. HealthCore's financial analysis of PCS use showed an average $545 savings on expenses related to the emergency visit and the first day of hospitalization. Furthermore, the costs of laboratory testing, cardiac catheterization, and medical and surgical supplies were reduced due to access to patient data.

The study formed the basis for MEDecision's marketing strategy in 2007. The company determined to advance its information exchange products into the mainstream of care management. Through collaboration with healthcare payers and providers, MEDecision hoped to take advantage of the efficiencies and cost-saving potential of information exchange. In particular, MEDecision began to develop the PCS tool in a manner that addressed workflow problems and requirements of healthcare providers. MEDecision formed the Center for Collaborative Health to analyze information usage at the point of care and to develop standards that met the workflow needs of healthcare professionals.

A related goal involved developing technologies capable of accessing information from as yet untapped sources of patient information. Toward this end, MEDecision formed the Interoperability Competency Center (ICC) with the intention of developing an open technology platform that would ease information exchange across a wide range of operating systems. The ICC would develop standards for healthcare information system engineers to follow in order to ensure comprehensive access to diverse bases of data, regardless of what company's software was in use. Although the secure circulation of patient health information would benefit all software companies involved, MEDecision formed the ICC to establish itself as a national leader in data exchange tools for the healthcare industry.

MEDecision promoted its cooperative approach through ongoing educational forums on collaborative healthcare systems. Customers and partners in collaborative projects participated in conducting these forums. Following from the new emphasis on collaboration, IMM for health payers and components for healthcare providers were combined as Collaborative Care Management Solutions. MEDecision organized software under four categories: (1) Data Gathering and Analytics, (2) Clinical Rules and Processes, (3) Advanced Medical

Management, and (4) Collaborative Data Exchange, which included PCS.

The collaborative approach to PCS implementation attracted new and existing clients. In May 2007, Lovelace Health Plan of New Mexico licensed Advanced Medical Management, Data Gathering and Analysis, Clinical Data Exchange, and Patient Clinical Summary. Lovelace Health Plan sought to personalize healthcare delivery for more effective healthcare outcomes. Blue Cross and Blue Shield of Minnesota implemented a comprehensive set of Collaborative Care technologies in July. Hawaii Medical Service Association, covering more than 700,000 members, began a 12-month PCS test project in September. Blue Cross and Blue Shield of Louisiana implemented a Collaborative Care Management suite of software following an agreement signed in November 2007. MEDecision completed several collaborative interoperability projects for PCS implementation with Health Care Service Corporation, a mutual insurance company servicing healthcare plans for Blue Cross and Blue Shield in Illinois, Oklahoma, Texas, and New Mexico.

MEDecision's promotion of PCS to healthcare providers, for point of care management, resulted in expansion of its standing relationship with Memphis Managed Care Corporation (MMCC), which purchased a PCS license on a six-month test basis. MMCC provided the technology to healthcare providers in both group and independent practices throughout west Tennessee. A state-funded program to improve healthcare performance supported the PCS test. In collaboration with Medem, Inc., MEDecision applied the PCS technology to that company's existing online technology, the iHealth system, which provided patient health records at the point of care.

LAUNCH OF ALINEO AND NEXALIGN

At the end of 2007, MEDecision decided to reorganize its product offering by consolidating the four collaborative care modules into two, simplified Collaborative Care Management brand categories, Alineo and NexAlign. NexAlign encompassed MEDecision's data exchange services, with PCS as the technological focus of information organization.

In January 2008, MEDecision announced that Alineo programs would be available on a state-of-the-art technology platform. The Alineo program simplified earlier architecture underlying MEDecision's software for easier workflow operability, and it improved the process of analyzing and applying best practices as well as automatically integrating new standards for practice.

The Alineo product offered all of the information software required for utilization, case, and disease management, such as Alineo Case Management Analytics, Alineo Clinical Intelligence, Alineo Clinical Summaries, and Alineo Clinical Criteria. Other components covered reporting, programs, correspondence, automated authorizations, and workflow management.

MEDecision continued to emphasize the development of its clinical summaries. MEDecision formed a partnership with NextGen Healthcare Information Systems, Inc., to share information, as allowed by law. Thus, MEDecision gained access to practice management and electronic medical records available through NextGen. The partnership comprised an initial step toward two-way information exchange intended to benefit clients of both companies with a wider array of data for clinical use.

Technology under development at MEDecision in 2008 would exceed the capabilities and data access of the PCS. If successful, MEDeWeaver would gather, analyze, and organize information from several sources, including PCS and the NextGen's electronic health record, and Cap Med's personal health record. With beta testing underway, MEDecision expected to release MEDeWeaver in 2009.

Mary Tradii

PRINCIPAL COMPETITORS

Health Management Systems, Inc.; IMS Health, Inc.; Landacorp, Inc.; McKesson Corporation; Microsoft Dynamics; QuadraMed, Inc.; The TriZetto Group, Inc.

FURTHER READING

"Automated Adjudication," *Managed Healthcare Executive,* September 2003, p. 53.

"Collaboration Aims to Amplify Clinical Impact of Integrated Medical Management," *Managed Care Weekly,* September 27, 2004, p. 4.

Geiger, Mia, "David St. Clair," *Philadelphia Business Journal,* January 12, 2001, p. 14.

"MEDecision Hires Dr. Henry DePhillips As Chief Medical Officer," *Managed Care Weekly,* May 3, 2004, p. 133.

"Medical Management Software Company Reports Record Growth in 2003," *Managed Care Weekly,* March 22, 2004, p. 47.

"Software Electronically Transfers Patient Information," *Product News Network,* February 24, 2005.

"Software Helps Ensure Best Health Care Practices," *Product Network News,* June 29, 2005.

"Software Offers Collaborative Health Care Management," *Product Network News,* January 29, 2008.

Merck & Co., Inc.

One Merck Drive
P.O. Box 100
Whitehouse Station, New Jersey 08889-0100
U.S.A.
Telephone: (908) 423-1000
Toll Free: (800) 672-6372
Fax: (908) 423-1043
Web site: http://www.merck.com

Public Company
Incorporated: 1927
Employees: 59,800
Sales: $24.2 billion (2007)
Stock Exchanges: New York Philadelphia
Ticker Symbol: MRK
NAIC: 325412 Pharmaceutical Preparation Manufacturing; 325199 All Other Basic Organic Chemical Manufacturing; 325411 Medicinal and Botanical Manufacturing; 325413 In-Vitro Diagnostic Substance Manufacturing; 325414 Biological Product (Except Diagnostic) Manufacturing; 541710 Research and Development in the Physical, Engineering, and Life Sciences

■ ■ ■

Merck & Co., Inc., is one of the largest pharmaceutical companies in the world. Among the company's most important prescription drugs are Singulair, a treatment for asthma and allergies; Cozaar, Hyzaar, Vasotec, and Vaseretic, hypertension medications; Vytorin, Zetia, and Zocor, used to modify cholesterol levels; Cosopt and Trusopt, used to treat glaucoma; Fosamax, for the treatment and prevention of osteoporosis; Primaxin and Cancidas, antibacterial/antifungal products; Januvia and Janumet, treatments for type-2 diabetes; Crixivan, a protease inhibitor used in the treatment of HIV; Maxalt, a migraine treatment; and Propecia, a hair loss remedy. Merck also produces a number of vaccines, including ProQuad, M-M-R II, chicken pox vaccine Varivax, and Gardasil, designed to prevent most cervical cancer caused by human papillomavirus.

In addition, Merck develops, manufactures, and markets pharmaceuticals through a number of joint ventures, including: a partnership with Johnson & Johnson that concentrates on designing and commercializing over-the-counter versions of prescription medications, such as Pepcid AC and Pepcid Complete; a venture with Schering-Plough Corporation that develops and markets prescription medications in the areas of cholesterol management (including Vytorin and Zetia) and allergy/asthma treatments (including a combination of Singulair and Schering-Plough's Claritin); a venture with Sanofi Pasteur S.A., a unit of Sanofi-Aventis, focusing on the European vaccine market; and another partnership with Sanofi-Aventis concentrating on animal health and poultry genetics.

Merck spends around $5 billion each year on pharmaceutical research and development and maintains research laboratories in Rahway, New Jersey; West Point, Pennsylvania; Boston; Seattle; San Francisco; Montreal, Canada; Hoddesdon, United Kingdom; Pomezia and Rome, Italy; Riom, France; Madrid, Spain; and Tokyo, Tsukuba, Menuma, and Okazaki, Japan. Merck products are sold in more than 140 countries around the world.

COMPANY PERSPECTIVES

The mission of Merck is to provide society with superior products and services by developing innovations and solutions that improve the quality of life and satisfy customer needs, and to provide employees with meaningful work and advancement opportunities, and investors with a superior rate of return.

About 40 percent of the company's sales are generated outside the United States, with about 21 percent originating in Europe, the Middle East, and Africa and 6 percent in Japan.

GERMAN ORIGINS

Merck's beginnings can be traced back to Friedrich Jacob Merck's 1668 purchase of an apothecary in Darmstadt, Germany, called "At the Sign of the Angel." Located next to a castle moat, this store remained in the Merck family for generations.

The pharmacy was transformed by Heinrich Emmanuel Merck into a drug manufactory in 1827. His first products were morphine, codeine, and cocaine. By the time he died in 1855, products made by his company, known as E. Merck AG, were used worldwide. In 1887 E. Merck sent a representative, Theodore Weicker, to the United States to set up a sales office. Weicker (who would go on to own drug powerhouse Bristol-Myers Squibb) was joined by George Merck, the 24-year-old grandson of Heinrich Emmanuel Merck, in 1891. In 1899 the younger Merck and Weicker acquired a 150-acre plant site in Rahway, New Jersey, and started production in 1903. Weicker left the firm the following year.

The manufacture of drugs and chemicals at this site began in 1903. This same location housed the corporate headquarters of Merck & Co. and four of its divisions, as well as research laboratories and chemical production facilities, into the 1990s. (The company headquarters were shifted 20 miles west to Whitehouse Station, New Jersey, in 1992.) Once known as "Merck Woods," the land surrounding the original plant was used to hunt wild game and corral domestic animals. In fact, George Merck kept a flock of 15 to 20 sheep on the grounds to test the effectiveness of an animal disinfectant. The sheep became a permanent part of the Rahway landscape.

The year 1899 also marked the first year the *Merck Manual of Diagnosis and Therapy* was published. In 2006 the manual entered its 18th edition. A *New York Times* review once rated it "the most widely used medical text in the world." By the early 21st century, a number of other Merck manuals were available, including a home edition, *The Merck Manual of Health and Aging,* and *The Merck Veterinary Manual,* as well as online versions of the manuals.

In 1917, upon the entrance of the United States into World War I, George Merck, fearing anti-German sentiment, turned over a sizable portion of Merck stock to the Alien Property Custodian of the United States. This portion represented the company interest held by E. Merck AG, thereby ending Merck & Co.'s connection to its German parent. At the end of the war, Merck was rewarded for his patriotic leadership; the Alien Property Custodian sold Merck shares, worth $3 million, to the public. George Merck retained control of the corporation, and by 1919 the company was once again entirely public-owned.

GROWTH THROUGH MERGERS AND R&D

By 1926, the year George Merck died, his son George W. Merck had been acting president for more than a year. The first major event of the younger Merck's tenure, which would last 25 years, was the 1927 merger with Philadelphia-based Powers-Weightman-Rosengarten, a pharmaceutical firm best known for anti-malarial quinine. Following the merger, Merck incorporated his company as Merck & Co., Inc. The merger enabled Merck & Co. to increase its sales from $6 million in 1925 to more than $13 million in 1929. With the resultant expansion in capital, Merck initiated and directed the Merck legacy for pioneering research and development. In 1933 he established a large laboratory and recruited prominent chemists and biologists to produce new pharmaceutical products. Their efforts had far-reaching effects. En route to researching cures for pernicious anemia, Merck scientists discovered vitamin B12. Its sales, both as a therapeutic drug and as a constituent of animal feed, were massive.

The 1940s continued to be a decade of discoveries in drug research, especially in the field of steroid chemistry. In the early 1940s, a Merck chemist synthesized cortisone from ox bile, which led to the discovery of cortisone's anti-inflammation properties. In 1943 streptomycin, a revolutionary antibiotic used for tuberculosis and other infections, was isolated by a Merck scientist.

Despite the pioneering efforts and research success under George W. Merck's leadership, the company struggled during the postwar years. There were no

KEY DATES

1668: Friedrich Jacob Merck purchases an apothecary in Darmstadt, Germany.

1827: Heinrich Emmanuel Merck transforms the pharmacy into a drug manufactory.

1887: E. Merck AG sets up a sales office in the United States.

1891: George Merck, grandson of Heinrich Merck, joins the U.S. branch, known as Merck & Company.

1899: The *Merck Manual of Diagnosis and Therapy* is first published.

1903: U.S. production begins at a site in Rahway, New Jersey.

1917: Entrance of United States into World War I leads to severing of relationship between Merck & Co. and E. Merck AG.

1925: George W. Merck takes over as president, succeeding his father.

1927: Company merges with Powers-Weightman-Rosengarten and is incorporated as Merck & Co., Inc.

1940s: Merck's laboratories make a series of discoveries: vitamin B12, cortisone, streptomycin.

1953: Company merges with Sharp & Dohme, Incorporated.

1965: Henry W. Gadsen is named CEO and launches an ill-advised diversification program.

1976: John J. Honran succeeds Gadsen and reemphasizes drug research.

1979: Company begins marketing Enalapril, a high-blood-pressure inhibitor whose annual sales eventually reach $550 million.

1982: Merck enters into a partnership with Astra AB to sell that company's products in the United States.

1985: Dr. P. Roy Vagelos takes over as CEO; Vasotec, a treatment for congestive heart failure, is introduced.

1988: Vasotec becomes Merck's first billion-dollar-a-year drug.

1989: Over-the-counter medication joint venture is created with Johnson & Johnson.

1992: Zocor, a cholesterol-fighter, is introduced and eventually becomes a blockbuster.

1993: Medco Containment Services Inc., a drug distributor, is acquired for $6.6 billion.

1994: Raymond V. Gilmartin is named chairman and CEO, becoming the first outsider so named.

1995: Company divests its specialty chemicals businesses.

1998: Marketing of the asthma/allergy treatment Singulair begins.

1999: Astra pays Merck $1.8 billion stemming from a joint venture between the companies and from Astra's merger with Zeneca; arthritis medication Vioxx makes its debut.

2000: Merck enters into a partnership with Schering-Plough Corporation to develop and market cholesterol-management and allergy/asthma medications.

2003: Merck-Medco is spun off to shareholders as Medco Health Solutions, Inc.

2004: Merck is forced to withdraw Vioxx from the market after the drug is linked to increased risk of heart attack or stroke.

2005: Richard T. Clark replaces Gilmartin as CEO.

2007: Company reaches a $4.85 billion settlement of a class-action lawsuit representing tens of thousands of Vioxx claimants.

promising new drugs to speak of, and there was intense competition from foreign companies underselling Merck products, as well as from former domestic consumers beginning to manufacture their own drugs. Merck found itself in a precarious financial position.

A solution arrived in 1953 when Merck merged with Sharp & Dohme, Incorporated, a drug company with a similar history and reputation. Sharp and Dohme began as an apothecary shop in 1845 in Baltimore, Maryland. Its success in the research and development of such important products as sulfa drugs, vaccines, and blood plasma products matched the successes of Merck. The merger, however, was more than the combination of two industry leaders. It provided Merck with a new distribution network and marketing facilities to secure major customers. For the first time, Merck could market and sell drugs under its own name.

At the time of George W. Merck's death in 1957, company sales had surpassed $100 million annually. Although Albert W. Merck, a direct descendant of Friedrich Jacob Merck, continued to sit on the board of directors into the 1980s, the office of chief executive was never again held by a Merck family member.

DIVERSIFICATION, THEN A REEMPHASIS ON RESEARCH

Henry W. Gadsen became CEO in 1965 and, as was fashionable at the time, initiated a program of diversification. Among the businesses acquired in the late 1960s and early 1970s were Calgon Corporation, a supplier of water treatment chemicals and services; Kelco, a maker of specialty chemicals; and Baltimore Aircoil, a maker of refrigeration and industrial cooling equipment. Many of these businesses were quickly divested after it was discovered that profits were hard to come by, but Calgon and Kelco remained part of Merck into the early 1990s. Under Gadsen's emphasis on diversification, Merck's pharmaceutical operations suffered.

In 1976 John J. Honran succeeded the 11-year reign of Gadsen. Honran was a quiet, unassuming man who had entered Merck as a legal counselor and then became the corporate director of public relations. However, Honran's unobtrusive manner belied an aggressive management style. With pragmatic determination Honran not only continued the Merck tradition for innovation in drug research but also improved a poor performance record on new product introduction to the market.

This problem was most apparent in the marketing of Aldomet, an antihypertensive agent. Once the research was completed, Merck planned to exploit the discovery by introducing an improved beta-blocker called Blocadren. Yet Merck was beaten to the market by its competitors. Furthermore, because the 17-year patent protection on a new drug discovery was about to expire, Aldomet was threatened by generic manufacturers. This failure to beat its competitors to the market is said to have cost the company $200 million in future sales. A similar sequence of events occurred with Indocin and Clinoril, two anti-inflammation drugs for arthritis.

Under Honran's regime, the company introduced a hepatitis vaccine, a treatment for glaucoma called Timoptic, and Ivomac, an antiparasitic for animals. In addition, while Honran remained strongly committed to

financing a highly productive research organization, Merck began making improvements on research already performed by competitors. In 1979, for example, Merck began to market Enalapril, a high-blood-pressure inhibitor, similar to the drug Capoten, which was manufactured by Squibb. Sales for Enalapril reached $550 million in 1986. Honran also embarked on a more aggressive program for licensing foreign products. In 1982 Merck purchased rights to sell products from Swedish firm Astra AB in the United States; a similar arrangement was reached with Shionogi of Japan. Two years later the Merck-Astra agreement was transformed into a joint venture, Astra Merck Inc.

Honran's strategy proved very effective. Between 1981 and 1985, the company experienced a 9 percent annual growth rate, and in 1985 the *Wall Street Transcript* awarded Honran the gold award for excellence in the ethical drug industry. He was commended for the company's advanced marketing techniques and its increased production. At the time of the award, projections indicated a company growth rate for the next five years of double the present rate.

In 1984 Honran claimed Merck had become the largest U.S.-based manufacturer of drugs in the three largest markets: the United States, Japan, and Europe. He attributed this success to three factors: a productive research organization; manufacturing capability that allowed for cost-efficient, high-quality production; and an excellent marketing organization. The following year, Honran resigned as CEO. In 1986 his successor, Dr. P. Roy Vagelos, a biochemist and the company's former head of research, also was awarded the ethical drug industry's gold award.

SURVIVING VARIOUS DIFFICULTIES

Although Merck's public image was generally good, it had its share of controversy. In 1974 a $35 million lawsuit was filed against Merck and 28 other drug manufacturers and distributors of diethylstilbestrol (DES). This drug, prescribed to pregnant women in the late 1940s and up until the early 1960s, ostensibly prevented miscarriages. The 16 original plaintiffs claimed that they developed vaginal cancer and other related difficulties because their mothers had taken the drug. Furthermore, the suit charged that DES was derived from Stilbene, a known carcinogen, and that no reasonable basis existed for claiming the drugs were effective in preventing miscarriages. (A year before the suit, the Food and Drug Administration [FDA] banned the use of DES hormones as growth stimulants for cattle because tests revealed cancer-causing residues of the substance in some of the animals' livers. The FDA, however, did not conduct public hearings on this issue; consequently, a federal court overturned the ban.)

Under the plaintiffs' directive, the court asked the defendants to notify other possible victims and to establish early detection and treatment centers. More than 350 plaintiffs subsequently sought damages totaling some $350 billion.

The DES lawsuit was not the only issue to beleaguer Merck. In 1975 the company's name was added to a growing list of U.S. companies involved in illegal payments abroad. The payoffs, issued to increase sales in certain African and Middle Eastern countries, came to the attention of Merck executives through the investigation of the Securities and Exchange Commission (SEC). While sales amounted to $40.4 million for that year in those areas of the foreign market, the report uncovered a total of $140,000 in bribes. Once the SEC revealed its report, Merck initiated an internal investigation and took immediate steps to prevent future illegal payments.

Later, Merck found itself beset with new difficulties. In its attempt to win hegemony in Japan, the second largest pharmaceutical market in the world, Merck purchased more than 50 percent of the Banyu Pharmaceutical Company of Tokyo. Partners since 1954 under a joint business venture called Nippon Merck-Banyu (NMB), the companies used Japanese detail men (or pharmaceutical sales representatives) to promote Merck products.

When NMB proved inefficient, however, Merck bought out its partner for $315.5 million, more than 30 times Banyu's annual earnings. The acquisition was made in 1982, and Merck was still in the process of bringing Banyu into line with its more aggressive and imaginative management style in the early 1990s.

Problems in labor relations surfaced during the spring of 1985 when Merck locked out 730 union employees at the Rahway plant after failing to agree to a new contract. For three months prior to the expiration of three union contracts, involving 4,000 employees, both sides negotiated a new settlement. When talks stalled, however, the company responded by locking out employees. The unresolved issues involved both wages and benefits. By June 5, all 4,000 employees participated in a strike involving the Rahway plant and six other facilities across the nation.

The strike proved to be the longest in Merck's history, but after 15 weeks an agreement was finally reached. A company request for the adoption of a two-tier wage system that would permanently pay new employees lower wages was rejected, as was a union demand for wage increases and cost-of-living adjust-

ments during the first year. Nevertheless, Merck's reputation as an exceptional, high-paying workplace remained intact, and its subsequent contract agreements were amicable. In fact, Merck was ranked as one of the "100 Best Companies to Work for in America" and one of *Working Mother* magazine's "100 Best Companies for Working Mothers" since that ranking's 1986 inception.

BLOCKBUSTER MEDICATIONS, JOINT VENTURES, MEDCO

During the late 1980s, double-digit annual sales increases catapulted Merck to undisputed leadership of the pharmaceutical industry. CEO Vagelos's research direction in the 1960s and 1970s laid the foundation for Merck's drug "bonanza" of the 1980s. Vasotec, a treatment for congestive heart failure, was introduced in 1985 and became Merck's first billion-dollar-a-year drug by 1988. Mevacor, a cholesterol-lowering drug introduced in 1987, and ivermectin, the world's top-selling animal health product, also contributed to the company's impressive growth. In the late 1980s, Merck was investing hundreds of millions of dollars in research and development (R&D), 10 percent of the entire industry's total. Over the course of the decade, Merck's sales more than doubled, its profits tripled, and the company became the world's top-ranked drug company as well as one of *Business Week*'s ten most valuable companies.

The company also was recognized for its heritage of social responsibility. In the 1980s Merck made its drug for "river blindness," a parasitic infection prevalent in tropical areas and affecting 18 million people, available at no charge. In 1987 the company shared its findings regarding the treatment of human immunodeficiency virus (HIV) with competitors. These efforts reflected George W. Merck's assertion: "Medicine is for the patients. It is not for the profits. The profits follow, and if we have remembered that, they have never failed to appear. The better we have remembered it, the larger they have been."

Growth did slow in the early 1990s, however, as Merck's drug pipeline dried up. Although the company maintained the broadest product line in the industry, its stable of new drugs was conspicuously absent of the "blockbusters" that had characterized the previous decade, with one exception. In 1992 Merck introduced Zocor, a cholesterol-fighting drug that eventually surpassed $1 billion in annual sales and became the company's top-selling drug and one of the most successful pharmaceuticals in history.

In the meantime, Merck entered into a number of joint ventures that created alternative avenues of product development and marketing. In 1989 Merck joined with Johnson & Johnson in a venture to develop over-the-counter (OTC) versions of Merck's prescription medications, initially for the U.S. market, later expanded to Europe and Canada. Two years later Merck and E.I. du Pont de Nemours and Company formed a joint venture to research, manufacture, and sell pharmaceutical and imaging agent products. Merck and Connaught Laboratories, Inc. (later part of Aventis S.A.), agreed in 1992 to develop combination vaccines in the United States. In 1994 Merck created a venture with a related company, Pasteur Mérieux Connaught (which was also later part of Aventis S.A.), to market combination vaccines in Europe.

In 1993 Merck acquired Medco Containment Services Inc. for $6.6 billion. Medco was a mail-order distributor of drugs that was previously acquired by Martin Wygod in the early 1980s for $36 million. With the help of infamous investment banker Michael Milken, Wygod built Medco into a mass drug distribution system with $2.5 billion in revenues and $138 million in profits by 1992. The acquired company soon was renamed Merck-Medco Managed Care.

The wisdom of the purchase was debated among analysts. On one hand, it was regarded as making Merck more competitive in a U.S. healthcare industry dominated by cost-cutting managed care networks and health maintenance organizations. On the other hand, some observers noted that Merck's newest subsidiary would necessarily distribute competitors' drugs and that it had been a major proponent of discounting, which threatened to cut into Merck's R&D funds.

The Medco acquisition also complicated Vagelos's plans for a successor. Vagelos's choice, Richard J. Markham, resigned unexpectedly in mid-1993, just months before the CEO's anticipated retirement. Some observers speculated that 54-year-old Wygod, with his cost-cutting tendencies and marketing forte, was a likely successor, but he, too, resigned in March 1994. In the end, other internal candidates were bypassed as well in favor of the first outsider in Merck history to take the top job, Raymond V. Gilmartin. Named CEO in June 1994 and chairman in November of that year, Gilmartin had helped turn around medical equipment maker Becton, Dickinson & Company as that firm's chairman and CEO.

RESTRUCTURING AND DIVESTMENTS

Although Vagelos had built Merck into its position of industry preeminence by the time of his retirement, the entire pharmaceutical sector was in upheaval stemming from the growth of managed care. Sales and earnings growth were on the decline. Industry pressure resulted in large mergers that created Glaxo Wellcome plc and Novartis AG and toppled Merck from its position as the world's biggest drugmaker to a tie for third place with Germany's Hoechst Marion Roussel. Merck also was suffering from the difficult 18 months it took to find Vagelos's successor and the "turf-conscious, defection-ridden" culture (so described by *Business Week*'s Joseph Weber) that Vagelos left behind. One of Gilmartin's first major tasks, then, was to restructure the company's management team. In September 1994 he set up a 12-member management committee to help him run the company and plot strategies for growth. The management team included sales executives in Europe and Asia, the heads of the veterinary and vaccine divisions, the president of Merck-Medco, and executives from the research, manufacturing, finance, and legal areas. The creation of this committee helped to streamline and flatten Merck's organizational structure, fostered a greater degree of company teamwork, and halted the exodus of top managers that occurred during the Vagelos succession.

One of the management committee's first acts was to create a mission statement for Merck, which affirmed that the company was primarily a research-driven pharmaceutical company. Gilmartin then launched a divestment program, which jettisoned several noncore units, including a generic-drug operation and a managed mental-health care unit. In 1995 Merck sold its Kelco specialty chemicals division to Monsanto Company for $1.1 billion, and its other specialty chemicals unit, Calgon Vestal Laboratories, went to Bristol-Myers Squibb Company for $261 million. These sales also helped Merck pay down the debt it incurred in acquiring Medco, a unit that Gilmartin retained.

There were also two significant divestments in the late 1990s. In July 1997 Merck exited from the agribusiness sector when it sold its crop protection unit to Novartis for $910 million. In July 1998 Merck sold its half-interest in its joint venture with E.I. du Pont to its partner for $2.6 billion. Merck also restructured its animal health unit by combining it with that of Rhone-Poulenc S.A. to form Merial, a stand-alone joint venture created in August 1997. At the end of the 1990s Merial stood as the world's largest firm focusing on the discovery, manufacture, and marketing of veterinary pharmaceuticals and vaccines. By that time, Merck's partner in Merial was Aventis S.A., which had been formed from the late 1999 merger of Rhone-Poulenc and Hoechst A.G. (Aventis later, in 2004, merged with Sanofi-Synthélabo to create Sanofi-Aventis.)

Another joint venture, the one formed with Astra in 1982, was restructured in the late 1990s. This venture's biggest success came with the December 1996 approval of Prilosec for the treatment of ulcers and heartburn. Prilosec went on to become a blockbuster. In July 1998 Merck and Astra agreed to transform the joint venture into a new limited partnership in which Merck would have no management control but would hold a limited partnership interest and receive royalty payments. This gave Astra more flexibility in terms of seeking a merger partner, and in April 1999 the company merged with Zeneca Group Plc to form AstraZeneca AB. Stemming from this merger and the 1998 agreement between Merck and Astra, Merck received from Astra two one-time payments totaling $1.8 billion.

LATE-CENTURY DRUG INTRODUCTIONS

From 1995 through 1999, Merck introduced a total of 15 new drugs. Gilmartin helped bring these new products to market, but credit for developing them fell to Dr. Edward M. Scolnick, the research chief under Vagelos who stayed with the firm even though he had vied to succeed Vagelos. Within 18 months of Gilmartin's arrival, Merck had launched a record eight drugs, including Crixivan, a protease inhibitor used in the treatment of HIV; Fosamax, used to treat osteoporosis; and hypertension medication Cozaar. The eight drugs accounted for more than $1 billion in sales in 1996, about 10 percent of the company's total drug sales. Through its joint venture with Johnson & Johnson, Merck also received U.S. approval in April 1995 for the antacid Pepcid AC, an OTC version of Merck's Pepcid.

As the 1990s continued, Merck faced the specter of the expiration of patent protection for some of its biggest-selling products; Vasotec and Pepcid were slated to expire in 2000, Mevacor and Prilosec in 2001. These core drugs generated $5.2 billion in U.S. sales in 1997. Under intense pressure to replace this looming lost revenue, Merck continued its torrid pace of product debuts. In 1998 the company introduced a record five drugs: Singulair for asthma, Maxalt for migraine headaches, Aggrastat for acute coronary syndrome, Propecia for hair loss, and Cosopt for glaucoma. Of these, Singulair eventually became the company's top-selling drug, with worldwide sales of nearly $3.6 billion by 2006.

Merck managed only one drug introduction in 1999, but it was an immediate blockbuster. Making its U.S. debut in May 1999, Vioxx was part of a new category of pain drugs, dubbed Cox-2 inhibitors. Cox-2, an enzyme present in various diseases, was blocked by the new drugs. As a treatment for arthritis, Vioxx was noteworthy for being effective while not irritating the stomach. Despite being second to market behind G.D. Searle & Company's Celebrex, Vioxx had a remarkable first seven months in which U.S. physicians wrote more than five million prescriptions. The new medication was expected to have sales in 2000 of more than $1 billion, a rapid rise to that level.

Merck headed into the uncertainty of the early 21st century riding a triumphant 1999 wave. In addition to its successful introduction of Vioxx, the company was heartened by the continued strength of its top-selling drug, Zocor, which was gaining market share despite intense competition, particularly from Warner-Lambert Company's Lipitor. Worldwide sales of Zocor topped $2.6 billion in 1999. Overall sales that year increased 22 percent, reaching $32.71 billion, while net income increased 12 percent to $5.89 billion. Merck's worldwide pharmaceutical sales totaled $12.55 billion in 1999, placing the company in the number one position.

Drug company megamergers, however, were creating ever-larger competitors. The year 2000, for example, saw two such deals consummated: the U.K. marriage of Glaxo Wellcome plc and SmithKline Beecham plc that created GlaxoSmithKline plc, and the U.S. coupling of Pfizer Inc. and Warner-Lambert. Merck's Gilmartin stated that he had no interest in such a merger, despite the looming patent expirations. One apparent reason for Gilmartin's go-it-alone approach was the company's rapidly growing Merck-Medco unit, which achieved 1999 sales of $15.23 billion. The unit had established the world's biggest Internet-based pharmacy, merckmedco.com, and formed an alliance with CVS Corporation in 1999 to sell OTC medicines and general health products through this site. Merck-Medco also was helping enhance the sales of Merck drugs, although the FDA launched an investigation in the late 1990s into the practices of pharmacy-benefit management (PBM) firms, including whether any illegalities were taking place in regard to the PBMs steering patients to drugs made by a particular firm. At the same time, Merck continued its commitment to R&D, spending $2.3 billion on drug development in 2000.

PARTNERSHIP WITH SCHERING-PLOUGH

Also in 2000, Merck entered into a joint venture with Schering-Plough Corporation to develop and market cholesterol-management and allergy/asthma medications. The first outcome of this partnership was the October 2002 FDA approval of ezetimibe (U.S. brand name Zetia), a compound developed by Schering-Plough that blocks absorption of cholesterol from food in the intestinal tract. This cholesterol-management method differed from that of statins, such as Zocor, which interfered with the production of cholesterol in the liver. Sales of Zetia in the United States reached $1.2 billion by 2005 in part because many doctors began prescribing Zetia for their patients instead of increasing the dose of a statin.

Anticipating that Zetia might be used in this way, Merck and Schering-Plough had begun investigating a single-pill combination of Zocor and Zetia even prior to Zetia's approval. The FDA approved this combination pill in July 2004, and the partners began marketing it as Vytorin. The introductions of Zetia and Vytorin were critical for Merck because it was facing the expiration of Zocor's patent in 2006. Zocor was the company's top-selling drug in the first years of the 21st century, with worldwide sales reaching nearly $5.2 billion by 2004. By 2007, however, sales of the now off-patent Zocor had plunged to less than $900 million. In the meantime, Merck and Schering-Plough were enjoying soaring sales of Zetia and Vytorin, more than $5 billion combined worldwide in 2007. Both drugs remained under patent protection until 2015 because that was the expiration date for Zetia's patent. During this same period, Merck and Schering-Plough were exploring another compound pill, a combination of Merck's asthma drug Singulair with Schering-Plough's allergy fighter Claritin in the hope of creating a highly effective asthma and allergy medication.

Other than the cholesterol medications developed with Schering-Plough, Merck's drug development outcomes were fairly thin in the first years of the 21st century. The bad news continued in 2003 when the company ended development of two once-promising drugs that had reached late-phase clinical trials; a treatment for depression had failed to show efficacy, while mice given a diabetes drug had developed malignant tumors. In addition, Vioxx failed to maintain its original heady growth rate. Sales plateaued at $2.6 billion in 2001 after concerns surfaced over possible cardiovascular risks. Merck nevertheless remained committed to its research-driven approach, eschewing the big mergers that had reshaped the landscape of the pharmaceutical industry and spending nearly $3.2 billion on R&D in 2003.

Under pressure from shareholders, Merck took a number of actions in 2003 to strengthen its position. Merck-Medco was spun off to shareholders as Medco Health Solutions, Inc., a move that turned Merck back into a pure pharmaceutical research company. Merck purchased full control of Banyu Pharmaceutical for $1.53 billion, solidifying its position in Japan, the world's second largest pharmaceutical market. The company also launched a cost-cutting initiative, one ele-

ment of which was a workforce reduction of more than 5,000 that was designed to slash annual expenses by $300 million.

THE VIOXX DEBACLE AND ITS AFTERMATH

Merck encountered a new crisis in 2004 when the concerns about Vioxx's cardiovascular risks were borne out. The company withdrew the painkiller from the worldwide market after a clinical trial found that patients on the drug were twice as likely to have a heart attack or stroke as those on a placebo. A wave of lawsuits ensued. By May 2005 more than 2,400 suits had been filed on behalf of patients or survivors of patients claiming Vioxx had caused heart attacks and other cardiovascular problems. That month Gilmartin was forced into early retirement. Richard T. Clark, most recently the head of Merck's manufacturing operations, was named the new CEO.

Under Clark, Merck aggressively defended itself against the Vioxx liability suits, winning some crucial early cases while losing a number of others as well. By late 2007 the company had spent $1.2 billion on litigation and hundreds of millions more in payouts to patients. At that time, Merck entered into a settlement of a class-action lawsuit representing tens of thousands of claimants, agreeing to pay a total of $4.85 billion. As part of a five-year plan to revitalize Merck, Clark also launched a major restructuring program in late 2005 that involved the elimination of 7,000 positions from the worldwide workforce (an 11 percent reduction) and the closure or sale of five of its 31 manufacturing facilities around the world. This streamlining was designed to yield pretax savings of as much as $5 billion by 2010.

Under the direction of Peter S. Kim, who had succeeded Scolnick as head of research in 2003, and with a more disease-focused approach instilled by Clark, Merck developed a more robust new product pipeline, with the initial results most evident in the area of vaccines. In 2005 the FDA approved the vaccine RotaTeq for the prevention of rotavirus gastroenteritis, while three more Merck vaccines gained FDA approval in 2006: Pro-Quad, the first U.S. vaccine to protect against the four diseases measles, mumps, rubella, and chicken pox in one shot; Zostavex, used to help prevent shingles in patients over age 60; and Gardasil, the first vaccine in the United States to guard against human papillomavirus, believed to be the leading cause of cervical cancer cases. Gardasil was considered the most important of these approvals, particularly after the Centers for Disease Control and Prevention recommended the vaccine for all women between the ages of 11 and 26. Sales of Gardasil approached $1.5 billion by 2007. The spate of introductions pushed Merck's overall vaccine revenues up to $4.28 billion by 2007, nearly four times the $1.1 billion total for 2005 and nearly 18 percent of the company's overall 2007 revenues.

Part of the improved productivity of Merck's R&D efforts during this period stemmed from Clark's decision to focus on nine key disease areas. In addition to vaccines, these included Alzheimer's disease, atherosclerosis, cancer, cardiovascular disease, diabetes, obesity, pain management, and sleep disorders. Another drug securing FDA approval in 2006 was Januvia, the first of a new class of diabetes drugs touted to enhance the body's natural ability to improve blood sugar control in patients with type-2 diabetes. Sales of Januvia totaled $667.5 million in 2007. In October 2007 the FDA approved Isentress, a new type of drug for patients with HIV who had developed resistance to other therapies. This approval came just months before another company challenge arose—the expiration of patent protection for osteoporosis treatment Fosamax, which garnered more than $3 billion in worldwide revenues in 2007.

Merck needed to find additional winners in its product pipeline to maintain its momentum and to replace the revenues soon to be lost from further patent expirations. Its hypertension medications Cozaar and Hyzaar, which raked in a combined $3.35 billion in revenues in 2007, were slated to lose patent protection in 2010, with asthma/allergy drug Singulair following two years later. In 2007 Singulair was Merck's top-selling single drug, with worldwide sales of $4.27 billion.

Merck's momentum, however, appeared to hit another significant roadblock in early 2008 when a panel of cardiologists recommended that widespread use of Vytorin and Zetia should be curtailed after a study found they were no better at fighting heart disease than the far-less expensive generic version of Zocor. On this damaging news for their blockbuster cholesterol-fighting drugs, Merck and Schering-Plough saw their stock prices plunge, with Merck's market capitalization slashed $14.3 billion in a single day. Doctors and public officials began raising allegations that the companies had delayed release of the study's results to protect their sales of Vytorin and Zetia, and a Congressional committee launched a probe. The companies denied these allegations and took exception to the panel's recommendation. Some researchers questioned the validity of the study's design and placed greater stock in a much larger study underway that was comparing how Vytorin stacked up against Zocor in preventing deaths and heart attacks in very high-risk patients. The results of this study were expected in 2011.

April Dougal Gasbarre
Updated, David E. Salamie

PRINCIPAL SUBSIDIARIES

Abmaxis Inc.; Banyu Pharmaceutical Company, Ltd. (Japan); Chibret Pharmazeutische GmbH (Germany); GlycoFi, Inc.; Hangzhou MSD Pharmaceutical Company Limited (China); Johnson & Johnson–Merck Consumer Pharmaceuticals Company (50%); Merck Cardiovascular Health Company; Merck Frosst Canada Ltd.; Merck Oncology Holdings, Inc.; Merck Respiratory Health Company; Merck Sharp & Dohme (Argentina) Inc.; Merck Sharp & Dohme (Asia) Limited (Hong Kong); Merck Sharp & Dohme (Australia) Pty. Limited; Merck Sharp & Dohme (China) Limited; Merck Sharp & Dohme (Europe) Inc.; Merck Sharp & Dohme (Holdings) B.V. (Netherlands); Merck Sharp & Dohme (Holdings) Limited (U.K.); Merck Sharp & Dohme (Italia) S.p.A. (Italy); Merck Sharp & Dohme (Middle East) Limited (Cyprus); Merck Sharp & Dohme (New Zealand) Limited; Merck Sharp & Dohme (Sweden) A.B.; Merck Sharp & Dohme (Switzerland) GmbH; Merck Sharp & Dohme B.V.; Merck Sharp & Dohme Bulgaria EOOD; Merck Sharp & Dohme d.o.o. (Croatia); Merck Sharp & Dohme de Espana, S.A. (Spain); Merck Sharp & Dohme de Mexico S.A. de C.V.; Merck Sharp & Dohme de Venezuela S.R.L.; Merck Sharp & Dohme Farmaceutica Ltda. (Brazil); Merck Sharp & Dohme GmbH (Austria); Merck Sharp & Dohme Ísland hf (Iceland); Merck Sharp & Dohme Limited (U.K.); Merck Sharp & Dohme Manufacturing (Ireland); Merck Sharp & Dohme Peru SRL; Merck Sharp & Dohme Pharmaceuticals LLC (Russia); Merck Sharp & Dohme Romania SRL; Merck Sharp & Dohme, Limitada (Portugal); Merck Sharp & Dohme Holdings de Mexico, S.A. de C.V.; Merck Sharp & Dohme Ilaclari Limited Sirketi (Turkey); Merial Limited (U.K.); Merial LLC; MSD (Norge) A/S (Norway); MSD (Proprietary) Limited (South Africa); MSD (Shanghai) Pharmaceuticals Consultancy Co., Ltd.; MSD (Thailand) Ltd.; MSD International Holdings, Inc.; MSD Korea Ltd.; MSD Limited (U.K.); MSD Magyarország Kft; MSD Overseas Manufacturing Co. (Ireland); MSD Pharmaceuticals Private Limited (India); MSD Polska Sp.z.o.o. (Poland); MSD Scandinavia AS (Norway); MSD Sharpe & Dohme GmbH (Germany); MSD Unterstutzungskasse GmbH (Germany); NovaCardia, Inc.; P.T. Merck Sharpe & Dohme Indonesia; Sharp & Dohme, S.A. (Spain); Sirna Therapeutics, Inc.;

The MSD Foundation Limited (U.K.); Variopharm Arzneimittel GmbH (Germany).

PRINCIPAL COMPETITORS

Pfizer Inc.; Novartis AG; Bristol-Myers Squibb Company; Sanofi-Aventis; GlaxoSmithKline plc; Bayer AG.

FURTHER READING

Abelson, Reed, "Out of the Merger Rush, Merck's on a Limb," *New York Times,* August 4, 2002, pp. B1+.

Baldo, Anthony, "Merck Plays Hardball," *Financial World,* June 26, 1990, pp. 22+.

Barrett, Amy, "Can Merck Grow Without a Megamerger?" *Business Week,* June 22, 1998, p. 40.

———, "Merck Could Use a Few Pep Pills," *Business Week,* December 17, 2001, pp. 128–29.

———, "Merck: Out of the Ivory Tower," *Business Week,* March 6, 2006, pp. 64–65.

Byrne, John A., "The Miracle Company," *Business Week,* October 19, 1987, pp. 84+.

Carreyrou, John, "Merck's Chief Leads a Revival, but Will It Last?" *Wall Street Journal,* November 13, 2006, p. B1.

Carreyrou, John, and Barbara Martinez, "Resistant Strain: Research Chief Stirs Up Merck by Seeking Aid from Outsiders," *Wall Street Journal,* June 7, 2006, pp. A1+.

Eklund, Christopher S., and Judith H. Dobrynski, "Merck: Pouring Money into Basic Research to Replace an Aging Product Line," *Business Week,* November 26, 1984, pp. 114+.

Freudenheim, Milt, "With Ties Lingering, Medco Leaves Merck," *New York Times,* August 20, 2003, p. C2.

Galambos, Louis, *Values and Visions: A Merck Century,* Rahway, N.J.: Merck & Co., 1991, 192 p.

Galambos, Louis, and Jane Eliot Sewell, *Networks of Innovation: Vaccine Development at Merck, Sharp, & Dohme, and Mulford, 1895–1995,* New York: Cambridge University Press, 1995, 273 p.

Gannes, Stuart, "Merck Has Made Biotech Work," *Fortune,* January 19, 1987, p. 58.

Harris, Gardiner, "Back to the Lab: Merck to Shed Medco, Its Drug-Benefits Unit, in Bid to Boost Stock," *Wall Street Journal,* January 29, 2002, pp. A1+.

———, "Cold Turkey: How Merck Intends to Ride Out a Wave of Patent Expirations," *Wall Street Journal,* February 9, 2000, pp. A1, A8.

———, "The Cure: With Big Drugs Dying, Merck Didn't Merge—It Found New Ones," *Wall Street Journal,* January 10, 2001, pp. A1+.

———, "Drug Makers Pair Up to Fight Key Patent Losses," *Wall Street Journal,* May 24, 2000, p. B1.

Hawthorne, Fran, *The Merck Druggernaut: The Inside Story of a Pharmaceutical Giant,* Hoboken, N.J.: Wiley, 2003, 290 p.

Johnson, Avery, "After a Revival, Merck CEO Clark Faces Trying Spring," *Wall Street Journal,* March 25, 2008, pp. B1, B2.

Koberstein, Wayne, "The Inner Merck: Chairman Ray Gilmartin Charts Pace-Setting Growth," *Pharmaceutical Executive,* January 2000, pp. 44–48+.

Kolata, Gina, "A Widely Used Arthritis Drug Is Withdrawn," *New York Times,* October 1, 2004, pp. A1, C4.

Landers, Peter, and Joann S. Lublin, "Under a Microscope: Merck's Big Bet on Research by Its Scientists Comes Up Short," *Wall Street Journal,* November 28, 2003, pp. A1+.

Langreth, Robert, "Merck Raises Its Estimate of Astra Sum," *Wall Street Journal,* December 10, 1998, p. B7.

Martinez, Barbara, "Merck Will Slash Work Force by 11%," *Wall Street Journal,* November 29, 2005, p. A3.

Martinez, Barbara, Anna Wilde Mathews, Joann S. Lublin, and Ron Winslow, "Expiration Date: Merck Pulls Vioxx from Market After Link to Heart Problems," *Wall Street Journal,* October 1, 2004, pp. A1+.

Martinez, Barbara, and Joann S. Lublin, "Change of Formula: Merck Replaces Embattled CEO with Insider Richard Clark," *Wall Street Journal,* May 6, 2005, pp. A1+.

"Mercky Waters," *Economist,* May 24, 1997, pp. 59–61.

Nossiter, Daniel D., "Blue Chip Bet on Research: Merck to Launch Raft of New Products," *Barron's,* November 8, 1982, pp. 16+.

O'Reilly, Brian, "Why Merck Married the Enemy," *Fortune,* September 20, 1993, pp. 60–64.

Petersen, Melody, "Pushing Pills with Piles of Money," *New York Times,* October 5, 2000, p. C1, C8.

Reingold, Jennifer, "Mercky Waters," *Financial World,* January 17, 1995, pp. 28–29.

Robertson, Wyndham, "Merck Strains to Keep the Pots Aboiling," *Fortune,* March 1976, p. 134.

Rubenstein, Sarah, "Merck Posts $1.63 Billion Loss on Vioxx Charges," *Wall Street Journal,* January 31, 2008, p. B6.

Rubenstein, Sarah, and Avery Johnson, "Merck to Pay over $650 Million to Settle Pricing Suits," *Wall Street Journal,* February 8, 2008, p. B4.

Scheibla, Shirley Hobbs, "Merck's Main Man: He Sees New Drugs Sparking Continued Growth," *Barron's,* November 11, 1985, pp. 13+.

Seiden, Carl, "Why Merck Has to Run Just to Stay in Place," *Medical Marketing and Media,* August 1998, pp. 38–40, 42, 44, 46.

Simons, John, "From Scandal to Stardom: How Merck Healed Itself," *Fortune,* February 18, 2008, pp. 94–96, 98.

———, "Merck's Man in the Hot Seat," *Fortune,* February 23, 2004, pp. 111–12, 114.

———, "Will R&D Make Merck Hot Again?" *Fortune,* July 8, 2002, pp. 89–90, 92, 94.

Simons, John, and David Stipp, "Will Merck Survive Vioxx?" *Fortune,* November 1, 2004, pp. 90–92+.

Smith, Lee, "Merck Has an Ache in Japan," *Fortune,* March 18, 1985, pp. 42+.

Tanouye, Elyse, "Drug Makers' PBM Strategy Produces Uneven Results," *Wall Street Journal,* February 11, 1998, p. B4.

————, "Gilmartin, Merck's New CEO, Expected to Try Approaches He Used at Becton," *Wall Street Journal,* June 13, 1994, p. B6.

Tanouye, Elyse, and Stephen D. Moore, "Novartis to Pay $910 Million for Merck Business," *Wall Street Journal,* May 14, 1997, p. A3.

Tesoriero, Heather Won, "Trouble Brews over Merck Product: As Closure Nears on Vioxx Claims, Fosamax Meets Challenges, Patent Loss," *Wall Street Journal,* January 30, 2008, p. A12.

Tesoriero, Heather Won, Sarah Rubenstein, and Jamie Heller, "Merck's Tactics Largely Vindicated As It Reaches Big Vioxx Settlement," *Wall Street Journal,* November 10, 2007, p. A1.

Vagelos, P. Roy, and Louis Galambos, *The Moral Corporation: Merck Experiences,* New York: Cambridge University Press, 2006, 185 p.

Warren, Susan, "DuPont Is Paying Merck $2.6 Billion to Buy Out 50% Stake in Drug Venture," *Wall Street Journal,* May 20, 1998, p. A4.

Weber, Joseph, "Merck Finally Gets Its Man," *Business Week,* June 27, 1994, p. 22.

————, "Merck Is Showing Its Age," *Business Week,* August 23, 1993, pp. 72–74.

————, "Merck Needs More Gold from the White Coats," *Business Week,* March 18, 1991, pp. 102+.

————, "Merck Wants to Be Alone—but with Lots of Friends," *Business Week,* October 23, 1989, p. 62.

————, "Mr. Nice Guy with a Mission," *Business Week,* November 25, 1996, pp. 132+.

————, "Suddenly, No Heir Is Apparent at Merck," *Business Week,* July 26, 1993, p. 29.

Weintraub, Arlene, "Is Merck's Medicine Working?" *Business Week,* July 30, 2007, pp. 66–68, 70.

"What the Doctor Ordered," *Time,* August 18, 1952.

Willatt, Norris, "Merck's Unlimited Medicine," *Management Today,* May 1981, pp. 82+.

Winslow, Ron, "Panel Deals Blow to Two Cholesterol Drugs," *Wall Street Journal,* March 31, 2008, p. B6.

Winslow, Ron, and Sarah Rubenstein, "Delays in Drug's Test Fuel Wider Data Debate," *Wall Street Journal,* March 24, 2008, pp. A1, A11.

————, "Study Deals Setback to Vytorin Cholesterol Drug," *Wall Street Journal,* January 15, 2008, p. A3.

MGA Entertainment, Inc.

—■—

16300 Roscoe Boulevard, Suite 150
Van Nuys, California 91406
U.S.A.
Telephone: (818) 894-2525
Toll Free: (800) 222-4685
Fax: (818) 894-8094
Web site: http://www.mgae.com

Private Company
Incorporated: 1998
Employees: 1,000
Sales: $2.5 billion (2006 est.)
NAIC: 339931 Doll and Stuffed Toy Manufacturing

■ ■ ■

MGA Entertainment, Inc., is the largest privately owned toy company in the world, a distinction it earned from its enormously successful line of Bratz fashion dolls. The company markets a variety of doll sets and action figures, including Alien Racers, Yummi-Land Soda Pop Girls, and Storytime Princesses, but the Bratz line of dolls and accessories drives its financial growth. The Bratz line includes playsets, vehicles, and accessories that the company distributes in more than 65 countries through more than 400 licensees.

THE EMERGENCE OF ISAAC LARIAN

In the early 21st century, a contentious battle took place in the toy industry. The world's largest publicly owned competitor was squaring off against the world's largest privately owned competitor. In the marketplace and in court, the venerable industry giant, Mattel, Inc., was fighting against the incursive threat of a relative upstart, its crosstown rival, MGA Entertainment. For Mattel, the might displayed by its new nemesis was a shock. When Mattel celebrated its 50th anniversary in 1995, MGA Entertainment, in name, did not exist. A decade later, Mattel executives were all too familiar with the name, both of the company and its founder and leader, Isaac Larian.

Born in Kashan, Iran, Larian immigrated to the United States in 1971, exactly 30 years before he would wreak havoc on Mattel's stalwart position in the fashion doll market. While a teenager in Iran, Larian helped his father run a retail textile business, an introduction to the entrepreneurial world that would have a lasting effect on the teenager. He arrived in the United States at age 17 with $750 in his pocket and a desire to further his education. He got a job washing dishes at a diner and eventually worked his way through college, earning a civil engineering degree in 1978 from California State University at Los Angeles.

Not long after leaving college, Larian began trying his luck as an entrepreneur. He never put his degree to use. "I have always been interested in the exhilarating nature of selling a product," he said in a November 21, 2007, interview published on www.america.gov, a U.S. Department of State web site. His interests varied early on as he tried to find a business that could develop some marketing muscle. First, he imported textiles and brassware through a mail-order company named ABC International Traders Inc. Next, in 1979, he founded a

---

company named Surprise Gift Wagon, an entity that marked his entry into the consumer electronics market. Larian began importing and distributing brand-name electronics products, a business that he used to forge important relationships with manufacturers in Japan.

Larian's ability to earn the esteem of Japanese manufacturers enabled him to record more than modest success with his business. He became a major importer of Sony Walkmans and registered his first big success in 1987, when he became the first U.S. licensor of hand-held LCD (liquid crystal display) games featuring characters created by Nintendo. His company eventually became known as Micro-Games of America Entertainment, Inc., the name it was operating under when he brokered his second major deal. In 1993, Larian secured the rights to Power Rangers action figures, giving his company a share in the market success of one of the most popular toys during the year's Christmas season.

SHIFTING STRATEGY IN 1997

Larian enjoyed sharing in the success of market winners, but it was not difficult to discern that licensors made considerably more money than licensees did. He decided to change his strategy. He moved away from electronics and securing licensing rights and geared his company to compete in the market for family entertainment products. In 1997, he introduced his first doll, Singing Bouncing Baby, and realized impressive success with his inaugural effort. Micro-Games of America sold one million dolls during the first year, which earned the company the Toy Association's "Family Fun Toy" of the year award. The following year, Larian changed the name of his company to MGA Entertainment, Inc., and began searching for his next big hit.

MEETING WITH CARTER BRYANT IN 2000

MGA Entertainment and the fashion doll industry changed substantially after Larian and a toy designer named Carter Bryant collaborated. In 2000, Bryant went to see Larian at MGA Entertainment's headquarters. He had some drawings of dolls, hoping to interest Larian in his designs, but Larian was unimpressed. The meeting would have ended there had not Larian's daughter, 11-year-old Jasmine, been asked for her opinion. Jasmine loved the drawings, which convinced her father to move forward with bringing Bryant's concept into production. The decision, which was rued by Mattel and celebrated by MGA Entertainment, had profound consequences. MGA Entertainment generated $110 million in revenue in 2000. A few years later, the company boasted annual revenues of $2.5 billion. For Mattel, the decision triggered the first genuine threat to the dominance of its Barbie doll, that was familiar to generations worldwide for more than 40 years as an American icon.

Introduced in 1959, blonde-haired, blue-eyed Barbie had held sway as the preeminent fashion doll for 40 years, rarely having to parry any serious threat by a rival doll. Over time, however, a weakness had developed, one that Larian intended to exploit. Changes in styles and tastes had narrowed the marketing range of Barbie to ages between three and six, as girls between the ages of 7 and 13 began to relate less with the image exuded by Barbie, a phenomenon in the toy industry known as "age compression."

When Larian decided to use Bryant's drawings to create a line of dolls called Bratz, he targeted the demographic that represented the soft underbelly of Barbie. "Up until Bratz dolls were first introduced in 2001, most people who tried to get into the fashion doll business basically took a Barbie figure and changed her hair and makeup, but really didn't tweak the form," an analyst explained in an April 28, 2003, interview with the *San Fernando Valley Business Journal*. "What MGA has done is kind of take a piece of MTV and bolt it onto a doll, and they came up with a whole new look that was much more sassy, much more appealing to this new mindset of young girls."

THE "DOLL WAR," BEGINS IN 2001

The competition between MGA Entertainment and Mattel began in June 2001, when Barbie faced not one but four new adversaries: Cloe, Sasha, Jade, and Yasmin. The Bratz lineup featured ten-inch dolls with different skin tones, shoes that could be snapped on and off, and proportions that were cartoonish: large heads, wide eyes, small noses, and short torsos. The dolls, marketed as "The Girls with a Passion for Fashion," were dressed in eclectic styles that included bell-bottom jeans, glittery

KEY DATES

1997: Isaac Larian introduces his first doll, Singing Bouncing Baby.

1998: Larian changes the name of his company from Micro-Games of America Entertainment to MGA Entertainment, Inc.

2000: Toy designer Carter Bryant shows Larian drawings of what will become the Bratz dolls.

2001: The original four Bratz dolls are released in June.

2006: After signing more than 400 licensing agreements, MGA Entertainment collects an estimated $2.5 billion in revenue.

miniskirts, chunky platform shoes, cropped shirts, and halter tops. The dolls retailed for $14.99 each.

Cloe, Sasha, Jade, and Yasmin captured the hearts of the "tweens" the dolls were created for, inundating Larian with orders. He realized he had struck gold and wasted little time before taking advantage of the popularity of the dolls. MGA Entertainment's sales shot up from $110 million to $200 million by the end of 2001, as manufacturers in China churned out as many of the dolls as they could, but in succeeding years the pace of financial growth accelerated, reaching a fever pitch. Revenues reached $500 million in 2002 and were projected to hit the $1 billion mark the following year, staggering growth that was fueled by Larian's aggressive activity in two areas: product line extension and licensing.

Larian, once the licensee, reveled in the opportunity to act as the licensor. The first four dolls were joined by ancillary dolls such as Lil' Bratz and the Bratz Babyz, while Cloe, Sasha, Jade, and Yasmin appeared on retail shelves in numerous reincarnations such as the Play Sportz line, which featured the dolls dressed for different sporting activities, and, with the addition of Roxxi and Meygan, and the Rock Angelz, a line of Bratz dolls dressed in 1970s inspired rock attire. Accessories such as playsets and vehicles were released, but the greatest proliferation of the brand occurred through a seemingly endless number of licensing agreements orchestrated by Larian. The Bratz brand diversified into consumer electronics, apparel, housewares, video games, books, and personal care products. Larian signed an agreement with Colgate-Palmolive Company to license a Bratz toothbrush and toothpaste line. A Bratz cartoon aired on cable television. A Bratz shoe and apparel line was released. Karaoke products based on the Bratz dolls were sold. A Bratz mobile telephone was released, featuring 50 minutes of nationwide airtime and exclusive Bratz wallpapers, voice ringtones, and screen savers. MGA Entertainment, in a joint effort with Avi Arad Productions and Crystal Sky Pictures, began producing a live-action, feature film based on the Bratz dolls.

A GLOBAL PHENOMENON AND LEGAL ISSUES

Within the first five years of the Bratz line's debut, Larian signed more than 400 licensing agreements with partners worldwide. Bratz enjoyed stunning success in markets in the United Kingdom, France, Germany, Italy, Australia, the Caribbean, South Africa, Canada, Puerto Rico, and in dozens of other countries. The dolls were a global force that caused a great deal of worry among Mattel executives who, for the first time in 40 years, watched a fashion doll chip away at Barbie's market share.

Mattel, headquartered a short drive south from MGA Entertainment, was forced to respond to the inroads made by Bratz dolls and accessories. The company revamped Barbie, giving her a trendier style, and signed sponsorship deals with teenage celebrities. Larian, emboldened by his success, shrugged off Barbie's makeover, belittling Mattel's attempt to rekindle the doll's appeal. "I don't care if they sign the Olsen twins and call it Bulimic Barbie," he said in a May 2, 2005, interview with *Business Week*. "Kids don't want to play with Barbies anymore."

The battle between MGA Entertainment and Mattel also occurred on a legal front. In one dispute with Larian's company, Mattel alleged Carter Bryant was a Mattel employee when he developed the Bratz drawings. In another legal salvo, Mattel claimed that three of its employees in Mexico had created a private e-mail account to correspond with MGA Entertainment and relay trade secrets. For its part, MGA Entertainment sued Mattel, accusing the company of unfair competition, intellectual property infringement, serial copycatting, and of harassing retailers and licensees for doing business with MGA Entertainment.

THE STAYING POWER OF BRATZ

Against the backdrop of the various legal tussles, the Bratz franchise was demonstrating impressive staying power. Revenues rose to an estimated $2.5 billion in 2006, a total largely collected from the plethora of Bratz merchandise sold by retailers in dozens of countries. As

Larian looked to the future, he continued to emphasize expanding the Bratz franchise—he opened sales offices in Europe in 2006 and planned to enter Latin America and Asia in 2007—and he also concluded deals to build MGA Entertainment's business in other areas. In late 2006, he announced he was acquiring The Little Tikes Co. Based in Hudson, Ohio, the company made toys, plastic furniture, inflatable bouncers, playhouses, and a variety of other products for infants, toddlers, and preschoolers. In mid-2007, MGA Entertainment acquired a majority stake in a French toy company, Smoby-Majorette.

Larian was exploring opportunities for the future, but as preparations were being made to celebrate the tenth anniversary of the MGA Entertainment name, his focus remained on the top-selling Bratz brand. In 2007, the year Bratz became the number one fashion doll in Canada, the list of new product introductions demonstrated that the Bratz franchise had yet to be exhausted. The company released Bratz Fashion Pixies Dolls, Bratz Xtreme Skateboarding RC Dolls, and the Bratz Babyz Mermaidz. In the years ahead, the list of merchandise was expected to grow longer, giving parents and their children myriad opportunities to bring the Bratz brand into their homes.

Jeffrey L. Covell

PRINCIPAL SUBSIDIARIES

The Little Tikes Company.

PRINCIPAL COMPETITORS

Mattel, Inc.; Hasbro, Inc.; JAKKS Pacific, Inc.

FURTHER READING

"Bratz Brand to Be Given Hi-Tech-Style Makeover," *Marketing Week,* September 13, 2007, p. 5.

"Bratz Mobile Phones Headed for Wal-Mart," *Wireless News,* January 26, 2006.

"Bratz Takes the Coveted No. 1 Fashion Doll Spot in Canada," *CNW Group,* April 11, 2007.

Fox, Jacqueline, "McDonald's Deal Feeds on Popularity of Bratz Dolls," *San Fernando Valley Business Journal,* April 28, 2003, p. 11.

Garcia, Shelly, "MGA Entertainment Buying Times Property," *San Fernando Valley Business Journal,* September 25, 2006, p. 41.

Garrahan, Matthew, "Barbie and Bratz Square Up for Court Battle," *Financial Times,* April 27, 2007, p. 22.

"Hand-Held Games," *Discount Store News,* November 8, 1999, p. 57.

Kandyba, Slav, "Successful Bratz Dolls Move into Hollywood," *San Fernando Valley Business Journal,* March 1, 2004, p. 5.

Palmeri, Christopher, "Totally Teed-Off Barbie," *Business Week,* December 18, 2006, p. 13.

"They Call It Puppy Love," *Playthings,* February 2000, p. 16.

"Videos to Support New Barbie, Bratz Lines," *DSN Retailing Today,* June 21, 2004, p. 23.

Weiss, Jeff, "MGA Expands in Europe," *San Fernando Valley Business Journal,* October 10, 2005, p. 9.

Wilensky, Dawn, "Doll Wars," *License!* June 2006, p. 48.

Zbar, Jeffery D., "Bratz, Isaac Larian, Founder-CEO, MGA Entertainment," *Advertising Age,* November 17, 2003, p. S17.

Murphy Oil Corporation

200 Peach Street
Post Office Box 7000
El Dorado, Arkansas 71731-7000
U.S.A.
Telephone: (870) 862-6411
Fax: (870) 864-6373
Web site: http://www.murphyoilcorp.com

Public Company
Incorporated: 1950 as Murphy Corporation
Employees: 7,539
Sales: $18.42 billion (2007)
Stock Exchanges: New York
Ticker Symbol: MUR
NAIC: 211111 Crude Petroleum and Natural Gas
     Extraction; 324110 Petroleum Refineries; 424710
     Petroleum Bulk Stations and Terminals; 447190
     Other Gasoline Stations

∎∎∎

Murphy Oil Corporation is a moderate-sized U.S.-based integrated oil company, with worldwide exploration and production activities and refining and marketing operations confined to the United States and the United Kingdom. Murphy conducts onshore and offshore oil and gas exploration and production mainly in the United States (particularly the Gulf of Mexico), western Canada and offshore eastern Canada, the United Kingdom's North Sea, Ecuador, Malaysia, and the Republic of Congo. The company owns two U.S. oil refineries located in Meraux, Louisiana, and Superior,

Wisconsin, and one in the United Kingdom at Milford Haven, Wales. On the marketing side, Murphy sells refined products through approximately 150 SPUR wholesale stations and more than 970 Murphy USA retail gasoline stations in 23 states in the southern and midwestern United States. Most of the Murphy USA outlets are located in the parking areas of discount retail giant Wal-Mart Stores, Inc. In the United Kingdom, Murphy sells refined products via nearly 400 gasoline stations, most of which operate under the MURCO name.

EARLY YEARS: FROM TIMBER TO OIL EXPLORATION

The Murphy story began in the early 1900s in El Dorado, Arkansas, where Charles H. Murphy Sr. started a lumber company with thousands of acres of timberland along the Arkansas-Louisiana border. Although he drilled his first oil well in the Caddo Pool of northern Louisiana in 1907, his primary efforts in oil exploration did not actually commence until 1936, when he and his associates discovered two large oilfields in southern Texas and Arkansas. At this time Murphy realized his land holdings were worth more for oil than for timber.

Murphy's business interests gradually expanded into a loose collection of partnerships, corporations, and individual holdings. In 1944, after he and his associates discovered their largest deposit near Delhi, Louisiana, they brought their diverse entities together as C.H. Murphy & Company.

Charles H. Murphy suffered a stroke late in the decade, and his son, 21-year-old Charles H. Murphy, Jr., was put in charge during his subsequent illness. With his new role in the company the younger Murphy was not able to attend college but eventually educated himself by reading the classics and learning foreign languages, and his ambitions grew with the goals of the company. He saw that corporate status would be necessary to achieve company objectives, so, in 1950 he incorporated C.H. Murphy & Company as Murphy Corporation, the direct predecessor of Murphy Oil Corporation.

During the early 1950s, Murphy continued to explore for oil on the more than 100,000 acres of company-owned land, which also contained timber and farming operations. In 1956, two years after Charles H. Murphy Sr. died, his son brought the company public, offering shares on the New York Stock Exchange.

CREATION OF AN INTEGRATED OIL COMPANY

Toward the end of the decade Murphy began an expansion program that eventually led to the company's status as an integrated oil company. He helped found the 51 percent owned Ocean Drilling and Exploration Company (ODECO), an outfit one reviewer called "one of the true pioneers and innovators in the off-shore drilling industry." In 1958 he exchanged 71,958 shares for Murphy's first refinery: Lake Superior Refining Company's Superior, Wisconsin, installation.

In 1960 Murphy continued to grow, acquiring Amurex Oil Co., River States Oil Co., and National Petroleum Corp. Most importantly, that year a merger took place with Spur Oil Co., an outfit whose extensive service station network would become Murphy's own.

After acquiring a second refinery in 1961—Ingram Oil and Refining Company's Meraux, Louisiana, installation—Murphy began expanding the company's drilling network. In 1962 he obtained the Western Natural Gas Company's Venezuelan properties and production. In the following years the company would begin exploring the Persian Gulf, Libya, the North Sea, the Louisiana shore, and other lands in the continental United States. It would also take large land positions in British Columbia, off the shore of Nova Scotia, in New Zealand's Tasman Sea, and off the coast of New South Wales in Australia.

As a result of this overwhelming concentration on fossil fuels, Murphy reorganized the company as Murphy Oil Corporation on January 1, 1964, placing the company's farm and timber interests, which included 200,000 owned acres and 100,000 acres managed for others, into a wholly owned subsidiary, Deltic Farm & Timber Co., Inc.

In the mid-1960s, the company scored large successes in Iran's Sassan Field and in Libya. Between 1964 and 1969 the company's production of crude oil and liquids increased from 16,000 barrels per day to 37,000 barrels per day, while refinery intake rose from 43,000 barrels per day to 90,000 barrels per day. Much of the gasoline refined by the company went to owned or independently operated gas stations using the SPUR name. By 1969 there were 942 leased and owned SPUR stations and 1,332 SPUR stations operated by others. Of these, 548 were in the United Kingdom, 315 in eastern Canada, and 127 in Sweden.

ODECO also grew during the late 1960s. Between 1964 and 1969, its revenues more than doubled from $12.4 million to $28.5 million. Of all drilling contractors ODECO was in a unique position to help its corporate parent. The company contracted work for itself in addition to farming some jobs out, and therefore received portions of successful leases on their proceeds, adding to Murphy's total reserves. By 1968 ODECO was operating 12 drilling barges and according to the *Wall Street Transcript* was considered "one of the best growth stocks in the oil industry."

About the only Murphy product that did not grow during the 1960s was natural gas production, which fell from a record 65.6 million cubic feet per day in 1962 to 60.3 cubic feet per day in 1969. Rising production, however, did not always translate into rising profits. Steep transportation costs, high exploration costs, weak refined products prices, and losses in Europe led to declining profits from 1967 through 1969, when net income fell from $8.2 million to $6.2 million.

Despite these losses, Murphy, who still controlled 51 percent of the stock, continued to expand the

KEY DATES

1944: Charles H. Murphy Sr. and associates form C.H. Murphy & Company.

1950: Company is incorporated as Murphy Corporation.

1956: Company is taken public on the New York Stock Exchange.

1958: First refinery, located in Superior, Wisconsin, is purchased.

1960: First service stations are acquired through acquisition of Spur Oil Co.

1961: Murphy acquires its second refinery, located in Meraux, Louisiana.

1964: Company is reorganized as Murphy Oil Corporation; farm and timber interests are placed into a wholly owned subsidiary, Deltic Farm & Timber Co., Inc.

1973: OPEC oil embargo leads to increased revenues and profits for the company.

1980: Revenues surpass $2 billion for the first time.

1983: Murphy Oil is reorganized as a holding company; Murphy Oil USA, Inc., is created to oversee domestic oil interests and Canadian marketing division is sold.

1986: Low crude prices lead to the layoff of 30 percent of the Murphy workforce and an annual loss of $194.7 million.

1996: Company launches alliance with Wal-Mart Stores, Inc., under which Murphy gas stations are added to the retailer's store properties; Deltic Farm & Timber is spun off to company shareholders.

2002: Murphy Oil announces its first major discovery in offshore Malaysia.

2005: Hurricane Katrina damages Murphy's Meraux refinery, leading to a major crude oil spill; the refinery remains shut down for around nine months.

2007: Murphy starts up production at the Kikeh field in Malaysia.

company. In 1969 he created Murphy Eastern Oil Company, in London, to monitor diversified overseas operations. The same year he signed off on ODECO's formation of Sub Sea International, Inc., to operate various undersea systems such as diving bells and underwater welding chambers.

In 1970, a year in which profits rose to $9.3 million, reflecting higher prices and lower ocean freight costs, Murphy Oil began drilling in the British North Sea through an 8 percent participation with Burmah Oil and Williams Bros. To finance this project as well as drilling barges for ODECO and additional acreage in the Gulf of Mexico, the company sold $34 million in convertible debentures in 1969 and 800,000 shares of common stock in June 1971.

By 1971, the company as a whole was reporting revenues of $300 million. While two-thirds of its crude reserves were in Iran, Libya, and Venezuela, it had also created Murphy Oil Company, Ltd., which oversaw exploration, production, and marketing operations in Canada and was headquartered in Calgary, Alberta.

PROFITING FROM HIGH OIL PRICES IN POST-EMBARGO PERIOD

The OPEC oil embargo of 1973 was a boon for Murphy Oil. Sales shot up from $377.6 million in 1972 to $499 million and $862 million in 1973 and 1974, respectively. At the same time profits ballooned from $14.3 million to $48.5 million and $60.9 million. In 1977 the company surpassed $1 billion in sales for the first time, selling $1.11 billion worth of fossil fuel products and services.

Prices remained high at the end of the decade. In 1979, after North Sea drilling paid off in the huge Ninian Field (the United Kingdom's third largest), the company racked up three consecutive years of record sales and income. Revenues surpassed $2 billion for the first time in 1980 while in 1981 profits reached $163 million despite a total $119 million increase in American, Canadian, and British crude oil excise taxes.

Throughout the industry, high prices made higher cost and higher risk exploration activities economically viable. Murphy invested heavily in prospects in Alaska and off the coast of Spain, and although he balanced these more risky plays with leases near established properties in the Gulf of Mexico, the company's activities reflected those of an industry that was taking more chances and using more drilling rigs. This was good news at ODECO, where executives ordered several new platforms to satisfy demand.

On February 15, 1982, the company experienced a tragedy inherent in the ocean drilling business. During a severe storm off the coast of Newfoundland, ODECO's semisubmersible Ocean Ranger sank. Eighty-four people were on board and all were lost.

Although margins, particularly for refined products, narrowed in the early 1980s, Murphy remained highly profitable. In 1983 the company began pumping oil from the Gaviota field off the north coast of Spain. The same year, it reorganized as a holding company, creating Murphy Oil USA, Inc., to oversee domestic oil interests and selling its Canadian marketing division, consisting of 100 owned or leased SPUR stations, a dealer network, and three product terminals.

RIDING OIL INDUSTRY CYCLICALITY

In 1984 Charles H. Murphy Jr., while retaining his role as the company's chairperson, turned the positions of CEO and president over to Robert J. Sweeney, an engineering physicist with a long career at Murphy. Sweeney faced an industry in which overcapacity and conservation had begun to pressure crude prices, and, consequently, refining and drilling margins. For example, as crude prices fell from $34 a barrel to $27 a barrel, there were periods in which the cost of products refined at company facilities were $2 higher than the same products on the spot cargo market.

In the fourth quarter of 1985, crude prices fell into the $15 to $20 range. Given reasonable returns for much of the year, Sweeney was able to salvage profits of $79.7 million, but in 1986 continued low prices forced him to take drastic economic measures. He slashed exploration budgets, terminated scientist positions, reduced support personnel by 15 percent, and let hundreds go at ODECO. Overall, he laid off over 1,600 employees, almost 30 percent of the company's total. Despite these efforts, the company lost $194.7 million, in what Sweeney in his annual report called "a terrible year."

Prices began to rise again in 1987, and all of the company's sectors rebounded except for ODECO, which suffered in a generally poor drilling climate. Because ODECO's capital costs were very high, underutilization of rigs meant heavy losses. In 1987 ODECO lost $61 million and at one point during the year was using only 29 percent of capacity. Excluding ODECO's figures, Murphy made $18 million that year; taking ODECO's losses into account, the company lost $44 million.

During these low years, management retained its credibility with stockholders by maintaining a $1 per share dividend. Moreover, Sweeney did make some moves toward growth. He used company land holdings to enter the real estate business in Little Rock, Arkansas, where the company was building homes and a PGA-quality golf course. In 1986 he bought ten drilling rigs, reasoning that a shakeup was underway and that ODECO might profit from being one of the few surviving firms. In 1987 he bought out the 23 percent minor-

ity interest in Murphy Oil Company, Ltd., Murphy's London-based subsidiary. That year the company also replaced its oil and gas reserves on an energy equivalent basis.

In 1988 Jack W. McNutt succeeded Sweeney as CEO. Like Sweeney, McNutt presided over a basically profitable company whose drilling subsidiary was what the *Arkansas Gazette* called the "monkey" on its back. ODECO was one of the nation's top three drilling companies, but like the industry as a whole, it had overbuilt and was carrying too many underutilized rigs.

During his first year, McNutt tried to gain more leverage in ODECO by buying out its minority owners. Although unsuccessful in this endeavor, Murphy reported a net income of $39 million in 1988, the first profit in three years. By 1990 the company had made a major rebound. Because of higher prices induced by Iraq's invasion of Kuwait, sale of the Sub Sea International (ODECO's diving segment), and divestment of a share of its interest in Ninian Field, Murphy reported net income of $114 million, the best overall result since 1983.

The year 1990 was also marked by an industrywide trend toward increased production of natural gas, a fuel whose environmental benefits many believed would prove valuable to utility and automotive companies in the future. At Murphy this trend was evidenced by record production and by the fact that for the first time natural gas production exceeded liquid hydrocarbon production on an energy equivalent basis.

In 1991 McNutt finally disposed of Murphy's ODECO problem. After several unsuccessful attempts, he acquired the minority interest in ODECO through a tax-free exchange of shares and then sold ODECO for $372 million to Diamond M Corp., a contract drilling subsidiary of Loews Corporation. Although the deal was not actually consummated until January 30, 1992, it was reported in 1991 as an $83.9 million charge against earnings and resulted in a loss for the year of $11.2 million. The company gained a much stronger balance sheet as a result, however. Part of the proceeds was used to pay debt down to just $24 million by the end of 1992, leaving Murphy in a cash-rich position, with a little more than $300 million on hand.

LATE-CENTURY UPSTREAM INVESTMENTS AND RESTRUCTURING

In the mid-1990s Murphy Oil chose to invest this money in its exploration and production operations (the upstream side of the oil industry) rather than in refining and marketing (the downstream side). The company's upstream strategy was to purchase interests, largely non-operated, in high-risk, high-potential, very large global exploration ventures, balancing this with investment in lower risk prospects in the Gulf of Mexico and western Canada. In 1993, then, Murphy expanded its interests in North Sea production operations through the purchase of an 11.3 percent stake in the "T-Block" (a venture between Italy's AGIN, the field's operator, British Gas PLC, PetroFina S.A. of Belgium, and others) for about $145 million. Murphy also bought a 6.5 percent stake in the Hibernia field, which was located off Newfoundland and was a potential 615 million barrel find. Also in 1993, the company purchased from the province of Alberta a 5 percent interest, equivalent to 100 million barrels, in Syncrude, an oil shale project in the northern reaches of the province. Moreover, in late 1994 it acquired a 10.7 percent stake in the Terra Nova field, which had the potential of producing 400 million barrels and was located 20 miles southeast of Hibernia. Murphy Oil was also targeting several other areas for exploration, including fields in Peru, Ecuador, and China. By the end of 1994 the company had increased its proven reserves to 327.6 million barrels, a significant jump from the year-end 1992 figure of 187 million barrels.

Other key developments in 1994 involved the company's management. In October of that year, R. Madison Murphy, who had been serving as CFO, was named to the largely ceremonial post of chairman, replacing his father. That same month, McNutt was replaced as president and CEO by Claiborne P. Deming, a cousin of Madison who had been chief operating officer. Almost immediately, Murphy Oil became more visible to the press and the investment community, reflecting the influence of Deming. Under Charles Murphy Jr.'s leadership, the company had kept a very low profile for a public company.

Deming proceeded with several major restructuring moves. In 1995 the company reported a net loss of $118.6 million that was entirely attributed to write-downs of previously overvalued assets. In August 1996 Deming sold 48 U.S. onshore oil and gas fields to a group of institutional investors for more than $47 million. At year-end 1996, in a move aimed at refocusing the company on its core petroleum operations, Murphy Oil spun off to its shareholders Deltic Farm & Timber, its farm, timber, and real estate subsidiary, which was reincorporated as Deltic Timber Corporation.

Deming also attempted to revive the company's long struggling downstream activities. In November 1996 Murphy Oil entered into an agreement to merge its U.K. refining and marketing interests with those of Chevron Corporation and France's Elf Aquitaine S.A. It withdrew from the merger in early 1997, however, choosing to go it alone in the difficult U.K. retailing environment. Murphy subsequently entered into an alliance with U.K. convenience chain Costcutter, whereby Costcutter stores were added to existing Murphy gas stations. The ensuing increase in volume helped turn the U.K. downstream operations from loss-making to profitable. Murphy Oil followed a similar strategy in the United States, where it joined with Wal-Mart Stores, Inc., to test the addition of gasoline stations to the retail giant's stores. The test proved so successful that Murphy had 145 stations operating on Wal-Mart parking lots by the end of 1999, with plans laid to more than double the amount by the end of 2000. The Wal-Mart program began in the Southeast, using gasoline from Murphy's Meraux, Louisiana, refinery, then expanded to the Upper Midwest, where the stations were serviced from the refinery in Superior, Wisconsin. Murphy Oil's commitment to its partnership with Wal-Mart was underscored by the announcement in August 1999 of the sale of 60 company-owned SPUR gas stations.

Meanwhile, an oil glut forced down the price of a barrel of crude by late 1998 to about $11, the lowest price in history with inflation factored in; just one year earlier, the price had been about $23. The oil glut was caused by a number of factors, principally the Asian economic crisis and the sharp decline in oil consumption engendered by it, and the virtual collapse of OPEC, which was unable to curb production by its own members. The low prices were the principal factor in a 20 percent decline in revenues for Murphy Oil in 1998, from the $2.13 billion figure of 1997 to $1.69 billion. The company also took a $57.6 million after-tax charge to write down the value of some of its properties, leading to a net loss for the year of $14.4 million. With oil prices bouncing back up in 1999, this appeared to be only a temporary setback. In late 1999 the company announced capital expenditures totaling $457 million for 2000, an 18 percent increase over 1999, with the bulk of the funds going toward exploration in the Gulf of Mexico, development of the Terra Nova field, and expansion of the Wal-Mart retailing program.

MALAYSIAN DISCOVERIES TAKE CENTER STAGE

Murphy Oil began the 21st century on a strong note, netting profits of nearly $300 million in 2000 on revenues of $4.64 billion, which was aided in part by rising natural gas prices. On the upstream side, the company made two significant finds in the deepwater Gulf of Mexico in 2001 that added a combined 79 million barrels of oil to the firm's reserves. Early the following year, production began at the Terra Nova field. The bigger news of 2002, however, was Murphy's major find in the deepwater Kikeh field located in the company's 4.1-million-acre concession off the northwest tip of Malaysia. The discovery, after around $150 million in capital expenditures off the coast of Malaysia, enabled Murphy to increase its estimate of the oil reserves it had discovered off Malaysia to between 400 million and 700 million barrels of oil.

The overall results for 2002 were disappointing as net income plunged nearly two-thirds largely because of lower crude oil and natural gas prices at the beginning of the year and weak refining and marketing margins throughout the year. Despite the downstream difficulties, Murphy continued its aggressive expansion of its alliance with Wal-Mart. The company had been opening more than 100 Murphy USA gas stations in the parking areas of Wal-Mart stores each year, and in the fourth quarter of 2002 the 500th such outlet was built. The growing demand for gasoline from these stations led to an expansion of the Meraux refinery's capacity from 100,000 to 125,000 barrels per day, a project completed late in 2003. During 2003, an additional 117 Murphy USA stations were opened, enabling the company to secure a 1 percent share of national retail fuel sales.

After making additional finds in Malaysia, Murphy Oil announced that its exploration and production activities would be concentrated primarily on its developments in Malaysia and the deepwater Gulf of Mexico. A number of upstream assets elsewhere were therefore divested. Most significantly, in the spring of 2004 Murphy sold the bulk of its western Canadian conventional oil and gas assets for net proceeds of roughly $583 million. The company nevertheless retained a number of assets outside its two core areas, and in early 2005 Murphy announced a discovery off the coast of the Republic of Congo that had the potential to produce more than 100 million barrels of oil. In the meantime, a 22 percent increase in oil and gas production, coupled with strong crude oil and natural gas prices, propelled the company to record heights in 2004—net income of $701.3 million on revenues of $8.36 billion. Also aiding the results was a profitable year for Murphy's downstream operations, which operated in the black for the first time since 2001.

DAMAGE TO MERAUX REFINERY FROM HURRICANE KATRINA

The devastating effects of Hurricane Katrina along the Gulf Coast in August 2005 included damage to the Meraux refinery, located in the heavily flooded St. Ber-

nard Parish. The floodwaters dislodged one of the refinery's storage tanks, leading to a spill of nearly 1.5 million gallons of crude oil. In addition to other settlements, Murphy in September 2006 agreed to pay $330 million to settle a class-action lawsuit filed by individuals whose homes and businesses had been inundated by floodwaters carrying the spilled oil. Final court approval of this agreement was reached in January 2007. The Meraux refinery remained closed for about nine months following the hurricane's impact, finally opening in mid-2006 after a cleanup and repair effort that cost Murphy nearly $200 million. The company's insurance covered much of the costs of the class-action settlement and a portion of the refinery repair expenses.

An important upstream development occurred in August 2007 when production started at the Kikeh field in Malaysia. This start-up helped push Murphy's average crude oil and natural gas production up to an average of more than 113,000 barrels per day during the fourth quarter of 2007, a 36 percent increase over the previous year. The company expected its production over the following few years to nearly double to an average of more than 200,000 barrels per day due not only to the Kikeh field but also to other developments anticipated to start up in 2008 and 2009. These included natural gas production from the Tupper area in western Canada and the Sarawak project in offshore Malaysia and crude oil production from the Azurite Marine field off the coast of the Republic of Congo and the Thunder Hawk field in the Gulf of Mexico. Revenues were thus expected to soar even higher after having leaped 29 percent in 2007 to $18.44 billion, an advance stemming not only from the increase in production but also from record-high oil prices. Net income for 2007 totaled $766.5 million, up 19 percent from the 2006 total.

Murphy Oil's refining and marketing operations generated record profits of $205.7 million in 2007. At the end of the year, the company was operating nearly 1,000 Murphy USA stations. During the year, Murphy purchased from Wal-Mart the real estate underlying most of these stations. Over in the United Kingdom, Murphy had been a minority partner in a refinery in Milford Haven, Wales, for more than 26 years. In December 2007 the company acquired full control of this refinery, which had a capacity of 108,000 barrels per day. The Milford Haven facility supported Murphy Oil's network of nearly 400 U.K. gas stations, most of which operated under the MURCO brand. Murphy owned about 160 of these stations, the rest of which were branded dealers.

Jordan Wankoff
Updated, David E. Salamie

PRINCIPAL SUBSIDIARIES

Murphy Eastern Oil Company (U.K.); Murphy Exploration & Production Company; Murphy Oil Company, Ltd. (Canada); Murphy Oil USA, Inc.; Murphy Sarawak Oil Co. Ltd. (Malaysia); Murphy Sabah Oil Co. Ltd. (Malaysia); Murphy Peninsular Malaysia Oil Co. Ltd.

PRINCIPAL COMPETITORS

Exxon Mobil Corporation; Royal Dutch Shell plc; BP p.l.c.; Chevron Corporation; Marathon Oil Corporation; Petro-Canada; Apache Corporation; EnCana Corporation; RaceTrac Petroleum, Inc.

FURTHER READING

Bailey, Dan, "Far-Sighted Purchases Positioned Murphy Oil for Current Success," *Arkansas Business,* May 28, 2001, p. 1.

Biers, John M., "Can Murphy Oil Clean Up?" *Barron's,* October 24, 2005, p. M10.

"Chevron Corp., Elf, Murphy Oil to Merge Operations in U.K.," *Wall Street Journal,* November 6, 1996.

"Chevron, Elf, and Murphy's British Downstream Merger Is Not Surprising," *Petroleum Finance Week,* November 11, 1996.

Cole, Nancy, "Katrina Spill Costs Murphy $330 Million," *Arkansas Democrat-Gazette,* September 26, 2006, p. 1.

Dolan, Kerry A., "Oiled Machine," *Forbes,* May 13, 2002, pp. 110, 112.

Fan, Aliza, "Deming's New Management Style Lifts Murphy Oil's Traditional Veil of Secrecy," *Oil Daily,* September 27, 1995, p. 1.

Ford, Kelly, "Murphys Plan Transition: Madison Murphy to Direct El Dorado Oil Firm," *Arkansas Business,* June 6, 1994, p. 30.

Garner, W. Lynn, "Cash-Rich Murphy Oil Continues Search for Big Strike with Big Exploration Budget," *Oil Daily,* October 18, 1993, p. 1.

Gullage, Peter, "Hibernia Partners Are Mired in Lawsuits," *Platt's Oilgram News,* February 4, 1997, p. 2.

Horn, Deborah, "Murphy Oil: Global Company Plans to Stay Put in El Dorado," *Arkansas Business,* March 15, 2004, pp. S38+.

Johnston, David, "Murphy, Wal-Mart Face Ruling in Below-Cost Fuel Pricing Case," *Platt's Oilgram News,* May 3, 1999, p. 2.

Klump, Edward, "Murphy Banking on Malaysia," *Arkansas Democrat-Gazette,* September 13, 2003, p. 41.

———, "Murphy Basks in 'Upstream' Gains," *Arkansas Democrat-Gazette,* February 22, 2004, p. 60.

———, "Murphy Going Where Oil Leads—East to Malaysia," *Arkansas Democrat-Gazette,* February 23, 2003, p. 62.

———, "Murphy Optimistic Despite Dry Spell," *Arkansas Democrat-Gazette,* February 19, 2006, p. 79.

———, "Murphy Payouts Top $50 Million," *Arkansas Democrat-Gazette,* January 13, 2006, p. 1.

———, "Murphy Turns Oil Sands into Gravy," *Arkansas Democrat-Gazette,* March 21, 2004, p. 58.

———, "Wal-Mart Gas Alliance Is Gold: Hundreds of Murphy USA Pumps Sprouting Up at Stores," *Arkansas Democrat-Gazette,* January 18, 2004, pp. 59, 61.

Mack, Toni, "Roots: The Third Generation in His Family to Run Murphy Oil, Claiborne Deming Is Bringing It Back to the Business That Made the Murphys Rich," *Forbes,* October 7, 1996, p. 60.

McKay, Betsy, "Murphy Oil to Pay $330 Million in Katrina Class-Action Suit," *Wall Street Journal,* September 26, 2006, p. A12.

Merolli, Paul, "Murphy Sells Assets to Focus on Malaysia, U.S. Gulf," *Oil Daily,* June 24, 2003.

"Murphy Oil Corp.," *Oil and Gas Investor,* October 1, 1999, p. 16.

"Murphy Oil Finds Refining and Marketing Up-Side in Wal-Mart Parking Lots," *Petroleum Finance Week,* September 27, 1999.

"Murphy Oil Focus Remains U.S. Gulf," *Platt's Oilgram News,* March 31, 1993, p. 5.

Ozanian, Michael K., "Murphy Oil: A Great Way to Play Oil Prices," *Financial World,* July 19, 1994, p. 22.

Stevens, Laura, "Judge OKs Settlement in Oil Spill: Katrina-Hit Murphy to Pay $330 Million," *Arkansas Democrat-Gazette,* January 31, 2007, p. 1.

———, "Murphy Quarterly Earnings Shoot Up," *Arkansas Democrat-Gazette,* January 31, 2008, p. 27.

Toal, Brian A., "In Search of Greener Grass," *Oil and Gas Investor,* November 1995, pp. 33–35.

"Two Midcontinent Majors Reconfigure to Improve Their Wall Street Profiles," *Petroleum Finance Week,* September 16, 1996.

Washer, James, "Murphy Surviving As Niche Player in UK Retail Market," *Platt's Oilgram News,* March 19, 1998, p. 1.

Zipf, Peter, and Jim Washer, "Murphy out of Milford Haven Deal," *Platt's Oilgram News,* March 14, 1997, p. 1.

MYRIAD
Myriad Genetics, Inc.

320 Wakara Way
Salt Lake City, Utah 84108
U.S.A.
Telephone: (801) 584-3600
Fax: (801) 584-3640
Web site: http://www.myriad.com

Public Company
Incorporated: 1991
Employees: 900
Sales: $157.17 million (2007)
Stock Exchanges: NASDAQ
Ticker Symbol: MYGN
NAIC: 325412 Pharmaceutical Preparation Manufacturing; 325413 In-Vitro Diagnostic Substance Manufacturing

■ ■ ■

Myriad Genetics, Inc., is the leading provider in the United States of diagnostic testing services that can assess a person's genetic predisposition to certain forms of breast, colon, or skin cancer. One part of the company, Myriad Genetic Laboratories, Inc., conducts ongoing research, often in alliance with large pharmaceutical companies, into the underlying genetic causes of illness in the relatively new field of predictive medicine. The company's other wing, Myriad Pharmaceuticals, Inc., develops drugs for commercialization through collaborations and from its own laboratories. Pharmaceutical products in human clinical trials include Flurizan (Alzheimer's disease), Azixa (solid tumors and brain me-

tastases), MPC-2130 (blood cancers), and Vivecon (AIDS).

PIONEERING THE GENETIC INFORMATION BUSINESS

The founders of Myriad Genetics, Inc., began their enterprise in May 1991 in Salt Lake City, Utah, with a well-defined vision to understand the genetic basis of disease and use that information to develop diagnostic products and novel therapeutic drugs. With an educational background in chemistry, coupled with business and venture capital experience, founder Peter D. Meldrum became the company's first president and CEO. Dr. Mark Skolnick, a pioneer in the area of genetic mapping, was Myriad's scientific founder, and in March 1992, Dr. Walter Gilbert, winner of the 1980 Nobel Prize in Chemistry, joined the company as scientific cofounder.

Initially, Myriad focused on what it called "the genetic information business." After raising $10 million in April 1993 from a private investor, the company increased its research staff from 7 to more than 20 scientists and announced plans to build a DNA Diagnostic Center for research into the genetic links to hereditary cancers and heart disease. With Skolnick as the director of the nearby University of Utah Cancer Epidemiology Center, Myriad's scientists had easy access to a genealogical database of the health and medical histories of 1.2 million descendants of Mormon pioneers in Utah.

In July 1993, the company announced a three-year, $1.8 million agreement with Eli Lilly and Company, of

Indianapolis, to fund Myriad's search for the gene responsible for hereditary breast cancer. At the time, Lilly also made a $1 million equity investment in Myriad.

Myriad made its first breakout discovery in April 1994, when it identified MTS1 (for multiple tumor suppressor), a specific human gene involved in the formation of about half of the major kinds of cancer, including tumors of the lung, breast, brain, bone, skin (melanoma), bladder, kidney, ovary, and blood.

In September 1994, Myriad's research team, led by Skolnick, achieved a second milestone when it beat out at least a dozen major research labs to win a global race to isolate BRCA1, a gene responsible for roughly 5 percent of all breast cancers and about half of inherited breast cancers. Scientists knew of the existence of BRCA1, which stands for BReast CAncer 1 gene, for four years before Myriad-led researchers mapped the DNA sequences for all of the gene's 1,863 amino acids. The feat secured a U.S. patent for Myriad, the University of Utah Medical Center, and the National Institutes of Health. In November 1994, Myriad moved its 50 employees into its new DNA Diagnostic Center and more spacious administrative headquarters in the University of Utah Research Park.

BUILDING STRATEGIC ALLIANCES

The company took a great leap forward financially in 1995. In April, Myriad entered a five-year drug discovery collaboration worth up to $60 million with Novartis Pharmaceuticals Corporation, of Basel, Switzerland, to research genetic links to cardiovascular diseases. September brought a multiyear, $71 million deal with Bayer AG, of Leverkusen, Germany, aimed at discovering therapeutics for obesity, asthma, and

osteoporosis. Then, on October 6, Myriad raised $46.8 million in its initial public offering (IPO) of stock, trading under the ticker symbol "MYGN" on the NASDAQ. The company sold 2.6 million shares at $18 a share. Myriad closed the year by filing a patent application on a second breast-cancer gene, BRCA2.

When Myriad filed its first public annual financial report in August 1996, it showed research revenues from its strategic alliances with Novartis, Bayer, and Eli Lilly of $6.6 million for the fiscal year ended June 30, 1996, compared to $1.3 million in the prior year. The net loss totaled $5.9 million but the company ended the year with $70 million in cash. In October 1996, Myriad introduced its first commercial product to the public, a blood test available from a physician capable of assessing a woman's risk of developing breast or ovarian cancer based on detection of mutations in the BRCA1 gene. BRACAnalysis, according to the company, was the first predictive medicine product developed for a major common disease.

In April 1997, Myriad announced its fourth alliance with a major pharmaceutical company, a collaboration with Schering-Plough Corp., of Madison, New Jersey, for the discovery of new prostate cancer therapies. The five-year research agreement was potentially worth $60 million. In a deal similar to its existing partnerships, Myriad retained exclusive rights to all diagnostic products and services, while Schering-Plough received worldwide rights to all pharmaceutical products resulting from the partnership. In November 1997, Myriad landed a $54 million deal with Bayer to search for gene targets to treat dementia and depression. The contract was Myriad's first significant sale of ProNet, the company's database and proprietary technology used to identify human genes and protein interactions for major diseases.

In May 1998, Myriad was granted exclusive U.S. rights to its patents for its BRCA1 and BRCA2 breast and ovarian cancer genetic testing services, ending a year of back-and-forth litigation with Maryland-based OncorMed, Inc. According to fiscal 1998 results for the year ended June 30, 1998, as reported by the company in August, Myriad's genetic testing revenues were up 139 percent to $2.2 million. BRACAnalysis, the company said, was used by over 380 major cancer centers in the United States, and over 180 insurance companies and HMOs covered its $2,400 cost. October brought the company its second ProNet collaboration, a $51 million five-year deal with Berlin-based Schering AG for the discovery of drug targets for the treatment of asthma, osteoporosis, and obesity genes.

```
┌─────────────────────────────────────────┐
│                                           │
│              KEY DATES                    │
│         ──────────◆──────────             │
│                                           │
│  1991:  Peter D. Meldrum and Dr. Mark Skolnick │
│         form company to research genetic links to │
│         disease.                          │
│  1994:  Myriad researchers make breakout discovery │
│         of hereditary breast cancer gene. │
│  1995:  Company goes public; forms first major │
│         strategic alliances with Novartis, Bayer, and │
│         Eli Lilly.                        │
│  1996:  First commercial product, a test for hereditary │
│         breast cancer, makes it to market. │
│  2000:  Myriad acquires rights to commercialize │
│         R-flurbiprofen for prostate cancer treatment. │
│  2002:  Flurizan begins FDA testing process for treat- │
│         ment of Alzheimer's disease.      │
│  2006:  Diagnostic testing product revenues break │
│         $100 million mark.                │
│  2007:  Flurizan fails as prostate cancer drug but │
│         continues FDA clinical trials for Alzheimer's │
│         treatment.                        │
│                                           │
└─────────────────────────────────────────┘
```

THE BIOTECHNOLOGY RIDE

In April 1999, the company's newly formed subsidiary, Myriad Pharmaceuticals, Inc., began research focused on creating new drugs for arthritis and sleep disorders. Genetic testing revenue, a product of Myriad's other newly created subsidiary, Myriad Genetic Laboratories, Inc., more than doubled to $5.2 million in fiscal 1999, as reported by the company in August, but Myriad still lost $10 million on revenues of $25.3 million. In September the company landed another research partnership, a two-year, $33.5 million pact with Novartis to study the genetic structure of cereal crops. In September, Myriad also announced its discovery of a gene involved in the inherited susceptibility to insulin-dependent diabetes. On November 19, company stock that was selling for around $10 a share in August jumped $5 to close at $27 with Myriad's announced discovery of a new HIV drug target.

Calendar year 2000 was a wild ride for Myriad and the biotechnology industry. Advances in the Human Genome Project and investor flight from high-risk tech stocks into biotechnology combined to drive the Myriad share price to $130 by mid-February. The company's stock peaked on March 9 when it closed at $229.88 a share. Myriad's market value had grown in six months from $89 million to $2.4 billion. On March 14, however, President Bill Clinton and U.K. Prime Minister Tony Blair made remarks that called into question whether genes could be patented, which sent the NASDAQ biotechnology index, up 80 percent from year-end 1999, into a free-fall. Myriad's shares bottomed out at around $40 in early April.

Myriad's fortunes quickly turned around again. In June 2000, the company announced its discovery of a gene linked to prostate cancer and saw their resurgent share price jump over $28 to around $120. On August 16, Myriad declared a two-for-one stock split. In September, the company launched COLARIS, a predictive medical test for hereditary colon cancer, and in October, plans to test a new colon cancer drug were announced. In November, Myriad raised $41 million from the sale of restricted shares of common stock to Acqua Wellington, followed by more new collaborations with Hoffmann-La Roche and Hitachi, and expanded work with Schering AG and Pharmacia.

SUCCESSES AND CHALLENGES

In December 2000, Myriad acquired exclusive commercial rights to R-flurbiprofen, a compound developed and taken through federally regulated Phase I and Phase IIa human clinical trials as a treatment for colon cancer by Encore Pharmaceuticals, Inc., of Loma Linda. All potential drug candidates had to pass through three phases of human clinical trials before earning approval for the marketplace from the U.S. Food and Drug Administration (FDA). Myriad initially renamed the compound MPC-7869 and began shepherding it through a Phase IIb clinical trial for treatment of prostate cancer. The compound gave Myriad its first chance to bring a therapeutic drug to market, a goal since the company's founding.

After 18 months of around-the-clock efforts by 40 of the company's 400 employees, in January 2001 Myriad announced it had successfully sequenced the entire genetic code of rice, the world's most widely consumed food crop. The achievement, marking 50,000 different genes, written in about 430 million "letters" of DNA, represented the second largest genome to be sequenced at the time. In April the company formed a new subsidiary, Myriad Proteomics, a $185 million joint venture with computer giants Hitachi and Oracle, to map the identity and function of every protein in the human body.

In September 2001, Myriad's laboratories became part of an effort to identify victims, based on DNA analysis, of the September 11 terrorist attacks on New York City's World Trade Center. In November, the company launched its third diagnostic services product, MELARIS, designed to assess a person's risk of developing skin cancer.

In 2002, Myriad signed a $34 million drug discovery pact with Illinois-based Abbott Laboratories for the treatment of depression in March, and a $24 million molecular genetics technology agreement with DuPont in April. June 2002 saw company stock sink to a low of $16.30 a share from 2001's high of $81.75. Myriad's August financial report for fiscal 2002 showed a net loss of nearly $14 million, or almost double the loss from the prior year, despite revenue growth to a record $53.8 million, which included $26.8 million in predictive medicine revenues.

FLURIZAN'S ENCORE PERFORMANCE

In August 2002, the company submitted an Investigational New Drug application to federal regulators for a drug aimed at the treatment and prevention of Alzheimer's disease. Myriad originally acquired the license to market the compound R-flurbiprofen from Encore Pharmaceuticals in December 2000. It renamed the drug MPC-7869 and began developing it as a prostate cancer treatment. The proposed Phase I trial of drug safety and dosage levels for MPC-7869 as an Alzheimer's drug was expected to last one year and involve 48 healthy elderly volunteers. Concurrently, MPC-7869 was in the middle of an ongoing Phase II trial for early stage prostate cancer.

In February 2003, Myriad announced the discovery of DEP1, a gene responsible for depression, triggering a $1 million milestone payment from research partner Abbott and opening the possibility for a new class of antidepressants. In late June, Myriad began enrolling subjects for its 12-month, 200-patient Phase II clinical trial of MPC-7869 as an Alzheimer's treatment. In a trial slated for 30 different centers in Great Britain and Canada, the company hoped to demonstrate the effectiveness of MPC-7869 in lowering Abeta42, a primary component of the plaques found in the brains of Alzheimer's patients and the suspected cause of neurological damage associated with Alzheimer's-related senility.

With 16 different potential drug targets for cancer, Alzheimer's, and AIDS under development in preclinical studies and three ongoing human trials, therapeutic product development was beginning to emerge as the company's top priority and it showed in year-end financials. As reported in August 2003, research and development expenses for fiscal 2003 were up 31 percent to $47.6 million. In November 2003, preliminary positive results of MPC-7869's Phase II trials for Alzheimer's as well as progress in identifying a compound for treating genetically linked obesity drove company stock up 15 percent to $12.90 a share.

In June 2004, Myriad raised $50.2 million from the sale of 3.4 million shares of common stock, bringing the total number of outstanding shares in the company to 30.6 million. In July, Myriad acquired a $14.2 million research contract from the National Institutes of Health. Also in July, Phase I trial results for MPC-7869 were presented at the Ninth International Conference on Alzheimer's Disease and Related Disorders in Philadelphia. It was at this time that Myriad began calling MPC-7869 by the brand name "Flurizan" when referring to its Alzheimer's drug candidate.

Fiscal 2004 financial results, as reported by Myriad in August 2004, showed 27 consecutive quarters of increased revenues from the company's predictive medicine products, including $13.1 million from the fourth quarter ended June 30, 2004. While the company experienced a record net loss for the year of more than $40 million, or $1.49 a share, on $56.6 million in revenue, the books also showed that Myriad had about $142 million in cash and no debt.

FLURIZAN'S TRIALS

Mid-January 2005 brought an unexpected announcement from Myriad that it was beginning enrollment, with the FDA's permission, in the Phase III trial of its Alzheimer's drug, Flurizan, even though Phase II was just ending. The company's shares jumped 14 percent to $24.95 on the news. At the time, Flurizan was also in an ongoing Phase II clinical trial in the United States for the treatment of patients with premetastatic prostate cancer. The company also began Phase I trials of two anticancer drugs, MP-6827 and MPC-2130, in January.

According to an independent market study titled "Alzheimer's Disease," released in March 2005, Flurizan was forecast to emerge as one of two therapies that by 2013 would share more than 56 percent of the $4 billion Alzheimer's market in the United States, Western Europe, and Japan.

In May 2005, Myriad reported that Flurizan "failed to achieve statistical significance" in its Phase II trial of patients suffering from mild to moderate Alzheimer's disease. However, subjects with mild Alzheimer's who received the 800 milligrams twice-daily dose of the drug achieved between 34 percent and 45 percent slowing in decline of their mental faculties. Flurizan also showed notable improvement for moderate-level subjects in relieving the agitation, paranoia, and anxiety often experienced by Alzheimer's patients.

In August 2005, Myriad said enrollment in its Phase III trial of Flurizan was proceeding on schedule but with an FDA-approved modified protocol. The 18-month, 1,600-patient, 130-site clinical trial, expected to begin across the United States by mid-2006, was fine-tuned with results from Phase II in mind to target people diagnosed in the beginning stages of the disease with an 800 milligrams twice-daily dose. In September, Myriad announced its discovery of COB1, a gene with possible links to childhood obesity, and in mid-November said it found a gene linked to major depression.

In June 2006, Myriad reported encouraging results from a follow-up study of patients from the Phase II trial of Flurizan. Eighty percent of the subjects chose to continue the study and after two years, results for patients with mild Alzheimer's showed benefits in cognition, memory retention, global function, and activities of daily living continued to increase over 24 months. Data from the two-year mark also showed that psychiatric events such as aggression, depression, confusion, and agitation were reduced by 60 percent.

In August 2006, Myriad began enrollment in Europe for an 18-month, 800-patient, Phase III trial of Flurizan. On August 22, Myriad announced the official start of its Phase III trial of Flurizan in the United States, the largest placebo-controlled study conducted for the disease. Financial results for fiscal 2006 were released at the same time and showed mixed results. Revenues were up 39 percent to $114.3 million, with product revenues breaking $100 million for the first time, but the company still lost $38.2 million. In September, the company reported the successful conclusion of a Phase I clinical trial of its drug candidate Azixa (MPC-6827), a compound for treatment of tumors discovered by Tarrytown, New York-based EpiCept Corporation and licensed to Myriad.

TOWARD PROFITABILITY

In January 2007, Myriad announced that its prostate cancer drug candidate, MPC-7869, did not achieve its Phase II clinical trial goals and ended all plans to pursue further development of the compound for cancer. Myriad originally purchased commercial rights for MPC-7869 for development as a treatment for prostate cancer in December 2000 from Encore Pharmaceuticals. However, the drug, also known at the time as R-flurbiprofen, emerged in 2002 as Myriad's potential flagship product to treat Alzheimer's disease and altered the company's direction from an emphasis on external research collaborations to its own in-house drug development programs. It was given the brand name "Flurizan" in 2004, and in order to disassociate R-flurbiprofen from the similarly named ibuprofen, Myriad changed the compound's name to Tarenflurbil sometime in 2006.

In March 2007, the company sold three million shares of common stock and raised about $105 million. In April, Myriad announced the start of a Phase II human clinical trial to determine the safety profile of Azixa and its ability to improve the overall survival of patients with melanoma skin cancer and brain metastases. Financial results for fiscal 2007, as reported by Myriad in August, showed that revenues from the company's line of breast, colon, and skin cancer testing products increased 44 percent to a record $145.3 million. Gross profit margins on diagnostic product revenues also rose to a record 79 percent. Net loss for the year was down 8 percent to $38 million on total revenues of $157.1 million.

Investors continued to be attracted to Myriad as anticipation built over the Phase III trial results for Flurizan. Shares in late August 2007 traded around $42 and by the end of October had risen to $55, double the price from the previous year. In December 2007, Myriad submitted an Investigational New Drug application to the FDA to begin Phase I human clinical trials with its drug candidate Vivecon (MPC-9055), for the treatment of AIDS.

In what appeared to be a ramp-up for the company's anticipated commercial launch of products in its therapeutic pipeline, Flurizan and Azixa, Myriad began 2008 with a January expansion of its commercial and clinical infrastructure with new hires in every department, bringing its workforce total to over 900 people. Figures through December 31, 2007, released by the company in February, showed that for the second quarter of fiscal 2008, molecular diagnostics revenue was up 55 percent to $53.1 million, producing gross profits of $45.4 million. The company's net loss shrank to $5.1 million, compared with $8.8 million for the second quarter of fiscal 2007. On December 31, 2007, Myriad's books showed $303 million in cash, and still no debt.

At the end of the first quarter of calendar 2008, Myriad stood on the brink of realizing its dream goal as a company: having a blockbuster therapeutic drug on the market that addressed the causes, not just the symptoms, of a major common disease. The last clinical trial for Flurizan, the company's flagship Alzheimer's drug candidate, was over and results were expected in June 2008. Myriad's future looked rosy provided that the drug won final FDA approval and made it to market. If not, a strong cash position, combined with a surging revenue stream and high profit margins from its diagnostic products, appeared to guarantee the company at least a consolation prize of profitability in the near future.

Ted Sylvester

PRINCIPAL SUBSIDIARIES

Myriad Genetic Laboratories, Inc.; Myriad Pharmaceuticals, Inc.

PRINCIPAL COMPETITORS

Third Wave Technologies, Inc.; Wyeth Pharmaceuticals, Inc.; Elan Corporation, plc (Ireland); Genomics Health, Inc.; Affymetrix, Inc.; Incyte Corporation; Celera Group; Novartis Pharmaceuticals Corporation; Human Genome Sciences, Inc.

FURTHER READING

"Alzheimer Disease: Myriad Genetics Submits IND for R-flurbiprofen to the FDA," *Pain & Central Nervous System Week,* September 30, 2002, p. 9.

"Anti-Cancer Companies Suffering," *Deseret News,* June 16, 2002.

Boulton, Guy, "Slow Start, but Genetics Firm Grows," *Salt Lake Tribune,* September 24, 1999, p. B1.

"Breast Cancer: Data on 10,000 BRACAnalysis Tests Published," *Women's Health Weekly,* April 11, 2002, p. 9.

Clemens, Natalie, "New Hope in Alzheimer's," *Deseret Morning News,* June 20, 2005, p. B1.

"Genetic Code of Rice Cracked," *Hindu,* January 28, 2001.

"Launch of Alzhemed, Flurizan Will Drive Dementia Drug Market, Report Indicates," *Health & Medicine Week,* November 14, 2005.

Lorenzo, Aaron, "Flurizan Misses Major Phase II Endpoints, but Positives Seen," *BIOWORLD Today,* May 3, 2005.

Nii, Jenifer K., "Is Slide in Biotech Stocks at an End?" *Deseret News,* April 6, 2000, p. E1.

"Obesity: Myriad Genetics Discovers a Major Cause of Hereditary Obesity," *Obesity, Fitness & Wellness Week,* December 21, 2002, p. 3.

Osborne, Randall, "Myriad's Predictive Medicine, Therapy Push Go 'Hand in Hand,'" *BioWorld Financial Watch,* December 2, 2002, p. 1.

Pihl-Carey, Karen, "With Flurizan in Phase III, Myriad Bringing in $130 Million," *Bioworld Today,* November 7, 2005.

Pollack, Andrew, "Patent for U.S. Genetic Test Is Revoked in Europe," *New York Times,* May 20, 2004, p. 17.

Rhein, Reginald, "Myriad Wins Breast Cancer Gene Race, Patent Rights Prize," *Biotechnology Newswatch,* September 19, 1994, p. 1.

Saltus, Richard, "Gene Test for Cancer Risk Is Offered; Some Geneticists Dispute Its Value," *Boston Globe,* October 25, 1996, p. A1.

"Schizophrenia; Drug Markets in Cognitive Dysfunction Will Experience Dramatic Transformation As Total Sales Increase from $300 Million in 2006 to $3.7 Billion in 2016," *Pharma Business Week,* January 28, 2008.

Waldholz, Michael, "One Gene Spurs Many Cancers, Scientists Find," *Wall Street Journal,* April 14, 1994, p. B1.

National Fuel Gas Company

6163 Main Street
Williamsville, New York 14221
U.S.A.
Telephone: (716) 857-7000
Toll Free: (800) 365-3234
Fax: (716) 857-7413
Web site: http://www.nationalfuelgas.com

Public Company
Incorporated: 1902
Employees: 1,952
Sales: $2.04 billion (2007)
Stock Exchanges: New York
Ticker Symbol: NFG
NAIC: 211111 Crude Petroleum and Natural Gas Extraction; 221121 Electric Bulk Power Transmission and Control; 221122 Electric Power Distribution; 221210 Natural Gas Distribution; 486210 Pipeline Transportation of Natural Gas; 113310 Logging; 321113 Sawmills

■ ■ ■

National Fuel Gas Company (NFG) is a diversified energy company whose operating companies primarily explore, produce, store, market, and distribute natural gas. Seneca Resources Corporation, headquartered in Houston, explores for and develops oil and natural gas reserves in the Texas and Louisiana Gulf Coast region, as well as California, the Southwest, and the Appalachian region. Its publicly regulated utility, National Fuel Gas Distribution Corporation, serves more than 730,000 customers in western New York and northwestern Pennsylvania. National Fuel Gas Supply Corporation and Empire State Pipeline oversee National Fuel Gas Company's 28 storage facilities and more than 3,000 miles of pipeline for natural gas distribution. In addition to supplying National Fuel customers, the pipeline transports gas for 20 utility companies located along the Atlantic seaboard. National Fuel Resources handles energy marketing to commercial and industrial customers. A minor aspect of the company's operations involves timber logging and wood processing in New York and Pennsylvania.

BEGINNINGS FROM FIRST NATURAL GAS SERVICE PROVIDERS

National Fuel Gas Company (NFG) emerged from nearly a century of natural gas development, as several rudimentary ventures advanced ideas for the extraction and uses of natural gas. One predecessor to NFG, the Fredonia Gas Light Company, was the first company organized in the United States to provide the delivery of natural gas. In 1821, the Village of Fredonia, in the western-most area of New York state, tapped an accumulation of inflammable gas that was known to bubble up from the bed of the Canadaway Creek. William Aaron Hart, a local gunsmith, drilled a hole on the bank of the creek and collected the gas in a gasometer. He then laid lead pipe through the streets, allowing the gas, moved by its own natural pressure, to flow freely into 100 street lamps throughout the town.

COMPANY PERSPECTIVES

To Our Shareholders: We have developed a proud history of success, leadership and expertise in the energy industry during the last 105 years. Our competitive advantage rests in our experience and the assets that have been assembled into your Company.

After the Fredonia project proved successful, a separate contractor converted a lighthouse in Barcelona, New York, 20 miles west of Fredonia, from whale oil to natural gas. The contractor similarly tapped the reservoir of natural gas that bubbled through the Canadaway Creek, and piped it to the lighthouse. That lighthouse became the first navigational beacon light in the world to be lit with natural gas. While it operated for many years to guide ships that plied Lake Erie, the lighthouse eventually fell into disuse. However, it was relit for a time again in 1962 as a monument to the merchantmen who sailed the Great Lakes and to the forebears of the National Fuel Gas Company.

Additional natural gas discoveries evolved from an 1859 oil discovery in Titusville, Pennsylvania, 50 miles south of Fredonia. The discovery set off a frenzy of oil fever throughout the Appalachian region, and a group of investors from Bloomfield, New York, 75 miles east of Fredonia, organized a drilling project. The contractor hired to do the drilling hit natural gas at 480 feet and had to stop work for several weeks, until the gas subsided. The contractor finished drilling the well at 500 feet, but no oil was found and the project was abandoned. The well was set on fire, as gas then was considered an unprofitable and undesirable byproduct of the search for oil. The well burned until another group of investors bought it in 1870 and built a natural gas pipeline that transported fuel for street and residential lighting in Rochester, New York, a growing town 25 miles north. The pipe was made of bored pine logs connected with bands of iron and iron joints. That project failed within two years due to significant leakage in the wooden pipes and the low pressure in the lines.

Through the 1870s and 1880s, similar ventures developed natural gas production and transport in increments. One successful project involved a two-inch, wrought-iron pipeline that was laid in 1872 to carry natural gas from Newton, Pennsylvania, to Titusville. In 1886, an eight-inch wrought-iron pipeline was laid to carry natural gas 87 miles from McKean County, Pennsylvania, to Buffalo, New York. The latter pipeline, built by the United Natural Gas Company, based in Oil City, Pennsylvania, was recognized at its time as the longest natural gas pipeline in the world. (Portions of it remain as part of NFG's distribution system.)

United Natural Gas Company continued to make innovations through the 1890s. These included the use of internal combustion engines to drive compressors and pump natural gas at constant pressure throughout the distribution area. The company put the world's first 1,000 horsepower gas engine into service in 1899 to drive a compressor.

By 1900 natural gas became a proven commodity for heating, cooking, and lighting, and all of these ventures were eventually purchased or merged into the company that became NFG. United Natural Gas Company, Pennsylvania Gas Company, of Warren, Pennsylvania, and Buffalo Natural Gas Fuel Company constituted the major part of NFG when the company organized as a corporation in 1902 in the State of New Jersey. NFG acquired smaller gas utility companies through the Iroquois Natural Gas Company, which formed during the 1910s. The small utilities were not as well capitalized and had spent their gas sources. NFG built three parallel pipelines from Pennsylvania to Buffalo to match the original eight-inch line built in 1886.

UNDERGROUND STORAGE PROVIDES STABLE ENVIRONMENT

Through its Provincial Gas Company subsidiary, which operated in southern Ontario, Canada, across the Niagara River from Buffalo, NFG became the first natural gas company to experiment with underground gas storage. Underground gas storage relies on pockets, or "lenses", of porous rock that are surrounded by impervious rock to form reservoirs of gas. Those pockets were the same formations drilled for the original supplies of natural gas and from which gas was pumped to deplete them. With proper maintenance and drilling techniques, those pools were capable of storing new supplies of gas pumped into them, just as they were for storing reserves of prehistoric natural gas. In 1916, NFG's Iroquois Natural Gas Corporation subsidiary began operations at the Zoar field, 30 miles south of Buffalo. The site became the first successful underground storage field in the United States. Underground gas storage became a common practice that allowed utility companies to store large quantities of gas in spent or low pressure producing fields during periods of low demand. Such storage maintained high pressure for periods of increased demand.

Through the 1940s, the availability of natural gas in the Appalachian region ebbed while the demand for the fuel for home heating, water heating, and cooking.

KEY DATES

1821: The first natural gas well is drilled to light streetlamps in Fredonia, New York.

1870: Wooden natural gas pipeline supplies residential lighting in Rochester, New York.

1886: An 87-mile metal pipeline carries natural gas from McKean County, Pennsylvania, to Buffalo, New York.

1902: National Fuel Gas Company (NFG) is incorporated; company begins consolidation of gas utility companies.

1915: NFG experiments with underground storage of natural gas.

1962: Sales exceed $128 million as postwar economy feeds expansion of residential service.

1978: Energy crisis prompts NFG to diversify with natural gas exploration and production.

1990: Energy marketing subsidiary National Fuel Resources is formed.

1996: International expansion includes utility in Czech Republic.

2003: Acquisition of Empire State Pipeline significantly increases operations.

2007: Construction begins on 78-mile pipeline; natural gas drilling activity increases 52 percent.

ENERGY CRISIS PROMPTS DIVERSIFICATION

Due to the changing nature of the natural gas industry, in 1974 National Fuel reorganized its regional gas firms (United, Pennsylvania Gas, and Iroquois) into one utility (Distribution), regulated by state governments, and one interstate pipeline (Supply), regulated by the federal government. The energy crisis of the early 1970s had far reaching effects on NFG, as several factors restricted growth, including residential energy conservation measures and a decline in industrial usage. Also, fuel shortages required the company to restrict new residential hookups, just as NFG's residential service markets neared saturation. The Natural Gas Policy Act of 1978 stimulated natural gas producers to develop new reserves and supplies. However, the industry developed a surplus of natural gas by the mid-1980s which, in turn, led to reduced gas and oil well-head prices. Government deregulation brought pricing in alignment with marketplace demand, thus reducing the cost of natural gas.

While the industry experienced a restructuring through the 1980s that saw several companies retrench, NFG acted to diversify its business and to double its reserves of natural gas and oil. In the early 1980s, NFG augmented its traditional retail business with investments in the storage, transportation, and production of natural gas. In 1983, the company owned gas and oil reserves totaling 99 billion cubic feet. By 1987 the company's gas and oil reserves totaled 199.6 billion cubic feet, with assets located in the Gulf of Mexico, California, and Western Canada.

To expand its reserves, NFG sought to build a pipeline that would import gas from reserves in Alberta, Canada. First the company applied to the Federal Energy Regulatory Commission for permission, one of six utility holding companies to do so. Then, in 1986, NFG bought Utility Constructors Incorporated of Linesville, Pennsylvania, to provide the capacity. However, NFG lost the bid to build the Canadian pipeline. Nevertheless, Utility Constructors built other pipelines in NFG's service and distribution areas. These included a $67 million pipeline, completed in 1988, which allowed NFG to import more natural gas from Canada than the Alberta project would have allowed.

By the fiscal year ending September 30, 1991, NFG operated 14,335 miles of utility pipeline and 3,256 miles of transmission and storage pipeline, and the company delivered 256.7 billion cubic feet of gas. NFG operated 34 natural gas fields, including four joint

natural gas for industrial and residential uses increased, and the company experienced several shortages in its distribution area. Demand for natural gas increased sharply during World War II. Inflation and demand from war industries caused increases in the cost of coal and oil, while the cost of natural gas remained low. Postwar demand for natural gas as a home heating fuel skyrocketed. In response to the declining availability of gas in its original producing region, interstate natural gas pipelines, such as Texas Eastern, purchased emergency oil pipelines at government auctions. The Big Inch and Little Inch pipelines were converted for natural gas distribution, transporting fuel from Texas to New Jersey. The utility companies built pipelines to connect this supply of gas to their storage facilities and service areas in Appalachia.

During the postwar era, NFG experienced rapid growth. By 1962 sales exceeded $128 million. Supplying 565,000 customers, more than 80 percent of the company's sales were to residential customers who used ventures with other pipeline suppliers. The fields were served by an additional 508 miles of pipeline, and reservoir capacity stored more than 117 billion cubic feet of gas.

The supply, transmission, and storage of natural gas contributed $497 million in revenues, while the retail sale of natural gas brought $694 million. Approximately 50 percent of retail sales originated from utility service to 716,000 customers and the remainder primarily from commercial and industrial customers.

National Fuel Gas Company's exploration and production operations supplied about 9 percent of the company's pretax operating income. The company increased its drilling activity, drilling 36 wells that produced 3.3 billion cubic feet of gas in 1990. The company drilled or participated in drilling 28 net gas wells in 1991, of which 12 were producers, providing the discovery of approximately 1.6 billion cubic feet of natural gas, while 16 were plugged and abandoned as dry holes. NFG at the time operated 2,459 gas wells, of which 2,199 were in the Appalachian region, and 625 oil wells, of which 447 were on the West Coast.

ORGANIZING FOR CONTINUED DIVERSIFICATION AND EXPANSION

During the 1990s, NFG took steps to expand and streamline operations for sustained growth. The company formed National Fuel Resources in 1990 to oversee expansion of regional gas marketing to industrial, commercial, residential, and public customers. During the early 1990s, the nonregulated subsidiary opened offices in Clark, New Jersey; Greenville, Pennsylvania; and Chicago, Illinois. In July 1994, NFG consolidated its oil and gas exploration and production activities under Seneca Resources Corporation. The company formed the Horizon Energy Development subsidiary to pursue international opportunities in small to medium-sized utilities. In June 1996, the company acquired Power International, s.r.o., a developer of private power outlets in the Czech Republic.

NFG acquired several companies to expand its base of resource extraction. These included the June 1999 purchase of 36,300 acres of land for timber and oil and gas resource extraction in Pennsylvania and New York. The property was acquired jointly by NFG's Seneca Resources and Highland Land and Minerals subsidiaries. Seneca significantly increased its operations in western Canada, with the acquisitions of Tri Link Resources and

Player Petroleum Corporation, in 2000 and 2001, respectively.

In February 2003 NFG expanded its pipeline operations through the $180 million cash acquisition of the Empire State Pipeline from Duke Energy Corporation. The natural gas transmission pipeline ran from the Niagara River, near the U.S.-Canada border, to Buffalo, and then proceeded another 157 miles to Syracuse. With a capacity to distribute 525 million cubic feet of natural gas per day, the pipeline supplied major industrial corporations, utility companies, and power producers. NFG began organizing to add a 78-mile extension to Victor and Corning, New York.

Under pressure from shareholders, NFG divested noncore properties with marginal returns on investment in order to reduce debt and provide funds for investments with greater returns. In July 2003 NFG sold oil assets in southeast Saskatchewan for $80 million and 70,000 acres of timber property in Pennsylvania and New York for $186.3 million. After receiving several offers for its holdings in the Czech Republic, NFG divested the operations for $116 million. In late 2007, NFG sold its Seneca Energy Canada subsidiary, comprised of oil and natural gas properties in Canada, for $231.8 million, representing a nonrecurring gain of $120 million.

After several years of dealing with legal, environmental, agricultural, and other issues, NFG's construction on the Empire Pipeline began in late 2007. NFG expected to begin natural gas delivery in November 2008. In conjunction with the Millennium Pipeline projects to other areas of the northeast, the Empire Connector pipeline would deliver an additional 25,400 dekatherms of natural gas per day to growing markets in the northeastern United States.

Higher gas prices prompted NFG to focus attention on its Appalachian mineral resources. A revaluation of NFG's reserves showed 670 billion cubic feet of natural gas on the company's one million acres in New York and Pennsylvania, nearly triple the previous estimate. Drilling activity in shallow sands of the Denovian and Silurian formations increased 53 percent to 233 wells in 2007, and the company planned to drill 280 wells in the upper Devonian formation in 2008. Moreover, a study of NFG's Marcellus Shale formation revealed approximately 50 trillion cubic feet of recoverable natural gas. With higher gas prices and improved technology for specialized shale well drilling, the Marcellus formation suddenly became valuable. In partnership with EOG Resources, NFG initiated drilling of three wells (two vertical and one horizontal) in 2007, and planned to drill an additional 18 wells (ten horizontal) in 2008.

Bruce Vernyi
Updated, Mary Tradii

PRINCIPAL SUBSIDIARIES

National Fuel Gas Supply Corporation; National Fuel Gas Distribution Corporation; National Fuel Resources, Inc.; Empire Pipeline, Inc.; Upstate Energy Corporation; Horizon Power, Inc.; Horizon LFG; Highland Forest Resources; Leidy Hub, Inc.; Data-Track Account Services; Seneca Resources Corporation.

PRINCIPAL OPERATING UNITS

Utility; Pipeline and Storage; Exploration and Production; Energy Marketing, Timber.

PRINCIPAL COMPETITORS

Allegheny Energy, Inc.; Consolidated Edison, Inc.; Castle Oil Corporation; Niagara Mohawk Power Corporation; PPL Corporation; Rochester Gas and Electric Corporation; UGI Corporation.

FURTHER READING

Baker, Sharon, "National Fuel Forms Company to Market Natural Gas All Over," *Business First of Buffalo,* January 27, 1992, p. 10.

"Empire Connector Pipeline Project Moving Forward," *CNW Group,* August 6, 2007.

"National Fuel Signs Agreement to Sell Assets in Czech Republic," *Canadian Corporate News,* June 29, 2005.

Nichols, Stuart H., *The Natural Gas Story from the Ground Down: The History of the National Fuel Gas Company,* New York: Newcomen Society in North America, 1963.

"Otis Eastern Service Wins Empires Connector Contract," *Pipeline & Gas Journal,* September 2007.

Robinson, David, "National Fuel's Bernard Kennedy Dies: Retired CEO, 75, Led Company for 13 Years," *Buffalo News,* March 7, 2007, p. B1.

———, "National Fuel's Gas Reserves Extensive Consultant Reports About 3-Fold Increase from Previous Estimates," *Buffalo News,* February 9, 2008, p. D6.

———, "National Fuel's Profits Soar to $123 Million," *Buffalo News,* November 10, 2007.

———, "Shareholder Seeks Sale of Some National Fuel Operations: National Fuel's Appalachian Oils and Gas Fields Could Be Worth More Than $1 Billion," *Buffalo News,* September 19, 2007, p. B7.

———, "Write-Down of Gas Fields to Cut Profit at NFG," *Buffalo News,* November 3, 2006, p. D7.

Waples, David A. *The Natural Gas Industry in Appalachia: A History from the First Discovery to the Maturity of the Industry,* Jefferson, N.C.: McFarland and Company, 2005.

"What's in Play?" *Oil and Gas Investor,* November 1, 2007.

Nippon Electric Glass Co., Ltd.

Nippon Electric Glass Co. Ltd.

———————■———————

2-7-1, Seiran 2-chome
Otsu, Shiga 520-8639
Japan
Telephone: (+81-77) 537-1700
Fax: (+81-77) 534-4967
Web site: http://www.neg.co.jp

Public Company
Incorporated: 1944
Employees: 1,949
Sales: ¥336.41 billion ($2.85 billion) (2007)
Stock Exchanges: Tokyo
Ticker Symbol: NPEG F
NAIC: 327211 Flat Glass Manufacturing

■ ■ ■

Nippon Electric Glass Co. Ltd. (NEG) is a manufacturer of high-technology glass, used mainly in the production of optical displays, including cathode-ray tubes (CRTs), glass fiber, liquid crystal displays (LCDs), and plasma display panels. According to NEG, as of 2008 flat-panel display glass was its core product. Other applications for NEG's glass include automobiles, building materials, electronic devices such as cellular phones and digital cameras, and kitchen appliances.

FORMATIVE YEARS: 1944–59

Backed by an investment from NEC Corporation, NEG was established in Shiga, Japan, on October 31, 1944. After World War II, operations were temporarily halted when NEG's facilities were lent to NEC. Five years later, NEG cut ties with NEC and became a stand-alone enterprise.

During NEG's early years, the company concentrated on the manufacture of hand-blown vacuum bulbs. The large-scale manufacture of glass tubing commenced in 1951, and within five years had become NEG's main product, produced by means of a large tank furnace. At this time the company began making powder glass. Glass used for radiation shielding was introduced in 1958, followed by glass block manufacturing in 1959. During that year NEG's Fujisawa plant opened its doors.

CRT FOCUS: 1960–89

According to an extensive time line on NEG's web site, the 1960s was a significant decade in the company's history. It was then that NEG gained status as a world leader in the production of specialty glass. The company ushered in the 1960s with several new products, including a glass-ceramic called Neoceram that had super heat-resistant properties. In time, NEG would expand its offerings to include electronic glass materials, glass fiber, and glass blocks used by the construction industry.

The 1960s also marked NEG's entry into the cathode-ray tube (CRT) market. CRTs are a key component in television screens and computer monitors. One of the earliest developments in this area occurred in 1963, when technology used to produce Owens-Illinois Inc.'s CRT glass was introduced.

Midway through the decade, NEG brought its Shiga-Takatsuki plant online and began making glass for electrical components called diodes, used for conducting electricity in a particular direction. This was followed by more CRT-related developments, including the manufacture of black-and-white CRT glass production in 1965 and color CRT glass three years later.

Progress continued at NEG during the early 1970s. After the company opened its Notogawa plant in 1971, its stock was listed on the second sections of both the Osaka Securities Exchange and the Tokyo Stock Exchange in 1973.

NEG introduced a series of new products during the first half of the 1970s. Neopariés, a glass-ceramic building material, was unveiled in 1973, followed by a heat resistant glass named Neorex and thin sheet glass for LCDs in 1974.

During the late 1970s, NEG made some initial headway in the area of international growth. In mid-1978 it forged a ten-year deal with Owens-Illinois Inc. to provide technical support to two state-owned Czechoslovakian companies, Polytechna and Sklounion. In October of that year, NEG and Kanematsu-Gosho secured a $65 million deal from Tekhnopromimport, a Soviet trade group, to establish a color picture tube plant in the Soviet Union.

International growth continued during the early 1980s. In 1981 NEG joined Toshiba Corporation and Mitsui & Company Ltd. in a $400 million deal to build a color television tube plant for East Germany-based Industrieanlagen-Import. That same year, progress continued on the new product front as NEG commenced production of solar tube collectors, followed by glass capillaries for optical connectors in 1981.

Several important developments took place in 1983. Owens-Illinois Inc., which held a sizable stake in NEG, sold a portion of its ownership interest that year but remained a major partner and shareholder. It also was in 1983 that NEG's stock moved to the first section of both the Osaka Securities Exchange and the Tokyo Stock Exchange.

Extra-large (37-inch) CRT glass production began in 1985, and the company continued to expand its product base heading into the late 1980s. By this time NEG was making glass for kitchenware, medical devices, ball lenses, as well as thin sheet glass and fire-resistant glass-ceramics.

In 1987 NEG forged a ten-year licensing deal with Denver, Colorado-based Manville Corporation, in which NEG agreed to supply the fiberglass giant with technology related to fiberglass yarn production. It also was in 1987 that NEG, Sumitomo Trading Co., and Owens-Illinois Television Products Inc. formed an eight-year partnership to build a $65 million color television bulb parts facility in Anyang, China, near Henan Province. Only the second of its kind in China, the plant had the capacity to supply three Chinese television tube plants with approximately four million parts per year.

During the late 1980s, NEG continued to work with familiar corporate partners on new projects. In March 1988 the company again partnered with Owens-Illinois Inc., establishing a 50-50 joint venture to produce glass television components in the United States. Early the following year, a seven-year licensing deal for highly efficient plastic reinforcement glass fiber production was forged with Manville. The deal allowed Manville to make chopped strands of glass fiber that could be used to give plastics in cameras, cars, and home appliances greater strength and resistance to heat and electricity.

By the decade's end, NEG had become the second largest manufacturer of CRTs in the world. The company rounded out the decade by establishing a Precision Glass Center and forming a U.S. sales subsidiary named Nippon Electric Glass America Inc. in 1989. Based in Des Plaines, Illinois, the new business, which expected to generate sales of about $15 million during its first year, set the stage for further international growth by tapping into a burgeoning market for the company's products in North America.

INTERNATIONAL GROWTH: 1990–99

NEG ushered in the 1990s by forging a new long-term licensing deal with partner Manville Corporation. This time, the deal gave Manville the rights to develop and market products incorporating all of NEG's various fiberglass reinforcement technologies in North America and Europe.

Two important developments unfolded in 1991. In addition to forming Nippon Electric Glass (Malaysia) Sdn. Bhd., the company brought its Wakasa-Kaminaka facility online. The following year marked the beginning of CRT glass production in Malaysia.

KEY DATES

■

1944: NEC Corporation helps to establish Nippon Electric Glass (NEG) in Shiga, Japan.

1949: NEG severs ties with NEC and becomes a stand-alone enterprise.

1973: The company's stock is listed on the second section of both the Osaka Securities Exchange and the Tokyo Stock Exchange.

1983: NEG's stock moves to the first section of both the Osaka Securities Exchange and the Tokyo Stock Exchange.

1993: The company buys Owens-Illinois Inc. out of the U.S.-based OI-NEG TV Products Inc. joint venture for $100 million, and OI-NEG TV becomes a wholly owned subsidiary.

1994: OI-NEG TV Products is renamed Techneglas Inc.

2004: After eliminating 1,100 jobs and shuttering operations in Columbus and Perrysburg, Ohio, and Pittston, Pennsylvania, Techneglas files for Chapter 11 bankruptcy.

2005: Techneglas emerges from bankruptcy as a sales and distribution operation with 40 employees.

In 1993 NEG agreed to buy Owens-Illinois Inc. out of the OI-NEG TV Products Inc. joint venture the two companies had formed in 1988. Since then, the operation had relocated from Toledo, Ohio, to Columbus, Ohio, and had benefited from investments totaling about $300 million. The $100 million deal made OI-NEG TV Products a wholly owned subsidiary of NEG, which adopted the name Techneglas Inc. in 1994.

According to a May 8, 1995, *Columbus Dispatch* article by Darris Blackford, by mid-1995 Techneglas was operating around the clock, seven days a week, employing approximately 1,300 people. The plant, which supplied components to Zenith, Toshiba, Sony, RCA, Philips, Mitsubishi, Matsushita, and Hitachi, was capable of making glass picture tube parts for TVs in the 19- to 35-inch range, and had made preparations to produce parts for the high-definition TVs that would hit the market in the coming years.

Techneglas's Columbus plant underwent an expansion effort costing approximately $65 million during the mid-1990s that resulted in new office space, a cafeteria, and a wellness facility. At this time the company also had operations in Perrysburg, Ohio, and Pittston, Pennsylvania. In late 1995 the company was honored with two Pennsylvania state environmental awards. Techneglas received an Environmental Partnership Award from the Pennsylvania Environmental Council, as well as the 1995 Governor's Waste Minimization Award from the Pennsylvania Department of Environmental Protection (Large Business/Pollution Prevention Category).

International growth began to intensify midway through the decade. In early 1995, NEG formed Ocean Technical Glass Ltd. in the United Kingdom, and CRT glass production commenced in the country that year. In 1996 the company began producing glass tubing in Malaysia and CRT glass in Indonesia. That same year, NEG also began making glass tubing used in LCD backlights.

Growth continued into the latter part of the decade. In addition to a joint venture that saw CRT glass production begin in China's Hebei Province, NEG formed Nippon Electric Glass California Inc. and Nippon Electric Glass Mexico S.A. de C.V. in 1997. That year, the company's Ocean Technical Glass Ltd. business became Nippon Electric Glass (U.K.) Ltd., and NEG started producing small glass-ceramic parts called ferrules for optical connectors.

In 1998 NEG began CRT glass production in Mexico, as well as glass fiber production in Malaysia. In September of the following year, the company moved all of its heat-resistant glass production to Malaysia, where ¥1.5 billion was earmarked to upgrade facilities at its Nippon Electric Glass (Malaysia) Sdn. subsidiary. Among new products introduced around this time was a low-temperature adhesive sealant glass. NEG ended the 1990s by obtaining ISO 14001 certification for all of the company's Japanese plants.

FLAT-PANEL DISPLAY FOCUS: 2000–08

NEG ushered in the new millennium by capitalizing on rising demand for CRT glass in markets such as China and southeast Asia. The company announced plans to invest $138 million for the expansion of its Malaysian subsidiary's plant, and also commenced CRT glass production in China's Fujian Province. Late in the year, the company's Techneglas arm announced "temporary" layoffs for 355 workers, in what turned out to be an early sign of the operation's eventual demise.

The early 2000s also were marked by a number of business deals. In early 2001 NEG sold a 33 percent interest in Ando Electric Co. to Yokogawa Electric for $113.7 million. In April the company's Electric Glass

Sangyo Co. Ltd. arm merged with Electric Glass New-man Power Service Co. Ltd. and adopted the latter company's name. It also was in 2001 that NEG liquidated the operations of its Techno Medic Co. Ltd. business.

Growth continued into 2002, beginning with the formation of Nippon Electric Glass (Fujian) Co. Ltd. in Fuzhou, China, which enabled NEG to bolster its Chinese CRT glass business. Late in the year, NEG formed Nippon Electric Glass (Korea) Co. Ltd. Finally, Nippon Electric Glass Taiwan Co. Ltd. was formed in late 2003.

While NEG was faring well outside of the United States, its Techneglas operations were suffering. Stiff competition from China and Malaysia, as well as growing demand for non-CRT televisions, namely plasma and LCD units, was taking its toll. From early 2002 to mid-2003, the company had laid off more than 300 employees. In the midst of these difficulties, President and CEO L. T. Hickey retired after a 30-year career with the company and was succeeded by NEG executive Motoharu Matsumoto.

The hammer finally fell at Techneglas on August 3, 2004, when NEG announced it was eliminating the subsidiary's 1,100 employees and shuttering the firm's operations in Columbus and Perrysburg, Ohio, and Pittston, Pennsylvania. Techneglas filed for Chapter 11 bankruptcy on September 1, revealing that it owed $50.2 million to its 20 largest creditors.

After missing some $17 million in payments to its pension fund, Techneglas proceeded to sell off assets, and in 2005 the company reached a settlement with the union that represented its workers. It ironed out matters regarding severance pay and pension benefits, including an agreement to pay Pension Benefit Guaranty Corp., which had assumed responsibility for 2,800 of its employee pensions, $34.5 million. Another $25 million was set aside for the retirement benefits of Techneglas's salaried workers.

In late 2005, Techneglas announced it would emerge from bankruptcy as a sales and distribution operation with 40 employees. Headquarters remained in Columbus, and the Perrysburg plant was retained, where production shifted to semiconductor materials and scratch-resistant glass coatings.

In the midst of the Techneglas situation, NEG continued expanding elsewhere. The company began transitioning away from CRT glass production and moving into the production of glass for LCD screens. Beyond the shuttering of Techneglas's operations, CRT production stopped in Mexico in 2004. In August of that year NEG announced a new $24 million plant in

Taiwan. In addition, the company earmarked $184.6 million for a new furnace at its Takatsuki, Japan, plant, allowing it to ramp up LCD glass production there by 50 percent.

NEG pulled the plug on its European CRT glass operations in 2005. Early that year, a joint venture with LG Philips LCD Co. Ltd., in which NEG had a 60 percent stake, was announced. Named Paju Electric Glass Co. Ltd., the new venture involved the construction of a $35.3 million glass polishing and processing plant near Seoul, Korea. Completed in mid-2006, the facility had the ability to produce approximately 60,000 glass sheets per month.

Heading into the late 2000s, NEG shuttered more of its CRT glass operations, including production lines in Japan and its joint venture in China's Hebei Province. Production in Indonesia closed down the following year.

After forming an LCD glass plate joint venture with Sumitomo Corporation in mid-2006, a new $44.67 million plant was planned for Shanghai. Brought online in late 2007, the facility was expected to churn out approximately 200,000 square meters of glass plates per month.

NEG's new Shanghai plant was but one example of the company's transformation from a producer of CRT glass to LCD glass. Moving into the 21st century's second decade, NEG appeared to be well positioned for continued growth in the age of flat-panel televisions.

Paul R. Greenland

PRINCIPAL SUBSIDIARIES

Nippon Electric Glass (Fujian) Co. Ltd. (80%); Nippon Electric Glass (Malaysia) Sdn. Bhd.; Nippon Electric Glass (UK) Ltd.; P.T. Nippon Electric Glass Indonesia (75%); Shijiazhuang Baoshi Electric Glass Co. Ltd. (China; 41%); Techneglas Inc. (U.S.A.).

PRINCIPAL COMPETITORS

Asahi Glass Co. Ltd.; Corning Inc.; SCHOTT AG.

FURTHER READING

Blackford, Darris, "Picture Perfect; TV Picture Tube Maker Techneglas Has a Clear Vision of Its High-Definition Future," *Columbus Dispatch,* May 8, 1995.

Lynott, Jerry, "Techneglas, Union Approve Settlement," *Wilkes-Barre Times Leader,* May 19, 2005.

Matthews, Tom, "Techneglas to Exit Bankruptcy," *Columbus Dispatch,* October 11, 2005.

"Owens-Illinois Inc. Plans Joint Venture with Japanese Firm," *Wall Street Journal,* March 15, 1988.

Showalter, Kathy, "Techneglas Builds Rehabilitation Center with Factory Hurts in Mind," *Business First-Columbus,* March 22, 1996.

"Television Glass-Maker Techneglas Files for Bankruptcy," *Associated Press State & Local Wire,* September 1, 2004.

"TV Glass Maker to Close Three Plants," *Associated Press Online,* August 3, 2004.

"U.S.S.R. Concludes Foreign Deals," *Facts on File World News Digest,* October 27, 1978.

THE METALS COMPANY

O'Neal Steel, Inc.

744 41st Street North
Birmingham, Alabama 35222
U.S.A.
Telephone: (205) 599-8000
Toll Free: (800) 292-4090
Fax: (205) 599-8037
Web site: http://www.onealsteel.com

Private Company
Incorporated: 1921 as Southern Steel
Employees: 4,300
Sales: $2.3 billion (2006 est.)
NAIC: 421510 Metal Service Centers and Offices

■ ■ ■

Based in Birmingham, Alabama, O'Neal Steel, Inc., is the United States' largest family-owned metals service company and distributor, its slate of subsidiaries providing one-stop shopping to original equipment manufacturers, fabricators, and job shops. O'Neal offers a complete range of steel, aluminum, brass, and bronze products: sheet, plate, coil, pipe, beams, bars, and angles. The company maintains more than 70 operations in North America, Europe, and Asia, providing such services as laser cutting, flame cutting, coil processing, shearing, sawing, machining, rolling, forming, tube processing, welding, plasma cutting, and punching, drilling, and notching. The company is owned by the O'Neal family and a third-generation member, Craft O'Neal, serves as chairman of the board.

FOUNDED IN BIRMINGHAM: 1921

O'Neal Steel was founded in Birmingham in 1921 with $2,000 in borrowed money by Kirkman O'Neal as a small steel fabricating business under the name Southern Steel. A descendant of two Alabama governors, his grandfather and great-grandfather, O'Neal had graduated from the U.S. Naval Academy and later served during World War I. Following his discharge in 1919 he worked as a production engineer at Chicasaw Shipbuilding Company, followed by a stint with Ingalls Iron Works. After starting Southern Steel, he borrowed another $2,000 to buy raw materials after his new plant received its first order for a rotary coal dump and ventilation system from a local mine. The company quickly earned a reputation for quality workmanship and reliability, establishing customer relations that would help carry O'Neal Steel through the Great Depression of the 1930s.

Employees also played a key role in keeping the company afloat through these difficult times. O'Neal was able to win contracts by making lowball bids because of his workers' willingness to split the earnings as their pay. In addition, the company provided employees with rent-free housing, helping to ease the economic pain. O'Neal also adapted to the times by serving customers who were unable to place large enough orders with the major steel mills. In 1935 he opened the first metals service center in the South, using the high tonnage orders that the fabricating division placed with the mills to supply smaller companies.

The Great Depression came to an end in the early 1940s, fueled by defense spending due to World War II.

COMPANY PERSPECTIVES

We're an organization built on initiative, flexibility, and freethinking. We strive to partner with our customers, to anticipate their needs, to customize services for them, and to help them improve their profitability by utilizing our efficiencies.

Birmingham's population swelled as the area's iron and steel mills and other industries were put to use around the clock to produce the military materials needed to fight the war. For its part, O'Neal Steel turned out gun platforms, deckhouses for destroyer escorts, and five different kinds of general purpose bombs, all of which were used exclusively in the Pacific theater. Southern Steel played an important role in the defeat of the Japanese, able to turn out twice as many bombs as other companies in the same time frame.

EMMET O'NEAL JOINS COMPANY AND POSTWAR EXPANSION

Following the war, as O'Neal Steel returned to nonmilitary work, O'Neal's son, Emmet O'Neal, came to work for the company in 1946 as a vice-president. He had earned an engineering degree from Vanderbilt University and then served as a naval officer during the war, supervising ship repairs at Pearl Harbor. According to his obituary in the *Mobile Register,* Southern Steel "grew under his leadership as the demand for steel increased following the war. Rather than just selling steel, the company began welding it, forming it, cutting it and further preparing it for use."

As the demand for steel increased during the postwar period, Southern Steel expanded beyond Birmingham. In 1952 the company opened its first satellite district in Jackson, Mississippi. Other districts were to be added, either through acquisition or startup. Chattanooga, Tennessee, followed in 1955, and Atlanta, Georgia, was brought into the fold two years later. Districts were then opened in Jacksonville, Florida, in 1961; Tampa, Florida, in 1967, and Knoxville, Tennessee, in 1968. The service center business became so dominant that in 1969 the fabricating division in Birmingham was closed and the service center operations expanded.

O'Neal Steel grew further in the 1970s and 1980s. A Mobile, Alabama, district was added in 1973, and two years later districts were opened in Lafayette, Louisiana, and Little Rock, Arkansas. In addition,

O'Neal Steel moved into a new Birmingham headquarters in 1974. After a lull of several years, the company opened the Memphis, Tennessee, district in 1981. Two years later the Tampa office added a number of products, including cold-rolled and galvanized steel, aluminum sheet and floorplate, and aluminum plate and structurals, to accommodate the light manufacturing plants of south Florida.

THIRD GENERATION BECOMES INVOLVED: 1984

Kirkman O'Neal, by this time in his early 90s, remained active with the company, and in 1984 his grandson, Emmet's son Craft O'Neal, joined the family business. A graduate of Birmingham-Southern College with a degree in business and economics, he started out in sales. A year later he transferred to the Atlanta district to become assistant manager. After learning the ropes he was ready to become a district manager, taking over the Houston branch in 1990. He then returned to Birmingham as a manager in 1995.

Also in the 1980s, O'Neal Steel looked to expand its geographic reach. It acquired Shelby Steel Inc. in 1985, picking up service centers in five new markets: Evansville, Ft. Wayne, and Shelbyville, Indiana; Louisville, Kentucky; and Nashville, Tennessee. Not only did the geographic diversity of Shelby make it an attractive acquisition, the company's emphasis on plate and structurals made it compatible. Other O'Neal Steel products, aluminum and other nonferrous metals, were then added to Shelby's.

Further territory expansion took place in 1988 with the acquisition of Toledo, Ohio-based Wabash-LaGrange Steel Co. that brought with it operations in Toledo as well as Cincinnati and Masury, Ohio. Although O'Neal service centers operated in nearby areas there was only modest overlap in sales territories in Illinois, Indiana, and Ohio. Later in 1988 O'Neal Steel expanded westward, purchasing Dallas-based Liberty Steel Co., establishing a presence in the Texas flat-roll and structural tubing markets. Previously the company had to serve the Texas market from Louisiana and Arkansas branches, but this acquisition added operations in Dallas, Austin, Houston, and Lubbock, Texas. To close out the 1980s, O'Neal Steel gained a foothold in another targeted region of the country, the Carolinas. In 1989 a Greensboro, North Carolina, district was opened.

Following a recession in the early 1990s, O'Neal Steel resumed its growth pattern. In 1991 the Louisville branch expanded its facility, creating the Channel

```
┌─────────────────────────────────────────┐
│                                         │
│            KEY DATES                    │
│               ■                         │
│ ───────────────────────────────────     │
│                                         │
│  1921:  Kirkman O'Neal founds steel      │
│         fabricator as Southern Steel.    │
│  1935:  Metal services center opens.     │
│  1946:  O'Neal's son, Emmet O'Neal,      │
│         joins company.                   │
│  1952:  First satellite operation opens  │
│         in Jackson, Mississippi.         │
│  1969:  Fabricating division is closed.  │
│  1984:  Emmet O'Neal's son, Craft        │
│         O'Neal, joins company.           │
│  1997:  Metalwest Inc. is acquired.      │
│  2004:  Emmet O'Neal dies and is         │
│         succeeded as chairman by         │
│         Craft O'Neal.                    │
│  2005:  TW Metals is acquired.           │
│  2008:  TAD Metals is acquired.          │
│                                         │
└─────────────────────────────────────────┘
```

Manufacturing Center to convert channel steel into machined components for forklift manufacturers, a growing customer base for the unit. In that same year, O'Neal Steel bought a large facility in Houston from Pittsburgh's USX Corp., and the much smaller facility picked up in the Liberty acquisition was sold. A year later a Pittsburgh, Pennsylvania, district was established through the acquisition of Ambridge, Pennsylvania-based Levinson Steel Co. The addition of this branch was especially important because it was needed to replace the Youngstown, Ohio, facility, the lease of which had expired in 1991, forcing O'Neal Steel to serve Ohio, Pennsylvania, and West Virginia from other less strategically located branches.

ACQUISITION OF METALWEST: 1997

O'Neal Steel grew on a number of fronts in the mid- to late 1990s. The company extended its reach in the upper Midwest in 1995, acquiring Waterloo, Iowa-based Weissman Steel Supply. In operation for more than 40 years, primarily serving the agricultural machinery market, Weissman Steel a year earlier had expanded its warehouse, making it well suited to the addition of inventory from its new owners. O'Neal Steel expanded its Tuscaloosa, Alabama, center in 1997 with the opening of a 200,000-ton-capacity coil processing facility, taking advantage of the close proximity of a major supplier, Tuscaloosa Steel Corp. Also in 1997, O'Neal Steel completed a major acquisition in Denver-based Metalwest Inc., a major operator of light-gauge, flat-rolled steel, maintaining units in Dallas; Las Vegas; Ogden, Utah; and Wichita, Kansas. Later in the year, O'Neal

Steel added to its footprint in the Carolinas, purchasing four service centers from Carolina Steel Corp. in Wilson, North Carolina; Lynchburg, Virginia; and Abingdon, Virginia, and the inventory of a fifth center located in Greensboro. The company also picked up Carolina's Weldment unit, which included operations in Roanoke and Abingdon, Virginia, that fabricated subassemblies for major original equipment manufacturers in those markets. Weldment would add a center in Monterrey, Mexico, to supply manufacturers with operations in that market as well.

In 2000 O'Neal Steel named Bill Jones, a seasoned veteran of the company, as the new president and chief executive officer. A graduate of the University of Virginia, he started his career with O'Neal Steel in 1976. He was very familiar with the various operations of O'Neal Steel, having worked in six areas of the company. He began his tenure in Inside Sales in Birmingham, then moved to Tupelo, Mississippi, to work in Outside Sales. In 1981 he was named district manager of the Memphis unit, and six years later became manager of Marketing and Specialty Products. Jones then became vice-president of the Birmingham district before becoming executive vice-president in 1993 to be groomed for the top spot. The company would also have a new chairman of the board as well in the new century. Emmet O'Neal died at the age of 82 in 2004 and was replaced by his son, Craft O'Neal.

Emmet O'Neal had grown the business his father had founded into a $1 billion concern. He had rejected a number of offers to sell the company, preferring to keep it family owned. Even as the new generation was taking firm control in the early 2000s, the growth strategy he had pursued remained in effect. In 2000 a tube processing center was opened in Lebanon, Tennessee, in order to meet the needs of an area customer for such a specialized unit. In early 2002 O'Neal Steel made a major capital investment in the Birmingham operation, installing a new automated storage and retrieval system that not only improved productivity but provided greater worker safety because employees were no longer required to retrieve and move heavy materials. Instead, requested materials were delivered by "cassette" using a computer tracking and conveyor system.

The early 2000s was a difficult period for the U.S. steel industry. Some of the largest mills closed their doors in 2002 and 2003, leading to consolidation but not the reopening of older plants. As the economy improved and domestic demand for steel was matched by increasing demand from the fast growing economies of India and China, steel supplies shrank and prices escalated. O'Neal had to face the difficult challenge of maintaining relationships with longtime customers, keeping them supplied with metals while also keeping them informed about price hikes and product availability.

As the economy recovered, O'Neal Steel continued to expand its operations. In 2004 Aerodyne Ulbrich Alloys was acquired and renamed Aerodyne Alloys LLC. A distributor of bar, sheet, and plate made from nickel-based alloys, cobalt, titanium, and stainless steel, Aerodyne maintained facilities in South Windsor, Connecticut, and Fresno, California, mostly serving the aerospace and energy markets in both the United States and Asia. Early in the following year, O'Neal Steel added to its product line with the purchase of Darien, Illinois-based high-strength steel and alloy plate distributor Leeco Steel Products Inc., doing business throughout the United States, Europe, and Asia. Later in the year, O'Neal Steel acquired Pennsylvania-based TW Metals, a service center company with 17 U.S. locations that operated in the United Kingdom, France, and Poland under the Phillip Cornes Group name.

Further acquisitions followed in 2006. Colorado-based Timberline Steel was added in the spring, bringing Rocky Mountain region operations in Commerce City, Grand Junction, and Pueblo, Colorado, and Farmington, New Mexico. Later in the year, Ohio-based Ferguson Metals, which specialized in stainless steel and high-temperature alloys, was acquired, as was Cincinnati-based AIM International, an aerospace specialist, and an allied company, Supply Dynamics LLC.

Early in 2007 O'Neal Steel created O'Neal-HPMG (High-Performance Metals Group), a cooperative effort that combined the capabilities of TW Metals, Aerodyne Allows, Ferguson Metals, AIM International, and Supply Dynamics. A year later, Ferguson Metals and AIM International were brought together to create United Performance Metals. Also in 2008 O'Neal Steel acquired

TAD Metals, a New Jersey-based metals service chain with operations in New Jersey; Norwell, Massachusetts; Dallas, Houston, Laredo, and San Marcos, Texas; and Mississauga, Ontario, Canada.

Ed Dinger

PRINCIPAL SUBSIDIARIES

Aerodyne; Leecoo; Metalwest; Supply Dynamics; TAD Metals; Timberline Steel; TW Metals; United Performance Metals; O'Neal High-Performance Metals Group.

PRINCIPAL COMPETITORS

Reliance Steel & Aluminum Co.; Ryerson, Inc.; Worthington Industries, Inc.

FURTHER READING

"Birmingham Steel Boss O'Neal Dies," *Mobile (Ala.) Register,* November 4, 2004, p. A3.

Burgert, Philip, "O'Neal Beefs Up Holdings; Buys Two Ohio Firms," *American Metal Market,* November 22, 2006, p. 1.

Collier, Andrew, "O'Neal to Purchase Indiana's Shelby," *American Metal Market,* July 24, 1985, p. 1.

"86 Years Old and Still Growing," *Trumpf Express,* Vol. 2, 2007.

Nicholson, Gilbert, "O'Neal Steel Rides Out the Industry Roller Coaster," *Birmingham Business Journal,* October 4, 2004.

Regan, James G., "O'Neal Steel Expands Westward, Agrees to Acquire Liberty Steel," *American Metal Market,* October 11, 1988, p. 4.

Robertson, Scott, "O'Neal Buying Assets of Carolina's Centers," *American Metal Market,* November 14, 1997, p. 2.

Wilkinson, Kaija, "Family Builds Strong Foundation at O'Neal Steel," *Birmingham Business Journal,* June 16, 2006.

Williams, Roy L., "O'Neal Growing, Strong As Steel," *Birmingham News,* May 3, 2006, p. 1D.

Obagi Medical Products, Inc.

———————————————■———————————————

310 Golden Shore, Suite 100
Long Beach, California 90802
U.S.A.
Telephone: (562) 628-1007
Fax: (562) 628-1008
Web site: http://www.obagi.com

Public Company
Incorporated: 1988 as WorldWide Product Distribution, Inc.
Employees: 153
Sales: $77.99 million (2006)
Stock Exchanges: NASDAQ
Ticker Symbol: OMPI
NAIC: 325412 Pharmaceutical Preparation Manufacturing

■ ■ ■

Obagi Medical Products, Inc., is a pharmaceutical company competing in the aesthetic and therapeutic skin health markets. Obagi Medical's products use proprietary technologies the company calls "Penetrating Therapeutics" that improve the ability of prescription and over-the-counter agents to penetrate the skin barrier. The company's flagship product, which accounts for approximately 70 percent of sales, is the Obagi Nu-Derm System, a physician-dispensed and prescription-based topical skin health system that improves skin firmness, reduces wrinkles, and increases the formation of elastin and collagen by transforming skin at the cellular level. Other products include the CLENZIderm

M.D. System, used to treat acne, the ELASTIderm System, used to increase the elasticity and skin tone of the eyes and face, the Obagi-C Rx System, which reduces the early effects of sun damage, and Professional-C and Cffectives, used to provide antioxidant protection. Obagi Medical relies on a domestic sales force and foreign distribution partners to market its products to dermatologists and plastic surgeons. The company's products are available in more than 35 countries.

ORIGINS: A SCIENTIFIC APPROACH

Nearly two decades after he introduced his company's flagship product, Dr. Zein Obagi savored his accomplishments in an April 2, 2007, interview with the *Los Angeles Business Journal.* "It's truly turned out as I envisioned when I set out to create science-based products that would improve the cellular function of the skin," he said. Obagi had realized his entrepreneurial dream, developing a product that attracted customers, primarily female, from more than 35 countries.

Obagi focused his work on the largest organ in the body, the skin. His research addressed the changes that occurred in the two primary layers of skin, the thin outer layer called the epidermis, and the thicker inner layer called the dermis. Within the epidermis, two types of specialized cells functioned in ways pertinent to Obagi's research. Keratinocytes formed in the epidermis, where, during a six-week maturation cycle, they traveled up through the layers of the epidermis and were exfoliated. Rough, thick, and dry skin, characteristics

Obagi sought to eliminate, resulted from a buildup of excess keratinocytes. Keratinocytes constituted 90 percent of epidermal cells. Melanocytes composed the remaining percentage. Located in the bottom layer of the epidermis, melanocytes produced melanin through a process called melanogenesis, yielding a pigment that determined skin color and protected the body against ultraviolet radiation.

Obagi's work also centered on the functions within the dermis, the layer of skin beneath the epidermis. Connective tissues composed much of the dermis, tissues made of collagen and elastin. Elastin was the protein that gave skin its ability to hold its shape and maintain healthy skin tension, that enabled it to snap back when pulled or stretched. Of particular concern to Obagi was the degradation of elastin, which the body produced in decreasing quantities after puberty. The degradation of elastin correlated with the signs of aging: skin tone and elasticity diminished, creating loose, sagging skin. Collagen, the main component of ligaments, tendons, bone, and teeth, also played a vital role in the skin's elasticity, giving it strength and resiliency. The degradation of collagen led to the wrinkles associated with aging.

DEBUT OF OBAGI NU-DERM SYSTEM: 1988

Obagi's mission was to combat the natural elements that attacked the dermis and epidermis. Age, hormones, stress, diet, disease, and a number of other influences waged a war from within the body against healthy skin.

External forces (pollutants, radiation from the sun) assaulted skin from the outside. Obagi sought to deliver a science-based, noninvasive system to prevent and possibly reverse the effects of the internal and external forces that damaged skin. His response was the Obagi Nu-Derm System, a product released commercially in 1988 that became his entrée into the aesthetic and therapeutic skin health markets.

The Obagi Nu-Derm System became the flagship product of Obagi's company. A physician-dispensed, prescription-based skin care system, the Obagi Nu-Derm System consisted of a combination of six prescription and over-the-counter drugs, including cleansers, exfoliating creams, and products that contained the drug hydroquinone in a 4 percent prescription concentration. The drugs penetrated deep into the skin, transforming skin at the cellular level. Cellular turnover was increased, normalizing the production of new melanin in the epidermis and increasing the formation of collagen and elastin. The system promised to improve skin firmness, tone, and clarity, as well as reduce wrinkles, delivering benefits that supported Obagi's company in the aesthetic segment of the skin care market. The Obagi Nu-Derm System also competed in the therapeutic segment. Radiation from the sun in the form of ultraviolet (UV) rays, both UVA and the more pernicious UVB, caused premature aging and skin cancer. The Obagi Nu-Derm System offered protection from both UVA and UVB rays.

Obagi also introduced another product in 1988, which, along with the Obagi Nu-Derm System, constituted essentially his entire product line for his first decade in business. The Obagi Blue Peel, like the Obagi Nu-Derm System, was prescribed and monitored by physicians, who recommended the product for its ability to reduce fine lines, wrinkles, hyperpigmentation (patchy discoloration), and laxity (looseness). The Obagi Blue Peel was a topical system that aided in the application of trichloroacetic acid (TCA) chemical peels, which removed the thin surface layers of aged and damaged skin, clearing the way for a new thin layer of healthy skin cells. Although the Obagi Blue Peel was marketed as a complementary treatment to the Obagi Nu-Derm System, it was not dispensed for daily home use, which limited its revenue-producing potential.

CHANGING NAMES

The Obagi Nu-Derm System and Obagi Blue Peel debuted in 1988, as did Obagi's company. His company was founded as WorldWide Product Distribution, Inc., the name it operated under for its first decade of business. A series of corporate moves led to the adoption of the corporate title used by the company in the 21st

KEY DATES

1988: Dr. Zein Obagi introduces the Obagi Nu-Derm System and Obagi Blue Peel.

2002: The release of tretinoin marks the company's entry into the acne market.

2004: Obagi Medical launches the Obagi-C Rx System, the first prescription-strength vitamin C and hydroquinone system.

2006: Obagi Medical completes its initial public offering of stock in December; the ELASTI-derm line debuts.

2008: During its 20th anniversary, Obagi Medical releases the ELASTIderm Decolletage System.

century. In October 1997, OMP Acquisition Corporation was formed to acquire WorldWide Product. In December 1997, OMP Acquisition changed its name to Obagi Medical Products, Inc. Next, OMP, Inc., was formed in November 2000 and two months later merged into Obagi Medical Products, with OMP, Inc., emerging as the surviving corporation. In December 2004, OMP, Inc., stockholders exchanged their shares for shares in a newly formed holding company named Obagi Medical Products, Inc.

SALES AND DISTRIBUTION MODEL

Although the company would broaden its product line, its initial phase of development was devoted primarily to the Obagi Nu-Derm System. During its first decade on the market, the system was steadily refined, as Obagi built a customer base. The company sold its products directly to physicians, relying on its own direct sales force to sell Obagi branded products to the medical-professional field. As the company expanded into international markets, it relied on agreements with foreign distribution partners to promote its product to physicians overseas. The company eventually struck accords with a dozen foreign distribution partners, enabling it to widen its operating territory to encompass markets in more than 35 countries.

Obagi Medical sold its products to physicians, but ultimately the company catered to the end user of its products. Women between the ages of 35 and 65 represented the company's primary customer, a demographic whose growth worked in Obagi Medical's favor. According to the U.S. Census Bureau, the number of women between the ages of 35 and 65

increased 35 percent between 1990 and 2004, creating ideal market conditions for the company's growth during its first phase of development. An expanding customer base enabled Obagi Medical to gain its footing. Once established, the company promoted the advantages of the Obagi Nu-Derm System, spreading word of its rejuvenating capabilities domestically and internationally to a growing number of target customers. After expanding both at home and abroad, the company began diversifying its product line, lessening its dependence on the Obagi Nu-Derm System.

PRODUCT LINE EXPANSION

By 2001, Obagi Medical's revenues had climbed to $35.6 million, the result of 13 years of growth. Within the next five years, the company's annual volume would nearly double as it began to broaden its presence in the aesthetic and therapeutic skin health markets. In part, the financial growth was attributable to the release of several new products during the period. In 2002, the company introduced tretinoin, the generic equivalent of Retin-A—among the most widely used acne treatments for the previous 25 years—which marked its entry into the fiercely competitive acne segment of the therapeutic market. Obagi Medical made the leap in the acne segment by reaching an exclusive licensing agreement with Triax Pharmaceuticals, LLC, giving it the right to distribute the topical cream in the United States. In 2004, Obagi Medical released the Obagi-C Rx System, the first prescription-strength vitamin C and hydroquinone system. The Obagi-C Rx System comprised a combination of four prescription and over-the-counter drugs that treated skin conditions resulting from sun damage. In 2005, the company launched Professional-C, a nonprescription, vitamin C-based serum that helped reverse the adverse effects of UV radiation and other environmental influences.

OBAGI MEDICAL GOES PUBLIC IN 2006

As Obagi Medical's 20th anniversary approached, the company's Long Beach, California, main offices were alive with activity. After operating in the private sector for nearly two decades, the company decided to make its public debut, filing for an initial public offering (IPO) of stock in September 2006. In December 2006, Obagi Medical completed the offering, selling 5.35 million shares at $11 per share.

By the time Obagi Medical became a publicly traded company, investors were greeted with several new additions to the company's product line. In July 2006, the company introduced Obagi Nu-Derm Condition and Enhance, a system that was designed for use after soft tissue filler injections such as Botox. In October 2006, the company released the first product of its new ELASTIderm line, ELASTIderm Eye Cream, a night-time eye cream for treatment of skin laxity around the eye. Products in the ELASTIderm line were formulated with a bi-mineral complex developed by the company that used the body's natural ability to increase epidermal thickness and elastin levels. By the end of the year, the newly public Obagi Medical could point to impressive financial totals, ensuring shareholders remained pleased with the company's progress. For the year, the company generated nearly $78 million in revenue and posted $6.1 million in net income.

New products continued to debut after Obagi Medical's IPO. In February 2007, a second product was added to the ELASTIderm line, ELASTIderm Eye Gel, which was designed to be used during the day in conjunction with ELASTIderm Eye Cream as a comprehensive eye therapy system. The month also marked the introduction of CLENZIderm M.D., another product developed to treat acne. CLENZIderm M.D. used a special formulation of Benzoyl Peroxide, which enabled the product to penetrate deep into the skin follicle and kill bacteria.

TURNING 20 IN 2008

Obagi Medical celebrated its 20th anniversary in 2008 in a fashion reflecting its newfound penchant for expansion. The company introduced a new product. In January 2008, a third member of the ELASTIderm family entered the market, the ELASTIderm Decolletage System. Developed to treat hyperpigmentation and wrinkles, the system replenished elasticity and built collagen on the chest and neck area. The company had the data to back up its claims. At the 2007 annual meetings of the American Academy of Dermatology and the American Society of Plastic Surgeons, Obagi Medical presented findings related to its ELASTIderm products that showed 49 percent improvement in skin elasticity and 68 percent reduction in fine lines and wrinkles around the eyes. The study, conducted over the course of nine weeks, involved 33 subjects.

In the years ahead, the roster of Obagi Medical products was set to expand around its core product, the Obagi Nu-Derm System. The company's flagship product continued to account for the bulk of its revenue—70 percent in 2006—but as more and more Obagi branded products entered the market, Obagi Medical could look forward to a more balanced corporate profile.

Jeffrey L. Covell

PRINCIPAL SUBSIDIARIES

OMP, Inc.

PRINCIPAL COMPETITORS

Skin Medica, Inc.; Valeant Pharmaceuticals International; L'Oréal SA.

FURTHER READING

"Correcting and Replacing," *Business Wire,* March 31, 2004, p. 5514.

Crowe, Deborah, "Obagi Sets Sights on Broadening Profile in Cosmeceuticals," *Los Angeles Business Journal,* April 2, 2007, p. 5.

"The Long Term Effects of a 'Healthy Tan,'" *Business Wire,* April 27, 2004, p. 6021.

"Obagi Medical Products and Revance Therapeutics Announce License Agreement for New, Proprietary Skin Products Targeting Elastin," *Internet Wire,* January 24, 2006.

"Obagi Medical Products Announces Pricing of Its Initial Public Offering," *Business Wire,* December 14, 2006.

"Obagi Medical Products Expands in the Middle East," *Canadian Corporate News,* July 9, 2004.

"Obagi Medical Products, Inc. Launches CLENZIderm M.D. Penetrating Acne Therapeutic System," *Business Wire,* January 29, 2007.

"Obagi Medical Products Introduces the New ELASTIderm Decolletage System," *PR Newswire,* January 23, 2008.

Prior, Molly, "Sephora Boutiques to Open in Greece's Notos Galleries," *WWD,* September 18, 2006, p. 25.

Omrix
Biopharmaceuticals, Inc.

650 Fifth Avenue, 22nd Floor
New York, New York 10111
U.S.A.
Telephone: (212) 887-6500
Fax: (212) 887-6550
Web site: http://www.omrix.com

Public Company
Incorporated: 1995 as Omrix Pharmaceuticals S.A.
Employees: 180
Sales: $61.7 million (2007)
Stock Exchanges: NASDAQ
Ticker Symbol: OMRI
NAIC: 325414 Biological Product (Except Diagnostic)
    Manufacturing

∎ ∎ ∎

Maintaining its corporate headquarters in New York City, Omrix Biopharmaceuticals, Inc., is a former Belgium-based company that develops and manufactures products at its facility in Tel Aviv, Israel. Relying on its proprietary protein purification technology, the NASDAQ-listed biopharmaceutical firm concentrates on two markets, biosurgery and passive immunotherapy. Derived from human plasma, the proteins are purified yet retain the biological benefits of their natural structure. Omrix's biosurgical products focus on the surgical sealant market, which uses the purified plasma product to control bleeding (hemostasis). The sealants are marketed under the CROSSEAL and Evicel brands

in the United States and Quixil in Europe and other parts of the world.

Providing about 65 percent of sales, however, are the company's passive immunotherapy products, which use protein purification to produce antibody-rich substances. They are intended for the treatment of smallpox vaccine complications (in the event terrorists unleash smallpox on a world in which young people have not been vaccinated for the former scourge) and primary immune deficiencies, as well as the prevention of Hepatitis B reinfection in transplanted livers. In addition to its Tel Aviv and New York operations, Omrix maintains an office in Cologne, Germany, to handle European regulatory affairs and provide logistical and marketing support. The founder and chief executive officer of Omrix, Robert Taub, owns about one-quarter of the company's stock.

BEGINNINGS IN BELGIUM: 1995

Robert Taub founded Omrix in Belgium in 1995. After receiving an undergraduate degree in languages from the University of Antwerp, he earned an M.B.A. from the European Institute of Business Administration in Fontainebleau, France. He then held a variety of sales and marketing and management positions with Armour Pharmaceutical, Revlon Health Care Group, Baxter Travenol Laboratories, Inc., and Monsanto Company. In 1983 he struck out on his own, teaming up with Wolfgang Marguerre to form a Swiss-Austrian company called Octapharma A.G., which used blood plasma fractionation (breaking down plasma into components) to develop pharmaceutical products.

COMPANY PERSPECTIVES

We aim to develop novel technologies to provide safer and more effective options to patients in areas with substantial unmet medical needs, particularly in the areas of biosurgical and passive immunotherapy products. We are utilizing our proprietary protein purification technology, innovative development capabilities, and manufacturing know-how to develop these product lines, often through collaborations with companies whose marketing and sales expertise are a complement to our own areas of specialty.

The initial goal of Octapharma was to produce a virally safe, extremely pure plasma product. Because of the HIV crisis that soon visited the plasma refractionation industry, the development of the product was fast-tracked by Octapharma partners and put on the market. Later the company developed a virus inactivated transfusion plasma and a number of other plasma derivatives. During his time at Octapharma, Taub established a research and development group to pursue a biological fibrin sealant product that could stop bleeding and therefore eliminate the need for blood transfusions and avoid possible infection.

When his partner decided to withdraw from the sealant project, Taub left Octapharma in 1995 to pursue the research himself. He formed Omrix Pharmaceuticals S.A. in Belgium in July 1995, and two months later reached an agreement with Octapharma and an Israeli nonprofit company, Magen David Adom (MDA), to obtain the rights to the sealant technology and related products in the Octapharma pipeline. Taub relocated the research and development effort to Tel Aviv, where work was conducted at Nes Ziona Science Based Industries Park and later production was done at a facility at the Tel-Hashomer Sheba Hospital. Taub told the Tel Aviv newspaper *Globes,* "The decision to establish the plant in Jerusalem was taken on the basis of the high quality personnel relative to their price, because plants in Israel meet international quality standards, because of the tax laws, and because we already had one plant in the country."

DELAWARE INCORPORATION: 1998

Taub did not, however, turn to Israeli venture capitalists for funding. Initially he relied on his own money and later turned to investors he had nurtured during his time in Belgium and the United States. Such connections led to the 1998 investment of BRM Capital of Boston, opening the door to additional U.S. investment. It was also in December 1998 that Omrix was incorporated in the state of Delaware.

Omrix researchers used plasma fractionation to find the most basic components of blood plasma, and then combined them in search of a way to stem bleeding or at least hasten clotting. A breakthrough came when they discovered that the combination of plasma constituents fibrinogen and thrombin created a biological glue that when applied to bleeding tissue caused almost immediate clotting. Because it was a natural product, it did not face rejection from the body. Also helpful was that over time the resulting clot dissolved on its own. The glue, which would take the commercial name Quixil, was successfully tested by orthopedic surgeons during knee and hip replacement surgery in both Israel and the United Kingdom. In November 1998 Quixil received approval by Israel's Ministry of Health and a year later the sealant was licensed in the United Kingdom, followed by regulatory approval in South Africa, Ireland, Finland, and Italy. In the meantime, Quixil was being tested at Johns Hopkins in Baltimore and appeared to be well on its way to receiving approval from the U.S. Food and Drug Administration (FDA). The market for the product was estimated to be more than $500 million a year. These positive developments were key to Omrix's ability to attract the interest of U.S. investors.

IPO POSTPONEMENT: 2000

Sales of Quixil accounted for less than $2 million in the $18 million in sales Omrix recorded in 1999, most of the revenues coming from the sale of immunoglobulins sold for use in pharmaceutical products. With its incorporation in Delaware and likely FDA approval for its sealant, Omrix made plans in 2000 to conduct an initial public offering (IPO) of stock in hopes of raising $50 million and achieving a market capitalization of $150 million to $200 million. Unfortunately, world events intervened to derail those plans and disrupt the entire Israel biotech sector.

A resumption of Israeli-Palestinian hostilities that began in 2000 prevented FDA inspectors from confirming the acceptable manufacturing practices of the Omrix plant in Tel Aviv because Israel appeared on the U.S. State Department's list of travel advisories. The company offered to purchase extra insurance and to hire security guards for the inspectors, and it tried to apply pressure on the State Department through the Israeli Ministry of Trade as well as through U.S. congressmen, but nothing worked and the company's attempt to sell

```
┌─────────────────────────────────────────────┐
│  ┌─────────────────────────────────────────┐ │
│  │             KEY DATES                   │ │
│  │                 ■                       │ │
│  └─────────────────────────────────────────┘ │
│                                               │
│   1995:  Company is founded in Belgium.       │
│   1998:  Omrix is incorporated in Delaware.   │
│   2003:  FDA approves CROSSEAL for use in     │
│          liver surgery.                       │
│   2006:  Initial public offering of stock is  │
│          completed.                           │
│   2008:  Evicel is approved for general       │
│          surgery uses.                        │
│                                               │
└─────────────────────────────────────────────┘
```

Quixil in the all-important U.S. market and take the company public was put on hold.

RECEIVING FDA APPROVAL: 2003

Despite the problems with the FDA, Omrix was able to grow sales. In 2002 product sales increased to $11.8 million and total revenues reached $12.2 million. A year later Omrix was finally able to secure FDA approval for its sealant, under the name CROSSEAL, for use in liver surgery. The American Red Cross also agreed to distribute the product in the United States under a long-term marketing and distribution contract. With CROSSEAL making a partial contribution in 2003, revenues improved to about $15 million. The company enjoyed other successes in the United States during this period. In 2003 it became the first Israeli company to receive a research grant from the U.S. National Institutes of Health (NIH). The two-year, $3 million grant was earmarked for the development of an anti-bioterror injection to combat any attempts made by terrorists to unleash smallpox on a population that was no longer vaccinated against the disease to the extent it once had been. In addition, Omrix and NIH signed a cooperation agreement to study an anti–West Nile fever intravenous immunoglobulin preparation.

Total revenues approached $20 million in 2004, when in the third quarter of the year, Johnson & Johnson Wound Management of ETHICON, Inc., acquired the exclusive marketing and distribution rights for CROSSEAL. A year earlier Johnson & Johnson had secured the rights to market and distribute QUIXIL in Europe. With the help of its much larger partner, Omrix grew revenues to $27.5 million in 2005, and despite a loss on the year it turned a profit in the fourth quarter.

PUBLIC OFFERING: 2006

According to press reports, Johnson & Johnson made a bid for Omrix but the two sides had been unable to settle on a price. With a second generation sealant being considered for FDA approval, Omrix decided instead to take advantage of its momentum and finally tap the U.S. equity market with an IPO. The company filed the offering in January 2006 with UBS Securities LLC, CIBC World Markets Corp., Leerink Swann & Company, and Oppenheimer & Co. serving as underwriters. Omrix hoped to sell up to $80.5 million in common stock, but Wall Street was not especially receptive to drug and medical-device makers that spring, forcing the company to cut its offering to $55 million and then to $34 million when the IPO took place in April 2006. The shares quickly rose above the IPO price of $10, eventually topping $39 before returning to a more realistic price in the $14 range.

A major reason for the strong performance of Omrix stock was the continuation of good news. In July 2006 the FDA approved the company's second generation sealant product, Evicel, which unlike CROSSEAL did not contain a stabilizer. Like CROSSEAL, Evicel was approved for use in liver surgery, but late-phase trials were already underway using the product in a wide variety of surgical procedures, including cardiovascular surgery, spine procedures, and general surgery or post-traumatic procedures. The price of Omrix stock also rose on rumors that Johnson & Johnson was again interested in buying the company. While nothing came of the acquisition talk, Omrix was able to take advantage of the positive environment to make a secondary offering of stock in December 2006, raising about $51.4 million, the money expected to be used to market its sealants as they received approval for additional uses.

When the numbers were tallied for 2006, Omrix posted product sales of $56.9 million and total revenues of $63.8 million, resulting in net income of $23 million. After more than a decade of effort, and a number of rough patches, Omrix had clearly turned the corner and proved that it was a viable player in its field. As expected, additional FDA approvals for the sealants were received in 2007. In May the FDA approved Evicel for use in vascular surgery. In August the company received approval on another product, Evithrom. Developed in collaboration with Johnson & Johnson, it was a human plasma-derived alternative to bovine protein-based thrombin, a bleeding control product that was causing some problems with patients who developed antibodies to bovine-derived thrombin. Early in 2008 Evicel was also approved for general hemostasis in all types of surgical procedures when standard techniques proved ineffective or impractical.

Despite an abundance of positive developments, the financial results of 2007 were not as good as the company had anticipated, due in large part to problems encountered during the second quarter. Not only were sales of intravenous immunoglobulin lower than expected outside of Israel, but Omrix also had to deal with an FDA delay in the approval for the purchase of cryo, a crucial raw material the company needed to produce Evicel. As a result, total revenues dipped to $61.7 million in 2007 and net income decreased to $11.9 million. Nevertheless, Omrix appeared to be well positioned for ongoing growth as its products gained approval for further uses and were poised to capture greater market share. Other product candidates were also in the final development stages, including Adhexil, an anti-adhesion product, and Fibrin Patch, intended to address severe, or "brisk," bleeding.

Ed Dinger

PRINCIPAL SUBSIDIARIES

Omrix Pharmaceuticals S.A.; Omrix Pharmaceuticals Ltd.

PRINCIPAL COMPETITORS

Baxter International Inc.; CryoLife, Inc.; CSL Behring.

FURTHER READING

Ben-Israel, Adi, "Sales Delays Weigh on Omrix," *Globes* (Tel Aviv, Israel), August 9, 2007.

"Biological Glue Approved in Israel," *Israel High-Tech Investment Report,* December 1997.

Machlis, Avi, and Adrian Michaels, "Israeli Biotech Suffers Lack of Inspections," *Financial Times,* March 22, 2002, p. 28.

Weinreb, Gali, "'We Want Omrix to Be a Big Israeli Company,'" *Globes* (Tel Aviv, Israel), June 28, 2006.

Openwave Systems Inc.

2100 Seaport Boulevard
Redwood City, California 94063
U.S.A.
Telephone: (650) 480-8000
Fax: (650) 480-8100
Web site: http://www.openwave.com

Public Company
Incorporated: 2000
Employees: 1,270
Sales: $290.3 million (2007)
Stock Exchanges: NASDAQ
Ticker Symbol: OPWV
NAIC: 511210 Software Publishers

■ ■ ■

Openwave Systems Inc. is a leading developer of software that enables services to be delivered to mobile telephones. The company develops server software that is integrated in the networks operated by wireless carriers. Openwave also develops client software that is installed on mobile telephones, enabling handset manufacturers to provide mobile browsing, messaging, and content services. The company helped develop the Wireless Application Protocol (WAP), the communications standard for software applications used by wireless devices that access the Internet.

ORIGINS

Openwave was born a giant. On its first day of business, the company employed more than 1,700 workers in 27

offices. It operated subsidiaries and offices in 15 countries. Its technology was regarded as the industry standard, used by more than 150 communications service providers who, in turn, served more than 500 million subscribers. The company was a newcomer as far as its name was concerned, but its creation was six years in the making, the result of the persistence and vision of one of Silicon Valley's serial entrepreneurs, Alain Rossmann, the father of WAP.

Born and raised in France, Rossmann immigrated to the United States and settled in California's Silicon Valley in 1981. He was a member of the early development team working on Apple Computer's Macintosh computer, an experience that gave him the confidence to strike out on his own. Rossmann founded or cofounded roughly a half dozen companies, including Radius Inc. Formed in 1986, Radius was a computer hardware firm that sold and developed processor upgrade cards, graphics accelerators, high-end video adapters, and monitors. Radius became the first licensed Macintosh clone vendor.

THE GROWTH OF PHONE.COM

Of all his entrepreneurial efforts, none required more of Rossmann's determination than his fourth venture, a company founded as Unwired Planet that gained fame as Phone.com. He started the company in 1994, at a time when many of his peers were preaching about the boundless opportunities to be created by providing broadband access to the Internet. Rossmann's interests ran in the opposite direction, focused instead on services that utilized narrowband access to the Internet. He foresaw the mobile telephone as playing a pivotal part in the wide-ranging multimedia future that countless people were forecasting. "There's something unique about a small device that you have with you all the time," he said in a March 1, 2000, interview with the *Financial Times.*

Rossmann wanted to connect the Internet to the mobile phone. To help make his vision a reality, Rossmann approached Charles Parrish, the general manager of mobile data for GTE Mobile Communications, one of the leading mobile phone network operators in the United States. He showed Parrish drawings he made of his idea, he showed him animations on a laptop computer, and he set up a system with a modem that demonstrated a mobile phone receiving stock quotes from the Internet. Parrish was impressed. "I didn't have much of an idea at the time of how successful it would be," he said in a March 15, 2000, interview with the *Financial Times,* "but I liked the idea. And I knew that if it was successful it would be good for the industry, so I introduced him to people in the sector."

Parrish's fascination with Rossmann's concept grew. When he left GTE Mobile, he turned down a chance to become chief executive officer of a well-known company to become executive vice-president of Rossmann's fledgling outfit. Together, the two men would tackle the numerous challenges ahead, as they began to develop software to deliver services such as the original stock quote idea as well as a range of entertainment, banking, and mobile commerce services.

THE DEVELOPMENT OF WAP

Rossmann and Parrish set up their office in Redwood City, along the water's edge of San Francisco Bay. They faced many daunting challenges, but none greater than developing a way to deliver Internet content to mobile telephones. The crux of the problem was to ensure data could flow through many different communications systems and come out correctly on a user's handset. The

solution to the problem became Phone.com's crowning achievement and arguably the single greatest professional contribution made by Rossmann. Instead of developing his own, proprietary way of delivering data, Rossmann encouraged rival companies to develop a worldwide standard. "We were quick to recognize the value of a standard to 'grow' the opportunity," Parrish recounted in his March 15, 2000, interview with the *Financial Times.* "We knew our share would have to go down from 100 percent, but we thought it was better to have a smaller piece of a much larger market."

After deciding to pool his company's technology with others, Rossmann spearheaded a gathering of wireless manufacturers, seeking to develop a protocol that would be accepted and used worldwide before commercial deployment of services to mobile telephones began. In 1997, Phone.com collaborated with Ericsson, Motorola, and Nokia. The meetings, which occurred in several rounds of talks, gave birth to the Wireless Application Protocol, or WAP. Although he was not alone in the effort, Rossmann was considered the architect of WAP, making him a genuine industry pioneer.

STOCK OFFERING IN 1999

Once WAP was established, Rossmann pressed forward, built a product line, and developed a customer base. He forged relationships with wireless network operators and handset manufacturers, marketing Phone.com's Up.Link Server Suite to network operators and the company's Up.Browser technology to handset manufacturers. By the time he was ready to take Phone.com public, Rossmann had signed agreements with 17 network operators in the United States and Europe and 18 handset manufacturers. The company gave away its microbrowser for free and tied its fortunes to the licensing fees it charged for its server software. Phone.com completed its initial public offering (IPO) of stock in June 1999, debuting at $16 per share. By the end of its first day of trading, the company's stock soared 151 percent, reaching $40 per share.

A global acquisition campaign followed the IPO, as Rossmann acquired the pieces to make his company the preeminent WAP software developer. In a little more than six months after Phone.com's stock offering, Rossmann acquired four companies, which triggered a sevenfold increase in the company's stock value, giving it a market capitalization of $8 billion and making Rossmann's stake worth nearly $1 billion. The companies acquired included @Motion, a $285 million, all-stock purchase that gave Phone.com voice processing software, making it possible to turn data into voice and vice versa. For $500 million, Phone.com purchased Paragon Software, a British company that developed synchroniza-

KEY DATES

1994: Alain Rossmann founds what will become Phone.com.

1997: Rossmann spearheads efforts to develop the Wireless Application Protocol (WAP).

1999: Phone.com completes its initial public offering of stock.

2000: Phone.com merges with Software.com, creating Openwave Systems Inc.

2006: Openwave acquires Musiwave.

2007: Robert Vrij is named chief executive officer.

tion software that coordinated data between mobile devices and personal computers. Phone.com purchased Onebox.com, a small unified messaging company based in San Mateo, California. It acquired a Danish mobile Internet software company named Angelica Wireless. While the acquisitions were being completed, Rossmann continued striking accords with telecommunications carriers. By March 2000, the company had relationships with more than 50 carriers, including AT&T and Sprint in the United States and Omnitel and Mannesmann in Europe.

THE MARRIAGE OF PHONE.COM AND SOFTWARE.COM IN 2000

For Rossmann, the biggest transaction was yet to come. In August 2000, he revealed his intention to acquire Software.com. In the metrics of the go-go days of the dot-com sector, the all-stock merger was valued at a staggering $6.4 billion. Software.com was founded in 1993 by four graduates of the University of California at Santa Barbara. The founders started the business to develop software that managed the delivery of e-mail, eventually developing applications for e-mail and messaging that were sold to wireline customers, including traditional telephone companies, Internet service providers, and cable companies. The combination of the two enterprises, which was consummated in November 2000, created a company with more than 1,700 employees and 27 offices in 15 countries. It also created a need for a new corporate title, giving birth to the name Openwave Systems Inc. "We wanted a name that was consistent with a communications company that's going to be in partnership with other companies," Openwave's senior manager of branding and advertising explained in a November 27, 2000, interview with *InfoWorld.* "We also wanted to convey approachability as well as boldness and innovation."

DON LISTWIN ASSUMES LEADERSHIP OF OPENWAVE

Rossmann became chairman of the newly constituted company and hired Don Listwin to serve as Openwave's chief executive officer and president. Listwin left his job at networking giant Cisco Systems to join Openwave, bringing with him considerable experience in completing acquisitions. As Openwave set out, it was expected to stay active on the acquisitions front. "The name of the game is to build bulk as quickly as you can," *Info-World* noted in its November 27, 2000, issue. In the November 20, 2000, issue of *Canadian Corporate News,* Listwin offered his view of the role Openwave would play in the coming months. "The next wave of communications is not about personal computers versus appliances, or short-messaging versus the mobile Internet," he said. "It is about connecting people with what is important to them—anywhere, anytime, over any device. It is communications without limits."

Openwave embarked on an acquisition campaign following its formation, but it did so without the architect of its creation. Rossmann, who initially assumed the responsibilities of chairman, resigned in mid-2001 to become chief executive officer of Secret Seal Inc., a security infrastructure software company. Listwin added the duties of chairman to his responsibilities after Rossmann's departure.

Listwin engineered several acquisitions during his tenure. In mid-2002, Openwave acquired SignalSoft for $59 million, which gave it location-based applications such as Friend Finder, software that allowed users to determine the geographic location of friends. At roughly the same time, the company purchased download management technology from wireless application developer Ellipsus Systems, which increased Openwave's ability to handle Java-based content, such as games and multimedia.

LACKLUSTER FINANCIAL PERFORMANCE

Acquisitions added to the suite of services Openwave could provide, but the company struggled to turn its promise into financial success. After recording a numbing $690 million loss in its first year, a deficit largely the result of merger- and acquisition-related charges, the company was a consistent money loser. Openwave did not record its first profitable quarter until the first quarter of fiscal 2004, when Listwin resigned from the company to devote all his energies to a nonprofit venture he founded, Canary Fund, that raised money to help in the early detection of cancer. David Peterschmidt, the former chief executive officer of an Internet search company, Inktomi, took his place, but he too struggled to turn a profit. Despite a promising start to the year, 2004 ended with another substantial loss of $30 million.

There was no doubt Openwave products were widely used. In 2005, its software products delivered more than one trillion mobile data transactions to consumers, a staggering volume recorded by managing more than three billion transactions daily, but its lackluster financial results continued to be a glaring weakness. The company ended 2005 saddled with another distressing blemish on its financial record, posting a net loss of nearly $63 million.

Openwave tried to find a way out of its financial morass, but it proved to be a difficult challenge. In 2006, the company acquired Musiwave, a Paris, France-based provider of music and entertainment applications, but Openwave put the company up for sale a year later, failing to realize the benefits of the acquisition. There was a glimmer of hope at the end of 2006, when for the first time Openwave posted an annual profit, registering $5.2 million in net income. By the end of the following year, however, the mood soured at headquarters, as the company announced a $196 million loss, which was partly attributable to counting Musiwave as a discontinued operation.

As Openwave prepared for the future, it still had much to prove. Peterschmidt resigned in 2007 and was replaced by Robert Vrij, who was promoted from his post as executive vice-president of Openwave's worldwide field operations. Vrij inherited control over a company struggling to find its footing. During Vrij's first two months in charge, Openwave retained the services of Merrill Lynch & Co. as its financial adviser to explore strategic alternatives, including the possible sale of the company. "Despite expressions of interest," Openwave noted in its 2007 annual filing with the U.S. Securities and Exchange Commission, "no binding proposals to acquire the company were submitted and we ceased soliciting any such proposals." Much remained for Vrij and his successors to accomplish for Rossmann's vision to be transformed into a financial success, which constituted the overriding objective Openwave pursued as it plotted its future course.

Jeffrey L. Covell

PRINCIPAL SUBSIDIARIES

Openwave Systems (Argentina) S.R.L.; Openwave Systems Pty. Ltd. (Australia); Openwave Systems Brasil Ltda. (Brazil); Openwave Systems (Canada) Limited; Magic 4 France; Musiwave SA (France); Openwave Systems Holdings (France) SAS; Openwave Systems (France) SAS; Openwave Systems (Deutschland) GmbH (Germany); Musiwave Asia Limited (Hong Kong); Openwave Systems (H.K.) Ltd. (Hong Kong); Openwave Systems Service India Private Limited; Openwave Systems (Italia) S.r. l. (Italy); Nihon Openwave Systems K.K. (Japan); Openwave Systems Mexico S. de R.L. de C.V.; Openwave Systems B.V. (Netherlands); Openwave Systems (New Zealand) Limited; Openwave Systems (Ireland) Limited (U.K.); Openwave Systems (NI) Limited (U.K.); Openwave Systems (ROI) Limited (Ireland); Openwave Systems (Singapore) Pte. Ltd.; Openwave Systems (South Africa) (Pty) Limited; Openwave Systems Co., Ltd. (South Korea); Openwave Systems (Espana), S.L. (Spain); Openwave Systems (Sweden) AB; Openwave Systems (Switzerland) SARL; Openwave Systems Taiwan Limited; Magic4 Limited (U.K.); Openwave Systems (Europe) Limited (U.K.); Openwave Systems (Holdings) Limited (U.K.); Openwave Systems Limited (U.K.); Widerweb Limited (U.K.); Magic4 US Inc.; Openwave Aries Inc.; Openwave ScriptEase Inc.; Openwave Systems International Holdings Inc.; Openwave Systems International Inc.; Openwave Technologies Inc.; Paragon Software, Inc.; Signalsoft Corporation; Solomio Corporation.

PRINCIPAL COMPETITORS

Nokia Corporation; Teleca Systems GmbH; Comverse Technology, Inc.

FURTHER READING

April, Carolyn A., "Merger: Phone.com Finishes Software.com Deal," *InfoWorld,* November 27, 2000, p. 16.

Benesh, Peter, "Wireless Technology: Openwave Looks to Recapture Wireless Excitement," *Investor's Business Daily,* December 19, 2000, p. A6.

Brown, Ken Spencer, "Openwave Struggles to Find Fans for Wireless Data Standard," *Silicon Valley/San Jose Business Journal,* June 22, 2001, p. 17.

Bruno, Antony, "Phone.com Rings Up Successful IPO," *RCR-Radio Communications Report,* June 21, 1999, p. 14.

Costello, Sam, "Openwave Goes on Buying Spree," *Infoworld. com,* May 29, 2002.

Freeman, Tyson, "Openwave Grabs Avogadro for $100M," *Daily Deal,* May 10, 2001.

Gibbs, Colin, "Openwave Loses CEO, Explores Possible Sale of Company," *RCR Wireless News,* March 26, 2007, p. 1.

Lee, Dan, "CEO Steps Down at Software Firm Openwave," *San Jose Mercury News,* November 5, 2004.

McElligott, Tim, "Openwave Investors Look to Install Board Members by Proxy," *Telephony,* December 29, 2006.

Meyer, Cheryl, "Openwave Bulks Up and Waits," *Daily Deal,* June 4, 2002.

"Openwave Acquires Magic4," *Wireless News,* May 16, 2004.

"Openwave Acquires WiderWeb," *Wireless News,* March 1, 2007.

"Openwave Appoints Robert Vrij As CEO and Announces Exploration of Strategic Alternatives," *Wireless News,* March 25, 2007.

"Openwave Launch Marks Combination of Phone.com and Software.com," *AsiaPulse News,* November 27, 2000, p. 0695.

Orman, Neil, "Growth in Wireless Sector Rings Openwave's Bells," *San Francisco Business Times,* January 26, 2001, p. 28.

Purton, Peter, "Persistence Paid Off for Frenchman with an Idea That Was Not So Crazy," *Financial Times,* March 15, 2000, p. 29.

Schmeiser, Lisa, "Openwave Systems Inc.," *Investor's Business Daily,* February 6, 2006, p. A6.

Waters, Richard, "Huge Potential in the Wireless Internet World," *Financial Times,* March 1, 2000, p. 2.

Pengrowth Energy Trust

2100, 222 Third Avenue Southwest
Calgary, Alberta T2P 0B4
Canada
Telephone: (403) 233-0224
Toll Free: (800) 223-4122
Fax: (403) 265-6251
Web site: http://www.pengrowth.com

Public Company
Incorporated: 1988 as Pengrowth Gas Income Fund
Employees: 600
Sales: CAD 1.21 billion (2006)
Stock Exchanges: Toronto New York
Ticker Symbols: PGF.UN; PGH
NAIC: 211111 Crude Petroleum and Natural Gas Extraction; 533110 Owners and Lessors of Other Non-Financial Assets; 551112 Offices of Other Holding Companies

■ ■ ■

Pengrowth Energy Trust is an oil and gas investment trust that distributes nearly all its earnings to its shareholders, referred to as unitholders. The trust, managed by Pengrowth Management Limited, has an average 62 percent working interest in 200 oil and gas properties that compose a portfolio split evenly between oil and gas. The properties are located in Alberta, British Columbia, Saskatchewan, and off Nova Scotia's coast. Daily production at all of the trust's properties is approximately 86,000 barrels of oil equivalent. Pengrowth

Energy Trust distributes its income to unitholders on a monthly basis.

THE OPERATION OF AN ENERGY TRUST

During its first 20 years of operation, Pengrowth Energy Trust relied on the leadership of one individual, its founder, James S. Kinnear. Kinnear, a 1969 graduate of the University of Toronto, worked in the securities sector for more than a decade before striking out as an entrepreneur. After college, he was employed as a securities analyst in Toronto and London, England, gaining the experience that would lead to his appointment as research director and partner of a securities firm in Montreal. In 1982, he began blazing his own trail, forming Pengrowth Management Limited, a specialty fund manager that provided advisory, management, and administrative services related to oil and natural gas assets.

Pengrowth Management Limited served as the manager for Pengrowth Gas Corporation, which later changed its name to Pengrowth Corporation, and Pengrowth Gas Income Fund, which later changed its name to Pengrowth Energy Trust. Kinnear's affiliated companies were structured to give retail investors an opportunity to invest in the energy sector. Pengrowth Corporation functioned as the administrator of Pengrowth Energy Trust, acquiring, owning, and operating interests in oil and natural gas properties. The corporation generated cash flow from oil and gas properties, which it distributed to the trust in the form of a royalty: 99 percent of the production revenue, less operating

COMPANY PERSPECTIVES

Pengrowth intends to continue its focus on seeking out high quality, value-adding acquisitions. Although the acquisition market remains competitive, Pengrowth has a number of key advantages. These include access to both domestic and international capital, the increased size of the trust, solid relationships with the major and supermajor oil companies and a strong track record of closing and financing deals which includes over 55 acquisitions since inception. These factors are expected to enhance Pengrowth's ability to complete significant transactions well into the future.

expenses, general and administrative costs, and management fees. The trust, exempt from taxes at the corporate level provided nearly all earnings were distributed to investors, converted the royalty units into trust units, distributing them to its investors, or unitholders.

Energy trusts, as the September 20, 2002, edition of the *Oil Daily* observed, were "the great white sharks of the Canadian oil patch." Trusts did not explore for oil or gas. They left the business of wildcatting to others. Instead, trusts acquired mature, producing oil and gas properties to harvest the cash they distributed to unitholders, earning their reputations as predators because they dominated merger and acquisition activity in Canadian oil and gas markets. Once certain properties began to suffer declines in production, new properties were acquired to offset the depleting asset base. The steady stream of acquisitions required trusts to raise capital nearly every year, and it gave individual investors the chance to participate in the ownership of a large portfolio of crude oil and natural gas properties. Investors also enjoyed a tax break on their investment because a portion of the distributions to unitholders was considered a return of capital by the Canadian government and exempted from taxation.

PUBLIC OFFERING IN 1988

Kinnear set up the framework for Pengrowth Energy Trust's operation in the late 1980s. Pengrowth Gas Corporation was created under the laws of the Province of Alberta in December 1987. One year later, in December 1988, the trust was formed, debuting as Pengrowth Gas Income Fund. Of the 1,100 Pengrowth Gas Corp. shares, the trust owned 1,000 with the remainder owned by the trust's manager, Pengrowth Management

Ltd. The trust gained its first supply of capital from an initial public offering of stock of $12.5 million, a modest start for an entity that would become one of the largest energy trusts in North America.

As the name of the trust and the corporation suggested, Kinnear's efforts initially were limited to natural gas properties. The trust's sole property at its formation was a 2.65 percent interest in the Dunvegan Gas Unit No. 1. The property was located near Fairview, Alberta, 270 miles northwest of Edmonton. Production at the property started in 1973, and included more than 120 producing well zones in an 82-square-mile area by the time the trust acquired its working interest in the property. In 1989, the first full year the trust operated, Pengrowth Gas Income Fund generated CAD 1.4 million net revenue, enabling it to distribute CAD 0.48 per unit.

ACQUISITION CAMPAIGN BEGINNING IN 1991

Pengrowth Gas Income Fund relied entirely on the Dunvegan property until it completed its second acquisition in 1991. In September, the trust purchased a 0.93 percent interest in Nipisi Gilwood Unit No. 1, using a bank loan to complete the CAD 3.6 million deal. Located 180 miles northwest of Edmonton, the Nipisi property originally belonged to Amoco Canada Petroleum Company Ltd., which began production at the site in 1969. By the time Kinnear purchased his stake, the Nipisi property had more than 185 producing wells, wells that produced light, sweet crude oil, marking Kinnear's first foray into the oil sector. The Nipisi property was capable of producing 17,500 barrels of oil per day.

RAPID GROWTH IN THE LATE NINETIES

After a slow start on the acquisition front, the trust began to expand more aggressively, although at a more measured pace than it would grow in later years. By the time it changed its name to Pengrowth Energy Trust in 1996, the trust had increased its interests in its first two properties and acquired stakes in dozens of other properties primarily in western Canada. Between 1991 and 1996, the trust's proven reserves increased 16-fold to 44.2 million barrels of oil equivalent (boe), a measurement used to express both oil and gas quantities (one barrel of oil is equal to approximately 5,650 cubic feet of natural gas). The trust's interests in more than 60 oil and gas producing properties generated CAD 77.8 million in revenue in 1996, more than double the total recorded the previous year, enabling it to pay CAD 1.92 per trust unit, a record high.

KEY DATES

1988: Pengrowth Gas Income Fund is formed.
1991: The trust's second acquisition, a stake in Nipisi Gilwood Unit No. 1, marks its entry into the oil sector.
1996: Pengrowth Gas Income Fund changes its name to Pengrowth Energy Trust.
1997: Judy Creek/Swan Hills acquisition casts Pengrowth Energy Trust as an operator for the first time.
2002: Pengrowth Energy Trust begins trading on the New York Stock Exchange.
2007: Pengrowth Energy Trust completes the purchase of CAD 1.04 billion worth of oil and gas assets from ConocoPhillips, the largest acquisition ever by a Canadian energy trust.

The year Pengrowth Energy Trust changed its name served as a benchmark for the growth achieved in ensuing years. In the decade following the name change, the trust's growth would be measured by increases in daily production, or boe per day (boe/d), total established reserves, and revenues, while its success in managing such growth would be expressed in the amount of distributable income it provided to unitholders. The figures in each category as they stood in 1996—9,397 boe/d, established reserves of 44,236 mboe (thousand barrels of oil equivalent), $77.8 million in revenue, CAD 1.92 per trust unit—increased robustly in the years to follow, beginning with a significant year in 1997.

THE TRUST AS AN OPERATOR

In 1997, Pengrowth Energy Trust began touting itself as "The Benchmark of Energy Trusts," a claim it made good on by completing a massive acquisition during the year. The trust spent CAD 496 million acquiring primarily oil properties in the Judy Creek/Swan Hills region in central Alberta, purchasing the properties from Imperial Oil Resources. It was the largest property acquisition in the history of the Canadian oil industry, more than tripling the value of the trust's established reserves. The purchase more than doubled the trust's stock market value, making it the largest publicly owned royalty trust in Canada, and it ushered in significant changes in the way the trust operated. Before the acquisition, the trust was managed by only two dozen

people at Pengrowth Management Limited, but afterwards the payroll swelled to more than 100. Part of the reason for the dramatic increase in personnel stemmed from a significant aspect of the acquisition. For the first time in its history, the trust assumed the role of an operator in one of its properties. Instead of relying on industry partners, Pengrowth Energy Trust took responsibility for running the Judy Creek assets.

After the Judy Creek/Swan Hills acquisition, daily production increased to 14,716 boe/d, revenue increased nearly 60 percent to CAD 122 million, and established reserves shot up 228 percent to 144,962 mboe. Unitholders shared in the growth, receiving CAD 2.02 per unit. The figures represented impressive growth, but in the years ahead the totals would be dwarfed by the numerous acquisitions orchestrated by Kinnear.

ACQUISITIONS FUEL EXPANSION

The Judy Creek/Swan Hills purchase left Pengrowth Energy Trust heavily dependent on oil. After the acquisition, the trust's portfolio comprised 82 percent oil and 18 percent gas, an imbalance Kinnear addressed in the years to follow. One of the trust's biggest gas purchases occurred in 2001, when Kinnear purchased the Sable Offshore Energy Project assets belonging to Nova Scotia Resources Limited. Pengrowth Energy Trust spent CAD 265 million to purchase the assets, an addition hailed by Kinnear in a May 21, 2001, interview with *Market News Publishing*. "Pengrowth," he said, "is enthusiastic about becoming a partner in the Sable Offshore Energy Project, one of the most exciting energy plays in the world. This adds a new dimension to the trust, diversifying our portfolio beyond our western Canadian assets and significantly increasing the proportion of natural gas production in Pengrowth's portfolio from 22 percent to 32 percent."

By the end of 2001, the figures representing Pengrowth Energy Trust's stature had increased substantially. Established reserves had increased to 210,500 mboe, daily production had risen to 40,300 boe/d, and revenues had climbed to CAD 469.9 million. Distributable income reached CAD 3.01 per unit. The trust's exposure to potential investors increased in 2002 when it began trading on the New York Stock Exchange. In the United States, energy trusts were prohibited from buying new properties when existing properties were exhausted, which limited their life spans and made them unattractive to long-term investors. "If you're going to significantly expand your business, you've got to look at the international capital markets," Kinnear said in an April 8, 2002, interview with the *Financial Times*. "We have a few holders in the

United States ... but it's easier for them to follow your company if it's listed."

New investors in the United States were treated to an aggressive display of acquisitive might in the years following the trust's listing on the New York Stock Exchange. In September 2002, Pengrowth Energy Trust acquired nearly all the oil and gas properties in British Columbia owned by San Jose, California-based Calpine Corp. The purchase, estimated at CAD 300 million, included 171 billion cubic feet of gas in proven reserves. In 2004, Kinnear spent CAD 550 million to buy oil and gas properties from Murphy Oil Company Ltd. The acquisition increased the trust's production base by 33 percent, adding 43,600 mboe of proved reserves and 15,000 boe/d.

A BANNER YEAR IN 2006

Kinnear was completing one major deal after another. He was swallowing up oil and gas properties in massive batches, making deals that, in retrospect, were merely a prelude to a year of frenetic activity. In 2006, Pengrowth Energy Trust displayed the appetite of a ravenous shark, completing and initiating deals that made the year by far the most active in its 18-year history. In mid-2006, the trust merged with a rival, natural gas-focused Esprit Energy Trust, a CAD 950 million deal that added 53,500 mboe of proved reserves and balanced the trust's portfolio almost evenly between oil and gas. In September, the trust closed on the acquisition of Exxon Mobil Canada's 89 percent stake in oil and gas properties in Carson Creek, Alberta, near the trust's Judy Creek/Swan Hills assets. Kinnear paid CAD 475 million for the Carson Creek properties, gaining 5,100 boe/d.

On the acquisition front, the biggest was yet to come. In late 2006, Pengrowth Energy Trust announced it was acquiring assets in western Canada belonging to ConocoPhillips. The deal was valued at CAD 1.04 bil-

lion, the largest acquisition ever by a Canadian energy trust. The acquisition, which closed in January 2007, included light crude, shallow gas, and coal bed methane properties that were roughly evenly split between oil and gas, increasing Pengrowth Energy Trust's daily production by 27 percent. Kinnear, approaching his 20th year at the helm of Pengrowth Energy Trust, showed no signs of curbing his desire to add to the trust's portfolio. In the years ahead, further advances were expected by one of North America's most aggressive energy trusts.

Jeffrey L. Covell

PRINCIPAL SUBSIDIARIES

Pengrowth Corporation.

PRINCIPAL COMPETITORS

Baytex Energy Trust; Bonavista Energy Trust; Provident Energy Trust.

FURTHER READING

Beard, Alison, "Oil Group That Cannot Be Sapped Dry Comes to US," *Financial Times,* April 8, 2002, p. 23.

Darbonne, Nissa, "Fire!" *Oil and Gas Investor,* September 2004, p. 66.

Gosmano, Jeff, "Murphy Unloads Bulk of Canadian Operations," *Oil Daily,* April 12, 2004.

———, "Shopping Spree Resumes for Canada's Trusts," *Oil Daily,* July 25, 2006.

Kelly, Andrew, "Pengrowth Energy Trust Snapping Up Conoco's Burlington Properties," *Natural Gas Week,* December 4, 2006, p. 16.

———, "Trusts Still Alive and Kicking As Pengrowth Buys Conoco Assets," *Oil Daily,* November 30, 2006, p. 2.

Merolli, Paul, "Fire Sales Blaze on at Battered Merchants Calpine, NRG," *Oil Daily,* September 20, 2002.

"New Financings," *Oil and Gas Investor,* December 1, 2006.

Petit Bateau

—■—

BP 525
15 rue Lieutenant Pierre Murard
Troyes, F-10081 Cedex
France
Telephone: (33 03) 25 71 36 36
Fax: (33 03) 25 72 36 15
Web site: http://www.petitbateau.fr

Wholly Owned Subsidiary of Yves Rocher Group
Founded: 1918
Employees: 1,325
Sales: $237.1 million (2005)
NAIC: 315231 Women's and Girls' Cut and Sew Lingerie, Loungewear, and Nightwear Manufacturing; 315223 Men's and Boys' Cut and Sew Shirt (Except Work Shirt) Manufacturing; 315232 Women's and Girls' Cut and Sew Blouse and Shirt Manufacturing; 315291 Infants' Cut and Sew Apparel Manufacturing; 422330 Women's, Children's, and Infants' Clothing and Accessories Wholesalers; 448130 Children's and Infants' Clothing Stores; 454111 Electronic Shopping

■ ■ ■

Petit Bateau is renowned throughout France and worldwide for its high-quality clothing for infants, children, and young women. Esteemed for softness, comfort, durability, and ease of washing, all clothing is produced using natural fibers, such as 100 percent cotton, a bamboo-cotton blend, and a wool and cotton blend. Customers take pleasure in the fit and classic styling of the company's clothing, available primarily in solid colors, polka dots, and Petit Bateau's signature milleraies stripes. For infants, Petit Bateau offers underwear, layettes, pajamas, sweaters, jumpers, and one-piece body suits in a variety of seasonal styles. Infant accessories include blankets, bibs, towels, hats, and cotton toy rabbits. Children's clothing includes pants, skirts, jumpers, and jackets. Petit Bateau is particularly famous for its T-shirts for infants and children as well as women. The company offers a limited selection of clothing for young women, including leggings and underwear.

Petit Bateau clothing is available at upscale chain department stores, independent retail stores, and company-operated boutiques worldwide. Petit Bateau owns more than 130 retail shops in France and more than 40 international stores, including its flagship stores in exclusive shopping areas of London, Brussels, Berlin, Barcelona, Milan, and Tokyo. Boutiques in the United States are located in upscale neighborhoods in Boston; New York City; and Hackensack, New Jersey. The company operates a discount outlet store near Chicago and a showroom in New York City. Petit Bateau clothing is available online through several clothing retailers and through the company's web sites.

INADVERTENT INVENTION OF CHILDREN'S UNDERPANTS

Petit Bateau originated as a unit of Valton-Quinquarlet & Sons, a hosiery company in Troyes, Champagne, France, founded in 1893. The company established its reputation for quality when it produced long underwear for French soldiers during World War I. In 1918, while contemplating a pair of children's long underwear, Pierre Valton cut off the legs, an act said to have created the first pair of children's underpants. Two years later, he gave the children's *culottes* the name Petit Bateau, meaning "little boats." The inspiration for the name occurred when he heard his young son singing, *"Maman, las p'tits bateaux qui vont sur l'eau ont-ils jambs?"* In English, it translated as "Mommy, do the little boats on the sea have legs?" In 1920, Valton registered the name Petit Bateau along with a boat trademark, a line drawing of a small boat with large masts shown at sea. Advertising featured a drawing of a female character, Marinette, who modeled the underwear.

The *petit culottes,* as the company referred to them, were introduced to a worldwide audience in 1937, at the International Exhibition for Art Technology in Modern Life, held in Paris that year. Petit Bateau was recognized for its innovation in children's clothing.

PRODUCT DEVELOPMENT

Over the years, succeeding generations of the Valton family adjusted the style of the infant clothing to new fabrics and methods of construction. Product development made the company's infantwear more attractive to

mothers and more comfortable to babies. In 1950, Petit Bateau integrated cutaway shoulders into the construction of its infant clothing. By sewing the sleeve into the shirt at an angle, the style provided more elasticity, making it easier for mothers to dress their babies. The company incorporated the use of terry-cloth knit fabric into its two-piece underwear and T-shirt sets in 1960.

As the market for fashionable children's clothing began to develop, Petit Bateau created its own classic styles. In 1970 Petit Bateau invented the milleraies stripe, a fine, colored stripe that could be washed, even in hot water, without bleeding. The clothing became a classic French style as children throughout the country wore milleraies stripes.

The growing trend to dress children in more fashionable clothing led Petit Bateau to enter the retail market. In 1978 Petit Bateau opened its first retail store, at the Parly II Shopping Mall in Versailles. After several years of marketing its products through fine boutiques and department stores in New York City, Petit Bateau opened a store in New York City, called Pat Rick, in upper Manhattan's Madison Avenue shopping district. The store offered Petit Bateau clothing for infants and children up to eight years old. Petit Bateau opened a brand-name store on Boston's Newbury Street. A 1983 licensing agreement to produce and market clothing for Tartine et Chocolat expanded Petit Bateau's retail offering.

Exports significantly contributed to overall sales and profit increases. In 1982 Petit Bateau experienced sales and profit growth of 16 percent. Sales rose to FRF 499.1 million ($64.2 million) and profit to FRF 13.1 million ($1.68 million). With strong sales growth occurring in the United States, revenues from exports alone increased 21 percent, to FRF 173 million ($22.2 million). On the strength of the Tartine et Chocolat brand, Petit Bateau USA sales increased 25 percent in 1983. The company opened a plant in Beaufort, South Carolina, in 1984 to produce the Tartine line.

Petit Bateau updated its boat trademark continually to fit with changing aesthetic trends. In the late 1950s, the new design reflected the modern, postwar sensibility with a simpler line structure and the flared, finlike styling of the multiple masts. During the 1980s, Petit Bateau updated its "little boat" logo with softer curves for the masts and a simpler boat overall, with only two masts. The boat was carved into an abstract block of blue floating on a wave that merged into a circle around the whole picture, with some parts exceeding the space of the circle. The Petit Bateau name arced in a semicircle below the picture.

FINANCIAL SHIFTS LEAD TO NEW OWNERSHIP

Despite the company's successes, short-term debt and the need for capital prompted Petit Bateau to restructure its finances. The company reduced short-term debt by shifting the burden of interest to liabilities paid over the long term. Then changes in France's financial trading laws allowed Petit Bateau to seek financial support for growth on the Paris Bourse stock exchange without relinquishing a significant portion of ownership. Taking advantage of the lower minimum offer requirement, reduced from 25 percent to 10 percent of equity, Petit Bateau opted to offer 31,454 shares for its first public offering of stock in July 1983. As demand increased to more than three million shares, the Paris Bourse increased the offering to 40,000 shares. Introduced at FRF 270 ($34.70) per share, Petit Bateau stock rose as high as FRF 382 ($49.10) per share on opening day. After completion of the offering, share value continued to increase.

By 1985, a 20 percent decline in sales of children's underpants, compounded with previous liabilities, led to several years of financial troubles. While certain sectors turned a profit, the parent company, Petit Bateau Valton, started losing money overall. Workforce reductions proved only a stopgap measure. The persistent financial misfortunes of the company prompted Laboratoires Yves Rocher, a French cosmetics firm, to acquire a majority ownership in the company in early 1988 on the advice of Banque Nationale de Paris (BNP). Yves Rocher acquired a 56.66 percent interest through the Paris Bourse and gained a total of 89 percent ownership through a tender offer to shareholders. Hence, Yves Rocher purchased Petit Bateau from the Valton family and BNP. However, according to Yves Rocher, BNP provided misleading information about the financial condition of Petit Bateau, which carried losses of FRF 110 million ($17.6 million) in 1988.

It took several years for Yves Rocher to bring the company back to profitability. In 1989, during a temporary resolution of a dispute with the BNP, the bank granted Yves Rocher a five-year deferment on debt payments. Also, a FRF 220 million loan, participatory to stock ownership, kept Petit Bateau in operation while Yves Rocher restructured. Petit Bateau streamlined its workforce, cutting redundant jobs. The company discontinued its licensing agreement to produce children's clothing for the Tartine et Chocolat brand. Yves Rocher sold or closed its other clothing subsidiaries, as well as the retail stores in the United States. The company focused on restoring Petit Bateau to profitability. Toward that end, the company invested FRF 50 million to update production equipment at the plant in Troyes.

FASHION TRENDS AFFIRM BRAND REPUTATION

New product development affirmed Petit Bateau's reputation for quality and comfort and facilitated a turnaround at Petit Bateau. During the 1980s, the company's new one-piece body suit for babies became a popular item. In 1990, Petit Bateau introduced a wool and cotton blend fabric that provided babies with the luxurious softness of cotton on the inside of the clothing, with the warmth of wool from the outside.

Petit Bateau's entry into women's clothing occurred through unexpected publicity in 1996, when runway models wore Petit Batcau baby T-shirts under $5,000 Chanel suits. The fashion show launched the bare-belly look that became popular among young women during the 1990s. The look spurred unusual demand for Petit Bateau clothing by fashionably sleek women able to wear the company's tank tops and T-shirts in children's sizes. Capitalizing on the social cachet generated by the publicity, Petit Bateau added several new colors and styles to its line of T-shirts. Also, women's interest in boys' clothing led the company to urge upscale retailers, such as Henri Bendel, Bergdorf Goodman, and Barneys, to carry or expand their offering of Petit Bateau's boys' clothing. Eventually, Petit Bateau began to produce T-shirts for young women, using a 12-year-old to 18-year-old sizing scheme, corresponding to women's sizes from extra small to large. The quality and softness of the cotton fabric and the feminine fit attracted women customers of all ages. Petit Bateau's sales in the United States tripled over the two years following the fashion show.

In other product development, Yves Rocher combined its expertise in cosmetics to create a line of bath care and perfumes for babies for sale in Europe. In June 1999, Petit Bateau introduced Queue Eau, a bath gel that can be used as a shampoo and body soap. Also, the company offered Ça Me Lave les Cheveau shampoo and Ça Me Lave le Corps bath gels in watermelon, pear, and licorice fragrances. Petit Bateau launched three perfumes, Ça Me Parfume, a scent similar to pencil lead, Drôle de Biscuit, of the aroma of cookies, and Comme la Poire, with the fragrance of pears.

INTERNATIONAL BOUTIQUES SPREADING PETIT BATEAU'S REPUTATION

Vincent Huguenin, managing director of Petit Bateau since 1993, was instrumental in widespread international expansion during the late 1990s and early 2000s. The company expanded its international presence in two ways. First, the company began offering a wider range of its products to retailers. In the United States, Petit Bateau expanded its longstanding relationship with Madeleine Wolcott by providing the childrenswear importer with a full range of styles. Also, the company opened a marketing and promotional office in Pennsylvania, near Wolcott's office.

The second means of expansion involved opening Petit Bateau boutiques in fashionable shopping districts of the major world capitals. The company's first overseas store opened in Tokyo, Japan, in 1998, and flagship stores followed in Berlin, Barcelona, London, Brussels, and Milan. In England, Petit Bateau began with a shop-in-shop concession at Selfridges, offering a limited range of children's clothing. In July 2001, Petit Bateau opened a flagship store on King's Road, a residential shopping area in the Chelsea district of London that attracts families to the many childrenswear outlets in the area. Over the next two years the company opened stores in Chiswick, and on South Molton Street, both in London. In 2002, Petit Bateau opened one of its largest stores on posh Toison d'Or Avenue in Brussels, Belgium. Petit Bateau opened several stores in Italy, where parents are known for being particularly devoted to their children. By the end of 2003, the company operated ten stores, including stores that opened in Monza and Parma that year.

Petit Bateau opened three boutiques in the United States, offering clothing from newborns to size 18. The 3,000-square-foot flagship store in New York City opened in the chic Upper East Side neighborhood of Manhattan in the fall of 2001. A new store opening followed on Newbury Street in Boston. In September 2006 Petit Bateau opened in The Shops at Riverside, in Hackensack, New Jersey, a location chosen for its base of affluent families in Bergen County.

New store development in France included a boutique on the Champs-Elysées, which opened in 2000. The 100th store in the company's home country opened in Toulouse Labège in 2002. Expansion continued, and by 2007 the company operated more than 130 retail stores throughout France.

Petit Bateau successfully launched online shopping sites for customers in Japan and the United States in 2004 and 2005, respectively. Following the success of those ventures, the company launched its French web site in 2006.

New marketing and promotional initiatives included redesigning store interiors to resemble the comfort of home. Playfulness and creativity included cabin-themed fitting rooms. A modern look, with white block shelving, increased the focus on the products offered. The company tested the concept at two locations in Italy and France before renovating its network of 180 stores in 2005. Along with the new store concept, the company introduced a new logo. The color logo featured yellow masts with a blue boat and circle enclosure.

The popularity of Petit Bateau's soft cotton children's wear among Hollywood celebrities furthered Petit Bateau's reputation. Gwyneth Paltrow was frequently seen shopping for her two children at Petit Bateau shops in London. Tom Cruise and Katie Holmes appeared in the September 2006 issue of *Vanity Fair* magazine with their daughter Suri Cruise, who wore a Petit Bateau onesie.

Mary Tradii

PRINCIPAL SUBSIDIARIES

Petit Bateau Belgique (Belgium); Petit Bateau England (U.K.); Petit Bateau IBERICA s.l. (Spain); Petit Bateau Italia (Italy); Petit Bateau Japan; Petit Bateau Kinderbekleidung GmbH (Germany); Petit Bateau USA.

PRINCIPAL COMPETITORS

Christian Dior SA; Bonpoint; Groupe Zannier S.A.; Le Marchand d'Étoiles; Little VIP; Monoprix; Groupe Naf Naf; Ovale.

FURTHER READING

Ashworth, Anne, "Even on Holiday Frenchwomen Know How to Push the Boat Out; Chain Reaction," *Times* (London), August 3, 2007, p. 9.

"Baby Shipping Line," *Soap Perfumery & Cosmetics*, May 1999, p. 11.

Clack, Erin, "Opening Doors," *Children's Business*, November 2001, p. 30.

———, "Petit Bateau," *Children's Business*, September 2001, p. 9.

De La Rocque, Jean-Pierre, "Yves Rocher—BNP: ca se gate," *L'Express International*, March 7, 1996, p. 14.

"Fashion with a French Accent," *New York Times*, May 16, 1976, p. 370.

"French Petit Bateau Appoints Guy Flament CEO," *French Digest News*, October 3, 2002.

"French Petit Bateau Opens 10th Store in Italy," *French Digest News*, June 17, 2002.

Gould, Kate, "First Standalone for Petit Bateau," *Drapers Record*, July 21, 2001, p. 9.

"International Update EC," *Children's Business,* August 2000, p. 102.

Kraus, J. Russell, "Family-Owned French Textile Firms Go Public," *Daily News Record,* January 17, 1984, p. 7.

"The Operation Launched by the Yves Rocher Group to Acquire the Balance of Shares of Petit Bateau That It Does Not Yet Own Was to Be Launched in the First Half of December," *Cosmetics International,* December 12, 2003, p. 9.

"Petit Bateau Belgium Counts on Diversity to Increase Turnover for 2002," *Belgian Digest News,* July 15, 2002.

"Petit Bateau Goes from Strength to Strength," *La Tribune,* July 12, 2006.

"The Petit Bateau Group of France Is Forecasting Sales for 1984 of FFr 650m (+15%)," *Les Echos,* December 4, 1984.

"Petit Bateau Hits Paris Exchange," *WWD,* July 19, 1983, p. 16.

"Petit Bateau Plans 140 Redundancies," *Les Echos,* July 1, 1991, p. 13.

"Petit Bateau Reports Loss in Half," *WWD,* November 25, 1991, p. 8.

"Petit Bateau Suffers Loss in 1992," *Les Echos,* May 25, 1993, p. 11.

"Petit Bateau UK Store," *Retail Week,* June 21, 2002, p. 4.

"Petit Bateau Valton of France Is to Cut 175 of Its Workforce of 2,600," *Le Monde,* July 27, 1985.

"Rocher, Banque Nationale Will Arbitrate Dispute," *WWD,* November 9, 1989, p. 6.

"Rocher Looks to Settle Score with BNP in Petit Bateau Affair," *Le Monde,* February 25, 1996, p. 24.

"Rocher Unit Stops Making Tartine et Chocolat Line," *WWD,* September 7, 1993, p. 15.

Taylor, Angela, "For Children: New World on Madison Avenue," *New York Times,* March 19, 1983, p. 148.

Tieman, Ross, "Petit Bateau Finds Its Production Plan Is Not Child's Play," *Evening Standard,* May 22, 2002, p. 41.

"A Twist on Playing Dress-Up; Women in Kids' Stuff," *New York Times,* August 16, 1998.

Verdon, Joan, "Where the Best-Dressed Kiddies Get Their $25 Onesies; Upscale French Clothier Opens a Bergen Store," *Record* (Bergen County, N.J.), September 2, 2006, p. B01.

"World: Gallery," *Campaign,* March 26, 2004, p. 22.

Petrofac Ltd.

4th Fl., 117 Jermyn Street
London, SW1Y 6HH
United Kingdom
Telephone: (+44 020) 7811 4900
Fax: (+44 020) 7811 4901
Web site: http://www.petrofac.com

Public Company
Founded: 1981
Employees: 9,500
Sales: $2.4 billion (2007)
Stock Exchanges: London
Ticker Symbol: PFC
NAIC: 213112 Support Activities for Oil and Gas Field
Exploration; 333132 Oil and Gas Field Machinery
and Equipment Manufacturing

■ ■ ■

Petrofac Ltd. is a London-based, Jersey-registered supplier of support services to the global oil and gas industry. The company operates through three primary divisions. The largest is the Engineering & Construction division, which focuses on supplying EPC (engineering, procurement, and construction) services, including turnkey development and construction of offshore oil platforms and other support facilities for oil and gas producers. This division, which is especially active in the Middle East, as well as in India, North Africa, Kazakhstan, Austria, and elsewhere, generated more than 58 percent of Petrofac's revenues of $2.4 billion in 2007. Petrofac's second largest division is Operations Services

and Resources, which operates through two primary business units: Petrofac Facilities Management and Petrofac Training. The former provides both facilities management and support services, including operations, staffing, and maintenance, as well as brownfield engineering services. The training component provides a critical function in the historically understaffed offshore industry. Based in Aberdeen, Scotland, and Sharjah, United Arab Emirates (UAE), the Operations Services and Resources division accounted for 37 percent of Petrofac's revenues in 2007.

The company's third division is its Resources branch, which provides investment support to offshore development projects. By acquiring significant stakes, as much as 10 percent or more, in some of the projects served by its other divisions, Petrofac becomes directly involved in the success of these projects. Petrofac was originally founded in the United States in 1981, but shifted its focus to international development in the 1990s. The company sold its U.S. operations in the early 2000s, then listed its shares on the London Stock Exchange. Petrofac is led by CEO Ayman Asfari, a Syrian-born, British citizen.

TEXAS BEGINNINGS IN 1981

Petrofac was founded in 1981 in order to provide support services to the U.S. oil industry. From its base in Tyler, Texas, the company focused on providing engineering services (specifically engineering, procurement, and fabrication, or EPF) for the construction and operation of oil platforms. The international nature of the oil industry led the company to develop activities beyond the United States almost from the start, with a first project for Hunt Oil Company in Yemen in the early 1980s. The company extended its operations into the Persian Gulf region in the mid-1980s, notably with an entry into Qatar in 1986. Syria also became an early Middle East market for the company. In 1987 the company scored a new major contract, in Oman, for the United States' Occidental Petroleum Corporation.

The increasing shift in Petrofac's operations toward the Middle East led the company to develop a dedicated presence in the region in the early 1990s. For this, the company brought in 33-year-old Ayman Asfari, who formed a new subsidiary, Petrofac International. Born in Syria, but a British citizen, Asfari set up operations in Sharjah, in the United Arab Emirates. Petrofac International focused its own operations on the region's EPC market. Asfari himself became a major shareholder in the company, building up a stake of more than 30 percent. He also placed a personal stake in the group's growth, and was reported to have invested more than £1 million in the company into the early 2000s.

Asfari's efforts paid off, as the Sharjah operation came to represent the focal point of Petrofac's operations through the 1990s. By the beginning of the next decade, approximately 50 percent of Petrofac's operations originated with its Middle East division.

INVESTING IN GROWTH IN 1997

Part of Petrofac's success into the middle of the first decade of the 2000s came from its early commitment to expanding its range of services. A key element to this expansion occurred in 1997 with the creation of Petrofac Resources. This division developed investment capital and other asset management and financial services that enabled the company to extend client relationships into full-fledged partnerships. In this way, Petrofac was able to expand its operations into the earliest stages of new projects. It also provided the company with increased incentive for its EPC work.

The development of Petrofac Resources, which later became known as Petrofac Energy Developments, also

led the group to expand its Engineering & Construction (E&C) division beyond the EPC market to include new engineering and consulting capacity. In 2001, the company began offering front-end engineering and design services, including early stage engineering, field facilities and development planning, and related consulting operations. As part of this extension of its E&C operations, the company opened a new office in Woking, England. The move into the United Kingdom, which later became the company's headquarters, also provided Petrofac with an entry into the growing North Sea oil market.

By 2002, Petrofac's investment interests had led it to become a founding partner in the development of the Ohanet gas field development in Algeria, together with Sonatrach, Japan National Oil Company, and Woodside Petroleum. Petrofac's willingness to invest in the project also became a key factor in the success of its decision to seek outside capital for the first time.

The early 2000s marked a shift in the global oil and gas industry, as the rising economies in China, India, and elsewhere placed new demands on available fuel supplies. Exploration had come to play an increasingly critical role for oil companies. In turn, more and more companies began to adopt an outsourcing model in order to support their own operations.

Petrofac sought to position itself as a primary partner for this changing market. For this, the company turned to venture capital group 3i, which through its office in Aberdeen, Scotland, had developed a strong expertise in investments in the oil and gas industry. As 3i's director of oil and gas told the *Glasgow Herald,* "Petrofac came to 3i because the company needed more than just investment—it needed access to networks, knowledge, and influence." 3i, impressed by Petrofac's own investments through Petrofac Resources, agreed to acquire a 13 percent stake in the company.

The entry of 3i led Petrofac to expand its range of outsourcing services for the oil and gas industry. This effort was given a jump-start in 2002, with the acquisition of Aberdeen-based PGS Production. That operation was then renamed Petrofac Facilities Management, providing the core for the Operations Services division. The division, centered in Aberdeen, then added offices in Sharjah as well.

GOING PUBLIC IN 2005

If the Middle East provided the largest part of Petrofac's revenues into the 2000s, the company moved to establish a presence in other increasingly important oil and gas production regions, notably in Russia, Kazakhstan, and the North Sea. In keeping with its new

KEY DATES

1981: Petrofac is founded in Tyler, Texas.

1991: Ayman Asfari leads team forming Petrofac International subsidiary in the United Arab Emirates, focused on engineering, procurement, and construction (EPC) market.

1997: Company launches Petrofac Resources oilfield investment division.

2002: Company acquires PGS to add facilities management services.

2003: Petrofac sells U.S. operations to focus on expansion in Middle East, North Sea, and other markets.

2005: Petrofac goes public on London Stock Exchange.

2007: Company acquires SPD Group to add oil well operations management services.

geographic interests, Petrofac decided to exit the U.S. market. This led the company to sell its Tyler, Texas, EPF operations to Chicago Bridge & Iron Company in 2003. Asfari by then had become CEO of the entire company.

Petrofac moved to expand its list of services. The company acquired U.K.-based RGIT Montrose in 2004. That company, formed in 1979, specialized in providing training services, including fire, safety, and survival training, for offshore platform employees. RGIT Montrose's operations were then renamed Petrofac Training.

Petrofac expanded its training operations again in 2005, with the purchase of Rubicon Response, a specialist in emergency response and crisis management. Following that acquisition, Petrofac merged its facilities management and personnel training business into a new division, Petrofac Operations Services. By then, the company's outsourcing services division neared one-third of Petrofac's total revenues.

Petrofac had achieved impressive growth at this stage. The group's revenues skyrocketed during the first half of the decade, rising from $391 million in 2002 to $950 million in 2004, before jumping again to nearly $1.5 billion in 2005. The company and its employee-shareholders, including Asfari, moved to cash in on the company's success. In September 2005, Petrofac completed a highly successful public offering on the London Stock Exchange.

The offering helped confirm Petrofac's rise into the major ranks of the international oilfield services sector.

Petrofac also began successfully competing for large-scale contracts, such as two EPC contracts worth nearly $800 million in Kuwait. The company broke into the fast-growing Caspian Sea region with a contract from Kazakhstan's North Caspian Operation Company worth $500 million. At the same time, Petrofac stepped up its investment business. At the end of 2006, for example, the company paid $30 million to acquire a 45 percent share of the Chergui gas field concession off the coast of Tunisia. The company also bought approximately 50 percent of the Don Southwest and West Don gas fields in the North Sea from BP and ConocoPhillips in 2006. As part of that investment, Petrofac prepared to spend more than $350 million developing the fields, which were believed to hold more than 26 million barrels of oil.

Petrofac added to its range of services again in 2007 through the acquisition of Aberdeen-based SPD Group Ltd. The two companies had begun working together after Petrofac hired SPD to provide its specialist well operations management services for Petrofac's Kuwait operations. Petrofac soon recognized the advantage of adding SPD's skill set to its own range of services, buying 51 percent of SPD for $7 million.

The surge in global demand for oil, and the corresponding explosion of the price of oil promised a new intensification of the oilfield services sector through the end of the decade. Petrofac itself profited strongly, nearly doubling its workforce to 9,500, and boosting its revenues past $2.4 billion in 2007. With its commitment to direct investments, and an order book valued at nearly $4.5 billion, Petrofac had emerged as a leading player in the global oilfield services market.

M. L. Cohen

PRINCIPAL SUBSIDIARIES

Atlantic Resourcing Limited; Monsoon Shipmanagement Limited (Cyprus); Monsoon Shipmanagement Limited (Jersey); Petrofac Caspian Limited (Azerbaijan); Petrofac E&C International Limited (U.A.E.); Petrofac Engineering (India) Private Limited; Petrofac Engineering Limited; Petrofac Engineering Services (India) Private Limited; Petrofac Facilities Management Group Limited; Petrofac Facilities Management Limited; Petrofac FZE United Arab Emirates n/a; Petrofac Inc. (U.S.A.); Petrofac International (Nigeria) Ltd.; Petrofac International Ltd. (Jersey); Petrofac Iran (PJSC); Petrofac Norge AS (Norway); Petrofac Offshore Management Limited (Jersey); Petrofac Pars (PJSC) (Iran); Petrofac Resources Limited; Petrofac Services Inc. (U.S.A.); Petrofac Training Limited; Petrofac UK Holdings

Limited; Petroleum Facilities E & C Limited (Jersey); PFMAP Sendirian Berhad (Malaysia); Plant Asset Management Limited; RGIT Montrose Inc. (U.S.A.); Sakhalin Technical Training Centre (Russia).

PRINCIPAL COMPETITORS

Bechtel Group Inc.; Technip SA; KBR Inc.; John Wood Group PLC; AMEC PLC; Snamprogetti S.p.A.

FURTHER READING

Beckman, Jeremy, "Petrofac Expands Operations Portfolio," *Offshore,* January 2007, p. 14.

———, "Petrofac Finds Role for Northern Producer," *Offshore,* February 2008, p. 16.

Dutta, Ashok, "Joining the Big League," *MEED Middle East Economic Digest,* January 20, 2006, p. 8.

Eley, Jonathan, "Petrofac ups the Ante Again," *Investors Chronicle,* June 25, 2007.

Gribben, Roland, "Petrofac Upbeat As It Slips Out of Bid Limelight," *Daily Telegraph,* March 11, 2008.

Hamilton, Douglas, "Petrofac Trounces City Forecasts with Net Earnings of $188.7m," *Herald,* March 11, 2008, p. 27.

Hope, Christopher, "Fast-Growing Petrofac Plans Flotation Within Five Years," *Herald,* May 27, 2002, p. 15.

Maksoud, Judy, "Petrofac Ltd. Has Agreed to Acquire a 45% Interest in the Chergui Concession, Tunisia, for $30 Million," *Offshore,* December 2006, p. 12.

"More Strong Growth at Petrofac," *Investors Chronicle,* March 10, 2008.

O'Sullivan, Daniel, "Petrofac Boosts Profitability," *Investors Chronicle,* September 7, 2007.

"Rising Oil Prices Set to Help Petrofac $1bn London IPO," *Euroweek,* September 2, 2005, p. 21.

Williamson, Mark, "Petrofac Snaps Up Controlling Interest in SPD Group for $7m," *Herald,* January 17, 2007, p. 22.

Pier1 imports®

Pier 1 Imports, Inc.

---

100 Pier 1 Place
Fort Worth, Texas 76102-2600
U.S.A.
Telephone: (817) 252-8000
Fax: (817) 252-8174
Web site: http://www.pier1.com

Public Company
Founded: 1962 as Cost Plus
Employees: 15,000
Sales: $1.51 billion (2008)
Stock Exchanges: New York
Ticker Symbol: PIR
NAIC: 442299 All Other Home Furnishings Stores;
    442110 Furniture Stores

■ ■ ■

Pier 1 Imports, Inc., is a leading specialty retailer, operating around 1,100 casual home furnishing stores across the United States and Canada and in Mexico and Puerto Rico. The vast majority operate as stand-alone Pier 1 Imports stores, while the operations in Mexico and Puerto Rico consist of "store within a store" outlets in Sears stores. The U.S. and Canadian stores are typically freestanding units located near major shopping centers or malls or are positioned within major shopping centers, and they feature about 7,900 square feet of selling space. The stores offer a wide selection of merchandise, including about 3,000 items imported from more than 40 countries worldwide (the bulk coming from Asia), with the principal categories consisting

of furniture, decorative accessories, housewares, bath and bedding accessories, candles, and seasonal items. Pier 1 aims to offer its customers a "treasure hunt" type of experience through its stores' collection of unique, affordable, and internationally flavored merchandise.

FOUNDED IN 1962

Charles Tandy and Luther Henderson opened the precursor to Pier 1 shops in 1962 under the name Cost Plus. Henderson was serving as treasurer for Tandy's burgeoning Tandy Corporation, which became best known for its Radio Shack chain. Pier 1 was inspired by the owner of a rattan furniture importer and wholesaler in San Mateo, California, who was having credit problems. To help liquidate costly inventory, the shop owner opened a liquidation outlet in 1958 called Cost Plus. Impressed by the shop's success, Tandy offered the owner of Cost Plus a loan to start a retail Cost Plus outlet. At the same time, Tandy secured the rights to open and operate additional stores under the Cost Plus name.

The concept behind Tandy's Cost Plus chain plan was relatively simple: A strong U.S. dollar would allow him to import items, including rattan furniture, brass candlesticks, specialty textiles, and other items, at rock-bottom prices from countries such as Mexico, India, and Thailand. Even with large markups the goods would seem relatively inexpensive in the United States. Furthermore, items that did not sell well could be easily liquidated by cutting their price to near cost. Although most of the merchandise was second-rate in comparison to U.S. or European-made goods, it was popular with the large baby-boom generation, most of whom were first-time buyers of furnishings.

Tandy opened 16 Cost Plus retail outlets between 1962 and 1965. By 1966, however, Tandy's growing Radio Shack enterprise began to take much of his attention away from his Cost Plus venture. On February 10, 1966, a group of 30 investors led by Henderson bought Tandy's Cost Plus operation. They changed the name to Pier 1 Imports to reflect the store's import emphasis and embarked on a mission to expand the concept nationally. At the same time, the company's headquarters were shifted to Fort Worth, Texas. The original Cost Plus outlet remained under separate ownership and eventually grew into the nationwide Cost Plus chain of the early 21st century, one of Pier 1's competitors.

By 1967, Pier 1's sales had reached $4.5 million annually, and growth accelerated throughout the remainder of the decade. By 1969, the chain had grown to 42 stores and demand for Pier 1's goods was increasing. Pier 1 went public in 1970 to raise money for continued expansion. The company's stock was initially listed on the American Stock Exchange, before moving to the New York Stock Exchange two years later. Pier 1 had multiplied its chain to 123 stores, which represented sales growth of more than 100 percent since 1968. Among Pier 1's shops were stores that had been opened in Australia and England in 1971. During the following two years the chain also branched out into France, West Germany, the Netherlands, and Belgium.

Pier 1 prospered during the late 1960s and early 1970s by focusing on the baby-boom generation, members of whom were looking for interesting, exotic goods such as love beads, incense, leather sandals, and serapes. "You could characterize a lot of our customers as flower children," recounted Pier 1 CEO Clark Johnson in the *Dallas-Fort Worth Business Journal.* "Our

stores had the look of an old grocery store ... and, at that time, the appeal was heavily toward cost." As the "flower children" rushed to Pier 1 to decorate their dormitory rooms, bedrooms, and apartments, company sales rose to $68 million and earnings to $3.8 million by 1973.

REORGANIZING AND RESTRUCTURING

After an explosive decade of growth, Pier 1's fortunes began to change in the mid-1970s. Importantly, global inflation and exchange rate fluctuations exposed Pier 1's unique vulnerability to worldwide financial changes. Foreign goods became much more expensive, thus diminishing Pier 1's important cost advantage. Furthermore, other retail chains and department stores began to vie for some of Pier 1's market share by offering many of the same imported goods. To make matters worse, the core group of customers upon which Pier 1 had focused its energy was changing; baby boomers were becoming more sophisticated by the mid- and late 1970s and were increasingly interested in more mainstream goods. According to some critics, Pier 1 lost touch with its patrons and failed to change its inventory to meet market demands.

In an attempt to buoy sales and profits, Pier 1 mounted several reorganization campaigns and new marketing strategies during the mid-1970s. The company even tested different types of stores, including specialty retail outlets, art supply centers, rug stores, and fabric shops. Pier 1 also diversified into several wholesale operations such as Singapore Candle Company, Southwestern Textile Company, Rug Corporation of America, and Pasha Pillows. Many of its retail and wholesale experiments languished, and Pier 1 eventually jettisoned most of them.

Although the company failed to sustain the rampant growth it had achieved during its first ten years, Pier 1's balance sheet had improved slightly by the late 1970s. By 1979, the chain included approximately 300 stores worldwide, while sales and profits had stabilized. Pier 1 merged with Cousins Mortgage and Equity Investments (CMEI) in 1979 in an effort to boost its capital. Then, in 1980, the board of directors brought in Robert Camp to help improve the company's performance.

Camp had successfully operated his own chain of Pier 1 stores in Canada and had a knack for retailing. Camp forced Pier 1 to reevaluate its buying operations and store location strategies. He also focused on improving visual merchandising techniques. During 1981 and 1982, Pier 1 consolidated its retail import operations, closed marginal stores, opened larger outlets in more

KEY DATES

1962: Charles Tandy and Luther Henderson open their first Cost Plus store.

1966: A group of investors led by Henderson buys Tandy's Cost Plus operation and changes the name to Pier 1 Imports; headquarters are moved to Fort Worth, Texas.

1970: Company goes public.

1971: International expansion begins with the opening of stores in Australia and England.

1979: Chain includes approximately 300 stores worldwide.

1985: Intermark purchases a majority interest in Pier 1; new efforts are made to win back customer base and reposition the company.

1989: Number of stores exceeds 550.

1991: Intermark sells its stake in Pier 1, returning Pier 1 to true public ownership.

1993: Pier 1 "stores within a store" are launched in Mexico; partnership is forged to operate "The Pier" chain in England.

1999: For the fiscal year ending in February, net ales exceed $1 billion for the first time.

2000: An online store is launched at the company web site.

2001: Pier 1 acquires children's furniture chain Cargo Furniture, Inc. (later renamed Pier 1 Kids).

2006: Company sells its Pier stores in the United Kingdom and Ireland.

2007: Company shutters its e-commerce site and begins winding down the operations of the Pier 1 Kids chain.

2008: Pier 1 posts its first quarterly profit in three years.

profitable locations, and shifted from novelty items to higher-quality goods. Investors were impressed by Camp's initiatives. Within two years, sales increased 41 percent to $165 million and operating income jumped 66 percent, to $6 million. Pier 1's stock price quickly rose from about $1 in 1980 to more than $7 by 1982.

REFOCUSING ON THE CUSTOMER

Just as Pier 1 began to build momentum under the direction of Camp, control of the company changed hands. Under the leadership of Charles (Red) Scott, La Jolla, California-based Intermark, Inc., a billion-dollar holding company with a reputation for turning ailing companies around, bought a majority interest in Pier 1. Camp eventually left, and Scott hired Clark Johnson to run Pier 1 in 1985. Johnson, who was known as an aggressive and sociable businessman, had a varied background that included experience in both the furniture and sporting goods industries. He had also managed lumberyards and had partnered with Jack Nicklaus to run MacGregor Golf Company. As president of Wickes Furniture he had engineered the turnaround of that company during the mid-1970s. Likewise, he boosted sales at MacGregor from $17 million to $50 million in just five years.

Like Camp, Johnson initiated numerous changes within the Pier 1 organization. He immediately sold Pier 1's two major subsidiaries, Sunbelt Nursery Group Inc. and Ridgewood Properties Inc. He also jettisoned the mail-order business, which lost more than $1 million in 1985 alone. In addition, Johnson developed plans to modernize Pier 1's computer information systems, upgrade advertising and marketing programs, and consolidate its North American management offices. Furthermore, between 1985 and 1989 he closed more than 60 marginal stores and refurbished most of the company's existing outlets at an average cost of $190,000 each. More aggressive managers were brought in and given the freedom to make critical decisions.

Perhaps Johnson's most notable strategic contribution during the mid-1980s was improving Pier 1's attentiveness to its customer base. "It was clear that there was a huge audience out there which had once felt a tremendous allegiance to Pier 1," recalled Johnson in *Adweek's Marketing Week,* adding "I believed we could rekindle that allegiance if we showed them that we were in tune with their new values." Johnson retained New York PR agency Makovsky & Company to conduct what it termed "the most comprehensive study of the American home ever undertaken."

The study was designed with two goals in mind: (1) to determine whether or not Pier 1 was on track with the values it was emphasizing in its stores, and (2) to generate publicity as the sponsor of the study. Among other statistics, survey findings indicated that 92 percent of college-educated Americans were satisfied with their homes; 86 percent decorated their homes themselves; 57 percent believed that their homes were nicer than what they had grown up in; and an overwhelming majority described their home interior as casual. As hoped, the media reported the survey's findings and brandished Pier 1's name on the cover of major national newspapers and on television screens.

Confident of his strategy to win back Pier 1's customer base and reposition the company, Johnson embarked on an aggressive program of growth in 1986. He set a goal of doubling the total number of Pier 1 outlets by 1990 and increasing the average floor space and annual sales of the stores. Pier 1 achieved its goal one year early. By 1989 the company had doubled its chain to include more than 550 outlets worldwide. In addition, profit margins increased and the average ticket value of store items rose to $25 (from just $5 in the early 1980s), aided by the 1988 introduction of the Pier 1 Preferred Customer Card, the chain's proprietary credit card. As a result, sales leaped from $173 million in 1985 to $517 million by 1990. More importantly, profits soared from $60 million to $210 million during the same time period.

Encouraged by Pier 1's success, Johnson boldly proposed expansion plans for the next decade. "The best way to predict the future is to create it," Johnson stated in *Adweek's Marketing Week.* He continued: "Pier 1 Imports has a vision of the kind of company it would like to become. By the year 2000 Pier 1 will operate more than 1,000 stores, producing more than $1.25 billion in sales and serving more than 10 million customers."

STUMBLING THROUGH A RECESSION

Despite these grand plans, Johnson was forced to slow Pier 1's pace in 1990 after seven years of expansion. Economic sluggishness in the United States forced the slowdown. Although sales swelled to $562 million in 1991, net income shrunk as retail markets became increasingly competitive. Pier 1 repurchased Sunbelt Nursery Group late in 1990 in an effort to diversify and reduce its total dependence on retail markets. By early 1991, its chain included more than 650 stores, but Johnson planned to open only a few new stores during 1991 and to close several as part of a company consolidation plan. Pier 1 trimmed its home office staff, reorganized management, and brought its advertising activities in-house to save money. Johnson explained that the company was shifting its focus from growth to more acute management of its existing operations.

Although it stumbled in the early 1990s, Pier 1 was the bright spot on its parent's list of company holdings. Intermark's other major holdings consisted of many different kinds of companies, including Dynamark (a manufacturer of mag wheels), Liquor Barns (liquor stores), and Western Sizzlin (restaurants). Intermark's stock price plunged during 1991 from $12 to $1.37 per share as the company posted a loss of $67 million (on the heels of a $10 million loss in 1990). To avert

disaster, CEO Scott was forced to sell Pier 1, making Pier 1 a public company. Scott's responsibilities at Intermark were reduced as the company slid into debt-induced jeopardy. Intermark would declare bankruptcy in 1992, emerging in June 1993 as Triton Group Inc.

Economic sluggishness continued to hurt Pier 1 during 1992 and 1993. Although its growth in comparison to the late 1980s was meager, the company managed to sustain moderate revenue gains and to stabilize profits. Net income surged to about $25 million annually during 1992 and 1993 as sales climbed to $629 million. Unfortunately, Pier 1's long-term debt obligations also increased, from about $92 million in 1990 to $147 million by 1993. As part of a reorganization strategy, Pier 1 repositioned itself as "The Place to Discover" in 1992. It also decentralized operations to better serve its 600 stores. In an effort to generate capital, Pier 1 again sold its interests in Sunbelt Nursery.

Although Johnson's efforts at Pier 1 were generally lauded by industry observers, some critics characterized his management style as "glad-handing," while citing his salary as inflated. Moreover, some criticized Pier 1's financial condition. Of concern to analysts was Pier 1's excessive debt, which had multiplied fivefold since Johnson's arrival. In addition, Pier 1's operating costs had increased, significantly reducing the company's overall profitability compared to leaner retailers competing in the same market. Other criticisms addressed Pier 1's selection of inventory and marketing strategy.

Buffeting criticism, however, was a history of strong growth and relatively steady earnings. In addition, Pier 1 had boosted its image through charitable donations, which included a $785,000 gift to UNICEF in 1992. Pier 1 had started donating to UNICEF after Johnson's arrival in 1982 and had supplied over $3.3 million to the organization between 1985 and 1992 from the sale of greeting cards in Pier 1 outlets. The extremely successful fund-raiser was established by Marvin J. Girouard (pronounced "Gerard"), a Pier 1 veteran who was named president and chief operating officer of the company in 1988.

CONTINUING TO PURSUE GROWTH

Pier 1's sales surged to $685 million in 1994, an increase of about 8 percent over the previous year, which helped allay doubts about the company's overall approach. Pier 1 opened 48 new stores and closed 17 during 1994, bringing the total size of its international chain to 636. Pier 1's reach extended into most of the United States, with an emphasis on Florida, California, New York, Texas, and Ohio. It operated 30 stores in

Canada and was active in several joint ventures, particularly in Mexico and the United Kingdom.

Pier 1 continued to emphasize imports from low-cost producers in the mid-1990s. China, its largest supplier, contributed about one-third of its inventory in the early 1990s. Other major suppliers included India, Indonesia, Thailand, and the Philippines. Sales of furniture and kitchen goods each represented about one-quarter of the company's revenues in 1994. Textiles and jewelry each comprised about 13 percent of sales, and the remainder was attributable to miscellaneous gifts and accessories.

As revenues continued to increase in early 1995, Johnson reaffirmed his intent to pursue the ambitious growth plans he had proffered in 1989. He still wanted to build the Pier 1 chain to more than 1,000 stores by 2000 and to push sales past the $1 billion mark. Toward that end, Pier 1 was pursuing growth through a multifaceted strategy in the mid-1990s that highlighted international expansion. Johnson hoped to open 100 foreign stores by the end of the decade by buying into existing retail chains or setting up joint ventures. Pier 1 was already operating two Pier 1 "stores within a store" in Mexico through a joint venture with Sears de Mexico S.A. that was launched in 1993. In addition, the company entered into a partnership with a chain of ten retail import stores in the United Kingdom called "The Pier," a venture that began in 1993.

Pier 1 was also striving to boost sales through its credit card, which was reportedly used in about 14 percent of store purchases in 1994 (totaling $100 million), as well as through the creation of smaller, more conveniently located stores. To that end, Pier 1 was bucking the retail trend toward giant warehouse stores and was initiating a program of building multistore locations that provided a better shopping experience (better parking and customer service, and a more pleasant atmosphere). In addition, the company was experimenting with new advertising media, including television, in an effort to lure younger buyers. Pier 1 launched its first national television ads in July 1995.

Sales continued to increase in 1995 and 1996, reaching $810.7 million in the latter year. Aiding the increase was further tinkering with the product mix, most notably a cutting back on space devoted to the sluggish apparel category. By 1996 apparel accounted for only 6 percent of overall sales, and the following year the category was discontinued altogether. Management also continued to push the chain's remaining product offerings upmarket, as the household income of its average customer reached about $60,000 by 1996, compared to $26,600 a decade earlier. As an example of

the upscaling of Pier 1, Johnson told *HFN* in 1996 that the chain's most expensive basket sold for $129, compared to $4.95 in 1985. The average customer ticket total in mid-1996 was $44, a huge increase over the 1980 figure of $5.25.

LATE-TWENTIETH-CENTURY STRUGGLES

Unfortunately, the earnings picture was not nearly as bright as that of revenues. To wind down its investment in Sunbelt Nursery, Pier 1 was forced to take write-offs totaling $37.3 million, including a $14 million charge during the 1996 fiscal year. That same year the company suffered a large trading loss. Capital Insight, a firm Pier 1 had hired to invest its excess cash and short-term funds, lost $19.3 million making risky futures investments that went sour. Following 1995 net income of just $22.1 million, the financial setbacks led to just $10 million in net income the following year. The trading loss also led to the firing of Pier 1's longtime CFO, Robert G. Herndon, who was responsible for overseeing the investments. The company also pursued legal action to attempt to recover its loss, and subsequently received an $11 million settlement during the 1998 fiscal year.

International expansion continued in the late 1990s, although the company's Mexican operations suffered from the devaluation of the peso. During fiscal 1996 Pier 1 entered into an agreement with Sears Roebuck de Puerto Rico, Inc., to develop Pier 1 "stores within a store" in Sears outlets located in Puerto Rico, an arrangement similar to the one in Mexico. By early 1999 seven Sears Puerto Rico stores were offering Pier 1 merchandise. In 1997 Pier 1 entered into a joint venture with Akatsuki Printing Co., Ltd., and Skylark Group to open stores in Japan. By early 1999 there were 18 Pier 1 stores in that country. Also during this time, the company purchased an Omaha, Nebraska-based national bank, which was soon renamed Pier 1 National Bank and which held the credit card accounts for the company's proprietary card. The Pier 1 credit card was responsible for 28 percent of sales by the end of the decade.

Pier 1's earnings decline appeared to be only temporary, as the company rebounded by fiscal 1998 to post profits of $78 million on record sales of $1.08 billion. This also marked the first time sales had exceeded the $1 billion mark. In June 1998 Girouard was appointed CEO, taking over from the retiring Johnson. Girouard added the chairmanship as well in February of the following year. Although sales grew again in 1999, reaching $1.14 billion, this represented an increase of only 5.6 percent over the previous year, compared to the 13 to 17 percent increases of the previous three years.

With markets for new Pier 1 stores in the United States at a minimum, and with competition increasing from fast-growing discounters such as Cost Plus and such upscale housewares chains as Pottery Barn and Crate and Barrel, Pier 1 Imports appeared to be hitting a plateau, prompting Girouard to investigate alternative avenues of growth. He first considered opening a second chain that would offer discount merchandising, before deciding that the upscale markets held more potential. In mid-1999 the company entered negotiations to purchase the privately held Z Gallerie, a retail chain offering high-end home furnishings. The deal fell apart in August, however, leading to the immediate departure of another CFO, Stephen F. Mangum, who had championed the acquisition. In the aftermath, the company's stock plunged 33 percent in one day. Girouard subsequently placed his plans to open or acquire a second chain on the back burner, deciding instead to concentrate on revitalizing the Pier 1 concept by cutting prices, opening stores in smaller markets, and experimenting with larger formats.

SHORT-LIVED TURNAROUND

By early 2000 Pier 1 was solidly back on track. Prices at Pier 1 had drifted higher in the late 1990s, undermining the chain's traditional value orientation, and the return to value pricing provided the underpinnings for a same-store sales increase of more than 9 percent in the fourth quarter of fiscal 2000. Several initiatives were pursued in fiscal 2001 to sustain this momentum. In June 2000 the company added an e-commerce component to its web site, with this online store initially offering more than 1,500 items along with a bridal and gift registry and a clearance center. Shortly thereafter, Pier 1 launched a new national advertising campaign featuring actress Kirstie Alley and the tagline, "Get in touch with your senses." This marked the first time that the chain had employed a celebrity spokesperson. Growth remained on the agenda as well, as Pier 1 added a net 41 stores in North America during fiscal 2001.

Girouard's ambitions for a second chain as a platform for further growth were finally fulfilled in February 2001 when Pier 1 acquired Cargo Furniture, Inc., from Tandycrafts, Inc., for about $4 million. Based in Fort Worth, just like Pier 1, Cargo operated 21 children's furniture stores in the Dallas–Fort Worth, Houston, Atlanta, and Washington, D.C., metropolitan areas. While the stores had been known for their sturdy, wooden furniture, Pier 1 began repositioning the chain in 2002 as a specialty retailer offering value-oriented, fashionable children's furniture and accessories. Along with this repositioning came a name change to Cargokids.

As this revamp continued, Pier 1 Imports was in the midst of an aggressive expansion of its flagship chain, aiming to eventually have more than 1,500 Pier 1 stores up and running across North America. The 1,000th Pier 1 store opened in February 2003 during a fiscal year in which the chain grew a net 90 units. Eight new Cargokids outlets were opened that year as well. On the international stage, meantime, Pier 1 had retrenched a year earlier by not renewing its expiring Japanese joint-venture agreement.

A PROLONGED SLUMP

Results for fiscal 2003 were quite strong with record net sales and earnings of $1.75 billion and $129.4 million, respectively, and a same-store sales increase of 4.7 percent. Pier 1's fortunes soon turned south, however. The company blundered in 2004 when it signed Thom Filicia as its celebrity spokesperson, replacing Alley. The ads featuring Filicia, the resident decorator for the *Queer Eye for the Straight Guy* television show, failed to drive customers into the stores, and his stint as pitchman came to a quick end. The six-month period that followed in which Pier 1 ads disappeared from TV screens as plans for a new campaign were gestating came during the crucial holiday shopping season, further denting the firm's fiscal 2005 performance. While overall sales grew slightly to $1.83 billion thanks to the net addition of 67 Pier 1 stores during the year, same-store sales dropped 5.8 percent. Also during the year, the Cargokids outlets were renamed Pier 1 Kids.

Beyond its difficulties on the marketing front, Pier 1 faced a much larger problem: the undermining of its value orientation by competitors. Other retailers, including discounters Target Corporation and Wal-Mart Stores, Inc., had begun offering merchandise similar to that found in Pier 1 stores, and they were selling the items at lower prices. Net sales fell 2.7 percent in fiscal 2006, while same-store sales were again negative, down 7.1 percent. In addition, Pier 1 began operating in the red, suffering a net loss of $39.8 million that year. In the spring of 2006 Pier 1 attempted to spark a turnaround with a move upscale. Pricey modern furniture was introduced under the Modern Craftsman brand, but this effort was quickly scaled back when customers failed to respond.

Retrenching further, the company sold its Pier 1 stores in the United Kingdom and Ireland in March 2006 to Palli Limited for around $15 million. The expansion in North America was scaled back as well.

During fiscal 2007, although 34 new Pier 1 stores opened, closures included 57 Pier 1 stores and seven Pier 1 Kids stores. In November 2006 the company sold its private-label credit card operations to JPMorgan Chase & Co. for approximately $155 million. As Pier 1 headed toward an even larger net loss for fiscal 2007, Girouard in late 2006 announced his intention to retire from the beleaguered company at fiscal year-end. By the time of this announcement, Pier 1 Imports stock was trading at $6.60 a share, down 75 percent from its November 2003 high of $26.44.

TURNAROUND EFFORT UNDER NEW LEADERSHIP

Hired on as the new CEO was Alex W. Smith, a retail veteran who had spent the previous 12 years in management positions at TJX Companies, Inc., parent of T.J. Maxx, Marshall's, and other retail chains. Smith moved quickly to slash costs, cutting 175 jobs in March 2007, 100 at the company headquarters and 75 at field offices across the United States. Soon thereafter he launched additional turnaround initiatives, beefing up the merchandise-buying team, making the company's supply chain more efficient in part through a streamlining of distribution centers, and developing a more cost-effective marketing plan. Around 100 underperforming stores were earmarked for closure during fiscal 2008. In addition, Pier 1 in the summer of 2007 shut down its e-commerce business and began closing its Pier 1 Kids stores and its clearance outlets.

By the fall of 2007 Pier 1 had its most important turnaround initiative well underway: a revamping of the stores' merchandise mix. The Modern Craftsman merchandise was aggressively liquidated, creating room for an infusion of an eclectic mix of 2,000 new items affordably priced and designed to be reminiscent of the offbeat, international styles that had defined Pier 1 through the late 1990s. Both with the merchandise overhaul and with a more departmentalized layout in the stores, Smith sought to re-create the "treasure hunt" type of shopping atmosphere with which Pier 1 had traditionally been associated. By early 2008 the turnaround plan appeared to be gaining momentum. In the fourth quarter of fiscal 2008 Pier 1 posted a net profit of $13.4 million, its first quarter in the black in three years, while also enjoying its first gain in same-store sales in 17 quarters. Not all analysts were convinced, however, that the company could sustain this momentum in the midst of a severe downturn in the housing market that was hurting the entire spectrum of home furnishing retailers. During fiscal 2009 Pier 1 planned to continue its cost-containment efforts and close as many as 30 additional underperforming stores.

Dave Mote
Updated, David E. Salamie

PRINCIPAL SUBSIDIARIES

Pier 1 Assets, Inc.; Pier 1 Licensing, Inc.; Pier 1 Imports (U.S.), Inc.; Pier 1 Funding, LLC; Pier 1 Value Services, LLC; Pier Lease, Inc.; Pier-SNG, Inc.; PIR Trading, Inc.; Pier International Limited (Hong Kong); Pier Alliance Ltd. (Bermuda); Pier Group, Inc.; Pier 1 Holdings, Inc.; Pier 1 Services Company.

PRINCIPAL COMPETITORS

Cost Plus, Inc.; Williams-Sonoma, Inc.; Euromarket Designs, Inc.; Bed Bath & Beyond Inc.; Linens 'n Things, Inc.; Inter IKEA Systems B.V.; Restoration Hardware, Inc.; The Container Store Inc.; Target Corporation; Wal-Mart Stores, Inc.

FURTHER READING

Byrnes, Nanette, and Stephanie Anderson Forest, "Goldinger: He's Not the Man with the Midas Touch," *Business Week*, January 15, 1996, p. 34.

"Capital Insight's Bad Bets Caused Losses of over $36 Million for Pier 1, Others," *Wall Street Journal*, December 28, 1995, p. A3.

Chatham, Laura, "Pier 1 Inc. Well-Positioned to Appeal to Baby Boomers," *Dallas–Fort Worth Business Journal*, April 21, 1986, p. 2A.

Corral, Cecile B., "Pier 1 Feeling Pressure to Adapt," *Home Textiles Today*, June 21, 2004, pp. 1, 19.

———, "Pier 1 Looks to Change Corporate Image," *Home Textiles Today*, September 19, 2005, pp. 2, 27.

Erlick, June Carolyn, "The Trade Winds Are Up at Pier 1: Or How a Chain Turned a Five-Buck Sale into $130," *HFN–The Weekly Newspaper for the Home Furnishing Network*, July 22, 1996, p. 1.

Feldman, Amy, "But Who Is Minding the Store?" *Forbes*, November 22, 1993, p. 47.

Forest, Stephanie Anderson, "At Pier 1, a Search for Lost Cachet," *Business Week*, November 1, 1999, pp. 109, 112–13.

———, "Pier 1's Ship Comes In: Even a $20 Million Trading Loss Won't Spoil a Boffo Year," *Business Week*, January 22, 1996, p. 45.

Halkias, Maria, "Pier 1 Ends 'Truly Horrible Year,'" *Dallas Morning News*, April 13, 2007, p. 1D.

———, "Signs of Turnaround May Be Taking Hold," *Dallas Morning News*, December 21, 2007, p. 3D.

Helliker, Kevin, "Pressure at Pier 1: Beating Sales Numbers of Year Earlier Is a Storewide Obsession," *Wall Street Journal,* December 7, 1995, p. B1.

Henderson, Barry, "Pier 2?" *Barron's,* November 16, 1998, pp. 19–20.

Howell, Debbie, "Pier 1 Contemplates Upscale Expansion Through Acquisition," *Discount Store News,* May 24, 1999.

Hudson, Kris, "Pier 1 Chairman, CEO Girouard Sets Retirement for February," *Wall Street Journal,* October 2, 2006, p. B2.

———, "Pier 1 Plots Sales Turnaround," *Wall Street Journal,* August 2, 2005, p. B7.

"Intermark's CEO Actually Thrives on Failure," *San Diego Business Journal,* January 19, 1987, p. 1.

La Hood, Lila, "Back in Its Niche: How Pier 1 Recaptured Its Brand Identity and Customer Loyalty," *Fort Worth (Tex.) Star-Telegram,* July 17, 2000, p. 14.

———, "Cargo Acquired by Pier 1," *Fort Worth (Tex.) Star-Telegram,* February 3, 2001, Business sec., p. 1.

———, "Fantastic at 40: With Stock Price and Profits Soaring, Pier 1 Is in the Prime of Life," *Fort Worth (Tex.) Star-Telegram,* June 23, 2002, Business sec., p. 1.

Landy, Heather, "New CEO Feeling Peachy About Pier 1," *Fort Worth (Tex.) Star-Telegram,* June 29, 2007, p. C1.

———, "Pier 1 Cuts 175 Positions to Stem Losses," *Fort Worth (Tex.) Star-Telegram,* March 30, 2007, p. C1.

———, "Pier 1 Hires Veteran Merchant," *Fort Worth (Tex.) Star-Telegram,* January 31, 2007, p. C1.

———, "Pier 1 to Stop Selling Online," *Fort Worth (Tex.) Star-Telegram,* June 22, 2007, p. C1.

———, "'We Have Been Our Own Worst Enemy,' Pier 1 CEO Says," *Fort Worth (Tex.) Star-Telegram,* April 13, 2007, p. C1.

Lee, Louise, "Pier 1 Fires Financial Chief Herndon over Loss Tied to Goldinger's Collapse," *Wall Street Journal,* February 12, 1996, p. B4.

———, "Pier 1 Restates Net, Reflecting Investment Loss," *Wall Street Journal,* January 17, 1996, p. B5.

———, "Pier 1 to Take Charge on Money-Manager Trades," *Wall Street Journal,* December 27, 1995.

Lloyd, Mary Ellen, "After Years in Decline, Pier 1 Shows Signs of Life," *Wall Street Journal,* October 31, 2007, p. B5E.

———, "Investors Losing Patience with Pier 1," *Wall Street Journal,* November 2, 2005, p. B2E.

Lockwood, Herbert, "Has Intermark Bottomed Out? Scott Says So," *San Diego Daily Transcript,* July 30, 1991, p. A1.

Pasztor, Andy, Louise Lee, and Fred Vogelstein, "Goldinger's Bet on Rates Led to Losses of Up to $100 Million, Associates Say," *Wall Street Journal,* January 2, 1996, p. 3.

The Pier 1 Imports Story, Fort Worth, Tex.: Pier 1 Imports, Inc., 1992.

"Pier 1 Names Alex W. Smith As New CEO," *Wall Street Journal,* January 31, 2007, p. B15.

"Pier 1 Plots Aggressive Growth Strategy," *Home Textiles Today,* September 9, 2002, pp. 1, 19.

Sain, Ariane, "Pier 1's Ship Has Finally Come in As Baby Boomers Mature," *Adweek's Marketing Week,* January 9, 1989, p. 43.

Santoli, Michael, "Back in Fashion," *Barron's,* November 3, 2003, p. 17.

Schnurman, Mitchell, "Bricks and Mortar Are Weighing Pier 1 Down," *Fort Worth (Tex.) Star-Telegram,* June 25, 2006, p. F1.

———, "Chief Executive of Pier Next in Line for Departure," *Fort Worth (Tex.) Star-Telegram,* May 21, 1998, p. 1.

———, "'Pier 1 Had Everything I Wanted': Loyalty, Persistence Paid Off for Firm's New Chief Executive," *Fort Worth (Tex.) Star-Telegram,* June 29, 1998, p. 1.

———, "Pier 1 Plans 2nd Chain with Upscale Goods," *Fort Worth (Tex.) Star-Telegram,* June 25, 1999, p. 1.

Shlachter, Barry, "Turnaround Plan Puts Pier 1 Back in the Black," *Fort Worth (Tex.) Star-Telegram,* April 11, 2008, p. C1.

"A 60's Store Passes Pier Review; Pier 1 Imports Plays Catch Up with Its Customers," *Adweek's Marketing Week,* May 29, 1989, p. S8.

Steinberg, Brian, "Pier 1, Once Starstruck, Changes Focus," *Wall Street Journal,* March 15, 2005, p. B6.

Stringer, Kortney, "Pier 1 Imports Works to Get Its Housewares in Order," *Wall Street Journal,* June 27, 2000, p. B4.

PROBuild

Pro-Build Holdings Inc.

———— ■ ————

7595 Technology Way
Denver, Colorado 80237
U.S.A.
Telephone: (720) 488-2884
Fax: (720) 488-2354
Web site: http://www.pro-build.com

Private Company
Incorporated: 2006
Employees: 16,640
Sales: $5.96 billion (2006)
NAIC: 444190 Other Building Material Dealers; 423310 Lumber, Plywood, Millwork, and Wood Panel Merchant Wholesalers; 423320 Brick, Stone, and Related Construction Material Merchant Wholesalers; 423330 Roofing, Siding, and Insulation Material Merchant Wholesalers; 321999 All Other Miscellaneous Wood Product Manufacturing

■ ■ ■

Pro-Build Holdings Inc. is the largest supplier of building materials to professional builders in the United States. The company operates more than 520 lumber and building product distribution, manufacturing, and assembly centers in 41 states. Pro-Build sells lumber, plywood, engineered wood, and drywall products. It sells roofing materials, siding products, insulation materials, metal specialties, hardware, and tools. The company's manufacturing operations are involved in trusses, wall panels, millwork, pre-hung doors, and window fabrication. Pro-Build operates as a holding company for a family of regional companies, including The Contractor Yard, Dixieline Lumber & Home Centers, F.E. Wheaton, Home Lumber Company, Hope Lumber & Supply Company, Lumbermens, Spenard Builders Supply, The Strober Organization, Inc., United Building Centers, and US Components.

A GIANT FROM THE START

With more than 14,000 employees, annual revenues of roughly $5 billion, and more than 400 locations, Pro-Build, at its birth, was a towering giant, the largest chain of its kind in the country. When the Pro-Build name first appeared in 2006, it was new to the professional contractors who would constitute its customer base. Home builders were very familiar with the brands housed with Pro-Build, however, names such as Lumbermens, Lanoga, Strober, Dixieline, Hope Lumber, Spenard, and United Building Centers. For more than a century, contractors had been doing business with the properties controlled by Pro-Build, relying on building materials dealers whose operating territories stretched from Florida to Alaska.

Pro-Build was a product of industry consolidation, the most extensive example of acquisitive activity in the history of the professional dealer industry. When Pro-Build was formed as a holding company in 2006, it inherited the legacies of numerous operators, each with distinct histories, but there were two companies in particular that formed the framework around which the rest of Pro-Build was built. The oldest and largest of the two companies traced its heritage to the entrepreneurial efforts of three brothers, William, Matthew, and James Laird.

COMPANY PERSPECTIVES

Our collective strength combines unmatched national market coverage (40 states and counting) with local focus, benefiting both multi-regional production builders, local builders and contractors. Our 17,000 employees know that while superior customer service begins at each local yard, Pro-Build's unparalleled resources extend our service advantage through supply chain efficiencies, technology enhancements, and product diversification. The Pro-Build brands are names professional builders have known and trusted for decades. While part of a strong national network, each division employs experienced managers with the local knowledge, authority, and flexibility necessary to foster deep relationships with local customers, suppliers, and the community.

ORIGINS OF LANOGA

In 1855, the Laird brothers started their own sawmill in Winona, Minnesota, the geographic origination of Pro-Build. After the Laird brothers' cousins, the Nortons, joined the business in the 1860s, the enterprise was known as Laird Norton Co., a company whose growth was hitched to the country's westward migration. Laird Norton began establishing lumberyards along the railroad routes headed west, an expansion strategy that eventually led the company to move its headquarters from Minnesota to Washington.

Laird Norton flourished in the Pacific Northwest. The company grew as the region it served grew, becoming one of the major suppliers of building materials to contractors and the general public during a construction boom period that spanned decades. Laird Norton's growth during the 20th century reached a point that enabled the company to entertain the prospect of purchasing other companies in its industry. In terms of Pro-Build's future, one acquisition stood out in particular, the purchase of Spenard Builders Supply in 1978. Spenard, owned by Galco Distributing and the operator of four stores, was founded in 1952 by George Lagerquist, who built his Anchorage-based building materials company into one of Alaska's premier retailers.

By the 1970s, Laird Norton was firmly established in Washington—it had been for decades—but the company remained tied to its birthplace through a subsidiary. United Building Centers, an operator of lumberyards, distribution centers, and manufacturing

facilities in the Midwest, was based in Winona. When Laird Norton acquired Spenard, it merged the company with United Building Centers and formed a new company to control the two companies. Lanoga Corporation, whose name was a blend of Laird Norton and Galco Distributing, was formed in 1978, marking the creation of half the framework that would later constitute Pro-Build. Lanoga's first president, who also served as Laird Norton's president, was Booth Gardner, heir to the Weyerhaeuser fortune and Washington's governor from 1985 to 1993.

LUMBERMENS COMES ABOARD IN 1982

Lanoga did not sit idle in the years before joining the Pro-Build fold. It was a trait shared by nearly every company that became part of Pro-Build. The formation of Pro-Build represented a consolidating move in one massive stroke, but each of the primary companies could be labeled as consolidators themselves. Such was the case with Lanoga, which engineered a major acquisition not long after it was formed. In 1982, the company acquired a venerable regional force in the Pacific Northwest building materials scene, purchasing Lumbermens Building Centers, an operator of lumberyards and truss and door manufacturing facilities. Lumbermens was formed in 1895.

Lanoga, like Pro-Build, was known to its customers primarily by the names of the retail chains and manufacturing facilities that composed its operations. During the decade following the acquisition of Lumbermens, the company grew through the expansion of its divisions, with United Building Centers acquiring stores from more than a dozen competitors, Spenard purchasing stores from two Alaska competitors, and Lumbermens purchasing locations from 11 competitors in Washington and neighboring states. By the early 1990s, Lanoga ranked as the 13th largest chain of its kind in the country, boasting revenues that eclipsed $500 million. By the end of the decade, after acquiring the largest lumber dealer in the Denver, Colorado, market, the company ranked as the 10th largest home improvement concern in the country. Lanoga operated 193 locations in more than 20 states and had revenues of more than $1 billion.

HYLBERT TAKES THE HELM AT LANOGA IN 2000

In 2000, Lanoga appointed a new chief executive officer, bringing in one of the personalities that would play a crucial role in Pro-Build's formation. Paul Hylbert took over from Daryl Nagel, who had orchestrated

KEY DATES

1855: The opening of a sawmill in Winona, Minnesota, represents the earliest predecessor to Pro-Build.

1895: Lumbermens, a building materials supplier and manufacturer, is founded in Washington.

1912: The Strober Organization is founded in Brooklyn, New York.

1978: Lanoga Corporation, based in Washington, is formed.

1982: Lanoga acquires Lumbermens.

2003: Lanoga acquires Dixieline Lumber and Home Centers.

2004: Strober acquires The Contractor Yard, doubling its revenue volume.

2005: Negotiations for a merger between Lanoga and Strober begin.

2006: Pro-Build is formed to complete the merger.

2007: Paul Hylbert is named chief executive officer.

tremendous growth during his 14-year tenure, quadrupling the company's revenues. Hylbert would leave a lasting mark on the company's development as well, using his penchant for deal making to touch off a new era of existence for Lanoga. In the years before joining Lanoga, Hylbert led a fastener supplier named PrimeSource, a Carrolton, Texas, company he had created by consolidating a number of small building materials suppliers in the 1990s. He sold the company to a Japanese conglomerate named Itochu International in 1998, but the deal did not mark the end of his participation in the industry as a consolidator. He would broker the biggest deal of his life once he met his counterpart at another building materials company, the man who led the other half of the framework that constituted Pro-Build.

STROBER'S ROOTS

While Hylbert settled into his duties at Lanoga, Fred Marino busied himself in Brooklyn, New York, with the tasks of leading The Strober Organization, Inc. Strober, a supplier of building materials to professional builders and contractors in the northeast and mid-Atlantic regions, was founded in 1912. The company was under the third generation of Strober leadership when it converted to public ownership in 1986, by which time sales had grown to $92 million, a total collected from nine stores in New York, New Jersey, Connecticut, and Pennsylvania. The company operated as a public concern until 1997, when Marino partnered with a Boston, Massachusetts-based investment firm named Fidelity Capital Investors (later renamed Fidelity Equity Partners), a division of Fidelity Strategic Investments. Marino and Fidelity returned Strober to the private sector, which touched off an aggressive expansion campaign led by Marino.

STROBER'S ACQUISITION SPREE

Between 1997 and 2004, Marino went on a tear, turning Strober's nine-store presence in four states into a regional powerhouse with 72 locations in 15 states. During the time span, Strober's revenues leaped from $152 million to $1 billion. One of the biggest deals occurred at the end of the period when Strober acquired The Contractor Yard in 2004. Marino had 45 locations in seven states under his control when he reached an agreement to acquire The Contractor Yard, a division of Lowe's Companies, Inc. The Contractor Yard, based in Charlotte, North Carolina, operated in 26 locations in nine states, which, when combined with Strober's holdings, created a company with 71 locations extending along the Atlantic Seaboard from Connecticut to Florida and as far west as Mississippi and Ohio. The deal, which closed in January 2004, approximately doubled Strober's revenues, making it the seventh largest dealer servicing the professional marketplace in the United States.

In the West, while Marino was making deals in the East, Hylbert was demonstrating an ambitious nature as well, continuing to expand Lanoga during his first years in office. One of his biggest deals was the acquisition of Dixieline Lumber and Home Centers, a ten-unit chain with $230 million in sales based in San Diego, California. Acquired in 2003, Dixieline became Lanoga's fifth operating division, giving the company 320 locations in 24 states by the time Marino completed the acquisition of The Contractor Yard. Marino, meanwhile, continued to acquire. In November 2004, he engineered Strober's purchase of Moore's Lumber and Building Supply, a Roanoke, Virginia-based company with $185 million in annual sales. Founded in 1954, Moore's, partly owned by Rooney Holdings Inc., conducted business primarily with professional builders.

NEGOTIATIONS BETWEEN LANOGA AND STROBER

By the time Dixieline and Moore's deals were being negotiated, Hylbert and Marino knew each other. They were on a trout-fishing trip together in Montana, each invited by a fellow building materials executive, Carl Hedlund, who led ThermaTru Doors. During the trip in the summer of 2004, Marino turned to Hylbert, broaching the subject of a merger between Strober and Lanoga. The two executives began official negotiations in March 2005, working out the details of a merger that would combine Lanoga's 36 locations in 24 states with Strober's 91 locations in 15 states. Their talks involved the creation of a building material supplier with approximately $5 billion in annual revenue. Because of the distinct geographic orientations of the two companies, market coverage overlapped in only one town, Mansfield, Ohio.

DEBUT OF PRO-BUILD

In February 2006, the merger, announced by Fidelity Capital, was completed. Fidelity Capital completed the purchase through the newly created entity, Pro-Build Holdings Inc., combining Strober, the sixth largest professional building materials dealer in the country, with Lanoga, the nation's third largest professional building materials dealer. Together, the two companies operated in 420 locations in 38 states with revenues eclipsing $5 billion. Fidelity Capital's leader, Paul Mucci, became Pro-Build's chairman. Hylbert and Marino were named vice-chairmen, with Marino taking on the duties of chief executive officer. "This deal allows us to pursue larger builders in most markets without excluding the smaller builder," Marino said in a February 2006 interview with *Prosales*.

Although the merger of Lanoga and Strober represented the culmination of two companies' ambitious expansion plans, it did not signal the end of deal making under the Pro-Build banner. Pro-Build was a base, a very large base, that its management team intended to build upon.

EXPANSION CONTINUES

Company executives sent up a flare declaring their aggressive intentions in June 2006, when Pro-Build announced it was acquiring Hope Lumber and Supply Company. Based in Tulsa, Oklahoma, Hope Lumber was founded by George D. Hope during the oil boom era at the beginning of the 20th century. For decades, the company served contractors and consumers, but beginning in the mid-1980s, Hope Lumber narrowed its focus on professional clientele working in the residential construction industry. The company expanded into Texas in 1991, entered New Mexico and Colorado in 1995, and established a presence in Kansas in 1997, the year it became the operating partner of Moore's, the company Marino purchased in 2004. By the time Pro-Build acquired Hope Lumber in August 2006, the Oklahoma company operated 49 lumberyards and five

truss plants in nine states, widening Pro-Build's lead as the largest competitor in its industry.

HYLBERT TAKES OVER IN 2007

More acquisitions were to follow as the Pro-Build name started to become familiar among professional builders. At the beginning of 2007, the responsibilities of chief executive officer were passed from Marino to Hylbert. The transfer of power, far from signaling any sort of dissension or weakness within Pro-Build, was strategic in nature, reflecting the company's earnest desire to continue expanding in the years ahead. "I am pleased to transition leadership of the great company to Paul Hylbert as I concentrate my energies on finding new growth opportunities for us," Marino said in a January 25, 2007, company press release. Mucci offered his own take on the leadership change in the same press release. "These changes," he said, "position Pro-Build to grow significantly as we maximize the expertise resident within our executive ranks to capitalize on the many opportunities that exist in the market for a company of our size and resources." Pro-Build was on the prowl. In the years ahead, the nation's largest competitor was set to become even larger as it pursed an expansion strategy destined to make an industry behemoth even more formidable.

Jeffrey L. Covell

PRINCIPAL SUBSIDIARIES

The Contractor Yard; Dixieline Lumber Company; F.E. Wheaton; Home Lumber Company; Hope Lumber and Supply Company; Lumbermens; Spenard Builders Supply; The Strober Organization, Inc.; United Building Centers; US Components.

PRINCIPAL COMPETITORS

Building Materials Holding Corporation; HD Supply; American Builders & Contractors Supply Co., Inc.

FURTHER READING

Caulfield, John, "Perfect Couple," *Prosales*, February 2006, p. 26.

"Contractor Yard Buys Two Hope Yards," *Home Channel News NewsFax*, March 27, 2006, p. 1.

"Controlling Its Own Destiny," *Construction Today*, March–April 2005, p. 182.

"Hope Lumber Buys Big Tin's Texas Operations," *Building Supply Home Centers*, November 1995, p. 1.

"Lanoga Merges with Strober to Form Industry's Fourth Largest Retailer," *Do-It-Yourself Retailing,* February 2006, p. 12.

"Lumber Supplier Being Sold: Rooney Holdings Agrees to Shed Its Hope Lumber & Supply Co. Subsidiary," *Tulsa World,* June 17, 2006.

Park, Clayton, "Low-Profile Lanoga One of Area's Best-Kept Secrets," *Puget Sound Business Journal,* June 18, 1993, p. 46.

Rice, Faye, "Soaring Sales, Stalled Stock," *Fortune,* November 9, 1987, p. 172.

"Strober Acquires Moore's," *Home Channel News NewsFax,* November 15, 2004, p. 1.

"Strober Eyes New Markets As Q3 Income Rises," *Building Supply Home Centers,* December 1994, p. 1.

"The Strober Organization Acquires Contractor Yard Locations from Lowe's," *Roofing Contractor,* April 2004, p. 8.

Tice, Carol, "Lanoga's New CEO Has Insider's Perspective," *Puget Sound Business Journal,* December 22, 2000, p. 6.

———, "Lumber Retailer Responds to Changing Market," *Puget Sound Business Journal,* June 23, 2000, p. 42.

QRS Music Technologies, Inc.

2011 Seward Avenue
Naples, Florida 34109
U.S.A.
Telephone: (239) 597-5888
Fax: (239) 597-3936
Web site: http://www.qrsmusic.com

Public Company
Incorporated: 1900 as Q.R.S. Music Roll Co.
Employees: 60
Sales: $18.08 million (2006)
Stock Exchanges: OTC Bulletin Board
Ticker Symbol: QRSM
NAIC: 339992 Musical Instrument Manufacturing

■ ■ ■

QRS Music Technologies, Inc., makes automated musical instruments that include computer-controlled player pianos, a piano-based Nickelodeon that incorporates an array of percussion instruments, and a self-playing violin, as well as software and accessories. Once the world's leading maker of player piano rolls (which it continues to produce), QRS has embraced digital technology to offer a more accurate re-creation of a musical performance, as well as to expand its products' capabilities. These include a web-based music library and a playback system that can synchronize a piano with a commercial CD or DVD. QRS's flagship Pianomation system is sold to other piano manufacturers for installation in their products and also via the firm's own Story & Clark and Gulbransen lines, which are marketed through a network of about 240 independent dealers around the United States and in some foreign markets. Purchasers include individuals, institutions, and entertainment-themed restaurants, hotels, and casinos. A majority of the publicly traded firm is owned by board Chairman Richard Dolan.

BEGINNINGS

The story of QRS dates to 1900, when Melville Clark founded a piano manufacturing company near Chicago. Clark, born in Rome, New York, in 1853, had built reed organs in California until 1877 before moving to the Chicago area to make organs under the name Reed and Clark. In 1884 he joined with Hampton L. Story to found the Story & Clark Organ Company, which in 1895 also began to produce pianos, but in 1900 Clark split off to found the Melville Clark Piano Co. in De-Kalb, Illinois, with initial capitalization of $50,000.

Clark, a talented inventor, had begun working on an automated piano of a type that had begun appearing on the market, in which a perforated roll of paper was passed through a foot-pumped, vacuum-powered device that played a sequence of notes on the keyboard. Previous player pianos (also known as pianolas) had varied in size and design, but Clark was determined to create one that utilized the full 88-key range of a standard instrument. His first model appeared in 1902, and in 1908 the 88-key, 11¼-inch-wide roll it used was officially accepted as the industry standard.

At the same time that he founded the piano company, Clark formed an offshoot called Q.R.S. Music Roll Co. to make rolls, reportedly to distance the piano

---

COMPANY PERSPECTIVES

Today QRS is an industry leader in introducing fun innovations in home musical entertainment.

---

company from a round of patent lawsuits then dogging the industry. The new firm's name had no clear meaning, and according to a 1927 *Wall Street Journal* article had in fact been created on the spur of the moment when company officials met with an attorney to draw up incorporation papers. The roll subsidiary's name was considered unimportant because it was expected to be dissolved after the patent litigation was settled, so when he noted the lack of a name on the papers the attorney is reported to have suggested, "Oh, call it X.Y.Z. or Q.R.S."

In 1909 the firm's piano rolls won copyright protection as sound recordings, and in 1912 Clark introduced the Marking Piano, which recorded a faithful reproduction of a live performance by marking notes on a roll of paper as it was played. The resultant pencil marks were later cut out by technicians who could also correct mistakes or add notes. Rolls had heretofore been created by arrangers who interpreted the pattern of holes directly from a music score, and this method would continue to be used as well. In 1916 the firm also began printing song lyrics on its rolls so that people could sing along by watching it unspool above the piano's keyboard.

DEATH OF MELVILLE CLARK IN 1918; SALE OF PIANO FACTORY

In 1918 Melville Clark died and Tom Pletcher took over management of the firm. The DeKalb piano manufacturing operation was sold to Wurlitzer in 1919, and during the 1920s QRS branched out to offer a broader mix of products that included phonographs, records, radio tubes, and neon signs.

To create rolls the firm relied on a number of different arrangers, whose ranks were joined in 1921 by J. Lawrence Cook, a 22-year-old African-American pianist. Cook would ultimately become the most prolific piano roll arranger ever, producing as many as 20,000 rolls during a nearly 50-year career with QRS. Most were popular songs of the day but some were done "in the style of" famous jazz musicians, which Cook transcribed to piano roll from recordings. During the 1920s QRS also signed a number of well-known pianists to make

rolls including Zez Comfrey, Fats Waller, and James P. Johnson.

As QRS grew it began to buy up competitors, acquiring 25 of them by 1926, when it added Connorized Music Co. and VocalstyleMusic Co. During the year production hit an all-time peak of ten million rolls, and in 1927 QRS stock began trading on the New York Stock Exchange.

The company had operations in Chicago, San Francisco, New York, Canada, Europe, and Australia, and was adding up to 50 new rolls per month to a catalog that included thousands of titles. The number of player pianos in the United States reached 2.5 million by decade's end.

The late 1920s saw music roll sales fall off sharply, however, due to the U.S. economic downturn as well as new forms of home entertainment stemming from inexpensive, mass-produced radio sets and improved phonograph reproduction. Combined annual sales of player pianos and rolls fell from $6 million in the early 1920s to just $428,000 in 1931, and continued to slide as most player piano and roll makers quit the business.

NEW OWNER, MAX KORTLANDER: 1931

In 1931 QRS recording department head Max Kortlander, who was also one of its top arrangers, mortgaged his home to buy the firm's music roll business for $25,000 and took the title of company president. He centralized operations in the Bronx, New York, and changed the struggling company's name to Imperial Industrial Corp. so it could more easily branch out to produce such items as paper rolls for office equipment.

Although music roll sales in the 1930s were slow, they improved during World War II because of a union-mandated recording ban and the use of player pianos on military bases and at U.S.O. clubs. Sales grew from about 500,000 rolls in 1942 to one million at the end of the war, but then fell to 200,000 by the early 1950s.

During the 1950s growing numbers of nostalgia-minded Americans began restoring player pianos while a new model, the Hardman Duo (partly funded by Kortlander) was introduced, and QRS's roll sales grew 50 percent between 1957 and 1962. The firm continued to upgrade its catalog with titles including "The Peppermint Twist," with rolls priced at between 90 cents and $1.20 each.

In 1961 Max Kortlander died at his office in the Bronx, New York, and his brother Herman was hired to run the business. In 1966 the firm was purchased from Max's widow by attorney and player piano enthusiast

KEY DATES

1900: Melville Clark founds two DeKalb, Illinois-based firms to make pianos and music rolls.

1919: After Clark's death, piano factory is sold to Wurlitzer.

1927: Company goes public after production of piano rolls peaks at ten million.

1931: Max Kortlander buys now-struggling roll business, renames it Imperial Industrial.

1961: Kortlander dies; ownership of firm passes to his widow.

1966: Ramsi Tick buys company, moves operations from the Bronx to Buffalo, New York.

1987: Tick sells firm to Richard Dolan, who moves firm's headquarters to Florida.

1989: QRS unveils new digital player piano system, Pianomation.

1993: Bankrupt Classic Player Piano, maker of Story & Clark brand, is acquired.

1996: Company becomes QRS Music as stock begins trading on pink sheets.

1997: Name changes to QRS Music Technologies, Inc.

2002: Thomas A. Dolan is named president and CEO; Richard Dolan becomes chairman.

2003: Gulbranson brand and digital hymnal product is acquired; first foreign office opens.

pharmaceutical companies, but his passion for player pianos led him to buy QRS as a side venture. Dolan, a Naples, Florida resident, moved the firm's headquarters to his hometown, although roll production would remain in Buffalo.

DEBUT OF PIANOMATION: 1989

The company's new owner began working to develop products that would bring QRS into the modern age, and in 1989 introduced Pianomation. The new system could be attached to a standard piano to make it play automatically based on signals sent from a control unit to solenoid-activated hammers. The music was recorded on compact discs that used MIDI (musical instrument digital interface) standards, and some discs included prerecorded vocal or instrumental accompaniment that could be played at the same time over speakers. The firm would assemble Pianomation from components sourced from outside manufacturers, while also starting to build up a library of discs.

In 1993 QRS bought Classic Player Piano of Seneca, Pennsylvania, the last remaining player piano maker in the world. Its pianos (which also included console and institutional models) were sold under the name Story & Clark, bringing QRS full circle to owning a piano brand created by Melville Clark. The purchase price of the bankrupt firm was $425,000. For 1994, QRS's sales reached $6 million and it sold 250 Story & Clark roll pianos and 700 disc-based instruments.

On July 24, 1996, QRS Music, Inc., was formed through a merger with publicly traded Geneva American Group, Inc. The firm also completed a $2 million private stock sale to Kyoto Securities, Ltd., of the Bahamas. QRS stock would be traded on the pink sheets exchange, with Richard Dolan continuing to hold a majority ownership stake.

In 1997 QRS broadened foreign distribution which already extended to Europe, Asia, and Canada with ten additional distributors in Europe, Asia, the Middle East, and Mexico. By this time, more than 4,500 Pianomation units had been sold, as well as thousands of the accompanying compact discs, of which 1,000 titles were available. They included popular songs of the day as well as transfers of the piano roll recordings of legends including Liberace and George Gershwin. During the year the firm also expanded its 26,000-square-foot Pennsylvania piano manufacturing division by half and moved Pianomation manufacturing there from Florida. A $1 million order for Pianomation systems was received from Baldwin Piano & Organ Co., which would use the devices as original equipment in its

Ramsi Tick. Tick moved the firm to his hometown of Buffalo, New York, where it took over a historic brick building that had once housed a streetcar line power plant. He also changed its name to QRS Music Rolls, Inc., and saw to it that the long-mothballed Marking Piano was restored.

In 1970 a new Celebrity Series of piano rolls was launched with such stars as Liberace, Roger Williams, Eubie Blake, and Ferrante and Teicher. By 1980 annual sales had grown to 750,000 from the 1966 total of 300,000, with 3,000 different titles available. Rolls were priced at between $3.20 and $4.75, with celebrity performances going for the higher rate. QRS also sold souvenir T-shirts and coasters, as well as attachments for items including kazoos. The firm employed 40 and had annual sales of approximately $1 million.

In 1987 Ramsi Tick sold the company to Richard Dolan, who took the titles of president and chairman. Dolan, a chemist, had founded Alltech Associates of Chicago to sell chromatography products to

ConcertMaster Complete Player System. QRS also added a web site from which it sold products and downloads of Pianomation MIDI files.

New products for 1997 included Presto-Digitation, a digital keyboard that could bring life back to an old piano whose inner workings were beyond repair; a square 18th-century style piano with a digital Korg keyboard; a combined digital keyboard and computer workstation for composers; a nickelodeon-style piano with 12 automated percussion instruments and optional coin-operated capabilities; and an affordable imported acoustic piano. At year's end, the company's name was changed to QRS Music Technologies, Inc.

In February 1998 the firm unveiled the Virtuoso Violin, the world's first computer-controlled instrument of its type. Originally developed by Paroutaud Music Laboratories, it would be built at QRS's Florida research and development facility. Although priced at more than $10,000, the firm quickly received orders for 20 of the devices.

In 1999 a new analog MIDI controller was introduced that allowed integration of Pianomation with other home entertainment or computer-based systems and offered recording and editing capabilities for piano students. The firm also won two major customers for Pianomation, Korean piano makers Young Chang and Samick, who would offer the system under their own brands. For the fiscal year QRS reported sales of $10.3 million and net earnings of $343,000.

ADDITION OF LAS VEGAS PRODUCTION FACILITY: 2000

In 2000 the firm opened showrooms in Naples, Florida, and Las Vegas. The latter was in a new 9,000-square-foot facility which incorporated a warehouse, Virtuoso Violin/Nickelodeon manufacturing site, player piano restoration shop, and Pianomation installation shop. As the firm celebrated its first century in business, it continued to make several hundred thousand music rolls annually, keeping up to date with new releases including a medley of Britney Spears hits. Sales for the fiscal year ended June 30 topped $13.7 million, and net income was just under $800,000.

In the summer of 2001 QRS's stock was added to the over-the-counter bulletin board, but sales were dropping as the U.S. economy suffered from the dot-com implosion. During the year Pianomation customer Baldwin Piano filed for bankruptcy protection, while foreign clients cut back on orders. Production of pianos had been shifted to China, although the firm's Pennsylvania plant would continue to be used for manufacturing of other QRS products, dealer prep, and distribution.

In 2002 the company bought worldwide rights to a patent-pending self-tuning piano system from inventor Don Gilmore and introduced the $10,000 Psalmist, an automated device that could play a Hammond B3 organ. It had been adapted from a Pianomation offshoot called Playola, an external device that could play a piano by physically pushing down the keys.

During 2002 the QRS sales force was bolstered with additional personnel and Richard Dolan's son Thomas A. Dolan was named president and CEO. He had an engineering, business, and economics background and had been employed by the firm since 1994 to market and develop the Pianomation system.

ACQUISITION OF GULBRANSEN DIGITAL HYMNAL: 2003

In January 2003 QRS bought a digital hymnal system and brand name from Gulbransen, Inc., of San Diego. The device enabled users to choose from thousands of hymns that could be played instantly by entering a number. The company also reached an agreement with Roland to allow QRS discs to play on its line of grand pianos. New products included SyncAlong, in which a synchronized piano track played along with a commercial compact disc recording.

In the fall of 2003 the firm opened a showroom and distribution center in Sydney, Australia, and at year's end a partnership with NetPiano.com was announced that would allow Playmation piano owners online access to an extensive collection of MIDI music files by subscription. For the fiscal year the firm had sales of $14.9 million and net income of just over $1 million.

In 2004 QRS opened an office in the Netherlands to serve its European customers, and launched a new national distribution strategy for the Gulbransen piano line, adding the brand name to its Nickelodeon, Virtual Violin, and Bottle Organ products. The latter was a $33,000 automated device that played music by blowing air across the tops of tuned beer bottles. For the year sales grew to $18.5 million and net income increased to $1.3 million.

In early 2005 QRS agreed to pay approximately $200,000 to settle a legal dispute related to the bankruptcy of former customer Baldwin. New products included the Qtouch-Tablet, a wireless Internet-based device that could remotely control a Pianomation system and the NetPiano service, as well as an upgraded Pianomation controller. Dubbed the Ancho, its features included a flash card slot, DVD-ROM drive, and built-in sound card. For 2005 sales reached $20.2 million and net income of $970,000.

In 2006 QRS unveiled Qsync, which could synchronize a Pianomation-equipped piano with a live concert DVD. Initial offerings included performances by Barry Manilow, John Tesh, Diana Krall, and Yanni. The firm also signed a letter of intent to buy distributor National Education Music Co. of New Jersey in February, although like several other acquisition attempts, including that of Chinese piano maker Dongbei, the deal was not consummated.

For 2006, the company's sales fell to $18 million and net income dropped to $39,000. Pianomation accounted for more than 50 percent of the total, with imported pianos in the Story & Clark line about 40 percent; CDs and other music software about 5 percent; and music rolls slightly less than 2 percent.

In the fall of 2007 QRS announced that it was revamping the Story & Clark piano line. The new Signature Series featured a variety of different designs, all priced at under $20,000. At this time the firm was also notified by the National Association of Securities Dealers that trading of its stock would be suspended until it filed an annual report. QRS, which was classified as a small business issuer by the U.S. Securities and Exchange Commission, had issued delayed financial reports on several other occasions.

More than a century after Melville Clark began producing player pianos and rolls, QRS Music Technologies, Inc., was carrying on his vision of automated music reproduction. In addition to selling Pianomation-equipped pianos and discs, the firm offered other unique musical devices including the Nickelodeon, Bottle Organ, and Virtuoso Violin, and continued to make piano rolls on machines that Clark himself had helped create. Although sales were off in part because of the U.S. economic downturn, the company's distinctive product line gave it a unique position in the market, and it continued to be run by a dedicated team of owner/managers that had weathered other hard times.

Frank Uhle

PRINCIPAL SUBSIDIARIES

QRS Music Technologies (Australia); QRS Music Technologies HK Limited (Hong Kong).

PRINCIPAL COMPETITORS

Yamaha Corporation; Burgett, Inc.; Steinway Musical Instruments, Inc.; Young Chang Co., Ltd.; Samick Musical Instruments Co., Ltd.; Kawai Musical Instruments Manufacturing Co., Ltd.

FURTHER READING

Barnett, Lee, "Max Kortlander: King of the Player Piano," *Grand River Valley History Magazine,* Vol. 18, 2001.

Berry, Kate, "QRS Music Technologies Vows to Rebuild Interest in Pianos," *Dow Jones News Service,* January 8, 1998.

Brown, Ed, "Sing Me a Song, Mr. Piano Man ... Excuse Me, Orchestra," *Fortune,* March 15, 1999, p. 44.

"A Century of Marrying Technology & Music," *Music Trades,* October 1, 2000, p. 100.

"CEO Interview: Thomas Dolan—QRS Music Technologies Inc.," *Wall Street Transcript,* August 11, 2003.

Cropp, Ian, "The Smaller the Niche, the Better the Chance of Survival," *Buffalo News,* June 21, 2004, p. B8.

Ferretti, Fred, "Piano Rolls: Shuffling Down from Buffalo," *New York Times,* March 12, 1980, p. C19.

Gargan, Edward A., "Buffalo Concern Gives Pop Sound to Player Pianos," *New York Times,* May 20, 1985, p. B1.

Germain, David, "Piano-Roll Maker to Buy Manufacturer of Player Pianos," *Associated Press,* September 7, 1993.

Layden, Laura, "Naples-Based Company Lets Instruments Play Themselves," *Associated Press Newswires,* March 6, 2001.

MacDougall, Kent, "Look Ma, No Hands," *Wall Street Journal,* November 5, 1962, p. 1.

"QRS Acquires Gulbransen," *Music Trades,* March 1, 2003, p. 40.

"QRS Music Finishes Its Equity Financing," *Derrick,* December 13, 1996, p. A7.

"QRS Technologies—Where High-Tech and Tradition Converge," *Music Trades,* October 1, 2002, p. 102.

"Revolutionary QRS MIDI Controller," *Music Trades,* March 1, 1999, p. 196.

"Roll On, Imperial," *Time,* February 15, 1943.

"Off the Record," *Fortune,* December, 1934.

"Straws: The Tail Wags the Dog," *Wall Street Journal,* August 9, 1927, p. 2.

"A Study of Melville Clark and Automatic Expression Rolls," http://www.bluesrolls.com/BT_MelvilleClark.html, April 1, 2008.

Regent Inns plc

Rowley House
S Herts Office Campus
Elstree Way
Borehamwood, WD6 1JH
United Kingdom
Telephone: (+44 020) 8327 2540
Fax: (+44 020) 8327 2541
Web site: http://www.regentinns.co.uk

Public Company
Incorporated: 1977
Employees: 2,524
Sales: £148.9 million ($302.0 million) (2007)
Stock Exchanges: London
Ticker Symbol: REG
NAIC: 722410 Drinking Places (Alcoholic Beverages);
721110 Hotels (Except Casino Hotels) and Motels;
722110 Full-Service Restaurants

■ ■ ■

Regent Inns plc is one of the United Kingdom's leading operators of branded late-night entertainment bars. Regent's core bar brands are Walkabout and Jongleurs Comedy Clubs. The company also operates restaurants under the Old Orleans and Asha's formats. With more than 50 locations, Walkabout is Regent's flagship bar concept. Walkabout clubs provide live sports broadcasts, music, and DJs, as well as other entertainment events,

with an Australia-inspired theme. Walkabouts tend to be large-scale, multiroom venues, with prime city center locations. Jongleurs is the United Kingdom's leading chain of comedy clubs. There are 16 Jongleurs located throughout the United Kingdom. Like Walkabout, Jongleurs focuses on the city center market, with four Jongleurs operated as part of Walkabout complexes. Nine other Jongleurs are paired with Bar Risa, a multiple-room nightclub format. Regent Inns entered the restaurant sector in September 2006 with the purchase of the Old Orleans restaurant chain. The 29-strong chain features a New Orleans/American theme and menu. In 2007, Regent acquired the franchise rights to develop Asha's, an upscale Indian-food restaurant format for the United Kingdom and Ireland. That operation had just one restaurant, in Birmingham, at the time of the franchise acquisition. Regent also operates two other restaurants under the Quincy's name, acquired with the Old Orleans chain. Despite the move into restaurant operations, Entertainment Bars remains Regent's main division, accounting for 80 percent of its sales of £148.9 million ($302 million) in 2007. Like all of the U.K. bar and club sector, Regent has been confronted with the effects of the Smoking Ban enacted across the United Kingdom in 2007. At the beginning of 2008, Regent acknowledged that it had been approached with a number of buyout offers. In the meantime, the company remains listed on the London Stock Exchange and is led by Chairman Bob Ivell, Managing Director Russell Scott, and Chief Financial Officer John Leslie, all three of whom joined Regent from giant drinks and pubs group Scottish & Newcastle.

PUB OPERATIONS IN THE EIGHTIES

Founded by David Franks, Regent Inns started out as the operator of a single pub in 1977. Franks quickly expanded the business, and by 1980 Regent operated six pubs. The company grew again in 1983 when Franks partnered with husband-and-wife team John Davy and Maria Kempinska to found Jongleurs Comedy Club. A novelty in the United Kingdom at the time, Jongleurs pioneered the U.S.-style comedy and cabaret concept, opening its first locations in Battersea and Camden. Jongleurs, which also featured an attached nightclub concept, Bar Risa, quickly became an important part of the growing alternative theater circuit in the United Kingdom and later expanded to nine locations around the country. Regent remained a minority partner in the Jongleurs chain through 2000.

Looking for further expansion, Regent agreed to a takeover by Lockton Inns in 1988. Lockton had been set up under the U.K. government's Business Expansion Scheme program but had been struggling for profitability into the late 1980s. The merger of the two operations quickly revealed itself as a reverse takeover as the more robust Regent took control of the group with Franks at the helm.

Regent continued to be on the lookout for new properties. The company spotted its next opportunity in 1990, when it acquired a group of 11 pubs, raising its total number of properties to 36. These remained so-called unbranded outlets in that each pub operated under a separate name and design.

The breakup of the British pub system, which had traditionally been controlled by the country's brewers, in the early 1990s set the stage for a new era of growth for Regent. In preparation for its expansion, the company went public in 1993, listing its shares on the London Stock Exchange.

Regent then went scouting for new growth prospects. This led the company to pay Crossgate Holdings £6.3 million in order to acquire its Muswells group of café bars in 1996. The 11 pubs in the Muswells chain featured a sports bar concept centered on snooker. Also that year, Regent signed a six-year deal that gave it management control of the string of pubs owned by the Unchained Pub Group. These properties were primarily located in the London market.

Regent continued to add to its portfolio of properties, opening and/or acquiring pubs across England. By 1999, the company boasted 85 pubs in its estate. These included the first of a new entertainment bar format, called Walkabout, created by the company soon after its public offering. The Walkabout concept featured a large-scale sports bar format based on an Australian design motif. The first Walkabout quickly proved a highly popular meeting place for the United Kingdom's large Australian, New Zealand, and South African expatriate community. Through the 1990s, Regent continued to refine the Walkabout format, particularly with an emphasis on live broadcasts of sporting events. The Walkabout clubs, ranging up to 17,000 square feet in size, were positioned in prime city center locations, a factor that contributed to the brand's success.

UNCERTAINTY IN THE NEW MILLENNIUM

The late 1990s were marked by intense competition within the British pub and club sector, as a growing number of large-scale players competed for market share. The end of the decade was marked by a drive toward consolidation among the industry's top players. At the same time, the market showed signs of an increasing segmentation, with a number of companies choosing to focus their operations exclusively on nightclubs. Others narrowed their focus to the pub sector.

Regent remained a small player in the increasingly competitive market. In addition, the company's financial fortunes fell toward the end of the decade. By 1998, the company was forced to issue a profit warning, sending its shares into a free fall. Regent attempted to climb back out again the following year when it launched merger talks with smaller rival SFI Group, which operated 55 pubs. Those talks fell through, however.

With little prospect of imposing itself as a player in the pub sector, Regent switched tactics at the start of the new century. The company announced its intention to focus on its branded nightclub operators, anchored by its successful Walkabout chain. As David Franks retired, turning over the chief executive position to Stephen

KEY DATES

1977: David Franks founds Regent Inns with single pub.

1980: Company expands to six pubs.

1983: Regent becomes founding partner in Jongleurs Comedy Club.

1988: Company completes reverse takeover of Lockton Inns.

1993: Regent attains public listing on London Stock Exchange; company creates first branded nightclub, Walkabout.

2000: Regent acquires full control of Jongleurs and changes strategy to focus on branded nightclub operations.

2006: Company acquires Old Orleans restaurant chain.

2008: Company is rumored to have received takeover bids.

Haupt in 2000, the company announced plans to expand the Walkabout chain to as many as 50 sites.

Instead of placing all its eggs in one basket, Regent took steps to broaden its nightclub offering. In 2000, the company bought full control of the Jongleurs Comedy Club chain, paying £7 million. The addition of Jongleurs not only gave the company a second strong brand, but it also allowed it to operate more or less unchallenged in the comedy club niche market. In keeping with its new strategy, Regent announced that it intended to sell its entire estate of more than 70 non-branded pubs. That process was launched with the sale of 20 pubs to Wizard Inns in June 2002, raising nearly £28 million for the company.

By then, however, Regent's growth strategy had hit a number of new snags. In December 2000, the company found its shares suspended from the London Stock Exchange when the company's liquidity was called into question. Trading resumed on Regent's stock in June 2001. Soon after, Regent failed in a new expansion effort after the beleaguered Wolverhampton & Dudley group rejected its £62 million offer to acquire the Pitcher & Piano pub chain.

As a result, Regent attempted to develop a new nightclub concept in-house, launching the PALS club brand. A more food-oriented format, the PALS brand attempted to create a "private member" atmosphere. The first two PALS clubs opened in Croyden and Ipswich, with a third in development in Southend. The format

failed to excite club-goers, unfortunately, and the company shut down the effort by the middle of the decade.

In the meantime, Regent itself reached the edge of an abyss. The company had continued its pub disposal program, selling half of its holdings by 2002. Yet the company soon found itself weakened as a number of deals went sour. These included the sale of 17 pubs to Porter Black Holdings for £4.27 million in 2002. However, that company went bankrupt the following year, forcing Regent to take back the leases on the group of pubs. Soon after, the Unchained Pub Group folded as well, leaving some £1.8 million in fees to Regent unpaid. In order to shore up its finances, Regent issued a new share offering, raising £16.7 million at the end of 2003. The company also completed a number of sale-and-leaseback deals for several of its Walkabout properties. In one such deal, which included locations in Portsmouth, Wolverhampton, and Hertford, Regent raised £7.2 million.

RESCUE IN 2004

Regent still continued to reel from crisis to crisis toward the middle of the decade. The company's operations director resigned at the beginning of April 2004. In September of that year, CEO Haupt and CFO Simon Rowe suddenly quit after Regent announced it had experienced a severe drop in its like-for-like sales. Just four days later, the company defaulted on the terms of its bank loans, which resulted in a delay in the publication of the company's annual report. When finally released, the report revealed that the company had slipped into the red, with losses topping £6.6 million for the year. Regent's share price plummeted, sinking to just 30p per share, down from a high of nearly 400p per share in the 1990s.

On the verge of collapse, Regent brought in an entirely new management team, led by Bob Ivell, who became Regent's chief executive and then chairman, and John Leslie, who assumed the chief financial officer's position. Both Ivell and Leslie, as well as others on the new team, came from Scottish & Newcastle, where they had successfully developed a group of pubs, hotels, and restaurants acquired from Grand Metropolitan in 1992. Scottish & Newcastle sold most of these properties to Spirit Group, raising £2.5 billion, in 2003.

Ivell and Leslie renegotiated Regent's bank debt, helping to relieve the pressure. The new team then addressed a number of problems within Regent Inns itself, particularly its lack of such key financial controls as internal audits and profit targets. Ivell and Leslie also launched a refurbishment effort for the company's core

Walkabout brand, which in part involved a de-emphasis of the Australian theme.

POTENTIAL TAKEOVER TARGET IN 2008

By 2005, Regent Inns appeared to be back on track. The company once again began seeking expansion opportunities amid the movement toward a new wave of consolidation in the U.K. pub and nightclub sector. This led Regent to make an unsolicited takeover bid for Urbium, a rival operator of late-night bars. After Urbium rejected Regent's initial bid of 820p per share, Regent raised the price, finally topping out at 975p per share. When this bid was also rejected, Regent dropped the takeover attempt.

Regent next set its sights on the acquisition of Inventive Leisure, a company that had developed the Revolution vodka bar format. The company's bid fell short again, however. Instead, Inventive Leisure went to a management buyout backed by private equity firm Alchemy Partners. Soon after, Regent found itself at the receiving end of a takeover bid from Alchemy Partners. The company rejected that offer, however, as too low.

Regent Inns finally found success in 2006, when it reached an agreement with Punch Taverns to take over the Old Orleans restaurant chain. Regent paid £24.7 million for the 31-strong restaurant group, which had formerly been part of Scottish & Newcastle. The company then set out to revitalize the restaurant chain, revamping its interiors and upgrading its menu.

The move into restaurants came at a crucial time in the British pub and club sector. The first phase of the British government's ban on smoking in public places came into effect in 2006. By mid-2007, the ban had come into effect nationwide. Like most of its counterparts, Regent quickly felt the effect of the new legislation as business declined. The company hoped to counter the drop with a push into the restaurant sector. As part of this effort, the company acquired the U.K. and Ireland franchise rights to roll out the Asha's restaurant format featuring an upscale Indian menu and décor. The first Asha's opened in Birmingham, but failed to generate sufficient revenues, and Regent decided against a general rollout of the brand.

Meanwhile, Regent continued to bear the brunt of the smoking ban as sales remained low into early 2008. By then, the company was rumored to have been approached with a takeover offer by another company; Alchemy Partners, Laurel Group, and Novus Leisure were all rumored as potential candidates. With its sales hit again by a downturn in consumer spending, Regent Inns suggested it would remain open to takeover offers, potentially putting an end to more than 30 years as one of the United Kingdom's most successful independent pub and nightclub companies.

M. L. Cohen

PRINCIPAL SUBSIDIARIES

Brandasia Limited; Old Orleans Limited; Regent Inns Bar Risa Limited; Regent Inns Limited; Regent Inns Property Limited; Regent Inns Walkabout Limited; Swanarch Limited.

PRINCIPAL COMPETITORS

Compass Group PLC; Scottish and Newcastle plc; Whitbread Group PLC; Punch Taverns plc; Mitchells and Butlers PLC; Greene King plc; Enterprise Inns plc; J D Wetherspoon PLC; Marston's PLC; The Spirit Group Ltd.; Bett Ltd.; Luminar Plc.

FURTHER READING

"Bid Speculation at Regent Inns," *Investors Chronicle*, January 16, 2008.

Blitz, Roger, "Regent Inns Still Pursuing Bid Discussions," *Financial Times*, February 6, 2008, p. 22.

Felton-Smith, Paul, "Pulling Businesses Back from the Brink," *Finance Week*, July 20, 2005, p. 14.

Golding, Christina, "Regent to Add 20 New Walkabouts Next Year," *Caterer & Hotelkeeper*, September 12, 2002, p. 12.

"Hangover at Regent Inns," *Investors Chronicle*, October 9, 2007.

Hume, Neil, and Robert Orr, "Walkabout Owner Races Ahead," *Financial Times*, December 7, 2007, p. 42.

"Last Orders for Regent Inns?" *Investors Chronicle*, January 18, 2008.

"Regent Inns Cuts Jobs in Cost-Saving Drive," *Finance Week*, February 16, 2005, p. 1.

"Regent Inns Rethinks Brands," *Marketing*, April 25, 2007, p. 15.

"Regent Reveals Key Men to Reverse Slide," *Caterer & Hotelkeeper*, October 28, 2004, p. 8.

"Urbium Set for Bidding War As Regent Withdraws Offer," *Leisure Report*, August 2005, p. 8.

Walsh, Dominic, "Come Together, Right Now," *Leisure Report*, October 2006, p. 20.

Warwick-Ching, Lucy, "Late-Night Bar Scene Brings Little Merriment to Regent Inns," *Financial Times*, November 25, 2006, p. 17.

Rusty, Inc.

8495 Commerce Avenue
San Diego, California 92121
U.S.A.
Telephone: (858) 578-0414
Fax: (858) 578-0603
Web site: http://www.rusty.com

Private Company
Incorporated: 1985 as Rusty Cos.
Employees: 35
Sales: $50 million (2007 est.)
NAIC: 315999 Apparel Accessories and Other Apparel
Manufacturing; 423910 Sporting and Recreational
Goods and Supplies Merchant Wholesalers; 339920
Sporting and Athletic Good Manufacturing

■ ■ ■

Rusty, Inc., is a manufacturer of surfboards and apparel.
The company sells its products primarily to specialty
surf shops, although it also distributes a limited supply
of apparel to department stores and specialty chains.
Rusty, which sponsors a team of surfers, is controlled by
R. & Everything Else Inc., a Perth, Australia-based
company that formerly operated as Rusty's Australian
licensee.

SURFING JUNKIE

When Russell "Rusty" Preisendorfer enrolled at the
University of California, San Diego (UCSD) in 1971,
the hopes of his parents, particularly his father, were
undermined by the location of the university's campus.
Preisendorfer's father was a research mathematician at
UCSD who wanted nothing more than for his 18-year-
old son to apply himself seriously to academic life, but
the view from the school's grounds and classrooms
proved no match for a father's persuasion. The UCSD
campus was perched on a hill overlooking Black's Beach.
Preisendorfer, seduced by the power of the waves crash-
ing at UCSD's doorstep, dropped out before he finished
his freshman year. "I knew when the surf was good," he
said in a July 25, 1988, interview with the *San Diego
Business Journal.* "I could smell it."

Preisendorfer's love for the beach could be traced to
a decision made by his parents in 1966. Preisendorfer
was 13 years old and had spent all his years living in
inland San Diego. When his parents decided to move to
La Jolla, along the coast, Preisendorfer discovered what
would become the focal point of his life. As a teenager,
he began bodysurfing on Shores Beach, but the
recumbent style of riding a wave lost its attraction once
he observed surfers using long, shaped planks to harness
a wave's power. He began surfing at Shores Beach, joining a small, tight-knit community of surfers who soon
directed the newcomer to a surfing spot favored by
locals, a then relatively unknown location known as
"Black's." Off the 300-foot cliffs towering over Black's
Beach, an underwater canyon served as a surfer's best
friend, funneling water to the shore and creating the
most powerful beach breaks in Southern California.
Preisendorfer spent virtually all his time at Black's, taking only a short break while viewing his favorite
hangout from above, on the campus of UCSD.

HONING HIS SURFBOARD SHAPING SKILLS

Before enrolling at UCSD, Preisendorfer began what would become his life's work. In the winter of 1969, while attending La Jolla High School, he shaped his first surfboard. The following year, he spent Christmas in Hawaii, where the high school senior saw the some of the biggest waves and some of the best surfers in the world. After graduating from La Jolla High School the following summer, Preisendorfer enrolled at UCSD in the fall, but by October 1971, he began to be pulled away from academia, notwithstanding the proximity of Black's Beach. A major surfing competition, the World Contest, was held in San Diego, featuring an Australian professional surfer named Peter Townend. Preisendorfer was introduced to Townend and left the contest inspired to create his first label for the boards he was shaping, settling on "Starlight Surfboards" for his first brand.

In the summer of 1972, after dropping out of UCSD, Preisendorfer began living his dream full-time. He started riding and shaping for G&S Surfboards, a business relationship that allowed him to travel, appear in advertisements, and earn press coverage in two of the sport's rising publications, *Surfer* and *Surfing*. He appeased his parents by telling them he wanted to learn everything he could about shaping boards before returning to school. Experimenting with blends of Kevlar and epoxy as board-building materials, shaping boards on a freelance basis, and making a pilgrimage to Australia, Preisendorfer accomplished his goal and also met some of the luminaries of the surfing world. He started a second label, Music! Surfboards, but after three years of pursuing his goals in surfing, Preisendorfer felt the tug of his parents' demands for earning a degree. He

returned to UCSD, atop the bluff staring over Black's Beach, and resisted temptation. "I put blinders on and divorced myself from surfing," he recalled in a June 19, 1995, interview with *Forbes*. In 1978, he earned a degree in graphic arts and immediately immersed himself in the beach scene.

Preisendorfer's first job after college was with Canyon Glassing, the company that did the fiberglass work for his Music! Surfboards. The company hired the 25-year-old UCSD graduate to shape its boards at a time when its sponsorship of young surfers included two jewels, Wes Laine and Richard Kenvin. The competitive accomplishments of the surfers made a name for Canyon and for the designer of its boards. Preisendorfer's name was beginning to draw respect within the surfing community, which led to requests for him to judge surfing contests. For his career as a board shaper, the sight of him at the judges' table of high-profile surfing contests cemented his place within the community. It also motivated Preisendorfer to use his shaping skills to advance the art of board-making. "I went to Australia, Hawaii, and up and down the California coast," he said in his July 25, 1988, interview with the *San Diego Business Journal*. "I met professional surfers, but I didn't see anything special about their boards."

SATISFYING THE ENTREPRENEURIAL ITCH: 1985

Preisendorfer's entrepreneurial inclinations were coming to the fore, an arc in his professional development that was accelerated by his increasing frustration at Canyon. Through Preisendorfer's contacts within the surfing community and his talents as a shaper, Canyon was selling 100 Preisendorfer-shaped boards per month, collecting $140 for each board. Preisendorfer wanted to reap the benefits of his influence and work, but he was rebuffed by the company's owner. "I was real aggressive at building that business," he said in a June 19, 1995, interview with *Forbes*. "I was in demand. I kept pushing for ownership, but I knew I wasn't ever going to be more than just an employee. The owner had a house and two very nice cars, but the only thing I had to show for all that work was a truck. That's when the light bulb went off."

The disgruntled employee was transformed into a hopeful entrepreneur in the fall of 1985. Preisendorfer based his company in a garage in San Diego, but the modest trappings belied the strength of the start-up. By the time he formed his own shop, Preisendorfer was shaping boards for more than half of the world's top 16 surfers, including an Australian named Mark Occhilupo, who twice had won the Ocean Pacific Pro in Huntington Beach, California. "I'm not taking credit for Mark's success," Preisendorfer said in his July 25, 1988, interview with the *San Diego Business Journal.* "He is a great athlete. He said my board worked perfect for him. Most of the pros got boards from me to emulate the way he surfed, or ordered one to try to psych out and derail Occhilupo." Preisendorfer was flooded with orders, spurring him and his six apprentices to churn out 2,000 boards, each emblazoned with a stylized "R" logo, within the first year of the business. The boards ranged in price between $300 and $500.

LAUNCHING AN APPAREL BUSINESS

As board sales swelled, Preisendorfer started a sideline venture selling T-shirts. The shirts, decorated with the Rusty logo, represented his first foray into apparel, which opened his eyes to both the upside and downside of the clothing business. The shirts proved to be highly popular, selling at a pace that soon averaged 1,200 units per month. Preisendorfer's joy at the success of the shirt sales was amplified after he calculated the apparel was generating profit margins of 25 percent, significantly more than the 5 percent profit margins he was realizing with board sales. In response to the finding, he split his company into two divisions in 1988 and sold a 25 percent stake in the apparel unit to two friends for $50,000. He planned to use the proceeds to hire a designer to create a line of Rusty shorts, swim trunks, and shirts, but within three months he exhausted $400,000 trying to get a line developed and manufactured. To compound matters, his customers— surf shop owners—failed to pay their invoices in a timely manner, creating a financial headache for Preisendorfer.

TAKING ON A PARTNER IN 1988

Beset by financial and operational problems, Preisendorfer needed help, prompting him to seek the assistance of C&C Partners, an Irvine, California-based clothing manufacturer and wholesaler. In 1988, Preisendorfer reached an agreement with C&C to produce a Rusty apparel line, selling the company a license for $700,000 and a 3 percent royalty on C&C's wholesale revenues. Not long after resolving one crisis, Preisendorfer was confronted with another, far more distressing problem. Neon-colored fabrics, the rage during the 1980s and closely associated with surf apparel, quickly went out of style, delivering a decisive blow that slashed industry retail sales from $2 billion in 1989 to less than $1 billion by 1992. "We had retailers tell us to our face that they didn't want our products just because we were a surf company," Preisendorfer recalled in his June 19, 1995, interview with *Forbes.*

To help reverse plunging sales, Preisendorfer huddled with C&C officials and devised a response. The line was simplified, stripped of neon coloring, and marketed exclusively to specialty surf shops. By 1995, the line had recovered, bringing in roughly $300,000 in royalties annually from the sale of baggy flannel shirts and trunks. At the time, the entire Rusty enterprise was generating $57 million in revenue from the sale of boards and apparel, a volume that netted Preisendorfer close to $1 million. With the profits, the company branched out into the production of snowboards and skateboards.

REVAMPING THE BRAND IMAGE

By the end of the 1990s, Rusty's U.S. sales peaked near $50 million and began to flatten. A new vice-president of marketing, Mike Schillmoeller, was appointed in 2000 to revitalize the brand domestically, conceding in a December 17, 2001, interview with *Daily News Record* that the brand "needed to exude more perpetual youth energy." He narrowed the company's focus on surf and skate products at the expense of other board sports, such as snowboarding and wakeboarding. "We're trying to channel our focus into certain areas," he explained to *Daily News Record,* "and decided that we'd rather just be a really good surf and skate company than anything else." Despite Schillmoeller's efforts, the Rusty brand continued its downward spiral in the United States as opposed to its strong performance in Australia. The anemic state of the Rusty franchise became apparent five years after Schillmoeller talked with *Daily News Record,* when Preisendorfer announced he wanted to cash out on the venture he had started as a board shaper.

SELLING THE BUSINESS: 2006

Preisendorfer was 53 years old in 2006, the year he sold his majority stake in R ... & Everything Else, the entity that owned Rusty trademarks and its intellectual property rights. He sold his interest in the company to his Australian licensee, Rusty Australia/Vegas Entertainment, a Perth, Australia-based company led by Geoff Bachshall. As part of the deal, Preisendorfer retained worldwide rights in perpetuity for the manufacture of Rusty-brand surfboards. "By purchasing Preisendorfer's 52 percent interest in R ... & Everything Else," Bachshall explained in an August 14, 2006, interview with *Daily News Record,* "we now control the look of the brand globally and C&C reports to us. We see a lot of potential in the brand, and it hasn't been well managed as far as the design and quality of the product. We're a major player here in Australia, and we have a lot to offer as far as how to manage the design team and create the product."

Rusty Australia/Vegas Entertainment, which changed its name to R. & Everything Else Inc. following the investment, took control of a business that was struggling in the United States. Domestic sales had slumped to a reported $15 million from their peak in the late 1990s. Meanwhile, the company's performance in Australia offered little room for criticism, having increased to an estimated $30 million. With Bachshall leading the way, the Australian controllers of the brand hoped to breathe new life into Rusty in the United States, projecting sales to increase to $50 million by 2012. "They've got a great track record, and they really understand the culture of the brand," Preisendorfer said in an August 20, 2007, interview with *Daily News Record*. "We're all like-minded, we're all surfers. I think we've got a great future together."

Jeffrey L. Covell

PRINCIPAL COMPETITORS

Quiksilver, Inc.; Pacific Sunwear of California, Inc.; Billabong International Limited.

FURTHER READING

Bermudez, Andrea, "Rusty Repair," *Daily News Record,* December 17, 2001, p. 8S.

Hathcock, Jim, "Future of Surfing Takes Shape As Rusty Rage Runs Unabated," *San Diego Business Journal,* July 25, 1988, p. 1.

La Franco, Robert, "Beach Bum Makes Good," *Forbes,* June 19, 1995, p. 80.

Pallay, Jessica, "Rusty Back in the Courtroom," *Daily News Record,* October 1, 2007, p. 6.

———, "Rusty License Granted to La Jolla," *Daily News Record,* August 20, 2007, p. 7.

Tschorn, Adam, "Rusty Founder Sells Control to Aussie Licensee," *Daily News Record,* August 14, 2006, p. 15.

SANLUIS Corporación, S.A.B. de C.V.

Monte Pelvoux 220
Lomas de Chapultepec
Mexico, D.F. 11000
Mexico
Telephone: (52 55) 5229-5800
Fax: (52 55) 5202-6467
Web site: http://www.sanluisrassini.com.mx

Public Company
Incorporated: 1984 as Corporación Industrial SANLUIS, S.A. de C.V.
Employees: 5,190
Sales: MXN 8 billion ($717.6 million) (2007)
Stock Exchanges: Bolsa Mexicana de Valores NASDAQ
Ticker Symbols: SANLUIS; SLRPP or CISR
NAIC: 336330 Motor Vehicle Steering and Suspension (Except Spring) Manufacturing; 336340 Motor Vehicle Brake System Manufacturing; 336399 All Other Motor Vehicle Parts Manufacturing

■■■

SANLUIS Corporación, S.A.B. de C.V., is a Mexican-based company that designs and produces automotive parts for suspension and brake systems, through its SANLUIS Rassini brand. The company's suspension division manufactures leaf springs, coil springs, and torsion bars for manufacturers of motor vehicles, particularly the Big Three U.S. automakers. These components are used in automobiles, pickups, trucks, and trailers. SANLUIS is the world's largest designer and manufacturer of leaf springs. The brake division is a key designer of advanced brake systems components for the North American market. This segment of the business manufactures rotors, drums, hubs, assemblies, clutch housings, flywheels, and clutch pressure plates. SANLUIS has plants in Mexico, the United States, and Brazil.

A CENTURY OF MINING GOLD AND SILVER

SANLUIS started out in mining rather than auto parts. Founded in the late 1880s by San Luis Mining Company according to one account, or in 1890 by Compañia Minera Candaleria, according to another, the Tayoltita mine in the state of Durango became a major producer of silver, with gold as a byproduct. Mexico was then, and generally remains, the world's leading silver producing nation.

Tayoltita, in the Sierra Madre Occidental mountain range, was accessible year-round only by airplane, since a primitive road was usable only during the winter dry season. An aerial tramway carried ore to the valley below, where a cyanide mill extracted precious metals for smelting. Power was supplied by three company-owned hydroelectric stations, with a standby generator, fueled by diesel oil, used in the dry season.

The enterprise was renamed Minas de San Luis, S.A., in 1962. It was acquired by the Hearst Corporation in the 1960s. A group of Mexican investors purchased a majority stake in the company in 1979 for about $20 million. Its leader was Antonio Madero Bracho, a member of the wealthy family that produced Francisco Madero, who led the revolution that overthrew the dictatorial regime of Porfirio Díaz in 1911. An engineer and graduate of Harvard Business School, Madero Bracho became chief executive of a holding company, Industrias Luismin, that ran the mine. It was renamed Corporación Industrial SANLUIS, S.A. de C.V., in 1984.

During the inflationary climate of the late 1970s, gold and silver prices soared. Madero and his partners used the high profits of mining to take positions in an aluminum company and also in unrelated businesses. In partnership with F.W. Woolworth Co., SANLUIS held a chain of stores in Mexico and with Hyatt Hotels, a number of hotels in Mexico.

MINING AND AUTO PARTS:
1988–99

In 1988 SANLUIS, foreseeing the future North American Free Trade Association, purchased the Rassini auto parts company from the Mexican government for about $45 million. Rassini, which dated from 1929, had three plants in Mexico and an office of design, engineering, and customer service to the U.S. auto industry in Ann Arbor, Michigan (later moved to Plymouth, Michigan). Two of these plants were supplying the U.S. market with leaf springs and coil springs.

The mining business, now Minas Luismin, S.A. de C.V., was doing less well. By 1984 the company had dropped to sixth place in silver production. The following year it closed a mine because recovering the remaining ore was not profitable. In 1990 the Tayolita mine closed temporarily because of low prices and labor problems. Still, Minas Luismin remained one of Mexico's four largest mining companies.

This boom period for SANLUIS ended in 1991, when, besides the decline in mining, its hotels were suffering from a fall in the tourist trade due to a recession in the United States. The holding company owed its creditors $150 million. Madero sold the hotel business for very little money and the stores back to Woolworth for $8.5 million. He even sold the company's private plane and moved the corporate offices to a more modest location. While paying the company's more pressing

debts in cash, Madero made peace with the bankers by issuing them debentures convertible into stock.

Rassini was the keystone of the company. The leaf spring plant in Piedras Negras, Coahuila, close to the Rio Grande and the Texas border, was expanded in size, and the company began producing torsion bars as well. The number of plants at Piedras Negras grew to as many as eight, including a joint venture with Hendrickson International, the Canadian arm of Hendrickson USA, LLC, a subsidiary of Boler Co.

In 1994 SANLUIS acquired Bujes y Autopartes Autometrices S.A., a company with a plant in San Martín Texmelucan, Puebla. This company became Rassini Frenos, S.A. de C.V., producing brake components. Two years later, a 35 percent interest in this company was sold to Brembo S.p.A. of Italy for about $100 million. Brembo, which had become a strategic partner, was the world leader in the development and sale of components for high-technology brakes. In 1997 Rassini Frenos secured a $360 million contract to make rear wheel discs for a new General Motors line of utility vehicles and pickup trucks. The next year Rassini Frenos began sending brake components to Bayerische Motoren Werke AG (BMW) plants in Germany and North Carolina.

Corporación Industrial SANLUIS changed its name to SANLUIS Corporación in 1996, the year it raised some $60 million by selling American Depositary Receipts (ADRs). With this money in hand and Japanese partners, Madero entered Brazil by purchasing Industrias C. Fabrini S.A. of São Paulo and NHK Cinebra Industria de Molas LTDA. of Rio de Janeiro. These companies were supplying half the Brazilian demand for suspension components for light vehicles and trucks. By means of a joint venture with NHK Spring Co. of Japan, the two acquired companies were joined in Rassini NHK Autopeças S.A.

SANLUIS was the Mexican publicly traded enterprise most oriented toward exports, with 90 percent of its sales made to customers abroad. The manufacture of auto parts was highly profitable because the company was paying its workers only about $5.25 per day, while unionized U.S. workers were earning at least $150 per day. Rassini had become a major supplier for Ford Motor Co., General Motors Corp., Chrysler Corp., and Nissan Motor Co., Ltd., which were buying two-thirds of its production. It was supplying parts mainly for the rapidly growing market of minivans, pickup trucks, and sport utility vehicles in the United States and Canada and ranked second in sales of suspension components in these countries and Mexico. Leslie Crawford of the *Financial Times* called SANLUIS "a

KEY DATES

1890: The predecessor of SANLUIS has founded a gold and silver mine in the state of Durango.
1962: Enterprise is renamed Minas de San Luis, S.A.
1979: Mexican investors purchase a majority stake in company for about $20 million.
1988: SANLUIS purchases the Rassini auto parts business for about $45 million.
1994: Company acquires a plant converted to the manufacture of brake components.
1996: SANLUIS purchases two companies producing suspension components in Brazil.
2002: SANLUIS reduces its debt load by selling its mining subsidiary.
2003: Company restructures its debts, signing an agreement with 14 creditor banks.
2007: SANLUIS loses money for the fourth straight year due to interest on its debt load.

walking advertisement for the North American Free Trade Association."

SANLUIS sent its engineers to Detroit to get input from the Big Three automakers on how to design and develop the company's suspension and brake components, opening its new center for technological development in Plymouth, Michigan, in 1998. The company also sent its technicians overseas for training. "Our goal is to have our entire management and technical team proficient in English and computing by the turn of the century," Madero told Crawford.

In Mexico, the workers in the company's manufacturing plants studied satellite-transmitted material on quality control. To motivate the Piedras Negras workers, SANLUIS built a model community for its workers, offering mortgage loans well below bank rates, depending on the productivity of its personnel. The company's managers qualified for bonuses calculated on the basis of the performance of their departments.

Minas Luismin, although accounting for little more than one-quarter of company sales, was also doing well now. There were seven mines in three Mexican states. High productivity, based on individual incentives, allowed the enterprise to double the amount of gold turned out per man-hour, making it one of the lowest-cost gold producers in the world. It continued to rank fourth among Mexican mining groups. All of the

production went abroad, mostly to British and Swiss refineries.

21ST-CENTURY HANGOVER: 2000–07

Unfortunately for SANLUIS's expansion program, the company's debts were growing even faster than its sales. In 2000 the former figure outstripped the latter as the U.S. economy slid toward a recession the following year. To help buttress its financial position, SANLUIS sold a 49 percent stake in Fundimak, S.A. de C.V., the parent company of Rassini Frenos, for $56 million in 2000. In addition, a copper-zinc mine was sold the next year to Canada-based Teck Corp. for stock valued at $15.9 million.

Only nine days after the 2001 terrorist attacks on the United States, SANLUIS missed an interest payment on a $200 million bond marketed in Europe, and also on commercial paper also marketed in Europe. The company's remaining debt was immediately downgraded, and SANLUIS was said to be Mexico's most indebted conglomerate. In 2002 it sold Minas Luismin, which represented only 12 percent of company sales, to a Canadian company, Wheaton River Minerals Ltd., for $90 million in cash and stock. Also in 2002, SANLUIS sold its 51 percent interest in Hendrickson-Rassini, S.A. de C.V., for $7.1 million.

SANLUIS completed the restructuring of its debts, which had neared $560 million, in early 2003 by reaching agreement with 14 creditor banks. A new subsidiary, SANLUIS Co-Inter, S.A. de C.V., then issued new bonds expiring in 2010 and 2011. In addition, for the ninth year in a row, General Motors Corp. named SANLUIS "Supplier of the Year." Also in 2003, SANLUIS opened a factory producing coil springs in Montpelier, Ohio. In 2005 SANLUIS opened offices in Stuttgart, Germany, and Shanghai.

In 2006 SANLUIS made 62 percent of its sales to customers in the United States, 21 percent in Brazil, and 17 percent in Mexico. Leaf springs accounted for 68 percent, brake components for 16 percent, coil springs for 15 percent, and torsion bars for 1 percent. The company's principal customers were General Motors and its close partner, American Axle & Manufacturing Holdings, Inc., 34 percent; Ford, 25 percent; and DaimlerChrysler AG, 15 percent. Madero was the company's chief stockholder, with 16 percent of the shares.

SANLUIS's heavy debt load resulted in interest payments that ate into its operating profits and resulted in a net loss in 2002 and 2004 through 2007. Its debt was MXN 2.88 billion ($241 million) at the end of 2006, with long term debt accounting for MXN 2.5 billion ($209 million). In 2007 Rep Uno, S.A. de C.V., was established as a subsidiary to market company debt. Rep Uno offered to purchase for cash any and all outstanding 8 percent notes due in 2010 issued by SANLUIS Co-Inter and any and all outstanding 8.875 percent notes due in 2008 issued by SANLUIS Corporación. It also offered to purchase any and all of certain outstanding Euro commercial paper notes of SANLUIS.

Robert Halasz

PRINCIPAL SUBSIDIARIES

Rep Uno, S.A. de C.V.; SANLUIS Co-Inter, S.A., and its subsidiary, SANLUIS Rassini Autopartes, S.A. de C.V.

PRINCIPAL OPERATING UNITS

Brake Group; Suspension Group.

PRINCIPAL COMPETITORS

Grupo Industrial Saltillo, S.A.B de C.V.; Spicer, S.A. de C.V.; Tenedora Nemak, S.A. de C.V.

FURTHER READING

Aguilar, Alberto, "Nombres, nombres y … nombres," *Reforma* (Mexico City), June 13, 1997, p. 35.

Bogart, John R., "TAYOLTITA: Mexico's Most Important Silver-Gold Mining Operation," *Mining World,* June 1963, pp. 20–24, and July 1963, pp. 22–25.

Crawford, Leslie, "Sanluis Finds Growth Without Frontiers," *Financial Times,* May 14, 1998, p. 41.

Dolan, Kerry A., "Made in Mexico," *Forbes,* November 3, 1997, pp. 300–01.

"Heavy Weight Mexican Auto Parts Companies Are Going Global," *Ward's Auto World,* January 2005, p. 12.

Mandel-Campbell, Andrea, "Autoparts Makers' Productivity Drive," *Financial Times,* June 13, 1999, p. 11.

———, "Sanluis Blames Turmoil As It Defaults on Debt," *Financial Times,* September 24, 2001, p. 26.

Martínez, Jaime, "Vende Sanluis negocio minero," *El Norte* (Monterrey), April 25, 2002, p. 2.

Murphy, Tom, and Bill Siuri, "NAFTA Success Story," *Ward's Auto World,* August 1999, pp. 64+.

"Reestructura deuda Sanluis Corporación," *Palabra* (Mexico City), January 21, 2003, p. 4.

Rodiles, Janine, "Cuestión de honor," *AméricaEconomía,* September 1996, pp. 60–62.

Stok, Gustavo, "Curva peligrosa," *AméricaEconomía,* May 17, 2001, pp. 18–20.

SANYO Electric Co., Ltd.

———■———

2-5-5 Keihan-Hondori
Moriguchi City, Osaka 570-8677
Japan
Telephone: (+81-6) 6991-1181
Fax: (+81-6) 6992-0009
Web site: http://www.sanyo.com

Public Company
Founded: 1947 as SANYO Electric Works
Incorporated: 1950
Employees: 94,906
Sales: ¥2.22 trillion ($18.77 billion) (2007)
Stock Exchanges: Tokyo Osaka
Ticker Symbol: 6764
NAIC: 333313 Office Machinery Manufacturing; 333315 Photographic and Photocopying Equipment Manufacturing; 333415 Air-Conditioning and Warm Air Heating Equipment and Commercial and Industrial Refrigeration Equipment Manufacturing; 334119 Other Computer Peripheral Equipment Manufacturing; 334220 Radio and Television Broadcasting and Wireless Communications Equipment Manufacturing; 334310 Audio and Video Equipment Manufacturing; 334413 Semiconductor and Related Device Manufacturing; 334414 Electronic Capacitor Manufacturing; 334419 Other Electronic Component Manufacturing; 335211 Electric Housewares and Household Fan Manufacturing; 335222 Household Refrigerator and Home Freezer Manufacturing; 335224 Household Laundry Equipment Manufacturing; 335911 Storage Battery Manufacturing; 335912 Primary Battery Manufacturing

■ ■ ■

One of Japan's electronics conglomerates, SANYO Electric Co., Ltd., (Sanyo) places particular emphasis on environmentally friendly products, such as rechargeable batteries and solar cells. The firm ranks as the world leader in rechargeable batteries for portable devices such as laptop computers and mobile phones. Sanyo also makes appliances, including refrigerators, laundry equipment, and air conditioners for home use and refrigerator/freezer supermarket showcases and large air conditioners on the commercial side. Among the other products manufactured by the company are digital cameras, televisions, LCD projectors, car navigation systems, semiconductors, capacitors, and optical pickups for DVD players/recorders. Sanyo has about 250 subsidiaries and affiliates worldwide; approximately 57 percent of overall sales are generated outside of Japan, with about 29 percent originating elsewhere in Asia, about 17 percent in North America, and about 8 percent in Europe.

EARLY HISTORY: CREATION OUT OF MATSUSHITA ELECTRIC

Sanyo was born in the shadow of the giant Matsushita Electric Industrial Co., Ltd., one of Japan's largest industrial institutions. Sanyo's founder, Toshio Iue, was the brother-in-law of Konosuke Matsushita and an original partner in Matsushita Electric. Shortly after

COMPANY PERSPECTIVES

SANYO Electric Group, by developing unique technologies and offering excellent products and sincere services, seeks to become a corporation that is loved and trusted by people around the world. The Group seeks to become "as indispensable as the Sun" for the people of the world.

World War II, the occupation authority ordered Matsushita broken up into two smaller companies as part of its industrial decentralization policy. In 1947 several of Matsushita's operations were turned over to Iue, who set up his own company in Osaka to produce and export bicycle lamp generators. Dreaming of one day having 100 factories around the world, Iue called his company SANYO Electric Works, "Sanyo" being a somewhat generic name that means "three oceans," referring to the Pacific, Atlantic, and Indian Oceans. On April 1, 1950, after paying off its unsecured loans, the company was incorporated as SANYO Electric Co., Ltd. It went public in 1954.

The dynamic economic atmosphere in Japan after the Korean War raised personal incomes and stimulated consumer demand. Sanyo grew modestly at first, offering only a limited line of simple electrical appliances. To boost its sales through greater name recognition, Iue asked Matsushita for permission to use that company's brand name, National. With only minimal benefit from Matsushita's broad marketing network, Sanyo widened its product line in the early 1950s to include radios, tape recorders, and even televisions. The company later began marketing products under its own name through independent retailers.

Toshio Iue believed in a unique management philosophy called the "white paper" method. Similar to the process by which parliamentary governments announce general policy goals and invite criticism or discussion, the white paper system encouraged a consensus approach to management.

As the Japanese economy began to grow even faster during the mid-1950s, consumers, long deprived of even simple amenities, expressed increasing demand for household appliances. Sanyo was well established in the market and had great success in simple technology items such as washing machines, air conditioners, and improved radios. Iue did not regard other electrical manufacturers as his competition. Instead, he saw consumers—the ones who dictate the market—as

competitors. This philosophy generated a very high creative awareness that forced him to anticipate new markets.

Sanyo created a separate affiliate in 1959 called Tokyo Sanyo Electric, which Iue hoped would make it easier for the company to respond to market demand and to raise capital. Although Sanyo eventually maintained only a 20 percent interest in Tokyo Sanyo, the two companies frequently engaged in bouts of constructive competition, what Iue himself described as a "friendly rivalry."

INTERNATIONAL EXPANSION

In pursuit of his goal of running a worldwide company, Iue began to export Sanyo bike lamps to underdeveloped countries. He reasoned that as these countries developed, Sanyo's sales volume would grow accordingly, much as it had done in Japan. Most of these countries, however, lacked fundamental industrial bases, and although Sanyo outsold its European competitors, the growth he expected in these countries never materialized. In 1961 Sanyo established its first overseas factory in Hong Kong. Sanyo also entered into an agreement to market transistor radios in the United States with U.S. antenna manufacturer Channel Master in the 1950s. This arrangement later was expanded to include Sanyo televisions, tape recorders, and some home appliances.

In 1962 Sanyo marketed a revolutionary new type of battery called the Cadnica. Named for its cadmium and nickel components, the Cadnica was especially durable and also rechargeable. The battery became very popular at the high end of the market and represented a new and profitable product line.

During the mid-1960s Japan maintained such strong price competitiveness in certain market segments, especially textiles and consumer appliances, that these segments became the primary source of the country's exported growth. In 1965 Sanyo became a leading exporter, deriving an ever larger percentage of its profits from the United States.

Two years later, at the end of 1967, Toshio Iue relinquished the company presidency to his younger brother Yuro Iue. While the elder Iue continued to serve as chairman, Yuro made some important changes in the company's direction. He led the development of new divisions outside of the traditional consumer products markets and also placed a greater emphasis on Sanyo's internationalization.

Toshio Iue died in July 1969, leaving Yuro Iue in a dual role as president and chairman. At the end of

```
╔═══════════════════════════════════════════╗
║                                           ║
║            KEY DATES                      ║
║              ────■────                    ║
║                                           ║
╚═══════════════════════════════════════════╝
```

1947: Several operations of Matsushita Electric are turned over to Toshio Iue, who forms Sanyo Electric Works, based in Osaka, Japan.

1950: Company is incorporated as SANYO Electric Company, Ltd.

1950s: Early production of radios and televisions begins.

1954: Company goes public.

1959: Affiliate called Tokyo Sanyo Electric is created.

1961: First overseas factory is established in Hong Kong.

1962: Cadnica rechargeable battery is introduced.

1973: Sanyo begins working with U.S. firm Emerson Electric on reviving Fisher Corporation.

1977: Sanyo takes full control of Fisher.

1986: Sanyo Electric and Tokyo Sanyo merge.

1987: Sanyo's U.S. affiliate merges with Fisher to form Sanyo Fisher (U.S.A.) Corporation.

1988: Sanyo North America Corporation is created as Sanyo's U.S. headquarters.

1990: Nickel-metal hydride batteries are introduced; company develops CFC-free absorption-type chiller/heaters and refrigeration systems.

1994: Lithium-ion rechargeable batteries are marketed for the first time.

1995: Company's first digital still camera is introduced.

2004: An earthquake heavily damages Sanyo's semiconductor plant in the Niigata Prefecture.

2005: Major restructuring involving 14,000 job cuts is launched.

2006: Sanyo suffers its second straight year of record losses; a group led by Goldman Sachs Group, Inc., and Daiwa Securities SMBC makes a major investment in Sanyo to shore up its finances.

2008: Company sells its mobile-phone business to Kyocera Corporation.

1970, he turned over the presidency to another brother, Kaoru Iue. Kaoru introduced a new sales plan to Sanyo, known as the "one-third marketing strategy." Under this scheme, Sanyo would attempt to diversify its manufacturing capacity geographically into three equal sectors: domestic manufacture for the domestic market,

domestic manufacture for foreign markets, and foreign manufacture for additional foreign markets. Less a means to Toshio's "100 factories" than a method to reduce risks in the international trade structure, Kaoru's "one-third" plan nevertheless contributed to the balanced growth of the company on a global basis.

In 1973 the U.S.-based Emerson Electric asked Sanyo to help revive its Fisher Corporation subsidiary. Fisher, acquired by Emerson in 1965, had moved its manufacturing operations to Hong Kong because of high labor costs, but continued to suffer from quality problems. The cooperation between Emerson and Sanyo continued until May 1975, when Sanyo, which still had no U.S. manufacturing affiliate, engineered the transfer of several Fisher product lines to Japan and rehabilitated a Fisher speaker plant at Milroy, Pennsylvania. As 50-50 partners, Sanyo and Emerson were unable to resolve numerous differences of opinion in regard to Fisher. Finally, in May 1977 Emerson agreed to sell its share in Fisher to Sanyo. That year the newly profitable Fisher Corporation moved its headquarters from New York to Los Angeles.

Sanyo realized tremendous growth during the 1970s; sales grew from $71.4 million in 1972 to $855 million in 1978. Subsequent growth, particularly in the video sector, was slowed by the ill-fated decision to adopt Sony Corporation's Betamax VCR format instead of Matsushita's VHS. Although initially successful, the Betamax eventually became all but obsolete. Sanyo avoided further damage by switching to the VHS format.

During the same decade it became increasingly evident that to remain competitive in world electronics, Sanyo would have to move more decisively into high-technology markets. This process was begun in the mid-1970s, but pursued in earnest only in the late 1970s, when a variety of products and integrated systems, ranging from LED televisions to home solar energy systems, were introduced commercially. Several manufacturing facilities and sales organizations were established in Europe and China.

INCREASED EFFICIENCY VIA MERGERS IN 1985 AND 1986

In 1985 a research institute was inaugurated at Tsukuba, the Tsukuba Research Center. By the following year, in light of the increased industrial concentration of competitors and the rising value of the yen, the sibling rivalry between Sanyo Electric and Tokyo Sanyo had become uneconomic. It was decided at that time to merge the two companies to form the "New Sanyo

Electric." Similarly, the following year, Sanyo's U.S. affiliate merged with Fisher to become Sanyo Fisher (U.S.A.) Corporation (later renamed Sanyo Fisher Company). The mergers made the entire organization more efficient, but resulted in the departure of certain key executives, most notably Howard Ladd, a Fisher executive who first introduced the Sanyo name to the United States in the early 1970s.

Kaoru Iue resigned suddenly in 1986 as a demonstration of responsibility for the deaths of customers who died using faulty Sanyo kerosene heaters. He was succeeded by Toshio Iue's son, Satoshi Iue, and died two years later.

Sanyo's new president promised to expand the company's overseas production capacity. Already the largest Japanese manufacturer outside of Japan, Sanyo built refrigerators in Kenya, portable stereos in Zimbabwe, and air conditioners in Singapore, and operated a television factory in Argentina's desolate Tierra del Fuego. Despite labor problems at a large plant in Arkansas, Sanyo intended to expand in the United States. To that end, in 1988 Sanyo created Sanyo North America Corporation as its U.S. headquarters, with 24 subsidiaries and affiliates.

POST-BUBBLE RESTRUCTURING

When the Japanese economic bubble burst in 1991, a lengthy economic downturn occured. Sanyo, like most Japanese electronics firms, was hurt by the difficult economic operating environment at home, where consumer demand, particularly for audio-video equipment, went into a steep decline. Overseas, the electronics firms felt the effects of a high yen, which made Japanese exports more expensive, as did high Japanese labor costs. In late 1992, shortly after the company posted a net loss for the 1992 fiscal year, Satoshi Iue stepped down as president of Sanyo and assumed the mostly ceremonial role of chairman. Yasuaki Takano stepped in as president, having been promoted from the position of vice-president he had held since 1986. Takano assumed responsibility for implementing a sweeping restructuring, which included shifting additional production outside of Japan, adopting a decentralized management system that focused on discrete profit centers, and overhauling the company's audio-video and office automation businesses to cut costs and improve profits. In 1993 Sanyo revamped its research and development (R&D) activities by consolidating eight R&D facilities into five, creating an overall R&D system that consisted of 13 facilities.

Sanyo also aimed to focus more on value-added products, particularly in those areas in which the company was ahead of the competition. One such area was that of environmentally friendly products, such as rechargeable batteries. In 1990 Sanyo had extended its offerings to include nickel-metal hydride batteries, which offered 50 percent more energy output than nickel-cadmium batteries, lasted longer, and were free of cadmium, a toxic heavy metal. The even more powerful lithium-ion rechargeable battery was introduced in 1994.

Meanwhile, in 1990 Sanyo developed new CFC-free absorption-type chiller/heaters and refrigeration systems incorporating hydrogen-absorbing alloys. Such systems were used to heat and cool large buildings, and Sanyo was the clear world leader in such technology in the 1990s.

Solar energy continued to be a key area as well, and the company introduced a solar air conditioner in 1992. Three years later Sanyo's solar energy operations were bolstered through the establishment of Sanyo Solar Industries Co., Ltd. Another "clean energy" initiative was the development of high-tech waste processors, which Sanyo first introduced in 1994. Available in both home and commercial versions, these devices transformed organic trash—banana peels, coffee grounds, fish bones—into a soil-like substance that could be used as a fertilizer. Sales began to take off in 1997 when the prices of these appliances, which were initially available only in Japan, began to fall.

After posting another loss in 1993, Sanyo returned to the black in 1994 when it reported net income of $114.5 million on revenue of $17.12 billion. The following year Sanyo established Sanyo Electric (China) Co., Ltd., to serve as its headquarters subsidiary in China, where by the end of the decade the company had more than 30 subsidiaries and affiliates, 25 of which were manufacturing operations producing air conditioners, consumer electronics, semiconductors, compressors, home appliances, telecommunications equipment, and numerous other products.

Also in 1995 Sanyo introduced its first digital still camera, part of its drive to "enrich people's lives" through multimedia technologies. The company's digital cameras were well received in the market, and by early 1998 Sanyo was making about 30 percent of the world output, more than any other firm, including brands that Sanyo produced for other companies. In the 1990s Sanyo also successfully entered the field of LCD projectors, which were used to make computer-based presentations. By 1998 the company held 15 percent of the world market, placing it in the number two position. Among the company's other key multimedia products in the late 1990s were digital cellular telephones and other personal communications devices.

END-OF-CENTURY MANAGEMENT SHIFT AND REORGANIZATION

During the fiscal year ending in March 1999, another management change occurred; Takano was named vice-chairman while Sadao Kondo was promoted to president. Despite Sanyo's continuing innovation, troubles recurred in the late 1990s as a result of the continuing sluggishness of the Japanese economy and the Asian economic crisis that erupted in mid-1997. Profits fell during fiscal 1998, then the company posted a net loss of ¥25.9 billion ($216 million) for fiscal 1999. In the wake of this result, Sanyo announced in April 1999 a major reorganization that rearranged all of its operations into five newly created "truly independent" companies—Multimedia Company, Home Appliances Company, Commercial Equipment Systems Company, Semiconductor Company, and Soft Energy Company—each with its own president and its own business strategies tied to basic overall objectives of increasing sales, cutting costs, and utilizing human resources in the most effective manner. The company also reformed the role of its board of directors, making the board more action-oriented and giving it greater oversight powers; the membership of the board also was overhauled, most notably with the addition of Corazon C. Aquino, former president of the Philippines. At the same time, Sanyo announced that it would reduce its overall workforce by 6,000 by March 2002, seeking to save about ¥40 billion ($330 million) annually in labor costs.

Other initiatives that looked toward the new century included several alliances with leading global firms. Sanyo was working with Koninklijke Philips Electronics N.V. of the Netherlands on developing optical sensors used in digital still and digital video cameras. In February 1999 Sanyo entered into an alliance with Eastman Kodak Company to jointly develop next-generation organic electroluminescent flat-panel displays for use in digital cameras and personal digital assistants. In April 1999 Sanyo diversified into the financial securities industry through the purchase of a 55 percent stake in Osaka-based Yamagen Securities Co., Ltd., an integrated securities company focused on the retail market.

By early 2000 the Japanese economy had not yet fully recovered but other Asian economies were on the upswing and the U.S. and European markets continued to expand. In this environment Sanyo was able to bounce back with solid results for fiscal 2000 with net income of ¥21.7 billion ($204.6 million) on net sales of ¥1.94 trillion ($18.31 billion). By this time, Sanyo had announced plans to continue focusing on multimedia and clean energy. Within these fields, the company had identified three areas that it felt had great potential for growth: products related to a home-based information society, such as "smart" appliances; products related to healthcare, food hygiene control, and an aging society; and environmentally friendly products, such as rechargeable batteries for hybrid vehicles.

Sanyo suffered a setback later in 2000 when it was disclosed that the company had for two years knowingly sold defective solar cells. A few days after this disclosure, Sanyo was forced to recall 180,000 refrigerators that had been produced with faulty doors. In the wake of these embarrassments, Kondo resigned from the presidency and was replaced by Yukinori Kuwano. The new president had joined the company in 1992 as head of research and development and in the interim had headed such important areas as batteries and semiconductors and had led Sanyo's entry into cellular phones and digital cameras. At the same time, Satoshi Iue reassumed a more active role in his position as chairman and CEO.

STRONG BEGINNING TO 21ST CENTURY

Despite these troubles, Sanyo overall enjoyed a strong start to the 21st century. By 2001 the company was the world's largest and most profitable producer of batteries for digital devices, holding a 30 percent share of the market for lithium-ion batteries and more than 50 percent for the nickel-metal hydride variety. Sanyo further bolstered its battery operations in 2001 by acquiring Toshiba Corporation's nickel-metal hydride business. It also entered into agreements with Ford Motor Company and Honda Motor Co., Ltd., to supply rechargeable batteries for hybrid gas-electric vehicles. At the same time, the company maintained its position as the world's leading maker of digital cameras, while also standing as the global leader in optical pickups, the components that read data in CD and DVD players. In addition, Sanyo held the top global share in around 40 types of semiconductors.

Although Sanyo was criticized during this period for hanging onto some unprofitable businesses, most notably its home appliance division, the company did show a willingness to jettison some marginal operations. In April 2002, for example, Sanyo sold its loss-making vending machine business after concluding that it would be unable to overtake the market leader. For its troubled home appliance division, Sanyo undertook a multiyear restructuring effort that was concluded in fiscal 2004. Domestic production of home appliances was scaled back in favor of increased overseas production, particularly in low-cost China. Alliances remained on the agenda as well, including the formation in 2004 of a joint venture with Seiko Epson Corporation in the area of small and medium-sized LCD displays. This venture combined Sanyo's strength in digital-camera LCD panels with Seiko Epson's world-leading cellphone LCD business. Around this same time, Sanyo began a major push to capture a significant share of the global market for digital consumer electronics products, particularly LCD television sets. In North America, the company quickly became a major supplier of lower-end LCD TVs to discount giant Wal-Mart Stores, Inc.

Despite continued sluggishness in the Japanese economy, Sanyo enjoyed record sales of ¥2.51 trillion ($23.66 billion) in fiscal 2004. Operating profits jumped 21 percent to ¥95.55 billion ($901.4 million), but restructuring expenses hurt the bottom line with net income totaling only ¥13.4 billion ($126.4 million). By the time these results were released, Sanyo was garnering plaudits in the financial press for its development of several strong businesses in various areas of the electronics industry, but the firm's fortunes soon turned south.

A SEVERE DOWNTURN

In October 2004 Sanyo's semiconductor plant in the Niigata Prefecture was severely damaged by a strong earthquake. Through the end of fiscal 2005, the company suffered losses totaling ¥73.3 billion ($684 million) from damage to the plant and equipment and from sales lost while the plant stood idle. Sanyo attempted to turn this misfortune into an opportunity by launching a restructuring of its semiconductor operations that de-emphasized its general-purpose memory business, which had been undermined by fierce competition. The company intended to more narrowly focus on higher-margin areas, such as chips for mobile devices, power supplies, and automotive applications.

The Niigata earthquake was hardly Sanyo's only challenge at this time. Two areas that had been company strongholds, digital cameras and cellular phones, began slumping not only because of increased competition from lower-cost rivals that drove product prices down but also because some companies were beginning to produce their own products in these areas rather than rely on ones manufactured by Sanyo. The company thus had to depend more on Sanyo-branded products, which were at a competitive disadvantage in the market because the brand carried less clout than such names as Sony or Matsushita Electric's Panasonic. Concurrently, Sanyo's battery business was struggling as well thanks to fierce price competition, while its household appliance unit continued operating in the red.

As a result of these and other problems, including surging raw material costs, Sanyo recorded the largest

net loss in its history in fiscal 2005: a deficit of ¥171.54 billion ($1.6 billion). Shortly after the end of this fiscal year, Sanyo puzzled a number of analysts with a management shakeup highlighted by the appointment of Tomoyo Nonaka as chairwoman and CEO. Nonaka was a former broadcast journalist with little knowledge of electronics and no senior management experience, although she had served on some government advisory committees and corporate boards, including Sanyo's. A new president was named as well: Toshimasa Iue, grandson of the founder and son of Satoshi Iue. Toshimasa Iue was known for his leadership of Sanyo's battery unit, which remained the firm's most profitable business.

In July 2005 the new management team launched a major restructuring involving 14,000 job cuts, the closure or sale of one-fifth of Sanyo's factory floor space in Japan, and the slashing of interest-bearing debt in half. Later in the year, Sanyo pulled back from its foray into financial services by selling a significant stake in its majority-owned credit unit to New York investment bank Goldman Sachs Group, Inc. The move enabled Sanyo to remove this troubled unit from its consolidated balance sheet. Also in the later months of 2005, the company pared back its consumer electronics business, ending production of DVD players and recorders and VCRs, and announced plans to close two chip plants in Japan and to shift away from the lower end of the appliance business in favor of a greater concentration on high-end products. Three businesses with high growth potential were designated as core business at this time: commercial air conditioning equipment, batteries, and "personal mobile devices," namely mobile phones and digital cameras.

NEW INVESTORS, SLOW RECOVERY

By late 2005 Sanyo appeared on the brink of collapse as it neared the end of its second straight year of record losses. Mainly because of restructuring costs, the company ended up with a net loss of ¥205.66 billion ($1.76 billion) for fiscal 2006. To shore up its finances, Sanyo raised ¥300 billion ($2.56 billion) through the issuance of preferred stock to a group of outside investors in a deal concluded in March 2006. Goldman Sachs and Japanese brokerage house Daiwa Securities SMBC made the largest investments, each gaining 24.5 percent of the voting rights in Sanyo and two seats on the company board. They were expected to push Sanyo to quicken its pace of restructuring, mainly by offloading weaker units and noncore assets.

The overhaul, however, proceeded slowly. Sanyo announced plans to sell its cell phone and semiconductor businesses, but by the end of fiscal 2007 the only significant divestment that had been completed was the sale of the firm's stake in the LCD panel joint venture to partner Seiko Epson. Sanyo made further cuts in its workforce and took additional restructuring charges as it posted another, though smaller, loss for fiscal 2007 of ¥45.36 billion ($384.4 million). Net sales for the year fell 7.6 percent to ¥2.22 trillion ($18.77 billion).

In early 2007 Japanese regulators launched a probe into allegations that Sanyo had manipulated its accounts to conceal losses at several subsidiaries earlier in the decade. Nonaka soon resigned from the company, and the departure of Toshimasa Iue soon followed, effectively marking the end of the founding family's rule. Seiichiro Sano, a lifelong Sanyo employee who had previously headed the firm's human resources area, was named the new president.

Under Sano the pace of restructuring picked up somewhat, although a sale of the semiconductor business had to be shelved when the company was unable to secure a price it deemed sufficient. Sanyo placed some of the blame for this setback on the global credit squeeze. The company did manage to divest its struggling mobile-phone unit, which was sold to Kyocera Corporation for roughly ¥40 billion ($375 million) in a deal completed in April 2008.

In November 2007, meantime, Sanyo announced a new three-year business plan centering on the investment of ¥350 billion ($3.2 billion) into several core areas, with the largest outlays in the areas of batteries and solar cells. Other areas to receive infusions were semiconductors, digital products, commercial appliances, and electronic components. Overall, Sanyo aimed to double its operating profit to ¥100 billion by fiscal 2011. A month later, Sanyo restated its accounts for the six years from fiscal 2001 to fiscal 2006 after a review confirmed that mistakes had been made in the company's accounting. The restatements turned fiscal years 2001 and 2002 from profitable years into loss-making ones while trimming the losses reported in later years.

With this latest embarrassing chapter behind it, Sanyo appeared headed for its first full year in the black in four years. The company nevertheless continued to face numerous challenges, and a sustained turnaround was far from assured. Further clouding Sanyo's future were reports in the media in late April 2008 that Sanyo and Matsushita Electric were discussing a potential tie-up plan, with the possibility of an eventual merger (which would amount to a reunification, given Sanyo's origins). Both companies issued strong denials that any such talks were underway.

Updated, David E. Salamie

PRINCIPAL SUBSIDIARIES

Tottori Sanyo Electric Co., Ltd.; Shimane Sanyo Electric Co., Ltd.; Sanyo Tokyo Manufacturing Co., Ltd.; Sanyo Semiconductor Co., Ltd.; Sanyo Semiconductor Manufacturing Co., Ltd.; Kanto Sanyo Semiconductors Co., Ltd.; Sanyo Seimitsu Co., Ltd.; Sanyo Mediatec Co., Ltd.; Sanyo Energy Tottori Co., Ltd.; Sanyo Energy Twicell Co., Ltd.; Sanyo GS Soft Energy Co., Ltd.; Sanyo Semicon Device Co., Ltd.; Sanyo Electric Logistics Co., Ltd.; Sanyo TV International Corporation (U.S.A.); Sanyo E & E Corporation (U.S.A.); Sanyo Energy (U.S.A.) Corporation; Sanyo North America Corporation (U.S.A.); Sanyo Semiconductor (U.S.A.) Corporation; Sanyo Europe Ltd. (U.K.); Sanyo Component Europe GmbH (Germany); Sanyo Airconditioners Europe s.r.l. (Italy); Sanyo Electric (Shekou) Limited (China); Dalian Sanyo Refrigeration Co., Ltd. (China); Dalian Sanyo Cold-Chain Co., Ltd. (China); Korea Tokyo Silicon Co., Ltd.; Sanyo Electric (Hong Kong) Limited; Sanyo Semiconductor (H.K.) Co., Ltd. (Hong Kong); Sanyo Asia Pte., Ltd. (Singapore); Sanyo Energy (Singapore) Corporation Pte. Ltd.; Sanyo PT (M) Sdn. Bhd. (Malaysia); P.T. Sanyo Jaya Components Indonesia.

PRINCIPAL DIVISIONS

Component Business Group; Finished Goods Business Group.

PRINCIPAL COMPETITORS

Hitachi, Ltd.; Matsushita Electric Industrial Co., Ltd.; Sony Corporation; Royal Philips Electronics N.V.; Fujitsu Limited; Samsung Electronics Co., Ltd.; Sharp Corporation; LG Electronics Inc.; General Electric Company.

FURTHER READING

Alabaster, Jay, "Sanyo Electric Revises Parent-Company Earnings," *Wall Street Journal*, December 26, 1007, p. B3.

———, "The Spark's Back in Sanyo," *Barron's*, March 31, 2008, p. M9.

Alabaster, Jay, and Hiroyuki Kachi, "Sanyo Aims to Fuel Recovery with Solar, Batteries," *Wall Street Journal*, November 28, 2007, p. B8.

Anzai, Tatsuya, "Making It in China: Sanyo Electric," *Tokyo Business Today*, April 1992, p. 51.

Armstrong, Larry, "Sanyo Tries to Stay One Step Ahead of the Yen," *Business Week,* June 9, 1986, p. 46.

"Basic Training, Sanyo Style," *U.S. News & World Report,* July 13, 1992, p. 46.

"Consumer Electronics Industry Shows Path of Growth Strategy—Into the Abyss," *Tokyo Business Today,* October 1992, pp. 38–41.

Dvorak, Phred, "Sanyo Electric Finds Itself in the Spotlight," *Wall Street Journal,* October 21, 2003, p. C13.

Eisenstodt, Gale, "Unidentical Twins," *Forbes,* July 5, 1993, p. 42.

Ishibashi, Kanji, and Ginny Parker Woods, "Sanyo Plots Restructuring Course," *Wall Street Journal,* November 21, 2005, p. B4.

Kane, Yukari Iwatani, "Sanyo Ends Era of Family Rule," *Wall Street Journal,* March 29, 2007, p. B4.

———, "Sanyo Struggles to Rebound: Accounting Issues, Resignation Add to Turmoil," *Wall Street Journal,* March 21, 2007, p. C7.

Kunii, Irene M., "Futurama at Sanyo: It's Moving Fast into Solar, Fuel Cells, and Other Technologies," *Business Week* (international ed.), November 18, 2002, p. 124B.

Leung, Shirley, "Sanyo's Chief Departure Is a Loss for Maquiladoras," *Wall Street Journal,* April 7, 1999.

Martin, Neil A., "In Sony's Shadow: After 50 Years on the Fringes, Sanyo Electric May Be Ready to Shine," *Barron's,* February 5, 2001, pp. 17–18.

Morse, Andrew, "Goldman Group to Buy Sanyo Stake," *Wall Street Journal,* December 22, 2005, p. C3.

———, "Goldman's Lesson: No Quick Payoff in Japan," *Wall Street Journal,* January 29, 2008, p. C7.

Nakanishi, Toyoki, "Sanyo Chairman Leads Reform Efforts," *Nikkei Report,* May 12, 2003.

Nakanishi, Toyoki, and Takayuki Isogai, "Iue Influence Increases at Sanyo," *Nikkei Report,* March 18, 2003.

Nakaoto, Michiyo, "The Japanese Art of Performance: Sanyo Has Achieved Record Results and Market Dominance by Adopting a Rigorous GE-Style Investment Strategy," *Financial Times,* May 18, 2004, p. 12.

———, "The Rising Yen Means Pain for a Supplier," *Financial Times,* January 1, 1994, p. 3.

———, "Sanyo's 'Carly' Sets Out Her Stall," *Financial Times,* July 7, 2005, p. 28.

———, "Tough Times for Sanyo As Electronics Loses Its Spark," *Financial Times,* April 6, 1993, p. 24.

Parker, Ginny, "Sanyo's Job Shuffle Draws Criticism," *Wall Street Journal,* April 20, 2005, p. B8B.

Rodger, Ian, "Waiting for Its Day in the Sun," *Financial Times,* January 10, 1991, Sec. I, p. 8.

Rowley, Ian, and Hiroko Tashiro, "Sanyo's Surprise CEO," *Business Week* (international ed.), May 2, 2005, p. 22.

Sanchanta, Mariko, "Kyocera to Buy Sanyo's Mobile Arm," *Financial Times,* January 22, 2008, p. 18.

———, "Sanyo's Chairwoman Steps Down," *Financial Times,* March 20, 2007, p. 15.

Sanyo Denki sanjunen no ayumi, Osaka, Japan: Sanyo Electric Co., 1980, 651 p.

"Sanyo Sounds Out the Upscale Market," *Business Week,* June 11, 1984, p. 154L.

Scott, Arran, "Outlook for Sanyo Electric Likely to Turn Dimmer," *Asian Wall Street Journal,* April 7, 2005, p. M3.

Shimamura, Kazuhiro, "Sanyo to Cut Staff 15%, Shut Factories," *Wall Street Journal,* July 6, 2005, p. A3.

Turner, David, "Sanyo Increases Layoffs As Restructuring Widens," *Financial Times,* October 9, 2006, p. 20.

Scientific Learning
Corporation

◼

300 Frank H. Ogawa Plaza, Suite 600
Oakland, California 94612
U.S.A.
Telephone: (510) 444-3500
Toll Free: (888) 665-9707
Fax: (510) 444-3580
Web site: http://www.scientificlearning.com

Public Company
Incorporated: 1996 as Scientific Learning Principles
    Corporation
Employees: 215
Sales: $40.99 million (2006)
Stock Exchanges: NASDAQ
Ticker Symbol: SCIL
NAIC: 611699 All Other Miscellaneous Schools and
    Instruction

■ ■ ■

Scientific Learning Corporation develops software that
helps struggling, at-risk, and special education students
improve their academic performance. The company's
products, which consist of 15 Fast ForWord programs,
use a neuroscience-based approach to help language-
impaired children improve their speech and reading
skills. Fast ForWord is marketed primarily to elementary
and secondary schools in the United States. Scientific
Learning also sells Progress Tracker, an online data
analysis tool that allows educators to monitor learning
performance at the individual, classroom, school, and
district level.

DECADES OF RESEARCH BEFORE
PRODUCT LAUNCH

Scientific Learning was founded in 1996, but the roots
of the company stretched back three decades earlier,
originating in the scientific research conducted by its
four founders, Michael M. Merzenich, William M. Jenkins, Paula A. Tallal, and Steven L. Miller. The
preliminary years encompassed the development of the
company's first product, a process that followed the
career paths of each cofounder. When the professional
pursuits of the founding four intersected, Scientific
Learning was the result, a company whose commercial
debut represented one of the lengthiest product development efforts in U.S. business history. Fast ForWord was
30 years in the making, and the seeds for its creation
were planted in the early work of Michael Merzenich.

Born in rural Oregon in 1942, Merzenich excelled
as an academic. He attended the University of Portland,
where his interest in science became the foundation of
his professional career. Merzenich left the University of
Portland in the early 1960s, graduating at the top of his
class, and enrolled at Johns Hopkins University Medical
School, where he began pursing his doctorate degree in
neurophysiology. After earning his Ph.D., he completed
his postdoctoral studies at the University of Wisconsin,
which led to his appointment to the faculty at
University of California, San Francisco (UCSF).

Merzenich's research resulted in numerous
significant discoveries in how the brain functioned. He
secured more than 50 patents during his career,
published more than 200 articles, and enjoyed
mainstream fame by appearing on national television

COMPANY PERSPECTIVES

Scientific Learning applies advances in neuroscience and cognitive research to increase human potential. We produce unique products, tools, and implementation strategies that enable people to build the fundamental cognitive abilities required to read and learn. We use technology, as appropriate, to provide our customers with the applications that allow each learner to progress based on his or her individual needs.

programs such as *Good Morning America* and the *CBS Evening News.* His work also resulted in the formation of several commercial enterprises, including Advanced Bionics Corporation, which sold cochlear implants developed by the UCSF research team he led. In relation to Scientific Learning, Merzenich's research revealed discoveries about brain functions that would serve as the scientific underpinning for Fast ForWord.

At UCSF during the 1970s and 1980s, Merzenich divided his time between teaching—he headed the Otolaryngology department—and conducting research. He and other UCSF scientists explored how the brain responded to stimuli, launching a formal inquiry that included running a series of experiments. The experiments demonstrated that when the brain learned or experienced something new it changed physiologically, reconfiguring itself by a phenomenon known as "brain plasticity."

Merzenich's progress in the understanding of brain plasticity, particularly as it related to Scientific Learning, received a helpful boost after the arrival of William Jenkins. Jenkins spent his academic career at Florida State University, where he earned his bachelor's degree in psychology and his master's and doctorate degrees in psychobiology. Jenkins joined Merzenich at UCSF Medical Center in 1980, a partnership credited with the discovery that the adult brain also responded and adapted to behavioral stimuli. Jenkins also led the way in a study that demonstrated progressive training accelerated the rate at which the brain changed. Equally as important as his scientific work was Jenkins' expertise in computer science, which would be instrumental in Scientific Learning's formation and operation. During his career, Jenkins authored or coauthored 13 software products for commercial release.

A STUDY OF AUDITORY PROCESSING

While the Merzenich-Jenkins partnership covered significant ground in San Francisco, another scientist was hard at work in Cambridge, 50 miles northeast of London, England. Paula Tallal was pursuing a doctorate in experimental psychology at the University of Cambridge, continuing education that began at New York University. Tallal, who was on her way toward becoming a respected cognitive neuroscientist, was focusing her work on children suffering from language-learning difficulties. She theorized that speech and language problems were related to auditory processing problems, that, in some cases, the brain processed information too slowly, particularly rapid sounds such as the consonant sounds "ba," and "da." To test her hypothesis, Tallal extended the duration of rapid consonant sounds with a computerized speech synthesizer and played the modified sounds to language-impaired children. Children who had difficulty distinguishing between speech sounds showed a marked increase in their ability to distinguish quick sound changes. "This was a unique and completely novel finding," Tallal explained in a statement published on Scientific Learning's web site. "We were able to find the root of the difficulty in temporal-spectral processing, and you could manipulate the results by changing the duration of the sounds."

SCIENTISTS UNITING IN 1993

In simple terms, there was research that showed the brain changed physiologically when subjected to stimuli. Research also demonstrated that the brain in a language-impaired child responded positively to auditory changes that altered the way information was received. There was a certain interrelation in the research being conducted thousands of miles apart. The link that connected the theories being tested in the United States with the theories being tested in England was the Santa Fe Institute in New Mexico. The institute was an organization, according to its web site, that "was devoted to creating a new kind of research community, one emphasizing multidisciplinary collaboration in pursuit of understanding the common themes that arise in natural, artificial, and social systems." It was an ideal venue for Merzenich, Jenkins, and Tallal to meet. In 1993, the meeting occurred, by which time Tallal had another scientist in tow, Scientific Learning's fourth founder, Steven Miller.

When Tallal was invited to the Santa Fe Institute to make a presentation in 1993, along with her was a postdoctoral student named Steven Miller, who had made the trip to assist in Tallal's presentation. Miller's

KEY DATES

1993: After meeting each other at the Santa Fe Institute, Michael M. Merzenich, William M. Jenkins, Paula A. Tallal, and Steven L. Miller begin working together.

1994: The first tests of Fast ForWord are conducted at Rutgers University in July.

1996: The scientists form their own company.

1997: Fast ForWord is released in March.

2002: Robert C. Bowen is appointed chief executive officer.

2003: Scientific Learning posts its first annual profit.

2006: Scientific Learning celebrates its tenth anniversary.

academic background included an undergraduate degree in psychology from Bloomsburg University, a master's degree in neuroscience from the University of Hartford, and a doctorate in psychology from the University of North Carolina, Greensboro.

Slated to make their presentation at the same Santa Fe Institute event were Merzenich and Jenkins. It was not long before the two teams of two decided to become one team of four. "Bill Jenkins and I," Merzenich wrote on Scientific Learning's web site, "had discussed using our training tools, as applied to monkeys, for impaired human populations, and we both realized that Paula's kind of kid problem might be addressed with our kind of solution." Tallal's recollection on the company's web site was more succinct. "It really clicked that we should work together," she wrote.

TESTING OF FAST FORWORD BEGINNING IN 1994

Rigorous testing of the scientists' theories followed the meeting in Santa Fe. The scientists secured research funding and developed model training tools, relying on Jenkins' skills to create software that made neuroscience-based learning an entertaining experience for children. Once they had a prototype of Fast ForWord, Tallal and Miller conducted a four-week study with seven children at Rutgers University in July 1994. Merzenich and Jenkins were kept abreast of the results through a software-tracking tool that provided daily updates, enabling them to celebrate along with Tallal and Miller when six of the seven children made substantial progress at the end of the study. A second study with a larger group of children followed a year later, and again the use of

acoustically modified speech yielded remarkable results. Data from the study was published in *Science,* which led to an article in the *New York Times* about the groundbreaking study, igniting public interest. Rutgers University was flooded with calls from throughout the country, receiving an estimated 20,000 inquiries. Merzenich, Jenkins, Tallal, and Miller were ready to launch their business.

Scientific Learning was formed in early 1996. To lead the company, the scientists turned to Sheryle Bolton, hired as chief executive officer in November 1996. Bolton, whose son suffered from severe medical and learning problems, developed an interest in linguistics while serving in the Peace Corps in Tunisia during the late 1960s. When she returned home to Georgia, she obtained her teaching credentials and taught English and French to high school students before earning a master's degree in linguistics at the University of Georgia and an M.B.A. at Harvard University. A diverse collection of jobs followed, including stints at Home Box Office, Physicians Online, and a medical supply company named Becton, Dickinson. Bolton also served as a senior manager for the Rockefeller family's investment and philanthropic unit.

RELEASE OF FAST FORWORD: 1997

In March 1997, Scientific Learning released its first product, Fast ForWord Language, the first of more than a dozen programs that would be marketed under the Fast ForWord name. Users of the program showed improvement in speech processing and language ability, on average, of one to two years in children ages 4 to 12 after only six to seven weeks of training. "It's similar to what children with vision impairments experience when they first put on a new pair of glasses," Merzenich remarked, as quoted in the March 27, 1997, issue of *PR Newswire.* "This program is like glasses for the ears." Experts readily agreed with Merzenich's appraisal of Fast ForWord. "This is the only training program I've seen in 30 years of practice that is based on science," a speech pathologist said in the same issue of *PR Newswire.* "Until now, most methods have been largely based on anecdotes and the individual inventions and dedication of speech therapists."

Fast ForWord was an unequivocal success as an aid to language-impaired children, but the product did not make Scientific Learning an instant financial success. Increasing numbers of students were enrolling in the system, which fueled steady revenue growth, but profits were another matter. The company generated $10.2 million in revenue in 1999, $15.2 million in 2001, and $17.8 million in 2002, years in which it lost more than

$40 million. Originally, Scientific Learning used a clinical sales model to market its product, making Fast ForWord available through speech and language professionals who were trained, certified, and licensed to use the software program. By 2000, however, the company had altered its marketing approach in an effort to turn the critical success of its technology into a financial success. Scientific Learning began selling directly to schools, targeting institutions teaching grades kindergarten through high school, the K–12 market.

NEW LEADERSHIP IN 2002

The task of turning losses into profits fell to a new chief executive officer in June 2002, when Robert C. Bowen took the helm. A former high school math teacher, Bowen spent a dozen years working as a senior executive at National Computer Systems, a provider of educational assessment and administrative software. At the company, he rose to the position of president of NCS Education, a provider of enterprise software for K–12 school districts. During his first full year in charge of Scientific Learning, Bowen succeeded in stanching the company's losses. In 2003, the company reported its first annual profit, posting $2.1 million in net income, a year in which revenues reached $28.6 million.

After the introduction of the first Fast ForWord program, the company released 14 new products in the next nine years. The new releases, various versions of Fast ForWord Language, Fast ForWord Reading, and Fast ForWord Literacy, found a receptive audience among the nation's schools. By the time Scientific Learning celebrated its tenth anniversary in 2006, 840,000 children had used the company's products and roughly 4,500 schools had purchased at least $10,000 of Fast ForWord product licenses and services. Revenues climbed steadily, increasing from the $28.6 million collected in 2003 to $40.9 million in 2006. During the same period, Scientific Learning's net income totals reflected less constancy than its revenue totals, fluctuating from a $693,000 loss in 2004, a $5.5 million profit in 2005, and a $208,000 profit in 2006.

THE ROAD AHEAD

There was little doubt about the efficacy of the educational software developed by Merzenich, Jenkins, Tallal, and Miller. Fast ForWord's neuroscientific underpinning had demonstrated an impressive effectiveness for more than a decade, enabling language-impaired children to realize substantial gains in reading and speech proficiency in a short amount of time. Although Scientific Learning did not demonstrate an ability to record consistent profits year after year during its first decade of business, Bowen was confident a pattern of growth in both revenue and profits would be established during Scientific Learning's second decade of business. No one questioned the importance or significance of the company's work. Fast ForWord was an educator's, parent's, and child's salvation from dyslexia and other impairments suffered by at least 10 percent of all children.

Jeffrey L. Covell

PRINCIPAL COMPETITORS

Edusoft Ltd.; Renaissance Learning, Inc.; The American Education Corporation.

FURTHER READING

"Clover Park School District Expands Use of Fast ForWord," *Internet Wire,* September 7, 2004.

"Dallas Independent School District Selects Fast ForWord," *Internet Wire,* February 12, 2004.

"Firm's Revenues Rise, Stock Drops," *San Francisco Business Times,* July 14, 2000, p. 10.

"First Scientifically Proven Training Represents Breakthrough for Children with Language-Learning Impairments," *PR Newswire,* March 27, 1997, p. 327NYTH006.

Hall, Carl T., "CEO's Aid for Troubled Readers," *San Francisco Chronicle,* April 23, 1998, p. D3.

"Ohio Elementary School Reaps Rewards with Fast ForWord," *Internet Wire,* July 21, 2004.

"Scientific Learning Corp.—Common Stock Begins Trading on OTC Bulletin Board," *Market News Publishing,* July 24, 2002.

"Scientific Learning and Neuroscience Solutions Complete Transaction," *Internet Wire,* October 1, 2003.

"Scientific Learning Inks Major Deal with School District of Philadelphia," *Internet Wire,* June 29, 2004.

"Scientific Learning Names Andrew Myers," *Wireless News,* December 9, 2007.

"Scientific Learning Reaches Agreement with White Hat," *Internet Wire,* August 17, 2004.

"Scientific Learning Releases New Fast ForWord Product," *Internet Wire,* August 15, 2006.

"U.S. Company Develops New Method to Enhance English Learning," *Xinhua News Agency,* December 5, 2000.

Silver Lake Cookie Company Inc.

141 Freeman Avenue
Islip, New York 11751
U.S.A.
Telephone: (631) 581-4000
Fax: (631) 581-4510
Web site: http://www.silverlakecookie.com

Private Company
Incorporated: 1965
Employees: 250
Sales: $26.1 million (2007 est.)
NAIC: 311821 Cookie and Cracker Manufacturing

■ ■ ■

Silver Lake Cookie Company Inc. is a privately owned contract baker focusing on the production of private-label fancy cookies for such retail customers as Wal-Mart, Costco, and supermarket chains, as well as hospitality and foodservice customers. The Islip, New York-based company also offers sales and marketing advice to help customers develop and grow a cookie program. Silver Lake produces a wide variety of seasonal cookies, packaged or sold in bulk, to celebrate major holidays, including Valentine's Day, St. Patrick's Day, Easter, the Fourth of July, Halloween, Thanksgiving, Hanukkah, and Christmas, as well as platters of cookies and petits fours for such special occasions as weddings, anniversaries, Mother's Day, and Father's Day. Half the company's revenues are generated in the fourth quarter of the year, so that during the busy autumn period the

company's employment ranks swell with temporary workers.

In addition, Silver Lake offers traditional Italian cookies and biscotti, European-style cookies, and a variety of cookies aimed at children, including holiday-inspired treats as well as happy-face cookies, and animal and toy shapes. Specialty items include fruit marzipan, cannoli shells, and brandy bites. Silver Lake also sells Heritage brand cookies in two forms: ready-to-bake frozen dough and cookies that are already baked and frozen and need only to be thawed for retail sale. Varieties available in bulk packs or trays include chocolate chip, sugar, oatmeal raisin, peanut butter, chocolate fudge chip, white chocolate macadamia, and candy pieces. All baking and packaging is done at Silver Lake's 140,000-square-foot facility in Islip, built on the site of a former speedway. Silver Lake is owned by President Joseph Vitarelli III, who focuses on sales, and his brother, Rocco Vitarelli, executive vice-president in charge of manufacturing. Their father, Joseph Vitarelli Jr., founded the company.

COMPANY ORIGINS: 1965

Joseph Vitarelli Jr. was born and raised in New York City. He went into sales, working for Century Cookie, a contract cookie baker, in the borough of the Bronx. Because he knew the cookie business and had developed contacts with retail bakeries and caterers in the region, when Vitarelli decided to strike out on his own and start a business in his late 30s, it was not surprising that he chose to remain in the field he knew the best and become a premium cookie maker. In 1965 he cobbled together $600 in family loans and built a 2,500-square-foot bakery in Baldwin, New York, in Nassau County near Long Island's South Shore. For a name he drew on a local landmark that inspired more than one area business, Silver Lake, the cornerstone of the nine-acre, residential Silver Lake Park. Hence, his new venture became Silver Lake Cookie Company Inc., a name that would be retained even after the company was later relocated.

Joseph Vitarelli III was 18 years old and a recent high school graduate when his father launched Silver Lake. He was simply told by his father that he was going to work for the bakery, and without protest he agreed. "That's just the way it was back then," he explained in a 2008 phone interview. The younger Vitarelli was a "shop guy," tending the ovens, while his father used his sales experience to find buyers for the fancy cookies he and two other employees turned out: European-style cookies, pinch pockets, and frosted leaves. Serving retail bakeries and caterers with 25 kinds of cookies, the new contract baker generated revenues that were in the "tens of thousands." However, the company was enjoying steady growth, so that at the end of the first year the number of workers had increased to about a dozen.

A major spur to growth for Silver Lake later in the 1960s was the addition of in-store bakeries to supermarket chains. The Bohack chain became an important customer, followed by another popular Long Island chain, Hills/Korvett Food Centers. In time Silver Lake outgrew its space and in the late 1970s moved into a new 32,000-square-foot bakery, located about ten miles to the east on Long Island's Sunrise Highway (Route 27) in Amityville, New York (which around this time became known for a haunted house in the community that was the subject for a book and nine subsequent films).

DEATH OF FOUNDER: 1979

By this time a second son, Rocco Vitarelli was involved in the business, joining his father and brother in the mid-1970s. When Joseph Vitarelli Jr. died in 1979

Rocco was seasoned enough to take responsibility for manufacturing while Joseph Vitarelli III succeeded their father as president of Silver Lake and oversaw administration and marketing. Sales at this stage were in the $1 million to $1.5 million range, and the company employed about 80 people.

Under the leadership of the second generation, Silver Lake grew at an accelerated rate. In addition to retail bakeries, supermarket bakeries, department stores, delicatessens, and hotel chains in the United States and Canada, the company's sales force during this period developed a new steady customer, the U.S. military. Silver Lake began supplying cookie gift packages to commissaries for U.S. naval bases around the world.

Between 1981 and 1985 sales increased fourfold, from about $3 million to about $11 million, making Silver Lake and its 70 varieties of cookies the largest specialty cookie company in the United States. A major factor in the company's success was the nation's increasing appetite for cookies, especially the premium cookies that Silver Lake specialized in. To stay ahead of consumers' tastes, the company hired European master chefs to add flavor recipes from such countries as France, Italy, and Belgium. To improve appearance and shelf life, a full-time "cookie scientist" was hired to modify recipes.

ACQUISITION OF TWO BAKING COMPANIES: 1985

With demand quickly outstripping capacity, space once again became a problem. In 1982 a 12,000-square-foot warehouse in Amityville was taken over, followed by another 15,000-square-foot facility. Silver Lake then acquired a competing contract baker, 45-year-old Westbury Continental Confections Inc. in July 1985. Not only did Silver Lake gain a 25,000-square-foot plant, it inherited Westbury's customers and added the bakery's line of petits fours and specialty confections. Earlier in 1985 the company also acquired the Kookie Cookie division of Southern Foods, adding a number of specialty cookies to the mix, in particular gingerbread products.

Operating out of four separate locations was not an efficient way to do business, however. In the mid-1980s Silver Lake began to scout for a new location where it could build a new, much larger plant to combine all of its operations under a single roof. In 1985 the Vitarelli brothers settled on the Town of Islip, New York, which provided incentives to lure the baking company to its community, including a $4.5 million bond provided by Islip's Industrial Development Agency to help finance the construction of a new 100,000-square-foot

KEY DATES

1965: Company is founded in Baldwin, New York, by Joseph Vitarelli Jr.
1979: Vitarelli's sons take control upon his death.
1985: Century Confections Inc. is acquired.
1986: Company moves to Islip, New York.
1999: Ground is broken on plant addition.
2005: Frozen dough products are added.

manufacturing and warehousing facility on eight acres of land. The site was the town's major claim to fame, the former Islip Speedway, and before that Long Island's first municipal airport.

MOVE TO ISLIP: 1986

The 2/10th-mile Islip track, built in 1947, was the smallest track to ever host a NASCAR grand national race, which it did from 1964 to 1971, but it was better known as the birthplace of the "demolition derby" in 1958, which for years received a regular showing on ABC's *Wide World of Sports.* The track also hosted "Figure 8" races for ABC, combining racing and wrecks by forcing drivers to negotiate an intersection at the center of the track. While television viewers of Islip Speedway fare may have been amused by the noise, mayhem, and smoke, the track's neighbors were not unhappy to see it closed down in 1984. After Silver Lake moved into its new 97,000-square-foot facility, capable of turning out more than 250 million cookies a year, in October 1986, Joseph Vitarelli told the *New York Times,* "People seem to love it that we're moving here. I understand they weren't too happy with the speedway, all that noise and pollution." He added, "We're going to be creating new jobs, employing people from the local area—and we smell good, too."

Although Islip was less than 20 miles farther out on Long Island on Route 27, a large number of the unskilled employees did not follow the company to its new home. Through the rest of the 1980s Silver Lake had to contend with a labor shortage that curtailed growth, which had averaged close to 30 percent a year but in 1988 fell to just 7 percent. Long Island's main newspaper, *Newsday,* reported that in 1988 the company "turned away more than $2 million in cookie orders because the company didn't have the workers to make them." Sales people were reduced to "twiddling their thumbs," in the words of vice-president of sales John DiStephano.

To help solve the labor crunch Silver Lake tried to streamline the operation as much as possible. A pair of large flour silos were installed, each capable of holding 60,000 pounds. Connected to computerized controls they could release precise amounts, eliminating the need for people to constantly haul in 100-pound bags of flour. New equipment was also on order to increase productivity. Instead of 1,000 pounds of cookies an hour requiring as many as 20 workers, the new state-of-the-art systems allowed just four workers to produce six times as many cookies. However, because the company produced premium cookies, there was a limit to how much automation could help. "If we were making Oreos all day," Rocco Vitarelli told *Newsday,* "we could automate a lot more. But we have lots of short runs and assortments." As a result, Silver Lake was dependent on unskilled labor, for example, to individually pinch raspberry pockets or center fudged-filled cookies before they were stamped with confection.

To supplement the local pool of labor, Silver Lake bused in workers from Nassau County and as far away as Brooklyn and Queens. The Vitarellis also looked into the possibility of outsourcing some work to northern Illinois or setting up a packaging plant in North Carolina where labor was cheap and plentiful. Nothing came of these efforts, though, and the labor situation began to improve.

At the time of the move to Islip, Joseph Vitarelli told *Newsday* that he hoped the company might increase its profile, allowing for the development of its own cookie brand. "More than likely it would be Silver Lake," he said. However, branding never became a priority and Silver Lake was content to serve the private-label market and remain a "baker's baker."

At the start of the 1990s annual sales were about $12 million and the number of permanent employees had reached 150. As had been the case for years, Silver Lake continued to grow by following the market and taking advantage of an aggressive sales force. As consumers became more health conscious Silver Lake developed low-fat cookies and sugar-free cookies while adding new shapes and flavors. It also developed new sales channels. Big-box retailers including Wal-Mart and Costco became customers in the early 1990s. Silver Lake also began serving catalogers. As a result of its diverse mix of customers, no one accounted for more than 7 or 8 percent of sales, providing the company with a modicum of security.

PLANT EXPANSION: 2000

By the end of the 1990s, Silver Lake had once again outgrown its facility and the local government and the

Industrial Development Agency stepped in to provide an economic incentive package to help the company finance a 40,000-square-foot expansion to its facility, which would allow it to hire another 100 people. The incentives included exemptions from mortgage recording, abatements on real property taxes that would have been increased due to the expansion, as well as exemptions on sales and use taxes. Work began in May 1999 and the new section opened in 2000.

With sales around $20 million, Silver Lake enjoyed steady growth in the new century following the same recipe that had proven successful for many years: follow the market and apply technology to develop new products. In keeping with this philosophy, in 2005 it expanded into the frozen dough business. The company continued to be run by the Vitarelli brothers. No succession plans were in the works and Joseph Vitarelli indicated in a 2008 interview that while his daughters were not interested in pursuing the cookie trade there was a possibility that his nephews might one day carry on the family business.

Ed Dinger

PRINCIPAL COMPETITORS

George Weston Limited; Interbake Foods LLC; Ralcorp Holding, Inc.

FURTHER READING

Anastasi, Nick, "Cookie Firm to Expand, Add Jobs," *Long Island Business News,* May 7, 1999, p. 1A.

Ketcham, Diane, "Long Island Journal," *New York Times,* November 2, 1986.

Phillips, Braden, "Cookie Company Has a Bakery in the Oven," *Newsday,* September 9, 1985, p. 3.

Roel, Ronald E., "Islip Cookie Maker Needs Bakers by the Dozens," *Newsday,* December 11, 1988, p. 4.

Silver Wheaton Corp.

666 Burrard Street, Suite 3150
Vancouver, British Columbia V6C 2X8
Canada
Telephone: (604) 684-9648
Fax: (604) 684-3123
Web site: http://www.silverwheaton.com

Public Company
Incorporated: 1994 as Chap Mercantile Inc.
Employees: 9
Sales: $175.43 million (2007)
Stock Exchanges: Toronto New York
Ticker Symbol: SLW
NAIC: 212222 Silver Ore Mining

∎ ∎ ∎

Silver Wheaton Corp. is the largest publicly traded mining company in the world that derives 100 percent of its revenue from silver production. The company obtains its silver through purchase contracts with five mines, the Luismin and Penasquito mines in Mexico, the Yauliyacu mine in Peru, the Zinkgruvan mine in Sweden, and the Stratoni mine in Greece. Most of the silver produced is a byproduct from mining for gold, lead, and zinc. Silver Wheaton has proven and probable reserves of 362.2 million ounces of silver. The company sells approximately 15 million ounces of silver annually, a volume that is expected to grow to more than 26 million ounces by 2012.

BEGINNINGS AS CHAP MERCANTILE

Silver Wheaton's first decade of existence was spent in a business far removed from the sale of silver. The world's largest "pure play" silver company began its corporate life providing locksmith services. Silver Wheaton was incorporated in August 1994 as Chap Mercantile Inc., a company that existed in name only at its inception. Chap Mercantile was formed as a junior capital pool company, a type of corporate structure that only existed in Canada. The purpose of a junior pool company was to provide a way for start-up companies to raise capital from the public before establishing a line of business. Of all the types of corporate structures, junior pool companies were the most ephemeral, existing essentially as a declaration of intentions, without defining what those intentions were. The concept originated in Alberta, Canada, where the province's oil industry attracted widespread speculative interest. Provided founders invested a minimum of CAD 100,000, a junior pool company could sell shares to the public, thereby raising the capital to start its business.

Chap Mercantile's existence as a junior pool company made for a slow start in its business life. For a year-and-a-half, its only activity was searching for a business to invest its capital in, a prolonged search that must have seemed an eternity for its investors. In February 1996, the company made its move, becoming an active commercial enterprise for the first time by acquiring Dial Locksmith Ltd. Dial Locksmith, a private company that had been in operation for approximately 30 years, provided locksmith services in Edmonton, Alberta. After Chap Mercantile secured a business foundation, it later

Over 70 percent of all silver is produced as a by-product from either gold or base metal mines. Our goal is to partner with the best of these mines to obtain all or a portion of the silver that they produce. Partnering with the best operators and the lowest cost mines around the world, helps mitigate the geopolitical and operating risks faced by many mining companies today.

expanded its business by introducing home and industrial safes, which eventually accounted for 10 percent of its business. The company also made a leap into the communications sector, buying nearly one-third of an Internet service provider, Zero-Hype Technologies Inc., but the investment failed after a hopeful beginning.

FROM LOCKSMITH TO SILVER COMPANY IN 2004

In the context of the global business world, Chap Mercantile offered little to distinguish itself until the beginning of 2004, nearly ten years after it was formed. In January, the company announced it intended to sell Dial Locksmith for CAD 325,000. Once the sale was made, Chap Mercantile expected to have CAD 435,000 in cash, which it intended to use to pursue a mission similar to the one it pursued a decade earlier. According to a statement published in the January 28, 2004, issue of *Canadian Corporate News,* Chap Mercantile announced it would "be seeking new assets or opportunities in the resource sector."

Unlike its search in 1994, Chap Mercantile's efforts in 2004 had a target, the resource sector, and they did not take 18 months to reach fruition. The company made its move in July 2004, when it hitched its future course to the sale of silver. Chap Mercantile agreed to purchase the entire silver production from the Luismin mine in Mexico, a mine owned by a Vancouver, British Columbia-based gold producer named Wheaton River Minerals Ltd. The deal essentially marked a new start for Chap Mercantile, making it 75 percent owned by Wheaton River. It also prompted a name change, as Chap Mercantile Inc. became Silver Wheaton Corp. by the end of the year. The former junior pool company had become another type of corporate shell, one used by Wheaton River to exploit its resources more effectively. Ian Telfer, Wheaton River's chairman and chief executive officer, explained to *American Metal Market* in a

July 16, 2004, interview that the transaction was a "way to unlock the value" of Wheaton River's silver production. "Silver Wheaton," he said, using the new name of Chap Mercantile before it was officially adopted, "will be a pure silver play and Wheaton River will continue to own 75 percent of Silver Wheaton."

LUISMIN MINE PROVIDES FIRST SILVER REVENUES

The transaction involving the Luismin SA de CV operations in Mexico was completed in October 2004, when Chap Mercantile paid CAD 46 million and stock and agreed on a payment of $3.90 per ounce of delivered, refined silver. Eduardo Luna, president of Wheaton River's Luismin subsidiary and former chairman of the Silver Institute, was appointed interim chief executive officer of Chap Mercantile. Peter Barnes, executive vice-president and chief financial officer of Wheaton River, was appointed chief financial officer of the company set to become Silver Wheaton. On October 22, 2004, trading on the Toronto Stock Exchange under the symbol of "CPC" ceased, as Chap Mercantile began trading as "SLW," although it had yet to change its name officially to Silver Wheaton.

When Chap Mercantile officially changed its name to Silver Wheaton in December 2004, the last vestige of its years as a locksmith service provider was eliminated. In the years ahead, the company planned to become a leading competitor in the silver mining business, and it would expand its presence in its new market by reaching agreements similar to its accord with Luismin SA de CV and Wheaton River. Under the terms of each agreement, Silver Wheaton agreed to pay $3.90 for each ounce of silver delivered, earning its living by profiting from the fluctuating price of silver on the open market. Between 2004 and 2007, the years of Silver Wheaton's initial expansion, the average price of silver increased from $6.65 per ounce to $13.39 per ounce.

SILVER WHEATON TAPS INTO SWEDEN'S ZINKGRUVAN MINE

Silver Wheaton did not wait long before securing access to a second silver stream. One month after the Luismin transaction closed, the company reached an agreement with another Canadian mining company, Lundin Mining Corporation. The November 2004 agreement involved Lundin Mining's Zinkgruvan mine in Sweden, a property located 200 kilometers southwest of Stockholm that had been producing zinc, lead, and silver on a continuous basis since 1857. The Zinkgruvan mine was expected to produce approximately two million ounces of silver annually for a minimum of 19 years. The

KEY DATES

1994: Silver Wheaton is incorporated as Chap Mercantile.

1996: Chap Mercantile makes its first acquisition, Dial Locksmith Ltd.

2004: Chap Mercantile sells Dial Locksmith and by the end of the year becomes Silver Wheaton.

2006: Silver Wheaton signs an agreement for silver production from the Yauliyacu mine in Peru.

2007: Silver Wheaton signs an agreement for 25 percent of the silver production from Mexico's Penasquito mine.

2008: Goldcorp sells its 48 percent interest in Silver Wheaton.

transaction closed December 8, 2004, the same day Chap Mercantile officially became Silver Wheaton. With the agreement involving Zinkgruvan Mining AB, Silver Wheaton was expected to sell 9.5 million ounces of silver in 2005 and more than ten million ounces by 2006. The company operated as the only publicly traded company in the world that derived 100 percent of its revenue from silver production.

A NEW OWNER IN 2005

Although Silver Wheaton did not add a silver stream in 2005, the year did include an important event on the acquisition front. While the company was negotiating its agreement with the Luismin mine, its majority owner, Wheaton River, was in the midst of merger talks with Goldcorp Inc. Based in Vancouver, Goldcorp ranked as one of the largest gold producers in the world, possessing reserves of roughly five million ounces from operations in North, Central, and South America. In April 2005, Wheaton River and Goldcorp merged, with Goldcorp the surviving entity. The deal gave Silver Wheaton a new parent company, with Goldcorp holding a 62 percent stake in Silver Wheaton.

Silver Wheaton jumped back into acquisition mode in 2006, doing so under the direction of a new leader. Eduardo Luna assumed the duties of chairman, making room for the appointment of Peter Barnes as Silver Wheaton's new chief executive officer in March 2006. Prior to the announcement, Barnes had been serving as executive vice-president and chief financial officer of Goldcorp. Under Barnes's stewardship, Silver Wheaton added its third silver stream the same month it gained a new chief executive officer. The company's agreement

was with Glencore International AG, a Switzerland-based supplier of metals and minerals, crude oil and oil products, and coal and agricultural products to industrial consumers. One of Glencore's nearly two dozen operations was the Yauliyacu mine in Peru, which had been in continuous operation for more than a century. Silver Wheaton agreed to purchase 4.75 million ounces of silver annually for 20 years from Glencore's Yauliyacu mine, paying $285 million plus a payment of $3.90 per ounce of silver delivered to secure a third silver stream.

Barnes and his small staff (Silver Wheaton had fewer than ten employees) began another round of negotiations before the end of the year, but before they did so they celebrated a significant event in the company's development. In May 2006, Silver Wheaton's application to list its shares on the New York Stock Exchange was approved. The company began trading under the ticker symbol "SLW," the same symbol it used on the Toronto Stock Exchange. "As a rapidly expanding silver company," Barnes said in a statement published in the May 5, 2006, issue of *Internet Wire,* "we view this as a great achievement considering the company is so young. Our move to the New York Stock Exchange represents an opportunity to reach a broader investment base in the United States, and will help us gain greater exposure in this critical market."

Not long after enjoying the honor of ringing the opening bell at the New York Stock Exchange, Barnes sat down with Goldcorp executives. In September 2006, the two parties reached an agreement that gave Silver Wheaton first right of refusal on future silver production from the Penasquito Project, a zinc-gold-silver-lead deposit located in Zactecas, Mexico, that ranked as the largest undeveloped silver project in the world. (Under the terms of Silver Wheaton's Luismin agreement, Silver Wheaton was entitled to purchase a 49 percent interest in production, development, or exploration properties acquired by Goldcorp in Mexico until October 2007.)

SECURING PRODUCTION FROM PENASQUITO: 2007

The Penasquito mine, which was expected to begin operations in 2008, was owned by Glamis Gold Ltd., a company Goldcorp was in the process of acquiring. Goldcorp completed the acquisition of Glamis in November 2006. In April 2007, Goldcorp and Silver Wheaton reached an agreement on the Penasquito Project, which entailed a $485 million cash payment and the usual ongoing per-ounce operating cost payment of $3.90 for 25 percent of the silver production at Penasquito for the life of the mine. The transaction increased Silver Wheaton's proven and probable reserves by 144 million ounces, giving it a total of 278 million ounces. With the acquisition, the company anticipated selling 22 million ounces of silver in 2009 and more than 26 million by 2012.

Silver Wheaton added its fifth silver stream the same month it brokered the deal for the Penasquito mine. In April 2007, the company reached an agreement to acquire the silver production from the Stratoni mine in Greece. The mine was owned by Hellas Gold S.A., which was 65 percent owned by European Goldfields Limited and 35 percent owned by Aktor, a Greek construction company. Silver Wheaton paid $57.5 million to acquire the silver produced by the Stratoni mine, which was expected to produce one million ounces of silver in 2007 and two million ounces annually by 2010. Silver Wheaton's agreement covered the entire life of the mine.

GOLDCORP SELLS ITS STAKE IN 2008

As Silver Wheaton plotted its future course, further investments were expected for the largest pure play silver company in the world. Silver Wheaton was scouring the globe in search of silver deposits, and it had its existing relationships with silver producers to exploit. Its agreement with the Stratoni mine, for instance, included the right of first refusal on any future silver sales from mines owned or operated by European Goldfields or Hellas Gold. The rights included the Olympias project near the Stratoni mine and the Certej project in Romania, two likely candidates for future acquisition. As Silver Wheaton pressed ahead, it gained independence when Goldcorp decided to sell its stake in the company. In February 2008, Goldcorp sold its 48 percent interest in Silver Wheaton, gaining CAD 1.56 billion in gross proceeds from the sale, an amount that reflected the enormous growth achieved by Silver Wheaton in only four years. In 2007, the company's revenues reached $175 million, from which it posted an impressive $92 million in net earnings. Selling silver was a lucrative business, particularly considering Silver Wheaton's meager payroll. The financial totals recorded in 2007 translated into a profit of more than $10.2 million for each Silver Wheaton employee.

Jeffrey L. Covell

PRINCIPAL SUBSIDIARIES

Silver Wheaton (Caymans) Ltd. (Cayman Islands).

PRINCIPAL COMPETITORS

Coeur d'Alene Mines Corp.; Pan American Silver Corp.; Silver Standard Resources Inc.

FURTHER READING

Bresnick, Julie, "Wheaton Sets Silver Spinoff, Output Accord," *American Metal Market,* July 16, 2004, p. 1.

"Chap Mercantile Inc.," *Market News Publishing,* January 22, 2002.

"Chap Mercantile Inc.: Proposed Reorganization of the Company," *Canadian Corporate News,* January 28, 2004.

"Lundin Mining Corporation to Sell Silver Production of Zinkgruvan Mine in Sweden," *Nordic Business Report,* November 15, 2004.

"Lundin Mining Sells Part of Its Holdings in Silver Wheaton," *Canadian Corporate News,* September 30, 2005.

"Mr. Peter Barnes Is Appointed Chief Executive Officer and Director of Silver Wheaton," *Canadian Corporate News,* March 7, 2006.

"Silver Wheaton Acquires Silver Production from European Goldfields," *Canadian Corporate News,* April 23, 2007.

"Silver Wheaton Completes Glencore Transaction," *Canadian Corporate News,* March 24, 2006.

"Silver Wheaton Completes Zinkgruvan Silver Transaction," *Canadian Corporate News,* December 8, 2004.

"Silver Wheaton Granted Right of First Refusal on Penasquito Silver Production," *Canadian Corporate News,* September 27, 2006.

"Silver Wheaton to List on the New York Stock Exchange," *Internet Wire,* May 5, 2006.

"Wheaton River Minerals Ltd. and Chap Mercantile Inc.: Silver Wheaton Transaction Completed," *Canadian Corporate News,* October 17, 2004.

Star of the West Milling Co.

121 East Tuscola St.
Frankenmuth, Michigan 48734
U.S.A.
Telephone: (989) 652-9971
Fax: (989) 652-6358
Web site: http://www.starofthewest.com

Private Company
Incorporated: 1929
Employees: 202
Sales: $175.9 million (2007)
NAIC: 311211 Flour Milling; 422510 Grain and Field
  Bean Wholesalers

■ ■ ■

Star of the West Milling Co. ranks as the 14th largest
U.S. wheat flour miller, in terms of daily capacity. It
operates five mills in four different states. The
company's flagship product is Cardinal flour made of
soft red wheat grown in the Midwest. Star of the West
also processes edible beans into food-grade quality.
Eleven elevators support the company's operations and
serve farmers. Customers for its flour and edible beans
include food manufacturers, canners, and packagers.

OLD WEST

Frankenmuth, Michigan, took root as an Indian missionary colony, as new settlers pushed the boundary of
the growing nation westward. German immigrants Johann Mathias Hubinger and Johann Georg Hubinger

settled in Frankenmuth in 1846 when they were in their
early 20s. The brothers came to the United States
equipped with the milling know-how of their family
that had been passed down over a span of two centuries
in the business.

During 1846 and 1847, the Hubinger brothers
established their own milling operation. They put
$1,000 into the construction of a wooden dam on the
Cass River and another $3,000 into a waterwheel-
powered flour mill. A second business, a sawmill, was
built upstream for $1,500. The wooden dam, later
covered with concrete, would survive over the
subsequent decades. The early mills, though not as long-
lived, served as a growth magnet for Frankenmuth.

"Originally the town seemed to develop where St.
Lorenz Church located. All of the colonists and a couple
of businesses were started in that vicinity in the first
years. With the Hubingers moving to the river, one mile
from the church, it caused a commercial shift in Frankenmuth business developments," the company's online
history recalled.

COMMUNITY PILLARS: 1851–1902

By 1851, the locale had transformed from an Indian
missionary colony to a small village, depending on Hubinger businesses. The sawmill allowed settlers to build
homes of lumber instead of log, and the flour mill
provided a market for grain produced by area farmers.

The Hubinger family entered into other key businesses as well. In 1851, Johann Mathias sold his share of
the mills to his brother and opened a general store. The

store on the southeast corner of Main and Tuscola streets passed down to his son Gottfried Hubinger, and eventually to his granddaughter, Hedwig "Hattie" Hubinger. The store carried "groceries, clothes, shoes, pipes, tiles, yard goods and was an agent for windmills, books, furnaces, sewing machines and washing machines," the online history recounted.

Johann Mathias Hubinger reentered the milling business in 1870, with a steam-powered operation. The company was the namesake of a side-wheeled merchant steamer. The oceangoing vessel, running a route between New York and New Orleans, gained fame during the Civil War. The Union army chartered the vessel, in secret, to carry soldiers and supplies to the South.

Lorenz Hubinger, the son of Johann Mathias, headed the patriotically named mill beginning in 1876. During the 1880s and into the early 1900s, the younger Hubinger took the mill through a series of improvements. In 1886, for example, the business was rebuilt as a roller mill. Less efficient millstones, long used to process wheat, yielded a lower percentage of better-grade flour than the new technology.

Johann Georg's children, meanwhile, worked the sawmill business. The operation, while locally significant, did not reach the stature of sawmill companies on the nearby Saginaw River system.

Beyond the flour and sawmills and the general store, members of the Hubinger family had developed other realms of influence, such as noncommercial banking and holding public office. Moreover, the family had accumulated considerable personal wealth through property holdings and financial investments.

CHANGE OF HANDS

The line of family ownership in Star of the West ended with Lorenz Hubinger. His sole surviving son chose a path other than milling, prompting Hubinger exit the business. A group of 50 farmers formed a partnership in 1903 and bought the operation.

When faced with significant renovations to the mill, the farmer-owners settled on building a new plant. The facility, which went into operation in 1911, continued

to be used for years to come. In July 1929, the business was incorporated as Star of the West Milling Co. Upon the conversion, meeting minutes were switched from the German to the English language.

Even though the Hubinger tenure had come to a close, others in the company provided continuity during the first half of the 20th century. Miller and Manager Jacob Rummel worked at Star of the West for 60 years. His son, Otto Rummel, put in 25 years.

In 1947, a young Richard Kraft Jr. was hired as a bookkeeper. He led the company for much of the second half of the century, retiring as president in 1997 but continuing as chairman of the board. Art Loeffler replaced him as president. Loeffler had been hired as controller, the company's first, in 1979.

As a side note, a bit of Hubinger family legacy was reconnected to Star of the West in 1976. The company bought the building that had housed the Hubinger general store. Wallace Bronner, Hattie Hubinger's nephew, had owned the store since her death. "This completed a circle since 1851 where all the owners could trace their beginning to the original Hubinger family," the Star of the West history concluded.

NEW HORIZONS

Star of the West expanded outside Michigan through acquisitions of other mills. One such purchase took place in 1987. The 100-year-old operation was based in Noble County, Indiana. Ligonier Milling, later named Lyon and Greenleaf Mill, opened in 1886, as one of the nation's first steel-roller mills, according to the *Noble County (Ind.) News-Sun*. "It was considered the most modern mill in the country," General Manager Ken Schuman told the northeast Indiana paper.

While steeped in milling history, Star of the West had the future of the industry to attend to as well. With the onset of the North American Free Trade Agreement (NAFTA) looming in 1993, Michigan Governor John Engler, a proponent of the deal, led a delegation of his state's business executives to Mexico. Participants hoped Michigan goods, ranging from automobiles to agricultural products, would surge south of the border once NAFTA went into effect on January 1, 1994. Initially, they did. Unfortunately, a downturn in the Mexican economy, coupled with a complex political environment, dashed hopes.

"Joe Cramer, a sales manager for Star of the West Milling Co., in Frankenmuth, recalled the relentlessly upbeat mood of Engler's mission two years ago," Rick Haglund reported for the *Grand Rapids Press*. "'To some degree, we heard what we wanted to hear,' Cramer told me. 'Everyone on that trip was there because of their

KEY DATES

1846: Hubinger brothers settle in Frankenmuth, Michigan.
1847: The German immigrants undertake a milling operation.
1851: Johann Georg Hubinger buys his brother's share of the business.
1870: Johann Mathias Hubinger reenters the milling business with Star of the West.
1876: Lorenz Hubinger succeeds his father Johann Mathias as head of company.
1903: Star of the West is sold to a group of farmers.
1929: The partnership incorporates.
1947: Richard Kraft Jr., future company president, is hired as a bookkeeper.
1976: Company buys building that housed the Hubinger general store.
1987: Star of the West acquires Ligonier Milling, a 100-year-old Indiana milling business.
1997: Art Loeffler succeeds Kraft Jr. as president.
2007: Company expands storage facilities at its New York mill.

optimism about the Mexican market.'" Star of the West Milling opted to sell dry beans to a Texas company willing to risk resale on the Mexican market.

In 1998, Star of the West improved storage capacity at its Ligonier mill, building two 330,000 bushel towers. The 130-foot structures held wheat purchased from midwestern grain terminals, co-ops, and farmers.

The mill, which could produce 450,000 pounds of flour a day, provided full-time employment for 23 people. "Some of the mill's biggest customers include pretzel makers, and licorice producers, as well as Kellogg's cereals and Archway cookies," the *News-Sun* reported in 1999. The Ligonier mill's annual revenue was estimated at $14 million.

A THIRD CENTURY

Star of the West Milling reached a milestone in 2000, having been in operation through part or all of three different centuries. Although milling technology, food products, and the political environment changed over the years, one thing remained constant: weather-related perils.

Bean farmers in the company's home state were hit by drought conditions during the 2001 growing season.

The result was record low production yield. Many of the beans that were produced were stressed, diminishing their quality and desirability, the *Grand Rapids Press* explained.

Star of the West processed edible beans, such as navy beans, black beans, and pinto beans, to food-grade quality. Packagers and canners then bought them in quantity, including by 100-pound bag, one and two ton tote bags, and railroad car and truckloads.

The grain end of the business also faced weather-related challenges in the early years of the 21st century, a time when the implications of global climate change were heatedly discussed. Indiana farmers, among the country's top wheat producers, posted a double digit drop-off in their 2005 harvest, compared with 2004.

According to the *Fort Wayne (Indiana) Journal Gazette:* "Some farmers did not have enough time to plant winter wheat this fall, said Ken Schuman, plant manger for Star of the West Milling Co.'s Ligonier flour mill. Farmers typically harvest soybeans and then plant winter wheat in the same field. A late soybean crop last fall made it difficult for some farmers to plant wheat before the first frost, he said."

Also contributing to the 2005 production downturn were weak 2004 wheat prices. Farmers planted more corn and soybeans, in response. A storage expansion project at its Churchville, New York, facility met with some opposition in 2007, as residential and commercial needs weighed in during the approval process. One neighbor expressed concerns about the size of the new bins and the potential for increased truck traffic, according to Westside News Inc. The town's mill dated to 1810, although it had changed locations and owners over the years.

Star of the West received approval for the addition on the industrially zoned site. "'We have one ingredient, produce a wholesome product and we use all of it,' Manager François Lachance said in the Westside News publication. He added that there is no air or water pollution created by the process and nothing is wasted, every part of the wheat can be eaten by either people or animals."

In 2008, Star of the West produced 2.23 million pounds of wheat flour per day, placing it 14th among U.S. millers in terms of daily capacity. On a global level, the year was marked by skyrocketing agricultural commodity and crude oil prices and escalating fears of food shortages.

Kathleen Peippo

PRINCIPAL DIVISIONS

Flour Milling; Elevator.

PRINCIPAL COMPETITORS

Bay State Milling Company; FACT Corporation; Hodgson Mill, Inc.

FURTHER READING

Buttgen, Bob, "Mill a 'Star' Business in Ligonier," *Noble County (Ind.) News-Sun,* July 1999 special edition.

"Dry-Bean Crop May Be the Worst in Decades," *Grand Rapids (Mich.) Press,* October 28, 2001, p. B2.

Glenn, Jenni, "State Wheat-Crop Harvest Smaller, Ag Report Shows," *Fort Wayne (Ind.) Journal Gazette,* August 13, 2005, p. 1A.

Haglund, Rick, "Falling Peso Takes Bloom off NAFTA; Businesses That Bought Gov. Engler's Enthusiasm for Trade with Mexico Have Been Shocked into Reality," *Grand Rapids (Mich.) Press,* March 15, 1995, p. C8.

"Star of the West Milling Expands Storage Capacity," http://www.westsidenewsonline.com, September 2, 2007.

Superdrug Stores PLC

118 Beddington Lane
Croydon, CR0 4TB
United Kingdom
Telephone: (+44 020) 8684 7000
Fax: (+44 020) 8684 6102
Web site: http://www.superdrug.com

Subsidiary of AS Watson & Company
Incorporated: 1964
Employees: 7,000
Sales: £1 billion ($2.02 billion) (2005)
NAIC: 446110 Pharmacies and Drug Stores

■ ■ ■

Superdrug Stores PLC is the United Kingdom's second largest specialist drugstore operator, behind sector leading Alliance Boots. Superdrug is also the sixth largest in the U.K. drugstore and pharmacy market, including supermarkets groups Tesco, Sainsbury, ASDA, and Morrisons. The company operates more than 900 stores across the United Kingdom, including Scotland, Wales, and Northern Ireland. Superdrug also entered Ireland itself in the middle of the first decade of the 2000s. Most of Superdrug's stores are located in the United Kingdom's high street shopping districts. While primarily focused on health and beauty products, the company's stores also feature perfumes, food selections, and other items. More than 225 of the company's stores also house their own pharmacies. In a bid to increase its market share, Superdrug has launched an ambitious chainwide refurbishment program, adopting a new,

more upscale "pink" theme. At the same time, Superdrug has developed what it calls its "next generation" retail format, which focuses especially on perfumes and cosmetics. The company also operates an e-commerce web site. Superdrug is owned by AS Watson, the retail division of Hong Kong conglomerate Hutchison Whampoa, which acquired the company in 2002. AS Watson's other drugstore and retail holdings include Kruidvat in the Netherlands, Marrionnaud in France, and 40 percent of Rossmann, in Germany, among many others. Superdrug generates more than £1 billion ($2 billion) in sales each year.

BROTHERLY BEGINNINGS: 1964

Superdrug was founded by brothers and grocers Peter and Ronald Goldstein, who decided to extend their retailing experience into the health and beauty sector in 1964. The brothers established a new company, originally called Leading Supermarkets Ltd. By the end of that year, they had adopted the Superdrug name. In 1966, the company opened its first Superdrug-branded store, in Putney.

Superdrug focused its operations on the discount market, selling health and beauty products, paramedical and medicinal products, and other toiletry items. In its earliest phase, the company's stores did not feature their own pharmacies—quite common in the drugstore sector in United Kingdom and elsewhere in Europe.

At the end of the decade, the company had expanded its operations into Croydon and Streatham. The rising sales volumes led the Goldsteins to add their own warehouse facility in Wimbledon in 1968, which then served as its central distribution facility. Superdrug continued adding stores, outpacing the capacity of its first warehouse. This led the company to establish a new headquarters in 1970, in West Moseley, adding a 20,000-square-foot warehouse.

Superdrug began its march toward the top the following year, when it launched an association with Rite Aid, the U.S. drugstore giant. Rite-Aid acquired a 49 percent stake in Superdrug and backed its new expansion phase. This got off to a strong start with the purchase of the five-store Elgee drugstore chain in 1972. Most of the company's growth was organic, and by the following year, Superdrug had opened 40 stores.

Superdrug continued building up its warehousing and distribution capacity through the 1970s as it continued to expand its store network. By the end of the decade, the company operated close to 80 stores. Just one year later, the company had climbed past the 100-store mark. By 1983, when Superdrug floated 25 percent of its shares on the London Stock Exchange's Unlisted Securities Market, the company's store network was nearing 150.

Superdrug's store network was still largely focused on the London area and southeastern England into the middle of the 1980s. The public offering provided the group with the momentum to move toward national expansion, and the company had already opened its first stores in the Manchester region. The company then moved into Scotland in 1985. By then, its retail network topped 250 stores.

GROWTH SPURT THROUGH ACQUISITIONS IN THE EIGHTIES

Superdrug continued to post respectable growth, boosting its number of stores to 300 by the beginning of 1987. That year, however, marked a turning point for the company, when it accepted a buyout offer from British retail leader Woolworth Holdings Plc (which later became known as Kingfisher). The Goldstein brothers and Rite Aid accepted Woolworth's offer of £257 mil-

lion, although both Goldstein brothers remained as heads of the group's operations.

Woolworth backed Superdrug's most impressive expansion effort to date. Superdrug gained access to a number of unused Woolworth properties including a number of highly coveted high street sites. In this way, the Superdrug chain expanded to nearly 340 stores at the end of 1987. The company had also firmly established itself as a major player in the high street market.

Next, Superdrug went on a buying spree that transformed the company into the United Kingdom's second largest toiletries specialist in just two years. The company started with the £3 million purchase of Tip Top Drugstores, adding 110 stores to its portfolio. The Tip Top acquisition especially helped raise the company's profile in the north of England and Scotland. This purchase was soon followed by that of Share Drug, which operated primarily in the south of England. Share Drug added another 145 stores to Superdrug's network, at a cost of £2 million.

Superdrug's expansion drive continued into 1989, when parent Kingfisher bought another drugstore operator, Medicare, and its 86 stores. These were placed under Superdrug, which began converting the Medicare stores to the Superdrug format. By 1990, Superdrug's total network approached 700 stores.

NEW MARKETS IN THE NINETIES

The Goldsteins retired from the company in 1990, turning over operations to a new management team led by Alan Smith. Superdrug launched an entirely new strategy, based on organic growth and diversification. The first stage of this effort included a rationalization of the group's network, and especially a large number of the former Medicare sites. By the conclusion of this program, the company's total store network had dropped back to 650.

Superdrug then began an effort to transform its image from that of a discounter to a more sophisticated, and more upscale retail group. The company began upgrading its own label line, which in the early 1990s represented only a small share of the more than 4,000 items carried in an average Superdrug store. The new focus on brand products included a shift from copies of major brands to developing the company's own formulations. An example of this strategy was the launch of the Natural Selections brand of beauty aids and toiletries, designed to compete directly with the highly successful Body Shop brand.

Superdrug's image change also included the extension of its product range in the early 1990s. The

KEY DATES

1964: Ronald and Peter Goldstein form Superdrug Stores as a discount health and beauty chain; first store opens in Putney.

1971: Rite Aid, of the United States, acquires 49 percent of Superdrug and backs its expansion into national chain.

1983: Superdrug lists shares on Unlisted Securities Market.

1987: Woolworth Holdings (later Kingfisher) acquires Superdrug and launches acquisition drive, boosting chain to 700 stores.

1990: Goldsteins retire and Superdrug launches effort to convert stores to a more upscale format, adding pharmacies and perfumeries.

2001: Kruidvat, of the Netherlands, acquires Superdrug.

2002: AS Watson acquires Kruidvat.

2005: Superdrug launches five-year expansion program to top 1,000 stores by 2009.

2007: Company begins conversion of Savers stores to Superdrug format.

company added its first in-store pharmacy in 1992, in Cheltenham. The success of that effort led to a wider rollout, and by the end of the decade, Superdrug operated more than 200 pharmacies.

The company also targeted a new and fast-growing retail sector, adding its first in-store perfumeries in 1991, in Newcastle-upon-Tyne and Epsom. By the end of 1992, the company's perfumery operations had been extended to 20 of its stores. The shift into perfume sales became a source of controversy, however. The major perfume houses, seeking to protect the product's luxury image, refused to supply Superdrug directly. Instead, the company was forced to buy perfumes on the grey market. The company attempted to force the issue, appealing to the Mergers and Monopolies Commission (MMC). However, in 1993 the MMC ruled that the perfume companies did indeed have the right to refuse to sell to Superdrug.

The MMC ruling had, however, established a set of criteria that would allow Superdrug to purchase directly from the perfume houses. The company set out to redevelop the perfume counters at its stores. The company was then able to reach supply agreements with a number of major perfume groups, including Givenchy and Yves Saint Laurent.

Superdrug then pushed ahead with its perfumery rollout. By the end of 1993, Superdrug had outfitted more than 60 stores with perfumeries. The success of the perfumeries led the company to develop a new store format for its chain, which it began rolling out in 1995. By 1998, this effort included the launch of the group's first in-store hair salons. The first of these opened at the group's new 8,300-square-foot Oxford Street flagship store in London.

The flagship store also exemplified the group's efforts to shed the group's image as a discounter as it approached the new millennium. As part of this effort, Superdrug had replaced its former "one-size-fits-all" policy, by which all of its stores had the same look and product range, to develop a more diversified format tailored to specific locations. As such, while many of the group's locations retained a broad mix of toiletries, household products, and other items, other sites, including the Oxford Street flagship, adopted a selection wholly oriented toward health and beauty products. Accompanying Superdrug's "new look" was a major expansion of its own-brand product range. This topped 1,400 items at the end of the 1990s.

In the meantime, the company had expanded its perfumeries to 128 stores. By the end of the decade, Superdrug had gained credit for introducing a new level of competition in the perfume sector in the United Kingdom. As a result, prices on perfumes dropped sharply by 2000, making the major brands more accessible to a far wider market.

CHANGING HANDS IN THE NEW CENTURY

Superdrug continued to expand its in-store range into the new century. The company rolled out a new convenience foods section in 1998. Called Foodzone, the new department quickly became one of the group's strongest departments, leading to a broader rollout across the chain. By 2000, more than 400 of the company's stores featured a Foodzone section. In that year, Liz Wright took over as the company's managing director.

In 2001, Kingfisher, which had steadily expanded its other retail operations through the 1990s, decided to sell Superdrug in order to reduce its debt. By August 2001, Kingfisher had reached an agreement to sell Superdrug to Kruidvat BV, one of the Netherlands' leading retail groups. The addition of Superdrug transformed Kruidvat into a European leader in the retail health and beauty sector.

By 2002, Superdrug found itself part of an even larger group when AS Watson, the retail arm of Hong

Kong conglomerate Hutchison Whampoa, acquired Kruidvat. The new ownership brought in a new general manager, Gerard Hazelebach, who had been head of Kruidvat's ICI Paris XL perfumery operation. Another result of the new ownership was the appearance of a new in-store boutique, "3," selling Hutchison Whampoa's mobile telephone service. By 2008, the company had rolled out "3" boutiques in more than 200 stores.

Under Hazelebach, Superdrug launched a new five-year strategy in order to reposition itself more firmly upscale, with a stronger focus on the fashion-oriented health and beauty market. As part of that effort, Superdrug launched a major reformatting of the chain, with plans to spend more than £14.5 million to convert 720 stores, or roughly 85 of its total network, to the new more fashion-forward format.

AS Watson already owned the Savers drugstore group in the United Kingdom. In 2007, the company began converting 220 of its Savers stores to the Superdrug format. This conversion program formed part of Superdrug's overall strategy of boosting its total store network past 1,000 by 2009. At the same time, Superdrug continued its refurbishment effort, spending more than £46 million to upgrade 440 stores in 2007. Meanwhile, Superdrug had successfully expanded into Ireland, opening its first stores there in 2006.

Superdrug continued to develop new store concepts as well. The company launched its first Superdrug Health store in Brighton in October 2007. The new store, converted from a Savers discount shop, was the first in a proposed chain focused exclusively as retail pharmacy and health stores. If successful, the company expected to launch a broader rollout of the Superdrug Health format, targeting conversions of Saver stores located near existing Superdrug branches. The latter were then to be refocused as beauty aids specialist shops.

While Superdrug waited for the results of the Superdrug Health trial, it had achieved success with a second new format. The company opened the first of its new "pink look" stores in Uxbridge, in West London, in 2006. The new format, which featured a pink-based color scheme, proved so successful that by the end of 2007 the company had developed plans to roll out the pink look to 200 of its stores. With more than 900 stores at the beginning of 2008, Superdrug appeared well on its way to achieving its goal of 1,000 stores by 2009.

M. L. Cohen

PRINCIPAL COMPETITORS

Alliance Boots PLC; Lloyds Pharmacy Ltd.; Manchester Airport Group PLC; Scottish Midland Co-operative Society Ltd.; T J Morris Ltd.; Strathclyde (Pharmaceuticals) Ltd.; G R and M M Blackledge PLC; Paydens Ltd.; The Perfume Shop Ltd.

FURTHER READING

Clegg, James, "Superdrug Launches Spin-off Health Store," *Chemist & Druggist*, October 12, 2007, p. 18.

Harwood, Jonathan, "Neglected Superdrug Handed a #10m Tonic," *Marketing Week*, April 21, 2005, p. 25.

Matthews, Imogen, "Superdrug: Changing Tack," *European Cosmetic Markets*, May 1999, p. 207.

Meyer, Scot, "New No. 3 Drug Chain in Europe," *MMR*, December 17, 2001, p. 21.

Nagel, Andrea, and Brid Costello, "Superdrug Set for UK Expansion," *WWD*, January 9, 2006, p. 18.

"'Pink' Store Rollout," *MMR*, December 10, 2007, p. 14.

"Sale May Change Superdrug's Strategy," *European Cosmetic Markets*, August 2001, p. 278.

"Superdrug Heads for a Beauty Contest," *Chemist & Druggist*, September 30, 2000, p. 33.

"Superdrug to Sell Online As It Takes on High Street Rival Boots," *New Media Age*, November 23, 2006, p. 1.

Synaptics Incorporated

3120 Scott Boulevard, Suite 130
Santa Clara, California 95054
U.S.A.
Telephone: (408) 454-5100
Fax: (408) 454-5200
Web site: http://www.synaptics.com

Public Company
Incorporated: 1986
Employees: 312
Sales: $266.78 million (2007)
Stock Exchanges: NASDAQ
Ticker Symbol: SYNA
NAIC: 334119 Other Computer Peripheral Equipment
Manufacturing; 511210 Software Publishers

∎∎∎

Synaptics Incorporated is a leading developer of custom-designed, user-interface products for electronic devices. The company dominates the market for navigation devices used on notebook computers, selling TouchPad, a pressure-sensitive pad that senses the position and movement of a user's finger on its surface, and Touch-Styk, a self-contained pointing stick module. Synaptics also serves what it calls the digital lifestyles market, supplying user-interface devices for portable digital music players, mobile telephones, remote controls, and Global Positioning System (GPS) devices. The company sells its products to the manufacturers of computers and other electronic devices.

FOUNDER FEDERICO FAGGIN

Synaptics was founded by the man who did much of the work on one of the greatest inventions of the 20th century. Federico Faggin was largely responsible—entirely responsible according to some accounts—for developing the 8080, the first microprocessor powerful enough to serve as a central processor for a personal computer. The development of the 8080 was just one of Faggin's achievements, one chapter in a storied career that continuously saw Faggin explore new ideas and ask profound questions of science and technology. "He is a man who speaks sometimes like a mad scientist, sometimes like a philosopher, sometimes like a hard-nosed businessman, and sometimes like a driven engineer," the *Business Journal* wrote of Faggin in a September 21, 1992, article.

Born in Vicenza, Italy, during World War II, Faggin, the son of a philosophy professor, excelled in school. He began cultivating his passion for electronics while attending a technical high school, which led him to seek a job with Italian computer giant Olivetti after earning his diploma. By age 19, in 1961, he had designed his first computer, a project that required the help of three technicians. Following that, Faggin enrolled at the University of Padua. Faggan completed the doctorate program in physics that normally required six or seven years to complete in just four years. He graduated from the University of Padua with the highest honors bestowed by the institution and briefly joined its faculty as a professor. His departure was hastened by his preference for the business world. For Faggin, uniting the rigors of the science realm with the rigors of the commercial realm was ideal. "There's a necessity to

COMPANY PERSPECTIVES

As a global company in a rapidly expanding marketplace, Synaptics places great emphasis on reflecting our corporate values while maintaining a fast-paced and energetic workplace. Our values of maintaining a respectful and stimulating work environment, supporting creativity and initiative, and fostering exemplary customer partnerships gives us the foundation to succeed. Our employees are our most important resource.

deliver," he said in an interview published in the September 21, 1992, edition of the *Business Journal*. "And you can't fool the marketplace the way you can fool people just by writing papers that no one understands."

Faggin left academia and began working for a European subsidiary of Fairchild Semiconductor. In 1968, Fairchild Semiconductor sent the 26-year-old Faggin to the company's research-and-development laboratory in Palo Alto, California, as part of an exchange program. While in California, Faggin developed silicon gate technology: the first manufacturable high-speed system using silicon instead of metal to conduct electrical impulses on integrated circuits. Fairchild Semiconductor asked Faggin to remain in the United States after his momentous breakthrough.

Faggin stayed in the United States, but he did not remain at Fairchild Semiconductor. In 1970, he joined Intel Corporation and began work on the 4004, the first programmable silicon chip. Faggin collaborated with an engineer named Ted Hoff on the 4004, forming a partnership that also would produce the historic 8080, the central processing unit (CPU) for the first personal computer, the Altair. Faggin's contributions to the project would be played down, or omitted, in the years to follow because he left Intel in 1974 to found a rival company, his first entrepreneurial endeavor, ZiLOG, Inc. Stung by Faggin's departure, Intel officials made Hoff the hero when recounting the pioneering development of the 4004 and 8080.

Faggin enjoyed considerable success with ZiLOG. He designed the Z80 microprocessor, one of the first mass-produced eight-bit processors. Within a decade, ZiLOG built more than one billion Z80 chips. The company eventually was acquired by Exxon Corp., whose management quarreled with Faggin, prompting him to leave ZiLOG in 1982 and form a second

company, Cygnet Technologies. With his second entrepreneurial creation, Faggin attempted to marry telephone communications with computing, an idea that failed to realize any commercial success. He sold the company in 1986, the year he teamed up with a professor of computer science at the California Institute of Technology, Carver Mead, and founded Synaptics.

FORMATION OF SYNAPTICS

With the financial assistance of a venture capitalist named Kevin Kinsella, Faggin and Mead began working together in San Jose, California. Through Synaptics, Faggin began exploring metaphysical questions, proposing the development of an entirely new type of computer. "If a machine could think, could learn, we will have to ask, 'Then what are we? What makes us different?'" he asked in his September 21, 1992, interview with the *Business Journal*. "It is exactly this kind of technology that will lead man to recognize his humanity. Being an optimist, I believe that will be a magical time."

Faggin started Synaptics to develop chips that emulated the human brain's thought patterns. Instead of accomplishing his proposed feat by programming a computer or delving into artificial intelligence technology, Faggin planned to build chips that could be used in a neural network. When confronted with a challenge or problem, a traditional computer's CPU approached a single part of the problem and worked on solving the problem one step at a time. A computer based on neural networking approached a problem in a different way, eschewing the linear reasoning of a traditional computer. A neural network tackled numerous pieces of the problem in a parallel, like the brain, sending partial answers to other components of the network, with each new piece of data making different parts of the network smarter. In simple terms, a computer was programmed, whereas a neural network was self-learning.

Faggin's objective was to burn a neural network into the chip itself. His goal was hardware-based, not software-based. He envisioned virtually limitless applications for the technology, seeing armies of autonomous machines capable of everything from mining for coal to picking fruit, traffic lights that intelligently monitored fluctuations in traffic, and computers that responded to the hand gestures of its user. He and Mead spent their time conducting experiments in pattern recognition, working on technology that would enable a computer to recognize the face of the person using it, for instance. The pair secured dozens of patents on their work, which Faggin, ever mindful of the commercial needs of running a company, applied to products Synaptics could sell to fund further experiments in neural networking.

1986: Synaptics is founded by Federico Faggin and Carver Mead.

1992: Synaptics begins selling the I-1000, which operates as part of a check-reading device.

1994: Synaptics secures Apple Computer as a customer, supplying touchpads for notebook computers.

1999: Francis Lee is appointed president and chief executive officer.

2002: Synaptics completes its initial public offering of stock.

2005: Apple cuts its ties to Synaptics.

2006: Synaptics releases a mobile telephone that operates without buttons.

2008: Synaptics releases a universal remote control, Boomerang, that operates without buttons or keys.

The company's first product debuted in June 2002, a relatively mundane product considering the exotic research from which it was born. Synaptics began selling the I-1000, which read the routing number on swiped checks, selling the product as part of a check reader made by VeriFone Inc.

ENTERING THE PERSONAL COMPUTER MARKET IN 1992

A product more pertinent to Faggin's research gained traction the same year the I-1000 was released. Part of Faggin's vision of a computer that could recognize its user and respond to hand gestures called for the elimination of devices such as keyboards and mice. In 1992, Swiss computer peripherals maker Logitech International S.A. hired Synaptics to develop a chip for a touchpad, a device intended to replace trackballs, the primary input device used on notebook computers. For Faggin, the project brought his neural network-based, pattern-recognition research into the field of human-interface products. The agreement with Logitech fell apart, but Faggin and his small staff pressed forward with the development of a touchpad. Within a short time, the company developed a solid-state, touch- and motion-sensitive pad that was released in 1994, the same year it hitched its growth to the rise of an industry giant, Apple Computer Inc.

COURTING APPLE AND A PRICE WAR WITH LOGITECH

In 1994, Apple introduced its PowerBook notebook with a touchpad supplied by a small, Salt Lake City, Utah-based company named Cirque. Despite its relationship with Cirque, Apple was interested in Synaptics' touchpad. Apple put Synaptics through the rigors of its own manufacturing and quality assurance vetting process and gave Faggin's company its business. The agreement, which under the terms stipulated by Apple forbade Synaptics from revealing its relationship with Apple, represented a tremendous boon to Synaptics' business. The laptop market was growing robustly, giving Faggin's company its first taste of commercial success, but soon the dynamics of the market changed. The agent of change was Logitech.

Logitech, which had flirted with touchpad technology in 1992, entered the market aggressively in 1995. To gain market share, the company, which dwarfed Synaptics, began selling touchpads below cost, dumping $6 touchpads in a market that Synaptics made its living by selling $11 touchpads, the same price charged by Cirque. A price war began, forcing Faggin to lower costs by replacing two chips with one. Logitech eventually stumbled badly, suffering severe quality-control problems that forced the company out of the touchpad market entirely by 1999, but Faggin had had enough of the tribulations caused by Logitech before it made its exit. In 1998, he began to look for a successor.

Faggin found his mark in Francis Lee. Lee immigrated from Hong Kong in 1968, arriving in Sacramento, California, at age 16. Despite only a smattering of English, Lee did well in high school, enrolled at the University of California, Davis, and earned a degree in electrical engineering. He was recruited by National Semiconductor out of college and spent 20 years at the company, becoming head of logic chips and of quality control.

THE LEE ERA BEGINNING IN 1999

Lee took the helm at the beginning of 1999, inheriting control of a company generating roughly $30 million in annual revenue. Despite Faggin's frustration, Synaptics occupied an enviable position. Logitech exited the touchpad market during Lee's first year as president and chief executive officer and the company developed into the dominant player in the notebook market, using its proprietary TouchPad device to seize control of more than 40 percent of the notebook market. By the time the company completed its initial public offering (IPO) of stock in January 2002, it was generating $73.7 million in revenue, all from the sale of TouchPad and a pointing device named TouchStyk. Synaptics was selling 61 percent of all touchpad technology worldwide.

A primary objective for the years following the company's IPO was to lessen its dependence on the personal computer market by entering new markets with new types of user-interface products. Toward this end, Synaptics registered phenomenal success by supplying devices for the most popular electronic device of the period, Apple's iPod. The portable music player featured a "round control" developed by Synaptics, which enabled the company to share in the enormous commercial success of Apple's market winner. Synaptics' revenues reached the $100 million mark in 2003 and more than doubled within the next two years, reaching $208 million in 2005. Net income increased exponentially during the period, skyrocketing from $7.7 million to $37.9 million, which drove the company stock value up from its IPO price of $11 per share to roughly $40 per share.

SYNAPTICS AND APPLE PART WAYS

Synaptics' share of the iPod's success represented a massive boost to its business, that was sorely missed when Apple dropped the company as a supplier. When Wall Street learned of the decision in February 2005, Synaptics' stock fell to $15 per share. Apple's decision, which included the company's new G4 PowerBook laptop, represented a major loss of business, estimated to be 30 percent to 40 percent of Synaptics' annual sales total.

The loss of Apple as a customer hit Synaptics hard, but Lee was confident the company could recover. The financial loss was apparent—the company generated $184.5 million in 2006 as profits slipped to $13.7 million—but it could have been worse. Lee focused efforts on developing touchpads and related devices for a wide range of products and applications, hoping to continue the company's success in diversifying away from the personal computer market. He reduced the design cycle of the company's products from the 12 to 18 months required for a new customer to get a touchpad integrated into its product down to three months. He also concentrated on giving customers the opportunity to ask for their own, custom specifications.

A DIVERSIFIED FUTURE

As Synaptics prepared for the future, it was pursuing a plan to develop user-interface modules of all sizes for a variety of applications. Several new products introduced after the loss of Apple's business pointed to a bright future. In 2006, the company partnered with a designer named Pilotfish to introduce the prototype of a mobile telephone that operated without buttons. The device responded to signs and gestures through a touchpad covering most of its surface. The year also saw the release of a biometric TouchPad for notebooks that incorporated fingerprint-sensing technology. At the end of 2007, the company completed the development of Boomerang, a universal remote control that operated without buttons or keys. In the years ahead, more new products were expected as Synaptics focused its efforts on changing the way humans interacted with electronic devices.

Jeffrey L. Covell

PRINCIPAL SUBSIDIARIES

Synaptics International, Inc.; Synaptics (UK) Limited; Synaptics Hong Kong Limited; Synaptics Europe Sarl (Switzerland); Synaptics Holding GmbH (Switzerland); Synaptics LLC.

PRINCIPAL COMPETITORS

Alps Electric Co., Ltd.; NMB Technologies Corporation; Quantum Technology Management Company; Cypress Semiconductor Corporation.

FURTHER READING

Detar, James, "Sales Sing for Firms Selling Key iPod Parts," *Investor's Business Daily,* December 22, 2004, p. A4.

Espe, Erik, "Firm Develops Chinese Character-Recognition Software," *Business Journal,* July 27, 1998, p. 20.

Gondo, Nancy, "Synaptics Has the Right Touch with iPods, Rival Music Players," *Investor's Business Daily,* November 1, 2004, p. B2.

Kharif, Olga, "A Quantum Leap for Cell Phones," *Business Week Online,* August 21, 2006.

Menlow, David, "IPO Pick of the Week: Synaptics Inc.," *Daily Deal,* January 28, 2002.

Moore, Heidi, "Handheld Device Maker Registers Year's First IPO," *Daily Deal,* January 29, 2002.

Pitta, Julie, "Federico Faggin," *Forbes,* July 7, 1997, p. 312.

Seitz, Patrick, "Synaptics Taps into Market," *Investor's Business Daily,* April 9, 2002, p. A7.

———, "Touch Pad Firm Feels the Music," *Investor's Business Daily,* February 17, 2004, p. A7.

"Synaptics Targets Vision, Sound Processing, to Follow Touch-Pad Module," *Electronic News (1991),* October 31, 1994, p. 24.

Weisman, Jonathan, "Federico Faggin: Pioneer Strives to Teach Computers to Learn to Think," *Business Journal,* September 21, 1992, p. 12.

Whelan, David, "Touchy Touchy," *Forbes Global,* October 31, 2005, p. 66.

"Wireless Drivers Deliver Optimized User Interface," *Product News Network,* June 4, 2007.

Young, Margaret, "Researchers Hope to Copy Brain Functions," *Business Journal,* August 31, 1987, p. 1.

Synchronoss Technologies, Inc.

---

750 Route 202 South, Suite 600
Bridgewater, New Jersey 08807
U.S.A.
Toll Free: (866) 620-3940
Fax: (908) 547-1285
Web site: http://www.synchronoss.com

Public Company
Incorporated: 2000
Employees: 170
Sales: $123.5 million (2007)
Stock Exchanges: NASDAQ
Ticker Symbol: SNCR
NAIC: 541511 Custom Computer Programming
Services

■ ■ ■

Synchronoss Technologies, Inc., provides on-demand transaction management services to communication service providers (CSPs), making money on each transaction performed rather than employing a subscription model. Clients include cable television companies, such as Cablevision, Comcast, and Time Warner Cable; stand-alone voice over Internet protocol (VoIP) telephone companies such as Vonage and Level 3; ILECs (incumbent local exchange carriers), such as AT&T and Verizon; and wireless carriers, in particular AT&T, with which Synchronoss worked on the successful launch of iPhone with Apple Computer. The backbone of the company is the ConvergenceNow software suite that automates the ordering and management of CSP

products and services via the Internet. Modules include Orchestration Gateway to activate CSP services; ConvergedWorkflow Manager, coordinating with Orchestration Gateway to handle order validation, activation, and other information exchange between CSPs and their customers; and VisibilityNow Reporting Manager, providing clients with realtime business information. Synchronoss is a public company listed on the NASDAQ and based in Bridgewater, New Jersey. Cofounder Stephen G. Waldis serves as chairman, president, and chief executive officer.

WALDIS, 1989 SETON HALL GRADUATE

With his father stationed in Japan while serving in the Air Force, Stephen Waldis was born in Tokyo, but by the time he was ready to start school his family had moved to Cherry Hill, New Jersey, near Philadelphia. An athlete, he made the baseball team as a walk-on after enrolling at Seton Hall University and later earned a scholarship. He was talented enough to pitch in relief on a team that featured three future major leaguers—Craig Biggio, Mo Vaughn, and John Valentin—but fell short on the ability needed to turn professional. Instead, after earning a degree in corporate communications in 1989, Waldis went to work for AT&T in Bedminster, New Jersey, involved in technical and product management.

After three years with AT&T, Waldis decided to take a chance, leaving a giant corporation to join a small marketing company, Logical Design Solutions, where he became vice-president of sales and marketing. In just two years he grew sales from less than $2 million to more than $10 million. Then in 1994 he decided to strike out on his own and joined forces with another former AT&T employee, Jim McCormick, a computer science professional who had worked for Bell Laboratories. In 1988 McCormick had launched a software company called Vertek Corporation in Murray Hill, New Jersey. He and Waldis relaunched the business as a professional services and software company, each of them investing $5,000. Waldis served as chief operating officer.

The roots of Synchronoss grew out of a dinner conversation between Waldis and David E. Berry, another former AT&T employee, a software engineer who joined Vertek and like Waldis chaffed under the bureaucracy of a large company. "We always thought we could move faster and accomplish more if we got out from under the big corporation," Berry told the *Star-Ledger* of Newark, New Jersey. At a Bridgewater tavern, the two friends toyed with the idea of finding a better way to handle the customer transactions of telecommunications companies, like their former employer, AT&T. A few days later Waldis urged Berry, Vertek's lead software architect, to turn their musings into an actual business and to serve as the chief technology officer. "I always believed he could sell it," Berry told the *Star-Ledger*. "He always believed I could make it sail."

SYNCHRONOSS TAKES SHAPE: 2000

After developing a business plan, Waldis and Berry launched their new venture, which took the name Synchronoss Technologies, in 2000 under the wing of Vertek. It was not the best of times for the telecommunications industry, due to the sudden collapse of the entire technology sector, but tough times actually played to the benefit of a small start-up like Synchronoss because telecoms were looking for ways to cut costs, and outsourcing customer transactions was one obvious way to trim headcount and save money.

Synchronoss was still just a seven-employee operation when it was spun off from Vertek, with Waldis serving as CEO, and established offices in the Lehigh Valley Corporate Center in Northampton County, Pennsylvania. Both Waldis and Berry pledged their homes to back the loans needed to finance the business, and to cut corners Waldis even took out the trash for a time. But investors recognized that the company held promise, enough to attract $34 million in venture capital in 2001. The young company also attracted clients, in particular MCI Worldcom, resulting in revenues of $5.6 million in 2001.

MCI WORLDCOM BANKRUPTCY THREATENS COMPANY: 2002

Landing MCI Worldcom as its top client was a major development for Synchronoss that soon appeared to be a worst-case scenario. Mired in an accounting scandal, MCI Worldcom filed for Chapter 11 bankruptcy protection in July 2002, leaving Synchronoss unpaid. Some of the investors of the young company suggested that Waldis should simply shut down rather than throw good money after bad, but just a month later Synchronoss was able to convince the bankruptcy court that it should be designated a "critical vendor," the services of which were needed to keep the reorganizing company functioning. The court agreed, and as a result Synchronoss was paid in full for the services it rendered to MCI Worldcom as it went through bankruptcy. "We never lost a nickel," Waldis told the *Star-Ledger*.

While Synchronoss was working its way through the travails of the MCI Worldcom situation, it had already begun a small project with AT&T. This business grew larger in late 2002 when AT&T decided to use Synchronoss with AT&T Wireless, awarding the company another major contract. Sales totaled $8.2 million in 2002, but with the addition of AT&T for the entire year, that number swelled to $15 million in 2003. To keep pace with demand for its services, Synchronoss opened a pair of offices in 2003. One was located in Redmond, Washington, also the headquarters of AT&T Wireless. The other office was established in Branchburg, New Jersey.

A year later the corporate offices at the Lehigh Valley Corporate Center were converted into cubicles for customer service personnel, and the administrative staff was relocated to a new headquarters in Bridgewater, New Jersey. The extra space in Lehigh Valley was required to service the needs of new customers, much of it the result of the 2004 rollout of a VoIP-Enhanced Version of its ActivationNow platform, capable of end-to-end provision management, including order and

```
┌─────────────────────────────────────────┐
│                                           │
│            KEY DATES                      │
│            ─────■─────                     │
│  ┌─────────────────────────────────────┐ │
│  │ 2000: Synchronoss is founded in     │ │
│  │       Pennsylvania.                  │ │
│  │ 2001: Company raises $34 million    │ │
│  │       from venture capitalists.     │ │
│  │ 2004: Headquarters move to           │ │
│  │       Bridgewater, New Jersey.      │ │
│  │ 2006: Company goes public.           │ │
│  │ 2007: Synchronoss handles iPhone     │ │
│  │       activations.                   │ │
│  └─────────────────────────────────────┘ │
└─────────────────────────────────────────┘
```

inventory management, and local number portability (allowing consumers to use their old phone numbers with their new voice providers). One of the country's largest cable television systems, Cablevision, signed on, as did Level 3 Communications, a communications and services wholesaler whose network supported many of the United States' largest Internet service providers, plus cable TV companies (including AOL Time Warner), local carriers, and other companies offering VoIP LNP (local number portability) service.

Until this point most of Synchronoss's revenues came from wireless operators, and in 2004 the company was able to avoid losing the business of its major customer in this sector, AT&T Wireless, when it was acquired by Cingular Wireless. Instead of dropping the activation management service Synchronoss provided AT&T, Cingular was won over by the company's automatic online approach and awarded all of its business to Synchronoss. Given the cost savings of the Synchronoss approach, it was clearly not a difficult decision to make. Manual wireless activation services cost between $20 and $50. Using the Synchronoss online platform, the cost could be reduced to $8 to $10.

Revenues increased to $27.2 million in 2004 and the company narrowed its net loss to just $7,000. The following year sales nearly doubled to $54.2 million and Synchronoss turned profitable, netting $12.4 million. Synchronoss took advantage of its momentum to tap the equity market in 2006 and raise cash to fuel further growth. In addition to having the money needed to invest in technology and infrastructure, a strong balance sheet could also be used to reassure potential customers that Synchronoss was not a flash in the pan, a conclusion reinforced by a stellar roster of clients already trusting their business to Synchronoss. Moreover, with new services to market and increased competition, CSPs were eager to find ways to increase efficiency and save money.

IPO: 2006

With Goldman Sachs Group Inc. and Deutsche Bank AG acting as underwriters, the company's initial public offering (IPO) of stock was completed in June 2006, netting Synchronoss $53 million. However, Synchronoss was able to fetch only $8 a share, below its expected range of $9 to $11 due to a downturn in the tech sector. Waldis took a philosophical approach to the low IPO price, telling *NJBIZ,* "If you can get a deal done in a market like this, it becomes your friend. You should feel pretty good going forward because when it [the market] does correct itself, you'll be in pretty good shape down the road." Indeed, after dipping below the $8 opening price in subsequent weeks, the value of Synchronoss shares improved steadily, peaking above $48 per share in October 2007 before receding. For the year 2006 Synchronoss posted revenues of $72.4 million and net income of more than $10.1 million.

VALIDATION FOR COMPANY WITH IPHONE LAUNCH

The primary reason for the rise in the price of Synchronoss stock in 2007 was its participation in the much-hyped June launch of Apple's iPhone, done in conjunction with AT&T Wireless. According to *Forbes,* "Waldis first learned of the iPhone opportunity in the fall of 2006, when AT&T and Apple were in discussions to launch the device. Since Apple wanted to automate the activation system, Waldis says AT&T suggested using Synchronoss to develop the necessary back-office software." Once involved in the project, Synchronoss devoted months working with both Apple and AT&T to prepare for the launch, making sure it was ready to handle an unknown volume of activation transactions. The iPhone launch became a major event, so that during the peak hours of the weekend launch, Synchronoss was completing more than 1,000 activations each minute with very few problems. "It validated in a very public way what we already knew, what AT&T knew and what our employees knew: We have a very serious business model," Waldis told the *Star-Ledger.*

Shortly after the iPhone launch AT&T signed a multiyear contract with Synchronoss to continue supporting iPhone. Overall, the iPhone launch provided Synchronoss with the kind of publicity, including an interview of Waldis on CNBC, it could never hope to buy. The exposure opened doors to potential new customers who had previously required a good deal of courting before agreeing to a meeting. The company signed up Sprint Nextel, making it less dependent on its AT&T business. The iPhone connection also helped to pave the way for Synchronoss to begin operating in

Europe and other international markets in the fall of 2007.

For a while Synchronoss was a Wall Street darling, but after the price of its stock peaked in the autumn of 2007, investors began to have second thoughts, afraid in large part that the company was too dependent on AT&T, which accounted for 65 percent of revenue in 2006. That percentage would grow to 78 percent in the third quarter of 2007, inflated because of the 1.1 million iPhones the company activated between late June and mid-October. For the year, Synchronoss would record revenues of $123.5 million and net income of $23.8 million.

Some investors feared, and short-sellers hoped, that AT&T might decide to take subscriber activations in-house, a situation that could prove catastrophic. However, given the expense involved, and the complexity, it seemed unlikely AT&T would find it advantageous to sever its relationship with Synchronoss. Moreover, Synchronoss was committed to making sure the services it had to offer remained cost-effective, rendering it pointless to start an in-house operation. What was more likely was that Synchronoss would become less dependent on AT&T by growing its new relationship with Sprint Nextel, exploiting the triple- and quad-play packages offered by CSPs that were being embraced by residential customers, and expanding overseas, where it already had partners in place in

France, Germany, Spain, and the United Kingdom to launch its software platform.

Ed Dinger

PRINCIPAL COMPETITORS

Motive, Inc.; NeuStar, Inc.; VeriSign, Inc.

FURTHER READING

Bonner, Jeanne, "Hanover Township, Pa., Software Firm Makes Order Fulfillment More Efficient," *Allentown (Pa.) Morning Call,* November 5, 2003.

———, "Telecom Software Maker Moves from Hanover Township, Pa., to New Jersey," *Allentown (Pa.) Morning Call,* November 5, 2004.

"Go Public, Young Company," *NJBIZ,* July 24, 2006.

Johnson, Tom, "Striking It Big," *Newark (N.J.) Star-Ledger,* December 30, 2007.

Kitchens, Susan, "Hitched to Apple," *Forbes,* January 28, 2008, p. 56.

Perone, Joseph R., "AT&T Vet Finds Growth at Synchronoss," *Newark (N.J.) Star-Ledger,* June 22, 2006.

Philbin, Brett, "Synchronoss Aims Beyond iPhone," *Wall Street Journal,* January 16, 2008, p. B.3C.

Womack, Brian, "Buzz over Apple's iPhone Fuels Interest in Small Software Company," *Investor's Business Daily,* June 26, 2007.

TAQA North Ltd.

150 6th Avenue Southwest, Suite 5100
Calgary, Alberta T2P 3Y7
Canada
Telephone: (403) 234-6600
Toll Free: (877) 968-7878
Fax: (403) 266-2825
Web site: http://www.primewestenergy.com

Subsidiary of Abu Dhabi National Energy Company
Incorporated: 1996
Employees: 225
Sales: CAD 698.5 million (2006)
NAIC: 211111 Crude Petroleum and Natural Gas
Extraction; 533110 Owners and Lessors of Other
Non-Financial Assets; 551112 Offices of Other
Holding Companies

■ ■ ■

TAQA North Ltd., formerly known as PrimeWest
Energy Trust, is an oil and gas investment trust that
distributes nearly all its earnings to its shareholders,
referred to as unitholders. Through two affiliated
companies, PrimeWest Management Inc. and
PrimeWest Energy Inc., the trust acquires, develops,
produces, and sells crude oil and natural gas. TAQA
North ranks as one of the largest, natural gas-weighted
energy trusts in North America. The trust's properties
are located in western Canada, primarily in its home
province of Alberta, and in Montana, North Dakota,
and Wyoming. TAQA North's daily production is
66,000 barrels of oil equivalent. The trust's established

and probable reserves are 280 million barrels of oil
equivalent. TAQA North is a subsidiary of Abu Dhabi
National Energy Company, a company 74 percent
owned by the government of Abu Dhabi.

THE CONCEPT OF ENERGY TRUSTS

Energy trusts catered to an audience: the individual
investors they hoped to attract as unitholders. Exempt
from taxation at the corporate level, provided they
distributed nearly all their income to unitholders, energy
trusts emerged in Canada in the mid-1980s, giving
investors the opportunity to invest in the oil and gas
sector. Unit holders received dividend payments on a
quarterly or monthly basis, a portion of which was
exempt from taxation because it was considered a return
of capital by the Canadian government.

Initially, energy trusts received a lukewarm recep-
tion from industry pundits, considered by some to be a
dubious gimmick. The concept caught on, however,
eventually becoming a high-profile, well-respected
component of Canada's oil and gas industry. Less than
two decades after their debut, Canadian oil and gas
trusts accounted for one in every five barrels of production in the country. They also appeared often in the
headlines of the industry's press, attracting attention for
their heavy involvement in merger and acquisition
activity. The penchant for deal making exhibited by
trusts inspired the *Oil Daily*, in its September 20, 2002,
issue, to characterize energy trusts as "the great white
sharks of the Canadian oil patch." Trusts, typically, did
not explore for energy resources. Instead, they acquired

COMPANY PERSPECTIVES

PrimeWest's asset management strategy is to focus on its existing core areas and pursue depletion optimization strategies to maximize value. We control approximately 80 percent of our assets with the balance controlled by partner operators. This level of control allows us to use our existing infrastructure and create synergies within our core areas. It also allows us to control our costs and plan the timing of our capital investments and projects.

mature, producing properties, essentially functioning as a depleting asset that continually needed to acquire new reserves to sustain the flow of distributable earnings to its unitholders. Trusts were always on the move, scanning the industry for new properties to acquire to keep their operations afloat.

DEBUT OF THE PRIMEWEST FAMILY: 1996

Although energy trusts first appeared in Canada in 1986, the industry niche gained much of its recognition and population a decade later. Between 1996 and 1997, the concept of energy trusts became a popular idea, proliferating because of strong oil prices and dropping interest rates: the kindling for growth that the founders of PrimeWest Energy Trust exploited. In March 1996, the founders entered the fray, forming PrimeWest Management Inc., PrimeWest Energy Inc., and PrimeWest Energy Trust.

PrimeWest Energy Trust got its start with oil and gas properties purchased from Amoco Canada Petroleum. Except for one property located in British Columbia, the initial properties were located in PrimeWest Energy Trust's home province of Alberta. The properties, four primarily oil producers and three primarily gas producers, produced 7,512 barrels of oil equivalent (boe), a measurement used to express both oil and gas quantities as a single figure (one barrel of oil is equal to approximately 5,650 cubic feet of natural gas). The trust's largest source of oil revenue was the Kaybob Area in Alberta, which produced 1,567 boe per day (boe/d). The trust's largest source of gas revenue was the Crossfield property, also located in Alberta, which produced 1,330 boe/d. Investors were given their first chance to invest in the properties in October 1996, when the trust completed its initial public offering (IPO) of stock, raising proceeds of CAD 249 million.

THE STRUCTURE OF PRIMEWEST

As PrimeWest Energy Trust set out, it never made a move without the assistance of its two affiliated companies, PrimeWest Management Inc. and PrimeWest Energy Inc. The three companies were interdependent, each playing a specific role in turning oil and gas assets into income distributed to unitholders. PrimeWest Energy Inc. acquired the oil and gas properties and sold essentially all the economic interest in the properties to PrimeWest Energy Trust in the form of a royalty. PrimeWest Management Inc. functioned as the ringleader of the PrimeWest organization, taking responsibility for managing PrimeWest Energy Trust and PrimeWest Energy Inc., providing advisory, management, and administrative services to the two companies for which it collected management fees from the two companies. PrimeWest Management Inc. also performed another task, one that set the PrimeWest organization apart from nearly all other energy trusts. Instead of relying on industry partners to operate oil and gas properties, as most energy trusts did, the PrimeWest organization operated the assets it acquired, a responsibility assumed by PrimeWest Management Inc.

Amoco Canada operated the properties acquired by the PrimeWest organization for the last four months of 1996 and handed over control at the beginning of 1997. The year marked the first full year of PrimeWest Energy Trust's operation, and little time was wasted before the organization began to exhibit the predatory characteristics of its ilk. More than 350 percent of its oil and gas reserves were replaced during its first full year in business. PrimeWest Energy Trust intended to be heavily involved in merger and acquisition activity. The trust ended the year with production of 9,096 boe/d, which enabled it to pay distributable income of CAD 1.34 per unit.

PRIMEWEST LAUNCHES HOSTILE BIDS

PrimeWest Energy Trust made history in the energy trust sector during its second full year of operation, doing something none of the 18 energy trusts in operation had done. Through PrimeWest Energy Inc., the managers of the trust attempted to acquire two rivals, Starcor Energy Royalty Funds and Orion Energy Trust, both managed by Calgary-based Starvest Capital. The two trusts rebuffed PrimeWest Energy Trust's advances, which prompted management to launch the first hostile takeover in the industry in December 1998. The deal was completed the following year, a CAD 200 million transaction that lifted PrimeWest Energy Trust's established reserves from 45 million boe to 85 million

KEY DATES

1996: PrimeWest Energy Trust is formed.
1998: PrimeWest Energy Trust launches the first hostile takeover in the energy trust sector.
2001: Cypress Energy Inc. is acquired.
2004: The assets of Calpine Canada Natural Gas Partnership are acquired.
2006: PrimeWest Energy Trust enters the U.S. market for the first time.
2007: The combination of PrimeWest Energy Trust and Shiningbank Energy Income Fund is a CAD 1.25 billion merger.
2008: PrimeWest Energy Trust is acquired by Abu Dhabi National Energy Company, becoming TAQA North Ltd. as a result of the transaction.

boe and increased its production from 12,000 boe/d to 21,000 boe/d.

The trust's next major move occurred in early 2000, when an additional 34 percent interest was acquired in the Crossfield natural gas processing plant and associated gathering system in Alberta. The purchase, which increased ownership in the Crossfield property to 54 percent, made the trust's portfolio weighted toward gas holdings. The trust's emphasis on gas holdings was increased substantially the following year, when Cypress Energy Inc. was acquired in March 2001. The CAD 790 million acquisition vaulted PrimeWest Energy Trust into the upper echelon of energy trusts, adding production of 18,200 boe/d. The acquisition also made PrimeWest Energy Trust the largest, gas-weighted trust in Canada.

The trust's managers stayed on the offensive, steadily adding to their reserves to ensure PrimeWest Energy Trust remained a premier energy trust. In 2003, the trust's position as a gas-focused concern was strengthened with purchase of gas and oil properties in the Caroline and Peace River Arch areas of Alberta. The CAD 206 million transaction added 6,800 boe/d, 83 percent of which was gas. In 2004, two notable acquisitions were completed, beginning with purchase of Seventh Energy Ltd. in March. For CAD 34.8 million, PrimeWest Energy Trust gained 1,300 boe/d. In September, a purchase that rivaled the magnitude of the Cypress Energy acquisition was completed when the assets of Calpine Canada Natural Gas Partnership were acquired. The transaction, a CAD 740 million deal,

added 14,500 boe/d in production and 54 million boe in established and probable reserves.

On the eve of its tenth anniversary, PrimeWest Energy Trust could look back on a decade of substantial progress. Production increased from 7,512 boe/d at the trust's inception to 40,351 boe/d by 2005. Reserves during the period increased from 36.2 million boe to 154.6 million boe. The constant focus on increasing reserves and daily production totals lifted revenue to CAD 801.2 million in 2005, from which the trust paid CAD 3.66 per unit, an impressive increase from the CAD 1.34 per unit distributed at the end of 1996.

PrimeWest Energy Trust had momentum on its side as it completed its first decade of business, a decade that marked the end of an era for the Calgary-based organization. The trust tapped into the U.S. market for the first time in mid-2006, gaining entry through a $300 million acquisition of oil and gas assets in Montana, North Dakota, and Wyoming. The purchase increased production by 3,200 boe/d. International expansion would have been the biggest story of the year for PrimeWest Energy Trust, but the border-crossing move was overshadowed by a stunning announcement. PrimeWest Energy Trust, as well as every other energy trust in Canada, was shocked by the revelation that its days were numbered.

BAD NEWS IN 2006

In late 2006, in an announcement that must have soured tenth anniversary celebrations in Calgary, Canada's finance minister, Jim Flaherty, declared energy trusts would be subjected to taxation beginning in January 2011. The proliferation of energy trusts in the 1990s and the early 21st century, Flaherty argued, had stripped the Canadian government and provincial governments of vital tax receipts. Energy trusts, not surprisingly, were opposed to Flaherty's proposed legislation. A newly formed Coalition of Canadian Energy Trusts, a 40-member group of which PrimeWest Energy Trust was a member, was lobbying against the prospect of taxation, arguing the energy trusts exploited oil and gas reserves conventional corporations considered uneconomical.

The looming threat of taxation did nothing to diminish PrimeWest Energy Trust's interest in further deal making. In May 2007, the largest transaction in the trust's history was announced, a CAD 1.25 billion merger with Shiningbank Energy Income Fund. Primarily a gas producer, Shiningbank had proved reserves of 57.5 million boe in western Alberta. The combination of the two concerns created a major force in the oil and gas industry, boosting PrimeWest Energy Trust's proved and probable reserves to 280 million boe and lifting its production to 66,000 boe/d, 70 percent of which was natural gas.

PrimeWest Energy Trust barely had time to settle into its new arrangement before arguably the most significant event in its history radically altered its future course. For more than a decade, the PrimeWest organization had displayed a voracious appetite for swallowing up assets, but its efforts on the acquisition front paled in comparison to a relative newcomer in the oil and gas industry. Abu Dhabi National Energy Company, a company commonly referred to as "TAQA," was on a buying spree as PrimeWest Energy Trust and Shiningbank inked their deal, intent on becoming one of the world's largest oil and gas producers. Formed in 2005, TAQA was 75 percent owned by the government of Abu Dhabi. The company wasted little time before developing substantial interests in oil and gas, power and water generation, and infrastructure industries throughout the Middle East, Africa, India, Europe, and North America. By 2007, TAQA executives were determined to build a large presence in western Canada. Midway through the year, the company spent CAD 2 billion to acquire Calgary-based Northrock Resources. In August, TAQA paid CAD 540 million for the Canadian assets belonging to U.S.-based Pioneer Natural Resources. In September, the company set its sights on PrimeWest Energy Trust, announcing what would be its largest Canadian acquisition.

A new era began for the PrimeWest organization in January 2008, one that would be conducted under the name TAQA North. TAQA completed its acquisition of PrimeWest Energy Trust midway through the month, paying CAD 5 billion for the 12-year-old trust. The president and chief executive officer of PrimeWest Energy Inc. became the chief executive officer of TAQA North. As the process of integrating the assets was underway, a new oil and gas giant had emerged in western Canada, one that drew much of its might from the assets of the PrimeWest organization. TAQA North boasted reserves exceeding 480 million boe and produc-

tion of 105,000 boe/d, making it one of the ten largest companies in Canada in terms of proven natural gas reserves and one of the 12 largest in terms of oil and gas production.

Jeffrey L. Covell

PRINCIPAL SUBSIDIARIES

PrimeWest Energy Inc.; PrimeWest Petroleum Inc.; PrimeWest Energy Development ULC; PrimeWest Oil LLC.

PRINCIPAL COMPETITORS

Peyto Energy Trust; Baytex Energy Trust; Provident Energy Trust.

FURTHER READING

Gosmano, Jeff, "Deal Making Returns Among Canada's Trusts," *Oil Daily,* May 11, 2007.

Heckathorn, Mark E., "PrimeWest Buyout of Cypress Tops Recent M&A List in Canada," *Natural Gas Week,* April 2, 2001, p. 16.

Lehmann, Richard, "High-Dividend Oil Trusts," *Forbes,* October 17, 2005, p. 128.

Merolli, Paul, "Another Big Canada Buy for Abu Dhabi," *Oil Daily,* September 25, 2007.

———, "Fire Sales Blaze On at Battered Merchants Calpine, NRG," *Oil Daily,* September 20, 2002.

Pike, David, "Trust Takeover Attempt Sparks Battle in Canada," *Oil Daily,* January 7, 1999.

"PrimeWest Closes Purchase," *Oil Daily,* January 27, 2003.

"PrimeWest Closes US Deal," *Oil Daily,* July 10, 2006.

"PrimeWest Completes Acquisition," *Oil Daily,* January 7, 2000.

"PrimeWest Energy Trust Successful in Bid for Reserve Royalty Corporation," *Canadian Corporate News,* July 27, 2000.

"TAQA Completes Acquisition of PrimeWest Energy Trust," *Middle East and North Africa Business Report,* January 17, 2008.

Tarmac

Tarmac Limited

Millfields Road
Ettingshall
Wolverhampton, West Midlands WV4 6JP
United Kingdom
Telephone: (+44 1902) 353522
Fax: (+44 1902) 353920
Web site: http://www.tarmac.co.uk

Wholly Owned Subsidiary of Anglo American plc
Incorporated: 1903 as Tar-Macadam (Purnell Hooley's Patent) Syndicate Limited
Employees: 12,500
Sales: $4.59 billion (2007)
NAIC: 212312 Crushed and Broken Limestone Mining and Quarrying; 212319 Other Crushed and Broken Stone Mining and Quarrying; 212321 Construction Sand and Gravel Mining; 212322 Industrial Sand Mining; 237310 Highway, Street, and Bridge Construction; 238120 Structural Steel and Precast Concrete Contractors; 324121 Asphalt Paving Mixture and Block Manufacturing; 327310 Cement Manufacturing; 327320 Ready-Mix Concrete Manufacturing; 327331 Concrete Block and Brick Manufacturing; 327390 Other Concrete Product Manufacturing; 327410 Lime Manufacturing

∎ ∎ ∎

Tarmac Limited is the largest supplier of building materials in the United Kingdom and one of the leading companies in that sector in Europe. The firm produces a variety of products used in the construction of build-

ings, bridges, roads, ports, harbors, and airports, including aggregates, mortar, screeds, ready-mixed concrete, asphalt, and precast concrete products. In addition to supplying building materials, Tarmac is active in contracting as well, including the laying and maintaining of roadways and the provision of fencing, lighting, signage, and traffic management solutions. While the United Kingdom remains Tarmac's core market, the firm has additional operations in Belgium, the Czech Republic, France, Germany, Poland, Romania, Spain, Turkey, the Middle East, and China. Founded in 1903, Tarmac has operated as a wholly owned subsidiary of global mining and natural resources giant Anglo American plc since 2000.

FOUNDED THROUGH INVENTION OF TARMAC

In 1901 the county surveyor of Nottingham, E. Purnell Hooley, noticed a dustless, unrutted patch of road as he was leaving an ironworks. Inquiries revealed that a barrel of tar had burst and the spillage had been covered with slag. Immediately grasping its potential, Hooley began to experiment. A British patent for the process of mixing tar with slag was obtained in 1903, and by the middle of the year a length had been laid in an area where traffic was particularly heavy. In the following year a local newspaper, the *Newark Advertiser,* reported that the area was "as good today as when new." The new material was christened "tarmac."

In conjunction with John Parker, Hooley incorporated Tar-Macadam (Purnell Hooley's Patent) Syndicate Limited in June 1903 and became its chairman. Despite the support of the natural roadstone

COMPANY PERSPECTIVES

Our mission: To be the first choice for building materials that meet the essential needs for the sustainable development of the world in which we live.

industry, for whom Hooley's invention was simply a profitable way of selling aggregate, the syndicate began to fail. An agreement with Alfred Hickman Ltd., a large ironworks, forced Parker and Hooley to relinquish a large part of their holding in exchange for an injection of capital by Hickman. In 1905 Hickman took control and changed the syndicate's name to Tarmac Limited. Parker resigned, but Hooley was retained as a consultant on a large fee.

With increased use of automobiles at the beginning of the century, the road covering industry boomed. Unlike all its competitors, Tarmac Ltd. confined itself to one product: tarmac. When Douglas G. Comyn was made secretary in 1908, Tarmac was well established within the road building and slag industries. In 1913, to raise capital for the expansion of its transport stock, the company was liquidated and the assets transferred to a new company. As part of this reorganization, Tarmac was taken public with a listing on the Birmingham Stock Exchange.

Tarmac's profits fell 25 percent during World War I as a result of cuts in government road expenditure. Comyn's friendship with the head of the government's road board led to Tarmac's being given contracts to supply the crushed slag needed to build roads through French battlefields. Newly erected works in Yorkshire were handed over for military use, the acute labor shortage being compensated for by several hundred German prisoners of war.

By 1918 Tarmac was drawing up plans for large-scale expansion. The intention to build crushed-slag depots and adjacent tarmac plants on the south coast, owing to a fear of overproduction of slag in the northeast, was thwarted by the high cost of sea freight. Comyn was, however, generally optimistic about postwar demand, having determined government plans to increase road expenditure. In 1919 the company bought existing slag tips in the Midlands and erected new coating plants nearby. Tarmac's first natural stone quarry, Ffrith in north Wales, was acquired in 1919 but was never developed and was sold in 1951. In 1919 the company also began diversification within the construction industry. The acquisition of the patent on Vincu-

lum, a process for binding the raw materials of concrete using waste slag dust, led to a contract to build houses in Wolverhampton and Birmingham, and the Vinculum division was established.

The 1920s began with extensive geographical and production capacity expansion. This heavy spending on acquisitions and expansion of railroad stock created a need for more capital. At the same time, the price of tarmac was falling despite a sharp increase in the cost of tar caused in large part by the occupation of the Ruhr, which was a major source of this substance. Comyn refused to raise the price of tarmac, believing that the company and his business connections were sufficiently established to survive a period of poor sales, while Tarmac's smaller competitors would fail. Comyn retired in 1926 because of ill health in the only year that Tarmac made a loss until 1992.

EXPANDING INTO CIVIL ENGINEERING BETWEEN THE WARS

Comyn's successor, Cecil Martin, reacted to the decline in sales by halving directors' salaries and reducing head office staff numbers by 20 percent. The company was reorganized, and in 1929 a civil engineering division was established. It engaged in road construction and the building of military airfields. An experiment in shipping precoated tarmac from northeast plants to Gravesend was unsuccessful, and it was decided to revert to Comyn's plans to build coating plants on the south coast. Preemption by Tarmac's largest rival, Crow Catchpole, which it later acquired, left Tarmac owning only three seaboard plants and with too much slag to dispose of. A series of convoluted deals with rival companies averted potentially crippling losses.

The early 1930s proved to be a stable period for Tarmac. A new product, Settite (bitumen macadam), believed to be superior to slag-based tarmac for road covering, was introduced in 1932. Diversifications into gravel and asphalt production were not successful, but were compensated for by the new spirit of camaraderie among mutually dependent industries. An important feature of this period was the price cooperation among blacktop producers. Whereas Comyn had sought to outwit his competitors, Martin favored a more amicable approach and was respected in the industry as a man of integrity. His efforts to help create a federation of slag producers in 1934 were rewarded eventually by a price agreement that guaranteed profits on the northeast slag plants. This brought new and lucrative contracts to the company.

KEY DATES

1903: E. Purnell Hooley and John Parker form Tar-Macadam (Purnell Hooley's Patent) Syndicate Limited to commercialize Hooley's invention of tarmac, a road-building material made from slag and tar.

1905: Alfred Hickman takes control of the syndicate, which is renamed Tarmac Limited.

1913: Tarmac is reorganized and taken public with a listing on the Birmingham Stock Exchange.

1919: Company ventures into construction industry with purchase of the patent on Vinculum, a process for making reinforced concrete blocks using waste slag dust.

1929: Civil engineering division is established to engage in road construction and the building of military airfields.

1958: Tarmac finishes construction of Britain's first motorway.

1959: Company acquires Crow Catchpole, a London-based rival, and Tarslag, a major Midlands-based road materials company.

1968: Tarmac merges with Derbyshire Stone and William Briggs & Son to form Tarmac Derby.

1971: "Derby" is dropped from the company name; Tarmac becomes the largest road surfacing contractor and blacktop producer in the United Kingdom via acquisition of Limmer and Trinidad Limited.

1974: Company establishes a housing and properties division following the purchase of John McLean and Sons Limited, a leading U.K. house-builder.

1987: Following a string of acquisitions, Tarmac America is established as the firm's U.S. arm.

1996: Tarmac swaps its housing division for George Wimpey PLC's quarrying and contracting businesses, leaving the firm with two core businesses: heavy building materials and construction services.

1999: Tarmac demerges into a new Tarmac plc, which concentrates on heavy building materials, and Carillion plc, specializing in construction services.

2000: In a £1.1 billion ($1.9 billion) deal, Anglo American plc acquires Tarmac and makes it a wholly owned subsidiary under the name Tarmac Limited; Tarmac America is divested.

2007: Anglo American announces its intention to sell Tarmac.

2008: Anglo temporarily shelves its plan to divest Tarmac.

By 1935 Tarmac's three divisions—roadstone, civil engineering, and Vinculum—were well established, although the company image was still predominantly that of a slag business. Whereas World War 1 had been difficult for Tarmac, World War II infused new life into the company. The occupation of France presaged the need for more airports in the United Kingdom, and Tarmac gained contracts from the U.S. Army and Air Force. Because military demand for tarmac was greater than for asphalt, the company's profits rose by more than 30 percent in the first year of the war, and by 43 percent in the second. By this time, the company had plants in northern England, north Wales, and Scotland, as well as a large transport stock. The increased mechanization of its plants compensated for the labor shortage. The civil engineering division won government contracts of £6 million and produced five million tons of road and runway material during the war. The Vinculum division also benefited from government demand for concrete blocks to build air raid shelters.

Despite steadily declining orders after August 1944, Tarmac anticipated an upsurge in demand as a result of the government's rearmament program. Tarmac consequently embarked on a £2 million program of reinvestment and development. New plants were commissioned in Yorkshire in 1949, existing plants were reconstructed and mechanized, and the transport stock was entirely replaced.

POSTWAR EXPANSION

In 1954 the company pursued considerable and risky expansion. A new iron foundry was being built in the northeast, and Tarmac proposed to build a massive works, including a wharf for ships of up to 3,000 tons, to deal with the slag produced. In the same year the company stepped up its transport conversion program, replacing rail wagons with trucks. With the promise of a contract in 1956 to build Britain's first, eight-mile stretch of motorway, which the firm completed in December 1958, Tarmac was in need of capital. A rights issue raised £1 million to pay for this growth.

Cecil Martin decided to retire on his 65th birthday in 1957. No chairman was appointed during the period of reorganization that followed Martin's retirement, although his son, Robin, was made managing director of the roadstone division. It was decided to make Tarmac into a holding company with three main subsidiaries: Tarmac Roadstone, Tarmac Civil Engineering, and Tarmac Vinculum. Most of the group's profits came from Tarmac Roadstone. Robin Martin, who managed the subsidiary, had inherited a sound business, albeit one with geographical gaps and no natural stone resources.

A proposed merger of Tarmac and its largest rivals, Amalgamated Roadstone Corporation and Crow Catchpole (a large London-based tar distiller), broke down in 1958, but Tarmac bought Crow Catchpole the following year. With a toehold in London and the southeast, Tarmac entered another phase of growth. The 1959 acquisition of Tarslag, a major Midlands-based road materials company, marked Tarmac's first major quarrying venture, and the company rapidly became one of the three largest quarry owners in the Midlands. The consequent boost to Tarmac's construction activities led to the formation in 1960 of an industrial division. Further expansion was restricted during this period to allow the company to focus on internal restructuring and the formation of a series of localized construction teams.

Robin Martin became group managing director in 1963, when the worst winter weather in 100 years threatened to slow considerably the output of all Tarmac's divisions. Strains on finance and problems with integration of Tarmac's divided structure, coupled with government cuts in roadwork expenditure, dampened the optimism of the early 1960s. In anticipation of a decline in the availability of slag, Tarmac sought to strengthen its quarrying resources. The group's overdependence on slag sales was relieved by the acquisition in 1966 of three large granite quarries in the north. Having secured the market for natural stone, Tarmac concentrated on procuring supplies of bitumen, its other main raw material. The opening in conjunction with Phillips Petroleum of Oklahoma of a refinery in Cheshire secured Tarmac's supply of bitumen. In October 1968 the company merged with Derbyshire Stone and William Briggs & Son, a large bitumen and building materials supplier and contractor in Scotland. Following the merger, the company operated under the

name Tarmac Derby until early 1971. Over the decade of the 1960s, group profits increased sixfold.

FURTHER DIVERSIFICATION

With Tarmac's 1971 takeover of Limmer and Trinidad Limited, a London-based quarry products business with an asphalt lake in Trinidad, it became the largest road surfacing contractor and blacktop producer in the United Kingdom. The acquisition of Limmer marked the beginning of another period of diversification, particularly in Tarmac's quest to develop strength in the brick and concrete production markets. A growing need for a wider range of aggregates, including sand and gravel, and the acquisitions of several large hybrid companies, precipitated another company reorganization. The existing roadstone and bitumen divisions were renamed quarry products and building products, to more accurately reflect their activities. Two new divisions were formed from the construction division, and by the middle of the 1970s Tarmac was operating in five divisions: quarry products, building products, construction, properties and housing, and international. The regrouping reflected not only a new administrative strategy but also an attempt to change Tarmac's image. Known traditionally as a road surfacing contractor and producer of blacktop, the company was keen to reaffirm its position as a broad-based construction and building materials producer.

The company's activities during the 1970s are difficult to evaluate. It was a period of dramatic expansion against a background of economic instability in Britain. The housing and properties division was established in 1974, following the acquisition of John McLean and Sons Limited, a leading house-builder, at the beginning of the year. Within a few years, and without any major acquisitions, Tarmac became the third largest house-builder in Britain. Eric Pountain, chairman of the Tarmac group, joined the company as chief executive of McLeans and became chief executive of the housing division. Under his leadership and with a policy of slow expansion and rigid financial controls, the housing division thrived. By the end of the decade one-third of Tarmac's profits came from house-building. The division became the management model for the rest of the company and set the precedent for the decentralization program at the end of the decade. The housing division prospered despite adverse economic conditions. The construction division continued its program of rapid expansion and diversification throughout the 1970s.

On the other hand, with the potential for growth in the United Kingdom restricted by the threat of recession, Tarmac began bidding for companies with established assets overseas. Having developed specialist construction skills in marine, soft, and rock tunneling with the takeovers of Mitchell Construction and Kinear Moodie in 1971, Tarmac seemed well placed to expand abroad. The new international division was set up to oversee the group's foreign projects. Few of the construction division's efforts on this front were successful, and it was not until the mid-1980s that the division began to recover from the ill effects of entering too many high-risk ventures abroad. The acquisition of the Holland Hannen and Cubitts construction company in 1976 was a cautionary event in Tarmac's history of foreign investment; Cubitts Nigeria, a failing African asset that had been overlooked at the time of acquisition, had to be sold. It cost Tarmac £16 million.

Despite a successful joint venture with the Egyptian company Arab Contractors in 1977 to build a tunnel under the Suez Canal and participation in a long-term international consortium on an irrigation scheme in Peru, Tarmac withdrew from most of its overseas projects, having incurred several significant losses. By the end of the decade the performance of the construction division was threatening the stability of the Tarmac group. The company's growing dependence on its housing and quarry products divisions at a time when the almost static British economy was adversely affecting the construction industry precipitated a dramatic fall in the share price in 1977.

KEY REORGANIZATION: 1979

Overall, the events of the 1970s, although potentially disastrous for Tarmac, prompted the reorganization that made the company the largest in its field in the United Kingdom by the late 1980s. After a purge of top management in 1979, Eric Pountain was appointed chief executive of the Tarmac group. He had distinguished himself as director of the housing division, and it generally was accepted that the growth of this division, despite an unfavorable economy, was almost entirely attributable to Pountain's management style and commitment to decentralization. He was the only director with previous experience as chief executive of a public company. He had joined Tarmac, he said, to make a big business work like a small business. Pountain's was an attitude strongly endorsed by Prime Minister Margaret Thatcher's government when it came to power in 1979. In 1985 Pountain was knighted in recognition of his determination that Tarmac succeed despite the precarious economy of the early 1980s.

The most significant change at Tarmac under Pountain's leadership was the implementation of the decentralization program. Convinced that the company's difficulties in the previous decade were the result of poor management, Pountain implemented a strategy that made the housing division Britain's largest house-builder ten years after its inception. Believing that divisional managers were better placed to assess prospective acquisitions than a board of directors, responsibility for growth and diversification was handed down to individual divisions. Decentralized organization clearly benefited the company, with profits increasing tenfold over the decade.

Reluctant to depend on domestic markets alone, and in view of the slow growth potential for the construction and quarrying industries in the United Kingdom, Tarmac in 1980 embarked on an expensive and ambitious program of acquisitions and development in the United States. The acquisition of the Hoveringham Group in 1981 marked the company's entry into the brick, tile, building block, and concrete markets. Hoveringham owned quarries in the United States and its takeover gave Tarmac a firm quarrying base in the United States. The £150 million acquisition of Lone Star Industries' ready-mix and concrete block plants in Florida in 1984, and the takeover of a large underwater limestone quarry at Pennsuco, gave Tarmac control of 10 percent of Florida's total aggregate, or natural stone, output. With a source of stone assured, the company began buying ready-mix concrete and brick-building plants throughout the southern states. In 1986 Tarmac paid £263 million for a 60 percent share in Lone Star Industries, and the following year Tarmac America was established. Several smaller plant and quarry acquisitions followed, giving Tarmac a significant standing in the U.S. aggregates and concrete industries. Nevertheless, falling oil prices in Texas and severe weather conditions in Virginia in the late 1980s disrupted Tarmac America's activities, and by the end of the decade the division represented only one-fifth of the group's total turnover.

Over the same period the housing division increased its output from 4,000 homes in 1980 to 11,000 in 1987, contributing with the quarry products division more than three-quarters of the group's turnover. Diversification within the building products division led to the creation of the industrial products division with roofing, construction, and oil interests in both the United Kingdom and the United States.

SHARP DOWNTURN AND MAJOR RESTRUCTURING

By the late 1980s Tarmac's diversification strategy of the previous 20 years had given the company a leading presence in many industrial sectors. At the same time, however, the company's expansion into the U.K. housing market and its broad expansion in the United States turned nearly disastrous after the U.K. and U.S. construction markets collapsed in the late 1980s. The company's policy of decentralization also proved troublesome as central management was unable to respond quickly to the property recession and pull-back on land purchases for housing and commercial property joint ventures. The result was a 1992 pretax loss of £350.3 million, the largest ever recorded in the U.K. construction industry, a deep downfall from the heady days of 1988, when Tarmac posted pretax profits of £393 million. Early in 1992, Neville Simms was appointed chief executive, having previously served as head of the construction division. Pountain remained nonexecutive chairman until early 1994, when John Banham took over that position.

Simms was charged with restructuring the company and fixing a balance sheet that had become dangerously debt-loaded. Tarmac's new strategy involved a concentration on three core areas: house-building, construction, and quarry products. A number of peripheral businesses were sold and by early 1994, 21 businesses had been divested, representing nearly £1 billion in turnover. Among the jettisoned operations were the commercial property development activities. By mid-1995 Tarmac also had exited from brick making. Through severe cost-containment efforts and the divestment program, the company was able to effect a substantial reduction in debt, cutting it from £677 million. The company also reinstated a greater degree of central control over investments by its units.

1996 JETTISONING OF HOUSE-BUILDING DIVISION

Tarmac's results improved to an after-tax loss of £58.8 million in 1993, followed by an after-tax profit of £74.7 million in 1994. Nonetheless, the company was barely profitable in 1995 and 1996, and even more dramatic changes were to come as management attempted to turn the group's fortunes around. In August 1995 Tarmac announced that it would sell its house-building division to concentrate on its building materials and other construction activities. Then in November of that year Tarmac and George Wimpey PLC, a U.K. house-building firm, reached an agreement on a £600 million asset swap, completed in March 1996, whereby Tarmac exchanged its housing division for Wimpey's quarrying and contracting businesses. Through this one deal, Tarmac was able to exit from a sector that had nearly caused its collapse, while at the same time bolster its two remaining core areas.

Wimpey Minerals was one of the leading producers of U.K. construction materials and was the fifth largest aggregates producer and fifth largest coated stone producer in the United Kingdom. The unit also had significant operations in the United States, and smaller operations in the Republic of Ireland, the Czech Republic, the Middle East, and the Far East. Wimpey Minerals had revenues of £266.1 million and operating profits of £6.4 million in 1994. Wimpey Construction was one of the leading construction businesses in the United Kingdom, engaging in a wide range of building and civil engineering activities, with overseas activities in Canada and the Middle East. In 1994 the unit generated revenues of £667.7 million while posting an operating loss of £10.5 million. Soon after the swap, Tarmac cut more than 1,400 jobs from its workforce in a rapid rationalization of the merged businesses.

FAILED MERGER, THEN A DEMERGER OF CONSTRUCTION SERVICES

Tarmac returned to more robust profitability in 1997 and 1998, posting after-tax profits of £80.7 million and £92 million, respectively. Pressure from shareholders, who were concerned over a falling stock price, coupled with a trend toward consolidation in the building materials industry, led to discussions in late 1998 between Tarmac and rival U.K. building materials firm Aggregate Industries about a merger to create one of the largest U.K. building materials companies. These talks made substantial progress, including a plan to spin off Tarmac's construction division following the merger, but in December 1998 the deal fell apart, due in part to disagreements over Simms's role in what would have been called Tarmac Aggregate International. The acrimonious end to the proposal led to further shareholder rancor.

Continuing to feel pressure to increase shareholder value, the company responded in February 1999 with an announcement of a plan to demerge its two core areas, heavy building materials and construction services, into two separately traded public companies. When the demerger was completed on July 30, 1999, the heavy building materials unit retained the Tarmac plc name, with Banham serving as nonexecutive chairman and Roy Harrison, head of the unit, becoming chief executive. Simms was named chairman and chief executive of the new construction services company, Carillion plc. Shareholders received one share of the "new" Tarmac and one share in Carillion for every five shares of the "old" Tarmac they had held. Both companies' shares were listed on the London Stock Exchange.

ACQUISITION BY ANGLO AMERICAN IN 2000

The highly focused Tarmac launched a new phase of growth targeting smaller acquisitions adding up to no more than £100 million per year. This initiative had barely begun when the British/South African mining giant Anglo American plc began pursuing a takeover of Tarmac. The initial offer of £5.35 per share, or approximately £1.1 billion ($1.9 billion) in total, was rejected, but Tarmac in November 1999 accepted a sweetened offer of £5.85 per share. When this £1.2 billion deal was completed in March 2000, Tarmac began operating as a wholly owned subsidiary of Anglo American under the name Tarmac Limited.

Following the takeover, Tarmac was bolstered at home by amalgamating with Anglo's existing U.K. industrial minerals division. The head of this division, Robbie Robertson, was named chief executive of Tarmac. While Anglo intended to keep and build up Tarmac's continental European operations, Tarmac America was immediately identified as noncore and put up for sale. Tarmac America had generated revenues of $480 million in 1998 from the sale of aggregates, ready-mix concrete, cement, and concrete products. Anglo American sold the U.S. unit in the latter months of 2000 to Titan Cement S.A. of Greece for $636 million. The divestment of Tarmac America left Tarmac with operations in the United Kingdom, continental Europe, and Hong Kong/China.

Over the next few years, Tarmac used the deep pockets of its parent to complete dozens of acquisitions. Most of the acquired businesses were in the United Kingdom or continental Europe, including in Spain, France, Germany, the Czech Republic, and Poland. Among the most noteworthy purchases were those of the aggregates and ready-mix concrete assets of the Mavike Group in Spain (2002) and David W. Gordon Ltd. (2004), one of the leading concrete block producers in Scotland. The 2004 acquisition of Zapadokamen made Tarmac the leading supplier of high-quality construction aggregates in the Czech Republic.

Subsequent purchases bolstered the company's operations in both Poland and the Czech Republic, while its position in central Europe grew further in early 2006 with the acquisition of a majority stake in CMG srl, later renamed Tarmac SRL, a leading Romanian producer of aggregates and ready-mix concrete. Tarmac entered Turkey, another emerging market in Europe, also in 2006. In the meantime, organic growth was on the agenda as well, with the opening in 2004 of a new £110 million state-of-the-art cement plant in Buxton, England, that had an annual capacity of 800,000 metric tons. At the end of that year, production commenced at the firm's Yang Quarry, which was situated 140 kilometers from Shanghai and began filling China's burgeoning demand for top-quality asphalt aggregates.

In early 2006, after selling its concrete business in India, Tarmac announced plans to divest several other operations identified as "underperforming," including its Hong Kong business, some noncore assets in Germany, and its U.K. concrete paving business. The disposals were largely complete by the end of the year. This restructuring, which focused Tarmac principally on aggregates, asphalt, ready-mix concrete, and concrete products and also aimed to reduce the company's annual operating costs by $50 million, cost its Anglo parent $278 million in 2006, a year in which Tarmac's operating profit fell 7 percent to $315 million. Tarmac's revenues for 2006 were just over $4 billion, up 6 percent from the 2005 total. Robertson retired from the company at the end of 2006. Taking over as chief executive in October 2006 was David Weston, who had been president of Shell Products Canada Limited.

As Tarmac's overhaul was carried out, Anglo American itself was in the midst of a major restructuring through which it intended to more narrowly focus on mining base metals, platinum group metals, and iron ore. In August 2007 Anglo announced plans to sell Tarmac as the final stage of this restructuring. Bids of more than $6 billion were expected, with potential suitors including CRH plc of Ireland, France's Lafarge S.A., and the Mexican firm CEMEX S.A. de C.V., along with private-equity players. Anglo's plans, however, were undermined by the global credit crunch that arose around this same time, and in early 2008 the company announced its decision to postpone the sale of Tarmac until the return of more normal credit markets. Tarmac, in the meantime, operated strongly in 2007, posting an operating profit of $474 million, up 38 percent from 2006 (when taking out gains from exchange rate differences), on revenues of $4.59 billion. Looking forward, Tarmac was facing the prospect of a likely downturn in the U.K. housing market and a slowdown in road building but was anticipating a boost in business from construction projects related to the 2012 Olympics, slated for London.

Juliette Bright
Updated, David E. Salamie

PRINCIPAL SUBSIDIARIES

Tarmac Precast Limited; Tarmac Topfloor Limited; Tarmac Topblock Limited; United Marine Holdings Ltd.; Tarmac France SA; Lausitzer Grauwacke GmbH (Germany); Tarmac Iberia SA (Spain); WKSM SA (Poland); Tarmac CZ a.s. (Czech Republic); Tarmac SRL (Romania; 60%); Koca Beton Agrega Mining and Construction Industry and Trading Company Limited (Turkey).

PRINCIPAL OPERATING UNITS

Tarmac Aggregate Products; Tarmac Building Products; Tarmac International.

PRINCIPAL COMPETITORS

CRH plc; Aggregate Industries UK Limited; HeidelbergCement AG; Lafarge S.A.; Colas S.A.; Italcementi S.p.A.; CEMEX S.A. de C.V.

FURTHER READING

Bream, Rebecca, "Anglo to Launch Sale of Tarmac," *Financial Times,* August 3, 2007, p. 15.

Brodie, Sophie, "Anglo Shelves Sale of Tarmac," *Sunday Telegraph* (London), January 6, 2008, p. 2.

Davidson, Andrew, "Neville Simms," *Management Today,* March 1994, pp. 60–62.

Dyer, Geoff, "Ibstock Acquires Tarmac Brick," *Financial Times,* May 13, 1995, p. 8.

Earle, J. B. F., *Black Top: A History of the British Flexible Roads Industry,* Oxford: Asphalt & Coated Macadam Association, 1974.

———, *A Century of Road Materials: The History of the Roadstone Division of Tarmac Ltd.,* Oxford: Tarmac Ltd., 1971.

Fifty Years of Progress, 1903–1953, Ettingshall, Wolverhampton, England: Tarmac, 1953, 57 p.

Larsen, Peter Thal, "Tarmac Excavates to Uncover the Value Hidden from View," *Financial Times,* June 16, 1999, p. 34.

Malkani, Gautam, "Tarmac Agrees Bid from Anglo American," *Financial Times,* November 6, 1999, p. 17.

Parker, Akweli, "Greek Firm to Buy Tarmac," *Norfolk (Va.) Virginian Pilot,* August 29, 2000, p. D1.

Pretzlik, Charles, "Advisers Try to Revive Tarmac Aggregate Deal," *Financial Times,* January 28, 1999, p. 32.

———, "Jealousy Ruins the Construction of a Special Relationship," *Financial Times,* December 16, 1998, p. 25.

———, "Tarmac Rationalises by Splitting Units," *Financial Times,* February 3, 1999, p. 28.

———, "Twin Roles for Simms After Tarmac Split," *Financial Times,* March 17, 1999, p. 21.

Ritchie, Berry, *The Story of Tarmac,* London: James & James, 1999, 144 p.

Shand, David, "Tarmac Aims to Divide and Grow," *Scotsman* (Edinburgh), June 16, 1999, p. 25.

"Sir John Banham to Chair Tarmac," *Financial Times,* September 22, 1993, p. 21.

Taylor, Andrew, "Building Blocks but Not Houses," *Financial Times,* August 3, 1995, p. 20.

———, "Investors Test for Firm Foundations," *Financial Times,* November 8, 1996, p. 21.

———, "Preparing to Rebuild on More Substantial Foundations," *Financial Times,* April 28, 1993, p. 23.

———, "Reshaped Tarmac Returns to the Black," *Financial Times,* September 24, 1997, p. 24.

———, "Swap Lays Strong Foundations," *Financial Times,* November 16, 1995, p. 31.

———, "Tarmac and ARC to Merge Quarries," *Financial Times,* November 19, 1996, p. 24.

———, "Tarmac Mounts Swift Revamp," *Financial Times,* September 25, 1996, p. 30.

———, "Tarmac Sale Plan Deals New Blow to Housing Industry," *Financial Times,* August 3, 1995, p. 1.

———, "Tarmac's Recuperation at a Critical Point," *Financial Times,* November 3, 1993, p. 23.

———, "Tarmac Swaps Tiles for Bricks," *Financial Times,* October 23, 1993, p. 10.

———, "Wimpey and Tarmac Swap Asset Details," *Financial Times,* February 10, 1996, p. 8.

———, "Wimpey and Tarmac Swap Divisions," *Financial Times,* November 16, 1995, p. 27.

"Titan Cement to Acquire Tarmac America, Sell Portion to Vulcan," *Pit and Quarry,* October 2000, p.14.

Tennant Company

701 North Lilac Drive
Post Office Box 1452
Minneapolis, Minnesota 55440-1452
U.S.A.
Telephone: (763) 540-1208
Toll Free: (800) 553-8033
Fax: (763) 540-1437
Web site: http://www.tennantco.com

Public Company
Founded: 1870
Incorporated: 1909
Employees: 2,774
Sales: $664.2 million (2007)
Stock Exchanges: New York
Ticker Symbol: TNC
NAIC: 333319 Other Commercial and Service Industry Machinery Manufacturing; 325612 Polish and Other Sanitation Good Manufacturing

■ ■ ■

Tennant Company is the world's foremost manufacturer of industrial floor maintenance equipment, including sweepers, scrubbers, and combination sweeper/scrubbers, in a variety of ride-on and walk-behind models. Other company products include carpet extractors, floor burnishers, vacuums, polishers, and outdoor cleaning equipment, as well as surface coatings for a variety of floors. Tennant machines are used to clean and coat indoor and outdoor surfaces in factories, warehouses, office buildings, stadiums, parking garages, airports,

schools, hospitals, and retail outlets. The company maintains manufacturing facilities in Minneapolis; Holland, Michigan; Northampton, United Kingdom; Uden, the Netherlands; and Shanghai, China. It sells its products directly in 15 countries and through independent distributors in an additional 80. Around 62 percent of revenues are generated in North America, with Europe accounting for roughly 26 percent.

EARLY HISTORY

Tennant Company was founded in Minneapolis in 1870 by an Irish immigrant named George Henry Tennant. Tennant had opened a sawmill and woodshop to supply the growing number of houses with hardwood floors, wooden downspouts, and rain gutters. Over the next 30 years the woodworking shop expanded, surviving several fires, and becoming one of the leading manufacturers of hardwood flooring in the Upper Midwest. Many of the original G. H. Tennant hardwood floors can still be found in the stately homes along the main streets of Minneapolis and St. Paul. The company was incorporated in 1909.

The innovation that would shape Tennant's business and revolutionize floor care was a classic example of ingenuity born of frustration. In 1932 Ben Casper, a local junior high school janitor weary of laboring over floors on his hands and knees, discovered a way to dry clean his floors. Casper fashioned a scouring contraption from a coffee can wrapped in steel wool that he hooked up to an old washing machine motor. The janitor demonstrated his idea to a neighbor, who just happened to be a shop foreman at Tennant. Tennant acquired the

```
┌─────────────────────────────────────────┐
│                                         │
│   COMPANY PERSPECTIVES                  │
│                ■                        │
│  ─────────────────────────────────────  │
│   Through innovative solutions, industry-leading service │
│   and a world-renowned reputation for quality and │
│   manufacturing excellence, Tennant is committed to │
│   helping our customers create a cleaner, safer world. │
│                                         │
└─────────────────────────────────────────┘
```

rights to manufacture the machine, and within a few years, a variation of the janitor's model formed the backbone of the company's business.

Tennant had developed a floor finishing and treating system based on oils and sealers to be applied with a buffer. Along with the floor-care machine, the Tennant Floor Maintenance System flourished, and by 1940, over 100,000 square feet of wooden floors in bakeries, schools, and factories were maintained with its products. In the 1940s, treatment products were developed for concrete floors.

The outbreak of World War II ushered in a new era for Tennant. As defense plants sprang up, heavy-duty machines were required to keep those installations immaculate. Tennant responded with the production of the Model K, a much larger machine with a wider cleaning path. The product line was expanded to include scarifiers, a series of outdoor machines that could be used to route and loosen up the surfaces of airport ramps, bridges, and highways. Tennant also participated in the war effort by subcontracting parts for the Norden bombsight manufactured by Honeywell. During this period, sales went from $330,000 in 1938 to $1 million in 1945.

POSTWAR GROWTH

The postwar period witnessed a continuation of Tennant's explosive growth. Ongoing innovations in equipment created increased demand, and the market for scrubbers and sweepers rapidly expanded. A landmark event was the invention of the first vacuumized power sweeper in 1947 by Ralph Peabody, a Tennant Company engineer. The sweeper revolutionized industrial floor maintenance by controlling dust dispersion during sweeping. The Model 36, as it was called, formed the prototype of a long line of sweepers, scarifiers, and scrubbers. The year 1950 marked the introduction of sweepers with front-wheel steering, and in 1953 Tennant launched the first mechanically raised hopper, followed by the first hydraulically driven sweeper in 1961.

As a result of Tennant's rapid expansion in the 1950s, the company outgrew its plant in Minneapolis and relocated to a larger headquarters in suburban Minneapolis in 1957. Tennant later added five other facilities in the greater suburban area of the Twin Cities. In 1969 Tennant went public with its first stock offering and made its first major acquisition with the purchase of Taylor Material Handling in Michigan.

The 1960s and 1970s were decades of prosperous growth for Tennant. In the early 1960s, Tennant took the first steps to carve out a stronger niche for the company's products in Europe by granting a license to its importer, R.S. Stokvis Company, to manufacture the company's products in Holland. By 1970, Tennant had bought out the license agreement from Stokvis in a takeover of Stokvis/De Nederlandsche Kroon Rijwiefabrieken and formed a wholly owned subsidiary, Tennant NV, based in Uden, the Netherlands.

Looking toward expansion in the Asia-Pacific region, Tennant embarked on a joint venture with Fuji Heavy Industries in Japan in 1964. In the long term, this relationship did not live up to its initial promise as Fuji was less than aggressive in promoting and distributing Tennant's products. In Australia, too, during this same period, sales failed to advance as expected under Tennant's national distributor, Clark Equipment. In the mid-1970s, Tennant phased out Clark and began selling directly. Sales increased from $750,000 in 1976 to $11 million by 1994.

In the United States, Tennant further solidified its position as an industry leader by introducing service and parts through authorized service dealers around the country. Unlike its major competitors, Tennant also maintained its own direct sales force, which actively sought new markets and customer feedback. In this way, the sales force not only sold Tennant's products and services but also served as a sounding board for customer concerns. Tennant's sales force promoted the company's complete product line out of three regions (western, central, and eastern), and worked in tandem with service representatives in these areas.

1979–89: QUALITY IMPROVEMENT CAMPAIGN

A major turning point for Tennant Company took place in 1979, when the company launched an all-out quality improvement campaign after a thorough evaluation of the company's operations by quality expert Philip Crosby. While Tennant's sales were booming at the time, CEO Roger Hale and other senior managers were keenly aware that American companies were quickly losing their competitive edge in the global marketplace. At the same time, Hale was detecting warning signs about Tennant's quality as complaints came in from Japanese

KEY DATES

1870: George Henry Tennant founds a company specializing in the manufacture of wood flooring.

1909: Company is incorporated.

1932: Local janitor develops a machine to dry clean his floors; Tennant later acquires the rights to manufacture the machine.

1945: Sales reach $1 million.

1947: A company engineer invents the first vacuumized power sweeper.

1969: Company goes public.

1970: Company forms a wholly owned manufacturing subsidiary in the Netherlands.

1976: Roger Hale takes over leadership of the company.

1979: Company launches a major quality improvement campaign.

1992: Preeminence 2000 campaign is launched.

1994: Castex Inc., a maker of commercial floor and carpet cleaning equipment, is acquired.

1999: Paul Andra KG, a German maker of commercial floor maintenance equipment, is acquired; Janet M. Dolan is named CEO of the company.

2005: Chris Killingstad succeeds Dolan as CEO.

2007: An environmentally friendly floor-cleaning technology called ech2o is introduced.

2008: Tennant acquires Applied Sweepers, producer of the Green Machines brand of subcompact outdoor sweeping machines.

customers about sweepers leaking hydraulic oil. Strangely enough, U.S. customers had not bothered to protest the same leaks, which Hale took as an indication of American complacency to issues of quality. Then came the news that Toyota Motor Corporation's lift-truck division was planning to enter the floor sweeper business. With a formidable Japanese competitor looming on Tennant's horizon, Hale and other Tennant executives moved quickly to explore dramatic quality improvements.

Tennant's extensive rework stations were the first target. These areas, where 20 of the company's top mechanics worked overtime to get faulty machines ready for shipping, took up 15 percent of assembly space, and an average of 33,000 hours was spent annually on manufacturing rework, a practice that was considered

standard across U.S. industry. Resolving to do it right the first time, Hale transferred rework mechanics to assembly to catch mistakes on the line from the beginning.

Tennant's vast number of suppliers posed another problem. Supplied parts represented 65 percent of the average cost of a sweeper or scrubber, and with so many suppliers, there were inevitable inconsistencies in parts and inadequate training for assemblers. Tennant carefully weeded out its suppliers and reduced their numbers from 1,100 in 1980 to 250 in 1992. The number of defects dropped dramatically. Employees were also trained in statistical process control (SPC), a method of monitoring defects and setting goals to reduce them. According to *Training* in 1990, SPC allowed the company to cut by half the number of inspectors of parts manufacturing.

In a further effort to reduce errors, small teams of managers and workers were formed to focus on how procedures could be improved. These small groups became a way of life at Tennant and encouraged regular employee feedback in all areas of the business. Management also relied on the team process to stay in touch with day-to-day operations. The 1993 edition of *The 100 Best Companies to Work for in America* gave Tennant high marks for management responsiveness and general working conditions. The report also highlighted the incentive programs and recognition program that helped prompt greater employee participation in the quality improvement campaign.

Roger L. Hale, a great-grandson of Tennant's founder, who had led the company since 1976, embraced the quality philosophy with the fervor of a missionary. His account of how the company transformed itself, *Quest for Quality: How One Company Put Theory to Work,* published in 1989, became required reading for other companies interested in quality management. Tennant also sponsored an annual conference on quality. In addition to the extensive training introduced for company employees, a department was created to run external training programs for companies eager to emulate Tennant's approach.

Tennant's quality campaign not only produced savings for the company but also translated into tangible benefits for its customers. Tennant's products were more reliable, and during the 1980s prices on some machines actually went down. Warranty coverage was extended. Tennant's sweepers and scrubbers were featured in *Fortune's* 1988 roundup of top-notch U.S. products in an article titled "What America Makes Best." According to *Management Accounting* in 1992, Tennant significantly improved product quality and reduced total quality costs from 17 percent of sales in 1980 to 2.5 percent of sales in 1988.

As part of its ongoing quality improvement campaign, Tennant was investing what *Barron's* called an incredibly high level of revenues, close to 5 percent, in new product research and development. By the mid-1990s, the company had cut its product development cycle in half, from four to two years. Some of the more innovative products to emerge in this period were environmentally safe resurfacing coatings and a heavy-duty machine for use in airports to pick up and recycle the deicing fluids sprayed on planes before takeoff.

DIVERSIFICATION AND OVERSEAS EXPANSION

Tennant weathered the recession of the early 1990s with minor layoffs and a slump in sales of its floor coatings products. Overall sales in 1991 dropped 6 percent to $144 million and earnings were off by approximately 25 percent. As a way to invigorate its quality efforts, Tennant launched a Preeminence 2000 campaign in 1992 to define a strategy to propel the company into the next century. The company's mission was to be the preeminent company in the industry with the goal of doubling sales by the millennium. Continued diversification and expansion of overseas sales seemed to be the key to prosperity despite a stagnant market at home.

Under Hale's leadership, Tennant had moved to expand international sales, initially concentrating on Europe. Using its base in the Netherlands as a springboard, Tennant had gradually assumed ownership of the Stokvis organizations in Germany (1978), the United Kingdom (1982), and France (1994), establishing direct sales and service operations in all four countries. A fifth direct sales office in Spain got its start in 1991 and had more than doubled in size four years later.

Tennant Australia, a wholly owned subsidiary, became a full sales, marketing, and service organization and the first to offer service 24 hours a day, seven days a week. In 1989, after ending its 25-year joint venture with Fuji Heavy Industries, Tennant formed Tennant Japan K.K. and with its master distributor, Nippon Yusoki Company, Ltd., initiated direct imports from the United States to Japan. In 1992 Tennant formed Tennant Company Japan Branch to sell commercial floor care equipment. In 1994 overseas sales accounted for $72 million, or 25 percent of revenues.

Tennant's significant inroads into the commercial market were enhanced by the acquisition in February 1994 of Castex Industries, Inc., the world leader in carpet maintenance equipment, for $26.8 million. Castex itself had widened its scope in 1989 by taking over Nobles Industries, which offered much broader established distribution channels for its line of hard floor maintenance equipment. Castex/Nobles was integrated with Tennant Trend, which had been formed in 1982, and these operations were consolidated in a new manufacturing facility in Holland, Michigan. Castex complemented Tennant's product line with a wide range of walk-behind scrubbers, sweepers, and wet/dry vacuums, as well as carpet extractors and floor polishers, appropriate for use in commercial settings such as office buildings, hospitals, and supermarkets.

Tennant's ambitious program to dominate the commercial floor equipment market was further bolstered with the purchase, also in 1994, of Eagle Floor Care, Inc., a manufacturer of propane burnishers. By the end of 1994, commercial floor maintenance equipment sales had more than tripled since the year before thanks to marketplace acceptance of the new acquisitions.

The year 1994 was a high point for Tennant in more ways than one. Sales of $281 million were up 27 percent over 1993, with sales in North America registering a 33 percent increase. That same year, Tennant was the first non-*Fortune* 500 company to receive *Purchasing* magazine's Medal of Professional Excellence. Other recipients of the award included Motorola, Inc., Hewlett-Packard Company, Chrysler Corporation, and General Electric Company. *Purchasing* made special note of the company's outstanding performance in the areas of supplier relations, product teams, and quality.

A PERIOD OF STEADY GROWTH TO END THE CENTURY

The late 1990s were a period of steady growth in sales and profits for Tennant, growth fueled both by the expansion into the commercial sector and heightened new product development. In 1998 alone, the company introduced three new commercial products and five industrial products. Among the latter were two products designed for outdoor cleaning: the Model 830-II street sweeper and the 4300 All-Terrain Litter Vacuum, a riding vehicle used to pick up small pieces of garbage. Tennant products had long been used outdoors, but these models were among the company's first to be designed specifically for such use. In addition to pursuing the outdoor niche, Tennant also identified a second niche market as a key growth opportunity, that of contract cleaners. Businesses everywhere were increasingly outsourcing their floor maintenance, and Tennant aimed to supply contract cleaners with the equipment they needed.

By the late 1990s Tennant had also completed a total overhaul of its worldwide computer systems, an initiative that began in 1994. By linking all operations and customer information, the company hoped to improve customer service, sell more efficiency to its customers, and design products and services that better met customer needs.

In April 1998 Janet M. Dolan was named president and chief operating officer at Tennant, having previously served as general counsel, head of the floor coatings division, and then head of the company's entire North American operations. One year later, Dolan became the first company CEO not descended from the founder when Roger Hale stepped down from that position after 23 years at the helm. In January 1999 Tennant made an important European acquisition when it paid almost $7 million for Paul Andra KG, a German, privately owned maker of commercial floor maintenance equipment, including single-disk machines, wet/dry vacuum cleaners, and vacuumized scrubbers. The company, which maintained a manufacturing facility in Waldhausen, Germany, sold about $27 million in products on an annual basis, mainly under the Sorma brand name, with 75 percent of sales occurring in Germany and Austria. This acquisition not only provided Tennant with a strong position in the key country of Germany, it also provided a base for extending the Sorma and Tennant commercial product lines into other countries.

In October 1999 Tennant announced a restructuring intended to position the company for greater growth and profitability in the 21st century. Aiming to reduce operating costs by $5 million per year, Tennant consolidated some operations and facilities and divested certain units, including the Eagle Floor Care line of burnishing equipment. About 150 jobs were trimmed from the workforce. Tennant also began moving from a "build-to-stock" manufacturing system to a "build-to-order" manufacturing capacity—according to the company, the first in the industry to take this ambitious step. Longer term, Tennant set financial goals for itself of annual sales increases of 10 to 12 percent and an increase in its operating margin to more than 10 percent. (This margin had ranged from 9.2 percent to 9.7 percent from 1995 to 1998.)

PRODUCT INNOVATION, RESTRUCTURING, AND ACQUISITIONS IN EARLY 21ST CENTURY

After switching its stock from the NASDAQ to the New York Stock Exchange in October 2000, Tennant entered a rough stretch in which its sales and earnings were depressed by the sharp downturn in the industrial economy. The nadir was reached in 2001 when the firm earned just $4.6 million on sales of $422.4 million, the latter representing a drop of nearly 7 percent. Tennant nevertheless maintained its aggressive pursuit of new product development. In 2002, for instance, the company unveiled its first full-size street sweeper, dubbed the Centurion, which featured a waterless dust-control system designed to help customers comply with more stringent environmental regulations. During this same period, Tennant launched a number of cost-cutting efforts. The firm shut down its plant in Waldhausen, Germany, shifting production to a contract manufacturer in the Czech Republic. In North America, Tennant transferred its distribution operations from a network of company-operated centers to a third-party logistics service provider operating two leased facilities.

By 2004 Tennant had recovered to post net earnings of $13.4 million, while revenues jumped nearly 12 percent, hitting a record $507.8 million. In January of that year, the company acquired Walter-Broadley Machines Limited, a privately owned U.K.-based producer of cleaning equipment that operated a manufacturing plant in Northampton and had annual revenues of around $13 million. In 2005 Tennant's history of innovation continued with the introduction of a line of carpet-cleaning machines featuring a technology called ReadySpace that enabled them to scrub dirt out of carpets using little water, greatly reducing drying time. Carpets cleaned using traditional machines could take as much as 18 hours to dry, compared to the 10- to 30-minute drying time of the ReadySpace line. These new machines became the company's best-selling carpet-cleaning devices. Dolan retired in late 2005 as Tennant president and CEO and was succeeded by Chris Killingstad. Before joining the company in April 2002 as its North American vice-president, Killingstad had spent ten years in management positions at the Pillsbury Company.

Seeking an eventual increase in Tennant's sales past the $1 billion mark, Killingstad carried forward the international expansion of his predecessor. In 2006 Tennant opened a manufacturing facility in Shanghai both to broaden the firm's global sourcing network and to facilitate sales of walk-behind floor scrubbers and sweepers in China and other Asian markets. The company's European expansion continued via the July 2006 purchase of the Dutch firm Hofmans Machinefabriek B.V. for $8.6 million. Hofmans specialized in compact, outdoor street-cleaning machines. In February 2007 Tennant acquired the Scottish cleaning equipment maker Floorep Limited for $3.6 million. Tennant enjoyed its best year ever in 2007, reporting net earnings of nearly $40 million on revenues of $664.2 million.

Tennant during this period was making a concerted effort to develop more environmentally friendly cleaning technologies. In October 2007 the company announced what it considered a breakthrough "green" technology, dubbed ech2o (and pronounced "echo"). Scrubbing machines equipped with this technology were able to clean floors using only tap water. An electrical current divided the water into separate streams of electrically charged acidic and alkaline water that served as a cleaning solution. Soon after their creation, these streams changed back into plain water, leaving only regular water and dirt in the recovery tank. Ech2o was touted not only for being environmentally friendly but also for its potential to lower customer costs because chemical-based cleaners were not needed and because the technology used 70 percent less water than traditional cleaning methods. Full production of ech2o-equipped machines began in the spring of 2008.

In February 2008, meantime, Tennant returned to the acquisition trail to purchase Applied Sweepers of Falkirk, Scotland, for around $68 million. Garnering annual sales of $40 million, Applied Sweepers produced the Green Machines brand of subcompact outdoor sweeping machines, which led its sector in the United Kingdom. Applied Sweepers also maintained overseas subsidiaries in the United States, France, and Germany. Also in February 2008, Tennant agreed to acquire Sociedade Alfa Ltda., the leading maker of commercial cleaning machines in Brazil under the Alfa brand. Through such acquisitions and its ongoing dedication to developing innovative new products, Tennant appeared firmly on the path toward reaching Killingstad's goal of $1 billion in annual revenues.

Leslie D. Hyde
Updated, David E. Salamie

PRINCIPAL SUBSIDIARIES

Tennant Sales and Service Company; Tennant Holding B.V. (Netherlands); Tennant N.V. (Netherlands); Tennant UK Limited.

PRINCIPAL COMPETITORS

Minuteman International, Inc.; Nilfisk-Advance A/S; Alfred Kärcher GmbH & Co. KG; Federal Signal Corporation.

FURTHER READING

Black, Sam, "Tennant CEO Touts Turnaround," *Minneapolis/St. Paul Business Journal*, April 20, 2007.

Brammer, Rhonda, "Gleaming Prospects," *Barron's*, September 20, 1999, pp. 22, 24–25.

Brat, Ilan, "How a Firm Got Smart to Fight Grime, Rivals," *Wall Street Journal*, January 28, 2008, pp. B1, B3.

Carr, Lawrence, and Thomas Tyson, "Planning Quality Cost Expenditures," *Management Accounting*, October 1992, pp. 52–56.

DePass, Dee, "Low Rollers Mean High Revenue," *Minneapolis Star Tribune*, August 29, 2005, p. 8D.

———, "Pillsbury Vet Named to Succeed Dolan at Tennant," *Minneapolis Star Tribune*, October 7, 2005, p. 1D.

———, "Tennant Goes Green and Global," *Minneapolis Star Tribune*, September 8, 2006, p. 1D.

Ewen, Beth, "Pacing Herself: Tennant's New CEO Wants Big Growth a Little at a Time," *Corporate Report-Minnesota*, June 1999, pp. 14+.

Gibson, Richard, "Tennant Hopes It Can Clean Up Once the Economic Slump Ends," *Wall Street Journal*, June 19, 2002, p. B6B.

Hale, Roger L., "Tennant Company: Instilling Quality from Top to Bottom," *Management Review*, February 1989, p. 65.

Hale, Roger L., Donald D. Carlton, Ronald E. Kowal, and Tim K. Sehnert, *Made in the U.S.A.: How One American Company Helps Satisfy Customer Needs Through Strategic Supplier Quality Management*, Minneapolis: Tennant Company, 1991, 145 p.

Hale, Roger L., Douglas R. Hoelscher, and Ronald E. Kowal, *Quest for Quality: How One Company Put Theory to Work*, Minneapolis: Tennant Company, 1987, 148 p.

Hequet, Marc, "Selling In-House Training Outside," *Training*, September 1991, pp. 51–56.

Kennedy, Patrick, and John J. Oslund, "Cleaning Up," *Minneapolis Star Tribune*, July 1, 2002, p. 1D.

Knowlton, Christopher, "What America Makes Best," *Fortune*, March 28, 1988, pp. 40–53.

Levering, Robert, and Milton Moskowitz, *The 100 Best Companies to Work for in America*, New York: Doubleday, 1993, pp. 447–50.

Oberle, Joseph, "Employee Involvement at Tennant," *Training*, May 1990, pp. 73–79.

Palmer, Jay, "Come the Recovery … and Tennant Seems Poised to Clean Up," *Barron's*, February 3, 1992, pp. 17, 36.

Peterson, Susan E., "Tennant Co. Promotes Janet Dolan to President, Chief Operating Officer," *Minneapolis Star Tribune*, April 8, 1998, p. 3D.

Porter, Anne Millen, "Does Quality Really Affect the Bottom Line?" *Purchasing*, January 16, 1992, pp. 61–64.

Raia, Ernie, "Medal of Excellence: Swept Away by Tennant," *Purchasing*, September 22, 1994, pp. 37–45.

St. Anthony, Neal, "Tennant Bounces Back by Focusing on Innovation," *Minneapolis Star Tribune*, June 21, 2002, p. 1D.

"Sweeper Manufacturer Writes the Book on Quality," *Diesel Progress, Engines and Drives*, April 1993, p. 18.

Tennant Anniversary Book, 1870–1995, Minneapolis: Tennant Company, 1995, 38 p.

Tianjin Flying Pigeon
Bicycle Co., Ltd.

———————■———————

Mendaokou, Xiqing District
Tianjin, 300385
China
Telephone: (0086-22) 83966887
Fax: (0086-022) 83960503
Web site: http://www.flying-pigeon.cn

Private Company
Incorporated: 1936 as Changho Works
Employees: 700
Sales: $50 million (2004 est.)
NAIC: 336991 Motorcycle, Bicycle, and Parts Manufacturing

■ ■ ■

Tianjin Flying Pigeon Bicycle Co., Ltd., is one of the largest bike manufacturers in one of the world's largest bicycle-producing nations. The Flying Pigeon brand was launched at an existing bicycle plant in the port city of Tianjin soon after the Communist Revolution in 1949. The durable bikes it produced by the millions were an anchor of Chinese life for decades.

The company struggled as economic reforms of the 1990s opened the door to a slew of new competitors. In response, it began developing dozens of new models, even making them available in colors besides the traditional black. However, the heavy, workhorse models that made it famous still account for one-fifth of sales.

After a partial management buyout in 1998 the company was relaunched with a greatly scaled back workforce and a new, modernized plant. Since then, revenues and employment have steadily increased and the company has begun to turn a profit in spite of the industry's razor-thin margins.

FOREIGN ORIGINS

The first bicycles arrived in China within a couple of years of their invention in France in the mid-1860s, but they remained a rare sight until around 1900. Bicycles started to become popular as transportation for the masses in the 1920s, but were largely imported from abroad.

In 1936 a Japanese entrepreneur built the Changho Works bicycle factory in the North China port city of Tianjin, China. The factory originally produced bikes under the Anchor brand, and later the Victory and Zhongzi nameplates after the Kuomintang (Chinese Nationalists) took over the plant.

The Communists came to power in 1949 and soon embraced the bicycle as an egalitarian mode of transport. The Changho factory resumed production the next year with 300 employees. This time it was making a new brand that was exclusive to the People's Republic: *Fei Gi* or Flying Pigeon. The bird in the name could also be translated as "dove," and is a symbol of peace. The first Flying Pigeon bicycles were completed on July 5, 1950.

The name became synonymous with models such as the PA-02, a heavy but practical machine built for a long, productive life. The design was based on a Japanese interpretation of a British-made Raleigh. It had only one speed, keeping costs down, and its large 28-

KEY DATES

1936: Japanese entrepreneur builds Changho Works bicycle factory in Tianjin, China.

1950: Flying Pigeon brand is launched at the Tianjin plant after the Communist Revolution.

1985: The factory is making about three million bikes a year.

1998: Company is restructured after a partial management buyout, moves into new factory.

2001: Flying Pigeon makes its 70 millionth bicycle.

2003: Company posts a modest profit as annual production exceeds one million bicycles.

inch wheels helped it glide over bumpy roads. It weighed in at about 45 pounds (most modern steel mountain bikes weigh between 25 and 35 pounds), and was strong enough to tote a pig under the double top tubes. Such attributes earned it the nickname "iron donkey." It was available in just one color, black. Until the 1980s such bikes sold for CNY 150 to CNY 160, or two to four months' salary for the average worker.

POLITICAL SIGNIFICANCE

The spindle of a sewing machine, the face of a watch, and the wheels of a bicycle made up the "three rounds" expected to be found in the home of every citizen. Flying Pigeons in particular played a politically significant role in the People's Republic from the beginning. Chairman Mao Zedong himself visited the plant in August 1958. In the 1970s future Premier Deng Xiaoping promised not a chicken in every pot, but "a Flying Pigeon in every household."

In 1989 a pair of Flying Pigeon bicycles were presented to newly elected President George H. W. Bush, who had become familiar with the brand during his days as an ambassador in Beijing, when he made headlines by cycling around town. The tradition continued in 2006 with Italian Prime Minister Romano Prodi, who received one of the company's new racing style road bikes.

Fidel Castro was also a recipient, but as a fellow Communist his dealings with the company were more extensive. In the early 1990s, China sold more than a million discounted bicycles to Cuba, which was reeling from reductions in oil shipments from post-Soviet Russia. In addition to being a friendship gesture between two of the last remaining Communist governments, this helped to dispose of as many as a million

surplus bikes that were stacking up at the Flying Pigeon plant. (China's two other main bike brands, Phoenix and Forever, were also included in the deal.)

ECONOMIC REFORM

Thanks to central planning, Flying Pigeon was able to thrive for decades with neither a sales force nor a research and development department. It kept churning out the same basic black bike by the hundreds of thousands, and they remained highly valued due to rationing. The company was not the only bicycle manufacturer in China; its most notable rivals, Forever and Phoenix, were based in Shanghai. However, in the "Kingdom of Bicycles," Flying Pigeon ruled the roost.

Its production reached an incredible three million bikes per year in the mid-1980s, when the plant was running around the clock. There were then 15,000 employees. By the end of the decade, China had nearly 300 million bicycles. Flying Pigeons were very durable, lasting ten years or more, and the market was not conditioned with a replacement mentality.

In 1986 Flying Pigeon became the first Chinese company to raise capital from private citizens. Purchasers of special coupons did not receive any equity, but rather the right to buy bicycles, which were still being rationed by the government. In spite of such progressive moves as the public fund-raising, Flying Pigeon would have a hard time navigating the bumpy road of economic reform to come.

China was greatly increasing production capacity with plans to sell the surplus overseas. Flying Pigeon sold about 350,000 bikes in international markets in 1985, with aims to more than double this figure by the end of the decade. However, a huge glut developed in the early 1990s.

INTENSE COMPETITION

Different factors converged to make life difficult for Flying Pigeon. It was facing new competition in a liberalized economic environment: the number of bicycle manufacturers increased to 150 by the early 1990s. Some of these were private citizens who began building bikes in their living rooms. Old rivals such as Shenzhen's China Bicycle and Shanghai's Forever and Phoenix remained a factor as well; in fact they had each become publicly listed companies. As the economy opened to foreign investment under Deng Xiaoping, international investors funded new competing factories with state-of-the-art equipment.

At the same time as the competition was growing, the bike market in China was shrinking, largely due to the growth of the automobile. The government was orienting its transportation plans toward cars as a means to grow a modern industrial society. At some point, certain big cities even banned bicycles from downtown areas. When the younger generations of Chinese did want to buy a bicycle, they were more interested in the latest styles and colors rather than the monochrome workhorse that was so closely identified with the Flying Pigeon brand.

Flying Pigeon formed a new subsidiary in 1993 to develop and manufacture new styles. It also made some initiatives to expand its international marketing and production, such as buying a factory in Germany and setting up an Indonesian joint venture.

Although its workforce was shrinking, Flying Pigeon was still the largest employer in the industry into the mid-1990s, with 8,000 workers. However, it was struggling to remain relevant. By the late 1990s, the company was selling only 200,000 bicycles a year, according to *BusinessWeek.* As was the case throughout the Chinese bike industry, its profit margins had been decimated within a few years.

A NEW BEGINNING: 1998

A handful of managers led by former Deputy General Manager Sha Yunshu took over the company in 1998, relocating to a new, modern plant on the outskirts of town. The enterprise started anew with only 300 employees, and a pay structure weighted toward performance incentives. New designs, such as mountain bikes, were also part of the equation for the restructured company.

Flying Pigeon also began making an electric bike called Wanda. The company's traditional black iron workhorses were reduced to one-fifth of the total output. Within a few years, annual production was back above one million units.

Flying Pigeon made its 70 millionth bicycle in 2001. Of these, six million had been sold abroad (the company also exported components such as flywheels). Revenues were about $38 million in 2003 and growing, Sha told *BusinessWeek,* and the company managed to turn a profit of $750,000. It produced 1.2 million bicycles during the year.

Meanwhile, some of the country's 300 other bike manufacturers were collapsing under the strain of uncomfortably tight profit margins. Ironically, in a country that exported more than two-thirds of its total bike production the company was considering outsourcing manufacturing to even lower-wage countries in Asia or Africa. (Although 90 percent of bicycles sold in the United States were made in China, Flying Pigeons were not imported there in significant numbers. The brand was available in certain big city boutiques.)

Just as the biking public was beginning to embrace cycling for recreation rather than practical transportation, so did the latest incarnation of the company bear striking differences to its early days. It was producing eight series of bicycles, totaling 200 different styles, with price points ranging from $35 to more than $1,000. Only half of its production was under its own brand.

Frederick C. Ingram

PRINCIPAL SUBSIDIARIES

Tianjin Flying Pigeon Bicycle Research & Manufacture Corp.

PRINCIPAL COMPETITORS

Shanghai Phoenix Import & Export Company Ltd.; Shanghai Forever Company, Ltd.; Giant Company; Tianjin Fushida Bicycle Company, Ltd.

FURTHER READING

Browne, Andrew, "China's Flying Pigeon Bicycles Pedal Hard to Compete," *Reuters News,* November 16, 1992.

Browne, Andrew, and Kersten Zhang, "A Legend's Bumpy Ride—Nearly Left for Roadkill on China's Path to Prosperity, a Bike-Industry Veteran Shifts Gears to Compete at Home," *Wall Street Journal,* April 29, 2006, p. A1.

Chan, Elaine, "Bicycle Makers Hope for New Dawn As Sunset Approaches," *South China Morning Post* (Hong Kong), October 10, 1996, p. 4.

Higgins, Andrew, "Jiang's Gamble Downs a Flying Pigeon," *Guardian* (London), Foreign Page, September 18, 1997, p. 15.

Koeppel, Dan, "Flight of the Pigeon," *Bicycling,* January/February 2007, pp. 60–66.

MacDougall, Colina, "Chinese Factory Raises Capital by Selling Shares," *Financial Times* (London), Sec. I, Overseas News, August 6, 1986, p. 2.

"Modern China Pedals Away from Iconic Bicycles," *Agence France Presse,* April 14, 2007.

Rocks, David, "This Pigeon Is Really Taking Wing," *BusinessWeek,* November 1, 2004, p. 18.

Rocks, David, and Chen Wu, "A Phoenix Named Flying Pigeon; The Storied Bikemaker Has Shed Weight, Added Models, and Regained Lost Sales," *BusinessWeek* (Asian Business ed.), September 20, 2004.

Simpson, Peter, "As Stylish Mountain Bikes Become the People's Choice, Production of the Country's Iconic Black

Bicycle Could Soon Be Outsourced Overseas," *Sunday Telegraph* (London), International Sec., May 21, 2006, p. 30.

Tefft, Sheila, "Market Throws State Firms over Handlebars in China," *Christian Science Monitor,* February 23, 1996, p. 1.

"Tianjin: Local Benefits Attract Suppliers," *Global Sources,* December 4, 2007.

Zhang Xunhai, "Enterprise Response to Market Reforms: The Case of the Chinese Bicycle Industry," *Australian Journal of Chinese Affairs* (28), July 1992, pp. 111–39.

Transammonia Group

---

320 Park Avenue
New York, New York 10022-6815
U.S.A.
Telephone: (212) 223-3200
Fax: (212) 759-1410
Web site: http://www.transammonia.com

Private Company
Incorporated: 1965
Employees: 347
Sales: $8.3 billion (2007)
NAIC: 424910 Farm Supplies Merchant Wholesalers;
424720 Petroleum and Petroleum Products
Merchant Wholesalers

■ ■ ■

Privately held Transammonia Group is a New York City-based group of merchandising and trading companies dealing in fertilizers, liquefied petroleum gas (LPG), and petrochemicals. The flagship unit, operating under the Transammonia name, deals in fertilizers and raw materials, including nitrogen-based, phosphate-based, sulfur-based, and potash-based products. It is the leading private firm in its field, the world's largest independent marketer and transporter of anhydrous ammonia, and among the world's top producers of ammonia. Transammonia is the world's largest trader of sulfuric acid, and also maintains a fleet of rail cars to deliver liquid sulfur to U.S. customers.

The Trammochem unit focuses on petrochemicals: MTBE (methyl tertiary-butyl ether), benzene, methanol, olefins, styrene monomer, toluene, and xylenes and isomers. The subsidiary operates out of Darien, Connecticut, and maintains offices in Altendorf, Switzerland; Moscow, Russia; and Singapore. Another Transammonia division, Trammo Gas, is based in Houston, Texas, where it merchandises and trades LPG products in the United States, including propane, ethane, butane, iso butane, and natural gasoline. Trammo Gas International, Inc., is a global transporter of LPG for third parties. Focusing on the northeastern and southeastern United States, Sea-3, Inc., supplies LPG to residential and business customers as well as to schools, hospitals, and industries. It is also involved in gas marketing on the Gulf Coast and some other markets. Finally, Trammo Petroleum, Inc., based in Houston, deals in crude oil, natural gas, and refined products, including gasoline, gasoline blend stocks, heating oil, diesel fuel, jet fuel, and naphtha. Transammonia also offers merchandising and trading services, as well as financing and transportation services. With revenues of $5.7 billion in 2006, Transammonia was ranked number 33 on *Forbes* magazine's list of the 500 largest private companies in the United States. Serving as chairman and chief executive officer is the company's founder, Ronald P. Stanton.

FOUNDER, GERMAN-BORN: 1928

Ronald Stanton was born in 1928 in Wiesbaden, Germany, and raised in Mainz with his mother, Hedi Steinberg, who had divorced his father when he was an infant. With the Nazi Party taking power in 1933, Germany became an increasingly hostile country for people of Jewish heritage like Stanton, and so at age nine he and his mother immigrated to the United

COMPANY PERSPECTIVES

Transammonia is an international merchandising and trading company that markets, trades, distributes and transports fertilizer materials, liquefied petroleum gas (LPG), petrochemicals (chiefly aromatics), methanol, crude oil and oil products.

States, settling in New York City. They became members of Congregation Shearith Israel, an upper westside Manhattan Spanish and Portuguese synagogue, where Stanton made a favorable impression on Rabbi David de Sola Poole.

When Stanton was 14 years old Rabbi Poole offered to pay for the boy's education at Yeshiva University and held out the possibility that Stanton might one day succeed him as the head of the synagogue. Instead Stanton decided on a business career, but his association with the school would one day make international news. Like many New Yorkers, especially Jewish children, in the post–World War II era, Stanton opted for a free, but quality, education at the City College of New York, the "poor man's Harvard."

After graduating in 1950 with a degree in economics Stanton worked, in his words, as a "soda jerk" before becoming involved in the fertilizer business with an Occidental Petroleum Corporation subsidiary based in New York City, International Ore and Fertilizer Corporation (Interore), eventually rising to the rank of vice-president. It was in this capacity that in 1963 he was indicted by a federal grand jury, along with Interore's president, Interore itself, and four phosphatic fertilizer companies. They were accused of illegal price fixing and allocating sales to export customers in violation of antitrust laws. Interore was eventually dropped from the antitrust suit.

TRANSAMMONIA FORMED: 1965

In 1965 Stanton struck out on his own forming Transammonia out of a former unit owned by Oklahoma City-based Apco Oil Company. Apco had been formed five years earlier to acquire the refining, marketing, and transportation assets of Anderson-Prichard Oil Corporation. By 1967 Transammonia became a global merchandiser and trader in fertilizer.

A decade later Transammonia began to expand beyond fertilizer. In 1978 the company became involved in the trading of LPG on a worldwide basis, forming Trammo Gas International Inc. Traditionally LPG had been a regional business, but in the second half of the 1970s Middle Eastern suppliers greatly increased capacity, which almost tripled between 1975 and 1980, and were eager to find new buyers. Additional supplies were coming from new LPG plants opened in Algeria, Australia, Indonesia, the North Sea, and Venezuela. To transport LPG supplies, massive ships were also being built to accommodate what was becoming a global export business. Serving as the hub for the international trading of LPG, at least for a while, was New York City, where Transammonia made its headquarters. One of the veterans of the LPG world, Louis Nielsen, joined forces with Transammonia to form Trammo Gas. Handling the transport of LPG around the world was subsidiary Trammo Navigation. Trammo made its mark by establishing a floating storage and transhipment facility off Vlissingen in Holland, which it operated for several years supplying LPG during the winter months.

SEA-3 ACQUIRED: 1985

Transammonia entered the retail distribution business in the United States in 1985, acquiring Sea-3, Inc. The Newington, New Hampshire-based company imported propane gas, mostly from Algiers, Norway, Russia, Scotland, and Venezuela. It then delivered the fuel throughout Northern New England, its market including most of New Hampshire, parts of Vermont, southern Maine, and eastern Massachusetts. Delivering about 750,000 gallons a day, Sea-3 provided about one-third of the propane used in the region.

During the 1980s Transammonia moved into other fields as well. In 1986 the company began dealing in sulfur in the United States, establishing a sulfur removal and marketing system. A year later, Transammonia became involved in petrochemicals, establishing Trammochem to operate as a global trader and merchandiser of petrochemicals. The new unit set up a small operation in Darien, Connecticut, and began dealing in such petrochemicals as MTBE, benzene, methanol, olefins, styrene monomer, toluene, and xylenes and isomers. Transammonia did not neglect its core ammonia business in the 1980s, however. The company acquired an ammonia terminal in Meredosia, Illinois, in 1989. Transammonia enjoyed so much success that it became a regular member of the 500 Largest Private Companies, as ranked by *Forbes* magazine. By the mid-1980s Transammonia generated about $750 million in annual sales.

CHINESE JOINT VENTURE: 1992

Revenues increased further in the first half of the 1990s as Transammonia continued to grow both internally and externally. In 1992 it became involved in the Chinese

KEY DATES

1965:	Ronald Stanton founds company.
1978:	Trammo Gas International Inc. is formed.
1985:	Sea-3, Inc., is acquired.
1992:	Beaumont, Texas, methanol plant is acquired.
2000:	Trammochem unit begins dealing in olefins.
2006:	Revenues top $6 billion.

fertilizer market through the creation of a joint venture with Sinochem Corporation, a state-owned company that was the largest provider of fertilizer in China. In the United States in that same year, Trammochem expanded its business through Transammonia's acquisition of the largest capacity methanol plant in the United States, capable of producing 280 million gallons of methanol each year. Built in Beaumont, Texas, in the 1960s by E.I. du Pont, the operation was renamed Beaumont Methanol Corporation. Trammochem would market the plant's methanol until the business was sold to Terra Industries Inc. two years later, and continued to market the plant's methanol for a time after that.

In the mid-1990s Transammonia's LPG business enjoyed its own share of growth. Sea-3's Newington terminal added an eight-million-gallon refrigerated propane storage tank, which opened in 1997, to increase storage capacity to 27 million gallons. The extra capacity helped to alleviate problems with peak demand during times of severe winter weather. Later in the decade Sea-3 looked to a new market, Tampa, Florida, where the company held a lease on a 12-acre parcel of land. In early 1999 work began on a $17.75 million facility, which included offices and a 111-foot-tall refrigerated tank with a 27-million-gallon capacity. Florida was an ideal market for Sea-3 because other than Texans, Floridians used more propane than residents of any other state, about 400 million gallons a year. Sea-3 chose Tampa because of its central location, with promising markets to both the north and the south. The company hoped to sell 180 million gallons of propane each year within a 135-mile radius of its storage facility, which opened in 2000. Also in the mid-1990s, Trammo Gas began the domestic trading and merchandising of LPG, operating out of Houston.

Despite these accomplishments, the second half of the 1990s proved challenging to Transammonia. In 1996 the company posted revenues of nearly $2.5 billion, netting $8 million in profits, providing it with a number 48 ranking on the *Forbes* list of the largest

private companies. Yet sales and profits would steadily erode as commodity prices fell over the next few years. Revenues dipped to $2.4 billion in 1997, $2.1 billion in 1998, and less than $1.4 billion in 1999, when Transammonia was ranked number 126 by *Forbes*. Profits during this period also fell to $5 million.

PURCHASE OF WEST COAST OPERATION: 2002

Transammonia looked to diversify and develop new sources of revenues. It began merchandising and trading sulfuric acid in 1999. The following year Trammochem started to merchandise and trade olefins. Trammo Petroleum also pursued this diversification strategy. In 2002 it acquired the West Coast refined products marketing business of Energy Operating Limited Partnership, a subsidiary of EOTT Energy Partners, L.P., a company in need of cash. The company was 37 percent owned by Houston-based Enron, which had filed for bankruptcy, its contracts with EOTT thus rendered worthless. Operating out of Long Beach, California, the new Trammo Petroleum unit pursued the wholesale marketing of refined products in California and the Pacific Northwest markets. It was also in 2002 that Trammo Petroleum began operating in Houston, merchandising and trading crude oil and refined products. A year later Trammo Petroleum became involved in the crude oil gathering and marketing business in the United States.

On the international scene, Trammo Gas in late 2002 acquired the London-based LP trading and transportation unit operated by Dynegy Global Liquids, a subsidiary of Dynegy Inc. In another development in 2002, Transammonia arranged to buy the entire output of ammonia and urea from a fertilizer plant scheduled to open in the Gulf state of Oman in 2005.

As a result of diversity, Transammonia's revenues rebounded at the start of the new century, totaling $2.45 billion in 2000. Poor economic conditions resulted in sales dipping to $2.3 billion in 2002, but a year later the company enjoyed a surge as revenues approached the $4 billion mark, making Transammonia *Forbes'* 39th largest private company in 2003. That sales number would grow to $6.1 billion in 2005, before slipping to $5.4 billion in 2006. In the meantime, Stanton, well into his 70s, finally turned over the chief executive function to Transammonia's president and chief operating officer, Peter Baumann, although he stayed on as chairman of the board.

While growing Transammonia into a multibillion-dollar company, Stanton had also devoted a considerable amount of time to philanthropic endeavors. He served as a member of the boards of New York Presbyterian Hospital and Lincoln Center, and as a trustee of his synagogue, making financial contributions to all three, but most of his generosity was bestowed upon Yeshiva University. In 1976 he was elected to the school's board of trustees. He became vice-chairman in 1992 and chairman of the board in 2002. He was instrumental in the hiring of a new president, Richard Joel, who was eager to improve Yeshiva's standing among private universities in the United States. Stanton was also a financial benefactor of the school. He donated $10 million to the university's undergraduate library which took the name of his mother, Hedi Steinberg, and then in 2006 made an even more generous contribution.

After being offered a variety of naming opportunities at Yeshiva, Stanton declined all of them in favor of donating $100 million to establish a fund that was both a working fund and an endowment. It was structured to provide the school with flexibility, a revolving fund that could be used for any project and then replenished as donations came in. The $100 million donation made headlines because it was the largest gift ever to a Jewish organization. Stanton told the *New York Jewish Week,* that he wanted the publicity to spur further donations. "I'm hoping that we can raise $1 billion, that this will raise the bar," he said. "There are lots of gifts of $1 million or $2 million, but now we want to get people to stretch a little bit. If we get to that point the university

can become much more influential outside of its immediate circle. The potential is definitely there."

Ed Dinger

PRINCIPAL SUBSIDIARIES

Transammonia, Inc.; Transammonia AG; Sea-3, Inc.; Trammo Petroleum, Inc.; Trammochem; Trammogas.

PRINCIPAL COMPETITORS

Cargill, Incorporated; ConAgra Foods, Inc.; Norsk Hydro ASA.

FURTHER READING

Arenson, Karen W., "Yeshiva University Gets $100 Million Gift," *New York Times,* September 13, 2006, p. B9.

Cohen, Debra Nussbaum, "$100 Million Gift to Yeshiva University," *New York Jewish Week,* September 15, 2006, p. 1.

"'Extra' Propane Tanker Arrives in Portsmouth," *New Hampshire Union Leader,* December 30, 1989, p. 18.

Forgrieve, Janet, "New York-based Propane Company Enters Florida Market to Build Tank," *Tampa Tribune,* January 22, 1999.

"4 Fertilizer Concerns Indicted on Violations of Sherman Act," *New York Times,* November 8, 1963.

"Sea-3 Set to Build," *New Hampshire Union Leader,* November 15, 1996.

True Temper Sports, Inc.

◾

8275 Tournament Drive, Suite 200
Memphis, Tennessee 38125-8881
U.S.A.
Telephone: (901) 746-2000
Toll Free: (800) 355-8783
Fax: (901) 746-2160
Web site: http://www.truetemper.com

Private Company
Incorporated: 1902 as American Fork and Hoe Company
Employees: 821
Sales: $108 million (2006 est.)
NAIC: 339920 Sporting and Athletic Goods Manufacturing

■ ■ ■

True Temper Sports, Inc., is a private manufacturing company that specializes in golf club shafts and high-end bicycle products. Golfing products is True Temper's signature division. The company provides both steel and composite shafts to almost all of the major club makers, including Callaway, PING, Titleist, and TaylorMade. Clubs using True Temper shafts have been a mainstay on the PGA professional golf tournament tour since the 1930s. Bicycle products, used by professional racers, include forks, handlebars, stems, seat posts, and bottle cages. True Temper also uses its steel manufacturing capabilities to make other sports products, such as hockey and lacrosse sticks, as well as automobile antennas. The company maintains its corporate offices in Memphis, Tennessee, overlooking the Tournament Players Club at Southwind, where each year the PGA holds the St. Jude Classic. Steel shaft and tubing manufacturing is conducted at a 335,000-square-foot plant in Amory, Mississippi, while composite shaft production is also done at facilities located in El Cajon and San Diego, California, and in China. Graphite golf shafts are also designed and engineered at the El Cajon location, which in addition houses the company's Performance Sports division, responsible for bicycle, hockey, and lacrosse products. True Temper maintains a test facility in Robinsonville, Mississippi.

EARLY 20TH-CENTURY ROOTS

True Temper grew out of the "tool trust" of the early 1900s, the American Fork and Hoe Company, incorporated in New Jersey in August 1902 by George H. Kelly, George G. Whitcomb, Joseph G. Russell, and Arthur B. Rust. The Cleveland-based company brought together a number of forging companies that produced agricultural implements and other tools (pitchforks, hoes, rakes, potato hooks, scythes) made from iron and steel, generally merging metal heads with a wooden handle. It was a combination that would naturally lead the company to the golf club business. The company reincorporated in Ohio in 1910, acquired other hand tool companies, and was by 1930 manufacturing about 90 percent of all farm-oriented hand tools.

BEGINNING OF GOLF CLUB SHAFT PRODUCTION: 1923

In 1923 American Fork and Hoe applied its expertise in forging to begin producing steel golf shafts. It was a good time to become involved in the sport, the popularity of which grew due to the exploits of wunderkind golfer Bobby Jones, who in 1923 won his first U.S. Open and then dominated golf for the rest of the decade, albeit with clubs using hickory shafts. In 1924 the United States Golf Association permitted steel shafts. American Fork and Hoe patented its step-down process to produce the shafts in 1928, but it was not until 1930 that the international arbiters of all things golf at the time, the Royal and Ancient Order of Saint Andrews, finally ruled that clubs with steel shafts could be used in tournament play. American Fork and Hoe began marketing the shafts under the True Temper brand. Within a year True Temper shafts were the market leader and a staple on the PGA tour.

Also in 1930 American Fork and Hoe grew larger through a $20 million merger that brought into the fold Charleston, West Virginia-based Kelley Axe and Tool Company and Dunkirk, New York-based Skelton Shovel Company. By this time making a broad range of steel products for both agricultural and industrial use, American Fork and Hoe was taken public in 1939.

The company continued in the 1940s to be an innovator in golf shaft design. In 1941 it introduced the first shafts available in the full range of flex categories, determined largely by the swing speed of the user, so that suitable shafts were available for women as well as male golfers desiring stiff and extra-stiff shafts. A year later the True Temper Dynamic line of shafts made its way to the PGA tour. By this point, however, the United States had entered World War II and, like most manufacturers, American Fork and Hoe had to contend with steel shortages while converting most of its production to war materials. Hence, the company produced such items as entrenching tools, bayonets, and machetes.

ADOPTION OF TRUE TEMPER NAME: 1949

Following the war, American Fork and Hoe resumed production of hand tools and golf club shafts. In 1949 the company changed its name to True Temper Corporation. It did especially well during the postwar years catering to the new suburbs that cropped up

around the United States as returning servicemen married and began raising children as well as gardens, which needed the kind of garden implements (hoes, rakes, shovels) that True Temper had been producing for farmers for many years. By the mid-1960s True Temper, with its 17 U.S. and four international plants, was generating record sales.

True Temper continued to produce golf shafts as well and in 1964 invested in the research and development of new shaft designs that made use of aluminum, fiberglass, and composite materials. The company also looked to apply its expertise to other sports, such as tennis. In 1965 the massive Armory, Mississippi, plant was opened. By this time True Temper was a major supplier of metal tennis rackets, and a year later became involved in the ski equipment industry through the acquisition of a manufacturing plant in Alliance, Nebraska.

MERGER WITH ALLEGHENY LUDLUM: 1967

In 1967 True Temper merged with Allegheny Ludlum Steel Corporation. The company continued to develop its golf business. In that same year, its researchers developed a golf robot to test clubs called Iron Byron, named after famed golfer Byron Nelson. The robot helped the company develop complete product lines in 1972 for women, juniors, and seniors.

Allegheny Ludlum sold True Temper to Wilkinson Sword Ltd. in 1978 for a 44.4 percent stake in Wilkinson. Two years later True Temper returned to Allegheny Ludlum, which had become Allegheny International, when the Pittsburgh, Pennsylvania-based conglomerate acquired the rest of Wilkinson Sword. A year later, in 1981, Allegheny acquired Sunbeam Corporation, taking on more debt than it could handle. In 1985 Allegheny was on its way to losing $109 million on revenues of $2.1 billion. In an effort to trim some of that debt, the company looked to divest some of its subsidiaries, including True Temper. In 1985 True Temper was sold to the Emhart Corporation for $102 million. At the time, True Temper was generating about $140 million in annual sales. Its product lines fit in nicely with Farmington, Connecticut-based Emhart, which operated hardware stores and home centers, and controlled such brands as Kwikset locks, Bostik adhesives, and Price Pfister faucets.

Under Emhart's ownership, True Temper invested in composite golf shafts and in 1986 opened a plant in Olive Branch, Mississippi, to produce the new shafts. True Temper's stint with Emhart lasted until 1989, when the parent company became the subject of a hostile takeover bid from Topper L.P., a New York

KEY DATES

1902: American Fork and Hoe is formed.

1923: American Fork and Hoe introduces steel golf shafts.

1930: True Temper brand is applied to golf shafts.

1949: American Fork and Hoe changes name to True Temper Corporation.

1967: Allegheny Ludlum acquires True Temper.

1985: True Temper is sold to Emhart Corporation.

1989: Black & Decker Corporation acquires company.

1998: Cornerstone Equity Investors acquires True Temper.

2001: Alpha Q bicycle fork line is acquired.

2007: Plant in China opens.

investment group headed by Gordon Getty, the son of the legendary oil baron J. Paul Getty. Rather than be acquired by Topper, Emhart sought a white knight in Towson, Maryland-based Black & Decker Corporation, which found the combination of the two concerns so inviting that it outbid Topper and acquired Emhart, along with True Temper.

In the fall of 1990 Black & Decker sold True Temper's hardware division for about $55 million to the Huffy Corporation of Dayton, Ohio, as well as three other divisions, in order to meet payments on the nearly $4 billion in debt it took on to acquire Emhart. Black & Decker retained True Temper Sport, the focus of which remained golf club shafts. Under Black & Decker's ownership, True Temper learned from the parent company's marketing skill to transform itself from a mere manufacturer to a significant consumer brand.

True Temper celebrated its 50th anniversary with the PGA in 1991 and continued to invest in research and development. In 1995, for example, the company introduced the Determinator fitting system, a system that measured a golfer's swing speed in order to determine the shaft offering the most appropriate flex. A year later True Temper introduced the Dynamic Gold Graphite line of shafts that relied on frequency matching to fit a golfer with proper shaft stiffness as well as length and weight, and used Sensicore Steel to absorb shock and provide a golfer with a more solid feel.

While golf equipment was making strides on a number of fronts in the early to mid-1990s, the game itself was losing popularity. As a result, True Temper's Seneca, South Carolina, steel shaft manufacturing facil-

ity was closed and production was handled in one plant. Golf's image would receive a much needed boost in August 1996 when Tiger Woods, the game's new wunderkind, turned professional. Woods quickly made his mark on the PGA tour, becoming rookie of the year in a limited number of appearances while displaying his prowess as a marketing magnet. Everyone connected to golf benefited, including True Temper. The company looked to golf-mad Asia to grow the business, establishing True Temper Japan in 1997. In that same year, the company introduced Shaftlab, a computerized system to develop an individual swing profile to help select the best shafts for a particular golfer.

SALE BY BLACK & DECKER: 1998

In the late 1990s Black & Decker decided to cut costs and focus on its core business, power tools, by divesting some of its assets, including True Temper Sports. The unit was generating about $90 million in revenues each year, 80 percent of which came from golf shafts. The remaining sales came from the application of the company's tubing technology to bicycles, BB gun barrels, and antennas. In June 1998 Black & Decker sold 94 percent of True Temper to a management group backed by New York City-based Cornerstone Equity Investors LLC for $202.7 million in cash and $4 million in stock. A few months after becoming an independent company, True Temper grew through acquisition. In October 1998 it acquired an El Cajon, California, manufacturer and distributor of composite golf club shafts, Graffaloy Corporation, a subsidiary of The American Materials & Technologies Corporation. Graffaloy brought with it the Attacklite, ProLite, and ProLogic brands of ultra-lightweight and performance graphite shafts, and bolstered True Temper's position in the growing graphite shaft market.

True Temper's golf business continued to grow in the new century. The company's Tri-Gold line of steel shafts was introduced in 2000. A year later the BiMatrix shaft was unveiled, combining a graphite shaft with a steel alloy tip, thus providing the distance and feel afforded by a graphite upper shaft along with the straighter shots delivered from increased head stability furnished by a tapered steel tip. In 2002 the company introduced what it billed as the world's lightest steel shaft, the TX-90. To help in further research and development efforts, the company opened a state-of-the-art testing facility in Robinsville, Mississippi, in 2003.

ACQUISITION OF FORK LINE: 2001

In the early 2000s, True Temper looked to expand its slate of other sports products beyond hockey and lacrosse sticks and bicycle tubing. In 2001 it acquired the Alpha Q bicycle fork line from AME, owned by Kyu Lee. True Temper had considered starting a fork operation from scratch but in the end decided to buy into the business. Moreover, Lee was well advanced in the technology of all-carbon fiber forks, having developed a patented carbon-rooting process. He started the business in San Leandro, California, in 1994, turning out handcrafted forks before employing carbon rooting. Despite receiving a patent on the technology, Lee watched as his designs were widely copied following their introduction in 1997. Because AME was too small to adequately defend the patent, or market his products, Lee decided to sell the business to True Temper and operate AME as a pure composite research and development company in order to develop additional bike components as well as pursue products for other industries. True Temper moved the production of the Alpha Q fork line to its El Cajon facility. It also looked to further develop the fork line and other composite components. Handlebars, stems, and seat posts were subsequently introduced.

In the autumn of 2003 Cornerstone was interested in taking a profit by selling True Temper, and hired investment bank Goldman Sachs & Co. to auction off the asset. It was not the most advantageous time to sell the business, however. Despite interest in Tiger Woods, the number of rounds of golf played nationally dipped in 2003, although international sales in the retail golf industry enjoyed a surge. In March 2004 Cornerstone was finally able to sell True Temper to a management group backed by Gilbert Global Equity Partners.

Sales grew from $98.4 million in 2004 to $117.6 million in 2005. True Temper looked to increase its market share in high-end golf shafts in June 2006 through the purchase of Royal Precision, which had gone out of business earlier in the year. True Temper picked up Royal Precision's Rifle and Project X brands

of golf shafts as well as manufacturing equipment, inventories, and other intellectual properties. In order to help meet increased production demands that came with the Royal Precision lines, as well as to bolster its presence in Asia, True Temper in March 2007 acquired CN Precision, a steel golf shaft manufacturer based in Suzhou, China. The two-year-old company was on the verge of production, and in October of that year the plant came on line under the auspices of True Temper.

Ed Dinger

PRINCIPAL SUBSIDIARIES

True Temper Sports—Europe; True Temper Sports—South Pacific; True Temper Sports—Japan.

PRINCIPAL COMPETITORS

Aldila Inc.; Graphite Design International Inc.; Toray Industries, Inc.

FURTHER READING

"Black & Decker to Sell 4 Units," *New York Times,* October 5, 1990.

Conner, Charles, "Golf Firm Primed for a Bid War," *Memphis Commercial Appeal,* February 1, 1998, p. C1.

Crenshaw, John, "True Temper Acquires Golf Maker, Aims to Boost Sales," *Bicycle Retailer and Industry News,* July 15, 2006, p. 8.

Somerville, Sean, "Black & Decker Says It Will Sell True Temper Unit to Cornerstone," *Baltimore Sun,* June 30, 1998, p. 1C.

"True Temper Buys Chinese Manufacturer," *Memphis Business Journal,* March 1, 2007.

Welsh, Jonathan, "Black & Decker to Shed Some Lines and Focus on Tools," *Wall Street Journal,* January 28, 1998, p. 1.

Wiebe, Matt, "True Temper Buys Carbon Fiber Fork Company," *Bicycle Retailer and Industry News,* November 1, 2001, p. 9.

Vestey Group Ltd.

---

16 St. John's Lane
London, EC1M 4AF
United Kingdom
Telephone: (+44 020) 7248 1212
Fax: (+44 020) 7250 3159
Web site: http://www.vesteyfoods.com

Private Company
Incorporated: 1897 as Union Cold Storage Company
Employees: 940
Sales: £460 million ($918 million) (2007 est.)
NAIC: 424470 Meat and Meat Product Merchant Wholesalers; 311612 Meat Processed from Carcasses

■ ■ ■

Vestey Group Ltd. has been a major force in the U.K. and European food sector for more than a century. Vestey Foods Group, the company's largest operation, is involved in the import, storage, and wholesale distribution of primarily meats and seafood, as well as convenience items. This division is comprised of 12 companies operating in the United Kingdom, Denmark, France, Germany, Switzerland, Japan, Korea, and Dubai. This geographic spread enables the company to reach more than 70 countries worldwide. Vestey Foods Group generates approximately £350 million ($700 million) of Vestey Group's total revenues of £460 million ($918 million). Vestey's Fine Foods division operates through subsidiary Classic Fine Foods and acts as a wholesale distributor of fresh and perishable foods, including

pastry, in the United Kingdom, Dubai, France, and a number of Asian markets. The company's third division is its Farms division, which operates cattle ranches and other farms in Brazil and Venezuela. Founded in 1897, Vestey Group remains a privately held company controlled by the founding Vestey family.

COLD STORAGE PIONEERS IN 1897

The Vestey family's involvement in the British food trade began in the mid-19th century, when Samuel Vestey founded a business importing and selling goods from North America. Vestey's oldest son, William, born in 1859, joined him in the business, and at the age of 17 was sent to the United States. Vestey traveled to Chicago in order to purchase and ship meats, cheese, and other goods for the Liverpool business.

Vestey quickly saw an opportunity to develop a business in canning meats. Backed by his father's capital, Vestey founded his own canning factory, where he began producing corned beef for shipment to Liverpool. By using cheaper cuts of meat, especially waste that would otherwise be discarded, Vestey's canning factory proved highly profitable, forming the basis of the family's later fortune.

Vestey was joined by his younger brother Edmund, born in 1866 as Samuel Vestey's fifth child. Edmund Vestey was also just 17 years old when he arrived in Chicago in 1883. William Vestey later turned over management of the Chicago cannery to Edmund, while he went in search of new business opportunities.

William Vestey's search soon took him to South America, especially to Argentina, which was gaining a reputation for its beef production. Vestey began acquiring cattle ranches there; the family later grew into one of the largest cattle ranchers in that country. Argentina was also a source for partridges, highly prized as part of traditional British holiday meals. Vestey's first operations there involved shipping partridges to England.

Transporting products, particularly perishable meats, from Argentina to the United Kingdom remained an obstacle. In 1890, William Vestey, joined by brother Edmund, decided to invest in new refrigeration technologies, developing cold storage facilities in Argentina and in Liverpool. This was the start of what became known as Union Cold Storage Company. Formally incorporated in 1897, Union Cold Storage became the basis of the later Vestey Group.

The success of the first cold storage facilities led the family to expand these operations to London, Glasgow, and Hull. By 1900, Union Cold Storage Company had added facilities in Moscow, Saint Petersburg, Vladivostock, and Riga, as well as in New York, Paris, and Johannesburg. The company also expanded its range of products, to include Russian poultry, dairy goods, and eggs.

INTEGRATING OPERATIONS BEFORE WORLD WAR I

In order to meet demand, the company added a new egg processing facility in Hankin, China, in 1905. Before long, the company had added four more processing facilities, and became one of the leading sources of eggs and powdered egg products not only in the United Kingdom, but in the rest of Europe and in North America.

The need to transport goods from China led the Vestey family into a new area of operations: shipping. In 1909, the company bought two tramp steamers and began converting them to refrigerated vessels. By 1911, the company's first refrigerated shipments set sail, under the soon-to-become famous Blue Star Line.

The Vesteys added another five ships to the Blue Star Line in the years leading up to World War I. At the same time, the company began investing elsewhere by buying a meat packing plant in England, then acquiring a chain of butcher shops there. The company also established packing and freezing operations in Australia and New Zealand during this time. Meanwhile, the Vesteys continued to build up their cattle ranching interests, notably in Venezuela, Brazil, and Australia. In this way, the Vestey family ensured highly integrated operations.

World War I represented a more shadowy period for the family, however. In 1914, the British government passed a new Finance Act that significantly raised taxes. The Vesteys, who felt that they should be exempt from such tax hikes, decided to go into exile. The family moved first to Chicago, then later established homes in Argentina.

The family preferred to live in England. After appealing unsuccessfully to the government to restore taxes to their pre-1915 levels, the Vesteys and their accountants instead set out to exploit a loophole in the tax law through a complex arrangement that involved transferring the leases on the family's holdings to Union Cold Storage Company, which then paid a fee to a trust fund set up in Paris. The trust fund then funneled this money into a holding company, Western United Investment Company, controlled by the Vestey family. Western United was then free to turn over the money to the Vesteys, who received these payments tax-free. The system was perfectly legal under British law, and remained in place for more than 60 years before the loophole was finally closed. During that time, the Vestey family reportedly paid just £10 per year, despite possessing one of England's greatest fortunes.

Living once again in England, both William and Edmund Vestey became barons in 1921 in recognition of their role in supplying meat to the British forces during the war years. The following year, William went a step further, and reportedly paid £25,000 to the government, then under P.M. David Lloyd George, to gain a peerage, becoming Lord Vestey.

EXPANSION BEFORE WORLD WAR II

In the meantime, the Vesteys had not neglected their ever-growing business empire. The company's butcher business grew strongly, and soon numbered close to 2,500 retail shops. In support of these operations, Union Cold Storage continued to expand its network of cold storage facilities as well. The company continued to prosper, even while many of its competitors struggled during the Depression era. This opened new opportunities for growth for the company. In 1934, for example, Union became a major player in the Australian market

KEY DATES

1897: William and Edmund Vestey found food trading and cold storage business Union Cold Storage Company.

1911: Company branches out into shipping, founding Blue Star Line.

1934: Company acquires Angliss, a meats trader in Australia, for £1.5 million.

1991: Near collapse of Vestey Group and Union International forces restructuring of operations.

1996: Union International goes into liquidation; company begins streamlining its holdings.

1998: Sell-off of Blue Star Line completes refocusing as food trading group, through subsidiary Angliss International.

2002: Company acquires 41 percent of Rari Food in Germany (raised to 92 percent in 2006).

2007: Company completes rebranding of Angliss and other food trading operations under Vestey Food Group.

when it paid £1.5 million to take over the Angliss meats company. Angliss then became a major company within the Vestey Group, growing into a multinational business with operations in the United Kingdom, Europe, and elsewhere.

The Blue Star Line continued to add ships, operating a dozen vessels through World War I. Following the war, the company began a major shipbuilding program, launching the first of its "Star" vessels, which included the *Almeda Star,* the *Andalucia Star,* and the *Avelona Star.* The Blue Star Line by then had expanded to include passenger vessel operations as well. Among the most noted of its vessels was the *Arandora Star,* which provided passenger transport between the Mediterranean, the Baltics, and the West Indies.

Most of the company's prewar growth was the work of Ronald Vestey, son of Edmund, described by the *Daily Telegraph* as: "a business autocrat who, after his father and uncle retired, controlled every detail of the family empire down to the arrangement of meat cuts in Dewhursts' shop displays, and expanded it with great success in the years before the Second World War."

By the end of the 1930s, Blue Star's fleet neared 40 vessels. These were soon pressed into service by the British government, providing food transport in support of the country's war effort. However, the hazards of war

caught up with the company's fleet. By the end of the war, the company had lost 29 of its ships.

William Vestey did not live to see the damage to the group's fleet, having died in 1940. His place was taken by his son, Samuel, born in 1882. Edmund Vestey remained chairman of the company until his own death in 1953, and his son, Ronald Vestey, born in 1898, became the group's chairman.

EXPANSION THEN NEAR COLLAPSE 1950–1995

The 1950s saw a period of new expansion for the family's holdings, both in its cold storage and distribution business, which became known as Union International, and its retail business, the Dewhurst butchers network. The company's shipping business also grew strongly, as Blue Star set out to rebuild its fleet through the 1950s. For this, the company combined both new buildings and secondhand purchases. Many of the company's ships featured both cargo transport and passenger accommodations, and became popular especially with Europeans wintering in South America.

The growth of the passenger airline industry during the 1960s and 1970s eventually put an end to Blue Star's passenger service. Instead, the company began converting its operations to containerships. Leading that company was Edmund Vestey, son of Ronald, who became head of Blue Star in 1971, before becoming the head of the family fortune following his father's death.

Through the 1970s, the Vestey family's operations remained one of the largest privately controlled business empires in the United Kingdom. The family, whose worth was valued at more than £2 billion, maintained significant operations both in the United Kingdom and abroad, including more than 250,000 head of cattle in South America. The company also diversified its holdings, adding insurance businesses, while also investing in real estate.

The family experienced a wave of negative publicity at the beginning of the 1980s, when their longstanding tax avoidance scheme came to light. While entirely legal, the scheme provoked an outcry among British taxpayers. In response, Edmund Vestey was reported to say: "Let's face it, no one pays more tax than they have to. ... I believe that it has been to the benefit of this country." Despite the outcry, the loophole that had permitted the scheme was finally closed only in 1991.

By then, the Vesteys' own fortunes appeared to be contracting. A series of ill-timed real estate investments during the boom of the 1980s proved to be the family's Achilles heel as the building market collapsed and the

United Kingdom slipped into recession in the early 1990s. By 1991, Union International, crippled by more than £430 million in debt, was on the verge of bankruptcy. Even the Vestey Group itself, set up as the holding company for the range of Vestey family businesses, began showing signs of breaking as the recession deepened.

Edmund was forced to turn over leadership of the Vestey Group to his son Tim Vestey, then just 31 years old. The younger Vestey in turn brought in outside management for the first time in order to sort out the problems at Union International. The family, whose worth had slipped back to £1.4 billion, also appointed a merchant bank to help restructure the Vestey Group's own debts with its nearly 100 banks around the world.

The restructuring at both Union International and Vestey Group helped slash the companies' debt, and, in the case of Union International restore it to profitability as early as 1992. However, the Vestey family continued to struggle with the effects of the recession, which lingered on toward the middle of the decade in the United Kingdom. In 1995, Edmund Vestey managed to force his eldest son Tim out of the Vestey Group leadership, and instead placed power in the hands of his two younger sons, George and Robin, in January 1995. Both were active in the company, with George working at the Dewhurst butcher chain, and Robin part of Blue Star Shipping.

The Dewhurst chain had become a new weak point in the family's operations. The company had been unable to respond to the shift away from traditional butchers in favor of the supermarket channel. This trend had only been exacerbated during the difficult recession years. Despite Union International's success in cutting its debt back to £100 million, the Dewhurst chain became a major source of losses. After losing £33 million in just six months at the end of 1995, Vestey Group was forced to place Union International, and Dewhurst, in receivership.

REBIRTH AS FOOD IMPORTER FOR THE NEW CENTURY

Vestey Group began streamlining its highly diversified holdings, starting with the sale of its insurance operations, completed in 1996. By 1998, the company had sold the Blue Star Line as well. That sale, to P&O Nedlloyd, not only raised £60 million for Vestey Group, but also brought the company back into profitability for the first time since earlier that decade.

By then, Vestey had begun refocusing itself as a food importer and distributor. This process began in 1997, when the company created Angliss International

Group, which became the holding company for more than 30 trade companies around the world.

Vestey then began expanding that business via a series of acquisitions. These included a 51 percent stake in Germany's Rari Food International. In Japan, the company formed a joint venture with a local wholesale partner in Yokohama in 2000. The company entered Switzerland in 2002, founding a trading company based in Chiasso. The following year, the company added two operations in France, Volagel, a global trading company established in 1947; and Serviandes, based near Nantes, which combined import and meat processing operations. Rounding out the group's acquisitions that year was the purchase of the United Kingdom's Global Group Trading Ltd.

In 2006, Vestey acquired an additional 41 percent of Rari. By the end of 2007, the company had completed the integration of its various acquisitions. In September of that year, Vestey Group carried out a rebranding exercise for all of its food trading companies, which all took on the Vestey name as part of the company's core Vestey Food Group division. With sales of nearly £460 million, Vestey remained a prominent name in the global food trade.

M. L. Cohen

PRINCIPAL SUBSIDIARIES

Classic Fine Foods Ltd.; Vestey Foods Denmark A/S; Vestey Foods Dubai; Vestey Foods France SA; Vestey Foods Germany GmbH; Vestey Foods International SAS; Vestey Foods Japan Ltd.; Vestey Foods Korea Inc.; Vestey Foods Production SA; Vestey Foods Switzerland SA; Vestey Foods UK Ltd.; Vestey Foods UK Ltd.

PRINCIPAL COMPETITORS

Unilever; Grampian Country Food Group Ltd.; Brake Brothers Ltd.; Northern Foods PLC; Uniq PLC; Bernard Matthews Ltd.; Cranswick PLC; Farmfoods Ltd.; Kerry Foods Ltd.; Tulip Ltd.; Warburtons Ltd.; Roach Foods Ltd.; Prize Foods Group Ltd.

FURTHER READING

Beresford, Philip, "Rejuvenated Vestey Looks at Flotation," *Sunday Times,* January 15, 1995, p. 2.

Buckingham, Lisa, "Dewhurst Collapse Hits Vestey Family Fortune," *Guardian,* March 23, 1995, p. 1.

"Edmund Vestey," *Daily Telegraph,* November 11, 2007.

"Edmund Vestey: On the Wrong Side of History," *Sydney Morning Herald,* December 8, 2007.

Hamilton, Kirstie, "Vestey Heir 'Disinherited' by Father," *Sunday Times,* January 29, 1995, p. 2.

Miller, Robert, "Vestey Sells Insurance Business to Reduce Debt," *Times,* January 15, 1996, p. 37.

Nelson, Fraser, "Blue Star Sale Puts Vestey Back into the Black," *Times,* February 10, 1998, p. 28.

"UK Meat Giant Hit by Land Reform in Venezuela," *Agra Europe,* September 9, 2005, p. N8.

"Vestey Group Ltd., London Acquires Additional 41% of Rari Food International GmbH, Germany," *M&A International,* January 2006.

"Vestey Restructures," *Food Trade Review,* July 1991, p. 378.

Wacker Construction Equipment AG

Preussenstrasse 41
Munich, 80809
Germany
Telephone: (+49-893) 54020
Fax: (+49-893) 5402390
Web site: http://www.wackergroup.com

Public Subsidiary of Wacker Neuson SE
Incorporated: 1848
Employees: 2,837
Sales: EUR 742.1 million (2007)
Stock Exchanges: Frankfurt
Ticker Symbol: WACGn.DE
NAIC: 333120 Construction Machinery Manufacturing; 811310 Construction and Industrial Machinery and Equipment (Except Automotive and Electronic) Repair and Maintenance

■ ■ ■

Wacker Construction Equipment AG is a major producer of equipment for the construction, landscaping, agriculture, and civil engineering sectors. The company manufactures and distributes more than 250 products, organized into three primary groups: Compact Construction Machines; Light Equipment; and Services. The Compact Construction Machines division produces wheel loaders, trench rollers, and related equipment. This division produces approximately 14 percent of the group's total sales. The Light Equipment division, is the company's largest, generating more than 60 percent of revenues. This division oversees the company's range of

tools and other equipment including soil and asphalt compactors, electric rammers and hammers, and pumps. Wacker's Services division backs up its product sales with logistics support, 24-hour repair and spare parts services, and maintenance and rental services. The Services division contributes approximately 23 percent to Wacker's revenues. Wacker operates subsidiaries in more than 30 countries. Wacker's international operations are grouped under Wacker Corporation in the United States, and Wacker Machinery in Hong Kong, while the group's Munich headquarters oversees its European, African, Russian, and Middle Eastern operations. The Wacker group merged with Austria's Neuson Kramer, specializing in compact machinery, forming the larger Wacker Neuson SE in 2007. Wacker Construction Equipment is that company's largest subsidiary, and maintains its listing on the Frankfurt Stock Exchange. In 2007, Wacker posted revenues of EUR 742.1 million. The founding Wacker family, led by Ulrich Wacker, remains the group's majority shareholders.

BLACKSMITH BEGINNINGS IN 1848

Johann Wacker founded the future Wacker Construction Equipment group as a blacksmith's shop in Dresden in 1848. Yet the company's development into an industrial company came only later, when Wacker's son Robert Wacker inherited the business. In 1875, the younger Wacker converted the company's operations from a manual workshop to full-scale industrial production.

COMPANY PERSPECTIVES

Mission: Successful companies must attract customers, advise them, and give them new reasons to be excited every single day. This insight is nothing new in itself, but it does require a high level of steady sustained commitment from everyone involved. But the company also gains a lot from such relationships, for example the feeling of being needed and the chance to participate in small and large-scale projects around the world. To achieve this, we learn the language of our customers and respond to their requests in a decentralized and flexible manner.

The Wacker family's operations continued to grow over the next decades, with the third generation taking over the company's leadership in 1907. The group's breakthrough, however, came under the family's fourth generation, as Hermann Wacker reoriented the group as a producer of light equipment. The main impetus for this specialization was the company's invention of the gasoline-powered rammer, used for soil and concrete compaction. The device provided something of a revolution in the industry, where traditional rammers had been tied to steam and electric power generators.

Wacker's focus on the light equipment sector, with a special emphasis on ground preparation, enabled it to grow strongly both in Germany and internationally through the 1930s. The company created a dedicated international sales operation in 1938. At the same time, Wacker continued to develop innovative equipment and technology, such as the use of high-frequency-based internal vibrators.

The bombing of Dresden toward the end of World War II, however, completely destroyed Wacker's operations. At war's end, the family was forced to start again. At first, the Wackers opened a production facility in Kulmbach. In 1951, however, Wacker moved to its permanent headquarters in Germany.

ENTERING THE UNITED STATES IN 1957

The need to rebuild much of Germany and Western Europe provided fertile ground for Wacker's growth in the postwar era. The company remained buoyant through the economic boom years of the 1950s and 1960s. Wacker also targeted further growth on the international front, and in 1957 opened its first foreign subsidiary, Wacker Corporation, in Hartford, Wisconsin. The company started off with just six employees, with Hermann and brother Peter the acting salesmen for the company's gasoline rammer. The company soon succeeded in establishing its rammer as something of standard equipment on U.S. construction sites. With the growth in sales, the company developed its own service and repairs facilities, before launching its first U.S. production facilities in the Milwaukee region.

In 1960, the family's fifth generation, led by Klaus Wacker, joined the company. Ulrich Wacker, who became head of the entire Wacker group, joined the company in 1971. By then, Wacker had launched a new expansion, led by the construction of a new factory in Reichertshofen in 1964. In the United States, Wacker targeted further growth by supplying the plant hire sector, as well as its own direct sales force, starting in 1968.

Wacker's growth remained steady through the 1980s under the leadership of CEO Ulrich Wacker. The company's U.S. operations were strengthened with the expansion of the company's Milwaukee area plant in 1986. The Menomonee Falls operations grew to a surface area of more than 440,000 square feet. It also became the company's U.S. headquarters.

Wacker also continued to invest in developing its technologies. This led to the launch of new remote control steering systems, using infrared guidance controls, in 1992. Among other technology breakthroughs made by the company was the launch of its "Magic" electric hammer in 2001. This tool, destined for the demolition market, featured a brushless motor, cutting down greatly on maintenance and repair downtime.

RESTRUCTURING FOR THE NEW CENTURY

Through the 1990s, Wacker's international sales grew strongly, leading the company to institute a new global logistics platform in 1995. Wacker had also begun to plan a further geographic expansion of its sales and production operations, targeting especially the fast-growing Far East markets. The company established a third regional headquarters, in Hong Kong. This was backed up by the construction of a new factory in Manila, in the Philippines.

Wacker then carried out a restructuring of its operations in 2002. The company adopted a regional operation structure, based on its headquarters in Munich, the United States, and Hong Kong. As part of this restructuring, the company changed its name to Wacker Construction Equipment AG.

Wacker entered the new century a solid company with strong sales and profits. Nonetheless, the company

---

KEY DATES

1848: Johann Wacker founds a blacksmith's shop in Dresden, Germany.

1875: Son Robert expands business into industrial production.

1930: Under Hermann Wacker, company develops new gasoline rammer, revolutionizing the construction market.

1945: Company's operations are destroyed at the end of World War II.

1951: Wacker transfers operations to Munich.

1957: Company enters United States, establishing sales and production subsidiary in Wisconsin.

1966: Wacker builds new production facility in Reichertshofen, Germany.

1968: Wacker begins sales to plant hire and rental sector in the United States.

1986: Company carries out expansion of Milwaukee-area factory.

1999: Company opens production subsidiary in Manila, the Philippines.

2005: Wacker acquires Weidemann as part of expansion into compact machinery.

2007: Company agrees to merge with Austria's Neuson Kramer, creating Wacker Neuson SE.

---

struggled to develop a clear strategy for its future. As a result, the family-owned company turned to an outside investor, selling a 31.5 percent stake to the United States' Lindsay, Goldberg & Bessemer (LGB), which already had strong expertise in the equipment and machinery sector.

With LGB's backing, Wacker put in place a new set of objectives for the new century. The company, which focused especially on the light equipment market, targeted an expansion of its services operations. These included 24-hour repair and spare parts services, as well as maintenance services. The company also began emphasizing rental services, as plant hire, rather than sales, became an increasingly important part of the construction equipment market. In support of this, Wacker developed its own network of rental outlets, focused especially in Germany, and elsewhere in Europe. By the middle of the decade, Wacker's services division accounted for more than 20 percent of the group's sales.

Another important part of Wacker's new strategy was the decision to push for growth in the compact machinery—such as wheel movers, and other smaller

onsite vehicles—market. This effort took off in 2005, when Wacker reached an agreement to acquire fellow German group Weidemann, a leading European producer of compact machinery, especially small and midsized front end loaders, for the agricultural, landscaping, and other sectors. Wacker and Weidemann had built up a prior relationship, with Weidemann supplying its front end loaders to Wacker's rental network. Following the Weidemann purchase, Ulrich Wacker turned over the company's leadership to Georg Sick, who had joined the company in 1994, and became the company's chairman and CEO.

MERGERS IN 2007

Wacker continued targeting acquisitions as it put into place its new strategy. In 2006, the company completed two new purchases, buying Switzerland's Drillfix and the United States' Ground Heaters Inc. Drillfix added its own light equipment line, focused on tool and binder production. Similarly, Ground Heaters broadened Wacker's equipment catalog with its range of portable hydronic heating equipment.

With Wacker's new strategy and new management in place, LGB cashed out its holding in the company in 2006. The shares were placed in a new holding vehicle owned jointly by the Wacker family and the company's management. LGB's divestment came as part of Wacker's run-up to a public offering. This was completed in May 2007, with a listing on the Frankfurt Stock Exchange, marking the end of nearly 160 years as a privately held, family-owned company. The Wacker family nonetheless retained a controlling stake in the company.

The public offering came at the same time as the company announced that it had reached an agreement with Austria's Neuson Kramer Baumaschinen to merge their operations. The addition of Neuson Kramer came as part of Wacker's efforts to expand its compact machinery division. Founded in 1981, Neuson Kramer had specialized in such compact machinery as mini-excavators, site dumpers, and drive loaders. The businesses' operations, both in terms of product range and geographic sales, proved highly complementary.

The merger was completed in October 2007, creating a new holding company, Wacker Neuson SE. Wacker Construction Equipment formed the largest part of the new operation, which maintained the Neuson Kramer and Weidemann brands as well. The company's combined sales were expected to top EUR 1 billion at the end of its first full year in operation in 2008. After a century and a half as a leading German equipment manufacturer, Wacker Construction Equipment had taken a step toward ensuring its future as a major global construction equipment and machinery group.

M. L. Cohen

PRINCIPAL SUBSIDIARIES

Drillfix AG; OOO Wacker Construction Equipment GUS (Russia); Wacker (Great Britain) Limited; Wacker Baumaschinen AG (Switzerland); Wacker Baumaschinen GmbH (Austria); Wacker Belux S.A. (Belgium); Wacker Benelux B.V. (Netherlands); Wacker Byggmaskiner AB (Sweden); Wacker Corporation (U.S.A.); Wacker Danmark A/S (Denmark); Wacker Épít gépek Hungária Kft.; Wacker France S.A.; Wacker Iberica Construction Equipment S.A. (Spain); Wacker Macchinari Italia S.r.l. (Italy); Wacker Machinery (HK) Ltd. (Hong Kong); Wacker Makinalari Limited Şirketi (Turkey); Wacker Maskiner Norge AS (Norway); Wacker Maszyny Budowlane Sp. z o.o. (Poland); Wacker South Africa (Proprietary) Ltd.; Wacker stavební stroje spol. s r.o. (Czech Republic); Wacker-Koneet Finland Oy.

PRINCIPAL COMPETITORS

Atlas Copco AB; Caterpillar Inc.; Deere & Company; Doosan Infracore Co. Ltd.; Gehl Company; Ingersoll-Rand Company; Kubota Corporation; Manitou BF; Takeuchi Mfg Co. Ltd.; Terex Corporation.

FURTHER READING

Geske, Dawn M., "Wacker Adds Weidemann," *Diesel Progress North American Edition,* June 2005, p. 6.

"Wacker Merges with Neuson Kramer," *Western Builder,* October 15, 2007, p. 20.

"Wacker, Neuson Kramer," *Underground Construction,* November 2007, p. 54.

"Wacker to Build Ground Heaters Factory," *Rental Equipment Register,* July 20, 2007.

"Wacker to Merge with Austrian Manufacturer Neuson Kramer," *Rental Equipment,* May 1, 2007.

Weingarten Realty Investors

—■—

2600 Citadel Plaza Drive, Suite 300
Houston, Texas 77008
U.S.A.
Telephone: (713) 866-6000
Fax: (713) 866-6049
Web site: http://www.weingarten.com

Public Company
Incorporated: 1948 as Weingarten Markets Realty
Employees: 485
Sales: $599.05 million (2007)
Stock Exchanges: New York
Ticker Symbol: WRI
NAIC: 525930 Real Estate Investment Trusts

■ ■ ■

Weingarten Realty Investors is a real estate investment trust that acquires, manages, and develops shopping centers and industrial properties. The company operates in two segments, retail and industrial, but primarily concentrates on retail properties. Its portfolio comprises 335 retail properties with 55.5 million square feet of building space and 77 industrial properties with 17.1 million square feet of building space. Weingarten Realty's retail business focuses on shopping centers that are anchored by largely recession-proof tenants such as supermarkets or national, value-oriented retailers. The company's revenues are generated primarily from leasing space to tenants. Weingarten Realty operates in 23 states. Its greatest concentration of holdings is in its

home state of Texas, where it owns 167 properties with 25.7 million square feet of building space.

FROM POLAND TO TEXAS

The Weingarten family succeeded twice in the business world, starting two different companies from scratch and developing them into formidable competitors in their markets. Discipline, dedication, and a keen business sense underpinned the family's success on both occasions, enabling the Weingartens, who left Eastern Europe in the late 19th century in search of greater opportunities, to find precisely what they were looking for in the state of Texas.

The patriarch of the Weingarten family was Harris Weingarten, born in 1854 in a small village in the Galicia region of Poland. Not long after his wife gave birth to the couple's first son, Joseph, in 1884, Harris Weingarten made the biggest decision of his life. He decided to make the long and arduous journey to the United States, where the promise of prosperity offered the hope of a better life for his family. The Weingartens emigrated from Poland before the end of the decade, settling at first in Richmond, Texas, before moving to Houston. The city was on the verge of enjoying an economic boom period, creating ideal conditions for Harris Weingarten to realize his dreams.

FIRST WEINGARTEN STORE IN 1901

In 1901, the discovery of oil near Beaumont, 80 miles east of Houston, set the region's economy afire. The

COMPANY PERSPECTIVES

Weingarten has a record of success across diverse business cycles, and we are well positioned to weather—and capture opportunities—in a downturn. With a focus on retail properties that provide food and other basic necessities, we are less susceptible to the effects of business cycles and likely to outperform other REIT categories in a weakening economy.

bustle of commerce equated to a deafening roar, as Houston, the railroad center of Texas, became the thriving hub of the state's oil business. The year oil was discovered at the Spindletop oilfield also was the year Weingarten, with the help of 17-year-old Joseph, opened a dry goods store in downtown Houston. The business marked the beginning of what became a retail empire for the Weingartens.

At first, there was little indication that a century-long family business had been launched. The store prospered, to be sure, but it did not begin to rise to prominence until Joseph Weingarten took full control of the family business. In 1914, he formed J. Weingarten, Incorporated, taking the first step toward creating a more ambitious enterprise. In 1920, he opened a second store and began promoting his stores with the slogan, "Better Food for Less." He was credited with pioneering the concept of self-service, cash-and-carry shopping in Texas, a concept he used to establish a chain of grocery stores in Texas, Arkansas, and Louisiana. By 1926, he had opened six stores. During the next dozen years, he doubled the size of the chain. By 1951, there were 25 discount grocery stores under his command.

DIVERSIFYING INTO REAL ESTATE IN 1948

As the Weingarten retail chain expanded, Joseph Weingarten steered the family in a new business direction. In a move aimed at vertically integrating his operations, Weingarten formed a real estate sister company in 1948, christening the venture Weingarten Markets Realty. Through the real estate company, Weingarten built the supermarkets J. Weingarten, Inc., would operate, giving the family further control over its operations.

The two companies grew side by side for more than 30 years, each feeding off the growth of the other. During the first decade of the new arrangement, the third generation of the Weingarten family joined the business.

Stanford Alexander, Harris Weingarten's grandson, joined the company in 1955. He entered on the supermarket side of the family's operations, completing an executive training program at J. Weingarten, Inc., but his future was in the real estate side. He was named president of the realty company in 1962, taking command of the company as it began to venture into a new business area. Its initial responsibility for building the family's supermarkets broadened into the development of shopping centers, which became the sole focus of the realty operations in later years.

Joseph Weingarten died in 1967, leaving behind him a chain of 70 supermarkets. His foray into real estate also had developed into a substantially sized business, boasting 45 properties in Texas, Arkansas, and Louisiana, the same three states where the supermarket chain operated.

The family's interests remained divided between operating supermarkets and developing shopping centers until 1980, a year of profound change for the Weingartens. Stanford Alexander decided to exit the supermarket business and focus the family's efforts exclusively on developing shopping centers. J. Weingarten, Inc., had developed into a chain of 104 stores in a five-state operating territory by the time it was sold to an Elmwood Park, New Jersey-based company named Grand Union. In 1984, Grand Union sold the Weingarten stores to three competitors (Safeway, Randall's, and Gerland's Food Fair), which marked the end of the association of the Weingarten name with supermarkets.

THE STANFORD ALEXANDER ERA

Stanford Alexander benefited from the legacy of his family in the supermarket business as he pressed ahead with Weingarten Realty Inc., the name of the company after it expanded into shopping center development. He would use his relationships with retailers—the supermarket, drugstore, and discount store operators he had come to know—to establish reliable tenants for his shopping centers. To aid him in his efforts, he relied on two individuals in particular. Martin Debrovner, who eventually became Weingarten Realty's vice-chairman, proved a valuable partner in orchestrating the expansion of the realty business. Debrovner had joined the realty business in 1968, one year after Joseph Weingarten's death, and he would play an instrumental role in converting the company into a real estate investment trust (REIT). Stanford Alexander also relied on the contributions of his son, Andrew "Drew" Alexander, who joined Weingarten Realty in 1978 as a leasing executive in the retail division. In 1984, Drew Alexander was named vice-president of the company.

KEY DATES

1901: Harris Weingarten opens a dry goods store in Houston.

1914: J. Weingarten, Incorporated, the entity in charge of the Weingartens' supermarket business, is formed.

1920: Joseph Weingarten opens a second grocery store and begins to develop a retail chain.

1948: To help build their supermarket chain, the Weingarten family forms a real estate company, Weingarten Markets Realty.

1980: The Weingartens, led by Stanford Alexander (grandson of the founder), exit the supermarket business to focus exclusively on real estate development.

1985: After converting to a real estate investment trust, Weingarten Realty completes its initial public offering of stock.

2001: Stanford Alexander's son, Andrew Alexander, is appointed chief executive officer.

2007: Revenues reach a record high of $599 million, a total drawn from 415 properties in 23 states.

PUBLIC DEBUT IN 1985

Not long after deciding to concentrate exclusively on the real estate business, the company made a significant change to its structure. Stanford Alexander and Martin Debrovner decided to restructure Weingarten Realty as a REIT, a tax designation for a company investing in real estate. As a REIT, Weingarten Realty avoided taxation on a corporate level provided it distributed 90 percent of its profits to investors. After converting to a REIT, the company completed its initial public offering (IPO) of stock, debuting on the New York Stock Exchange in August 1985.

Weingarten Realty's status as a publicly traded entity allowed for greater scrutiny of the operations headed by Stanford Alexander. More industry observers came to know the company, whose personality aped that of its leader. Weingarten Realty and Alexander moved methodically, taking measured, carefully calculated steps forward. "I've seen glaciers move faster than Weingarten," an investment banker commented in a July 24, 1989, interview with *Forbes*. Stanford Alexander typically studied more than 100 real estate properties before finding one candidate that met his criteria. He built or acquired only shopping centers ranging between 100,000 and 300,000 square feet, eschewing regional malls and strip shopping centers. He never began development of a property until at least 50 percent of the space was pre-leased. Further, he invested for the long-term, having divested no more than a handful of properties during a quarter-century of investing in real estate. Most important, he secured anchor tenants whose businesses typically were able to withstand anemic economic conditions, preferring supermarkets and national retail chains that tended to perform well during recessions.

By the end of the 1980s, Weingarten Realty owned nearly 120 properties in six states, nearly all of which were shopping centers. The company dabbled in the industrial sector, owning nine industrial properties. The majority of Weingarten Realty's shopping centers, which generated 90 percent of its revenues, were located in Texas, primarily in Houston. The concentration of properties in Houston offered evidence that Stanford Alexander employed an effective investment strategy. The city's economy was suffering at the end of the decade, feeling the sting of a recession, but Weingarten Realty's 61 shopping centers in Houston were 94 percent occupied. By comparison, the company's competitors in the Houston market averaged occupancy rates of 78 percent.

EXPANSION IN THE NINETIES

Stanford Alexander's disciplined investment strategy was cause for both joy and concern among Weingarten Realty's shareholders. The chief executive officer, "as shrewd as anyone I've ever met in real estate," a colleague noted in a July 24, 1989, interview with *Forbes*, was the architect of the company's success, which raised questions about the future success of Weingarten Realty after it lost Stanford Alexander. By the beginning of the 1990s, when Stanford Alexander was in his early 60s, speculation concerning his successor had begun to surface in the business press. Likely candidates to replace the company's most prominent personality were Martin Debrovner and Drew Alexander, but the selection process would have to wait. Stanford Alexander had no intention of retiring at the start of the decade. Instead, he was preparing to expand, armed with unused lines of credit that he intended to use to extend the company's presence across the southwestern, southeastern, and central United States.

During the 1990s, Stanford Alexander led the company's charge into new markets while fleshing out its presence in existing markets. The number of properties owned by the company increased from fewer than 120 to nearly 250 during the decade, giving Weingarten Realty a portfolio of 196 shopping centers, 50 industrial properties, one apartment complex, and one office building. Expansion during the 1990s, which was achieved according to Stanford Alexander's exacting standards, increased the company's operating territory from six states to 14 states. Annual revenues during the period leaped upward, increasing from $76 million in 1990 to $245 million in 2000, making Stanford Alexander's last decade in charge the period during which Weingarten Realty realized its greatest growth.

FROM FATHER TO SON IN 2001

In 2000, when Stanford Alexander was 73 years old, the issue of succession was settled. Drew Alexander was selected to lead the company, his promotion effective on the first day of 2001, 100 years after his great-grandfather opened the family's first store in Houston. Before the end of the month, the 44-year-old chief executive officer completed his first deal, acquiring Weingarten Realty's first properties in California. The deal, distinguished from Stanford Alexander's usual practice of buying only one property at a time, was massive, including 19 shopping centers anchored by supermarkets. Weingarten Realty purchased the properties from Burnham Pacific Properties, paying $145 million in cash and taking on a $132 million loan.

Under Drew Alexander's stewardship, Weingarten Realty outpaced the rate of expansion recorded during the 1990s. Between 2001 and 2007, the company's revenues climbed from $309 million to $599 million. Its operating territory stretched to include 23 states. The company's retail segment comprised 335 neighborhood and community shopping centers stretching from coast to coast. Industrial properties numbered 77 by 2007, situated in California, Florida, Georgia, Tennessee, Texas, and Virginia. In total, Weingarten Realty owned 415 properties that contained 72.8 million square feet of building space. As the company looked beyond 2007, it had 42 projects under development in ten states, with

more likely to follow. Considering the pace of expansion during the 1990s and 2000s, Weingarten appeared to be driving toward the $1-billion-in-sales mark, a total that would ensure the company remained one of the largest REITs in the United States.

Jeffrey L. Covell

PRINCIPAL SUBSIDIARIES

Weingarten Realty Management Company; Weingarten/ Investments, Inc.; WRI/Lone Star, Inc.

PRINCIPAL DIVISIONS

Retail; Industrial.

PRINCIPAL COMPETITORS

Developers Diversified Realty Corporation; Kimco Realty Corporation; Regency Centers Corporation.

FURTHER READING

"Aimed at Clearly Defined Targets: Leading Acquirers Grow Portfolios," *Chain Store Age,* May 1997, p. 88.

Greer, Jim, "Weingarten Realty Stock Price Soars As Market Continues to Skid," *Houston Business Journal,* November 2, 2001, p. 16.

Mendes, Joshua, "A Vehicle for Riding the Texas Rebound," *Fortune,* September 10, 1990, p. 24.

Shinkle, Kirk, "Weingarten Realty Investors," *Investor's Business Daily,* October 3, 2001, p. A10.

Taylor, John H., "Discipline, Discipline, Discipline," *Forbes,* July 24, 1989, p. 42.

"Weingarten Realty Investors," *Houston Business Journal,* November 21, 1988, p. 35.

"Weingarten Realty to Get New CEO; Drew Alexander to Replace Father," *Houston Chronicle,* September 7, 2000, p. 2.

"Weingarten to Buy 19 California Centers," *Houston Chronicle,* January 18, 2001, p. 3.

Whiting-Turner
Contracting Company

300 East Joppa Road
Baltimore, Maryland 21286-3020
U.S.A.
Telephone: (410) 821-1100
Toll Free: (800) 638-4279
Fax: (410) 337-5770
Web site: http://www.whiting-turner.com

Private Company
Incorporated: 1909
Employees: 1,900
Sales: $3.34 billion (2006 est.)
NAIC: 236220 Commercial and Institutional Building
    Construction; 236210 Industrial Building
    Construction

∎ ∎ ∎

Whiting-Turner Contracting Company is one of the largest construction companies in the United States. The employee-owned company is based in Baltimore, Maryland, but maintains about 25 offices across the country, including Boston, Massachusetts; Bridgewater, New Jersey; North Carolina's Triangle area; Atlanta, Georgia; Orlando, Florida; Cleveland, Ohio; Houston and Dallas, Texas; Las Vegas, Nevada; Denver, Colorado; and San Diego and Irvine, California. Whiting-Turner offers a full range of services, from feasibility studies and design, to construction and closeout. The company participates in virtually all types of building projects: cultural, educational, entertainment, healthcare, hospitality, industrial, life sciences, mixed use, office, parking, residential, retail, senior living, transportation, utilities and power, warehouses, and wastewater. Whiting-Turner is known for its practice of using engineers to run the company as much as possible. The company's longtime chief executive, Willard Hackerman, is an engineer by training who has also proven to be an adept, and sometimes controversial, developer. He rarely gives interviews and keeps the inner-workings of Whiting-Turning as private as possible.

FOUNDED ON FRIENDSHIP: 1900

The men behind the Whiting-Turner name were friends George William Carlyle Whiting and LeBaron Turner. While Turner may have contributed his name, the contracting company was very much Whiting's enterprise. Born in Baltimore in 1885, Whiting met Turner at the Massachusetts Institute of Technology (MIT), where he completed his studies in civil engineering after spending two years at Johns Hopkins University. After returning to Baltimore Whiting decided to start his own construction company, developing the idea with his friend and fellow MIT alumnus Turner. In 1909 they established Whiting-Turner Contracting, but Turner never worked for the company because, according to company sources, he was afraid of jeopardizing their friendship. A year later Whiting bought out Turner, but as a testament to his close friend, he retained Turner's name.

COMPANY PERSPECTIVES

The mission of Whiting-Turner is to build on our reputation for integrity, excellence, experience and leadership as the nation's finest construction organization by: continuously improving the quality of our work and services; constantly striving to exceed each client's expectations; maintaining our dedication to the highest moral principles; providing our people with a challenging, secure and safe environment in which to achieve personal career goals.

HACKERMAN JOINS FIRM: 1938

Whiting-Turner started out specializing in the building of sewer lines. Later the company added bridge-building to its repertoire. It took on one project at a time and was still a two-engineer outfit in 1938 when Hackerman joined the company. Also a Baltimore native, Hackerman, the son of a factory manager, got a head start on his engineering education by enrolling in Baltimore Polytechnic Institute, a public high school that offered an illustrious engineering program. Thus, Hackerman was able to trim the time required for his college engineering degree. As it was, Hackerman graduated from Poly at age 16. He then graduated from Johns Hopkins at age 19.

Whiting hired Hackerman at a salary of $35 a week, starting him out as a timekeeper, but from the very beginning Hackerman claimed that he knew that eventually he would become president of the company. At the time, the prize was not so illustrious, however. The country was in the midst of the Great Depression and contracting work was difficult to find. Whiting-Turner was fortunate to win a $187,000 contract to build a drawbridge in Cambridge, Maryland, Hackerman's first job. He soon graduated from his role as timekeeper to become a practicing engineer, and was tasked to find new areas of construction for the company to pursue beyond sewer lines and bridges. With the coming of World War II, which revived the U.S. economy, and the postwar business boom, there would be no shortage of opportunities for Whiting-Turner in the years to come.

HACKERMAN SUCCEEDS WHITING: 1955

In 1955 Whiting turned over the reins of the company to the 37-year-old Hackerman, who had been groomed for the post for many years. Whiting imparted a number of lessons, including the use of engineers in as many roles as possible, such as project managers or supervisors. Hackerman told the *Baltimore Business Journal* in a rare interview, granted in 1994, "Mr. Whiting stressed that for a company to succeed, you must have the highest levels of integrity." His mentor also told him, "If you can run Whiting-Turner without borrowing, do it." Hackerman followed the advice, telling the *Journal* that the firm had not borrowed any money since 1938.

Whiting died in 1974. Five years later the Johns Hopkins School of Engineering, which he and his wife had supported generously over the years, was named in his honor. Hackerman played an important part in arranging for half of Whiting's estate to be donated to the school. Hackerman would also contribute money to the engineering school as well as the School of Medicine. Moreover, Hackerman, after working a typical 12-hour day, found time to sit on about 60 boards over the years, including Johns Hopkins, the Associated Jewish Charities and Welfare Fund, and the Baltimore Symphony Orchestra. He also raised funds for numerous charities and once brokered the settlement of a five-month strike of the orchestra.

Aside from following the advice of his predecessor, Hackerman established his own basic guidelines, according to the *Journal:* "Diversifying, developing relationships, hiring the best people." Hackerman was especially adept at currying favor with state and local politicians, contributing lavishly to their campaign chests, to open doors for contracts to major building projects, including some of Baltimore's most recognizable landmarks. In the words of the *Baltimore Sun,* "He tied his fortunes to then [Baltimore]-Mayor William Donald Schaefer in the 1970s and 1980s, when Whiting-Turner was selected to build structures such as the National Aquarium, the Baltimore Convention Center and the Meyerhoff Symphony Hall." In addition, there was the IBM Tower at 100 East Pratt Street, virtually every bridge on Interstate 95 in the area, and the entrance gate at the Dundalk Marine Terminal. Over the years, Hackerman expanded Whiting-Turner's portfolio, according to a profile in *Johns Hopkins Engineer* magazine, "to include some of America's most prominent shopping malls, elegant embassies, high-tech cleanrooms, and well-known landmarks."

The list of Whiting-Turner's corporate clients was also impressive, including Frito-Lay Inc., International Business Machines Corporation, Bethlehem Steel Corp., Chrysler Corporation, Ford Motor Company, and General Motors. Even more importantly they became repeat customers, the result of the firm consistently

KEY DATES

1909: George Whiting and LeBaron Turner found company.
1910: Whiting buys out Turner.
1938: Willard Hackerman joins company.
1955: Hackerman succeeds Whiting as president.
1974: Whiting dies.
1994: Revenues grow to $700 million, branch offices to nine.
1998: Revenues top $1 billion.
2006: Revenues top $3 billion.

completing projects on time and within budget. Whiting-Turner also built a reputation for being able to handle the most complex construction jobs. "At one time," Hackerman told *Baltimore Business Journal,* "the top 15 *Fortune* 500 companies were repeat customers at Whiting-Turner."

WEATHERING THE 1989 BUILDING SLUMP

This repeat business led to Whiting-Turner opening offices around the country to serve the needs of its loyal customers. When the construction industry suffered through a severe slump in 1989, Whiting-Turner was able to bank on the solid relationships with customers, who directed whatever work they had to the firm. As a result, while other construction companies went under, Whiting-Turned did not even suffer a single layoff. As the industry picked up in the early 1990s, Whiting-Turner increased annual revenues to $700 million by 1994, when it was operating nine branch offices. At the age of 76 Hackerman was well past retirement age, but made it clear he had no intention of stepping down. "They're gonna have to hit me with a baseball bat to get me out of here," he told the *Baltimore Business Journal.* "I enjoy being the boss and I think I'm doing a good job."

Along the way, in addition to running a construction firm and being a philanthropist, Hackerman became a developer, directing work to Whiting-Turner while also gaining a reputation as a "savvy businessman," in the words of the *Baltimore Sun,* "who sometimes stretches the boundaries of ethics, one who benefits from the access to political leaders that copious campaign donations can earn." In 1981, for example, Hackerman acquired a trash incinerator from the city of Baltimore for $41 million, a deal that was lauded at the time as a way to allow private enterprise to improve an

inefficient operation. Not only did Hackerman receive a tax break in the deal, he negotiated a long-term contract with the city to make use of the incinerator. Soon it became apparent that the city was locked into a poor deal, in which it was paying three times more than necessary to dispose of the garbage.

Hackerman also gained some notoriety related to the building of Orioles Park at Camden Yards, Baltimore's new Major League Baseball stadium. In 1984 Mayor Schaefer named Hackerman to a panel that would decide the location of the new ballpark. A year earlier Hackerman and partner Morton Macks acquired the former B&O Railroad warehouse at Camden Yards in Baltimore for $3.8 million. Soon after Hackerman joined the panel, the list of potential sites was reduced to just two, one of which was Camden Yards. Hackerman recused himself at that point and began lobbying for Camden Yards, the project gaining steam when Schaefer was named Maryland's governor.

Hackerman and Whiting-Turner won some prominent state contracts following Schaefer taking over as governor. Kelly-Springfield Tire Co., based in Cumberland, Maryland, was on the verge of moving out when Schaefer, even before taking office, arranged a deal by which the state would invest $9 million in new facilities and road improvements to keep the company in Maryland. What was not known until later was that Whiting-Turner received a no-bid contract to do the work, which in the end cost taxpayers $15 million. The secrecy was troubling to competitors because two years earlier Whiting-Turner had received a no-bid contract to manage the construction of an addition to the convention center. Only after other construction companies complained about the arrangement did the city of Baltimore put the project up for bid and another construction firm won the contract.

It was against the backdrop of politically connected deals that the Camden Yards project played out. In 1986 the Maryland Stadium Authority decided to build the new ballpark at Camden Yards. Hackerman and Macks contended that this decision killed their plans to turn the warehouse into an outlet mall and office building. Hence, they asked for $18 million for the property. The Stadium Authority, on the other hand, maintained the property was worth $7.5 million and that the building plans for the site were unrealistic for a number of reasons: the location, minus a ballpark, was far from desirable, the economy was too sluggish, and the building was too long and narrow to accommodate the kind of use Hackerman and Macks said they planned. The two sides bickered over the price, and in 1989 the Stadium Authority, after having its $10 million offer rejected, moved to seize the property through eminent domain. The matter went to court and eventually the two sides settled on an $11 million price. The ballpark project went forward and the old B&O warehouse became a signature feature of Orioles Park at Camden Yards.

After Schaefer left office, Whiting-Turner continued to win a large number of public projects, albeit with far less controversy, including university and hospital buildings. By the late 1990s the company was generating more than $1 billion in annual revenues, briefly making it Baltimore's largest private company.

As Whiting-Turner entered the new century, its owner, in his 80s, continued to serve as chief executive officer and grow the company. Additional construction offices opened across the country, while Hackerman pursued more development projects and drew more adverse publicity. He succeeded in building an 18-story office building, the first downtown Baltimore skyscraper in more than a decade. However, Hackerman also drew criticism for another state-related deal. In this one, he arranged to acquire 836 acres of environmentally sensitive land in St. Mary's County for the same price, $2.5 million, that the state had paid a year earlier. Not only did Hackerman not have to guarantee in writing that he would conserve the land, he received a tax break of some $7 million and received the development rights to the property. What made the situation even more noteworthy was that for months state documents related to the negotiations referred to him as the "benefactor," whom officials refused to identify until required by law. Hackerman also engendered some ill will in the early 2000s when he wanted to demolish a retail and office complex in Baltimore County to make way for a chain drugstore, leading to community protests.

NEW CENTURY, CONTINUED GROWTH

In the meantime, Whiting-Turner continued its steady growth. In 2001 revenues totaled $2.3 billion, the result of a wide variety of projects spread across the country: a $400 million plant in Hopewell Junction, New York; a pair of semiconductor plants; a neuroscience center in Bethesda, Maryland; a $160 million Las Vegas mall; and a $90 million facility in Manassas, Virginia. As the decade progressed, Whiting-Turner continued to win more than its share of contracts, such as those for a Dell Inc. plant in Winston-Salem, North Carolina; a nanoscience research facility at the University of Florida; and repair of the runway at the Marine Corps Base in Quantico, Virginia. As a result, the company's revenues, according to estimates, topped the $3 billion level in 2006.

Ed Dinger

PRINCIPAL COMPETITORS

Clark Enterprises, Inc.; Skanska USA Building Inc.; The Turner Corporation.

FURTHER READING

Banisky, Sandy, "Judge Sets Formula for Price Haggling Today over Stadium Site," *Baltimore Sun,* April 17, 1991, p. 1B.

Kline, Alan, "Hackerman: Still on Top, Still Breaking New Ground," *Baltimore Business Journal,* November 11, 1994, p. 1.

Koch, Nora, "A Span Seven Decades Strong," *Johns Hopkins Engineer,* Fall 2005, p. 2.

Nitkin, David, "Developer Often Helps—And He Often Gains," *Baltimore Sun,* November 7, 2004, p. 1A.

Willkie Farr & Gallagher LLP

---

787 Seventh Avenue
New York, New York 10019-6099
U.S.A.
Telephone: (212) 728-8000
Fax: (212) 728-8111
Web site: http://www.willkie.com

Private Company
Founded: 1888 as Hornblower and Byrne
NAIC: 541110 Offices of Lawyers

■ ■ ■

Willkie Farr & Gallagher LLP is a New York City-based law firm employing more than 600 attorneys, operating branch offices in Washington, D.C., Paris, London, Milan, Rome, Frankfurt, and Brussels. Practice groups include antitrust and competition; business reorganization and restructuring; corporate and financial services; environmental, health, and safety; executive compensation and employee benefits; government relations; intellectual property; litigation; private clients group; real estate; tax; and telecommunications. The firm also does a great deal of pro bono work for the Legal Aid Society, representing clients unable to afford legal representation; Volunteer Lawyers for the Arts; Habitat for Humanity; Women in Need; City Harvest; and other organizations. Well respected but often flying below the radar, Willkie Farr became more visible to the general public after former New York Governor Mario Cuomo joined the firm in 1995 after leaving office. The firm has since aggressively expanded its operations, especially in Europe, where four offices have opened since 2000.

PREDECESSOR FIRM: 1888

Willkie Farr traces its history to the New York firm of Hornblower & Byrne. The lead attorney, William Butler Hornblower, was one of the most celebrated trial lawyers of his day and a member of prominent families on both his father and mother's side. He was born in Paterson, New Jersey, the great-grandson of Josiah Hornblower, a judge who was also a member of the Congress of the Confederation, the predecessor to the U.S. Congress during the country's formative years. His mother, Matilda Butler, descended from a number of Revolutionary leaders and colonial judges. Hornblower's father studied law but became a Presbyterian minister and professor of sacred rhetoric. Ironically, William Hornblower planned to study for the ministry but under the influence of a pair of uncles, one a U.S. Supreme Court justice and the other a U.S. circuit judge, the young man attended law school at Columbia University, graduating in 1875. Within two years he was a junior partner for the firm of Carter & Eaton, bankruptcy lawyers. The senior partners did not care for the courtroom, leaving Hornblower to serve as the firm's trial lawyer and allowing him to become well connected with both the bench and the bar, paving the way for an illustrious career.

At the age of 38 Hornblower established his own firm with a Harvard Law School graduate, James Byrne, six years his junior. Edward Sanford and Mark Potter served as law clerks. The firm represented such major clients as New York Life Insurance Company; Grant &

COMPANY PERSPECTIVES

Willkie Farr & Gallagher LLP was founded more than 115 years ago upon principles that still characterize our practice today. Our founders and memorable colleagues, like Wendell Willkie and Felix Frankfurter, established a strong foundation of integrity, innovation, pragmatism, flexibility and intellectual agility designed to continually meet the ever-changing business needs of our clients. These values form our approach to providing legal and business advisory services today.

Ward, the brokerage firm of former President Ulysses S. Grant; Otis Elevator Company; and famed inventor Thomas A. Edison. Hornblower was also personal counsel to newspaperman Joseph Pulitzer. In 1893 Hornblower was nominated by President Grover Cleveland, a political ally, to be an associate justice of the U.S. Supreme Court. Despite his obvious qualifications for the post, Hornblower would be denied with the appointment blocked by a political enemy, New York Senator David B. Hill.

LATE 19TH-CENTURY NAME CHANGES

In 1890 the firm took a new name, Hornblower, Byrne & Taylor, to recognize new partner Howard A. Taylor, and four years later became Hornblower, Byrne, Taylor & Miller with the addition of William Wilson Miller as partner. Specializing in corporate law, Miller would play a prominent role in the firm for the next 40 years, both as rainmaker and manager. One of the original associates, Mark Potter, left in 1894 to become a member of the firm Cole & Potter, but returned in 1898 to become a rail and coal specialist for what became Hornblower, Byrne, Miller & Potter a year later. Aside from its roster of illustrious partners, the firm during the early 1900s included associates Charles Evans Hughes and Felix Frankfurter, future Supreme Court justices.

HAROLD GALLAGHER JOINS FIRM: 1917

In 1907 the firm was renamed Hornblower, Miller & Potter. Seven years later William Hornblower died, but his name was retained by the firm, which became known as Hornblower, Miller, Potter & Earle. Two years later a prominent partner came to the firm, Lindley

Garrison, the Secretary of War for President Woodrow Wilson. In 1917 one of the namesake attorneys of the present-day Willkie Farr & Gallagher, Harold John Gallagher, joined the firm as an associate. Seven years later he became a partner. He would play an active role in the American Bar Association and a key part in bringing the lead name to the firm, Willkie. However, a number of other developments would take place before then.

In the same year Gallagher became a partner, the firm opened a Paris office to pursue the foreign loan business. Due to the Great Depression, the office would be shut down in 1932. Also during the mid-1920s, the firm opened short-lived offices in Berlin and Havana. The firm, by this time known as Hornblower, Miller & Garrison, underwent a major change in January 1930. Not only did Garrison leave because of poor health, the firm merged with another well-known New York firm, Miller, Otis & Farr, which included former New York Governor Nathan L. Miller and then president of the American Bar Association. The new firm, with a dozen partners and 24 associates, took the name Hornblower, Miller, Miller & Boston. The firm represented such prominent clients as Allied Chemical Corporation, Continental Can Company, and the United States Steel Corporation. During the early 1930s the firm established a longstanding relationship representing Major League Baseball owners when Governor Miller advised National League President Ford Frick on matters related to radio broadcasts.

WENDELL WILLKIE, PARTNER: 1941

It was not until 1935, more than 20 years after his death, that Hornblower's name was removed and the firm became Miller, Boston & Owen. Governor Miller would leave the firm in 1939 to serve as general counsel for U.S. Steel. Gallagher led the firm, albeit on an informal basis. He also became heavily involved in the presidential campaign of Republican Wendell L. Willkie, and after Willkie's loss to President Franklin Roosevelt in 1940, Gallagher invited Willkie to join the firm. He accepted and became a partner in April 1941. The firm became known as Willkie, Owen, Otis & Bailly, and a year later became Willkie, Owen, Otis, Farr & Gallagher. Although Willkie's name became a fixture, his tenure with the firm was brief. At the age of 52 he died of a heart attack in October 1944.

In the 1940s the firm continued to represent the interests of industrial and railroad companies while deepening its ties to baseball and developing a significant practice in private placements for insurance companies, serving Aetna, Connecticut General, Equitable, John Hancock, Metropolitan Life Insurance

KEY DATES

1888: William Hornblower and James Byrne form law practice.

1914: Hornblower dies.

1925: Harold J. Gallagher is named partner.

1931: Firm merges with Miller, Otis & Farr.

1941: Wendell Willkie joins firm.

1968: Firm takes name Willkie Farr & Gallagher.

1971: Paris office opens.

1981: Washington, D.C., office opens.

1995: Former New York Governor Mario Cuomo joins firm.

2000: Three European offices open.

2003: Firm is reorganized as limited liability partnership.

Company, New York Life, Prudential, and others. One of the firm's, and the country's, top railroad lawyers, Walter H. Brown, Jr., became a partner in 1943. Walston S. Brown, who had previously worked for the Roosevelt administration, became a partner in 1947 and brought with him as a client Kaiser Steel.

During the postwar period Robert B. Hodes, a tax lawyer, was named partner in 1956. William FitzGibbon joined the firm in 1958, resulting in another name change: Willkie Farr Gallagher Walton & FitzGibbon. In 1962 the growing firm moved to offices in the new 1 Chase Manhattan Plaza, one of the world's tallest buildings. (It would remain home until 1998 when the firm moved to new offices at 787 Seventh Avenue.) Also of note in 1962, future Chairman Jack H. Nusbaum joined the firm as an associate. Although he would eventually become a senior partner, the firm would not bear his name, because in 1968 the firm settled on Willkie Farr & Gallagher as its permanent moniker.

MERGER ADDS SEVEN PARTNERS: 1976

After a half-century, Willkie Farr resumed its practice in France, opening a Paris office in 1971. The decade also saw the firm complete its first merger in more than 40 years. In 1976 it joined with the New York firm of Sykes, Galloway & Dikeman, picking up seven partners and seven associates and a major municipal bond practice. Willkie Farr quickly became one of the top bond counsels to municipalities in New York state and public power authorities across the United States.

In 1981 Harold Gallagher died at the age of 87, the last link to the "old Hornblower firm." With 50 partners, as opposed to nine in 1917 when Gallagher became one of ten associates, Willkie Farr continued to grow in the 1980s. An office was opened in Washington, D.C., early in the decade and grew steadily, especially enjoying success with its telecommunications practice. In 1985 the office expanded by taking over much of the international trade practice of Wald, Hardraker & Ross, picking up five partners and nine associates. In 1989 an environmental regulation practice was established.

In New York during the 1980s, the firm's corporate lawyers were kept busy by a rash of hostile takeovers. The decade also brought the 1988 opening of a three-lawyer office in London, England, primarily to serve the interests of U.S. clients, and the expansion of the Paris office in late 1989 through the hiring of four partners from the Paris firm of Salans Hertzfeld & Heilbronn who handle mergers and acquisitions and leveraged buyouts. Although Willkie Farr had no particular aspirations for the Paris office, it turned into a powerhouse operation. Also, in 1988 Nusbaum and Hodes became co-chairmen, with Nusbaum taking the lead in plotting the firm's future course. He would become sole chair in 1995 after Hodes resigned at the age of 70.

In the 1980s the firm became too dependent on one client, the Shearson securities firm and its different manifestations. The relationship began in the 1960s when Nusbaum began doing work for First Cogan Berlind Weill & Levitt, which became Shearson Loeb Rhodes, Shearson/American Express, and finally Shearson Lehman Hutton Inc. By the late 1980s Shearson accounted for one-third of Willkie Farr's revenues, a risky commitment to a single revenue stream. Realizing its exposure, the firm established a bankruptcy practice in 1989 that would prove to be a wise hedge against the future. In 1990 business with Shearson began to decrease when Shearson's CEO and Nusbaum's close friend, Peter Cohen, was ousted. As a result the firm had to lay off 22 associates in 1990. The situation grew even worse three years later after The Travelers Companies acquired Shearson. Moreover, tough economic conditions had dried up opportunities in the mergers and acquisition and corporate finance markets, leading to a steady drop in partner profits, from $805,000 in 1989 to $605,000 in 1991. Yet tough times also benefited the new bankruptcy practice, which thrived and helped the firm weather a difficult stretch and begin to rebuild profits while diversifying. By 1999 profits exceeded $900,000, and no one client contributed more than 5 percent of revenues. One of those clients was Michael Bloomberg, who began working with Willkie Farr in 1987 through partner Richard

DeScherer, who helped Bloomberg build his media empire in the 1990s. DeScherer would become co-chair of the firm in 2002.

Another important partner to join the firm was New York State Governor Mario Cuomo. After Cuomo lost his reelection bid in 1994, partners John D'Alimonte and Nusbaum began to wonder if the governor had any post-office plans and quickly arranged a meeting. Cuomo made it clear to Nusbaum that he truly wanted to practice law, not simply act as a figurehead. Both men were impressed with one another and a month later Cuomo agreed to become a partner at Willkie Farr after he left office in February 1995. The addition of Cuomo helped raise the profile of the firm and generate more business. In 1996 the firm posted gross revenues of $209 million. In that same year the Paris office enjoyed another growth spurt and included seven partners, three special counsels, and 16 associates.

NEW CENTURY BRINGS EUROPEAN EXPANSION

The success of the Paris office and the trend toward globalization in the practice of law prompted Willkie Farr to expand its European footprint in the new century. Using Paris as the model, the firm opened three offices in 2000: Frankfurt, Milan, and Rome. At the same time, the firm beefed up its London office, and in 2004 added another continental office in Brussels to specialize in mergers and acquisitions, corporate finance and securities, commercial litigation, and business reorganization. The firm was also reorganized in the new century, in 2003 becoming a limited liability partnership under the name Willkie Farr & Gallagher LLP.

Ed Dinger

PRINCIPAL COMPETITORS

Dewey & LeBoeuf LLP; Fried, Frank, Harris, Shriver & Jacobson LLP; Wachtell, Lipton, Rosen & Katz.

FURTHER READING

"Big Law Firms to Merge," *New York Times,* December 4, 1930.

Herman, Eric, "The Stealth Firm," *American Lawyer,* September 1997, p. 58.

"Judge Hornblower," *New York Times,* June 17, 1914.

Lipman, Harvy, "Wall Street Law Firm Makes Cuomo a Partner," *Albany Times Union,* February 8, 1995, p. A1.

"Mark Potter, 76, Head of Coal Firm," *New York Times,* August 13, 1942.

"Mr. Hornblower's Career," *New York Times,* September 20, 1893.

"William W. Miller," *New York Times,* July 17, 1940.

"Willkie Farr in European Push," *Corporate Financing Week,* March 27, 2000, p. 5.

Zachry Group, Inc.

—————■—————

527 Logwood
San Antonio, Texas 78221-1738
U.S.A.
Telephone: (210) 475-8000
Fax: (210) 475-8060
Web site: http://www.zachry.com

Private Company
Incorporated: 1924 as H.B. Zachry Company
Employees: 15,000
Sales: $1.94 billion (2007)
NAIC: 237310 Highway, Street, and Bridge Construction; 237990 Other Heavy and Civil Engineering Construction

■ ■ ■

Zachry Group, Inc., is a family-owned private holding company based in San Antonio, Texas, the flagship unit of which is Zachry Construction Corporation offering construction, design-build, and project management services. Projects includes highways, bridges, dams, power generation plants, chemical refineries, retrofit air quality control systems, as well as U.S. embassies and other specialty projects. Zachry serves both public and private clients including such *Fortune* 500 companies as Abbott Laboratories, Bank of America Corp., ChevronTexaco Corp, Exxon Mobil, Hilton Hotels Corp., Monsanto Company, Pfizer Inc., and United States Steel. The firm works for the branches of the U.S. military and the State Department, U.S. municipalities and transportation authorities, and a number of foreign

governments. Also included in Zachry Group is Zachry Engineering Corp., Capitol Aggregates Ltd., Zachry Project Management & Consulting, and Zachry Remediation Services, LLC. The company is owned and managed by the second and third generations of the Zachry family.

FOUNDER, TEXAS BORN: 1901

The Zachry family of companies was founded by Henry Bartell "Pat" Zachry, born in Uvalde, Texas, in 1901, the son of Colonel John H. Bartell, an Army officer and successful banker. A well-rounded student, the younger Bartell earned a scholarship to Texas A&M University, intending to study animal husbandry to prepare himself for a career as a rancher. Due to World War I, the school was not offering the classes he wanted, however, and Zachry decided instead to major in civil engineering. After graduating in 1922, he was unable to take a job with the United States Geodetic Survey in Panama because his mother was ill, and he moved to Laredo, Texas, where his father was president of the Merchants State Bank.

Zachry went to work as a surveyor for the Texas Highway Department, drawing up the plans for the first highway in Webb County, providing access to an oilfield. After the Highway Department took on the construction project, he formed his own company in 1924, H.B. Zachry Company, to bid on the building of the road's only bridge. He won the $40,000 contract and set up shop over a Laredo drugstore. With a completed project under its belt, Zachry's construction business was established and within two years was generating more than $200,000 in revenues.

COMPANY PERSPECTIVES

Our Genuine Know-how positively impacts the delivery of Zachry's services, and fuels our success and continued growth. Zachry's commitment to excellence leads us to raise performance standards, reach out to the community, and provide better solutions for our customers.

COMPANY SURVIVES THE GREAT DEPRESSION

Zachry expanded beyond Highway Department contracts in 1927, adding commercial construction and remodeling projects. He would have to diversify even further in the 1930s with the country mired in the Great Depression. He won a few modest Highway Department jobs and a street paving contract from the U.S. Army Corps of Engineers, which was building Randolph Airfield, but soon Zachry was forced to look further afield for projects. He began building stock water tanks, which were being subsidized for farmers and ranchers by the U.S. Agriculture Department, work that allowed the company to scrape by during the early 1930s. Highway work eventually picked up, as the state and federal government began investing in projects to put people back to work, so that in 1935 and 1936 Zachry received 37 contracts from the Highway Department. A year later he established a department to focus on building construction and soon won a contract to build a pair of dormitory buildings for the Texas State Hospital System in Austin. By the end of the decade, the unit completed more than 20 building projects.

As the 1940s dawned, Europe was engulfed in war and Japan had invaded China, prompting the United States to begin a military buildup for the country's inevitable involvement in the worldwide conflict. Well before the Pearl Harbor attack on December 7, 1941 that led to the United States' entry into World War II, Zachry's company was focusing on defense work, including the expansion of Fort Bliss and Biggs Field in El Paso. During the war years, Zachry completed about $50 million worth of military-related construction projects, earning a reputation as a contractor that could produce good work in a timely fashion. For example, the company built the Hondo Navigation School, which included classrooms, barracks, mess halls, chapels, a hospital, hangars, shops, as well as runways and aprons,

streets, water wells, and utilities—the work completed in a mere three months.

The company's road and bridge work also prospered during this period because highways were needed to transport troops and material. Yet even as the founder was starting to take on defense work, he was taking advantage of the petrochemical industry that was developing the oil reserves in the Coastal Bend area of Texas. In 1940 he established a subsidiary to build, own, and operate a recycling plant in Grapeland, Texas, followed a year later by another plant in Francitas, Texas.

POSTWAR EXPANSION

After the war ended in 1945, the economy dipped into a mild recession before roaring back to life, leading to a boom that benefited H.B. Zachry, which also underwent a reorganization in 1945. In that year, Pat Zachry took on the titles chairman and chief executive officer. During the postwar years, his company was involved in a wide range of projects in addition to roads and bridges, including dams, airports, pipelines, processing plants, hospitals, railroads, and a variety of commercial buildings. H.B. Zachry also became involved in real estate development and housing, which experienced a great deal of demand during the postwar period as returning servicemen married and raised the baby boom generation. When the war came to a close in 1945, H.B. Zachry was posting revenues of $2 million; ten years later that number grew to $30 million.

H.B. Zachry outgrew Laredo, and in 1952 relocated its headquarters to San Antonio. It was also during the early 1950s that H.B. Zachry completed its first large pipeline job, laying 95 miles of 30-inch pipe in Tennessee and Kentucky. In addition, the company became involved in the power industry, building and upgrading power plants. Later in the decade Zachry added a sand and gravel unit to help in making the concrete needed to rebuild the runways at Austin's Bergstrom Air Force Base. It would be the start of Capitol Aggregates. Also of importance in the 1950s, the company became participated in a joint venture to build an antimissile test facility in the Marshall Islands, a project that led to almost $250 million in similar projects over the next 25 years.

BARTELL ZACHRY, CEO: 1965

In 1957 Zachry's son, H. B. "Bartell" Zachry Jr., joined the company, having already become familiar with the business during his high school and college years. Like his father he earned a degree in civil engineering from Texas A&M, graduating in 1954. He then spent a three-year stint in the U.S. Air Force, becoming a pilot. In 1965 he succeeded his father as CEO, although the elder Zachry stayed on as chairman and remained actively involved. Earlier in the decade the company had done a good deal of work in the power industry, completing a number of projects, including a nuclear plant in Spain, and under the leadership of Bartell Zachry, the company grew its heavy construction business. In 1966 it was part of a group involved in the massive Yuba River dam project in northern California. H.B. Zachry also built the 500-room, 21-story Hilton Palacio del Rio Hotel in San Antonio in 1968, completed in little more than six months (202 working days) in order to be ready for the World's Fair (the HemisFair) to be held that year. The company used innovative modular building techniques on the hotel, techniques it would employ to reduce construction times on apartment, condominium, dormitory, hospital, hotel, industrial plant, and prison projects. Pat Zachry also played a major role with the HemisFair, serving as chairman and CEO and covering hundreds of thousands of dollars in losses.

H.B. Zachry continued to win large contracts in a variety of areas in the 1970s. Industrial construction projects in the early part of the decade included seven coal power plants and the 1974 completion of the Union Carbide Olefins Complex in Louisiana. Airport work included paving the Dallas–Fort Worth International Airport runway. The company also helped construct the Trans-Alaska Pipeline in the 1970s as well as a number of international projects, including a dam in Canada and power plants in Puerto Rico.

DEATH OF FOUNDER: 1984

The 1980s was a period of transition for the company and the Zachry family. In September 1984 Pat Zachry

died. He was a man who was not only well respected as a businessman but also as a philanthropist. He served on the board of scores of educational and civic organizations and endowed scholarships at both Texas A&M and St. Mary's University. Because of his unassuming nature, it was impossible to gauge the full scope of his generosity. A few months before his death a grandson, John Zachry, joined the company he founded after graduating from Texas A&M with a degree in civil engineering. His brother, David Zachry, graduated a year later from Texas A&M with a civil engineering degree, and he too joined his father and brother at H.B. Zachry.

Aside from the introduction of the third generation of the Zachry family, the 1980s saw the company add to its reputation as a reliable contractor, one capable of tackling major projects. It completed the largest project in the history of the Texas Highway Department, the $63.5 million reconstruction of a major Interchange near San Antonio that called for new bridges, wider roadways, reengineered curves, new frontage roads, and other features. Another major project of the decade was the $64 million Richland Creek Dam, one of several dam projects the company took on. In addition, H.B. Zachry constructed eight power plants and 75 major industrial facilities.

At the start of the 1990s, H.B. Zachry was generating annual revenues of more than $700 million. After the country overcame a recession in the beginning of the decade, the economy roared and the company continued to win large contracts, leading to a steady increase in revenues. Some of the noteworthy projects during this time included the $1 billion Lyondell Citgo Refinery expansion; a $400 million joint venture to build a dam at the Eastside Reservoir in California; the BASF/FINA/NAFTA Region Olefins complex in Port Arthur, Texas; and the Dallas High Five Project, the largest single highway contract ever awarded by the Texas Department of Transportation. A new source of international projects also developed in the late 1990s, the reconstruction of U.S. embassies around the world, the result of the 1998 terrorist attacks on U.S. embassies in Kenya and Tanzania. The U.S. State Department budgeted about $16 billion to improve the security in the country's diplomatic facilities around the world. With its capabilities and international experience, H.B. Zachry was able to win its share of these contracts, including the reconstruction of the U.S. embassy in Moscow, Russia, which opened in 2000.

Because of its expanding operations, in 1998 H.B. Zachry was reorganized and new leadership roles given to the new generation as Bartell Zachry reached 65 years of age. To focus on construction and management projects, Zachry Construction Corporation (ZCC) was formed with John Zachry serving as president. David Zachry became president of the ZCC Civil Group.

In the early years of the new century, ZCC completed the construction of 25 power projects and grew its industrial maintenance services businesses. The company also won contracts to build new U.S. embassies in Cambodia and China in 2003, Nicaragua in 2004, and Ecuador in 2005. By 2004 ZCC was generating sales in the $1.5 billion range.

Further realignment took place in 2004 when David Zachry replaced his brother as president and chief operating officer of ZCC and John Zachry took over as CEO, replacing Bartell Zachry, who stayed on as chairman. David's role was to oversee day-to-day operations while John focused on long-range strategy and other areas. John also became chair of Capitol Aggregates. Part of the planning responsibilities included acquisitions. In 2005 Zachry Group acquired the Denver-based Utility Engineering Corp. of Xcel Energy Inc., picking up three subsidiaries, which designed and managed power plants.

REALIGNMENT ANNOUNCED: 2007

In November 2007 Zachry Group announced plans to further realign the companies. According to the *San Antonio Express-News,* instead of housing ZCC, Zachry Engineering, and Capitol Aggregates, the new plan called for Zachry Group to house just two: Zachry Engineering and Capitol Aggregates. ZCC operations would be split between the two, with industrial building and the maintenance of power plants and refineries falling under Zachry Engineering, and highway construction, infrastructure, commercial buildings, and river expansion projects assigned to Capitol Aggregates. John Zachry would take charge of Zachry Engineering while David Zachry would oversee Capitol Aggregates. The newspaper maintained that the changes were slated to take place in 2008 with Zachry Engineering likely to as-

sume a new name. The company assured clients, however, that the change would have no material impact on the way the Zachry family had always done business. "We're still the same company, doing the same thing," spokesperson Vicky Waddy told the newspaper. "It's just something we're doing at the high corporate level." A few months later, however, the company insisted the changes cited by the newspaper were inaccurate although some reorganization was expected to take place in 2008.

Ed Dinger

PRINCIPAL SUBSIDIARIES

Capitol Aggregates Ltd.; Zachry Construction Corporation; Zachry Engineering Corp.; Zachry Project Management & Consulting; Zachry Remediation, LLC.

PRINCIPAL COMPETITORS

Bechtel Group, Inc.; Fluor Corporation; Foster Wheeler Ltd.

FURTHER READING

"Family Tradition Continues," *ZachryWay,* Issue 4, 2004, p. 2.

Pfister, Bonnie, "San Antonio's Zachry Construction Vies to Build Embassy in Beijing, China," *San Antonio Express-News,* October 30, 2003.

Welch, Creighton A., "Zachry Group Streamlining Construction Operations into 2 Segments," *San Antonio Express-News,* November 8, 2007.

"Zachry Agrees to Buy Utility Engineering Firm," *San Antonio Business Journal,* March 3, 2005.

"Zachry, Henry Bartell," *The Handbook of Texas Online,* http://www.tshaonline.org.

"Zachry Lands Two State Department Contracts," *San Antonio Business Journal,* October 13, 2005.

"Zachry Presence Continues to Be Felt on Many High-Profile Projects Throughout Texas," *Texas Construction,* April 1, 2003, p. 39.

Zapf Creation AG

Moenchroedener Str 13
Roedental, D-96472
Germany
Telephone: (+49 09563) 72 51 0
Fax: (+49 09563) 72 51 116
Web site: http://www.zapf-creation.com

Public Company
Incorporated: 1932 as Max Zapf Puppen-und Spiel-
    warenfabrik
Employees: 336
Sales: EUR 116.1 million ($160.1 million) (2006)
Stock Exchanges: Frankfurt
Ticker Symbol: ZPF
NAIC: 339931 Doll and Stuffed Toy Manufacturing

■ ■ ■

Zapf Creation AG is one of Europe's leading doll
makers. The Roedental, Germany-based company leads
the European market in sales of play and functional
dolls, and holds a significant share of the plush dolls
category as well. Zapf's flagship brands include the Baby
Born doll line of functional dolls—that is, dolls that
exhibit lifelike functions, such as eating, drinking, wetting, and crying. While the Baby Born line is battery-
free, Zapf has also developed a second, battery-powered
branded line, Baby Annabell, with advanced features
such as sounds and facial movements. The Chou Chou
line includes plush dolls both with and without
functions. The more advanced dolls in the Chou Chou
line include Love Me Chou Chou, capable of kicking its

feet, sucking a bottle, facial movements, and sound; and
Rock-a-Bye Chou Chou, which yawns and can be put
to sleep by rocking. Since the early 2000s, Zapf has also
become a leading European developer in the 12-
centimeter-tall minidoll category, through the Baby
Born Miniworld line. Zapf also markets the My Model
fashion doll line for older girls.

Other doll lines include My Lovely Baby, for
children ages newborn to three, and the Maggie Raggies
fabric dolls, for ages one through eight. In addition to
the dolls themselves, Zapf also produces a wide range of
accessories for each doll family, including clothing and
props, such as strollers and high chairs. Founded in
1932, Zapf has been listed on the Frankfurt Stock
Exchange since 1999. Since 2006, the company has
developed a distribution partnership with major
shareholder MGA Entertainment, based in the United
States, which holds more than 24 percent of the
company. Harald Rieger serves as the company's
chairman. In 2006, Zapf posted revenues of EUR 116
million ($160 million).

DOLL MAKER IN 1932

Zapf Creation originated as a small toy workshop
founded by Max and Rosa Zapf in Roedental, Germany,
in 1932. The company, Max Zapf Puppen-und Spiel-
warenfabrik, quickly developed doll making as a
specialty. The company's earliest dolls were made of
papier-mâché by Rosa Zapf herself. The company soon
began hiring homeworkers in Roedental to produce its
dolls, while Max Zapf served as the company's salesman.

COMPANY PERSPECTIVES

Zapf Creation AG is Europe's leading brand manufacturer of play and functional dolls including accessories. The Company's most popular brands are Baby Born, Baby Annabell and Chou Chou. All branded play concepts share a high standard in terms of design, quality, safety and play value. The Company's branded play concepts are sold in more than 65 countries throughout the world.

Zapf later developed its own factory, and began producing celluloid-based dolls. The outbreak of World War II and the increasing difficulty in acquiring raw materials cut severely into the company's production, however.

The company's fortunes picked up again in the postwar period, as Germany entered a new period of economic prosperity and political stability. The company remained largely focused on the domestic market throughout the 1950s. This changed when the next generation of the Zapf family, led by Willi Zapf, took over the leadership of the company. Under Willi and Brigitte Zapf, the company began to develop its international sales for the first time. The neighboring German-speaking markets, particularly Austria and Switzerland, became strong markets for the company. The company also developed strong sales in the Benelux region and elsewhere in Europe.

A major milestone for the company came with its decision to launch production of plastic dolls in 1960. In this way, Zapf became one of the first to produce dolls with the new materials, which were much less fragile (and less flammable) than celluloid, while also easier to mold. Zapf was thus able to differentiate its dolls with increasingly lifelike features. By the end of the decade, the Zapf brand had become one of the most popular doll brands in Europe.

The 1960s also marked an attempt by Zapf to develop operations in other toy categories. Again, the group's move into plastic provided the basis for the company's growth. In the late 1960s, for example, the company launched a line of inflatable swim toys, under the Maritime brand. While never a major part of Zapf's overall revenues, the Maritime line nonetheless remained a part of the company's catalog until the end of the century.

NEW OWNERS IN THE NINETIES

Into the early 1980s, Zapf also recognized an important shift not only in the toy market, but in the global manufacturing sector. By then, an increasing number of manufacturing companies had begun to redevelop themselves as brand-holders, while outsourcing their production to low-wage markets in Asia and elsewhere. Zapf became one of the first of the European toy manufacturers to begin outsourcing its production. The shift toward an outsourcing model initially led the company to seek manufacturing partners in lower-wage markets in Europe.

Quickly, however, the Far East, with its far lower wages, came to represent the most promising manufacturing market. Zapf developed relationships with a number of Hong Kong-based manufacturers, especially King Creation, Wah Shing, and Gallant. These three manufacturers began producing the bulk of Zapf's dolls and other toys; in turn, Zapf represented more than 60 percent of these companies' revenues. In order to become closer to its suppliers, Zapf established a dedicated Hong Kong subsidiary in 1991.

By the end of the decade, approximately 92 percent of Zapf's production requirements were carried out overseas. The company nonetheless maintained a manufacturing base in Roedental. This was, in part, in order to maintain a level of manufacturing know-how within the company. At the same time, the Roedental facility specialized in high-end production, such as the Zapf Design Collection of collectible and limited edition dolls. These often sold for prices as high as $750 and more.

By the end of the 1990s, Zapf had firmly established itself as the leading European doll maker and the world's number one producer in the large-size doll category. The company had also completed its transition from family ownership.

That process was launched in 1992, when Willi Zapf agreed to sell 90 percent of the company to IMM Spielwaren-und-Freizeilartikel, the holding company for the toy operations of German conglomerate Triumph Adler. As such, Zapf joined Triumph Adler's other European toy brands, including Germany's Europlay, and France's Ideal and Majorette brands. The agreement included a plan to transition management of the company from the Zapf family to a new team brought in by Triumph Adler. That process was finally completed in 1997, when the Zapf family sold their remaining holding in the company.

BABY BORN SUCCESS

The new ownership and management structure came at a critical time for Zapf. In 1991, the company had

---

KEY DATES

1932: Max and Rosa Zapf set up toy company in Roedental, Germany, producing papier-mâché dolls by hand.

1958: Son Willi Zapf takes over as head of the company, leading international development and extending production into plastics.

1980: Company begins outsourcing production to lower-wage markets.

1991: Highly successful Baby Born functional doll line debuts.

1992: Triumph Adler acquires 90 percent of company.

1999: Zapf lists on the Frankfurt Stock Exchange.

2006: Company agrees to distribution partnership with MGA Entertainment, which acquires 24 percent stake.

---

launched what was to become its flagship brand, the Baby Born line of functional dolls. The Baby Born dolls represented an important breakthrough in the doll market, offering a range of highly lifelike features. These included "real" tears and the ability to be bottle-fed with a corresponding delayed wetting system. Importantly, the Baby Born line featured a wide range of accessories, from clothing to strollers, high chairs, and other items used in a child's pretend play. By the end of the decade, these accessories accounted for 75 percent of the Baby Born brand's total sales. The launch of accessories also permitted Zapf to balance out its sales beyond the traditional Christmas season.

The launch of the Baby Born brand coincided with another significant moment in the German toy industry. The deregulation of the German television broadcasting sector at the start of the 1990s introduced advertisements for the first time. Backed by Triumph Adler, Zapf spent heavily on developing its own television advertising campaign. As a result, Baby Born sales surged. By 1995, the line had captured the lead among all doll sales in Germany. By 1998, the Baby Born doll brand posted the highest sales of any toy in Germany, excluding video games. The brand also accounted for more than 60 percent of Zapf's total revenues.

Zapf's success encouraged Triumph Adler in its own plans to refocus its operations, and exit the toy industry, at the end of the 1990s. In 1999, Zapf went public, listing its shares on the Frankfurt Stock Exchange's SMAX index. Triumph Adler maintained a 25 percent stake,

however, in part to shield Zapf from the possibility of a takeover offer. Under Germany's rules, a takeover could be completed only if a prospective buyer was able to acquire more than 75 percent of a takeover target.

NEW PARTNERS IN THE NEW CENTURY

With the capital generated by its public offering, Zapf launched a new effort to increase its international presence. The Baby Born doll proved the group's flagship, especially as it sought to establish a presence in the U.S. market. The company had entered that country during the 1990s; in 1999, Zapf decided to set up its own dedicated distribution subsidiary for the United States, based in Florida.

By then, the company had also developed significant sales in the United Kingdom, where it launched a distribution subsidiary in Corby, England. Into the new century, Zapf added sales subsidiaries for a number of other European markets, including Australia, Italy, and the Czech Republic in 2001. In 2002, the company created a Spanish subsidiary, followed by a subsidiary in Poland in 2003.

Zapf backed up its expansion with the launch of a number of new doll brands. The company extended its functional doll technology with the creation of the highly sophisticated Baby Annabell line in 2001. The new doll line featured a variety of technology, such as infrared sensing and sound recognition. The doll proved a strong success: in the United Kingdom, the Baby Annabell line became the best-selling toy of the year.

Zapf also enjoyed success with its Chou Chou plush doll line. The launch of Rock-a-Bye Chou Chou in 2001 gave the company the number one position in the Duracell Kids' Choice Toy Survey in the United States. In 2002, Zapf entered the minidoll category, as exemplified by Barbie, launching the Baby Born Miniworld line.

While Zapf's European operations remained strong through the middle of the decade, its U.S. business stumbled. The company had begun experiencing difficulties generating orders from that market's major toy retailers, especially Toys 'R' Us and Wal-Mart. Part of the reason behind this was the strong and sudden success of the Bratz doll brand, marketed by California's MGA Entertainment. The success of Bratz tipped doll sales toward the fashion doll segment, and away from Zapf's core functional doll category. Yet Zapf itself was partially to blame for the slip in sales, as the company failed to launch a new doll for the 2003 year. At the same time, Zapf was unable to replicate the European success of the Miniworld line in the United States, against the perennial success of the Barbie brand.

Zapf slipped into losses at mid-decade. The company began looking for a larger partner and in 2006 reached an agreement to allow itself to be acquired by Japanese toy giant Bandai for EUR 10.50 per share. However, that deal soon hit a snag when MGA Entertainment announced that it had acquired more than 18 percent of Zapf. As a result, Zapf's share price surged, leading the supervisory board to believe that the Bandai offer undervalued the company.

At the same time, MGA's shareholding all but blocked Bandai's ability to assume control of Zapf under Germany's takeover rules. MGA then proposed a distribution partnership with Zapf, in which MGA would take responsibility for Zapf's sales in the United States, while gaining access to Zapf's strong distribution network in Europe. Following a boardroom struggle, and the resignation of a number of directors, Zapf agreed to MGA's offer. MGA subsequently increased its holding in Zapf to more than 24 percent.

One early result of the partnership was an increase in Zapf's U.S. distribution by more than 50 percent. The company was also able to shut down its money-losing U.S. subsidiary. The MGA partnership also allowed Zapf to retain its status as one of Europe's and the world's leading independent toy companies.

M. L. Cohen

PRINCIPAL SUBSIDIARIES

Zapf Creation (Central Europe) GmbH & Co. KG; Zapf Creation (France) S.A.R.L., Limonest; Zapf Creation (H.K.) Ltd. (Hong Kong); Zapf Creation (Italy) S.R.L.; Zapf Creation (Spain) S.L.; Zapf Creation (UK) Ltd.; Zapf Creation AG; Zapf Creation Logistics GmbH & Co. KG.

PRINCIPAL COMPETITORS

Mattel Inc.; GMA Accessories Inc.; Hasbro Inc.; JAKKS Pacific Inc.; Ty Inc.; Jumbo S.A.; Russ Berrie and Company Inc.; Dorel France S.A.; Cesar S.A.; Playmates Holdings Ltd.; Groupe Berchet S.A.; Dream International Ltd.; Chicco Espanola S.A.

FURTHER READING

Betts, Paul, "German Baby Dolls Play Hard to Get," *Financial Times,* July 12, 2006, p. 16.

Cottrill, Ken, "Out of the Box," *Traffic World,* August 12, 2002, p. 15.

"Custody Battle," *Economist,* July 22, 2006, p. 62US.

"Dolls and Accessories Sales Bolstered by Marketing Campaigns," *Retail Merchandiser,* October 2003, p. 22.

"It's a Doll World After All for Zapf Creation," *Playthings,* February 2002, p. 96.

Mendelson, Seth, "Zapf Gets Dolled Up," *Grocery Headquarters,* March 2003, p. 68.

Wassener, Bettina, "Zapf Creation Looks to Capture US Hearts," *Financial Times,* December 24, 2002, p. 22.

Wiesmann, Gerrit, "Bandai Drops out of Zapf Bidding," *Financial Times,* August 5, 2006, p. 17.

———, "Zapf Directors Start to Play Tough," *Financial Times,* July 11, 2006, p. 24.

Wilensky, Dawn, "An Executive Team at MGA Entertainment, Inc. Acquired a Significant Minority Interest in Zapf Creation AG," *License!* August 2006, p. 9.

"Zapf Makes Better Dolls, Helps Retailers Sell Them," *Chain Drug Review,* June 9, 2003, p. 108.

Cumulative Index to Companies

Actividades de Construcción y Servicios S.A. (ACS), **55** 179
Activision, Inc., **32** 8–11; **89** 6–11 (upd.)
Actuant Corporation, **94** 1–8 (upd.)
Acuity Brands, Inc., **90** 13–16
Acumos, **11** 57
Acushnet Company, **64** 3–5
Acuson Corporation, **10** 15–17; **36** 3–6 (upd.)
Acxiom Corporation, **35** 15–18
AD-AM Gas Company, **11** 28
AD South Africa, Inc., **60** 34
Ad Vantage Computer Systems Inc., **58** 273
Adaco, **70** 58
Adage Systems International, Inc., *see* Systems & Computer Technology Corp.
Adam, Meldrum & Anderson Company (AM&A), **16** 61–62; **50** 107
Adam Opel AG, **7** 6–8; **21** 3–7 (upd.); **61** 6–11 (upd.)
Adams/Cates Company, **21** 257
Adams Childrenswear Ltd., **95** 14–19
The Adams Express Company, **86** 1–5
Adams Golf, Inc., **37** 3–5
Adams Media Corporation *see* F&W Publications, Inc.
Adaptec, Inc., **31** 3–6
Adar Associates, Inc. *see* Scientific-Atlanta, Inc.
ADC of Greater Kansas City, Inc., **22** 443
ADC Telecommunications, Inc., **10** 18–21; **30** 6–9 (upd.); **89** 12–17 (upd.)
Addison Communications Plc, **45** 272
Addison Corporation, **31** 399
Addison Structural Services, Inc., **26** 433
Addison Wesley, **IV** 659
Adecco S.A., **36** 7–11 (upd.)
Adeletom Aviation L.L.C., **61** 100
Adelphia Communications Corporation, **17** 6–8; **52** 7–10 (upd.)
Ademco *see* Alarm Device Manufacturing Co.
Adero Inc., **45** 202
ADESA, Inc., **71** 7–10
Adesso-Madden, Inc., **37** 372
ADI Group Limited *see* AHL Services, Inc.
Adia S.A., **6** 9–11 *see also* Adecco S.A.
Adiainvest S.A. *see* Adecco S.A.
adidas Group AG, **14** 6–9; **33** 7–11 (upd.); **75** 12–17 (upd.)
Aditya Birla Group, **79** 1–5
Adler, **23** 219
Adler Line *see* Transatlantische Dampfschiffahrts Gesellschaft.
ADM *see* Archer Daniels Midland Co.
ADME Bioanalyses SAS *see* Eurofins Scientific S.A.
Administaff, Inc., **52** 11–13
Administracion Corporativa y Mercantil, S.A. de C.V., **37** 178
Administración Nacional de Combustibles, Alcohol y Pórtland, **93** 23–27

Admiral Co. *see* Maytag Corp.
ADNOC *see* Abu Dhabi National Oil Co.
Adobe Systems Incorporated, **10** 22–24; **33** 12–16 (upd.)
Adolf Würth GmbH & Co. KG, **49** 13–15
Adolfo Dominguez S.A., **72** 3–5
Adolph Coors Company, **I** 236–38; **13** 9–11 (upd.); **36** 12–16 (upd.) *see also* Molson Coors Brewing Co.
Adolphe Lafont, *see* Vivarte SA.
ADP *see* Automatic Data Processing, Inc.
Adria Produtos Alimenticios, Ltd., **12** 411
Adrienne Vittadini, **15** 291
ADS *see* Aerospace Display Systems.
Adstaff Associates, Ltd., **26** 240
Adsteam, **60** 101
ADT Automotive, **71** 8–9
ADT Ltd., **26** 410; **28** 486; **63** 403
ADT Security Services, Inc., **12** 9–11; **44** 6–9 (upd.)
Adtran Inc., **22** 17–20
Adtranz *see* Bombardier Inc.
Advacel, **18** 20; **43** 17
Advance Auto Parts, Inc., **57** 10–12
Advance Circuits Inc., **49** 234
Advance Gems & Jewelry Co., Ltd., **62** 371
Advance/Newhouse Communications, **42** 114
Advance Publications Inc., **IV** 581–84; **19** 3–7 (upd.)
Advanced Aerodynamics & Structures Inc. *see* Mooney Aerospace Group Ltd.
Advanced Broadband, L.P., **70** 325
Advanced Casino Systems Corporation, **21** 277
Advanced Circuits Inc., **67** 3–5
Advanced Colortech Inc., **56** 238
Advanced Communications Engineering *see* Scientific-Atlanta, Inc.
Advanced Communications Inc. *see* Metrocall, Inc.
Advanced Data Management Group S.A., **23** 212
Advanced Fiberoptic Technologies, **30** 267
Advanced Fibre Communications, Inc., **63** 3–5
Advanced Gravis, **28** 244; **69** 243
Advanced Logic Research, Inc., *see* Gateway, Inc.
Advanced Marine Enterprises, Inc., **18** 370
Advanced Marketing Services, Inc., **34** 3–6
Advanced Medical Optics, Inc., **79** 6–9
Advanced Metallurgy, Inc., **29** 460
Advanced Micro Devices, Inc., **6** 215–17; **30** 10–12 (upd.)
Advanced Neuromodulation Systems, Inc., **73** 14–17
Advanced Parking Systems Ltd., **58** 184
Advanced Plasma Systems, Inc., **48** 299
Advanced Pollution Instrumentation Inc., **62** 362
Advanced Semiconductor Engineering, **73** 301
Advanced Structures, Inc., *see* Essef Corp.

Advanced System Applications, **11** 395
Advanced Technology Laboratories, Inc., **9** 6–8
Advanced Telecommunications, Inc. *see* Eschelon Telecom, Inc.
Advanced Tissue Sciences Inc., **41** 377
Advanced Web Technologies, *see* Miner Group Int.
AdvanceMed LLC, **45** 146
AdvancePCS, Inc., **63** 336
Advanstar Communications, Inc., **57** 13–17
Advanta Corporation, **8** 9–11; **38** 10–14 (upd.)
Advanta Partners, LP, **42** 322
Advantage Company, *see* LDDS-Metro Communications, Inc.
The Advantage Group, Inc., *see* Habersham Bancorp.
Advantage Health Plans, Inc., **11** 379
Advantage Health Systems, Inc., **25** 383
Advantage Publishers Group, **34** 5
Advantest Corporation, **39** 350, 353
Advantica Restaurant Group, Inc., **27** 16–19 (upd.)
Advantra International NV *see* Punch International N.V.
Adventist Health, **53** 6–8
The Advertising Council, Inc., **76** 3–6
Advertising Unlimited, Inc., *see* R.L. Polk & Co.
The Advisory Board Company, **80** 1–4 *see also* The Corporate Executive Board Co.
Advo, Inc., **6** 12–14; **53** 9–13 (upd.)
Advocat Inc., **46** 3–5
AEA *see* United Kingdom Atomic Energy Authority.
AEA Investors Inc., **22** 169, 171; **28** 380; **30** 328
AECOM Technology Corporation, **79** 10–13
AEG A.G., **I** 409–11
AEG Hausgeräte, **53** 128
Aegean Marine Petroleum Network Inc., **89** 18–21
Aegek S.A., **64** 6–8
Aegis Group plc, **6** 15–16
AEGON N.V., **III** 177–79; **50** 8–12 (upd.) *see also* Transamerica–An AEGON Company
AEI Music Network Inc., **35** 19–21
Aeneas Venture Corp., **26** 502
AEON Co., Ltd., **V** 96–99; **68** 6–10 (upd.)
AEP *see* American Electric Power Co.
AEP Industries, Inc., **36** 17–19
Aer Lingus Group plc, **34** 7–10; **89** 22–27 (upd.)
Aera Energy LLC, **41** 359
Aérazur, **36** 529
Aereos Del Mercosur, **68** 365
Aerial Communications Inc., **31** 452
Aeries Health Care Corporation, **68** 299
Aero Mayflower Transit Company *see* Mayflower Group Inc.
Aero O/Y *see* Finnair Oy.

American Lightwave Systems, Inc., *see* ADC Telecommunications, Inc.

American Limousine Corp., **26** 62

American Linen Supply Company *see* Steiner Corp.

American Locker Group Incorporated, **34** 19–21

American Lung Association, **48** 11–14

American Machine and Metals, *see* AMETEK, Inc.

American Machine and Tool Co., Inc., **57** 160

American Machinery and Foundry, Inc., **57** 85

American Maize-Products Co., **14** 17–20

American Management Association, **76** 22–25

American Management Systems, Inc., **11** 18–20

American Materials & Technologies Corporation, **27** 117

American Media, Inc., **27** 41–44; **82** 10–15 **(upd.)**

American Medical Association, **39** 15–18

American Medical Disposal, Inc. *see* Stericycle, Inc.

American Medical Holdings, **55** 370

American Medical International, Inc., **III** 73–75

American Medical Response, Inc., **39** 19–22

American Medical Services, *see* TW Services, Inc.

American Metal Climax, Inc. *see* AMAX.

American Metals and Alloys, Inc., **19** 432

American Metals Corporation *see* Reliance Steel & Aluminum Co.

American Modern Insurance Group *see* The Midland Co.

American Motors Corp., **I** 135–37 *see also* DaimlerChrysler AG.

América Móvil, S.A. de C.V., **80** 5–8

American MSI Corporation *see* Moldflow Corp.

American Multi-Cinema *see* AMC Entertainment Inc.

American National Can Co., *see* Pechiney SA.

American National Insurance Company, **8** 27–29; **27** 45–48 **(upd.)**

American Natural Snacks Inc., **29** 480

American Olean Tile Company, *see* Armstrong Holdings, Inc.

American Optical Co., **38** 363–64

American Oriental Bioengineering Inc., **93** 45–48

American Pad & Paper Company, **20** 18–21

American Paging, *see* Telephone and Data Systems, Inc.

American Patriot Insurance, **22** 15

American Payment Systems, Inc., **21** 514

American Petrofina, Inc., *see* FINA, Inc.

American Pfauter, *see* Gleason Corp.

American Pharmaceutical Partners, Inc., **69** 20–22

American Phone Centers, Inc., **21** 135

American Pop Corn Company, **59** 40–43

American Port Services (Amports), **45** 29

American Power & Light Co., **6** 545, 596–97; **49** 143

American Power Conversion Corporation, **24** 29–31; **67** 18–20 **(upd.)**

American Premier Underwriters, Inc., **10** 71–74

American Prepaid Professional Services, Inc. *see* CompDent Corp.

American President Companies Ltd., **6** 353–55 *see also* APL Ltd.

American Printing House for the Blind, **26** 13–15

American Prospecting Equipment Co., **49** 174

American Public Automotive Group, **37** 115

American Publishing Co., *see* Hollinger International Inc.

American Re Corporation, **10** 75–77; **35** 34–37 **(upd.)**

American Recreation Company Holdings, Inc., **16** 53; **44** 53–54

American Red Cross, **40** 26–29

American Reprographics Company, **75** 24–26

American Residential Mortgage Corporation, **8** 30–31

American Residential Services, **33** 141

American Restaurant Partners, L.P., **93** 49–52

American Retirement Corporation, **42** 9–12 *see also* Brookdale Senior Living.

American Rice, Inc., **33** 30–33

American Rug Craftsmen, *see* Mohawk Industries, Inc.

American Safety Razor Company, **20** 22–24

American Salt Co., **12** 199

American Satellite Co., **15** 195

American Savings Bank, *see* Hawaiian Electric Industries, Inc.

American Science & Engineering, Inc., **81** 22–25

American Sealants Company *see* Loctite Corp.

American Seating Company, **78** 7–11

American Seaway Foods, Inc, *see* Riser Foods, Inc.

American Securities Capital Partners, L.P., **59** 13; **69** 138–39

American Service Corporation, **19** 223

American Ships Ltd., **50** 209

American Skiing Company, **28** 18–21

American Sky Broadcasting, **27** 305; **35** 156

American Smelting and Refining Co. *see* ASARCO.

American Society for the Prevention of Cruelty to Animals (ASPCA), **68** 19–22

The American Society of Composers, Authors and Publishers (ASCAP), **29** 21–24

American Software Inc., **22** 214; **25** 20–22

American Standard Companies Inc., **III** 663–65; **30** 46–50 **(upd.)**

American States Water Company, **46** 27–30

American Steamship Company *see* GATX.

American Steel & Wire Co., *see* Birmingham Steel Corp.

American Steel Foundries, **7** 29–30

American Stores Company, **II** 604–06; **22** 37–40 **(upd.)** *see also* Albertson's, Inc.

American Sugar Refining Company *see* Domino Sugar Corp.

American Sumatra Tobacco Corp., **15** 138

American Superconductor Corporation, **41** 141

American Surety Co., **26** 486

American Teaching Aids Inc., **19** 405

American Technical Ceramics Corp., **67** 21–23

American Technical Services Company *see* American Building Maintenance Industries, Inc.; ABM Industries Inc.

American Telephone and Telegraph Company *see* AT&T.

American Television and Communications Corp., **IV** 675

American Thermos Bottle Company *see* Thermos Co.

American Threshold, **50** 123

American Tile Supply Company, **19** 233

American Tissue Company, **29** 136

American Tobacco Co. *see* American Brands Inc.; B.A.T. Industries PLC.; Fortune Brands, Inc.

American Tool Companies, Inc., **52** 270

American Tourister, Inc., **16** 19–21 *see also* Samsonite Corp.

American Tower Corporation, **33** 34–38

American Trans Air, **34** 31

American Transitional Hospitals, Ltd., **65** 307

American Transport Lines, **6** 384

American Twist Drill Co., **23** 82

American Vanguard Corporation, **47** 20–22

American VIP Limousine, Inc., **26** 62

American Water Works Company, Inc., **6** 443–45; **38** 49–52 **(upd.)**

American Woodmark Corporation, **31** 13–16

American Yard Products, **22** 26, 28

American Yearbook Company, *see* Jostens, Inc.

Americana Entertainment Group, Inc., **19** 435

Americana Foods, LP, *see* TCBY Enterprises Inc.

Americana Healthcare Corp., **15** 522

Americana Ships Ltd., **50** 210

AmeriCares Foundation, Inc., **87** 23–28

Americom, **61** 272

Americrown Service Corporation *see* International Speedway Corp.

Ameridrive, **58** 67

AmeriGas Partners, L.P., **56** 36

Angele Ghigi, **II** 475

Angelica Corporation, 15 20–22; **43** 28–31 (upd.)

Angelo's Supermarkets, Inc., *see* Supermarkets General Holdings Corp.

ANGI Ltd., **11** 28

AngioDynamics, Inc., 81 26–29

Anglian Water Plc, **38** 51

Angliss International Group *see* Vestey Group Ltd.

Anglo-Abrasives Ltd. *see* Carbo PLC.

Anglo American Industrial Corporation, **59** 224–25

Anglo American PLC, IV 20–23; **16** 25–30 (upd.); **50** 30–36 (upd.)

Anglo-Canadian Telephone Company of Montreal *see* British Columbia Telephone Co.

Anglo-Dutch Unilever group, **9** 317

Anglo Energy, Ltd., **9** 364

Anglo Industries, Inc., *see* Nabors Industries, Inc.

Anglovaal Industries Ltd., **20** 263

Anheuser-Busch Companies, Inc., I 217–19; **10** 99–101 (upd.); **34** 34–37 (upd.)

ANI America Inc., **62** 331

Anixter International Inc., 88 13–16

Anker BV, 53 45–47

ANMC *see* Amedisys, Inc.

Ann Street Group Ltd., **61** 44–46

Anne Klein & Co., **15** 145–46; **40** 277–78; **56** 90

Annecy Béon Carrières, **70** 343

Anneplas, **25** 464

Annie's Homegrown, Inc., 59 48–50

AnnTaylor Stores Corporation, 13 43–45; **37** 12–15 (upd.); **67** 33–37 (upd.)

Anocout Engineering Co., **23** 82

ANR Pipeline Co., 17 21–23

Anritsu Corporation, 68 28–30

The Anschutz Company, 12 18–20; **36** 43–47 (upd.); **73** 24–30 (upd.)

Ansco & Associates, LLC, **57** 119

Ansell Ltd., 60 35–38 (upd.)

Anselmo L. Morvillo S.A., **19** 336

Ansett Australia, *see* Air New Zealand Ltd.

Ansoft Corporation, 63 32–34

Answer Products, Inc., **76** 237

ANSYS Technologies Inc., **48** 410

Antalis, **34** 38, 40

AntarChile S.A., **69** 141, 143

Antares Capital Corp., **53** 213

Antares Electronics, Inc., *see* Control Data Systems, Inc.

Antenna Company, **32** 40

Anteon Corporation, 57 32–34

ANTEX *see* American National Life Insurance Company of Texas.

Anthem Electronics, Inc., 13 46–47

Anthem P&C Holdings, **15** 257

Anthony & Sylvan Pools Corporation, 56 16–18

Anthony Industries Inc. *see* K2 Inc.

Anthracite Industries, Inc. *see* Asbury Carbons, Inc.

Anthropologie, Inc. *see* Urban Outfitters, Inc.

Antinori *see* Marchesi Antinori SRL.

The Antioch Company, 40 42–45

Antique Street Lamps, **19** 212

ANTK Tupolev *see* Aviacionny Nauchno-Tehnicheskii Kompleks im. A.N. Tupoleva.

Antofagasta plc, 65 46–49

Antonio Puig, S.A. *see* Puig Beauty and Fashion Group S.L.

Antonov Design Bureau, 53 48–51

ANZ *see* Australia and New Zealand Banking Group Ltd.

AO Sidanco, **45** 50

AO VimpelCom, **59** 300

Aohata Corporation, **57** 202, 204

AOK-Bundesverband (Federation of the AOK), 78 12–16

Aoki Corporation, **9** 547, 549; **29** 508

AOL Time Warner Inc., 57 35–44 (upd.)

AP *see* The Associated Press.

AP&L *see* American Power & Light Co.

Apache Corporation, 10 102–04; **32** 42–46 (upd.); **89** 58–65 (upd.)

APACHE Medical Systems, Inc., **16** 94

Apanage GmbH & Co. KG, **53** 195

Apartment Furniture Rental, **26** 102

Apartment Investment and Management Company, 49 24–26

Apasco S.A. de C.V., 51 27–29

Apax Partners Worldwide LLP, 89 66–69

APB *see* Atlantic Premium Brands, Ltd.

APCOA/Standard Parking *see* Holberg Industries, Inc.

Apex Digital, Inc., 63 35–37

Apex Oil, **37** 310–11

Apex One Inc., **31** 137

APH *see* American Printing House for the Blind.

APi Group, Inc., 64 29–32

APL Limited, 61 27–30 (upd.)

Aplex Industries, Inc., **26** 363

APLIX S.A. *see* Velcro Industries N.V.

APM Ltd. *see* Amcor Limited

APN *see* Affiliated Physicians Network, Inc.

Apogee Enterprises, Inc., 8 34–36

Apogee Sound International LLC, **62** 39

Apollo Advisors L.P., **16** 37; **26** 500, 502; **43** 438

Apollo Group, Inc., 24 40–42

Apollo Heating & Air Conditioning Inc., **15** 411

Apollo Investment Fund Ltd., **31** 211; **39** 174

Apollo Ski Partners LP of New York, *see* Vail Associates, Inc.

Apothekernes Laboratorium A.S., **12** 3–5

Appalachian Travel Services, Inc., *see* Habersham Bancorp.

Apparel Ventures, Inc. *see* The Jordan Company, LP.

Appetifrais S.A., **51** 54

Applause Inc., 24 43–46 *see also* Russ Berrie and Co., Inc.

Apple & Eve L.L.C., 92 5–8

Apple Bank for Savings, 59 51–53

Apple Computer, Inc., III 115–16; **6** 218–20 (upd.); **36** 48–51 (upd.); **77** 40–45 (upd.)

Apple Corps Ltd., 87 29–34

Apple Orthodontix, Inc., **35** 325

Apple South, Inc. *see* Avado Brands, Inc.

Applebee's International Inc., 14 29–31; **35** 38–41 (upd.)

Applera Corporation, **74** 71

Appliance Recycling Centers of America, Inc., 42 13–16

Applica Incorporated, 43 32–36 (upd.)

Applied Beverage Systems Ltd., **21** 339

Applied Biomedical Corp., **47** 4

Applied Bioscience International, Inc., 10 105–07

Applied Biosystems, **74** 72

Applied Communications, Inc., **6** 280; **29** 477–79

Applied Data Research, Inc., **18** 31–32

Applied Engineering Services, Inc. *see* The AES Corp.

Applied Films Corporation, 48 28–31

Applied Industrial Materials Corporation, *see* Walter Industries, Inc.

Applied Laser Systems, **31** 124

Applied Learning International, **IV** 680

Applied Materials, Inc., 10 108–09; **46** 31–34 (upd.)

Applied Micro Circuits Corporation, 38 53–55

Applied Network Technology, Inc., **25** 162

Applied Power Inc., 9 26–28; **32** 47–51 (upd.) *see also* Actuant Corp.

Applied Signal Technology, Inc., 87 35–38

Applied Technology Solutions *see* RWD Technologies, Inc.

Applied Thermal Technologies, Inc., **29** 5

Apria Healthcare Inc., **43** 266

Aprilia SpA, 17 24–26

Aprolis, **72** 159

APS *see* Arizona Public Service Co.

APSA, **63** 214

AptarGroup, Inc., 69 38–41

Aqua Alliance Inc., 32 52–54 (upd.)

Aqua Cool Pure Bottled Water, **52** 188

Aqua de Oro Venture, **58** 23

Aquafin N.V., **12** 443; **38** 427

aQuantive, Inc., 81 30–33

Aquarion Company, 84 12–16

Aquarius Group *see* Club Mediterranee SA.

Aquarius Platinum Ltd., 63 38–40

Aquatech, **53** 232

Aquila Energy Corp., **6** 593

Aquila, Inc., 50 37–40 (upd.)

Aquitaine *see* Société Nationale des Petroles d'Aquitaine.

AR Accessories Group, Inc., 23 20–22

ARA *see* Consorcio ARA, S.A. de C.V.

ARA Services, II 607–08 *see also* Aramark.

The Austin Company, 8 41–44; 72 14–18 (upd.)

Austin Nichols, *see* Pernod Ricard S.A.

Austin Powder Company, 76 32–35

Austin Quality Foods, 36 313

Austins Steaks & Saloon, Inc. *see* WesterN SizzliN Corp.

Australia and New Zealand Banking Group Limited, II 187–90; 52 35–40 (upd.)

Australian Airlines *see* Qantas Airways Ltd.

Australian and Overseas Telecommunications Corporation *see* Telecom Australia.

Australian Consolidated Press, 27 42; 54 299

Australian Mutual Provident Society, IV 61, 697

Australian Tankerships Pty. Ltd., 25 471

Australian Telecommunications Corporation, 6 342

Australian Wheat Board *see* AWB Ltd.

Austria Tabak, 55 200

Austrian Airlines AG (Österreichische Luftverkehrs AG), 33 49–52

Austrian Star Gastronomie GmbH, 48 63

Authentic Fitness Corp., 20 41–43; 51 30–33 (upd.)

Auto Helloes Co. Ltd., 76 37

Auto Parts Wholesale, 26 348

Auto Shack *see* AutoZone, Inc.

Auto Value Associates, Inc., 25 26–28

Autobacs Seven Company Ltd., 76 36–38

Autobytel Inc., 47 32–34

Autocam Corporation, 51 34–36

Autodesk, Inc., 10 118–20; 89 78–82 (upd.)

Autogrill SpA, 49 31–33

Autoliv, Inc., 65 53–55

Autologic Information International, Inc., 20 44–46

Automated Loss Prevention Systems, 11 445

Automated Sciences Group, Inc. *see* CACI International Inc.

Automated Security (Holdings) PLC, *see* Sensormatic Electronics Corp.

Automatic Coil Corp., 33 359, 361

Automatic Data Processing, Inc., III 117–19; 9 48–51 (upd.); 47 35–39 (upd.)

Automatic Liquid Packaging, 50 122

Automatic Payrolls, Inc. *see* Automatic Data Processing, Inc.

Automatic Retailers of America, Inc., *see* Aramark Corporation

Automatic Sprinkler Corp. of America *see* Figgie International, Inc.

Automatic Toll Systems, 19 111

Automatic Voting Machine Corporation *see* American Locker Group Inc.

AutoMed Technologies, Inc., 64 27

Automobiles Citroën, 7 35–38

Automobili Lamborghini Holding S.p.A., 13 60–62; 34 55–58 (upd.); 91 25–30 (upd.)

Automotive Diagnostics, *see* SPX Corp.

Automotive Group *see* Lear Corp.

Automotive Industries Holding Inc., 16 323

AutoNation, Inc., 50 61–64

Autonet, 6 435

Autonom Computer, 47 36

Autoridad del Canal de Panamá, 94 45–48

Autoroutes du Sud de la France SA, 55 38–40

Autosite.com, 47 34

Autotote Corporation, 20 47–49 *see also* Scientific Games Corp.

AutoTrader.com, L.L.C., 91 31–34

Autoweb.com, 47 34

AutoZone, Inc., 9 52–54; 31 35–38 (upd.)

Auvil Fruit Company, Inc., 95 32–35

AVA AG (Allgemeine Handelsgesellschaft der Verbraucher AG), 33 53–56

Avado Brands, Inc., 31 39–42

Avalon Correctional Services, Inc., 75 40–43

Avalon Publishing Group *see* Publishers Group, Inc.

AvalonBay Communities, Inc., 58 11–13

Avantel, 27 304

Avantium Technologies BV, 79 46–49

Avaya Inc., 41 287, 289–90

Avco *see* Aviation Corp. of the Americas.

Avco Corp., 34 433

Avco Financial Services Inc., 13 63–65 *see also* Citigroup Inc.

Avdel, 34 433

Avecia Group PLC, 63 49–51

Avecor Cardiovascular Inc., 22 360

Avecor, Inc. *see* M. A. Hanna Co.

Aveda Corporation, 24 55–57

Avedis Zildjian Co., 38 66–68

Avendt Group, Inc., *see* Marmon Group, Inc.

Aventine Renewable Energy Holdings, Inc., 89 83–86

Aventis Pharmaceuticals, 34 280, 283–84; 38 378, 380; 63 232, 235

Avery Communications, Inc., 72 39

Avery Dennison Corporation, IV 251–54; 17 27–31 (upd.); 49 34–40 (upd.)

AvestaPolarit, 49 104

Avex Electronics Inc., 40 68

Avgain Marine A/S, 7 40; 41 42

Avia Group International, Inc. *see* Reebok International Ltd.

Aviacionny Nauchno-Tehnicheskii Komplex im. A.N. Tupoleva, 24 58–60

Aviacsa *see* Consorcio Aviacsa, S.A. de C.V.

Aviall, Inc., 73 42–45

Avianca Aerovías Nacionales de Colombia SA, 36 52–55

Aviation Corp. of the Americas, 9 497–99

Aviation Inventory Management Co., 28 5

Aviation Sales Company, 41 37–39

Aviation Services West, Inc. *see* Scenic Airlines, Inc.

Avid Technology Inc., 38 69–73

Avimo, 47 7–8

Avionics Specialties Inc. *see* Aerosonic Corp.

Avions Marcel Dassault-Breguet Aviation, I 44–46 *see also* Groupe Dassault Aviation SA.

Avis Group Holdings, Inc., 6 356–58; 22 54–57 (upd.); 75 44–49 (upd.)

Avista Corporation, 69 48–50 (upd.)

Aviva PLC, 50 65–68 (upd.)

Avnet Inc., 9 55–57

Avocent Corporation, 65 56–58

Avon Products, Inc., III 15–16; 19 26–29 (upd.); 46 43–46 (upd.)

Avon Rubber plc, 23 146

Avondale Industries, Inc., 7 39–41; 41 40–43 (upd.)

Avonmore Foods Plc, 59 205

Avril Alimentaire SNC, 51 54

Avstar, 38 72

Avtech Corp., 36 159

AVTOVAZ Joint Stock Company, 65 59–62

AVX Corporation, 67 41–43

AW Bruna Uitgevers BV, 53 273

AW North Carolina Inc., 48 5

AWA *see* America West Holdings Corp.

AWA Defence Industries (AWADI) *see* British Aerospace plc.

AwardTrack, Inc., 49 423

AWB Ltd., 56 25–27

Awesome Transportation, Inc., 22 549

Awrey Bakeries, Inc., 56 28–30

AXA Colonia Konzern AG, III 210–12; 49 41–45 (upd.)

AXA Financial, Inc., 63 26–27

AXA Private Equity *see* Camaïeu S.A.

AXA UK plc, 64 173

Axcan Pharma Inc., 85 25–28

Axcelis Technologies, Inc., 95 36–39

Axe-Houghton Associates Inc., 41 208

Axel Johnson Group, I 553–55

Axel Springer Verlag AG, IV 589–91; 20 50–53 (upd.)

Axsys Technologies, Inc., 93 65–68

Ayala Corporation, 70 182

Ayala Plans, Inc., 58 20

Aydin Corp., 19 30–32

Aynsley China Ltd. *see* Belleek Pottery Ltd.

Ayres, Lewis, Norris & May, Inc., 54 184

AYS *see* Alternative Youth Services, Inc.

AZA Immobilien AG, 51 196

Azcon Corporation, 23 34–36

Azerbaijan Airlines, 77 46–49

Azerty, 25 13

Azienda Generale Italiana Petroli *see* ENI S.p.A.

AZL Resources, *see* Tosco Corp.

Azlan Group Limited, 74 338

Aznar International, 14 225

Azon Limited, *see* Illinois Tool Works Inc.

AZP Group Inc., 6 546

Aztar Corporation, 13 66–68; 71 41–45 (upd.)

Boots & Coots International Well Control, Inc., 79 70–73
Booz Allen & Hamilton Inc., 10 172–75
Boplan Ingénierie S.A.S. *see* SNC-Lavalin Group Inc.
Boral Limited, III 672–74; **43** 72–76 (upd.)
Borden, Inc., II 470–73; **22** 91–96 (upd.)
Border Fine Arts, **11** 95
Border Television, **41** 352
Borders Group, Inc., 15 61–62; **43** 77–79 (upd.)
Borders, Perrin and Norrander, **23** 480
Borealis AG, 94 83–86
Borg Instruments, **23** 494
Borg-Warner Australia, **47** 280
Borg-Warner Automotive, Inc., 14 63–66; **32** 93–97 (upd.)
Borg-Warner Corporation, III 438–41 *see also* Burns International.
BorgWarner Inc., 85 38–44 (upd.)
Borland International, Inc., 9 80–82
Borneo Airways *see* Malaysian Airlines System BHD.
Boron, LePore & Associates, Inc., 45 43–45
Borregaard Osterreich AG, *see* Orkla ASA.
Borror Corporation *see* Dominion Homes, Inc.
Borsheim's, *see* Berkshire Hathaway Inc.
Bosch *see* Robert Bosch GmbH.
Boscov's Department Store, Inc., 31 68–70
Bose Corporation, 13 108–10; **36** 98–101 (upd.)
Bosert Industrial Supply *see* W.W. Grainger, Inc.
Bossa, **55** 188
Bost Sports Clubs *see* Town Sports International, Inc.
Boston Acoustics, Inc., 22 97–99
The Boston Beer Company, Inc., 18 70–73; **50** 111–15 (upd.)
Boston Celtics Limited Partnership, 14 67–69
Boston Chicken, Inc., 12 42–44 *see also* Boston Market Corp.
The Boston Consulting Group, 58 32–35
Boston Edison Company, 12 45–47
Boston Gas Company *see* Eastern Enterprises.
Boston Globe, *see* Affiliated Publications, Inc.
Boston Market Corporation, 48 64–67 (upd.)
Boston Pizza International Inc., 88 33–38
Boston Popcorn Co., **27** 197–98; **43** 218
Boston Professional Hockey Association Inc., 39 61–63
Boston Properties, Inc., 22 100–02
Boston Scientific Corporation, 37 37–40; **77** 58–63 (upd.)
The Boston Symphony Orchestra Inc., 93 95–99

Boston Technology, **43** 117
Boston Ventures Management, Inc., **27** 41, 393; **65** 374
Boston Whaler, Inc. *see* Reebok International Ltd.
Bostrom Seating, Inc., **23** 306
BOTAS *see* Türkiye Petrolleri Anonim Ortakliği.
Boticas Fasa S.A., **72** 128
Botswana General Insurance Company, **22** 495
Bott SA, **72** 221
Bottu, **II** 475
BOTWEB, Inc., **39** 95
Bou-Matic, 62 42–44
Bougainville Copper Pty., **IV** 60–61
Boulanger, **37** 22
Boulder Creek Steaks & Saloon, **16** 447
Boulet Dru DuPuy Petit Group *see* Wells Rich Greene BDDP.
Boulton & Paul Ltd., **31** 398–400
Boundary Gas Inc., **6** 457; **54** 260
Bountiful Psychiatric Hospital, Inc., **68** 299
Boundary Healthcare, **12** 327
Bourbon *see* Groupe Bourbon S.A.
Bourjois, *see* Chanel.
Bourbon Corporation, 82 49–52
Bouverat Industries, **51** 36
Bouwmar N.V., **68** 64
Bouygues S.A., I 562–64; **24** 77–80 (upd.)
Bovis, *see* Peninsular and Oriental Steam Navigation Company (Bovis Division)
Bovis Construction, **38** 344–45
Bovis Lend Lease, **52** 222
Bow Bangles, *see* Claire's Stores, Inc.
Bow Flex of America, Inc. *see* Direct Focus, Inc.
Bow Valley Energy Inc., **47** 397
Bowater PLC, IV 257–59
Bowdens Media Monitoring Ltd., **55** 289
Bowers and Merena Galleries Inc., **48** 99
Bowes Co., *see* George Weston Ltd.
Bowling Green Wholesale, Inc. *see* Houchens Industries Inc.
Bowman Gum, Inc., **13** 520
Bowne & Co., Inc., 23 61–64; **79** 74–80 (upd.)
Bowthorpe plc, 33 70–72
The Boy Scouts of America, 34 66–69
Boyd Bros. Transportation Inc., 39 64–66
Boyd Coffee Company, 53 73–75
Boyd Gaming Corporation, 43 80–82
The Boyds Collection, Ltd., 29 71–73
Boyer Brothers, Inc., **14** 17–18
Boyer's International, Inc., **20** 83
Boyles Bros. Drilling Company *see* Christensen Boyles Corp.
Boyne USA Resorts, 71 65–68
Boys & Girls Clubs of America, 69 73–75
Bozell, Jacobs, Kenyon, and Eckhardt Inc. *see* True North Communications Inc.
Bozell Worldwide Inc., 25 89–91
Bozkurt, **27** 188
Bozzuto's, Inc., 13 111–12

BP Canada *see* Talisman Energy Inc.
BP p.l.c., 45 46–56 (upd.)
BPB plc, 83 46–49
BPI Communications, Inc., **7** 15; **19** 285; **27** 500; **61** 241
BR *see* British Rail.
Braathens ASA, 47 60–62
Brabants Dagblad BV, *see* N.V. AMEV.
Brach's Confections, Inc., 15 63–65; **74** 43–46 (upd.)
Braden Manufacturing, **23** 299–301
Bradford & Bingley PLC, 65 77–80
Bradford Exchange Ltd. Inc., **21** 269
Bradington-Young LLC *see* Hooker Furniture
Bradlees Discount Department Store Company, 12 48–50
Bradley Air Services Ltd., 56 38–40
Bradley Lumber Company, *see* Potlatch Corp.
Bradstreet Co. *see* The Dun & Bradstreet Corp.
Brady Corporation, 78 50–55 (upd.)
Bragussa, **IV** 71
Braine L'Alleud Bricolage BV, **68** 64
BRAINS *see* Belgian Rapid Access to Information Network Services.
Brake Bros plc, 45 57–59
BRAL Reststoff-Bearbeitungs-GmbH, **58** 28
Bramac Dachsysteme International GmbH, **70** 363
Bramalea Ltd., 9 83–85
Brambles Industries Limited, 42 47–50
Brammer PLC, 77 64–67
The Branch Group, Inc., 72 43–45
Brand Companies, Inc., *see* Chemical Waste Management, Inc.
Branded Restaurant Group, Inc., *see* Oscar Mayer Foods Corp.
Brandeis & Sons, **19** 511
BrandPartners Group, Inc., 58 36–38
Brandt Zwieback-Biskuits GmbH, **44** 40
Brandywine Asset Management, Inc., **33** 261
Brandywine Holdings Ltd., **45** 109
Brandywine Valley Railroad Co., *see* Lukens Inc.
Braniff Airlines, **36** 231
Brannock Device Company, 48 68–70
Brascan Corporation, 67 71–73
Brasfield & Gorrie LLC, 87 72–75
Brasil Telecom Participaçoes S.A., 57 67–70
Brass-Craft Manufacturing Co. *see* Masco Corp.
Brass Eagle Inc., 34 70–72
Braud & Faucheux *see* Manitou BF S.A.
Brauerei Beck & Co., 9 86–87; **33** 73–76 (upd.)
Braun GmbH, 51 55–58
Brauns Fashions Corporation *see* Christopher & Banks Corp.
Brazcot Limitada, **53** 344
Brazil Fast Food Corporation, 74 47–49
Brazos Gas Compressing, *see* Mitchell Energy and Development Corp.
Brazos Sportswear, Inc., 23 65–67

Broderbund Software, Inc., **13** 113–16; **29** 74–78 (upd.)

Les broderies Lesage, **49** 83

Brok SA, **54** 315, 317

Broken Hill Proprietary Company Ltd., **IV** 44–47; **22** 103–08 (upd.) *see also* BHP Billiton.

Bronco Drilling Company, Inc., 89 118–21

Bronner Brothers Inc., 92 29–32

Bronner Display & Sign Advertising, Inc., 82 53-57

Bronson Laboratories, Inc., **34** 460

Bronson Pharmaceuticals, **24** 257

Brookdale Senior Living, 91 69–73

Brooke Bond, **32** 475

Brooke Group Ltd., 15 71–73 *see also* Vector Group Ltd.

Brooke Partners L.P., **11** 275

Brookfield International Inc., **35** 388

Brookfield Properties Corporation, 89 122–25

Brooklyn Union Gas, 6 455–57 *see also* KeySpan Energy Co.

Brooks Brothers Inc., 22 109–12

Brooks Fashion, **29** 164

Brooks Sports Inc., 32 98–101

Brookshire Grocery Company, 16 63–66; **74** 50–53 (upd.)

Brookstone, Inc., 18 81–83

Brose Fahrzeugteile GmbH & Company KG, 84 34–38

Brother Industries, Ltd., 14 75–76

Brother International, **23** 212

Brother's Brother Foundation, 93 100–04

Brothers Gourmet Coffees, Inc., 20 82–85 *see also* The Procter & Gamble Co.

Brotherton Chemicals, **29** 113

Brotherton Speciality Products Ltd., **68** 81

Broughton Foods Co., 17 55–57 *see also* Suiza Foods Corp.

Brouwerijen Alken-Maes N.V., 86 47–51

Brown & Brown, Inc., 41 63–66

Brown & Haley, 23 78–80

Brown & Root, Inc., 13 117–19 *see also* Kellogg Brown & Root Inc.

Brown & Sharpe Manufacturing Co., 23 81–84

Brown and Williamson Tobacco Corporation, 14 77–79; **33** 80–83 (upd.)

Brown Boveri *see* BBC Brown Boveri.

Brown Brothers Harriman & Co., 45 64–67

Brown Cow West Corporation, **55** 360

Brown-Forman Corporation, I 225–27; **10** 179–82 (upd.); **38** 110–14 (upd.)

Brown Group, Inc., V 351–53; **20** 86–89 (upd.) *see also* Brown Shoe Company, Inc.

Brown Institute, **45** 87

Brown Jordan International Inc., 74 54–57 (upd.)

Brown Printing Company, 26 43–45

Brown Shipbuilding Company *see* Brown & Root, Inc.

Brown, Shipley & Co., Limited, **45** 65

Brown Shoe Company, Inc., 68 65–69 (upd.)

Browning-Ferris Industries, Inc., V 749–53; **20** 90–93 (upd.)

Browning International, **58** 147

Broyhill Furniture Industries, Inc., 10 183–85

BRS Ltd. *see* Ecel plc.

Bruce Foods Corporation, 39 67–69

Bruce Power LP, **49** 65, 67

Bruckmann, Rosser, Sherill & Co., **40** 51 *see also* Jitney-Jungle Stores of America, Inc.; Lazy Days RV Center, Inc.

Bruegger's Corporation, 63 79–82

Brugman, *see* Vorwerk & Co.

Bruno's Supermarkets, Inc., 7 60–62; **26** 46–48 (upd.); **68** 70–73 (upd.)

Brunswick Corporation, III 442–44; **22** 113–17 (upd.); **77** 68–75 (upd.)

Brunswick Mining, **64** 297

Brush Electrical Machines, *see* Hawker Siddeley Group PLC.

Brush Engineered Materials Inc., 67 77–79

Brush Wellman Inc., 14 80–82

Bruster's Real Ice Cream, Inc., 80 51–54

Bruxeland S.P.R.L., **64** 91

Brylane Inc., **29** 106–07; **64** 232

Bryn Mawr Stereo & Video, **30** 465

BSA *see* The Boy Scouts of America.

BSC *see* Birmingham Steel Corporation; British Steel Corp.

BSH Bosch und Siemens Hausgeräte GmbH, 67 80–84

BSkyB, **IV** 653; **29** 369, 371; **34** 85

BSN Groupe S.A., II 474–75 *see also* Groupe Danone

BSN Medical, **41** 374, 377

BT Group plc, 49 69–74 (upd.)

BTG, Inc., 45 68–70

BTG Plc, 87 80–83

BTM *see* British Tabulating Machine Co.

BTR Dunlop Holdings, Inc., **21** 432

BTR plc, I 428–30

BTR Siebe plc, 27 79–81 *see also* Invensys PLC.

B2B Initiatives Ltd. *see* O.C. Tanner Co.

Bubbles Salon *see* Ratner Companies.

Bublitz Case Company, **55** 151

Buca, Inc., 38 115–17

Buck Consultants, Inc., 55 71–73

Buck Knives Inc., 48 71–74

Buckaroo International *see* Bugle Boy Industries, Inc.

Buckbee-Mears Company *see* BMC Industries, Inc.

Buckeye Partners, L.P., 70 33–36

Buckeye Technologies, Inc., 42 51–54

Buckhorn, Inc., *see* Myers Industries, Inc.

The Buckle, Inc., 18 84–86

BUCON, Inc., **62** 55

Bucyrus International, Inc., 17 58–61

Bud Bailey Construction, **43** 400

The Budd Company, 8 74–76 *see also* ThyssenKrupp AG.

Buderus AG, 37 46–49

Budgens Ltd., 59 93–96

Budget Group, Inc., 25 92–94 *see also* Cendant Corp.

Budget Rent a Car Corporation, 9 94–95

Budgetel Inn *see* Marcus Corp.

Budweiser Budvar, National Corporation, 59 97–100

Budweiser Japan Co., **21** 320

Buena Vista Home Video *see* The Walt Disney Co.

Buena Vista Music Group, **44** 164

Bufete Industrial, S.A. de C.V., 34 80–82

Buffalo Grill S.A., 94 87–90

Buffalo News, *see* Berkshire Hathaway Inc.

Buffalo Paperboard, **19** 78

Buffalo Wild Wings, Inc., 56 41–43

Buffets Holdings, Inc., 10 186–87; **32** 102–04 (upd.); **93** 105–09 (upd.)

Bugaboo Creek Steak House Inc., **19** 342

Bugatti Automobiles S.A.S., 94 91–94

Bugle Boy Industries, Inc., 18 87–88

Buhrmann NV, 41 67–69

Buick Motor Co. *see* General Motors Corp.

Build-A-Bear Workshop Inc., 62 45–48

Builders Concrete *see* Vicat S.A.

Builders Square *see* Kmart Corp.

Building Materials Holding Corporation, 52 53–55

Building One Services Corporation *see* Encompass Services Corp.

Building Products of Canada Limited, **25** 232

Buitoni SpA, *see* Nestlé S.A.

Bulgari S.p.A., 20 94–97

Bull *see* Compagnie des Machines Bull S.A.

Bull S.A., 43 89–91 (upd.)

Bulletin Broadfaxing Network Inc., **67** 257

Bulley & Andrews, LLC, 55 74–76

Bullock's, **31** 191

Bulova Corporation, 13 120–22; **41** 70–73 (upd.)

Bumble Bee Seafoods L.L.C., 64 59–61

Bundall Computers Pty Limited, **56** 155

Bundy Corporation, 17 62–65

Bunge Ltd., 62 49–51

Bunzl plc, IV 260–62; **31** 77–80 (upd.)

Burbank Aircraft Supply, Inc., **14** 42–43; **37** 29, 31

Burberry Group plc, 17 66–68; **41** 74–76 (upd.); **92** 33–37 (upd.)

Burda Holding GmbH. & Co., 23 85–89

Burdines, Inc., 60 70–73

Bureau de Recherches de Pétrole, **21** 203–04

The Bureau of National Affairs, Inc., 23 90–93

Bureau Veritas SA, 55 77–79

Burelle S.A., 23 94–96

Burger King Corporation, II 613–15; **17** 69–72 (upd.); **56** 44–48 (upd.)

Burgess, Anderson & Tate Inc., *see* U.S. Office Products Co.

Carlisle Companies Inc., **8** 80–82; **82** 58–62 (upd.)

Carlisle Memory Products, **14** 535

Carlon, *see* Lamson & Sessions Co.

Carlova, Inc., **21** 54

Carlsberg A/S, 9 99–101; **29** 83–85 (upd.)

Carlson Companies, Inc., 6 363–66; **22** 125–29 (upd.); **87** 88–95 (upd.)

Carlson Restaurants Worldwide, 69 82–85

Carlson Wagonlit Travel, 55 89–92

Carlton and United Breweries Ltd., I 228–29 *see also* Foster's Group Limited

Carlton Cards Retail, Inc., **39** 87; **59** 34–35

Carlton Communications plc, 15 83–85; **50** 124–27 (upd.)

Carlton Foods Corporation, **57** 56–57

Carlton Investments L.P., **22** 514

Carlyle & Co. Jewelers *see* Finlay Enterprises, Inc.

The Carlyle Group, **14** 43; **16** 47; **21** 97; **30** 472; **43** 60; **49** 444; **73** 47; **76** 315

Carlyle Management Group, **63** 226

Carma Laboratories, Inc., 60 80–82

CarMax, Inc., 55 93–95

Carmichael Lynch Inc., 28 66–68

Carmike Cinemas, Inc., 14 86–88; **37** 62–65 (upd.); **74** 64–67 (upd.)

Carmine's Prime Meats, Inc. *see* CBRL Group, Inc.

Carnation Company, II 486–89 *see also* Nestlé S.A.

CarnaudMetalBox, *see* Crown, Cork & Seal Company, Inc.

Carnegie Corporation of New York, 35 74–77

Carnegie Group, **41** 371–72

Carnival Corporation, 6 367–68; **27** 90–92 (upd.); **78** 65–69 (upd.)

Caro Produce and Institutional Foods, **31** 359–61

Carolina Energies, Inc., **6** 576

Carolina First Corporation, 31 85–87

Carolina Freight Corporation, 6 369–72

Carolina Paper Board Corporation *see* Caraustar Industries, Inc.

Carolina Power & Light Company, V 564–66; **23** 104–07 (upd.) *see also* Progress Energy, Inc.

Carolina Telephone and Telegraph Company, 10 201–03

Carolinas Capital Funds Group, **29** 132

Carpenter Investment and Development Corporation, **31** 279; **76** 222

Carpenter Technology Corporation, 13 139–41; **95** 81–86 (upd.)

Carpets International Plc., *see* Interface, Inc.

Carpro, Inc., **65** 127

CARQUEST Corporation, 29 86–89

Carr-Gottstein Foods Co., 17 77–80

Carrabba's Italian Grill, *see* Outback Steakhouse, Inc.

CarrAmerica Realty Corporation, 56 57–59

Carre Orban International, **34** 248

Carrefour SA, 10 204–06; **27** 93–96 (upd.); **64** 66–69 (upd.)

Carrera-Optyl Group, **54** 319–20

Carrera y Carrera, **52** 147, 149

The Carriage House Companies, Inc., 55 96–98

Carriage Services, Inc., 37 66–68

Carrier Access Corporation, 44 68–73

Carrier Corporation, 7 70–73; **69** 86–91 (upd.)

Carrington Laboratories, **33** 282

Carrington Viyella, **44** 105

Carroll County Electric Company, **6** 511

Carroll's Foods, Inc., 46 82–85

Carrols Restaurant Group, Inc., 92 48–51

Carrows, **27** 16, 19

The Carsey-Werner Company, L.L.C., 37 69–72

Carsmart.com, **47** 34

Carso Global Telecom S.A. de C.V., 34 362

Carson, Inc., 31 88–90

Carson Pirie Scott & Company, 15 86–88

Carswell Insurance Group *see* Plamer & Cay, Inc.

CART *see* Championship Auto Racing Teams, Inc.

Cartem Wilco Group Inc., **59** 350

CarTemps USA *see* Republic Industries, Inc.

Carter & Sons Freightways, Inc., **57** 278

Carter Hawley Hale Stores, V 29–32

Carter Holt Harvey Ltd., 70 41–44

Carter Lumber Company, 45 90–92

Carter-Wallace, Inc., 8 83–86; **38** 122–26 (upd.)

Cartier, *see* Vendôme Luxury Group plc.

Cartier Monde, 29 90–92

Cartiera F.A. Marsoni, **IV** 587

Cartocor S.A. *see* Arcor S.A.I.C.

Carton Titan S.A. de C.V., **37** 176–77

Cartotech, Inc., **33** 44

Carvel Corporation, 35 78–81

Carver Bancorp, Inc., 94 106–10

Carver Boat Corporation LLC, 88 43–46

Carvin Corp., 89 140–43

Cary-Davis Tug and Barge Company *see* Puget Sound Tug and Barge Co.

CASA *see* Construcciones Aeronautics S.A.

Casa Bancária Almeida e Companhia *see* Banco Bradesco S.A.

Casa Cuervo, S.A. de C.V., 31 91–93

Casa Herradura *see* Grupo Industrial Herradura, S.A. de C.V.

Casa Ley, S.A. de C.V. *see* Safeway Inc.

Casa Saba *see* Grupo Casa Saba, S.A. de C.V.

Casablanca Records, **23** 390

Casalee, Inc., **48** 406

Casarotto Security, **24** 510

Casas Bahia Comercial Ltda., 75 86–89

Cascade Communications Corp., **20** 8

Cascade Corporation, 65 90–92

Cascade Fertilizers Ltd., **25** 232

Cascade General, Inc., 65 93–95

Cascade Natural Gas Corporation, 9 102–04

Cascade Steel Rolling Mills, Inc., *see* Schnitzer Steel Industries, Inc.

Cascades Inc., 71 94–96

Cascadian Farm *see* Small Planet Foods, Inc.

CasChem, Inc. *see* Cambrex Corp.

Casco Northern Bank, 14 89–91

Casden Properties, **49** 26

Case Corporation *see* CNH Global N.V.

Case Technologies, Inc., **11** 504

Casey's General Stores, Inc., 19 79–81; **83** 58–63 (upd.)

Cash & Go, Inc., **57** 139

Cash America International, Inc., 20 113–15; **61** 52–55 (upd.)

Cash Systems, Inc., 93 133–36

Cash Wise Foods and Liquor, **30** 133

Casino, **23** 231; **26** 160

Casino America, Inc. *see* Isle of Capri Casinos, Inc.

Casino Frozen Foods, Inc., **16** 453

Casino Guichard-Perrachon S.A., 59 107–10 (upd.)

Casinos International Inc., **21** 300

CASIO Computer Co., Ltd., III 448–49; **16** 82–84 (upd.); **40** 91–95 (upd.)

Casite Intraco LLC, **56** 156–57

Caspian Pipeline Consortium, **47** 75

Cassa Risparmio Firenze, **50** 410

Cassandra Group, **42** 272

Cassco Ice & Cold Storage, Inc., **21** 534–35

CAST Inc., **18** 20; **43** 17

Cast-Matic Corporation, **16** 475

Castel MAC S.p.A., **68** 136

Castex, **13** 501

Castings, Inc., **29** 98

Castle & Cooke, Inc., II 490–92; **20** 116–19 (upd.) *see also* Dole Food Company, Inc.

Castle Cement, **31** 400

Castle Harlan Investment Partners III, **36** 468, 471

Castle Rock Entertainment, **23** 392; **57** 35

Castle Rubber Co., *see* Park-Ohio Industries Inc.

Castleton Thermostats *see* Strix Ltd.

Castorama S.A. *see* Groupe Castorama-Dubois Investissements.

Castro Convertibles *see* Krause's Furniture, Inc.

Castro Model Ltd., 86 61–64

Casual Corner Group, Inc., 43 96–98

Casual Male Retail Group, Inc., 52 64–66

Casual Wear Española, S.A., **64** 91

Caswell-Massey Co. Ltd., 51 66–69

CAT Scale Company, **49** 329–30

Catalina Lighting, Inc., 43 99–102 (upd.)

Catalina Marketing Corporation, 18 99–102

Catalogue Marketing, Inc., *see* Hickory Farms, Inc.

Cenex Cooperative, **21** 342

Cenex Harvest States Cooperative *see* CHS Inc.

Cenex Inc., **19** 160

Centaur Communications, **43** 204, 206

Centel Corporation, **6** 312–15 *see also* EMBARQ Corp.

Centennial Communications Corporation, **39** 74–76

Centennial Technologies Inc., **48** 369

Center Co., Ltd., **48** 182

Center of Insurance, **51** 170

Center Rental & Sales Inc., **28** 387

Centerior Energy Corporation, **V** 567–68

CenterMark Properties, **57** 156

Centerplate, Inc., **79** 96–100

Centerpulse AG, **68** 362

Centex Corporation, **8** 87–89; **29** 93–96 **(upd.)**

Centocor Inc., **14** 98–100

CenTrade, a.s., **64** 73

Central Alloy Steel Corporation *see* Republic Engineered Steels, Inc.

Central and South West Corporation, **V** 569–70

Central Arizona Light & Power Company, **6** 545

Central Bancshares of the South, Inc. *see* Compass Bancshares, Inc.

Central Detallista, S.A. de C.V., **12** 154; **16** 453

Central Electric & Gas Company *see* Centel Corp.

Central Electric and Telephone Company, Inc. *see* Centel Corp.

Central Elevator Co., **19** 111

Central European Distribution Corporation, **75** 90–92

Central European Media Enterprises Ltd., **61** 56–59

Central Florida Investments, Inc., **93** 137–40

Central Florida Press, **23** 101

Central Freight Lines, Inc., **53** 249

Central Garden & Pet Company, **23** 108–10; **58** 57–60 **(upd.)**

Central Hudson Gas And Electricity Corporation, **6** 458–60

Central Illinois Public Service Company *see* CIPSCO Inc.

Central Independent Television, **7** 78–80; **23** 111–14 **(upd.)**

Central Indiana Power Company, **6** 556

Central Investment Corp., **12** 184

Central Japan Railway Company, **43** 103–06

Central Maine Power, **6** 461–64

Central Mining and Investment Corp., **IV** 79, 95–96, 524, 565

Central National-Gottesman Inc., **95** 87–90

Central Newspapers, Inc., **10** 207–09 *see also* Gannett Company, Inc.

Central Ohio Mobile Power Wash *see* MPW Industrial Services, Inc.

Central Parking Corporation, **18** 103–05

Central Plains Steel Company *see* Reliance Steel & Aluminum Co.

Central Research Laboratories, **22** 194

Central Soya Company, Inc., **7** 81–83

Central Sprinkler Corporation, **29** 97–99

Central Supply Company *see* Granite Rock Co.

Central Telephone & Utilities Corporation *see* Centel Corp.

Central Trust Co., **11** 110

Central Vermont Public Service Corporation, **54** 53–56

Central West Public Service Company *see* Centel Corp.

Centrale Verzorgingsdienst Cotrans N.V., **12** 443

Centre de Diffusion de l'Édition *see* Éditions Gallimard.

Centre Investissements et Loisirs, **48** 107

Centre Partners Management LLC, **70** 337

Centrepoint Properties Ltd., **54** 116–17

Centric Group, **69** 153

Centrica plc, **29** 100–05 **(upd.)**

Centron DPL Company, Inc., **25** 171

Centros Commerciales Pryca, **23** 246, 248

Centrum Communications Inc., **11** 520

Centuri Corporation, **54** 57–59

Centurion Brick, **14** 250

Century Aluminum Company, **52** 71–74

Century Bakery *see* Dawn Food Products, Inc.

Century Brewing Company *see* Rainier Brewing Co.

Century Business Services, Inc., **52** 75–78

Century Casinos, Inc., **53** 90–93

Century Communications Corp., **10** 210–12

Century Development *see* Camden Property Trust.

Century Manufacturing Company, **26** 363

Century Papers, Inc., *see* National Sanitary Supply Co.

Century Supply Corporation, **39** 346

Century Telephone Enterprises, Inc., **9** 105–07; **54** 60–63 **(upd.)**

Century Theatres, Inc., **31** 99–101

Century 21 Real Estate, **21** 97; **59** 345; **61** 267

Century Union (Shanghai) Foods Co., **75** 372

Century Wood Door Ltd., **63** 268

CenturyTel *see* Century Telephone Enterprises, Inc.

Cenveo Inc., **71** 100–04 **(upd.)**

CEP Industrie, **55** 79

CEPA *see* Consolidated Electric Power Asia.

CEPAM, **21** 438

CEPCO *see* Chugoku Electric Power Company Inc.

Cephalon, Inc., **45** 93–96

Cepheid, **77** 93–96

CEPSA *see* Compañia Española de Petroleos S.A.

Cera Trading Co. *see* Toto Ltd.

Ceradyne, Inc., **65** 100–02

Ceramconsult AG, **51** 196

Ceramesh, **11** 361

Ceramic Tile International, Inc., **53** 176

Cerberus Capital Management LP, **73** 289

Cerberus Group, **69** 261

Cerberus Limited *see* Elektrowatt AG.

Cerco S.A., **62** 51

Cereal and Fruit Products, **32** 519

Cereal Industries, *see* Associated British Foods plc.

Cereal Partners Worldwide, **10** 324; **36** 234, 237; **50** 295

Cereol SA, **36** 185; **62** 51

CERES, **55** 178

Cerestar, *see* Cargill, Inc.

Ceresucre, **36** 185

Ceridian Corporation, **38** 58; **71** 262 *see also* Control Data Systems, Inc.

Cerner Corporation, **16** 92–94; **94** 111–16 **(upd.)**

Cerprobe Corporation *see* Kulicke and Soffa Industries, Inc.

Cerro de Pasco Corp., **40** 411

Cerro E.M.S. Limited *see* The Marmon Group, Inc.

CertainTeed Corporation, **35** 86–89

Certegy, Inc., **63** 100–03

Certified Grocers of Florida, Inc., **15** 139

Cerulean, **51** 249, 251

Cerus, **23** 492

Cerveceria Cuahtémoc Moctezuma, **25** 281

Cerveceria Moctezuma, **23** 170

Cerveceria Polar, **I** 230–31 *see also* Empresas Polar SA.

Cerveceria y Malteria Quilmes S.A.I.C.A. y G., **70** 62

Ceska Nezavisla Televizni Spolecnost, **61** 56

Ceská Sporitelna a.s. *see* Erste Bank der Osterreichischen Sparkassen AG

Ceské aerolinie, a.s., **66** 49–51

Cesky Telecom, a.s., **64** 70–73

Cessna Aircraft Company, **8** 90–93; **27** 97–101 **(upd.)**

CET *see* Compagnie Européenne de Télésecurité.

CET 21, **61** 56, 58

Cetelem S.A., **21** 99–102

Cetus Corp., **41** 201; **50** 193

CeWe Color Holding AG, **76** 85–88

CFC Investment Company, **16** 104

CFM *see* Compagnie Française du Méthane.

CFP *see* Compagnie Française des Pétroles.

CFR Corporation *see* Tacony Corp.

CG&E *see* Cincinnati Gas & Electric Co.

CGE *see* Alcatel Alsthom.

CGIP, **57** 380

CGM *see* Compagnie Générale Maritime.

CGR Management Corporation, **51** 85

CH Mortgage Company I Ltd., **58** 84

Chace Precision Metals, Inc., **29** 460–61

Chaco Energy Corporation *see* Texas Utilities Co.

Dolmar GmbH, **59** 272

Dolomite Franchi SpA, **53** 285

Dolphin Book Club, *see* Book-of-the-Month Club.

Dolphin Services, Inc., **44** 203

Dom Perignon, **25** 258

Domain.com, Inc. *see* StarTek, Inc.

Domain Home Fashions *see* Aga Foodservice Group PLC.

Domaine Carneros, **43** 401

Domaines Barons de Rothschild, **36** 113, 115

Doman Industries Limited, 59 160–62

Dome Petroleum, Ltd., **IV** 401, 494; **12** 364

Dominick & Dominick LLC, 92 93–96

Dominick International Corp., **12** 131

Dominick's Finer Foods, Inc., 56 87–89

Dominion Bond Rating Service Ltd., **65** 244

Dominion Bridge Company, Limited, *see* United Dominion Industries Ltd.

Dominion Homes, Inc., 19 125–27

Dominion Industries Ltd., **15** 229

Dominion Resources, Inc., V 596–99; **54** 83–87 **(upd.)**

Dominion Salt Ltd., **62** 307

Dominion Textile Inc., 12 117–19

Domino S.p.A., **51** 324

Domino Printing Sciences PLC, 87 136–139

Domino Sugar Corporation, 26 120–22

Domino's, Inc., 7 150–53; **21** 177–81 **(upd.); 63** 133–39 **(upd.)**

Domtar Corporation, IV 271–73; **89** 185–91 **(upd.)**

Don Canham Enterprises *see* School-Tech, Inc.

Don Massey Cadillac, Inc., 37 114–16

Don's Foods, Inc., **26** 164

Donaldson Company, Inc., 16 178–81; **49** 114–18 **(upd.)**

Donaldson, Lufkin & Jenrette, Inc., 22 188–91

Donaldson's Department Stores, **15** 274

Donatos Pizzeria Corporation, 58 96–98

Donegal Parian China Ltd. *see* Belleek Pottery Ltd.

Dong Guan Highsonic Electronic Products Company, **62** 150

Dong Yang Department Store Company, **62** 174

Dong-Myung Industrial Company Ltd., **64** 270

DongGuan Leeway Footwear Company Ltd., **68** 69

Dongguan Shilong Kyocera Optics Co., Ltd., **21** 331

Dongguan Xinda Giftware Co. Ltd., **60** 372

Dongil Frozen Foods Co., *see* Nippon Suisan Kaisha, Ltd.

Dönkasan, **55** 188

Donna Karan International Inc., 15 145–47; **56** 90–93 **(upd.)**

Donnellon McCarthy Inc., **12** 184

Donnelly Coated Corporation, **48** 28

Donnelly Corporation, 12 120–22; **35** 147–50 **(upd.)**

Donning Company Publishers *see* Walsworth Publishing Company, Inc.

Donnkenny, Inc., 17 136–38

Donohue Inc., *see* Quebecor Inc.

Donohue Meehan Publishing Co., *see* Penton Media, Inc.

Donruss Playoff L.P., 66 81–84

Dooney & Bourke Inc., 84 111–114

Dorel Industries Inc., 59 163–65

Dorenbecher Properties, **19** 381

Doric Corp., **19** 290

Dorling Kindersley Holdings plc, 20 194–96 *see also* Pearson plc.

Dorman Products of America, Ltd., **51** 307

Dorney Park, *see* Cedar Fair, L.P.

Dornier GmbH, *see* Daimler-Benz Aerospace AG

Dorothy Hamill International, *see* International Family Entertainment Inc.

Dorr-Oliver Inc., **35** 134–35

Dorset Capital, **49** 189

Dorsey & Whitney LLP, 47 96–99

Doskocil Companies, Inc., 12 123–25 *see also* Foodbrands America, Inc.

Dot Foods, Inc., 69 134–37

Dot Hill Systems Corp., 93 185–88

Dot Wireless Inc., **46** 422

Doty Agency, Inc., **41** 178, 180

Double A Products Co., **23** 82–83; **74** 320

Double-Cola Co.-USA, 70 74–76

DoubleClick Inc., 46 154–57

Doubleday Book Shops, Inc., **25** 31; **30** 68

Doubleday-Dell, **IV** 594, 636

Doubletree Corporation, 21 182–85

Doughty Handson, **49** 163

Douglas & Lomason Company, 16 182–85

Douglas Aircraft Co., *see* McDonnell Douglas Corp.

Douglas Dynamics L.L.C., **41** 3

Doulton Glass Industries Ltd., **IV** 659

Douwe Egberts, *see* Sara Lee Corp.

Doux S.A., 80 93–96

Dove International, *see* Mars, Inc.

Dover Corporation, III 467–69; **28** 101–05 **(upd.); 90** 162–67 **(upd.)**

Dover Downs Entertainment, Inc., 43 139–41

Dover Publications Inc., 34 148–50

Dovrat Shrem, **15** 470

The Dow Chemical Company, I 323–25; **8** 147–50 **(upd.); 50** 160–64 **(upd.)**

Dow Corning *see* Corning Inc.; Dow Chemical Co.; Wright Medical Group, Inc.

Dow Jones & Company, Inc., IV 601–03; **19** 128–31 **(upd.); 47** 100–04 **(upd.)**

Dow Jones Telerate, Inc., 10 276–78 *see also* Reuters Group PLC.

DOW Stereo/Video Inc., **30** 466

DowElanco, **21** 385, 387

Dowell Schlumberger *see* Schlumberger Ltd.

Down River International, Inc., **15** 188

Dowty Aerospace, *see* TI Group plc.

Dowty Group plc, **58** 345

Doyle Dane Bernbach *see* Omnicom Group Inc.

Doyle Hotel Group, **64** 216

DP&L *see* Dayton Power & Light Co.

DP World, 81 115–18

dPi Teleconnect LLC, **75** 336–37

DPL Inc., 6 480–82

DPPI *see* Distribuidora de Produtos de Petróleo Ipiranga.

DQE, 6 483–85; **38** 40

Dr. August Oetker KG, 51 102–06

Dr. E. Fresenius KG *see* Fresenius Aktiengesellschaft.

Dr. Gerhard Mann Pharma, **25** 56

Dr Hans Kraus d.o.o, **72** 221

Dr. Ing he F. Porsche GmbH, *see* Porsche AG.

Dr. Karl Thomae GmbH, **39** 72–73

Dr. Martens, **23** 399, 401

Dr Pepper/Seven Up, Inc., 9 177–78; **32** 154–57 **(upd.)**

Dr. Reddy's Laboratories Ltd., 59 166–69

The Dr. Robert C. Atkins Foundation, **58** 8–9

Dr. Solomon's Software Ltd., **25** 349

Dr Specht & Partner GmbH, **70** 90

Drackett Professional Products, 12 126–28 *see also* S.C. Johnson & Son, Inc.

Draftfcb, 94 164–68

DraftDirect Worldwide, **22** 297

Draftline Engineering Co., *see* Defiance, Inc.

Dragados y Construcciones *see* Grupo Dragados SA.

Drägerwerk AG, 83 111–114

Dragoco *see* Symrise GmbH and Company KG.

Dragon Genomics Co. Ltd., **62** 347

Dragonair *see* Hong Kong Dragon Airlines Ltd.

Drake Beam Morin, Inc., 44 155–57

Draper Corporation, **15** 384

Draper Fisher Jurvetson, 91 149–52

Draw-Tite, Inc., *see* TriMas Corp.

Dräxlmaier Group, 90 168–72

DreamLand *see* Etablissements Franz Colruyt N.V.

DreamWorks SKG, 43 142–46

The Drees Company, Inc., 41 131–33

Dreher Breweries, **24** 450

Drescher Corporation *see* Dor Foods, Inc.

Dresden Papier GmbH, **64** 275

Dresdner Bank A.G., II 281–83; **57** 110–14 **(upd.)**

Dresdner Kleinwort Wasserstein, 60 110–13 **(upd.)**

Dresdner RCM Global Investors, **33** 128

The Dress Barn, Inc., 24 145–46

Dresser Industries, Inc., III 470–73; **55** 129–31 **(upd.)**

Dresser Power, **6** 555

E-mu Systems, Inc., **57** 78–79

E-Pet Services, **74** 234

E-Stamp Corporation, **34** 474

E-Systems, Inc., 9 182–85

E*Trade Financial Corporation, 20 206–08; **60** 114–17 (upd.)

E-II Holdings Inc. *see* Astrum International Corp.

E-Z Serve Corporation, 17 169–71

E-Z-EM Inc., 89 196–99

E A Rosengrens AB, **53** 158

E.B. Badger Co., **11** 413

E.B. Eddy Forest Products, *see* George Weston Ltd.

e.Biscom *see* FASTWEB S.p.A.

E.F. Hutton Group, *see* Shearson Lehman Brothers Holdings Inc.

E H Booth & Company Ltd., 90 173–76

E.I. du Pont de Nemours and Company, I 328–30; **8** 151–54 (upd.); **26** 123–27 (upd.); **73** 128–33 (upd.)

E.J. Brach & Sons *see* Brach and Brock Confections, Inc.

E.J. Longyear Company *see* Boart Longyear Co.

E. Katz Special Advertising Agency *see* Katz Communications, Inc.

E.M. Warburg Pincus & Co., **16** 319; **29** 262

E. Missel GmbH, **20** 363

E.On AG, 50 165–73 (upd.)

E.piphany, Inc., 49 123–25

E.R.R. Enterprises, **44** 227

E. Rosen Co., **53** 303–04

E.S. International Holding S.A. *see* Banco Espírito Santo e Comercial de Lisboa S.A.

E.V. Williams Inc. *see* The Branch Group, Inc.

E.W. Howell Co., Inc., 72 94–96 *see also* Obayashi Corporation

The E.W. Scripps Company, IV 606–09; **7** 157–59 (upd.); **28** 122–26 (upd.); **66** 85–89 (upd.)

E. Witte Verwaltungsgesellschaft GmbH, **73** 326

EADS N.V. *see* European Aeronautic Defence and Space Company EADS N.V.

EADS SOCATA, 54 91–94

Eagel One Industries, **50** 49

Eagle Airways Ltd., **23** 161

Eagle Distributing Co., **37** 351

Eagle Family Foods, Inc., **22** 95

Eagle Floor Care, Inc., *see* Tennant Co.

Eagle Gaming, L.P., **16** 263; **43** 226; **75** 341

Eagle Global Logistics *see* EGL, Inc.

Eagle Hardware & Garden, Inc., 16 186–89 *see also* Lowe's Companies, Inc.

Eagle Industries Inc., *see* Great American Management and Investment, Inc.

Eagle Managed Care Corp., *see* Rite Aid Corp.

Eagle-Picher Industries, Inc., 8 155–58; **23** 179–83 (upd.) *see also* PerkinElmer Inc.

Eagle Sentry Inc., **32** 373

Eagle Trading, **55** 24

Eagle-Tribune Publishing Co., 91 153–57

Earl Scheib, Inc., 32 158–61

Earle M. Jorgensen Company, 82 99–102

Early Learning Centre, **39** 240, 242

Earth's Best, Inc., **21** 56; **36** 256

The Earthgrains Company, 36 161–65

EarthLink, Inc., 36 166–68

EAS *see* Engineered Air Systems, Inc.; Executive Aircraft Services.

Easco Hand Tools, Inc., **7** 117

Easi-Set Industries, Inc., **56** 332

Eason Oil Company, **6** 578

East African Gold Mines Limited, **61** 293

East Japan Railway Company, V 448–50; **66** 90–94 (upd.)

The East New York Savings Bank, *see* First Empire State Corp.

East Penn Manufacturing Co., Inc., 79 154–57

East Tennessee Steel Supply Inc. *see* Siskin Steel & Supply Co.

East-West Federal Bank, **16** 484

East West Motor Express, Inc., **39** 377

Easter Enterprises *see* Nash Finch Co.

Easter Seals, Inc., 58 105–07

Eastern Air Group Co., 31 102

Eastern Airlines, I 101–03

Eastern Aviation Group, **23** 408

The Eastern Company, 48 140–43

Eastern Enterprises, 6 486–88

Eastern Industries, Inc. *see* Stabler Companies Inc.

Eastern Kansas Utilities, **6** 511

Eastern Market Beef Processing Corp., **20** 120

Eastern Platinum Ltd. *see* Lonmin plc.

Eastern Shore Natural Gas Company, **56** 62

Eastern Software Distributors, Inc., **16** 125

Eastern Texas Electric *see* Gulf States Utilities Co.

Eastern Wisconsin Power, **6** 604

Eastern Wisconsin Railway and Light Company, **6** 601

EastGroup Properties, Inc., 67 149–51

Eastland Shoe Corporation, 82 103–106

Eastman Chemical Company, 14 174–75; **38** 178–81 (upd.)

Eastman House *see* Chittenden & Eastman Co.

Eastman Kodak Company, III 474–77; **7** 160–64 (upd.); **36** 169–76 (upd.); **91** 158–69 (upd.)

Easton Sports, Inc., 66 95–97

Eastpak, Inc., **30** 138; **70** 136

Eastport International Inc., **63** 318

Eastwynn Theatres, Inc., **37** 63

easyJet Airline Company Limited, 39 127–29; **52** 330

Eatco, Inc., **15** 246

Eateries, Inc., 33 138–40

Eaton Corporation, I 154–55; **10** 279–80 (upd.); **67** 152–56 (upd.)

Eaton Vance Corporation, 18 150–53

EAudio, Inc., **48** 92

EBA Holding S.A., **63** 180

EBASCO *see* Electric Bond and Share Co.

eBay Inc., 32 162–65; **67** 157–61 (upd.)

EBCO, **55** 302

Ebara Corporation, 83 119-122

Eberhard Manufacturing Company, **48** 141

EBIC *see* European Banks' International Co.

EBS *see* Electric Bond & Share Company; Electronic Bookshelf.

EBSCO Industries, Inc., 17 151–53; **40** 158–61 (upd.)

EC Delaware Incorporated, **72** 117

EC Erdolchemie GmbH, *see* Deutsche BP AG.

ECAD Inc., **48** 75

ECC *see* Educational Credit Corp.

ECC Group plc, III 689–91 *see also* English China Clays plc.

ECC International Corp., 42 122–24

Ecce, **41** 129

ECCO *see* Adecco S.A.

Ecco Sko A/S, 62 109–11

Echlin Inc., I 156–57; **11** 83–85 (upd.) *see also* Dana Corp.

Echo Bay Mines Ltd., IV 75–77; **38** 182–85 (upd.)

The Echo Design Group, Inc., 68 128–30

Les Echos, **IV** 659

EchoStar Communications Corporation, 35 155–59

EchoStar Satellite Corp., **39** 400

ECI Telecom Ltd., 18 154–56

Eckerd Corporation, 9 186–87 *see also* J.C. Penney Company, Inc.

Eckes AG, 56 100–03

Eclipse Aviation Corporation, 87 148–151

Eclipse Candles, Ltd., *see* Blyth, Inc.

Eclipse Telecommunications, Inc., **29** 252

Eco Hotels, **14** 107

Eco SA, **48** 224

Eco-Tech Company Inc., **60** 272

Ecoiffier, **56** 335

Ecolab Inc., I 331–33; **13** 197–200 (upd.); **34** 151–56 (upd.); **85** 97–105 (upd.)

eCollege.com, 85 106–09

Ecology and Environment, Inc., 39 130–33

Econo Lodge *see* Choice Hotels International, Inc.

Economist Group, **15** 265

The Economist Group Ltd., 67 162–65

Economy Fire & Casualty, **22** 495

Ecopetrol *see* Empresa Colombiana de Petróleos.

EcoSystems Software, Inc., *see* Compuware Corp.

EcoWater Systems, Inc., *see* The Marmon Group, Inc.

Fabri-Centers of America Inc., 16
    197–99 *see also* Jo-Ann Stores, Inc.
Fabritec GmbH, **72** 221
Fabtek Inc., **48** 59
Facebook, Inc., 90 184–87
Facet International, **61** 66
Facom S.A., 32 183–85
Façonnable S.A., **67** 279–80
Facts on File, Inc., **22** 443
FactSet Research Systems Inc., 73
    148–50
FAE Fluid Air Energy SA, **49** 162–63
Fafnir Bearing Company, *see* The
    Torrington Co.
FAG—Kugelfischer Georg Schäfer AG,
    62 129–32
Fagerdala World Foams, **54** 360–61
Fair Grounds Corporation, 44 177–80
Fair, Isaac and Company, 18 168–71
Fairchild Camera and Instrument Corp.,
    21 122
The Fairchild Corporation, **37** 30; **76** 318
Fairchild Dornier GmbH, 9 205–08; 48
    167–71 (upd.)
Fairchild Industries, **14** 43; **15** 195; **34**
    117
Fairchild Publications, **59** 133–34
Fairchild Semiconductor Corporation, **II**
    63–65; **41** 201
Fairclough Construction Group plc, I
    567–68
Faircy Industries Ltd., **IV** 659
Fairfax Financial Holdings Limited, 57
    135–37
Fairfax Media Ltd., 94 202–08 (upd.)
Fairfield Communities, Inc., 36 192–95
The Fairfield Group, **33** 259–60
Fairfield Resorts *see* Outrigger Enterprises,
    Inc.
Fairmont Foods Co., **15** 139
Fairmont Hotels & Resorts Inc., 69
    161–63
Fairmont Insurance Co., **26** 487
Fairway Outdoor Advertising, Inc., **36**
    340, 342
Faiveley S.A., 39 152–54
Falcon Drilling Co. *see* Transocean Sedco
    Forex Inc.
Falcon Microsystems, Inc., **57** 172–73
Falcon Products, Inc., 33 149–51
Falconbridge Limited, 49 136–39
The Falk Corporation *see* Rexnord Corp.
Fallon Worldwide, 22 199–201; 71
    157–61 (upd.)
Falmouth Fertilizer Company *see* Griffin
    Industries, Inc.
Family Bookstores *see* Family Christian
    Stores, Inc.
Family Channel *see* International Family
    Entertainment Inc.
Family Christian Stores, Inc., 51
    131–34
Family Dollar Stores, Inc., 13 215–17;
    62 133–36 (upd.)
Family Golf Centers, Inc., 29 183–85
Family Mart Group, **V** 188; **36** 418, 420
Family Preservation Services, Inc., **64** 311

Family Restaurants, Inc., *see* Foodmaker,
    Inc.
Family Steak Houses of Florida, Inc. *see*
    Ryan's Restaurant Group, Inc.
Famous Atlantic Fish Company, **20** 5
Famous-Barr, **46** 288
Famous Brands Ltd., 86 144–47
Famous Dave's of America, Inc., 40
    182–84
Famous Footwear *see* Brown Shoe
    Company, Inc.
Famous Restaurants Inc., **33** 139–40
Fanafel Ltda., **62** 348, 350
Fannie Mae, 45 156–59 (upd.)
Fannie May Confections Brands, Inc.,
    80 114–18
Fansteel Inc., 19 150–52
Fantastic Sam's, **26** 476
Fanthing Electrical Corp., **44** 132
Fanuc Ltd., III 482–83; 17 172–74
    (upd.); 75 137–40 (upd.)
Fanzz, **29** 282
FAO Schwarz, 46 187–90
Faprena, **25** 85
Far-Ben S.A. de C.V., **72** 128
Far Eastern Air Transport, Inc., **23** 380
Far Eastern Bank, **56** 363
Farah Incorporated, 24 156–58
Farben *see* I.G. Farbenindustrie AG.
Farberware, Inc., *see* Lifetime Brands, Inc.
Farbro Corp., **45** 15
FAREC Fahrzeugrecycling GmbH, **58** 28
Farihault Foods, Inc., 89 212–15
Farley Northwest Industries Inc., I
    440–41
Farley's & Sathers Candy Company,
    Inc., 62 137–39
Farm Electric Services Ltd., **6** 586
Farm Family Holdings, Inc., 39 155–58
Farm Fresh Catfish Company, **54** 167
Farm Journal Corporation, 42 131–34
Farm Power Laboratory, **6** 565; **50** 366
Farm Progress Group *see* Rural Press Ltd
Farmacias Ahumada S.A., 72 126–28
Farmacias Ahumada S.A., **69** 312
Farmcare Ltd., **51** 89
Farmer Bros. Co., 52 117–19
Farmer Jack Supermarkets, 78 109–13
Farmer Mac *see* Federal Agricultural
    Mortgage Corp.
Farmers Insurance Group of
    Companies, 25 154–56
Farmers Petroleum, Inc., **48** 175
Farmland Foods, Inc., 7 174–75
Farmland Industries, Inc., 48 172–75
Farmstock Pty Ltd., **62** 307
FARO Technologies, Inc., 87 164–167
Farouk Systems, Inc., 78 114–17
Farrar, Straus and Giroux Inc., 15
    158–60
FAS Acquisition Co., **53** 142
FASC *see* First Analysis Securities Corp.
Fasco Consumer Products, **19** 360
FASCO Motors *see* Tecumseh Products
    Co.
Fashion Bug, *see* Charming Shoppes, Inc.

Fashion Fair Cosmetics *see* Johnson
    Publishing Company, Inc.
Fashion Resource, Inc. *see* Tarrant Apparel
    Group.
Fasint Ltd., **72** 128
Fasson *see* Avery Dennison Corp.
Fast Air, **31** 305
Fast Fare, *see* Crown Central Petroleum
    Corp.
Fast Trak Inc. *see* Ultimate Electronics,
    Inc.
Fastenal Company, 14 185–87; 42
    135–38 (upd.)
FASTWEB S.p.A., 83 147-150
Fat Bastard Wine Co., **68** 86
Fat Face Ltd., 68 147–49
FAT KAT, Inc., **51** 200, 203
Fatburger Corporation, 64 122–24
Fate S.A., **74** 10
Fateco Förlag, **14** 556
FATS, Inc., *see* Firearms Training Systems,
    Inc.
Faultless Starch/Bon Ami Company, 55
    142–45
Fauquet, **25** 85
Faurecia S.A., 70 91–93
FAvS *see* First Aviation Services Inc.
Fay's Inc., 17 175–77
Faydler Company, **60** 160
Fayette Tubular Products, *see* Danaher
    Corp.
Faygo Beverages Inc., 55 146–48
Fayva, *see* Morse Shoe Inc.
Fazoli's Management, Inc., 27 145–47;
    76 144–47 (upd.)
FB&T Corporation, **14** 154
FBC *see* First Boston Corp.
FBO *see* Film Booking Office of America.
FBR *see* Friedman, Billings, Ramsey
    Group, Inc.
FBS Fuhrpark Business Service GmbH,
    58 28
FC Holdings, Inc., **26** 363
FCA Ltd. *see* Life Time Fitness, Inc.
FCC *see* Federal Communications
    Commission.
FCI *see* Framatome SA.
FDIC *see* Federal Deposit Insurance Corp.
Featherlite Inc., 28 127–29
Feature Enterprises Inc., **19** 452
FECR *see* Florida East Coast Railway,
    L.L.C.
Fedders Corporation, 18 172–75; 43
    162–67 (upd.)
Federal Agricultural Mortgage
    Corporation, 75 141–43
Federal Cartridge, **26** 363
Federal Deposit Insurance Corporation,
    93 208–12
Federal Express Corporation, V 451–53
    see also FedEx Corp.
Federal Home Life Insurance Co., **IV** 623
Federal Home Loan Mortgage Corp. *see*
    Freddie Mac.
Federal Insurance Co., *see* The Chubb
    Corp.
Federal Laboratories, **57** 230

Fording Inc., **45** 80

FORE Systems, Inc., 25 161–63 *see also* Telefonaktiebolaget LM Ericsson.

Forefront Communications, **22** 194

Forefront Petroleum Company, **60** 160

Foreign & Colonial, **64** 303

Foremost-McKesson Inc. *see* McKesson Corp.

FöreningsSparbanken AB, 69 177–80

Forest City Auto Parts, **23** 491

Forest City Enterprises, Inc., 16 209–11; **52** 128–31 (upd.)

Forest E. Olson, Inc., **21** 96

Forest Laboratories, Inc., 11 141–43; **52** 132–36 (upd.)

Forest Oil Corporation, 19 161–63; **91** 182–87 (upd.)

Forestal Mininco S.A. *see* Empresas CMPC S.A.

Forestal Quiñenco S.A. *see* Madeco S.A.

Forestry Corporation of New Zealand, **19** 156

Förctagsfinans, **25** 464

Forethought Group, Inc., *see* Hillenbrand Industries, Inc.

Forever Living Products International Inc., 17 186–88

Forever 21, Inc., 84 127–129

Forge Books *see* Tom Doherty Associates Inc.

Forjas Metalicas, S.A. de C.V. (Formet), **44** 193

FormFactor, Inc., 85 128–31

Formica Corporation, 13 230–32

Formonix, **20** 101

Formosa Plastics Corporation, 14 197–99; **58** 128–31 (upd.)

Formtec Inc., **62** 350

Formulabs, Inc., **52** 307

Forrester Research, Inc., 54 113–15

Forstmann Little & Co., 38 190–92

Fort Bend Utilities Company, *see* Imperial Sugar Co.

Fort Garry Brewery, **26** 304

Fort Howard Corporation, 8 197–99 *see also* Fort James Corp.

Fort James Corporation, 22 209–12 (upd.) *see also* Georgia-Pacific Corp.

Fort Mill Manufacturing Co. *see* Springs Industries, Inc.

Forte Plc, **15** 46; **29** 443; **64** 340

Fortis, Inc., 15 179–82; **47** 134–37 (upd.); **50** 4–6

Fortum Corporation, 30 202–07 (upd.) *see also* Neste Oil Corp.

Fortum Oil and Gas Oy, **68** 125–26

Fortun Foods, **26** 59

Fortune Brands, Inc., 29 193–97 (upd.); **68** 163–67 (upd.)

Fortunoff Fine Jewelry and Silverware Inc., 26 144–46

Forward Air Corporation, 75 147–49

Forward Industries, Inc., 86 152–55

The Forzani Group Ltd., 79 172–76

Fosgate Electronics, **43** 322

Foss Maritime Co., *see* Totem Resources Corp.

Fossil, Inc., 17 189–91

Foster Forbes, **16** 123

Foster Grant *see* FosterGrant, Inc.

Foster Management Co., *see* NovaCare, Inc.

Foster Poultry Farms, 32 201–04

Foster-Probyn Ltd., **38** 501

Foster Wheeler Corporation, 6 145–47; **23** 205–08 (upd.); **76** 152–56 (upd.)

Foster's Group Limited, 7 182–84; **21** 227–30 (upd.); **50** 199–203 (upd.)

FosterGrant, Inc., 60 131–34

Fougerolle, *see* Eiffage.

Foundation Fieldbus, **22** 373

Foundation Health Corporation, 12 175–77

Founders of American Investment Corp., **15** 247

Fountain Powerboats Industries, Inc., 28 146–48

Four Leaf Technologies *see* Groupe Open.

Four Media Co., **33** 403

Four Paws Products, Ltd., 58 60

Four Queens Hotel and Casino *see* The Elsinore Corp.

Four Seasons Hotels Inc., 9 237–38; **29** 198–200 (upd.)

Four-Ten Corporation, **58** 378

Four Winds, **21** 153

4Kids Entertainment Inc., 59 187–89

Fournier Furniture, Inc., **12** 301

4P, **30** 396–98

Fourth Financial Corporation, 11 144–46

Fowler, Roenau & Geary, LLC, **37** 224

Fox and Hound English Pub and Grille *see* Total Entertainment Restaurant Corp.

Fox & Jacobs, *see* Centex Corp.

Fox Broadcasting Company, **21** 25, 360

Fox Children's Network, **21** 26

Fox Entertainment Group, Inc., 43 173–76

Fox Family Worldwide, Inc., 24 170–72 *see also* ABC Family Worldwide, Inc.

Fox Film Corp. *see* Twentieth Century Fox Film Corp.

Fox, Inc., *see* Twentieth Century Fox Film Corp.

Fox Network, **29** 426

Fox Paine & Company L.L.C., **63** 410, 412

Fox Ridge Homes, **70** 208

Foxboro Company, 13 233–35

Foxconn International, Inc. *see* Hon Hai Precision Industry Co., Ltd.

FoxHollow Technologies, Inc., 85 132–35

FoxMeyer Health Corporation, 16 212–14 *see also* McKesson Corp.

Foxmoor, **29** 163

Foxworth-Galbraith Lumber Company, 91 188–91

Foxx Hy-Reach, **28** 387

Foxy Products, Inc., **60** 287

FP&L *see* Florida Power & Light Co.

FPA Corporation *see* Orleans Homebuilders, Inc.

FPK LLC, **26** 343

FPL Group, Inc., V 623–25; **49** 143–46 (upd.)

Fracmaster Ltd., **55** 294

Fragrance Corporation of America, Ltd., **53** 88

Fragrance Express Inc., **37** 271

Framatome SA, 19 164–67 *aee also* Alcatel S.A.; AREVA.

Franc-Or Resources, **38** 231–32

France-Loisirs, **IV** 615–16, 619

France Quick, **12** 152; **26** 160–61

France Télécom Group, V 291–93; **21** 231–34 (upd.)

Franchise Finance Corp. of America, **37** 351

Franciscan Vineyards, Inc., **34** 89; **68** 99

Francisco Partners, **74** 260

Franco-American Food Company *see* Campbell Soup Co.

Francodex Laboratories, Inc., **74** 381

Francotyp-Postalia Holding AG, 92 123–27

Frank & Pignard SA, **51** 35

Frank & Schulte GmbH, *see* Stinnes AG.

Frank H. Nott Inc., *see* The David J. Joseph Co.

Frank Holton Company, **55** 149, 151

Frank J. Zamboni & Co., Inc., 34 173–76

Frank Russell Company, 46 198–200

Frank Schaffer Publications, **19** 405; **29** 470, 472

Frank W. Horner, Ltd., **38** 123

Frank's Nursery & Crafts, Inc., 12 178–79

Franke Holding AG, 76 157–59

Frankel & Co., 39 166–69

Frankfurter Allgemeine Zeitung GmbH, 66 121–24

Franklin Brass Manufacturing Company, **20** 363

Franklin Coach, **56** 223

Franklin Corp., **41** 388

Franklin Covey Company, 11 147–49; **37** 149–52 (upd.)

Franklin Electric Company, Inc., 43 177–80

Franklin Electronic Publishers, Inc., 23 209–13

The Franklin Mint, 69 181–84

Franklin Mutual Advisors LLC, **52** 119, 172

Franklin National Bank, **9** 536

Franklin Plastics *see* Spartech Corp.

Franklin Resources, Inc., 9 239–40

Frans Maas Beheer BV, **14** 568

Franz Inc., 80 122–25

Franzia *see* The Wine Group, Inc.

Frape Behr S.A. *see* Behr GmbH & Co. KG.

Fraport AG Frankfurt Airport Services Worldwide, 90 197–202

Fraser & Neave Ltd., 54 116–18

Fray Data International, **14** 319

Frazer & Jones, **48** 141

FRE Composites Inc., **69** 206

Fred Campbell Auto Supply, **26** 347

Gulistan Holdings Inc., **28** 219
Gulton Industries Inc., *see* Mark IV
    Industries, Inc.
Gum Base Asia Ltd., **72** 272
Gum Tech International *see* Matrixx
    Initiatives, Inc.
Gunderson, Inc. *see* The Greenbrier
    Companies.
Gunite Corporation, 51 152–55
The Gunlocke Company, 23 243–45
Gunnebo AB, 53 156–58
Gupta, **15** 492
Gurwitch Bristow Products, LLC, **49** 285
GUS plc, 47 165–70 **(upd.)**
Gustav Schickendanz KG *see* Karstadt
    Quelle AG.
Guthy-Renker Corporation, 32 237–40
Guttenplan's Frozen Dough Inc., 88
    151–54
Gutzeit *see* W. Gutzeit & Co.
Guy Degrenne SA, 44 204–07
Guy Maunsell International Limited *see*
    AECOM Technology Corporation
Guy Pease Associates, **34** 248
Guyenne et Gascogne, 23 246–48
Guyomarc'h, **39** 356
GVN Technologies, **63** 5
Gwathmey Siegel & Associates
    Architects LLC, 26 186–88
GWC *see* General Waterworks Corp.
GWK GmbH, **45** 378
GWR Group plc, 39 198–200
Gymboree Corporation, 15 204–06; **69**
    198–201 **(upd.)**
Gynecare Inc., **23** 190
Gynetics, Inc., **26** 31

H

H&D *see* Hinde & Dauch Paper Co.
H&D Holdings, **64** 79
H&R Block, Inc., 9 268–70; **29** 224–28
    (upd.); 82 162–69 **(upd.)**
H.B. DeViney Company, Inc., *see* The
    J.M. Smucker Co.
H.B. Fenn and Company Ltd., **25** 485
H.B. Fuller Company, 8 237–40; **32**
    254–58 **(upd.); 75** 179–84 **(upd.)**
H. Betti Industries Inc., 88 155–58
H.C. Prange Co., **19** 511–12
H Curry & Sons *see* Currys Group PLC.
H.D. Lee Company, Inc. *see* Lee Apparel
    Company, Inc.
H.D. Vest, Inc., 46 217–19
H. E. Butt Grocery Company, 13
    251–53; **32** 259–62 **(upd.); 85**
    164–70 **(upd.)**
H.E. Moss and Company Tankers Ltd.,
    23 161
H.F. Ahmanson & Company, II
    181–82; **10** 342–44 **(upd.)** *see also*
    Washington Mutual, Inc.
H.F.T. Industrial Ltd., **62** 150
H.G. Anderson Equipment Corporation,
    6 441
H. Gringoire S.A.R.L., **70** 234
H.H. Brown Shoe Company, *see* Berkshire
    Hathaway Inc.
H.H. Cutler Company, *see* VF Corp.

H.H. Robertson, Inc., **19** 366
H.H. West Co., **25** 501
H.I.G. Capital L.L.C., **30** 235
H.J. Heinz Company, II 507–09; **11**
    171–73 **(upd.); 36** 253–57 **(upd.)**
H.J. Justin & Sons *see* Justin Industries,
    Inc.
H.J. Russell & Company, 66 162–65
H.L. Yoh Company *see* Day &
    Zimmerman, Inc.
H. Lundbeck A/S, 44 208–11
H.M. Byllesby & Company, Inc., **6** 539
H.M. Payson & Co., 69 202–04
H.M. Spalding Electric Light Plant, **6**
    592; **50** 37
H N Norton Co., **11** 208
H.O. Systems, Inc., **47** 430
H-P *see* Hewlett-Packard Co.
H.P. Foods, **II** 475
H.P. Hood, **7** 17–18
H.S. Trask & Co. *see* Phoenix Footware
    Group, Inc.
H. Samuel Plc, **61** 326
H.W. Johns Manufacturing Co. *see*
    Manville Corp.
H.W.S. Solutions, **21** 37
The H.W. Wilson Company, 66 166–68
Ha-Lo Industries, Inc., 27 193–95
Häagen-Dazs, *see* Nestlé S.A.
Haan Crafts Corporation, **62** 18
Haarmann & Reimer *see* Symrise GmbH
    and Co. KG
The Haartz Corporation, 94 223–26
Haas, Baruch & Co. *see* Smart & Final,
    Inc.
Haas Publishing Companies, Inc., **22** 442
Haas Wheat & Partners, **15** 357; **65**
    258–59
Habersham Bancorp, 25 185–87
Habitat for Humanity International, 36
    258–61
Habitat/Mothercare PLC *see* Mothercare
    plc.
Hach Co., 18 218–21
Hachette Filipacchi Medias S.A., 21
    265–67
Hachette S.A., IV 617–19 *see also*
    Matra-Hachette S.A.
Haci Omer Sabanci Holdings A.S., 55
    186–89 *see also* Akbank TAS
Hacker-Pschorr Brau, **35** 331
Hackman Oyj Adp, 44 212–15
Hadco Corporation, 24 201–03
Hadron, Inc. *see* Analex Corp.
Haeger Industries Inc., 88 159–62
Haemocell, **11** 476
Haemonetics Corporation, 20 277–79
Haftpflichtverband der Deutschen
    Industrie Versicherung auf
    Gegenseitigkeit V.a.G. *see* HDI
    (Haftpflichtverband der Deutschen
    Industrie Versicherung auf
    Gegenseitigkeit V.a.G.).
Hagemeyer N.V., 39 201–04
Hagemeyer North America, **63** 289
Haggar Corporation, 19 194–96; **78**
    137–41 **(upd.)**
Haggen Inc., 38 221–23

Hägglunds Vehicle AB, **47** 7, 9
Hagoromo Foods Corporation, 84
    175–178
Hahn Automotive Warehouse, Inc., 24
    204–06
Hahn Department Stores *see* Allied Stores
    Corp.
Haier Group Corporation, 65 167–70
Haights Cross Communications, Inc.,
    84 179–182
The Hain Celestial Group, Inc., 27
    196–98; **43** 217–20 **(upd.)**
Hair Club For Men Ltd., 90 222–25
Hair Cuttery *see* Ratner Companies.
Hake Group, Inc. *see* Matrix Service Co.
Hakone Tozan Railway Co., Ltd., **68** 281
Hakuhodo, Inc., 6 29–31; **42** 172–75
    (upd.)
HAL Inc., 9 271–73 *see also* Hawaiian
    Airlines, Inc.
Hale and Dorr, **31** 75
Hale-Halsell Company, 60 157–60
Haleko Hanseatisches Lebensmittel
    Kontor GmbH, **29** 500
Halewood, **21** 246
Half Price Books, Records, Magazines
    Inc., 37 179–82
Halfords Ltd., *see* Alliance Boots plc.
Halkin Holdings plc, **49** 338–39
Hall Bros. Co. *see* Hallmark Cards, Inc.
Hall, Kinion & Associates, Inc., 52
    150–52
Hall Laboratories, Inc., **45** 209
Hall-Mark Electronics, **23** 490
Hallhuber GmbH, **63** 361, 363
Halliburton Company, III 497–500; **25**
    188–92 **(upd.); 55** 190–95 **(upd.)**
Hallmark Cards, Inc., IV 620–21; **16**
    255–57 **(upd.); 40** 228–32 **(upd.); 87**
    205–212 **(upd.)**
Hallmark Chemical Corp., *see* NCH
    Corp.
Hallmark Holdings, Inc., **51** 190
Hallmark Investment Corp., **21** 92
Hallmark Residential Group, Inc., **45** 221
Halo Lighting, **30** 266
Haloid Company *see* Xerox Corp.
Halstead Industries, **26** 4; **52** 258
Halter Marine, **22** 276
Hambrecht & Quist Group, **26** 66; **31**
    349
Hambro Countrywide Security, **32** 374
Hambros Bank, **16** 14; **43** 7
Hamburg-Amerikanische-Packetfahrt-
    Actien-Gesellschaft *see* Hapag-Lloyd
    AG.
Hamburgische Electricitaets-Werke AG,
    57 395, 397
Hamelin Group, Inc. *see* Spartech Corp.
Hamer Hammer Service, Inc., **11** 523
Hamersley Holdings, **IV** 59–61
Hamil Textiles Ltd. *see* Algo Group Inc.
Hamilton Beach/Proctor-Silex Inc., 17
    213–15
Hamilton Group Limited, **15** 478
Hamilton/Hall-Mark, **19** 313
Hamilton Oil Corp., **IV** 47; **22** 107
Hamilton Sundstrand, **76** 319

Hospira, Inc., 71 172–74
Hospital Central Services, Inc., 56 166–68
Hospital Corporation of America, III 78–80 *see also* HCA - The Healthcare Co.
Hospital Cost Consultants, 11 113
Hospital Management Associates, Inc. *see* Health Management Associates, Inc.
Hospital Specialty Co., 37 392
Hospitality Franchise Systems, Inc., 11 177–79 *see also* Cendant Corp.
Hospitality Worldwide Services, Inc., 26 196–98
Hosposable Products, Inc. *see* Wyant Corp.
Hoss's Steak and Sea House Inc., 68 196–98
Host America Corporation, 79 202–06
Hot Dog Construction Co., 12 372
Hot Dog on a Stick *see* HDOS Enterprises.
Hot Sam Co. *see* Mrs. Fields' Original Cookies, Inc.
Hot Shoppes Inc. *see* Marriott.
Hot Stuff Foods, 85 171–74
Hot Topic Inc., 33 202–04; 86 190–94 (upd.)
Hotel Properties Ltd., 71 175–77
Hotel Reservations Network, Inc., 47 420
Hotels By Pleasant, 62 276
HotJobs.com, Ltd. *see* Yahoo! Inc.
HotRail Inc., 36 124
HotWired, 45 200
Houbigant, 37 270
Houchens Industries Inc., 51 168–70
Houghton Mifflin Company, 10 355–57; 36 270–74 (upd.)
Houlihan's Restaurant Group, 25 546
House of Blues, 32 241, 244
House of Fabrics, Inc., 21 278–80 *see also* Jo-Ann Stores, Inc.
House of Fraser PLC, 45 188–91 *see also* Harrods Holdings.
House of Miniatures, 12 264
House of Prince A/S, 80 151–54
Household International, Inc., II 417–20; 21 281–86 (upd.) *see also* HSBC Holdings plc.
Housing Development Finance Corporation, 20 313
Housmex Inc., 23 171
Houston Airport Leather Concessions LLC, 58 369
Houston Electric Light & Power Company, 44 368
Houston Industries Incorporated, V 641–44 *see also* Reliant Energy Inc.
Houston Oil & Minerals Corp., *see* Seagull Energy Corp.
Houston Pipe Line Company, 45 21
Hovnanian Enterprises, Inc., 29 243–45; 89 254–59 (upd.)
Howard B. Stark Candy Co., 15 325
Howard Flint Ink Company, *see* Flint Ink Corp.
Howard Hughes Corporation, 63 341

Howard Hughes Medical Institute, 39 221–24
Howard Johnson International, Inc., 17 236–39; 72 182–86 (upd.)
Howard Research and Development Corporation, 15 412, 414
Howard Schultz & Associates, Inc., 73 266
Howard, Smith & Levin, 40 126
Howden *see* Alexander Howden Group.
Howe & Fant, Inc., 23 82
Howmedica, 29 455
Howmet Corporation, 12 253–55 *see also* Alcoa Inc.
Hoyle Products, 62 384
HP *see* Hewlett-Packard Co.
HPI Health Care Services, 49 307–08
HQ Global Workplaces, Inc., 47 331
HQ Office International, *see* Office Depot Inc.
HRB Business Services, 29 227
HSBC Holdings plc, 12 256–58; 26 199–204 (upd.); 80 155–63 (upd.)
HSG *see* Helikopter Services Group AS.
Hsiang-Li Investment Corp., 51 123
HSN, 64 181–85 (upd.)
HSS Hire Service Group PLC, 45 139–41
HTH, 12 464
HTM Goedkoop, 26 278–79; 55 200
Hua Bei Oxygen, 25 82
Hua Yang Printing Holdings Co. Ltd., 60 372
Huawei Technologies Company Ltd., 87 228–231
Hub Group, Inc., 38 233–35
Hub International Limited, 89 260–64
Hub Services, Inc., *see* Dynegy Inc.
Hubbard Broadcasting Inc., 24 226–28; 79 207–12 (upd.)
Hubbard Construction Co., 23 332
Hubbell Inc., 9 286–87; 31 257–59 (upd.); 76 183–86 (upd.)
Huck Manufacturing Company, *see* Thiokol Corp.
The Hudson Bay Mining and Smelting Company, Limited, 12 259–61
Hudson Foods Inc., 13 270–72 *see also* Tyson Foods, Inc.
Hudson I.C.S., 58 53
Hudson Pharmaceutical Corp., 31 347
Hudson River Bancorp, Inc., 41 210–13
Hudson's *see* Target Corp.
Hudson's Bay Company, V 79–81; 25 219–22 (upd.); 83 187–194 (upd.)
Huf-North America, 73 325
Huffman Manufacturing Company, *see* Huffy Corp.
Huffy Corporation, 7 225–27; 30 239–42 (upd.)
Hughes Aircraft Company, *see* GM Hughes Electronics Corp.
Hughes Electronics Corporation, 25 223–25
Hughes Helicopter, 26 431; 46 65
Hughes Hubbard & Reed LLP, 44 230–32
Hughes Markets, Inc., 22 271–73 *see also* Kroger Co.

Hughes Network Systems Inc., 21 239
Hughes Space and Communications Company, 33 47–48
Hughes Supply, Inc., 14 246–47
Hughes Tool Co. *see* Baker Hughes Inc.
Hugo Boss AG, 48 206–09
Hugo Neu Corporation, 19 381–82
Hugo Stinnes GmbH, *see* Stinnes AG.
Huhtamäki Oyj, 64 186–88
HUK-Coburg, 58 169–73
The Hull Group, L.L.C., 51 148
Hulman & Company, 44 233–36
Hüls A.G., I 349–50 *see also* Degussa-Hüls AG.
Hulsbeck and Furst GmbH, 73 325
Hulton Getty, 31 216–17
Human Services Computing, Inc. *see* Epic Systems Corp.
Humana Inc., III 81–83; 24 229–32 (upd.)
The Humane Society of the United States, 54 170–73
Humanetics Corporation, 29 213
Humanities Software, 39 341
Humberside Sea & Land Services, 31 367
Humble Oil & Refining Company *see* Exxon.
Hummel International A/S, 68 199–201
Hummel Lanolin Corporation, 45 126
Hummel-Reise, 44 432
Hummer, Winblad Venture Partners, 36 157; 69 265; 74 168
Humongous Entertainment, Inc., 31 238–40
Humps' n Horns, 55 312
Hunco Ltd., IV 640; 26 273
Hungarian-Soviet Civil Air Transport Joint Stock Company *see* Malév Plc.
Hungarian Telephone and Cable Corp., 75 193–95
Hungry Howie's Pizza and Subs, Inc., 25 226–28
Hungry Minds, Inc. *see* John Wiley & Sons, Inc.
Hunt Consolidated, Inc., 7 228–30; 27 215–18 (upd.)
Hunt Manufacturing Company, 12 262–64
Hunt-Wesson, Inc., 17 240–42 *see also* ConAgra Foods, Inc.
Hunter Fan Company, 13 273–75
Hunting plc, 78 163–16
Huntingdon Life Sciences Group plc, 42 182–85
Huntington Bancshares Incorporated, 11 180–82; 87 232–238 (upd.)
Huntington Learning Centers, Inc., 55 212–14
Huntleigh Technology PLC, 77 199–202
Hunton & Williams, 35 223–26
Huntsman Chemical Corporation, 8 261–63
Huntstown Power Company Ltd., 64 404
Hurd & Houghton, *see* Houghton Mifflin Co.
Huron Consulting Group Inc., 87 239–243

IHS Inc., **78** 167–70

IIS, **26** 441

IJ Holdings Corp., **45** 173

IK Coach, Ltd., **23** 290

IKEA Group, V 82–84; 26 208–11 (upd.); 94 248–53 (upd.)

IKON Office Solutions, Inc., 50 236–39

Il Fornaio (America) Corporation, 27 225–28

Ilaco, **26** 22

ILC Dover Inc., **63** 318

ILFC *see* International Lease Finance Corp.

Ilitch Holdings Inc., 37 207–210; 86 195–200 (upd.)

Illco Toy Co. USA, **12** 496

Illinois Bell Telephone Company, 14 251–53

Illinois Central Corporation, 11 186–89

Illinois Lock Company, **48** 142

Illinois Power Company, 6 504–07 *see also* Ameren Corp.

Illinois Tool Works Inc., III 518–20; 22 280–83 (upd.); 81 186–91 (upd.)

Illumina, Inc., 93 246–49

Illuminet Holdings Inc., **47** 430

illycaffè SpA, 50 240–44

Ilwaco Telephone and Telegraph Company *see* Pacific Telecom, Inc.

ILX Resorts Incorporated, 65 174–76

Image Business Systems Corp., **11** 66

Image Entertainment, Inc., 94 254–57

Image Industries, Inc., *see* The Maxim Group.

Image Technologies Corporation, **12** 264

Imageline Inc., **25** 348

ImageTag Inc., **49** 290

Imaginarium Toy Centers, Inc., **57** 374

Imagine Entertainment, 91 255–58

Imagine Foods, Inc., 50 245–47

Imagine Manufacturing Solutions Inc., **48** 410

Imagine Technology Group, Inc., **73** 165

ImagiNet, **41** 97

Imaging Technologies, **25** 183

Imaje, S.A., **28** 104

IMAKE Software and Services, Inc., **49** 423–24

IMall Inc., **26** 441

Imasa Group, *see* ASARCO Inc.

Imasco Limited, V 401–02

Imation Corporation, 20 301–04 *see also* 3M Co.

Imatra Steel Oy Ab, 55 215–17

Imatran Voima Oy *see* Fortum Corporation

IMAX Corporation, 28 205–08; 78 171–76 (upd.)

IMC *see* Intertec Marine Corp.

IMC Fertilizer Group, Inc., 8 264–66

IMC Global Inc., **57** 149

ImClone Systems Inc., 58 178–81

IMCO Recycling, Incorporated, 32 270–73

IMED Corp., **38** 364

Imerys S.A., 40 176, 263–66 (upd.)

Imetal S.A., IV 107–09

IMG, 78 177–80

Imhoff Industrie Holding GmbH, **53** 315

IMI plc, 9 288–89; 29 364

IMIWeb Bank, **50** 410

Imlo, **26** 22

Immeon Networks LLC, **54** 407

Immersion Corporation, **28** 245

Immobilier Batibail, **42** 152

Immucor, Inc., 81 192–96

Immunex Corporation, 14 254–56; 50 248–53 (upd.)

Imo Industries Inc., 7 235–37; 27 229–32 (upd.)

Imo Pump, **58** 67

Impala Platinum Holdings Ltd., **IV 91–93; 63 38–39**

Impark Limited, **42** 433

IMPATH Inc., 45 192–94

Imperial Airways *see* British Overseas Airways Corp.

Imperial Business Forms, **9** 72

Imperial Chemical Industries plc, I 351–53; 50 254–58 (upd.)

Imperial Commodities Corporation *see* Deli Universal NV.

Imperial Feather Company, **19** 304

Imperial Holly Corporation, 12 268–70 *see also* Imperial Sugar Co.

Imperial Industries, Inc., 81 197–200

Imperial Metal Industries Ltd. *see* IMI plc.

Imperial Oil Limited, IV 437–39; 25 229–33 (upd.); 95 196–203 (upd.)

Imperial Packing Co. *see* Beech-Nut Nutrition Corp.

Imperial Parking Corporation, 58 182–84

Imperial Products, Inc., **62** 289

Imperial Sports, **19** 230

Imperial Sugar Company, 32 274–78 (upd.)

Imperial Tobacco Company *see* B.A.T. Industries PLC.

Imperial Tobacco Group PLC, 50 259–63

Implantes Y Sistemas Medicos, Inc., **72** 262

Implats *see* Impala Platinum Holdings Ltd.

IMPO Import Parfumerien, **48** 116

Imported Auto Parts, Inc., **15** 246

Impressions Software, **15** 455

Impulse Airlines Pty Ltd. *see* Qantas Airways Ltd.

Impulse Designs, **31** 435–36

IMRA America Inc., **48** 5

IMRS *see* Hyperion Software Corp.

IMS Health, Inc., 57 174–78

IMX Pharmaceuticals, **59** 285

In Focus Systems, Inc., 22 287–90

In-N-Out Burgers Inc., 19 213–15; 74 153–56 (upd.)

In-Sink-Erator, 66 195–98

INA Corporation *see* CIGNA Corp.

INA-Holding Schaeffler KG, **62** 129

InaCom Corporation, 13 276–78

Inalca S.p.A. *see* Cremonini S.p.A.

Inamed Corporation, 79 213–16

Incentive Group, **27** 269

Inchcape PLC, III 521–24; 16 276–80 (upd.); 50 264–68 (upd.)

INCO-Banco Indústria e Comércio de Santa Catarina, **13** 70

Inco Limited, IV 110–12; 45 195–99 (upd.)

Incon Research Inc., **41** 198

InControl Inc., **11** 460

Incredible Universe, **12** 470; **36** 387

Incyte Genomics, Inc., 52 174–77

Indel, Inc., 78 181–84

Indemnity Insurance Company *see* CIGNA Corp.

Independent Delivery Services, Inc., **37** 409

Independent Election Corp. of America, **47** 37

Independent Exhibitions Ltd., *see* Penton Media, Inc.

Independent Grocers Alliance *see* IGA.

Independent News & Media PLC, 61 129–31

Independent Print Media Group, **74** 283

Independent Stave Company, **28** 223

India Exotics, Inc., *see* Celebrity, Inc.

Indian Airlines Corporation *see* Air-India.

Indian Airlines Ltd., 46 240–42

Indian Archery and Toy Corp., *see* Escalade, Inc.

Indian Iron & Steel Company Ltd. *see* Steel Authority of India Ltd.

Indian Oil Corporation Ltd., IV 440–41; 48 210 13 (upd.)

Indiana Bell Telephone Company, Incorporated, 14 257–61

Indiana Electric Corporation, **6** 555

Indiana Energy, Inc., 27 233–36

Indiana Gaming Company, **21** 40

Indiana Gas & Water Company, **6** 556

Indiana Parts and Warehouse, **29** 86, 88

Indiana Power Company, **6** 555

Indiana Protein Technologies, **55** 233

Indiana Tube Co., **23** 250

Indianapolis Brush Electric Light & Power Company, **6** 508

Indianapolis Cablevision, **6** 508–09

Indianapolis Light and Power Company, **6** 508

Indianapolis Motor Speedway Corporation, 46 243–46

Indianapolis Power & Light Company, **6** 508–09

Indianapolis Pump and Tube Company, *see* Arvin Industries, Inc.

IndianOil Companies *see* Indian Oil Corporation Ltd.

Indigo Books & Music Inc., 58 185–87

Indigo NV, 26 212–14 *see also* Hewlett-Packard Co.

Indigo Systems Corp. *see* FLIR Systems, Inc.

The Inditex Group *see* Industria de Diseño Textil S.A.

Indo Mobil Ltd., **48** 212

Indosat *see* PT Indosat Tbk.

Indresco, Inc., **22** 285; **52** 215

Induba, S.A. de C.V., **39** 230

Induban, **II** 196

Indura SA Industria Y Commercio, **25** 82
Indus International Inc., 70 127–30
Industri Kapital, **27** 269; **68** 125–26
Industri Kapital 2000 Ltd., **64** 17
**Industria de Diseño Textil S.A.
   (Inditex), 64** 193–95
Industrial & Commercial Bank, **56** 363
Industrial Air Tool, **28** 387
Industrial Airsystems Inc., **56** 247
Industrial Bank of Japan, Ltd., II
   300–01
Industrial Chemical and Equipment, **16**
   271
Industrial Circuits, **IV** 680
Industrial Development Corp. of Zambia
   Ltd., *see* Zambia Industrial and Mining
   Corp. Ltd.
Industrial Development Corporation, **57**
   185
Industrial Devices Inc., **48** 359
Industrial Exportadora Famian, S.A. de
   C.V., **62** 353
Industrial Gases Lagos, **25** 82
Industrial Instrument Company *see*
   Foxboro Co.
Industrial Light & Magic, *see* Lucasfilm
   Ltd.
Industrial Powder Coatings, Inc., **16** 475
Industrial Publishing Company, *see*
   Pittway Corp.
Industrial Resources, **6** 144
Industrial Services Group, Inc., **56** 161
Industrial Services of America, Inc., 46
   247–49
Industrial Tectonics Corp., **18** 276
Industrial Tires Limited, **65** 91
Industrial Trade & Consumer Shows Inc.
   see Maclean Hunter Publishing Ltd.
Industrias Bachoco, S.A. de C.V., 39
   228–31
Industrias del Atlantico SA, **47** 291
Indústrias Klabin de Papel e Celulose S.A.
   see Klabin S.A.
Industrias Nacobre, **21** 259
Industrias Negromex, **23** 170
Industrias Penoles, S.A. de C.V., 22
   284–86
Industrias Resistol S.A., **23** 170–71
Industrie Natuzzi S.p.A., 18 256–58
**Industrie Zignago Santa Margherita
   S.p.A., 67** 210–12
Industriförvaltnings AB Kinnevik, **26**
   331–33; **36** 335
AB Industrivärden, **32** 397
Induyco *see* Industrias y Confecciones,
   S.A.
Indy Lighting, **30** 266
Indy Racing League, **37** 74
Inet Technologies Inc. *see* Tektronix Inc.
Infineon Technologies AG, 50 269–73
Infinity Broadcasting Corporation, 11
   190–92; **48** 214–17 (upd.)
Infinity Enterprises, Inc., **44** 4
Infinity Partners, **36** 160
Inflight Sales Group Limited, **11** 82; **29**
   511
InfoAsia, **28** 241
Infocom, **32** 8

InfoCure Corporation *see* AMICAS, Inc.
InFocus Corporation, 92 172–75
Infogrames Entertainment S.A., 35
   227–30
Infonet Services Corporation *see*
   Belgacom.
Informa Group plc, 58 188–91
Information Access Company, 17
   252–55
Information Builders, Inc., 22 291–93
Information Consulting Group, *see*
   McKinsey & Company, Inc.
Information, Dissemination and Retrieval
   Inc., **IV** 670
Information Holdings Inc., 47 183–86
Information International *see* Autologic
   Information International, Inc.
Information Management Reporting
   Services *see* Hyperion Software Corp.
Information Please LLC, **26** 216
Information Resources, Inc., 10 358–60
Information Spectrum Inc., **57** 34
Informix Corporation, 10 361–64; **30**
   243–46 (upd.) *see also* International
   Business Machines Corp.
Infoseek Corporation, **27** 517; **30** 490
InfoSoft International, Inc. *see* Inso Corp.
InfoSonics Corporation, 81 201–04
InfoSpace, Inc., 91 259–62
Infostrada S.p.A., **38** 300
Infosys Technologies Ltd., 38 240–43
Infotech Enterprises, Ltd., **33** 45
Infotel, Inc., **52** 342
Inframetrics, Inc., **69** 171
Infun, S.A., **23** 269
ING Australia Limited, **52** 35, 39
ING, B.V., **14** 45, 47; **69** 246, 248
Ing. C. Olivetti & C., S.p.A., III
   144–46 *see also* Olivetti S.p.A
ING Groep N.V., **63** 15
Ingalls Shipbuilding, Inc., 12 271–73
Ingefico, S.A., **52** 301
**Ingenico—Compagnie Industrielle et
   Financière d'Ingénierie, 46 250**–52
Ingenious Designs Inc., **47** 420
Ingersoll-Rand Company, III 525–27;
   15 223–26 (upd.); **55 218**–22 (upd.)
Ingka Holding B.V. *see* IKEA
   International A/S.
Ingleby Enterprises Inc. *see* Caribiner
   International, Inc.
Inglenook Vineyards, *see* Canandaigua
   Brands, Inc.
Ingles Markets, Inc., 20 305–08
Inglis Ltd. *see* Whirlpool Corp.
Ingram Book Group, **30** 70
Ingram Industries, Inc., 11 193–95; **49**
   217–20 (upd.)
Ingram Micro Inc., 52 178–81
AB Ingredients, *see* Associated British
   Foods plc.
Ingres Corporation, **9** 36–37
Ingwerson and Co., **II** 356
INH *see* Instituto Nacional de
   Hidrocarboros.
Inha Works Ltd., **33** 164
INI *see* Instituto Nacional de Industria.
Initial Electronics, **64** 198

Initial Security, 64 196–98
Initial Towel Supply *see* Rentokil Initial
   Plc.
Inktomi Corporation, 45 200–04
Inland Container Corporation, 8
   267–69 *see also* Temple-Inland Inc.
Inland Paperboard and Packaging, Inc., **31**
   438
Inland Steel Industries, Inc., IV 113–16;
   19 216–20 (upd.)
Inland Valley, **23** 321
Inmac, Inc., *see* Micro Warehouse, Inc.
Inmobiliaria e Inversiones Aconcagua S.A.,
   71 143
Inmotel Inversiones, **71** 338
InnCOGEN Limited, **35** 480
The Inner-Tec Group, **64** 198
InnerCity Foods Joint Venture Company,
   16 97
Inno-BM, **26** 158, 161
Inno-France *see* Societe des Grandes
   Entreprises de Distribution,
   Inno-France.
Innova International Corporation, **26** 333
Innovacom, **25** 96
Innovation, **26** 158
Innovative Marketing Systems *see*
   Bloomberg L.P.
Innovative Products & Peripherals
   Corporation, **14** 379
**Innovative Solutions & Support, Inc.,
   85 175**–78
Innovative Sports Systems, Inc., **15** 396
Innovative Valve Technologies Inc., **33**
   167
Innovex Ltd. *see* Quintiles Transnational
   Corp.
Innovo Group Inc., 83 195-199
Inovoject do Brasil Ltda., **72** 108
Inpaco, *see* Liqui-Box Corp.
Inprise/Borland Corporation, **33** 115; **76**
   123–24
Input/Output, Inc., 73 184–87
INS *see* International News Service.
Insa, **55** 189
Inserra Supermarkets, 25 234–36
Insight Enterprises, Inc., 18 259–61
Insight Marques SARL IMS SA, **48** 224
Insignia Financial Group, Inc. *see* CB
   Richard Ellis Group, Inc.
Insilco Corporation, 16 281–83
Inso Corporation, 26 215–19
Inspiration Resources Corporation, *see*
   Terra Industries.
Inspirations PLC, **22** 129
Insta-Care Holdings Inc., **16** 59
Instant Auto Insurance, **33** 3, 5
Instant Interiors Corporation, **26** 102
Instapak Corporation, *see* Sealed Air Corp.
Instinet Corporation, 34 225–27
Insituform Technologies, Inc., 83
   200-203
Institute for Professional Development, *see*
   Apollo Group, Inc.
Institution Food House *see* Alex Lee Inc.
Institutional Financing Services, **23** 491
Instituto Bancario San Paolo di Torino, **50**
   407

Iowa Beef Processors, *see* IBP, Inc.
Iowa Mold Tooling Co., Inc., **16** 475
Iowa Public Service Company, **6** 524–25
Iowa Telecommunications Services, Inc.,
  85 187–90
IP Services, Inc., **IV** 597
IP Timberlands Ltd., *see* International
  Paper Co.
IP&L *see* Illinois Power & Light Corp.
IP Vista, **74** 143
Ipalco Enterprises, Inc., 6 508–09
IPC *see* International Publishing Corp.
IPC Communications, Inc., **15** 196
IPC Magazines Limited, 7 244–47
IPD *see* International Periodical
  Distributors.
Iphotonics Inc., **48** 369
Ipiranga S.A., 67 216–18
Ipko-Amcor, **14** 225
IPL Energy Inc. *see* Enbridge Inc.
IPM *see* International Pharmacy
  Management, Inc.
IPS Praha a.s., **38** 437
IPS Publishing, **39** 341–42
IPSCO Inc. *see* SSAB Svenskt Stål AB.
Ipsen International Inc., 72 192–95
Ipsos SA, 48 221–24
Ipswich Bancshares Inc., **55** 52
iQuantic Buck, **55** 73
IQUE, Inc., **21** 194
IranAir, 81 214–17
Irdeto, **31** 330
Irex Contracting Group, 90 245–48
IRI *see* Instituto per la Ricostruzione
  Industriale.
Iridcon, Inc., **35** 435
Iridian Asset Management LLC, **52** 172
Irish Agricultural Wholesale Society Ltd.
  see IAWS Group plc.
Irish Air *see* Aer Lingus Group plc.
Irish Life & Permanent Plc, 59 245–47
Irish Life Assurance Company, **16** 14; **43**
  7
Irkut Corporation, 68 202–04
iRobot Corporation, 83 212-215
Iron and Steel Industrial Corporation, **59**
  224
Iron City Brewing Company *see*
  Pittsburgh Brewing Co.
Iron Mountain, Inc., 33 212–14
Ironside Technologies Inc., **72** 197
IronUnits LLC, **62** 74
Iroquois Gas Corporation, **6** 526
IRSA Inversiones y Representaciones
  S.A., 63 212–15
Irvin Aerospace, Inc. *see* Airborne Systems
  Group.
Irvin Feld & Kenneth Feld Productions,
  Inc., 15 237–39 *see also* Feld
  Entertainment, Inc.
Irving Tanning Company, *see* Fuqua
  Enterprises, Inc.
Irwin Financial Corporation, 77 213–16
Irwin Lehrhoff Associates, *see* NovaCare,
  Inc.
Irwin Toy Limited, 14 265–67
Isagro S.p.A., **26** 425
Isbank *see* Turkiye Is Bankasi A.S.

Iscor *see* Iron and Steel Industrial Corp.
Iscor Limited, 57 183–86
Isdin, **60** 246
Isetan Company Limited, V 85–87; **36**
  289–93 (upd.)
Ishikawajima-Harima Heavy Industries
  Company, Ltd., III 532–33; **86**
  211–15 (upd.)
Isis Distributed Systems, Inc., *see* Stratus
  Computer, Inc.
Island Def Jam Music, **57** 359
The Island ECN, Inc., 48 225–29
Island Equipment Co., **19** 381
Island Pictures Corp., **23** 389
Island Records, **23** 389
Isle of Capri Casinos, Inc., 41 217–19
Isokauf *see* SIG plc.
Isosceles PLC, **24** 270; **47** 367–68
Ispat Inland Inc., 30 252–54; **40**
  267–72 (upd.)
Israel Aircraft Industries Ltd., 69
  215–17
Israel Chemicals Ltd., 55 226–29
ISS A/S, 49 221–23
ISS Securitas, **42** 165, 167
ISSI *see* Integrated Silicon Solutions Inc.
Istante Vesa s.r.l., *see* Gianni Versace SpA.
Istituto Farmacologico Serono S.p.A. *see*
  Serono S.A.
Istituto Mobiliare Italiano S.p.A., **50** 407,
  409
Istituto per la Ricostruzione Industriale
  S.p.A., I 465–67; **11** 203–06 (upd.)
Isuzu Motors, Ltd., 9 293–95; **23**
  288–91 (upd.); **57** 187–91 (upd.)
IT Group, **28** 203
IT International, **V** 255
IT-Software Companies, **48** 402
Italcimenti Group, **40** 107–08
Italianni's, **22** 128
Italstate *see* Societa per la Infrastrutture e
  l'Assetto del Territoria.
Italtel, **V** 326–27
Itaú *see* Banco Itaú S.A.
Itaúsa *see* Investimentos Itaú S.A.
ITC Holdings Corp., 75 206–08
Itek Corp., *see* Litton Industries Inc.
Itel Corporation, 9 296–99
Items International Airwalk Inc., 17
  259–61
Ithaca Gas & Electric *see* New York State
  Electric and Gas.
ITI Education Corporation, **29** 472
ITM Entreprises SA, 36 294–97
Ito Gofuku Co. Ltd. *see* Matsuzakaya
  Company Ltd.
Ito-Yokado Co., Ltd., V 88–89; **42**
  189–92 (upd.)
Itochu and Renown, Inc., **12** 281
ITOCHU Corporation, 32 283–87
  (upd.)
Itochu Housing, **38** 415
Itoh *see* C. Itoh & Co.
Itoham Foods Inc., II 518–19; **61**
  138–40 (upd.)
Itoman & Co., **26** 456
Itron, Inc., 64 202–05

The Itsy Bitsy Entertainment Company,
  51 309
ITT *see* International Telephone and
  Telegraph Corp.
ITT Aerospace, **33** 48
ITT Automotive Inc. *see* Valeo.
ITT Educational Services, Inc., 33
  215–17; **76** 200–03 (upd.)
ITT Sheraton Corporation, III 98–101
  see also Starwood Hotels & Resorts
  Worldwide, Inc.
iTurf Inc., **29** 142–43
ITV PLC, **71** 368
ITW *see* Illinois Tool Works Inc.
i2 Technologies, Inc., 87 252–257
IU International, **23** 40
IURA Edition, **14** 556
IV Therapy Associates, **16** 440
IVACO Industries Inc., *see* IVAX Corp.
Ivanhoe, Inc., *see* Steinberg Inc.
Ivar's, Inc., 86 216–19
IVAX Corporation, 11 207–09; **55**
  230–33 (upd.)
IVC Industries, Inc., 45 208–11
iVillage Inc., 46 253–56
Ivy and Mader Philatelic Auctions, Inc.,
  60 146
Ivy Mortgage Corp., **39** 380, 382
Iwerks Entertainment, Inc., 34 228–30
IXC Communications, Inc., 29 250–52
IXI Ltd., **38** 418–19
Ixos Software AG *see* Open Text
  Corporation
IYG Holding Company of Japan, *see*
  7-Eleven, Inc.
The IZOD Gant Corporation, *see*
  Phillips-Van Heusen Corp
Izod Lacoste, *see* Crystal Brands, Inc.
Izukyu Corporation, **47** 408
Izumi Fudosan *see* Sumitomo Reality &
  Development Co., Ltd.

J

J & J Snack Foods Corporation, 24
  240–42
J&L Industrial Supply, *see* Kennametal,
  Inc.
J&L Steel *see* Jones & Laughlin Steel
  Corp.
J & M Laboratories, **48** 299
J&R Electronics Inc., 26 224–26
J&W Hardie Ltd., **62** 347
J. & W. Seligman & Co. Inc., 61
  141–43
J.A. Jones, Inc., 16 284–86
J. Alexander's Corporation, 65 177–79
J.B. Hunt Transport Services Inc., 12
  277–79
J.B. Ivey & Company *see* Dillard's Inc.
J.B. Lippincott & Company, *see* Wolters
  Kluwer NV.
J.B. McLean Publishing Co., Ltd. *see*
  Maclean Hunter Publishing Ltd.
J.B. Wolters Publishing Company, *see*
  Wolters Kluwer NV.
J. Baker, Inc., 31 270–73
J Bibby & Sons, *see* Barlow Rand Ltd.
J. Boag & Son Limited, **57** 306

J. Bulova Company *see* Bulova Corp.
J C Bamford Excavators Ltd., 83 216-222
J.C. Baxter Co., **15** 501
J.C. Hillary's, **20** 54
J.C. McCormic, Inc., **58** 334
J. C. Penney Company, Inc., V 90–92; 18 269–73 (upd.); 43 245–50 (upd.); 91 263–72 (upd.)
J.C. Potter Sausage Company, **57** 56–57
J. Crew Group, Inc., 12 280–82; 34 231–34 (upd.); 88 203–08
J.D. Bassett Manufacturing Co. *see* Bassett Furniture Industries, Inc.
J.D. Edwards & Company, 14 268–70 *see also* Oracle Corp.
J.D. Power and Associates, 32 297–301
J. D'Addario & Company, Inc., 48 230–33
J.E. Sirrine *see* CRSS Inc.
J.F. Corporation *see* Isetan Company Ltd.
J.F. Shea Co., Inc., 55 234–36
J.H. Findorff and Son, Inc., 60 175–78
J.H. Heafner Co., **20** 263
J.H. Westerbeke Corp. *see* Westerbeke Corp.
J.H. Whitney & Company, **32** 100
J. Homestock *see* R.H. Macy & Co.
J. Horner's, **48** 415
J.I.C. Group Limited, **61** 233
J.I. Case Company, 10 377–81 *see also* CNH Global N.V.
J.J. Farmer Clothing Inc., **51** 320–21
J.J. Keller & Associates, Inc., 81 2180–21
J.J. Kenney Company, Inc., **51** 244
The J. Jill Group, Inc., 35 239–41; 90 249–53 (upd.)
J.K. Starley and Company Ltd, *see* Rover Group Ltd.
J.L. Clark, Inc. *see* Clarcor Inc.
J.L. French Automotive Castings, Inc. *see* Onex Corp.
J.L. Hammett Company, 72 196–99
J.L. Hudson Company *see* Target Corp.
J.L. Shiely Co. *see* English China Clays Ltd.
J Lauritzen A/S, 90 254–57
J.M. Huber Corporation, **40** 68
The J. M. Smucker Company, 11 210–12; 87 258–265 (upd.)
J.M. Tull Metals Co., Inc., *see* Inland Steel Industries, Inc.
J.M. Voith AG, 33 222–25
J-Mar Associates, **31** 435–36
J.P. Morgan Chase & Co., II 329–32; 30 261–65 (upd.); 38 253–59 (upd.)
J.P. Stevens Inc., *see* WestPoint Stevens Inc.
J.R. Brown & Sharpe *see* Brown & Sharpe Manufacturing Co.
J.R. Simplot Company, 16 287–89; 60 179–82 (upd.)
J Sainsbury plc, II 657–59; 13 282–84 (upd.); 38 260–65 (upd.); 95 212–20 (upd.)
J. Sears & Company *see* Sears plc.
J. Spiegel and Company *see* Spiegel, Inc.

J.U. Dickson Sawmill Inc. *see* Dickson Forest Products, Inc.
J.W. Bateson, *see* Centex Corp.
J.W. Charles Financial Services Inc., 25 542
J.W. Childs Associates, L.P., 46 220; 64 119
J.W. Childs Equity Partners LP, **40** 274
J.W. Foster and Sons, Inc. *see* Reebok International Ltd.
J. W. Pepper and Son Inc., 86 220–23
J.W. Spear, **25** 314
J.W. Wassall Ltd. *see* Wassall PLC.
J. Walter Thompson Co. *see* JWT Group Inc.
Jabil Circuit, Inc., 36 298–301; 88 209–14
Jack Daniel's *see* Brown-Forman Corp.
Jack Eckerd Corp., **19** 467
Jack Henry and Associates, Inc., 17 262–65; 94 258–63 (upd.)
Jack in the Box Inc., 89 265–71 (upd.)
Jack Morton Worldwide, 88 215–18
Jack Schwartz Shoes, Inc., 18 266–68
Jackpot Enterprises Inc., 21 298–300
Jackson & Perkins *see* Bear Creek Corp.
Jackson Furniture of Danville, LLC, 48 246
Jackson Hewitt, Inc., 48 234–36
Jackson Mercantile Co. *see* Jitney-Jungle Stores of America, Inc.
Jackson National Life Insurance Company, 8 276–77
Jacmar Companies, 87 266–269
Jaco Electronics, Inc., 30 255–57
Jacob Leinenkugel Brewing Company, 28 209–11
Jacobs Brake Manufacturing Company, *see* Danaher Corp.
Jacobs Engineering Group Inc., 6 148–50; 26 220–23 (upd.)
Jacobs Suchard (AG), II 520–22 *see also* Kraft Jacobs Suchard AG.
Jacobson Stores Inc., 21 301–03
Jacoby & Meyers, **20** 435
Jacor Communications, Inc., 23 292–95
Jacques Borel International, **49** 126
Jacques Chocolaterie S.A., **53** 315
Jacques Whitford, 92 184–87
Jacquot *see* Établissements Jacquot and Cie S.A.S.
Jacuzzi Brands Inc., 23 296–98; 76 204–07 (upd.)
Jade KK, **25** 349
JAFCO Co. Ltd., 79 221–24
Jafra Cosmetics, **15** 475, 477
Jaguar Cars, Ltd., 13 285–87
JAIX Leasing Company, **23** 306
JAKKS Pacific, Inc., 52 191–94
JAL *see* Japan Airlines Company, Ltd.
Jalate Inc., 25 245–47
Jaluzot & Cie *see* Pinault-Printemps-Redoute S.A.
Jamaica Water Supply Company *see* JWP Inc.
Jamar Company, **64** 30, 32
Jamba Juice Company, 47 199–202
Jamdat Mobile *see* Electronic Arts Inc.

James Avery Craftsman, Inc., **76** 208–10
James Beattie plc, 43 242–44
James Burn/American, Inc., *see* Standex International Corp.
The James C. Heintz Company, *see* Myers Industries, Inc.
James Felt Realty, Inc., **21** 257
James Fison and Sons *see* Fisons plc.
James G. Fast Company *see* Angelica Corp.
James Galt & Co. Ltd., **60** 124
James Hardie Industries N.V., 56 174–76
James Heekin and Company, *see* Heekin Can Inc.
James Industries, Inc., **61** 298
James McNaughton Ltd., *see* PWA Group.
James Original Coney Island Inc., 84 197–200
James Purdey & Sons Limited, 87 270–275
James River Corporation of Virginia, IV 289–91 *see also* Fort James Corp.
James Wellbeloved, **39** 354, 356
Jamestown Insurance Co. Ltd., **55** 20
Jamestown Publishers, *see* Tribune Co.
Jamesway Corporation, **23** 177
Jamie Scott, Inc., **27** 348
Jan Bell Marketing Inc. *see* Mayor's Jewelers, Inc.
Janata Bank, **31** 219
Janco Overseas Limited, **59** 261
Jane Jones Enterprises, **16** 422; **43** 309
Janesville Electric, **6** 604
Jani-King International, Inc., 85 191–94
Janin, S.A., **36** 163
Janna Systems Inc., **38** 433
Janssen Pharmaceutica N.V., 80 164–67
Janson Publications, *see* Tribune Co.
JanSport, Inc., 70 134–36
JANT Pty. Ltd., *see* Honshu Paper Co. Ltd.
Jantzen Inc. *see* VF Corp.
Janus Capital Group Inc., 57 192–94
Japan Airlines Company, Ltd., I 104–06; 32 288–92 (upd.)
Japan Brewery *see* Kirin Brewery Company, Ltd.
Japan Broadcasting Corporation, 7 248–50
Japan Elanco Company, Ltd., **17** 437
Japan Energy Corporation, **14** 206, 208; **59** 375
Japan Food Corporation, *see* Kikkoman Corp.
Japan Leasing Corporation, 8 278–80
Japan Medico, **25** 431
Japan Photo Holding Norge AS, **76** 85, 87
Japan Pulp and Paper Company Limited, IV 292–93
Japan Rifex Co., Ltd., **64** 261
Japan Tobacco Inc., V 403–04; 46 257–60 (upd.)
Japan Trustee Services Bank Ltd., **53** 322
Japan Vilene Company Ltd., **41** 170–72
Japan Xanpak Corporation *see* JSP Corp.

K.H. Wheel Company, *see* Hayes
Lemmerz International, Inc.
K. Hattori & Co., Ltd. *see* Seiko Corp.
K.J. International Inc., **70** 74, 76
k.k. Staatsbahnen *see* Österreichische
Bundesbahnen GmbH.
K Line *see* Kawasaki Kisen Kaisha, Ltd.
K-Line Pharmaceuticals Ltd. *see* Taro
Phramaceutical Industries Ltd.
K.O. Lester Co., **31** 359, 361
K.P. American, **55** 305
Kabelvision AB, **26** 331–33
Kable News Company *see* AMREP Corp.
Kafte Inc., **28** 63
Kagoshima Central Research Laboratory,
21 330
Kaiser + Kraft GmbH, *see* GEHE AG
Kaiser Aluminum Corporation, IV
121–23; 84 212–217 (upd.)
Kaiser Foundation Health Plan, Inc., 53
184–86
Kaiser Packaging, **12** 377
Kaiser Permanente Corp. *see* Kaiser
Foundation Health Plan, Inc.
Kaiser Steel, **IV** 59
Kaiser's Kaffee Geschäft AG, *see*
Tengelmann Group.
Kajima Corporation, I 577–78; 51
177–79 (upd.)
Kal Kan Foods, Inc., 22 298–300
Kalamazoo Limited, **50** 377
Kaldveer & Associates, **14** 228
Kaliningradnefteprodukt, **48** 378
Kaman Corporation, 12 289–92; 42
204–08 (upd.)
Kaman Music Corporation, 68 205–07
Kamewa Group, *see* Vickers plc.
Kaminski/Engles Capital Corp. *see* Suiza
Foods Corp.
Kammer Valves, A.G., *see* Duriron Co.
Inc.
Kampgrounds of America, Inc., 33
230–33
Kamps AG, 44 251–54
Kana Software, Inc., 51 180–83
Kanagawa Chuo Kotsu Co., Ltd., **68** 281
Kanan Enterprises Inc., **74** 167
Kanebo, Ltd., 53 187–91
Kanematsu Corporation, IV 442–44; 24
259–62 (upd.)
Kangaroo *see* Seino Transportation
Company, Ltd.
Kanpai Co. Ltd., **55** 375
Kansai Paint Company Ltd., 80 175–78
The Kansai Electric Power Company,
Inc., V 645–48; 62 196–200 (upd.)
Kansai Plast Corporation, **74** 163
Kansallis-Osake-Pankki, II 302–03
Kansas City Ingredient Technologies, Inc.,
49 261
Kansas City Power & Light Company,
6 510–12 *see also* Great Plains Energy
Inc.
Kansas City Southern Industries, Inc., 6
400–02; 26 233–36 (upd.)
The Kansas City Southern Railway
Company, 92 198–202

Kansas City White Goods Company *see*
Angelica Corp.
Kansas Fire & Casualty Co., *see* Berkshire
Hathaway Inc.
Kansas Sand and Concrete, Inc., **72** 233
Kansas Utilities Company, **6** 580
The Kantar Group, **48** 442
Kao Corporation, III 38–39; 20 315–17
(upd.); 79 225–30 (upd.)
Kaolin Australia Pty Ltd. *see* English
China Clays Ltd.
Kapalua Land Company, Ltd., **29** 307–08
Kaplan Educational Centers, **12** 143
Kaplan, Inc., 42 209–12; 90 270–75
(upd.)
Kaplan Musical String Company, **48** 231
Kapok Computers, **47** 153
Kar Nut Products Company, 86 233–36
Karan Co. *see* Donna Karan Co.
Karastan Bigelow, **19** 276
Karl Kani Infinity, Inc., 49 242–45
Karl Schmidt Unisia, Inc., **56** 158
Karlsberg Brauerei GmbH & Co KG,
41 220–23
Karmann *see* Wilhelm Karmann GmbH.
Karrosseriewerke Weinsberg GmbH *see*
ASC, Inc.
Karstadt Aktiengesellschaft, V 100–02;
19 234–37 (upd.)
Karstadt Quelle AG, 57 195–201 (upd.)
Karsten Manufacturing Corporation, 51
184–86
Kasco Corporation, **28** 42, 45
Kash n' Karry Food Stores, Inc., 20
318–20
Kashi Company, 89 282–85
Kashima Chlorine & Alkali Co., Ltd., **64**
35
Kaspare Cohn Commercial & Savings
Bank *see* Union Bank of California.
Kasper A.S.L., Ltd., 40 276–79
Kasuga Radio Company *see* Kenwood
Corp.
Kasumi Co., Ltd., **68** 9
Kat-Em International Inc., **16** 125
Katabami Kogyo Co. Ltd., **51** 179
Kate Industries, **74** 202
kate spade LLC, 68 208–11
Katharine Gibbs Schools Inc., **22** 442
Katherine Beecher Candies, Inc. *see*
Warrell Corp.
Katies, **V** 35
Kativo Chemical Industries Ltd., *see* H. B.
Fuller Co.
Katokichi Company Ltd., 82 187–90
Katy Industries Inc., I 472–74; 51
187–90 (upd.)
Katz Communications, Inc., 6 32–34 *see*
also Clear Channel Communications,
Inc.
Katz Media Group, Inc., 35 245–48
Kaufhalle AG, **V** 104; **23** 311; **41** 186–87
Kaufhof Warenhaus AG, V 103–05; 23
311–14 (upd.)
Kaufman and Broad Home
Corporation, 8 284–86 *see also* KB
Home.

Kaufmann Department Stores, Inc. *see*
The May Department Stores Co.
Kaufring AG, 35 249–52
Oy Kaukas Ab *see* UPM-Kymmene
Kaukauna Cheese Inc., **23** 217, 219
Kawai Musical Instruments
Manufacturing Co.,Ltd., 78 189–92
Kawasaki Heavy Industries, Ltd., III
538–40; 63 220–23 (upd.)
Kawasaki Kisen Kaisha, Ltd., V 457–60;
56 177–81 (upd.)
Kawasaki Steel Corporation, IV 124–25
Kawsmouth Electric Light Company *see*
Kansas City Power & Light Co.
Kay-Bee Toy Stores, 15 252–53 *see also*
KB Toys.
Kay Jewelers Inc., **61** 327
Kaydon Corporation, 18 274–76
Kaye, Scholer, Fierman, Hays & Handler,
47 436
Kayex, *see* General Signal Corp.
Kaytee Products Incorporated, **58** 60
KB Home, 45 218–22 (upd.)
AO KB Impuls, **48** 419
KB Investment Co., Ltd., **58** 208
KB Toys, Inc., 35 253–55 (upd.); 86
237–42 (upd.)
KBLCOM Incorporated, **V** 644
KC *see* Kenneth Cole Productions, Inc.
KC Holdings, Inc., *see* Kimco Realty
Corp.
KCI Konecranes International, **27** 269
KCK Tissue S.A., **73** 205
KCPL *see* Kansas City Power & Light Co.
KCS Industries, **12** 25–26
KCSI *see* Kansas City Southern Industries,
Inc.
KCSR *see* Kansas City Southern Railway.
KD Acquisition Corporation, **34** 103–04;
76 239
KD Manitou, Inc. *see* Manitou BF S.A.
KDI Corporation, **56** 16–17
Keane, Inc., 56 182–86
Keck's *see* Decorator Industries Inc.
The Keds Corp., **37** 377, 379
Keebler Foods Company, 36 311–13
Keene Packaging Co., **28** 43
KEG Productions Ltd., **IV** 640; **26** 272
Keio Teito Electric Railway Company, V
461–62
The Keith Companies Inc., 54 181–84
Keithley Instruments Inc., 16 299–301
Kelco, **34** 281
Kelda Group plc, 45 223–26
Keliher Hardware Company, **57** 8
Kelkoo S.A. *see* Yahoo! Inc.
Kelley Blue Book Company, Inc., 84
218–221
Keller Builders, **43** 400
Keller-Dorian Graveurs, S.A., *see* Standex
International Corp.
Keller Group PLC, 95 221–24
Kelley Drye & Warren LLP, 40 280–83
Kellock Holdings Ltd., *see* The Governor
and Company of the Bank of Scotland.
Kellogg Brown & Root, Inc., 62
201–05 (upd.)

MacMark Corp., **22** 459

Macmillan & Co. Ltd., **35** 452

MacMillan Bloedel Limited, IV 306–09
see also Weyerhaeuser Co.

Macmillan, Inc., 7 284–86

**The MacNeal-Schwendler Corporation,
25 303–05**

**MacNeil/Lehrer Productions, 87
296–299**

Macquarie Bank Ltd., 69 246–49

Macromedia, Inc., 50 328–31

MACSTEEL Monroe, Inc., **62** 289

Macy's, Inc., 94 284–93 (upd.)

Mad Dog Athletics, **19** 385

Mad River Canoe *see* Confluence
Holdings Corp.

MADD *see* Mothers Against Drunk
Driving.

Madden's on Gull Lake, 52 231–34

Madeco S.A., 71 210–12

**Madeira Wine Company, S.A., 49
255–57**

Maderin ECO S.A., **51** 6

Madge Networks N.V., 26 275–77

Madison Dearborn Partners LLC, **46** 289;
49 197; **51** 131, 282, 284; **69** 197

Madison Furniture Industries, *see* Shelby
Williams Industries, Inc.

**Madison Gas and Electric Company, 39
259–62**

Madison-Kipp Corporation, 58 213–16

Madison Park Press *see* Bookspan.

Madrange SA, 58 217–19

Maersk Oile, **22** 167; **65** 316–17

Maersk Sealand *see* A.P. Møller - Maersk
A/S.

Macs Group Breweries, **II** 475

Maeva Group *see* Club Mediterranee SA.

Mafco Holdings, Inc., **28** 248; **38** 293–95

Mag Instrument, Inc., 67 240–42

MagCorp, **28** 198

Magee Company, **31** 435–36

Magella Healthcare Corporation, **61** 284

**Magellan Aerospace Corporation, 48
274–76**

Magellan Corporation, **22** 403; **60** 137

Magellan et Bergerat, **72** 159

MaggieMoo's International, 89 312–16

Magic Chef Co. *see* Maytag Corp.

Magic City Food Products Company *see*
Golden Enterprises, Inc.

Magic Marker, **29** 372

Magic Years Child Care, **51** 198

Magicsilk, Inc., *see* Celebrity, Inc.

Maglificio di Ponzano Veneto dei Fratelli
Benetton *see* Benetton.

Magma Copper Company, 7 287–90 *see
also* BHP Billiton.

**Magma Design Automation Inc., 78
203–27**

Magma Power Company, 11 270–72

Magna Computer Corporation, *see* EMC
Corp.

Magna Distribuidora Ltda., **43** 368

Magnaflux, *see* Illinois Tool Works Inc.

Magnavox Co., *see* Philips Electronics.

**MagneTek, Inc., 15 287–89; 41 241–44
(upd.)**

**Magneti Marelli Holding SpA, 90
286–89**

Magnetic Peripherals Inc., **19** 513–14

Magnivision, Inc., *see* American Greetings
Corp.

Magnum Hunter Resources, Inc. *see*
Cimarex Energy Co.

Magro, **48** 63

Magyar Telekom Rt, 78 208–11

Magyar Viscosa, **37** 428

Mahalo Air, **22** 252

Mahir & Numan A.S., **48** 154

MAI PLC, **28** 504

MAI Systems Corporation, 11 273–76

Maid-Rite Corporation, 62 235–38

**Maidenform, Inc., 20 352–55; 59
265–69 (upd.)**

**Mail Boxes Etc., 18 315–17; 41 245–48
(upd.)** *see also* U.S. Office Products Co.

Mail.com Inc., **38** 271

Mail Coups, Inc., **53** 13

Mail Finance, **53** 239

Mail Marketing Systems Inc., **53** 13

Mail-Well, Inc., 28 250–52 *see also*
Cenveo Inc.

MailCoups, Inc., **53** 9

Mailtek, Inc., *see* Total System Services,
Inc.

MAIN *see* Makhteshim-Agan Industries
Ltd.; Mid-American Interpool Network.

Main Plaza Corporation, **25** 115

Main Street Advertising USA, **IV** 597

**Maine & Maritimes Corporation, 56
210–13**

**Maine Central Railroad Company, 16
348–50**

**Maines Paper & Food Service Inc., 71
213–15**

Mainline Industrial Distributors, Inc., *see*
Bearings, Inc.

Maison Blanche Department Stores
Group, **35** 129

Maison de Valérie, **19** 309

Maison Louis Jadot, 24 307–09

**Majesco Entertainment Company, 85
225–29**

Majestic Industries, Inc., **43** 459

**The Major Automotive Companies, Inc.,
45 260–62**

Major SA, **53** 179

Major Video Concepts, **6** 410

Major Video Corporation, *see* Blockbuster
Inc.

**Makhteshim-Agan Industries Ltd., 85
230–34**

**Makita Corporation, 22 333–35; 59
270–73 (upd.)**

Makivik Corporation, **56** 38–39

Makoff R&D Laboratories, **56** 375

Malapai Resources, **6** 546

Malayan Banking Berhad, 72 215–18

**Malaysian Airlines System Berhad, 6
100–02; 29 300–03 (upd.)**

Malcolm Pirnie, Inc., 42 242–44

**Malden Mills Industries, Inc., 16
351–53**

Malév Plc, 24 310–12

Malew Engineering, **51** 354

Malibu, **25** 141

Mall.com, **38** 271

Mallard Bay Drilling, Inc., **28** 347–48

Mallinckrodt Group Inc., 19 251–53

Malmö Aviation, **47** 61

Malmö Woodworking Factory *see* Tarkett
Sommer AG.

Malone & Hyde, Inc., **14** 147 *see also*
AutoZone, Inc.; Fleming Companies,
Inc.

**Malt-O-Meal Company, 22 336–38; 63
249–53 (upd.)**

Malterie Soufflet *see* Groupe Soufflet SA

Mama Fu's Noodle House, Inc., **64**
327–28

Mama's Concept, Inc., **51** 229

Mameco International, *see* RPM Inc.

Mammoet Transport B.V., 26 278–80

Man Aktiengesellschaft, III 561–63

MAN Gutehoffnungshütte AG, **15** 226

**MAN Roland Druckmaschinen AG, 94
294–98**

**Management and Training Corporation,
28 253–56**

Management By Information Inc., **48** 307

Management Recruiters International *see*
CDI Corp.

Manatron, Inc., 86 260–63

**Manchester United Football Club plc,
30 296–98**

Manco, Inc. *see* Henkel Manco Inc.

Mancuso & Co., **22** 116

Mandabach & Simms, **6** 40

Mandalay Pictures, **35** 278–80

**Mandalay Resort Group, 32 322–26
(upd.)**

Mandarin, Inc., **33** 128

Mandarin Oriental International Limited,
47 177

Mandom Corporation, 82 205–08

Manetta Home Fashions, Inc., *see*
Pillowtex Corp.

Manhattan Associates, Inc., 67 243–45

Manhattan Bagel Inc., **63** 80

Manhattan Construction Company *see*
Rooney Brothers Co.

Manhattan Drug Company *see* Integrated
BioPharma, Inc.

Manhattan Group, LLC, 80 228–31

Manhattan International Limousine
Network Ltd., **26** 62

Manheim, 88 244–48

**Manila Electric Company (Meralco), 56
214–16**

Manischewitz Company *see* B.
Manischewitz Co.

**Manitoba Telecom Services, Inc., 61
184–87**

Manitou BF S.A., 27 294–96

**The Manitowoc Company, Inc., 18
318–21; 59 274–79 (upd.)**

Mann's Wine Company, Ltd., *see*
Kikkoman Corp.

Mannatech Inc., 33 282–85

**Mannesmann AG, III 564–67; 14
326–29 (upd.); 38 296–301 (upd.)** *see
also* Vodafone Group PLC.

Merrill Corporation, 18 331–34; 47 241–44 (upd.)

Merrill Lynch & Co., Inc., II 424–26; 13 340–43 (upd.); 40 310–15 (upd.)

Merrill Lynch Capital Partners, 47 363

Merrill Lynch Investment Managers *see* BlackRock, Inc.

Merrill, Pickard, Anderson & Eyre IV, 11 490

Merrill Publishing, 29 57

Merrimack Services Corp., 37 303

Merry-Go-Round Enterprises, Inc., 8 362–64

Merry Group *see* Boral Ltd.

Merry Maids *see* ServiceMaster Inc.

Merryhill Schools, Inc., 37 279

The Mersey Docks and Harbour Company, 30 318–20

Mervyn's California, 10 409–10; 39 269–71 (upd.) *see also* Target Corp.

Merz Group, 81 253–56

Mesa Air Group, Inc., 11 298–300; 32 334–37 (upd.); 77 265–70 (upd.)

Mesaba Holdings, Inc., 28 265–67

Messerschmitt-Bölkow-Blohm GmbH., I 73–75 *see also* European Aeronautic Defence and Space Company EADS N.V.

Mestek, Inc., 10 411–13

Met Food Corp. *see* White Rose Food Corp.

Met-Mex Penoles *see* Industrias Penoles, S.A. de C.V.

META Group, Inc., 37 147

Metal Box plc, I 604–06 *see also* Novar plc.

Metal-Cal *see* Avery Dennison Corp.

Metal Casting Technology, Inc., 23 267, 269

Metal Management, Inc., 92 247–50

AB Metal Pty Ltd, 62 331

Metalcorp Ltd, 62 331

Metales y Contactos, 29 461–62

Metaleurop S.A., 21 368–71

MetalExchange, 26 530

Metallgesellschaft AG, IV 139–42; 16 361–66 (upd.)

MetalOptics Inc., 19 212

Metalúrgica Gerdau *see* Gerdau S.A.

Metalurgica Mexicana Penoles, S.A. *see* Industrias Penoles, S.A. de C.V.

Metaphase Technology, Inc., *see* Control Data Systems, Inc.

Metatec International, Inc., 47 245–48

Metcalf & Eddy Companies, Inc., 6 441; 32 52

Metcash Trading Ltd., 58 226–28

Meteor Film Productions, 23 391

Meteor Industries Inc., 33 295–97

Methane Development Corporation, 6 457

Methanex Corporation, 40 316–19

Methode Electronics, Inc., 13 344–46

MetLife *see* Metropolitan Life Insurance Co.

MetPath, Inc., *see* Corning Inc.

Metra Corporation *see* Wärtsilä Corp.

Metra Steel, 19 381

Metragaz, 69 191

Metrastock Ltd., 34 5

Metric Constructors, Inc., 16 286

Metric Systems Corporation, *see* Tech-Sym Corp.

Metris Companies Inc., 56 224–27

Metro AG, 50 335–39

Metro Distributors Inc., 14 545

Metro-Goldwyn-Mayer Inc., 25 326–30 (upd.); 84 263–270 (upd.)

Metro Holding AG, 38 266

Métro Inc., 77 271–75

Metro Information Services, Inc., 36 332–34

Metro International S.A., 93 309–12

Metro-Mark Integrated Systems Inc., 11 469

Metro-North Commuter Railroad Company, 35 292

Metro Pacific, *see* First Pacific Co. Ltd.

Metro Southwest Construction *see* CRSS Inc.

Metro Support Services, Inc., 48 171

Metrocall, Inc., 41 265–68

Metrol Security Services, Inc., 32 373

Metroland Printing, Publishing and Distributing Ltd., 29 471

Metromail Corp., IV 661; 18 170; 38 370

Metromedia Company, 7 335–37; 14 298–300 (upd.); 61 210–14 (upd.)

Metronic AG, 64 226

Metroplex, LLC, 51 206

Métropole Télévision S.A., 76 272–74 (upd.)

Metropolis Intercom, 67 137–38

Metropolitan Baseball Club Inc., 39 272–75

Metropolitan Clothing Co., 19 362

Metropolitan Edison Company, *see* GPU, Inc.

Metropolitan Financial Corporation, 13 347–49

Metropolitan Life Insurance Company, III 290–94; 52 235–41 (upd.)

The Metropolitan Museum of Art, 55 267–70

Metropolitan Opera Association, Inc., 40 320–23

Metropolitan Reference Laboratories Inc., 26 391

Metropolitan Tobacco Co., 15 138

Metropolitan Transportation Authority, 35 290–92

MetroRed, 57 67, 69

Metrostar Management, 59 199

METSA, Inc., 15 363

Metsä-Serla Oy, IV 314–16 *see also* M-real Oyj.

Metsec plc, 57 402

Metso Corporation, 30 321–25 (upd.); 85 269–77 (upd.)

Mettler-Toledo International Inc., 30 326–28

Metwest, 26 391

Metz Baking Company, 36 164

Metzdorf Advertising Agency, 30 80

Metzeler Kautschuk, 15 354

Mexican Metal Co. *see* Industrias Penoles, S.A. de C.V.

Mexican Restaurants, Inc., 41 269–71

Meyer International Holdings, Ltd., 87 312–315

Meyerland Company, 19 366

Meyers Motor Supply, 26 347

Meyers Parking, *see* Central Parking Corp.

The Meyne Company, 55 74

Meyr Melnhof Karton AG, 41 325–27

M4 Data (Holdings) Ltd., 62 293

M40 Trains Ltd., 51 173

MFS Communications Company, Inc., 11 301–03 *see also* MCI WorldCom, Inc.

MG&E *see* Madison Gas & Electric.

MG Holdings *see* Mayflower Group Inc.

MGA Entertainment, Inc., 95 279–82

MGD Graphics Systems *see* Goss Holdings, Inc.

MGIC Investment Corp., 52 242–44

MGM *see* McKesson General Medical.

MGM Grand Inc., 17 316–19

MGM Mirage *see* Mirage Resorts, Inc.

MGM Studios, 50 125

MGM/UA Communications Company, II 146–50 *see also* Metro-Goldwyn-Mayer Inc.

MGN *see* Mirror Group Newspapers Ltd.

MGT Services Inc. *see* The Midland Co.

MH Alshaya Group, 28 96

MH Media Monitoring Limited, 26 270

MHI Group, Inc., 16 344

MHS Holding Corp., 26 101

MHT *see* Manufacturers Hanover Trust Co.

MI *see* Masco Corp.

MI S.A., 66 244

Mi-Tech Steel Inc., 63 359–60

Miami Computer Supply Corporation *see* MCSi, Inc.

Miami Herald Media Company, 92 251–55

Miami Power Corporation *see* Cincinnati Gas & Electric Co.

Miami Subs Corp., 29 342, 344

Mich-Wis *see* Michigan Wisconsin Pipe Line.

Michael Anthony Jewelers, Inc., 24 334–36

Michael Baker Corporation, 14 333–35; 51 245–48 (upd.)

MICHAEL Business Systems Plc, *see* Control Data Systems, Inc.

Michael C. Fina Co., Inc., 52 245–47

Michael Foods, Inc., 25 331–34

Michael Joseph, IV 659

Michael Page International plc, 45 272–74

Michaels Stores, Inc., 17 320–22; 71 226–30 (upd.)

MichCon *see* MCN Corp.

Michelin *see* Compagnie Générale des Établissements Michelin.

Michie Co., 33 264–65

Michigan Automotive Compressor, Inc., *see* Toyoda Automatic Loom Works, Ltd.

Modern Controls, Inc. *see* Mocon, Inc.
Modern Food Industries Limited *see* Hindustan Lever Limited
Modern Furniture Rentals Inc., **14** 4
Modern Handling Methods Ltd., **21** 499
Modern Times Group AB, 36 335–38
Modern Woodmen of America, 66 227–29
Modine Manufacturing Company, 8 372–75; **56** 243–47 **(upd.)**
Modis Professional Services *see* MPS Group, Inc.
MoDo *see* Mo och Domsjö AB.
MoDo Paper AB, **28** 446; **52** 164
Modtech Holdings, Inc., 77 284–87
ModusLink Corporation *see* CMGI, Inc.
Moe's Southwest Grill, LLC, **64** 327–28
Moen Incorporated, 12 344–45
Moët-Hennessy, I 271–72 *see also* LVMH Moët Hennessy Louis Vuitton SA.
Mogen David *see* The Wine Group, Inc.
The Mogul Metal Company *see* Federal-Mogul Corp.
Mohasco Corporation, **15** 102; **26** 100–01
Mohawk Carpet Corp., **26** 101
Mohawk Industries, Inc., 19 274–76; **63** 298–301 **(upd.)**
Mohawk Rubber Co. Ltd., *see* The Yokohama Rubber Co., Ltd.
Mohegan Tribal Gaming Authority, 37 254–57
Mojave Foods Corporation, *see* McCormick & Company, Inc.
Mojo MDA Group Ltd., **11** 50–51; **43** 412
Moksel *see* A. Moskel AG.
Mokta *see* Compagnie de Mokta.
MOL *see* Mitsui O.S.K. Lines, Ltd.
MOL Rt, 70 192–95
Molabe S.A. Espagne *see* Leroux S.A.S.
Moldflow Corporation, 73 227–30
Molerway Freight Lines, Inc., **53** 250
Molex Incorporated, 11 317–19; **14** 27; **54** 236–41 **(upd.)**
Molfino Hermanos SA, **59** 365
Moliflor Loisirs, 80 252–55
Molinera de México S.A. de C.V., **31** 236
Molinos Nacionales C.A., *see* International Multifoods Corp.
Molinos Río de la Plata S.A., 61 219–21
Molins plc, 51 249–51
Mölnlycke AB, **36** 26
The Molson Companies Limited, I 273–75; **26** 303–07 **(upd.)**
Molson Coors Brewing Company, 77 288–300 **(upd.)**
Momentum Worldwide, **73** 279
Momentus Group Ltd., **51** 99
Mon-Dak Chemical Inc., *see* Hawkins Chemical, Inc.
Mona Meyer McGrath & Gavin, **47** 97
MONACA *see* Molinos Nacionales C.A.
Monaco Coach Corporation, 31 336–38
Monadnock Paper Mills, Inc., 21 381–84

Monarch Air Lines, *see* Frontier Airlines Holdings Inc.
Monarch Casino & Resort, Inc., 65 239–41
The Monarch Cement Company, 72 231–33
Monarch Development Corporation, **38** 451–52
Monarch Foods, **26** 503
Mondadori *see* Arnoldo Monadori Editore S.p.A.
Mondi Foods BV, **41** 12
Moneris Solutions Corp., **46** 55
Monet Jewelry, *see* Crystal Brands, In.
Money Access Service Corp., **11** 467
Money Management Associates, Inc., **53** 136
MoneyGram International, Inc., 94 315–18
Monfort, Inc., 13 350–52
Monitor Dynamics Inc., **24** 510
Monitor Group Inc., **33** 257
Monk-Austin Inc., **12** 110
Monnaie de Paris, 62 246–48
Monneret Industrie, **56** 335
Monnoyeur Group *see* Groupe Monnoyeur.
Monogram Aerospace Fasteners, Inc., **11** 536
Monongahela Power, **38** 40
Monoprix S.A., 86 282–85
Monro Muffler Brake, Inc., 24 337–40
Monrovia Nursery Company, 70 196–98
Monsanto Company, 1 365–67; **9** 355–57 **(upd.); 29** 327–31 **(upd.); 77** 301–07 **(upd.)**
Monsoon plc, 39 287–89
Monster Cable Products, Inc., 69 256–58
Monster Worldwide Inc., 74 194–97 **(upd.)**
Montabert S.A., **15** 226
Montana Alimentaria S.p.A., **57** 82
Montana Coffee Traders, Inc., 60 208–10
Montana-Dakota Utilities Co., *see* MDU Resources Group, Inc.
Montana Group, **54** 229
Montana Mills Bread Co., Inc., **61** 153
The Montana Power Company, 11 320–22; **44** 288–92 **(upd.)**
Montana Refining Company, *see* Holly Corp.
MontBell America, Inc., **29** 279
Montblanc International GmbH, 82 240–44
Monte Paschi Vita, **65** 71–72
Montedison S.p.A., I 368–69; **24** 341–44 **(upd.)**
Montefina, **IV** 499; **26** 367
Monterey Homes Corporation *see* Meritage Corp.
Monterey Mfg. Co., **12** 439
Monterey Pasta Company, 58 240–43
Monterey's Acquisition Corp., **41** 270
Monterrey, Compania de Seguros sobre la Vida *see* Seguros Monterrey.

Monterrey Group, **19** 10–11, 189
Montgomery Elevator Company *see* KONE Corporation.
Montgomery Ward & Co., Incorporated, V 145–48; **20** 374–79 **(upd.)**
Montinex, **24** 270
Montreal Engineering Company, **6** 585
Montres Rolex S.A., 13 353–55; **34** 292–95 **(upd.)**
Montrose Capital, **36** 358
Montupet S.A., 63 302–04
Moody's Corporation, 65 242–44
Moody's Investors Service,
Moog Inc., 13 356–58
Moog Music, Inc., 75 261–64
Mooney Aerospace Group Ltd., 52 252–55
Mooney Chemicals, Inc. *see* OM Group, Inc.
Moonlight Mushrooms, Inc. *see* Sylvan, Inc.
Moonstone Mountaineering, Inc., **29** 181
Moore Corporation Limited, IV 644–46 *see also* R.R. Donnelley & Sons Co.
The Moore Group Ltd., **20** 363
Moore-Handley, Inc., 39 290–92
Moore Medical Corp., 17 331–33
Moquin Breuil *see* Smoby International SA.
Moran Towing Corporation, Inc., 15 301–03
Morana, Inc., *see* International Flavors & Fragrances Inc.
More Group plc *see* JCDecaux S.A
Moretti-Harrah Marble Co. *see* English China Clays Ltd.
Morgan & Banks Limited, **30** 460
The Morgan Crucible Company plc, 82 245–50
Morgan Grampian Group, **IV** 687
Morgan Grenfell Group PLC, II 427–29 *see also* Deutsche Bank AG.
The Morgan Group, Inc., 46 300–02
Morgan Guaranty Trust Company *see* JPMorgan Chase & Co.
Morgan, Lewis & Bockius LLP, 29 332–34
Morgan, Lewis, Githens & Ahn, Inc., **6** 410
Morgan Schiff & Co., **29** 205
Morgan Stanley Dean Witter & Company, II 430–32; **16** 374–78 **(upd.); 33** 311–14 **(upd.)**
Morgans Hotel Group Company, 80 256–59
Morguard Corporation, 85 287–90
Moria Informatique, **6** 229
Morinaga & Co. Ltd., 61 222–25
Morinda Holdings, Inc., 82 251–54
Morino Associates, *see* Legent Corp.
Mormac Marine Group, **15** 302
Morning Star Technologies Inc., *see* Ascend Communications, Inc.
Morning Sun, Inc., **23** 66
Morningstar Inc., 68 259–62
Morningstar Storage Centers LLC, **52** 311

Morris Communications Corporation,
36 339–42

Morris Travel Services L.L.C., 26
308–11

Morrison & Co. Ltd., 52 221

Morrison & Foerster LLP, 78 220–23

Morrison Homes, Inc., 51 138

Morrison Knudsen Corporation, 7
355–58; 28 286–90 **(upd.)** *see also*
The Washington Companies.

Morrison Restaurants Inc., 11 323–25

Morrow Equipment Co. L.L.C., 87
325–327

Morse Industrial, *see* Borg-Warner
Automotive, Inc.

Morse Shoe Inc., 13 359–61

Morse's Ltd., **70** 161

Mortgage Guaranty Insurance Corp. *see*
MGIC Investment Corp.

MortgageRamp Inc. *see* OfficeTiger, LLC.

Morton Foods, Inc., *see* Kerry Group plc.

Morton International, Inc., 9 358–59
(upd.); 80 260–64 (upd.)

Morton Thiokol Inc., I 370–72 *see also*
Thiokol Corp.

Morton's Restaurant Group, Inc., 30
329–31; 88 262–66 **(upd.)**

Mos Magnetics, **18** 140

The Mosaic Company, 91 330–33

Mosby-Year Book, Inc., *see* Times Mirror
Co.

Moscow Bank for Reconstruction &
Development, **73** 303–04

Mosinee Paper Corporation, 15 304–06
see also Wausau-Mosinee Paper Corp.

Moss Bros Group plc, 51 252–54

Moss-Rouse Company, **15** 412

Mossgas, **IV** 93

Mossimo, Inc., 27 328–30

Mostek Corp., **20** 175; **29** 323

Mostjet Ltd. *see* British World Airlines
Ltd.

Móstoles Industrial S.A., **26** 129

Mostra Importaciones S.A., **34** 38, 40

Motel 6, 13 362–64; 56 248–51 (upd.)
see also Accor SA

Mothercare plc, 17 334–36; 78 224–27
(upd.)

Mothers Against Drunk Driving
(MADD), 51 255–58

Mothers Work, Inc., 18 350–52

Motion Factory, Inc., **38** 72

Motion Picture Association of America,
37 353–54

Motiva Enterprises LLC, **41** 359, 395

MotivePower *see* Wabtec Corp.

The Motley Fool, Inc., 40 329–31

Moto Photo, Inc., 45 282–84

Moto S.p.A., **57** 84

Motor Cargo Industries, Inc., 35
296–99

Motor Club of America Insurance
Company, **44** 354

Motor Coaches Industries International
Inc., **36** 132

Motor Wheel Corporation, *see* Hayes
Lemmerz International, Inc.

Motorcar Parts & Accessories, Inc., 47
253–55

Motoren-und-Turbinen-Union, **I** 151; **15**
142; **34** 128, 131, 133

Motorola, Inc., II 60–62; 11 326–29
(upd.); 34 296–302 (upd.); 93
313–23 **(upd.)**

Motorsports International Corporation, **74**
157

Motospecs *see* Repco Corporation Ltd.

Motown Records Company L.P., 26
312–14

Mott's Inc., 57 250–53

Moulinex S.A., 22 362–65 *see also*
Groupe SEB.

Mound Metalcraft *see* Tonka Corp.

Mount *see also* Mt.

Mount Isa Mines, **IV** 61

Mount Vernon Group, *see* Albany
International Corp.

Mount Washington Hotel *see* MWH
Preservation Limited Partnership.

Mountain Air Cargo, Inc. *see* Air T, Inc.

Mountain Fuel Supply Company *see*
Questar Corp.

Mountain High Casino *see* Ameristar
Casinos, Inc.

Mountain Safety Research, *see* Recreational
Equipment, Inc.

Mountain States Mortgage Centers, Inc.,
29 335–37

Mountain States Power Company *see*
PacifiCorp.

Mountain Valley Indemnity Co., **44** 356

Mountain West Bank, **35** 197

Mouvement des Caisses Desjardins, 48
288–91

Movado Group, Inc., 28 291–94

Mövenpick Holdings, **63** 328

Movie Gallery, Inc., 31 339–41

Movie Star Inc., 17 337–39

Movies To Go, Inc., *see* Blockbuster Inc.

Movil@ccess, S.A. de C.V., **39** 25, 194

Moving Co. Ltd. *see* Marui Co., Ltd.

The Moving Picture Company, **15** 83; **50**
124, 126

The Mowry Co., **23** 102

Moy Park Ltd., 78 228–31

MP3.com, **43** 109

MPB Corporation, *see* The Timken Co.

MPI *see* Michael Page International plc.

MPRG *see* Matt Prentice Restaurant
Group.

MPS Group, Inc., 49 264–67

MPW Industrial Services Group, Inc.,
53 231–33

Mr. Bricolage S.A., 37 258–60

Mr. Coffee, Inc., 15 307–09

Mr. Donut, **21** 323

Mr. Gasket Inc., 15 310–12

Mr. Gatti's, LP, 87 321–324

Mr. Payroll Corporation, **20** 113; **61**
52–54

MRD Gaming, **51** 206–07

M-real Oyj, 56 252–55 (upd.)

MRJ Technology Solutions, **54** 396

MRN Radio Network, **19** 223

Mrs. Baird's Bakeries, 29 338–41

Mrs. Fields' Original Cookies, Inc., 27
331–35

Mrs. Giles Country Kitchens, **63** 69, 71

Mrs. Grossman's Paper Company Inc.,
84 277–280

Mrs. Paul's Kitchens *see* Campbell Soup
Co.

Mrs. Smith's Frozen Foods *see* Kellogg
Company

Mrs. Winner's Chicken & Biscuits, **58**
324

MS&L *see* Manning Selvage & Lee.

MS-Relais GmbH *see* Matsushita Electric
Works, Ltd.

MSAS Cargo International *see* Excel plc.

MSC *see* Material Sciences Corp.

MSC Industrial Direct Co., Inc., 71
234–36

MSE Corporation, **33** 44

MSI Data Corp., **15** 482

M6 *see* Métropole Télévision S.A..

MSK Corporation *see* Suntech Power
Holdings Company Ltd.

MSL Industries, *see* Alleghany Corp.

MSNBC, **28** 301

MSP, Inc., **57** 231

MSR *see* Mountain Safety Research.

MSU *see* Middle South Utilities.

Mt. *see also* Mount.

Mt. Beacon Insurance Co., **26** 486

Mt. Goldsworthy Mining Associates, **IV**
47

Mt. Olive Pickle Company, Inc., 44
293–95

MTA *see* Metropolitan Transportation
Authority.

MTC *see* Management and Training Corp.

MTel *see* Mobile Telecommunications
Technologies Corp.

MTG *see* Modern Times Group AB.

MTM Entertainment Inc., *see*
International Family Entertainment Inc.

MTR Foods Ltd., 55 271–73

MTR Gaming Group, Inc., 75 265–67

MTS *see* Mobile TeleSystems.

MTS Inc., 37 261–64

MTV, **31** 239

MTV Asia, **23** 390

MTVi Group, **37** 194

Muehlens KG, **48** 422

Mueller Co. *see* Tyco International Ltd.

Mueller Furniture Company, *see* Haworth
Inc.

Mueller Industries, Inc., 7 359–61; 52
256–60 **(upd.)**

Muench Woodworking, Inc., **68** 133

Muffler Corporation of America, **56** 230

Muir Glen *see* Small Planet Foods, Inc.

Mulberry Group PLC, 71 237–39

Mule-Hide Products Co., **22** 15

Mullen Advertising Inc., 51 259–61

Multex Systems, **21** 70

Multi-Color Corporation, 53 234–36

Multicanal S.A., **67** 200–01

Multicare Companies *see* NeighborCare,
Inc.

Multicom Publishing Inc., **11** 294

Multiflex, Inc., **63** 318

National Pig Development Co., **46** 84
National Power Corporation, **56** 214–15
National Power PLC, 12 349–51 *see also* International Power PLC.
National Presto Industries, Inc., 16 382–85; **43** 286–90 (upd.)
National Propane Corporation, *see* Triarc Companies, Inc.
National Public Radio, 19 280–82; **47** 259–62 (upd.)
National Publishing Company, **41** 110
National R.V. Holdings, Inc., 32 348–51
National Railroad Passenger Corporation (Amtrak), 22 375–78; **66** 238–42 (upd.)
National Ready Mixed, **70** 343
National Realty Trust *see* NRT Inc.
National Record Mart, Inc., 29 348–50
National Register Publishing Co., **23** 442
National Reinsurance Corporation *see* General Re Corp.
National Research Corporation, 87 332–335
National Restaurants Management, Inc., **38** 385–87
National Revenue Corporation, **22** 181
National Rifle Association of America, 37 265–68
National Sanitary Supply Co., 16 386–87
National Sea Products Ltd., 14 339–41
National Security Containers LLC, **58** 238
National Semiconductor Corporation, II 63–65; **6** 261–63; **26** 327–30 (upd.); **69** 267–71 (upd.)
National Service Industries, Inc., 11 336–38; **54** 251–55 (upd.)
National-Southwire Aluminum Company, **11** 38
National Standard Co., 13 369–71
National Starch and Chemical Company, 49 268–70
National Steel Corporation, 12 352–54 *see also* FoxMeyer Health Corp.
National System Company, **11** 469
National Tea Co., *see* George Weston Ltd.
National TechTeam, Inc., 41 280–83
National Telecommunications of Austin, *see* LDDS-Metro Communications, Inc.
National Telephone and Telegraph Corporation *see* British Columbia Telephone Co.
National Thoroughbred Racing Association, 58 244–47
National Transcommunications Ltd. *see* NTL Inc.
National Weather Service, 91 345–49
National Westminster Bank PLC, II 333–35
National Wine & Spirits, Inc., 49 271–74
Nationale-Nederlanden N.V., III 308–11
Nationale Portefeuille Maatschappij (NPM) *see* Compagnie Nationale à Portefeuille.

NationsBank Corporation, 10 425–27 *see also* Bank of America Corporation
NationsRent, **28** 388
Nationwide Cellular Service, Inc., **27** 305
Nationwide Credit, Inc. *see* First Financial Management Corp.
Nationwide Logistics Corp., *see* TNT Freightways Corp.
Nationwide Mutual Insurance Co., **26** 488
NATIOVIE, **II** 234
NATM Buying Corporation, **10** 9, 468
Natref *see* National Petroleum Refiners of South Africa.
Natrol, Inc., 49 275–78
NatSteel Electronics Ltd., **48** 369
NatTeknik, **26** 333
Natura Cosméticos S.A., 75 268–71
Natural Alternatives International, Inc., 49 279–82
Natural Gas Clearinghouse *see* NGC Corp.
Natural Gas Pipeline Company, **6** 530, 543
Natural Ovens Bakery, Inc., 72 234–36
Natural Selection Foods, 54 256–58
Natural Wonders Inc., 14 342–44
NaturaLife International, **26** 470
Naturalizer *see* Brown Shoe Company, Inc.
Naturally Fresh, Inc., 88 272–75
The Nature Company, *see* Discovery Communications, Inc.
The Nature Conservancy, 28 305–07
Nature's Path Foods, Inc., 87 336–340
Nature's Sunshine Products, Inc., 15 317–19
Nature's Way Products Inc., **26** 315
Naturin GmbH *see* Viscofan S.A.
Naturipe Berry Growers, **62** 154
Natuzzi Group *see* Industrie Natuzzi S.p.A.
NatWest Bancorp, **38** 393
NatWest Bank *see* National Westminster Bank PLC.
Naumes, Inc., 81 257–60
Nautica Enterprises, Inc., 18 357–60; **44** 302–06 (upd.)
Nautilus International, Inc., **30** 161
Navaho Freight Line, **16** 41
Navajo LTL, Inc., **57** 277
Navajo Refining Company, *see* Holly Corp.
Navajo Shippers, Inc., **42** 364
Navan Resources, **38** 231
Navarre Corporation, 24 348–51
Navigant International, Inc., 47 263–66; **93** 324–27 (upd.)
The Navigators Group, Inc., 92 261–64
Navire Cargo Gear, **27** 269
Navisant, Inc., **49** 424
Navistar International Corporation, I 180–82; **10** 428–30 (upd.) *see also* International Harvester Co.
NAVTEQ Corporation, 69 272–75
Navy Exchange Service Command, 31 342–45
Navy Federal Credit Union, 33 315–17

Naylor, Hutchinson, Vickers & Company *see* Vickers PLC.
NBC *see* National Broadcasting Company, Inc.
NBC Bankshares, Inc., **21** 524
NBC/Computer Services Corporation, **15** 163
NBD Bancorp, Inc., 11 339–41 *see also* Bank One Corp.
NBGS International, Inc., 73 231–33
NBSC Corporation *see* National Bank of South Carolina.
NBTY, Inc., 31 346–48
NCB *see* National City Bank of New York.
NCC Industries, Inc., **59** 267
NCC L.P., **15** 139
NCH Corporation, 8 385–87
nChip, **38** 187–88
NCI Building Systems, Inc., 88 276–79
NCL Corporation, 79 274–77
NCL Holdings *see* Genting Bhd.
NCNB Corporation, II 336–37 *see also* Bank of America Corp.
NCO Group, Inc., 42 258–60
NCR Corporation, III 150–53; **6** 264–68 (upd.); **30** 336–41 (upd.); **90** 303–12 (upd.)
NCS *see* Norstan, Inc.
NCS Healthcare Inc., **67** 262
nCube Corp., **14** 15; **22** 293
NDB *see* National Discount Brokers Group, Inc.
NDL *see* Norddeutscher Lloyd.
NE Chemcat Corporation, **72** 118
NEA *see* Newspaper Enterprise Association.
Neatherlin Homes Inc., **22** 547
Nebraska Book Company, Inc., 65 257–59
Nebraska Furniture Mart, Inc., 94 323–26
Nebraska Light & Power Company, **6** 580
Nebraska Public Power District, 29 351–54
NEBS *see* New England Business Services, Inc.
NEC Corporation, II 66–68; **21** 388–91 (upd.); **57** 261–67 (upd.)
Neckermann Versand AG *see* Karstadt AG.
Nedcor, **61** 270–71
Nederland Line *see* Stoomvaart Maatschappij Nederland.
Nederlands Talen Institut, *see* Koninklijke Vendex KBB N.V. (Royal Vendex KBB N.V.)
Nederlandsche Electriciteits Maatschappij *see* N.E.M.
Nederlandsche Handel Maatschappij, **26** 242
Nederlandsche Heidenmaatschappij *see* Arcadis NV.
N.V. Nederlandse Gasunie, V 658–61
Nedlloyd Group *see* Koninklijke Nedlloyd N.V.
NedMark Transportation Services *see* Polar Air Cargo Inc.

Needham Harper Worldwide *see* Omnicom Group Inc.
Needleworks, Inc., **23** 66
Neenah Foundry Company, 68 263–66
Neenah Printing, *see* Menasha Corp.
NEES *see* New England Electric System.
Neff Corp., 32 352–53
Neff GmbH, **67** 81
NEG Micon A/S, **73** 375
Negromex, **23** 171–72
NEI *see* Northern Engineering Industries PLC.
Neico International, Inc., **67** 226
NeighborCare, Inc., 67 259–63 (upd.)
Neilson/Cadbury, *see* George Weston Ltd.
The Neiman Marcus Group, Inc., 12 355–57; **49** 283–87 (upd.)
Nektar Therapeutics, 91 350–53
Nelson Entertainment Group, **47** 272
Nelson Publications, **22** 442
Nelsons *see* A. Nelson & Co. Ltd.
NEMF *see* New England Motor Freight, Inc.
Neo Products Co., **37** 401
Neogen Corporation, 94 327–30
Neopost S.A., 53 237–40
Neos, **21** 438
Nepera, Inc., **16** 69
Neptun Maritime Oyj, **29** 431
Neptune Orient Lines Limited, 47 267–70
NER Auction Group, **23** 148
NERCO, Inc., 7 376–79 *see also* Rio Tinto PLC.
NES *see* National Equipment Services, Inc.
Nesco Inc., **28** 6, 8
Nespak SpA, **40** 214–15
Neste Oil Corporation, IV 469–71; **85** 295–302 (upd.)
Nestlé S.A., II 545–49; **7** 380–84 (upd.); **28** 308–13 (upd.); **71** 240–46 (upd.)
Nestlé Waters, 73 234–37
Net Investment S.A., **63** 180
NetApp *see* Network Appliance, Inc.
NetCom Systems AB, 26 331–33
NetCreations, **47** 345, 347
NetEffect Alliance, **58** 194
Netezza Corporation, 69 276–78
Netflix, Inc., 58 248–51
NETGEAR, Inc., 81 261–64
Netherlands Trading Co *see* Nederlandse Handel Maatschappij.
NetHold B.V., **31** 330
NetIQ Corporation, 79 278–81
NetMarket Company, **16** 146
NetPlane Systems, **36** 124
Netscape Communications Corporation, 15 320–22; **35** 304–07 (upd.)
NetStar Communications Inc., **24** 49; **35** 69
Nettingsdorfer, **19** 227
Nettle Creek Corporation, *see* Pillowtex Corp.
Net2Phone Inc., **34** 224
NetWest Securities, **25** 450
Network Appliance, Inc., 58 252–54
Network Associates, Inc., 25 347–49

Network Communications Associates, Inc., **11** 409
Network Equipment Technologies Inc., 92 265–68
Network Solutions, Inc., **47** 430
Network Ten, **35** 68–69
NetZero Inc. *see* United Online, Inc.
Netzip Inc., **53** 282
Neuberger Berman Inc., 57 268–71
Neuer Markt, **59** 153
Neuro Navigational Corporation, **21** 47
NeuStar, Inc., 81 265–68
Neutrogena Corporation, 17 340–44
Nevada Bell Telephone Company, 14 345–47 *see also* AT&T Corp.
Nevada Community Bank, **11** 119
Nevada Power Company, 11 342–44
Nevada Savings and Loan Association, **19** 412
Nevada State Bank, **53** 378
Nevamar Company, 82 255–58
Nevex Software Technologies, **42** 24, 26
New Access Communications, **43** 252
New Asahi Co., *see* Asahi Breweries, Ltd.
New Balance Athletic Shoe, Inc., 25 350–52; **68** 267–70 (upd.)
New Bauhinia Limited, **53** 333
New Belgium Brewing Company, Inc., 68 271–74
New Brunswick Scientific Co., Inc., 45 285–87
New Century Energies, **73** 384
New Century Equity Holdings Corporation, **72** 39
New Century Network, **13** 180; **19** 204, 285
New Clicks Holdings Ltd., 86 295–98
New CORT Holdings Corporation *see* CORT Business Services Corp.
New Daido Steel Co., Ltd., **IV** 62–63
New Dana Perfumes Company, 37 269–71
New Dimension Software, Inc., **55** 67
New England Audio Company, Inc. *see* Tweeter Home Entertainment Group, Inc.
New England Business Service, Inc., 18 361–64; **78** 237–42 (upd.)
New England Confectionery Co., 15 323–25
New England CRInc, *see* Wellman Inc.
New England Electric System, V 662–64 *see also* National Grid USA.
New England Motor Freight, Inc., **53** 250
New England Mutual Life Insurance Co., III 312–14 *see also* Metropolitan Life Insurance Co.
New England Paper Tube Co., **54** 58
New England Power Association *see* National Grid USA.
New Flyer Industries Inc., 78 243–46
New Galveston Company, Inc., **25** 116
New Hampton Goldfields Ltd., **63** 182, 184
New Hampton, Inc., *see* Spiegel, Inc.
New Haven District Telephone Company *see* Southern New England Telecommunications Corp.

New Haven Electric Co., **21** 512
New Holland N.V., 22 379–81 *see also* CNH Global N.V.
New Hotel Showboat, Inc. *see* Showboat, Inc.
New Impriver NV *see* Punch International N.V.
New Jersey Devils, 84 281–285
New Jersey Educational Music Company *see* National Educational Music Co. Ltd.
New Jersey Resources Corporation, 54 259–61
New Jersey Shale, **14** 250
New Jersey Tobacco Co., **15** 138
New Laoshan Brewery, **49** 418
New Line Cinema, Inc., 47 271–74
New Look Group plc, 35 308–10
New Market Development Company *see* Cousins Properties Inc.
New Materials Ltd., **48** 344
New Orleans Saints LP, 58 255–57
The New Piper Aircraft, Inc., 44 307–10
New Plan Realty Trust, 11 345–47
New Seasons Market, 75 272–74
New South Wales Health System, **16** 94
New Street Capital Inc., 8 388–90 (upd.) *see also* Drexel Burnham Lambert Inc.
New Times, Inc., 45 288–90
New Toyo Group, **19** 227
New Trading Company *see* SBC Warburg.
New Valley Corporation, 17 345–47
New Vanden Borre, *see* Kingfisher plc.
New Ventures Realty Corporation, **58** 272
New World Coffee-Manhattan Bagel, Inc., **32** 15
New World Communications Group, **22** 442; **28** 248
New World Development Company Limited, IV 717–19; **38** 318–22 (upd.)
New World Pasta Company, 53 241–44
New World Restaurant Group, Inc., 44 311–14
New York Capital Bank, **41** 312
New York Central Railroad Company, **10** 43–44, 71–73
New York City Health and Hospitals Corporation, 60 214–17
New York City Off-Track Betting Corporation, 51 267–70
New York Community Bancorp, Inc., 78 247–50
New York Daily News, 32 357–60
New York Electric Corporation *see* New York State Electric and Gas.
New York Envelope Co., **32** 346
New York Eye and Ear Infirmary *see* Continuum Health Partners, Inc.
New York Gas Light Company *see* Consolidated Edison Company of New York.
New York Health Care, Inc., 72 237–39
New York Life Insurance Company, III 315–17; **45** 291–95 (upd.)

Nippon Express Company, Ltd., V 477–80; **64** 286–90 (upd.)

Nippon Foundation Engineering Co. Ltd., **51** 179

Nippon Gakki Co., Ltd *see* Yamaha Corp.

Nippon Global Tanker Co. Ltd., **53** 116

Nippon Gyomo Sengu Co. Ltd., **IV** 555

Nippon Hatsujo Kabushikikaisha *see* NHK Spring Co., Ltd.

Nippon Helicopter & Aeroplane Transport Co., Ltd. *see* All Nippon Airways Company Ltd.

Nippon Hoso Kyokai *see* Japan Broadcasting Corp.

Nippon Idou Tsushin, **7** 119–20

Nippon K.K *see* Nikon Corp.

Nippon Kogaku K.K. *see* Nikon Corp.

Nippon Kogyo Co. Ltd *see* Nippon Mining Co. Ltd.

Nippon Kokan K.K. *see* NKK Corp.

Nippon Life Insurance Company, III 318–20; **60** 218–21 (upd.)

Nippon Light Metal Company, Ltd., IV 153–55

Nippon Meat Packers, Inc., II 550–51; **78** 255–57 (upd.)

Nippon Mining Co., Ltd., IV 475–77

Nippon Mitsubishi Oil Corporation, **49** 216

Nippon Oil Corporation, IV 478–79; **63** 308–13 (upd.)

Nippon Paper Industries Co., Ltd., **57** 101

Nippon Phonogram, **23** 390

Nippon Reizo Co. *see* Nichirei Corp.

Nippon Seiko K.K., III 589–90

Nippon Sekiyu Co *see* Nippon Oil Company, Ltd.

Nippon Sheet Glass Company, Limited, III 714–16

Nippon Shinpan Co., Ltd., II 436–37; **61** 248–50 (upd.)

Nippon Soda Co., Ltd., 85 303–06

Nippon Steel Corporation, IV 156–58; **17** 348–51 (upd.)

Nippon Suisan Kaisha, Limited, II 552–53; **92** 269–72 (upd.)

Nippon Telegraph and Telephone Corporation, V 305–07; **51** 271–75 (upd.)

Nippon Tire Co., Ltd. *see* Bridgestone Corp.

Nippon Unipac Holding, **57** 101

Nippon Yusen Kabushiki Kaisha (NYK), V 481–83; **72** 244–48 (upd.)

Nippondenso Co., Ltd., III 591–94 *see also* DENSO Corp.

NIPSCO Industries, Inc., 6 532–33

NiSource, Inc., **38** 81

Nissan Motor Company Ltd., I 183–84; **11** 350–52 (upd.); **34** 303–07 (upd.); **92** 273–79 (upd.)

Nissay Dowa General Insurance Company Ltd., **60** 220

Nisshin Seifun Group Inc., II 554; **66** 246–48 (upd.)

Nisshin Steel Co., Ltd., IV 159–60

Nissho Iwai K.K., I 509–11

Nissin Food Products Company Ltd., 75 286–88

Nisso *see* Nippon Soda Co., Ltd.

Nissui *see* Nippon Suisan Kaisha.

Nitches, Inc., 53 245–47

Nittsu *see* Nippon Express Co., Ltd.

Niugini Mining Ltd., **23** 42

Nixdorf Computer AG, III 154–55 *see also* Wincor Nixdorf Holding GmbH.

Nixdorf-Krein Industries Inc. *see* Laclede Steel Co.

Nizhny Novgorod Dairy, **48** 438

NKI B.V., **71** 178–79

NKK Corporation, IV 161–63; **28** 322–26 (upd.)

NL Industries, Inc., 10 434–36

NLG *see* National Leisure Group.

NLI Insurance Agency Inc., **60** 220

NLM City-Hopper, *see* Koninklijke Luchtvaart Maatschappij N.V.

NM Acquisition Corp., **27** 346

NMC Laboratories Inc., *see* Alpharma Inc.

NMT *see* Nordic Mobile Telephone.

NNG *see* Northern Natural Gas Co.

Noah's New York Bagels *see* Einstein/Noah Bagel Corp.

Nob Hill Foods, **58** 291

Nobel Drilling Corporation, **26** 243

Nobel Industries AB, 9 380–82 *see also* Akzo Nobel N.V.

Nobel Learning Communities, Inc., 37 276–79; **76** 281–85 (upd.)

Noble Affiliates, Inc., 11 353–55

Noble Broadcast Group, Inc., **23** 293

Noble Roman's Inc., 14 351–53

Nobleza Piccardo SAICF, 64 291–93

Noboa *see also* Exportadora Bananera Noboa, S.A.

Nobody Beats the Wiz *see* Cablevision Electronic Instruments, Inc.

Nocibé SA, 54 265–68

Nocona Belt Company, **31** 435–36

Nocona Boot Co. *see* Justin Industries, Inc.

Noel Group, Inc., *see* Lincoln Snacks Co.

NOF Corporation, 72 249–51

NOK Corporation, **41** 170–72

Nokia Corporation, II 69–71; **17** 352–54 (upd.); **38** 328–31 (upd.); **77** 308–13 (upd.)

Nokian Tyres PLC, **59** 91

NOL Group *see* Neptune Orient Lines Ltd.

Noland Company, 35 311–14

Nolo.com, Inc., 49 288–91

Nolte Mastenfabriek B.V., *see* Valmont Industries, Inc.

Nomura Securities Company, Limited, II 438–41; **9** 383–86 (upd.)

Nomura Toys Ltd., *see* Hasbro, Inc.

Non-Stop Fashions, Inc., *see* The Leslie Fay Companies, Inc.

Noodle Kidoodle, 16 388–91

Noodles & Company, Inc., 55 277–79

Nooter Corporation, 61 251–53

NOP Research Group, **28** 501, 504

Nopri *see* GIB Group.

Norampac Inc., **71** 95

Norand Corporation, **72** 189

Noranda Inc., IV 164–66; **7** 397–99 (upd.); **64** 294–98 (upd.)

Norandex, *see* Fibreboard Corp.

Norbro Corporation *see* Stuart Entertainment Inc.

Norcal Pottery Products, Inc., **58** 60

Norcal Waste Systems, Inc., 60 222–24

Norcon, Inc., *see* VECO International, Inc.

Norcore Plastics, Inc., **33** 361

Nordbanken, **9** 382

Norddeutsche Affinerie AG, 62 249–53

Norddeutscher-Lloyd *see* Hapag-Lloyd AG.

Nordea AB, 40 336–39

Nordic Baltic Holding *see* Nordea AB.

Nordica S.r.l., **15** 396–97; **53** 24

NordicTrack, 22 382–84 *see also* Icon Health & Fitness, Inc.

Nordisk Film A/S, 80 269–73

Nordson Corporation, 11 356–58; **48** 296–99 (upd.)

Nordstrom, Inc., V 156–58; **18** 371–74 (upd.); **67** 277–81 (upd.)

Nordwestdeutsche Kraftwerke AG *see* PreussenElektra AG.

Norelco Consumer Products Co., 26 334–36

Norelec, *see* Eiffage.

Norex Leasing, Inc., **16** 397

Norfolk Shipbuilding & Drydock Corporation, **73** 47

Norfolk Southern Corporation, V 484–86; **29** 358–61 (upd.); **75** 289–93 (upd.)

Norge Co., *see* Fedders Corp.

Noric Corporation, **39** 332

Norinchukin Bank, II 340–41

Norlin Industries, **16** 238–39; **75** 262

Norm Thompson Outfitters, Inc., 47 275–77

Norma AS *see* Autoliv, Inc.

Norman BV, **9** 93; **33** 78

Normandy Mining Ltd., **23** 42

Normark Corporation *see* Rapala-Normark Group, Ltd.

Norment Security Group, Inc., **51** 81

Normond/CMS, *see* Danaher Corp.

Norrell Corporation, 25 356–59

Norris Cylinder Company, *see* TriMas Corp.

Norris Oil Company, **47** 52

Norshield Corp., **51** 81

Norsk Aller A/S, **72** 62

Norsk Helikopter AS *see* Bristow Helicopters Ltd.

Norsk Hydro ASA, 10 437–40; **35** 315–19 (upd.)

Norsk Rengjorings Selskap a.s., **49** 221

Norske Skog do Brasil Ltda., **73** 205

Norske Skogindustrier ASA, 63 314–16

Norstan, Inc., 16 392–94

Nortek, Inc., 34 308–12

Nortel Inversora S.A., **63** 375–77

Nortel Networks Corporation, 36 349–54 (upd.)

Nortex International, **19** 338

Paulaner Brauerei GmbH & Co. KG, 35 330–33

Pauls Plc, *see* Elementis plc.

Pavex Construction Company *see* Granite Rock Co.

Pawnee Industries, Inc., 19 415

Paxson Communications Corporation, 33 322–26

Pay 'N Pak Stores, Inc., 9 399–401

Pay 'n Save Corp., 15 274

Paychex, Inc., 15 347–49; 46 333–36 (upd.)

PayConnect Solutions, 47 39

Payless Cashways, Inc., 11 384–86; 44 330–33 (upd.)

Payless DIY *see* The Boots Company PLC.

PayLess Drug Stores, *see* Thrifty PayLess, Inc.

Payless ShoeSource, Inc., 18 413–15; 69 288–92 (upd.)

PayPal Inc., 58 266–69

PBF Corp. *see* Paris Corp.

PBL *see* Publishing and Broadcasting Ltd.

PBS *see* Public Broadcasting Stations.

The PBSJ Corporation, 82 269–73

PC Connection, Inc., 37 300–04

PC Globe, Inc., *see* Broderbund Software, Inc.

PC Home Publishing, 61 246

PCA *see* Packaging Corporation of America.

PCA-Budafok Paperboard Ltd., 12 377

PCA International, Inc., 62 263–65

PCAS *see* Dynaction S.A.

pcBoat.com, 37 398

PCC *see* Papel e Celulose Catarinense S.A.

PCC Natural Markets, 94 348–51

PCI NewCo Inc., 36 159

PCI Services, Inc. *see* Cardinal Health, Inc.

PCL Construction Group Inc., 50 347–49

PCM Uitgevers NV, 53 270–73

PCO *see* Corning Inc.

PCS *see* Potash Corp. of Saskatchewan Inc.

PCS Health Systems Inc., 12 333; 47 115, 235–36

PCX *see* Pacific Stock Exchange.

PDA Engineering, 25 305

PDA Inc., 19 290

PDI, Inc., 52 272–75

PDL BioPharma, Inc., 90 322–25

PDO *see* Petroleum Development Oman.

PDQ Food Stores Inc., 79 310–13

PDQ Machine, 58 75

PDS Gaming Corporation, 44 334–37

PDV America, Inc., 31 113

PDVSA *see* Petróleos de Venezuela S.A.

Peabody Energy Corporation, 10 447–49; 45 330–33 (upd.)

Peabody Holding Company, Inc., IV 169–72

Peace Arch Entertainment Group Inc., 51 286–88

Peachtree Doors, 10 95

Peak Audio Inc., 48 92

Peak Oilfield Service Company, *see* Nabors Industries, Inc.

The Peak Technologies Group, Inc., 14 377–80

Peapod, Inc., 30 346–48

Pearl Health Services, I 249

Pearl Musical Instrument Company, 78 297–300

Pearle Vision, Inc., 13 390–92

Pearson plc, IV 657–59; 46 337–41 (upd.)

Peasant Restaurants Inc., 30 330

Pease Industries, 39 322, 324

Peat Marwick *see* KPMG Peat Marwick.

Peavey Electronics Corporation, 16 408–10; 94 352–56 (upd.)

Peavey Paper Mills, Inc., 26 362

Pechenganickel MMC, 48 300

Pechiney S.A., IV 173–75; 45 334–37 (upd.)

PECO Energy Company, 11 387–90 *see also* Exelon Corp.

Pecom Nec S.A., 72 279–80

Pediatric Services of America, Inc., 31 356–58

Pediatrix Medical Group, Inc., 61 282–85

Pedigree Petfoods, *see* Kal Kan Foods, Inc.

Peebles Inc., 16 411–13; 43 296–99 (upd.)

Peek & Cloppenburg KG, 46 342–45

Peekskill Chemical Works *see* Binney & Smith Inc.

Peet's Coffee & Tea, Inc., 38 338–40

Peg Perego SpA, 88 300–03

Pegasus Solutions, Inc., 75 315–18

PEI *see* Process Engineering Inc.

Pei Cobb Freed & Partners Architects LLP, 57 280–82

Pei Wei Asian Diner, Inc. *see* P.F. Chang's China Bistro, Inc.

Pelican Homestead and Savings, 11 107

Pelican Products, Inc., 86 331–34

Pelikan Holding AG, 92 296–300

Pella Corporation, 12 384–86; 39 322–25 (upd.); 89 349–53 (upd.)

Pelmorex, Inc., 52 402

Pelto Oil Corporation, 44 362

PEM International Ltd., 28 350

Pemco Aviation Group Inc., 54 283–86

Pemex *see* Petróleos Mexicanos.

Pen Computing Group, 49 10

Penaflor S.A., 66 252–54

Penauille Polyservices SA, 49 318–21

Penda Corp., 19 415

Pendaflex *see* Esselte.

Pendaries Petroleum Ltd. *see* Ultra Petroleum Corp.

Pendle Travel Services Ltd. *see* Airtours Plc.

Pendleton Grain Growers Inc., 64 305–08

Pendleton Woolen Mills, Inc., 42 275–78

Penford Corporation, 55 296–99

Pengrowth Energy Trust, 95 323–26

The Penguin Group, 46 337

Penguin Publishing Co. Ltd., IV 659

Penhaligon's Ltd, *see* Intimate Brands, Inc.

Peninsula Stores, Ltd. *see* Lucky Stores, Inc.

The Peninsular and Oriental Steam Navigation Company, V 490–93; 38 341–46 (upd.)

Peninsular and Oriental Steam Navigation Company (Bovis Division), I 588–89 *see also* DP World.

Peninsular Power, 6 602

Penn Central Corp., 10 71, 73, 547; 70 34

Penn Champ Co., *see* BISSELL, Inc.

Penn Corp., *see* Western Publishing Group, Inc.

Penn Engineering & Manufacturing Corp., 28 349–51

Penn National Gaming, Inc., 33 327–29

Penn Traffic Company, 13 393–95

Penn Virginia Corporation, 85 324–27

Penn-Western Gas and Electric, 6 524

PennEnergy, 55 302

Penney's *see* J.C. Penney Company, Inc.

Pennington Seed, Inc. of Delaware, 58 60

Pennon Group Plc, 45 338–41

Pennsy Supply, Inc., 64 98

Pennsylvania Blue Shield, III 325–27 *see also* Highmark Inc.

Pennsylvania Dutch Candies Company *see* Warrell Corp.

Pennsylvania Electric Company, *see* GPU, Inc.

Pennsylvania Farm Bureau Cooperative Association, 7 17–18

Pennsylvania Gas and Water Company, 38 51

Pennsylvania General Insurance Company, 48 431

Pennsylvania House, Inc., 12 301

Pennsylvania International Raceway *see* Penske Corp.

Pennsylvania Power & Light Company, V 693–94

Pennsylvania Railroad, 10 71–73; 26 295

Pennsylvania Steel Foundry and Machine Co., 39 32

Pennwalt Corporation, I 382–84

PennWell Corporation, 55 300–03

Penny Curtiss Baking Co., Inc., *see* Penn Traffic Co.

Pennzoil-Quaker State Company, IV 488–90; 20 418–22 (upd.); 50 350–55 (upd.)

Penobscot Shoe Company, 70 221

Penske Corporation, V 494–95; 19 292–94 (upd.); 84 305–309 (upd.)

Pentair, Inc., 7 419–21; 26 361–64 (upd.); 81 281–87 (upd.)

Pental Insurance Company, Ltd., 11 523

Pentastar Transportation Group, Inc. *see* Dollar Thrifty Automotive Group, Inc.

Pentax Corporation, 78 301–05

Pentech International, Inc., 29 372–74

Pentes Play, Inc., *see* PlayCore, Inc.

Pentland Group plc, 20 423–25

Penton Media, Inc., 27 360–62

Pentzer Corporation *see* Avista Corp.

Precision Software Corp., **14** 319

Precision Spring of Canada, Ltd., **55** 305

Precision Stainless Inc., **65** 289

Precision Standard Inc. *see* Pemco Aviation Group Inc.

Precision Tool, Die & Machine Company Inc., **51** 116–17

Precisionaire *see* Flanders Corp.

Precoat Metals, **54** 331

Predica, **II** 266

Prefco Corporation, **57** 56–57

Preferred Medical Products *see* Ballard Medical Products.

Preferred Products, Inc., *see* Supervalu Inc.

PREINCO Holdings, Inc., *see* Transatlantic Holdings, Inc.

PREL&P *see* Portland Railway Electric Light & Power Co.

Premark International, Inc., III 610–12 *see also* Illinois Tool Works Inc.

Premcor Inc., 37 309–11

Premier Cement Ltd., **64** 98

Premier Industrial Corporation, 9 419–21

Premier Insurance Co., **26** 487

Premier Medical Services, **31** 357

Premier Milk Pte Ltd., **54** 117

Premier One Products, Inc., **37** 285

Premier Parks, Inc., 27 382–84 *see also* Six Flags, Inc.

Premier Radio Networks, Inc., **23** 292, 294

Premier Rehabilitation Centers, **29** 400

Premier Sport Group Inc., **23** 66

Premiere Labels Inc., **53** 236

Premium Standard Farms, Inc., 30 353–55

PremiumWear, Inc., 30 356–59

Premix-Marbletite Manufacturing Co. Inc. *see* Imperial Industries, Inc.

Prentice Hall Inc., **I** 453; **IV** 672; **19** 405; **23** 503

Prescott Investors, **14** 303; **50** 311

Preserver Group, Inc., 44 354–56

President Baking Co., **36** 313

President Casinos, Inc., 22 438–40

President Riverboat Casino-Mississippi Inc., **21** 300

Presidents Island Steel & Wire Company *see* Laclede Steel Co.

Presley Cos., **59** 422

Presses de la Cité *see* Groupe de la Cité.

Pressman Toy Corporation, 56 280–82

Presstar Printing, **25** 183

Presstek, Inc., 33 345–48

Pressware International, **12** 377

Prestage Farms, **46** 83

Prestel Verlag, **66** 123

Prestige Fragrance & Cosmetics, Inc., **22** 158

The Prestige Group plc., *see* Gallaher Group Plc.

Prestige International, **33** 284

Prestige Leather Creations, **31** 435–36

Prestige Properties, **23** 388

Presto Products, Inc., *see* Reynolds and Reynolds Co.; Reynolds Metals Co.

Preston Corporation, 6 421–23

Prestone Products Corp., **22** 32; **26** 349

Prestwick Mortgage Group, **25** 187

Pret A Manger, 63 280, 284–85

Pretty Good Privacy, Inc., **25** 349

Pretty Neat Corp., *see* Goody Products, Inc.

Pretty Paper Inc., *see* Thomas Nelson Inc.

Pretzel Time *see* Mrs. Fields' Original Cookies, Inc.

Pretzelmaker *see* Mrs. Fields' Original Cookies, Inc.

Pretzels Inc., *see* J & J Snack Foods Corp.

Preussag AG, 17 378–82; 42 279–83 (upd.)

PreussenElektra Aktiengesellschaft, V 698–700 *see also* E.On AG.

Preval, **19** 49–50

Previews, Inc., **21** 96

PreVision Marketing LLC *see* Valassis Communications Inc.

PRG-Schultz International, Inc., 73 264–67

Priba, **26** 158, 160

Pribina, **25** 85

Price & Pierce International Inc. *see* Gould Paper Corporation

Price Chopper Supermarkets *see* The Golub Corp.

Price Communications Corporation, 42 284–86

Price Company Ltd *see* Abitibi-Consolidated, Inc.

The Price Company, V 162–64 *see also* Costco Wholesale Corp.

Price Enterprises, Inc., **14** 395

Price, McCormick & Co., **26** 451

Price Pfister, Inc., 70 236–39

Price Rite, **25** 67

Price Waterhouse LLP, 9 422–24 *see also* PricewaterhouseCoopers

PriceCostco, Inc., 14 393–95 *see also* Costco Wholesale Corp.

Pricel *see* Chargeurs.

Priceline.com Incorporated, 57 296–99

Priceline.com Inc., **58** 118–19

Pricesearch Ltd Co, **48** 224

PriceSmart, Inc., 71 287–90

PricewaterhouseCoopers, 29 389–94 (upd.)

PRIDE Enterprises *see* Prison Rehabilitative Industries and Diversified Enterprises, Inc.

Pride International, Inc., 78 319–23

Pride Petroleum Services *see* DeKalb Genetics Corp.

Prima Gold International Company Limited *see* Pranda Jewlry plc.

Prima S.A., **67** 201

Primagas GmbH, **55** 347

Primark Corp., 13 416–18 *see also* Thomson Corp.

Primary Coatings, Inc., **51** 190

Prime Capital Services, Inc. *see* Gilman & Ciocia, Inc.

Prime Care International, Inc., **36** 367

Prime Computer, Inc. *see* Computervision Corp.

Prime Hospitality Corporation, 52 280–83

Prime Motor Inns Inc., **IV** 718; **11** 177

Prime Service, Inc., **28** 40

Prime Telecommunications Corporation, *see* LDDS-Metro Communications, Inc.

Primedex Health Systems, Inc., 25 382–85

Primedia Inc., 22 441–43

Primera Group, **71** 151, 153

Primergy Corp., **39** 261

Primerica Corporation, I 612–14

Primerica Financial Services, Inc., **30** 124; **59** 121, 125

PriMerit Bank, **19** 412

PrimeSource, **26** 542

Primestar, **38** 176

PRIMESTAR Partners L.P., **28** 241

PrimeWood, Inc., **61** 398

Primex Fibre Ltd., *see* Sanyo-Kokusaku Pulp Co., Ltd.

Prince Co., *see* Borden, Inc.

Prince Gardner Company, **23** 21

Prince Golf International, Ltd., **23** 450

Prince Holding Corporation, **26** 231; **59** 252

Prince Sports Group, Inc., 15 368–70

Prince William Bank, **II** 337

Princes Ltd., 76 312–14

Princess Cruise Lines, 22 444–46

Princess Hotel Group, **21** 353

Princess Hotels International Inc., **45** 82

Princess Metropole, **21** 354

Princeton Gas Service Company, **6** 529

The Princeton Review, Inc., 42 287–90

Princeton Telecommunications Corporation, **26** 38

Principal Health Care, **59** 139

Principal Mutual Life Insurance Company, III 328–30

Print Technologies, Inc., *see* Miner Group Int.

PrintNation Inc., **58** 275

Printpack, Inc., 68 293–96

Printrak, A Motorola Company, 44 357–59

Printronix, Inc., 18 434–36

Priority Records, **22** 194; **69** 351

Pripps Ringnes AB, *see* Orkla ASA.

Prison Rehabilitative Industries and Diversified Enterprises, Inc. (PRIDE), 53 277–79

Prisunic SA *see* PPR SA.

Pritchard Corporation *see* Black & Veatch, Inc.

Private Colleges and Universities, Inc., **55** 15

PrivatPort, **70** 311

Prize Energy, **59** 336

Pro-Build Holdings Inc., 95 344–48 (upd.)

Pro-Fac Cooperative, Inc., *see* Birds Eye Foods, Inc.

Pro-Lawn, **19** 250

Pro-Line Corporation, **36** 26

Pro-optik AG, **31** 203

Probe Exploration Inc., **25** 232

Probe Technology Corporation, **76** 231

Rewe-Beteiligungs-Holding National GmbH, **53** 179; **54** 295–96
Rewe Group, **37** 241
Rewe-Liebbrand, **28** 152
Rex Re Insurance Ltd., **51** 143
REX Stores Corp., **10** 468–69
Rexall Drug Co., **50** 487
Rexall Sundown, Inc., **37** 340, 342
Rexam PLC, **32** 380–85 (upd.); **85** 353–61 (upd.)
Rexel, Inc., **15** 384–87
Rexene Products Co., **IV** 457
Rexham Inc., *see* Rexam PLC.
Rexnord Corporation, **21** 429–32; **76** 315–19 (upd.)
Rexroth Mecman GmbH, **74** 321
Reycan, **49** 104
Reydel Industries, **23** 95–96
Reyes Holdings, Inc., **24** 388
The Reynolds and Reynolds Company, **50** 376–79
Reynolds Metals Company, **IV** 186–88; **19** 346–48 (upd.) *see also* Alcoa Inc.
RF Micro Devices, Inc., **43** 311–13
RFC Franchising LLC, **68** 317–19
RFF *see* Réseau Ferré de France.
RFI Group, Inc., **54** 275
RGI *see* Rockefeller Group Inc.
RHD Holdings, **23** 413
Rheem Manufacturing, **52** 398–99; **71** 269–70
Rheem South Africa Ltd., **59** 226
Rheinbraun A.G., **73** 131
Rheinische Metallwaaren- und Maschinenfabrik AG, *see* Rheinmetall Berlin AG.
Rheinmetall Berlin AG, **9** 443–46
Rhenus-Weichelt AG *see* Schenker-Rhenus AG.
RHI AG, **53** 283–86
RHI Entertainment Inc., **16** 257
Rhino Entertainment Company, **18** 457–60; **70** 276–80 (upd.)
RHM *see* Ranks Hovis McDougall.
Rhodes Inc., **23** 412–14
Rhodia SA, **38** 378–80
Rhône Moulage Industrie, **39** 152, 154
Rhône-Poulenc S.A., **I** 388–90; **10** 470–72 (upd.)
RhoxalPharma Inc., **69** 209
Rhymney Iron Company, **31** 369
Rica Foods, Inc., **41** 328–30
Ricardo Gallo *see* Vidrala S.A.
Ricardo plc, **90** 352–56
Rich Products Corporation, **7** 448–49; **38** 381–84 (upd.); **93** 368–74 (upd.)
Rich's Inc., *see* Federated Department Stores Inc.
Richard A. Shaw, Inc., *see* Dean Foods Co.
Richard D. Irwin Inc. *see* Dow Jones & Company, Inc.
Richard Ginori 1735 S.p.A., **73** 248–49
Richard R. Dostie, Inc. *see* Toll Brothers Inc.
Richards & O'Neil LLP, **43** 70
The Richards Group, Inc., **58** 300–02
Richardson Company, **36** 147

Richardson Electronics, Ltd., **17** 405–07
Richardson Industries, Inc., **62** 298–301
Richardson-Vicks Company *see* The Procter & Gamble Company
Richardson's, **21** 246
Richfood Holdings, Inc., **7** 450–51; *see also* Supervalu Inc.
Richman Gordman Half Price Stores, Inc. *see* Gordmans, Inc.
Richmond Cedar Works Manufacturing Co., **19** 360
Richmond Corp., **15** 129
Richmond Paperboard Corp., **19** 78
Richton International Corporation, **39** 344–46
Richtree Inc., **63** 328–30
Richwood Building Products, Inc., *see* Ply Gem Industries Inc.
Rickel Home Centers, *see* Supermarkets General Holdings Corp.
Rickenbacker International Corp., **91** 408–12
Ricoh Company, Ltd., **III** 159–61; **36** 389–93 (upd.)
Ricola Ltd., **62** 302–04
Ricolino, **19** 192
Riddarhyttan Resources AB *see* Agnico-Eagle Mines Ltd.
Riddell Inc., **33** 467
Riddell Sports Inc., **22** 457–59; **23** 449
Ridder Publications *see* Knight-Ridder, Inc.
Ride, Inc., **22** 460–63
Ridge Tool Co., *see* Emerson.
Ridgewell's Inc., **15** 87
Ridgway Co., **23** 98
Ridley Corporation Ltd., **62** 305–07
Riedel-de Haën AG, **22** 32; **36** 431
The Riese Organization, **38** 385–88
Rieter Holding AG, **42** 315–17
Riggs National Corporation, **13** 438–40
Right Associates, **27** 21; **44** 156
Right Management Consultants, Inc., **42** 318–21
Right Source, Inc., **24** 96
RightPoint, Inc., **49** 124
RightSide Up, Inc., *see* AHL Services, Inc..
Rijnhaave Information Systems, **25** 21
Riken Kagaku Co. Ltd., **48** 250
Riklis Family Corp., **9** 447–50
Rimage Corp., **89** 369–72
Rinascente S.p.A., **71** 308–10
Ring King Visibles, Inc., *see* HNI Corp.
Ring Ltd., **43** 99
Ringnes Bryggeri, *see* Orkla ASA.
Rinker Group Ltd., **65** 298–301
Rio de Janeiro Refrescos S.A., **71** 140
Rio Grande Industries, Inc., **12** 18–19
Rio Grande Servaas, S.A. de C.V., **23** 145
Rio Sportswear Inc., **42** 269
Rio Sul Airlines *see* Varig, SA.
Rio Tinto plc, **19** 349–53 (upd.) **50** 380–85 (upd.)
Riocell S.A. *see* Klabin S.A.
Ripley Entertainment, Inc., **74** 273–76
Ripotot, **68** 143

Riser Foods, Inc., **9** 451–54 *see also* Giant Eagle, Inc.
Risk Management Partners Ltd., **35** 36
Risk Planners, *see* Supervalu Inc.
Ritchie Bros. Auctioneers Inc., **41** 331–34
Rite Aid Corporation, **V** 174–76; **19** 354–57 (upd.); **63** 331–37 (upd.)
Riteway Distributor, **26** 183
Rittenhouse Financial Services, **22** 495
Ritter Co. *see* Sybron Corp.
Ritter Sport *see* Alfred Ritter GmbH & Co. KG.
Ritter's Frozen Custard *see* RFC Franchising LLC.
Ritz Camera Centers, **34** 375–77
The Ritz-Carlton Hotel Company, L.L.C., **9** 455–57; **29** 403–06 (upd.); **71** 311–16 (upd.)
Ritz-Craft Corporation of Pennsylvania Inc., **94** 365–68
Riunione Adriatica di Sicurtà SpA, **III** 345–48
Riva Group Plc, **53** 46
Riva Fire *see* Gruppo Riva Fire SpA.
The Rival Company, **19** 358–60
Rivaud Group, **29** 370
River City Broadcasting, **25** 418
River Metals Recycling LLC, **76** 130
River North Studios *see* Platinum Entertainment, Inc.
River Oaks Furniture, Inc., **43** 314–16
River Ranch Fresh Foods LLC, **88** 322–25
River Thames Insurance Co., Ltd., **26** 487
Riverdeep Group plc, **41** 137
Riverside Insurance Co. of America, **26** 487
Riverside Press, *see* Houghton Mifflin Co.
Riverside Publishing Company, **36** 272
Riverwood International Corporation, **11** 420–23; **48** 340–44 (upd.)
Riviana Foods, **27** 388–91
Riviera Holdings Corporation, **75** 340–43
Riviera Tool Company, **89** 373–76
Riyadh Armed Forces Hospital, **16** 94
Rizzoli Publishing, **23** 88
RJMJ, Inc., **16** 37
RJR Nabisco Holdings Corp., **V** 408–10 *see also* R.J Reynolds Tobacco Holdings Inc., Nabisco Brands, Inc.; R.J. Reynolds Industries, Inc.
RK Rose + Krieger GmbH & Co. KG, **61** 286–87
RKO *see* Radio-Keith-Orpheum.
RM Auctions, Inc., **88** 326–29
RMC Group p.l.c., **III** 737–40; **34** 378–83 (upd.)
RMH Teleservices, Inc., **42** 322–24
Roadhouse Grill, Inc., **22** 464–66
Roadmaster Industries, Inc., **16** 430–33
Roadmaster Transport Company, **18** 27; **41** 18
RoadOne *see* Miller Industries, Inc.
Roadstone-Wood Group, **64** 98
Roadway Express, Inc., **V** 502–03; **25** 395–98 (upd.)

SAI *see* Stamos Associates Inc.
Saia Motor Freight Line, Inc., **6** 421–23; **45** 448
Saibu Gas, **IV** 518–19
SAIC *see* Science Applications International Corp.
SAIC Velcorex, *see* Groupe DMC (Dollfus Mieg & Cie).
Saiccor, **IV** 92; **49** 353
SalesLink Corporation *see* CMGI, Inc.
Sainco *see* Sociedad Anonima de Instalaciones de Control.
Sainsbury's *see* J Sainsbury PLC.
St. Alban Boissons S.A., **22** 515
Saint-Gobain *see* Compagnie de Saint Gobain S.A.
Saint-Gobain Weber *see* Weber et Broutin France.
St. Ives Laboratories Inc., **36** 26
St Ives plc, 34 393–95
St. James Associates, **32** 362–63
St. James's Place Capital, plc, 71 324–26
The St. Joe Company, 31 422–25
St. Joe Corporation, **59** 185
St. Joe Gold, **23** 40
St. Joe Minerals Corp., *see* Flour Corp.
St. Joe Paper Company, 8 485–88
St. John Knits, Inc., 14 466–68
St. JON Laboratories, Inc., **74** 381
St. Jude Medical, Inc., 11 458–61; **43** 347–52 (upd.)
St. Laurent Paperboard Inc., **30** 119
St. Lawrence Cement Inc., *see* Holnam Inc.
Saint Louis Bread Company, **18** 35, 37; **44** 327
St. Louis Concessions Inc., **21** 39
St. Louis Music, Inc., 48 351–54
St. Louis Post-Dispatch LLC, **58** 283
St. Luke's-Roosevelt Hospital Center *see* Continuum Health Partners, Inc.
St. Martin's Press, **25** 484–85; **35** 452
St. Mary Land & Exploration Company, 63 345–47
St. Michel-Grellier S.A., **44** 40
St. Paul Bank for Cooperatives, 8 489–90
St. Paul Book and Stationery, Inc., **47** 90
St. Paul Fire and Marine Insurance Co. *see* The St. Paul Companies, Inc.
The St. Paul Travelers Companies, Inc., III 355–57; **22** 492–95 (upd.); **79** 362–69 (upd.)
St. Paul Venture Capital Inc., **34** 405–06
St. Regis Paper Co., **12** 377
salesforce.com, Inc., 79 370–73
Saipem S.p.A. *see* ENI S.p.A.
SAirGroup, **29** 376; **33** 268, 271; **37** 241; **46** 398; **47** 287
SAirLogistics, **49** 80–81
Saison Group, **V** 184–85, 187–89; **36** 417–18, 420; **42** 340–41
Sakae Printing Co., Ltd., **64** 261
Sako Ltd., **39** 151
Saks Inc., 24 420–23; **41** 342–45 (upd.)
Sakura Bank *see* Sumitomo Mitsui Banking Corp.

Salant Corporation, 12 430–32; **51** 318–21 (upd.)
Sale Knitting Company *see* Tultex Corp.
Salem Broadcasting, **25** 508
Salem Sportswear, **25** 167
Salick Health Care, Inc., 53 290–92
Salient Partners & Pinnacle Trust Co., **70** 287
Salinas Equipment Distributors, Inc., **33** 364
Salix Pharmaceuticals, Ltd., 93 384–87
Sallie Mae *see* SLM Holding Corp.; Student Loan Marketing Association.
Sally Beauty Company, Inc., 60 258–60
Salomon Inc., II 447–49; **13** 447–50 (upd.) *see also* Citigroup Inc.
Salomon Worldwide, 20 458–60 *see also* adidas-Salomon AG.
Salon Cielo and Spa *see* Ratner Companies.
Salon Plaza *see* Ratner Companies.
Salt River Project, 19 374–76
Salton, Inc., 30 402–04; **88** 343–48 (upd.)
Salvagnini Company, **22** 6
The Salvation Army USA, 32 390–93
Salvatore Ferragamo Italia S.p.A., 62 311–13
Salzgitter AG, IV 200–01
SAM *see* Sociedad Aeronáutica de Medellín, S.A.
Sam & Libby Inc., **30** 311
Sam Ash Music Corporation, 30 405–07
Sam Goody, **63** 65
Sam Levin Inc., 80 328–31
Sam's Club, 40 385–87
Samancor Ltd., **IV** 92–93
Samaritan Senior Services Inc., **25** 503
Samas-Groep N.V., **47** 91
Samcor Glass *see* Corning Inc.
Samedan Oil Corporation, *see* Noble Affiliates, Inc.
Sames, S.A., **21** 65–66
Samick Musical Instruments Co., Ltd., 56 297–300
Samim, **IV** 422
Sammy Corp., **54** 16; **73** 291
Samna Corp., **6** 256; **25** 300
Sampoerna PT, **62** 96–97
Sampson Supermarkets, Inc., *see* Hannaford Bros. Co.
Samson Technologies Corp., **30** 406
Samsonite Corporation, 13 451–53; **43** 353–57 (upd.)
Samsung Display Co., Ltd., **59** 81
Samsung Electronics Co., Ltd., 14 416–18; **41** 346–49 (upd.)
Samsung Group, I 515–17
Samuel Austin & Son Company, *see* The Austin Co.
Samuel Cabot Inc., 53 293–95
Samuel Meisel & Company, Inc., *see* Duty Free International, Inc.
Samuels Jewelers Incorporated, 30 408–09
San Antonio Public Service Company *see* City Public Service.

San Diego Gas & Electric Company, V 711–14 *see also* Sempra Energy.
San Diego Padres Baseball Club L.P., 78 324–27
San Francisco Baseball Associates, L.P., 55 340–43
San Francisco Maillots, **62** 228
San Giorgio Macaroni Inc., **53** 242
San Jose Water Company *see* SJW Corp.
San Miguel Corporation, 15 428–30; **57** 303–08 (upd.)
San Paolo IMI S.p.A., **63** 52–53
Sanborn Hermanos, S.A., 20 461–63
Sanborn Manufacturing Company, **30** 138
Sanborn Map Company Inc., 82 321–24
The Sanctuary Group PLC, 69 314–17
Sandals Resorts International, 65 302–05
Sandcastle 5 Productions, **25** 269–70
Sanders Morris Harris Group Inc., 70 285–87
Sanderson Farms, Inc., 15 425–27
Sandia National Laboratories, 49 345–48
Sandiacre Packaging Machinery Ltd., **51** 249–50
Sandoz Ltd., I 671–73 *see also* Novartis AG.
Sandusky Plastics, Inc., *see* Envirodyne Industries, Inc.
Sandusky Portland Cement Company, *see* Medusa Corp.
Sandvik AB, IV 202–04; **32** 394–98 (upd.); **77** 367–73 (upd.)
Sandwell, Inc., **6** 491
Sandwich Chef, Inc. *see* Wall Street Deli, Inc.
Sandy's Pool Supply, Inc. *see* Leslie's Poolmart, Inc.
Sanford C. Bernstein Inc., **63** 27
Sanford L.P., 82 325–29
Sanford-Brown College, Inc., **41** 419–20
Sanitation Systems, Inc. *see* HMI Industries.
Sanitec Corporation, 51 322–24
Sanko Peterson Corporation, **55** 306
Sankyo Company, Ltd., I 674–75; **56** 301–04 (upd.)
Sanlam Ltd., 68 331–34
SANlight Inc., **62** 293
SANLUIS Corporación, S.A.B. de C.V., 95 362–65
Sano Corporation, **63** 142
The Sanofi-Synthélabo Group, I 676–77; **49** 349–51 (upd.)
SanomaWSOY Corporation, 51 325–28
Sanpaolo IMI S.p.A., 50 407–11
Sanrio Company, Ltd., 38 413–15
Sansone Group, **69** 120
Santa Barbara Restaurant Group, Inc., 37 349–52
The Santa Cruz Operation, Inc., 38 416–21
Santa Fe Gaming Corporation, 19 377–79 *see also* Archon Corp.
Santa Fe Gold Corporation, **38** 232
Santa Fe Industries, **12** 19; **28** 498

Sevenson Environmental Services, Inc., 42 344–46

Seventh Generation, Inc., 73 294–96

Seventh Street Corporation, 60 130

Severn Trent PLC, 12 441–43; 38 425–29 (upd.)

Severonickel Combine, 48 300

Severstal Joint Stock Company, 65 309–12

Sextant In-Flight Systems, LLC, 30 74

Seyfarth Shaw LLP, 93 388–91

Seymour International Press Distributor Ltd., IV 619

Seymour Press, IV 619

SF Bio, 52 51

SF Recycling & Disposal, Inc., 60 224

SFI Group plc, 51 334–36

SFIC Holdings (Cayman) Inc., 38 422

SFIM Industries, 37 348

SFNGR see Nouvelles Galeries Réunies.

SFS Bancorp Inc., 41 212

SFX Broadcasting Inc., 24 107

SFX Entertainment, Inc., 36 422–25

SG Cowen Securities Corporation, 75 186–87

SG Racing, Inc., 64 346

SGC see Supermarkets General Corp.

SGE see Vinci.

SGI, 29 438–41 (upd.)

SGL Carbon Group, 40 83; 46 14

SGS-Thomson Microelectronics, 54 269–70

Shakespeare Company, 22 481–84

Shakey's Pizza, see Jacmar Companies.

Shaklee Corporation, 12 444–46; 39 361–64 (upd.)

Shampaine Industries, Inc., 37 399

Shamrock Broadcasting Inc., 24 107

Shamrock Holdings, 25 268

Shan-Chih Business Association, 23 469

Shana Corporation, 62 142

Shandong Nichirei Foods Company Ltd. see Nichirei Corp.

Shandwick International, 47 97

Shanggong Co. Ltd., 65 134

Shanghai Asia Pacific Co., 59 59

Shanghai Autobacs Paian Auto Service Co., 76 38

Shanghai Baosteel Group Corporation, 71 327–30

Shanghai Dajiang, 62 63

Shanghai General Bearing Co., Ltd., 45 170

Shanghai International Finance Company Limited, 15 433

Shanghai Kyocera Electronics Co., Ltd., 21 331

Shanghai Petrochemical Co., Ltd., 18 483–85

Shanghai Shesuo UNF Medical Diagnostic Reagents Co., 61 229

Shanghai Tobacco, 49 150, 153

Shangri-La Asia Ltd., 71 331–33

Shanks Group plc, 45 384–87

Shannon Aerospace Ltd., 36 426–28

Shannon Group, Inc., see Manitowoc Co., Inc.

Shansby Group, 27 197; 43 218; 64 265

Shanshin Engineering Company Ltd., 60 236

Shared Financial Systems, Inc., 10 501

Shared Medical Systems Corporation, 14 432–34 see also Siemens AG.

ShareWave Inc., 48 92

Shari Lewis Enterprises, Inc., 28 160

Sharmoon, 63 151

Sharp Corporation, II 95–96; 12 447–49 (upd.); 40 391–95 (upd.)

Sharp Water, Inc., 56 62

The Sharper Image Corporation, 10 486–88; 62 321–24 (upd.)

Sharples Separator Company, 64 17

Shasta Beverages see National Beverage Corp.

Shato Holdings, Ltd., 60 357

Shaw Communications Inc., 26 274; 35 69

The Shaw Group, Inc., 50 427–30

Shaw Industries, Inc., 9 465–67; 40 396–99 (upd.)

Shaw's Supermarkets, Inc., 56 315–18

Shea Homes see J.F. Shea Co., Inc.

Sheaffer Group, 23 54, 57

Sheaffer Pen Corporation, 82 340–43

Shearer's Foods, Inc., 72 323–25

Shearman & Sterling, 32 419–22

Shearson Lehman Brothers Holdings Inc., II 450–52; 9 468–70 (upd.)

Shedd Aquarium Society, 73 297–99

Sheetz, Inc., 85 387–90

Sheffield Exploration Company, 28 470

Sheffield Forgemasters Group Ltd., 39 32

Sheffield Silver Company, 67 322–23

Shekou Container Terminal, 16 481; 38 345

Shelby Steel Processing Co., 51 238

Shelby Williams Industries, Inc., 14 435–37

Sheldahl Inc., 23 432–35

Shelf Life Inc. see King Kullen Grocery Co., Inc.

Shell see Royal Dutch/Shell Group; Shell Oil Company; Shell Transport and Trading Company p.l.c.

Shell Canada Limited, 32 45

Shell Chemical Corporation, IV 531–32, 540

Shell Forestry, 21 546; 50 58

Shell France, 12 153

Shell Oil Company, IV 540–41; 14 438–40 (upd.); 41 356–60 (upd.)

Shell Transport and Trading Company p.l.c., IV 530–32 see also Royal Dutch Petroleum Company; Royal Dutch/Shell.

Sheller-Globe Corporation, I 201–02 see also Lear Corp.

Shells Seafood Restaurants, Inc., 43 370–72

Shelly Brothers, Inc., 15 65

Shenandoah Telecommunications Company, 89 390–93

Shenhua Group see China Shenhua Energy Company Limited

Shenzhen Namtek Co., Ltd., 61 232–33

Shepherd Neame Limited, 30 414–16

Shepherd Products Ltd., see The Marmon Group, Inc.

Sheraton Corp. of America, see ITT Sheraton Corp.

The Sheridan Group, Inc., 86 357–60

Shermag, Inc., 93 392–97

Sherr-Gold, 23 40

The Sherwin-Williams Company, III 744–46; 13 469–71 (upd.); 89 394–400 (upd.)

Sherwood Brands, Inc., 53 302–04

Sherwood Equity Group Ltd. see National Discount Brokers Group, Inc.

Sherwood Medical Group, see American Home Porducts.

Sherwood Securities, 66 308

Shiara Holdings, Inc., 53 88

Shidler Group see First Industrial Realty Trust, Inc.

Shihen Technical Corporation, 60 272

Shihlin Electric & Engineering Group, 49 460

Shikoku Electric Power Company, Inc., V 718–20; 60 269–72 (upd.)

Shiley, Inc., 38 361

Shillito's, 31 192

Shimano Inc., 64 347–49

Shimizu Construction Company Ltd., 44 153

Shin-Nihon Glass Co., see Asahi Breweries, Ltd.

Shinko Rayon Ltd. see Mitsubishi Rayon Co., Ltd.

Shinko Securities Co. Ltd., 58 235

Shinwa Pharmaceutical Co. Ltd., 48 250

Shionogi & Co., Ltd., III 60–61; 17 435–37 (upd.)

Shipley Co. Inc., 26 425

Shipper Group, 16 344

Shiseido Company, Limited, III 62–64; 22 485–88 (upd.); 81 364–70 (upd.)

Shizuoka Itaku Co., Ltd., 64 261

SHL Systemhouse Inc., 27 305

Shobiz, Inc., 60 143

Shochiku Company Ltd., 74 302–04

Shockley Electronics, 20 174

Shoe Carnival Inc., 14 441–43; 72 326–29 (upd.)

Shoe Pavilion, Inc., 84 346–349

Shoe-Town Inc., 23 310

Shonac Corporation see DSW Inc.

Shoney's, Inc., 7 474–76; 23 436–39 (upd.)

Shop 'n Save Warehouse Foods Inc., 63 129

Shop At Home Network LLC see The E.W. Scripps Co.

SHOP Channel, 64 185

Shop Rite Foods Inc. see Big V Supermarkets, Inc.

ShopKo Stores Inc., 21 457–59; 58 329–32 (upd.)

Shoppers Drug Mart Corporation, 49 367–70

Shoppers Food Warehouse Corporation, 66 290–92

Shoppers World Stores, Inc. see LOT$OFF Corp.

The Strober Organization, Inc., 82
357–60 *see also* Pro-Build Holdings
Inc.
Stroehmann Bakeries, Inc., *see* George
Weston Ltd.
The Stroh Brewery Company, I 290–92;
18 499–502 (upd.)
Strombecker Corporation, 60 289–91
Stroock & Stroock & Lavan LLP, 40
418–21
Strouds, Inc., 33 383–86
Structural Fibers, Inc. *see* Essef Corp.
Struebel Group, 18 170
Strydel, Inc., *see* The Ohio Art Co.
Stryker Corporation, 11 474–76; 29
453–55 (upd.); 79 400–05 (upd.)
Stuart & Sons Ltd., 34 493, 496
Stuart C. Irby Company, 58 333–35
Stuart Entertainment Inc., 16 470–72
Stuart Medical, Inc., *see* Owens & Minor,
Inc.
Student Loan Marketing Association, II
453–55 *see also* SLM Holding Corp.
StudioCanal, 48 164–65
Studley Products Inc., *see* Ply Gem
Industries Inc.
Stuffit Co., IV 597
Stuller Settings, Inc., 35 405–07
Sturm, Ruger & Company, Inc., 19
430–32
Stussy, Inc., 55 361–63
Style Magazine BV, 48 347
Styleclick.com, Inc., 47 420
SU214, 28 27, 30
Suave Shoe Corporation *see* French
Fragrances, Inc.
Sub-Zero Freezer Co., Inc., 31 426–28
Suber Suisse S.A., 48 350
Subic Bay Energy Co., Ltd, 56 290
The SubLine Company, Inc., 53 340
SubLogic, 15 455
SUBperior Distribution Systems, Inc., 53
340
Suburban Propane Partners, L.P., 30
440–42
Subway, 32 442–44 *see also* Doctor's
Associates Inc.
Successories, Inc., 30 443–45
Sucden *see* Compagnie Financière Sucres
et Denrées.
Sucesora de Jose Puig y Cia C.A., 60 246
Suchard Co. *see* Jacobs Suchard.
Sudamericana Holding S.A., 63 180
Sudbury Inc., 16 473–75
Sudbury River Consulting Group, 31 131
Südzucker AG, 27 436–39
Suez Lyonnaise des Eaux, 36 456–59
(upd.)
Suez Oil Processing Co., IV 413–14; 51
113
Sugar Entertainment, 51 288
Sugar Mount Capital, LLC, 33 355
Sugarland Industries *see* Imperial Holly
Corp.
SugarLoaf Creations, Inc. *see* American
Coin Merchandising, Inc.
Sugarloaf Mountain Corporation, 28 21
Suge Knight Films, Inc., 69 350–51

The Suit Company, 51 253
Suito Sangyo Co., Ltd. *see* Seino
Transportation Company, Ltd.
SUITS *see* Scottish Universal Investments.
Suiza Foods Corporation, 26 447–50 *see
also* Dean Foods Co.
Sukhoi Design Bureau Aviation
Scientific-Industrial Complex, 24
463–65
Sullivan & Cromwell, 26 451–53
Sullivan-Schein Dental Products Inc. *see*
Henry Schein Inc.
Sulpetro Limited, 25 232
Sulzer Ltd., III 630–33; 68 358–62
(upd.)
Sumergrade Corporation, 19 304; 41 300
Sumisho Electronics Co. Ltd., 18 170
Sumitomo Bank, Limited, II 360–62;
26 454–57 (upd.)
Sumitomo Chemical Company Ltd., I
397–98
Sumitomo Corporation, I 518–20; 11
477–80 (upd.)
Sumitomo Electric Industries, II 104–05
Sumitomo Heavy Industries, Ltd., III
634–35; 42 360–62 (upd.)
Sumitomo Life Insurance Company, III
365–66; 60 292–94 (upd.)
Sumitomo Metal Industries Ltd., IV
211–13; 82 361–66 (upd.)
Sumitomo Metal Mining Co., Ltd., IV
214–16
Sumitomo Mitsui Banking Corporation,
51 356–62 (upd.)
Sumitomo Realty & Development Co.,
Ltd., IV 726–27
Sumitomo Rubber Industries, Ltd., V
252–53
Sumitomo Trading, 45 8
The Sumitomo Trust & Banking
Company, Ltd., II 363–64; 53
320–22 (upd.)
Summa International, 56 284
Summer Paper Tube, 19 78
SummerGate Inc., 48 148
Summers Group Inc., 15 386
The Summit Bancorporation, 14
472–74 *see also* FleetBoston Financial
Corp.
Summit Constructors *see* CRSS Inc.
Summit Family Restaurants Inc., 19
433–36
Summit Systems Inc., 45 280
Summit Technology Inc., 30 485
Sumolis, 54 315, 317
Sun Alliance Group PLC, III 369–74 *see
also* Royal & Sun Alliance Insurance
Group plc.
Sun Apparel Inc., 39 247
Sun Capital Partners Inc., 63 79
Sun Chemical Corp. *see* Sequa Corp.
Sun Communities Inc., 46 377–79
Sun Company, Inc., IV 548–50 *see also*
Sunoco, Inc.
Sun Country Airlines, I 30 446–49
Sun-Diamond Growers of California, 7
496–97 *see also* Diamond of California.
Sun Distributors L.P., 12 459–461

Sun Electric, 15 288
Sun Equities Corporation, 15 449
Sun Financial Group, Inc., 25 171
Sun Gro Horticulture Inc., 49 196, 198
Sun Healthcare Group Inc., 25 455–58
Sun Hydraulics Corporation, 74 319–22
Sun International Hotels Limited, 26
462–65 *see also* Kerzner International
Ltd.
Sun Life Financial Inc., 85 409–12
Sun Life Group of America, *see*
SunAmerica Inc.
Sun Live Co., 56 201
Sun-Maid Growers of California, 82
367–71
Sun Mark, Inc., 21 483
Sun Media, 29 471–72; 47 327
Sun Men's Shop Co., Ltd. *see* Nagasakiya
Co., Ltd.
Sun Microsystems, Inc., 7 498–501; 30
450–54 (upd.); 91 455–62 (upd.)
Sun Oil Co., IV 424, 548–50; 11 35; 36
86–87 *see also* Oryx Energy Co;
Sunoco, Inc.
Sun Optical Co., Ltd. *see* Nagasakiya Co.,
Ltd.
Sun Pac Foods, 45 161
Sun Pharmaceutical Industries Ltd., 57
345–47
Sun-Rype Products Ltd., 76 336–38
Sun Shades 501 Ltd., 21 483
Sun Ship, IV 549
Sun Sportswear, Inc., 17 460–63
Sun State Marine Services, Inc. *see* Hvide
Marine Inc.
Sun Techno Services Co., Ltd. *see*
Nagasakiya Co., Ltd.
Sun Technology Enterprises, *see* Sun
Microsystems, Inc.
Sun Television & Appliances Inc., 10
502–03
Sun Valley Equipment Corp., 33 363
Sun World International, LLC, 93
426–29
SunAir, 11 300
SunAmerica Inc., 11 481–83 *see also*
American International Group, Inc.
Sunbeam-Oster Co., Inc., 9 484–86
Sunbelt Beverage Corporation *see* The
Charmer Sunbelt Group.
Sunbelt Coca-Cola Bottling Co., *see*
Coca-Cola Bottling Co. Consolidated.
Sunbelt Nursery Group, Inc., 12 179,
200, 394
Sunbelt Rentals Inc., 34 42
Sunbird *see* Nagasakiya Co., Ltd.
Sunburst Hospitality Corporation, 26
458–61
Sunburst Shutters Corporation, 78
370–72
Sunburst Technology Corporation, 36 273
Sunco N.V., 22 515
Suncoast Motion Picture Company, 63 65
Suncoast Toys, Inc., 74 14
SunCor Development Company, 6
546–47
Suncor Energy Inc., 54 352–54
Suncorp-Metway Ltd., 91 463–66

TNT Grading Inc., **50** 348

TNT Limited, V 523–25

TNT Post Group N.V., 27 471–76 (upd.); 30 461–63 (upd.) *see also* TPG N.V.

Toa Tanker Co. Ltd., **IV** 555

Tobacco Group PLC, **30** 231

Tobias, **16** 239

Tobu Railway Co Ltd, 6 430–32

Today's Man, Inc., 20 484–87

Todays Computers Business Centers *see* Intelligent Electronics, Inc.

The Todd-AO Corporation, 33 400–04 *see also* Liberty Livewire Corp.

Todd Shipyards Corporation, 14 507–09

TODCO, 87 439–442

Toden Real Estate Company Inc., **74** 348

Todhunter International, Inc., 27 477–79

Todito.com, S.A. de C.V., **39** 194, 196

Toei Co. Ltd., **9** 29–30; **28** 462

Tofa, *see* Koç Holding A.S.

Tofte Industrier, **63** 315

Toftejorg Group, **64** 18

Tofutti Brands, Inc., 64 382–84

Togo's Eatery, **29** 19

Tohan Corporation, 84 402–405

Toho Co., Ltd., 28 461–63

Tohoku Alps, *see* Alps Electric Co., Ltd.

Tohoku Anritsu Co., Ltd. *see* Anritsu Corp.

Tohuku Electric Power Company, Inc., V 726–28

Tokai Aircraft Co., Ltd. *see* Aisin Seiki Co., Ltd.

The Tokai Bank, Limited, II 373–74; 15 494–96 (upd.)

Tokai Kogyo Co. Ltd., **I** 615; **48** 42

Tokheim Corporation, 21 493–95

Tokio Marine and Fire Insurance Co., Ltd., III 383–86 *see also* Millea Holdings Inc.

Tokiwa shokai Ltd., **64** 261

Tokos Medical Corporation, *see* Matria Healthcare, Inc.

Tokushima Automobile Service Company Inc., **60** 272

Tokyo City Finance, **36** 419 20

Tokyo Disneyland, **6** 176

Tokyo Electric Power Company, V 729–33; 74 343–48 (upd.)

Tokyo Gas Co., Ltd., V 734–36; 55 372–75 (upd.)

Tokyo Maritime Agency Ltd., **56** 181

Tokyo Motors *see* Isuzu Motors, Ltd.

Tokyo Stock Exchange, **34** 254

Tokyo Telecommunications Engineering Corp *see* Tokyo Tsushin Kogyo K.K.

TOKYOPOP Inc., 79 415–18

Tokyu Corporation, V 526–28; 47 407–10 (upd.)

Tokyu Department Store Co., Ltd., V 199–202; 32 453–57 (upd.)

Tokyu Land Corporation, IV 728–29

Toledo Edison Company *see* Centerior Energy Corp.

Toledo Milk Processing, Inc., **15** 449

Toledo Scale Corp., **30** 327

Toll Brothers Inc., 15 497–99; 70 323–26 (upd.)

Tollgrade Communications, Inc., 44 424–27

Tom Brown, Inc., 37 389–91

Tom Doherty Associates Inc., 25 483–86

Tom Snyder Productions, **29** 470, 472

Tom Thumb, **40** 365–66

Tom's Foods Inc., 66 325–27

Tom's of Maine, Inc., 45 414–16

Toman Corporation, **19** 390

The Tomatin Distillery Co., Ltd., **62** 347

Tombstone Pizza Corporation, 13 515–17 *see also* Kraft Foods Inc.

Tomcan Investments Inc., **53** 333

Tomen Corporation, IV 224–25; 24 488–91 (upd.)

Tomkins plc, 11 525–27; 44 428–31 (upd.)

Tommy Armour Golf Co., **32** 446–47

Tommy Bahama *see* Viewpoint International, Inc.

Tommy Hilfiger Corporation, 20 488–90; 53 330–33 (upd.)

TomTom N.V., 81 388–91

Tomy Company Ltd., 65 341–44

Tone Brothers, Inc., 21 496–98; 74 349–52 (upd.)

Tone Coca-Cola Bottling Company, Ltd., *see* Kikkoman Corp.

Tonen Corporation, IV 554–56; 16 489–92 (upd.)

TonenGeneral Sekiyu K.K., 54 380–86 (upd.)

Tong Yang Cement Corporation, 62 366–68

Tonka Corporation, 25 487–89

Tonkin, Inc., **19** 114

Tony Lama Company Inc., **19** 233

Tony Roma's, A Place for Ribs Inc. *see* Romacorp, Inc.

Tony Stone Images, **31** 216–17

Too, Inc., 61 371–73

Toolex International N.V., 26 489–91

Tootsie Roll Industries, 12 480–82; 82 392–96 (upd.)

Top End Wheelchair Sports, **11** 202

Top Glory International Group Company, **76** 89–90

Top Tool Company, Inc., **25** 75

Topack Verpackungstechnik, **60** 193

The Topaz Group, Inc., 62 369–71

Topco Associates LLC, 60 302–04

Topcon Corporation, 84 406–409

Topkapi, *see* Claire's Stores, Inc.

Toppan Printing Co., Ltd., IV 679–81; 58 340–44 (upd.)

The Topps Company, Inc., 13 518–20; 34 446–49 (upd.); 83 400–406 (upd.)

Topps Markets, **16** 314

Tops Appliance City, Inc., 17 487–89

Tops Markets LLC, 60 305–07

TopTip, **48** 116

Tor Books *see* Tom Doherty Associates Inc.

Toray Industries, Inc., V 383–86; 51 375–79 (upd.)

Torchmark Corporation, 9 506–08; 33 405–08 (upd.)

Toresco Enterprises, Inc., 84 410–413

Torfeaco Industries Limited, *see* Pillowtex Corp.

The Toro Company, 7 534–36; 26 492–95 (upd.); 77 440–45 (upd.)

Toromont Industries, Ltd., 21 499–501

The Toronto-Dominion Bank, II 375–77; 49 395–99 (upd.)

Toronto Maple Leafs *see* Maple Leaf Sports & Entertainment Ltd.

Toronto Raptors *see* Maple Leaf Sports & Entertainment Ltd.

Toronto Sun Publishing Company *see* Sun Media.

Torrent Systems, Inc., **59** 56

The Torrington Company, 13 521–24 *see also* Timken Co.

Torstar Corporation, 29 470–73 *see also* Harlequin Enterprises Ltd.

Tosco Corporation, 7 537–39 *see also* ConocoPhillips.

Toshiba Corporation, I 533–35; 12 483–86 (upd.); 40 435–40 (upd.)

Toshin Building Co. Ltd., **74** 348

Toshin Kaihatsu Ltd. *see* Takashimaya Co., Ltd.

Tosoh Corporation, 70 327–30

Tostem *see* Toyo Sash Co., Ltd.

Total Beverage Corporation, *see* Dart Group PLC.

Total Compagnie Française des Pétroles S.A., IV 557–61 *see also* Total Fina Elf S.A.

Total Entertainment Restaurant Corporation, 46 427–29

Total Filtration Services, Inc., **61** 66

Total Fina Elf S.A., 50 478–86 (upd.)

Total Global Sourcing, Inc., *see* Staples, Inc.

Total Home Entertainment (THE), **39** 240, 242

Total Petroleum Corporation, **21** 500

TOTAL S.A., 24 492–97 (upd.)

Total System Services, Inc., 18 516–18

Totem Resources Corporation, 9 509–11

Totino's Finer Foods, **26** 436

TOTO LTD., III 755–56; 28 464–66 (upd.)

Tottenham Hotspur PLC, 81 392–95

Touch America Inc., **37** 127; **44** 288

Touch-It Corp., **22** 413

Touche Remnant Holdings Ltd., **II** 356

Touche Ross *see* Deloitte Touche Tohmatsu International.

Touchstone Films *see* The Walt Disney Co.

Toupargel-Agrigel S.A., 76 354–56

Le Touquet's, SA, **48** 197

Touristik Union International GmbH. and Company K.G., II 163–65 *see also* Preussag AG.

Tourtime America, **56** 223

TOUSA *see* Technical Olympic USA, Inc.

U.S. Plywood Corp *see* United States Plywood Corp.

U.S. Premium Beef LLC, 91 487–90

U.S. RingBinder Corp., *see* General Binding Corp.

U.S. Robotics Corporation, 9 514–15; 66 339–41 (upd.)

U.S. Satellite Broadcasting Company, Inc., 20 505–07 *see also* DIRECTV, Inc.

U.S. Shoe Corporation, **43** 98; **44** 365

U.S. Software Inc., **29** 479

U.S. Steel Corp *see* United States Steel Corp.

U.S. Timberlands Company, L.P., 42 397–400

U.S. Trust Corp., 17 496–98

U.S. Venture Partners, **15** 204–05

U.S. Vision, Inc., 66 342–45

U S West, Inc., V 341–43; 25 495–99 (upd.)

U.S. Windpower, *see* Kenetech Corp.

U.S. Xpress Enterprises, Inc., **75** 148

UA *see* Metro- Goldwyn-Mayer Inc., MGM/UA Communications Company; United Artists Corp.

UAA *see* EgyptAir.

UAL Corporation, 34 462–65 (upd.)

UAP *see* Union des Assurances de Paris.

UAP Inc., **45** 179

UARCO Inc., **15** 473–74

UAT *see* UTA.

UAW (International Union, United Automobile, Aerospace and Agricultural Implement Workers of America), 72 354–57

Ube Industries, Ltd., III 759–61; 38 463–67 (upd.)

Ubi Soft Entertainment S.A., 41 407–09

Ubique Ltd, **25** 301

UBL Educational Loan Center, **42** 211

UBS AG, 52 352–59 (upd.)

UCAR International, Inc., **40** 83

UDRT *see* United Dominion Realty Trust, Inc.

UDV *see* United Distillers and Vintners.

Ueda Kotsu Company, **47** 408

UETA Inc., **29** 510–11

Ufa Sports, **44** 190

UFA TV & Film Produktion GmbH, 80 382–87

UFJ Bank, **61** 250

Ugg Holdings, Inc., *see* Deckers Outdoor Corp.

UGI *see* United Gas Improvement.

UGI Corporation, 12 498–500

Ugine S.A., 20 498–500

Ugly Duckling Corporation, 22 524–27 *see also* DriveTime Automotive Group Inc.

UHU GmbH *see* Bolton Group B.V.

UI International, **6** 444

UIB *see* United Independent Broadcasters, Inc.

UICI, 33 418–21 *see also* HealthMarkets, Inc.

Uinta Co., **6** 568

UIS Co., **15** 324

Uitgeversmaatschappij Elsevier *see* Reed Elsevier plc.

Uitzendbureau Amstelveen *see* Randstad Holding n.v.

Ukbetting Plc *see* 365 Media Group plc.

UKF *see* Unie van Kunstmestfabrieken.

Ukrop's Super Market's, Inc., 39 402–04

UL *see* Underwriters Laboratories, Inc.

Ullrich Copper, Inc. *see* Foster Wheeler Corp.

Ullstein Langen Müller, **IV** 591

ULN *see* Union Laitière Normande.

Ulstein Holding ASA, *see* Vickers plc.

Ulster Television PLC, 71 366–68

Ulta Salon, Cosmetics & Fragrance, Inc., 92 471–73

Ultimate Electronics, Inc., 18 532–34; 69 356–59 (upd.)

Ultimate Leisure Group PLC, 75 383–85

Ultra Mart, **16** 250

Ultra Pac, Inc., 24 512–14

Ultra Petroleum Corporation, 71 369–71

UltraCam *see* Ultrak Inc.

UltraCare Products, *see* Drypers Corp.

Ultrak Inc., 24 508–11

Ultralife Batteries, Inc., 58 345–48

Ultramar Diamond Shamrock Corporation, IV 565–68; 31 453–57 (upd.)

ULVAC, Inc., 80 388–91

Umberto's of New Hyde Park Pizzeria, **16** 447

Umbro plc, 88 414–17

UMC *see* United Microelectronics Corp.

UMG *see* Universal Music Group.

UMI Company, **29** 58

NV Umicore SA, 47 411–13

Umpqua Holdings Corporation, 87 443–446

Unadulterated Food Products, Inc., *see* Snapple Beverage Corp.

Unbrako Socket Screw Company Ltd., **30** 429

UNCF *see* United Negro College Fund, Inc.

Uncle Ben's Inc., 22 528–30

Uncle Ray's LLC, 90 417–19

Under Armour Performance Apparel, 61 381–83

Underberg AG, 92 388–393

Underwriter for the Professions Insurance Company, **55** 128

Underwriters Laboratories, Inc., 30 467–70

Underwriters Reinsurance Co., *see* Alleghany Corp.

Unefon, S.A., **39** 194, 196

UNELCO *see* Union Electrica de Canarias S.A.

UNG *see* United National Group, Ltd.

Ungaro SA, **62** 313

Uni-Cast *see* Sturm, Ruger & Company, Inc.

Uni-Marts, Inc., 17 499–502

Uni-President Group, **49** 460

Unibail SA, 40 444–46

Unibanco Holdings S.A., 73 350–53

Unibank, **40** 336; **50** 149–50

Unic *see* GIB Group.

Unica Corporation, 77 450–54

Unicapital, Inc., **15** 281

UNICARE, *see* WellPoint Health Networks Inc.

Unicco Security Services, **27** 22

Unice, **56** 335

UNICEF *see* United Nations International Children's Emergency Fund (UNICEF).

Unicel *see* Rural Cellular Corp.

Unicer, *see* Carlsberg A/S.

Unicharm Corporation, 84 414–417

Unicom Corporation, 29 486–90 (upd.) *see also* Exelon Corp.

Unicoolait, **19** 51

UNICOR *see* Federal Prison Industries, Inc.

Unicord Company, **64** 60

UniCredito Italiano, **50** 410

Unidrive, **47** 280

Uniface Holding B.V., *see* Compuware Corp.

Unifi, Inc., 12 501–03; 62 372–76 (upd.)

Unified Energy System of Russia *see* RAO Unified Energy System of Russia.

Unified Grocers, Inc., 93 474–77

Unified Western Grocers, **31** 25

UniFirst Corporation, 21 505–07

Uniflex Corporation, **53** 236

Uniforce Services Inc., **40** 119

Unigate PLC, II 586–87; 28 488–91 (upd.) *see also* Uniq Plc.

Uniglory, **13** 211

Unigro *see* Laurus N.V.

Unigroup, **15** 50

UniHealth America, **11** 378–79

Unijoh Sdn, Bhd, **47** 255

Unik S.A., **23** 170–171

Unilab Corp., **26** 391

Unilever, II 588–91; 7 542–45 (upd.); 32 472–78 (upd.); 89 464–74 (upd.)

UniLife Insurance Co., *see* CompDent Corp.

Unilog SA, 42 401–03

Uniloy Milacron Inc., **53** 230

UniMac Companies, **11** 413

Unimetal, **30** 252

Union Aéromaritime de Transport *see* UTA.

Union Bag–Camp Paper Corp. *see* Union Camp Corp.

Union Bank *see* State Street Boston Corp.

Union Bank of California, 16 496–98 *see also* UnionBanCal Corp.

Union Bank of Switzerland, II 378–79 *see also* UBS AG.

Union Biscuits *see* Leroux S.A.S.

Union Camp Corporation, IV 344–46

Union Carbide Corporation, I 399–401; 9 516–20 (upd.); 74 358–63 (upd.)

Union Colliery Company *see* Union Electric Co.

Union Commerciale, **19** 98

Voith Sulzer Papiermaschinen GmbH *see* J.M. Voith AG.
Volcan Compañia Minera S.A.A., **92** 403–06
Volcom, Inc., **77** 477–80
Volga-Dnepr Group, **82** 411–14
Volition, Inc., **39** 395
Volkswagen Aktiengesellschaft, **I** 206–08; **11** 549–51 (upd.); **32** 501–05 (upd.)
Volt Information Sciences Inc., **26** 518–21
Volume Distributors *see* Payless ShoeSource, Inc.
Volume Service Company *see* Restaurants Unlimited, Inc.
Volume Services America, Inc. *see* Centerplate, Inc.
Volume Shoe Corporation *see* Payless ShoeSource,Inc.
Volunteer Leather Company, *see* Genesco Inc.
Volunteers of America, Inc., **66** 360–62
AB Volvo, **I** 209–11; **7** 565–68 (upd.); **26** 9–12 (upd.); **67** 378–83 (upd.)
Volvo-Penta, **21** 503
Von Maur Inc., **64** 405–08
von Roll, **6** 599
Vonage Holdings Corp., **81** 415–18
The Vons Companies, Incorporated, **7** 569–71; **28** 510–13 (upd.)
Vornado Realty Trust, **20** 508–10
Voroba Hearing Systems, **25** 56
Vortex Management, Inc., **41** 207
Vorwerk & Co., **27** 502–04
Vosper Thornycroft Holding plc, **41** 410–12
Vossloh AG, **53** 348–52
Votorantim Participaçoes S.A., **76** 375–78
Vought Aircraft Industries, Inc., **49** 442–45
Vox, **58** 195
Voyageur Travel Insurance Ltd., **21** 447
VR&P *see* Virginia Railway and Power Co.
Vratislavice A.S., **38** 77
VRG International *see* Roberts Pharmaceutical Corp.
Vriesco Plastics B.V., **53** 221
Vroom & Dreesmann, *see* Koninklijke Vendex KBB N.V. (Royal Vendex KBB N.V.).
VSA *see* Vendors Supply of America, Inc.
VSB Groep, *see* N.V. AMEV.
VSD Communications, Inc., **22** 443
VSK Group *see* The Allied Defense Group, Inc.
VSM *see* Village Super Market, Inc.
VST *see* Vision Technology Group Ltd.
VTech Holdings Ltd., **77** 481–84
VTR Incorporated, **16** 46; **43** 60
Vu-Tech Communications, Inc., **48** 54
Vulcan Materials Company, **7** 572–75; **52** 392–96 (upd.)
Vulcan Ventures Inc., **32** 145; **43** 144
Vulcraft, *see* Nucor Corp.
VW&R *see* Van Waters & Rogers.

VWR Textiles & Supplies, Inc., **11** 256
VWR United Company, *see* Univar Corp.
Vycor Corporation, **25** 349
Vyvx, **31** 469

W

W&A Manufacturing Co., LLC, **26** 530
W & J Sloane Home Furnishings Group, **35** 129
W + K *see* Wieden + Kennedy.
W de Argentina–Inversiones S.L., **63** 377
W.A. Whitney Company, **53** 353–56
W. Atlee Burpee & Co., **27** 505–08
W.B Doner & Co., **56** 369–72
W.B. Saunders Co., **IV** 623–24
W.C. Bradley Co., **69** 363–65
W.C.G. Sports Industries Ltd. *see* Canstar Sports Inc.
W.E. Dillon Company, Ltd., **21** 499
W.F. Kaiser, **60** 364
W.F. Linton Company, *see* Newell Rubbermaid Inc.
W.G. Yates & Sons Construction Company *see* The Yates Companies, Inc.
W.H. Brady Co., **16** 518–21 *see also* Brady Corp.
W. H. Braum, Inc., **80** 407–10
W.H. Gunlocke Chair Co. *see* Gunlocke Co.
W.H. Smith & Son (Alacra) Ltd., **15** 473
W H Smith Group PLC, **V** 211–13
W Jordan (Cereals) Ltd., **74** 382–84
W.L. Gore & Associates, Inc., **14** 538–40; **60** 321–24 (upd.)
W.M. Bassett Furniture Co. *see* Bassett Furniture Industries, Inc.
W.P. Carey & Co. LLC, **49** 446–48
W.R. Berkley Corporation, **15** 525–27; **74** 385–88 (upd.)
W.R. Case & Sons Cutlery Company *see* Zippo Manufacturing Co.
W.R. Grace & Company, **I** 547–50; **50** 522–29 (upd.)
W.S. Barstow & Company, **6** 575
W.W. Grainger, Inc., **V** 214–15; **26** 537–39 (upd.); **68** 392–95 (upd.)
W.W. Norton & Company, Inc., **28** 518–20
Waban Inc., **13** 547–49 *see also* HomeBase, Inc.
Wabash National Corp., **13** 550–52
Wabash Valley Power Association, **6** 556
Wabtec Corporation, **40** 451–54
Wachbrit Insurance Agency, **21** 96
Wachovia Bank of Georgia, N.A., **16** 521–23
Wachovia Bank of South Carolina, N.A., **16** 524–26
Wachovia Corporation, **12** 516–20; **46** 442–49 (upd.)
Wachtell, Lipton, Rosen & Katz, **47** 435–38
The Wackenhut Corporation, **14** 541–45; **63** 423–26 (upd.)
Wacker-Chemie GmbH, **35** 454–58
Wacker Construction Equipment AG, **95** 438–41

Wacker Oil Inc., *see* Seagull Energy Corp.
Wacoal Corp., **25** 520–24
Waddell & Reed, Inc., **22** 540–43
Wade Smith, **28** 27, 30
Wadsworth Inc., *see* The Thomspn Corp.
WaferTech, **18** 20; **43** 17; **47** 385
Waffle House Inc., **14** 544–45; **60** 325–27 (upd.)
Wagers Inc. (Idaho Candy Company), **86** 416–19
Waggener Edstrom, **42** 424–26
Wagner Castings Company, **16** 474–75
Wagon plc, **92** 407–10
Wagonlit Travel, *see* Carlson Wagonlit Travel.
Wagons-Lits, **27** 11; **29** 443; **37** 250–52
Wah Chang, **82** 415–18
Waha Oil Company *see* National Oil Corp.
Wahl Clipper Corporation, **86** 420–23
AB Wahlbecks, **25** 464
Waitrose Ltd. *see* John Lewis Partnership plc.
Wakefern Food Corporation, **33** 434–37
Wako Shoji Co. Ltd. *see* Wacoal Corp.
Wal-Mart de Mexico, S.A. de C.V., **35** 459–61 (upd.)
Wal-Mart Stores, Inc., **V** 216–17; **8** 555–57 (upd.); **26** 522–26 (upd.); **63** 427–32 (upd.)
Walbridge Aldinger Co., **38** 480–82
Walbro Corporation, **13** 553–55
Walchenseewerk AG, **23** 44
Waldbaum, Inc., **19** 479–81
Waldenbooks, **17** 522–24; **86** 424–28 (upd.)
Waldorf Corporation, **59** 350
Walgreen Co., **V** 218–20; **20** 511–13 (upd.); **65** 352–56 (upd.)
Walk Haydel & Associates, Inc., **25** 130
Walk Softly, Inc., **25** 118
Walker Dickson Group Limited, **26** 363
Walker Digital, **57** 296–98
Walker Manufacturing Company, **19** 482–84
Walkers Shortbread Ltd., **79** 464–67
Walkers Snack Foods Ltd., **70** 350–52
Wall Drug Store, Inc., **40** 455–57
Wall Street Deli, Inc., **33** 438–41
Wallace & Tiernan Group, **11** 361; **52** 374
The Wallace Berrie Company *see* Applause Inc.
Wallace Computer Services, Inc., **36** 507–10
Wallace International Silversmiths, *see* Syratech Corp.
Wallin & Nordstrom *see* Nordstrom, Inc.
Wallis *see* Sears plc.
Wallis Arnold Enterprises, Inc., **21** 483
Wallis Tractor Company, **21** 502
Walnut Capital Partners, **62** 46–47
Walrus, Inc., *see* Recreational Equipment, Inc.
Walsworth Publishing Company, Inc., **78** 445–48

The Walt Disney Company, II 172–74;
6 174–77 (upd.); 30 487–91 (upd.);
63 433–38 (upd.)
Walter Bau, *see* Eiffage.
Walter Herzog GmbH, *see* Varlen Corp.
Walter Industries, Inc., III 765–67; 22
544–47 (upd.); 72 368–73 (upd.)
Walter Kidde & Co., **73** 208
Walter Wilson, **49** 18
Walter Wright Mammoet, **26** 280
Walton Monroe Mills, Inc., 8 558–60
see also Avondale Industries.
WaMu *see* Washington Mutual, Inc.
Wanadoo S.A., 75 400–02
Wang Global, **39** 176–78
Wang Laboratories, Inc., III 168–70; 6
284–87 (upd.) *see also* Getronics NV.
WAP, **26** 420
Warbasse-Cogeneration Technologies
Partnership, **35** 479
Warburg Pincus, **14** 42; **61** 403; **73** 138
Warburg USB, **38** 291
Warburtons Ltd., 89 487–90
Ward's Communications, **22** 441
Wards *see* Circuit City Stores, Inc.
Waremart *see* WinCo Foods.
WARF *see* Wisconsin Alumni Research
Foundation.
Warman International *see* Weir Group
PLC.
The Warnaco Group Inc., 12 521–23;
46 450–54 (upd.) *see also* Authentic
Fitness Corp.
Warner Chilcott Limited, 85 446–49
Warner Communications Inc., II
175–77 *see also* AOL Time Warner Inc.
Warner Electric, **58** 67
Warner-Lambert Co., I 710–12; **10**
549–52 (upd.) *see also* Pfizer Inc.
Warner Music Group Corporation, 90
432–37 (upd.)
Warner Roadshow Film Distributors
Greece SA, **58** 359
Warners' Stellian Inc., 67 384–87
Warrantech Corporation, 53 357–59
Warrell Corporation, 68 396–98
Warren Apparel Group Ltd., **39** 257
Warren Bancorp Inc., **55** 52
Warren Frozen Foods, Inc., **61** 174
Warren, Gorham & Lamont, *see* The
Thomson Corp.
Warren Petroleum, *see* Dynegy Inc.
Warrick Industries, **31** 338
Warrington Products Ltd. *see* Canstar
Sports Inc.
Warwick International Ltd., *see* Sequa
Corp.
Warwick Valley Telephone Company, 55
382–84
Wasatch Gas Co., **6** 568
Wascana Energy Inc., 13 556–58
Washburn Graphics Inc., **23** 100
The Washington Companies, 33 442–45
Washington Federal, Inc., 17 525–27
Washington Football, Inc., 35 462–65
Washington Gas Light Company, 19
485–88
Washington Inventory Service, **30** 239

Washington Mutual, Inc., 17 528–31;
93 483–89 (upd.)
Washington National Corporation, 12
524–26
Washington Natural Gas Company, 9
539–41 *see also* Puget Sound Energy
Inc.
The Washington Post Company, IV
688–90; **20** 515–18 (upd.)
Washington Public Power Supply System,
50 102
Washington Railway and Electric
Company, **6** 552–53
Washington Scientific Industries, Inc.,
17 532–34
Washington Sports Clubs *see* Town Sports
International, Inc.
Washington Steel Corp., *see* Lukens Inc.
Washington Water Power Company, 6
595–98 *see also* Avista Corp.
Washtenaw Gas Company *see* MCN
Corp.
Wassall Plc, 18 548–50
Waste Connections, Inc., 46 455–57
Waste Control Specialists LLC, *see* alhi,
Inc.
Waste Holdings, Inc., 41 413–15
Waste Management, Inc., V 752–54
Water Pik Technologies, Inc., 34
498–501; **83** 450–453 (upd.)
The Waterbury Companies, *see* Talley
Industries, Inc.
Waterford Foods Plc, **59** 206
Waterford Wedgwood plc, 12 527–29;
34 493–97 (upd.)
Waterhouse Investor Services, Inc., 18
551–53
Waterman Marine Corporation, *see*
International Shipholding Corporation,
Inc.
The Waterman Pen Company *see* BIC
Corp.
Watermark Paddlesports Inc., **76** 119
Waterpark Management Inc., **73** 231
WaterPro Supplies Corporation *see* Eastern
Enterprises.
Waters Corporation, 43 453–57
Waterstone's, **42** 444 *see also* HMV
Group plc.
Watkins-Johnson Company, 15 528–30
Watsco Inc., 52 397–400
Watson & Philip *see* Alldays plc.
Watson Group, **55** 52
Watson-Haas Lumber Company, **33** 257
Watson-Marlow Bredel, **59** 384
Watson Pharmaceuticals Inc., 16
527–29; **56** 373–76 (upd.)
Watson Wyatt Worldwide, 42 427–30
Watt & Shand, **16** 61; **50** 107
Watt AG, **6** 491
The Watt Stopper, **21** 348, 350
Wattie Industries, **52** 141
Wattie's Ltd., 7 576–78
Watts Industries, Inc., 19 489–91
Watts of Lydney Group Ltd., 71 391–93
Watts/Silverstein, Inc., **24** 96
Waukesha Engine Servicenter, **6** 441

Wausau Sulphate Fibre Co. *see* Mosinee
Paper Corp.
Wausau-Mosinee Paper Corporation, 60
328–31 (upd.)
Waverly, Inc., 16 530–32
Waverly Pharmaceutical Limited, **11** 208
Wawa Inc., 17 535–37; **78** 449–52
(upd.)
**The Wawanesa Mutual Insurance
Company, 68** 399–401
Waxman Industries, Inc., 9 542–44
Wayfinder Group Inc., **51** 265
Waymaker Oy, **55** 289
Wayne Home Equipment *see* Scott Fetzer
Co.
WAZ Media Group, 82 419–24
WB *see* Warner Communications Inc.
WBI Holdings, Inc., **42** 249, 253
WCI Holdings Corporation, V 223; **41**
94
WCM Beteiligungs- und Grundbesitz
AG, **58** 202, 205
WCPS Direct, Inc., **53** 359
WCRS Group plc *see* Aegis Group plc.
WD-40 Company, 18 554–57; **87**
455–460 (upd.)
We Energies *see* Wisconsin Energy Corp.
WearGuard, *see* Aramark Corp.
The Weather Channel Companies, 52
401–04 *see also* Landmark
Communications, Inc.
Weatherford International, Inc., 39
416–18
Weaver Popcorn Company, Inc., 89
491–93
Webb Corbett and Beswick, **38** 402
Webber Oil Company, 61 384–86
WeBco International LLC, **26** 530
Webco Securities, Inc., **37** 225
Weber, **16** 488
Weber Aircraft Inc., **41** 369
Weber et Broutin France, 66 363–65
Weber Metal, **30** 283–84
Weber-Stephen Products Co., 40
458–60
WebEx Communications, Inc., 81
419–23
WebLogic Inc., **36** 81
WebMD Corporation, 65 357–60
WebTrends Corporation, **76** 189
Webvan Group Inc., **38** 223
Weddingpages, Inc. *see* The Knot, Inc.
Wedgwood *see* Waterford Wedgewood
Holdings PLC.
Weeres Industries Corporation, 52
405–07
Weetabix Limited, 61 387–89
Weg S.A., 78 453–56
Wegener NV, 53 360–62
Wegert Verwaltungs-GmbH and Co.
Beteiligungs-KG, **24** 270
Wegmans Food Markets, Inc., 9
545–46; **41** 416–18 (upd.)
Weichenwerk Brandenburg GmbH, **53**
352
Weider Health and Fitness, Inc., **38** 238
Weider Nutrition International, Inc., 29
498–501

Oy Wilh. Schauman AB *see* UPM-Kymmene

Wilh. Wilhelmsen ASA, 94 459–62

Wilhelm Karmann GmbH, 94 463–68

Wilhelm Weber GmbH, 22 95

Wilhelm Wilhelmsen Ltd., 7 40; 41 42

Wilkinson Hardware Stores Ltd., 80 416–18

Wilkinson Sword Ltd., 60 349–52

Willamette Falls Electric Company *see* Portland General Corp.

Willamette Industries, Inc., IV 357–59; 31 465–68 (upd.) *see also* Weyerhaeuser Co.

Willamette Valley Vineyards, Inc., 85 465–69

Willbros Group, Inc., 56 381–83

Willcox & Gibbs Sewing Machine Co., 15 384

Willey Brothers, Inc. *see* BrandPartners Group, Inc.

William Benton Foundation, *see* Encyclopaedia Britannica, Inc.

The William Brooks Shoe Company *see* Rocky Shoes & Boots, Inc.

William Byrd Press Inc., 23 100

William Cory & Son Ltd., 6 417

William Esty Company, 16 72

William George Company, 32 519

William Grant & Sons Ltd., 60 353–55

William Hewlett, 41 117

William Hill Organization Limited, 49 449–52

William Hodges & Company, 33 150

William Hollins & Company Ltd., 44 105

William L. Bonnell Company, Inc., 66 372–74

William Lyon Homes, 59 420–22

William Morris Agency, Inc., 23 512–14

William P. Young Contruction, 43 400

William Penn Life Insurance Company of New York, *see* Legal & General Group plc.

William Reed Publishing Ltd., 78 467–70

William Underwood Co., *see* Pet Inc.

William Zinsser & Company, Inc., 58 365–67

Williams & Connolly LLP, 47 445–48

Williams & Wilkins *see* Waverly, Inc.

Williams Advanced Materials Inc., *see* Brush Wellman Inc.

Williams Communications Group, Inc., 34 507–10

The Williams Companies, Inc., IV 575–76; 31 469–72 (upd.)

Williams Electronics Games, Inc., 15 539

The Williams Manufacturing Company, *see* Escalade, Inc.

Williams/Nintendo Inc., 15 537

Williams Oil-O-Matic Heating Corporation, 21 42

Williams plc, 44 255

Williams Printing Company *see* Graphic Industries Inc.

Williams Scotsman, Inc., 65 361–64

Williams-Sonoma, Inc., 17 548–50; 44 447–50 (upd.)

Williamsburg Restoration, Incorporated, 53 106

Williamson-Dickie Manufacturing Company, 14 549–50; 45 438–41 (upd.)

Williamsport Barber and Beauty Corp., 60 287

Willie G's, 15 279

Willis Corroon Group plc, 25 537–39

Willis Group Holdings Ltd., 73 36

Willis Stein & Partners, 21 404; 58 318, 321; 73 397

Williston Basin Interstate Pipeline Company, *see* MDU Resources Group, Inc.; WBI Holdings, Inc.

Willkie Farr & Gallagher LLPLP, 95 450–53

Wilmington Trust Corporation, 25 540–43

Wilsdorf & Davis, *see* Montres Rolcx S.A.

Wilshire Real Estate Investment Trust Inc., 30 223

Wilshire Restaurant Group Inc., 28 258

Wilson Bowden Plc, 45 442–44

Wilson Brothers, *see* Triarc Companies, Inc.

Wilson Foods Corp., *see* Doskocil Companies, Inc.

Wilson Greatbatch Technologies Ltd *see* Greatbatch Inc.

Wilson Jones Company, 7 4–5

Wilson Sonsini Goodrich & Rosati, 34 511–13

Wilson Sporting Goods Company, 24 530–32; 84 431–436 (upd.)

Wilson's Supermarkets, *see* Hannaford Bros. Co.

Wilsons The Leather Experts Inc., 21 525–27; 58 368–71 (upd.)

Wimbledon Tennis Championships *see* The All England Lawn Tennis & Croquet Club.

Win-Chance Foods, *see* H.J. Heinz Co.

Winbond Electronics Corporation, 74 389–91

Wincanton plc, 52 418–20

Winchell's Donut Houses Operating Company, L.P., 60 356–59

WinCo Foods Inc., 60 360–63

Wincor Nixdorf Holding GmbH, 69 370–73 (upd.)

Wind River Systems, Inc., 37 419–22

Windmere Corporation, 16 537–39 *see also* Applica Inc.

Windmere-Durable Holdings, Inc., 30 404

WindowVisions, Inc., 29 288

Windsong Exports, 52 429

Windsor Forestry Tools, Inc., 48 59

Windstar Sail Cruises *see* Carnival Corp.

Windstream Corporation, 83 462-465

Windsurfing International, 23 55

Windswept Environmental Group, Inc., 62 389–92

Windward Capital Partners, 28 152, 154

The Wine Group, Inc., 39 419–21

Winegard Company, 56 384–87

Winfire, Inc., 37 194

Wingate Partners, *see* United Stationers Inc.

Winget Ltd. *see* Seddon Group Ltd.

Wings & Wheels Express, Inc., *see* Air Express International Corp.

WingspanBank.com, 38 270

Winkelman Stores, Inc., *see* Petrie Stores Corp.

Winlet Fashions, 22 223

Winmark Corporation, 74 392–95

Winn-Dixie Stores, Inc., II 683–84; 21 528–30 (upd.); 59 423–27 (upd.)

Winnebago Industries Inc., 7 589–91; 27 509–12 (upd.)

Winners Apparel Ltd. *see* The TJX Companies, Inc.

Winning International, 21 403

WinsLoew Furniture, Inc., 21 531–33 *see also* Brown Jordan International Inc.

Winston & Strawn, 35 470–73

Winston Furniture Company, Inc., 21 531–33

Winter Hill Frozen Foods and Services, 55 82

WinterBrook Corp., 26 326

Winterflood Securities Limited, 39 89, 91

Wintershall AG, IV 485; 38 408

Winterthur Group, III 402–04; 68 402–05 (upd.)

Winyah Concrete & Block, 50 49

Wipro Limited, 43 465–68

Wire and Plastic Products PLC *see* WPP Group PLC.

Wireless Hong Kong *see* Hong Kong Telecommunications Ltd.

Wireless Management Company, 11 12

The Wiremold Company, 81 428–34

Wiretel, 76 326–27

Wiron Prefabricados Modulares, S.A., 65 363

Wirtz Corporation, 72 374–76

Wisconsin Alumni Research Foundation, 65 365–68

Wisconsin Bell, Inc., 14 551–53 *see also* AT&T Corp.

Wisconsin Central Transportation Corporation, 24 533–36

Wisconsin Dairies, 7 592–93

Wisconsin Energy Corporation, 6 601–03; 54 417–21 (upd.)

Wisconsin Gas Company, 17 22–23

Wisconsin Power and Light, 22 13; 39 260

Wisconsin Public Service Corporation, 9 553–54 *see also* WPS Resources Corp.

Wisconsin Steel, *see* Envirodyne Industries, Inc.

Wisconsin Wire and Steel, *see* FinishMaster, Inc.; Maxco Inc.

Wise Foods, Inc., 79 468–71

Wise Solutions, Inc. *see* Altiris, Inc.

Wispark Corporation, 6 601, 603

Wistron Corporation *see* Acer Inc.

Wisvest Corporation, 6 601, 603

WiSys Technology Foundation, 65 367

Zayre Corp., *see* The TJX Companies, Inc.
ZCE Platinum, **63** 40
ZCMI *see* Zion's Cooperative Mercantile Institution.
ZDF, **41** 28–29
ZDNet, **36** 523
Zealand Mines S.A., **23** 41
Zebco Corp. *see* W.C. Bradley Co.
Zebra Technologies Corporation, **14** 569–71; **53** 371–74 (upd.)
Zecco, Inc., **6** 441
Zed Group, **93** 498–501
Zee Medical, Inc., **47** 235
ZeFer, **63** 151
Zell Bros., *see* Zale Corp.
Zellers *see* Hudson's Bay Co.
Zellstoff-und Papierfabrik Rosenthal Gmbh & Co KG., **64** 275
Zeneca Group PLC, **21** 544–46 *see also* AstraZeneca PLC.
Zengine, Inc., **41** 258–59
Zenit Bank, **45** 322
Zenith Data Systems, Inc., **10** 563–65
Zenith Electronics Corporation, **II** 123–25; **13** 572–75 (upd.); **34** 514–19 (upd.); **89** 494–502 (upd.)
Zenith Media, **42** 330–31
Zentralsparkasse und Kommerzialbank Wien, **23** 37
Zentronics, **19** 313
Zep Manufacturing Company, **54** 252, 254
Zeppelin Luftschifftechnik GmbH, **48** 450
Zerex, **50** 48
Zergo Holdings, **42** 24–25
ZERO Corporation, **17** 563–65; **88** 443–47 (upd.)
Zero First Co Ltd., **62** 245
Zero Plus Dialing, Inc. *see* Billing Concepts Corp.

Zetor s.p., **21** 175
Zeus Components, Inc., *see* Arrow Electronics, Inc.
Zexel Valeo Compressor USA Inc. *see* Valeo.
ZF Friedrichshafen AG, **48** 447–51
Zhenjiang Zhengmao Hitachi Zosen Machinery Co. Ltd., **53** 173
Zhong Yue Highsonic Electron Company, **62** 150
Zhongbei Building Material Products Company, **26** 510
Zhongde Brewery, **49** 417
Zicam LLC *see* Matrixx Initiatives, Inc.
Ziebart International Corporation, **30** 499–501; **66** 379–82 (upd.)
The Ziegler Companies, Inc., **24** 541–45; **63** 442–48 (upd.)
Ziff Davis Media Inc., **12** 560–63; **36** 521–26 (upd.); **73** 397–403 (upd.)
Zignago Vetro S.p.A., **67** 210–12
Zila, Inc., **46** 466–69
Zildjian *see* Avedis Zildjian Co.
Zilkha & Company, **12** 72
ZiLOG, Inc., **15** 543–45; **72** 377–80 (upd.)
Zimmer Holdings, Inc., **45** 455–57
Zinc Products Company, **30** 39
Zindart Ltd., **60** 370–72
Zingerman's Community of Businesses, **68** 406–08
Zinifex Ltd., **85** 474–77
Zinsser *see* William Zinsser & Company, Inc.
Zio's Italian Kitchens *see* Mazzio's Corp.
Zion Foods, **23** 408
Zion's Cooperative Mercantile Institution, **33** 471–74
Zions Bancorporation, **12** 564–66; **53** 375–78 (upd.)
Zipcar, Inc., **92** 429–32

Zippo Manufacturing Company, **18** 565–68; **71** 394–99 (upd.)
Zipps Drive-Thru, Inc., *see* Rally's.
Zodiac S.A., **36** 527–30
Zolfo Cooper LLC, **57** 219
Zoll Foods, **55** 366
Zoloto Mining Ltd., **38** 231
Zoltek Companies, Inc., **37** 427–30
Zomba Records Ltd., **52** 428–31
Zondervan Corporation, **24** 546–49; **71** 400–04 (upd.)
Zones, Inc., **67** 395–97
Zoom Technologies, Inc., **18** 569–71; **53** 379–82 (upd.)
Zoran Corporation, **77** 489–92
Zotos International, Inc., *see* Shiseido Company, Ltd.
ZPT Radom, **23** 427
Zuari Cement, **40** 107, 109
Zuellig Group N.A., Inc., **46** 226
Zuffa L.L.C., **89** 503–07
Zuivelcooperatie De Seven Provincien UA, **59** 194
Zuka Juice, **47** 201
Zumiez, Inc., **77** 493–96
Zumtobel AG, **50** 544–48
Zurich Financial Services, **III** 410–12; **42** 448–53 (upd.); **93** 502–10 (upd.)
Zurich Insurance Group, **15** 257
Zvezda Design Bureau, **61** 197
Zweckform Büro-Produkte G.m.b.H., **49** 38
Zycad Corp., **11** 489–91; **69** 340–41
Zycon Corporation, *see* Hadco Corp.
Zygo Corporation, **42** 454–57
ZymoGenetics Inc., **61** 266
Zytec Corporation, **19** 513–15 *see also* Artesyn Technologies Inc.

Index to Industries

Aerospace

Airlines

Beverages

Bio-Technology

Chemicals

Conglomerates

Construction

Containers

Viatech Continental Can Company, Inc., 25 (upd.)
Vidrala S.A., 67
Vitro Corporativo S.A. de C.V., 34

Drugs & Pharmaceuticals

A. Nelson & Co. Ltd., 75
A.L. Pharma Inc., 12
Abbott Laboratories, I; 11 (upd.); 40 (upd.); 93 (upd.)
Actelion Ltd., 83
Akorn, Inc., 32
Albany Molecular Research, Inc., 77
Allergan, Inc., 77 (upd.)
Alpharma Inc., 35 (upd.)
ALZA Corporation, 10; 36 (upd.)
American Home Products, I; 10 (upd.)
American Oriental Bioengineering Inc., 93
American Pharmaceutical Partners, Inc., 69
AmerisourceBergen Corporation, 64 (upd.)
Amersham PLC, 50
Amgen, Inc., 10; 89 (upd.)
Amylin Pharmaceuticals, Inc., 67
Andrx Corporation, 55
AstraZeneca PLC, I; 20 (upd.); 50 (upd.)
Axcan Pharma Inc., 85
Barr Pharmaceuticals, Inc., 26; 68 (upd.)
Bayer A.G., I; 13 (upd.)
Berlex Laboratories, Inc., 66
Biovail Corporation, 47
Block Drug Company, Inc., 8
Boiron S.A., 73
Bristol-Myers Squibb Company, III; 9 (upd.); 37 (upd.)
BTG Plc, 87
C.H. Boehringer Sohn, 39
Caremark Rx, Inc., 10; 54 (upd.)
Carter-Wallace, Inc., 8; 38 (upd.)
Celgene Corporation, 67
Cephalon, Inc., 45
Chiron Corporation, 10
Chugai Pharmaceutical Co., Ltd., 50
Ciba-Geigy Ltd., I; 8 (upd.)
D&K Wholesale Drug, Inc., 14
Discovery Partners International, Inc., 58
Dr. Reddy's Laboratories Ltd., 59
Elan Corporation PLC, 63
Eli Lilly and Company, I; 11 (upd.); 47 (upd.)
Endo Pharmaceuticals Holdings Inc., 71
Eon Labs, Inc., 67
Express Scripts Inc., 44 (upd.)
F. Hoffmann-La Roche Ltd., I; 50 (upd.)
Fisons plc, 9; 23 (upd.)
Forest Laboratories, Inc., 52 (upd.)
FoxMeyer Health Corporation, 16
Fujisawa Pharmaceutical Company Ltd., I
G.D. Searle & Co., I; 12 (upd.); 34 (upd.)
Galenica AG, 84
GEHE AG, 27
Genentech, Inc., I; 8 (upd.); 75 (upd.)
Genetics Institute, Inc., 8
Genzyme Corporation, 13, 77 (upd.)
Glaxo Holdings PLC, I; 9 (upd.)
GlaxoSmithKline plc, 46 (upd.)

Groupe Fournier SA, 44
Groupe Léa Nature, 88
H. Lundbeck A/S, 44
Hauser, Inc., 46
Heska Corporation, 39
Hexal AG, 69
Hospira, Inc., 71
Huntingdon Life Sciences Group plc, 42
ICN Pharmaceuticals, Inc., 52
Immucor, Inc., 81
Integrated BioPharma, Inc., 83
IVAX Corporation, 55 (upd.)
Janssen Pharmaceutica N.V., 80
Johnson & Johnson, III; 8 (upd.)
Jones Medical Industries, Inc., 24
The Judge Group, Inc., 51
King Pharmaceuticals, Inc., 54
Kinray Inc., 85
Kos Pharmaceuticals, Inc., 63
Kyowa Hakko Kogyo Co., Ltd., 48 (upd.)
Laboratoires Arkopharma S.A., 75
Leiner Health Products Inc., 34
Ligand Pharmaceuticals Incorporated, 47
MannKind Corporation, 87
Marion Merrell Dow, Inc., I; 9 (upd.)
Matrixx Initiatives, Inc., 74
McKesson Corporation, 12; 47 (upd.)
Medicis Pharmaceutical Corporation, 59
MedImmune, Inc., 35
Merck & Co., Inc., I; 11 (upd.); 34 (upd.); 95 (upd.)
Merz Group, 81
Miles Laboratories, I
Millennium Pharmaceuticals, Inc., 47
Monsanto Company, 29 (upd.), 77 (upd.)
Moore Medical Corp., 17
Murdock Madaus Schwabe, 26
Mylan Laboratories Inc., I; 20 (upd.); 59 (upd.)
Myriad Genetics, Inc., 95
Nadro S.A. de C.V., 86
Nastech Pharmaceutical Company Inc., 79
National Patent Development Corporation, 13
Natrol, Inc., 49
Natural Alternatives International, Inc., 49
Nektar Therapeutics, 91
Novartis AG, 39 (upd.)
Noven Pharmaceuticals, Inc., 55
Novo Nordisk A/S, I; 61 (upd.)
Obagi Medical Products, Inc., 95
Omnicare, Inc., 49
Omrix Biopharmaceuticals, Inc., 95
Par Pharmaceutical Companies, Inc., 65
PDL BioPharma, Inc., 90
Perrigo Company, 59 (upd.)
Pfizer Inc., I; 9 (upd.); 38 (upd.); 79 (upd.)
Pharmacia & Upjohn Inc., I; 25 (upd.)
Pharmion Corporation, 91
PLIVA d.d., 70
PolyMedica Corporation, 77
POZEN Inc., 81
The Quigley Corporation, 62
Quintiles Transnational Corporation, 21
R.P. Scherer, I
Ranbaxy Laboratories Ltd., 70

ratiopharm Group, 84
Reckitt Benckiser plc, II; 42 (upd.); 91 (upd.)
Roberts Pharmaceutical Corporation, 16
Roche Bioscience, 14 (upd.)
Rorer Group, I
Roussel Uclaf, I; 8 (upd.)
Salix Pharmaceuticals, Ltd., 93
Sandoz Ltd., I
Sankyo Company, Ltd., I; 56 (upd.)
The Sanofi-Synthélabo Group, I; 49 (upd.)
Schering AG, I; 50 (upd.)
Schering-Plough Corporation, I; 14 (upd.); 49 (upd.)
Sepracor Inc., 45
Serono S.A., 47
Shionogi & Co., Ltd., 17 (upd.)
Sigma-Aldrich Corporation, I; 36 (upd.); 93 (upd.)
SmithKline Beecham plc, I; 32 (upd.)
Solvay S.A., 61 (upd.)
Squibb Corporation, I
Sterling Drug, Inc., I
Stiefel Laboratories, Inc., 90
Sun Pharmaceutical Industries Ltd., 57
The Sunrider Corporation, 26
Syntex Corporation, I
Takeda Chemical Industries, Ltd., I
Taro Pharmaceutical Industries Ltd., 65
Teva Pharmaceutical Industries Ltd., 22; 54 (upd.)
The Upjohn Company, I; 8 (upd.)
Vertex Pharmaceuticals Incorporated, 83
Virbac Corporation, 74
Vitalink Pharmacy Services, Inc., 15
Warner Chilcott Limited, 85
Warner-Lambert Co., I; 10 (upd.)
Watson Pharmaceuticals Inc., 16; 56 (upd.)
The Wellcome Foundation Ltd., I
Zila, Inc., 46

Electrical & Electronics

ABB ASEA Brown Boveri Ltd., II; 22 (upd.)
ABB Ltd., 65 (upd.)
Acer Incorporated, 16; 73 (upd.)
Acuson Corporation, 10; 36 (upd.)
ADC Telecommunications, Inc., 30 (upd.)
Adtran Inc., 22
Advanced Micro Devices, Inc., 30 (upd.)
Advanced Technology Laboratories, Inc., 9
Agere Systems Inc., 61
Agilent Technologies Inc., 38; 93 (upd.)
Agilysys Inc., 76 (upd.)
Aiwa Co., Ltd., 30
AKG Acoustics GmbH, 62
Akzo Nobel N.V., 13; 41 (upd.)
Alienware Corporation, 81
Alliant Techsystems Inc., 30 (upd.); 77 (upd.)
AlliedSignal Inc., 22 (upd.)
Alpine Electronics, Inc., 13
Alps Electric Co., Ltd., II
Altera Corporation, 18; 43 (upd.)
Altron Incorporated, 20
Amdahl Corporation, 40 (upd.)

American Power Conversion Corporation, 24; 67 (upd.)
American Technical Ceramics Corp., 67
Amkor Technology, Inc., 69
AMP Incorporated, II; 14 (upd.)
Amphenol Corporation, 40
Amstrad plc, 48 (upd.)
Analog Devices, Inc., 10
Analogic Corporation, 23
Anam Group, 23
Anaren Microwave, Inc., 33
Andrew Corporation, 10; 32 (upd.)
Anixter International Inc., 88
Anritsu Corporation, 68
Apex Digital, Inc., 63
Apple Computer, Inc., 36 (upd.); 77 (upd.)
Applied Power Inc., 32 (upd.)
Applied Signal Technology, Inc., 87
Argon ST, Inc., 81
Arotech Corporation, 93
ARRIS Group, Inc., 89
Arrow Electronics, Inc., 10; 50 (upd.)
Ascend Communications, Inc., 24
Astronics Corporation, 35
Atari Corporation, 9; 23 (upd.); 66 (upd.)
ATI Technologies Inc., 79
Atmel Corporation, 17
ATMI, Inc., 93
AU Optronics Corporation, 67
Audiovox Corporation, 34; 90 (upd.)
Ault Incorporated, 34
Autodesk, Inc., 10; 89 (upd.)
Avnet Inc., 9
AVX Corporation, 67
Axcelis Technologies, Inc., 95
Axsys Technologies, Inc., 93
Ballard Power Systems Inc., 73
Bang & Olufsen Holding A/S, 37; 86 (upd.)
Barco NV, 44
Bell Microproducts Inc., 69
Benchmark Electronics, Inc., 40
Bicoastal Corporation, II
Blonder Tongue Laboratories, Inc., 48
Blue Coat Systems, Inc., 83
BMC Industries, Inc., 59 (upd.)
Bogen Communications International, Inc., 62
Bosc Corporation, 13; 36 (upd.)
Boston Acoustics, Inc., 22
Bowthorpe plc, 33
Braun GmbH, 51
Broadcom Corporation, 34; 90 (upd.)
Bull S.A., 43 (upd.)
Burr-Brown Corporation, 19
BVR Systems (1998) Ltd., 93
C-COR.net Corp., 38
Cabletron Systems, Inc., 10
Cadence Design Systems, Inc., 48 (upd.)
Cambridge SoundWorks, Inc., 48
Canon Inc., 18 (upd.); 79 (upd.)
Carbone Lorraine S.A., 33
Cardtronics, Inc., 93
Carl Zeiss AG, III; 34 (upd.); 91 (upd.)
Cash Systems, Inc., 93
CASIO Computer Co., Ltd., 16 (upd.); 40 (upd.)

CDW Computer Centers, Inc., 52 (upd.)
Celestica Inc., 80
Checkpoint Systems, Inc., 39
Chi Mei Optoelectronics Corporation, 75
Chubb, PLC, 50
Chunghwa Picture Tubes, Ltd., 75
Cirrus Logic, Inc., 48 (upd.)
Cisco Systems, Inc., 34 (upd.); 77 (upd.)
Citizen Watch Co., Ltd., III; 21 (upd.); 81 (upd.)
Clarion Company Ltd., 64
Cobham plc, 30
Cobra Electronics Corporation, 14
Coherent, Inc., 31
Cohu, Inc., 32
Color Kinetics Incorporated, 85
Compagnie Générale d'Électricité, II
Concurrent Computer Corporation, 75
Conexant Systems, Inc., 36
Cooper Industries, Inc., II
Cray Inc., 75 (upd.)
Cray Research, Inc., 16 (upd.)
Cree Inc., 53
CTS Corporation, 39
Cubic Corporation, 19
Cypress Semiconductor Corporation, 20; 48 (upd.)
D&H Distributing Co., 95
D-Link Corporation, 83
Dai Nippon Printing Co., Ltd., 57 (upd.)
Daiichikosho Company Ltd., 86
Daktronics, Inc., 32
Dallas Semiconductor Corporation, 13; 31 (upd.)
De La Rue plc, 34 (upd.)
Dell Computer Corporation, 31 (upd.)
DH Technology, Inc., 18
Dictaphone Healthcare Solutions 78
Diehl Stiftung & Co. KG, 79
Digi International Inc., 9
Diodes Incorporated, 81
Directed Electronics, Inc., 87
Discreet Logic Inc., 20
Dixons Group plc, 19 (upd.)
Dolby Laboratories Inc., 20
Dot Hill Systems Corp., 93
DRS Technologies, Inc., 58
Dynatech Corporation, 13
E-Systems, Inc., 9
Electronics for Imaging, Inc., 15; 43 (upd.)
Elma Electronic AG, 83
Elpida Memory, Inc., 83
Emerson, II; 46 (upd.)
Emerson Radio Corp., 30
ENCAD, Incorporated, 25
Equant N.V., 52
Equus Computer Systems, Inc., 49
ESS Technology, Inc., 22
Essex Corporation, 85
Everex Systems, Inc., 16
Exabyte Corporation, 40 (upd.)
Exar Corp., 14
Exide Electronics Group, Inc., 20
Finisar Corporation, 92
First Solar, Inc., 95
Fisk Corporation, 72
Flextronics International Ltd., 38

Fluke Corporation, 15
FormFactor, Inc., 85
Foxboro Company, 13
Freescale Semiconductor, Inc., 83
Frequency Electronics, Inc., 61
FuelCell Energy, Inc., 75
Fuji Electric Co., Ltd., II; 48 (upd.)
Fuji Photo Film Co., Ltd., 79 (upd.)
Fujitsu Limited, 16 (upd.); 42 (upd.)
Funai Electric Company Ltd., 62
Gateway, Inc., 63 (upd.)
General Atomics, 57
General Dynamics Corporation, I; 10 (upd.); 40 (upd.); 88 (upd.
General Electric Company, II; 12 (upd.)
General Electric Company, PLC, II
General Instrument Corporation, 10
General Signal Corporation, 9
Genesis Microchip Inc., 82
GenRad, Inc., 24
GM Hughes Electronics Corporation, II
Goldstar Co., Ltd., 12
Gould Electronics, Inc., 14
GPS Industries, Inc., 81
Grundig AG, 27
Guillemot Corporation, 41
Hadco Corporation, 24
Hamilton Beach/Proctor-Silex Inc., 17
Harman International Industries Inc., 15
Harris Corporation, II; 20 (upd.); 78 (upd.)
Hayes Corporation, 24
Herley Industries, Inc., 33
Hewlett-Packard Company, 28 (upd.); 50 (upd.)
Holophane Corporation, 19
Hon Hai Precision Industry Co., Ltd., 59
Honeywell Inc., II; 12 (upd.); 50 (upd.)
Hubbell Incorporated, 9; 31 (upd.)
Hughes Supply, Inc., 14
Hutchinson Technology Incorporated, 18; 63 (upd.)
Hypercom Corporation, 27
IDEO Inc., 65
IEC Electronics Corp., 42
Illumina, Inc., 93
Imax Corporation, 28
In Focus Systems, Inc., 22
Indigo NV, 26
InFocus Corporation, 92
Ingram Micro Inc., 52
Innovative Solutions & Support, Inc., 85
Integrated Defense Technologies, Inc., 54
Intel Corporation, II; 10 (upd.); 75 (upd.)
Intermec Technologies Corporation, 72
International Business Machines Corporation, III; 6 (upd.); 30 (upd.); 63 (upd.)
International Rectifier Corporation, 31; 71 (upd.)
Intersil Corporation, 93
Ionatron, Inc., 85
Itel Corporation, 9
Jabil Circuit, Inc., 36; 88 (upd.)
Jaco Electronics, Inc., 30
JDS Uniphase Corporation, 34
Johnson Controls, Inc., 59 (upd.)
Juno Lighting, Inc., 30

THOMSON multimedia S.A., II; 42
(upd.)
THQ, Inc., 92 (upd.)
The Titan Corporation, 36
TomTom N.V., 81
Tops Appliance City, Inc., 17
Toromont Industries, Ltd., 21
Trans-Lux Corporation, 51
Trimble Navigation Limited, 40
TriQuint Semiconductor, Inc., 63
Tweeter Home Entertainment Group,
Inc., 30
Ultimate Electronics, Inc., 69 (upd.)
Ultrak Inc., 24
Universal Electronics Inc., 39
Varian Associates Inc., 12
Veeco Instruments Inc., 32
VIASYS Healthcare, Inc., 52
Viasystems Group, Inc., 67
Vicon Industries, Inc., 44
Victor Company of Japan, Limited, II; 26
(upd.); 83 (upd.)
Vishay Intertechnology, Inc., 21; 80
(upd.)
Vitesse Semiconductor Corporation, 32
Vitro Corp., 10
VLSI Technology, Inc., 16
VTech Holdings Ltd., 77
Wells-Gardner Electronics Corporation,
43
Westinghouse Electric Corporation, II; 12
(upd.)
Winbond Electronics Corporation, 74
Wincor Nixdorf Holding GmbH, 69
(upd.)
Wyle Electronics, 14
Xerox Corporation, 69 (upd.)
Yageo Corporation, 16
York Research Corporation, 35
Zenith Data Systems, Inc., 10
Zenith Electronics Corporation, II; 13
(upd.); 34 (upd.); 89 (upd.)
Zoom Telephonics, Inc., 18
Zoran Corporation, 77
Zumtobel AG, 50
Zytec Corporation, 19

Engineering & Management Services

AAON, Inc., 22
Aavid Thermal Technologies, Inc., 29
AECOM Technology Corporation, 79
Alliant Techsystems Inc., 30 (upd.)
Altran Technologies, 51
Amey Plc, 47
American Science & Engineering, Inc., 81
Analytic Sciences Corporation, 10
Arcadis NV, 26
Arthur D. Little, Inc., 35
The Austin Company, 8; 72 (upd.)
Babcock International Group PLC, 69
Balfour Beatty plc, 36 (upd.)
BE&K, Inc., 73
Birse Group PLC, 77
Brown & Root, Inc., 13
Bufete Industrial, S.A. de C.V., 34
C.H. Heist Corporation, 24
CDI Corporation, 6; 54 (upd.)

CH2M Hill Ltd., 22
The Charles Stark Draper Laboratory,
Inc., 35
Coflexip S.A., 25
Corrections Corporation of America, 23
CRSS Inc., 6
Dames & Moore, Inc., 25
DAW Technologies, Inc., 25
Day & Zimmermann Inc., 9; 31 (upd.)
Donaldson Co. Inc., 16
Dycom Industries, Inc., 57
Edwards and Kelcey, 70
EG&G Incorporated, 8; 29 (upd.)
Eiffage, 27
Essef Corporation, 18
Exponent, Inc., 95
FKI Plc, 57
Fluor Corporation, 34 (upd.)
Forest City Enterprises, Inc., 52 (upd.)
Foster Wheeler Corporation, 6; 23 (upd.)
Foster Wheeler Ltd., 76 (upd.)
Framatome SA, 19
Fraport AG Frankfurt Airport Services
Worldwide, 90
Gale International Llc, 93
Georg Fischer AG Schaffhausen, 61
Gilbane, Inc., 34
Great Lakes Dredge & Dock Company,
69
Grupo Dragados SA, 55
Halliburton Company, 25 (upd.)
Harding Lawson Associates Group, Inc.,
16
Harza Engineering Company, 14
HDR Inc., 48
HOK Group, Inc., 59
ICF Kaiser International, Inc., 28
IHC Caland N.V., 71
Jacobs Engineering Group Inc., 6; 26
(upd.)
Jacques Whitford, 92
The Judge Group, Inc., 51
JWP Inc., 9
The Keith Companies Inc., 54
Keller Group PLC, 95
Klöckner-Werke AG, 58 (upd.)
Kvaerner ASA, 36
Layne Christensen Company, 19
The MacNeal-Schwendler Corporation, 25
Malcolm Pirnie, Inc., 42
McDermott International, Inc., 37 (upd.)
McKinsey & Company, Inc., 9
Michael Baker Corporation, 51 (upd.)
Nooter Corporation, 61
Oceaneering International, Inc., 63
Odebrecht S.A., 73
Ogden Corporation, 6
Opus Group, 34
PAREXEL International Corporation, 84
Parsons Brinckerhoff, Inc., 34
The Parsons Corporation, 8; 56 (upd.)
The PBSJ Corporation, 82
Petrofac Ltd., 95
Quanta Services, Inc., 79
RCM Technologies, Inc., 34
Renishaw plc, 46
Ricardo plc, 90
Rosemount Inc., 15

Roy F. Weston, Inc., 33
Royal Vopak NV, 41
Rust International Inc., 11
Sandia National Laboratories, 49
Sandvik AB, 32 (upd.)
Sarnoff Corporation, 57
Science Applications International
Corporation, 15
Serco Group plc, 47
Siegel & Gale, 64
Siemens AG, 57 (upd.)
SRI International, Inc., 57
SSOE Inc., 76
Stone & Webster, Inc., 13; 64 (upd.)
Sulzer Ltd., 68 (upd.)
Susquehanna Pfaltzgraff Company, 8
Sverdrup Corporation, 14
Tech-Sym Corporation, 44 (upd.)
Technip 78
Tetra Tech, Inc., 29
ThyssenKrupp AG, IV; 28 (upd.); 87
(upd.)
Towers Perrin, 32
Tracor Inc., 17
TRC Companies, Inc., 32
Underwriters Laboratories, Inc., 30
United Dominion Industries Limited, 8;
16 (upd.)
URS Corporation, 45; 80 (upd.)
U.S. Army Corps of Engineers, 91
VA TECH ELIN EBG GmbH, 49
VECO International, Inc., 7
Vinci, 43
The Weir Group PLC, 85
Willbros Group, Inc., 56
WS Atkins Plc, 45

Entertainment & Leisure

A&E Television Networks, 32
Aardman Animations Ltd., 61
ABC Family Worldwide, Inc., 52
Academy of Television Arts & Sciences,
Inc., 55
Acclaim Entertainment Inc., 24
Activision, Inc., 32; 89 (upd.)
AEI Music Network Inc., 35
Affinity Group Holding Inc., 56
Airtours Plc, 27
Alaska Railroad Corporation, 60
All American Communications Inc., 20
The All England Lawn Tennis & Croquet
Club, 54
Alliance Entertainment Corp., 17
Alternative Tentacles Records, 66
Alvin Ailey Dance Foundation, Inc., 52
Amblin Entertainment, 21
AMC Entertainment Inc., 12; 35 (upd.)
American Golf Corporation, 45
American Gramaphone LLC, 52
American Kennel Club, Inc., 74
American Skiing Company, 28
Ameristar Casinos, Inc., 33; 69 (upd.)
AMF Bowling, Inc., 40
Anaheim Angels Baseball Club, Inc., 53
Anchor Gaming, 24
AOL Time Warner Inc., 57 (upd.)
Applause Inc., 24
Apple Corps Ltd., 87

Financial Services: Banks

Financial Services: Excluding Banks

Food Products

Utz Quality Foods, Inc., 72
Van Camp Seafood Company, Inc., 7
Ventura Foods LLC, 90
Vestey Group Ltd., 95
Vienna Sausage Manufacturing Co., 14
Vilmorin Clause et Cie, 70
Vion Food Group NV, 85
Vista Bakery, Inc., 56
Vlasic Foods International Inc., 25
W Jordan (Cereals) Ltd., 74
Wagers Inc. (Idaho Candy Company), 86
Walkers Shortbread Ltd., 79
Walkers Snack Foods Ltd., 70
Warburtons Ltd., 89
Warrell Corporation, 68
Wattie's Ltd., 7
Weaver Popcorn Company, Inc., 89
Weetabix Limited, 61
Weis Markets, Inc., 84 (upd.)
Wells' Dairy, Inc., 36
Wenner Bread Products Inc., 80
White Lily Foods Company, 88
White Wave, 43
Wilbur Chocolate Company, 66
Wimm-Bill-Dann Foods, 48
Wisconsin Dairies, 7
Wise Foods, Inc., 79
WLR Foods, Inc., 21
Wm. B. Reily & Company Inc., 58
Wm. Wrigley Jr. Company, 7; 58 (upd.)
World's Finest Chocolate Inc., 39
Worthington Foods, Inc., 14
Yamazaki Baking Co., Ltd., 58
Yarnell Ice Cream Company, Inc., 92
Yeo Hiap Seng Malaysia Bhd., 75
YOCREAM International, Inc., 47
Young's Bluecrest Seafood Holdings Ltd., 81
Zacky Farms LLC, 74
Zatarain's, Inc., 64

Food Services & Retailers

A. F. Blakemore & Son Ltd., 90
Advantica Restaurant Group, Inc., 27 (upd.)
AFC Enterprises, Inc., 32 (upd.); 83 (upd.)
Affiliated Foods Inc., 53
Albertson's, Inc., II; 7 (upd.); 30 (upd.); 65 (upd.)
Aldi Einkauf GmbH & Co. OHG, 13; 86 (upd.)
Alex Lee Inc., 18; 44 (upd.)
Allen Foods, Inc., 60
Almacenes Exito S.A., 89
Alpha Airports Group PLC, 77
America's Favorite Chicken Company, Inc., 7
American Restaurant Partners, L.P., 93
American Stores Company, II
Andronico's Market, 70
Applebee's International, Inc., 14; 35 (upd.)
ARA Services, II
Arby's Inc., 14
Arden Group, Inc., 29
Argyll Group PLC, II
Ark Restaurants Corp., 20

Asahi Breweries, Ltd., 20 (upd.)
ASDA Group Ltd., II; 28 (upd.); 64 (upd.)
Associated Grocers, Incorporated, 9; 31 (upd.)
Association des Centres Distributeurs E. Leclerc, 37
Atlanta Bread Company International, Inc., 70
Au Bon Pain Co., Inc., 18
Auchan, 37
Auntie Anne's, Inc., 35
Autogrill SpA, 49
Avado Brands, Inc., 31
B.R. Guest Inc., 87
Back Bay Restaurant Group, Inc., 20
Back Yard Burgers, Inc., 45
Bashas' Inc., 33; 80 (upd.)
Bear Creek Corporation, 38
Ben E. Keith Company, 76
Benihana, Inc., 18; 76 (upd.)
Bertucci's Corporation, 64 (upd.)
Bettys & Taylors of Harrogate Ltd., 72
Big Bear Stores Co., 13
The Big Food Group plc, 68 (upd.)
Big V Supermarkets, Inc., 25
Big Y Foods, Inc., 53
Blimpie International, Inc., 15; 49 (upd.)
Bob Evans Farms, Inc., 9; 63 (upd.)
Bob's Red Mill Natural Foods, Inc., 63
Boddie-Noell Enterprises, Inc., 68
Bon Appetit Holding AG, 48
Boston Market Corporation, 12; 48 (upd.)
Boston Pizza International Inc., 88
Brazil Fast Food Corporation, 74
Briazz, Inc., 53
Brinker International, Inc., 10; 38 (upd.); 75 (upd.)
Brookshire Grocery Company, 16; 74 (upd.)
Bruegger's Corporation, 63
Bruno's Supermarkets, Inc., 7; 26 (upd.); 68 (upd.)
Buca, Inc., 38
Budgens Ltd., 59
Buffalo Wild Wings, Inc., 56
Buffets Holdings, Inc., 10; 32 (upd.); 93 (upd.)
Burger King Corporation, II; 17 (upd.); 56 (upd.)
Busch Entertainment Corporation, 73
C&K Market, Inc., 81
C & S Wholesale Grocers, Inc., 55
C.H. Robinson, Inc., 11
Caffè Nero Group PLC, 63
California Pizza Kitchen Inc., 15; 74 (upd.)
Captain D's, LLC, 59
Cargill, Incorporated, II; 13 (upd.); 40 (upd.); 89 (upd.)
Caribou Coffee Company, Inc., 28
Carlson Companies, Inc., 6; 22 (upd.); 87 (upd.)
Carlson Restaurants Worldwide, 69
Carr-Gottstein Foods Co., 17
Carrols Restaurant Group, Inc., 92
Casey's General Stores, Inc., 19; 83 (upd.)

Casino Guichard-Perrachon S.A., 59 (upd.)
CBRL Group, Inc., 35 (upd.); 86 (upd.)
CEC Entertainment, Inc., 31 (upd.)
Centerplate, Inc., 79
Chart House Enterprises, Inc., 17
Checkers Drive-In Restaurants, Inc., 16; 74 (upd.)
The Cheesecake Factory Inc., 17
Chi-Chi's Inc., 13; 51 (upd.)
Chicago Pizza & Brewery, Inc., 44
Chick-fil-A Inc., 23; 90 (upd.)
Chipotle Mexican Grill, Inc., 67
Church's Chicken, 66
Cinnabon Inc., 23; 90 (upd.)
The Circle K Corporation, II
CKE Restaurants, Inc., 19; 46 (upd.)
Coborn's, Inc., 30
The Coffee Beanery, Ltd., 95
Coffee Holding Co., Inc., 95
Cold Stone Creamery, 69
Coles Group Limited, V; 20 (upd.); 85 (upd.)
Compass Group PLC, 34
Comptoirs Modernes S.A., 19
Consolidated Products Inc., 14
Controladora Comercial Mexicana, S.A. de C.V., 36
Cooker Restaurant Corporation, 20; 51 (upd.)
The Copps Corporation, 32
Cosi, Inc., 53
Cost-U-Less, Inc., 51
Coto Centro Integral de Comercializacion S.A., 66
Country Kitchen International, Inc., 76
Cracker Barrel Old Country Store, Inc., 10
Cremonini S.p.A., 57
CulinArt, Inc., 92
Culver Franchising System, Inc., 58
D'Agostino Supermarkets Inc., 19
Dairy Mart Convenience Stores, Inc., 7; 25 (upd.)
Daniel Thwaites Plc, 95
Darden Restaurants, Inc., 16; 44 (upd.)
Dean & DeLuca, Inc., 36
Del Taco, Inc., 58
Delhaize "Le Lion" S.A., 44
DeMoulas / Market Basket Inc., 23
DenAmerica Corporation, 29
Denner AG, 88
Deschutes Brewery, Inc., 57
Diedrich Coffee, Inc., 40
Dierbergs Markets Inc., 63
Distribución y Servicio D&S S.A., 71
Doctor's Associates Inc., 67 (upd.)
Dominick's Finer Foods, Inc., 56
Domino's, Inc., 7; 21 (upd.); 63 (upd.)
Donatos Pizzeria Corporation, 58
E H Booth & Company Ltd., 90
Eateries, Inc., 33
Ed S.A.S., 88
Edeka Zentrale A.G., II; 47 (upd.)
Einstein/Noah Bagel Corporation, 29
El Chico Restaurants, Inc., 19
El Pollo Loco, Inc., 69
Elior SA, 49

Health & Personal Care Products

VHA Inc., 53

VIASYS Healthcare, Inc., 52

Vion Food Group NV, 85

VISX, Incorporated, 30

Vitamin Shoppe Industries, Inc., 60

Water Pik Technologies, Inc., 34; 83 (upd.)

Weider Nutrition International, Inc., 29

Weleda AG 78

Wella AG, III; 48 (upd.)

West Pharmaceutical Services, Inc., 42

Wright Medical Group, Inc., 61

Wyeth, 50 (upd.)

Zila, Inc., 46

Zimmer Holdings, Inc., 45

Health Care Services

Acadian Ambulance & Air Med Services, Inc., 39

Adventist Health, 53

Advocat Inc., 46

Almost Family, Inc., 93

Alterra Healthcare Corporation, 42

Amedysis, Inc., 53

The American Cancer Society, 24

American Healthways, Inc., 65

American Lung Association, 48

American Medical Association, 39

American Medical International, Inc., III

American Medical Response, Inc., 39

American Red Cross, 40

AMERIGROUP Corporation, 69

AmeriSource Health Corporation, 37 (upd.)

AmSurg Corporation, 48

Applied Bioscience International, Inc., 10

Assisted Living Concepts, Inc., 43

ATC Healthcare Inc., 64

Baptist Health Care Corporation, 82

Beverly Enterprises, Inc., III; 16 (upd.)

Bon Secours Health System, Inc., 24

Brookdale Senior Living, 91

C.R. Bard, Inc., 65 (upd.)

Cancer Treatment Centers of America, Inc., 85

Capital Senior Living Corporation, 75

Caremark Rx, Inc., 10; 54 (upd.)

Catholic Health Initiatives, 91

Children's Comprehensive Services, Inc., 42

Children's Hospitals and Clinics, Inc., 54

Chronimed Inc., 26

COBE Laboratories, Inc., 13

Columbia/HCA Healthcare Corporation, 15

Community Health Systems, Inc., 71

Community Psychiatric Centers, 15

CompDent Corporation, 22

CompHealth Inc., 25

Comprehensive Care Corporation, 15

Continental Medical Systems, Inc., 10

Continuum Health Partners, Inc., 60

Coventry Health Care, Inc., 59

Cystic Fibrosis Foundation, 93

DaVita Inc., 73

Easter Seals, Inc., 58

Erickson Retirement Communities, 57

Express Scripts Incorporated, 17

Extendicare Health Services, Inc., 6

Eye Care Centers of America, Inc., 69

FHP International Corporation, 6

Fresenius AG, 56

Genesis Health Ventures, Inc., 18

Gentiva Health Services, Inc., 79

GranCare, Inc., 14

Group Health Cooperative, 41

Grupo Ángeles Servicios de Salud, S.A. de C.V., 84

Hamot Health Foundation, 91

Hazelden Foundation, 28

HCA - The Healthcare Company, 35 (upd.)

Health Care & Retirement Corporation, 22

Health Management Associates, Inc., 56

Health Risk Management, Inc., 24

Health Systems International, Inc., 11

HealthSouth Corporation, 14; 33 (upd.)

Henry Ford Health System, 84

Highmark Inc., 27

The Hillhaven Corporation, 14

Holiday Retirement Corp., 87

Hooper Holmes, Inc., 22

Hospital Central Services, Inc., 56

Hospital Corporation of America, III

Howard Hughes Medical Institute, 39

Humana Inc., III; 24 (upd.)

Intermountain Health Care, Inc., 27

Jenny Craig, Inc., 10; 29 (upd.); 92 (upd.)

Kinetic Concepts, Inc. (KCI), 20

LabOne, Inc., 48

Laboratory Corporation of America Holdings, 42 (upd.)

LCA-Vision, Inc., 85

Life Care Centers of America Inc., 76

Lifeline Systems, Inc., 53

LifePoint Hospitals, Inc., 69

Lincare Holdings Inc., 43

Manor Care, Inc., 6; 25 (upd.)

March of Dimes, 31

Marshfield Clinic Inc., 82

Matria Healthcare, Inc., 17

Maxicare Health Plans, Inc., III; 25 (upd.)

Mayo Foundation, 9; 34 (upd.)

McBride plc, 82

Médecins sans Frontières, 85

Medical Management International, Inc., 65

Medical Staffing Network Holdings, Inc., 89

Memorial Sloan-Kettering Cancer Center, 57

Merge Healthcare, 85

Merit Medical Systems, Inc., 29

MeritCare Health System, 88

Myriad Genetics, Inc., 95

National Health Laboratories Incorporated, 11

National Medical Enterprises, Inc., III

National Research Corporation, 87

New York City Health and Hospitals Corporation, 60

New York Health Care, Inc., 72

NewYork-Presbyterian Hospital, 59

NovaCare, Inc., 11

NSF International, 72

Operation Smile, Inc., 75

Option Care Inc., 48

Orthodontic Centers of America, Inc., 35

Oxford Health Plans, Inc., 16

PacifiCare Health Systems, Inc., 11

Palomar Medical Technologies, Inc., 22

Pediatric Services of America, Inc., 31

Pediatrix Medical Group, Inc., 61

PHP Healthcare Corporation, 22

PhyCor, Inc., 36

PolyMedica Corporation, 77

Primedex Health Systems, Inc., 25

Providence Health System, 90

The Providence Service Corporation, 64

Psychemedics Corporation, 89

Psychiatric Solutions, Inc., 68

Quest Diagnostics Inc., 26

Radiation Therapy Services, Inc., 85

Ramsay Youth Services, Inc., 41

Renal Care Group, Inc., 72

Res-Care, Inc., 29

Response Oncology, Inc., 27

Rural/Metro Corporation, 28

Sabratek Corporation, 29

St. Jude Medical, Inc., 11; 43 (upd.)

Salick Health Care, Inc., 53

The Scripps Research Institute, 76

Select Medical Corporation, 65

Shriners Hospitals for Children, 69

Sierra Health Services, Inc., 15

Smith & Nephew plc, 41 (upd.)

Special Olympics, Inc., 93

The Sports Club Company, 25

SSL International plc, 49

Stericycle Inc., 33

Sun Healthcare Group Inc., 25

Sunrise Senior Living, Inc., 81

Susan G. Komen Breast Cancer Foundation 78

SwedishAmerican Health System, 51

Tenet Healthcare Corporation, 55 (upd.)

Twinlab Corporation, 34

U.S. Healthcare, Inc., 6

U.S. Physical Therapy, Inc., 65

Unison HealthCare Corporation, 25

United HealthCare Corporation, 9

United Nations International Children's Emergency Fund (UNICEF), 58

United Way of America, 36

Universal Health Services, Inc., 6

Vanguard Health Systems Inc., 70

VCA Antech, Inc., 58

Vencor, Inc., 16

VISX, Incorporated, 30

Vivra, Inc., 18

Volunteers of America, Inc., 66

WellPoint Health Networks Inc., 25

World Vision International, Inc., 93

YWCA of the U.S.A., 45

Hotels

Accor S.A., 69 (upd.)

Amerihost Properties, Inc., 30

Ameristar Casinos, Inc., 69 (upd.)

Archon Corporation, 74 (upd.)

Aztar Corporation, 13; 71 (upd.)

Bass PLC, 38 (upd.)

Information Technology

Wipro Limited, 43
Witness Systems, Inc., 87
Wolters Kluwer NV, 33 (upd.)
WordPerfect Corporation, 10
Wyse Technology, Inc., 15
Xerox Corporation, III; 6 (upd.); 26 (upd.)
Xilinx, Inc., 16; 82 (upd.)
Yahoo! Inc., 27; 70 (upd.)
YouTube, Inc., 90
Zanett, Inc., 92
Zapata Corporation, 25
Ziff Davis Media Inc., 36 (upd.)
Zilog, Inc., 15

Insurance

AEGON N.V., III; 50 (upd.)
Aetna Inc., III; 21 (upd.); 63 (upd.)
AFLAC Incorporated, 10 (upd.); 38 (upd.)
Alexander & Alexander Services Inc., 10
Alfa Corporation, 60
Alleanza Assicurazioni S.p.A., 65
Alleghany Corporation, 10
Allianz AG, III; 15 (upd.); 57 (upd.)
Allmerica Financial Corporation, 63
The Allstate Corporation, 10; 27 (upd.)
AMB Generali Holding AG, 51
American Family Corporation, III
American Financial Group Inc., III; 48 (upd.)
American General Corporation, III; 10 (upd.); 46 (upd.)
American International Group, Inc., III; 15 (upd.); 47 (upd.)
American National Insurance Company, 8; 27 (upd.)
American Premier Underwriters, Inc., 10
American Re Corporation, 10; 35 (upd.)
N.V. AMEV, III
AOK-Bundesverband (Federation of the AOK) 78
Aon Corporation, III; 45 (upd.)
Arthur J. Gallagher & Co., 73
Assicurazioni Generali SpA, III; 15 (upd.)
Assurances Générales de France, 63
Assured Guaranty Ltd., 93
Atlantic American Corporation, 44
Aviva PLC, 50 (upd.)
Axa, III
AXA Colonia Konzern AG, 27; 49 (upd.)
B.A.T. Industries PLC, 22 (upd.)
Baldwin & Lyons, Inc., 51
Bâloise-Holding, 40
Benfield Greig Group plc, 53
Berkshire Hathaway Inc., III; 18 (upd.); 42 (upd.); 89 (upd.)
Blue Cross and Blue Shield Association, 10
British United Provident Association Limited (BUPAL), 79
Brown & Brown, Inc., 41
Business Men's Assurance Company of America, 14
Capital Holding Corporation, III
Catholic Order of Foresters, 24
China Life Insurance Company Limited, 65

ChoicePoint Inc., 65
The Chubb Corporation, III; 14 (upd.); 37 (upd.)
CIGNA Corporation, III; 22 (upd.); 45 (upd.)
Cincinnati Financial Corporation, 16; 44 (upd.)
CNA Financial Corporation, III; 38 (upd.)
Commercial Union PLC, III
Connecticut Mutual Life Insurance Company, III
Conseco Inc., 10; 33 (upd.)
The Continental Corporation, III
Crawford & Company, 87
Debeka Krankenversicherungsverein auf Gegenseitigkeit, 72
The Doctors' Company, 55
Empire Blue Cross and Blue Shield, III
Enbridge Inc., 43
Endurance Specialty Holdings Ltd., 85
Engle Homes, Inc., 46
The Equitable Life Assurance Society of the United States Fireman's Fund Insurance Company, III
ERGO Versicherungsgruppe AG, 44
Erie Indemnity Company, 35
Fairfax Financial Holdings Limited, 57
Farm Family Holdings, Inc., 39
Farmers Insurance Group of Companies, 25
Federal Deposit Insurance Corporation, 93
Fidelity National Financial Inc., 54
The First American Corporation, 52
First Executive Corporation, III
Foundation Health Corporation, 12
Gainsco, Inc., 22
GEICO Corporation, 10; 40 (upd.)
General Accident PLC, III
General Re Corporation, III; 24 (upd.)
Gerling-Konzern Versicherungs-Beteiligungs-Aktiengesellschaft, 51
GraceKennedy Ltd., 92
Great-West Lifeco Inc., III
Groupama S.A., 76
Gryphon Holdings, Inc., 21
Guardian Financial Services, 64 (upd.)
Guardian Royal Exchange Plc, 11
Harleysville Group Inc., 37
HDI (Haftpflichtverband der Deutschen Industrie Versicherung auf Gegenseitigkeit V.a.G.), 53
HealthExtras, Inc., 75
HealthMarkets, Inc., 88 (upd.)
Hilb, Rogal & Hobbs Company, 77
The Home Insurance Company, III
Horace Mann Educators Corporation, 22; 90 (upd.)
Household International, Inc., 21 (upd.)
Hub International Limited, 89
HUK-Coburg, 58
Irish Life & Permanent Plc, 59
Jackson National Life Insurance Company, 8
Jefferson-Pilot Corporation, 11; 29 (upd.)
John Hancock Financial Services, Inc., III; 42 (upd.)

Johnson & Higgins, 14
Kaiser Foundation Health Plan, Inc., 53
Kemper Corporation, III; 15 (upd.)
LandAmerica Financial Group, Inc., 85
Legal & General Group plc, III; 24 (upd.)
The Liberty Corporation, 22
Liberty Mutual Holding Company, 59
LifeWise Health Plan of Oregon, Inc., 90
Lincoln National Corporation, III; 25 (upd.)
Lloyd's, 74 (upd.)
Lloyd's of London, III; 22 (upd.)
The Loewen Group Inc., 40 (upd.)
Lutheran Brotherhood, 31
Manulife Financial Corporation, 85
Marsh & McLennan Companies, Inc., III; 45 (upd.)
Massachusetts Mutual Life Insurance Company, III; 53 (upd.)
MBIA Inc., 73
The Meiji Mutual Life Insurance Company, III
Mercury General Corporation, 25
Metropolitan Life Insurance Company, III; 52 (upd.)
MGIC Investment Corp., 52
The Midland Company, 65
Millea Holdings Inc., 64 (upd.)
Mitsui Marine and Fire Insurance Company, Limited, III
Mitsui Mutual Life Insurance Company, III; 39 (upd.)
Modern Woodmen of America, 66
Munich Re (Münchener Rückversicherungs-Gesellschaft Aktiengesellschaft in München), III; 46 (upd.)
The Mutual Benefit Life Insurance Company, III
The Mutual Life Insurance Company of New York, III
National Medical Health Card Systems, Inc., 79
Nationale-Nederlanden N.V., III
The Navigators Group, Inc., 92
New England Mutual Life Insurance Company, III
New York Life Insurance Company, III; 45 (upd.)
Nippon Life Insurance Company, III; 60 (upd.)
Northwestern Mutual Life Insurance Company, III; 45 (upd.)
NYMAGIC, Inc., 41
Ohio Casualty Corp., 11
Old Republic International Corporation, 11; 58 (upd.)
Oregon Dental Service Health Plan, Inc., 51
Palmer & Cay, Inc., 69
Pan-American Life Insurance Company, 48
PartnerRe Ltd., 83
The Paul Revere Corporation, 12
Pennsylvania Blue Shield, III
The PMI Group, Inc., 49
Preserver Group, Inc., 44

Legal Services

Manufacturing

WMS Industries, Inc., 15; 53 (upd.)
Wolverine Tube Inc., 23
Wood-Mode, Inc., 23
Woodcraft Industries Inc., 61
Woodward Governor Company, 13; 49 (upd.)
Wright Medical Group, Inc., 61
Württembergische Metallwarenfabrik AG (WMF), 60
Wyant Corporation, 30
Wyman-Gordon Company, 14
Wynn's International, Inc., 33
X-Rite, Inc., 48
Xerox Corporation, 69 (upd.)
Yamaha Corporation, III; 16 (upd.)
The Yokohama Rubber Company, Limited, V; 19 (upd.); 91 (upd.)
The York Group, Inc., 50
York International Corp., 13
Young Innovations, Inc., 44
Zapf Creation AG, 95
Zebra Technologies Corporation, 53 (upd.)
ZERO Corporation, 17; 88 (upd.)
ZiLOG, Inc., 72 (upd.)
Zindart Ltd., 60
Zippo Manufacturing Company, 18; 71 (upd.)
Zodiac S.A., 36
Zygo Corporation, 42

Materials

AK Steel Holding Corporation, 19
American Biltrite Inc., 16
American Colloid Co., 13
American Standard Inc., III
Ameriwood Industries International Corp., 17
Apasco S.A. de C.V., 51
Apogee Enterprises, Inc., 8
Asahi Glass Company, Limited, III
Asbury Carbons, Inc., 68
Bairnco Corporation, 28
Bayou Steel Corporation, 31
Blessings Corp., 19
Blue Circle Industries PLC, III
Bodycote International PLC, 63
Boral Limited, III
British Vita PLC, 9
Brush Engineered Materials Inc., 67
California Steel Industries, Inc., 67
Callanan Industries, Inc., 60
Cameron & Barkley Company, 28
Carborundum Company, 15
Carl Zeiss AG, III; 34 (upd.); 91 (upd.)
Carlisle Companies Inc., 8; 82 (upd.)
Carter Holt Harvey Ltd., 70
Cementos Argos S.A., 91
Cemex SA de CV, 20
Century Aluminum Company, 52
CertainTeed Corporation, 35
Chargeurs International, 6; 21 (upd.)
Chemfab Corporation, 35
Cimentos de Portugal SGPS S.A. (Cimpor), 76
Cold Spring Granite Company Inc., 16; 67 (upd.)
Columbia Forest Products Inc. 78

Compagnie de Saint-Gobain S.A., III; 16 (upd.)
Cookson Group plc, III; 44 (upd.)
Corning Inc., III; 44 (upd.); 90 (upd.)
CSR Limited, III; 28 (upd.); 85 (upd.)
Dal-Tile International Inc., 22
The David J. Joseph Company, 14; 76 (upd.)
The Dexter Corporation, 12 (upd.)
Dickten Masch Plastics LLC, 90
Dyckerhoff AG, 35
Dynamic Materials Corporation, 81
Dyson Group PLC, 71
ECC Group plc, III
Edw. C. Levy Co., 42
84 Lumber Company, 9; 39 (upd.)
ElkCorp, 52
Empire Resources, Inc., 81
English China Clays Ltd., 15 (upd.); 40 (upd.)
Envirodyne Industries, Inc., 17
Feldmuhle Nobel A.G., III
Fibreboard Corporation, 16
Filtrona plc, 88
Florida Rock Industries, Inc., 46
Foamex International Inc., 17
Formica Corporation, 13
GAF Corporation, 22 (upd.)
The Geon Company, 11
Giant Cement Holding, Inc., 23
Gibraltar Steel Corporation, 37
Granite Rock Company, 26
Groupe Sidel S.A., 21
Harbison-Walker Refractories Company, 24
Harrisons & Crosfield plc, III
Heidelberger Zement AG, 31
Hexcel Corporation, 28
Holderbank Financière Glaris Ltd., III
Holnam Inc., 39 (upd.)
Holt and Bugbee Company, 66
Homasote Company, 72
Howmet Corp., 12
Huttig Building Products, Inc., 73
Ibstock Brick Ltd., 14; 37 (upd.)
Imerys S.A., 40 (upd.)
Imperial Industries, Inc., 81
Internacional de Ceramica, S.A. de C.V., 53
International Shipbreaking Ltd. L.L.C., 67
Joseph T. Ryerson & Son, Inc., 15
Lafarge Coppée S.A., III
Lafarge Corporation, 28
Lehigh Portland Cement Company, 23
Loma Negra C.I.A.S.A., 95
Manville Corporation, III; 7 (upd.)
Material Sciences Corporation, 63
Matsushita Electric Works, Ltd., III; 7 (upd.)
McJunkin Corporation, 63
Medusa Corporation, 24
Mitsubishi Materials Corporation, III
Nevamar Company, 82
Nippon Sheet Glass Company, Limited, III
North Pacific Group, Inc., 61
Nuplex Industries Ltd., 92
OmniSource Corporation, 14

Onoda Cement Co., Ltd., III
Otor S.A., 77
Owens-Corning Fiberglass Corporation, III
Pacific Clay Products Inc., 88
Pilkington Group Limited, III; 34 (upd.); 87 (upd.)
Pioneer International Limited, III
PolyOne Corporation, 87 (upd.)
PPG Industries, Inc., III; 22 (upd.); 81 (upd.)
Redland plc, III
Rinker Group Ltd., 65
RMC Group p.l.c., III
Rock of Ages Corporation, 37
Rogers Corporation, 80 (upd.)
Royal Group Technologies Limited, 73
The Rugby Group plc, 31
Schuff Steel Company, 26
Sekisui Chemical Co., Ltd., III; 72 (upd.)
Severstal Joint Stock Company, 65
Shaw Industries, 9
The Sherwin-Williams Company, III; 13 (upd.); 89 (upd.)
The Siam Cement Public Company Limited, 56
SIG plc, 71
Simplex Technologies Inc., 21
Siskin Steel & Supply Company, 70
Solutia Inc., 52
Sommer-Allibert S.A., 19
Southdown, Inc., 14
Spartech Corporation, 19; 76 (upd.)
Ssangyong Cement Industrial Co., Ltd., III; 61 (upd.)
Steel Technologies Inc., 63
Sun Distributors L.P., 12
Symyx Technologies, Inc., 77
Tarmac Limited, III, 28 (upd.); 95 (upd.)
Tilcon-Connecticut Inc., 80
TOTO LTD., III; 28 (upd.)
Toyo Sash Co., Ltd., III
Tuscarora Inc., 29
U.S. Aggregates, Inc., 42
Ube Industries, Ltd., III
United States Steel Corporation, 50 (upd.)
USG Corporation, III; 26 (upd.); 81 (upd.)
Usinas Siderúrgicas de Minas Gerais S.A., 77
Vicat S.A., 70
voestalpine AG, 57 (upd.)
Vulcan Materials Company, 7; 52 (upd.)
Wacker-Chemie GmbH, 35
Walter Industries, Inc., III
Waxman Industries, Inc., 9
Weber et Broutin France, 66
Wienerberger AG, 70
Wolseley plc, 64
ZERO Corporation, 17; 88 (upd.)
Zoltek Companies, Inc., 37

Mining & Metals

A.M. Castle & Co., 25
Acindar Industria Argentina de Aceros S.A., 87
Aggregate Industries plc, 36
Agnico-Eagle Mines Limited, 71

678

Personal Services

Petroleum

Publishing & Printing

Rubber & Tires

Telecommunications

Textiles & Apparel

Wright Express Corporation, 80
Yamato Transport Co. Ltd., V; 49 (upd.)
Yellow Corporation, 14; 45 (upd.)
Yellow Freight System, Inc. of Delaware, V
YRC Worldwide Inc., 90 (upd.)

Utilities

AES Corporation, 10; 13 (upd.); 53 (upd.)
Aggreko Plc, 45
Air & Water Technologies Corporation, 6
Alberta Energy Company Ltd., 16; 43 (upd.)
Allegheny Energy, Inc., V; 38 (upd.)
Ameren Corporation, 60 (upd.)
American Electric Power Company, Inc., V; 45 (upd.)
American States Water Company, 46
American Water Works Company, Inc., 6; 38 (upd.)
Aquarion Company, 84
Aquila, Inc., 50 (upd.)
Arkla, Inc., V
Associated Natural Gas Corporation, 11
Atlanta Gas Light Company, 6; 23 (upd.)
Atlantic Energy, Inc., 6
Atmos Energy Corporation, 43
Avista Corporation, 69 (upd.)
Baltimore Gas and Electric Company, V; 25 (upd.)
Bay State Gas Company, 38
Bayernwerk AG, V; 23 (upd.)
Berlinwasser Holding AG, 90
Bewag AG, 39
Big Rivers Electric Corporation, 11
Black Hills Corporation, 20
Bonneville Power Administration, 50
Boston Edison Company, 12
Bouygues S.A., 24 (upd.)
British Energy Plc, 49
British Gas plc, V
British Nuclear Fuels plc, 6
Brooklyn Union Gas, 6
California Water Service Group, 79
Calpine Corporation, 36
Canadian Utilities Limited, 13; 56 (upd.)
Cap Rock Energy Corporation, 46
Carolina Power & Light Company, V; 23 (upd.)
Cascade Natural Gas Corporation, 9
Centerior Energy Corporation, V
Central and South West Corporation, V
Central Hudson Gas and Electricity Corporation, 6
Central Maine Power, 6
Central Vermont Public Service Corporation, 54
Centrica plc, 29 (upd.)
Chesapeake Utilities Corporation, 56
China Shenhua Energy Company Limited, 83
Chubu Electric Power Company, Inc., V; 46 (upd.)
Chugoku Electric Power Company Inc., V; 53 (upd.)
Cincinnati Gas & Electric Company, 6
CIPSCO Inc., 6

Citizens Utilities Company, 7
City Public Service, 6
Cleco Corporation, 37
CMS Energy Corporation, V, 14
The Coastal Corporation, 31 (upd.)
Cogentrix Energy, Inc., 10
The Coleman Company, Inc., 9
The Columbia Gas System, Inc., V; 16 (upd.)
Commonwealth Edison Company, V
Commonwealth Energy System, 14
Companhia Energética de Minas Gerais S.A. CEMIG, 65
Compañia de Minas Buenaventura S.A.A., 93
Connecticut Light and Power Co., 13
Consolidated Edison, Inc., V; 45 (upd.)
Consolidated Natural Gas Company, V; 19 (upd.)
Consumers Power Co., 14
Consumers Water Company, 14
Consumers' Gas Company Ltd., 6
Covanta Energy Corporation, 64 (upd.)
Dalkia Holding, 66
Destec Energy, Inc., 12
The Detroit Edison Company, V
Dominion Resources, Inc., V; 54 (upd.)
DPL Inc., 6
DQE, Inc., 6
DTE Energy Company, 20 (upd.)
Duke Energy Corporation, V; 27 (upd.)
E.On AG, 50 (upd.)
Eastern Enterprises, 6
Edison International, 56 (upd.)
El Paso Electric Company, 21
El Paso Natural Gas Company, 12
Electrabel N.V., 67
Electricidade de Portugal, S.A., 47
Electricité de France, V; 41 (upd.)
Electricity Generating Authority of Thailand (EGAT), 56
Elektrowatt AG, 6
The Empire District Electric Company, 77
Empresas Públicas de Medellín S.A.E.S.P., 91
Enbridge Inc., 43
ENDESA S.A., V; 46 (upd.)
Enersis S.A., 73
ENMAX Corporation, 83
Enron Corporation, V; 46 (upd.)
Enserch Corporation, V
Ente Nazionale per L'Energia Elettrica, V
Entergy Corporation, V; 45 (upd.)
Environmental Power Corporation, 68
EPCOR Utilities Inc., 81
Equitable Resources, Inc., 6; 54 (upd.)
Exelon Corporation, 48 (upd.)
Florida Progress Corporation, V; 23 (upd.)
Florida Public Utilities Company, 69
Fortis, Inc., 15; 47 (upd.)
Fortum Corporation, 30 (upd.)
FPL Group, Inc., V; 49 (upd.)
Gas Natural SDG S.A., 69
Gaz de France, V; 40 (upd.)
General Public Utilities Corporation, V
Générale des Eaux Group, V
GPU, Inc., 27 (upd.)

Great Plains Energy Incorporated, 65 (upd.)
Gulf States Utilities Company, 6
Hawaiian Electric Industries, Inc., 9
Hokkaido Electric Power Company Inc. (HEPCO), V; 58 (upd.)
Hokuriku Electric Power Company, V
Hong Kong and China Gas Company Ltd., 73
Hongkong Electric Holdings Ltd., 6; 23 (upd.)
Houston Industries Incorporated, V
Hyder plc, 34
Hydro-Québec, 6; 32 (upd.)
Iberdrola, S.A., 49
Idaho Power Company, 12
Illinois Bell Telephone Company, 14
Illinois Power Company, 6
Indiana Energy, Inc., 27
International Power PLC, 50 (upd.)
IPALCO Enterprises, Inc., 6
ITC Holdings Corp., 75
The Kansai Electric Power Company, Inc., V; 62 (upd.)
Kansas City Power & Light Company, 6
Kelda Group plc, 45
Kenetech Corporation, 11
Kentucky Utilities Company, 6
KeySpan Energy Co., 27
Korea Electric Power Corporation (Kepco), 56
KU Energy Corporation, 11
Kyushu Electric Power Company Inc., V
LG&E Energy Corporation, 6; 51 (upd.)
Long Island Lighting Company, V
Lyonnaise des Eaux-Dumez, V
Madison Gas and Electric Company, 39
Magma Power Company, 11
Maine & Maritimes Corporation, 56
Manila Electric Company (Meralco), 56
MCN Corporation, 6
MDU Resources Group, Inc., 7; 42 (upd.)
Middlesex Water Company, 45
Midwest Resources Inc., 6
Minnesota Power, Inc., 11; 34 (upd.)
The Montana Power Company, 11; 44 (upd.)
National Fuel Gas Company, 6; 95 (upd.)
National Grid USA, 51 (upd.)
National Power PLC, 12
Nebraska Public Power District, 29
N.V. Nederlandse Gasunie, V
Nevada Power Company, 11
New England Electric System, V
New Jersey Resources Corporation, 54
New York State Electric and Gas, 6
Neyveli Lignite Corporation Ltd., 65
Niagara Mohawk Holdings Inc., V; 45 (upd.)
Nicor Inc., 6; 86 (upd.)
NIPSCO Industries, Inc., 6
North West Water Group plc, 11
Northeast Utilities, V; 48 (upd.)
Northern States Power Company, V; 20 (upd.)
Northwest Natural Gas Company, 45
NorthWestern Corporation, 37
Nova Corporation of Alberta, V

NRG Energy, Inc., 79
Oglethorpe Power Corporation, 6
Ohio Edison Company, V
Oklahoma Gas and Electric Company, 6
ONEOK Inc., 7
Ontario Hydro Services Company, 6; 32
   (upd.)
Osaka Gas Company, Ltd., V; 60 (upd.)
Österreichische Elektrizitätswirtschafts-AG,
   85
Otter Tail Power Company, 18
Pacific Enterprises, V
Pacific Gas and Electric Company, V
PacifiCorp, V; 26 (upd.)
Panhandle Eastern Corporation, V
PECO Energy Company, 11
Pennon Group Plc, 45
Pennsylvania Power & Light Company, V
Peoples Energy Corporation, 6
PG&E Corporation, 26 (upd.)
Philadelphia Electric Company, V
Philadelphia Gas Works Company, 92
Philadelphia Suburban Corporation, 39
Piedmont Natural Gas Company, Inc., 27
Pinnacle West Capital Corporation, 6; 54
   (upd.)
PNM Resources Inc., 51 (upd.)
Portland General Corporation, 6
Potomac Electric Power Company, 6
Power-One, Inc., 79
Powergen PLC, 11; 50 (upd.)
PPL Corporation, 41 (upd.)
PreussenElektra Aktiengesellschaft, V
Progress Energy, Inc., 74
PSI Resources, 6
Public Service Company of Colorado, 6
Public Service Company of New
   Hampshire, 21; 55 (upd.)
Public Service Company of New Mexico,
   6
Public Service Enterprise Group Inc., V;
   44 (upd.)
Puerto Rico Electric Power Authority, 47
Puget Sound Energy Inc., 6; 50 (upd.)
Questar Corporation, 6; 26 (upd.)
RAO Unified Energy System of Russia, 45
Reliant Energy Inc., 44 (upd.)
Rochester Gas and Electric Corporation, 6
Ruhrgas AG, V; 38 (upd.)
RWE AG, V; 50 (upd.)
Salt River Project, 19
San Diego Gas & Electric Company, V
SCANA Corporation, 6; 56 (upd.)
Scarborough Public Utilities Commission,
   9
SCEcorp, V
Scottish and Southern Energy plc, 66
   (upd.)
Scottish Hydro-Electric PLC, 13
Scottish Power plc, 19; 49 (upd.)
Seattle City Light, 50

SEMCO Energy, Inc., 44
Sempra Energy, 25 (upd.)
Severn Trent PLC, 12; 38 (upd.)
Shikoku Electric Power Company, Inc., V;
   60 (upd.)
SJW Corporation, 70
Sonat, Inc., 6
South Jersey Industries, Inc., 42
The Southern Company, V; 38 (upd.)
Southern Connecticut Gas Company, 84
Southern Electric PLC, 13
Southern Indiana Gas and Electric
   Company, 13
Southern Union Company, 27
Southwest Gas Corporation, 19
Southwest Water Company, 47
Southwestern Electric Power Co., 21
Southwestern Public Service Company, 6
Suez Lyonnaise des Eaux, 36 (upd.)
TECO Energy, Inc., 6
Tennessee Valley Authority, 50
Tennet BV 78
Texas Utilities Company, V; 25 (upd.)
Thames Water plc, 11; 90 (upd.)
Tohoku Electric Power Company, Inc., V
The Tokyo Electric Power Company, 74
   (upd.)
The Tokyo Electric Power Company,
   Incorporated, V
Tokyo Gas Co., Ltd., V; 55 (upd.)
TransAlta Utilities Corporation, 6
TransCanada PipeLines Limited, V
Transco Energy Company, V
Trigen Energy Corporation, 42
Tucson Electric Power Company, 6
UGI Corporation, 12
Unicom Corporation, 29 (upd.)
Union Electric Company, V
The United Illuminating Company, 21
United Utilities PLC, 52 (upd.)
United Water Resources, Inc., 40
Unitil Corporation, 37
Utah Power and Light Company, 27
UtiliCorp United Inc., 6
Vattenfall AB, 57
Vereinigte Elektrizitätswerke Westfalen
   AG, V
VEW AG, 39
Viridian Group plc, 64
Warwick Valley Telephone Company, 55
Washington Gas Light Company, 19
Washington Natural Gas Company, 9
Washington Water Power Company, 6
Westar Energy, Inc., 57 (upd.)
Western Resources, Inc., 12
Wheelabrator Technologies, Inc., 6
Wisconsin Energy Corporation, 6; 54
   (upd.)
Wisconsin Public Service Corporation, 9
WPL Holdings, Inc., 6
WPS Resources Corporation, 53 (upd.)

Xcel Energy Inc., 73 (upd.)

Waste Services

Allied Waste Industries, Inc., 50
Allwaste, Inc., 18
American Ecology Corporation, 77
Appliance Recycling Centers of America,
   Inc., 42
Azcon Corporation, 23
Berliner Stadtreinigungsbetriebe, 58
Biffa plc, 92
Brambles Industries Limited, 42
Browning-Ferris Industries, Inc., V; 20
   (upd.)
Chemical Waste Management, Inc., 9
Clean Harbors, Inc., 73
Copart Inc., 23
Darling International Inc., 85
E.On AG, 50 (upd.)
Ecolab Inc., I; 13 (upd.); 34 (upd.); 85
   (upd.)
Ecology and Environment, Inc., 39
Empresas Públicas de Medellín S.A.E.S.P.,
   91
Fuel Tech, Inc., 85
Industrial Services of America, Inc., 46
Ionics, Incorporated, 52
ISS A/S, 49
Jani-King International, Inc., 85
Kelda Group plc, 45
MPW Industrial Services Group, Inc., 53
Newpark Resources, Inc., 63
Norcal Waste Systems, Inc., 60
1-800-GOT-JUNK? LLC, 74
Onet S.A., 92
Pennon Group Plc, 45
Philip Environmental Inc., 16
Philip Services Corp., 73
Republic Services, Inc., 92
Roto-Rooter, Inc., 15; 61 (upd.)
Safety-Kleen Systems Inc., 8; 82 (upd.)
Saur S.A.S., 92
Sevenson Environmental Services, Inc., 42
Severn Trent PLC, 38 (upd.)
Servpro Industries, Inc., 85
Shanks Group plc, 45
Shred-It Canada Corporation, 56
Stericycle, Inc., 33; 74 (upd.)
TRC Companies, Inc., 32
Valley Proteins, Inc., 91
Veit Companies, 43; 92 (upd.)
Waste Connections, Inc., 46
Waste Holdings, Inc., 41
Waste Management, Inc., V
Wheelabrator Technologies, Inc., 60
   (upd.)
Windswept Environmental Group, Inc.,
   62
WMX Technologies Inc., 17

Geographic Index

Germany

United States

McLeodUSA Incorporated, 32
McMenamins Pubs and Breweries, 65
McNaughton Apparel Group, Inc., 92
  (upd.)
MCN Corporation, 6
MCSi, Inc., 41
McWane Corporation, 55
MDU Resources Group, Inc., 7; 42 (upd.)
The Mead Corporation, IV; 19 (upd.)
Mead Data Central, Inc., 10
Mead Johnson & Company, 84
Meade Instruments Corporation, 41
Meadowcraft, Inc., 29
MeadWestvaco Corporation, 76 (upd.)
Measurement Specialties, Inc., 71
Mecklermedia Corporation, 24
Medarex, Inc., 85
Medco Containment Services Inc., 9
MEDecision, Inc., 95
Media Arts Group, Inc., 42
Media General, Inc., 7; 38 (upd.)
Mediacom Communications Corporation,
  69
MediaNews Group, Inc., 70
Medical Information Technology Inc., 64
Medical Management International, Inc.,
  65
Medical Staffing Network Holdings, Inc.,
  89
Medicis Pharmaceutical Corporation, 59
MedImmune, Inc., 35
Medis Technologies Ltd., 77
Meditrust, 11
Medline Industries, Inc., 61
Medtronic, Inc., 8; 30 (upd.); 67 (upd.)
Mcdusa Corporation, 24
Megafoods Stores Inc., 13
Meier & Frank Co., 23
Meijer Incorporated, 7; 27 (upd.)
Mel Farr Automotive Group, 20
Melaleuca Inc., 31
Melamine Chemicals, Inc., 27
Mellon Bank Corporation, II
Mellon Financial Corporation, 44 (upd.)
Mellon-Stuart Company, I
The Melting Pot Restaurants, Inc., 74
Melville Corporation, V
Melvin Simon and Associates, Inc., 8
MEMC Electronic Materials, Inc., 81
Memorial Sloan-Kettering Cancer Center,
  57
Memry Corporation, 72
The Men's Wearhouse, Inc., 17; 48 (upd.)
Menard, Inc., 34
Menasha Corporation, 8; 59 (upd.)
Mendocino Brewing Company, Inc., 60
The Mentholatum Company Inc., 32
Mentor Corporation, 26
Mentor Graphics Corporation, 11
Mercantile Bankshares Corp., 11
Mercantile Stores Company, Inc., V; 19
  (upd.)
Mercer International Inc., 64
Merck & Co., Inc., I; 11 (upd.); 34
  (upd.); 95 (upd.)
Mercury Air Group, Inc., 20
Mercury General Corporation, 25
Mercury Interactive Corporation, 59

Mercury Marine Group, 68
Meredith Corporation, 11; 29 (upd.); 74
  (upd.)
Merge Healthcare, 85
Meridian Bancorp, Inc., 11
Meridian Gold, Incorporated, 47
Merillat Industries Inc., 13
Merillat Industries, LLC, 69 (upd.)
Merisant Worldwide, Inc., 70
Merisel, Inc., 12
Merit Medical Systems, Inc., 29
MeritCare Health System, 88
Meritage Corporation, 26
Merix Corporation, 36; 75 (upd.)
Merrell Dow, Inc., I; 9 (upd.)
Merriam-Webster Inc., 70
Merrill Corporation, 18; 47 (upd.)
Merrill Lynch & Co., Inc., II; 13 (upd.);
  40 (upd.)
Merry-Go-Round Enterprises, Inc., 8
Mervyn's California, 10; 39 (upd.)
Mesa Air Group, Inc., 11; 32 (upd.); 77
  (upd.)
Mesaba Holdings, Inc., 28
Mestek Inc., 10
Metal Management, Inc., 92
Metatec International, Inc., 47
Meteor Industries Inc., 33
Methode Electronics, Inc., 13
Metris Companies Inc., 56
Metro Information Services, Inc., 36
Metro-Goldwyn-Mayer Inc., 25 (upd.); 84
  (upd.)
Metrocall, Inc., 41
Metromedia Company, 7; 14; 61 (upd.)
Metropolitan Baseball Club Inc., 39
Metropolitan Financial Corporation, 13
Metropolitan Life Insurance Company,
  III; 52 (upd.)
The Metropolitan Museum of Art, 55
Metropolitan Opera Association, Inc., 40
Metropolitan Transportation Authority, 35
Mexican Restaurants, Inc., 41
MFS Communications Company, Inc., 11
MGA Entertainment, Inc., 95
MGIC Investment Corp., 52
MGM Grand Inc., 17
MGM/UA Communications Company, II
Miami Herald Media Company, 92
Michael Anthony Jewelers, Inc., 24
Michael Baker Corporation, 14; 51 (upd.)
Michael C. Fina Co., Inc., 52
Michael Foods, Inc., 25
Michaels Stores, Inc., 17; 71 (upd.)
Michigan Bell Telephone Co., 14
Michigan National Corporation, 11
Michigan Sporting Goods Distributors,
  Inc., 72
Micrel, Incorporated, 77
Micro Warehouse, Inc., 16
MicroAge, Inc., 16
Microdot Inc., 8
Micron Technology, Inc., 11; 29 (upd.)
Micros Systems, Inc., 18
Microsemi Corporation, 94
Microsoft Corporation, 6; 27 (upd.); 63
  (upd.)
MicroStrategy Incorporated, 87

Mid-America Apartment Communities,
  Inc., 85
Mid-America Dairymen, Inc., 7
Midas Inc., 10; 56 (upd.)
The Middleby Corporation, 22
Middlesex Water Company, 45
The Middleton Doll Company, 53
The Midland Company, 65
Midway Airlines Corporation, 33
Midway Games, Inc., 25
Midwest Air Group, Inc., 35; 85 (upd.)
Midwest Grain Products, Inc., 49
Midwest Resources Inc., 6
Mikasa, Inc., 28
Mike-Sell's Inc., 15
Mikohn Gaming Corporation, 39
Milacron, Inc., 53 (upd.)
Milbank, Tweed, Hadley & McCloy, 27
Miles Laboratories, I
Millennium Pharmaceuticals, Inc., 47
Miller Brewing Company, I; 12 (upd.)
Miller Industries, Inc., 26
Miller Publishing Group, LLC, 57
Milliken & Co., V; 17 (upd.); 82 (upd.)
Milliman USA, 66
Millipore Corporation, 25; 84 (upd.)
The Mills Corporation, 77
Milnot Company, 46
Milton Bradley Company, 21
Milton CAT, Inc., 86
Milwaukee Brewers Baseball Club, 37
Mine Safety Appliances Company, 31
The Miner Group International, 22
Minerals Technologies Inc., 11; 52 (upd.)
Minnesota Mining & Manufacturing
  Company (3M), I; 8 (upd.); 26 (upd.)
Minnesota Power, Inc., 11; 34 (upd.)
Minntech Corporation, 22
The Minute Maid Company, 28
Minuteman International Inc., 46
Minyard Food Stores, Inc., 33; 86 (upd.)
Mirage Resorts, Incorporated, 6; 28 (upd.)
Miramax Film Corporation, 64
Misonix, Inc., 80
Mississippi Chemical Corporation, 39
Mitchell Energy and Development
  Corporation, 7
MITRE Corporation, 26
Mity Enterprises, Inc., 38
MIVA, Inc., 83
MNS, Ltd., 65
Mobil Corporation, IV; 7 (upd.); 21
  (upd.)
Mobile Mini, Inc., 58
Mobile Telecommunications Technologies
  Corp., 18
Mocon, Inc., 76
Modern Woodmen of America, 66
Modine Manufacturing Company, 8; 56
  (upd.)
Modtech Holdings, Inc., 77
Moen Incorporated, 12
Mohawk Industries, Inc., 19; 63 (upd.)
Mohegan Tribal Gaming Authority, 37
Moldflow Corporation, 73
Molex Incorporated, 11; 54 (upd.)
Molson Coors Brewing Company, 77
  (upd.)

Stratus Computer, Inc., 10
Strauss Discount Auto, 56
Strayer Education, Inc., 53
The Stride Rite Corporation, 8; 37 (upd.); 86 (upd.)
Strine Printing Company Inc., 88
The Strober Organization, Inc., 82
The Stroh Brewery Company, I; 18 (upd.)
Strombecker Corporation, 60
Stroock & Stroock & Lavan LLP, 40
Strouds, Inc., 33
Stryker Corporation, 11; 29 (upd.); 79 (upd.)
Stuart C. Irby Company, 58
Stuart Entertainment Inc., 16
Student Loan Marketing Association, II
Stuller Settings, Inc., 35
Sturm, Ruger & Company, Inc., 19
Stussy, Inc., 55
Sub-Zero Freezer Co., Inc., 31
Suburban Propane Partners, L.P., 30
Subway, 32
Successories, Inc., 30
Sudbury Inc., 16
Suiza Foods Corporation, 26
Sullivan & Cromwell, 26
The Summit Bancorporation, 14
Summit Family Restaurants, Inc. 19
Sun Communities Inc., 46
Sun Company, Inc., IV
Sun Country Airlines, 30
Sun-Diamond Growers of California, 7
Sun Distributors L.P., 12
Sun Healthcare Group Inc., 25
Sun Hydraulics Corporation, 74
Sun-Maid Growers of California, 82
Sun Microsystems, Inc., 7; 30 (upd.); 91 (upd.)
Sun Sportswear, Inc., 17
Sun Television & Appliances Inc., 10
Sun World International, LLC, 93
SunAmerica Inc., 11
Sunbeam-Oster Co., Inc., 9
Sunburst Hospitality Corporation, 26
Sunburst Shutter Corporation 78
Sundstrand Corporation, 7; 21 (upd.)
Sundt Corp., 24
SunGard Data Systems Inc., 11
Sunglass Hut International, Inc., 21; 74 (upd.)
Sunkist Growers, Inc., 26
Sunoco, Inc., 28 (upd.); 83 (upd.)
SunPower Corporation, 91
The Sunrider Corporation, 26
Sunrise Greetings, 88
Sunrise Medical Inc., 11
Sunrise Senior Living, Inc., 81
Sunterra Corporation, 75
SunTrust Banks Inc., 23
Super 8 Motels, Inc., 83
Super Food Services, Inc., 15
Supercuts Inc., 26
Superior Essex Inc., 80
Superior Energy Services, Inc., 65
Superior Industries International, Inc., 8
Superior Uniform Group, Inc., 30
Supermarkets General Holdings Corporation, II

SUPERVALU Inc., II; 18 (upd.); 50 (upd.)
Suprema Specialties, Inc., 27
Supreme International Corporation, 27
Susan G. Komen Breast Cancer Foundation 78
Susquehanna Pfaltzgraff Company, 8
Sutter Home Winery Inc., 16
Sverdrup Corporation, 14
Swales & Associates, Inc., 69
Swank, Inc., 17; 84 (upd.)
SwedishAmerican Health System, 51
Sweet Candy Company, 60
Sweetheart Cup Company, Inc., 36
The Swett & Crawford Group Inc., 84
SWH Corporation, 70
Swift & Company, 55
Swift Energy Company, 63
Swift Transportation Co., Inc., 42
Swinerton Inc., 43
Swisher International Group Inc., 23
Swiss Valley Farms Company, 90
Sybase, Inc., 10; 27 (upd.)
Sybron International Corp., 14
Sycamore Networks, Inc., 45
Sykes Enterprises, Inc., 45
Sylvan Learning Systems, Inc., 35
Sylvan, Inc., 22
Symantec Corporation, 10; 82 (upd.)
Symbol Technologies, Inc., 15
Syms Corporation, 29; 74 (upd.)
Symyx Technologies, Inc., 77
Synaptics Incorporated, 95
Synchronoss Technologies, Inc., 95
SYNNEX Corporation, 73
Synopsys, Inc., 11; 69 (upd.)
SynOptics Communications, Inc., 10
Synovus Financial Corp., 12; 52 (upd.)
Syntel, Inc., 92
Syntex Corporation, I
Sypris Solutions, Inc., 85
SyQuest Technology, Inc., 18
Syratech Corp., 14
SYSCO Corporation, II; 24 (upd.); 75 (upd.)
System Software Associates, Inc., 10
Systemax, Inc., 52
Systems & Computer Technology Corp., 19
T-Netix, Inc., 46
T. Marzetti Company, 57
T. Rowe Price Associates, Inc., 11; 34 (upd.)
TAB Products Co., 17
Taco Bell Corporation, 7; 21 (upd.); 74 (upd.)
Taco Cabana, Inc., 23; 72 (upd.)
Taco John's International, Inc., 15; 63 (upd.)
Tacony Corporation, 70
Tag-It Pacific, Inc., 85
Take-Two Interactive Software, Inc., 46
The Talbots, Inc., 11; 31 (upd.); 88 (upd.)
Talk America Holdings, Inc., 70
Talley Industries, Inc., 16
TALX Corporation, 92
Tambrands Inc., 8

Tandem Computers, Inc., 6
Tandy Corporation, II; 12 (upd.)
Tandycrafts, Inc., 31
Tanger Factory Outlet Centers, Inc., 49
Tanox, Inc., 77
Tapemark Company Inc., 64
Target Corporation, 10; 27 (upd.); 61 (upd.)
Tarragon Realty Investors, Inc., 45
Tarrant Apparel Group, 62
Taser International, Inc., 62
Tasty Baking Company, 14; 35 (upd.)
Tattered Cover Book Store, 43
Taubman Centers, Inc., 75
Taylor Corporation, 36
Taylor Guitars, 48
Taylor Made Golf Co., 23
Taylor Publishing Company, 12; 36 (upd.)
TB Wood's Corporation, 56
TBWA/Chiat/Day, 6; 43 (upd.)
TCBY Enterprises Inc., 17
TCF Financial Corporation, 47
Teachers Insurance and Annuity Association-College Retirement Equities Fund, III; 45 (upd.)
TearDrop Golf Company, 32
Tech Data Corporation, 10; 74 (upd.)
Tech-Sym Corporation, 18; 44 (upd.)
TechBooks Inc., 84
TECHNE Corporation, 52
Technical Olympic USA, Inc., 75
Technitrol, Inc., 29
Technology Research Corporation, 94
Technology Solutions Company, 94
TECO Energy, Inc., 6
Tecumseh Products Company, 8; 71 (upd.)
Tee Vee Toons, Inc., 57
Tejon Ranch Company, 35
Tekelec, 83
Tektronix Inc., 8; 78 (upd.)
Telcordia Technologies, Inc., 59
Tele-Communications, Inc., II
Teledyne Technologies Inc., I; 10 (upd.); 62 (upd.)
Telephone and Data Systems, Inc., 9
Tellabs, Inc., 11; 40 (upd.)
Telxon Corporation, 10
Temple Inland Inc., IV; 31 (upd.)
Tempur-Pedic Inc., 54
Tenet Healthcare Corporation, 55 (upd.)
TenFold Corporation, 35
Tennant Company, 13; 33 (upd.); 95 (upd.)
Tenneco Inc., I; 10 (upd.)
Tennessee Valley Authority, 50
TEPPCO Partners, L.P., 73
Teradyne, Inc., 11
Terex Corporation, 7; 40 (upd.); 91 (upd.)
The Terlato Wine Group, 48
Terra Industries, Inc., 13; 94 (upd.)
Tesoro Petroleum Corporation, 7; 45 (upd.)
The Testor Corporation, 51
Tetley USA Inc., 88
Tetra Tech, Inc., 29
Texaco Inc., IV; 14 (upd.); 41 (upd.)